# Trade, Travel, and Exploration in the Middle Ages

Garland Reference Library of the Humanities (Vol. 1899)

# Advisory Board

# Trade, Travel, and Exploration in the Middle Ages
## *An Encyclopedia*

*Editors*

John Block Friedman

Kristen Mossler Figg

*Associate Editor*

Scott D. Westrem

*Collaborating Editor*

Gregory G. Guzman

GARLAND PUBLISHING, INC.
A MEMBER OF THE TAYLOR & FRANCIS GROUP
NEW YORK & LONDON
2000

Published in 2000 by
Garland Publishing, Inc.
A member of the Taylor & Francis Group
29 West 35th Street
New York, NY 10001

10  9  8  7  6  5  4  3  2  1


**Library of Congress Cataloging-in-Publication Data**

Trade, travel, and exploration in the Middle Ages : an encyclopedia / editors, John Block
   Friedman, Kristen Mossler Figg ; associate editor, Scott D. Westrem ; collaborating
   editor, Gregory G. Guzman.
         p. cm. — (Garland reference library of the humanities ; 1899)
      Includes bibliographical references and index.
      ISBN 0-8153-2003-5 (alk. paper)
      1. Commerce—History—Encyclopedias.   2. Travel—History—Encyclopedias.
   I. Friedman, John Block, 1934–   II. Figg, Kristen Mossler, 1952–   III. Scott D. Westrem
   IV. Guzman, Gregory G.   V. Series.

HF1001.T72000
909.07'03—dc21                                                                00-037575

Printed on acid-free, 250-year-life paper
Manufactured in the United States of America

# Contents

# Introduction

*Trade, Travel, and Exploration in the Middle Ages: An Encyclopedia* is an introduction to the history of travel, exploration, discovery, and mercantile activity in Europe, Asia, Africa, and the New World. We have sought to present in a single, convenient reference work important information and perspectives on travel, trade, and exploration, much of which is currently to be found only in monographs and scholarly articles. These sources are often difficult to access, principally because a good deal of work on the subject has been written in languages other than English, but also because they are not intended for use by readers without specialized knowledge. The subject matter we treat here is complex and vast, and we therefore make no claims for completeness. We hope, however, to have provided a balanced, informative, and up-to-date reference work that, although primarily directed toward students and the general reader, will also provide a useful starting point for investigation by scholars in various disciplines.

The 435 entries by 177 contributors range from brief mentions of an issue (around 100 words) to probing studies of concepts (more than 5,000 words). Shorter entries provide ready reference, while longer entries give overviews of major movements, peoples, economic developments, concepts, and technologies. The encyclopedia has a cross-disciplinary focus that promotes the integration of historical, scientific, and literary perspectives, provides a synthetic view of parallel developments in East and West, and encourages immediate connections—through a detailed system of "See also" cross-references—among topics, writers, and geographical areas often viewed in isolation. Though

experts in the subjects here covered will be familiar with the basic information and bibliography contained in some articles, they will find, through the bibliography at the end of each entry, information from disciplines other than their own that is indispensable for general orientation, careful interpretation, and further study. A general bibliography at the end of the encyclopedia contains materials frequently referred to in individual entries in abbreviated form, as well as a variety of titles that have appeared since the project was undertaken and entries were first submitted in 1995. The index at the end of the volume—tied to the cross-referencing system already mentioned—is designed to encourage exploration of the various aspects of, and approaches to, a topic.

The terms "travel," "trade," "exploration," and "Middle Ages" all warrant some definition. By "Middle Ages," we mean the millennium between the fall of the Roman Empire—with the decline of such Roman legacies as geographical speculation, established trade routes, mapmaking, roads, bridges, and navigable waterways—and the so-called "Age of Discovery" at the end of the fifteenth century. It is a period in which a new conception of the world and mankind's ability to reach all parts of it was formed. Although we originally conceived this encyclopedia as spanning the period from 525 to 1495 C.E., we found it necessary, in order to provide an appropriate context for major developments, to include some articles (like those on Huns) dealing with a slightly earlier period and a few (like that on Bartolomé de Las Casas) dealing with events and ideas that follow the voyages of Christopher Columbus. We understand "travel" to mean the movements of individuals from their homes to other places, some close and some extremely distant, whether the travel was undertaken for religious reasons (as with pilgrims or ascetics), for personal and political gain (as with merchants or colonizers), out of simple intellectual curiosity (as is demonstrated in the travel reports of Ibn Battūta), or out of a mix of motives (as several entries here indicate was true of European crusaders). "Trade" involves the exchange of goods for money or barter between or among peoples, usually, though not always, distant. "Exploration" is broadly conceived as an intellectual and practical curiosity which encourages travel, either armchair or actual, on the part of voyagers on land and over water, to learn about or experience regions of the world new to them, though often mentioned in works of the ancient Greek and Roman geographers in sensationalizing and garbled ways. This volume attempts to cover as universal a geographical area as possible, including the Near East, the Far East, Inner or Central Asia, Africa, Scandinavia, and the new worlds of the Americas, as well as purely fabulous regions.

As is to be expected in an encyclopedia, entries are arranged alphabetically. There are blind entries where needed, as in "*Arin*, see Center of the Earth." In the listings of literary works, preference has been given to the names of the authors, whenever known, rather than to the titles of the works. Thus *Divisament dou monde* will be found under Marco Polo. It has frequently proven problematic to determine what spelling (and diacritics) to use for proper nouns; this has been especially true with names of Mongol rulers (Tamerlane/Tīmūr), the names of Asian battle sites (which have been transliterated from non-Roman alphabets), and certain commercial terms like "*fondaco*." At the start of the project it was the editors' intention to use the spellings favored by the author of each entry, but it soon became apparent that there were so many ways to spell Khubilai Khân or Karakorum, and so many variants for the names of cities like Almaligh, that both scholars and general readers would be disoriented by having to face an array of spellings and unfamiliar diacritical marks. We reached a compromise by deciding to include the form of each name most familiar to scholars (usually, in Arabic names, retaining the macron if the name is commonly found without it in English dictionaries) or by choosing the form most likely to be in the Library of Congress and standard reference works. Thus, if a city or a person (Giovanni de Pian di Carpine) has a name widely known to English readers, we have tried to choose the more familiar form of the name (John of Plano Carpini).

A further complicating factor was whether to alphabetize under the given name or the cognomen/surname. When cognomens began to appear, mainly in the eleventh century and later, they were originally loconyms; the personal name remained the individual's chief identification. By the fourteenth century, family names competed with cognomens in identifying persons. Many people in the later Middle Ages are more readily identified by their surnames than by their personal names (Geoffrey Chaucer). Thus it turned out that many individuals active before the fourteenth century were best alphabetized by their personal names (Jordan of Giano), while those who were active later were better alphabetized under their family names (Behaim, Martin). However, the most important guiding principle was common usage for whatever single name was used most often by scholars after first reference (Jordan of Sévérac, but Sacrobosco, John of).

The volume contains illustrations, maps, lists of frequently mentioned leaders, lists of related topics, and a chart showing the sequence of major events and documents. In all cases, our intent is not to be exhaustive, but to add a visual or schematic dimension that will help to clarify unfamiliar topics and inform the reader, especially where other reference books may not cover such specialized details. The Index at the end of the volume is intended to guide users to topics that either lack their own entry or are cited repeatedly throughout the volume. The bibliographies appended to the entries are not intended to be exhaustive but instead provide reference materials that will enable the student and the scholar to move quickly and confidently into the matter at hand. The nature of our subject is such that many of the topics treated in this work have engaged the attention of writers whose language is not English. While it may seem that there is a great deal of reference material in French, German, Italian, and other languages, this is simply a fact of the state of scholarship on trade, travel, and exploration in the Middle Ages.

A work of this magnitude required the collaboration and cooperation of many persons over the six years of its creation and production. Our deepest gratitude goes in the first place to the many colleagues who graciously gave of their time and knowledge to write the articles that are at the very heart of this undertaking; their names are listed both at the beginning of the volume and after the articles which they contributed. One, Delno C. West, did not live to see his contributions in print. We are especially grateful to Gary Kuris, formerly of Garland

Publishing, under whose aegis this project began, and also Joanne Daniels, who helped us through the early stages of the volume's development. Richard Steins and Andrea Johnson more recently have given the greatest attention to the production of the book. Errors are ours and not theirs. In addition to writing key articles, several scholars provided special assistance in reviewing lists of entries and defining coverage for specific areas. Our Advisors, Anna-Dorothee von den Brincken, Chandra Richard de Silva, John Parker, J.R. Seymour Phillips, Jean Richard, and Denis Sinor, often contributed in this manner, and some read over entries and offered ideas for additional topics. We are especially grateful to our fellow editor Scott Westrem, who provided us with ideas for articles in areas in which we had little initial knowledge. He also painstakingly checked facts in the articles and contributed to the occasional rewriting of articles by contributors whose first language was not English. Our collaborating editor, Gregory Guzman, was generous with his vast knowledge of Mongol lore.

The editors wish to thank the many libraries and institutions that granted permission to reproduce items in their collections; individual acknowledgments are provided in the captions. We also wish to thank the Department of English at the University of Illinois at Urbana-Champaign and Kent State University Salem Campus for providing research assistance and other services to the editors.

John B. Friedman and Kristen M. Figg

# Topics

# Sequence of Events

| | Major Expansions & Explorations | Encyclopedists & Cosmographers<br>(*date indicates major work*) |
|---|---|---|
| **100** B.C.E. | Roman Empire, 27 B.C.E.–476 C.E. | Pomponius Mela, 33–34 C.E.<br>Pliny the Elder, before 79 C.E. |
| **100** C.E. | | |
| **200** | | Solinus, *c.* 230/240 |
| **300** | | |
| **400** | Hunnish Incursions into Western Europe,<br>376–453 | Macrobius, *c.* 400 |
| **500** | | Cosmas Indikopleustes, *c.* 540 |
| **600** | Islamic Expansion as far as Spain and<br>India, 632–750 | Isidore of Seville, *c.* 636 |
| **700** | | Aethicus Ister, *c.* 700 |
| **750** | | |
| **800** | Viking Discoveries, late 8th to mid-11th century | al-Kwarizmi, early 9th century |
| **850** | | |
| **900** | | |
| **950** | | |
| **1000** | Empire of Seljuk Turks, 986–1092 | |
| **1050** | | Adam of Bremen, *c.* 1073–1076 |
| **1100** | Crusades, 1095–1464 | Honorius Augustodunensis, *c.* 1110<br>Lambert of St. Omer, 1112–1121 |
| **1150** | | al-Idrīsī, *c.* 1154 |

| Travelers & Travel Narratives | Maps | |
|---|---|---|
| | Sallust Maps, 86–*c.* 34 B.C.E. | **100** B.C.E. |
| | Agrippa's World Map, 44 B.C.E. | **100** C.E. |
| | | **200** |
| Earliest Pilgrims to the Holy Land: Bordeaux Pilgrim, 333 C.E. | | **300** |
| Egeria, 384 Antoninus, late 6th century | Macrobius's zonal (climate) map, 5th century | **400** |
| St. Brendan, legendary 6th-century Irish seafarer | Madaba Map, mosaic map of the Near East, 6th century | **500** |
| Arculf, Merovingian bishop, visited Byzantine Empire and the Holy Land, *c.* 680–683 | Isidorean Maps, 7th–15th century | **600** |
| | | **700** |
| | | **750** |
| | Beatus Maps, late 8th–12th century | **800** |
| | | **850** |
| | | **900** |
| Ibrāhīm Ibn Yaʿqūb al-Isrāʾīli, Hispano-Arab Jewish traveler to France, Germany, and Eastern Europe, 960s | | **950** |
| | | **1000** |
| | Cotton (Anglo-Saxon) Map, *c.* 1050 | **1050** |
| | *Liber Floridus,* with circular world map, early 12th century | **1100** |
| Benjamin of Tudela, Jewish traveler from Spain to the Middle East, d. 1173 | Jerome Maps of Asia and of the Near East, 12th century | **1150** |
| | *Continued* | |

| | Major Expansions & Explorations | Encyclopedists & Cosmographers<br>(*date indicates major work*) |
|---|---|---|
| **1175** C.E. | | |
| **1200** | Mongol Expansion, 1206–1368 | Gervase of Tilbury, 1211/1214 |
| **1220** | Dominance of Italian City States,<br>1204–1500 | Thomas of Cantimpré, 1228–1244 |
| **1240** | | Bartholomaeus Anglicus, 1245 |
| **1260** | | Vincent of Beauvais, *c.* 1244–*c.* 1260<br>Brunetto Latini, *c.* 1265 |
| **1280** | | |
| **1300** | Ottoman Expansion, 1302–1566 | |
| **1320** | | Paulinus Minorita of Venice, *c.* 1321–1344 |
| **1340** | | |
| **1360** | | |
| **1380** | | |
| **1400** | Zheng He's Maritime Expeditions,<br>1405–1433 | Ptolemy's *Cosmographia,* Latin translation, *c.* 1407 |
| **1420** | | Pierre d'Ailly, *c.* 1410 |
| **1440** | Portuguese Expansion, 1415–1550 | |
| **1460** | | |
| **1470** | | |
| **1480** | | Paolo dal Pozzo Toscanelli, 1474, 1480 |
| **1490** | Christopher Columbus reaches the<br>Americas, 1492 | |
| **1500** | | |

| Travelers & Travel Narratives | Maps | |
|---|---|---|
| | | **1175** C.E. |
| Ibn Jubayr, Muslim pilgrim and traveler from Granada to the Middle East, 1183–1185 | Henry of Mainz World Map, late 12th century | |
| | | **1200** |
| | | **1220** |
| John of Plano Carpini, papal ambassador to Great Khân in Mongolia, 1245–1247 | | |
| Simon of Saint-Quentin, papal envoy to Mongols in the Middle East, 1240s | Ebstorf Map, c. 1240 | **1240** |
| Andrew of Longjumeau, envoy to Middle East, 1243–1254 | Matthew Paris, maps of Britain, Mediterranean (often called world map), and Palestine; itineraries; c. 1250 | **1260** |
| | London Psalter Map, c. 1250 | |
| William of Rubruck, missionary to Mongol court at Karakorum, 1253–1255 | Duchy of Cornwall Map, 1283 | **1280** |
| | Hereford Map, c. 1290 | |
| Marco Polo, Venetian traveler to Mongol Empire, 1271–1295 | Portolan Charts, beginning in late 13th century | **1300** |
| Ricold of Monte Croce, missionary to Middle East; treatise on Islam, c. 1300 | Pietro Vesconte, sea charts and atlases, 1310–1330 | |
| | | **1320** |
| John of Monte Corvino, first Christian missionary to China, 1291–1328 | | **1340** |
| Odoric of Pordenone, missionary to Mongol Qipchaks, Persia, East Asia, d. 1331 | | |
| *The Book of John Mandeville, c. 1360* | Gough Map of Britain, c. 1360 | **1360** |
| Ibn Battūta, Moroccan traveler to India, China, and Asia Minor, d. 1368 | | **1380** |
| Johannes Witte de Hese, fictional pilgrimage to eastern Asia, c. 1389–1392 | | |
| | Maps of Ptolemy introduced to Western Europe, c. 1406 | **1400** |
| | Vienna-Klosterneuburg Map Corpus, cartographic material, including geographical coordinates, 1420s–1430s | **1420** |
| | Borgia Map, round *mappamundi* engraved on copper plate, c. 1430. | **1440** |
| Felix Fabri, pilgrim to the Holy Land, 1441/2–1502 | Bell, Walsperger, and Zeitz maps, c. 1450–1470 | **1460** |
| | Fra Mauro World Map, c. 1459 | |
| | Petrus Roselli, nautical charts, 1447–1468 | **1470** |
| | Bartolomeo da li Sonetti, *Isolario*, collection of island maps, printed in Venice in 1485 | **1480** |
| | Martin Behaim, globe, 1492 | |
| Bernhard von Breydenbach, pilgrimage account prepared with woodcuts for the printing press, 1486 | Erhard Etzlaub, woodcut versions of road map of Central Europe, from the Baltic to Italy, c. 1500 and 1501 | **1490** |
| | | **1500** |

# Kings, Popes, and Rulers

*(regnal dates)*

**Great Khâns**
Chinggis Khân (d. 1206–1227)
Ögödei (1229–1241)
Güyük (1246–1248)
Möngke (1251–1259)
Khubilai (1260–1294)

**Khâns of the Golden Horde
(Qipchak Khanate)**
Batu (1227–1255)
Berke (1257–1266)
Möngke-Temür (1266–1280)
Töde Möngke (1280–1287)
Töle-Buka (1287–1290)
Toktu (1290–1312)
'Abd Allah Khân Özbeg (1313–1341)
Khân Janibeg (1340–1357)
Berdibeg (1357–1359)
Toktamish (1377–1395)

**Il-khâns of Persia**
Hülegü (1256–1265)
Abagha (1265–1281)
Arghun (1284–1291)
Ghaikatu (1291–1295)
Ghazan (1295–1304)

**Popes** *(as mentioned in articles)*
Leo I (440–461)
Gregory I (590–604)
Zacharias (741–752)
Nicholas I (858–867)
Sylvester II (999–1003)
John XVIII (1003-1009)
Leo IX (1049–1054)
Gregory VII (1073–1085)
Urban II (1088–1099)
Calixtus II (1119–1124)
Eugenius III (1145–1153)
Alexander III (1159–1181)
Innocent III (1198–1216)

Honorius III (1216–1227)
Gregory IX (1227–1241)
Innocent IV (1243–1254)
Clement IV (1265–1268)
Gregory X (1271–1276)
Nicholas IV (1288–1292)
Boniface VIII (1294–1303)
Clement V (1305–1314)
John XXII (1316–1334)
Benedict XII (1334–1342)
Clement VI (1342–1352)
Innocent VI (1352–1362)
Gregory XI (1370–1378)
Boniface IX (1389–1404)
Eugenius IV (1431–1447)
Nicholas V (1447–1455)
Pius II (1458–1464)
Alexander VI (1492–1503)

**Portuguese Kings**
Dom Afonso I Henriques (1139–1185)
Dom Sancho I (1185–1211)
Dom Afonso II (1211–1223)
Dom Sancho II (1223–1248)
Dom Afonso III (1248–1279)
Dom Dinis (1279–1325)
Dom Afonso IV (1325–1357)
Dom Pedro I (1357–1367)
Dom Fernando I (1367–1383)
Dom João I (1383–1433) (father of
    Prince Henry the Navigator)
Dom Duarte (1433–1438)
Dom Afonso V (1438-1481)
Dom João II (1481-1495)
Dom Manuel I (1495–1521)

**Dukes of Burgundy** (Valois line)
Philip the Bold (1363–1404)
John the Fearless (1404–1419)
Philip the Good (1419–1467)
Charles the Bold (1467–1477)

# Contributors

Gloria Allaire
*Gettysburg College*

Reuven Amitai-Preiss
*The Hebrew University of Jerusalem*

Alfred J. Andrea
*University of Vermont*

Thomas S. Asbridge
*University of Reading*

Bryan Atherton
*Western Michigan University*

Germaine Aujac
*Université de Toulouse Le Mirail*

Spurgeon Baldwin
*University of Alabama*

John W. Barker
*University of Wisconsin*

Lars Berggren
*University of Lund*

Werner Bergmann
*Ruhr-Universität Bochum*

Jonathan P. Berkey
*Davidson College*

Nancy Bisaha
*Vassar College*

Sarah Blick
*Kenyon College*

Dorothy A. Bray
*McGill University*

Anna-Dorothee von den Brincken
*Universität zu Köln*

Joseph P. Byrne
*Belmont University, Nashville*

Michael Camille
*University of Chicago*

Mary Baine Campbell
*Brandeis University*

Brian Catlos
*Toronto*

Leonid S. Chekin
*Washington, D.C.*

Key Ray Chong
*Soka University, Tokyo*

Arne Emil Christensen
*University of Oslo*

**Willene B. Clark**
*Marlboro College*

**Esther Cohen**
*Hebrew University of Jerusalem*

**Jeffrey Jerome Cohen**
*George Washington University*

**William E. Coleman**
*City University of New York*

**Charles W. Connell**
*Northern Arizona University*

**Olivia Remie Constable**
*University of Notre Dame*

**Kathy Curnow**
*Cleveland State University*

**Linda Kay Davidson**
*University of Rhode Island*

**Michael T. Davis**
*Mount Holyoke College*

**Jacqueline de Weever**
*Brooklyn College*

**Juliette Dor**
*Université de Liège*

**John E. Dotson**
*Southern Illinois University*

**Maryjane Dunn**
*Lufkin, Texas*

**Marsha L. Dutton**
*Ohio University*

**Bruce S. Eastwood**
*University of Kentucky–Lexington*

**Siân Echard**
*University of British Columbia*

**Ivana Elbl**
*Trent University*

**Martin Malcolm Elbl**
*Trent University*

**Steven A. Epstein**
*University of Colorado*

**Dwight Ferguson**
*West Georgia College*

**Kristen Mossler Figg**
*Kent State University–Salem*

**Nona C. Flores**
*University of Illinois at Chicago*

**Gladys Frantz-Murphy**
*Regis University*

**Paul H. Freedman**
*Yale University*

**John Block Friedman**
*University of Illinois–Urbana-Champaign and
Kent State University–Salem*

**Daniel Getz**
*Bradley University*

**Peter B. Golden**
*Rutgers University*

**Andrew Colin Gow**
*University of Alberta*

**Aryeh Grabois**
*University of Haifa*

**Kathryn L. Green**
*California State University–San Bernardino*

**Gregory G. Guzman**
*Bradley University*

**Thomas G. Hahn**
*University of Rochester*

Kenneth R. Hall
*Ball State University*

Mary Hamel
*Mount St. Mary's College*

Donald J. Harreld
*University of Minnesota*

Paul D. A. Harvey
*University of Durham*

Peter S. Hawkins
*Yale Divinity School*

Iain M. Higgins
*University of British Columbia*

Cynthia Ho
*University of North Carolina–Ashville*

Hoberman, Barry
*Cambridge, MA*

Laura F. Hodges
*Houston, Texas*

Bonnie D. Irwin
*Eastern Illinois University*

Kurt Villads Jensen
*Odense University*

Jenny Jochens
*Towson State University*

Lynn Jones
*Philadelphia, Pennsylvania*

Michael C.E. Jones
*University of Nottingham*

Timothy S. Jones
*Augustana College, Sioux Falls*

William R. Jones
*University of New Hampshire*

William Chester Jordan
*Princeton University*

Benjamin Z. Kedar
*Hebrew University of Jerusalem*

Kathleen Coyne Kelly
*Northeastern University*

Douglas A. Kibbee
*University of Illinois–Urbana-Champaign*

Adam Knobler
*Trenton State College*

Allan T. Kohl
*Minneapolis College of Art and Design*

Désirée Koslin
*Fashion Institute of Technology*

Adam Kosto
*Columbia University*

Z.J. Kosztolnyik
*Texas Agricultural and Mechanical University*

Barbara M. Kreutz
*Rosemont, Pennsylvania*

Margaret Wade Labarge
*Carleton University, Ottawa*

Maura K. Lafferty
*Villanova University*

Annette Landen
*University of Lund*

John L. Langdon
*University of Alberta*

Jennifer Lawler
*Lawrence, Kansas*

Teresa Leslie
*Emory University*

Amalia Levanoni
*Haifa University*

R.L.A. van Leeuwen
*University of Amsterdam*

Nehemia Levtzion
*Hebrew University of Jerusalem*

Juris G. Lidaka
*West Virginia State College*

Ora Limor
*Open University, Israel*

Malcolm C. Lyons
*Cambridge University*

Roger T. Macfarlane
*Brigham Young University*

Thomas F. Madden
*Saint Louis University*

Jerome Mandel
*Tel Aviv University*

Pierre Maraval
*Université de Strasbourg II*

Z.R.W.M. von Martels
*University of Groningen*

James V. McMahon
*Emory University*

Laurel Means
*McMaster University*

Yoko Miyamoto
*Chicago, Illinois*

Jo Ann Hoeppner Moran (Cruz)
*Georgetown University*

Margot Mortensen
*University of Alberta*

Lawrence V. Mott
*University of Minnesota*

Carolyn A. Muessig
*University of Bristol*

Anneke B. Mulder-Bakker
*University of Groningen*

James Muldoon
*Rutgers University Camden
and John Carter Brown Library, Brown University*

Richard G. Newhauser
*Trinity University*

Joseph F. O'Callaghan
*Norwalk, Connecticut*

Erhard P. Opsahl
*McFarlane, Wisconsin*

Robert Ousterhout
*University of Illinois–Urbana-Champaign*

John Parker
*University of Minnesota*

Joseph D. Parry
*Brigham Young University*

Robert Penkett
*University of Reading*

Richard V. Pierard
*Indiana State University*

Scott R. Pilarz, SJ
*Georgetown University*

James M. Powell
*Syracuse University*

John H. Pryor
*University of Sydney*

Susan A. Rabe
*Loyola Marymount University*

**Lynn Tarte Ramey**
*University of Montevallo*

**Kathryn L. Reyerson**
*University of Minnesota*

**Jean Richard**
*Institut de France*

**Louise Buenger Robbert**
*University of Missouri–St. Louis*

**Elizabeth Rodini**
*The David and Alfred Smart Museum of Art,
Chicago*

**Timothy J. Runyan**
*Eastern Carolina University*

**James D. Ryan**
*Bronx Community College*

**Debra Salata**
*University of Minnesota*

**Alauddin Samarrai**
*St. Cloud, Minnesota*

**Alessandro Scafi**
*The Warburg Institute, University of London*

**Daniel E. Schafer**
*Belmont University, Nashville*

**Brenda Deen Schildgen**
*University of California at Davis*

**Gary D. Schmidt**
*Calvin College*

**Felicitas Schmieder**
*J.W. Goethe-Universität, Frankfurt*

**Juergen Schulz**
*Brown University*

**Sandra Sider**
*Sotheby's, New York*

**Chandra Richard de Silva**
*Old Dominion University*

**Rudolf Simek**
*Universität Bonn*

**Walter Simons**
*Dartmouth College*

**Denis Sinor**
*Indiana University*

**John Masson Smith, Jr.**
*University of California–Berkeley*

**Julian A. Smith**
*University of Toronto*

**Laura Ackerman Smoller**
*University of Arkansas–Little Rock*

**Marina Smyth**
*University of Notre Dame*

**Elliot Sperling**
*Indiana University*

**Alan M. Stahl**
*American Numismatic Society*

**Gretchen D. Starr-LeBeau**
*University of Kentucky–Lexington*

**Walter Stephens**
*Johns Hopkins University*

**Lorraine Kochanske Stock**
*University of Houston*

**Jerzy Strzelczyk**
*Uniwersytet Adama Mickiewicza, Poznan*

**Van Jay Symons**
*Augustana College, Rock Island*

**Vicki Ellen Szabo**
*Cornell University*

# Maps

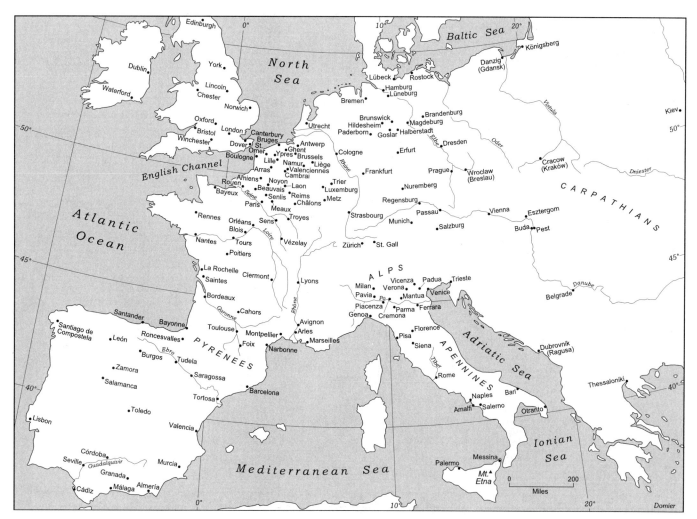

European Towns and Cities after 1200

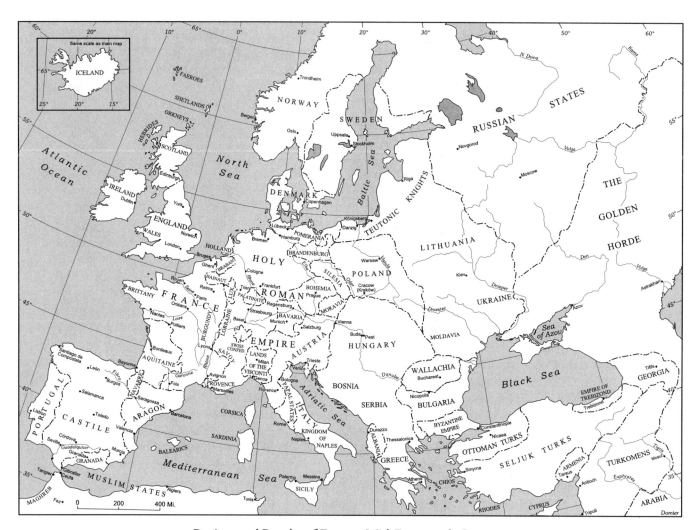

Regions and Peoples of Europe, Mid-Fourteenth Century

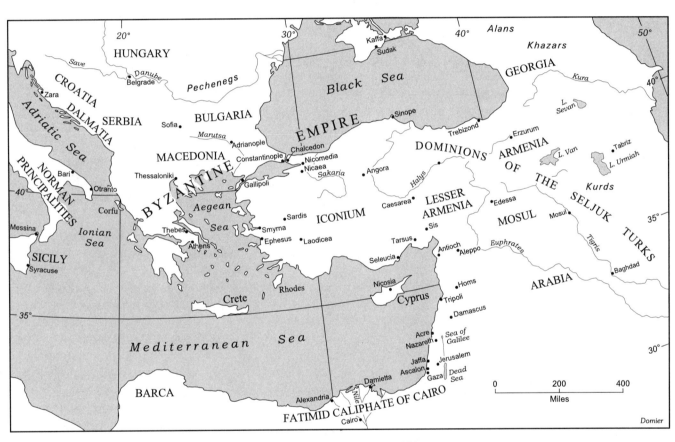

Mediterranean Regions, Early Twelfth Century

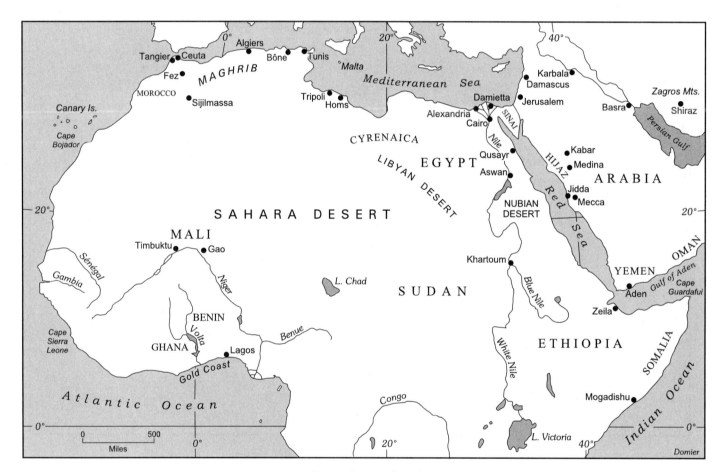

Northern Africa and Arabia

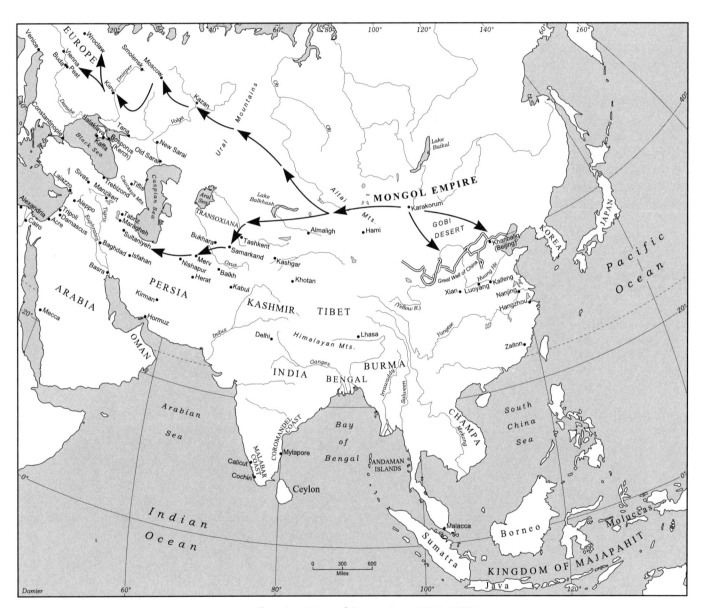

Asia, Showing Mongol Expansions 1211–1239

# A

## Abagha (r. 1265–1282)

Hülegü's son and successor as il-khân (subject khân or regional ruler) of Persia, and promoter of cooperation between his khanate and Europe.

When Hülegü died in 1265, he left his newly founded kingdom surrounded by enemies. Facing the hostility of the Golden Horde in the north and that of the Mamluk sultan in the south, and threatened by his cousins in Transoxiana from the east, Abagha reasserted his authority to rule by seeking and obtaining from Khubilai (r. 1260–1294) a *yarlik* (an official grant of authority) that allowed him to exercise jurisdiction in the great khân's name. Nonetheless, the war with the Muslim khân of the Golden Horde, Berke (1257–1267), resumed immediately at the commencement of Abagha's reign and lasted until Berke's death in 1267, while friction with the Mongols of Transoxiana occupied Abagha until 1270. When he was finally able to turn his full attention to the south, Abagha sought an alliance with Western Crusaders to counter the Mamluks of Egypt who occupied Syria. Having been in correspondence with Pope Clement IV since 1265, Abagha wrote in 1273 to Pope Gregory X and to the king of England, proposing an alliance against the Mamluk sultan of Egypt. No one in the West responded to this offer. Abagha decided to act alone and died on his way to Syria in 1282.

Abagha showed his statesmanship in welding his kingdom into an effective unit while fending off external foes. Under his reign, international trade through Persia grew. The friendly disposition of the khâns fostered mutual commerce between the il-khânate of Persia and the domain of the great khân, China. Abagha's capital, Tabriz, became a major emporium for Asian goods. Because of Abagha's friendliness toward the Christians, trade between Persia and the Mediterranean through the kingdom of Little Armenia (Lesser Armenia) also flourished, and Italian merchants' trade establishments grew rapidly in Tabriz. Thus, in the late thirteenth century, Tabriz became the hub of trade between Asia and Europe.

### BIBLIOGRAPHY

Boyle, J.A., ed. *The Seljuq and Mongol Periods.* Vol. 5 of *The Cambridge History of Iran.* Cambridge: Cambridge UP, 1968.

Grousset, René. *The Empire of the Steppes.* New Brunswick, NJ: Rutgers UP, 1970.

Saunders, J.J. *The History of Mongol Conquests.* London: Routledge, 1971.

Spuler, Bertold. *The Muslim World: A Historical Survey.* Pt.2: *The Mongol Period.* Leiden: Brill, 1960.

*Yoko Miyamoto*

### SEE ALSO

Armenia; Bukhara; China; Egypt; Golden Horde; Hülegü; Mamluks; Merchants, Italian; Mongols; Yuan Dynasty

## Accommodations, Inns and

*See* Inns and Accommodations

## Acre [Akko]

The main port of entry to Palestine. The ancient Phoenician coastal city of Akko ("'Aak" in the tribute lists of Thothmes III [1500 B.C.E.]; "Ake" in Greek;

# A

"Akko" in Hebrew; called "Akre" in the Latin of Josephus; "Acre" in French) occupies a point of land that creates two protected harbors at the northern end of Haifa Bay. The triumphant Alexander the Great established a royal mint at Acre after capturing Jerusalem and Tyre in 332 B.C.E. In 267 B.C.E., Ptolemy II Philadelphus renamed the city Ptolemais, the name by which it was known until the Arab invasion of the 630s. Acre became a Roman colony under Claudius I (41–54 C.E.). The Romans paved the road from Gaza to Acre and connected it with Antioch in the north and Egypt to the south, thus firming its commercial and political connections.

Although overshadowed as a port in late Roman times by Herod's new port city of Caesarea, Acre remained Galilee's main harbor, providing the easiest access to the interior of Palestine through a series of connecting valleys. A Greek legend (repeated by Pliny and Josephus) locates the accidental invention of glass in the dunes south of Acre. The area was rich in glass factories and was a center for glass exports from the Hellenistic period through the Middle Ages. The fair at Acre was one of the three most famous in Palestine, and the plenitude of fisheries gave rise to the saying "bring fish to Acre" as the ancient equivalent of "carrying coals to Newcastle."

The location of a large Samaritan community, Acre was also one of the earliest Christian communities (visited by St. Paul, Acts 12:7) and, in Byzantine times, the seat of a bishopric. The point of disembarkation for Jewish and Christian pilgrims and for immigrants to Palestine, Acre was captured by the Arabs in 638 and taken by the Crusaders in 1104. The Crusaders, who generally eschewed the agricultural countryside and used port cities as their main residential centers, made Acre their chief port in Palestine. Italian maritime cities supplied men and material for the crusading efforts through Acre; remains of the port area built by and reserved for the Pisans can still be seen. The town was retaken by Saladin in 1187, besieged by Guy de Lusignan, king of Jerusalem, in 1189, and recaptured by Richard the Lionheart and Philip Augustus in 1191, when it became capital of the Second Crusader Kingdom for a hundred years. It was the headquarters of the Hospitalers and the Templars and, in 1219, the site of the first Franciscan convent in the Holy Land. Burchard of Mt. Sion used Acre as the geographical "center" for his *Descriptio Terrae Sanctae* (*c.* 1280), in which he located sites in four blocks of territory radiating out

from this port. In 1291, al-Malik al-Ashraf, the Mamluk sultan of Egypt, massacred the Christian and Jewish inhabitants of Acre, drove the Crusaders from the country, and completely destroyed the town, ending European political authority in the Holy Land. The Turks who occupied the town in 1517 found little but ruins.

BIBLIOGRAPHY
Dichter, B[ernard]. *Akko, A Bibliography.* Akko: Municipality of Akko, 1979.
———. *The Orders and Churches of Crusader Acre.* Akko: Municipality of Akko, 1979.
Makhouly, Na'im. *Guide to Acre.* Jerusalem: Azriel, 1941.
Reuven and Idit Hekht Museum. *Mound and Seas: Akko and Caesarea Trading Centres.* Haifa: U of Haifa P, 1986.
Wilson, Charles William, Sir, ed. *The Land of Galilee and the North.* Jerusalem: Ariel, 1975.

Jerome Mandel

SEE ALSO
Ain Jalut; Benjamin of Tudela; Burchard of Mount Sion; Buscarello de' Ghisolfi; Crusades, First, Second, and Third; Crusade, Fifth; Exploration and Expansion, European; Fairs; Franciscan Friars; Holy Land; Ludolf of Suchem; Mamluks; Military Orders; Pisa; William of Tripoli

## Adam of Bremen (*c.* 1040–*c.* 1085)

Teacher and author of an historical work invaluable for knowledge about north Germany and Scandinavia in the tenth and eleventh centuries, distinguished by its extensive utilization of contemporary sources and, especially, geographical materials.

Adam was born in eastern Franconia, probably near Würzburg, and perhaps educated at Bamberg. Other details of his life are extremely sketchy, but it is known that Archbishop Adalbert in 1066 or 1067 invited him to Bremen where he became canon of the cathedral chapter and had responsibility for the cathedral school. Soon after arriving, Adam began gathering material for the *Gesta Hammaburgensis ecclesiae pontificum* (History of the Archbishops of Hamburg-Bremen), which he wrote between 1073 and 1076. Adam was well acquainted with classical authors and such early medieval Christian writers as Gregory of Tours, Einhard, and Bede, and he made abundant use of monastic annals, biographies, and papal documents. He also drew upon oral sources, especially Danish king Svein [Sweyn] Estrithson, whom he visited personally to obtain information about missionary work in Scandinavia. Moreover, Adam was not only a first-rate historian but also the first noteworthy geographer in medieval Germany.

The *History* is divided into four books. The first covers the history of Christianity in Lower Saxony to 936. The second details the careers of the archbishops of Hamburg-Bremen to 1045, surveys developments among the Slavic peoples and their lands, and comments on the conflicts between the church and the Saxon aristocracy. Book III is largely dedicated to the episcopate of Adalbert (1043–1072) and contains a brilliant biographical sketch of Adam's patron. Also noteworthy in this book is the description of Danish expansion under Canute the Great; the lives of St. Olaf, Magnus the Good, and Harold Hardrada in Norway; the battle of Stamford Bridge and the Norman Conquest in England in 1066; and the spread of Christianity among the Slavic peoples.

Book IV, subtitled "A Description of the Islands of the North," is probably the most important part of the *History.* It is the best factual and critical account of Scandinavia and its peoples to be found in Western literature to this time. Adam provides many details about Denmark, Sweden, Norway, the Baltic regions and their peoples, the Orkney Islands, Iceland, Greenland, and Vinland. The account of pagan worship at Uppsala is remarkable in its precision, as is the description of the endless days and nights north of the Arctic Circle. He also indicated an awareness that the earth was round, but was unable to explain the tides.

After completing the work in 1076, Adam undertook a revision and added considerable new material. Some of the copyists in the years following his death utilized the original text while others drew from the revised version, thus leading to wide variations among the surviving manuscripts of the *History.* In the early twentieth century the distinguished German medievalist Bernhard Schmeidler carefully reevaluated all the variant texts and produced a critical version that has been accepted as authoritative.

**BIBLIOGRAPHY**

Adam of Bremen. *Hamburgische Kirchengeschichte.* Ed. Bernhard Schmeidler. Hanover and Leipzig: Hahn, 1917; 2nd edition. Leipzig: Dyk, 1926; 3rd edition. Hanover: Hahn, 1977.

———. *History of the Archbishops of Hamburg-Bremen.* Ed. and trans. Francis J. Tschan. New York: Columbia UP, 1959.

Kimble, George H.T. *Geography in the Middle Ages.* London: Methuen, 1938.

Kohlmann, Philipp W. *Adam von Bremen, ein Beitrag zur mittelalterlichen Textkritik und Kosmographie.* Leipzig: Quelle & Meyer, 1926.

Schmeidler, Bernhard. *Hamburg-Bremen und Nordost-Europa vom 9. bis 11. Jahrhundert; kritische Untersuchungen zur hamburgischen Kirchengeschichte des Adam von Bremen, zu Hamburger Urkunden und zur nordischen und wendischen Geschichte.* Leipzig: Dieterich, 1918.

*Richard V. Pierard*

**SEE ALSO**
Bede; Hungary; Iceland; Viking Discoveries and Settlements

## Adamnan [Adomnan] (625?–704)

Author of the *Vita Columbae,* as well as *De locis sanctis,* an unusually vivid and detailed transcription of a pilgrimage narrative by the Merovingian bishop Arculf. Born in Donegal, Ireland, into a branch of the family of St. Columba, Adamnan studied at Clonard before entering the important Columban monastic community at Iona, where he was made abbot in 679. After his death he became a minor saint in the Irish and Scottish calendars, whose cult was linked closely to that of his kinsman Columba, founder and first abbot of Iona.

Adamnan's fame is largely based, in modern times, on his *Vita* of Columba, usually judged the best hagiographical "life" composed in the early Middle Ages. The *De locis sanctis,* however, is also a book of real importance, one of very few accounts we possess of the Holy Land from the early medieval period. Adamnan produced these works despite heavy administrative duties and was active politically as well. He conducted at least two diplomatic missions to Northumbria (on one of which he presented *De locis sanctis* to the Northumbrian king Aldfrith) and was also, during one of several lengthy visits to Ireland, instrumental in instituting the so-called "Law of the Innocents," which legally protected women, children, and clerics from performing military service.

A traveler himself, around and among the British islands, Adamnan seems to have been interested in pilgrimage as both an idea and a reality. Scholars consider his edited transcription of Arculf's narrative to show considerable knowledge of the Holy Land and adjacent territories, although his grasp of geographical theory was not particularly strong (he seems to have believed Arculf's claim that a pillar set up in Jerusalem would cast no shadow at midday on the summer solstice). A characteristically Irish notion of pilgrimage as an ascetic act without particular destination lies behind

# A

several uses of the narrative motif in the *Vita Columbae;* in his account of Arculf's pilgrimage in *De locis sanctis,* he is less interested in the spiritual action than in the details it provides for home-bound interpreters of Scripture. An eleventh-century example of the medieval genre "visions of heaven and hell" is ascribed to Adamnan (*Fin Adamnain*); although he did not write this work, the linkage of the text to him attests to an interest in miraculous travel as part of his legend.

About Arculf little is known beyond what Adamnan's text tells us. He was a Merovingian Gaul, shipwrecked near Iona (according to Bede) on his way home from almost three years' voyaging; in addition to Jerusalem and the "holy places" generally, he visited Constantinople, Alexandria, Tyre, and Sicily, probably during the years 679–682. The account is full of wonders and quasi-magical objects of veneration that attest to the growing power of holy images and relics in the decades before the outbreak of Iconoclasm, a movement advocating the systematic destruction of such images. His close observation of architectural and monumental detail has been useful to historians of early Christian art and ritual; indeed, the earliest good manuscript (Vienna, Österreichische Nationalbibliothek, Cod. Lat. 458, from the ninth century) is illustrated with architectural plans of four monumental sites, copied from sketches made by Arculf on wax tablets (*De locis sanctis* i.ii): the Church of the Holy Sepulchre and its surroundings, the Basilica on Mt. Sion, the Church of the Ascension, and the Church of Jacob's Well (in Nablus).

In composing his text from notes on Arculf's testimony, Adamnan seems to have relied on a number of onomastic works, especially Jerome's *On Hebrew Names,* of which he transcribed or paraphrased whole passages, as well as Sulpicius Severus's *Chronicon.* At least one critic has considered the work a response to Augustine's call in *De doctrina christiana* for reference works on factual matters useful for interpreting Scripture, while others have seen signs of a notable interest in secular and natural phenomena on the parts of both Arculf and Adamnan. Whatever its original motives, the account was epitomized by Bede in his *Historia ecclesiastica* and in that form became the standard account of Holy Land geography for several centuries.

## BIBLIOGRAPHY

Campbell, Mary B[aine]. *The Witness and the Other World: Exotic European Travel Writing, 400–1600.* Ithaca: Cornell UP, 1988, pp. 33–45.

Colgrave, Bertram, and R.A.B. Mynors, eds. *Bede's Ecclesiastical History of the English People.* Oxford: Oxford UP, 1969.

Harley-Woodward. *A History of Cartography.* Vol. 1, pp. 466–469, 473. See Gen. Bib.

Meehan, Denis, ed. and trans. *Adamnan's* De locis sanctis. Scriptores Latini Hiberniae No. 3. Dublin: Dublin Institute for Advanced Studies, 1958.

O'Loughlin, Thomas. "The Exegetical Purpose of Adomnan's *De locis sanctis.*" *Cambridge Medieval Celtic Studies* 24 (Winter 1992): 37–53.

*Mary Campbell*

SEE ALSO

Arculf; Bede; Holy Land; Irish Travel; Pilgrimage, Christian

## Aeneas Silvius
*See* Pius II

## Aethicus Ister, *Cosmographia*

A fictional world-travelogue dating from the late seventh or eighth century. The *Cosmographia* purports to be a Latin-language translation or summary of Aethicus's Greek by one "Hieronymus Presbyter" (pretending to be St. Jerome), who speaks of Aethicus in the third person. A second *Cosmographia* by another Aethicus (not "Ister"), of uncertain date but probably earlier, is found in a number of manuscripts; this is a catalogue of geographic features adapted principally from Julius Honorius and Orosius.

"Aethicus Ister" is not otherwise known: his name associates him with Istria, though he claims to be from Scythia, and some have found Irish traits in his Latin. It has been argued that the name was a pseudonym used by the Irish-born bishop Virgil of Salzburg (d. 784), but this claim is not now generally accepted (Herren 237–238). Aethicus's "travels" take him from Ireland to India, including places such as Ceylon, Spain, Britain, Thule, Germany, Asia Minor, Armenia, and Greece (in roughly that order), and among peoples such as the Turks and other "nations whom the Old Testament does not mention." Some descriptions are based on Solinus, Isidore, and other writers, some on stories of Alexander the Great; others are apparently made up.

Aethicus has been more widely cited in travel literature than actually read. Like the nearly contemporary *Liber Monstrorum,* the *Cosmographia* is written in a style often so ornate as to suggest deliberate obfuscation, with many words fancifully invented or adapted from the Greek, and including "riddles" other "philosophers" cannot solve. Sentences are at times telegraphic, with verbs omitted, fragmentary clauses, and notable failures of agreement; heavy alliteration in some passages overwhelms sense. The pretense of Latin translation nevertheless allows the narrator to praise Aethicus not only for his daring travels and his wisdom, but for his clear and beautiful style ("et plane et pulchre scripsit," I.17 [Wuttke 9]). Thus the work may have an ironic intention that was not well understood by the many medieval writers and compilers of maps who used it as a source.

**BIBLIOGRAPHY**

Dopsch, Heinz, and Roswitha Juffinger, eds. *Virgil von Salzburg: Missionar und Gelehrter.* Salzburg: Amt der Salzburger Landesregierung, 1985.

Herren, Michael W. Review of Prinz, *Die Kosmographie des Aethicus. Journal of Medieval Latin* 3 (1993): 236–245.

Prinz, Otto, ed. *Die Kosmographie des Aethicus.* Quellen zur Geistesgeschichte des Mittelalters 14. Munich: MGH, 1993.

Riese, Alexander, ed. *Geographi Latini minores.* Heilbronn, 1878; rpt. Hildesheim: Olms, 1964.

Wuttke, Heinrich, ed. *Die Kosmographie des Istrier Aithikos im lateinischen Auszüge des Hieronymus.* Leipzig: Dyk, 1853.

*Mary Hamel*

**SEE ALSO**

Isidore of Seville; *Liber Monstrorum;* Orosius; Scythia; Solinus, Julius Gaius; Thule; Virgil of Salzburg, St.

## Aetna, Mount
*See* Etna, Mount

## Africa, Gold Trade in
*See* Gold Trade in Africa

## Africa, Ivory Trade in
*See* Ivory Trade

## African Slave Trade
*See* Slave Trade, African

## African Trade (Non-Mediterranean)

For thousands of years Africans have carried out exchanges of goods among themselves. Great increases in the intensity and variety of exchanges, of both raw and manufactured goods, however, occurred during the medieval period, largely as a result of expanded Muslim Arab contacts. Throughout much of this era, caravan routes crisscrossed northern Africa north of the Benue River from Tangier to the Red Sea. Little is known in detail of this activity, but at least bare outlines may be discerned from references in Arab sources. The two regions with which this article is most concerned are West Africa, demarcated roughly by the Atlantic, Lake Chad, the Sahara and the Benue River; and southeastern Africa from Lake Victoria to the Limpopo River. From the 600s, Arab Muslims controlled the exploitation and trade of Ethiopia and Somali lands, and too little is known of the Bantu states of Central Africa, which apparently retained a largely pastoral economy in any case, to warrant treatment prior to the Portuguese contact beginning in 1482.

West Africa was arguably the most dynamic region of medieval Africa. South of the Niger and Senegal Rivers the extensive gold fields of Bambuk, Bure, the Akan Forest, and the Black Volta supported all of the region's medieval empires. The Mande-speaking Soninkes established the empire of Ghana around the fourth century C.E. between the upper Senegal and Niger Rivers north of the Bambuk and Bure fields, over which they gained control. Sanhaja Berbers from North Africa established caravan routes that carried gold, slaves, and salt northward to Mogador and Tangier, and manufactured metal goods, dates, figs, horses, and Islam into Ghana. By the mid-twelfth century Ghana was at its zenith of wealth and power, but in the decades that followed it was crippled by external attacks and the decline of the Almoravid empire to the north, and by 1240 Ghana had been absorbed into the rapidly expanding Islamic state of Mali to the south.

The Kangaba kingdom, from which Mali emerged, had been founded along the upper reaches of the Niger in the mid-eighth century and was converted to Islam by Moroccan traders by the early twelfth century. Led by Sundiata, in the mid-thirteenth century Mali defeated and absorbed most of Ghana and gained control of the lower trade routes northward from Lake Chad to the Bambuk fields. By around 1325, mining and trade in a wide range of goods, including slaves, leatherwork, and

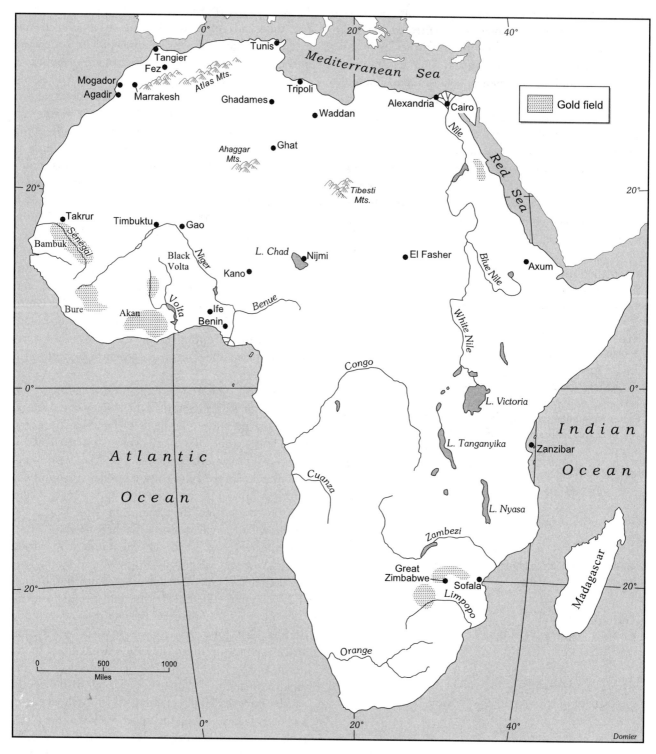

African Trade, Showing Gold Fields

gold, made Mali both the richest and largest empire yet to exist in West Africa. The empire of Mali at its height stretched from the Atlantic coast (from south of the mouth of the Gambia to north of that of the Senegal) to Tadmakka, northeast of Gao. Late in the fourteenth century Mali's gold supply shifted eastward from Bure and Bambuk to the Black Volta and Akan Forest fields, and the northward trade routes likewise shifted eastward through Timbuktu. When resurgent Songhay took Timbuktu in 1464, Mali began its long decline, being finally absorbed by Songhay by the later sixteenth century.

Songhay was founded along the Niger River by North African merchants during the mid-eighth century, and its people were converted to Islam by aggressive Almoravids during the twelfth century. Songhay lost its major city, Gao, to Mali around 1240, but regained it a century later. Under Sunni 'Ali in the later fifteenth century, Songhay armies swept north and west along the arc of the Niger and north to the Sahara, restricting Mali to the uplands around Kangaba, and gaining control of the trade in gold from the Akan and Black Volta fields. After Ghana and Mali, Songhay was the third most powerful empire of West Africa. In all three cases, empire was predicated upon control of the gold fields and the trade routes northward to the Mediterranean littoral.

Smaller states, such as the seven Mossi states that lay along the White Volta, thrived by raiding and slaving near the gold fields and along the trade routes south to the Gold Coast. Between the Sahara and the Gambia Rivers, especially along the Atlantic coast and Senegal River, small states that traded with Arabs and Berbers emerged as early as the ninth century. Gold, salt, and slaves dominated commerce, and these states were periodically submerged by the expanding empires, and left to thrive as they contracted.

By the fifteenth century, the trading state of Jolof, along the Atlantic coast between the Senegal and Gambia Rivers, had expanded in the western shadow of powerful Songhay, forming the Wolof empire. Trade with North Africa, and soon the Portuguese, fueled Wolof ambitions until the empire disintegrated into its constituent states in the mid-sixteeth century. Little is known of the peoples of the lower Niger before European contact, but trade in slaves, cloth, beads, and palm oil certainly took place; and after 1450, under the aggressive Ewuare the Great, Benin became the major regional power and broker for slaves, ivory, gold, and pepper to the Portuguese.

Stretching northward from Lake Chad along the main routes to Tripoli lay the empire of Kanem. Origi-

nally at the nexus of trade from North Africa, East Africa, and the Niger basin, it shipped out ivory, gold, leather, and slaves while importing salt, metal and metal tools, cowrie shells, corals, pearls, and horses. Between the mid-twelfth and mid-thirteenth centuries, Kanem (later Kanem-Bornu) extended almost a thousand miles northward across the Sahara and into the Fezzán region, subsequently contracting but retaining control over the corridor of trade. Between Kanem-Bornu and Songhay, a number of Hausa city-states established themselves after about 1000 along east-west trade routes and developed a commerce in their distinctively dyed cloth. After more direct routes northward developed, the cities fought amongst themselves for control of these, and eventually came to be ruled from the former Songhay region of Kebbi.

In general, the opening of port cities along the Atlantic to European raiders and traders in the later fifteenth century drained the vitality from the trans-Saharan caravan routes, and shifted the flow of West African resources from the Muslim world to the European.

Southern Africa presents a rather different picture of trade and relations with the Muslim world. Gold fields between the Zambezi and Limpopo Rivers in southeast Africa drew Arab traders from at least the tenth century. When the Bantu-speaking Shona people migrated into the region in the following century, they created a thriving civilization on the Zimbabwe plateau that controlled the trade in gold and copper from their urban center, a major settlement known as the Great Zimbabwe. When the local gold fields played out in the mid-fifteenth century, the Shona abandoned the Great Zimbabwe, migrated northward, and repeated their commercial successes. Corals, cowrie shells, sugar, spices, porcelains, and textiles moved along the coastal routes from the Gulf of Aden to the Zambezi and into the interior from Mozambique, Zanzibar, and Mombasa. Extensive iron and mineral salt deposits and ivory drew traders inland between Lakes Nyassa and Victoria as far as Lake Tanganyika, and copper and gold mines attracted them to the upper Zambezi. Muslim merchants connected southeastern Africa with ports as far afield as southern Europe and the South China Sea, though there is little evidence of this network extending south of the Limpopo River.

**BIBLIOGRAPHY**
Bennett, Norman P. *Africa and Europe from Roman Times to the Present.* New York: Africanus Publishing Company, 1975.

# A

Freeman-Grenville, G.S.P. *The New Atlas of African History.* New York: Simon and Schuster, 1991.

Oliver, Roland. *The African Experience.* New York: Harper-Collins, 1992.

———. *Cambridge History of Africa.* III: *From c. 1050 to c. 1600.* New York: Cambridge UP, 1982.

Reader, John. *Africa: Biography of the Continent.* New York: A.A. Knopf, 1998.

*Joseph P. Byrne*

**SEE ALSO**

Caravans; Ethiopians; Gold Trade in Africa; Ham's Curse and Africans; Ivory Trade; Muslim Travelers and Trade; Pepper; Portuguese Trade; Slave Trade, African

## Africans, Ham's Curse and
*See* Ham's Curse and Africans

## Agrippa's World Map

A physical and political world map, probably rectangular, attributed to Marcus Vipsanius Agrippa (*c.* 63–12 B.C.E.); it included ornamental pictures and was accompanied by an extensive geographical treatise (*commentarii*), both of which are now lost.

Agrippa, who was admiral under Caesar Augustus (then Octavian) at the battle of Actium (31 B.C.E.) and later his son-in-law, took on the responsibility for the design of a world map. He had completed the *commentarii,* but not the map, when he died, so his sister and Augustus himself made use of the written text to finish the map. It was completed around 7 B.C.E. and was subsequently displayed in the Porticus Vipsania, a colonnade named for Agrippa. Pliny clearly regarded the cartography as the work of Agrippa himself (*Natural History* 3.17).

The combination of Hellenistic geographic theory with current Roman topographical data made Agrippa's scientific accomplishment perhaps the most significant of the Augustan Age, but the map's purpose was probably to project the expansion of the empire, a concern that also drove the geographical surveys instituted by Julius Caesar. The *commentarii* apparently offered the latest measurements for the entire *oikoumene,* from Ireland and the northern Ocean to the Seres (Silkmen) in the East and from the Vistula into the Sahara. Pliny cites the map and commentary frequently in his geographical books (*NH* 3–6); likewise, when Strabo refers to a certain *chorographia,* he may mean Agrippa's map.

The map and its attendant treatise may well have been the basis for the Peutinger Table and other medieval maps, including the Hereford *mappamundi.*

Two subsequent geographical treatises, the *Dimensuratio provinciarum* (*c.* 400) and the *Divisio orbis terrarum* (*c.* 435) use Agrippa's data, though many measurements are corrupted. Dicuil, in his preface to the *De mensura orbis terrae* (*c.* 814–825), tells how Theodosius II (Emperor of the East, 408–450) dispatched cartographers and supposes that their task was to update Agrippa's map. Orosius's geographical data (*Historiarum adversus paganos* 1.2), as well as Dicuil's, are based ultimately on Agrippa. Albertus Magnus, in a discussion of the torrid zone, refers to an Augustan expedition to equatorial Africa, which was recorded, he says, in Augustus's survey of the world (*De natura locorum* 1.7).

**BIBLIOGRAPHY**

Dilke, O.A.W. *Greek and Roman Maps.* Ithaca: Cornell UP, 1985.

———. "Maps in the Service of the State: Roman Cartography to the End of the Augustan Era." In Harley-Woodward, Vol. 1, pp. 201–211. See Gen. Bib.

Klotz, Alfred. "Die geographischen Commentarii des Agrippa und ihre Überreste." *Klio* 25 (1931): 38–58; 386–466 (fragments).

Kubitschek, W. "Karten." In Pauly-Wissowa, *Realencyclopädie der classischen Altertumswissenschaft* § 60–66 (Agrippa). See Gen. Bib.

Riese, Alexander, ed. *Geographi Latini minores.* Rpt. Hildesheim: Olms, 1964.

*Roger T. Macfarlane*

**SEE ALSO**

Albertus Magnus; Climate; Dicuil; Geography in Medieval Europe; Hereford Map; *Mappamundi;* Maps; *Oikoumene;* Peutinger Table; Pliny the Elder

## Ailly, Pierre d' [Petrus de Alliaco] (1350–1420)

A noted French cardinal and academic whose writings had a profound influence on fifteenth-century intellectuals and explorers, including Christopher Columbus. The author of treatises on theology, philosophy, logic, ecclesiology, and astrology, d'Ailly also composed a series of geographical works in the years after 1410. His *Imago mundi* (*Image of the World,* 1410) contains an important world map, while the two treatises forming his *Compendium cosmographiae* (probably 1410) were based on Ptolemy's *Geography,* which had recently been translated from Greek into Latin.

D'Ailly was born in Compiègne and enrolled in the University of Paris in 1363 or 1364. He received his licentiate in arts in 1367 and became a doctor of theology in 1381. D'Ailly was named chaplain to King Charles VI (1380–1422) and chancellor of the University of Paris in 1389 preceding his illustrious student, Jean Gerson (1363–1429), then held the bishoprics of Le Puy (1395), Noyon (1396), and Cambrai (1397). His career spanned the years of the Great Schism (1378–1414), and he became one of the leading proponents of the conciliar solution to the problem of two competing popes. He was among the group of dissident churchmen who elected a third pope at the Council of Pisa in 1409; that pope's successor, the antipope John XXIII (1410–1415), named d'Ailly cardinal in 1411. D'Ailly was a leading voice at the Council of Constance (1414–1417) that ended the Schism, after which he retired to Avignon, where he died in 1420.

After the Council of Pisa, d'Ailly retreated to his bishopric of Cambrai, where he composed a series of treatises on cosmographical and astrological subjects. He com-

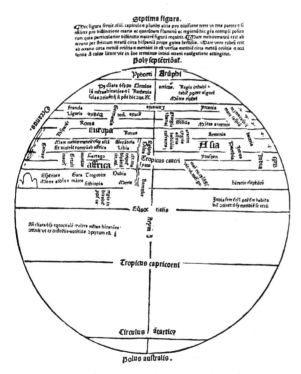

Climate Map. *Imago Mundi* of Pierre d'Ailly. *Tractatus de Imagine Mundi et Varia Ejusdem Auctoris et Joannis Gersonis Opuscula.* Louvain: Johannes Paderborn de Westphalia, 1483. Fig. 7.

pleted the first of these, the *Imago mundi,* on August 12, 1410. In this work's sixty chapters, d'Ailly presented a description of the heavens and earth drawn from such authors as Pliny the Elder (23–79), Solinus (fl. 230–240), Orosius (fl. 418), Isidore of Seville (*c.* 560–636), Honorius Augustodunensis (*c.* 1075/1080–*c.* 1156), Vincent of Beauvais (*c.* 1190–1264), Johannes Sacrobosco (John of Holywood, *c.* 1200–1256), and, especially, Roger Bacon (1220–1292), whose writings also profoundly influenced d'Ailly's thought on astrology in the years after 1409. D'Ailly appended eight figures illustrating his text, of which the seventh was a world map. D'Ailly's map is a north-oriented zone-type map, of the sort ultimately derived from Macrobius's *Commentary on the Dream of Scipio* (*c.* 399–422).

Like most of his contemporaries d'Ailly understood the earth to be a sphere. The map portrays a globe divided by horizontal lines marking the Arctic and Antarctic circles, the tropics, the equator, and seven climates in the Northern Hemisphere. On this framework, text (but no graphic representation) identifies the world's major features: Europe, Asia, and Africa (the three divisions of the T-O maps [see Maps]); important waterways (both oceans and rivers); mountains; and regions and cities (including Rome and Carthage, but not Jerusalem). The map contains sixty place names (twenty-five in Asia, twenty in Africa, and fifteen in Europe). A vertical line labeled "Arym" (the supposed center of the world in Islamic thought) bisects the globe; its position as central meridian points to the Arabic sources that ultimately underlie d'Ailly's (and Roger Bacon's) thought, as does the prominence given to the seven climates (which were important in Arabic astrological thought as well).

Probably the most noteworthy feature of d'Ailly's description of the world in the *Imago mundi* is his insistence on the relatively small size of the ocean separating the westernmost point of Africa and the easternmost point of Asia, an opinion he adopted from Roger Bacon and one that later bolstered Columbus's faith in his own enterprise. D'Ailly stressed that India (by which he meant, in effect, the "Far East") was immense, some one-third of the habitable world, extending southward to the tropic of Capricorn, and eastward much farther than others had thought. Also of interest in the *Imago mundi* is d'Ailly's treatment of questions about the habitability of various regions of the earth. Although astrologers supposed the seven climates depicted on d'Ailly's map to contain the entire habitable world,

# A

d'Ailly noted that many peoples were known to inhabit the "anteclimates" and "postclimates" to the south and the north of the seven climates of his map (save the region around the equator, uninhabitable due to excessive heat). The extreme north and south contained races of monsters and cannibals, d'Ailly added, as did India. In an appended *Epilogus mappae mundi* (also from 1410), he opined that, according to the considerations of natural philosophy, there should be a habitable region south of the equator comparable to the known habitable world (thus arguing emphatically, if theoretically, for the existence of the antipodes).

Shortly after completing the *Imago mundi,* d'Ailly composed two treatises entitled *Compendium cosmographiae.* These two treatises were based on a reading of Ptolemy's *Geography,* first translated into Latin in 1406–1407 by Jacobus Angelus in Tuscany. It is likely that d'Ailly obtained a copy of this newly translated work while he was at the Council of Pisa in 1409; his friend Guillaume Fillastre later oversaw the production of a series of maps to accompany the *Geography.* In these treatises, d'Ailly gave his readers instructions for devising a map according to Ptolemy's method and provided tables of locations with their latitudes and longitudes to serve anyone wishing to construct such a map. In keeping with his conclusions in the *Imago mundi,* d'Ailly rejected Ptolemy's calculation of the distance from western Africa to eastern India in favor of his own smaller estimate. Indeed, he asserted that the ocean could be crossed in only a few days with a favorable wind.

D'Ailly's treatises enjoyed a wide audience in the fifteenth century among readers grateful for his encyclopedic surveys, some two hundred manuscript copies of the *Imago mundi* survive. This large number of handwritten copies of a fifteenth-century book is especially remarkable because the geographical works, along with many of d'Ailly's astrological compositions and related writings by Jean Gerson, were printed around 1483 at Louvain by Johannes de Westphalia. Columbus's copy of this volume survives and is covered with his own holograph annotations: 875 in all, 546 on the geographical works and 329 on d'Ailly's astronomical and astrological treatises. In addition to their considerable importance in confirming Columbus's belief in the feasibility of a westerly route to the Indies, the descriptive portions of d'Ailly's treatises also appear to have influenced the admiral's perceptions of the New World, including his descriptions of the marvels, monsters, and products he saw there and his search for the Terrestrial Paradise. D'Ailly's astrological texts, concerned in part with calculating the end of the world, helped fuel Columbus's millenarian interpretation of his own mission.

**BIBLIOGRAPHY**
Ailly, Pierre d'. Imago mundi *by Petrus de Aliaco (Pierre d'Ailly) with Annotations by Christopher Columbus.* Facsimile edition. Boston: Massachusetts Historical Society, 1927.
———. *Imago mundi.* Trans. E.F. Keever. Wilmington, NC: Linprint Co., 1948.
Beaune, Colette. "La notion d'Europe dans les livres d'astrologie du XVe siècle." In *La conscience Européene au XVe et au XVIe siècle.* Collection de l'École Normale Supérieure de Jeunes Filles, 22. Paris: École Normale Supérieure de Jeunes Filles, 1982, pp. 1–7.
Buron, Edmond, ed. Ymago mundi *de Pierre d'Ailly. Texte latin et traduction française des quatre traités cosmographiques de d'Ailly et des notes marginales de Christophe Colombe. Étude sur les sources de l'auteur.* 3 vols. Paris: Maisonneuve frères, 1930.
Flint, Valerie I.J. *The Imaginative Landscape of Christopher Columbus.* Princeton, NJ: Princeton UP, 1992.
Guenée, Bernard. *Between Church and State: The Lives of Four French Prelates in the Late Middle Ages.* Trans. Arthur Goldhammer. Chicago: U of Chicago P, 1991.
Smoller, Laura. *History, Prophecy, and the Stars: The Christian Astrology of Pierre d'Ailly, 1350–1420.* Princeton, NJ: Princeton UP, 1994.
Watts, Pauline Moffit. "Prophecy and Discovery: On the Spiritual Origins of Christopher Columbus's 'Enterprise of the Indies.'" *American Historical Review* 90 (1985): 73–102.

*Laura A. Smoller*

**SEE ALSO**
Antipodes; Cartography, Arabic; Center of the Earth; Climate; Columbus, Christopher; Honorius Augustodunensis; Isidore of Seville; *Mappamundi;* Orosius; Ptolemy; Sacrobosco, John of; Solinus, Julius Gaius; Vincent of Beauvais

# Ain Jalut

Location in Palestine, also known as Goliath's Well, and site of a significant defeat of the Mongols in 1260.

After having established direct control over Persia and Persian Iraq, Hülegü (d. 1265), the il-khân (regional ruler, subject to the great khân) of Persia marched on to conquer Syria. In the first half of 1260 the Mongols invaded Syria, sacked Aleppo, subjugated Damascus, and destroyed the Muslim principalities of Syria and Palestine. The Mamluks of Egypt, to whom Hülegü offered the alternative of submission or war, decided to fight. Thanks to the benevolence of the Franks of Acre, the Mamluks obtained safe passage through the coastal area still held by the Crusaders, and penetrated into Jordan. On September 3, 1260, the Mamluks defeated the Mongols at Ain Jalut (Goliath's Well) in Palestine, thus allowing them to expel the Mongols and occupy Syria. Though the Mongols repeatedly threatened and invaded Syria until a little beyond 1300, they never again occupied Syria for more than a short period of time.

The battle of Ain Jalut can be said to have marked the turning point in the history of Mongol expansion in the Middle East. Since it marked the first Mongol defeat on the battlefield, it shattered the myth of Mongol superiority based on divine support for their world conquest. Some historians consider this battle as a "missed opportunity" for the Crusaders; had they formed an alliance with the Mongols, they might have defeated the Muslims and regained the Holy Land.

The Mongol defeat at Ain Jalut is traditionally attributed to the numerical superiority of the Mamluks. The death of the Great Khân Möngke (1251–1259) and the incipient succession struggle had forced Hülegü and the bulk of his troops to withdraw from Syria; thereafter, the hostility of the Golden Horde prevented the Mongols of Persia from mobilizing their full military power for the conquest of Syria. Recent studies suggest that an inadequate supply of water and pastureland was a major reason for the repeated Mongol failure to occupy Syria after the battle of Ain Jalut; the Mongols' traditional nomadic tactics required a larger number of horses than could be supported on the sparse water and pasture available in Syria.

**BIBLIOGRAPHY**
Amitai-Preiss, Reuven. *Mongols and Mamluks: The Mamluk-Ilkhanid War, 1260–1281.* Cambridge Studies in Islamic Civilization. Cambridge and New York: Cambridge UP, 1995.
Morgan, David. *The Mongols.* The Peoples of Europe Series. Oxford and New York: Blackwell, 1986.
Smith, John Masson, Jr. "Ayn Jalut: Mamluk Success or Mongol Failure?" *Harvard Journal of Asiatic Studies* 44 [2] (1984): 307–345.
Spuler, Bertold. *The Muslim World: A Historical Survey.* Pt. 2: *The Mongol Period.* Leiden: Brill, 1960.

*Yoko Miyamoto*

SEE ALSO
Golden Horde; Hülegü; Mamluks; Mongols; Nomadism and Pastoralism

## Albertus Magnus [Albert the Great] (*c.* 1200–1280)

Dominican scholar proficient in all branches of science, and author of *De natura locorum,* an important work on geographical theory. Known by the epithets *Doctor universalis* and *Doctor expertus,* Albert popularized Aristotelian thought, just becoming available to the Latin West through translations from the Arabic. The teacher of St. Thomas Aquinas, he was also instrumental in introducing the works of Arabo-Islamic thinkers and making philosophy a necessary part of the Dominican university curriculum. Indeed, the only contemporary who matched Albert as a scientist was Roger Bacon (*c.* 1213–*c.*1293).

Albert was born in Lauingen (Bavarian Swabia) of a knightly family, probably between 1183 and 1206. He first studied at Padua, where he early demonstrated scientific aptitude, marked powers of observation, and a willingness to travel. He entered the Dominican order in 1223, embarking on theological studies at Cologne, which became the center of his intellectual activities. By 1228 he was a lector in theology and taught at Dominican houses in Cologne and elswhere. About 1241 he undertook further study at Paris, where he became the first German Dominican to earn a master's degree in theology (in 1245). It was during his Parisian studies that Albert first encountered Averröes's commentaries on the works of Aristotle. In 1248 he returned to Cologne to teach and to prepare paraphrases of Aristotle's works, beginning with the *Physics* and continuing systematically through all of the natural scientific works, completing the project in 1270.

Besides being an able scientist, Albert was also a skilled administrator and negotiator. He served as prior of the German Dominicans in the Teutonic province of the order in 1253–1256, and as bishop of Regensburg in 1260–1262, mediating a long-standing feud between the archbishop and citizens of Cologne and defending the mendicant orders at the papal court in

**A**

1256. Albert was beatified in 1622, canonized as a Doctor of the Church in 1931, and officially recognized as the patron saint of natural scientists in 1941.

Albert was an inveterate traveler and exhibited marked curiosity about the world. Partly, this was due to his responsibilities as a provincial, for his territory included all of Germany, Austria, Bohemia, Switzerland, Alsace, Lorraine, Luxemburg, Belgium, Holland, and parts of Poland, Lithuania, and Latvia. The scope and frequency of Albert's travels were extraordinary for one so preoccupied with the sedentary act of writing, but they are even more remarkable in the light of the Dominican rules against travel by carriage or on horseback except in extraordinary circumstances. Indeed, his sturdy laced walking shoes gave him the title "Bishop the Boots." Many of Albert's observations of the natural world must have been made on these foot journeys. Thus, he witnessed an earthquake in Lombardy in 1222, saw a comet in Saxony in 1240, and made visits to mines in search of fossils and minerals.

Much of his observation appeared in or affected his very important geographical treatise *De natura locorum,* compiled for teaching purposes between 1248 and 1252; the text remains untranslated and is the only one of his books not inspired directly by Aristotle. This work contains the most elaborate discussion of geographical theory with relation to human culture since Hippocrates' *Airs, Waters, Places.* Albert indicates some interest in practical geography as well, reportedly producing a round world map, now lost; the Vienna manuscript of the *De natura locorum* refers to a rectangular map, oriented to the east. Much of his treatise—which like many such medieval works was largely a compilation from authorities—was borrowed from the works of earlier cosmographers such as Julius Honorius (*c.* 400), Aethicus Ister, and the Spaniard Paulus Orosius (*c.* 418), the first Chistian historian to offer the tripartite conception of the earth reflected in the T-O maps (see Maps). None of these authors is named by Albert, who quotes Orosius almost verbatim. In addition to Aristotle's geographical thinking, Albert also mentions (though almost certainly not all from direct knowledge) Hesiod, Democritus, Socrates, Plato, Ptolemy, Porphyrius, Boethius, and the Muslim scholars Avicenna, Averröes, and Albumasar.

The *De natura locorum* treats the theoretical foundations of physical geography and discusses a variety of experimental phenomena. The first and second parts owe a debt to Aristotle's *Physics.* Part three contains a Ptolemaic description of the inhabited world. Albert was particularly interested in such issues as the distinctions between habitable and uninhabitable places, the influence of terrain and plants on climate, and the question of the antipodes. Albert often corrects Aristotle by way of Islamic scholars, affirming the earth's sphericity but rejecting, for example, the Greek thinker's measurement of its circumference in favor of estimates made by Arab mathematicians. He notes that "Averröes agrees with Aristotle" regarding the possibility of life in the antipodes, and that Ptolemy and Avicenna agree that the "the torrid zone is not in all places torrid." An awareness of historical change and cultural relativism is also evident in the use of toponyms postdating the rise of Islam (*Mare Arabicum* for the Indian Ocean, *Sinum Arabicum* for the Red Sea) and in historical comments such as one about "great cities . . . first subject to the Greeks and later to the Romans. Later, however, they were seized by the Saracens, very many of them were destroyed and others of different names were built and their names were changed."

For his introduction of Arab thought, his wide-ranging observation of the natural history of Germany, and his inexhaustible curiosity about the trades, customs, and practices of his contemporaries, Albert has few equals in the history of medieval travel.

**BIBLIOGRAPHY**

Albertus Magnus. *Opera omnia, ad fidem codicum manuscriptorum edenda.* Ed. Bernhard Geyer et al. Münster: Aschendorff, 1951–1982.

Gobbo, Ida, O.P. *Il Pensiero geographico di S. Alberto Magno.* Torino: Editore Gheroni, 1950.

Hossfeld, Paul. *Albertus Magnus als Naturphilosoph und Naturwissenschaftler.* Bonn: Albertus-Magnus Institut, 1983.

Kovach, Francis J., and Robert W. Shahan, eds. *Albert the Great: Commemorative Essays.* Norman: U of Oklahoma P, 1980.

Tilman, Sister Jean Paul. *An Appraisal of the Geographical Works of Albertus Magnus and His Contribution to Geographical Thought.* Michigan Geographical Publications 4. Ann Arbor: U of Michigan Geographical Publications, 1971.

Weisheipl, James A., ed. *Albertus Magnus and the Sciences: Commemorative Essays.* Studies and Texts 49. Toronto: Pontifical Institute, 1983.

Zambelli, Paola. *The Speculum astronomiae and Its Enigma: Astrology, Theology and Science in Albertus Magnus and His Contempories.* Dordrecht and Boston: Kluwer, 1992.

*Marina A. Tolmacheva*

## *Alexandreis*
**See** Walter of Châtillon

## Alfonso X [of Castile] (1221–1284)

King of Castile, an area now in north-central Spain,
from 1252 to 1284. Because of his patronage of scholars and his own erudition, he was known as "the
Learned King." His policies helped to develop trade
and travel in the Iberian Peninsula.

Urging his people to take pride in their country and
to improve it, he declared that roads and bridges should
be erected where necessary and that all routes, including
rivers and harbors, should be kept free of barriers in
order to encourage the free flow of persons and goods
throughout his kingdom (see *Siete Partidas,* 2.11.1–3;
2.12. Prologue; 2.20.1–8). Pilgrimage to the shrine of
St. James of Compostela in Galicia had long brought
many northern European travelers to the peninsula. In
the *Fuero real* ("Royal Statute," 1.23.1–4), the *Siete Partidas* ("Seven Divisions," 1.24.1–4), and in a constitution enacted in 1254, the king assured pilgrims of safe
passage and security for their lives and property.

Nevertheless, the recent reconquest of Seville
(1248), long a major seaport, although it stood several
miles up the Guadalquivir River from the Mediterranean Sea, had given the kingdom a new orientation
from north to south. Alfonso X hoped to broaden his
access to the Mediterranean by acquiring control of
ports on the Moroccan side of the Straits of Gibraltar
(an enterprise that failed) and by developing Cádiz and
El Puerto de Santa María on the Gulf of Cádiz (a plan
that had limited success in his lifetime). He welcomed
foreigners who wished to settle there, giving merchants
a variety of privileges to encourage them to do so.
Genoese merchants who had settled in Seville continued to enjoy benefits accorded them by the king's
father, Fernando III (1217–1252).

Alfonso also furthered the development of fairs, creating nineteen new ones in addition to six already in
existence. Seville, for example, was authorized to hold
two annual fairs, where Christians, Muslims, and Jews,
whether natives of the kingdom or foreigners, were
guaranteed protection and exempted from certain tolls.

Law on payment to clergy from law code of Alfonso X.
London, British Library MS Add. 20787, fol. 112v, late 13th
century. Courtesy of the British Library.

Following the policy of his immediate predecessors, the
king decreed in the *cortes* of Seville in 1252 (art.
19–21) and in 1261 (art. 15), and in the assembly of
Jerez in 1268 (art. 14), limitations or prohibitions on
the export of certain types of goods (the so-called *cosas
vedadas*), such as iron, horses, other animals, hides,
foodstuffs, gold, and silver. In order to maintain a
favorable balance of trade, the king required merchants
to export goods equal in value to those imported.

Trade was controlled and duties were levied at customs houses established at the ports on the Bay of Biscay,
on the Atlantic coast of Galicia, and on the Mediterranean, as well as along the land frontiers with Portugal,
Navarre, and Aragón. These restrictions aroused opposition, however, and prompted the king in 1281 to grant
three privileges to merchants. They were exempted from
the payment of local tolls and internal customs duties
and had to pay only one duty on goods brought into or

# A

taken out of the kingdom. In return for a major financial contribution, he pardoned merchants for previous violations of the law in these matters. Even though he was deprived of royal authority in 1282 when his son Sancho assumed power (maintaining only the royal title until his death two years later), Alfonso's successors continued to follow his policies for generations.

**BIBLIOGRAPHY**

Jiménez, Manuel González. *Alfonso X, 1252–1284.* Palencia, Diputación Provincial de Palencia, 1993.

O'Callaghan, Joseph F. *The Learned King: The Reign of Alfonso X of Castile.* Philadelphia: U of Pennsylvania, 1993.

———. "Paths to Ruin: The Economic and Financial Policies of Alfonso the Learned." In *The Worlds of Alfonso the Learned and James the Conqueror.* Ed. Robert I. Burns, S.J. Princeton: Princeton UP, 1985, pp. 41–65.

*Joseph F. O'Callaghan*

**SEE ALSO**

Brunetto Latini; Cádiz; Córdoba; Fairs; *Nao*; Navigation; Pilgrimage Sites, Spanish; Portolan Charts; Seville; Spain and Portugal; Transportation, Inland

## al-Idrīsī (1100–1165)

Greatest medieval Arab geographer; collector of geographical information and mapmaker. Abū 'Abd Allāh Muhammad ibn 'Abd Allāh ibn Idrīs al-'Ali bi-Amr Allāh was born around A.H. 493 (1100 C.E.) and died around 560 (1165 C.E.). A descendant of the prophet Muhammad, this Muslim Arab scholar was titled al-Sharīf al-Idrīsī, but in the West he was known for a long time as *Geographus Nubiensis,* "the Nubian geographer." Born in Morocco and educated in Córdoba, he worked in Palermo at the court of the Norman king Roger II (r. 1130–1154). His most important book is a world geography, *Nuzhat al-mushtāq fī 'khtirāq al-āfāq* "Entertainment for One Desiring to Travel Far" (1154); it is also called *Kitāb Rujjār,* "Book of Roger." He later wrote a shorter geography, known under a variety of Arabic titles and usually referred to as "the Little Idrisi." Both are extensively illustrated with maps; the maps in *Nuzhat al-mushtāq* are oriented to the south, while the maps in the latter book are smaller and often oriented to the east.

Al-Idrīsī traveled in Asia Minor, Europe, and North Africa; in Sicily he was able to consult both European and Islamic sources procured from books and travel reports. Thus, his *Geography* is a synthesis of information and cartographic traditions emanating from Islamic and European cultures. For sheer volume and detail of description, it is unsurpassed as a medieval text both in narrative geography and cartography. The approach is eclectic and occasionally anachronistic; Ptolemy's influence is felt and acknowledged, but there are also contemporary data, independent research, and innovative thinking. Al-Idrīsī's work sometimes has been judged unoriginal, but he used a new type of projection that is still not fully understood and he introduced a new type of map that strongly affected later cosmographers and thinkers like Ibn Khaldun. It is possible that European Mediterranean cartographers of the fourteenth century had some familiarity with his maps.

Al-Idrīsī produced more regional maps of the world than any other medieval cartographer, and his description of certain regions remote from Sicily, such as the Balkans or northern Europe, is remarkably precise. His information on Africa, although sometimes confused, remained an important source for Islamic and, later, European cosmographers into the seventeenth century. In the Islamic academic tradition, al-Idrīsī's impact was mostly limited to the descriptive genre; his cartography and his narrative method followed a new, distinctive pattern, and therefore it is possible to identify later imitations as works in the manner of the "Idrīsī school." In Europe, his work may have been the only Islamic universal geography known before the mid-sixteenth century. It became the first secular Arabic work printed in Europe (Rome, 1592), and a Latin translation was published in 1619 in Paris.

Al-Idrīsī credited his patron Roger with commissioning the collection of scientific data and the construction of a large map of the world; the work, however, was done by al-Idrīsī. The map was engraved on a silver disk, taking the form of a planisphere, although some have interpreted the description to mean a relief map. The accompanying text describes the work in detail. This world map was supposed to follow that of Marinus and its later, Arabic version created under the caliph al-Ma'mūn (813–833), since lost. The silver prototype was also lost, but the text was accompanied by a round, schematic map of the world and seventy detailed, colored, rectangular maps of the seventy parts into which al-Idrīsī had divided the world. Ten manuscripts of *Nuzhat al-mushtāq* survive, eight of them with maps; there is no complete good translation.

Al-Idrīsī's geographical system was built on a Ptolemaic foundation, adopted by the early Islamic scholars, whereby the round earth is divided into quarters and only the inhabited quarter is described. It is astronomically divided into seven latitudinal belts, called "climates," between the extreme north and equatorial south. Although familiar with coordinates, al-Idrīsī did not use them; in addition to the parallel boundaries of the climates, he introduced, instead of meridians, ten longitudinal divisions. Thus, the map with its corresponding narrative was divided into seventy sections.

Climates are numbered from south to north, with sections numbered west to east, both signs of Greek influence. Following this arrangement, the text proceeds, after a brief general introduction, to delineate each climate and then list and describe its important geographical features by section: cities, mountains, rivers, seas, and islands, progressing eastward to the farthest reaches of Asia. Al-Idrīsī names only ten of his sources in the Introduction, and contemporary information is mixed indiscriminately with data collected from Greek, Latin, and earlier Islamic sources.

Each subsequent chapter begins with the description of the next climate to the north and its first section from the west. Peoples, trade goods, the environment, and regional curiosities are described. Within this wealth of detail, al-Idrīsī's book offers the largest number of toponyms since Ptolemy's *Geography*, written some 1,000 years earlier, and it considerably updates the geographical inventory found in earlier Arabic works. All locations get more or less equal attention, although chapters dealing with the northern climates provide less detail. Many of the locations al-Idrīsī identifies are described for the first time in geographical literature. The narrative is pieced together by following itineraries, and an element of measurement is introduced by travel distances expressed in miles (*mil*), *farsakh* units (3 miles), caravan stages (*marhala*), day marches, or days of sailing.

The earth is depicted as encircled by the Encircling Sea, al-Bahr al-Muhīt (the Greek Ocean). Africa extends eastward to form the southern coast of the Indian Ocean which, however, remains open at its eastern extreme. Several African locations, including the sources of the Nile, are placed south of the equator; the southern limit of the inhabited world is north of the equator in *Nuzhat al-mushtāq*, but south of the equator in the treatise called *Little Idrīsī*. The southern portion of the round world map is filled with the African landmass, which is not shown on sectional maps. The western limit is the prime meridian drawn through the westernmost part of Africa, but the Fortunate Isles in the Atlantic are included. The easternmost country is *Sīlā* (Korea), supposedly at 180 degrees. The northern limit is 64 degrees, practically coinciding with the Arctic (Polar) Circle. The maps are color-coded and demonstrate a thoughtful and somewhat artistic approach, but neither degrees nor itineraries are drawn on them, and their practical value is doubtful.

### BIBLIOGRAPHY

Ahmad, S. Maqbul. "Cartography of al-Sharīf al-Idrīsī." *A History of Cartography*. Ed. Harley-Woodward, 2:156–174. See Gen. Bib.

al-Idrīsī, Abū Abdallāh Muhammad. *Opus geographicum; sive, "Liber ad eorum delectationem qui terras peragrare studeant."* Ed. Enrico Cerulli et al. 9 vols. Naples: Istituto Universitario Orientale di Napoli, and Rome: Istituto Italiano per il Medio ed Estremo Oriente, 1970–1984.

Miller, Konrad. *Mappae Arabicae. Arabische Welt- und Landkarten.* 6 vols. Stuttgart: Miller, 1926–1927. Vols. 1 [2] and 6.

Tolmacheva, Marina. "The Medieval Arabic Geographers and the Beginnings of Modern Orientalism." *International Journal of Middle East Studies* 27 [2] (1995): 141–156.

*Marina A. Tolmacheva*

### SEE ALSO

African Trade; Caravans; Cartography, Arabic; Climate; Córdoba; Geography in Medieval Europe; Maps; *Mare Oceanum;* Muslim Travelers and Trade; *Oikoumene;* Ptolemy

## Almaligh

A key city (variant spellings include Amaliq, Almalik, Almalygh, Almalyq, Almalyk) on the route from the Mongol court to the Black Sea region. Known as the "Apple Orchard," this important city of the medieval Mongol Empire was located in the valley of the Ili River, southeast of Lake Balkash in Central Asia, along one of the major routes between the Mongol court at Karakorum and Samarkand. In the early fourteenth century, Almaligh was also a commercial station, where Italian merchants operated, and a Christian episcopal center for the conversion of the Mongols. In 1250 c.e., the il-khân Arghun celebrated his marriage for a month or so in the region of Almaligh, and in the late fourteenth century it

# A

was one of the sites destroyed by Tamerlane in his attempt to block the caravan routes from the Black Sea to China.

Almaligh is perhaps best known for its place in the tumultuous power struggle over the Central Asiatic khânate of Chaghatai, named for its founder, the second son of Chinggis Khân, who had established Mongol control over the Uighur country and Transoxiana on the death of his father in 1227. Chaghatai enjoyed great prestige among the Mongols, ruling until his death in 1242, but was known to be bitterly hostile to the Muslims within his territory. The Chaghatai khânate survived under the rule of his descendants until the death of Tamerlane in 1405.

Caught between the Mongols and Muslims were Western Christian missionaries and merchants. In 1333, Nicholas of Botras was named to succeed John of Monte Corvino as archbishop of Khanbaliq. He began his journey to the Mongol court, but was forced to halt in Almaligh in 1334. There, some of the twenty-six friars who accompanied him decided to stay with the Franciscan Richard of Burgundy, whom Pope Benedict XII appointed bishop of Almaligh in 1338. A church was built for Nicholas's companions by two Alan (Iranian nomadic) Christian courtiers of the il-khân, and one of the friars became the tutor for the khân's son, who was later baptized. However, an uprising of the Muslim subjects in Almaligh occurred in 1339, and several Christians were martyred, including Bishop Richard, a Genoese merchant called William of Modena, and another prominent Franciscan, Paschal of Vittoria, who had written letters in 1338 warning of the dangers of the troubles in Almaligh.

The violence of 1339 did not end the Western presence there. In 1340, John of Marignolli stopped on his way to China and was able to preach without restriction. He built a new church and reported baptizing new converts. However, by the 1360s, conditions had become very dangerous for Christians once again. The last report from the region came in 1362, when James of Florence was executed and two other friars were starved to death in prison. Almaligh thus represents much of the frustration of Western missionary efforts in Central Asia during the waning days of the Mongol Empire. Though there were no systematic anti-Christian efforts by local or regional rulers, anti-Christian feeling was always present among the Muslim inhabitants of the Mongol Empire and could erupt into violence at any time.

**BIBLIOGRAPHY**

Petech, Luciano. "Les Marchands italiens dans l'Empire Mongol." *Journal Asiatique* 201 (1962): 549–574.

Phillips, J.R.S. *The Medieval Expansion of Europe.* Oxford: Oxford UP, 1988.

de Rachewiltz, Igor. *Papal Envoys to the Great Khans.* Stanford: Stanford UP, 1971.

Richard, Jean. *La Papauté et les missions d'Orient au moyen âge (XIIIe–XVe siècle).* Collection de l'École Française de Rome 33. Rome: École Française de Rome, 1977.

Saunders, J.J. *The History of the Mongol Conquests.* London: Routledge, 1971.

Setton, Kenneth, ed. "Missions to the East in the Thirteenth and Fourteenth Centuries." In *History of the Crusades,* Vol. 5, Chap. 10. 2nd edition. Madison: U of Wisconsin P, 1985.

*Charles W. Connell*

**SEE ALSO**

Caravans; Chaghatai; Chaghatai Khânate; China; John of Marignolli; John of Monte Corvino; Karakorum; Khanbaliq; Merchants, Italian; Missionaries to China; Mongols; Samarkand; Tamerlane

# Amalfi

A small port in southern Italy that made significant contributions to European seafaring.

Clinging to a mountainous peninsula south of Naples, Amalfi owed its rise to geography. It lacked a good natural harbor, but in the early Middle Ages it could benefit from its location. Safely distant from the domination of the Carolingian Empire, which was centered in France and, later, Germany, Amalfi lay more or less on the boundary between East and West. And when the Arabs took Sicily from the Byzantines, a conquest completed in 878, Amalfi found itself conveniently close to the Islamic world.

Initially, Amalfi had been only a minor settlement, subordinate to Naples, which was under Byzantine influence. But by the early ninth century Amalfi had achieved independence, while retaining a loose but commercially useful Byzantine connection. By then, since their peninsula lacked arable land, the Amalfitans had taken to the sea. They also had connections with neighboring Salerno, the most stable of the Lombard principalities then dominating much of southern Italy. And now, in addition, Amalfi began trading with the Muslims.

Evidence for all of this comes from many sources. In the early Carolingian period, there are merely generalized references to the Amalfitans as seafarers and traders. By the late ninth century, however, Amalfitan merchants are specifically reported in Muslim North Africa, and in the tenth century we hear of them not only at Constantinople, but also in Muslim Egypt and Muslim Spain. In this period, no other "Western" port, not even Venice, had ships ranging so widely.

Legends of Amalfi's "invention" of the compass must be treated with skepticism; at best, Amalfi may have helped to popularize that instrument. Yet in several ways this city-state did prepare the ground for later Italian achievements at sea, and not only in relation to trans-Mediterranean contacts. Since Amalfi's harbor offered little protection, Amalfitan ships could not have been large. Yet they were said to be swift, and it is notable that they carried the lateen sails then coming into favor throughout the Mediterranean. So, too, Amalfi seems to have been advanced in maritime law: the surviving version of the *Tavola Amalfitana,* a maritime code, comes from the fourteenth century, but some sections are thought to date back to Amalfi's prime period.

The Norman conquests in southern Italy in the latter eleventh century presaged the end of Amalfitan independence. Amalfi managed to avoid surrender until 1131, but thereafter its citizens, as subjects of the Norman rulers, could no longer voyage at will. In the next century, they are mentioned only as grain merchants in southern Italy's province of Apulia. Their great period had come to an end.

**BIBLIOGRAPHY**
Citarella, Armand O. "The Relations of Amalfi with the Arab World before the Crusades." *Speculum* 42 (1967): 299–312.
Del Treppo, Mario, and Alfonso Leone. *Amalfi medioevale.* Naples: Giannini, 1977.
Kreutz, Barbara M. *Before the Normans: Southern Italy in the Ninth and Tenth Centuries.* Philadelphia: U of Pennsylvania P, 1991, Chap. 5.
———. "Ghost Ships and Phantom Cargoes: Reconstructing Early Amalfitan Trade." *Journal of Medieval History* 20 (1994): 347–357.

*Barbara M. Kreutz*

**SEE ALSO**
Byzantine Empire; Compass, Magnetic; Constantinople; Law, Maritime; Merchants, Italian; Venice

**Amazons**

A nation of warrior women located at the end of the known world. From the classical tradition of the Amazons, passed on, for example, in Trogus Pompeius's *Historiae Philippicae* (*c.* first century C.E.) by way of the *Historia adversus paganos libri VII* of the fifth-century Spanish historian Orosius (I.15), comes the idea of an autonomous community of women ruled by one or more queens and associated with the Scythians. The earliest accounts locate Amazonia in western Asia, as far west as Cappadocia and as far east as the Caspian Sea. The people took their name from *a-mazos,* "without breast"; this reflects the belief that the Amazons seared off the right breast in order to pull their bows further back and gain more power, an idea repeated in Isidore's *Etymologies* (IX.2.64). They were thought to be skilled at riding, hunting, and archery, and to reproduce as the result of periodic meetings with the men of neighboring regions. Accounts of their exploits highlight their bravery and their cruelty.

These classical traditions of the Amazons were widely adapted in the medieval period. They appear regularly in chronicles from the sixth through the twelfth century such as those of Jordanes and Otto of Freising. Amazons figure prominently in romances and epic cycles such as the French *Roman d'Eneas* and *Roman de Troie* and in Alexander literature (texts concerning the military and geographical adventures of the Macedonian ruler Alexander the Great) in many languages. Boccaccio's *Teseida* and Chaucer's *Knight's Tale* both begin with Theseus's return from his victory over the Amazons. In the work of encyclopedic authors such as Brunetto Latini, Thomas of Cantimpré, and Vincent of Beauvais, the Amazons form part of a panoply of monstrous races of the world. They are depicted alongside even more exotic peoples on the early *mappaemundi,* including the Henry of Mainz, Ebstorf, and Hereford maps, as well as on the Catalan Atlas.

Traditions concerning the Amazons multiplied quickly. A new name appeared for the Amazon homeland in some sources: *Femenie* (e.g., in the Prester John letter). Medieval authors also introduced new types of political organizations for the Amazons: a segregated dual community, where the women are closely associated with a nearby group of men, or an integrated nation ruled by women. A variety of stories developed about the fate of their male issue, whom they were believed to have killed, maimed for use as slaves, or exiled. In some of the maps the illustrators separated the Amazons from the

Amazons. *Secretz de la Nature.* New York, The Pierpont Morgan Library MS M. 461, fol. 55, 1460. Courtesy of The Pierpont Morgan Library.

traditional monstrous races of India, Africa, and the antipodes by keeping them in their traditional location in Asia, but in others they occupied a more northerly clime. The same geographical variation appears in the written sources: Adam of Bremen, for example, places the land of the Amazons in Scandinavia.

Travel writers and illustrators set the Amazons apart morally as well as geographically from most other monstrous races among whom they were frequently found in medieval encyclopedias. Typically, the Amazons were grouped with such benevolent and wise races as the Gymnosophisti and Bragmanni, and a Talmudic legend makes them—like the Bragmanni—teach Alexander the Great wisdom; he leaves their land saying that he was a fool until instructed by women. Picture cycles from Alexander's adventures show them clothed and fighting with swords, shields, spears, and other chivalric weapons; in the *Secretz de la Nature* (1460), they wear elegant Burgundian costume and are treated with admiration by the artist. Their purported geographical and cultural proximity to Europe attracted the attention of

writers, who used them as exempla to illustrate Christian moral truths. Thus, according to Jacques de Vitry in his *Historia Orientalis,* their military prowess was attributable to their chastity: "since so much bodily energy is consumed in frequent copulation, so all the more rarely do they conjoin with their mates; in such a way are these female warriors stronger and greatly suited to fighting." The twelfth-century abbot Peter the Venerable paired the Amazon Penthesilea (a legendary queen who fought at Troy and was killed by Achilles) with Deborah as positive classical and Old Testament models, and the *Letter of Prester John* claimed they were prepared to fight on behalf of Christendom. This idea is also developed in Thomas of Cantimpré's account of them; an illuminated manuscript of his work depicts aristocratic Amazons in armor (Valenciennes, Bibliothèque Municipale MS 320, fol. 44r) next to the Gymnosophisti. Indeed, according to Johannes Witte de Hese's *Itinerarius,* the Amazon community is fully Christian, marrying their mates and attending mass. The *Book of John Mandeville* has the queen of the Amazons guarding the enclosed nations of Gog and Magog to keep them from erupting into Christendom.

The positive connotations of the term "Amazon" extended to its use as an honorific. Several prominent medieval women, such as Isabel de Conches-Toesny as described by Orderic Vitalis and Constance of France as described by Andrew of Fleury, were likened to Amazons because of their decisiveness of character or their participation in battle.

**BIBLIOGRAPHY**

DiMarco, Vincent. "The Amazons and the End of the World." In *Discovering New Worlds.* Ed. Scott D. Westrem, pp. 69–90. See Gen. Bib.

Friedman, John B. *The Monstrous Races in Medieval Art and Thought.* Cambridge, MA: Harvard UP, 1981; rpt. New York: Syracuse UP, 2000.

Petit, Aimé. "Le traitement courtois du thème des Amazones d'après trois romans antiques: *Enéas, Troie,* et *Alexandre." Le Moyen Age* 89 (1983): 63–84.

Salvat, Michel. "Amazonia: Le Royaume de Femmenie." In *La Réprésentation de l'antiquité au Moyen Age: Actes du colloque des 26, 27, et 28,* ed. Danielle Buschinger and André Crepin. *Université de Picardie. Centre d'études médiévales.* Vienna: Karl M. Halosar, 1982, pp. 229–241.

Wallach, Luitpold. "Alexander the Great and the Indian Gymnosophists in Hebrew Tradition." *Proceedings of the American Academy for Jewish Research* 11 (1941): 51, 54, 58.

*Adam Kosto*

## Ambassadors

Envoys, couriers (*nuncii*), or procurators and legates
who relayed messages between rulers and polities.
Though envoys had no power beyond their authority
to deliver the information with which they had
been entrusted, procurators or legates (*procuratores,
legati*) were invested with *plena potestas,* or what would
come to be called plenipotentiary powers, to transact
business on behalf of their authorizing party, or principal, a status derived from the traditions of Roman
civil law.

The authority to dispatch emissaries empowered in
either or both capacities was not initially limited to
sovereign states in the Middle Ages. Indeed, much of
the precedent for conducting diplomacy in the Christian West was set by the Roman pontiffs, who,
throughout the Middle Ages, dispatched clerics of
varying ranks to convert heathen peoples and represent
the pope at various ecclesiastical councils and foreign
courts as *missi, legati apostolicae sedis,* and semi-resident
*apocrisiarii.* Byzantine emperors made extensive use of
diplomatic envoys as negotiators and sources of information from late antiquity until the fall of Constantinople (1453). Umayyad, Abbasid, and Fatimid
caliphs, together with Seljuk, Mamluk, and Ottoman
emirs and sultans, utilized emissaries in a similarly flexible manner, showing particular interest in the commercial affairs of their neighbors.

The role of diplomatic envoys in the conduct of
relations between Western European territorial states
and civic polities, by contrast, took increasingly complex forms between 500 and 1500. European narrative
sources for the period between 500 and 1100, such as
the *Royal Frankish Annals* (compiled 787–831), indicate that Anglo-Saxon, Viking, Merovingian, and Carolingian rulers of Western and Eastern Europe initially
employed envoys primarily as couriers alone, reserving
the settlement of matters requiring negotiations for
personal meetings between principals or high-ranking
representatives. Legal sources from this early period,

King Clotharius II receiving Lombard ambassadors. *Grandes
Chroniques de France*, Paris, Bibliothèque Nationale MS fr.
2608, fol. 77, *c.* 1400. Courtesy of the Bibliothèque Nationale.

such as the Burgundian *Lex Gundobada* (524–532),
indicate that such representatives enjoyed a privileged
status as travelers in the West.

Between 900 and 1300, the commercial and territorial expansion of Western Europe led secular powers to
rely increasingly upon diplomatic emissaries with procu-
ratorial authority to negotiate settlements with foreign
governments and advocate for compatriots abroad. In
contrast to the Byzantine emperors, who restricted diplomatic appointments to high nobility, Western European,
Mongol, and Muslim powers also dispatched lower-
ranking clerics and nobles trained in Roman and canon
or Islamic law, as well as merchants (particularly Italians)
with a specialized knowledge of their destination.

The rise of the European territorial state led to increasingly precise distinctions among the powers, privileges,

and grades of diplomatic emissaries in the West between 1300 and 1500. It is during this period that the term *ambaxator* may first be noted in Italian archival sources as a designation for representatives of foreign polities as distinct from the procurators who acted for private citizens. By the mid-fifteenth century, the service of diplomatic envoys dispatched to treat specific matters was complemented by the representation of resident ambassadors, who transacted daily business with a foreign power while furnishing current information concerning the disposition of foreign affairs to their authorizing government. The Byzantine emperor Manuel II (1391–1425) is credited with having dispatched the earliest of these ambassadors to the court of the Ottoman ruler Mehmed I (1413–1421). Resident embassies were thereafter established in and by the Italian republics of Florence, Venice, and Milan, and were found throughout the rest of Europe by the beginning of the early modern period.

The wealth of sources for medieval diplomacy dramatizes the wide implications of the ambassador's evolving role in politics, administration, law, and cultural imagination during the Middle Ages. The actions and mentality of those who served as foreign emissaries constructs the context for much medieval narrative, composed as it was primarily by Byzantine, Muslim, and Western European authors with diplomatic experience. The *Relatio de legatione Constantinopolitana* of Liudprand of Cremona (920–972); the *Historia Mongalorum* of John of Plano Carpini (1247); and the *Mémoires* of Philippe de Commynes (1447–1511) offer valuable first-person accounts of individual diplomatic missions. Ambassadors also figure in works of fiction, hagiography, and art. Prescriptive texts such as the *De administrando imperio* of the Byzantine emperor Constantine VII Porphyrogenitus (913–959), the *Speculum judiciale* of the legist William Durand (1237–1296), and the *Ambaxiator breviloquus* of Bernard du Rosier (1436) document the evolution of the ambassador's office in law and ideal. Treaties, letters of introduction or credence (*litterae credentie*) and instruction, safe-conducts, embassy dispatches, the financial records of medieval Europe's sovereign polities, and the deliberations of their governing councils, preserved in the state and municipal archives of Europe, correct and complement contemporary literary testimony, simultaneously documenting the development of medieval international relations, the individuals who conducted them, and the burgeoning institutions of government by which they were administered.

BIBLIOGRAPHY

Commynes, Philippe de. *Mémoires.* Ed. Joseph Calmette. 3 vols. Paris: H. Champion, 1924–1925.

Cuttino, G.P. *English Diplomatic Administration, 1259–1339.* Oxford: Clarendon Press, 1971.

Ganshof, François L. *The Middle Ages: A History of International Relations.* Trans. Remy Inglis Hale. New York: Harper and Row, 1968.

Hrabar, Vladimir E. *De legatis et legationibus tractatus varii.* Dorpat: Mattieson, 1906.

Queller, Donald E. *The Office of Ambassador in the Middle Ages.* Princeton, NJ: Princeton UP, 1967.

Shepard, Jonathan, and Simon Franklin, eds. *Byzantine Diplomacy: Papers from the Twenty-Fourth Spring Symposium of Byzantine Studies, Cambridge, Massachusetts, March, 1990.* London: Ashgate, 1992.

*Emily Sohmer Tai*

SEE ALSO

Byzantine Empire; Commynes, Philippe de; Diplomacy; Fātimids; John of Plano Carpini; Liudprand of Cremona; Merchants, Italian; Mongols; Ottoman Empire; Popes; Seljuk Turks; Venice; Viking Age

## Americas, Indians and the
*See* Indians and the Americas

## Andrew of Longjumeau (c. 1200–c. 1270)

Dominican linguist, missionary, and envoy to schismatic Christians, Muslims, and Mongols. After joining the recently established Order of Preachers, Andrew studied Eastern languages in order to be better able to convert Eastern infidels. He was selected by King Louis IX (1226–1270) to go to Constantinople in 1238 to accompany a major relic, the Crown of Thorns, on its trip to France. Around 1244, Andrew was chosen by Pope Innocent IV (1243–1254) to lead a mission to dissident Christian groups in the Middle East. Leaders of the Jacobite and Nestorian Christians sent back letters of submission; these schismatic Christians accepted the pope's appeal for Christian unity, since they were caught between the hostile Muslims and unpredictable Mongols. Andrew reported back to Innocent IV in Lyons in June of 1247; the dissident Christian letters of submission, as well as letters from Muslim sultans in Syria, are entered in the Pontifical Register between papal bulls dated June 4 and June 17 of 1247. While it is not clear whether Andrew personally met with Eljigidei, the leader of the Mongol forces in the Middle East, he did pass along papal letters to a Mongol army detachment near Tabriz. Nevertheless, Andrew's contacts and letters from his embassy in the Middle East brought back useful information to the Pope and the Christian West; parts of his report on the Mongols have been preserved in Matthew Paris's *Chronica Majora*.

Shortly thereafter, Andrew was again associated with a Mongol mission, accompanying King Louis IX's crusade to the Middle East as an interpreter. He was on Cyprus with Louis IX when two Mongol envoys named David and Mark arrived in December of 1248. Andrew recognized David from his earlier meeting with the Mongols near Tabriz. These envoys carried a letter from the Mongol general Eljigidei, now commander of all the Mongols forces in western Asia. Andrew translated this letter from the Persian for the French king; the authenticity of this letter has been questioned since only the Latin version in the papal register has survived. Eljigidei offered his protection to all Christian groups in the Middle East, and he offered Louis IX an alliance against the Muslims, their common enemy. The letter also refers to an oral message that the two Mongol envoys carried to Louis IX: they told the French king that both Eljigidei and Güyük Khân had been baptized as Christians, and that they intended to help the Western Crusaders free Jerusalem. Scholars are not sure if the two envoys made up these stories or whether they had been ordered to tell them by the clever Eljigidei. Part of this story was somewhat confirmed by reports from independent Armenian sources, which also stressed the influence of high-ranking Christians at the Mongol court.

King Louis IX and the papal legate immediately wrote letters to Eljigidei and Güyük to acknowledge their conversions and to commend their support for Christians. Andrew was selected to lead the French embassy that carried letters and presents to the khân and to accompany the Mongol envoys back to Eljigidei's camp; his previous meeting with the Mongols near Tabriz and his knowledge of Eastern languages made him the obvious choice. Scholars assume Andrew also carried an oral message from Louis IX to Eljigidei concerning the proposed Mongol-Frankish military alliance. This mission left Cyprus in late January of 1249 and reached Eljigidei's encampment near Tabriz in the spring. The reception of this Frankish mission was not, however, what they had expected. Major changes had occurred in the Mongol world between the departure of David and Mark and the

arrival of Andrew's embassy. The Great Khân Güyük had died, and there was a major power struggle at the Mongol court. The line of Tolui (Chinggis's youngest son), supported by Batu, khân of the powerful Golden Horde in Russia, was in the process of outmaneuvering the line of Ögödei, led by Güyük's widow, the official regent until the next election. As an appointee of Güyük, Eljigidei realized he was in a very precarious position, so he sent Andrew and his mission directly to the Mongol court. The regent acknowledged the Frankish envoys bearing gifts as a sign of homage from a vassal—that is, of the formal submission of the Christian West to Mongol authority—in order to strengthen her position in the courtly power struggle. Her letter to Louis IX contained the usual Mongol formula for a vassal ruler and threatened punishment if he did not obey. There was no mention of conversions to Christianity nor of the Mongol-Frankish military alliance. Unfortunately, Andrew's account of his travels across Central Asia and the arrival and events of his embassy in the regent's camp in early 1250 have been lost.

Andrew and his companions reported back to Louis IX in Caesarea in Palestine in March/April of 1251. Andrew's account of the embassy's reception and the tone of the regent's letter shocked Louis IX, for the letter clearly referred to Frankish subservience to Mongol rule; Louis IX said that he deeply regretted ever having sent the embassy. Still, despite not fulfilling its immediate objectives, Andrew's mission did achieve other noteworthy results. Not only was it the second Western diplomatic mission that traveled to and from the heart of Mongol Central Asia (after John of Plano Carpini, but before William of Rubruck), but it confirmed the influence of high-ranking Christians at the Mongol royal court, and it was the first positive response from the West to the idea of a Mongol-Christian alliance against the Muslims in the Middle East.

Despite the questionable success of his earlier missions, Andrew was not deterred from his individual commitment to convert infidels to Christianity. He returned to the West with Louis IX and was soon involved in the Dominican mission in Tunisia. He eventually returned to France but, because of his advanced age, did not accompany Louis on his crusade to Tunisia in 1270. The exact date and year of his death are not known. Andrew's linguistic skills (he undoubtedly knew Arabic, Syriac, and Persian) attest to his intelligence and missionary dedication, and his ongoing friendship with King Louis IX, later canonized Saint Louis, suggests

# A

virtue and integrity as well. As one of the earliest envoys to the Mongols, Andrew and his embassies were known to and mentioned by William of Rubruck, Salimbene, and Vincent of Beauvais, among others.

**BIBLIOGRAPHY**

Altaner, Berthold. *Die Dominikanermissionen des 13. Jahrhunderts.* Habelschwerdt: Franke, 1924, pp. 52–58, 128–137.

Guzman, Gregory G. "Simon of Saint-Quentin and the Dominican Mission to the Mongol Baiju: A Reappraisal." *Speculum* 46 (1971): 232–249.

Kaeppeli, Thomas. *Scriptores ordinis praedicatorum medii aevi.* Rome: S. Sabina, 1970, 1:70.

Matthew Paris. *Chronica Majora.* In *Rerum Britannicarum Medii Aevi Scriptores.* Ed. H.R. Luard. London, 1872–1873, 57 (in seven parts). [This account has been translated into English by J.A. Giles under the title *Matthew Paris's English History.* London 1852–1854, 3 vols; rpt. Millwood, NY: Kraus Reprint. See 57, pt. IV, 76–78 (Giles 1:312–314), 109–112 (Giles 1:338–342), and 337–339 (Giles 1:522–523); pt. V, 37–38 (Giles 2: 280) and 80 (Giles 2:314); and pt. VI, 113–115 and 163–165 No. 84 (Giles 3:419–420).]

*The Mission of Friar William of Rubruck: His Journey to the Court of the Great Khan Möngke 1253–1255.* Trans. Peter Jackson, with notes and introduction by Peter Jackson and David Morgan. Hakluyt Society, 2nd series, 173, pp. 32–39. London: Hakluyt Society, 1990.

Pelliot, Paul. "Les Mongols et la papauté." *Revue de l'Orient chrétien* 23 (1922–1923): 3–30; 24 (1924–1925): 225–335; and 28 (1931–1932): 3–84.

de Rachewiltz, Igor. *Papal Envoys to the Great Khans.* Stanford: Stanford UP, 1971, pp. 112–115, 119–124.

Rastoul, Armand. "André de Longjumeau." In *Dictionnaire d'histoire et de géographie ecclésiastiques.* Paris: L. Letouzey, 1914, 2:1677–1681.

*Les Registres d'Innocent IV.* Ed. E. Berger. Paris: E. Thorin, 1884, 1: nos. 3031–3039.

Saunders, J.J. "Matthew Paris and the Mongols." In *Essays in Medieval History Presented to Bertie Wilkinson.* Ed. T.A. Sandquist and M.R. Powicke, pp. 116–132. Toronto: U of Toronto P, 1969.

Vincent of Beauvais. *Speculum quadruplex: naturale, doctrinale, morale, historiale.* 4 vols. Douai, 1624; rpt. Graz: Akademische Druck-u. Verlag, 1964–1965. 4: Bk. 29, Chap. 70; and Bk. 31, Chaps. 89–94.

*Gregory G. Guzman*

**SEE ALSO**

Ambassadors; Diplomacy; Dominican Friars; Eastern Christianity; Inner Asian Trade; Inner Asian Travel; Innocent IV; John of Plano Carpini; Louis IX; Matthew Paris; Mongols; Nestorianism; Vincent of Beauvais; William of Rubruck

## Andrew, Son of Guido of Perugia (d. *c.* 1332)

A Franciscan friar and lector of theology, early missionary to China, and third bishop of Zaiton. Andrew was one of seven suffragan bishops sent by Pope Clement V to Peking in 1307 at the request of John of Monte Corvino, the founder of the Chinese mission. These Franciscans form an historical link between William of Rubruck's earlier Mongol mission in 1253–1255 and the later Jesuit missionary activities of the sixteenth and seventeenth centuries.

Andrew, the highest-ranking member of the mission, and his group most likely took the sea route through Ormuz in the Persian Gulf to arrive in India. It was probably during their sojourn there that three bishops—Andrutius of Assisi, Nicholas of Bonzia, and Ulrich of Seydrisdorf—died due to the extreme heat. A fourth member, William of Villeneuve, apparently returned to Italy. Only Andrew, Gerard Albuini, and Peregrine of Castello reached their assigned goal, arriving at the Mongol capital of Khanbaliq (modern-day Beijing) around 1308. They consecrated John of Monte Corvino archbishop of the East, as ordered by Clement.

Andrew and the others remained at Khanbaliq for almost five years. During that period, another mission was established at Zaiton, where a rich Armenian woman endowed it with a great cathedral. In 1318, on the death of the first bishop, Gerard Albuini, Andrew was selected to be bishop of Zaiton. He refused the appointment, which then passed to Peregrine of Castello. Andrew's presence at the Zaiton mission during this period is attested by a letter of Peregrine's dated January 1318. Only on the death of Peregrine in 1322 did Andrew finally accept the see.

In January 1326, Andrew wrote from Zaiton to his superiors in the monastery at Perugia. His letter furnishes much of what is known about the medieval Christian church in China. In his missive, Andrew recalls the sufferings and difficulties faced on the initial voyage eastward. He relates how the missionaries had at first lived in Khanbaliq, thanks to the munificent support of the emperor, and describes the different types of people he encountered there. By 1318, four years before the death of Bishop Peregrine, Andrew had decided to transfer to Zaiton. There he was again accorded great honor and an annual allowance from the great khân estimated by Genoese merchants to be worth about 100 gold florins. Andrew used this sum to execute the former bishop's plans to construct a church and a small house for twenty-two religious in a grove outside the city. As bishop, he divided his time between the cathedral and the country retreat. The letter concludes with a comment on the coexistence of different religions within the empire, a fact that allowed the Franciscans to preach relatively unhindered.

When the medieval walls at Zaiton were torn down in 1938, Andrew's gravestone was discovered. In his letter of 1326, Andrew had described himself as white-haired and elderly, although still in good health. The damaged inscription combined with his own statement indicates that he must have died between 1330 and 1332. There appears to have been only one successor to Andrew, Jacob of Florence, who, together with Friar William of Campania, was martyred in 1362.

**BIBLIOGRAPHY**

Dawson, Christopher, ed. *The Mongol Mission.* See Gen. Bib.

Foster, John. "Crosses from the Walls of Zaitun." *Journal of the Royal Asiatic Society* (1954): 1–25.

Golubovich, P. Girolamo. *Biblioteca Bio-bibliografica della Terra Santa e dell'Oriente francescano.* Vol. 3. Florence: Quaracchi, 1906.

Moule, A.C. *Christians in China before the Year 1550.* London: SPCK, 1930.

Wadding, Luke, ed. *Annales Minorum seu Trium ordinum a S. Francisco Institutorum.* Rev. edition. P. Bonaventure Marrani. Vols. 6 and 7. Florence: Quaracchi, 1931.

Yule-Cordier. *Cathay and the Way Thither.* See Gen. Bib.

*Gloria Allaire*

**SEE ALSO**

John of Monte Corvino; Khanbaliq; Missionaries to China; William of Rubruck; Zaiton

## Anglo-Saxon Map

*See* Cotton World Map

## Animals, Exotic

Animals not indigenous to Europe, but known to medieval Europeans through bestiaries, natural history compendia, noble menageries, and the reports of travelers.

The authority of tradition frequently played a more important role than firsthand observation when it came to describing, classifying, and depicting (in words or art) exotic animals. The main sources for bestiaries and compendia included Aristotle's *Historia animalium* (fourth century B.C.E.), Pliny's *Historia Naturalis* (first century C.E.), the *Physiologus* (fourth century), and Isidore's *Etymologies* (seventh century). In medieval texts, exotic animals, by evoking a host of associations with the remote and the marvelous, frequently function as metonyms for the "East."

Medieval Europeans who traveled to the Muslim world and to Byzantium could see exotic animals both in the wild and in menageries; Byzantine emperors traditionally kept rare animals at Constantinople. In Muslim Spain, Abderrahman III (912–961) established a garden at Zahra (outside of Córdoba) in which he kept exotic animals. This is considered to be the first zoological garden in Europe. Holy Roman Emperor Frederick II (1212–1250) kept a famous zoo at his court at Palermo.

Henry I of England (1100–1135) kept lions, leopards, and camels at his Woodstock menagerie; Henry III of England (1216–1272) kept lions, leopards, and other animals in the Tower menagerie. Edward III (1327–1377) also possessed a number of exotic animals. Both William of Malmesbury and Alexander Neckham note that sovereigns often gave exotic animals as lavish gifts; in fact, Frederick II gave Henry III a camel, and Louis IX of France (1226–1270) presented him with an elephant.

Apes and crocodiles were among the animals that exercised a special fascination. The ape (Latin *simia*) of medieval Western European literature is most likely the

Crocodile. Bestiary, Oxford, Bodleian Library MS Douce 88, fol. 96v, 13th century. Courtesy of the Bodleian Library, Oxford.

# A

tailless Barbary ape of the African coast, or in some cases, the tailed ape of tropical Africa. The marmoset is mentioned in English customs records. Baboons were probably also known in medieval England. The two species of baboon that medieval Europeans are most likely to have been acquainted with are the *Hamadryas,* native to Arabia and Ethiopia, and the *Gelada B.,* native to Ethiopia.

The crocodile (Latin *crocodilus;* OF *cocodrille;* ME *cocodrille*) could have been either the fresh-water crocodile of the Nile valley or the saltwater crocodile of India. Mandeville says crocodiles are found in Sille [Cille]: a kind of "serpens" with four feet, short legs, and two enormous eyes; when they eat the flesh of men, they weep. He adds that the king of Silha (Ceylon) permits the poor people of his country to retrieve precious stones in a lake formed by the tears of Adam and Eve; they rub themselves with lemon juice just to keep the monsters away. One fifteenth-century traveler, John Poloner, says that the Nile "breeds . . . crocodiles innumerable, which are shaped like lizards, having four feet, thick short legs, sharp claws like a bear, and a head like a lizard." Arnold von Harff (who went on a pilgrimage from 1496 to 1499) draws a crocodile, and comments on the great strength of its tail—and on the fact that, "having no fundament, it is forced to eject what remains out its mouth."

Through a curious chain of lexical confusions, the *cockatrice* (Latin *calcatrix;* Greek *ichneumon*), described by Pliny as the enemy of the crocodile, became identified with the fabulous basilisk (Latin *basiliscus* or *regulus*), and then with the crocodile itself. After the fourteenth century, it is not always clear what is meant by the words *basilisk* (ME and OF *basilicoc*), *cockatrice,* and *crocodile.* There are numerous depictions of the crocodile in medieval European art; often they are seen devouring humans or graphically symbolizing the mouth of hell.

The hippopotamus, native to central and southern Africa, was found on the banks of the Nile. *The Book of John Mandeville* says (after Vincent of Beauvais) that the man-eating hippopotamus, half man and half horse, is found in Bactria (the northern part of modern Afghanistan); John of Trevisa gives its home as Egypt, while Alexander Neckam classifies it as a fish. The poet of *Kyng Alisaunder* (*c.* 1300), following Pliny, depicts it as a huge, man-eating creature with tusks like a boar's.

As is the case with other exotic animals, one must wonder what the word "tiger" meant to a medieval Western European audience; often, depictions of the lion were substituted for it in manuscript illumination. A fourteenth-century English knight, John of Norwich, added a tiger to his coat of arms, but it looks more like a lion with a moustache to modern eyes.

Reports of the existence of the one-horned Indian rhinoceros are commonly thought to have contributed to the legend of the unicorn (which undoubtedly drew as well on accounts of the African oryx, a species of antelope, and the narwhal). Marco Polo accurately describes a rhinoceros, and sadly concludes that this "unicorn," wallowing in the mud as it does, is nothing like the fabulous beast of legend.

Of all the animals known to Europeans, perhaps the one that was considered most desirable for display was the giraffe. The species of giraffe most likely known to medieval Europeans was the *Giraffa reticulata* of northeast Africa. However, because of the common European confusion of Ethiopia and India, the animal was generally thought to live in India. Throughout the Middle Ages, Western Europeans would have had to visit one of the famous Byzantine or Muslim zoos to see a giraffe, but a small number of these beasts apparently were brought to southern Europe, usually in the form of East-West royal gifts. Vincent of Beauvais says that the "Sultan of Babylon" presented an *orasius,* or giraffe, to Frederick II (1212–1250), and the Mamluk Sultan Baybars I (1260–1277) sent a giraffe to Manfred, king of Naples and Sicily (*c.* 1232–1266). The desire to possess a giraffe consumed Anne de Beaujeu, the daughter of French King Louis XI (d. 1483), who also had a passion for collecting animals. In 1489, she wrote Lorenzo di Medici, reproaching him for breaking his promise to send her as a gift the giraffe presented to him by al-Ashraf Kait (1468–1496), the Mamluk sultan of Egypt. Lorenzo apparently kept his giraffe.

Perhaps because the giraffe was not a part of medieval Western European bestiaries (Aristotle, an important source for the bestiary, never mentions it), it remained a mysterious creature, and went by a variety of names in different encyclopedias. When ancient writers do mention the giraffe, they usually compare its body parts to those of other, better-known animals such as the horse, camel, sheep, deer, lion, and leopard. This tradition of description-by-analogy continued into the Middle Ages.

Pliny (*c.* 23–79 C.E.) and late antique writers refer to the giraffe as *camelopardus,* a term that enters the medieval lexicon through Solinus (fl. 230/240) and

Isidore of Seville (*c.* 560–636). Jerome translates the Hebrew word for one of the "clean" animals of Deuteronomy 14:5 as *camelopardalum*. John Wycliffe, in translating this passage in the later 1300s, uses the word *camelion;* a compound apparently based on the analogy of *camelopardus.* He inserts a gloss for those unfamilar with the beast: "that is, a beast like a camel in the head, in the body like a panther, and in the neck like a horse, in the feet like a water buffalo and a small panther."

As Western Europeans began to have more direct contact with Muslim culture, they borrowed the Arabic word for giraffe, *zarafa,* adapted in OF and ME as *orafle.* Albertus Magnus (1200–1280) gives *Seraph* as the giraffe's Arabic name, and Vincent of Beauvais (1190–1264) refers to the giraffe as *Anabulla, camelopardus,* and *Orasius* in three different chapters of the *Speculum naturale,* apparently without realizing that these names denoted the same animal. (He also observes that the giraffe, once it becomes aware of people looking at it, turns completely around so that it can be admired from every angle.) In 1336, William of Boldensele, describing a recent visit to Cairo, reports having seen there an "animal of India" named "Jeraffa," whose neck is so long it could eat from the roof of a normal-sized house. The author of *The Book of John Mandeville* rather uncharacteristically does *not* appropriate William's remarks, although near the end of his account he locates giraffes in India. The fourteenth-century English translation of Mandeville's *Book* gives the first English reference to the giraffe (*orafles*), saying that its name in Arabic is *gerfauntz,* perhaps a compound coined through an analogy with Middle English *olifaunt,* elephant.

Cosmas Indikopleustes (*Christian Topography, c.* 547), Bernhard von Breydenbach (*Peregrinations into the Holy Land,* 1486), and Arnold von Harff (who went on pilgrimage from 1496 to 1499), provide illustrations of the giraffe. Cosmas writes: "in the palace [at Axum, in Ethiopia], they have one or two which they have tamed . . . When milk or water to drink is given to these creatures in a dish, as is done in the king's presence, they cannot reach the vessel . . . except by straddling with their forelegs, owing to the great length of their legs and height of the chest and neck above the ground." Marco Polo (*c.* 1295) seems quite impressed by the beauty of the giraffe (though it is not clear that he ever actually saw one). In his account written sometime after 1406, Ruy González de Clavijo, the Spanish ambassador to the court of Tamerlane (Timur), was astonished at the sight of the *Jornufa* (from Persian *surnapa*) presented to the ruler by a Mamluk embassy. Pero Tafur (*Travels and Adventures, c.* 1435–1439) says that the giraffe has a neck "as long as a good-sized tower is high," adding that the one that he saw had been in Cairo for more than two hundred years.

**BIBLIOGRAPHY**

Boltz, William G. "Leonardo Olschki and Marco Polo's Asia (with an Etymological Excursus on *giraffe*)." *Romance Philology* 23 [1] (1969): 1–16.

Clavijo, Ruy González de. *Embassy to Tamerlane 1403–1406.* Trans. Guy Le Strange. New York and London: Harper, 1928.

Druce, George C. "The Symbolism of the Crocodile in the Middle Ages." *Archaeological Journal* 66 (1909): 311–338.

Janson, H.W. *Apes and Apelore in the Middle Ages and the Renaissance.* London: Warburg Institute, University of London, 1952.

Klingender, Francis D. *Animals in Art and Thought to the End of the Middle Ages.* Ed. Evelyn Antel and John Harthan. Cambridge, MA: MIT Press, 1971.

Laufer, Berthold. "The Giraffe in History and Art." Field Museum of Natural History, Anthropology Leaflet 27. Chicago, 1928.

Lloyd, Joan Barclay. *African Animals in Renaissance Art and Literature.* Oxford: Clarendon, 1971.

*Marco Polo: The Description of the World.* 2 vols. Ed. A.C. Moule and Paul Pelliot. London: G. Routledge, 1938; rpt. New York: AMS Press, 1976.

Rowland, Beryl. *Blind Beasts: Chaucer's Animal World.* Kent, OH: Kent State UP, 1971.

Tafur, Pero. *Pero Tafur: Travels and Adventures 1435–1439.* Trans. and ed. Malcolm Letts. London: Routledge, 1926.

Warmington, E.H. *The Commerce between the Roman Empire and India.* Cambridge, 1928; rpt. London: Curzon, 1974.

*Kathleen Coyne Kelly*

**SEE ALSO**

Albertus Magnus; Ambassadors; Barnacle Goose; Bartholomaeus Anglicus; Baybars I; Birds, Exotic; Breydenbach, Bernhard von; Camels; Cosmas Indikopleustes; Diplomacy; Elephants; Frederick II; Isidore of Seville; Louis IX; *Mandeville's Travels*; Pliny the Elder; Tamerlane; Trevisa, John; Vincent of Beauvais

## Anonymous of the Lower Rhine or of Cologne (*c.* 1345–1355)

The first author to write a geographical description of Asia in German.

# A

The anonymous author of this description of western and central Asia is associated with the Lower Rhine in part because he wrote in the Ripuarian dialect of that region; he also demonstrates some local knowledge of Cologne and Aachen. The author shows specific interest in the three "Magi ex oriente" recorded in the New Testament (Matthew 2:1–9; see also Psalms 71: 10–11). Medieval Europeans believed the Magi to be kings from Central Asia; their relics were venerated in the cathedral at Cologne following their celebrated translation there in 1164. Thus, the text's interest in the geographical origins of the Magi constitutes another reason to suppose it was written in Cologne, probably by a native of the city or its vicinity.

This author shows particular interest in the theological and liturgical similarities and differences between Roman and Eastern Christianity, but he also attentively describes the customs, the trading, the flora and the fauna of the Eastern region. Because the author wrote in German and not Latin, he is thought to have been a layman, perhaps a merchant, who was acquainted with a wide range of missionary texts and commercial records, including works by Thietmar, Jacques de Vitry, Hetoum, and the *Letter of Prester John.* He mentions his own experiences in Egypt (1338–1341), Tabriz (1340), Damascus (1341), and Armenia (before 1348). The work is not, however, the report of a journey, but a description of the conditions found in the Near East, not only in Jerusalem and Palestine, but also in the surrounding countries, including Egypt, Syria, Mesopotamia, Persia, and Mongolia. According to the New Testament (Acts 2:1–11), people from all over the world were "filled with the Holy Spirit" when they were gathered in Jerusalem on Pentecost. Medieval Europeans believed them to have carried the truth of Christianity to their native regions, and this idea is reflected in the author's attention to Christian inhabitants of India, Nubia, Tarsis, Syria, and Greece.

The story of the three kings was of continuing interest to medieval Europeans since, according to the *Annales Marbacenses,* written about 1238 and concerning the year 1222, the Mongol military movement westward had as one of its goals the recovery of the bones of the Magi from Cologne. The most influential account of the Magi story was John of Hildesheim's *Legend of the Holy Three Kings* (*Historia Trium Regum, c.* 1370), which derives much information from the text written by Anonymous of the Lower Rhine. Both books document a vivid European interest in Asian societies and, in particular, the Christians living at the edges of the earth.

**BIBLIOGRAPHY**

Röhricht, Reinhold, and H. Meisner, eds. "Ein niederrheinischer Bericht über den Orient." *Zeitschrift für Deutsche Philologie* 19 (1887): 1–86.

von den Brincken, Anna-Dorothee. *Die "Nationes Christianorum Orientalium" im Verständnis der lateinischen Historiographie von der Mitte des 12. bis in die zweite Hälfte des 14. Jahrhunderts.* Kölner Historische Abhandlungen 22. Köln/Wien: Böhlau, 1973.

von Hildesheim, Johannes. *Die Legende von den Heiligen Drei Königen.* Ed. Elisabeth Christern. München: Dt. Taschenbuchverlag 164, 1963.

*Anna-Dorothee von den Brincken*

**SEE ALSO**

Armenia; Damascus; Eastern Christianity; Edges of the World; Egypt; Hetoum; India; Jacques de Vitry; Jerusalem; Mongols; Prester John

## Antillia

A mythical Atlantic island often identified with the legendary Island of the Seven Cities. The name is a composite of *ante* (Latin and Portuguese) meaning "before" and *ilha* (Portuguese) meaning "island"—the island before, or opposite. The earliest appearance of the word and the island are on the Nautical Chart of 1424 now housed in the James Ford Bell Library at the University of Minnesota. It reflects the concept of an island or islands in the Atlantic west of the Canary Islands and the Azores, a location that undoubtedly resulted from Spanish, Portuguese, French, or Majorcan ships storm-driven beyond these islands in the fourteenth century. The association of Antillia with the Island of the Seven Cities legend came about in the fifteenth century with the appearance of Antillia on charts. The legend tells of the escape to sea by seven Portuguese bishops in the eighth century when Moslem invaders overran Portugal and Spain. In his globe of 1492, Martin Behaim perpetuates the legend by placing an island labeled Antillia in the Atlantic Ocean. Portuguese sources placed it some 200 leagues west of the Canary Islands and the Azores.

Antillia was significant to Columbus's first transatlantic voyage in that Paolo de Pozzo Toscanelli included the location of it in his letter to Columbus concerning his intended route. Toscanelli placed it at or near the Tropic of Cancer about thirty-five degrees west of the

Canary Islands, therefore along Columbus's proposed route to Japan. On fifteenth-century maps and charts, Antillia was usually grouped with three other islands bearing the names Satanazes, Saya, and Ymana, with variant spellings, and sometimes with islands named Toumar, Rosellia, Rollio, and Tammay, also with variant spellings. On Antillia itself are sometimes found seven place-names indicative of the Seven Cities legend. Despite the emergence on maps of the New World continents, the search for Antillia continued into the sixteenth century without any such island being found. The name, however, survives in "Antilles," the islands at the forefront of the American continents.

**BIBLIOGRAPHY**
Babcock, William H. "Antillia and the Antilles." Chap. 10 in *Legendary Islands of the Atlantic.* New York: American Geographical Society, 1922.
Cortesão, Armando. *The Nautical Chart of 1424.* Coimbra: U of Coimbra P, 1954.
Morison, Samuel Eliot. "Flyaway Islands and False Voyages, 1100–1492." Chap. 4 in *The European Discovery of America: The Northern Voyages, A.D. 500–1600.* New York: Oxford UP, 1971.

*John Parker*

**SEE ALSO**
Azores; Behaim, Martin; Canary Islands; Portuguese Expansion; Toscanelli, Paolo dal Pozzo

## Antipodes

Creatures who put the soles of their feet against our own, that is, those who live on the opposite ("anti") side of the globe; by extension, the territory they inhabit.

The existence of antipodean people, which testifies to early knowledge of the spherical shape of the earth, had been familiar to the Greek natural philosophers since Pythagoras (second half of the sixth century B.C.E.) or at least since Parmenides (fl. *c.* 480 B.C.E.). The term *antipode* was created by Plato (Timaeus 63 A: *antipous*), and it denotes the inhabitants of a place or region situated diametrically opposite to the user of the word (originally assumed to be an Athenian) on the southern hemisphere of the globe; in a broader sense it also stands for people living very far away, as well as those belonging to a different world.

If the world is conceived of as a disc, the idea of the antipodes leads to strange, even grotesque conceptions. Amused by that, Lactantius (*c.* 240–*c.* 320 C.E.), a baptized teacher of rhetoric at the court of Constantine I, composed a masterpiece of rhetorical entertainment in his *Institutiones* (III, 24) that has often been cited erroneously in order to demonstrate that a flat earth was part of Christian dogma, although Lactantius did not cite the Bible in his argument.

The theory of the antipodes is derived from the Stoic idea of the earth as a sphere divided into four symmetrical parts by two zones of ocean crossing each other at right angles; each quarter forms an island continent. For those living in the world of Asia, Europe, and Africa, only their *oikumenic* continent is accessible, inhabited, and known; the *perioikumenic* continent on the backside of the northern hemisphere has differing periods of daylight, whereas the *anteoikumenic* continent on the southern hemisphere has other seasons, and the *antichthonic* continent on the southern backside of the globe, which is the antipodal area in its restricted sense as shown on the map of Lambert of Saint-Omer, differs in daylight hours as well as in seasons.

Crates of Mallos (second century B.C.E.) refined (and, by constructing a large terrestrial globe, depicted) the theory of the antipodes in the Hellenistic world; Cicero demonstrates familiarity with the concept by

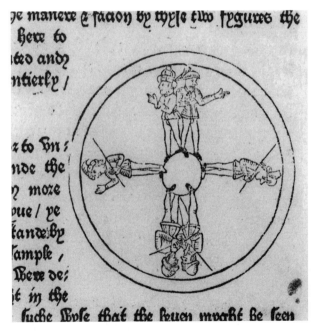

Two men going in opposite directions from Europe meet at the Antipodes. William Caxton, tr. *Mirrour of the World* (Westminster: Caxton, 1481) sig. D6r. Minneapolis, MN. By permission of the James Ford Bell Library, University of Minnesota.

# A

speaking of those "qui adversis vestigiis stant contra nostra vestigia"; and it was Macrobius (beginning of the fifth century), who eventually imparted the doctrine to the Latin West during the Middle Ages: his commentary on Cicero's *Somnium Scipionis* could be found in nearly every monastic or church library in medieval Europe.

Apart from Lactantius, who did not refer to the Bible, and the Nestorian Cosmas Indikopleustes (sixth century), who wrote in Greek and interpreted the universe as a tabernacle according to the Bible, early Christians approved the spherical shape of the earth, but they had difficulty accepting the idea of the antipodes. Saint Augustine considered the issue thoroughly (*De civitate Dei* 16.7–9): he was not concerned with the shape of the earth, but rather with the existence of human beings who did not derive from Adam or Noah living in some distant region of the earth and how their presence could be harmonized with the witness of the Book of Genesis. Augustine could find no reference to any antipodes in the Bible, and he argued that even deformed people were said to be descended from Noah and to take part in any blessing prepared for Noah's offspring. Thus, Augustine assumed that there could be only ocean on the reverse side of the globe.

These objections to the existence of antipodes did not prevent Isidore of Seville (*c.* 560–636) from introducing a fourth continent in addition to Asia, Europe, and Africa (*Etymologies* 14, 5, 17), inaccessible because of the heat of the sun, where he located remarkable antipodes. Pope Zacharias, in a letter to Saint Boniface (*c.* 748), criticized a certain Virgil, who suggested the existence of another world and other people under the earth, under the sun, and under the moon; but the original statement of this Virgil (possibly Virgil of Salzburg?) is lost. Nevertheless, all versions of the maps of Beatus of Liébana (after 776 C.E.) presented this fourth continent in accordance with Isidore, and characterized it as inaccessible and inhabited by fabulous antipodal creatures.

Lambert of Saint-Omer (*c.* 1112–1115), in his marvelously illustrated encyclopedia *Liber floridus,* offered among other maps a hemispheric world map based on Macrobius and Martianus Capella, which, oriented to the east, presented the inhabited world on the left and a note concerning the antecumenical part on the right. At the top, to the east of the inhabited world, we find the star-shaped Earthly Paradise, connected with Asia by the Four Rivers of Paradise; at the bottom of the map in the extreme west, there is an island understood to be on the reverse side of the hemisphere, which is accompanied by a legend identifying this as home to "the antipodes," who experience different daytime hours and seasons from people in the known world.

In his *Otia imperialia* (*c.* 1214), written for Emperor Otto IV, Gervase of Tilbury introduced an anecdote about a pig breeder in England who lost one of his pigs on a cold and stormy day (III, 45). By following it in the subterranean paths of a castle, he finally came to a pleasant place with lovely warm weather, where he found his pig with her progeny: obviously, this pig breeder had discovered the other side of the earth and crossed the interior of the globe by entering it at the edge of the known world, where it was not so far to travel to the unknown.

On the maps of the thirteenth century, this fabulous and unknown world is graphically represented by galleries of monsters, which are usually placed on the right side in southern Africa behind Ethiopia near the equator; examples include the London Psalter map, the Ebstorf map, and the Hereford map, on which appear a series of humanlike creatures with numerous defects and deformities: people without a face or mouth, with only one eye or with four eyes, with their eyes on their chest, with a dog's head, or backward-facing feet, or a gigantic foot used as sunshade, or six arms, or gigantic ears, or horns, or necks of cranes, and so forth. These creatures had already been described in antique fables, but now, in the Middle Ages, were presumed to inhabit specific, though little known, parts of the earth.

An important piece of evidence for a theory of the antipodes is the extremely popular and widespread record of the fantastic travels gathered in *The Book of John Mandeville,* in which the earth is described as round and circumnavigable; while there are people "who live under us, foot against foot [dessouz nous . . . pie contre pie]" in geographical opposition to Mandeville's European audience, they are not described as monstrous nor are they clearly part of the list of *"monstruosi populi"* Mandeville introduces in his description of East Asia.

Thus, in general, the term *antipodes* can refer to creatures who live far away and differ by strange behavior, but who nevertheless belong to the human race.

**BIBLIOGRAPHY**

Kauffmann, Georg. "Antipoden." In Pauly-Wissowa, *Realencyclopädie der classichen Altertumswissenschaft* 12 (1894), cols. 2531–2533. See Gen. Bib.

von den Brincken, Anna-Dorothee. *Fines Terrae. Die Enden der Erde und der vierte Kontinent auf mittelalterlichen*

*Weltkarten.* Schriften der Monumenta Germaniae Historica 36. Hanover: Hahn, 1992.

*Anna-Dorothee von den Brincken*

**SEE ALSO**

Beatus Maps; Climate; Cosmas Indikopleustes; Ebstorf Map; Four Rivers of Paradise; Geography in Medieval Europe; Gervase of Tilbury; Ham's Curse and Africans; Hereford Map; Isidore of Seville; *Liber Floridus; Mandeville's Travels;* Maps; Monstrosity, Geographical; *Oikoumene;* Psalter Map; Virgil of Salzburg, St.

## Antonine Itinerary [*Itinerarium provinciarum Antonini Augusti*]

A copious list of place-names and some 255 routes throughout the Roman world, including the *Imperatoris Antonini Augusti itinerarium maritinum,* a briefer listing of sea routes and islands. Though the *Itinerary* is named after one of the Antonine emperors of Rome who reigned between 138 and 222 C.E., specific attribution to Antoninus Pius or to Caracalla has been proposed but remains unproved. Indeed, several place-names suggest a date of origin not before Diocletian's administrative reforms in 280.

*Itineraria* in general supplied soldiers, government officials, and other travelers with information on staging-points, distances, and points of interest along the roads of the empire. The routes treated in the *Antonine Itinerary* stretched from Mauritania to Samosata on the Euphrates and went as far south as Hiera Sycaminos above Aswan on the Nile to points beyond Hadrian's Wall in Britain in the north. Gaul, Dacia, and much of Greece are given disproportionately brief treatment; fortunately for later historians and geographers, the accounts of Britain and the Italian peninsula are more thorough. Recording distances in Roman miles (*milia pedum*), except in Gaul where the native *leuga* is frequently used, the *Itinerary* covers nearly 53,000 total miles.

Because the text contains so many numerals, the document was especially susceptible to textual corruption by copyists. Nevertheless, since antiquity, the *Itinerary* has proven itself important for locating ancient sites and for tracing lost roadways. It was also employed by medieval cartographers, including the maker[s] of the Hereford *mappamundi.*

**BIBLIOGRAPHY**

Cuntz, Otto, ed. *Itineraria Romana.* Leipzig: Teubner, 1929.

Dilke, O.A.W. *Greek and Roman Maps.* Ithaca: Cornell UP, 1985.

Pauly-Wissowa. *Realencyclopädie der classichen Altertumswissenschaft.* 9.2308–9.2363, s.v. "Itinerarien." See Gen. Bib.

Rivet, A.L.F. "The British Section of the Antonine Itinerary." *Britannia* 1 (1970): 34–82.

*Roger T. Macfarlane*

**SEE ALSO**

Guido; Hereford Map; *Mappamundi;* Maps; Nicholas of Cusa

## Antonini Placentini Itinerarium ["Antoninus's Travel"]

A work written by an anonymous pilgrim from the northern Italian town of Piacenza in the second half of the sixth century. The author is also known as "Anonymous of Piacenza" or "The Pilgrim of Piacenza," or, probably wrongly, "Antonius Martyr." The erroneous identification of the author as Antoninus Placentinus is due to medieval copyists' misreading the first sentence in the work.

The tract exists in two versions. The first, of which there are two manuscripts, lacks many of the details given in the second, which survives in sixteen manuscripts, and is more smoothly written and longer. Until recently it was commonly believed that the second version is the original one, while the first is an abridgment or digest. Today it is thought that the first version is the original, or at least closer to the original, while the second is a reworked text, probably done in the Carolingian period (751–987). Based on various data in the text, the journey in question has been dated to around 570.

"Antoninus's Travel" is a first-person narrative describing a trip undertaken by a group, accompanied by a local guide. The pilgrim set out from Constantinople to Cyprus and thence to Syria; traveling south down the coast, he turned inland at Acre and proceeded to the holy places of Galilee. Reaching the Sea of Galilee, he then visited the holy sites around the lake and the sources of the Jordan. He next turned south to Bethshean and Samaria, traveling down the Jordan to the Place of the Baptism. He visited famous sites on both sides of the Jordan, as well as Jericho, before an extended stay at Jerusalem.

The description of Jerusalem, the most detailed part of the work, attests to the magnificence of the city after the completion of Justinian's construction projects. The traveler now made Jerusalem his point of departure for further trips. He went south to Bethlehem and Hebron, returned to Jerusalem and traveled to Sinai

# A

and Egypt; subsequently, he returned to Jerusalem for the third time and went north to Syria and Mesopotamia, whence he presumably set out on the return trip. The entire trip was obviously well planned in advance, taking the dates of feast-days and the liturgy of the holy sites into consideration.

The traveler from Piacenza was an ardent collector of wonders and miracles, and he untiringly lists the unique qualities of the sacred objects in the Holy Land and describes the various customs that the pilgrims practiced *pro benedictione* ("for a blessing"). He returned home with many souvenir objects with miraculous properties, mainly remedial. While particularly interested in the exotic, the traveler does not ignore the landscape or the inhabitants of the places through which he passes. In this respect the work departs from earlier itineraries, throwing light on the popular experience of Christian pilgrimage in late antiquity.

## BIBLIOGRAPHY

*Antonini Placentini Itinerarium.* In *Itineraria et alia Geographica.* Ed. P. Geyer. Corpus Christianorum: Series Latina 175. Turnholt: Brepols, 1965, pp. 127–174.

Gildemeister, Johann. *Antonini Placentini Itinerarium in unentstellten Text mit deutscher Übersetzung.* Berlin: H. Reuther, 1889.

Milani, Celestina. *Itinerarium Antonini Placentini. Un viagio in Terra Santa del 560–570 d.C.* Milan: Vita e Pensiero, 1977.

Wilkinson, John. *Jerusalem Pilgrims before the Crusades.* Jerusalem: Ariel Publishing House, 1977, pp. 79–89.

Ora Limor

SEE ALSO

Acre; Catherine in the Sinai, Monastery of St.; Constantinople; Holy Land; Jerusalem; Pilgrim Souvenirs; Pilgrimage, Christian


## Arab Navigation

*See* Navigation, Arab


## Arabic Cartography

*See* Cartography, Arabic


## Ararat, Mount

The biblical resting place of Noah's ark, according to some medieval writers. The legend of a great flood inundating much or all of the earth's surface appears in the "genesis" traditions of many different peoples. Such a story, for example, was already many centuries old and preserved in the Mesopotamian epic poem Gilgamesh (*c.* 2000 B.C.E.) when it was attached to Noah and included in the Hebrew Bible, which became, with the spread of Christianity, the most widely distributed version of the story.

According to Genesis 8:4, Noah's ark came to rest on the "mountains of Ararat," a toponym whose exact geographical location gave rise to much dispute. In post-biblical times the highest peak in the area, which lies between the Black and Caspian seas in what is now eastern Turkey, came to be called Mount Ararat. Great Ararat, a domed mountain with a peak 16,945 feet above sea level, was scaled only in very recent times. Though the *Book of John Mandeville* spoke of Ararat in Armenia, a seven-mile-high "hill called Ararat . . . where Noah's ship rested after the flood," there was some disagreement from the intertestamental and patristic periods onward as to what mountain was intended by Genesis 8. In his commentary on Isaiah, St. Jerome identified Ararat as the Armenian Mount Taurus, a view later held by Roger Bacon in the *Opus Maius.*

A variety of apocryphal traditions relating to Ararat also developed where the Garden of Eden was believed to be located in the valley of the Araxes and Noah's wife was said to be buried in the nearby city of Marand in what is now northwestern Iran. Noah himself was said to have planted the first vineyard at Arghuri, where a monastery to St. James was built. The monks believed that no one was permitted to reach the top of Ararat with its sacred remains. The monastery (destroyed by lightning in 776 C.E.) and a mosque were built there to commemorate the "relics" of the ark found in the area, according to Mandeville, when a monk "through the grace of God, went there and brought back a timber of the ship, which is still in an abbey at the foot of the mountain," though in keeping with the myth of inaccessibility, the monk was given the timber by God and never actually reached the peak in spite of repeated attempts.

The nature of the medieval debate on the location of Mount Ararat may perhaps best be characterized by the work of the great Jesuit biblical commentator Athanasius Kircher in his definitive *Arca Noe.* Published in 1675, this work detailed many of the disparate traditions about the mountain and applied a type of scientific analysis in scrutinizing them. He points out that since Ararat was a much lower mountain than some, such as those in the Taurus range, the waters would have had to subside by some fifteen cubits before the ark could have rested on Ararat, which it did, he concludes, for exactly seventy-seven days.

**BIBLIOGRAPHY**
Allen, Don Cameron. *The Legend of Noah.* Urbana: U of Illinois P, 1963.
Parrot, André. *The Flood and Noah's Ark.* Studies in Biblical Archaeology No. 1. New York: Philosophical Library, 1955.

*Jerome Mandel*

**SEE ALSO**
Armenia; Caspian Sea; *Mandeville's Travels;* Paradise, Travel to

## Arculf

A Merovingian bishop and traveler to the Byzantine Empire and the Holy Land, in about 680–683. The Venerable Bede, in his eighth-century *Ecclesiastical History* (V,15), relates that Arculf journeyed to the East, visiting the Holy Land and other regions, some in the Byzantine Empire and some under Muslim rulers. On his return to Gaul, his ship was carried by a storm to the west coast of England; after some adventures, he found refuge with Adamnan, abbot of Iona in the years 679–704 and author of the biography of Saint Columba. Adamnan heard the story of Arculf's travels and wrote it down. The resulting work, *De locis sanctis,* is based on Arculf's story, with the addition of certain information that Adamnan had acquired through his reading of earlier authors, such as Jerome and Eucherius. The gift of the finished work to King Aldfrith on his visit to the monastery presumably promoted its fame and distribution. It was well known in medieval Europe, has survived in numerous manuscripts, and has been used by various authors (in particular, the Venerable Bede, in his *De locis sanctis*).

Adamnan's work consists of three parts. The first deals with Jerusalem and its environs; the second with Bethlehem, Hebron, Jericho, Jordan, Galilee, Damascus, and Alexandria; and the third with Constantinople and a few other topics. The first and third books are based almost exclusively on Arculf's report, but in the second, Adamnan also relies on other sources. Adamnan learned a good deal about the holy places from Arculf (who, by Adamnan's testimony, reinforced by Bede, was an educated person). He pays particular attention to the architecture of the great churches that Arculf saw in the East, furnishing invaluable evidence about the state of the holy places just after the Muslim conquest of the Holy Land in 638; the account provides a kind of summing-up of the Byzantine period and the reconstruction of churches after the Persian invasion. Included in the work are plans of churches that Arculf drew for Adamnan—a contribution unparalleled at that time or, for that matter, for many centuries to come.

It is now believed that Arculf's journey was undertaken around 680 and took two or perhaps even three years. On his own evidence, Arculf stayed in Jerusalem for nine months. It was apparently then that he took trips out of the city to Bethlehem and Hebron, Jordan, Jericho, the Dead Sea, and Galilee. In Galilee he met a monk from his own country, Peter of Burgundy, who acted as his guide there. From Galilee Arculf went on to Damascus, then traveling to Tyre and returning to Jerusalem, before he again departed, this time for Egypt. He sailed from Jaffa to Alexandria, and via Crete to Constantinople. On his way home from Constantinople he found time to visit Sicily and intended to visit Rome.

**BIBLIOGRAPHY**
*Adamnani De locis sanctis.* In *Itineraria et alia Geographica.* Ed. L. Bieler, Corpus Christianorum: Series Latina 175. Turnholt: Brepols, 1965, pp. 175–234.
*Adamnan's* De locis sanctis. Ed. Denis Meehan. Scriptores Latini Hiberniae 3. Dublin: The Dublin Institute for Advanced Studies, 1958.
Wilkinson, John. *Jerusalem Pilgrims Before the Crusades.* Jerusalem: Ariel Publishing House, 1979, pp. 93–116.

*Ora Limor*

**SEE ALSO**
Adamnan; Bede; Byzantine Empire; Constantinople; Damascus; Dead Sea; Egypt; Holy Land; Itineraries and *Periploi;* Jerusalem; Pilgrimage, Christian

## *Arin*

*See* Center of the Earth

## Armenia

A culturally distinct region that during the Middle Ages was geographically defined, at its greatest extent,

# A

by the high Anatolian plateau bounded to the north by the Pontic and Lesser Caucasus mountains, to the south and west by the Tigris valley and the Taurus mountains, and to the east by the Araxes River. Today this land is divided between Turkey, Georgia, Armenia, Azerbaijan, and Iran.

Armenia's strategic location made it an attractive target for foreign ambitions and aggression, resulting in an almost continual shifting of its national boundaries. In 428 C.E., Sasanid Persia conquered Armenia and eradicated the ruling Armenian Arsacid dynasty, ending Armenian independence. When Persia was defeated by Islam, Armenia became a vassal state of the caliphate. The weakening of the caliphate in the tenth century allowed incursions into Armenian territory by the Byzantine Empire, Armenia's western neighbor, and by Arab successor states. A brief period (884–908) of unified rule by an Armenian king was ended by internal disputes among Armenian nobility, or *nakharars,* which divided the country into the southern kingdom of Vaspurakan and the northern kingdom of Armenia. Continuing civil wars further partitioned Armenia and greatly weakened its defensive capabilities.

The eastward expansion of Byzantium in the first half of the eleventh century resulted in the loss of Vaspurakan, Ani, and Kars, with displaced *nakharars* receiving Byzantine titles and lands in Cappadocia. This westward Armenian diaspora increased during the Seljuk invasion of the mid-eleventh century. Armenian resettlement west of the Euphrates resulted in the formation of the Armenian kingdom of Cilicia (1198–1375) between the Taurus and Amanus mountains on the modern-day Turkish Mediterranean coast. Like its eastern predecessor, Cilicia was not autonomous, falling under the jurisdiction of both the Holy Roman Empire and Rome. While Armenian reconquest of some northern regions, including Ani, was achieved in the early thirteenth century, the end of that century saw the absorption of Cilicia and northern Armenia into the Mongol Empire. The rise of the Ottoman Empire in the fourteenth and fifteenth centuries further isolated the remaining Armenian communities.

While medieval Armenia's strategic location was ultimately fatal to its political stability, it did ensure its development as a thriving center of trade. During the eighth through tenth centuries, goods from the Muslim east were transported across Armenia on trade routes leading to Islamic cities in Upper Mesopotamia, and to Baghdad. During the period of the Armenian Bagratid dynasty (880s to mid-eleventh century), northern trade routes were further developed by the rulers of Ani, Duin, and Kars for the transport of international goods to Byzantium and the Islamic successor states. The eleventh-century expulsion of Armenians from the main cities along these routes, and from Vaspurakan, effectively ended Armenian control of international trade in its historic lands. Armenian-produced goods, however, remained in great demand throughout the Middle Ages. Arab and Byzantine historians note the high quality of Armenian woodwork, glazed ceramics, glassware, and metalwork. Particular praise is reserved for Armenian dyed-wool products, including woven and embroidered carpets. Armenian carpets are unvaryingly present in lists of luxury gifts presented to Byzantine and Islamic rulers. During the Cilician period the city of Lajazzo (Ayas) was the main trading port of the eastern Mediterranean. Here, goods from Cilicia, Byzantium, the Muslim world, and the Latin Crusader states were bought and sold by Western European merchants. Lajazzo also served as the point of entry for travelers journeying further eastward, including Marco Polo.

Recent scholarship suggests that Armenia converted to Christianity in 314, establishing it as the earliest Christian nation. The Armenian Church broke with the Church of Byzantium in 451 over doctrinal issues, rejecting the decrees issued by the Eastern Orthodox Church at the council of Chalcedon. Two centuries later Armenia separated from the Georgian Church, which also espoused Eastern Orthodoxy. During the period of Islamic domination, Byzantium periodically and unsuccessfully pursued union with the Armenian Church. In the early Cilician period the Armenian Church agreed to unification with the Latin Church of Rome; increasing Latin pressure to alter traditional Armenian doctrine and liturgy split this union in 1361. The Catholicos was the spiritual head of the Armenian Church; as the sole authority recognized by all *nakharars,* he also served an important political function. In the fourteenth century the Armenian bishop of Jerusalem adopted the title of patriarch; the Ottomans later granted the same title to the Armenian bishop in Constantinople.

Weakened by internal political divisions and torn asunder by foreign invasions, medieval Armenia found unity in language and religion. The invention of the

Armenian alphabet is attributed to the monk, and later saint, Mashtots' in the early fifth century C.E. The ability to compose literary works in their native language and to translate texts—especially the Bible—into Armenian did much to create a single Armenian cultural identity. This identity, deeply rooted in religion, was strengthened by the burgeoning construction of churches and monasteries during the medieval period. Armenian architects were internationally renowned; in 989, Trdat, builder of the Cathedral of Ani, was summoned by the Byzantine emperor to repair the fallen dome of Hagia Sophia in Constantinople.

Monastic complexes included scriptoria, where monks copied religious texts and decorated them with painted images, or illuminations. While Armenian artists also excelled in sculpture and monumental painting, it was the medium of illuminated manuscripts, with their unique mix of Armenian language, theology, and art, which transmitted and preserved Armenian cultural identity throughout the upheavals of the Middle Ages. During the Cilician period, proximity with the Latin West and renewed contacts with the Muslim East influenced manuscript illumination. This period saw the fullest flowering of the Armenian national style. The finest Cilician paintings are by T'oros Roslin, who combined imaginative, playful forms with a newly muted palette and delicacy of line. The fall of Cilicia, and subsequent Mongol and Ottoman domination, resulted in the increasing isolation of monastic centers and the emergence of regional styles.

## BIBLIOGRAPHY

Boase, Thomas S.R., ed. *The Cilician Kingdom of Armenia.* Edinburgh: Scottish Academic P., 1978.

Der Nersessian, Sirarpie. *The Armenians.* London: Thames and Hudson, 1969.

Manandian, Hakob A. *The Trade and Cities of Armenia in Relation to Ancient World Trade.* Trans. Nina G. Garsoïan. Lisbon: Livraria Betrand, 1965.

Mathews, Thomas, and Roger S. Wieck, eds. *Treasures in Heaven. Armenian Illuminated Manuscripts.* New York: Pierpont Morgan Library, 1994.

*Lynn Jones*

## SEE ALSO

Baghdad; Byzantine Empire; Constantinople; Eastern Christianity; Hetoum; Lajazzo; Marco Polo; Masons and Architects as Travelers; Mongols; Ottoman Empire; Seljuk Turks; Textiles, Decorative

## Asia, Jerome Map of
*See* Jerome Map of Asia

## Asian Trade, Inner
*See* Inner Asian Trade

## Asian Travel, Inner
*See* Inner Asian Travel

## Assassins

The name, synonymous with political murderers, by which a small sect of the Isma'ili branch of the Shi'ite minority within Islam is known in the West.

The myth of the Assassins, propagated in Europe by medieval chroniclers of the Crusades, projected a secret garden of sensuous delight reserved on earth and in heaven for the fanatical adherents of a secret society absolutely devoted to their master, often called "The Old Man of the Mountain." The name in medieval Latin, *assassinus,* derives from the Arabic *hashashin,* the name by which they were known in Syria, which reflects the belief that the Assassins' master—the "Old Man"—would dispatch them, drugged on hashish, against his enemies or sell them to his allies for use against their enemies. These legends reflect medieval fears and the awareness that political autocracies are most easily subverted by the murder of the autocrat. Political assassination existed long before and continued long after the Assassins gave their name to the phenomenon. They were, however, without precedent in the planned, systematic, long-term use of terror as a political weapon, which they employed almost exclusively against the Sunni Muslim political, military, bureaucratic, and religious establishment before they were effectively neutralized at the end of the thirteenth century.

The history of the Assassins begins in 1090 when Hasan ibn Sabbah seized control of Alamut, a Daylami fortress held by the Seljuk sultanate in the mountains south of the Caspian Sea in Persia (now northern Iran). For the next thirty-five years, from this redoubt and others subsequently captured, Hasan ibn Sabbah sent agents to subvert the political power of the Seljuk Turks, and he dispatched missionaries to convert the surrounding areas of Sunni orthodoxy to his version of Isma'ili Shi'ism. When words did not work, they used

**A**

murder. The assassination of the vizier Nizam al-Mulk in 1092 was their first great success in a calculated war of terror that brought sudden death to political figures who opposed them or Sunni religious figures who preached against them.

The Persian Isma'ilis thrived in the political chaos that attended the disintegration of the Seljuk sultanate in the middle of the twelfth century. In this period of wars, raids, and assassinations, they extended their faith to India. In the thirteenth century, when Mongol horsemen invaded Muslim lands and penetrated western Iran, Hülegü, the grandson of Chinggis Khân, captured, looted, and burned Baghdad and, in 1258, persuaded the Assassins, their temporary allies, to abandon Alamut, which the Mongols then destroyed.

Hasan ibn Sabbah had sent missionaries to Syria, which had recently suffered foreign invasion by Crusaders who established Latin kingdoms in Edessa, Antioch, Tripoli, and Jerusalem. The assassination in 1103 of Janah al-Dawla, ruler of Homs, in the city mosque by Persians disguised as Sufis is the first of the religious and political murders that characterize the history of the Syrian Isma'ilis. Since their struggle was still against the masters, not the enemies of Islam, they would occasionally seek refuge in areas controlled by the Crusaders. Although they murdered Count Raymond II of Tripoli in 1130 and (disguised as Christian monks) the Marquis Conrad of Montferrat, king of Jerusalem, in 1192, they also made two attempts on the life of Saladin (between 1174 and 1176) before establishing an uneasy truce with him.

The end of the Assassins as an extremist, messianic, reformative, religious movement and a political terrorist organization came under the double onslaught of Baybars I, the Mamluk sultan of Egypt, and the Mongols. By 1273, all the Assassin castles in Syria had fallen to Baybars, after which no further murders by Syrian Assassins acting for the sect are authenticated. The Assassins stagnated as a minor heresy in Persia and Syria and all but disappeared. The modern descendants of Hasan ibn Sabbah's sect of Isma'ili Shi'ism who survived in Persia and India, much domesticated and civilized, recognize the imam Karim Aga Khân IV (1936–) as their spiritual leader.

**BIBLIOGRAPHY**
Hammer-Purgstall, Joseph von. *The History of the Assassins.* Trans. Oswald Charles Wood. London, 1835; rpt. New York: Franklin, 1968.

Hodgson, Marshall G.S. *The Order of Assassins. The Struggle of the Early Nizari Isma'ilis against the Islamic World.* The Hague: Mouton, 1955.
Lewis, Bernard. *The Assassins. A Radical Sect in Islam.* London: Weidenfeld and Nicolson, 1967.

*Jerome Mandel*

**SEE ALSO**
Baybars I; Caspian Sea; Crusades, First, Second, and Third; Hülegü; Mongols; Saladin; Seljuk Turks; Shi'ism; Sunnism

## Astrological Influence on Travel

Medieval astrology held that the world was a microcosm reflecting the celestial macrocosm and, therefore, travel on earth was strongly influenced by the movements of the heavenly bodies. Judicial astrology provided guidance in the form of prognostics about what activities should or should not be undertaken according to celestial conditions. Thus, choosing the right time for a journey could theoretically allow one to avoid such risks as shipwreck, storms, or fruitless mercantile ventures.

Such prognostics depended on two central factors, the first regarding the heavenly bodies themselves and the second the twelve zodiacal signs. The nature or property of heavenly bodies could be hot, cold, dry, moist, masculine, or feminine; their position or aspect within the 360-degree circle of the universe could range from opposition (at 180 degrees) to conjunction (at 0 degrees); other determinants would be movement, whether rising, falling, or retrograde. In addition, the 360-degree circle was divided into twelve signs (Aries, Taurus, Gemini, Cancer, Leo, Virgo, Libra, Scorpio, Sagittarius, Capricorn, Aquarius, and Pisces), each likewise affected by property and aspect, as well as the quality of movement, whether mobile, fixed, or mixed. The interworking of heavenly bodies with zodiacal signs, each with capacity for a combination of different attributes, constituted a very complex "map" of the universe and determined human conditions on the terrestrial "map."

Travel was especially affected by the astrological concept of *houses*, based on a second twelve-part division of the 360-degree celestial circle. Because the seasons also reflect celestial conditions, they, too, had to be taken into account in a full prognostication. Alternatively, the potential traveler might consult conditions predicted only for the proposed time of travel, and a large body of Latin and vernacular matter from at least the twelfth century developed to aid anyone wishing to use this simpler approach.

In the medieval West, theoretical formulations about travel are attributed to Ptolemy (fl. 121–151 C.E.) and Firmicus Maternus (fl. 330–354 C.E.). Ptolemy's *Tetrabiblos* devotes one whole chapter to travel (IV.8) and is especially interested in the moon's influence because of its nearness to the earth and its influence on tides. Ptolemy specifies a number of predictors, including whether the "good" planets (Jupiter, Venus, and Mercury) as opposed to the "bad" ones (Saturn and Mars) were in favorable or unfavorable aspect with the essential third and ninth houses governing travel. The visual imagery associated with the zodiacal sign present at the proposed time of travel would also be influential: a watery Aquarius might cause shipwreck.

Such travel prognostica were elaborated through Arab writers, then translated into Latin from the twelfth century onward (many of them by John of Spain, fl. 1135–1170). Most influential were Messahala's *De testimoniis luni* (c. 800), Haly Embrani's *De electionibus horarum* (c. 955), and Haly Albohazen's *De judiciis astrorum* (c. 1020). Much was collected into popular Latin compendia, like Guido Bonatti's *Liber astronomicus* (c. 1277), from which astrological matter descended into more simplified, vernacular texts.

Theories about astrological influence on travel continued to develop throughout the fourteenth and fifteenth centuries, and came to include the division of the world into quadrants, each governed by a particular zodiacal sign and planet and serving as point of origin for one of the four winds. This system established not only the racial color of its inhabitants, but also their disposition and propensity for travel. For example, in *The Book of John Mandeville,* the "English" author observes of his own countrymen that they are destined to travel because of the influence of the moon on the seventh climate—the one in which England is found. In contrast to those people, for example, who live under Saturn and have no desire to travel, the English are natural voyagers since the moon "is swiftly and easily moving and the planet of freedom and passage. And for this reason it gives us a natural desire to move swiftly and to go on various roads and to seek exotic things and other diversities in the world." The idea was sufficiently popular to appear in the works of another, actual Englishman, John Gower.

Because of the potential for complexity in calculating all the factors necessary for greatest accuracy (including not only positions and movements of heavenly bodies, but time of year, horoscope of the traveler, destination, and reason for the journey), many of the more popular works tended to select only certain referents for travel. The moon became the primary predictor and gave rise to treatises called *lunaries* that offered general prognostics on life, health, agriculture, and phlebotomy, as well as rather simple ones on travel. A tenth-century Latin lunary observes that, on the first day of the moon "it is a risk to go by water, but, if one escapes, one will live long."

According to other sources, the moon's influence on travel could depend upon its position within the zodiac. A fifteenth-century Middle English example, whose prognostics are based ultimately on the Arabic *De judiciis astrorum,* proposes that before any journey is undertaken, the traveler must first take his horoscope, assessing whether the moon is in a moveable sign and hence favorable. All other signs being good and "with God's presence," the traveler will achieve "a safe and profitable journey." Another Middle English example concludes optimistically that, with the moon in Pisces, "if you go poor, you will not return poor"; it adds a unique example of a travel charm alluding to Christ's going out among the people.

The form of travel prognostication that was perhaps the most important for pilgrims, merchants, and others who made long, arduous journeys was the *questionary,* a work that could produce answers as to the most advantageous times for an undertaking and its final results. Based on a combination of astrological and numerological devices, these derive primarily from Messahalla's *De receptione planetarum siue de interrogationibus* (c. 800) through the twelfth-century translation by John of Spain, or from Michael Scot's *Liber introductorius.* The inquirer, seeking answers to such questions as "Will I return safe from my journey to Rome?" calculates the ascendant sign and planet for a house, then works out their aspect and other astrological conditions to find the answers. Methods of calculating the answers to *questions* fell into several categories, including those that focused on *houses,* those that involved casting *figures* through patterns of dots, and those that relied on the device known as the *Pythagorean Wheel.* Travel questions could be quite general, asking "whether the absent or pilgrim shall come home," "to know of a long journey," and "of

# A

going by land or water," or they could serve commercial interests specifically, as in examples from Martin of Spain's *De geomancia* (*c.* 1319), where merchants could ask about the acquiring of goods, the repayment of loans, and even the stability of currency in Spain.

## BIBLIOGRAPHY

Carmody, Francis J. *Arabic Astronomical and Astrological Sciences in Latin Translation: A Critical Bibliography.* Berkeley and Los Angeles: U of California P, 1956.

Charmasson, Thérèse. *Recherches sur une technique divinatoire: La géomancie dans l'occident médiéval.* Centre de Recherches d'histoire de la Philosophie de la IVe Section de l'Ecole Pratique des Hautes Etudes 44. Paris: Champion, 1980.

Curry, Patrick, ed. *Astrology, Science, and Society: Historical Essays.* Woodbridge, Suffolk: Boydell, 1987.

Förster, Max. "Vom Fortleben antiker Sammellunare im Englischen und in anderen Volksprachen." *Anglia* 67 (1944): 1–171.

Means, Laurel. "Electionary, Lunary, Destinary, and Questionary: Toward Defining Categories of Middle English Prognostic Material." *Studies in Philology* 89 (1992): 367–403.

*Medieval Lunar Astrology: A Collection of Representative Middle English Texts.* Lewiston/Queenston/Lampeter: Mellen, 1993.

*Popular and Practical Science of Medieval England.* Ed. Lister M. Matheson. East Lansing, MI: Colleagues P, 1994.

Ptolemy, Claudius Ptolemaeus. *Tetrabiblos.* Ed. and trans. F.E. Robbins. Cambridge, MA: Harvard UP, 1971.

*Laurel Means*

## SEE ALSO
*Mandeville's Travels;* Ptolemy

## Atlas

A collection of maps organized according to a preconceived system. The term was first used by the Flemish cartographer Gerard Mercator near the end of the sixteenth century, and is, consequently, an anachronism when employed to describe medieval map collections. Very few such collections survive. Of the extant maps from the Middle Ages, the overwhelming majority stood alone and show no sign of having been designed as part of a collection. Even those rare medieval maps that resemble books (such as Abraham Cresques's so-called "Catalan Atlas" of 1375) are most often single-sheet world maps that have been folded for ease of examination or storage. For most of the Middle Ages,

the role of modern atlases was filled by the large single-sheet world maps known today as *mappaemundi* and by the many prose descriptions of world geography and history.

Books of maps—or at least books that contain a number of maps—became more common during the fifteenth century. The earliest are the books of islands (*Isolarii*) that began to appear in Italy at the end of the 1300s. These books contain descriptions of the major islands of the world, and are often decorated with crude maps. Similarly, manuscripts of Gregorio Dati's cosmographical poem *La Sfera,* probably composed at Florence around 1420, are often decorated with maps derived from the nautical charts of the Mediterranean known today as portolans. In both the *Isolarii* and *La Sfera,* the maps are clearly subservient to the text. A more remarkable series of maps by Pietro Vesconte—including *mappaemundi* and a chart of the Holy Land, as well as *portolani,* oriented to the north—appear as ideological and practical images accompanying Marino Sanudo's polemical treatise advocating a crusade (*Liber secretorum fidelium crucis* [1307–1321]). Not an atlas in the geographically comprehensive sense the term has today, Vesconte's contributions are, in Tony Campbell's formulation, "a cartographic supplement to Sanudo's text."

Most important among the new map collections of the 1400s was Claudius Ptolemy's *Geography.* Compiled at Alexandria, Egypt, in the second century C.E., the *Geography* was brought to Italy from Constantinople around 1400. A purely geographical work, Ptolemy's book comprises an enormous list of geographical coordinates (latitude and longitude marks), instructions on how to draw maps, as well as a set of maps. The text was first printed at Vicenza, in 1475, without maps; the first edition with maps appeared at Bologna on June 23, 1477, with twenty-six maps derived from Ptolemy's text. Maps based on more recent geographical knowledge were added to the collection beginning with editions printed in 1482 (at Ulm, on July 16 [woodcuts] and Florence, before September [copperplate engravings]). The *Geography* provided the direct model for the modern atlas.

## BIBLIOGRAPHY

Akerman, James R. "From Books with Maps to Books as Maps: The Editor in the Creation of the Atlas Idea." In *Editing Early and Historical Atlases.* Ed. Joan Winearls. Toronto: U Toronto P, 1995, pp. 3–48.

Harley-Woodward. *A History of Cartography.* Vol 1., especially David Woodward, "Medieval Mappaemundi" (pp. 286–370); Tony Campbell, "Portolan Charts from the Late Thirteenth Century to 1500" (pp. 371–463); and P.D.A. Harvey, "Local and Regional Cartography in Medieval Europe" (pp. 464–501). See Gen. Bib.

*Ben Weiss*

**SEE ALSO**
Benincasa, Grazioso; Cresques, Abraham; Geography in Medieval Europe; *Mappamundi;* Maps; Portolan Charts; Ptolemy; Vesconte, Pietro/Perrino

## Attila (d. 453)

The ruler under whom the Hunnic empire reached its greatest extent. His name is not Hunnic, but Gothic, a diminutive of *atta* ("father"). He and his brother Bleda became co-rulers of the Huns in 433 and ruled together until Attila murdered Bleda in 445. Attila then ruled alone until his death in 453. We know that his father's name was Mundzuch (spelling may vary) and that his chief wife was called Erka or Helche (*r* and *l* are interchangeable, and many variant spellings are recorded).

Our most complete picture of Attila and his people comes from the account of the Greek historian Priscus, who accompanied an ambassador of the Eastern emperor to Attila's headquarters in 449 and 450. In this account, which has come down to us through Cassiodorus and Jordanes, he describes, in great detail, not only the official activities of the embassy, but also a plot to assassinate Attila, and how it was foiled. Physically, Attila is described by Jordanes as short and stocky, with a large head, small eyes, a thin beard, a flat nose, and a swarthy complexion. He is also described as ferocious but subtle, a ruler who fought with craft before he made war. In one legend, found in stories from Gaul and Italy and echoed in some Old Norse sources, he was said to be descended from a dog.

Attila first appeared on the scene in 435, when he and Bleda concluded a treaty with emissaries from the Eastern Empire at Margus on the lower Danube. Five years later, taking advantage of a temporary weakening of the Roman frontier garrison, the Huns crossed the Danube and destroyed several towns. In the next few years they continued their marauding, finally forcing the Romans to sue for peace and agree to pay large sums of gold as tribute. In 447, the Huns again descended on the Eastern Empire, but were turned back by an imperial army before they could reach Constantinople.

By 451, Attila was in control of a large territory stretching from the Balkans to the Baltic and was able to turn his attention westward. He attacked Gaul first, conquering, among other towns, Trier and Metz, and besieging Orléans. Though the Huns were actually defeated in a climactic battle at a place (now unidentifiable) in the neighborhood of Troyes called the Catalaunian fields or the *locus Mauriacus,* they were allowed to retreat instead of being destroyed because the Roman general Aetius needed them as the outside threat that kept the barbarian tribes in league with Rome from attacking each other or the empire.

The next year Attila attacked northern Italy, destroying Aquileia, Pavia, and Milan before being halted, not by military resistance, but by a famine that made it too difficult to find food for his army and fodder for its horses. This campaign in Italy won for Attila the title of "Scourge of God," God's chosen weapon for punishing the sinful people of Italy. Pope Leo, leading an embassy from Rome, met with Attila and is believed to have persuaded him to go no further south. Legend says that Attila saw a gigantic apparition of St. Peter armed with a sword standing behind the pope. We cannot know what arguments the pope used, but he may well have only pointed out that conditions were no better in the south. Attila returned to Pannonia, and soon threatened to attack the Eastern Empire, but when he no longer had the military might to make good on his threat, the empire stopped sending tribute.

In 453, Attila decided to take a new bride, a Germanic maiden named Ildico. At the wedding he drank too much, and after going to bed with his bride he suffered a nosebleed while lying in a stupor on his back. The blood flowed into his windpipe and he suffocated. When he did not appear the next morning, his retainers finally forced the door of his chamber open and discovered him dead in the arms of his weeping bride. It was specifically noted that he had not been wounded in any way, but later accounts claimed that his Germanic bride had slain him with a knife, for personal or political reasons. Acting as allies of the Romans, the Huns had defeated the Burgundians in 437. Although Attila had not taken part in this battle, later stories maintained that his bride was a Burgundian and that she slew him to avenge the defeat of her people. This version of his death gave rise eventually to all the stories of revenge that revolve around him in the German *Nibelungenlied* and the Norse *Poetic Edda.*

# A

Not surprisingly, the stories about Attila vary according to whether they were related by friends (that is, members of allied or subjugated peoples) or enemies (victims of his marauding). All the stories that originated in Gaul and Italy depict him as a demonic conqueror, while many (but not all) of the stories from German territories make him a stern but benevolent ruler. The stories from Gaul and Italy tend to be accounts of how a given city suffered when the Huns attacked, and the role played by some saintly citizen, such as St. Anianus at Orléans.

The stories of Germanic origin are grouped around several themes. One group of stories is centered on Dietrich von Bern (the historical Theodoric the Great [454–526]). Although Attila and Theodoric were not contemporaries, and Theodoric was never driven into exile, the stories—including the *Hildebrandslied* (Song of Hildebrand), the *Rabenschlacht* (The Battle of Ravenna), *Das Buch von Bern* (The Book of Verona), also called *Dietrichs Flucht* (Theodoric's Flight) and the Latin poem *Waltharius Manu Fortis* (Walter Stronghand)—all relate how Dietrich was forced out of his kingdom by his evil uncle and took refuge with Attila, a wise, just, generous, and powerful ruler who helped him return to his kingdom.

The first part of the *Nibelungenlied* tells the story of Siegfried, Brynhild, and the Burgundian royal house, but the second part, dealing with Kriemhild's revenge, tells how Kriemhild married Etzel (the Middle High German form of Attila) and used his Huns to exact vengeance on her brothers for killing Siegfried. Here Etzel is very noble but quite inactive, a mere onlooker until the very end.

In Norse stories Attila is called Atli. In several lays of the *Poetic Edda,* most notably the *Atlakvitha* (The Lay of Atli) and the *Atlamal in Groenlenzko* (The Greenland Lay of Atli), he is the brother of Brynhild and the enemy of the Burgundian kings. When he kills them, his wife, their sister, gets revenge, first by killing their children and serving them to him as food, and then by killing him. Quite different from the *Nibelungenlied* version, the Norse versions recall the story that Attila was slain by his wife for personal or political reasons.

The *Thidrekssaga* (Saga of Theodoric) portrays Atli in contradictory fashion: sometimes he is noble, generous, and kind, and at other times he is cruel, cowardly, and avaricious. This may be one indication that the *Thidrekssaga* had more than one author. Oddly, in this story Attila is not a Hun, but a Frisian who becomes king of the Huns by conquering Hunland.

The contradictory depictions of Attila in the Norse stories may reflect the lines of communication, and hence of trade, in early medieval Europe. The Goths and the other East Germanic peoples had migrated from Scandinavia through eastern Europe to the Black Sea before turning west and moving across all of southern Europe. It is likely that the favorable stories about Attila, which had their origin among these peoples, spread back along the migration route to Scandinavia, while the unfavorable ones, which originated in Latin territories, probably spread north along western trade routes, especially the Rhine. Thus the Norse stories, composed after the two traditions had converged, contain elements of both.

**BIBLIOGRAPHY**
Gordon, C.D. *The Age of Attila: Fifth-Century Byzantium and the Barbarians.* Ann Arbor: U of Michigan P, 1972.
Jordanes. *The Gothic History of Jordanes.* Intro. Charles Christopher Mierow. Princeton, NJ: Princeton UP, 1915.
Maenchen-Helfen, Otto. *The World of the Huns: Studies in Their History and Culture.* Ed. Max Knight. Berkeley: U of California P, 1973.
Thompson, E.A. *A History of Attila and the Huns.* Oxford: Clarendon P, 1948.

James V. McMahon

**SEE ALSO**
Byzantine Empire; Huns; German Literature, Travel in

## Avars

A people, probably of Asian origin, who appeared in Chinese territory around the year 400, moved to western Mongolia in the 450s, and settled in the area of the lower Danube in the early sixth century, later occupying Pannonia and invading eastern Europe before their defeat by Charlemagne and their decline in the ninth century.

The Byzantine emperors had, beginning in the sixth century, a policy of concluding alliances with rulers of neighboring but less developed peoples so that they might turn their new allies on others who threatened the empire's security. Justinian (527–565) hoped in this way to use the Avars against the Uturgurs (a people living between the Volga and the Don), whom Bajan, the Avar khagan, had subjugated.

Bajan dispatched envoys to Justinian in 562 to request land for settlement in exchange for such military aid, and the emperor began to negotiate the transfer to the Avars of Pannonia, a part of which was inhabited by the Longobards, a Germanic people who later settled in northern Italy and gave their name to Lombardy. The Avars had, in the meantime, defeated the Slavs of the Vistula-Elbe-Oder region, as well as Sigibert of Austrasia (the eastern Merovingian Empire), with whom they afterward formed an alliance in 566.

When the Longobards moved to Italy in 568, Bajan occupied their remaining territories as well, and moved his headquarters next to the Tisza River. He had in effect established the Avar kingdom. In 570, he concluded peace with Justin II (565–578) in exchange for an annual tribute. By then his empire had spread from the Elbe and the eastern Alps to the Don River.

The Avars were not necessarily nomads, but a people of advanced military tactics, who in times of peace would pursue ice fishing in winter and hunt for other food in the spring and fall. They ate fish and roasted spiced animal meat, using animal skins to make their own clothing and footwear. They grew their own wheat and hay during the summer. Their economic trade routes expanded over the region north, northwest, and northeast of the Black Sea, reaching to the Far East, Mongolia, and China.

Avar power began to decline in the 630s. On the eastern Frankish border, the Frank Samo (625–660) had organized the Slavs to shake off the Avar yoke. In 637, the Bulgarians in Pannonia—descendants of the peoples who had accepted the rule of Bajan—revolted against the Avars and by 660 were independent. At the same time, the Byzantine emperor Heraclius (610–641) isolated the Avars by settling Croats and Serbs from the Elbe-Oder region on the lower Danube; the Serbs accepted Christianity and became Byzantine subjects, but were allowed to retain their native customs and self-rule in the area.

In the early 790s, the Avars aided the Bavarians against Charlemagne, who, in turn, led three campaigns against Avar country. East of Vienna the Avars fought the Franks and were badly defeated. The Avars now killed their khagan, and named as their leader Prince Tudun, who was eager to conclude peace with the Franks and accept Christianity. Two Frankish armies, however, pursued the war effort, reached the main Avar camp on the Tisza, and captured much treasure, which they took to Aachen. Indeed, on raiding the "rings" where the Avars had deposited large amounts of precious metals, coins, and other treasures, the Franks, who had been so poor, now suddenly

became rich, wrote Einhard, Charlemagne's biographer—perhaps revealing Charlemagne's real reason for hostility toward the Avars. Pannonia came under Frankish administration, though Tudun was allowed to keep his territory east of the Tisza. The Avars revolted against the provisions of the agreement and were decimated by the Frankish forces between 799 to 803. In the Treaty of Verdun, 843, all Avar territory came under the Franks' rule, and though the politically and culturally advanced Avars had no further historical importance of their own, their treasures, when invested, greatly furthered the development of trade and industry during the Carolingian era.

**BIBLIOGRAPHY**

Bury, J.B. *History of the Later Roman Empire.* 2 vols. New York: Dover, 1958. 2:314–316.

Hóman, Bálint. *Geschichte des ungarischen Mittelalters.* 2 vols. Berlin: de Gruyter, 1940–1943. Vol 1: esp. 84–85.

Kollautz, A. "Die Awaren." *Saeculum* 5 (1954): 129–178.

Köpeczi, Béla, et al., eds. *History of Transylvania.* Trans. Adrianne Chambers-Makkai, Eva Pálmai, and Christopher Sullivan. Budapest: Akadémiai Kiadó, 1994, pp. 90–97.

*Z.J. Kosztolnyik*

**SEE ALSO**

Byzantine Empire; Inner Asian Trade; Muslim Travelers and Trade; Nomadism and Pastoralism

## Ayas
*See* Lajazzo

## Ayyūbids

A Kurdish people among the first of the displaced, non-sedentary Eastern populations being forced westward by the movement of Turks and then Mongols. They formed a contingent of the Seljuqid Turkish forces that invaded and ruled Syria beginning in the early eleventh century just before the First Crusade. Under their leader Saladin they became a dynasty that ruled Egypt, Syria-Palestine, northern Mesopotamia, and the Yemen from 1169 to 1252.

The founder of the Ayyūbid dynasty, Saladin (Salāh ed-Dīn Yūssuf ibn Ayūb, 1137–1193), known as the Scourge of the Crusaders, began his military career in Damascus when Syria united in its efforts to defeat the recently arrived Western Christian armies. Sent to Egypt in the service of his Seljuqid overlords, he took power and restored Sunnism. Establishing Egypt as his power base, he used his Kurdo-Turkish forces to achieve his primary objective of securing control of Syria from rival Seljuqid Turks while at the same time prosecuting the war against the Third Crusade.

Among the Ayyūbid innovations in Egypt was the eastern *iqtāʿ*, military tax-farming system, introduced by Saladin. This system of military land grants had serious repercussions on agriculture and on the economy of Egypt. Egyptian agricultural revenues were harnessed to the needs of a military machine focused on the conquest of Syria from rival Seljuqid princes and the expulsion of the Crusaders. While fighting the Crusaders and contending with the westward expansion of the Seljuqid Turks, the Ayyūbids had also to deal with the advancing Mongols.

The most significant pressure against the Ayyūbid dynasty came from the Crusaders, who understood that they could not maintain themselves in Palestine as long as Egypt was a power. The fall of Constantinople in 1204 to the Fourth Crusade left the Ayyūbids separated from their natural ally, the Turks. And in 1217, with the capture of the important Egyptian port of Damietta, Egypt became the target of crusading activity. As a result of continual Crusader attacks on Egypt's coastal cities, the Ayyūbids focused increasingly on the Red Sea, abandoning the Mediterranean and intensifying what had always been Egypt's Red Sea-Yemen commercial and strategic focus.

Although Egypt remained the focus of Crusader activity until the Crusaders' final defeat and expulsion from the Middle East in 1291, the Ayyūbids were able to maintain important commercial activities throughout their reign. Crusaders had tried to establish themselves in the Red Sea in 1182, probably for commercial reasons but also to interdict the flow of war materiel to the Ayyūbids via Yemen and the East, especially from India, which was a major supplier of swords and weaponry to the "Near" West during this period. The Crusaders were never successful in their efforts, however, since warfare makes good business. Ayyūbid commercial relations with Pisans, Genoese, and Venetians intensified in the later decades of the dynasty, with southern Italy becoming a source of wood for the reconstruction of an Egyptian navy. French, Italian, and Catalan merchants remained active in Egypt and Syrian ports despite continuing warfare, and Italian merchants expanded their business to supply both sides with war materiel. They also provisioned resident Crusaders and Franks, who were never able to expand beyond their coastal enclaves to secure provisions from the interior of Syria-Palestine.

Egyptian merchants, particularly the Kārimī, who dominated the spice trade from their centers in Cairo and Damascus, continued to be active in the Red Sea and Indian Ocean, leaving the Mediterranean to Europeans. The Kārimī merchants' presence is noted from the late Fatimid period through the fifteenth century. They functioned as a banking house providing forced loans to Egypt's sultans.

Under the early Ayyūbids a bulk export was unprocessed flax, later displaced by sugar cane. Since sugar cane and flax competed for the same cropland, and both competed with grain, the expansion and eventual preeminence of sugar exports correlates with the decline of the linen textile industry in Egypt.

The later Ayyūbid period (1238–1252) saw intermittent cooperation between the Crusaders and Ayyūbids as both were pressured by the continuing influx of Turco-Mongols pushing westward. The Ayyūbids and Crusaders were ultimately displaced by invading Turco-Mongols, who replaced the Ayyūbid with the Mamluk dynasty (1252–1517).

**BIBLIOGRAPHY**

Cahen, Claude. "Ayyūbids." *Encyclopaedia of Islam,* New edition, Vol. 1, pp. 796–807. Leiden: Brill, 1979.

Garcin, Jean-Claude. "Kūs." *Encyclopaedia of Islam,* New edition, Vol. 5, pp. 514–515. Leiden: Brill, 1986.

Goitein, Shelomo D. "Mediterranean Trade in the Eleventh Century: Some Facts and Problems." In *Studies in the Economic History of the Middle East.* Ed. M.A. Cook. London: Oxford, 1970, pp. 51–77.

Halm, Heinz. "Misr, 4. The Ayyūbid Period 1171–1250." *Encyclopaedia of Islam,* New edition, Vol. 2, pp. 164–165. Leiden: Brill, 1983.

Labib, Subhi. "Kārimī." *Encyclopaedia of Islam,* New edition, Vol. 4, pp. 640–643. Leiden: Brill, 1978.

*Gladys Frantz-Murphy*

**SEE ALSO**

Constantinople; Crusade, Fourth; Fātimids; Genoa; Mamluks; Merchants, French; Merchants, Italian; Mongols; Pisa; Red Sea; Saladin; Seljuk Turks; Venice

## Azores

An archipelago located midway between Europe and the Americas. Discovered by Prince Henry the Navigator in 1427, who found them uninhabited, the nine islands of the Azores quickly became central to Portugal's transatlantic and Euro-African trade. Through much of the fifteenth century, the three most important (and easternmost) islands of Santa Maria, San Miguel, and Terceira served as supply and trading centers for ships returning from Portuguese excursions to Africa and later Spanish explorations in the Americas. Exploration of the Azores also provided important information on the Atlantic and set the stage for Columbus's voyage to the Americas.

At the beginning of the fifteenth century, the recently discovered Madeira Islands were on the trade route south to Africa, and allowed ships to resupply on the way. By bearing northwest on the return voyage, sailors heading back to Europe could use the Azores for the same purpose. This enabled Portuguese caravels to travel farther than would have otherwise been possible with their limited space for fresh water and other supplies. The Azores quickly expanded beyond a simple way station, however. Although the first settlers had been petty criminals, the wealth passing through the Azores soon attracted Portuguese nobles and colonists from throughout Europe. These volcanic islands, especially Santa Maria, sold food and goods to returning sailors. The Azores also became an important site of sugar production in the late medieval world.

The Azores, positioned midway between the European and American continents, also helped set the stage for later transatlantic journeys. The Azorean population included a number of nobles, explorers, and sailors who were familiar with the winds and currents of the mid-Atlantic, information important for later Portuguese and Spanish explorations. Columbus and many of his sailors had experience in the Azores, which provided a template not only for the mechanics of transatlantic travel, but also for developing new colonies in the Americas.

**BIBLIOGRAPHY**

Afonso, João. *Bibliografia geral dos Açores: seqüência do dicionário bibliográfico português.* 2 vols. Angra do Heroismo, Azores: Secretaria Regional da Educação e Cultura, 1985.

Guill, James H. *A History of the Azores Islands.* Menlo Park, CA: n.p., 1972.

Marques, Antonio Henriques R. de Oliveira. *History of Portugal.* 2 vols. New York: Columbia UP, 1972.

Santos, João Marinho dos. *Os Açores nos séculos XV e XVI.* 2 vols. Maia, Azores: Serafim Silva, 1989.

*Gretchen D. Starr-LeBeau*

**SEE ALSO**

African Trade; Antillia; Behaim, Martin; Brasil; Caravel; Columbus, Christopher; Exploration and Expansion, European; Genoa; Henry the Navigator; Portuguese Expansion; Spain and Portugal

# B

## Baghdad

Capital city of Iraq, located on the middle Tigris. Medieval Arabic authors frequently try to derive the name from Persian, but it seems to exist (Hudadu/Bagdadu) in Old Babylonian, and the Babylonian Talmud mentions "Bagdatha." There is also a close resemblance to the name Agade, the capital city of Sargon I, king of Akkad, who reigned from about 2340 to 2305 in the twenty-fourth century B.C.E.

Medieval Baghdad was founded by the second Abbasid caliph Abu-Jafar al-Mansūr (754–775). When they overthrew the Umayyads in 750, the Abbasids moved their capital to Iraq. Kūfah, al-Anbār, and al-Hāshimiyyah preceded Baghdad as capital cities.

Al-Mansūr commenced the building of Baghdad in 762 and completed it in 766. The city, named Madinat al-Salām (City of Peace) was situated on the western side of the Tigris. Its circular shape points to Persian influence in city planning. It was protected by double walls and a water-filled moat; four equidistant gates, with heavy iron doors, connected the Round City to the outside.

As the capital of a prosperous empire, Baghdad rapidly expanded to the eastern side of the river. Baghdad reached its height of influence during the caliphate of Hārūn al-Rashīd (786–809), who maintained friendly diplomatic relations with Charlemagne, including the exchange of presents.

Harun was succeeded by his son al-Amīn (809–813), who was challenged by his half brother al-Ma'mūn. A destructive civil war ensued, resulting in the murder of al-Amīn. The reign of al-Ma'mūn (813–833) was a period of great intellectual progress. The caliph sponsored a vigorous program of translation. He estab-

lished the Bayt al-Hikmah (House of Wisdom), where Syriac Christian scholars translated into Arabic all the Greek scientific and philosophical works they could find. Also, much of the Persian and Indian intellectual heritage became available in Arabic. During this period, al-Khwārizmi (780–c. 850) made his important contributions to mathematical knowledge, especially his book on algebra, later to be translated into Latin.

The Abbasids soon began to depend on foreign mercenaries. The unruly conduct of the Turkish soldiers in Baghdad forced al-Mu'tasim (833–842) to move the capital in 836 to Samarra, some 65 miles north northwest from Baghdad, on the Tigris. Al-Mu'tadid (892–902) returned the capital to Baghdad in 892.

In 756, a Umayyad prince established a rival dynasty in Spain. Other territories, east and west, became independent of Baghdad. The Abbasid caliphs themselves were reduced to the status of virtual puppets, first by the Persian Shi'ite Buwayhids from 945, then by the Sunnite Seljuk Turks from 1055.

By the twelfth century, Baghdad was in serious decline. Nevertheless, the Spanish Jewish traveler Benjamin of Tudela, who visited the city during the reign of al-Mustanjid (1160–1170), paints a glowing picture of prosperity and tolerance. The city's Jewish inhabitants, numbering around 40,000, "dwell in security, prosperity and honour under the great Caliph." The exilarch, who traces his ancestry to David, enjoys enormous prestige among Jews and Muslims alike. On the other hand, another Spanish traveler, the Muslim Ibn Jubayr, who visited Baghdad in 1184, depicts a gloomy picture of physical and moral decay. Baghdad, Ibn Jubayr laments, "is like an effaced ruin, a remain washed out, or the

# B

statue of a ghost. It has no beauty that attracts the eye. . . ." He denounces the hypocrisy of the Baghdadis who "affect humility, but who yet are vain and proud. They are dishonest in business dealings and they despise the stranger." Nevertheless, the oratorical finesse of Baghdad's *imāms* greatly impressed Ibn Jubayr.

On February 10, 1258, the Mongolian Hülegü, a grandson of Chinggis Khân, conquered Baghdad. The last Abbasid caliph, al-Musta'sim (1242–1258), his entire family, and tens of thousands of the city's inhabitants were murdered. Much of the city was destroyed. The descendants of Hülegü (the il-khâns) were succeeded by the Mesopotamian dynasty of the Jalāyirids. Tamerlane (1336–1405), who claimed descent from Chinggis Khân, conquered Baghdad in 1401, slaughtered almost the entire population, and effected the almost total destruction of the city. Tamerlane's biographer, Ibn 'Arabshah (d. 1450), relates that the Mongol leader ordered the erection of one hundred and twenty towers made of the skulls of Baghdadis. Medieval Baghdad, for all intents and purposes, ceased to exist.

## BIBLIOGRAPHY

Duri, A.A. "Baghdad." *Encyclopaedia of Islam,* New Edition, Vol. I, pp. 894–908. Leiden: Brill, 1979.

Hitti, Philip K. *History of the Arabs.* 6th edition. London: Macmillan, 1958.

———. *Capital Cities of Arab Islam.* Minneapolis: U of Minnesota P, 1973.

Le Strange, Guy. *Baghdad during the Abbasid Caliphate.* Oxford: Oxford UP, 1924.

*Alauddin Samarrai*

## SEE ALSO
Benjamin of Tudela; Damascus; Holy Land; Hülegü; Ibn Jubayr; Jerusalem; Mecca; Muslim Travelers and Trade; Nestorianism; Ptolemy; Red Sea; Ricold of Monte Croce; Saladin; Silk Roads; Sindbad the Sailor; Sunnism; Tamerlane; Women Travelers, Islamic

## Balsam Garden

A well-known attraction for medieval pilgrims at Materea, outside Cairo, where the Holy Family supposedly rested after fleeing the persecution of Herod the Great (c. 73–4 B.C.E.).

According to the German traveler William of Boldensele (1336), the garden marks the spot where Mary washed Jesus's diapers, the water from which was said to have subsequently generated balsam trees. The author of *Mandeville's Travels,* who used Boldensele as a source for his own book (*c.* 1360), adds that the well was made by the imprint of Christ's foot as he played with his companions as a child, asserting further that only Christians can harvest the balsam from the small trees (he cannot confirm the claims that "le baulme" also grows in India, and he offers a method for determining whether the balm is genuine). Ogier D'Anglure, in his pilgrimage account of 1395, says that the well of pure water in the Balsam Garden was made by the infant Christ as he drummed his heels upon the ground. He repeats Boldensele's assertion that the balsam bushes sprang from water used to wash Jesus's clothes. Similar information can be found in works by Burchard of Mount Sion (*c.* 1285), Marino Sanudo (1306–1321), Ludolph of Suchem (*c.* 1350), and John of Hildesheim (*c.* 1370). The Dominican Felix Fabri, who traveled to Egypt in 1483, compares Materea to Paradise and describes in detail the miraculous well and surrounding buildings designed to accommodate visitors.

Balsam, or in some European vernacular languages *baum,* was an expensive commodity, and pilgrims paid dearly for it, especially if it was thought to come from the famous Balsam Garden.

## BIBLIOGRAPHY

Fabri, Felix. *The Wanderings of Felix Fabri.* Trans. Aubrey Stewart. Palestine Pilgrim Text Society 7–10. London, 1887–1897; rpt. New York: AMS Press, 1971.

*Mandeville's Travels.* Ed. Peter Hamelius. EETS: OS 153, 154. 1919, 1923; rpt. London: Oxford UP, 1961, 1973. [Cotton MS]

Letts, Malcolm. *Sir John Mandeville: The Man and His Book.* London: Batchworth, 1949.

Ogier D'Anglure. *Le Saint Voyage de Jerusalem par le Baron d'Anglure.* Au Bureau de la Bibliothèque Catholique. Paris: Pouget-Coulon, 1858.

Prescott, H.F.M. *Once to Sinai: The Further Pilgrimage of Father Felix Fabri.* New York: Macmillan, 1958.

*Kathleen Coyne Kelly*

## SEE ALSO
Burchard of Mount Sion; Egypt; Fabri, Felix; Holy Land; India; Ludolf of Suchem; *Mandeville's Travels;* William of Boldensele

## Banana

A fruit known since antiquity. Pliny, building on Theophrastus's account, names the tree *pala* ("banana palm") and the fruit *ariena* (XII.12). Of Spanish or Portuguese origin, the word *banana* came into general use after the sixteenth century, replacing various vernacular words for "fig," such as the Portuguese *figo da India* and *figo de Adão* ("Adam's fig").

In the early fourteenth century, the Franciscan John of Marignolli gives an accurate account of the banana as he saw it in Sri Lanka. He adds that, when one slices open the fruit, one finds the figure of a crucified man inside. He refers to the banana as a "fig," and asserts that Adam and Eve did not wear fig leaves, but banana leaves. William of Boldensele (1336) describes "oblong apples, called 'paradises'" (*poma oblonga, que paradisi nuncupantur*) in Cairo, adding that the fruit, no matter which way it is cut, lengthwise or across, and no matter into how many pieces, reveals the symbol of the cross within. He later describes a similar fruit in the land of "Cadisle" [or "Caldilhe"] beyond Cathay. Boldensele's information was appropriated by the writer of the book attributed to Sir John Mandeville (*c.* 1360), who points out that "long apples" (or perhaps plantains, closely related to the banana) rot quickly, which is why they cannot be transported to Europe.

**BIBLIOGRAPHY**

John of Marignolli. *Itinera et Relationes Fratrum Minorum Saeculi XIII et XIV.* Vol. 1 of *Sinica Franciscana.* Ed. Anastasius van den Wyngaert. Quaracchi-Firenze: Collegio di S. Bonaventura, 1929.

———. *Travels.* In *Cathay and the Way Thither,* 2nd series. Ed. Yule-Cordier. pp. 33, 37, 38, 41. See Gen. Bib.

*Mandeville's Travels.* Ed. Peter Hamelius. EETS: OS 153, 154. 1919, 1923; rpt. London: Oxford UP, 1973, 1961. [Cotton MS]

Reynolds, P.K. "Earliest Evidence of Banana Culture." *Journal of the American Oriental Society.* Suppl. 12 (1951): 6–11.

Stover, R.H., and N.W. Simmonds. *Bananas.* 3rd edition. London: Longman, 1987.

*Kathleen Coyne Kelly and Barry Hoberman*

**SEE ALSO**
John of Marignolli; *Mandeville's Travels;* William of Boldensele

## Barca

A type of ship most notably associated with the earliest Portuguese explorations along the coasts of Morocco and Western Sahara. It was in a *barca* that, according to the Portuguese court chronicler Azurara, the navigator Gil Eanes passed the famous Cape Bojador for the first time in 1434. As exploration workhorses, *barca*s were quickly replaced by caravels after 1440. In European waters, they nonetheless continued to play a significant role as smaller-sized cargo carriers well into the second half of the fifteenth century.

*Barca*s are well documented in Portugal from the twelfth century onward, but little is known about their features. Belonging to the same family of vessels as northern barges and various Mediterranean barques, the *barca* seems to have had one or two square rigged masts (as shown in the seal of the Cabido da Sé of Lisbon [1255] or in the escutcheon of the town of Peniche), and may have used oars for alternative propulsion. Of varying sizes, but rarely heavier than 30 to 50 metric tons burden, medieval Portuguese *barca*s served as fishing boats, and carried merchandise between the Iberian Peninsula and northwestern Europe.

The better documented Mediterranean barques of the early 1400s carried, by contrast, up to three masts and had lateen (triangular) sails. It remains uncertain which type of rig—lateen or square—was used in the Portuguese *barca*s of the early fifteenth century. The *barca*s resupplying the Portuguese Moroccan fortress town of Ceuta in the 1450s were from 40 to 70 tons burden, while typical contemporary Mediterranean barques ranged from 15 to 70 tons. *Barca*s remained a common sight in the harbor of Oporto in the 1460s, and carried sugar from Madeira to the Mediterranean as late as 1498. Mediterranean barques of up to 150 tons still sailed the Levant and Flanders routes in the 1500s.

**BIBLIOGRAPHY**

Albuquerque, Luís de. "Barca." In *Dicionário de história de Portugal.* Ed. Joel Serrão. Vol. 1. A–D. Lisbon: Iniciativas Editoriais, 1963, p. 299.

Elbl, Martin M. "The Portuguese Caravel and European Shipbuilding: Phases of Development and Diversity." *Revista da Universidade de Coimbra* 33 (1985): 543–572.

Fonseca, Quirino da. *Os navios do Infante D. Henrique.* 2nd edition. Lisbon: Comissão Executiva das Comemorações do Quinto Centenário da Morte do Infante, 1958.

Lopes de Mendonça, Henrique. *Estudos sobre navios portuguezes dos séculos XV e XVI.* Lisbon: Academia Real das Sciencias, 1892.

*Martin Malcolm Elbl*

**SEE ALSO**
Bojador, Cape; Caravel; Portuguese Expansion; Ships and Shipbuilding

# B

## Barcelona

A key western Mediterranean seaport and the religious, administrative, and economic metropolitan center of medieval Catalonia. Briefly occupied by the Visigoths in 415, Barcelona [Barcino] remained an Ibero-Roman community well into the 470s. Having served as the Visigothic capital from 531 to 548, Barcelona lost the position to Toledo in 573. After the Muslim Berber invasion of the Iberian Peninsula in 711, the city retained partial autonomy, coming under Islamic rule only from 719 to 720, and in 801 it fell to Carolingian troops led by William of Gotha. As a key Christian base, it sustained repeated Muslim attacks, and was plundered by the 'Āmirid first minister al-Mansūr in 985. In 988, it became the capital of the independent county of Barcelona.

By 1010, the city was poised to become a lively hub of seaborne trade, and around 1050, its merchants abandoned the old mediocre Roman port in favor of the open strand around the estuary of the Rambla stream. The dynastic union of Catalonia and Provence in 1112 promoted maritime ambitions. Under Ramon Berenguer III (1097–1134), Barcelona supported early Christian efforts to conquer the Balearic Islands from the Muslims (1114–1116). The consolidation of the *Principat de Catalunya* opened up a hinterland that further expanded when Barcelona's counts became sovereigns of Aragon (1137). Its merchants received important privileges between 1118 and 1232, and in 1252, they began to appoint their own overseas consuls. Out of the urban power struggles of the later 1200s emerged a mature municipal organization, documented in the privilege (charter of rights) *Recognoverunt proceres* of 1284. Work on new fortifications to encompass the expanding city started in 1285. By the early 1300s, Barcelona's commercial ties reached from England in the west to the Levant in the east.

The year 1333 brought the first severe economic downturn, and the Black Death of 1348–1349 inflicted the next blow. Perils of war aggravated the perils of disease during the War of the Union (1347–1348) and the Catalan war with Castile and Genoa (1356–1365). In 1359, when Barcelona became the target of a Castilian naval offensive, the city had 7,631 hearths, or around 38,000 inhabitants. Subsequent outbreaks of pestilence made further ravages, and despite peasant immigration the hearth count sank to 6,565 by the century's end. The bank failures and social strife of the 1380s foreshadowed a deep recession, and

in 1391, popular fury vented itself on Barcelona's Jews. The recovery of the early 1400s was short-lived, but prosperity returned in the early 1420s. The 1430s registered a new decline, aggravated by difficulties in the Levant trade, the competition facing Catalan shipping and cloth exports, and the impoverishment of North African markets. The attempts by Alfonso V of Catalonia/Aragon to conquer Naples, coupled with aggressive policies to protect Catalan trade, did more harm than good. The resulting internal tensions exploded in a struggle between the "popular" and often monarchist Busca party and the oligarchical and regionalist Biga. The Busca came to power in 1453, with the onset of another recession, but its protectionist measures failed, and it was ousted when the Catalan civil war broke out in 1462.

The city suffered heavily during the ten-year-long conflict that pitted Catalonia against King Joan II (with the Biga, the nobility, the church, and a sizeable popular following arrayed against royalists, enserfed peasants, and Busca supporters). The hearth count fell to 4,000, representing some 20,000 inhabitants, foreign markets were lost, and overseas consulates closed. A slow recovery began only after the union of the crowns of Castile and Catalonia/Aragon under Ferdinand and Isabella, but in 1479, the loss of Barcelona's position as a seat of the royal court further eroded its regional hegemony. Ferdinand's centralizing tendencies antagonized the city, and the Second *Remença* (Peasant) War of 1484–1485 temporarily paralyzed trade. Against considerable local opposition, the Inquisition was introduced in its full rigor to Barcelona in 1486–1487, sparking off an emigration of *conversos* (Christianized Jews) and a flight of capital. Relative prosperity returned in 1493–1504, as commerce with the Atlantic seaboard grew, but Barcelona proved unable to tap the new channels of American trade and remained confined to nursing old Mediterranean connections and developing protected markets in southern Italy and Sicily.

**BIBLIOGRAPHY**

Batlle y Gallart, C. *La crisis social y económica de Barcelona a mediados del siglo XV.* 2 vols. Barcelona: Institución Milà y Fontanals, 1973.

Bensch, Stephen P. *Barcelona and Its Rulers, 1096–1291.* New York: Cambridge UP, 1995.

Carrère, Cl. *Barcelone, centre économique à l'époque des difficultés, 1380–1462.* EPHE–6. Civilisations et sociétés. Paris: Mouton, 1967.

Fernández-Armesto, Felipe. *Barcelona: A Thousand Years of the City's Past.* Oxford: Oxford UP, 1992.

Shneidman, J. Lee. *The Rise of the Aragonese Catalan Empire, 1200–1350.* New York: New York UP, 1970.

Sobrequés Vidal, S., and Sobrequés Callicó, J. *La guerra civil catalana del segle XV.* 2 vols. Barcelona: Edicions 62, 1973.

Vicens Vives, J. *Ferran II i la ciutat de Barcelona, 1479–1516.* 3 vols. Barcelona: Tipografia Emporium, 1936–1937.

*Martin Malcolm Elbl*

**SEE ALSO**

Benjamin of Tudela; Black Death; Cog; Law, Maritime; Mediterranean Sea; Pilgrimage Sites, Spanish; Saffron; Spain and Portugal

Barnacle goose from Book of Wonders. Paris, Bibliothèque Nationale MS fr. 2810, fol. 210v, *c.* 1440. Courtesy of the Bibliothèque Nationale.

## Barnacle Goose

A marvelous bird, thought to be generated either from rotting wood that floated upon the sea, or from the fruit of a tree or a shell attached to a tree, or to be actually growing from the tree, attached by its bill.

According to the book widely known as *Mandeville's Travels,* in a certain land beyond Cathay (China) named *Cadisle* [or *Caldilhe*], tiny lambs grow within certain gourds, and people eat both the fruit and the beast. The writer of the *Travels* goes on to borrow from Vincent of Beauvais, recounting the story of an equally marvelous creature, native to Europe, sometimes called the barnacle goose. According to this tale, if the bird hatches and falls into the water, it lives and flies away, but if it falls to earth, it dies and can then be eaten.

The goose *Branta leucopsis,* first identified and located in 1907, has its nesting grounds on the high cliffs of Greenland and Spitzbergen Island, and winters in northern Europe. Medieval people who saw this species of goose appear fully grown each winter and then disappear, without nesting, the following spring, must have sought some explanation for this curious behavior. Some medieval observers, including scholars interested in natural science, thought that the common barnacle, a general term for a variety of crustaceans (order *Cirripedia*), was an early stage in the life cycle of the barnacle goose. In profile, the barnacle's shell (the stalk by which it is attached to driftwood) and its cirri (the feathery arms used to comb the water for food) look remarkably like a small goose-like bird. Since the barnacle goose was often classified as a fish in the Middle Ages, some churchmen argued that it was permissible to eat during Lent.

The origin of the word *barnacle* (Med. Lat. *bernaca;* OF *bernaque;* ME *bernake, bernekke*) is unknown, though etymologies have been offered. It may be related to the Latin *pernacula,* an unattested diminutive of *perna,* a kind of shellfish. Another theory connects the word *bernakes* to *Hibernicula* (literally, "little Ireland"), arguing that Irish priests seemed particularly willing to accept the goose as a kind of shellfish. More convincingly, the word has been traced to Gaelic *bairneach* or Welsh *brenig,* "limpet." The barnacle goose is discussed by Bede, Alexander Neckam, Gerald of Wales, and John Trevisa; Albertus Magnus and Roger Bacon completely reject the connection between crustacean and bird.

There are distant analogues to the barnacle goose: al-Biruni (A.H. 362/973 C.E.–after A.H. 442/1050 C.E.) tells a story of bees that are supposedly generated from the leaves of a tree; the *Thousand and One Nights* includes references to the mythical land of Wak-wak, where trees are supposed to generate maidens who hang by the hair of their heads.

**BIBLIOGRAPHY**

Donoghue, Daniel. "An *Anser* for Exeter Book Riddle 74." In *Words and Works: Studies in Honour of Fred C. Robinson.* Ed. Peter S. Baker and Nicholas Howe. Toronto: U of Toronto P, 1998, pp. 45–58.

Heron-Allen, Edward. *Barnacles in Nature and in Myth.* London: Oxford UP, 1928.

*Mandeville's Travels.* Ed. Peter Hamelius. EETS: OS 153, 154. 1919, 1923; rpt. London: Oxford UP, 1973, 1961. [Cotton MS]

# B

Müller, F. Max. *The Science of Language.* London: Longmans, Green & Co., 1891.

Kathleen Coyne Kelly

SEE ALSO
Albertus Magnus; Bede; Gerald of Wales; *Mandeville's Travels;* Trevisa, John; Vincent of Beauvais

## Bartholomaeus Anglicus

English author of a thirteenth-century encyclopedia generally demonstrating the Christian significance of phenomena; the work includes a substantial chapter on geography.

Very little is known about Bartholomaeus Anglicus (sometimes called "de Glanville") except that he was of English nationality, presented the cursory lectures on the Bible at Paris, and was sent in 1231 to be the *lector* of the Franciscan provincial *studium* in Magdeburg. Thereafter, he rose to be the provincial minister of Austria, probably in 1247, and of Saxony in 1262, a post he held until his death in 1272. Alexander IV may also have named him papal legate to Bohemia, Moravia, Poland, and Austria, where he was to propagandize for the Crusades and protect converts (even against excesses by the Teutonic Knights).

Around 1245, he finished his encyclopedia, *De proprietatibus rerum,* the structure of which followed the order of the Great Chain of Being: God, the angels, the soul of man, the body of man, and so forth. Perhaps because of Magdeburg's remote location, it took a while for the encyclopedia to attain any popularity—it is not mentioned until a surge of citations beginning after 1275. But from that time its popularity was assured, as it multiplied in manuscripts and printed books until the beginning of the seventeenth century, in Latin and in many vernacular translations (such as John Trevisa's into Middle English, *c.* 1386–1390). His intention was to explain "properties" of things mentioned in the Bible, so that the unlearned might begin to understand the spiritual meanings intended; thus, he compiled definitions and commentaries from saints and philosophers, as he says, adding little or nothing of his own.

In Book XV, on the provinces of the world, Bartholomaeus presents one of the larger geographical sections found in any medieval encyclopedia. The compilation is conservative in that Bartholomaeus intended only to repeat the wisdom of established

T-O Map of the World with the Four Elements. Jean Corbechon's translation of *De proprietatibus rerum.* James Ford Bell Library MS 1400/fBa, beginning of Chapter 9. Minneapolis, MN. By permission of the James Ford Bell Library, University of Minnesota.

authors. Thus, for example, he includes a discussion of Pannonia, even though it had ceased to exist more than a century before his time, and of Gallia Senonensis. In fact, another century would pass before cartographers turned from repeating traditional information to reflecting modern geographical realities. Despite his reliance on sources, however, Bartholomaeus does at times appear to add new information, whether on his own or from an otherwise unknown contemporary whom he calls "Erodotus," for discussions of many lands and a few cities, most of them European: Almania, Andegavia (Anjou), Apulia, Aquitania, Aragon, Asturia, Belgium, Bohemia, Brittany, Burgundy, Carinthia, Champagne, Dacia (Denmark), Finland, Flanders, France, Franconia, Frisia, Gallia, Gascony, Gotland (in "Gothia"), Holland, Iceland, Ireland, Italy, Kent, Lectonia (Lithuania), Livonia, Lothringen (Lorraine), perhaps Mauritania, Mide (in Ireland), Missena (Meissen in Germany), Narbonne, Normandy, Norway, the Orcades, Pannonia, Paris, Picardy, Poitiers, the Pyrenees, Rencia and Rintonia (in Germany), Reval (in Estonia), Rumania, Rus', Sambra (Samland), Savoy, Saxony, Scotland, Semigallia (Zemgale in Latvia),

Slavia, Suecia (Sweden), Swabia, Syria, Thuringen, Touraine, Tuscany, Vironnia (Estonia), Vitria (the Isle of Wight), Westphalia, and Zeeland.

Often, these additions merely aver that the fields are good for various crops, but other times more interesting material is added. In Iceland, for example, polar bears break holes in the ice and dive in after fish. The best salt comes from Saxony. Gypsum in the ground around Paris is burned and mixed with water, and then it solidifies until it is hard as stone; this cement is used for walls, buildings, vaulting, and even pavements. And in Livonia, Bartholomaeus notes, the Germans turned the people from the false faith of fiends to the worship and faith of one God, no doubt thinking of the Teutonic Knights (of whose actions he later had personal experience), and discouraged the Livonian funerary tradition that placed wives, slaves, and such on the pyres of the dead.

Since the encyclopedia was finished before Bartholomaeus's career was well under way in northeast Europe, it is not surprising that much of his information was secondhand. However, it does seem peculiar that, despite his origin and university education, his descriptions of England, France, and Paris are generally little more than pastiches of well-known material. Only his discussion of Kent lacks any known source, perhaps suggesting personal acquaintance with the area. It is unfortunate that he did not revise his geography to include information on the Mongol khânate to the east, based on the reports of John de Plano Carpini (Franciscan provincial minister of Saxony, 1232–1239), who returned in 1247 and lectured widely, not far from where Bartholomaeus was living. Nonetheless, Bartholomaeus's information—both original and secondhand—is helpful for understanding the names and legends on medieval *mappaemundi*.

## BIBLIOGRAPHY

Bartholomaeus Anglicus. *De genuinis rerum* [*De proprietatibus rerum*]. Frankfurt, 1601; rpt. Frankfurt am Main: Minerva, 1964.

Delisle, Léopold. "Traités divers sur les *Propriétés des choses.*" *Histoire littéraire de la France.* Paris, 1888, 30:334–388, esp. 353–365.

Greetham, D.C. "The Concept of Nature in Bartholomaeus Anglicus (fl. 1230)." *Journal of the History of Ideas* 41 (1980): 663–677.

Meyer, Heinz. "Bartholomäus Anglicus *De proprietatibus rerum:* Selbstverständnis und Rezeption." *Zeitschrift für Deutsches Altertum und Deutsche Literatur* 99 (1988): 237–274.

Seymour, M.C., et al., eds. *Bartholomaeus Anglicus and His Encyclopedia.* Aldershot: Variorum, 1992.

Trevisa, John, trans. *On the Properties of Things: John Trevisa's Translation of Bartholomaeus Anglicus' De proprietatibus rerum.* Ed. M.C. Seymour, et al. 3 vols. Oxford: Clarendon P, 1975–1988.

Twomey, Michael W. "Medieval Encyclopedias." In *Medieval Christian Literary Imagery: A Guide to Interpretation,* Ed. R.E. Kaske, Arthur Groos, and Michael W. Twomey. Toronto Medieval Bibliographies 11. Toronto: U of Toronto P, 1988. pp. 182–215.

*Juris G. Lidaka*

## SEE ALSO
Franciscan Friars; Geography in Medieval Europe; John of Plano Carpini; Teutonic Order; Trevisa, John

## Bartolomé de Las Casas
*See* Las Casas, Bartolomé de

## Bartolomeu Dias
*See* Dias, Bartolomeu

## Bartholomew of Cremona (d. after 1254)
A thirteenth-century friar who accompanied fellow Franciscan William of Rubruck on his mission to the Mongols in the area north of the Gobi desert (1253–1255).

In the early 1240s, some Christian leaders saw the Mongols who were then invading eastern Europe as potential allies against the Egyptian Mamluks and the Turks. Bartholomew and a certain Friar Thomas, another Franciscan, arrived in the Gobi desert around 1250, possibly sent there by King Louis IX of France, then engaged in the Sixth Crusade, to urge John III Vatatzes (Byzantine emperor at Nicaea) to join in the campaign against the Muslims. In 1253, Bartholomew joined Friar William as he passed through Constantinople on a similar mission to carry letters from Louis and from Baldwin II, the Latin emperor at Constantinople, to the Mongol khâns in Central Asia. Although most scholars emphasize the political and diplomatic implications of these letters proposing a Franco-Mongol alliance, Friar William's own account of the journey insists on its religious purpose: to instruct the Mongol chieftains, rumored to have been converted, in the doctrines of the true faith, and to minister to German captives of the Mongols. Despite this ostensibly religious purpose, the mission did not really accomplish anything for the church: the friars did not effect mass conversions, and, after living among the Mongols for a year, William baptized only six persons.

William's account is the only surviving primary source about the expedition and its members. It is not a travel diary in the modern sense, but provides a glimpse of the physical hardships they endured and their attempts at preaching to Nestorians, Muslims, and *Tuins* (Buddhists). A few details about Bartholomew are found in William's narrative. On the voyage through the steppes, he was so hungry he could no longer recall when he had last eaten. Following the precepts of their order, the Franciscans traveled barefoot until their toes froze due to the severe winter. Unaware of a Mongol law that forbad anyone to touch the threshold of a dwelling upon entering, Bartholomew was once arrested and narrowly escaped execution for stumbling on the threshold of Möngke Khân's dwelling. When William departed for the West in July 1254, the ailing Bartholomew, knowing that he could not survive the return journey, begged the khân to be allowed to remain in Karakorum. He probably ended his life ministering to its few Christian residents, members of a small colony of European craftsmen held captive there.

**BIBLIOGRAPHY**

*Les frères mineurs et l'église grecque orthodoxe au XIIIe siècle (1231–1274). Biblioteca Bio-Bibliografica della Terra e dell'Oriente francescano,* series 4: Studi, no. 2. Cairo: Centre d'Etudes Orientales, 1954.

*The Mission of Friar William of Rubruck. His Journey to the Court of the Great Khan Möngke 1253–1255.* Trans. Peter Jackson, with notes and introduction by Peter Jackson and David Morgan. Hakluyt Society, 2nd series, 173. London: Hakluyt Society, 1990.

Olschki, Leonardo. *Marco Polo's Precursors.* Baltimore: Johns Hopkins UP, 1943.

Van den Wyngaert, Anastasius. *Sinica Franciscana, I. Itinera et relationes Fratrum Minorum saeculi XIII et XIV.* Florence: Quaracchi, 1929.

*Gloria Allaire*

**SEE ALSO**
Buddhism; Diplomacy; Franciscan Friars; Louis IX; Mamluks; Missionaries to China; Nestorianism; William of Rubruck

## Bartolomeo da li Sonetti

A late-fifteenth-century Venetian shipmaster and cartographer. Bartolomeo da li Sonetti acquired justifiable fame as the man responsible for an *isolario,* or collection of island maps, printed in Venice in 1485; they are among the first printed maps in history and constitute the first printed collection of charts. "Da li Sonetti" is a nickname, referring to the descriptive sonnets in Venetian dialect that accompany his maps. He has been incorrectly identified as Bartolomeo Zamberti, who was only thirteen when the *isolario* was printed. It has also been suggested that he was the Bartolomeo Turco named in Leonardo da Vinci's notebooks as a supplier of information about the Black and the Caspian seas.

Bartolomeo's *Isolario* was largely indebted to the unpublished, but widely circulated, *Liber Insularum Archipelagi* (*c.* 1420) by Cristoforo Buondelmonte. Bartolomeo's cartography is not entirely uninfluenced by his own practical experience, however. As an officer and later as a ship's captain, he traveled to the Greek archipelago fifteen times. The forty-nine charts of his *Isolario* include the Greek islands, Crete, and Cyprus. These charts are noteworthy for being created from firsthand observation by Italian mariners, without dependence on Ptolemy. They were produced by means of a compass, not by a system of projection. Like earlier Italian nautical maps, some charts employ distance scales and the eight-pointed compass rose, although they are not uniformly oriented by direction. Rocks are conventionally noted by the use of a cross, and shoals by a line of single dots. None of the maps bears names of cities: the only features shown are sketches of scattered churches, castles, and hills.

Although Bartolomeo's maps have been judged as insignificant in terms of their technical achievements, they have the distinction of being both the earliest printed sea charts and the first printed map collection. The work was published in Venice in a woodcut edition without a title page *c.* 1485 by Guglielmo da Trino, called "Anima Mia" (Hain 2538-14890). A cryptogram embedded in the prologue's opening three lines dedicates the book to Giovanni Mocenigo, doge of Venice (1478–1485). Most of the islands fill a single page, although Crete and Negroponte each cover facing pages. Although the outline of each individual island is clearly recognizable, none bears any caption, being described instead in the accompanying verses. The unlettered woodcuts may have been intended for hand coloring and finishing. In 1528, Bartolomeo's *Isolario* was enlarged by Benedetto Bordone, who added the Baltic and portions of America in his *Libro de Tutte l'Isole del Mondo.* It was also imitated by Camocio, Porcacchi, and others. It received a second Venetian edition with woodcut illustrations in 1532; this was printed with the addition of Francesco Rosselli's oval projection world map, which was produced around 1508.

**BIBLIOGRAPHY**

Bartolommeo dalli Sonetti. *Isolario. Venice 1485.* Intro. Frederick R. Goff. Series of Atlases in Facsimile, 6th series, 1. Amsterdam: Theatrum Orbis Terrarum, 1972.

Bühler, Curt F. "Variants in the First Atlas of the Mediterranean." In *Gutenberg-Jahrbuch* (1957): 94–97.

Campbell, Tony. *The Earliest Printed Maps 1472–1500.* Berkeley: U of California P, 1987.

Howse, Derek, and Michael Sanderson. *The Sea Chart. An Historical Survey Based on the Collections in the National Maritime Museum.* New York: McGraw-Hill, 1973.

Turner, Hilary Louise. "Christopher Buondelmonti and the Isolario." *Terrae Incognitae* 19 (1987): 11–28.

*Gloria Allaire*

**SEE ALSO**

Compass, Magnetic; Maps; Portolan Charts; Rosselli, Francesco; Venice

## Baybars I (r. 1260–1277)

An extremely influential sultan of Egypt and ruler of the Mamluks, a military body originally composed of Turkish slaves, that seized the throne of Egypt in 1250.

Although Baybars [Al-Malik al-Zāhir Rukn al-Dīn al-Bundukdārī] was the fourth sultan to reign over the Mamluks of Egypt and Syria, later generations nevertheless considered him the true founder of the Mamluk sultanate and looked upon the structures he put into place and the policies he established as a venerated ideal. In establishing religious institutions, Baybars was careful to follow Muslim political tradition, which viewed the task of government as defending Islam from its enemies from without and ruling the country according to the dictates of the *sharīʿa* (Muslim law) from within. In keeping with these objectives, Baybars restored in 1261 the Abbasid caliphate that medieval Islam theoretically esteemed as the source of religious and political authority. He also established a judicial system based on the four Muslim legal schools, which, while ostensibly in accordance with the *sharīʿa*, divided the judicial system in such a way as to weaken its status and subordinate the religious establishment to the Mamluk government.

In another and equally influential undertaking, the independent and innovative approach Baybars took in reorganizing the army and restructuring its adminisration was much in keeping with the Mamluks' newly acquired status as rulers of the sultanate. He first created a discrete framework for a single uniform army that he made subordinate to the central Mamluk government. He then supplied the equipment his Mamluks needed out of the sultan's treasury, and introduced standard training procedures, as well as a fixed system of military ranks and well-defined principles for apportioning fiefs (*iqtāʿāt*), revenues that served the Mamluks as remuneration. In times of both war and peace, Baybars maintained his army at a very high level of professionalism and readiness through strict discipline, intensive training exercises, and wide-ranging maneuvers.

But clearly, Baybars' most direct contribution to trade and travel was the efficient system of intelligence and mail service (*al-barīd*) that he introduced. Well known in the Islamic world from the Umayyad period, this system was based on waystations that housed fully equipped horses and homing pigeons taking messages to and from the sultan. During his reign the system was so efficient, the sources tell us, that Baybars could be playing polo in Cairo the first half of the week and in Damascus the second half; it also made control of Syria easier, which was of great strategic importance to the Mamluk sultanate against the Mongol il-khâns who ruled in Mesopotamia and Persia.

With his highly disciplined army and sophisticated system of communications, Baybars conducted very effective military campaigns against the Crusaders, razing cities like Caesarea, Haifa, and Jaffa, and pushing the Crusaders' presence into a narrow strip along the Syrian shore. These campaigns culminated in 1268, when Antioch—the major Crusader princedom—was conquered and completely destroyed. With the fall of Antioch, Frankish control of the Syrian coast collapsed, clearing the way to the final elimination of the Crusader presence in Syria and Palestine. Baybars also destroyed the mountain strongholds of the Assassins, who had enjoyed Crusader protection, weakened the Armenians, and used superior intelligence services and careful military strategy to stabilize the border along the Euphrates that separated Mamluk and Mongol territories.

At the same time, Baybars employed diplomacy against the Mongol il-khâns. In 1261, a conflict within the Mongol camp provided him with the opportunity

# B

of forging an alliance with Berke Khân, the Mongol khân of the Golden Horde (r. 1256–1266), who had recently converted to Islam, against his Persian il-khân opponents. Beyond the purely military advantage of harassing the Mongol il-khâns on two fronts simultaneously, the alliance with the Golden Horde also reinforced the Mamluk sultanate by ensuring Egypt an uninterrupted supply of Mamluks from the slave markets in territory controlled by the Golden Horde.

The renewal of friendly relations between Egypt and Byzantium allowed the conduct of commerce between the Mamluk sultanate and the Golden Horde along the maritime trade routes, after the traditional overland routes that went through eastern Anatolia had passed into the hands of the Mongol il-khâns, their Seljuk vassals, and their Christian allies from Lesser Armenia (*Bilad Sis*). As part of these friendly relations, the emperor of Byzantium, Michael Palaeologus, who also viewed the Mongol il-khâns and their Seljuk vassals in Anatolia as a threat to his territory, agreed to allow passage through the Bosporus of Genoese vessels carrying goods to Egypt, including the majority of the Qipchaq Mamluks from the Golden Horde.

To ensure Egypt's commercial interests in Europe, Baybars sought allies in that region. In 1261, he sent a delegation to Manfred, son of Frederick II, king of Sicily, who was a sworn enemy of the papacy. A commercial agreement was signed in 1262 with James of Aragon, and similar agreements were later signed with a number of Italian naval states. In 1264, in Cairo, Baybars received a delegation from Charles of Anjou, brother of Louis IX, who was the papacy's candidate to succeed the Hohenstaufens. This delegation symbolized recognition of the power of the Mamluk sultan by the European rulers.

Toward the end of his rule, Baybars devoted his efforts to consolidating the influence of the Mamluk sultanate beyond its southern borders. In 1276, he exploited the outbreak of conflicts within the Nubian ruling family to intervene in that country's internal affairs and to draw it into the Mamluk sphere of influence, thus renewing Nubian-Egyptian commercial relations that had been disrupted in 1272. At his death on June 17, 1277, after seventeen years of rule, Baybars left his successors a well-organized army and government and a far-flung empire stretching from Nubia in the south to the Taurus in the north, and from the Euphrates in the east to Cyrenaica (*Barka*) in the west.

## BIBLIOGRAPHY

Amitai-Preiss, Reuven. *Mongols and Mamluks.* Cambridge: Cambridge UP, 1995.

Levanoni, Amalia. *A Turning Point in Mamluk History.* Leiden: Brill, 1995.

Thorau, P. *The Lion of Egypt: Sultan Baybars I and the Near East in the Thirteenth Century.* Trans. P.M. Holt. London: Longman, 1992.

*Amalia Levanoni*

## SEE ALSO

Animals, Exotic; Armenia; Assassins; Byzantine Empire; Egypt; Golden Horde; Holy Land; Krak des Chevaliers; Mamluks; Mongols; Seljuk Turks; Spies; Yasa

## Beatus Maps

*Mappaemundi* illuminating some fourteen manuscripts of the *Commentarium in Apocalypsin* written in the last decades of the eighth century by the Spanish monk, Beatus of Liébana. Representative of what has been called the "golden age of Church cartography," these maps are one of the important sources of *mappaemundi* of the period between the eighth and the twelfth century. They are unusual in their innovative character, both for their technical conception and their symbolic meaning, and they present a thoughtful conceptualization of the structure, content, and meaning of the world.

The *mappaemundi* appear in the prologue to Book II, which describes the mission of the Apostles to evangelize the world. That Beatus himself included such a map in his original commentary is evident in his textual reference to it, *subiectae formulae pictura demonstrat.* In itself, this is an indication of the central importance of the topic of evangelization for the overarching themes of Beatus's commentary. This is above all a map of salvation history in which the Gospel is brought to the four corners of the earth.

With few exceptions, these maps are of large format, spread across two folios, and oriented toward the east. There are two different versions of the map, one oval in shape and one rectangular, reflecting the two broad families of Beatus manuscripts. This manuscript tradition is controversial, as are questions of sources and filiation. Overall, however, it can be said that the oval map, found for example in the Beatus manuscript today in Burgo de Osma, represents the manuscript Branch I, and the rectangular, simplified map, represented among others by the Beatus of Gerona or the famous Morgan Beatus, today in the Pierpont Morgan Library, characterizes Branch II.

The Osma map is oval in shape and highly detailed. The Ocean Sea, in which various fish swim, frames the map. At the top right lies Paradise, represented by the biblical Four Rivers that flow from it. The basic distribution of land masses is in the tau-omega (T-O) form characteristic of Isidorean *mappaemundi,* in which the world is divided into three continents arranged as a T within a circle or O. Asia stands at the top, by far the largest land mass; Europe inhabits the bottom left, and Africa the bottom right. A fourth continent, unknown because of the heat of the sun, stands as an island at the far right, and in the Osma map (and those related to it) is inhabited by a sciapod, a "shadow-foot" or antipod, whose one huge foot serves as a canopy to shade him from the sun. Most noteworthy in the Osma version is the depiction of busts of the Apostles at the sites of their evangelization and burial, underscoring the central theme of Beatus's text at this point.

The Branch II map, on the other hand, is rectangular in shape and simplified in detail, particularly in the elimination of some place-names and the busts of the Apostles. In five of the Branch II manuscripts (Branch IIb), the Apostles are depicted separately on folios preceding the map. A drawing of Adam and Eve in the Garden of Eden replaces the Four Rivers of Paradise at the top right. An unusual feature of both branches, given their overarching spiritual intent, is the fact that

the world is Greek, centered on Constantinople, and it is this city, not Jerusalem, that lies at the geographical center of the world.

Because the archetype is now lost, there is no way of knowing what the original looked like, since there is significant variation both in generalities and detail among the various examples. As the Osma map so clearly illustrates Beatus's text, scholars have taken it to be the closest representative of the original map. The representation of the sciapod in the fourth continent, on the other hand, is an innovation more akin to the eleventh century, when the manuscript itself was produced. Given what is now known about the evolution of the manuscript texts and illluminations, it seems unlikely that the Osma map can be taken for anything but an eleventh-century development, from which the other Beatus maps in this style likely also stem. Even the two-folio format may have developed later.

A number of sources have been proposed for Beatus's map, but given both the traditional T-O distribution of land masses and the fact that Isidorean texts accompany the map at this point in the commentary, it is likely that the source was an *Etymologies* map. Such a map, found in MS Vat. lat. 6018 (Biblioteca Apostolica Vaticana), bears such close resemblance to the Beatus map that a common archetype has been proposed. Isidore's *Etymologies* XI.iii.23 also seems to be the source of inspiration for the sciapod, since tenth-century *Etymologies* maps depict a zone in Africa as *terra de pedes latos,* or "the land of wide

World map from Beatus's *Commentary on the Apocalypse.* Spain, Burgo de Osma, Archivo de la Catedral MS 1, fols. 35v-36, *c.* 1086. Courtesy Burgo de Osma Cathedral.

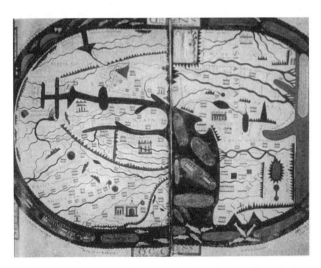

World map from Beatus's *Commentary on the Apocalypse.* Paris, Bibliothèque Nationale MS lat. 8878, fol. 45r, *c.* 1058. Courtesy of the Bibliothèque Nationale.

# B

feet." Indeed, in the various Beatus maps diverse inscriptions from the *Etymologies* define the fourth continent, the most interesting drawn precisely from *Etymologies* XI cited above: *Sciopodum gens . . . singulis cruribus et celeritate mirabili . . . per aestum in terra resupini jacentes, pedum suorum magnitudine adumbrentur.*

Despite the considerable geographical and ethnographic interest of its innovations, the intent of the Beatus *mappaemundi* is symbolic: to represent the progress of salvation history through the apostolic mandate to carry the Gospel to the four corners of the earth. In this sense the map also underscores other related themes of Beatus's commentary. Beatus wrote in the years shortly following the Muslim conquest of Spain, and made a direct connection between the macrocosmic events of the Apocalypse and the immediate circumstances of the fall of the Visigoths due to the faithlessness and apostasy of their priests and kings. Concomitantly, the rebirth of Spain would come through faithfulness and the renewed preaching of the true faith. One of the most interesting and innovative elements of the Beatus text and *mappaemundi* is that they make one of the earliest known associations between St. James and the evangelization of Spain, an affirmation that would later be of great importance for the political and spiritual reconquest of the peninsula. Thus, Beatus maps are exceptional representatives of the early medieval worldview as much for their spiritual as for their physical topography.

## BIBLIOGRAPHY

Harley-Woodward. *History of Cartography.* Vol. 1. See Gen. Bib.

Klein, Peter. *Der ältere Beatus-Kodex Vitr. 14-1 der Biblioteca Nacional zu Madrid: Studien zur Beatus-Illustration und der spanischen Buchmalerei des 10. Jahrhunderts.* Hildesheim: Olms, 1976.

Miller, Konrad. *Die Weltkarte des Beatus.* Vol. 1 of *Mappae Mundi. Die ältesten Weltkarten.* Stuttgart: Roth, 1895.

von den Brincken, Anna-Dorothee. "Das Weltbild der lateinischen Universalhistoriker." *Popoli e Paesi nella Cultura Altomedievale. Settimane di Studio del Centro Italiano di Studi sull'alto Medioevo* 29 (1983): 386–408.

———. "Mappa Mundi und Chronographia." *Deutsches Archiv für die Erforschung des Mittelalters* 24 (1968): 118–186.

Williams, John. *The Illustrated Beatus: A Corpus of the Illustrations of the Commentary on the Apocalypse.* London: Harvey Miller, 1994.

*Susan A. Rabe*

## SEE ALSO

Center of the Earth; Constantinople; Four Rivers of Paradise; Isidore of Seville; *Mappamundi;* Maps; Monstrosity, Geographical; *Terra Australes; Terra Incognita*

## Bede (673–735)

An English historian, interested in natural and geographical phenomena. At the age of seven, Bede entered the monastery of St. Peter and St. Paul at Wearmouth under Abbot Benedict Biscop. Sometime afterward he was transferred to the monastery at Jarrow under Abbot Ceolfrith. Except for short trips to Lindisfarne and York, Bede never left his assigned monastery. But if his travels were limited, his range of interests was not. He excelled in an astonishing variety of academic disciplines. He wrote commentaries on the Gospel of Luke, the Book of Acts, and many Old Testament books; educational treatises on subjects including poetry, natural science, orthography, and chronography, as well as biographies, hagiographies, and homilies; and the work for which he is best known, *The Ecclesiastical History of the English People,* which he completed in 731.

Though he himself never left England, in his *Ecclesiastical History,* Bede praised the pilgrimages of men like Benedict Biscop and Ceolfrith; he also wrote a guide to the Holy Land, though he never traveled there. In fact, Bede demonstrated his interest in the Holy Land by writing three works about it, two of them explications of biblical toponyms in Palestine. The first, *Nomina locorum ex beati Hieronimi presbiteri et Flavi Iosephi collecta opusculis,* is a compendium of material Bede gathered from the work of Jerome and Flavius Josephus; it is attached to his commentary, *In primam partem Samuhelis.* The second, *Nomina regionum atque locorum de Actibus Apostolorum,* attached to his commentary on the Book of Acts, is a geographical dictionary of sites associated with Luke's history.

Bede's most important work of this type is his abridgment of Adamnan's *De locis sanctis.* Adamnan wrote his text based on information received from Bishop Arculf, who had been a pilgrim to Jerusalem, Damascus, and Constantinople, before being shipwrecked on the shore of Britain. Bede included selections from his version of Adamnan's work in his *Ecclesiastical History* (Book 5, chapters 15–17).

Bede included the most crucially significant sites in Christian history, describing the churches built to enshrine them. He begins with a description of Bethlehem and the Church of the Nativity. The Church of St. Mary in Bethlehem marks the spot where her milk fell on paving stones and "can be seen today." In Jerusalem, he discusses the Church of the Holy Sepulchre, with its specific chapels marking the sites of the discovery of the True Cross, the Crucifixion (Golgotha), and the Resurrection (the Anastasis), where twelve lamps burn day and night. In a church on the Mount of Olives, the site of Jesus's Ascension, pilgrims can see "His last footprints, exposed to the sky above." Bede records no miracles associated with these places except for the rush of wind that strikes the Mount of Olives and knocks people to the ground on the anniversary of the Ascension. Before concluding his summary, Bede describes the tombs of the patriarchs at Hebron.

Bede thought these passages would be "useful" to the reader of his *Ecclesiastical History,* and he compiled a book of extracts from pilgrimages to the Holy Land entitled *De locis sanctis,* after Adamnan's work, which is its principal source. It includes selections from Eucherius's (*c.* 410–*c.* 499) *Epitome about Certain Holy Places* and Hegesippus's (d. 180) commentary on Acts. Bede harmonizes the material and styles of these texts in a unified work of his own.

**BIBLIOGRAPHY**

Bede. *De locis sanctis.* Ed. F. Fraipont. In *Itineraria et alia geographica.* Corpus Christianorum Series Latina 175. Turnhout, Belgium: Brepols, 1965, pp. 245–280.

———. *A History of the English Church and People.* Trans. Leo Sherley-Price. Harmondsworth: Penguin, 1978.

———. *In Primam Partem Samuhelis Libri III.* Ed. D. Hurst, Corpus Christianorum Series Latina 119. Turnhout, Belgium: Brepols, 1962, pp. 1–287.

Brown, George Hardin. *Bede the Venerable.* Boston: Twayne, 1987.

Eucherius. *The Epitome of S. Eucherius about Certain Holy Places.* Trans. Aubrey Stewart. London: Palestine Pilgrims' Text Society, 1890; rpt. New York: AMS Press, 1971.

Hunter Blaire, Peter. *The World of Bede.* London: Secker and Warburg, 1970.

Meehan, Denis, ed. *Adamnan's De locis sanctis.* Scriptores Latini Hiberniae 3. Dublin: Dublin Institute for Advanced Studies, 1958.

Sharpe, Richard. *A Handlist of the Latin Writers of Great Britain and Ireland before 1540.* Turnhout, Belgium: Brepols, 1997, pp. 70–76.

*Gary D. Schmidt*

**SEE ALSO**
Adamnan; Arculf; Holy Land; Jerusalem

# Behaim, Martin (*c.* 1459–1507)

A German cloth merchant who produced, before 1492, a remarkable globe that may have encouraged early exploration. Born around 1459 in Nuremberg, Behaim claimed to have sailed as far south as the Guinea coast in 1484–1485 as captain of one of Diogo Cão's ships, and it is likely that he sat as a member of the *Junta dos mathematicos* in the court of Portugal's King John in 1484 or 1485. The king knighted him in Lisbon on February 14, 1485.

Behaim is best known for the globe he helped fashion in Nuremberg sometime before 1492, now the oldest extant globe. He is remembered by historians—perhaps erroneously and through his own self-promotion—as "the Navigator." As an experienced geographer, cosmographer, and cartographer, he has been credited with influencing Columbus's and Magellan's explorations and with furthering the navigational arts by introducing into Portugal the planispheric astrolabe for use by seamen, the sundial, the cross-staff (Jacob's staff), and Johann Müller's *Ephemerides.* Some of these claims and attributions lack historical certainty.

On Behaim's return to Nuremberg from Portugal in 1490, George Holzschuher of the town council, intermediary between Behaim and the lords of Nuremberg's treasury, suggested that "the Navigator" be commissioned to construct a globe illustrating his knowledge of recent Portuguese discoveries. Although it was made according to his "indications," the exact nature of which are unclear, and although he generally is assumed to be the source of its inscriptions, Behaim's precise role in the globe's construction is unknown. He was paid for "a printed *mappa mundi* embracing the whole world," which was meant later to hang in Nuremberg's town hall, and for painting, mounting, and framing the map. The provision of this *mappamundi,* which has not been found, and the globe's inscriptions were Behaim's main contributions. The world map and globe's sources include Ptolemy, Isidore of Seville, Marco Polo, Sir John Mandeville, portolan charts, Toscanelli, Strabo, Pomponius Mela, Diodorus Siculus, Herodotus, Pliny, Dionysius, Pierre d'Ailly, and Portuguese pilots' charts that Behaim would likely have seen. The sphere, essentially papiermâché, was constructed by Kalperger, coated with whiting, and then covered by the map gores, which the miniature painter Georg Glockenthon illustrated. The globe, on display since 1907 in Nuremberg's Germanisches Nationalmuseum, measures 63.6 inches (1,595

# B

mm) in circumference and 20.28 inches (507 mm) in diameter.

Behaim's globe represents the equator and the ecliptic, the circles of the tropics, the Arctic, and the Antarctic; it is studded with signs of the zodiac. Its only meridian is drawn from pole to pole 80 degrees west of Lisbon. Behaim's reliance on Ptolemy meant that he extended Asia so far eastward that his Atlantic Ocean was about 100 degrees narrower than its true width of 229 degrees. The sea is dark blue, and the land bright brown or buff with patches of green and silver, which represent the forests and regions supposedly buried beneath permanent ice and snow. Glockenthon painted 111 miniatures and filled the empty Antarctic Circle with the Nuremberg eagle and virgin's head, along with the arms of the three chief captains by whose authority it was made: Paul Volckamer, Gabriel Nützel, and Nikolaus Groland. Forty-eight flags and fifteen coats of arms with heraldic colors, including a faulty version of the Portuguese arms, are represented. Following the medieval cartographic tradition, the globe also depicts creatures of legend: a merman and mermaid near the Cape Verde Islands, two sciapodes in south-central Africa, sirens, and satyrs. Men with dogs' heads appear in some of Behaim's legends, which are painted in black, red, gold, and silver. There is no Garden of Eden (this is not a didactically Christian globe), but there are more than 1,100 places named—many of them in duplicate. During two restorations (1823 and 1847) a number of the place-names were corrupted beyond recognition.

Behaim likely had a fair knowledge of reading, writing, mathematics, and Latin, although the particulars of his education are unknown. He boasted of having studied under Johann Müller of Königsberg (also known as Regiomontanus [Köningsberg is today Kalingrad]), one of the premier mathematicians and astronomers of the age. This claim, recorded by João Barros, seems to have been the basis of his immediate and historical reputation as cosmographer, geographer, and cartographer. There is no other evidence to show that either this tutelage or his reputation was based in any way on historical fact. There is also no record of Behaim's distinguishing himself in the navigational arts; indeed, his first real sea experience did not come until 1484, when he sailed to Lisbon from Antwerp. All of this makes his claim to have been appointed captain of one of Diogo Cão's two vessels, which set sail from Portugal in 1484 to explore the west coast of Africa, even more suspect. Nonetheless, Gerald Crone thought that Behaim must have had "some fairly detailed record of Cão's second voyage" (124), which he used in writing the legends for his globe. This was likely the information that prompted Holzschuher to lobby in Behaim's favor with the Nuremberg treasurers. Behaim announced in 1494 that he was returning to Portugal and the Azores from Nuremberg. After this announcement, there is only a brief mention of his name, found in a legal document in which his wife was charged with adultery. Nothing else was heard of him until he died impoverished in Lisbon on July 29, 1507.

E.G. Ravenstein, still Behaim's best—if biased—biographer, includes a fine four-sheet, original-scale reproduction of the globe's gores, and Rand McNally has produced a single-sheet copy, *Martin Behaim's Erdapfel, 1492*. Elly Decker and Peter van der Krogt provide an excellent reproduction of the entire globe (p. 26, pl. 2), and Charles Bricker gives a close-up view of Behaim's Africa (p. 29). In her study of Columbus's mental map, Valerie I.J. Flint sketches a map of his first two voyages onto a Behamian projection (p. 147, fig. 1).

## BIBLIOGRAPHY

Bricker, Charles, Gerald Roe Crone, and R.V. Tooley. *Landmarks of Mapmaking: An Illustrated Survey of Maps and Mapmakers.* New York: Thomas Y. Crowell, 1976.

Crone, Gerald Roe. "Martin Behaim, Navigator and Cosmographer; Figment of Imagination or Historical Personage?" *Acts of the Congresso Internacional de Historia dos Descobrimentos* 2 (1961): 117–133.

Decker, Elly, and Peter van der Krogt. *Globes from the Western World.* London: Zwemmer, 1993.

Flint, Valerie I.J. *The Imaginative Landscape of Christopher Columbus.* Princeton: Princeton UP, 1992.

*Martin Behaim's Erdapfel, 1492.* Chicago: Rand McNally, 1960.

Ravenstein, Ernest George. *Martin Behaim: His Life and His Globe, With a Facsimile of the Globe Printed in Colours, Eleven Maps and Seventeen Illustrations.* London: George Philip, 1908.

Stefoff, Rebecca. *The British Library Companion to Maps and Mapmaking.* London: The British Library, 1995.

Winter, Heinrich. "New Light on the Behaim Problem." *Acts of the Congresso Internacional de Historia dos Descobrimentos* 2 (1961): 399–410.

*Daniel P. Terkla*

**SEE ALSO**

Ailly, Pierre d'; Columbus, Christopher; Geography in Medieval Europe; Isidore of Seville; *Liber Floridus;*

*Mandeville's Travels; Mappamundi;* Maps; Marco Polo; Pliny the Elder; Mela, Pomponius; Portolan Charts; Portuguese Expansion; Ptolemy; Toscanelli; *Wonders of the East*

## Bell *Mappamundi*

A *mappamundi* prepared *c.* 1450 by a scribe from southern Germany, and housed since 1960 in the James Ford Bell Library at the University of Minnesota.

The Bell *mappamundi* is a product of the Vienna-Klosterneuburg school of geographic and cartographic knowledge, which flourished in central Europe in the early to mid-1400s. Along with the Walsperger and Zeitz maps, it is one of only a few surviving visual examples of the intellectual innovations of this school, whose thinkers were influenced by Arabic and Ptolemaic concepts of mapmaking, during the century immediately preceding Europe's expansion both east and west. It is oriented to the south, has a fairly accurate Mediterranean coastline, and describes the Canary Islands as having been "recently discovered [*inventa*]." The Bell *mappamundi*'s 152 legends reveal direct influence of the cosmographical material copied by the monk Fridericus Amann (Munich, Bayerische Staatsbibliothek Clm. 14583 [transcribed by Dana Bennett Durand in his Appendix 14]). Although invaluable as an image based on careful geographical tables, the Bell exemplar is a fragment—the vellum surface today measures approximately 9 to 9½-by-13¼ inches (223/238-by-330/334 mm), but all evidence indicates that the originally square surface was some 24 inches (590/600 mm) on a side. The fragment retains all of what modern map-readers would call Africa, Europe from the Mediterranean to a line extending from north of the Black Sea to Yorkshire, and a sliver of the Arabian Peninsula. Place-names such as "Salzepurk" strongly suggest that the scribe was from southern Germany.

The intellectual tradition that produced the map sought to establish exact coordinates for locations for the first time on European world maps: cities are located precisely by means of inked dots (some are also displayed in architectural designs, topped by crescents or crosses to indicate the official local religion, most prominently Cairo, the Isle of the Blest off the west coast of Africa, and an unnamed place at the southern tip of Ireland). The Mediterranean region, both north and south, is particularly rich in toponyms. Sub-Saharan Africa, however, is represented as a region inhabited by people with lion heads and fox tails, governments whose kings are elected for one year and then decapitated, and religions whose adherents worship the sun. Unlike the Walsperger and Zeitz maps, the Bell *mappamundi* depicts several of these peoples, some of whom are shown in stylish costumes of red and blue (blue is also used for water and names of waterways; brown for mountains and promontories; red for regional and population names; and silver to decorate the facades of buildings in the architectural designs). The display contradicts somewhat modern assumptions about the delineation of continents and shows that even the scientific advances of the Vienna-Klosterneuburg school could not completely overcome traditional associations of remote parts of the world with monstrous races of humans.

**BIBLIOGRAPHY**

Destombes, Marcel, ed. *Mappemondes. Imago Mundi,* supp. 4, pp. 214–217 [52.11]. See Gen. Bib.

Durand, Dana Bennett. *The Vienna-Klosterneuburg Map Corpus of the Fifteenth Century. A Study in the Transition from Medieval to Modern Science.* Leiden: Brill, 1952. (The Bell *mappamundi* is not mentioned by Durand, but his Appendix 14 [pp. 391–456] contains transcriptions closely related to legends on it.)

Parker, John. "A Fragment of a Fifteenth-century Planisphere in the James Ford Bell Collection." *Imago mundi* 19 (1965): 106–107.

*Scott D. Westrem*

**SEE ALSO**

Canary Islands; Cartography, Arabic; Geography in Medieval Europe; Klosterneuburg Map Corpus; *Mappamundi;* Maps; Monstrosity, Geographical; Portolan Charts; Ptolemy; Walsperger, Andreas; Zeitz Map

## Benedict the Pole (fl. 1240s)

Companion of John of Plano Carpini when they traveled as papal ambassadors to the great khân in Mongolia between 1245 and 1247.

A Franciscan friar who joined John of Plano Carpini in Wrocław (German Breslau) in Silesia, Benedict accompanied John on one of the first papal embassies sent to the Mongols by Pope Innocent IV. Benedict was a valuable companion for John since he was fluent in Slavic languages and could thus serve as a translator for a substantial part of their journey and help gather information from Russians and other Eastern Europeans at

# B

the great khân's court. He also had contacts with key Christian rulers in Eastern Europe. Nothing about the rest of Benedict's life is known, except that he presumably accompanied John to confer with the pope at Lyons, arriving in November 1247.

Friar Benedict left behind a brief account of his travels and experiences, comprising only around 1,400 words in the Latin, about one-twelfth the length of John's complete *Ystoria Mongalorum.* Given the title *Relatio,* the work was evidently dictated by Benedict in Cologne in late September 1247 upon the embassy's return from Karakorum, the emerging Mongol capital. Composed in the third person with occasional first-person plural interruptions reflecting a scribal point of view, it contains certain information not found in John's longer history, including some geographical data (about the salt desert near the Sea of Azov) and the observation that some 3,000 envoys and 5,000 princes and lords attended the Mongol court for the election and coronation of a new khân. Benedict also echoes John's report about the presence of monstrous races of humans in Central Asia. Perhaps most significantly, the work has at its conclusion a short version of Güyük Khân's reply letter to Innocent IV, ordering the pope and other "Christian princes" to surrender.

The *Relatio,* which is known from two manuscripts in which it precedes John's account (and is untitled), does not, however, constitute Benedict's principal contribution to Western knowledge about the Mongols and Central Asia. Benedict was the main oral source for a much longer account written in Poland or Bohemia (Kråkow, Wrocław, and Prague have been suggested) by a Franciscan named C. de Bridia, who finished his *Historia Tartarorum* (*Tartar Relation* in English) on July 30, 1247; this work was discovered and first studied by modern scholars in the mid-1950s. While he got a few items from John, de Bridia obtained nearly all his information directly from Benedict in a context that has been compared to a "press conference" or a "lecture tour." Benedict apparently spoke in his native Polish, which C. de Bridia translated into Latin.

Unlike the first-person account of John and the dictated work by Benedict, C. de Bridia's *Historia* did not record much about the travel and adventures of the friars. The primary focus of C. de Bridia's text is Mongol history: their conquests, character, way of life, social customs, religious beliefs, and future plans and intentions. These topics were of practical importance to Europeans, who greatly feared a second Mongol invasion—a fear that was only fanned by Güyük Khân's ultimatum or challenge in his reply to the pope. While much of John's material came from Christian captives living among the Mongols, Benedict's sources were often the Mongols themselves, and he cites them repeatedly. Along with John, Benedict—through his own brief *Relatio* and C. de Bridia's longer *Historia*—provided thirteenth-century Europe with one of its first reliable, eyewitness accounts of the geography, people, and political status of Central Asia, especially of the rise and conquests of the Mongols.

## BIBLIOGRAPHY

Dawson, Christopher, ed. *The Mongol Mission.* See Gen. Bib.

Olschki, Leonardo. *Marco Polo's Precursors.* Baltimore: Johns Hopkins UP, 1943; rpt. 1972.

Rachewiltz, Igor de. *Papal Envoys to the Great Khans.* Stanford: Stanford UP, 1971.

Sinor, Denis. "Mongol and Turkic Words in the Latin Versions of John of Plano Carpini's *Journey to the Mongols* (1245–1247)." In *Mongolian Studies.* Ed. Louis Ligeti. Budapest: B.R. Grüner, 1970, pp. 537–551. Reprint in *Inner Asia and Its Contacts with Medieval Europe.* London: Variorum, 1977.

Skelton, R.A., T.E. Marston, and G.D. Painter. *The Vinland Map and the Tartar Relation.* 1965; 2nd edition. New Haven: Yale UP, 1995, pp. 19–106, 247–249.

van den Wyngaert, Anastasius. *Sinica Franciscana.* Quarrachi-Firenze: Collegium S. Bonaventurae, 1929. 1:135–143.

*Gregory G. Guzman*

## SEE ALSO

Bridia, C. de; Franciscan Friars; Golden Horde; Inner Asian Trade; Inner Asian Travel; Innocent IV; John of Plano Carpini; Karakorum; Mongols; Vincent of Beauvais; Vinland Map; William of Rubruck

## Benincasa, Grazioso (c. 1410–after 1482) and Andrea (after 1435–after 1513)

Patrician father and son, important Italian cartographers. Grazioso is considered "one of the main conduits through whom the details of Portuguese discoveries reached the portolan [charts]" (Harley 411). Little is known of either man, since the city records of their native Ancona were destroyed in the sixteenth century.

Grazioso was active as a merchant ship master (*patrono*) in the Mediterranean and Black seas until he lost a ship to Genoese pirates off of Tunis in 1460. From 1435 to 1445, he kept careful notes in his "portolan" on the coastline and ports from Venice to the Black Sea. In 1461, while in Genoa, he turned to mapmaking. Between 1461 and 1482, he produced atlases, of which seventeen signed copies survive, and at least six nautical charts; these account for two-thirds of the extant and datable maps for the period. He made fourteen of these in Venice between 1462 and 1474, three atlases in Rome in 1467, three other works in Genoa, and three in Ancona, where, presumably, he died.

His early atlases generally had five sheets, one each for the eastern, central, and western Mediterranean Sea, and two for Atlantic Europe. His six-sheet atlas of 1468 is notable for its inclusion of the West African discoveries of Alvise Cadamosto along the coast of Gambia and the Rio Grande (1455–1456), the earliest clear appearance on an extant map of the Cape Verde Islands (Cadamosto, 1460), and Pietro da Sintra's discoveries south to Sierra Leone (1462). This sheet also displays a problem of early African cartography: the scale of its southern reaches is about four times that of its northern.

Andrea, Grazioso's oldest son, apparently remained in Ancona, where he was captain of the port and responsible for its fortifications in 1496. His atlas of 1476 and charts of 1490 and 1508 survive. They follow closely the content and artistic style of his father's works.

**BIBLIOGRAPHY**

Caraci, Giuseppe. "An Unknown Nautical Chart of Grazioso Benincasa, 1468." *Imago Mundi* 7 (1950): 18–31.

Emiliani, Marina. "Le carte nautiche dei Benincasa." *Bolletino della Reale Società Geografica Italiana* 73 (1936): 485–510.

Harley-Woodward. *History of Cartography.* Vol. 1. See Gen. Bib.

Spadolini, Ernesto. "Il portolano di Grazioso Benincasa." *Acta Geographica* 11 (1971): 384–450.

*Joseph P. Byrne*

**SEE ALSO**

Atlas; Genoa; Maps; Portolan Charts; Venice

## Benjamin of Tudela (?–1173)

The greatest medieval Jewish traveler. Benjamin of Tudela described Jewish and non-Jewish life from Spain to Baghdad in a unique book, written in Hebrew and subsequently translated into almost every European language; it remains an important source for medieval historians.

Sometime between 1159 and 1168, during a period of renewed Muslim expansionism and increasing resistance to Frankish rule in the Holy Land, Benjamin, the son of Jonah, left Tudela in northern Spain (Navarre) on a journey that may have lasted between five and fourteen years. His *Itinerary* or *Book of Travels* provides unequalled insight into the lives of the Jewish and non-Jewish communities he visited. From Barcelona, he traveled through coastal Provence and Italy, crossing the Adriatic from Otranto to Corfu. He traveled through Greece to Constantinople, down the Mediterranean coast, and stopped at Rhodes and Cyprus before coming to the Holy Land. Visiting the important sites in the area (Acre, Haifa, Caesarea, Nablus, Jerusalem, Bethlehem, Hebron, Jaffa, Ashkelon, Tiberias), he then continued to Damascus and Baghdad. Although the travel book records his journeys in India, Ceylon, and China, these seem based on the tales of other travelers. Benjamin probably did not venture far into Persia; most likely he took ship at Basra, circumnavigated the Arabian Peninsula, paused at Aden, Cairo, and Alexandria, then returned to Spain via Sicily in 1172–1173. His book ends with a utopian picture of Jewish life in northern Europe, based, like his journey to the East, more on hearsay than experience.

Although the object of his travels is unknown, he may have been a gem merchant in search of markets (he shows a lively interest in mercantile and commercial matters, especially the occupations of Jews—dyers, silkweavers, tanners, glassworkers), or he may have been looking for a place of asylum for Jews persecuted in Spain (he describes with particular delight those places where Jews maintained independent communities), or he may simply have had a pious interest in Palestine. He apparently spent a long time in Rome, where he describes the antiquities in detail; in Constantinople, which he denigrates for hiring "barbarians" to fight their wars; in Baghdad, where he describes the court of the caliph and the organization of the talmudic academies that remained; and finally in Cairo and Alexandria, of which he left a characteristically detailed account. He is the earliest non-Arab writer on the Druse; he provides important information about the Ghuzz Turks and the Islamic sect of Assassins, as well as the Samaritans, the Karaites, the black Jews of Malabar, and the false Messiah, David

# B

Alroy. While primarily interested in the location and number of inhabitants in the Jewish communities along his route, Benjamin of Tudela provided a lively and objective—in many ways an unparalleled—account of the cities, the scholars, and the political and economic life of the Mediterranean basin in the later twelfth century.

**BIBLIOGRAPHY**

Adler, Marcus Nathan. *The Itinerary of Benjamin of Tudela. Critical Text, Translation, and Commentary.* London: Oxford UP, 1907; rpt. New York: Feldheim, [1966?].

Benjamin of Tudela. *The Itinerary of Benjamin of Tudela.* Introductions by Michael A. Signer (1983), Marcus Nathan Adler (1907), and A. Asher (1840). Malibu, CA: J. Simon, Pangloss P, 1987.

Benjamin, Sandra, ed. *The World of Benjamin of Tudela: A Medieval Mediterranean Travelogue.* Madison, NJ: Fairleigh Dickinson UP and London: Associated UP, 1995.

Komroff, Manuel, ed. *Contemporaries of Marco Polo.* New York: Liveright, 1928.

Levanon, Yosef. *The Jewish Travelers in the Twelfth Century.* Lanham, MD: UP of America, 1980.

Prawer, Joshua. *The History of Jews in the Latin Kingdom of Jerusalem.* Oxford: Clarendon P, 1988.

*Jerome Mandel*

**SEE ALSO**

Acre; Assassins; Baghdad; Constantinople; Egypt; Holy Land; Itineraries and *Periploi;* Merchants, Jewish

## Bernard the Wise (fl. 865)

A ninth-century traveler to Palestine who has been confused with at least two other Bernards who traveled extensively in the same period. What is known is that Bernard the Wise is the author of a short tract describing a journey to Egypt and Palestine, a tract cited by William of Malmesbury in his *Gesta Regum Anglorum.*

This tract indicates that Bernard was probably French, that he set out for Palestine from Rome sometime between 863 and 867 after having received the blessing of Pope Nicholas I, that he traveled by way of the regular trade routes through Egypt, and that he returned first to Italy before proceeding to the Monastery of Mont Saint Michel in Brittany.

Bernard traveled during a time of aggressive Muslim activity, so that he found himself in the difficult position of needing the help of his enemies in order to complete his journey. He traveled to the Levant by way of

routes all in Muslim hands, and finally reached Alexandria aboard a Muslim vessel transporting—by his somewhat exaggerated account—9,000 Christian slaves to Africa; he was allowed to disembark only after paying a bribe of six gold pieces. Similar bribes were extorted at each city; for a time he was imprisoned in Cairo, despite letters of introduction and safe conduct. He descended the Nile to Tanis, set out across the desert, and passed Gaza, where finally he entered Palestine.

Bernard's account of Palestine itself is brief. He enumerates several miracles and sacred sites—the Holy Fire kindled by an angel in the Church of the Holy Sepulchre, the stone rolled away from Jesus' tomb, Solomon's Temple, the prison door through which Peter was escorted by an angel, the four tables of the Last Supper, and the pool where Lazarus bathed after his resurrection; the descriptions are so short as to suggest that they are derived as much from earlier travelers' accounts (particularly Bede's abridged account of Adamnan's *De locis sanctis*) as they are from personal visits. He devotes considerable space to a description of the library of Charlemagne, collected in the Church of St. Mary in Jerusalem; his account makes it clear that places established at the beginning of the century for pilgrims (some of them women) to the Holy Land were falling into disrepair.

After a visit to Bethlehem, he explored the mountains of Judea and the monasteries associated with them, then returned to Jerusalem, and from there traveled back to the Mediterranean and home. It is a return marked with some regret; his relief at the end of a difficult homeward journey is diminished by his awareness of the contrast between the relative peace and order of the Islamic world and the disorder of Italy, where Rome itself is anarchic, where robbers threaten all travelers, and where civil war and feuds dominate. The end of his account is marked by the tension between his Christian fealty and his impression of Islamic order.

**BIBLIOGRAPHY**

Bernard the Wise. *The Itinerary of Bernard the Wise.* Trans. John Henry Bernard. London: Palestine Pilgrims' Text Society, 1893; rpt. New York: AMS Press, 1971.

Runciman, Steven. "The Pilgrimages to Palestine before 1095." In *A History of the Crusades.* Ed. Kenneth M. Setton. Vol. 1. Philadelphia: U of Pennsylvania P, 1955.

Wright, Thomas, ed. *Early Travels in Palestine.* London, 1848; rpt. New York: AMS Press, 1969.

*Gary D. Schmidt*

SEE ALSO
Adamnan; Bede; Egypt; Holy Land; Pilgrimage, Christian

## Bestiaries

Medieval collections of allegorized lore about animals, plants, and stones, with frequent references to particular geographic locations and ethnic groups.

Medieval bestiaries, like the ancient Greek treatise on animals known as the *Physiologus,* comprise individual entries that first describe animals (real and legendary) and then find in them and their behavior religious or moral meaning. Thus, natural history provides object lessons in the conflict between evil/sin and good/salvation, so as to communicate memorably the Christian doctrine of redemption. Owing to their popularity, bestiaries and the *Physiologus* together equipped Western

Siren. France, Crypt of St. Parize-le-Châtel, *c.* 1150. Photo by John B. Friedman.

Ass playing lyre. France, Crypt of St. Parize-le-Châtel, *c.* 1150. Photo by John B. Friedman.

Europe with a rich lexicon of lore and symbolism about animals from throughout the Old World—as well as about animals from outside the real world altogether.

The word *Physiologus* is today used as the title of a book, but in the original Greek it was a compound that meant roughly "philosopher of the natural world" and designated an anonymous author who probably flourished in the second century C.E. Although some suppose that he lived in Syria, most situate him in cosmopolitan Alexandria, in part because both real and fabulous beasts of Egypt are particularly well represented in his book. The author was not, however, parochial in his purview: although the facts are sometimes distorted, the text reflects knowledge of, and legends about, foreign fauna from the whole Mediterranean and even from the Far East.

The Greek *Physiologus* achieved a wide diffusion, spreading to the farthest bounds of Christendom. It

Goat and bull. Bestiary, London, British Library MS Royal 12 C. xix, fol. 31r, *c.* 1200. Courtesy of the British Library.

was translated into Latin sometime between the fifth and the ninth centuries, with added extracts from Isidore of Seville (including entries on familiar animals, such as wolves and dogs; on exotic ones, such as crocodiles and ibexes; and on the purely fabulous, such as dragons). Despite being "blacklisted" in the so-called *Decretum Gelasianum* (supposedly dated 494, but in fact a later "false decretal"), the *Physiologus* did not merely survive: it formed the core of one of the most popular and widely read medieval books.

By no later than the twelfth century, the Latin *Physiologus* had been reorganized and expanded with new animals, such as Ireland's "barnacle geese," taken from the observations of Gerald of Wales. Yet for all the innovations, these later texts—written first in Latin, then in Old French and other Romance languages, and eventually in all major European vernacular languages—often manifest a clearer sense of order and structure than appears in the *Physiologus*. Many of these texts were referred to by the general term "bestiary" (*liber bestiarius* means "a book of beasts").

In the *Physiologus* only a few geographical locations merit explicit mention: the antelope drinks from "the terrible Euphrates River"; piroboli rocks exist only in the East; the phoenix lives "in the land of India," enters "the wood of Lebanon," and signals "the priest of Heliopolis [a holy city in Egypt]"; and the peridexion tree is found in India. No geographical site is specified for creatures of the Nile such as the niluus, crocodile, or echinemon: their habitat is apparently considered self-evident.

By contrast, references to particular places and peoples are far more common in bestiaries. Geographical and ethnographic associations appear in both descriptions and interpretations of animals, though more often in the former. Among the peoples mentioned in a typical bestiary are Greeks, Syrians, Persians, Medes, Indians, Garamantes, and Sarmatians. Rivers range from the Tiber and Nile in the Mediterranean region, through the Tigris and Euphrates in the Fertile Crescent, and beyond to the Ganges in India. The spectrum of toponyms includes Africa, Antioch, Arabia, Arcadia, Asia, Bactria, Ethiopia, Hyrcania, Hyperborea, the Indies, Numidia, Scythia, and Sodom.

Although the earliest extant copy of an illustrated *Physiologus* dates from no earlier than the ninth century, its pictorial style reveals indebtedness to ancient models that seem no longer to exist. Bestiaries were even more frequently produced as picture books. The influence of bestiary texts and illustrations on medieval understandings of world geography and ethnography can be seen clearly on *mappaemundi:* the Hereford and Ebstorf Maps, for example, include both pictures and descriptions of creatures from the bestiary.

**BIBLIOGRAPHY**

Clark, Willene B., and Meradith T. McMunn. *Beasts and Birds of the Middle Ages. The Bestiary and Its Legacy.* Philadelphia: U of Pennsylvania P, 1989.

Curley, Michael J. *Physiologus.* Austin: U of Texas P, 1979.

James, Montague Rhodes. *The Bestiary, Being a Reproduction in Full of the Manuscript Ii.4.26 in the University Library, Cambridge.* Oxford: Oxford UP, 1928.

McCulloch, Florence. *Medieval Latin and French Bestiaries.* U of North Carolina Studies in Romance Languages and Literatures 33. Chapel Hill: U of North Carolina P, 1962.

White, T.H. *The Bestiary: A Book of Beasts, Being a Translation from a Latin Bestiary of the Twelfth Century.* New York: Putnam, 1960.

*Jan M. Ziolkowski*

## Birds, Exotic

Species of birds native to Asia and Africa—and thus
"exotic" to Europeans—which are described by Western medieval writers or depicted in medieval art.

Medieval Europeans possessed very limited knowledge of birds native to other parts of the world. Exotic
species of birds commonly found in medieval Western
records include only the ring-necked parakeet (*psittac-
ula krameri;* India, east central Africa); the ostrich
(*struthio camelus;* Egypt, Middle East, north and central Africa); and the peacock (*pavo cristatus;* east Asia,
domesticated in Europe by the Romans). Two familiar
domesticated farmland birds, the pheasant (*phasianus
colchicus;* Asia) and guinea fowl (*numida meleagaris;*
Africa), were sometimes recognized as exotics.

Europeans, beginning with the Romans, imported
ring-necked parakeets for pets, a custom observed by
Pliny (*Nat. hist.* 10.58.117) and later by Isidore of Seville
(*Etymologies* 12.7.24). Medieval writers speak of the
"popinjay" or "papagai," both almost certainly the ring-
neck, which is the only member of the parrot family to
appear in text and picture in bestiaries, as well as in the
border ornament of thirteenth and fourteenth-century
manuscripts (e.g., British Library, MS Royal 1.D.1, fol.
5r). A rare lutino (yellow) ring-neck occurs in Jean de
Berri's *Grandes Heures* (1409; Paris, Bibliothèque
Nationale, MS lat. 919, fol. 45r). Psittacines appear,
although without reference to species, in a few medieval
poems and romances, most notably the several late
medieval works collectively entitled *Roman de papagai.*

As early as the third century B.C.E. Aristotle describes
the ostrich (*De Partibus animalium* 4.13); the Romans
kept ostriches in menageries, and Thomas Aquinas (d.
1280; *De anim.* 23.24.102) wrote that many people had
seen one. Recognizable medieval portrayals occur in
some bestiaries such as Canterbury Cathedral MS Lit.
D.10, f. 16r, and in Hugh of Fouilloy's *Aviarium* (Cambrai, Bibl. Mun. MS 259, f. 198r), as well as in the Liège
*Tacuinum sanitatis* (University Lib. MS 1041, f. 42r).
They are also found in wallpaintings, as in the late
medieval Longthorpe Tower (Northants.) and in a fifteenth-century church fresco at Bressanone, in the Tirol.

Ostrich. Cloister Fresco, Nineteenth Arcade, Bressanone, Tirol,
*c.* 1450. Photo by Nona C. Flores.

The most familiar exotic bird was the peacock, mentioned by Greek and Roman writers, and an early symbol of Christ's resurrection. Great lords kept peacocks
to decorate their gardens and to eat, and the bird is a
frequent motif in medieval art and literature. The
Romans also kept guinea fowl, and occasionally pheasants, for pleasure and food; pheasants figured in northern European menageries by around 800.

Several other exotic birds were known to a limited
number of Europeans. Frederick II (1194–1250) received a white cockatoo (probably *cacatua galerita
galerita* or *sulphurea sulphurea;* south Pacific; see Vatican MS Pal. lat. 1071, fol. 18v) as a gift. Marco Polo (*c.*
1254–1324) claims to have observed several unfamiliar
cranes, possibly the Siberian crane (*grus leucogeranus*)
and Sarus crane (*grus antigone*), and all-white parrots
with red feet and bills, perhaps a white morph of the

# B

ring-necked parakeet, which produces color mutations, has a red bill, and with the albino factor could have pink feet. In the Getty Museum's early-sixteenth-century Flemish Spinola Hours (MS IX.18, f. 256v) several multicolored, crested birds resemble turacos (*tauraco porphyeolophus* or *johnstoni;* east central Africa); and a gray-crested bird could be the white bellied go-away (*corythaixoides leucogaster;* central and south Africa). Non-European birds of prey were brought home by Crusaders returning from the Middle East and imported as gifts for princes.

While there are numerous references to birds in medieval texts and they appear frequently in images, there are usually too few descriptive details to allow species identification of non-native birds. For lack of data, the routes by which most exotics came to medieval Europe, either on the wing or by importation, are also little known.

**BIBLIOGRAPHY**

Hutchinson, G. Evelyn. "Attitudes toward Nature in Medieval England: The Alphonso and Bird Psalters." *Isis* 65: 226 (1974): 35–37.

Loisel, Gustave. *Histoire des ménageries de l'antiquité à nos jours.* Paris: Doin et Fils/Henri Laurens, 1912.

Sauvage, André. *Étude des thèmes animaliers dans la poésie latine.* Brussels: Latomus, 1975.

Vaurie, Charles. "Birds in the Prayer Book of Bonne of Luxembourg." *Metropolitan Museum of Art Bulletin* 29 [6] (1971): 279–281.

Yapp, W.B. "The Illustrations of Birds in the Vatican Manuscript of *De arte venandi cum avibus* of Frederick II." *Annals of Science* 40 (1983): 597–634.

*Willene B. Clark*

## Black Death

The popular name for the second major outbreak of bubonic plague, a disease that spread throughout the medieval world in two pandemics, one in the sixth through eighth century and the other, and better known, in the mid-fourteenth century. In both instances, travel and trade were crucial modes of transmission.

Caused by the bacillus *Yersinia pestis,* bubonic plague is a disease that settles in the lymph nodes, causing swelling of the groin, armpits, and throat; blood pooling and darkening beneath the surface of the skin gives the infected person a distinctive mottled look. The dis-

ease has a complex etiology. It is transmitted to humans primarily by infected fleas linked with rodent populations. It is also transmitted, to some extent, from person to person through a more virulent pneumonic form. In all cases, travel (of fleas in clothing and cargo, or of rats in grain supplies or on ships, or of infected humans) contributes to the spread of the disease.

The first pandemic (sometimes called Justinian's Plague) arose in East Africa and spread throughout the Middle East, North Africa, and Europe beginning in the 540s. It did not subside until the late seventh and early eighth centuries, leaving behind two long-standing reservoirs of plague bacillae in the Caucasus region of southern Russia and in East Africa. Sources are sufficient to identify this plague as bubonic and to estab-

Avenging angel and plague victims. Horae, Copenhagen, Det Kongelige Bibliothek, Samling MS 50, fol. 26v, 15th Century. Courtesy Det Kongelige Bibliothek.

Burial of plague victims. *Annals* of Gilles li Muisis 1349–1352. Tournai, Pierart dou Tielt. Brussels, Bibliothèque Royale Albert 1er MS 1307—1377, fol. 24v, *c.* 1553. Courtesy Bibliothèque Royale Albert 1er.

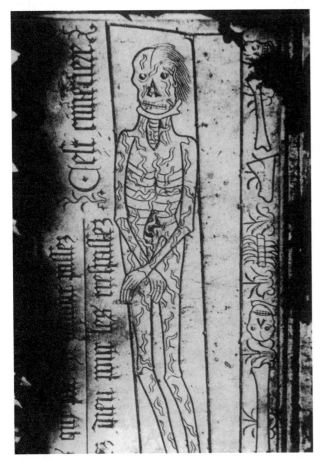

Plague imagery on grave stone. France, Musée Municipale de Beauvais, courtyard, *c.* 1400. Photo by John B. Friedman.

lish that it followed commercial routes in its expansion, reaching England, for example, in 544, 664, and 682.

Some historians have suggested that bubonic plague continued to strike Europe, attacking Rome in 1167 and 1230, Florence in 1244, and Spain and southern France in 1320 and 1333. St. Roch of Languedoc, the patron saint of plague, was thought to have contracted the disease on a pilgrimage to Rome in 1333. There is no clear evidence that these episodes were bubonic plague, and there appears not to have been an established animal reservoir of plague in medieval Europe. To the degree that bubonic plague was present, it must have been repeatedly reintroduced into Europe through trade and travelers, especially with the establishment of permanent trade routes and the revival of pilgrimages that brought vessels and people back and forth from Europe to Asia from the eleventh century on.

The second pandemic (traditionally labeled the Black Death) arose in the steppes of southern Russia and spread through Europe, Russia, North Africa, and the Middle East between 1347 and 1352, killing an estimated one-third to one-half the population of Europe and Russia and perhaps one-third the population of Egypt and Syria. The Muslim traveler Ibn Battuta (1304–1368) first encountered news of bubonic plague from travelers reaching Aleppo in June 1348; he passed through Damascus, Palestine, Egypt, and Mecca in the midst of plague. When he returned home to Morocco in 1349, he did so in the wake of the disease. In Europe, plague spread everywhere, sparing only Iceland, parts of the Pyrenees and southeastern Europe, and a few cities. Particular populations sustained different rates of mortality; between 35 and 45 percent of the beneficed clergy of England, 68 percent of the notaries of Perpignan, 5 to 10 percent of the theologians at Oxford, and 50 percent of the population of Florence died. Some households and villages lost entire populations, while others were nearly unaffected. The disease returned at regular intervals throughout the fourteenth and fifteenth centuries, producing sustained population decline.

There are conflicting explanations for the high mortality rates of the fourteenth and fifteenth centuries. Some argue for the role of other diseases such as influenza, typhus, smallpox, and anthrax; others argue for disease combined with Malthusian causes or a deteriorating climate. To the extent that the 30 to 50 percent death rate and sustained population decline were due to epidemic disease, human vectors are a possibility and contact over geographical space becomes a variable.

# B

From its likely origin in Mongol territories northwest of the Caspian Sea, the bubonic plague moved along caravan routes through the cities of southern Russian, perhaps carried in the grain supplies. Several medieval chroniclers report that it reached the Crimea in 1346 where Genoese soldiers, infected during a siege, carried it to Messina in Sicily. From there it spread to Pisa, Genoa, Venice, and Marseilles. Armies and ships, merchants, pilgrims, fairgoers, transient laborers, and other travelers carried it throughout Europe, at first following pilgrimage and trade routes and then dispersing it into the countryside. Nearly all medieval chroniclers of the 1348 plague cite the role of merchants and sailors in spreading plague. Contemporary accounts describe plague-bearing ships anchoring in ports, spreading the disease, and moving on. Legends from Scandinavia tell of plague arriving on drifting or stranded ships or via foreign merchants, wandering old men, women, and even children. Medieval writers did not understand the crucial role played by rats, rat fleas, and grain supplies. Nor did they understand that rural environments could be even more conducive to plague than were urban environments, as is evident from the very high mortality rates in smaller and more widely dispersed populations.

Europeans received reports of approaching plague from the East "attested by merchants and travelers who regularly visited those distant countries" (Gilles li Muisis in Horrox). Travelers and pilgrims carried reports of plague to England and the Low Countries a year in advance of its arrival. In preparation, ecclesiastical authorities encouraged prayers, processions, and pilgrimages. Various municipal provisions for plague control and containment were put in place in Italy and parts of Spain, France, England, and Germany, including fines for travelers from infected areas, forbidden entry to people and goods from infected areas, and the incarceration of sick foreigners and burning of their goods. Medieval Dubrovnik (Ragusa), an Adriatic port, was the first to institute a quarantine, in 1379, of thirty days for all travelers, no matter what their point of origin or state of health. After the 1450s, quarantines and the active hospitalization and isolation of the sick became more widespread. These actions suggest belief in a theory of contagion, a belief shared by most chroniclers but not taken up in the medical literature, which favored theories of transmission through corrupted air and planetary influences. In Muslim countries, plague was also not generally understood in terms of contagion theory. Traditional, authoritative Islamic texts emphasized plague as a martyrdom from which one should not flee.

There were no such theological constraints on Christians, many of whom tried to escape the disease. Guy de Chauliac, the papal physician in 1348, counseled individuals to "flee quickly, go far, and come back slowly." Chroniclers were nearly unanimous in recounting large numbers who left, in lieu of any better remedy, and Boccaccio's *Decameron* presents a contemporary literary depiction of the phenomenon in focusing on ten storytellers who sought refuge from the plague in the countryside near Florence. While many fled, others joined a movement of flagellants, especially in Italy and northern and central Europe. Flagellants traveled about beating themselves with whips, repenting their sins. Another extremist response to plague was the destruction of Jewish communities in Provence, Catalonia, Aragon, Switzerland, southern Germany, and the Rhineland, since Jews were believed to have spread the disease by poisoning wells; the attacks on their communities resulted in a shift of the surviving Jewish population toward eastern Europe.

When the plague abated in 1350, Pope Clement VI declared it a jubilee year, and multitudes of penitents streamed into Rome to receive a plenary indulgence for their sins.

## BIBLIOGRAPHY

Biraben, Jean-Noel. *Les hommes et la peste en France et dans les pays européens et mediterranéens.* Vol. 1. Hague: Mouton, 1975.

———, and J. LeGoff. "The Plague in the Early Middle Ages." In *Biology and Man in History.* Ed. Robert Forster and Orest Ranum. Baltimore: Johns Hopkins UP, 1975.

Dols, Michael. *The Black Death in the Middle East.* Princeton: Princeton UP, 1977.

Gottfried, Robert S. *The Black Death: Natural and Human Disaster in Medieval Europe.* New York: Free Press, 1983.

Horrox, Rosemary, trans. and ed. *The Black Death.* Manchester, England: Manchester UP, 1994.

Twigg, Graham. *The Black Death: A Biological Reappraisal.* New York: Schocken, 1985.

Ziegler, Philip. *The Black Death.* New York: Harper & Row, 1969.

*Jo Ann Hoeppner Moran (Cruz)*

## SEE ALSO

Expulsion, Corporate; Ibn Battūta, Abu Abdallah; Pilgrimage, Christian

## Bofeti, Pericciolo di Anastasio (fl. 1284–1304)

A Pisan nobleman, merchant, and diplomat who lived in Persia. A citizen of one of the great seafaring Italian city states, Bofeti [commonly called Zolus the Pisan or Isol the Pisan] lived in the late thirteenth and early fourteenth centuries. While hundreds of Genoese and Venetian sailors, merchants, and mercenaries traveled, worked, and fought in the Middle East, Bofeti is a rare, documented case of a Pisan operating at Tabriz, in Persia. Thanks to the active interest of the il-khâns, this city was a center of international commerce by the 1280s. Bofeti held high positions in the courts of Arghun (1284–1291), Ghaikatu (1291–1295), and Ghazan (1295–1304). His influence enabled him to provide important support to the Christian efforts to recolonize the Holy Land and maintain political relations between East and West in the years preceding and following the fall of Acre (1291).

Few sources survive to demonstrate the role Bofeti or his family may have played in his homeland; yet he certainly led an active life in the East. Like Marco Polo, he may have begun his career abroad as a merchant or adventurer and ended up earning a position of trust in the Mongol Empire.

Diverse documents containing various spellings of his name, or mentioning a European in the il-khânid court, render him somewhat mysterious. "Sir Tchol" served as godfather when the future il-khân Öljeitü, Ghazan's brother, received baptism at Arghun's court in 1288. Chronicles of the Cypriot naval expedition against Rosetta in 1300 describe his participation under the name "sire Chiol." The Persian historian Rashid al-Din refers to him as *Gol Bahadur*. Pope Nicholas IV wrote him letters in 1289 and 1291, addressing him as *Jolus* or *Ozolus*. These various spellings are Persian transliterations or Latinate diminutive forms of the common Pisan name *Perizolus* or *Pericciolus*. He is recorded in the notarial acts written by the Genoese Lamberto di Sambuceto in 1300 and 1301. Here his name appears as "dominus Zolus de Anastasio " and "nobilis vir Ciolus Bofeti de Pisis." The titles and surname indicate that he must have come from a high-ranking family.

The content of these documents reveals that Bofeti had denounced to Boniface VIII (1294–1303) several European merchants who were running contraband shipments of arms and supplies to the Egyptian Mamluks in spite of papal interdiction of all trade after the fall of Acre. His awareness of mercantile activities and shipping routes suggests that he had a practical knowledge of these trades. John of Monte Corvino, en route to China, carried a papal missive of 1289 addressed to Bofeti at the Persian court. A document of 1300, which contains a papal bull, gives him the impressive title "vicarius Sirie ac Terre Sancte a Casano imperatore Tartarorum" ("Vicar of Syria and the Holy Land to Ghazan the Emperor of the Tartars"), while in the act of 1301 he is called *misaticus* (envoy) of Ghazan. Although the definition of his duties as "vicar" remains elusive, the term may be more than just a formula applied to the document by a chancery scribe. Persian documents indicate a repartition of the government of Syria at about this time. This political restructuring may have occurred after Bofeti left on his ambassadorial mission to King Henry II of Cyprus (1285–1324); thus, he may have been referred to as *vicarius* of a territory no longer intact. On the other hand, the title may reflect not the actualities of Persian government but the Roman church's designation of the whole group of territories that had been occupied during the Crusades as "Syria," and the ancient kingdom of Jerusalem as the "Holy Land." When Ghazan came to power, he was willing to abide by earlier treaty agreements between his predecessors and the West to allow the Frankish recolonization of the area. Bofeti held a doubly influential position in this project, being invested with power by both Eastern and Western leaders, Ghazan and Boniface VIII, to oversee the resettlement.

In addition to his numerous commercial, political, and military contributions, Bofeti may have furnished the Persian historian Rashid al-Din much of the information regarding the West that appeared in the Frankish history section of his *Universal History.*

**BIBLIOGRAPHY**

Heyd, W. *Histoire du commerce du Levant au Moyen-Age.* Rev. ed. Furcy Raynaud. Vol. 2. Leipzig, 1885–1886; rpt. Amsterdam: Adolf M. Hakkert, 1967.

Pelliot, Paul. "Chrétiens d'Asie centrale et d'Extrême-Orient." *Toung pao* 15 (1914): 623–644.

———. "Isol le Pisan." *Journal Asiatique* 187, series 11[6] (1915): 495–497.

Petech, Luciano. "Les marchands italiens dans l'Empire Mongol." *Journal Asiatique* 250 (1962): 549–574.

Richard, Jean. "Isol le Pisan: un aventurier franc gouverneur d'une province mongole?" *Central Asiatic Journal* 14 (1970): 186–194.

Wadding, Luke, ed. *Annales Minorum seu Trium ordinum a S. Francisco Institutorum.* Rev. ed. P. Bonaventura Marrani. Florence: Quaracchi, 1931, 5:220–221.

*Gloria Allaire*

# B

SEE ALSO

Acre; Ambassadors; Diplomacy; Holy Land; John of Monte Corvino; Mamluks; Mongols; Pisa

## Bojador, Cape

The geographical feature of the northwestern coast of Africa that, according to fifteenth-century Portuguese sources, represented the limit of European navigation in that area. Gomes Eanes de Zurara (*c.* 1410–*c.* 1474), the author of *The Discovery and Conquest of Guinea*, insisted that the Portuguese did not dare to sail beyond this point because of navigational hazards, the inhospitable nature of the supposedly uninhabited coast, and fear that return voyage might be impossible. Zurara claims that Cape Bojador frustrated the exploratory expeditions for twelve years until it was finally passed in 1434 by Gil Eanes, who, after having failed the year before, was under severe pressure from Prince Henry the Navigator (1394–1460) to succeed. Many historians consider the passing of Cape Bojador the initial point of the Portuguese overseas explorations.

The actual geographical location of the fifteenth-century Cape Bojador has been much debated. What today is called Cape Bojador is relatively easy to pass and does not display the dangerous features about which Duarte Pacheco Pereira, a pilot and naval officer in the service of Kings João II and Manuel I, warned when he admonished his peers to sail by the Cape at least 8 *leguas* (*c.* 48 km) out to sea. He claimed that the rocks and shoals of the low-lying, sand-covered cape protruded some 36–40 km into the sea and were difficult to notice. The modern Cape Juby (Yubi), located some 320 km to the northeast, fits this description much better. The latitude that Pacheco Pereira gives for Cape Bojador, 27°10' N, also approximates that of Cape Juby. However, the fact that Cape Juby directly faces the Canaries, an archipelago well known to European sailors since the fourteenth century, makes this theory doubtful. Most historians believe that the modern Cape Bojador is indeed the "Cape Bojador" of Portuguese sources, and that the chief difficulty in rounding it was the fear of the unknown.

### BIBLIOGRAPHY

Albuquerque, Luis de. *Gil Eanes.* Lisbon: CEHCA, 1987. Separ. 186.

———. "Navegações além do Cabo Bojador no tempo do Infante D. Henrique: o seu Objectivo." In *Portugal no Mundo.* Ed. Luis de Albuquerque. Lisbon: Alfa, 1989 1:137–149.

Diffie, Bailey W., and George D. Winius. *Foundations of the Portuguese Empire, 1415–1580.* Minneapolis: U of Minnesota P, 1977.

Pereira, Duarte Pacheco. *Esmeraldo de Situ Orbis.* Lisbon: Sociedade de Geografia, 1905; rpt. 1975.

Zurara, Gomes Eanes de. *Crónica dos feitos notáveis que se passaram na conquista de Guiné.* Ed. Torquato de Sousa Soares. Lisbon: Academia Portuguesa da História, 1978.

*Ivana Elbl*

SEE ALSO

Canary Islands; Henry the Navigator; Portuguese Expansion

## Bordeaux Pilgrim

Supposed author of the earliest known Christian account (*Itinerarium burdigalense*) of a visit to the Holy Land in 333 C.E.

Although the author does not identify himself in his work, he lists sites on the way to and from the Holy Land; since the first location mentioned on this itinerary is Bordeaux, it is probable that the author lived there. The pilgrimage may be dated by the names of the Roman consuls referred to in the text: the pilgrim was in Chalcedon on May 30, 333, and returned there on December 25 or 26 of the same year. The account was written only nine years after the Holy Land came under Christian rule and provides a literary impression of the revolutionary changes that had occurred, such as ambitious construction of churches, clear identification of holy places, and increased numbers of pilgrims visiting those destinations.

The *Itinerarium* combines two distinct purposes and types of contents. First, the author lists, in the form of an itinerary, stations (*mansiones*) and changing posts for horses (*mutationes*) from Bordeaux to the holy sites and back, including the distances between them. This list opens the work and ends it. Second, he describes the holy places. This description is located between the list of stations at the beginning and the list of stations at the end of the *Itinerarium*. Most likely, the list of stations—presumably a known, standard list, at the disposal of travelers all over the empire—was the basis for the entire work, and to that the author simply added information about the holy sites as a guide for the pilgrim. This part perhaps resembles the itineraries with descriptions of important places popular among travelers in the Roman Empire but not widely used by

Christians. In this respect, the Bordeaux Pilgrim contributes to the developing genre of the Christian travel itinerary.

The writer proposes a land route from the south of France to northern Italy, then through the Balkans on to Constantinople, and finally through Syria to Palestine by way of Sidon. The return route is by sea and land, passing through Constantinople and Macedonia to Rome and Milan. The pilgrim reaches Palestine from the north. He skirts the coast, turns east to Nablus, Samaria, and Beth-el, and then journeys up to Jerusalem. From Jerusalem he continues to Jericho, the Dead Sea, the river Jordan, Bethlehem, and Hebron. He does not visit the holy places in Galilee or in Trans-Jordan. The list of sites described is rather puzzling. Most of the traditions mentioned are rooted in the Old Testament, sparking various theories as to the author's identity and the nature of his sources. One suggestion is that the author, a devout Christian, received his information from a Jewish traveler who came to his city from Palestine. Some authorities have suggested that the work was written by a converted Jew. Nevertheless, the text seems to be a faithful reflection of the existing reality: new Christian traditions, still in the process of identification, and ancient local traditions from the Old Testament, current among both Jews and Christians, the latter viewing themselves as the legitimate heirs to the biblical text and its geography.

**BIBLIOGRAPHY**

*Itinerarium Burdigalense.* In *Itineraria et alia Geographica.* Ed. P. Geyer and O. Cuntz. Corpus Christianorum: Series Latina 175. Turnholt: Brepols, 1965, pp. 1–26.

Mommert, Carl. "Das Jerusalem des Pilgers von Bordeaux (333)." *Zeitschrift des deutschen Palästina-Vereins* 29 (1906): 177–193.

Wesseling, Peter. *Vetera Romanorum Itineraria.* Amsterdam, 1735.

Wilkinson, John. *Egeria's Travels in the Holy Land.* London: Society for the Promotion of Christian Knowledge, 1971, pp. 153–163.

———. "Jewish Holy Places and the Origins of Christian Pilgrimage." In *The Blessings of Pilgrimage.* Ed. Robert Ousterhout. Urbana and Chicago: U of Illinois P, 1990, pp. 41–53.

*Ora Limor*

**SEE ALSO**

Constantinople; Holy Land; Itineraries and *Periploi*; Jerusalem; Pilgrimage, Christian

## Borgia Map

A round *mappamundi,* probably of south German manufacture, engraved (anonymously) on a copper plate around 1430.

This world map, usually known as the Borgia map because it is housed in the Borgia Gallery (XVI) of the Biblioteca Apostolica Vaticana, is centered on the Black and Mediterranean seas. It follows ancient and medieval tradition and seems very medieval in form: the continents are compressed, Italy is rectangular, south is at the top. Nonetheless, the shape of Africa (to some extent) and of northern Asia, showing the Caspian Sea far inland and not open to the northern "Ocean," suggests the influence of Catalan atlases and the reception of post-Ptolemaic knowledge of the earth. The Portuguese "discoveries" and the west coast of Africa were still unknown to the mapmaker. This is the first map to list the *"iudei inclusi,"* whom it implicitly identifies as Gog and Magog, in accordance with the tradition that they were walled up by Alexander the Great behind an immense gate in the Caucasus.

**BIBLIOGRAPHY**

Campbell, Tony. *Early Maps.* New York: Abbeville Press, 1981.

Destombes, Marcel, ed. *Mappemondes.* [Borgia Map reproduced in Table XXIX]. See Gen. Bib.

Gow, Andrew. "Kartenrand, Gesellschaftsrand, Geschichtsrand: Die legendären *iudei clausi/inclusi* auf mittelalterlichen und frühneuzeitlichen Weltkarten." In *Förden und Bewahren. Studien zur europäischen Kulturgeschichte der frühen Neuzeit.* Ed. Helwig Schmidt-Glintzer. Wolfenbüttel: Herzog August Bibliothek, 1996, pp. 137–155; esp. 145.

Harvey, P.D.A. *Medieval Maps.* London: The British Library, 1991.

*Andrew Gow*

**SEE ALSO**

Atlas; Caspian Sea; Cresques, Abraham; Gog and Magog; Portolan Charts; Portuguese Expansion; Ptolemy; Red Jews

## Brasil [or Brazil]

An imaginary island in the Atlantic Ocean found on many late medieval and early Renaissance maps and charts. Variously spelled, the name appears to be Gaelic in origin: *breas-ail,* meaning "blessed," a possible reference to the voyages of medieval Irish monks in search of an "isle of the blessed." Some scholars have related it

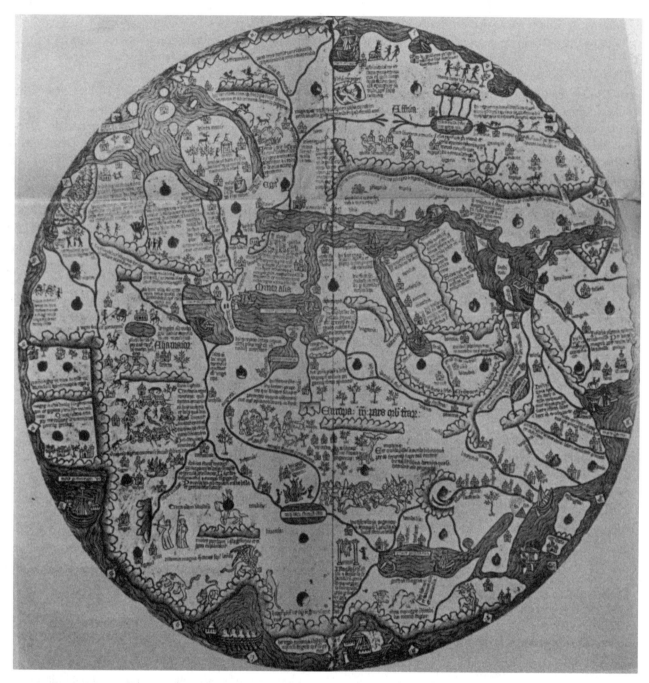

Borgia Map. A world map on metal, oriented to the south. Rome, Biblioteca Apostolica Vaticana, Borgia Gallery. After Marcel Destombes, ed. *Mappemondes A.D. 1200-1500. Catalogue préparé par la Commission des Cartes Anciennes de l'Union Géographique Internationale*. Vol. I of *Monumenta Cartographica Vetustioris Aevi A.D. 1200-1500*, ed. Roberto Almagià and Marcel Destombes, *Imago Mundi*, supp. 4. Amsterdam N. Israel, 1964, Pl. XXIX. Reproduced by permission of the Map Division, The New York Public Library (Astor, Lenox and Tilden Foundations).

to Hy-Brasil of Irish literature, a place where the blessed await entry into heaven.

The earliest known appearance of the island on a map is on the Angellino de Delorto chart of 1325, where it is located off the west coast of southern Ireland; this continued to be its most frequent location on subsequent maps, although it appears as far south as the Azores and as far north as near Greenland. Typically, the island is given a spherical form, often divided by a strait. On a Catalan map of 1375 it is a ring of islands enclosing nine smaller islands.

Brasil enters prominently into the Age of Discovery with the report in 1498 of Pedro de Ayala, Spain's ambassador to England, that "the people of Bristol have for the past seven years sent out two, three, or four ships in search of the island of Brazil and the Seven Cities." These expeditions led to the expedition of John Cabot to Newfoundland in 1497, and are indications of a concerted search by Bristol navigators for land in the northwestern Atlantic. Along with St. Brendan's Island and Antillia, Brasil was among the most persistent cartographic portrayals of medieval legends and fantasies regarding the Atlantic Ocean, but unlike the other two, Brasil has no surviving legend to account for it.

**BIBLIOGRAPHY**

Babcock, William H. "The Island of Brazil." Chap. 4 in *Legendary Islands of the Atlantic.* New York: American Geographical Society, 1922.

Quinn, David Beers. "The Argument for the English Discovery of America between 1480 and 1494." Chap. 1 in *England and the Discovery of America, 1481–1620.* New York: Alfred A. Knopf, 1974.

Westropp, T.J. "Brasil and the Legendary Islands of the North Atlantic: Their History and Fable." *Proceedings of the Royal Irish Academy* 30 [C] (1912–1913): pp. 223–260.

*John Parker*

**SEE ALSO**
Antillia; Azores; Brendan's Voyage, St.; Irish Travel

## Brendan's Voyage, St.

The fabled travels of a sixth-century Irish saint, also known as the Navigator, whose legends depict him as a seafarer and early explorer. The story of his fantastic voyage became one of the more popular tales in medieval literature.

Brendan was born *c.* 486 in Kerry and died in 577 or 583; his feast day is May 16. He was founder and abbot of the Monastery of Clonfert in county Galway, which existed into the sixteenth century. He apparently sailed to western Scotland and Iona and possibly to southern Britain and Brittany as well. At this time, Irish monks and clerics frequently undertook sea voyages, not only to visit other monasteries, but also as an ascetic act of penitence and devotion, either to expiate a sin or to get closer to God by abandoning all worldly ties. The legends of Brendan's voyage are probably based partly on this early movement of voluntary exile, begun in Brendan's own lifetime. Hagiographical sources for Brendan's voyage include several saint's lives, both in Latin and Irish, but most seem to have been conflated with, or elaborated from, the tale known as the *Navigatio Sancti Brendani Abbatis* (The Voyage of St. Brendan, the Abbot).

The *Navigatio* is a fictionalized account in Latin of Brendan's voyage and dates from the late ninth or early tenth century. Of unknown authorship and provenance, this work was most likely composed by an Irishman, perhaps on the Continent. The tale relates how St. Brendan and a group of monks set sail from Clonfert in a small boat made of oxhides in search of the Land of Promise of the Saints, a heavenly island somewhere to the west of Ireland. During the course of their voyage, the monks encounter many marvels, such as a crystal column in the ocean, a gryphon, an island of fallen angels in the form of birds, an island of demon blacksmiths, and Judas Iscariot. They also meet a great sea monster named Jasconius, which they mistake for an island and on which they celebrate Easter. Several of the islands they come across contain monastic communities or hermitages. Eventually, they reach the Promised Land, which is surrounded by a dense fog. There they find a land of eternal light and bliss, but are told by an angel to return to their monastery, where Brendan dies in the glory of God. The episodic structure of the narrative within a frame tale of voyaging from island to island, and its ecclesiastical perspective, place it in the tradition of the Irish sea-voyage tales known as *imrama*.

The tale contains enough realistic details to suggest that it may have been based on an actual voyage or a number of voyages, and its descriptions of early Irish shipbuilding and the existence of island monasteries and hermitages off the coast of Ireland can be confirmed from archaeological and textual sources. The geographical details have led some to attempt to recreate Brendan's route and to speculate that he and his monks reached the New World long before the Vikings or Columbus (Bray, Severin). The crystal column in the ocean is thus understood to be an iceberg, Jasconius a whale, and the mists surrounding the Land of Promise the dense fog off the Grand Banks of Newfoundland. There is no real evidence that Irish monks ever reached the shores of North America, but they did sail to the Hebrides and Orkneys, and as far north as the Faeroes and Iceland (which may have been the basis for the Island of Sheep and the volcanic Island of Smiths described in the *Navigatio*).

On an allegorical level, the *Navigatio* represents the ideal of monastic life; Brendan's goal of a promised land is a metaphor for the kingdom of heaven to which the monks aspire, and the journey follows a cyclical pattern based on the liturgical year. The author describes in detail the monks' devotions and prayers, their observance of the canonical hours, and their adherence to Brendan's rule. Translated into several vernacular European languages soon after its composition, the *Navigatio* made Brendan the most renowned Irish saint throughout Europe in the Middle Ages.

**BIBLIOGRAPHY**
Bray, Dorothy A. "Allegory in the *Navigatio Sancti Brendani.*" *Viator* 26 (1995): 1–10.
Bouet, Pierre. *La Fantastique dans la Littérature Latine du Moyen Age: La Navigation de Saint Brendan.* Caen: Centre d'Etudes et de Recherches pour l'Antiquité, 1986.
Mac Cana, Proinsias. "The Voyage of St. Brendan: Literary and Historical Origins." In *Atlantic Visions.* Ed. John de Courcy Ireland and David C. Sheehy. Dun Laoghaire: Boole, 1989, pp. 3–16.
O'Meara, John J., trans. *The Voyage of Saint Brendan: Journey to the Promised Land.* Mountrath, Portlaoise: Dolmen, and Atlantic Highlands, NJ: Humanities Press, 1976; rpt. 1985.
Selmer, Carl, ed. *Navigatio Sancti Brendani Abbatis from Early Latin Manuscripts.* Notre Dame, IN, 1959; rpt. Blackrock [County Dublin]: Four Courts, 1989.
Severin, Tim. *The Brendan Voyage.* London: Hutchinson, 1978.

*Dorothy A. Bray*

**SEE ALSO**
Brasil; Cockaigne, Land of; Columbus, Christopher; Exploration and Expansion, European; Four Rivers of Paradise; Geography in Medieval Europe; Iceland; *Imrama;* Irish Travel; *Mare Oceanum;* Navigation; New World; Paradise, Travel to; Pilgrimage, Christian; Viking Discoveries and Settlements; Witte de Hese, Johannes

## Breviator

Name given to the lay messenger hired by a medieval monastic institution to travel to other monasteries and religious institutions such as cathedral schools to announce the death of a member of the monastery and to ask for prayers for the soul of the deceased.

Typically, the breviator carried a short obituary notice, known as a mortuary brief, which was written in the scriptorium of the monastery sending the announcement. When a prominent person such as an abbot, abbess, or major patron died, a more elaborate document known as a mortuary roll might be produced and circulated. The parchment mortuary roll, sometimes called an obituary or bede roll, included an elegant obituary of the deceased, which was often beautifully illuminated.

Communities visited by a breviator with a mortuary roll were expected to say prayers for the dead and to write a memorial of some sort on the roll. A mortuary brief was delivered to each establishment the breviator visited, but when he carried a mortuary roll, it grew as he traveled and collected entries, ultimately returning the document to the monastery or nunnery that had issued it.

Breviators often carried more than one roll at a time in their travels, and might even be employed by more than one monastic house simultaneously. Breviators were, at least in some cases, issued credentials vouching for their character and attesting that they had been given the right to convey a particular roll for a given period of time, usually one or two years. Breviators were paid a small sum by the issuing monastery, which was supplemented by the charity of the monastic houses and cathedrals they visited. These institutions were also expected to provide food and lodging, when necessary, for the breviator.

In most instances, the monastery employing a breviator supplied him with an itinerary of houses he was to visit. Often, monasteries were linked by specific agree-

Signatures on breviator roll. Durham Dean and Chapter Library Locellus I.12. Courtesy Durham Dean and Chapter. Photo by John B. Friedman.

ments to pray for the souls of each other's dead, and a breviator might be hired to announce the death at the houses belonging to this confraternity. At other times, however, breviators were simply instructed to visit religious institutions within a specific geographical area or to circulate a roll for a specified amount of time. The area covered on a single journey was sometimes quite extensive, and the messenger might carry one roll for several years. For example, the breviator bearing the mortuary roll commemorating Abbess Mathilda, a prominent Norman abbess of the early twelfth century, traveled throughout Normandy, France, and England, visiting 253 monasteries, nunneries, and cathedrals.

Other titles used in medieval documents to refer to these messengers include *brevigulus, breviger, brevillator, gerulus, tomiger, rollifer,* and *rotulifer.*

BIBLIOGRAPHY

Delisle, Léopold, ed. *Rouleaux des morts du IXe au XVe siècle.* Paris: Jules Renouard for La Société de l'Histoire de France, 1866; rpt. New York: Johnson Reprint, 1968.

Dufour, Jean. "Les rouleaux des morts." *Codicologica* 3 (1980): 96–102.

Huyghebaert, N. *Les Documents Nécrologique.* Typologie des Sources du Moyen Age Occidental, fasc. 4. Turnhout: Brepols, 1972.

*Teresa Leslie*

SEE ALSO
Mortuary Roll

## Breydenbach, Bernhard von
## (*c.* 1440–1497)

Author of a detailed, highly literary pilgrimage account, prepared with accompanying woodcuts for the printing press. Bernhard von Breydenbach's *Peregrinatio in Terram Sanctam* was published in 1486, and was soon reprinted and translated into various languages. It contains a description of a pilgrimage to Jerusalem and Mount Sinai in 1483.

Von Breydenbach [Breidenbach] was born around 1440. Beginning in 1456, he studied law at the University of Erfurt. At the time of his pilgrimage to the Holy Land in 1483, and until his death on May 5, 1497, he was dean of the Cathedral of Mainz; he also held other offices.

Von Breydenbach's pilgrimage began on April 25, 1483. He was accompanied by Count Johann von Solms-Lich, Philipp von Bicken, and a number of servants. They joined a much larger group of pilgrims traveling over sea from Venice that included Felix Fabri, himself the author of a well-known pilgrimage account. After they arrived in the Holy Land on July 11, the group made short excursions to various holy places. On July 22, most pilgrims returned to their ship for Venice, but Breydenbach, Fabri, and others stayed in Jerusalem until August 24, when they traveled to the Monastery of St. Catherine in the Sinai desert. After a visit to Cairo, the pilgrims embarked from Alexandria for the return journey to Venice on November 5 or 15. Their arrival at Venice marks the end of von Breydenbach's report.

Soon after his return to Mainz, probably at the beginning of February 1484, he started to write a short

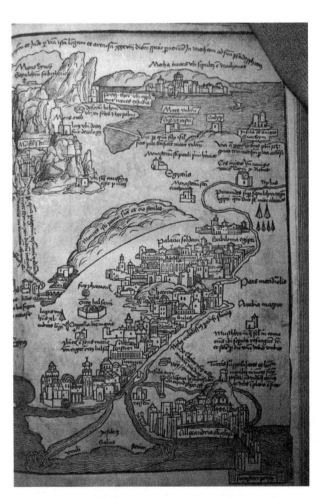

Bernhard von Breydenbach's *Peregrinatio in Terram Sanctam.* Mainz: Erhard Reuwich, 11 February 1486, n.p. n. sig. Map of the Holy Land, detail of Egypt, the Red Sea, and Mecca at top center. Reproduced by permission of the Map Division, The New York Public Library (Astor, Lenox and Tilden Foundations).

# B

instruction in German for pilgrims to the Holy Land at the request of Count Ludwig von Hanau-Lichtenberg. The *Peregrinatio in Terram Sanctam* appeared two years later in Mainz. Von Breydenbach himself is believed to have been the author of the actual report of the journey, whereas he commissioned the Dominican Martin Roth, *magister theologiae* at the University of Mainz, to write the many historical and theological digressions on peoples, towns, and events. These parts are based on a number of classical and medieval authors. Erhard Reuwich (of Utrecht), one of the servants of von Breydenbach and his two main companions, was responsible for the beautiful woodcuts that appeared in the many editions in Latin and vernacular languages. Before 1510, the book had been published at least four times in Latin, as well as in German, Dutch, French, and Spanish (an Italian version appeared later in the 1500s). The woodcuts are remarkable for the accuracy with which they portray Asian clothing styles and animals. An elaborate fold-out map shows a city plan of Jesusalem and records territory as far away as Mecca.

## BIBLIOGRAPHY

Breydenbach, Bernhard von. *Peregrinatio in terram sanctam.* Mainz: Erhard Reuwich, 1486.

—— *Die Reise ins Heilige Land. Ein Reisebericht aus dem Jahre 1473, mit 15 Holzschnitten, 2 Faltkarten und 6 Textseiten in Faksimile.* Ed. Elizabeth Geck. Wiesbaden: Pressler, 1961. [Based on the edition Mainz: Reuwich, 1486.]

Davies, Hugh William. *Bernhard von Breydenbach and His Journey to the Holy Land 1483–1484. A Bibliography.* London: Leighton, 1911; rpt. Utrecht: Haentjens, Dekker and Gumbert, 1968.

Orbán, Arpad P. "Bernhard von Breydenbach. *Peregrinatio in Terram Sanctam.*" *Ons geestelijk erf* 57 (1983): 180–190.

Röhrbacher. "Bernhard von Breydenbach und sein Werk 'Peregrinatio in Terram Sanctam' (1486)." *Philobiblion* 33 [2] (1989): 89–113.

Röhricht, Reinhold, and Heinrich Meisner. "Die Reiseinstruction des Bernhard von Breitenbach, 1483." In *Deutsche Pilgerreisen nach dem Heiligen Lande.* Berlin: Weidmann, 1880, pp. 120–145.

Weiss, Gerhard. "The Pilgrim as Tourist: Travels to the Holy Land as Reflected in the Published Accounts of German Pilgrims Between 1450 and 1550." In *The Medieval Mediterranean: Cross-Cultural Contacts.* Ed. Marilyn J. Chiat and Kathryn L. Reyerson. Medieval Studies at Minnesota 3. St. Cloud, MN: North Star Press, 1988, pp. 119–131.

*Z.R.W.M. von Martels*

SEE ALSO

Catherine in the Sinai, Monastery of St.; Costume, Oriental; Egypt; Fabri, Felix; Jerusalem; Mecca; Venice

## Bridia, C. de (fl. *c.* 1245 C.E.)

The Franciscan author of a report on the mission of John of Plano Carpini to the Mongols completed on July 30, 1247.

Little is known about "C. de Bridia," whose first name is abbreviated in the single manuscript copy of his account, and whose origins are uncertain (the place-name "Bridia" does not appear in Graesse's *Orbis Latinus;* it may be Brzeg [Brieg] in Silesia). He himself entitled his work *Historia Tartarum,* but it is today more familiarly known as the *Tartar Relation,* the name its editor gave it in 1965, when it was published with the Vinland Map.

In 1440, the *Tartar Relation* was included with a copy of Vincent of Beauvais's *Speculum Historiale* in a manuscript now in Yale University's Bcinecke Library. De Bridia's report is important because it helps scholars to understand how John of Plano Carpini and Nicholas the Pole compiled their better known works.

De Bridia wrote his account at the request of his superior, Friar Boguslaus, who was then minister of the Franciscan province of Bohemia and Poland. In 1247, John of Plano Carpini passed through Poland on a return journey to France from the Mongols with two companions, Benedict the Pole and Ceslaus of Bohemia. It appears that de Bridia spoke with all three friars about their adventures, and that his principal source was Benedict the Pole, who had already prepared a written brief.

The focus of de Bridia's report is the history and customs of the Mongols, not the story of the journey itself. The *Tartar Relation* is one of the most detailed of the Western accounts of Mongol history, genealogy, ethnography, and military methods. The work includes some speculation about future Mongol intentions, which were then of particular concern because of the Mongol invasions of Poland and surrounding regions in 1241 and 1242. It details the Mongol campaigns between the 1220s and 1240s, and it provides a list of the nations conquered by the Mongols. It is the only Western source that correctly attributes the Mongol campaign in Europe to Jochi, rather than Batu.

De Bridia's semi-historical account of Chinggis Khân's rise to power incorporates a considerable amount of myth and fable, including the khân's frightening encounter with Gog and Magog, here associated with the tradition of Alexander the Great romance, a body of late antique and medieval narrative detailing the eastward adventures of the Macedonian king. Thus, the *Tartar Relation* illustrates that amid the great amount of historically accurate and revealing information found in travel literature were explanations of unknown phenomena that borrowed from legendary material.

**BIBLIOGRAPHY**

Burnett, Charles S.W., and Patrick G. Dalché. "Attitudes toward the Mongols in Medieval Literature: The XXII Kings of Gog and Magog from the Court of Frederick II to Jean de Mandeville." *Viator* 22 (1991): 153–167.

Connell, C.W. "Western Views of the Origin of the 'Tartars': An Example of the Influence of Myth in the Second Half of the Thirteenth Century." *Journal of Medieval and Renaissance Studies* 3 (1973): 115–137.

Skelton, R.A., T.E. Marston, and G.D. Painter, eds. *The Vinland Map and the Tartar Relation*, 1965. 2nd edition. New Haven: Yale UP, 1995.

*Charles W. Connell*

**SEE ALSO**

Franciscan Friars; John of Plano Carpini; Mongols; Poland; Vincent of Beauvais; Vinland Map

## Brittany and Navigational Charts

The prominent position of Brittany (ancient Armorica), jutting into the Atlantic Ocean where it meets the English Channel, ensured that knowledge of its deeply indented and dangerous coasts was important to sailors from the earliest days of seafaring in the Northern Hemisphere. Phoenician traders bound for Cornwall as early as the sixth century B.C.E. observed that the inhabitants of the peninsula voyaged to Ireland in skin boats; brief written descriptions of conditions off the rocky capes and islands of Finistère were provided in Classical Greek *periploi,* sailing manuals, and accounts of voyages, from which they passed to Byzantium and the medieval world.

Maps accompanying the earliest known (thirteenth-century) manuscript copies of Ptolemy's *Geography,* probably based on much older sources, furnish recognizable outlines of Brittany's coast, a tradition that continues in the first published versions (for example, in the updated map of France [*tabula moderna*] added by Francesco Berlinghieri to his 1482 Florence edition). "Brittania" is also appropriately located with some topographical accuracy on the Cotton "Anglo-Saxon" Map (British Library, MS Cotton Tiberius B. v., fol. 56v), which has no demonstrable Ptolemaic influence. Likewise, Brittany is shown with some realism in Arabic sources starting with al-Idrīsī (fl. 1165 C.E.) and may be recognized without difficulty in *mappaemundi* from the thirteenth century onward, though Matthew Paris's world map (*c.* 1250) deprives it of all individuality. By the mid-fifteenth century, impressive large-scale depictions of the peninsula exist (for example, Fra Mauro's map of 1459).

With the rise of seaborne commerce and the extension of nautical charts beyond the Mediterranean after around 1300, cartographic knowledge of the Brittany coastline was greatly enhanced. Progress was rapid. The earliest surviving portolan chart, the Carta Pisana, provides only one Breton place-name, and the peninsula scarcely disturbs its rudimentary, flattened representation of western and northern France. But from the 1320s and 1330s, Italian and Catalan charts provide many toponyms, often twenty or more, including Nantes, St. Mathieu, and St. Malo, as well as a relatively detailed coastal outline that served sailors like the Castilian knight Pedro Niño as he rounded Brittany in 1406.

On Portuguese charts (which survive from only shortly before 1500) it became traditional to distinguish Brittany from France by a flag bearing ermines, a practice that continued after the duchy's absorption into France in 1532. Though Portuguese maps in contrast to Italian and Catalan ones often distort the peninsula by constricting its north-south dimensions, João Afonso's *Cosmography* (*c.* 1543) accurately represents the territory.

During the Middle Ages, northern sailors often had little alternative to oral tradition and use of lead and line for acquiring information on conditions along the peninsula's hazardous coasts with their powerful tides. Chaucer's Shipman was renowned for knowledge of "every cryk in Bretayne" based on personal experience. But around 1400, technical pilot manuals and sailing directions survive. The oldest native Breton contribution to this literature may be the description of various bottoms around Ushant, based on detailed local knowledge, incorporated in the earliest English rutter (route book), which appeared before 1461. Pierre Garcie's French equivalent, *Le grand routier de la mer* (manuscript versions from 1483; printed editions from 1502; illustrated English translation, 1538), acknowledges similar material provided by native pilots.

**BIBLIOGRAPHY**

Harley-Woodward. *The History of Cartography.* Vol. 1. See Gen. Bib.

Waters, D.W. *The Rutters of the Sea.* New Haven and London: Yale UP, 1967.

*Michael Jones*

**SEE ALSO**

Cartography, Arabic; Chaucer, Geoffrey; Cotton World Map; Itineraries and *Periploi; Mappamundi;* Maps; Matthew Paris; Mauro Map, [Fra]; Navigation; Portolan Charts; Ptolemy; Tides

## Broquière

*See* La Broquière, Bertrandon de

## Bruges [Brugge]

A city in present-day Belgium that was the main port of Flanders and a major center of trade in northern Europe during the later Middle Ages.

The history of Bruges has largely been determined by its accessibility to ships from the North Sea. Located at the boundary between the sandy plains and the coastal lowlands (*polders*) of Flanders, Bruges owes its origins and growth to several creeks that flow through the *polders* and allow access to the sea. It further benefited from the small estuary of the Reie, a freshwater river linking it to the Flemish hinterland.

While there is archeological evidence for navigation to the Bruges area dating from the beginning of Roman rule (first century C.E.), the settlement probably had a purely defensive military function by the fourth century. Nothing is known about its fate during the period of Frankish domination in the Merovingian era (500–757). When extant written sources first mention the city, in the eighth and ninth centuries, Bruges appears to have been serving primarily as a center for secular and ecclesiastical administration. In or before 851, a small fortress was erected in the central urban area, where Carolingian coins were minted before 875.

Yet even in those early years, some form of international trade at the site appears probable. Its Flemish name, *Brugge,* must be a conflation of the local river name *Reie* with the Old Norse *bryggja* (pier), which philologists date to the late eighth or early ninth century; such a blending of languages suggests intensive and peaceful contact between the local settlement and Scandinavia. What is known for certain is that merchants and craftsmen settled there in great numbers during the eleventh century. Galbert of Bruges, in his account of the murder of Charles the Good, count of Flanders, in 1127, portrays his hometown as a powerful political unit, conscious of its own interests and capable of concerted action against the Flemish nobility and even the French king. At this time the city acquired its first medieval walls and was granted its own jurisdiction, further widened by Count Philip of Alsace between 1165 and 1177.

Bruges grew to become one of the most important centers of trade in northern Europe by 1300. At that time the city had established direct links overseas not only with London, Gascony, and the Baltic nations (its traditional contacts), but also with the Rhône delta, Genoa, and soon with Venice. With an estimated population of 46,000 in the mid-fourteenth century, Bruges was slightly smaller than Ghent, Flanders's largest city, but it always was more prosperous and cosmopolitan. Merchants from the German Hanse, En-

Flemish single-masted clinker built coastal vessel with lee boards and centerline rudder. Bruges, 15th century. Photo by John B. Friedman.

Map of Bruges. Bruges City Archives Map and Plan #13. *C.* 1525. Courtesy Bruges City Archives.

which specialized in high-quality cloth, entered a slow but steady decline, eventually reducing the city's appeal to foreign merchants. Meanwhile, the passageway to the sea had started to silt up; as early as about 1200 a canal was dug three miles north to Damme, the first of several outports controlled by Bruges, to facilitate navigation in the area; by the late 1400s, however, even these subsidiary ports had become hard to reach and transfer of merchandise to Bruges exceedingly expensive. The city's prolonged conflict with Emperor Maximilian of Germany between 1484 and 1493 finally disturbed traffic at a crucial moment. Antwerp, with its excellent connections to the expanding Brabantine fairs, as well as to the land routes to southern Germany, succeeded Bruges and became one of the great world markets of the early modern era.

**BIBLIOGRAPHY**

Nicholas, David. *Medieval Flanders.* London and New York: Longman, 1992.

Ryckaert, Marc. *Brugge.* Brussels: Gemeentekrediet van België/Crédit communal de Belgique, 1991.

Strohm, Reinhard. *Music in Late Medieval Bruges.* 1985. Rev. ed., Oxford: Clarendon P, 1990.

*Walter Simons*

**SEE ALSO**

Fairs; *Fondaco;* Genoa; Ghent; Guilds; Hanse, The; Spain and Portugal; Stones and Timber, Scandinavian Trade in; Venice

gland, Scotland, Venice, Lucca, Genoa, Florence, Catalonia, Castile, and Portugal were organized in official corporations that enjoyed special privileges and played a major role in the Bruges market; these international contacts also turned the city into an important center of banking in northern Europe.

Partly because of its indigenous and foreign wealth, partly because the counts of Flanders (later the dukes of Burgundy) and their courts often resided there, Bruges attracted many artists in the later Middle Ages. It was especially well known for its patronage of music, manuscript illumination, embroidery, and the panel painting of Jan van Eyck and Hans Memling in the late fourteenth and fifteenth centuries.

Toward the end of the Middle Ages, Bruges's importance for northern European trade was eclipsed by Antwerp. In the early 1300s, the local textile industry,

## Brunetto Latini (*c.* 1220–1294)

Dante's teacher in thirteenth-century Florence and author of an enormously influential encyclopedic work that includes sections on geography.

Most modern readers know Brunetto Latini only through Dante's *Commedia,* where, in the circle of the Sodomites (*Inferno* 15), he and his *Book of the Treasure* (Livres dou Tresor) are treated with respect and admiration. Like Dante, Brunetto was a member of the spice and herb merchants' guild of Florence, an organization to which artists (because of their work with plant pigments) and physicians (because of their work with herbal medicines) both belonged. Following the overthrow of Florence's Ghibelline nobility in the late 1200s, their rivals, the Guelphs, established a government modeled on the plebeian genesis of the Roman republic. It was in this sociopolitical context that Latini rose to a career as "notary," a position rather like a

# B

modern attorney, the training for which prepared him to teach commerce and enabled him to assume a variety of administrative duties in the city.

As a respected and influential figure in the government, Brunetto undertook a mission to Spain in 1260 to seek assistance from King Alfonso X against the mounting aggression of Frederick II's son Manfred (king of Sicily 1258–1266) and the Sienese Ghibellines; the embassy failed to produce a promise of military aid, but Brunetto himself reaped an immense intellectual reward from his contact with Alfonso, who was known as the Learned King for his patronage of scholars and scholarship.

On crossing the Pyrenees, however, he learned from an encounter with a fellow Florentine of the defeat of the Guelph forces at Montaperti and of Brunetto's own exile, whereupon he abandoned the idea of returning to Florence, directing himself instead to centers of Italian economic, scribal, and intellectual community in France. He was to remain in France for the next six years, first in Montpellier, later in Arras and Bar-sur-Aube; following the defeat of the Ghibellines and the death of Manfred at Benevento in February of 1266, he returned to Florence, probably in the retinue of Charles of Anjou.

During his sojourn in France, Brunetto composed his *Book of the Treasure,* an encyclopedic, ethical, and political manual dedicated to a "*biaus dous amis*" ("handsome sweet friend") who was almost certainly Charles of Anjou; the volume, composed in French, first lays a foundation of basic knowledge (reflecting a long tradition of encyclopedic compilations: Cassiodorus, Boethius, and especially Martianus Capella), then proceeds to a translation of the *Nichomachean Ethics* of Artistotle and a rendition of Cicero's *De inventione,* followed by a brief outline of the technicalities of communal government; the ultimate goal is to summarize the intellectual, ethical, and rhetorical qualities needed to defend law and justice on behalf of the citizens of the commune. While it was conceived as a basic indoctrination for Charles (in the tradition of the "Mirrors for Princes" like the *Secretum secretorum*), a preparation for informed leadership of a communal government, the work's immense popularity in France and Italy (as well as on the Iberian Peninsula) throughout the next two centuries transcends the immediate circumstances of its composition.

Book 1 of the *Treasure* includes, in its eclectic lore, a description of the world that became an important source of basic geographical and astronomical informa-tion. Brunetto clearly knew key texts on the subject, both ancient and modern; these include Solinus, Orosius, Isidore of Seville, Honorius Augustodunensis, Peter Comestor, and Godfrey of Viterbo. From these authorities he took "scientific" data, such as the distance from earth to the firmament (taken from the works of Pseudo Maimonides), and reports on "mirabilia," which he wrote so filled the lands and seas that no one could comprehend them all.

The widely circulated *Treasure,* in turn, influenced the content of other books, including the encyclopedic work attributed to Sir John Mandeville, which borrows from Brunetto, among other things, in its passages on the Danube, Sicily, the burial place of John the Evangelist, the sultan's capital at Cairo, the inundation of the Nile, Heliopolis and the legend of the phoenix, and the Amazons.

Besides Brunetto's importance in geographical writings, scholarship has uncovered important new evidence connecting Brunetto Latini and Dante through the *Romance of the Rose;* the *Romance's* authors, Guillaume de Lorris and Jean de Meun, were from the area around Montpellier and Bar-sur-Aube, and documentation of Brunetto's literary activities there strengthens the case for his role in the transmission of that monument of French letters to Italy.

**BIBLIOGRAPHY**

Barrette, Paul, and Spurgeon Baldwin, trans. *Brunetto Latini: The Book of the Treasure (Li Livres dou Tresor).* New York: Garland, 1993.

Holloway, Julia Bolton. *Brunetto Latini, An Analytic Bibliography.* London: Grant and Cutler, 1986.

Latini, Brunetto. *Li Livres dou Tresor.* Francis J. Carmody, ed. Berkeley: U California P, 1948.

*Spurgeon Baldwin*

**SEE ALSO**

Alfonso X; Amazons; Frederick II; Godfrey of Viterbo; Guilds; Honorius Augustodunensis; Isidore of Seville; *Mandeville's Travels*; Merchants, Italian; Orosius; Solinus, Julius Gaius

## Bubonic Plague

*See* Black Death

## Buddhism

One of the great missionary religions of the world. Originating in northeast India around the fifth century

B.C.E., Buddhism subsequently spread throughout the rest of the Indian subcontinent and on to other parts of Asia where it played a formative role in the development of Asian civilizations while in turn being absorbed and transformed by those civilizations. In light of its evangelical orientation, Buddhism developed a close and mutually beneficial relationship with commerce and travel throughout Asia.

The missionary thrust of Buddhism is already clearly evident in the life of its historical founder Gautama (*c.* 563–483 B.C.E.). After having renounced the world and undergone an arduous search for spiritual liberation, Gautama at the age of thirty-five is recorded as having achieved enlightenment and become a Buddha (Awakened One). The newly liberated Buddha, though at first reluctant to share his experience, was persuaded by the god Brahma to spread his doctrine, the Dharma. He thereupon embarked on a ministry of teaching, preaching his first sermon to a band of five ascetics who became the first members of his order, the Sangha. This community came to consist of both monks and nuns who, abandoning their lives as householders, removed themselves from society and sought to reproduce in their persons the enlightenment experience of the Buddha through the threefold cultivation of moral discipline, meditation, and wisdom. For the next forty-five years, until his death at the age of eighty, the Buddha traveled about teaching and gathering followers, both renunciant and lay, who announced their discipleship by taking refuge in the Buddha, his Dharma, and the Sangha.

Since preaching the Dharma was the central focus of the Buddha's career, he instructed his renunciant disciples to do the same with the commission, "Go monks and travel for the welfare and happiness of people, out of compassion for the world, for the benefit, welfare, and happiness of gods and men. No two of you go the same way. Teach the Dharma, monks, and proclaim the pure holy life" (Vinaya I, 2). This mandate to spread the Dharma out of compassion has remained a primary motivational tenet in the essentially peaceful and noncoercive dissemination of Buddhism.

Despite a decided emphasis on the necessity of the renunciant life for the attainment of liberation, the Buddha in the course of his career also cultivated lay followers. In one version of his biography, even before he preached to the ascetics, the newly enlightened Buddha was encountered by merchants who made food offerings and did obeisance to him. This event presaged not only the indispensable function that the lay community was to serve in providing for the physical needs of the renunciant community, but also the essential role that traveling merchants, whether through caravans on the Silk Road or vessels on the South Seas, would play in the Buddhist missionary enterprise.

Significantly, the Buddha included royal figures among his lay followers, thereby foreshadowing the importance that civil authorities and state sponsorhip were to have in the promotion of Buddhism. Perhaps no person other than Gautama himself figured so prominently in the early history of Buddhism as the Indian ruler Asoka, who reigned in the middle of the third century B.C.E. and who, as a convert to Buddhism, became the quintessential universal ruler and exemplar for all subsequent Buddhist sovereigns. Among the notable events that took place during Asoka's reign were the dispaching of emissaries abroad and the sending forth of missionaries. Most prominent among these missionaries was Asoka's son Mahinda, who historically was credited with the establishment of Buddhism in Sri Lanka, where it later had a decisive influence on the development of the faith in Southeast Asia.

The nature of the Sangha also affected the spread of the religion. In the period following the Buddha's death the renunciant order remained, as it had been during the Buddha's life, an itinerant community wandering around homeless for nine months of the year, except during the rainy season when the order settled in fixed residences for an extended three-month retreat. Although the Sangha eventually came to reside for the most part in permanent monasteries, the role of the wandering renunciant never completely disappeared. Ironically, the establishment of fixed monasteries also provided a condition for furthering travel and commerce since monastic settlements often served as anchors on trade routes like the Silk Road. Furthermore, the building of monasteries and hermitages in isolated areas often had the effect of improving travel and communications to remote regions. In addition, since a valid ordination ceremony for monks required a quorum of previously ordained monks (ten in Buddhist regions and five in border areas), travel increased as a result of this religious duty.

After the Buddha's death, his original missionary mandate was supplemented by a number of other

# B

factors that further acted as stimuli to the expansion of Buddhism as well as to increased travel and trade throughout Asia. These include the practice of pilgrimage and relic veneration. The Buddha, before he died, had instructed that his remains be cremated and placed in reliquary monuments called stupas (*stūpa*s), which came to symbolize the continuing presence of the Buddha among the community. After his death, stupas were erected at places associated with major events in the Buddha's life. These became major pilgimage sites that drew devotees not only from other locations in India but also from afar. As the Buddhist message spread, so too did the cult of the Buddha's relics and the practice of building stupas. Relics and cultic images were transported abroad, sometimes as gifts from one king to another. Consequently, pilgrimage sites appeared throughout Buddhist regions attracting large numbers of pilgims. The monastic establishment often took responsibility for the care of these pilgrims, lodging them in monasteries or hostels constructed for their use along the pilgrimage routes.

The emergence of texts also fostered the spread of the Buddhist message and encouraged travel. The Dharma of the Buddha, at first preserved and transmitted orally, finally was committed to writing around the first century B.C.E. The existence of written scriptures and their steady proliferation required Buddhists in outlying areas to send out missions to bring back new scriptures, to retrieve lost or compromised texts, and to enlist competent translators from abroad. The conveyance of texts acquired even greater importance as the physical texts became cultic objects thought to possess numinous powers.

The diffusion of Buddhism was further enhanced by the emergence of the Mahayana movement around the beginning of the Christian era. This new orientation in Buddhism called itself the Great Vehicle (*Mahāyāna*) since it saw its path and teaching as superior to the older renunciant-centered schools of Buddhism that were referred to by the derogatory epithet *Hīnayāna* (Inferior Vehicle). Of these Hinayana schools, *Theravāda* was to become the sole surviving representative. In contrast to the Hinayana schools that held the self-striving Arhat (Perfected One) as their ideal, Mahayana posed the new ideal of the Bodhisattva, a being who, while seeking the ultimate goal of Buddhahood, was required to assist other sentient beings to that same end, thus increasing the emphasis on the missionary

vocation. Besides its positive influence on the spread of Buddhism, this Bodhisattva ideal also had a salutary effect on travel and trade, since lay and monastic adherents of Mahayana were enjoined to engage in public charitable activities that included the building of roads, fords, bridges, ferries, and hostels for travelers.

While the preceding factors were essential to the spread of Buddhism, no less importance should be attached to material, cultural, and historical conditions that made that diffusion possible. In particular, a long-standing access to East Asia through the Silk Road and increased ocean commerce throughout Southeast Asia were both essential prerequisites for the missionary success of Buddhism.

By the beginning of Europe's Middle Ages, Buddhism had almost passed its first millennium, during which significant expansion had taken place across Asia. The medieval period was a time for the domestication of Buddhism in cultures that had already accepted the faith, while the religion continued to expand into new areas, most notably Japan, Tibet, and Inner Asia. At the same time, the latter part of this period also witnessed the rising fortunes of Islam in south, southeast, and Central Asia, and the subsequent virtual disappearance of Buddhism from India, Malaysia, Indonesia, and Central Asia.

Southeast Asia during this period witnessed the creation of the classical monarchical states. These kingdoms arose within the context of a wider adaption of Indian customs and culture, in which Buddhism and Hinduism played formative roles by contributing not only their concept of kingship based on cosmology, but also their overall world view and value systems. Before the eleventh century, Buddhism, which according to traditional accounts had been introduced to Southeast Asia during Asoka's reign, existed in diverse and syncretic forms that included both Hinayana and Mahayana. The latter was heavily colored by the newly emerged Tantric religiosity, which was attractive to lay audiences because of its incorporation of popular religious practices. As the classical Southeast Asian states were established in the period from the eleventh to the fifteenth centuries, however, they gradually embraced Theravada Buddhism. It thus became the orthodox faith in Burma, Thailand, Cambodia, and Laos. Vietnam, in contrast, remained largely beholden to the Chinese Mahayanist model.

Tibet, due to its inaccessibility, was one of the latest Asian countries introduced to Buddhism: its conversion was roughly contemporaneous with the European medieval period. The Buddhism of Tibet was historically conditioned by that of all the surrounding countries, but its essence was ultimately determined by the Buddhism of medieval India, particularly its Mahayanist Tantric expression. Because of the paramount importance of the spiritual guide (lama; *bla-ma*) in this ritually oriented and intensely meditative religion, Tibetan Buddhism came to be known in the West through the misnomer "Lamaism."

Traditionally, the introduction of Buddhism in Tibet has been credited to the work of Indian missionaries and the patronage of Tibetan kings. Tibet also produced its own traveler-scholars who undertook the arduous journey to India for the sake of the Dharma. Most prominent of these was the great translator Marpa (1012–1096), who made three trips to India. After Buddhism was established in Tibet, the country became a base for launching the faith to other regions, particularly across the wastes of Inner Asia where the Mongols were eventually converted to the Tibetan tradition of Buddhism.

The entry of Buddhism into China, which occured during the Later Han dynasty (25–220 C.E.), marked a momentous occasion in the religion's history, as the civilization of India was brought into contact with that of China. Mahayana Buddhism eventually came to permeate and transform the civilizations of East Asia while itself being modified in the process. Unlike in other parts of Asia where the involvement of royal figures was crucial in the introduction and dissemination of Buddhism, Buddhism's early period in China coincided with a phase of declining imperial power. The religion was able to take hold only after the end of the Han dynasty when its ideological buttress of Confucianism had fallen into disrepute. This, of course, does not diminish the importance of later Chinese rulers in establishing contacts with foreign powers for the sake of the Dharma and in ultimately shaping the history of Chinese Buddhism. The initial appearance of Buddhism, however, was not in the company of official emissaries but in communities of foreign merchants, who were often accompanied by translator monks, one of the earliest of whom was the Parthian An Shigao [An Shih-kao] (fl. 184). He represented the first in a long line of foreign translators who during the next millennium journeyed to China from abroad, contributing to the enormous task of translat-

ing the vast Buddhist corpus from Indic languages into Chinese.

China during this period produced its own great traveler monks who went to India in pursuit of texts, learning, and pilgrimage. Coming from a highly literate and historically conscious culture, Chinese monks like Faxian [Fa-hsien] (339?–420?), Xüanzang [Hsüan-tsang] (602–664), and Yijing [I-ching] (635–713) produced noteworthy records of their journeys that are still extant. Of these men, the most famous was Xüanzang, who not only became one of Chinese Buddhism's most prolific and authoritative translators of Indian texts, but also produced a record of his travels that became one of the great classics in travel diaries. His *Records of the Western Region* (Da Tang Xiyü ji) contains copious information on Central Asia and India that has proved invaluable to modern historians and archaeologists.

Much as the expansion of Buddhism into Southeast Asia accompanied a general trend of Indian cultural influence, the transmission of the religion to Korea and Japan took place as part of a broad process of Sinification that spread the mantle of Chinese civilization over East Asia. Buddhism was introduced to Korea from China in the fourth century C.E. and to Japan from Korea in the sixth century C.E. This introduction occurred on an informal popular level through movement of merchants, artisans, and refugees, as well as on an official level through royal embassies. As elsewhere in the Buddhist world, Korean and Japanese rulers played a vital role both in the adoption and spread of the faith in their own domain and in continuing attempts to renew the Dharma through foreign contacts. Korea's geographical setting as a peninsula and Japan's as an island led to the development of extensive maritime capabilities that furthered the cause of Buddhist expansion while at the same time benefiting from the ongoing developments in the religion.

The steady stream of Korean and Japanese monks to the Chinese mainland, especially during the Tang (618–906) and Song (960–1279) periods, produced a number of individuals who were instrumental in bringing Chinese Buddhist scholastic systems and traditions back to their native countries. Korean and Japanese monk-travelers also left significant records of their trips to India and China. The Korean monk Hyech'o (eighth century) produced a travelogue of his journey through Central Asia and India, while the Japanese Tendai monk

# B

Ennin (794–864) produced a valuable eyewitness account of his stay in China during the turbulent period of the Huichang Suppression that reached its height in 845. Later, the Tendai monk Jojin (1011–1081) kept a diary through one year of travel in China during the Song dynasty (960–1279). These documents, in addition to their obvious contribution as historical sources, are eloquent testimonies to the positive role played by Buddhism in stimulating and facilitating travel and communication across Asia during the medieval period.

BIBLIOGRAPHY

Ch'en, Kenneth. *Buddhism in China: A Historical Survey.* Princeton: Princeton UP, 1964.

Gernet, Jacques. *Buddhism in Chinese Society: An Economic History from the Fifth to the Tenth Centuries.* Trans. Franciscus Verellen. New York: Columbia UP, 1995.

Gombrich, Richard. *Theravada Buddhism: A Social History from Ancient Benares to Modern Colombo.* London: Routledge and Kegan Paul, 1988.

Harvey, Peter. *An Introduction to Buddhism: Teachings, History and Practices.* Cambridge: Cambridge UP, 1990.

Thomas, Edward J. *The Life of the Buddha as Legend and History.* 3rd edition. London: Routledge and Kegan Paul, 1949.

*Daniel Getz*

SEE ALSO

China; Confucianism; India; Inner Asian Travel; Mongols; Pilgrimage, Christian; Silk Roads; Tibet

## Bukhara

Major commercial city of Transoxiana (the region north of the Oxus river, now Uzbekistan), and important center of both Sunni Islamic learning and the Neo-Persian *shu'ubiyya* movement. Bukhara exported local industrial goods and the produce of its oasis, and acted as a conduit for trade with Russia and Scandinavia, Central Asia, and China, India, and the Middle East. Its great prosperity in the tenth century, when it had some 75,000 inhabitants, was followed by a decline in the 1100s and 1200s.

The settlement dates back to the middle of the first millennium B.C.E., and is first mentioned in seventh-century sources of the Chinese, under whose influence its industry developed. Coinage of pure silver was minted here before the arrival of Islam (*c.* 710 C.E.) and the Arab conquest (728/729 C.E.). As the capital of the Iranian Samanids (875–999 C.E.), Bukhara reached its apogee, and under the Turkic Qarakhanids (999–1032 C.E.), was second in importance only to Samarkand. A high volume of trade with northeastern Europe is attested to by the discovery of numerous hordes of Samanid coins along the Volga route and in Scandinavia. As the purity of the coinage declined in the tenth century, so did this commerce. Muslim traders based in Bukhara carried on a barter trade with the Chinese and the nomads of the Asian interior. Borne by the caravans, Islam spread eastward. Tenth-century visitors remark on Bukhara's importance as a center for the trade of Turkish slaves, and of the cramped and unsanitary character of the city. Ibn Sīna, or Avicenna (980–1037), spent his youth here and marveled at the city's famous book market.

Civil disorder and desertification were preludes to the disasters of the thirteenth century. In 1220, the Mongols destroyed the city and massacred its inhabitants. Realignment of trade with the Mongol capital of Karakorum helped sponsor a revival, but Bukhara suffered devastation at Mongol hands again in 1273 and 1316, events from which it never recovered.

BIBLIOGRAPHY

Barthol'd, Vasili V. *Turkestan Down to the Mongol Invasion.* Trans. H.A.R. Gibb. Gibb Memorial Series, n.s. 5. London: Luzac, 1928; rpt. Philadelphia: Porcupine, 1977.

Frye, Richard Nelson, ed. and trans. *The History of Bukhara. Translated from a Persian Abridgment of the Arabic Original by Narshakhi.* Cambridge: Medieval Academy of America, 1954.

———. *Bukhara. The Medieval Achievement.* Norman OK: U of Oklahoma P, 1965.

*Brian Catlos*

SEE ALSO

Caravans; Coinage and Money; Inner Asian Trade; Inner Asian Travel; Karakorum; Mongols; Muslim Travelers and Trade; Nomadism and Pastoralism; Samarkand

## Burchard of Mount Sion (fl.1280)

German Dominican, pilgrim to the Holy Land and author of a travel narrative, *Descriptio Terrae Sanctae,* the first systematic description of the portion of Palestine west of the Jordan.

Nothing is known about Burchard's origins or life except that he joined the Dominican convent at

Magdeburg and by 1280 had undertaken his pilgrimage. Burchard stayed in Acre for some time and was connected with the Dominican convent of Mount Sion, from which his name is derived.

In 1283, Burchard wrote his travelogue, entitled *Descriptio Terrae Sanctae,* based on his recollections of the Christian holy sites he visited, of the topography, flora, and fauna, and of the sociopolitical conditions of the Holy Land, with a particular emphasis on Jerusalem.

He was an excellent observer, critical and empirical by nature; he often challenged statements made by previous authors no matter how authoritative, if their accounts were contradicted by his own observations. For example, during his visit on Mount Gilboa, he experienced a heavy rain, despite the account of King David's curse "neither let there be rain upon you" given in the magnificent passage in II Samuel 1:21; thus he challenged the interpretation of the biblical text. He also showed a very early interest in biblical archaeology. Having been aware of the historical evolution that had caused the destruction of many early Christian sites in Palestine, he recommended digging through the strata of ruins in order to reach the original holy places.

Burchard's description of Palestinian society is an important record of the ethno-social conditions of the region in the last generation of the Crusader presence. Among the Eastern Christian communities there, he praised the Armenians for their piety and vehemently criticized the Crusaders for their behavior, prophesying the loss of the Holy Land to Christendom "due to their sins."

**BIBLIOGRAPHY**
Burchard of Mount Sion. *Descriptio Terrae Sanctae.* Ed. C.J.J. Laurent. Leipzig: Akademie Verlag, 1864.
Grabois, Aryeh. "Christian Pilgrims in the Thirteenth Century and the Latin Kingdom of Jerusalem: Burchard of Mount Sion." In *Outremer: Studies in the History of the Crusading Kingdom of Jerusalem Presented to Joshua Prawer.* Ed. B.Z. Kedar et al. Jerusalem: Yad Izhak Ben-Zvi, 1982, pp. 285–296.

*Aryeh Grabois*

**SEE ALSO**
Acre; Armenia; Dominican Friars; Eastern Christianity; Holy Land; Jerusalem; Pilgrimage, Christian

## Buscarello de' Ghisolfi (d. after 1304)

A member of one of the foremost Genoese trading families in the Middle East, professional soldier, and diplomat.

Buscarello de' Ghisolfi's earliest documented activity was in 1274, when he participated in arming a galley. A notarial act of 1279 situates him at Lajazzo, in Lesser Armenia. For many years Buscarello served as a guard and confidant to the il-khâns of Persia. In spring 1289, he embarked for Europe at the head of an embassy sent by Arghun (1284–1291). Arghun's two previous ambassadors to the West had been Mongols assisted by interpreters fluent in Latin, but their messages had been coolly received; the il-khân may have thought it prudent to entrust the mission to a European. The letters that Buscarello carried proposed an allied crusade against the Mamluks in Egypt to begin at Acre in January 1291. Acknowledging the transportation problems faced by a sizeable armed force, Arghun offered to supply twenty to thirty thousand horses and the necessary supplies for a European landing in Syria.

In September 1289, Buscarello had an audience at Rieti with Pope Nicholas IV (1288–1292), who gave him letters of introduction to England's King Edward I (r. 1272–1307). In November or December, he presented Arghun's proposal to Philip IV of France (r. 1285–1314). He arrived in London on January 5, 1290, where he must have delivered the same message to Edward. After a twenty-day sojourn in England, he returned to the pope. There he was met by Arghun's fourth ambassador, the Mongol aristocrat Chagan [or Zagan], who took charge of the embassy's return. Buscarello was in Italy again in December 1290 on another of Arghun's missions.

The Franco-Mongolian campaign never materialized, and Acre fell in the spring of 1291. Buscarello's whereabouts are unknown at that time, but he was in Genoa the following August. Documents show that he borrowed a large sum of money from eight different people for an enterprise in what is now Romania. However, as was customary with Genoese merchant documents, no plan was stated. At some point, he encountered the envoy of Edward I, Sir Geoffrey of Langley, and accompanied him from Genoa on his mission to Arghun. Langley's travel account shows that Buscarello, joined by his brother Percivalle and his nephew Corrado, guided the entourage to Samsun, on the Black Sea, by way of Trebizond; thence the party followed the main caravan route to the Persian court.

# B

In the meantime, Arghun had died and was succeeded by his brother Gaikhatu (1291–1295). Before reentering Mongol territory, Buscarello sent Corrado ahead to obtain a safe conduct for him, to be sure of his position under the new sovereign. Granted permission to proceed (after some difficulty), Buscarello and the English entourage arrived at Gaikhatu's court, and later went to Tabriz. The mission was completed, and on September 22, 1292, the party departed for Trebizond; Buscarello returned to Genoa in January 1293.

During the next several years, Buscarello may have pursued his calling as a merchant while continuing to perform diplomatic services. He carried a message from Pope Boniface VIII (1294–1303) to Ghazan (1295–1304), the il-khân who aggressively sought to drive the Mamluks from Syria. In 1301, Buscarello relayed messages between Ghazan and the pope and, in 1302, between Ghazan and Edward I. In 1303, Buscarello carried a letter from Edward to the Nestorian patriarch Mar Jabalaha III.

Buscarello may have died in 1304, since subsequent Persian embassies were entrusted to others. A Genoese document of 1317 indicates that he was certainly dead by that year, survived by a son, Argone, whose name reveals the close ties between the Ghisolfi and the former khân. It is not known if Buscarello's descendants also served the il-khâns.

## BIBLIOGRAPHY

Balard, Michel. "Les Génois en Asie centrale et en Extrême-Orient au XIVe siècle: un cas exceptionnel?" In *Économies et Sociétés au Moyen Âge. Mélanges offerts à Edouard Perroy.* Publications de la Sorbonne, Études 5. Paris: Sorbonne, 1973, pp. 681–688.

Boyle, John Andrew. "The Il-Khans of Persia and the Princes of Europe." *Central Asiatic Journal* 20 (1976): 25–40.

Chabot, J.B. "Notes sur les relations du roi Argoun avec l'Occident." *Revue de l'Orient latin* 2 (1894): 566–638.

Grousset, René. *The Empire of the Steppes. A History of Central Asia.* Trans. Naomi Walford. New Brunswick, NJ: Rutgers UP, 1970.

Petech, Luciano. "Les marchands italiens dans l'empire mongol." *Journal Asiatique* 250 (1962): 549–574.

Sinor, Denis. "The Mongols and Western Europe." In *Inner Asia and Its Contacts with Medieval Europe.* Aldershot: Variorum Reprints, 1977, section 9, pp. 513–544.

*Gloria Allaire*

## SEE ALSO

Acre; Ambassadors; Armenia; Caravans; Diplomacy; Genoa; Lajazzo; Mamluks; Mongols; Nestorianism; Transportation, Inland; Trebizond

## Byzantine Empire

A term representing a political state of varying scope and geographic extent over a period of some eleven centuries, reckoned as beginning with Constantine the Great's transfer of the Roman Empire's capital to Constantinople in the early fourth century to the capture of that city by the Turks in 1453. By the fifth century, it would have embraced the eastern half of the Roman Empire's Mediterranean territories; at perhaps its fullest extent under Justinian (sixth century), it stretched from North Africa and Italy to the Caucasus and northern Mesopotamia; shrunk by the Arab conquests of the seventh century, it was reduced to a central core of the Balkan Peninsula and Asia Minor, with territories recovered thereafter in various directions; eroded anew by the Fourth Crusade (1199–1204), in its reconstituted form thereafter (thirteenth century) it shrank even further, and in its final decades consisted only of the area around the capital, the Peloponnesus, and a few islands. For most of its history, Byzantium was a multiethnic society, only in its final period coming to a more consciously Hellenic sense of identity in anything like modern "national" terms.

As in much of the medieval world, travel within Byzantium was rarely undertaken for reasons of pleasure or personal experience, but rather travelers set out with explicit objectives, mainly commercial, diplomatic, or religious. Though they are scattered, surviving sources testify vividly to these activities through the more than eleven centuries of the eastern Roman Empire's history.

Commercial movement involved both internal and external trade on a large scale, though in patterns affected by changing political and economic conditions over the centuries. One advantage from the outset was the establishment of a stable currency system, based on the gold *solidus* (*nomisma, hyperpyron, bezant*), which maintained its reliability from the fourth to the eleventh century. Though challenged along the way by the Arabic *dinar*, Byzantine coinage remained the preferred medium of international exchange for centuries, thereby giving the Empire a powerful advantage in trade.

Under the unified Roman Empire (first through fourth centuries) the eastern provinces had always enjoyed a fuller, more prosperous commercial life than that in the less developed western territories. It was through eastern regions that the Oriental luxury goods (such as silks, spices, and jewelry) so prized in the Mediterranean world were imported into its markets. Such traffic prospered, despite harassment by Vandal naval power in the fifth century and the liberating achievement of the Empire's own native silk industry in the sixth century. Just how far Byzantine commercial reach could extend is demonstrated by *The Christian Topography,* written by the early-sixth-century Alexandrian merchant Cosmas Indikopleustes ("the Sailor to India"), whose description of his travels was meant to argue his own curious cosmographical ideas. Such lively activity was then compromised by the upheavals of the Arab conquests in the seventh century, which disrupted both movement in the Mediterranean and the pattern of trade routes by land. Considerable constriction and readjustment marked the next two centuries, but trade flourished anew by the tenth. Some elements of economic self-sufficiency persisted, but internal traffic again stirred. And, with some competition from Thessaloniki and other cities, Constantinople became, more than ever, the center of a large international carrying trade, drawing merchants from numerous lands beyond the Empire.

The vitality of Byzantine commercial life was hampered by rigid state regulation, which exacted heavy tariffs, controlled the flow of goods and supplies of materials, licensed places of business, monopolized financial mechanisms, and generally served to discourage the development of capitalistic enterprise on any scale. The mechanics of this highly statist system are documented in the *Book of the Eparch,* from the early tenth century, which describes the duties of Constantinople's prefect (or eparch) in regulating the trade guilds of the capital, seeing to its security, and controlling the various groups of foreign merchants there. This statism helped guarantee rich revenues to the government, but it limited the growth of mercantile initiative and of a healthy merchant class. It also left the Byzantine economy vulnerable to the unfettered enterprise of Italian merchants, backed by their trade-oriented home governments (Venice, Genoa, Pisa), which were able to secure exceptional trading privileges within the Empire in the eleventh and twelfth centuries. Such status might

mesh to some extent with smaller-scale Byzantine trading activities, to mutual advantage in the short term. But, in the long term, it allowed the Italians to penetrate the Byzantine economy in general, subordinating it to their own advantages and agendas, while taking over from Constantinople the control of maritime trade and making themselves the new middlemen of international commerce. The once-unchallenged revenues of Constantinople were lost, denying the government a principal source of income, and thus contributing to Byzantium's increasing weakness and reduced political status. By the Empire's final centuries (thirteenth through fifteenth), its economic life was largely restricted to regional and local trade within and beyond its reduced borders: a trade, however, that still afforded considerable prosperity to Byzantine merchants. Indeed, even through the epochs of Italian penetration, local centers, such as the still-thriving Thessaloniki, operated widely attractive trade fairs and sustained healthy regional economies.

Notwithstanding such atypical voyagers as Cosmas, Byzantine mercantile travel rarely extended far beyond the Empire's borders, though allowing for locales such as Baghdad, Alexandria, and Cairo in the Islamic world, parts of Italy and the western Mediterranean basin, and the outer reaches of the Black Sea. By the same token, however, foreign merchants were, in Byzantium's heyday, powerfully drawn to its markets. Traders from everywhere were allowed relatively free short-term access, and selected groups of Syrian, Balkan, Russian, and then Italian merchants could be allowed continuing residence, the Italians eventually being granted permanent quarters in Constantinople and other Byzantine cities. Such international movement created the impression of cosmopolitanism conveyed in two twelfth-century texts: the Byzantine satire *Timarion,* which describes the great autumn fair at Thessaloniki; and the account of the Jewish traveler from Spain, Benjamin of Tudela, who gives an admiring picture of Constantinople.

Such imported cosmopolitanism, however, generally represented the extent of Byzantine interest in the world beyond its borders. The outside world was welcome to come to the Byzantines, but they themselves showed little curiosity about it, beyond gathering information useful to the government in dealing with neighboring peoples who were immediate or potential enemies. On private or commercial levels, there was little impulse toward what we understand as exploration. In the early fifteenth century, to be sure, a Byzantine traveler named Laskaris Kananos journeyed as far as Baltic Germany, Scandinavia, and Iceland—for reasons not known—and left a very brief account of his experiences, but he is an almost unique example of such seemingly private travel.

Official journeys, on the other hand, constituted an important category of Byzantine travel. The concept of permanent diplomatic representation in foreign centers was to be developed only in the late Middle Ages by the Italian mercantile cities, out of their experiences in Crusader lands and, especially, in Byzantium itself. During most of the medieval period, however, the Byzantines, like most others, understood ambassadors and embassies as sent abroad for an immediate and circumscribed negotiation only and not for permanent accreditation or long-term residence. Not only were they to transact the business of their immediate assignment, but they were to bring back any relevant information of use to the Byzantine intelligence agencies.

These embassies occasionally produced literary recollections, as in the case of Priscus of Panion's fascinating account of his visits to the court of Attila the Hun in the fifth century. But memoirs of this type are rare, even when, in the late era, such sophisticated scholar-ambassadors as Manuel Chrysoloras roamed through Western Europe on diplomatic assignments and could have told us much. In the final age of weakened Byzantium, however, emperors themselves belatedly undertook diplomatic travel. Three members of the Palaeologan house—John V (in 1369–1371), Manuel II (1371, 1400–1402), and John VIII (1423–1424, 1438–1439)—journeyed to Italy or beyond to negotiate variously for Western aid against the Turks. Indeed, the visits of Manuel II to Italy and France and of John VIII to the Council of Ferrara-Florence provoked great fascination among the host peoples, and especially among their artists. In their turn, the Byzantines had careful procedures for handling foreign diplomats who were to be processed through receptions, displays, and negotiations. A tenth-century Lombard ambassador, Liudprand of Cremona, a frequent visitor to Constantinople, left a sour account of his abortive final embassy (968), on behalf of German Emperor Otto I.

Internally, meanwhile, a highly efficient postal system was maintained by the Byzantine government, at least until its later breakdown, for communications between the capital and all parts of the Empire, and all government officials were entitled to free transportation and lodging wherever they went. For others, travel conditions varied with times and places. Roads were variably maintained, and security was not always assured: bandits, wild animals, and vagabonds posed recurrent dangers. While commercial inns were to be found here and there, their facilities were often crude (or disreputable) and their availability unpredictable. Many travelers would rely rather on the hospitality of monasteries, who were bound in Christian charity to maintain *xenodocheiai,* or guesthouses, for visitors. Travel by ship was preferable as an alternative, and the traffic of maritime merchants usually allowed for passenger service where explicitly organized sea transport was not arranged. Nevertheless, there were risks here as well, especially during the long period of Arab maritime menace (the ninth and tenth centuries), when piracy was a serious problem.

Among users of land and sea routes would be an important third category of travelers, those on religious journeys. One division of these, involving destinations beyond the Byzantine borders, was missionaries. Efforts to convert neighboring peoples to Christianity were rarely a matter of private pious enterprise but were usually functions of government policy and therefore partly linked to the Empire's diplomatic operations. There were various instances of officially organized missionary outreach, the most famous being the embassy of the brothers Constantine-Cyril and Methodius to Christianize the Moravians in the mid-ninth century, a venture that effectively launched the Christianization of the Slavic peoples in general.

The majority of individual religious travelers, however, were pilgrims, especially in the earlier centuries. It was St. Helena, the mother of the first avowed Christian emperor, Constantine the Great, who, in 326, identified the sites and relics of the Savior's Passion, and who initiated the practice of Christian pilgrimage to the sacred places in the Holy Land. The Arab conquests by no means halted the appeal or feasibility of that traffic, which drew pious Byzantines in consistent numbers. Well-established routes to Jerusalem (and other points in Syria-Palestine) were maintained, along with particular rituals of devotion, with hostelries en route, a literature of guidebooks and advice, and a range of holy trinkets and souvenirs available. Other sites within the Empire, identified with outstanding saints, also developed their own pilgrimage traffic (for example, the shrine of St. Demetrius in Thessaloniki).

And the vast accumulation of relics and holy objects within Constantinople itself made its innumerable churches and shrines a magnet for pilgrimage, both internal and international. Among the many foreign pilgrims, Russians in particular developed a lively tradition of visits to Byzantium. To this they added an equally lively tradition of writing accounts of their visits and experiences for audiences back home. These survive as immensely valuable sources for Byzantine spiritual life, as well as for topography and historical events.

Not all religious travelers were pilgrims in the narrow sense of visitors to major holy places. Monks, holy men, and people of religious vocations (almost invariably men, given the greater danger and lessened freedom for women) regularly understood spiritual travel as a part of their life's work, often in defiance of the formal requirement of stable monastic residence. Their journeys were varied: to lesser shrines, to seek new places of devotion and service in remote locales, and above all to find new venues for solitary meditation and ascetic devotion. This pattern of pious mobility characterized the entire span of Byzantine history and is amply documented in the *Lives* of numerous individual saints. It was an important feature of Byzantine society, especially in the hinterland, beyond the capital and major cities. Though such travel in the name of piety was also a feature transmitted to some extent to Slavonic, especially Russian, Orthodox cultures, and even had some counterparts in Western Europe, in the general medieval context its scale was a comparatively unique feature of the Byzantine world.

BIBLIOGRAPHY

Harvey, Alan. *Economic Expansion in the Byzantine Empire, 900–1200.* Cambridge: Cambridge UP, 1989.

Hendy, Michael F. *Studies in the Byzantine Monetary Economy, c. 300–1450.* Cambridge: Cambridge UP, 1985.

Heyd, Wilhelm von. *Histoire du commerce du Levant au Moyen Âge.* 2 vols. Leipzig, 1885–1886; rpt. Amsterdam: Adolf M. Hakkert, 1967.

Kazhdan, A.P., gen. ed. *The Oxford Dictionary of Byzantium.* 3 vols., Oxford: Oxford UP, 1991. Entries on "Commerce and Trade," "Pilgrimage," "Travel."

Laiou-Thomadakis, A.E. "The Byzantine Economy in the Mediterranean Trade System: Thirteenth–Fifteenth Centuries." *Dumbarton Oaks Papers,* 34–35 (1980–1981): 177–222.

Majeska, George. *Russian Travellers to Constantinople in the Fourteenth and Fifteenth Centuries.*

Malamut, Elisabeth. *Sur la route des saints byzantins.* Paris: Centre National de la Recherche Scientifique, 1993.

Vikan, Gary. *Byzantine Pilgrimage Art.* Washington, DC: Dumbarton Oaks, 1982.

Wilkinson, John. *Jerusalem Pilgrims: Before the Crusades.* Jerusalem: Ariel, and Warminster: Aris and Phillips, 1977.

*John W. Barker*

SEE ALSO

Ambassadors; Attila; Benjamin of Tudela; Coinage and Money; Constantinople; Cosmas Indikopleustes; Crusade, Fourth; Diplomacy; Eastern Christianity; Fairs; Genoa; Inns and Accommodations; Liudprand of Cremona; Merchants, Italian; Merchants, Jewish; Pilgrim Souvenirs; Pilgrimage Sites, Byzantine; Piracy; Pisa; Russia and Rus'; Spice Trade, Indian Ocean; Spies; Textiles, Decorative; Transportation, Inland; Venice

# C

## Cádiz

A port city located in southwest Castile. On an island at the mouth of the Guadalquivir river, Cádiz is strategically located at the intersection of Mediterranean, Atlantic, and African trade routes. The history of the city reflects the varying importance of those trade routes in Europe during the Middle Ages under the successive control of Rome, Constantinople, the Visigoths, the Umayyad caliphate, and Castile.

Founded as "Gadir" by the Phoenicians *c.* 1100 B.C.E. and taken by Carthage before 500 B.C.E., Cádiz was known during the Roman Republic as "Gades" and served as an important link in Roman trade routes. By the early Middle Ages, however, long-distance trade had greatly diminished, and with it Cádiz. From the period of Byzantine control through the Muslim conquest of the region in 712, Cádiz, known in Arabic as Yazira Qadis, languished as a backwater known only for its fishermen. Renewed links with North Africa during the Almoravid and Almohad regimes after the tenth century were the beginnings of the city's renaissance. Cádiz's importance further increased after the Almoravids shifted their trade center from Almería to Seville, upriver on the Guadalquivir.

In 1248, King Alfonso X reconquered Seville and much of southern Castile; he captured Cádiz in 1262. Alfonso saw the importance of an Atlantic port in his struggles with North Africa and Portugal, and worked to establish a strong Castilian presence in the city. By the fifteenth century, Cádiz was populated by an international business community of Genoese, Venetians, Catalans, and northern Europeans. In addition to its tuna fishing, the city's renewed links along the European and African Atlantic coasts and with the Berbers created a healthy trade in gold, slaves, copper, leather, wax, and honey. Strong ties to commercial Seville and the beneficent control of the Ponce de León family from 1466–1492 made Cádiz a substantial commercial center by the end of the Middle Ages.

### BIBLIOGRAPHY

Imamuddin, Syed M. *Some Aspects of the Socio-Economic and Cultural History of Muslim Spain: 711–1492.* Leiden: Brill, 1965.

Lomas Salmonte, Francisco Javier, and Rafael Sánchez Saus. *Entre la Leyenda e el Olvido. Épocas Antigua y Media. Historia de Cádiz,* Vol. I. Madrid: Sílex, 1991.

Sánchez Herrero, José. *Cádiz. La ciudad medieval y cristiana (1260–1525).* Córdoba: Monte de Piedad Caja de Ahorros, 1981.

Vicens Vives, Jaime, and Jordi Nadal Oller. *An Economic History of Spain.* Princeton: Princeton UP, 1969.

*Gretchen Starr-LeBeau*

### SEE ALSO

Alfonso X; Byzantine Empire; *Canarien, Le;* Ptolemy; Seville; Spain and Portugal

## Camels

Beasts of burden, essential to trade and travel in the arid regions of Asia and Africa because of their ability to bear heavy loads and to exist for long periods without water.

The Visigoths and other Germanic tribes brought the sturdy and useful camel westward with them, though not as part of any large herding enterprise; its

# C

name in Gothic, *ulbandus* (perhaps related to *elephant*) is not an obvious borrowing. Fredegarius, in his continuation of Gregory of Tours's *Historia Francorum*, reports that King Clotaire II (d. 629) paraded his wife Brunehaut before his army on the back of a camel before having her executed. In a later period, the camel (Lat. *camelus*, OF *cameil, chameil*; ME *camel, camayl, chamayle*; perh. orig. Arab. *jamal*) was known to Europeans through descriptions of returning crusaders, pilgrims, and merchants, and through firsthand observation in noble menageries. For example, the Holy Roman Emperor Frederick II (1212–1250) gave Henry III of England (1216–1272) a camel, which he kept in the Tower zoo. John of Trevisa distinguishes between the Arabian one-humped camel and the Bactrian two-humped camel. The dromedary (Lat. *dromas, dromadarius*; OF *dromedaire*; ME *dromodarye*) is a lighter and faster variety of the Arabian camel.

In addition to scriptural references to the camel (and various patristic and medieval commentaries on those passages), camels are mentioned in vernacular romances, especially in those with oriental settings. In the Middle English *Firumbras* (*c.* 1380), for example, the Muslim warrior Floripas puts out "wild fire" (probably Greek fire) with camel's milk mixed with vinegar. Camels also appear in the Alexander romance tradition; for example, in *Kyng Alisaunder*, Candace makes generous promises to Alexander about the number of exotic animals she will give him, and, when Alexander marches on India to fight with Porus, the seriousness of their lack of water is emphasized through a reference to "dromedaries, and other bestes" that are dying of thirst.

Two-humped Bactrian camels. Bestiary, Oxford, Bodleian Library MS Douce 88, fol. 78r, 13th century. Courtesy of the Bodleian Library.

Camels were best known in the bestiaries for their ability to bear heavy loads, a trait that figures often in Middle English imaginative literature. A well-known simile that draws on the bestiary description of the camel is found in the "Lenvoy de Chaucer" to *The Clerk's Tale*: "First among wives, stand at defense; / You are as strong as any great camel, / No need to endure what men do in offense."

**BIBLIOGRAPHY**

Bulliet, Richard W. *The Camel and the Wheel.* Cambridge, 1975; rpt. Cambridge: Harvard UP, 1977.

*Kathleen Coyne Kelly*

**SEE ALSO**

Animals, Exotic; Bestiaries; Caravans; Chaucer, Geoffrey; Frederick II; Gregory of Tours, St.; Trevisa, John

## Canarien, Le (c. 1405)

An account, written before 1420, of the Castilian conquest of the Canary Islands. The library of the fifteenth-century dukes of Burgundy was one of the largest in Europe, even surpassing the papal libraries at Rome. An important part of the collection was devoted to travel, particularly in the context of crusades to liberate the Holy Land, to combat heresy in Europe, or to convert pagans—such as those in the Baltic states—to Christianity. One of the most interesting manuscripts in the ducal library is *Le Canarien*. It is an account in French of the early fifteenth-century conquest (*c.* 1402) of the Canary Islands by Jean IV de Béthencourt (1360–1422) and Gadifer de La Salle (*c.*1340–1422).

The first version was written by Friar Pierre Boutier (or Bontier) and Chaplain Jean Le Verrier. Soon afterward, Gadifer incorporated their account into a polished version which entered the library before 1420 (it is named in the inventory of books drawn up after the death of John the Fearless in 1419). Today this Boutier-Le Verrier-Gadifer version is preserved in an illuminated manuscript in the British Library (MS Egerton 2709). There also exists an adumbrated, rewritten "corrupt" version of the exploits of Béthencourt and Gadifer that was put together around 1490 by a nephew of the former. It gives no important role to Gadifer, with whom Béthencourt had a falling out in the islands in 1405, after which each went his own way.

Béthencourt and Gadifer had had some crusading experience before their Canarian adventure. Gadifer populations. It recounts the internecine fights of the French and the Spanish, their treacheries, and their deeds of chivalry, as well as their subjugation of the inhabitants of the islands to the throne of Enrique III (1390–1406), king of Castile. A remarkable passage of the work is a five-paragraph section devoted to the Christian catechism that Boutier and Le Verrier wrote to instruct the converts after King Guadarfia of Lanzarote asked Béthencourt to allow him to be baptized under the name of Louis. Le Verrier performed this ceremony on February 29, 1404, and the entire population followed their king's example. This kind of colorful, imaginative scene presumably made *Le Canarien* attractive to the Burgundian court, although only one manuscript containing it survives.

**BIBLIOGRAPHY**

*Le Canarien.* Ed. Elías Serra Rafols and Alexandre Cioranescu. 3 vols. Las Palmas: La Laguna, 1959–1965 (includes the Egerton text and also the 1490 version).

Cioranescu, Alexandre. "La conquista bethencouriana." In *Historia general de las Islas Canarias.* Ed. Agustin Millares Torres. 2 vols. Las Palmas: Edirca, 1984, 2:23–89.

Krebs, A. "Gadifer de La Salle." In *Dictionnaire de biographie française* 15 (1982), 25–26.

Mollat, Michel. "La place de la conquête normande des Canaries." In *Études d'histoire maritime (1938–1975).* Ed. Michel Mollat. Torino: Bottega d'Erasmo, 1977, pp. 141–157.

*A.J. Vanderjagt*

**SEE ALSO**
Canary Islands; Canon Law and Subject Peoples; John the Fearless, Funeral Cortege of

*Le Canarien* Expedition to the Canary Islands. London, British Library MS Egerton 2709, fol. 2v, after 1404. Courtesy British Library.

joined the French crusade against Prussia in 1390, and together with Béthencourt he shortly afterward fought the Moors at Tunis. The account of the conquest of the Canaries begins with a statement of the goal of the voyage: to convert "the infidels of different laws and languages who live in these islands to the Christian faith." After leaving the port of La Rochelle on May 1, 1402, Béthencourt and his crew set out for Cádiz, from which, in the middle of July, they sailed to the Canary Islands.

*Le Canarien* gives a vivid account of the French exploits in the Canaries, describing at length the character of the individual islands and of their indigenous

## Canary Islands

An archipelago of seven major islands (Gran Canaria, Lanzarote, Tenerife, Gomera, Hierro, La Palma, Fuerteventura) and six smaller ones that extends for 300 miles westward from the northwest coast of Africa (off Cape Juby [Yubi]). Rediscovered in the fourteenth century, in the fifteenth they became the earliest target of European south Atlantic expansion and colonization, prototypical of many later colonial developments in the Western Hemisphere.

Known to Ptolemy and Pliny as the Fortunate Isles (including "Canaria"), the unpeopled islands had been colonized by Roman authorities with pre-Berber North Africans in the first centuries C.E. Medieval Europeans

# C

knew little about them and imagined the islands populated with sciapods and "big dogs" (*canes*), from which they get their name. Around 1336, the Genoese Lanzarote Malocello explored at least three islands, and Angelino Dulcert included these on his 1339 portolan chart. In 1341, a Portuguese-sponsored, Italian-led, and Castilian-manned expedition explored farther. News reached Italy from merchants in Seville. Majorcans under royal license sailed in 1342, and in 1351, Joan Doria and Jaume Segarra, armed with a bull from Pope Clement VI, established the first Canarian mission and later diocese (Fortunata). Aragon, which absorbed Majorca in 1343, claimed the islands, as did Castile in 1345. Expeditions, both missionary and mercantile, continued through the fourteenth century, though only a few settlements were attempted.

In 1346, Petrarch wrote that the islands were "close and familiar" to Europeans, but the natives were "savage in their customs, so similar to beasts" (*Vita solitaria*). Boccaccio, in arguably the first Atlantic travel narrative of the era, *De Canaria*, characterized the people as "robust of limb, courageous and very intelligent," praising their "faithfulness and honesty." The Guanches—technically only the natives of Tenerife—had a politically divided, neolithic, and pastoral society, which made them easy targets for slavers, and incapable of resisting European colonization and exploitation.

In 1402, the Norman Jean de Béthencourt began the century-long process of conquest under a Castilian royal license. His adventures were chronicled in *Le Canarien*, the first version of which was completed by 1420. Lanzarote, Fuertaventura, and Hierro fell within a decade in "the last Norman conquest" (Fernandez-Armesto), and acculturation of the enfeebled natives was swift. Subjugation of Gomera began in 1440 and was largely a matter of manipulating intertribal rivalries and treaty-making, leaving the native society intact until 1489. Following the Treaty of Alcaovas (1479), the Castilian crown directed the conquests of Gran Canaria, which took six years, La Palma (completed in 1492), and Tenerife (1496). Native resistance was surprisingly effective and funding of Spanish campaigns ineffective. Royal control ebbed as financial support and proprietary interests reverted to speculators and conquistadors.

The islands provided the dyestuffs orchil and dragon-tree sap, leather, slaves, and, after 1500, sugar and grapes. Initially, Canarians benefited materially from access to European tools, weapons, and clothing. Eventually, however, the native population was nearly eliminated due to sickness, war, and enslavement, and the Spanish Canary Islands became net importers of African and American slaves.

## BIBLIOGRAPHY

Cachey, Theodore J., Jr. "Petrarch, Boccaccio and the New World Encounter." *Stanford Italian Review* 10 (1991): 45–59.

Clavijo Hernández, Fernando J. "Canarias en el proceso de expansión europea del s.XV." In *Jornados de Estudios Canarias-América*, 7a. Santa Cruz de Tenerife: Confederatión de Cajas de Ahorro, 1985, pp. 7–36.

Fernández-Armesto, Felipe. *Before Columbus: Exploration and Colonization from the Mediterranean to the Atlantic, 1229–1492*. London: Macmillan, and Philadelphia: U of Pennsylvania P, 1987.

———. *The Canary Islands after the Conquest*. New York: Oxford UP, 1982.

Mercer, John. *The Canary Islanders: Their Prehistory, Conquest and Survival*. London: Collings, 1980.

Tejera Gaspar, Antonio, and Eduardo Anzar Vallejo. "Lessons from the Canaries: The First Contact between Europeans and Canarians c. 1312–1477." *Antiquity* 66 (1992): 120–129.

*Joseph P. Byrne*

**SEE ALSO**
*Canarien, Le;* Dyes and Pigments; Pliny the Elder; Portolan Charts; Portuguese Expansion; Ptolemy; Seville

## Cannibalism

The practice of eating the flesh of other humans, whether for survivalist, ritualistic, or nutritional reasons. The term *cannibalism* is derived from the Carib, a tribe in the West Indies who, according to Columbus, ate other humans. It is also called anthropophagy, derived from the Greek for "eating human flesh." The practice of cannibalism is as old as human history.

Cannibalism is divided into two basic types. Survival cannibalism describes the eating of human flesh by people who are starving to death. Learned cannibalism is unrelated to hunger and occurs for a variety of reasons, such as ritual, custom, medicine, morality, religion, and superstition.

The first humans in Africa were apparently cannibalistic, and their European descendants inherited the practice. Many Neanderthal caves in Yugoslavia, Italy, and France point to possible cannibalism between 50,000 and 100,000 years ago. Cro-Magnon caves, which contain cracked leg bones and base-broken skulls, also suggest that the practice continued until 30,000 years ago. Excavated homesites from the Mesolithic (10,000 B.C.E.) and Neolithic (2,000 B.C.E.) periods reveal almost without question that cannibalism continued long after the first civilizations were established.

From the beginning of recorded history, there have been references to cannibalism. In the Bible, God warns the Jews that they will be forced to eat their sons and daughters if they are disobedient (Leviticus 26:29). Greek mythology and history indicate that early Indo-Europeans practiced cannibalism. Herodotus in his *History,* written around 443–421 B.C.E., provides an eyewitness account of how the Massagetae, who lived north of the Caspian Sea around 450 B.C.E., killed and ate the old people of their tribes. This was confirmed by the Greek geographer and historian, Strabo. In his *Gallic Wars,* Julius Caesar wrote that the people of Alesia in Gaul, when besieged by the Roman army, ate women, old men, and others who could not fight. In 890 C.E., the women of Elvira, Spain, cut up and ate the body of Sauwer, an Arab leader who had ordered the massacre of their men.

Learned cannibalism was also reported in ancient and medieval Europe, as an activity that often resulted from war. Herodotus reports that the Scythians, who had lived on the lower Danube and the shores of the Black Sea, regularly sacrificed one out of each hundred prisoners taken on the battlefield and drank the blood of the first man they overthrew in war. In ancient Mesopotamia, prisoners were killed and eaten in temples. According to Herodotus, the Greeks did not eat other humans when they died, but the Callatians in India customarily ate their deceased fathers. According to St. Jerome, writing around 400, the Scottish moss-troopers who plundered the borderlands of England drank the blood of their defeated enemies.

Despite these historical precedents, medieval Europe, based largely on Christian dogma, came to view cannibalism as a practice associated only with non-Europeans or "infidels," a line of logic extended to all regions of the non-Western world. Christian accounts of the Mongols, written in the 1230s and 1240s, attribute to them cannibalistic practices, probably as part of a general effort to depict them in the worse possible light or out of fearful anxiety about them.

**BIBLIOGRAPHY**

Arens, William. *The Man-eating Myth: Anthropology and Anthropophagy.* New York and Oxford: Oxford UP, 1979.

Chong, Key Ray. *Cannibalism in China.* Wakefield, NH: Longwood Academic, 1992.

Guzman, Gregory. G. "Reports of Mongol Cannibalism in the Thirteenth-Century Latin Sources: Oriental Fact or Western Fiction?" In Westrem, *Discovering New Worlds,* pp. 31–68. See Gen. Bib.

Sanday, Peggy Reeves. *Divine Hunger: Cannibalism as a Cultural System.* Cambridge: Cambridge UP, 1986.

Tattersall, Jill. "Anthropophagi and Eaters of Raw Flesh in French Literature of the Crusade Period: Myth, Tradition, and Reality." *Medium Aevum* 57 (1988): 240–253.

*Key Ray Chong*

**SEE ALSO**
Columbus, Christopher; John of Plano Carpini; Mongols; Monstrosity, Geographical; *Wonders of the East*

Tartars eating human flesh. Matthew Paris, *Chronica Majora,* Cambridge, Corpus Christi College MS 16, fol. 167r, *c.* 1250. Permission Master and Fellows, Corpus Christi College, Cambridge.

## Canon Law and Subject Peoples

Although the canon law, the legal system of the medieval Catholic Church, dealt almost entirely with ecclesiastical administration, it did provide some basis for dealing with non-Christians who became subject to Christian rulers.

Both volumes of the law, the *Decretum* (1140) and the *Decretales* (1234), provided some discussion of the

# C

status of Jews and Muslims who lived within Christian societies. Beginning in the eleventh century, the expansion of Europe, especially in Spain and the Middle East, brought many Jews and Muslims under Christian rule. Expansion elsewhere similarly affected people of other religions—including some regarded by Europeans as "idolators." Christian rulers and lawyers were thus forced to consider a variety of specific situations that resulted from the daily interaction of Christians and non-Christians. On the one hand, because Catholic theology expressly forbade forced baptism and conversion of nonbelievers, Christian rulers could not require their Jewish, Muslim, and pagan subjects to convert. On the other hand, they could demand that their non-Christian subjects attend sermons where preachers would attempt to convince them of the truth of Christianity. Furthermore, Christian rulers could limit the religious activities of non-Christian subjects in various ways, such as forbidding the muezzin from calling the Muslim faithful to prayer. Finally, in order to protect Christians from "spiritual contamination" and to discourage religiously mixed marriages, at the Fourth Lateran Council (1215), Pope Innocent III (1198–1216) ordered that Jews and Muslims living in Christian lands wear distinctive garb. Some canonists also argued that Christian rulers were morally obligated to eliminate practices that violated natural law, such as the worship of idols, human sacrifice, and marriage between individuals related within the forbidden degrees of consanguinity. Pope Innocent IV (1243–1254) declared that the pope was the judge of all mankind, judging Christians by Christian law, Jews by Jewish law, and all others by natural law.

People considered to be heretics and schismatics, such as Orthodox Christians, also came under the jurisdiction of canon law when they became subject to a ruler who adhered to the practices of the Western church. The general policy of the papacy was to insist that these Christians adopt Roman liturgy, ritual practices, and marriage laws, and that their churches reconcile themselves with the Roman Church. The most significant example of this policy was the establishment of the Latin Patriarchate of Constantinople in 1204 after the city was seized during the Fourth Crusade.

The application of the canonists' theories was always limited by political and economic realities. For example, the rulers of the Spanish kingdoms where Muslim workers were an essential component of the labor force were inclined to give wider latitude to their Muslim subjects than the popes and the canonists authorized. Likewise, the status of Jews varied according to local circumstances.

The most important development and application of these canonistic theories about the rights of subject peoples came after Columbus reached the Americas and the Spanish monarchs began to impose their rule on the inhabitants. The Spanish debate about the legitimacy of the conquest of the Americas and about the rights of native people was based on the work of Innocent IV and the canon lawyers who followed his lead.

## BIBLIOGRAPHY

Kedar, Benjamin Z. *Crusade and Mission. European Approaches toward the Muslims.* Princeton: Princeton UP, 1984.

Muldoon, James. *Popes, Lawyers, and Infidels. The Church and the Non-Christian World, 1250–1550.* Philadelphia: U of Pennsylvania P, 1979.

Powell, James M., ed. *Muslims under Latin Rule.* Princeton: Princeton UP, 1990.

Synan, Edward A. *The Popes and the Jews in the Middle Ages.* New York: Macmillan, 1965.

*James Muldoon*

## SEE ALSO

Columbus, Christopher; Constantinople; Crusade, Fourth; Eastern Christianity; Indians and the Americas; Innocent IV; Las Casas, Bartolomé de

## Caravans

Convoys of merchants, pilgrims, travelers, and pack animals journeying together, usually for mutual protection in unpoliced or insecure areas. The term, derived from the Persian *karvan*, was originally used in reference to southwest and central Asia, but is now applied to Africa and the Americas as well. For over three millennia, caravans served as the main conduit for overland movement of merchants, commodities, religious ideas, pilgrims, and even disease.

Caravan trade has existed since antiquity. Convoys of pack donkeys regularly crossed the Syrian desert and the Taurus mountains as early as 2000 B.C.E., while the famous Silk Road route across Central Asia was established at the end of the last millennium B.C.E. The domestication in Mesopotamia of the single-humped dromedary for use as a baggage animal around 1000 B.C.E. and the taming of the two-humped Bactrian camel marked significant advances, since the camel's unique food- and water-storing capacities and its ability to walk on soft sand made it well suited to long-distance travel. An adult male camel could carry between 250 and 650 pounds (115–295 kilograms) and cover twenty to twenty-five miles (thirty-two to forty kilometers) per day. Camels greatly facilitated Asian trade and made possible the opening of regular trans-Saharan caravan links in the first centuries C.E.

The size of an individual caravan could vary tremendously, from a few dozen camels hired for a local journey to 1,000 or more pack animals in a vast Central Asian caravan. Mounting a large caravan posed significant challenges of forage, protection, and discipline. In southwest Asia, commercial transactions between cities were undertaken by merchants and carried out as joint ventures. Merchant families maintained houses or branches in a number of cities and used these to coordinate their caravan trade. As recently as the early twentieth century, the Chinese caravan master occupied a position much like that of a sea captain. His knowledge of the routes and skill in managing pack animals and men earned him the appointment and placed him in authority over the other travelers.

Caravan trade was frequently a high-risk venture. When crossing the Gobi or Taklamakan desert, it was essential to carry all one's food stocks. If supplies ran out before the desert ended, travelers would have to slaughter the baggage animals for food—this was a common business loss. Bandits, wars, and political instability were recurring dangers. When Ibn Battūta's pilgrim caravan left Tunis for the Hijaz in the early

Camel carrying casks. Matthew Paris, *Chronica majora*, Cambridge, Corpus Christi College MS 16, fol. ii.v, *c.* 1250. Permission Master and Fellows, Corpus Christi College, Cambridge.

fourteenth century, the escort consisted of several hundred horsemen and a detachment of archers. Caravans and the customs revenue they generated were critical resources for empire builders throughout Afro-Eurasia. They made possible the trading states of West Africa (Ghana, Mali, Songhay), provided great wealth for the nomadic empires of the Turks, Uighurs, and Mongols in Inner Asia, and were critical to the formation of the Arab Muslim empire.

Caravan halting places were often determined by the locations of towns, oases, and caravansarais—buildings specifically created to shelter caravans in southwest and central Asia. These structures, often fortified, were commonly constructed outside the walls of a town or village and provided water, lodging, an open central court for the pack animals, and sometimes food and provender. Usually a quadrangular structure, the typical caravansarai (also called "caravansary") was enclosed by a massive wall with a single gateway, through which animals and travelers entered. The paved central court on the ground floor was often large enough to contain 300 or 400 tethered camels or mules and was surrounded by cellular storage spaces for bales of merchandise. Lodging rooms were located on an arcaded second story, reached by broad, open stone stairways. Caravansarais were particularly common in Islamic lands, where traditional economic tracts enjoined rulers to facilitate trade by protecting merchants and travelers and by maintaining an infrastructure of bridges, roads, and shelters. During the eleventh through thirteenth centuries, individual princes and cities erected especially elaborate caravansarais on major trade routes in southwest Asia, particularly in Anatolia, eastern Iran, and northern Iraq. Larger caravan towns could supply all forms of commercial services: brokers, markets, bankers, transport animals, forage, and stabling. Many caravan cities in Arabia, Central Asia, and elsewhere derived their livelihood exclusively from long-distance trade, rising or falling according to shifts in the caravan routes.

Information concerning the costs of caravan trade is scarce, particularly for the medieval period. However, data about caravans in the sixteenth and seventeenth centuries suggest that pure transport costs for camel caravans were fairly low, cheaper even than transport by ship—on the order of three percent of the sales price for valuable commodities like silk carried from Persia to the Levant. Protection costs, customs duties, and bribes, on the other hand, were typically much higher,

# C

and this made caravan trade substantially more expensive than sea transport.

The caravan trade flourished throughout the medieval period, but gradually declined after the seventeenth century in competition with European-dominated seaborne trade and, more recently, transportation by truck and railroad. Nevertheless, some local caravan routes survive in the absence of alternative transport.

**BIBLIOGRAPHY**

Chaudhuri, K.N. *Trade and Civilization in the Indian Ocean: An Economic History from Rise of Islam to 1750.* Cambridge: Cambridge UP, 1985.

Clapp, Nicholas. *The Road to Ubar: Finding the Atlantis of the Sands.* Boston: Houghton Mifflin, 1998.

Dunn, Ross E. *The Adventures of Ibn Battūta: A Muslim Traveller of the Fourteenth Century.* Berkeley: U of California P, 1986.

Lattimore, Owen. *The Desert Road to Turkistan.* London, 1928; rpt. New York: Kodansha Globe, 1996.

Simkin, C.G.F. *The Traditional Trade of Asia.* London: Oxford UP, 1968.

Steensgaard, Niels. *The Asian Trade Revolution of the Seventeenth Century: The East India Companies and the Decline of the Caravan Trade.* Chicago: U of Chicago P, 1974.

Wriggins, Sally Hovey. *Xuanzang: A Buddhist Pilgrim on the Silk Road.* Boulder, CO: Westview, 1996.

*Daniel E. Schafer*

**SEE ALSO**

African Trade; Black Death; Camels; *Fondaco;* Gold Trade in Africa; Ibn Battūta, Abu Abdallah; Inner Asian Trade; Silk Roads; Sunnism

## Caravel

Light, sleek, shallow-draughted vessel, hoisting lateen (triangular fore-and-aft) sails on some or all masts. It was favored by many fifteenth- and early sixteenth-century Portuguese and Spanish explorers undertaking voyages in the Atlantic and the Indian Ocean. During the caravel's heyday, from about 1430 to about 1530, the ship type was adapted to local use in various maritime regions of Europe. The Iberian caravel of this era had two to four masts; was usually from 30 to more than 120 metric tons burden; and had a length-to-beam ratio between 3:1 and 5:1. The hull had a low silhouette, lacked a forecastle, and carried a low and long aftercastle or quarterdeck. Reputedly able to sail as much 45 or 50 degrees to the wind, the highly maneuverable but capricious caravel required alert and expert handling.

The caravel's origins go back to the thirteenth century, when small fishing boats designated by that name first appeared in Portugal and Castile. These were probably related to the *caravo* or *qārib,* a lateen-rigged craft used by Iberian and northwest African Muslims. Little is heard of caravels thereafter, until 1408–1409. By 1430, they were commonplace among Portuguese and Andalusian fishermen, and soon spread across southern Europe. By 1440–1450, Catalan, Sicilian, Genoese, and even Tuscan caravels sailed the Mediterranean. Toward the end of the century, caravel-like ships were a common sight in the Adriatic and were also used by Greek and Turkish mariners. In northern Europe the process of adoption was more halting, even though Philip the Good of Burgundy had three caravels built by Portuguese shipwrights as early as 1438–1439. English and Irish corsairs captured a number of Iberian caravels in the late 1440s and early 1450s. The caravel contributed to the northward spread of skeleton hull construction and carvel planking (joined edge to edge). An offshoot of this process was the three-masted full-rigged northern *carvel.* Although English, Irish, Flemish, Norman, Basque, and even Scottish *carvels* are documented in the later fifteenth century, the leaders in carvel-building were the Bretons.

The caravel owes its notoriety to the Portuguese explorations along the coasts of Africa, the Iberian charting of South America, and the early Portuguese Indian Ocean expeditions. Caravels were not specifically designed for exploration, however, and for the most part toiled as ordinary cargo carriers or worked the Iberian fisheries, from the Saharan coast to Newfoundland. They also served as patrol vessels in Iberian home waters, and as convoy escorts. The development of the caravel culminated in the early 1500s in the heavier and more stable four-masted *caravela de armada,* which carried a square spritsail, square sails on the foremast, and lateen sails on the remaining masts. This warship of 140 to 170 tons represented an uneasy compromise between full and lateen rig. In the 1530s, caravels began to disappear both from the Mediterranean and from the Spanish Atlantic shipping routes. They briefly returned to prominence, exclusively in the Iberian maritime sphere, from the 1570s to the 1620s.

**BIBLIOGRAPHY**

Elbl, Martin M. "The Caravel." In *Cogs, Caravels, and Galleons. The Sailing Ship, 1000–1650. Conway's History of the Ship.* Ed. R. Gardiner. London: Conway Maritime Press, 1994.

Edwards, Clinton. "Design and Construction of Fifteenth-Century Iberian Vessels." *The Mariner's Mirror* 78 (1992): 419–572.

Fonseca, Quirino da. *A caravela portuguêsa e a prioridade técnica das navegações Henriquinas.* Coimbra: Imprensa da Universidade, 1934.

Pastor, Xavier. *The Ships of Christopher Columbus.* London: Conway Maritime Press, 1992.

*Martin Malcolm Elbl*

**SEE ALSO**

*Barca;* Cog; Dias, Bartolomeu; Exploration and Expansion, European; *Nao;* Naval Warfare; Navigation; Piracy; Portuguese Expansion; Ships and Shipbuilding

## Carrack

A large seagoing cargo-carrying sailing ship that first appeared in the Mediterranean in the fourteenth century.

The name may come from an Arabic word for a ship of burden. The type was based on the tubby but capacious northern European cog, but with significant modifications. Mediterranean shipwrights built the carrack skeleton-first. The hull planks abutted one another, so the ship's strength came from the internal ribs and frames. The southern shipbuilders changed the rigging as well by adding to the large square sail on the mainmast at the middle of the ship a lateen sail near the stern on its own mast. The carrack was thus more maneuverable than earlier cogs and had more capacity than traditional Mediterranean round ships of the same length.

It proved ideal for carrying bulk cargoes economically. Riding higher in the water than any contemporary vessel, it also made a superior platform for hurling projectiles down on any attacker. It was not vulnerable to pirates and served as an effective warship in the Mediterranean and in the English Channel. Carracks were easily able to make trips back and forth from northern to southern Europe, negotiating the Straits of Gibralter in both directions. They served to improve direct trading connections by sea between the two parts of the Continent.

The carrack design in the late fourteenth and fifteenth century was among the earliest to take on the full rig of square sails on a foremast and on a mainmast and a lateen sail on a third or mizzen mast. Ships with

Two-masted Mediterranean vessel from Bernard von Breydenbach, *Bevaerden tot dat heilighe grafft* (Mainz, 1488). Courtesy of the Rijksmuseum Nederlands Scheepvaartmuseum, L.B.J. 235.

full-rig were both more economical and more reliable than their predecessors. The balanced rig made ships much more maneuverable and versatile and gave captains better control over their vessels. The design change also made possible the building of bigger ships with no increase in crew size. The greater payload possible on the three-masted carrack made it the choice for bulk trades and long-distance trades. It was the preferred type for shipping between Iberia and the Low Countries, as well as England, in the fifteenth and sixteenth centuries. The Portuguese carracks used in the trade to India were the largest wooden ships ever built, towering high above any contemporary ship and reaching 2,000 tons. The carrack fell out of use by the end of the sixteenth century, replaced in Europe by smaller and more lightly built cargo ships, and in the dangerous trades by galleons and later East Indiamen.

# C

**BIBLIOGRAPHY**

Bass, George, ed. *A History of Seafaring Based on Underwater Archaeology.* London: Thames and Hudson, 1972.

Hattendorf, John B., ed. *Maritime History in the Age of Discovery: An Introduction.* Malabar, FL: Krieger, 1995.

Hutchinson, Gillian. *Medieval Ships and Shipping.* Rutherford, NJ: Fairleigh Dickinson UP, 1994.

Pryor, J.H. *Geography, Technology and War: Studies in the Maritime History of the Mediterranean 649–1571.* Cambridge: Cambridge UP, 1988.

Scammell, G.V. *The World Encompassed: The First European Maritime Empires, c. 800–1650.* Berkeley: U of California Press, 1981.

*Richard W. Unger*

**SEE ALSO**

*Barca;* Cog; Naval Warfare; Piracy; Portuguese Expansion; Ships and Shipbuilding

## Cartography, Arabic

A by-product of Islamic astronomy and geography. Synthesizing the geographical knowledge developed during the early centuries of the Islamic era and several astronomical and cosmographical traditions that preceded the rise of Islam, Arabic cartography in turn influenced Persian and, to a lesser extent, Turkish cartography. The impact of Arab cartography on medieval European maps appears to have been slight, but the subject has not been well explored. Nor is it clear if there was any interaction between Arabic and Byzantine traditions. The most important contributions of Arabic cartography were to synthesize earlier Greek and Persian traditions, to record detailed data on both Near Eastern and European geography, and to transmit knowledge to the West through Latin and Hebrew translators.

The earliest record of Arab ability to make maps dates to A.H. 83/702 C.E., but the majority of extant maps are found in copies of the thirteenth and later centuries, with a few dating as early as the eleventh century. Arabic maps were designed to serve as illustrations to texts, and like their Western medieval counterparts, none can be used as a practical guide to location. Although a few authors give instructions for map production and some texts describe maps, cartography never became an independent branch of science in the Arab world. Indeed, the massive factual knowledge accumulated by Muslim travelers and geographers on places as distant as Ireland and the British Isles was never translated into cartographic detail, even though extensive narratives existed. Although degrees of latitude had sometimes been measured with great precision and some later maps have grids, Arabic cartography did not use graticules to create a systematic representation of latitudinal and longitudinal lines.

In form, Arabic maps typically included round world maps and rectangular regional maps; there are also a few oval and semicircular maps. In addition, there were maps of seas, special Islamic maps of the Ka'ba for orienting the viewer to the *qibla* (sacred direction) from any location, small maps of astronomically determined zones, cosmographical diagrams, and maps of the heavens. City plans must have existed, but the ones we have are from the sixteenth century and later. There are no topographical maps. Sailing charts reportedly existed but none survives. The extant charts of the Mediterranean show strong influence of European *portolani*. All maps are drawn in ink, mostly on paper, often with coloring; there are no printed maps from this period.

Scientific cartography in Islam began in the late eighth century when the Abbasid court (750–1258 C.E.) sponsored an extensive campaign of translations into Arabic, supported especially by the caliph al-Ma'mūn (813–833 C.E.). Greek, Persian, and Indian works of astronomical, mathematical, and geographical content were translated (often via Syriac) and became the bases for Arabic learned treatises. Greek and Persian ideas of mapmaking had the strongest and most widely acknowledged influence on Arab cartography, and they were often intermixed in complex ways. Certain Indian cosmological concepts (such as Mount Meru as the center of the earth) continued to be considered valid but had little practical effect on maps. The influence of Qur'anic cosmogony (inherited from Semitic and ancient Arabian traditions) was largely limited to showing Mount Qaf surrounding the Encircling Ocean. Few maps reflect the mythic Arab concept of the earth as a bird with spread wings, but frequent orientation to the east probably followed this and the ancient Semitic traditions. As their geographical knowledge expanded, Islamic cartographers became less dependent on foreign sources, but there was little conceptual innovation. Even the practical knowledge of travelers and scholars did not significantly affect map content and presentation.

The two main schools of early Arab cartography are the Greek, or Greco-Muslim, and the Balkhi school, also called the *Atlas of Islam* school. Both of these date to the ninth and tenth centuries and have later followers. Two other, later schools are represented by the concepts and maps of al-Bīrūnī (d. *c.* A.H. 442/1050 C.E.) and al-Idrīsī (d. A.H. 560/1165 C.E.). There are no clearcut boundaries; the same cartographer might produce maps in more than one style, and his narrative may refer to a different type of map than the illustration provided in the work. The Greco-Muslim school owes its ideas, and much of the early data, to Claudius Ptolemy (fl. 127–145 C.E.). Several early translation efforts resulted in the first Arabic tables of geographical coordinates of many of the hundreds of locations listed by Ptolemy, with corrections to the coordinates provided, in some cases, by Arabic scholars. The extant version closest to Ptolemy's original belongs to the astronomer al-Battānī (d. A.H. 317/929 C.E.). Several scholars also translated (and abridged) Ptolemy's *Geography;* the single surviving Arabic version was made by the great mathematician al-Khwārazmī (d. *c.* A.H. 232/846–7 C.E.). The main cartographic aspects inherited from Ptolemy are the depiction of the inhabited part of the earth as defined by the Greek thinkers; the division of the inhabited quarter into latitudinal zones, usually numbering seven, according to the length of day (Arabic *aqālīm*, sing. *iqlīm*, from the Greek κλίμα); degrees of latitude and longitude; and the representation of Africa stretched out to the east and forming the south shore of the Indian Ocean. However, not all of these features were adopted by all authors equally or consistently, and the four maps contained in the unique eleventh-century manuscript of al-Khwārazmī are not like any of the European Ptolemaic maps.

Some of the Greco-Muslim maps show the world centered on modern-day Iraq (a remnant of pre-Islamic Persian, maybe even Babylonian, influence); for that reason, some scholars group them and the related texts in the "Iraqi school" of Islamic geography. The lost map of the caliph al-Ma'mūn apparently combined Greek and Persian features as well. By contrast, the Balkhī school, which expressed the Islamic worldview, placed Mecca in the center of its world maps and oriented them to the south. No maps by al-Balkhī (d. A.H. 322/934 C.E.) survive; the pattern set by him was followed by al-Istakhrī (fl. A.H. 340/951 C.E.), Ibn Hawqal (d. *c.* A.H. 378/988 C.E.), and al-Muqaddasī (d. *c.* A.H. 390/1000 C.E.). These maps come in sets of twenty-one and, in addition to the round world map, contain three maps of seas and seventeen of the provinces of the Abbasid caliphate, reflecting the school's politico-administrative concerns. The landmass is surrounded by the Encircling Ocean (*al-Bahr al-Muhīt*); the Mediterranean and the Indian Ocean represent its two gulfs. The seas and other geographical features are given highly geometric shapes. The maps of provinces (also called *iqlīm*, in translation of the Persian *kishvar*, or region) show the ethnic divisions, boundaries, cities, rivers, mountains, and roads. This type of map prevailed in the Muslim East.

The Greco-Muslim tradition found its best and most original interpreter in al-Idrīsī (d. A.H. 560/1165 C.E.), who worked at the court of the Norman rulers of Sicily and had access both to European and Muslim sources. He reportedly had a world map, inspired by those of both Ptolemy and al-Ma'mūn, engraved on silver. That map did not survive, but numerous copies of his work *Nuzhat al-mushtāq fī khtirāq al-āfāq* (Entertainment for One Desirous of Travel Far) contain a round map of the world (although undistinguished, it was later adopted by Ibn Khaldun) and 70 sectional maps accompanied by texts that describe the map and cite itineraries and distances for travel in the territories represented.

Al-Idrīsī's wealth of geographical information was unsurpassed anywhere in the world during his lifetime, and his work is the pinnacle of medieval Arab and Muslim cartography. In essence, he adopted Ptolemy's map of the world and superimposed on it an enormous amount of new information gathered from books and travelers. Especially valuable are the data on Asia and Europe. Al-Idrīsī's maps give the first realistic representation of northern Europe by an Islamic scholar. There are significant differences from Ptolemy as well: al-Idrīsī does not use his conical projection; the Indian Ocean is never completely enclosed; and the prime meridian is drawn through the westernmost point of Africa, that is, ten degrees east of Ptolemy's prime meridian, which went through the Fortunate Isles (Canaries). Although al-Idrīsī discussed the coordinates in his narrative, they are not used on the map. The grid is formed by eight straight lines of latitude, marking the equator and boundaries of the seven climates, and by vertical lines dividing the 180 degrees of longitude into ten sections (without degree marks). This pattern accommodated the inhabited quarter of the earth (the land south of the equator was considered uninhabitable) in seventy sections. Correspondingly,

# C

there were seventy page-size sectional maps accompanied by seventy chapters of text.

Al-Idrīsī is one of the few Arabic scholars who provided instructions for map production (although the projection is never explained) and discussed distance measures. While few scholars imitated his maps, his system affected the structure of many later geographical narratives, and his information was repeated (often without acknowledgment) by numerous cosmographers. This, combined with the introduction of the grid and al-Idrīsī's almost complete independence from the outdated content and tables of Ptolemy, constitutes a major reason for setting him apart from the early Arabic imitators of Greek geography.

The most original thinker among Islamic scientists, al-Bīrūnī (d. after A.H. 442/1050 C.E.) was the first to articulate the idea of the Atlantic communicating with the Indian Ocean. Although only one of his maps survives, al-Bīrūnī's ideas about the distribution of water and land drastically revised the cartography of Africa and the Indian Ocean. His round world sketch-map shows the Southern Hemisphere almost completely covered with water and the African continent much reduced. Africa, Arabia, Persia, and India form four peninsular protrusions into the ocean, increasing in size from west to east. The Indian Ocean occupies about one-third of the whole and communicates in the west and east with the Encircling Ocean. This scheme was followed in the maps of some later cosmographers, especially of the Persian tradition (al-Bīrūnī worked in India and Central Asia and wrote some of his works in Persian).

However, this realistic cartographic innovation did not greatly influence mainstream Islamic geographical theory or narratives. Though al-Bīrūnī argued, for example, that Africa is inhabited south of the equator, cosmographers went on repeating classical Greek geographers' assertions that the heat made life impossible there. This is especially curious in light of the fact that Arab navigators regularly sailed to southwest Africa with the monsoon and came back to tell stories, many of which were recorded and circulated. One of these travelers and navigators was Ibn Fatima, the informer of the geographer Ibn Saʿīd (d. A.H. 685/1286 C.E.) who improved on al-Idrīsī by adding the coordinates to the distances in the text. A map formerly attributed to Ibn Saʿīd shows Africa somewhat realistically: the continent curves along the round rim of the map only some of the way east, leaving much of the space to the south for the ocean filled with islands. (This map is found in a manuscript dated A.H. 977/1570 C.E. and has recently been attributed to a later Maghriban author). Another map contained in a sixteenth-century copy of the fourteenth-century work by Ibn Fadlallāh al-ʿUmarī (d. A.H. 749/1349 C.E.) shows the Indian Ocean extending both east and south, with Africa south of the equator occupying all of the southwest quarter and reaching into the south-southeast portion of the circle. Some scholars have proposed that this is a version of al-Maʾmūn's map, but others see in it a derivation of the Idrīsī-Ibn Saʿīd cartographic tradition. In any case, since realistic maps were not produced independently but were copied with the old texts, their relevance, limited to begin with, declined ever more. This explains their easy and rapid displacement by European-style maps in the post-Renaissance era. On the other hand, the so-called *qibla* maps, astronomically determined and truly original in their Islamic inspiration, continued to be produced as a needed and viable part of the sacred geography of Islam.

## BIBLIOGRAPHY

Ahmad, S. Maqbul. "Djughrāfiyā" and "Kharīta." *Encyclopaedia of Islam,* New edition, Vol. 2, pp. 575–587, and Vol. 4, 1077–1083. Leiden: Brill, 1960.

Harley-Woodward. *The History of Cartography.* Vol. 2, Book 1. See Gen. Bib.

Kamal, Youssouf [Yusuf]. *Monumenta cartographica Africae et Aegypti.* 5 vols. in 16 parts. Cairo, 1926–1951; rpt. in 6 vols. Ed. Fuat Sezgin. Frankfurt: Institut für Geschichte der Arabisch-Islamischen Wissenschaften, 1987.

Kennedy, Edward S., and Mary Helen Kennedy. *Geographical Coordinates of Localities from Islamic Sources.* Frankfurt: Institut für Geschichte der Arabisch-Islamischen Wissenschaften, 1987.

King, David A. "Makka: As the Centre of the World." *Encyclopaedia of Islam,* New edition, Vol. 6, pp. 180–187. Leiden: Brill, 1960.

———. "The Sacred Direction in Islam: A Study of the Interaction of Religion and Science in the Middle Ages." *Interdisciplinary Science Reviews* 10 (1985): 315–328.

Miller, Konrad. *Mappae arabicae: Arabische Welt- und Länderkarten des 9.-13. Jahrhunderts.* 6 vols. Stuttgart, 1926–1931; rpt. Frankfurt: Institut für Geschichte der Arabisch-Islamischen Wissenschaften, 1994.

Sezgin, Fuat. *The Contribution of the Arabic-Islamic Geographers to the Formation of the World Map.* Frankfurt: Institut für Geschichte der Arabisch-Islamischen Wissenschaften, 1987.

C

Tolmacheva, Marina. "The Medieval Arabic Geographers and the Beginnings of Modern Orientalism." *International Journal of Middle East Studies* 27 (1995): 141–156.

*Marina A. Tolmacheva*

SEE ALSO

al-Idrīsī; Canary Islands; Geography in Medieval Europe; Maps; *Mare Oceanum;* Muslim Travelers and Trade; Ptolemy

## Caspian Sea

A large salt lake known to ancient authors as *Mare Caspium* or *Mare Hyrcanium* and apparently called "sea" in the languages of all the peoples who inhabited surrounding territories. Herodotus (*c.* 485–425 B.C.E.) was the first European author to refer to it. The Greeks knew that the Caucasus Mountains separated the Caspian from the Black Sea and some thought that the two seas communicated underground. Beyond it lay Bactria. The term *Caspian Gate,* usually called "Iron Gate" in the Middle Ages, referred to the mountain pass where the Great Caucasus range meets the Caspian near Derbend.

Strabo (*c.* 64 B.C.E.–23 C.E.) considered the Caspian to be a northern gulf of the Ocean-Sea that surrounds the earth's landmass (Asia, Africa, and Europe); this concept is repeated in many medieval descriptions of the world (for example, in Isidore of Seville's *Etymologies* [14.3.31] from *c.* 636) as well as on *mappaemundi.* On the other hand, Ptolemy (*c.* 100–180), was confident that the Caspian was landlocked (it is so depicted on Ptolemaic maps) though, of course, his *Geography* was unknown to medieval Europe until the early 1400s. The Franciscan William of Rubruck (1255) pronounced Isidore wrong in his assertion that the Caspian "is a gulf from the ocean," declaring that, based on his own experience, the sea "is surrounded on all sides by land." The rivers Amu Darya (Oxus) and Syr Darya (Iaxartes) were thought to flow into the Caspian, and modern scholars have suggested that the Amu Darya may in fact have done so before the twelfth century (local legends argue for an even earlier date).

Italian navigators charted the sea in the fourteenth century, and at least one traditional round world map (*c.* 1500) shows the sea, with a north-south expanse exceeding its east-west distance. But most European maps (of those that did not make it an oceanic gulf) gave it the opposite proportions, as Ptolemy did. This is true, for example, of the Catalan Atlas (*c.* 1175–1255).

In Islamic geography, descriptions of the Caspian show a blend of borrowings from the Greeks with factual information from Middle Eastern sources. Arab geographers call the sea *Bahr al-Khazar* (Sea of the Khazar.) Derbend is called *Bāb al-Abwāb* (Gate of the Gates) and is sometimes associated with the mythical gate behind which Alexander reputedly walled up the tribes Gog and Magog. However, the Aral Sea was well known and shown on maps as the receptacle of the two great Central Asian rivers; it was called *Bahr al-Khwārazm* (Khorezmian Sea).

In antiquity, Caspians and Hyrcanians served in Xerxes' army; Persian influence remained dominant in regional trade and continued to be felt in the few important cities that were founded, mostly in the north, south, and southwest parts of the coast. Persian merchant ships (*busi*) took goods north to Astrakhan and up the Volga. Turkic peoples prevailed among the nomads to the north and east. Marco Polo (*c.* 1296) described the area as "completely surrounded by mountains and land [with] no connection with the main sea." He noted the presence of Genoese merchants sailing its waters and recorded several local names for it: "the Sea of Baku or of Ghel or Ghelan" and the "Sea of Sarai." The Russian traveler Afanasii Nikitin passed through Derbend, Shemakha, and Baku in the late 1460s. The Venetian Ambrosio Contarini sailed the sea twice, on his way to and from Persia (1473–1475). These travelers note the local and transit goods—silk, fish, salt, petroleum—and the "undying fire" (apparently the flames of natural gas) at Baku, site of a modern oil field.

Russians have sailed and traded on the Caspian since at least the late ninth century, but they did not settle in the area until after the conquest of Astrakhan by Ivan IV (1554).

BIBLIOGRAPHY

Morgan, E. Delmar, and C.H. Coote, eds. *Early Voyages and Travels to Russia and Persia, by Anthony Jenkinson and other Englishmen.* 2 vols. London: Hakluyt Society, 1886.

Rabino, Hyacinth Louis. *Les Provinces caspiennes de la Perse: le Guilan.* Paris: Ernest Leroux, 1917 (*Revue du Monde Musulman* 32; Kraus reprint 1974).

*Marina A. Tolmacheva*

SEE ALSO

Atlas; Cartography, Arabic; Genoa; Gog and Magog; Isidore of Seville; *Mappamundi;* Marco Polo; Ptolemy; Russia and Rus'; Silk Roads; Venice; William of Rubruck

# C

## Catherine in the Sinai, Monastery of St.

An important pilgrimage goal, marking the site where Moses encountered God, and possessing the relics of St. Catherine of Alexandria.

Founded in the sixth century, in the later years of Justinian's reign (527–565), the Monastery of St. Catherine was built, according to tradition, where God spoke to Moses from out of a burning bush (Exodus 3:1–5) at the base of Mount Sinai (Djebel Mousa). The identification of the precise site, as well as the authenticity of the ossuary of the Alexandrian martyr St. Catherine (on the peak known as Djebel Katrin), is a matter of scholarly controversy. Early Christian pilgrims, based on their understanding of the Bible, chose the present spot over Djebel Serbal, at the foot of which the oasis of Faran arguably corresponds better to the biblical record than does the arid region around the monastery. The monastery, originally dedicated to the Virgin Mary, was commissioned between 548 and 565, and had already been a destination for pilgrims and the site of a cenobitic community well before that time. The Burning Bush and the chapel maintained nearby by monks were visited by the fourth-century pilgrim Egeria (recorded in her *Peregrinatio*).

The site of the Burning Bush, now a chapel in which a slab marks the spot of the bush, was originally outdoors and featured a live bush (Egeria comments that it still was growing new shoots)—an ideal arrangement for an important pilgrimage. The fortified monastery, founded by Justinian as much for geopolitical as for pious reasons, was a frontier outpost both of Christianity and of the Byzantine Empire. The monastery, though essentially Greek in origin (as it remains to this day), was not cut off from the West by the schism of 1054. As part of the autocephalous Sinaitic Church (ruled over by an archbishop), the monastery continued its ties with the Western Church. During the tenth or eleventh century, the relics of St. Catherine were translated from the peak that bears her name to the monastery, at which time it was dedicated to her. According to late medieval sources, her body was brought to Sinai from Alexandria by angels. (Most of the relics were later sold to the Cathedral of Rouen.)

The church dates from the sixth century; the walls and many interior features of the basilica-church are original, including the monumental mosaic of the transfiguration of Christ above the sanctuary, the carved and gilded rafters of the nave, and the cypress-wood main portal. A dizzying succession of architectural, ornamental, and iconographic styles attests to the uninterrupted Christian presence and cult of the monastery. It is a tribute to Muslim cooperation and tolerance that St. Catherine's has survived largely unscathed through fourteen centuries of Muslim rule; there is even a mosque within the monastery itself. According to legend, it was built in haste during the eleventh century to dissuade the Fatimid caliph al-Hakim (r. 996–1021) from destroying the monastery as he did the Church of the Holy Sepulchre (1009); the mosque still serves Muslim guests of the monastery and its Bedouin servants.

During the twelfth century, crusaders came as visitors, but in the thirteenth, a colony of Latin monks resided in the monastery and built their own chapel, St. Catherine's of the Franks. Though the Latin monastic community disappeared after the fall of the Crusader Kingdom (1291), continuing contacts with the West made St. Catherine's a popular pilgrimage site. Western European coats of arms, dating from the fourteeth to the sixteenth centuries, are carved into the walls of many buildings. William of Boldensele dedicated nearly an entire chapter of his pilgrimage account (1336) to his visit to the monastery: he reports on the asceticism and hospitality of the large monastic community—"Arabs and a few Greeks"—and claims that no insect pests are found there. The less trustworthy accounts attributed to John Mandeville and Johannes Witte de Hese report on the miraculous burning of lamps coterminous with the life of individual monks and the participation of birds in the production of olive oil.

During his Egyptian campaign (1798–1799), Napoleon—in keeping with his imperial pretensions—sent Marshall Jean-Baptiste Kléber to the monastery to restore its partially dilapidated walls; he also granted it special privileges. Likewise, during the nineteenth century, Russian largesse, consonant (once again) with imperial ideology and the concept of Moscow as the Third Rome, enriched St. Catherine's and many other Middle Eastern religious foundations.

The churches that adhere to the Chalcedonian dogma of the two natures of Christ (451), including not only the Greek Orthodox Church but also other orthodox churches (the Melchite Syrian, Georgian, and Slavic) and at times the Roman Church, have had a strong influence on St. Catherine's; unrepresented in the monastery and its collections are the Monophysite confessions.

**BIBLIOGRAPHY**

Galey, John. *Sinai and the Monastery of St. Catherine.* London: Chatto and Windus, 1980.

Shevcenko, Ihor. "The Early Period of the Sinai Monastery in the Light of Its Inscriptions." *Dumbarton Oaks Papers* 20 (1966): 255–264.

*Andrew Gow*

**SEE ALSO**

Byzantine Empire; Eastern Christianity; Egeria; Egypt; Holy Land; *Mandeville's Travels;* Pilgrimage, Christian; William of Boldensele; Witte de Hese, Johannes

## Caxton, William (*c.* 1422–1491)

First person to establish a printing press in England, and publisher of books related to real and imagined travel. William Caxton translated and printed the works of many writers, as well as composing and printing texts of his own. Some of his most famous publications include Thomas Malory's *Morte Darthur,* and Geoffrey Chaucer's *The Canterbury Tales.* In 1481, he printed *Myrrour of the Worlde* (also known as *Image of the World*), a treatise he translated from the French *Image dou monde* of Gautier (or Gossuin) de Metz (itself based on Honorius Augustodunensis's *Imago mundi*). This book included several

Caxton, *Myrrour of the World* woodcut depicting the center of the earth as the center of the universe; a rock dropped into the earth from any of the four cardinal directions would, theoretically, come to rest at the planet's core and remain there. Westminster: William Caxton, 1490, sig. D3r. Reproduced by permission of the Map Division, The New York Public Library (Astor, Lenox and Tilden Foundations).

woodcuts, some illustrating geographical and astronomical principles, such as the circumnavigability of the earth and eclipses. These, with the two simple T-O maps he included (see Maps), are the first printed illustrations in any English book. Book dealers in Flanders exported beautifully crafted manuscripts; Caxton imported and even commissioned many of these, including the copy of the *Image du monde* that he translated.

Caxton's *Myrrour* is an encyclopedia beginning with an account of the Creation. It follows medieval cosmology fairly typically. Philosophy, astronomy, and the liberal arts are thoroughly detailed. The book includes descriptions of fabulous beasts, as well as geographical information that is presented in an explanatory way. For instance, in a passage on Iceland and its long winter months with little sunlight, Caxton offers clear reasons for this phenomenon. Some information is his own, such as the course of the Danube and a long list of countries Caxton says are in Europe, even though his source places them in Africa.

**BIBLIOGRAPHY**

Blake, Norman F. *Caxton's Own Prose.* London: Andre Deutsch, 1973.

————. *William Caxton and English Literary Culture.* London: Hambledon Press, 1991.

Childs, Edmund. *William Caxton. A Portrait in a Background.* London: Northwood Publications, Ltd., 1976.

Painter, George D. *William Caxton: A Quincentenary Biography of England's First Printer.* London: Chatto and Windus, 1976.

*Jennifer Lawler*

**SEE ALSO**

Honorius Augustodunensis; Iceland; *Mappamundi;* Maps

## Center of the Earth: *Arin*

The central point around which a map is organized. Erhard Etzlaub, the first German surveyor, chose Nuremberg as the center of his map ("Das ist der Rom Weg" [*c.* 1500]) because he was living there and working for its citizens.

World maps often reflect a view of life: many medieval cartographers chose to center their maps on a place of religious importance to them. St. Jerome (*c.* 342–420), noted exegete and translator of the Bible into Latin, declared Jerusalem the center of the earth, a decision he based on Ezekiel 5:5, where Jerusalem is called *in medio gentium;* Jerome expanded on this and

# C

called the Holy City the "umbilicus mundi," or "navel of the world."

It took a long time for cartographers to turn this knowledge into practice. Mapping always depends on models, and the Roman map, representing the Roman Empire and its trade routes in the Mediterranean world, was inherited by the medieval West. Therefore, maps of the Christian author Beatus of Liébana (776/786) were Romacentric. In his map attached to the *Imago mundi* of Honorius Augustodunensis (*c.* 1110), the mapmaker of Sawley placed the Greek island of Delos at the middle of the earth, following a Classical conviction that Delos or Delphi was the religious center of Greece (this map is Cambridge, Corpus Christi College, MS 66, p. 2). It might be a consequence of the crusader movement that the first map showing Jerusalem as center appears around 1100 (Oxford, St. John's College, MS 17).

A source of confusion for the makers of Western *mappaemundi* was inherent in a presentation based on the T-O system (the world disk—oriented to the East—is shaped like an ○ and is divided into the three continents—Asia, Europa, and Africa—by a ⊤, formed by the Mediterranean Sea as shaft and the rivers Don and Nile as crossbeam). If Asia got half the world above the crossbar, the exact center, the point of intersection, would fall in the waters of the eastern Mediterranean; in order to make Jerusalem the point of intersection, the T was sometimes moved slightly to the west. Most maps from the twelfth to the fifteenth centuries are designed in that way; only the Ptolemaic maps, dating from the beginning of land surveying, adopt a cartographical method that chooses the center based solely on geography.

One important exception is the Latin zone or climate map, which has a different arrangement. Whether oriented to the south (for example, the map of Petrus Alfonsi [1110]), to the east (for example, the map of John of Wallingford [*c.* 1258]), or to the north (for example, the map of Pierre d'Ailly [1417]), these maps are centered on a place named *Arin* or *Arym* or *Aren*. Nevertheless, this toponym is not regarded as the midpoint of the habitable world, but is situated on its edge. Maps of climates always offer the inhabited world divided into seven bandlike zones or climates up to the equator, where Arin is to be found. European cartographers inherited the toponym from the Islamic tradition, which places Arin on the prime meridian at the center of the inhabited world.

The name *Arin* is derived from Ujjain (modern Avanti), site of an ancient observatory in the Indian tradition. Some Asian maps extend the meridian from Mount Meru (Sumeru) in the north, through Ujjain to Lanka on the equator; all were important in the cosmography of Buddhism as well as Hinduism.

The oldest Turkish world map is in the encyclopedia of Mahmud al-Kashghari (1076 C.E.), a grammarian who worked at Baghdad. The world is oriented to the east and is centered on the town of Balasaghun, the capital of the Uighurs in the Tien Shan mountains. The rest of the world recedes from the areas of Central Asia in which Turkish was spoken.

A map's center is thus often a reliable indicator of the values its cartographer or patron holds dear.

**BIBLIOGRAPHY**

Harley-Woodward. *The History of Cartography.* Vol. 1: 334–357. See Gen. Bib.

*Anna-Dorothee von den Brincken*

**SEE ALSO**

Ailly, Pierre d'; Climate; Crusades, First, Second, and Third; Etzlaub, Erhard; Honorius Augustodunensis; Jerusalem; *Mappamundi;* Maps; Ptolemy

## Chaghatai (d. 1241/1242)

Second son of Chinggis Khân by his chief wife, Bortei, and founder of a dynasty that later ruled in Central Asia.

Chaghatai participated in Chinggis's campaigns in northern China (1211–1216) and against Khwārazm-shāh (1219–1224), and led the expedition into India (winter 1221–1222) against the shah's successor, Jalāl al-Dīn. About that time, Chinggis endowed Chaghatai with the land of the Uighurs, Karakitais, and the Khwarazmian Empire south of the Aral Sea—virtually all of Central Asia. His descendents ruled this *ulus* (patrimony) as Chaghatai khânate. Chaghatai closely resembled Chinggis in character; surviving sources paint him as stern, iron-willed, unsmiling, and able to inspire terror in his subjects. Although it was his younger brother, Ögedei, who succeeded as great khân, Chaghatai enjoyed enormous prestige as Chinggis's eldest surviving son. Unlike his brothers, he avoided drunkenness. He took Ögedei to task for overindulgence, and made him promise to limit his alcohol intake. After 1229, he took no part in military campaigns, dividing his time between his brother's court and his own peripatetic *ordu* (camp), which was generally on the banks of the river Ili. Almaligh [Almayq], near Yining in Xinjiang, where he camped in summer, later became the administrative center for Chaghatai khânate, and the Roman Church made it a bishopric in the fourteenth century.

Chaghatai was chief authority on the *yasa*, the Mongol customary law codified under Chinggis. Rigidly upholding Mongol law, he incurred his Muslim subjects' wrath. He punished them severely for following dictates of the Islamic *sharī'a*, or holy law, such as slaughtering animals by cutting their throats or performing ritual ablutions in running water, because these practices were contrary to the *yasa*. According to the Persian historian, Juwayni, no Muslim in his khânate dared slaughter a sheep properly, and many were forced to eat meat they considered carrion. Perhaps because of his opposition to Islam, the tradition developed, reported by Marco Polo, that Chaghatai had been baptized. Chaghatai died in his mid- to late-fifties, either shortly before or several months after (the sources differ) the death of Ögedei.

**BIBLIOGRAPHY**

Barthol'd, Vasili V. *Turkestan Down to the Mongol Invasion.* Trans. H.A.R. Gibb. Gibb Memorial Series, n.s. 5, London, 1928. 4th edition. Philadelphia: Porcupine, 1977.

Jackson, Peter. "The Dissolution of the Mongol Empire." *Central Asiatic Journal* 22 (1978): 186–243.

Morgan, David. *The Mongols.* London: Blackwell, 1986.

Rashid al-Din. *The Successors of Genghis Khan.* Trans. J.A. Boyle. New York: Columbia UP, 1971.

Spuler, Bertold. *History of the Mongols, Based on Eastern and Western Accounts of the Thirteenth and Fourteenth Centuries.* Trans. H. and S. Drummond. London: Routledge, 1972.

*James D. Ryan*

**SEE ALSO**

Almaligh; Chaghatai Khânate; Cumans; Karakitai; Marco Polo; Mongols; Yasa; Yuan Dynasty

## Chaghatai Khânate

The Mongol "Middle Kingdom" in Central Asia, created in the thirteenth century, originally the appanage of Chinggis Khân's second son, Chaghatai. Astride the silk roads, the khânate encompassed most of modern Xinjiang autonomous region (China), Kyrgyzstan, Tajikistan, and Uzbekistan, as well as parts of Kazakhstan, Turkmenistan, northern Afghanistan, and eastern Iran; it included major trading centers like Samarkand, Bukhara, and Tashkent.

Brief reigns and violent struggles for succession were frequent in Chaghatai, intermittently hindering trade and travel in Central Asia from the second half of the thirteenth century until the end of the Middle Ages. Although less is known concerning Chaghatai khânate than other Mongol realms, its historical outline is clear. Chaghatai and his descendants renounced urban living and followed the traditional Mongol nomadic life, which their cousins in China and Persia gradually abandoned. Their khânate, lacking administrative structure and without a real capital, was usually ruled from the banks of the river Ili, where the khâns pitched their camps. Chaghatai soon became a loose confederation of diverse peoples, including Turks, Uighurs, Karakitans, and Persians, ruled through intimidation by a militarily superior Mongol minority. Perhaps because it was less affected by urban civilization than Mongol kingdoms in more sedentary areas, Chaghatai khânate survived longer.

When Chaghatai died (1241/1242), his khânate was still an integral part of the Mongol Empire. As Chaghatai's progeny became embroiled in struggles between rivals for the office of great khân and as political fortunes changed, control over Central Asia was given to various of his heirs. During the civil war after Khubilai's election, Alighu (1260–1265/6), grandson of Chaghatai, rebelled and proclaimed Chaghatai khânate independent. His cousin, Mubarak Shah, the first of Chaghatai's line to adopt Islam, assumed power in 1266. Muslim historians glorified his brief reign, but it was an anomaly. Although Islam had been the state religion throughout Central Asia (except Uighur territory) before Mongol dominion, most Chaghataid khâns were shamanists, followed the *yasa* (Mongol law), and were tolerant of all religions. Some even favored Christianity over Islam.

After Alighu died, Qaidu, a grandson of Ögedei, reigned in Central Asia, waging war against both Yuan China and the Persian il-khâns until his death in 1303. Qaidu shared rule with Chaghatai's descendants, notably Barak (1266–1271) and his son Du'a (1282–1306/7), who were his satellites. Du'a wrested total control over Chaghatai from Qaidu's heirs around 1305, however, and six of his sons succeeded as Chaghataid khâns. As the itineraries of the Polos and

# C

missionaries to the great khân demonstrate, during these decades war disrupted commerce on the silk roads, and travelers were diverted to the sea route from Persia to China via India.

Originally, Chaghataid khâns and their warriors lived in the semi-arid east, and maintained both their ancestral, nomadic culture and their military supremacy over subject cities in the west. These they governed through Muslim intermediaries, with each Mongol prince allotted craftsmen in units called "thousands" or "workshops," to provide weapons and revenues. But under Du'a's sons, khâns had difficulty maintaining both the loyalty of nomadic warriors and control over the centers of wealth. In Esen-Buka's reign (1309–1318), armies from China made eastern Chaghatai unsafe, and his successor, Kebek (1318–1326), moved his court west, constructing a palace near Samarkand. His attraction to city life cost him support among nomad warriors, and his reign ended violently.

Because Muslim Turkic tribesmen, quartered near urban centers, had become a large part of the warrior class, religious issues now came to the fore. Eljigidai (1326), reported to have been baptized, was quickly overthrown by his Turkic emirs, and his successor, Tarmashirin (1326–1334), locating his court in the Muslim west, converted to Islam as 'Ala al-Dīn. Ibn Battūta spent time in his camp in 1333, reporting the khân a pious Muslim, humbly accepting admonishments from the sheik. Under Tarmashirin, persecution of non-Muslims wreaked havoc on Nestorian communities, which never recovered the importance they formerly enjoyed in the Mongol Empire. His neglect of the *yasa* and the eastern provinces alienated Mongol warriors there, however, and they raised his nephew, Buzan, to the khânate in 1333/34.

The khânate's history well illustrates how, in Mongol-Turkic society, clan leadership passed to the oldest male in the direct family line rather than automatically going to the eldest son. Many khâns died in violent revolts, but their successors were more often brothers or older nephews than sons. Thus two of Barak's brothers reigned before Du'a succeeded his father, and Du'a's six sons became khâns before any of their children. After Tarmashirin, no strong leader acceptable to both east and west emerged, and the khânate split into two states. Four khâns were elected in quick succession between 1334 and 1339, a period of general disorder and sectarian violence during which European missionaries were martyred in the khânate. Kazan

(1339–1346) restored stability in the east, but died doing battle against Turkish nobility in the west. Chaghatai khânate remained divided thereafter, its western reaches becoming Transoxiana, a Muslim state where the lineage of Chaghatai continued to rule (as puppets of the Turkic Muslim emirs) until Tamerlane assumed power in 1370. The eastern provinces became Mughulistan, where Mongol traditions were more generally preserved and Chaghatai's heirs reigned through the medieval period.

**BIBLIOGRAPHY**

Boyle, John Andrew. *The Mongol World Empire, 1206–1370.* London: Variorum Reprints, 1977.

Grousset, René. *The Empire of the Steppes.* Trans. N. Walford. New Brunswick, NJ: Rutgers UP, 1970.

Kwanten, Luc. *Imperial Nomads—A History of Central Asia, 500–1500.* Philadelphia: U of Pennsylvania P, 1979.

Manz, Beatrice Forbes. *The Rise and Rule of Tamerlane.* Cambridge: Cambridge UP, 1989.

Morgan, David. *The Mongols.* London: Blackwell, 1986.

Rossabi, Morris. *Khubilai Khan: His Life and Times.* Berkeley: U of California P, 1988.

*James D. Ryan*

**SEE ALSO**

Bukhara; Chaghatai; Hülegü; Ibn Battūta, Abu Abdallah; Karakitai; Mongols; Nestorianism; Nomadism and Pastoralism; Samarkand; Silk Roads; Tamerlane; Yasa; Yuan Dynasty

## Charts, Brittany and Navigational

*See* Brittany and Navigational Charts

## Charts, Portolan

*See* Portolan Charts

## Chaucer, Geoffrey (*c.* 1340–1400)

English poet best known for his celebrated work, *The Canterbury Tales,* which relates the stories told by a group of pilgrims on their way to the shrine of St. Thomas à Becket in the cathedral at Canterbury.

Chaucer himself was widely traveled. As a page attached to the household of the countess of Ulster, he journeyed throughout England to visit the outlying estates and to attend royal feasts. In a campaign with the earl of Ulster in 1360, he ventured into France where he was taken prisoner and ransomed. He went to

Spain six years later, either on a pilgrimage or as an emissary, possibly to Pedro of Castile (*c.* 1350–1366 and 1367–1369), and undertook nearly annual expeditions to France to subdue hostilities that were continually renewed. By the mid-1370s, he was a customs officer who went abroad frequently.

In his *Canterbury Tales,* Chaucer uses a novel frame story: his characters are on a pilgrimage. Chaucer had inherited a tradition of travel and pilgrimage narratives, but those accounts were predominantly edifying stories written by the clergy to detail miracles and marvels. Thus, he creates a pilgrimage both more realistic and more imaginative than any written about in actual first-person narratives. The collection of tales—and pilgrims did tell stories while traveling—reflects the range of human experience. The whole pilgrimage group is a microcosm of medieval society itself.

The pilgrims Chaucer describes do not seem to be penitent; none is poor, and instead of undertaking the journey on foot, they ride on horseback. The elegant Prioress, well-dressed Monk, and lewd Friar do not seem intent on a spiritual journey. The Wife of Bath goes on pilgrimage as a hobby, having visited Jerusalem three times. This colorful group contrasts with the traditional picture of the pilgrim on foot, bearing a staff and scrip, wearing a long coarse robe and a broad-brimmed hat. The pilgrims Chaucer describes are richly human and interesting as people, some apparently modeled on actual persons Chaucer's audience could recognize. Like the pilgrimage described by Felix Fabri, Chaucer's Canterbury journey is an important document for a view of the actual daily progress of a pilgrim, with distances traveled, references to accommodations, and ever-present conflict between members of the different classes and orders of religious who went on pilgrimages.

**BIBLIOGRAPHY**

Chaucer, Geoffrey. *The Riverside Chaucer.* 3rd edition. Ed. Larry D. Benson, et al. New York: Houghton-Mifflin, 1987.

Howard, Donald R. *Writers and Pilgrims. Medieval Pilgrimage Narratives and Their Posterity.* Berkeley: U of California P, 1980.

Loxton, Howard. *Pilgrimage to Canterbury.* London: David & Charles, 1978.

Pearsall, Derek. *The Life of Geoffrey Chaucer.* Oxford: Blackwell Publishers, 1992.

Zacher, Christian K. *Curiosity and Pilgrimage.* Baltimore and London: Johns Hopkins UP, 1976.

*Jennifer Lawler*

**SEE ALSO**

Fabri, Felix; Pilgrimage, Christian; Pilgrimage Sites, English; Pilgrimage Sites, Spanish

## China

An area of southern Asia that was home to an extremely sophisticated culture from ancient times but virtually unknown to Europeans prior to the thirteenth and fourteenth centuries, when the Mongol conquest of much of Eurasia created the opportunity for Italian merchants and Latin Christian missionaries to establish direct contact with the Far East.

Although Han China and the Roman Empire had traded with each other from before the beginning of the Common Era, this long-distance commerce was conducted through Persian, Arab, Turkish, and East Indian intermediaries, operating across the Silk Road through Central Asia or the maritime route around India, with limited encounters of the peoples at opposite ends of the Old World economic and cultural highways. The ancient Greeks and Romans knew the land and people of China by such vague names as "the realm of Sina," which derived from the dynastic title of the first imperial family, "the Ch'ins," or "the Seres of the land of Serica," which reflected Western belief that this was the place where silk was combed from trees. It is possible that ancient geographers did not recognize that these names referred to the same locale. On the other hand, equally vague names were applied by the Chinese to Western regions that seemed exotically distant and evoked similar feelings of mystery and romance. Although members of the merchant communities that exchanged trade goods along the silk and spice routes were undoubtedly familiar with the landscapes, races, and products of these regions, such information was seldom incorporated into formal geographical and ethnological learning. Indeed, medieval Europeans before the thirteenth century were probably better informed about India, at least the India of romance and legend, than they were about China, because of the former's connection with the adventures of Alexander the Great and the Apostle Thomas.

The China that was "discovered" by medieval European merchants and missionaries was the China of the Yuan emperors, the centerpiece of a vast steppe nomadic empire created by Chinggis Khân and his successors. In 1264, the Mongols pushed southward beyond the Great Wall to occupy North China; and in

# C

1279, Khubilai Khân concluded the conquest of the Sung kingdom of the south by annexing it to the northern state. The opportunity for the establishment of direct contact between China and Europe and for the exchange of more or less accurate information was the result of the convergence of Mongol domination with certain other strategic factors during the thirteenth and fourteenth centuries: the Mongol conquest of adjacent lands extending to Russia and Persia in the West; the presence in the Middle East of Italian merchants and European crusaders; the wishful thinking of some popes and princes concerning the possible conversion of the Mongols to Christianity and of an alliance with them against Islam; and, finally, the reinvigoration of the European economy with the result that it was able to play the role of a junior partner in a medieval "world system" that flourished from *c.* 1250 to 1350.

Information about China first began to reach the West after Mongol rampages in Poland and Hungary in the early 1240s prompted the pope to inaugurate a series of missions, undertaken mainly by Franciscans with a handful of Dominican friars, to persuade the Mongols to cease their depredations against the Christian West, consider conversion to Catholic Christianity, and form a military alliance. The circulation of the legend of the great Christian potentate of Asia, Prester John, and knowledge of the favor shown by the Mongols to the Nestorian Christians of their dominions strengthened hope for a rapprochement with Christian Europe. In 1247, a Franciscan friar, John of Plano Carpini, returned from a two-year journey to the court of the great khân at Karakorum in Mongolia where he had been sent by Pope Innocent IV (1243–1254). In his report to the pope, which was subsequently given publicity by its inclusion in Vincent of Beauvais's encyclopedia, the *Speculum historiale,* John offered a brief assessment of the civilization of "Cathay" (a name for north China derived from that of a non-Chinese people known as the Kitans or Kitai who had ruled from the tenth to the twelfth centuries as the dynasty of the Liao). He expressed admiration for the technological virtuosity of the Cathayans and for their great wealth. His Chinese informants at the Mongol court may have misled him as to the nature of their faith or he may have been confused in his understanding of Buddhism, which he presented as a kind of Christianity with several of the distinctive beliefs and practices of his own religion. A half-dozen years later,

in 1254, another Franciscan, William of Rubruck, reported to King Louis IX of France, who had dispatched him on a similar mission to the Mongol court at Karakorum, concerning the same Cathayans, whom he recognized as the Seres of classical fame. William's account, which was neglected in the Middle Ages despite its use by Roger Bacon in the *Opus majus* (*c.* 1269), showed the author's observational skills in its description of Chinese artistry, medical practice, and writing. Neither John of Plano Carpini nor William of Rubruck visited China, and both viewed it as simply a part of the greater Mongol Empire that was the real focus of their attention and concern.

The first European to visit China and to return home to write about it was the Venetian Marco Polo (*c.* 1254–1324), who spent seventeen years of his life as a servitor of the Great Khân Khubilai. Surviving in more than 100 manuscripts and a large number of printed editions, in a dozen vernacular languages and two Latin translations, Marco Polo's *Divisament dou monde* (Description of the World) provided medieval readers with an ostensibly authoritative description of the politics, society, and culture of Mongol China. Marco's admiration for Khubilai Khân and his enthusiasm for describing the wealth of Yuan China reflected his appreciation of the material advantages enjoyed by the premodern world's greatest civilization. During the Sung dynasty (960–1279), China became the most prosperous, populous, economically developed, and technologically sophisticated society in the Old World. The momentum that Sung prosperity had given China endured through the Mongol period, which continued the process of rapid urbanization, agricultural expansion, and population growth. Marco was especially impressed by the great coastal ports of Kinsai (Hangchou) and Zaiton (Chuanchou); and he extolled the attractiveness of the Mongol capital at Khanbaliq, which had been recently built.

Comparable to Marco Polo's book in its popularity and in its use of superlatives to describe Chinese civilization was the travelogue of Odoric of Pordenone, a Franciscan friar who spent three years in China during the 1320s. It has been pointed out that Odoric was fascinated with numbers: Canton was three times larger than Venice; there were two thousand cities in South China larger than Treviso or Vicenza; and the salt administration of Yangchou, where Marco Polo may have served as an official, was capable of generating more than seven million florins in revenue. Like

Marco's book, Odoric's memoir was reprinted during the Age of Discovery in accordance with the progress of exploration in the New World and the Far East during the late fifteenth and early sixteenth centuries; and it was a principal source for the author of John Mandeville's book of travels, the most famous work of travel fiction in medieval literary history.

The major Chinese coastal ports of Kinsai and Zaiton attracted communities of Genoese and Venetian merchants that provided congregations for the missionaries dispatched to China by popes of the fourteenth century. The appointment of John of Monte Corvino as archbishop of Beijing and his tenure of this office for twelve years until his death in 1328 revealed the effort by the papacy to organize the life of the church to benefit Catholic expatriates and Asian Christians resident in the religiously diverse empire of the khâns. On the other hand, since it was both dependent on the sponsorship of the Mongol government and subject to harassment by Nestorian Christians, who also enjoyed official status and protection, the Catholic Christian presence was tenuous and did not outlast the end of the Yuan imperial line.

The conditions across Eurasia that made possible the establishment of temporary contact between China and the West gradually dissolved during the late fourteenth and the fifteenth centuries: the nativist dynasty of the Ming displaced the Yuan and closed China to foreign commerce; the Genoese and Venetians withdrew to the Black Sea and the Crimea; the triumph of Islam and endemic civil war closed access to Central Asia; and a great pandemic of the Black Death depressed the economies of the Old World. Knowledge of China thus remained limited to that contained in the works of Marco Polo and the Latin missionaries. Only gradually in the sixteenth century did new information generated by Portuguese navigators and Jesuit missionaries clearly identify the recently encountered kingdom of China with medieval Cathay and the ancient land of the Seres. Traditional geographical lore long coexisted with the new empirical data generated by Portuguese explorers and Jesuit missionaries. Christopher Columbus, who cherished his Marco Polo and lamented the failure of the popes to take seriously the conversion of the Mongols, searched the New World for a great khân of the Indies. The loss of mastery of East Asian geography was clearly implied by the set of questions that representatives of the Portuguese crown were to pose to the "Chijns" whom they antici-

pated meeting in the port of Malacca: Are they merchants and how often do they come to market; what is their religion and how do they practice it; and what direction does their country lie and how do they reach it?

**BIBLIOGRAPHY**
Abu-Lughod, Janet L. *Before European Hegemony: The World System A.D. 1250–1350.* Oxford: Oxford UP, 1989.
Critchley, John. *Marco Polo's Book.* Aldershot: Variorum, 1992.
Curtin, Philip D. *Cross-Cultural Trade in World History.* Cambridge: Cambridge UP, 1984.
Phillips, J.R.S. *The Medieval Expansion of Europe.* Oxford and New York: Oxford UP, 1988.
———. "The Outer World of the European Middle Ages." In *Implicit Understandings: Observing, Reporting, and Reflecting on the Encounters between European and Other Peoples in the Early Modern Era.* Ed. Stuart B. Schwartz. Cambridge: Cambridge UP, 1994.
de Rachewiltz, Igor. *Papal Envoys to the Great Khans.* Stanford: Stanford UP, 1971.
Reichert, Folker. "Chinas Beitrag zum Weltbild der Europäer: Zur Reception der Fernostkenntnisse im 13. und 14. Jahrhundert." *Zeitschrift für Historische Forschung* 6 (1989): 33–57.
Rossabi, Morris. *Khubilai Khan: His Life and Times.* Berkeley, Los Angeles, and London: U of California P, 1988.

*William R. Jones*

**SEE ALSO**
Black Death; Buddhism; Dominican Friars; Franciscan Friars; Genoa; Great Wall; India; John of Monte Corvino; John of Plano Carpini; Karakitai; Karakorum; Khanbaliq; Louis IX; Malacca Straits; *Mandeville's Travels;* Marco Polo; Merchants, Italian; Missionaries to China; Mongols; Nestorianism; Odoric of Pordenone; Portuguese Expansion; Prester John; Silk Roads; Venice; Vincent of Beauvais; William of Rubruck; Yuan Dynasty; Zaiton

## China, Missionaries to
*See* Missionaries to China

## Chinese Navigation
*See* Navigation, Chinese

## Christianity, Eastern
*See* Eastern Christianity

# C

## Christians, Marriages between Muslims and Christians, Attitudes toward
**See** Marriages between Muslims and Christians, Attitudes toward

## City Plans

Medieval representations of entire cities. Although such representations are generally termed plans, few are true plans. Most of them are views of some sort: bird's-eye views, profile views, and hybrid projections that show some details in perspective, others in elevation, and still others in plan. Plans properly so named—that is, diagrams drawn to scale, projected from a zenithal viewing point (from straight above and an infinite height)—were also made, but have survived in much smaller numbers than have views.

All these modes of projection had been used since antiquity by cartographers (including the makers of city plans) and in planning or illustrating buildings. Sometimes the purpose of such documents was to establish a value-free record, delineating the layout of properties or projected buildings, itineraries or routes for travel, and so forth. Sometimes the purpose was to convey large, abstract ideas symbolically through the medium of a cartographic image. Plans tend to be found more often among record drawings, while views are found among images with a symbolic content, but a firm distinction cannot always be made.

Projections and functions developed in antiquity were not forgotten during the Middle Ages. For example, flat plans of buildings and complexes of buildings, serving as record drawings for architectural planning, continued to be made. Often destroyed through use or discarded after they had served their purpose, they are rare today, but some are extant: a ninth-century, precisely scaled plan for a typical monastery (St. Gall, Stiftsbibliothek, Codex 1092); a

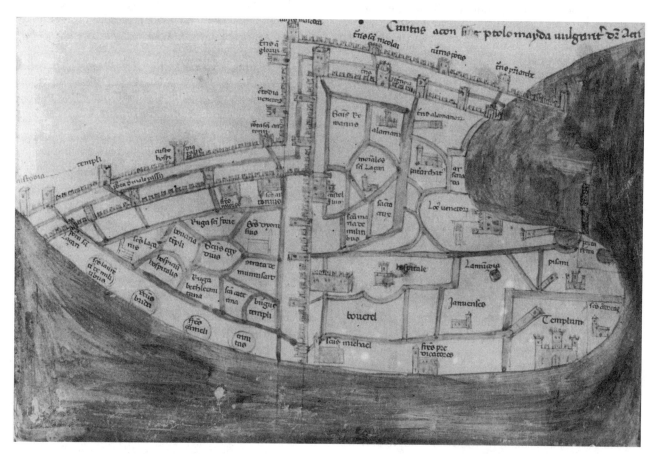

Fourteenth-century copy of a thirteenth-century plan of Acre. Oxford, Bodleian Library MS Tanner 190, fol. 207. Courtesy of the Bodleian Library, Oxford.

thirteenth-century, architectural model book containing many small, roughly scaled ground plans by Villard de Honnecourt (Paris, Bibliothèque Nationale, MS fr. 19093); and more than a dozen large, scaled plans of the late thirteenth and the fourteenth century, reproducing whole churches or portions of them in the workshop archives of major cathedrals in France (Strasbourg), Germany (Cologne), and Italy (Milan and Siena).

Flat plans of entire cities, made as records of systems of fortification or public rights of way, are even rarer than architectural plans because there was no incentive to keep them once they were outdated. Such plans were the twelfth-century plans of Venice and Jerusalem, a mid-thirteenth-century plan of Acre, and a fourteenth-century plan of Pavia, all known only through copies at Rome, Biblioteca Vaticana Apostolica MSS Palatine Lat. 1362 and 1993; Oxford, Bodleian Library MS Tanner 190; and Venice, Biblioteca Nazionale Marciana MS Lat. Z 399.

Preparation of a true plan requires the acquisition of accurate linear dimensions and—if the subject extends over a large area—accurate bearings. In both ancient times and the Middle Ages, the means for collecting or calculating such information were relatively primitive. However, the new enthusiasm for secular learning that arose in fourteenth-century Italy and traveled to northern Europe encouraged the development of more accurate measuring devices and more powerful algorithms for the calculation of unmeasurable dimensions. Thus, from the end of the fifteenth century, accurate plans lay increasingly within the power of architects, surveyors, and cartographers. The result was the appearance, by around 1500, of city plans that seem to be as precise as those prepared in our own day. An example is Leonardo da Vinci's famous plan of Imola (Windsor, Royal Library, MS 12284), prepared in 1502 in connection with a military campaign. The distinction between record drawings, most often projected in the form of true plans, and symbolically charged drawings, generally views, held good into the period of the Renaissance.

City views, like *mappaemundi* or other schematic maps, could also communicate symbolic meanings. Whether through its accompanying vignettes and inscriptions, or through the selection of features reproduced, a city view could characterize its subject as, among other things, a miraculous home to holy men and deeds, a reminder of the vanity of earthly pomp and glory, a member of a political alliance, or a site of significant events. Examples of these are, respectively, the many hybrid views of Jerusalem in twelfth- and thirteenth-century manuscripts; the large, painted, bird's-eye view of Rome of shortly before 1490 (Mantua, Palazzo Ducale, Saletta delle città); the mural, bird's-eye views of Florence, Genoa, Milan, Naples, Rome, and Venice, painted in 1484–1487 in the Belvedere villa at the Vatican (now mostly destroyed); and the numerous, early-sixteenth-century engraved bird's-eye views of towns in Germany and Italy, illustrating sieges and battles of the day, volcanic eruptions, and other events that had excited public curiosity.

**BIBLIOGRAPHY**

Harley-Woodward, *The History of Cartography.* Esp. P.D.A. Harvey, "Local and Regional Cartography in Medieval Europe," 1:464–501. See Gen. Bib.

Harvey, P.D.A. *The History of Topographical Maps: Symbols, Pictures and Surveys.* London: Thames and Hudson, 1980, esp. Chap. 4.

Schulz, Juergen. "Jacopo de' Barbari's View of Venice: Map Making, City Views and Moralized Geography Before the Year 1500." *Art Bulletin* 60 (1978): 425–474 and 744.

*Juergen Schulz*

**SEE ALSO**
Acre; Jerusalem; Jerusalem City Plans; *Mappamundi;* Maps; Venice

## City Plans, Jerusalem
*See* Jerusalem City Plans

## Clavus, Claudius (fl. 1424–1430)
A Danish geographer and mapmaker who influenced the development of cartography in southern Europe.

Born on the island of Fyn, Claudius Clavus [Clausson/Claussen Svart] is thought to have been living in Rome by 1424 and may have remained in Italy until at least 1430. He is best known for a map of northern Europe, displaying territory from Greenland to the Baltic coast, which he completed *c.* 1425. This map introduced—or at least confirmed—some awareness within southern geographical circles of the polar regions in general; more specifically, it is one of the earliest maps to show Greenland as lying west of Ireland but extending like a large peninsula from a northern landmass. Several copies of this map, as well as an

# C

accompanying descriptive text, are known today (a manuscript now in Vienna contains the text alone).

Clavus's cartography is noteworthy for several additional reasons. First, it is a regional map that is not a sea chart, which makes it something of a rarity for the Middle Ages. Second, Clavus sought to apply contemporary methods of quantitative map design to land area—that is, to represent actual space and its graphic counterpart proportionally, and to use graduated lines of latitude and longitude. This was no innovation for the 1420s, and Clavus may have learned these techniques in southern Europe, but he is remarkable for employing them to chart the North Atlantic and Baltic, a region that portolan charts even of this late date avoid (in part because Mediterranean mariners, the chief producers of *portolani,* were denied access to the Baltic after 1323). Third, a map by Clavus (drawn by him or under his direction) was included in the manuscript copy of Ptolemy's *Geography* made in 1427 for Guillaume Fillastre (*c.* 1400–1473), who carried it to France, where he became an influential cardinal; it is preserved at Nancy. Since a Latin translation of Ptolemy began to circulate only around 1406/1407, this is an early sign that fifteenth-century European scholars hoped to escape the limitations of a second-century world view that regarded as *terra incognita* everything above 64½°N. latitude. Fourth, a somewhat restyled Clavus map (based on Nicholas Germanus's revision of one—not Fillastre's—in *c.* 1466) entered the printed Ptolemaic atlas on July 16, 1482, when it appeared as one of five woodcut "modern maps" in the edition (entitled *Cosmographia*) of Lienhart Holle at Ulm. A reissue on July 21, 1486 (by Johann Reger for Justus de Albano) added an identifying rubric (that has been excised from some surviving copies): TABULA MODERNA PRUSSIE LIVONIE NORBEGIE ET GOTTIE (Modern Map of East Prussia, Lithuania/Latvia, Norway, and southern Sweden/Gotland/Finland). According to this map's own coordinate system, Europe is depicted from 55°N. to 71°N. latitude.

Nineteenth- and early-twentieth-century scholars praised Clavus for his learning, practical experience (he was reputed to have visited Greenland himself), and precise delineation of northern coastal areas. While he most likely was acquainted with John of Sacrobosco's *Tractatus de sphaera* (1220) and the *Book of John Mandeville* (*c.* 1360), he probably acquired much of his geographical and cartographical expertise in Italy; details about

Scandinavian topography might, for example, have come from the papal archives. His design recalls the representation of northern Europe on the *mappamundi* (*c.* 1351) in the Medici ("Laurentian") Atlas, now in Florence. His information about the north, moreover, is incomplete and peculiar, especially in the text of the Vienna manuscript. Thirteenth- and fourteenth-century treatises in Old Norse record the toponyms Markland, Helluland, and Vinland/Vínland (from the saga tradition) as being in the western Atlantic, but Clavus has no knowledge of them. On the other hand, his map legends identify various areas of the polar landmass as being inhabited by an obscure people named "Careli," one-legged mariners, pygmies, and griffons. He more plausibly locates a "land of wild Lapps" (*Wildhlappelandi*) on the shore of a gulf northeast of Sweden.

## BIBLIOGRAPHY

Bjørnbo, Axel A., and Carl Sophus Petersen. *Der Däne Claudius Claussøn Swart (Claudius Clavus). Der älteste Kartograph des Nordens.* Innsbruck: Wagner'sche Universitätsbuchhandlung, 1909.

Nansen, Fridtjof. *In Northern Mists: Arctic Exploration in Early Times.* Trans. Arthur G. Chater. 2 vols. London: Heinemann, 1911; rpt. New York: AMS Press, 1969.

Simek, Rudolf. "Elusive Elysia, or: Which Way to Glæsisvellir?" *Sagnaskemmtun* [Vienna] (1986): 247–275.

Skelton, R.A. "The Vinland Map." In *The Vinland Map and the Tartar Relation.* Ed. R.A. Skelton, Thomas E. Marston, and George D. Painter. New Haven: Yale UP, 1965; 2nd edition 1995, pp. 107–240.

Scott D. Westrem

## SEE ALSO
Iceland; *Mappamundi;* Ptolemy; Sacrobosco, John of; *Terra Incognita;* Viking Discoveries and Settlements; Vinland Map

# Climate

An astronomical and geographical concept, assuming the sphericity of the earth and identifying latitudinal bands around the earth, parallel to the equator. Writers vary in numbering them and in describing their characteristics. Our modern notion of climate as the meterological conditions of a particular region no longer conveys the fundamentally geometrical aspect of medieval climates, or *climata*.

Originated by Babylonians before the development of spherical astronomy by the Greeks, *clima* (the singular form of *climata*) means the inclination of the earth's axis to the observer's horizon plane. It is observed directly as the angle of the earth's pole. In the Hellenistic era the term came to have as much a geographical as an astronomical use. Hipparchus (*c.* 150 B.C.E.) was already familiar with *climata,* and various later writers, including Pliny the Elder (23–79 C.E.) and Ptolemy (fl. 127–145 C.E.), use the term with different meanings.

In astronomy a *clima* is a precise parallel around the earth, while in geography it is commonly a band between two parallels, where certain identifying phenomena are found. The early way to identify parallels, before trigonometric techniques were invented, was to measure the maximum length of the shadow cast by a gnomon (a rod or a triangular plate, such as the one in a sundial). This length would remain constant along the parallel. Although highly practical, this method was imprecise. Nonetheless, its correlate, the maximum numbers of hours of daylight along the parallel, was the usual identifying property.

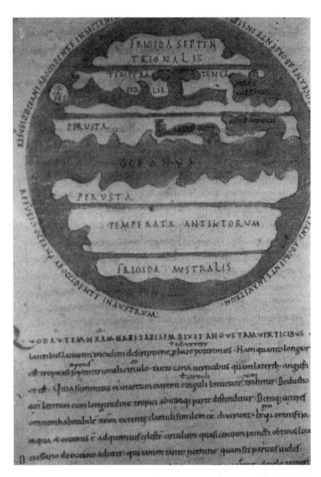

Macrobian zone map. Oxford, Bodleian Library MS D'Orville 77, fol. 100, 11th century. Courtesy of the Bodleian Library, Oxford.

Zone map from William of Conches, *De Philosophia Mundi.* Now Malibu, J. Paul Getty Museum MS XV.4, fol. 177v, 13th century. Formerly London, Sion College MS ARC L. 40.2/L. 28. Photo by John B. Friedman.

The number of *climata* to be identified was a question answered variously in the ancient sources available to the Middle Ages. Ptolemy, in *Almagest* II, 6, begins at the equator and describes thirty-three parallels at regular intervals up to the parallel where we first find twenty-four hours of maximum daylight at the time of summer solstice (66°, 8′, 40″ N.). He gives shadow lengths along each parallel at the different points of the year—that is, the equinoxes and solstices—and mentions notable or characteristic places. In some passages in the *Almagest* he uses only seven *climata;* these are a listing of seven latitudes that had become canonical long before. Beginning with Meroe, far to the south, with thirteen daylight hours, the list proceeds by half-hour intervals to the following places: Syene, Alexandria, Rhodes, Hellespont, mid-Pontus, and Borysthenes, the last having sixteen hours. There are other, somewhat different sets of seven *climata* in late

# C

antiquity, especially in the astrological literature, but all are rooted in an original Babylonian pattern.

In geographical applications, the *climata* came to be the zones between significant parallels. The Hellenistic system of seven *climata,* spread by the works of Ptolemy and others, had a long history into the Middle Ages. At the end of the sixth book of his *Natural History* (VI, 212–218), Pliny sets forth seven parallels, modifying details of the canonical seven, with the names of many places along each and the maximum lengths of gnomon shadows and daylight hours for each. Pliny's work was known at least from the time of Bede (*c.* 673–735). The seven *climata* were also reflected in pedagogical works like Martianus Capella's *Marriage of Mercury and Philology,* which was written in the early fifth century and used as a school text from the ninth century onward.

However, it was the notion of five latitudinal bands, or zones, around the earth that appeared most widely throughout the Middle Ages, perhaps because this pattern was usually presented in schematic as well as verbal form in the climate diagrams and maps of medieval manuscripts. This scheme of five bands was the simplest division of the globe and had been presented in the early fifth-century work of Macrobius, *Commentary on the Dream of Scipio.* It is created by a projection of four astronomically defined circles on the earth. In the first of a series of geographical chapters (Book II, chapter 5), Macrobius elaborates on the theme that the part of the globe that humans inhabit is by definition quite small. He first rules out the frigid, or Arctic and Antarctic, regions as being too cold, and then excludes the broad central band between the two tropics as being too hot to support human life. The two remaining temperate zones run from 24 degrees to 66 degrees of latitude in the Northern and Southern Hemispheres. The inhabitants of "our" (European) northern zone can infer by reason the existence of persons in the southern temperate zone, since the nature of that zone must be the same as "ours," given assumptions of cosmic and global symmetry.

Among the medieval delineations of space on the terrestrial globe, the five climates, or zones, outlined by Macrobius and other late antique writers offered a basis for ordering geography. The system came from and continued to suggest a correspondence between the celestial and the earthly realms. While the other common pattern for a world map in the early Middle Ages, the T-O design, identified three continents and was oriented to

the east (based in part on the position of Jerusalem or Paradise), the zonal map took the polar axis as its frame of reference and suggested a more naturalistic geography. The inferred existence of human life in the southern temperate zone led to many speculations about these inhabitants of the "antipodes." They were often supposed to be the home of different kinds of human races, almost always considered far removed in character and anatomy, as well as in space, from the familiarities of the Mediterranean world. Stories of strange people—headless, one-legged, long-eared, and so forth—were easily combined with the knowledge that an inhabitable but unreachable region existed far to the south. Pliny's *Natural History* gave details about such races as well as providing, with other Roman texts, much information about near and more distant parts of the northern temperate zone. Like Pliny and earlier writers, Macrobius describes the amount of heat in different parts of the habitable zone, refers to canonical locations like Meroe and Syene, and discusses climatic variations in different environments within the northern temperate zone as well as the borderline area of the torrid zone.

Isidore of Seville, in his *On the Nature of Things* (*c.* 613), devoted a chapter (Chap. 10) to the five zones, which he describes more succinctly than Macrobius. Unfortunately, Isidore's accompanying diagram makes the five bands into five small circles arranged in sequence around the inside of a large circle, which represents the earth. This image looks like a flat circular earth with the zones as five circular islands in sequence around the edge. Half a dozen of the Carolingian manuscripts add at the end of this work a T-O map, which is conceptually opposed to the zonal pattern and which must have misled many early medieval readers. In his *Etymologies* (*c.* 630), Isidore interprets the five parallel zones as celestial regions, then mentions that each region allows or disallows habitation below it because of the heat or cold of the zone (13.6.1–7). But he then proceeds (14.2.1–14.5.22) to describe the earth and its parts in terms of the T-O pattern, as if the habitable earth fills the space within the surrounding ocean. Isidore goes on to offer a large amount of traditional geographical lore about the three continents: Asia, Europe, and Africa. In manuscripts of the *Etymologies* copied throughout the early Middle Ages, a map organized according to this T-O pattern is consistently inserted at the beginning of Book 14.

Thus, from the early Hellenistic astronomical conception, the *climata,* as parallels around the earth, became a framework for geographical divisions, defined either as the seven canonical *climata* based on the maximum number of daylight hours or as the five parallel zones based on considerations of heat and habitability, and sometimes, from Macrobius and Isidore onward, modified to include the tripartite (the T-O) pattern and other elements. The Macrobian climates were a dominant pattern of world maps throughout the high Middle Ages, appearing in the five-zone form, for example, in the *De Philosophia Mundi* of William of Conches (1080–1145). Although by the end of the period the information provided by exploration had made the climate theory itself obsolete, the concept of climatic zones persisted as late as the fifteenth century, as, for example, in the world map of Andreas Walsperger (1448), which shows a world divided into seven climatic regions, but superimposes them on an empirically based representation of continents and geographical features.

**BIBLIOGRAPHY**

Harley-Woodward. *The History of Cartography.* Vol. 1. See Gen. Bib.

Honigmann, Ernst. *Die sieben Klimata und die Poleis Episemoi. Eine Untersuchung zur Geschichte der Geographie und Astrologie im Altertum und Mittelalter.* Heidelberg: Winter, 1929.

Isidorus Hispalensis. *Etymologiarum sive originum.* Ed. W.M. Lindsay. 1911; rpt. Oxford: Clarendon, 1985.

Macrobius Ambrosius Theodosius. *Commentary on the Dream of Scipio.* Trans. W.H. Stahl. New York: Columbia UP, 1952.

Neugebauer, Otto. *History of Ancient Mathematical Astronomy.* New York: Springer, 1975.

*Bruce S. Eastwood*

**SEE ALSO**

Antipodes; Geography in Medieval Europe; Isidore of Seville; Maps; Monstrosity, Geographical; *Oikoumene;* Pliny the Elder; Ptolemy; Walsperger, Andreas

## Cockaigne, Land of

A utopian country of effortless abundance and sensual pleasure that was a widespread motif in medieval folklore and literature; in English, one version survives, known as *The Land of Cockaigne.*

A single copy of the Middle English *Land of Cockaigne,* which is of Irish provenance and composition, is preserved in the British Library (MS Harley 913). In addition to items in French and Latin, this manuscript also collects seventeen works in English that are of central importance for our knowledge of medieval Hiberno-English. The manuscript is generally dated *c.* 1330; it is undoubtedly associated with the Franciscan order, possibly the house at Kildare.

The poem is set on an island, "Far in the sea, west of Spain." In the first fifty lines of the poem, Cockaigne is presented as an incomparable paradise. It is a marvelous patchwork and a successful combination of the ingredients of a wide range of Otherworlds described in a variety of texts. Throughout the poem's 190 lines, European folkloric features merge with motifs drawn from accounts of the Earthly Paradise and from the classical and Oriental traditions. Most notably, this Cloud-Cuckoo-Land is rich in echoes and parodies of Irish visions, *imrama,* and *echtrae.* The latter were tales of a human visit to the Otherworld; in the former a hero makes a sea-voyage from island to island (*imram* means literally "the rowing about"). The oldest *imrama* may go back to the eighth century and the most famous example is the Voyage of Mael Duin, probably the source of the *Navigatio Brendani* (St. Brendan's Voyage). Thus, the Cockaigne poem is firmly rooted in Irish literature.

The second section of the poem (ll. 51–100) focuses on the island's abbey, depicted in imagery drawn from the New Jerusalem of the Book of Revelation, medieval lapidaries and catalogues of *loci amoeni,* and from other works of Irish folklore. For example, the traditional Four Rivers of Paradise have become the abbey's four wells overflowing with treacle, *halwei* (healing potion), balm, and *piement* (a spiced drink made from wine and honey). The festive account of the monks' activities (ll. 101–182), however, employs a style of grotesque realism: young monks fly after their meal, and in order to call them back to earth, the abbot beats a young maiden's bottom as if it were a drum. Licentious activities are enhanced by the presence of a neighboring nunnery. On hot summer days, the young nuns throw themselves naked into a river of sweet milk. Then, each of the young monks catches one of them for a fabliau-like sexual initiation. An *envoi* adds that the addressees can also reach Cockaigne if they are willing to walk for seven years through swine dung.

Thus, for this poem, the phrase "world upside-down" is no mere cliché. The prevailing rule of Cockaigne seems to be a general suspension of norms (such as cosmic order, monastic hierarchy, and social prohibitions), and a comic merging of heaven and earth

# C

(heaven is on earth, roasted geese fly into the abbey, larks drop into the mouths of the monks, and monks fly). This imagery is subtly combined with an anticlerical satire in which Catholic ritual is parodied and the sacraments are burlesqued. The mock election of a clownish abbot who caricatures a monastic superior's prestige and teachings constitutes a pre-Rabelaisian carnivalesque overturning of hierarchies. The author cultivates burlesque stereotypes (the spanking of a sacrificial victim, sexual intercourse as "schooling," the carnival bells, and rewards going to the best sleeper) and images of the bodily functions (food, drink, sex, and defecation).

Although the Hiberno-English poem's relationship with the thirteenth-century Old French extant version (the misnamed *Fabliau de Cocaigne*) and the latter's two Middle Dutch analogues remains uncertain, the *Land of Cockaigne* cannot be a mere translation. While the idea of a land of abundance and sensual bliss may be traced to a number of sources, the additions, the tone, and the overall purpose of this early—if not the first—English utopia make it highly original. Its author, almost certainly a goliardic cleric, parodies not only a monk's paradise but the very myth of Cockaigne. Even the enigmatic etymology of the word has been employed to advantage: it is reminiscent of a Middle Dutch word meaning "small, very sweet cake sold to children at fairs" (*kokenje*), the famous abbot of the *Carmina Burana* ("Ego sum abbas Cucaniensis / et consilium meum est cum bibulis . . ."), and of Aristophanes' utopian city of *nephelo-kokkugia*. Such a convergence has generated a very innovative play of fools, in which the abbey has become a fair whose marketplace culture coexists with anticlerical satire.

**BIBLIOGRAPHY**

Bennett, J.A.W., and G.V. Smithers, eds. *Early Middle English Verse and Prose*. Oxford: Clarendon Press, 1966, pp. 136–144.

De Caluwé-Dor, Juliette. "L'anti-Paradis du *Pays de Cocagne*. Cocagne I, Etude et traduction [française] du poème moyen-anglais." In *Mélanges de philologie et de littératures romanes offerts à Jeanne Wathelet-Willem*. Liège: Marche Romane, 1978, pp. 103–123.

———. "L'Elément irlandais dans la version moyen-anglaise de *The Land of Cockaygne*." In *Mélanges de langue et littérature françaises du Moyen Âge et de la Renaissance offerts à Charles Foulon*. Vol. 1. Rennes: Institut français de l'Université de Haute-Bretagne, 1980, pp. 89–98.

———. "Carnival in Cokaygne: *The Land of Cokaygne* in Medieval English Literature." In *Gesellschaftsutopien im Mittelalter. Discours et figures de l'utopie au Moyen Âge*. Greifswald: Reineke, 1994, pp. 39–49.

Dillon, Myles. *Early Irish Literature*. Chicago and London: U of Chicago P, 1948, pp. 101–130.

Henry, P.L. "The Land of Cokaygne: Cultures in Contact in Medieval Ireland." *English Studies Today* 5 (1973): 175–203.

Tigges, Wim. "*The Land of Cockaygne*, Sophisticated Mirth." In *Companion to Early Middle English Literature*. Ed. N.H.G.E. Veldhoen and H. Aertsen. Amsterdam: Free University Press, 1988. pp. 97–104.

Vasvari, Louise O. "The Geography of Europe and Topsy-Turvy Literary Genres." In *Discovering New Worlds*. Ed. Westrem. pp. 178–192. See Gen. Bib.

*Juliette Dor*

**SEE ALSO**

Balsam Garden; Brendan's Voyage, St.; Four Rivers of Paradise; *Imrama;* Paradise, Travel to

# Cog

A sailing cargo vessel originating along the coasts of the North and Baltic seas. Associated in particular with the cities of the Hanseatic League, cogs are depicted on the seals of many northern European cities. In 1962, dredging crews working in the Weser River at Bremerhaven uncovered the nearly-complete hull of a late fourteenth-century cog. Since then several other cogs have been excavated. This combination of iconographic and archeological evidence makes the cog one of the best understood medieval ship types.

Short in proportion to its breadth, it had straight stem and sternposts with a centerline rudder hung from the sternpost. It was clinker-built, that is, each of the broad planks that made up the hull overlapped the one below it and was fastened to it by iron nails. Light superstructures, often called "castles," were raised on the hull—a relatively large one aft, and frequently a smaller one forward. Propulsion was by a single large square sail carried on a mast stepped amidships.

By 1200, the cog was the most common merchant vessel of the Hanse cities, and had spread quickly over the Baltic and North Sea area. By comparison to the descendants of Viking cargo ships, the cog's advantages were that it was cheaper to build and the stern rudder made it easier to handle. They were made of sawn rather than split planking, a technique that produced more planks from a tree and required less skilled labor; their simplified construction further reduced the cost.

Cog, showing the addition of a number of features of the hulk, the great seal of Gdansk, 1400. After Heino Wiechell. *Das Schiff auf Siegeln des Mittelalters und der beginnenden Neuzeit.* Lübeck: Kultusverwaltung, 1971.

Moreover, the rudder mounted on the sternpost and turned with a tiller was more efficient than steering oars for ships of this size (large cogs could reach 250 tons capacity).

Designed and built as carriers for bulk cargo, cogs were pressed into service as warships, transformed by the simple expedient of filling them with soldiers. Though cogs were neither fast nor maneuverable, their high sides were defensible, and the castles at either end provided elevated fighting platforms. Since the Hanse cities had no navy, and northern European kings maintained only a few royal ships, large numbers of merchant cogs could be armed and pressed into service when a fleet was needed. Crusaders from these northern seas certainly traveled in cogs into the Mediterranean in the thirteenth century, but the design apparently made little impression on the southern sailors, and the caravel-built, lateen-sail-powered "nef" continued to be the large sailing cargo vessel of the Mediterranean in the thirteenth century.

Around 1300—the Florentine chronicler Giovanni Villani specifically says that it was in the summer of 1304—cogs began to be used by sailors from Mediterranean ports. The first mention of a *cocha* (as cogs were called in Italian) at Venice was in 1315. By this time the cog was fully developed, and its virtues were perhaps more clearly apparent to the southern seamen than in

the preceding century. There were also changes in the Mediterranean maritime economy that made the cog an attractive alternative to the nef. The chief advantage of the cog was in its square sail. The lateen rig of the Mediterranean could, perhaps, sail a little closer to the wind than the square-rigged cog. But in tacking, the lateen yard had to be swung from one side of the mast to the other. These yards were huge, often longer than the ship itself, so this change required a large crew and was a dangerous operation. To shorten sail when the wind rose, it was necessary to lower the huge lateen yard to the deck and bend on a smaller sail; a large nef might carry two or three of these sails on as many masts. The cog's single square sail could present either edge to the wind (it was prevented from curling under by a bowline), eliminating the need to manhandle the yard. Reefpoints and bonnets made it possible to adjust the size of the sail to the force of the wind without changing the entire sail. Thus it was possible to sail a cog with a smaller, and therefore cheaper, crew than a comparably sized nef.

By the beginning of the fifteenth century, fleets of cogs were common in Italian mercantile city-state commerce. The adoption of the cog by the sailors of Barcelona, Genoa, Venice, and other Mediterranean ports marked the beginning of a dramatic cross-fertilization between the shipbuilding traditions of northern and southern Europe.

**BIBLIOGRAPHY**

Crumlin-Pedersen, Ole. "Danish Cog Finds." In *The Archaeology of Medieval Ships and Harbours in Northern Europe.* Ed. Sean McGrail. Oxford: British Archaeological Reports, 1979, pp. 17–34.

Dotson, John E. "Jal's *Nef X* and Genoese Naval Architecture in the Thirteenth Century." *The Mariner's Mirror* 59 (1973): 161–170.

Lane, Frederic C. *Venetian Ships and Shipbuilders of the Renaissance.* Baltimore: Johns Hopkins UP, 1934. Revised edition, *Navires et Constructeurs à Venise pendant la Renaissance.* Paris: S.E.V.P.E.N., 1965.

McGrail, Sean, ed. "The Cog of Bremen and Related Boats of the North Sea." In *The North Sea: A Highway of Economic and Cultural Exchange.* Ed. Arne Bang-Andersen, Basil Greenhill, and Egil Harald Grude, Stavanger: Norwegian UP, 1985.

Unger, Richard W., ed. *Cogs, Caravels, and Galleons: The Sailing Ship 1000–1650.* London: Conway Maritime Press, 1994.

Villain-Gandossi, Christiane, Salvino Busuttil, and Paul Adam, eds. *Medieval Ships and the Birth of Technological Societies, Vol. 1: Northern Europe.* Malta: European Coordination

# C

Centre for Research and Documentation in Social Sciences, 1989.

Wiechell, Heino. *Das Schiff auf Siegeln des Mittelalters und der beginnenden Neuzeit.* Lübeck: Kultusverwaltung, 1971.

John E. Dotson

**SEE ALSO**

*Barca;* Bruges; Galley; Ghent; Hanse, The; Mediterranean Sea; Navigation; Navigation, Viking; Ships and Shipbuilding

## Coinage and Money

Coinage of precious metal, chiefly gold and silver, stood at the base of much medieval trade. In some periods and regions, barter played an important role, and by the end of the Middle Ages transfer of money through letters became possible, but most transactions involved the use of metal of known fineness, either in ingots stamped with recognizable validating images or in coins.

Coins were always issued by an individual or group with recognized political standing, but in medieval Europe this could include bishops, abbots, and abbesses, as well as kings, dukes, counts, and communes. Each minting authority could issue coins of a fineness, weight, and appearance of its own choice, and coins of various issuers often circulated side by side. Individuals engaged in commerce would have had to recognize and know the value of a large number of coinages; money changers made a profession of such knowledge. In most periods, a few coinages were known and recognized well beyond the region of their minting and could stand as a means of exchange and a standard against which other coinages could be measured.

Late Roman coins, especially the gold *solidus,* stood at the basis of the Byzantine, Islamic, and European coinages that developed in the early centuries of the Middle Ages. The solidus of about 4.5 grams of fine gold continued unchanged in the Byzantine Empire, where it took on the name *nomisma* in Greek sources and *bezant* among Latins. Silver coinage was issued sporadically in the Byzantine system, but does not appear to have been of much importance in trade, and copper coinage was used only for low-level transactions.

Islamic rulers adapted the solidus by replacing the images with sacred texts for their coin, which they called a *dinar,* and which was referred to as a *mancus* in Europe. The Islamic silver coin, of significant use in commerce, was derived from that of the Sassanian Empire; it was known as a *dirham.* There was also a copper coinage called the *fals.* In some periods the coinage

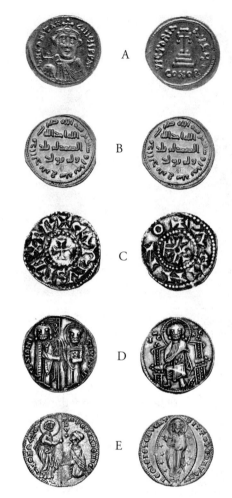

Fig. A) Byzantine gold solidus of Constans II (641–646).
Fig. B) Umayyad gold dinar A.H. 78 (687–698 C.E.).
Fig. C) Charlemagne (768–814) silver penny, Aachen mint.
Fig. D) silver grosso, Venice, doge Pietro Gradenigo (1289–1311). Fig. E) gold ducat, Venice, doge Pietro Ziani (1205–1229). Courtesy of the American Numismatic Society, New York.

was standard throughout the Islamic world, but at other times it varied from region to region. Islamic coins were usually weighed rather than counted in transactions.

The coinage of the early European rulers was based on the *tremissis,* one-third of the Roman solidus. In most European states, the gold tremissis was the only coinage minted in the sixth and seventh centuries. These coinages were gradually debased in alloy, and by the eighth century the coinage of Europe had become mainly silver, bringing an end to the age of gold.

The central Middle Ages was the period of the silver penny. Shortly before the year 800, Charlemagne reformed the coinage throughout his kingdom, which included much of continental Western Europe. He issued silver coins of a single standard, the *denarius* (penny), with occasional issues of half-pennies, *oboles*. These coins were counted in a system that used the term *solidus* (shilling) for twelve pennies and *libra* (pound) for 240 pennies. This system was taken up in England under Offa of Mercia (r. 757–796), and was introduced into northern and eastern Europe as coinage spread into these areas.

As the unity of the Carolingian Empire diminished in the ninth and tenth centuries, pennies originating in different regions of Europe took on individual identities in terms of appearance and standard. A few of these became recognized for a consistent value and served as the basis for long-range trade. After undergoing periodic recoinages through the Anglo-Saxon period, the coinage of England was fixed at an unchanging standard with the sterling penny of Henry II initiated in 1180, and its use eventually extended as far away as the Aegean. In France, the coinages of Tours and Melgueil (near Montpellier) were among the most important, while in Germany, that of Cologne set the standard. In Italy, the coinage of Lucca supplied the needs of Tuscany, while Pavia and Milan supplied those of Lombardy, and Verona those of the northeast. In the course of the twelfth century, new mints in Genoa, Pisa, and Bologna, among other cities, supplemented this coinage.

The coinage of Byzantium maintained its importance through the period, but the gold nomisma underwent a series of debasements in the eleventh century. Under Alexius I Comnenus (1081–1118), gold coinage was restored, based on the *hyperperon,* which was somewhat less fine than the earlier standard. In the Islamic world, the coinages of various dynasties became distinctive in terms of appearance and standard. Islamic coinage became so important in the trade of the Mediterranean that it was imitated by Christian rulers in Spain, southern France, Amalfi, Norman Sicily, and the crusader states of the Levant.

In contrast to earlier periods, the late Middle Ages was characterized by the diversity of denominations. The dominance of the penny was broken in Europe in the thirteenth century, as mints began to issue larger silver denominations and gold coins as well as low-value coins of almost pure copper. The move to heavy silver coins started in Italy, with the introduction of the *grosso* in Venice and Genoa around the year 1200 and from the mints of other city-states in succeeding decades. It spread northward with the *gros tournois,* to England with the *groat,* and to central and eastern Europe with the *groschen.* In southern Italy the silver *gigliato* became the standard coin of trade.

Gold coinage was reintroduced into Latin Europe by Frederick II Hohenstaufen with his *augustale,* initiated in 1231. In 1252, both Florence and Genoa initiated coinages in gold on the same standard: both the *florin* and the *genovino* were of pure gold and weighed just over 3.5 grams. Of the two, it was the florin that became dominant in trade, especially in Western Europe, the Rhineland, and even the North Sea area. In 1285, Venice introduced its own gold coin, the *ducat,* on virtually the same standard as the florin and the genovino. The ducat quickly became the basic coin of the trade of the eastern Mediterranean, eventually replacing the coinages of Byzantium and the Islamic mints in this commerce.

By the end of the Middle Ages, the coins used in European and Mediterranean trade were very diverse and variable, but all could be related to a single value, that of the florin and the ducat.

**BIBLIOGRAPHY**
Grierson, Philip. "Numismatics." In *Medieval Studies, An Introduction.* Ed. James M. Powell. 2nd edition. Syracuse: Syracuse UP, 1992, pp. 114–161.
———, and Mark Blackburn. *Medieval European Coinage, 1: The Early Middle Ages (5th–10th Centuries).* Cambridge: Cambridge UP, 1986.
Spufford, Peter. *Handbook of Medieval Exchange.* London: Royal Historical Society, 1986.
———. *Money and Its Use in Medieval Europe.* Cambridge: Cambridge UP, 1988.

*Alan M. Stahl*

**SEE ALSO**
Amalfi; Byzantine Empire; Economics and Trade; Frederick II; Genoa; Pisa; Venice

## Columbus, Christopher (1451–1506)

Sailor, first European known to have voyaged to the Americas, and author of several works about his experiences and geographical theories.

Christopher Columbus [Colón] was born in Genoa, Italy. He became a sea captain sailing and trading in the Atlantic Ocean from the shores of West Africa to the coast of Iceland. He is credited with the first sustained contact with the Western Hemisphere.

Medieval legends and seamen's lore told of lands across the Atlantic Ocean. For example, Arabic sources related

# C

reports of ocean voyages of exploration by West African fleets in the Middle Ages, while European fables told of early medieval travelers such as the Irish St. Brendan; material and literary evidence supports Viking attempts to explore and to establish a colony along the northeastern coast of North America. Columbus undoubtedly heard many of these and other stories of voyages to the West, which added to his desire to cross the great ocean.

Christopher Columbus's discovery of the New World was both an intellectual and a practical feat. By the end of the thirteenth century, the bulk of Greek, Roman, and Muslim science had been made available to and assimilated by European scholars. Columbus was well enough read in cosmographical, geographical, and travel literature to envision and plan a voyage across the Atlantic. He also held the requisite navigational and sailing skills to accomplish such a voyage. Transoceanic travel was safer by the late fifteenth century due to technological advancements in sail design, use of the Catalan rudder, compasses, trigonometric tables, nautical charts, and pilot books. Columbus was among the first to realize and exploit the implications

Christopher Columbus. *Eyn schön hübsch lesen von etlichen insslen.* Strasbourg: Bartholomäus Kistler, 30 September 1497, sig. A1r. Woodcut of title page of the German translation of Columbus' *Letter to Sanchez* showing Jesus Christ commissioning the King of Spain and Columbus to evangelize among native peoples of the Americas. Reproduced by permission of the Map Division, The New York Public Library (Astor, Lenox and Tilden Foundations).

of nautical science and technology developed during the late Middle Ages.

It is uncertain when Columbus first conceived his plan to cross the Atlantic Ocean to reach Asia. Most likely, it began to develop when he lived in Porto Santo in the Madeira Islands. Moving to Portugal and then to Spain after his wife died, he eventually settled at the Franciscan convent of La Rabída where he studied scientific and religious materials in the convent's large library and conversed with resident scholars. He began building his own library of books, in which he made careful marginal notations. From the books that survive today, it appears that Pierre d'Ailly's *Imago mundi* (*c.* 1410) and Aeneas Sylvius Piccolomini's *Historia rerum ubique gestarum* (*c.* 1460) made the strongest impressions on him. Both were compilations of medieval cosmology and geography. Also of great importance in his intellectual development concerning an Atlantic crossing were the correspondence and map drawings of the fifteenth-century Florentine humanist, physician, and geographer Paolo Toscanelli.

Once Columbus had assimilated information from the learned men of the past and of his own time, he distilled it through his own extensive experience as navigator, ship's captain, and ocean voyager. After being turned down in a request for support from the king of Portugal, he appealed to King Ferdinand and Queen Isabella of Castile and Aragón for government backing for his transatlantic voyage. They forwarded Columbus's appeal to a learned commission for advice.

It has long been popular to describe the learned council of theologians and university professors that met to discuss Columbus's proposal as having their collective heads in medieval sand. Columbus, on the other hand, has been portrayed as an avant-garde Renaissance activist frustrated by righteous, dogmatic, and superstitious "old guard" pedagogues. In reality, the learned commission had every right to be skeptical. Columbus presented them with a jumble of ancient and medieval cosmographical and geographical sources, data from dubious medieval travelers, and inaccurate mathematical calculations on the size of the world. The Salamanca Commission knew from the latest theories and mathematics that the world was much larger and the Atlantic Ocean much wider than Columbus was willing to admit. The commission also knew that fifteenth-century technology and logistics were inadequate for a proposed voyage from Iberia to Japan. They advised the monarchs against supporting Columbus's enterprise.

The commission had not considered other important factors, however. No one could have known that at approximately the location Columbus theorized for Japan lay a huge landmass that made the actual size of the earth a relatively insignificant issue for the survival of the fleet. The other factor was Columbus's strong credentials as a potential explorer. Although his theoretical knowledge was based on ancient and medieval scholarship, he was willing to challenge both texts and the lore of centuries. He was also a practical sailor with an extraordinary skill in navigation and a profound understanding of the Atlantic wind and current system. Furthermore, he held the sincere conviction that God had destined him to make the voyage.

Eventually rejecting the advice of their own commission, Ferdinand and Isabella gave Columbus the backing for a voyage, which by 1492 had been labeled the "Enterprise to the Indies." On August 3, 1492, Columbus set sail from Palos de la Frontera with three ships. Using his learning, skills, perseverance, and the latest technology, Columbus altered the course of world history. He sailed first to the Canary Islands and then headed straight west. On October 12, one of his sailors sighted an island in the Bahamas.

He sailed four times to the new hemisphere, never comprehending that he had discovered a new continental landmass, but believing himself to be among the outer islands off the coast of Asia. On the second voyage, he established a colony, La Isabela, on the north coast of Hispaniola (the island that now is divided into the Dominican Republic and Haiti), settling a population of approximately 1,500. On his third voyage, he reached the mainland of South America, and on his fourth voyage, he coasted up and down Mesoamerica.

Columbus, a man firmly rooted in, and sustained by, the medieval past, ended the isolation of the two hemispheres and ensured that humankind would henceforth be global in its culture, politics, and economy.

### BIBLIOGRAPHY

The Christopher Columbus Encyclopedia. Ed. Silvio Bedini. 2 vols. New York: Simon & Schuster, 1992.

The Diario of Christopher Columbus's First Voyage to America 1492–1493. Ed. and trans. Oliver Dunn and James Kelley. Norman: Oklahoma UP, 1989.

Fernández-Armesto, Felipe. Columbus. Oxford: Oxford UP, 1991.

Flint, Valerie I.J. The Imaginative Landscape of Christopher Columbus. Princeton: Princeton UP, 1992.

Henige, David. In Search of Columbus. Tucson: Arizona UP, 1991.

The Libro de las profecías of Christopher Columbus. Ed. and trans. Delno West and August Kling. Gainesville: UP of Florida, 1991.

Morison, Samuel Eliot. Admiral of the Ocean Sea: A Life of Christopher Columbus, 2 vols. Boston: Little, Brown, 1942.

Phillips, William, and Carla Phillips. The Worlds of Christopher Columbus. Cambridge, Cambridge UP, 1992.

Provost, Foster. Columbus: An Annotated Guide to the Scholarship on His Life and Writings 1750–1988. Detroit: Omnigraphics, 1991.

Taviani, Paolo. Christopher Columbus: The Grand Design. London: Orbis, 1985.

West, Delno. "Christopher Columbus and His Enterprise to the Indies: Scholarship of the Last Quarter Century." The William and Mary Quarterly 49 (1992): 254–277.

†Delno C. West

### SEE ALSO

Ailly, Pierre d'; Antillia; Azores; Behaim, Martin; Brendan's Voyage, St.; Canary Islands; Exploration and Expansion, European; Four Rivers of Paradise; Franciscan Friars; Genoa; Geography in Medieval Europe; Iceland; India; Indians and the Americas; Jewish Travelers; Las Casas, Bartolomé de; Lignum Aloes; Nao; Navigation; Navigation, Arab; New World; Nicholas of Lynn; Pius II; Popes; Portuguese Expansion; Ptolemy; Rosselli, Francesco; Ships and Shipbuilding; Spain and Portugal; Toscanelli, Paolo dal Pozzo; Viking Discoveries and Settlements; Vinland Sagas; Wild People, Mythical, and New World Relations

## Commercial Law

*See* Law, Commercial

## Commynes, Philippe de (*c.* 1447–1511)

Soldier, statesman, diplomat, and courtier, best known for his *Mémoires,* a first-person recollection of his experience in the service of Charles the Bold, duke of Burgundy (r. 1467–1477); Louis XI of France (r. 1461–1483); Charles VIII (r. 1483–1498); and Louis XII (r. 1498–1515).

Composed over three periods between 1489 and 1498, the *Mémoires* constitute an important source for the evolution of "new monarchy" and the balance of power in late-fifteenth-century England and continental Europe, providing narrative accounts of the pivotal contest between the Valois monarchs of France and the

# C

Duchy of Burgundy during the decades following the Hundred Years War; French relations with England during the final stage of the Plantagenet dynastic struggle (the so-called "War of the Roses") under Henry VI (r. 1422–1461), Edward IV (r. 1461–1483), Richard III (r. 1483–1485), and Henry VII (r. 1485–1509); and French involvement in the politics of Renaissance Italy, culminating in the ill-fated French invasion of the peninsula in 1494. In spite of this wealth of detail, the *Mémoires* must nevertheless be used with caution. Commynes routinely inverts chronology and omits facts that might tarnish the reputation of his principal patron, Louis XI, and expose the author's own role in several significant political intrigues, including Commynes's defection from the service of Charles the Bold to Louis XI between 1468 and 1472, and his later involvement, after Louis XI's death, in a conspiracy against the regent Princess Anne de Beaujeu (d. 1552) that resulted in a six-year period of imprisonment and political disgrace (1485–1491).

Although Books VII and VIII of the *Mémoires* contain lengthy discussions of political conditions and architectural landmarks in the Renaissance republics of Florence, Venice, and Genoa, Commynes demonstrates limited knowledge of areas outside Western Europe; he reflects the spirit of his time in being so preoccupied with politics that he excludes consideration of the role of commerce in the events he describes. The author freely admits ignorance of affairs in Asia and Africa, while his account of politics in the Ottoman sultanate (under Mohammed the Conqueror [r. 1451–1481]), and the kingdom of Hungary (under Ladislaus V [r. 1439–1457] and Matthias Corvinus [r. 1458–1490]) are overly reliant on rumor and gossip. The merchant fleet of the Hanseatic League is alluded to only in the context of Hanseatic privateering forays, and he mentions the burgeoning Portuguese slave trade in Africa only to argue that peoples of the East contend even more brutally with one another than do his fellow Europeans.

More significant than any facts Commynes chooses to record, then, is the wealth of insight his *Mémoires* afford into the mentality of Europeans during the fifteenth century, a transitional era during which medieval religious and political institutions were being challenged and reshaped by the rise of the modern territorial state. As expressed in his *Mémoires,* Commynes's outlook epitomizes these developments. A descendant of urban parvenus and minor Burgundian nobility, Commynes was typical of those within his class who sought advancement in the service of Renaissance monarchs. His analysis of contemporary European politics evinces a clear admiration for those who exercise power, tinged with a slight disdain for men of merchant estate (note, for example, his assessment of Lorenzo de Medici). Commynes's acute psychological awareness of his patrons as individuals, including the fatal impetuousness of Charles the Bold and the religious and political anxieties of Louis XI, are all keenly observed and reported.

The author's appreciation of the ways in which the course of events may fall hostage to the idiosyncrasies of great men furnishes a rationale, in Commynes's judgment, for their reliance on the assistance of savvy advisors such as himself, and on the emerging art of diplomacy to which he dedicated his career (note Books I.9; II. 6–8; V.7). His *Mémoires* represent arguably one of the richest vernacular sources for the mechanics of fifteenth-century European statecraft, containing numerous references to the diplomatic activity of ambassadors, envoys, and heralds, as messengers, negotiators, and spies (note Books II.2; III.8; IV.3–11; V.1, 16; VI.8, and VII.19–20). If Machiavelli's *Prince* offers a primer for politicians that appears to reject the ethical constraints of medieval mirrors for princes, the *Mémoires* of Philippe de Commynes can perhaps be considered a useful complement in providing a revealing synthesis of moral prescription and illustrative narrative.

## BIBLIOGRAPHY

Bittmann, Karl. *Ludwig XI und Karl der Kuhne: die Memoiren des Philippe de Commynes als historiche Quelle.* Gottingen: Vandenhoeck & Ruprecht, 1964.

Commynes, Philippe de. *Mémoires.* Ed. Joseph Calmette. 3 vols. Paris: H. Champion, 1924–1925.

Dufournet, Jean. *La destruction des mythes dans les mémoires de Philippe de Commynes.* Geneva: Droz, 1966.

Lettenhove, Kervyn de. *Lettres et negociations de Philippe de Commines.* 3 vols. Brussels: V. Devaux, 1867–1874.

*The Memoirs of Philippe de Commynes.* Ed. Samuel Kinser. Trans. Isabelle Cazeaux. 2 vols. Columbia, SC: U of South Carolina P, 1969.

*Emily Sohmer Tai*

SEE ALSO

Ambassadors; Diplomacy; Genoa; Hanse, The; Hungary; Slave Trade, African; Spies; Venice

## Compass, Magnetic

A navigational instrument that gives the direction or heading relative to the magnetic pole; it consists of a magnetized needle free to rotate above a circular plate inscribed with various directions (the "compass card"). In its original "wet" form (a magnetized needle floating in a bowl of water inscribed with directions), the compass was discovered by Chinese diviners between the first and sixth centuries C.E. The modern "dry" compass, which uses a pivot to position the needle above the compass card, was also developed in China, during the early twelfth century. Both types of compass appear in European records for the first time in the mid-twelfth century.

The first clear European references to the magnetic compass appear in the works of the English monk and scholar Alexander Neckam (1157–1217), the French poet Guyot de Provins (fl. 1184–1210), and the French historian and bishop Jacques de Vitry (c. 1165–1240). Neckam's *De nominibus utensilium* (c. 1175–1183) and *De naturis rerum* (c. 1197–1204) describe the use of a dry compass by sailors to establish direction when the skies are too cloudy to observe the sun or stars. Guyot's satirical *La Bible* (c. 1205) explains how mariners magnetized a needle by rubbing it against a lodestone; it was then placed inside a hollow straw, and carefully floated in a bowl of water, where it would indicate magnetic north (clearly a description of the "wet" compass). Jacques de Vitry briefly mentions the compass in his *Historia Orientalis seu Hierosolymitana* (c. 1218–1225), a history of the Holy Land.

No twelfth- or thirteenth-century author considers the magnetic compass a novelty. Most refer to its use onboard ships in a matter-of-fact way, leading historians to suggest that the instrument was already commonplace in Europe by the mid-twelfth century. Yet this knowledge was primarily empirical; theoretical explanations of the magnetic compass largely begin in the thirteenth century. Medieval scholars were divided about the reasons for the magnetic compass's activity; authors like Jacques de Vitry and the Flemish encyclopedist Thomas of Cantimpré (c. 1201–1270/2) attributed it to an attraction between the magnetic needle and Polaris, but rivals such as the French Dominican Vincent of Beauvais (c. 1190–1264) and the German theologian Albertus Magnus (c. 1200–1280) argued instead that the needle was attracted to the North Pole. Meanwhile, the English Franciscan philosopher and scientist Roger Bacon (c. 1213–1292) posited that the four cardinal points of the heavens all attracted the compass needle.

The most important discussion of magnetism and the compass in medieval European documents was the *Epistola Petri Maricourt ad Sygerum de Foucacourt Militem, de Magnete* (1269), written by the French mathematician and physicist Petrus Peregrinus (fl. 1261–1269). He described both "wet" and "dry" compasses in detail, explaining their behavior as the result of an attraction between the needle and the geographic or celestial pole. Peregrinus also demonstrated the fundamental law that like magnetic poles repel, and unlike ones attract. A triumph of experimental and theoretical reasoning, the *Epistola* also included descriptions of several additional magnetic instruments, including a "dry" compass with an attached scale, a combination "wet" compass and sighting tool, and even a magnetically powered perpetual motion machine.

Some historians have suggested that medieval accounts of compass needles following the small circle of Polaris and other objects indicate a primitive understanding of magnetic variation, but the documents are uncertain. The compass actually points toward the magnetic pole, not the geographical one, and the angle of difference between the two (the magnetic variation) depends on the observer's position. However, the first clear description of magnetic variation does not appear in European records (maps, documents, and sundials) until the mid-fourteenth century. Knowledge of variation in China begins in the late Tang period (eighth and ninth centuries C.E.), and the earliest Chinese account occurs in the chronicler Shen Gua's *Meng Qi Bi Than* (c. 1088).

It was not until the Scientific Revolution (1500–1700) that the modern explanation of the magnetic compass was developed. The English scientist William Gilbert (1544–1603) argued in his revolutionary *De Magnete* of 1600 that the earth was essentially a giant lodestone containing north and south magnetic poles, to which the compass needle was directed. The displacement of these poles from geographic north readily accounted for the phenomenon of magnetic variation.

**BIBLIOGRAPHY**

Mitchell, A. Chrichton. "Chapters in the History of Terrestrial Magnetism." *Terrestrial Magnetism and Atmospheric Electricity* 37 (1932): 105–146; 42 (1937): 241–280; 44 (1939): 77–80.

Mottelay, Paul Fleury. *Bibliographic History of Electricity and Magnetism.* London: Charles Griffin, 1922.

Peregrinus, Peter. *Epistola de Magnete.* Trans. H.D. Harrandon and Sydney Chapman. In "Archaeologica Geomagnetica," *Terrestrial Magnetism* 48 (1943): 1–17.

Smith, Julian. "Precursors to Peregrinus: The Early History of Magnetism and the Mariner's Compass in Europe." *Journal of Medieval History* 18 (1992): 21–74.

*Julian A. Smith*

# C

SEE ALSO
Albertus Magnus; Jacques de Vitry; Lodestone; Navigation;
Navigation, Arab; Navigation, Chinese; Thomas of
Cantimpré; Vincent of Beauvais

## Confucianism

A Western designation for an indigenous Chinese philosophy, cultic system, and bureaucratic order that for most of history provided the worldview, value system, and primary machinery of governance for China, as well as for other civilizations (Korea, Japan, and Vietnam) that came under its influence.

Confucianism derived its name from the Chinese philosopher Confucius [Kongfuzi / K'ung-fu-tzu, "Master K'ung"] (551–479 B.C.E.) who lived in the Zhou dynasty (1122–256 B.C.E.) during a period of increasing social and political upheaval. Confucius saw himself not as the creator of a new philosophy but as the transmitter of a revered tradition inherited from ancient sage kings. He was concerned with the restoration of societal harmony and balance through a return to the way of those sage kings who had governed righteously and had established a system of rituals and decorum that came to serve as a compass for life in a hierarchically ordered aristocratic and monarchical society. The Confucian teaching, then, was intensely humanistic, focusing primarily on the realm of familial, social, and political relationships. Civic, societal, and domestic harmony could be achieved through just and competent governance and through individual moral and ritual cultivation emphasizing learning, particularly the mastery of a select corpus of canonical texts. This Confucian canon was adopted as the basis for state ideology in the Han dynasty (206 B.C.E.–220 C.E.) and remained so for most of China's subsequent history. Entry into the bureaucracy and one's level within that administrative order eventually became contingent on one's performance in state-sponsored examinations that tested knowledge of those texts.

In view of this orientation, the Confucian approach to trade, travel, and exploration was ambivalent. On the one hand, since the tradition from the beginning was concerned primarily with governing the Chinese polity, it had little concern for what lay beyond China's borders. Held in the sway of this prevailing sinocentric attitude, Confucianism lacked the soteriological urgency and expansive concern for humanity that propelled missionary religions like Manichaeism, Christianity, Islam, and Buddhism outward across ethnic, cultural, and political boundaries. Confucians saw themselves as the conservators of Chinese civilization. Non-Chinese barbarians were welcome to learn and partake of the benefits of the Confucian system, but if they failed to do so, they alone in their obtuseness and intransigence bore the blame. From the Confucian perspective, the barbarian world beyond China had little to offer other than tribute and recognition of China's superiority and hegemony. Furthermore, the Confucian emphasis on moral rectitude that disregards pecuniary or utilitarian considerations meant that in the scheme of societal occupations, merchants and commerce were, at least theoretically, held in low esteem. Consequently, the Confucian tradition was not inherently disposed to promoting the aspirations of the commercial class.

This standard, but admittedly one-sided, view of Confucianism as being indifferent, if not obstructive, to trade, travel, and exploration must be balanced, however, by the fact that, given its rational and pragmatic approach to the world, Confucianism as the main bureaucratic and literary tradition of China was concerned with both the proper administration of the empire and ultimately its economic welfare. Consequently, Confucians made significant contributions to the creation of a dynamic commercial civilization, the production of a vast geographical literature, and the development of a sophisticated cartography, all of which facilitated commerce and communication in East Asia.

Following centuries of division between a barbarian-occupied north and a Han-dominated south, the reunification of China under a centralized Chinese state in the Sui dynasty (581–617 C.E.) and the subsequent creation of a cosmopolitan empire under the Tang (618–907 C.E.) were characterized by a greater prominence accorded to Confucian learning and administrative principles. The new Confucian state brought about political and economic integration through the completion of the Grand Canal, providing a commercial and administrative link between the political centers of the north and the increasingly prosperous Yangtze valley in the south. Furthermore, by promulgating new law codes and instituting civil service examinations based on the Confucian classics, the Sui and Tang dynasties created a politically stable environment in which trade prospered. The militarily expansive Confucian state of the early Tang contributed further to this prosperity by opening the Central Asian silk route and by attracting trade and tribute missions from surrounding states. Confucianism during this period further acted as a catalyst in the creation of a greater East Asian civilization by drawing into China's cultural orbit surrounding states like Korea and Japan that sought to adopt Confucian learning and system of government.

In the Song dynasty (960–1279), Confucianism played an even greater role in Chinese society as the government became more strongly centralized, the civil service examination system was expanded, and Confucianism revitalized itself (through the movement known as Neo-Confucianism) by creating its own metaphysical underpinning, thereby rivaling the systems of Buddhism and Taoism. During this period, Confucianism, through governmental policies and efficient local administration, helped create an unprecedented dynamic commercial culture that predated similar economic advancements in Europe by centuries. Confucianism must thus be acknowledged for its role in creating the prosperous civilization and fabulous wealth that was witnessed by European observers in the subsequent Yuan dynasty (1271–1367), and that consequently became a key impetus inspiring the age of European outreach and exploration.

Travel within China itself appeared to have dramatically improved with the expansion of the economy that took place in the Song period. One measure of this improvement was an increase in religious pilgrimages to sacred sites. Although Confucianism cannot be said to be the inspirational force behind such pilgrimages, imperial sponsorship of many of these sites, particularly of the Five Sacred Peaks, in which Mount Tai Shan occupied the most prestigious position, was an essential element in the development of such pilgrimages. Confucian scholar-officials were not averse to visiting, writing about, and painting sacred sites that were Buddhist or Taoist in inspiration. Yet Confucian literati also created and frequented in great numbers their own places of remembrance, such as the tomb of Confucius and the White Deer Hollow Academy in Kiangsi, which was founded by the great Neo-Confucian Zhu Xi [Chu Hsi] (1130–1200).

The Mongol rule of China in the Yuan period was characterized by the adoption of a Confucian system of government, a process that in no small measure was due to the persuasion of a Kitan aristocrat and former Jin (1115–1234) official, Yelü Chucai [Yeh-lü Ch'u-ts'ai] (1190–1244). Famous for his promotion of the Confucian cause under three Mongol khâns (Chinggis, Ögedei, and Khubilai), Yelü Chucai is also celebrated for his contributions to astronomy and to travel and exploration. His *Record of a Journey to the West* (*Xiyou lu*) documented an expedition to Persia that he made in the company of Chinggis Khân between 1219 and 1224.

The role played by Confucianism in Chinese exploration of course far exceeded this one instance. Exploration was frequently a by-product of the Chinese empire's military and diplomatic dealings with the outside world. During the Tang dynasty, for example, the source of the Yellow River was confirmed by a military operation and a diplomatic mission to Tibet. Perhaps the most famous exploration was that associated with the seven imperially sponsored maritime expeditions led between 1405 and 1438 by Zheng He [Cheng Ho], a eunuch admiral of the Ming period (1368–1644). Although he came from a Muslim background, his enterprise was nonetheless an expression of a self-confident Confucian state seeking international recognition of its power and prestige. Zheng He's flotillas, consisting of dozens of large ships bearing tens of thousands of men, secured tribute states throughout southeast Asia and reached all the way across the Indian Ocean to the east coast of Africa. The far-reaching nature of these expeditions attested not only to the seemingly ubiquitous nature of Chinese maritime commerce but also to the expansive vision of the early Ming state before it retreated into a defensive posture in the latter half of the fifteenth century, which left the seas open for the Western expansion of the sixteenth century.

The aforementioned developments in Chinese trade and travel were accompanied by and contingent on an exponential increase in geographical knowledge, beholden in part to the Confucian tradition. The origins of Chinese geographical literature can be traced back to a Zhou dynasty Confucian canonical text, the *Classic of History* (*Shu Jing*), which contains the Yü Gong (Tribute of Yü) chapter, describing the types of soils, characteristic products, and waterways of the traditional nine provinces. The concerns evidenced in this classic were addressed and broadened in subsequent periods through the production of a seemingly unbroken and voluminous stream of geographical literature in diverse genres, including entries in the official histories, anthropological geographies, descriptions of the

# C

southern regions and foreign countries, travel accounts, hydrographic books, geographical encyclopedias, and local topographies (gazetteers).

The growth of geographical literature was also accompanied by advances in cartography that produced scientifically based land maps constructed on grids as well as accurate navigational charts. Although advances with regard to geographical knowledge were made in all periods of Chinese history, those that took place through the work of scholars like Jia Dan [Chia Tan] (fl. 770) and Shen Gua [Shen Kua] (1031–1095) during the Tang and Song periods are especially noteworthy since they far outpaced the comparatively meager advancements of medieval Europe both in terms of quantity and quality.

**BIBLIOGRAPHY**

Gernet, Jacques. *A History of Chinese Civilization.* 2nd edition. Cambridge: Cambridge UP, 1996.

Graham, A.C. *Disputers of the Tao: Philosophical Argument in Ancient China.* La Salle, IL: Open Court, 1989.

Naquin, Susan, and Chün-fang Yü, eds. *Pilgrims and Sacred Sites in China.* Berkeley: U of California P, 1992.

Needham, Joseph. *Science and Civilisation in China.* Vols. 2, 3. 1953; rpt. Cambridge UP, 1962.

*Daniel Getz*

**SEE ALSO**

Buddhism; China; Karakitai; Manichaeism; Mongols; Navigation, Chinese; Silk Roads; Taoism; Tibet; Yuan Dynasty; Zheng He, Admiral

## Constantinople

Capital of the Roman Empire in the East (Byzantine Empire) and one of the most popular destinations of medieval travelers from the East and West. The city's wealth, opulence, and enormous storehouse of relics drew a constant stream of merchants, mercenaries, pilgrims, and sightseers.

Constantinople stood at one of the most important crossroads in the Western world. It not only commanded the Bosporus, the only seaway between the Mediterranean and Black seas, but was also perched on the tip of Thrace, making it the most convenient overland crossing between Europe and Asia. Western pilgrims to Jerusalem often passed through Constantinople, and it therefore became an important entry in travelers' accounts and guidebooks. Even those who made the trip by sea often stopped at Constantinople,

either because they were aboard merchant vessels that had business there, or because they did not want to miss the spectacle of the greatest city in Christendom.

For those who sailed up the Bosporus and caught their first glimpse of it, Constantinople did not disappoint. Surrounded on two of its three sides by water, the city rose out of the Bosporus, spilling, into the distance, across its seven broad hills. After the sixth century, a traveler would first notice Justinian's magnificent church, Hagia Sophia, visible from every direction. Sailing closer, the visitor would make out more churches, and then palaces, and then the forest of monumental pillars rising from the city at various points. Those who approached at night would see the blazing lighthouse that bellowed loud warnings during high winds, and the brightly lit dome of Hagia Sophia.

Most important for Western pilgrims were the churches, monasteries, and relics that Constantinople safeguarded. No city, not even Jerusalem or Rome, had so large a collection of holy objects. Byzantine guides not only ushered travelers between churches but also pointed out the vast forums, the enormous walls, the crowds of bronze statues, and the monumental hippodrome. Travelers who wrote of their experience did their best to relate the city's wonders, but were unable to do them justice. Robert of Clari's sentiments, in the *Conquête de Constantinople* (c. 1205), are typical: "If anyone should recount to you the hundredth part of the richness and the beauty and the nobility that was found in the abbeys and in the churches and in the palaces and in the city, it would seem like a lie and you would not believe it."

Travelers' accounts describing Constantinople do not begin until the eighth century, and are not very numerous before the twelfth century. Among the earliest Western narratives are those of Arculf's travels to the Holy Land (probably c. 680), and the legations of Liudprand of Cremona (940–968). Constantinople also figures highly in the travels of Sigurd, the future king of Norway, who visited the city on his way to Jerusalem about 1111. More informative is the *Itinerary* of Benjamin of Tudela, who was in Constantinople around 1170; he described Hagia Sophia, the hippodrome, the city's great wealth, and the condition of Constantinople's Jewish population. He is also remembered for his indictment of the citizens of the city for their lavish lifestyle and disdain for martial skill.

Arab travelers also frequently visited the city. Harūn-ibn-Yahya was a reluctant traveler, having been captured by Byzantine troops in Syria in 911; nevertheless, he wrote a useful account of the city. Marvazi, an Arab naturalist who traveled around 1030, described in great detail the Byzantine army, administration, religion, sciences, and arts. He also recorded the state of women in Constantinople and described the city's festivals and the games in the hippodrome. A century later another Arab, al-Idrīsī, journeyed from his home in Morocco to Constantinople to collect material for a geographical compendium. Around 1170, the Arab traveler ʿAlī al-Harawī also sailed to Constantinople and left a written record of his travels.

The last medieval traveler to describe Constantinople before its devastation by the Fourth Crusade in 1204 was Robert of Clari, himself one of the crusaders. Robert's description of the "marvels" of the city was the most complete at that time. With a naive willingness to believe anything the Greeks told him, Clari marveled over the many churches and relics and statues he saw. Like other Westerners before and after him, Clari believed that many of the pagan relics of antiquity were filled with powerful spirits. In the years after Clari, travelers tended to avoid Constantinople. The Latin Empire was in a permanently bad state, always teetering on the brink of destruction. Most of the city's attractions, its relics and great wealth, had been shipped to the West in 1204. The population of the city shrank to about one-tenth its previous level.

Despite its dilapidated state, Constantinople drew travelers from the West after the restoration of the Byzantine Empire in 1261. William of Boldensele visited the city in the 1330s, and his description of it became the basis for the prominent account in *The Book of John Mandeville*. Ludolph von Suchem visited the city around 1340, remarking on Hagia Sophia, the colossal statue of Justinian, and the ruins of the old imperial palace (he too was indebted to William's book). Fourteenth- and fifteenth-century Russian travelers also made their way south to visit the seat of the Orthodox faith. Stephen of Novgorod, the Anonymous Russian, Ignatius of Smolensk, and Alexander the Clerk visited Constantinople between 1349 and 1395, and wrote their own descriptions of the city.

Even as the Byzantine capital was shorn of its empire by the Ottomans, it remained a favorite destination for Westerners. As Renaissance ideas took hold in Europe, Constantinople's ancient past began to displace its remaining relics as its greatest attraction. Ruy Gonzales de Clavijo visited Constantinople in October 1403 on his way to meet with Tamerlane on behalf of King Enrique III of Castille. Cristoforo Buondelmonti, a Florentine priest, visited the city in order to include it in his geographical studies, which included the earliest surviving map of Constantinople. Others, like Johann Schiltberger, Bertrandon de la Broquière, Zosima the Deacon, and Pero Tafur, also visited Constantinople in the years preceding its conquest by the Ottomans in 1453.

**BIBLIOGRAPHY**

Ebersolt, Jean. *Constantinople byzantine et les voyageurs du Levant.* Paris: Leroux, 1919.

Majeska, George P. *Russian Travelers to Constantinople in the Fourteenth and Fifteenth Centuries.* Washington, DC: Dumbarton Oaks, 1984.

Van der Vin, J.P.A. *Travelers to Greece and Constantinople. Ancient Monuments and Old Traditions in Medieval Travelers' Tales.* Leiden: Nederlands Historisch-Archaeologisch Instituut te Istanbul, 1980.

Wright, Thomas, ed. *Early Travels in Palestine.* London, 1848; rpt. New York: AMS Press, 1969.

*Thomas F. Madden*

**SEE ALSO**

al-Idrīsī; Arculf; Benjamin of Tudela; Byzantine Empire; Crusade, Fourth; Eastern Christianity; La Broquière, Bertrandon de; Liudprand of Cremona; Ludolf of Suchem; *Mandeville's Travels;* Muslim Travelers and Trade; Ottoman Empire; Pilgrimage, Christian; Pilgrimage Sites, Byzantine; Schiltberger, Johann; Tamerlane; William of Boldensele

## Córdoba

A city in the southern Spanish region of Andalusia, on the river Guadalquivir, 82 miles (131 km) upstream from Seville. The capital of Muslim Spain in the tenth and eleventh centuries and a noted center of crafts and learning, Córdoba became a strategic urban military base after its reconquest by the Christians in 1236, and remained a commercial crossroads between the south of Spain, Muslim Granada, and Castile.

The prosperous Roman agricultural colony of Corduba declined in the fourth century C.E., losing to Hispalis (Seville) its position as the capital of Roman Baetica. It came under Visigothic control in 459, but soon regained virtual independence, finally falling to the Visigoths only in 584. Córdoba remained a lesser regional center until its conquest by a detachment of

# C

the army of Tāriq ibn Ziyād in 711. In 717, it regained its political primacy, becoming the capital of Muslim Spain (al-Andalūs), but economic growth was delayed by factional strife and a Berber revolt that erupted around 740.

Córdoba flourished under the Umayyads (756–1016), who made it the seat of the western caliphate in 929. Home to at least 100,000 inhabitants, it was the most populous urban center in Western Europe, renowned above all for its luxury crafts (leatherworking, woodcarving, glazed tiles, pottery). Intellectual tolerance during the prosperous reigns of 'Abd al-Rahmān III (912–961) and al-Hakam II (961–976) also made Córdoba a focal point for manuscript copying and for the dissemination of scientific knowledge. Of Córdoba's many private and institutional libraries, that of al-Hakam II reputedly held 400,000 volumes. Yet the city's position as a dynastic power center and a crossroads for goods, people, and ideas also made it a hotbed of social, cultural, and religious unrest. In 818, the suburb of Shaqunda was obliterated after an uprising of *muladí* artisans and merchants (Christian converts to Islam). In 850–859, a revolt of the Mozarabs (subject Christians) shook Córdoba, and from 886 to 928 another *muladí* rebellion wracked southern Spain. Disaster struck when the power of 'Āmirid first ministers (976–1009) collapsed, leaving the city open to siege and plundering by insurgent Berbers in 1010–1013. The economic wounds healed only slowly under the weak regimes that ruled the city until 1069–1070, when it was annexed by the 'Abbādids of Seville.

The southward push of the Christian reconquest and the loss of Toledo by the Muslims in 1085 began Córdoba's fundamental transformation. From a dynastic court capital with a capacity to attract from all directions luxury goods, foreign merchants, learned men, poets, and musicians, the city sheltered by the northern mountain rampart of the Sierra Morena gradually became a key rear base for Muslim defense and a regional gateway for north-south communication between Muslim and Christian Spain. The arrival, in 1091, of the reforming North African sect of the Almoravids (al-Murābitūn) helped ease the Christian military pressure. Almoravid rule brought religious intolerance, but also political stability. Córdoba prospered once again, chiefly owing to links with North Africa, and its most splendid Umayyad monuments were finally completed. Briefly garrisoned by Alfonso VII of Castile in 1146, Córdoba remained Muslim for

another ninety years thanks to the North African Almohads (al-Muwahhidūn). In 1162–1163, the declining city became one last time the capital of al-Andalūs, but under the last Almohad caliph it sank into disarray and fell to King Ferdinand III in 1236.

Christian Córdoba fulfilled many of the functions of its Muslim predecessor, although some had become reversed. While the city remained a gateway for north-south trade, it now became a rear base for Christian thrusts directed southward against Muslim Granada. Quickly repopulated after its evacuation by the Muslims, it lost some settlers to Jaén and Seville when those were in turn conquered. The revolt of the Mudéjars (subject Muslims) in 1264, and the civil war between Sancho IV and his father, Alfonso X of Castile, in 1281–1284, sorely tested Córdoba's economy, as did warfare with Granada in 1326–1341. The subsequent spell of relative peace and unhindered commercial intercourse with Granada favored the city, however. It experienced modest growth despite the plagues of the later fourteenth century. The new quarter of Alcázar Viejo was founded in 1399, and a century later Córdoba had some 40,000 inhabitants. In 1439–1476, the city suffered during the struggles between the oligarchic nobility and partisans of royal centralization in Castile. Urban factional strife accompanied the conflict between Infante Don Alfonso and Henry IV of Castile in 1465–1468, and the contest over Henry IV's succession. Under the Catholic monarchs Ferdinand and Isabella, Córdoba remained an important interregional trade node between the Spanish south, Extremadura, and Castile. It enjoyed a reputation for fine crafts, wine, and horses, but the conquest of Granada in 1492 relegated it to the status of a quiet backwater.

## BIBLIOGRAPHY

Arjona Castro, A. *Andalucía musulmana, estructura político-administrativa.* Cordoba: Monte de Piedad y Caja de Ahorros de Córdoba, 1980.
———. *El reino de Córdoba durante la dominación musulmana.* Cordoba: Excma. Diputación Provincial, 1982.
Edwards, J. *Christian Córdoba. The City and Its Region in the Late Middle Ages.* Cambridge: Cambridge UP, 1982.
Knapp, Robert C. *Roman Córdoba.* Berkeley: U of California P, 1983.
Nieto Cumplido, Manuel. *Historia de Córdoba. Islam y Cristianismo.* Cordoba: Publicaciones del Monte de Piedad y Caja de Ahorros de Córdoba, 1984.

Scales, Peter C. *The Fall of the Caliphate of Córdoba: Berbers and Andalusia in Conflict*. Leiden: Brill, 1994.

Wolf, Kenneth Baxter. *Christian Martyrs in Muslim Spain*. Cambridge: Cambridge UP, 1988.

*Martin Malcolm Elbl*

SEE ALSO

Alfonso X; Black Death; Seville; Spain and Portugal


## Corporate Expulsion

*See* Expulsion, Corporate


## Cosmas Indikopleustes [Cosmas the "Indian Sea Traveler"] (fl. 540 C.E.)

The name used to refer to Constantine of Antioch, a merchant probably of Syrian birth who lived in Alexandria. A convert to Nestorian Christianity, Cosmas was the author of the *Christian Topography*, which attacked the idea of a spherical world as pagan and posited instead a universe shaped like an oblong and vaulted building.

Cosmas's book, written in Greek, survives in three manuscript copies and was almost certainly unknown to any geographer in the medieval West. Cosmas wrote his twelve-book *Topography* in the mid sixth-century, when theological disputes about the nature of Christ divided Christians into several groups, depending on the degree to which they recognized the divinity and/or humanity of Jesus (those believing in the dual nature of Christ were known as "dyophysites" in opposition to "monophysites" who believed in a single nature). At the same time, Christian theologians were attempting to reconcile Christian knowledge inerrantly recorded in the Bible with non-Christian (pagan) learning.

The author of the *Topography* actually signed his work with the name "Christian," perhaps preferring to disseminate his unconventional ideas anonymously. The name "Cosmas Indikopleustes" did not appear until the eleventh century, in manuscripts containing fragments of his commentaries on the Psalms and the Gospels, as well as geographical extracts from books of the *Topography*.

It is important to stress at the outset that Cosmas's complete book title (*Christian Topography of the Entire Universe*) underscores the author's intentions to describe cosmic space in a way that corresponds to Nestorian eschatological representations; the title does not refer particularly to the work's geographical contents. In calling his work a "Christian" topography, Cosmas makes it clear that he is proposing a system of the world in opposition to the theories of pagans and, worse yet, "false" Christians who espoused Greek scientific thought and advocated the idea of a spherical earth. Cosmas particularly attacks, without naming him, Johannes Philoponos, a monophysite commentator on Aristotle, whose *De opificio mundi* appeared as a rebuttal to the *Topography*.

Cosmas argued that "before the creation of the world" God ordained that human beings would need to pass through two stages of development: a kind of schooling or apprenticship and a state of happiness and perfect knowledge. To accommodate this development, God fashioned a universe as a "receptacle" to shelter these two stages. Cosmas relied on literal exegesis of the Bible, as conceived by the school of Antioch: in discussing the structure of the universe, he maintains that it can be ascertained from the specific description of the Holy Place, the Tabernacle of Exodus 25:10–21. The table within the Holy Place, nearly twice as long as it is wide, is our inhabited part of the earth; the molding of gold that surrounds it is the sea; the cornice is the earth beyond the ocean; and so on.

The universe is an "immense house" (*oikos pammegethis*), "vaulted and oblong." Divided into two regions or zones by the firmament (following the model of the Tabernacle divided by the veil into the Holy Place and the Most Holy of Holies), the universe is suited to sheltering the two states of humanity; the lower space is reserved for the "present condition"; the higher space is prepared for those people waiting to be resurrected from "among the dead" following the example of Christ, the only one to have ascended into the heavenly space during the time of the present condition.

Cosmas appears to have traveled a great deal and gathered firsthand information from people he saw, as well as from the merchants and Nestorian missionaries who came from the Orient to the Red Sea ports. He combined this experience with theological training to produce a cosmographical description of the "world here below." The geographical content of the work is, in the end, no more than a *parergon*, an appetizer in a universal chronicle that unites God, humans, and the universe in a single indivisible whole.

Blending the Bible with "scientific theory" badly understood, Cosmas represents the earth "suspended in

# C

nothingness," twice as long as it is wide. The earth, he contends, rises progressively from south to north, so that the rising altitude screens the movement of the sun around the earth, which is why it cannot be seen at night on a flat earth. The earth is divided by a sea into two parts, the *oikoumene* (inhabited world) and the "opposing world" or the "world beyond the ocean" (which Greek cosmographers called *antichthone* and medieval writers refer to as the antipodes) in the eastern part of which is Paradise. Humans inhabited that landmass until the Flood when Noah and his family miraculously sailed to "this" part of the world. The ocean, now uncrossable, surrounds the inhabited earth and intrudes on the mainland as four "gulfs": the "Romaic Gulf" (the Mediterranean Sea), the "Arabian Gulf" (the Red Sea); the "Persian Gulf" (the Indian Ocean, which reaches all the way to "Zingion," located at the frontier of Ethiopia and Barbary); and the "Hyrcanian Gulf" (Caspian Sea). Cosmas claims to have sailed into the first three of these gulfs. One day, approaching "interior India" (southern Arabia or modern-day India), he got dangerously close to the ocean, so that he was nearly pulled into the inescapable seas by the current.

The inhabited world is divided into three parts: "India" (Asia), "Lybia" (Africa), and Europe. It extends from "Tzinista" (China) to "Gaidera" (Cádiz) and measures (east to west) 400 days of thirty-mile walks, and (north to south) 200 days of thirty-mile walks from the far north to "Sassou" in southern Ethiopia, beyond which there is nothing but the ocean. Thus, Cosmas's *oikoumene* distinctly recalls the geographical information found in Eratosthenes (c. 275–194 B.C.E.) and Strabo (c. 64/63 B.C.E.–21 C.E.), while rejecting the earth's sphericity. Cosmas has not questioned such tenets of classical geography as the earth's east-west expanse doubling the north-south extent and the four great sea gulfs, of which the (landlocked) Caspian is one.

Cosmas joined to the polemics of this work descriptions of countries and the activities of their inhabitants, some more detailed than others. He merely mentions "Tzinista," which is found "in the most interior India of all," far beyond the Persian Gulf, and the island called Silediva by the Indians and "Taprobane" (presumably Sri Lanka) by the Greeks. He pauses to digress at length on the Red Sea basin, the country of the Himyarit, and Ethiopia with Sassou ("country of incense") rich in gold mines at its interior. Nearby, the inhabitants of Barbary mine gold and produce aromat-

ics, which they send to "Adoulia" near India and Persia. The merchants of Alexandria form convoys of some 500 men, transporting herds of cattle, blocks of salt, and iron, which they trade for gold nuggets in a speechless barter with an extremely reticent people (another story found in classical sources). On a voyage (c. 518–527) that brought him to the great empire of Axum [Aksum] (c. 1st–8th century) in northern Ethiopia, Cosmas transcribed two inscriptions, one telling of the exploits of Ptolemy Euergetes (246–221 B.C.E.), and the other relating to an Auxumite king.

The second-to-last book of the *Topography*, Book 11, is probably a version of the Book of Geography that Cosmas mentions in Prologue 1 (the work is now lost). In the Geography, evidently, Cosmas offered a description of "the entire earth, the part beyond the Ocean and this part (where we live) as well as all the countries." The book has two parts; in the first, Cosmas treats "Indian animals and trees": rhinoceros, buffalo, giraffe, yak, musk ox, unicorn, hippopotamus, seal, dolphin, tortoise, pepper plant, and the Indian walnut tree. Many of these animals are not native to India, but most are to Ethiopia, and thus Cosmas probably is not writing about the Indian subcontinent, but, like his contemporaries, using "India" as a toponym referring generally to Asia (including the west coast of the Red Sea). In the second part of Book 11, Cosmas describes the "Isle of Taprobane," the principal intermediary port in the commerce between China and "other markets." He lists the many exotic and precious commodities of the East and names principal ports for traders. He also reports on the "hyacinth" (jacinth) stone in a temple on Ceylon, Christians whose allegiance is to the church in Persia, the "White Huns" and their king, Gollias, and the use of elephants in making both war and spectacles.

Despite Cosmas's picturesque narratives, it remains uncertain if he ever personally visited India (the subcontinent). His report, a rather haphazard blend of travel experiences and poorly digested reading, comes with fragmentary documentation (at best), and its imprecise language lends itself to contradictory interpretations. Cosmas is not a geographer, nor did he intend to write a treatise on political and economic geography. A self-educated man who did not receive (and thus was not led astray by) "complete instruction for outsiders" (pagans of the Greek culture), a man "ignorant of the art of rhetoric," Cosmas was a devout man viscerally attached to the beliefs of his religious movement, which imposed a certain vision of the universe and of humanity. He lived on the borderline between two worlds and two cultures—Alexandria and Antioch, science and biblical revelation, Nestorianism and monophysism—and thus recorded a view of the world that is far from characteristic of geographical thought as it was developing in the medieval West.

Three magnificently illustrated manuscript copies of Cosmas's book are known: Rome, Biblioteca Apostolica Vaticana MS Vat. gr. 699 (a ninth-century copy made at Constantinople); Mount Sinai, Monastery of St. Catherine MS Sinaïticus gr. 1186 (an eleventh-century copy made in Cappadocia); and Florence, Biblioteca Laurenziana MS Plut. 9.28 (an eleventh-century copy made on Mount Athos).

**BIBLIOGRAPHY**
Cosmas Indicopleustes. *The Christian Topography of Cosmas Indicopleustes*. Ed. E.O. Winstedt. Cambridge: Cambridge UP, 1909.
————. *Topographie Chrétienne. Introduction, texte critique, illustration, traduction et notes*. Ed. Wanda Wolska-Conus. Paris: Editions du Cerf, 1968, 1970, 1973.
Wolska-Conus, Wanda. "La 'Topographie Chrétienne' de Cosmas Indicopleustès: hypothèses sur quelques thèmes de son illustration." *Revue des Etudes Byzantines* 48 (1990): 155–190.

*Wanda Wolska-Conus*

**SEE ALSO**
Animals, Exotic; Antipodes; Cádiz; Caspian Sea; China; Eastern Christianity; Elephants; Ethiopians; Geography in Medieval Europe; Gold Trade in Africa; India; Maps; Measurement of Distances; Nestorianism; *Oikoumene;* Paradise, Travel to; Pepper; Red Sea; Taprobane

## Costume, Oriental

Clothing that conveyed to the West the sense of remote and exotic cultures and that was minutely described in medieval travel narratives of journeys to the Orient or depicted in manuscript illuminations of such cultures.

Oriental visual arts from this period corroborate the styles these travelers claim to have seen and often provide additional information, giving precise and realistic details of length, color, and cut. A fifteenth-century copy of a Rashid al-Din *History of the World* manuscript providing an accurate record of a variety of Oriental clothing and hat styles is Paris, Bibliothèque Nationale MS Suppl. persan 1113. Especially interesting is folio 126v, which depicts Chinggis Khân, his wives, sons, and servants in ceremonial Chinese costume.

In contrast, European depictions of Asians often show them wearing European clothing styles, fanciful costumes drawn from the painter's imagination, or dress based loosely on Persian or Indian costumes that are used "generically" or as synecdoche for all foreign costume. Thus, the turbans oriental figures so often wear in European paintings actually belong not to the entire East, but rather to Indian, Persian, or Arabian costume, as seen, for example, in the early thirteenth-century illumination in Paris, Bibliothèque Nationale MS arabe 6094, fol. 68r; alternatively, these turbans may be derived from medieval gypsy costume, as some scholars have argued. The illuminations in the early-fifteenth-century *Le livre des merveilles,* Paris, Bibliothèque

Exotic hybrid Asian costume: Turban, Thracian boots, Asian scimitar. Veit Stoss, Vockamer monument, Church of St. Sebaldus, Nuremberg, Germany, c. 1499.

# C

Nationale MS, fr. 2810, associated with the Boucicaut workshop, and containing among other texts *The Book of John Mandeville,* often portray Asians dressed in slightly altered European styles, except for their hat styles, which are imaginatively exotic.

Mitter discusses the problem, in Western pictorial tradition, of visual stereotypes that were derived from classical accounts of the East, which resulted in Oriental costume being portrayed inaccurately in Western medieval manuscripts; an anonymous illuminator in the early fifteenth century, the Boucicaut Master, for example, paints Indian subjects wearing Western dress in Paris, MS fr. 2810. An additional distortion often occurs when travelers' reports, interpreted visually by illuminators, result in negative and even diabolic characteristics being used to sensationalize the scenes. A case in point is the late-fourteenth-century Italian manuscript now London, British Library MS Additional 27695, Folio 13, where the illuminator of Khubilai Khân at a banquet paints the Mongol ruler as an allegorical figure, Gluttony.

As with other Eastern products like ivory and spices, Asian costume and fabrics also became fashionable and influenced Western styles, sometimes provoking hostility. For example, the *escoffion,* the two-horned headdresses popular from 1380 to around 1410, and the fifteenth-century *hennin,* a tall, conical women's headdress with a thin veil waving from its peak, were based on similar headdresses worn by noble Chinese ladies. Their lavish character and strangeness made them a target for moralists, and they were regularly denounced as evil in medieval sermons and poems satirizing extremes in costume. Similarly, moralists denounced Oriental patterned fabric and embroidery, and Dante describes the diabolical Geryon's flanks painted with knots and circles like colorful Tartar and Turkish fabrics in *Inferno* 17.14–17.

Medieval travelers report costumes made in a variety of colors and fabrics, and even metallic materials. Dyestuffs were a prized commodity in Mongol culture since, according to Odoric of Pordenone, the colors worn in the khân's court revealed the status of the wearer; in order of descending status, garments were dyed green, red, and yellow. Indeed, his travel account indicates that everybody dressed in a single color on feast days, with the colors changed on succeeding days. On the occasion of his birthday, Khubilai Khân wore a robe of beaten gold, and his court followed suit. And every medieval traveler to the Orient describes costly

dyestuffs such as purple, which came from the New Sur area near Acre. Citing a priest in Cathay who wore a robe of lovely red cloth, William of Rubruck says that such fabrics might be dyed purple or scarlet employing the blood of wild men who could be captured when they were drunk on mead provided by hunters. These wild people in Tartar territory wore clothing of camel-hair felt, according to John of Plano Carpini, although William says that their bodies were covered with hair.

Fabrics mentioned for Oriental garments are silk in many colors, purple cloths, fine Persian linen, cotton, brocade or "baldakin," samite, cloth of gold, *mosulin* made in the kingdom of Mosul (southeast of Armenia), *nasich, nakh,* and "cramoisy" (a luxury fabric with decorative beasts and birds made in Baghdad), Persian silk called *yazdi* that the women embroider with bird and animal motifs, sendal from the province of Ch'êng-tu-fu, the world's finest camlets (made of camel hair, or of white wool called white camlets) from Kalachan in Egrigaia (province of Tangut) in Cathay, a variety of woolen fabrics, fine Indian buckrams, and Tibetan fustian.

According to travelers such as Marco Polo and Benjamin of Tudela, the finer fabrics of Asian costume were often decorated with gold and costly gems, some mythical. Marco Polo lists a variety of precious jewels, most commonly pearls but especially balass rubies, as well as lapis lazuli, jasper, and chalcedony. William of Rubruck speaks of a girdle decorated with a jewel that protects the wearer from thunder and lightning.

Oriental garment styles varied according to geographic area and the wearer's station in life. For example, Mongol men and women wore the same styles: thigh-length gowns made of material having a hairy side showing, with a back opening. Over these they wore buckram, scarlet, or brocade jackets of unusual design. It was forbidden to wash these garments, according to John of Plano Carpini; the women's garments were somewhat longer, and William of Rubruck states that married Tartar women wore a hooded nun-like garment that tied under the right arm. Marco Polo reported on poor Turcomans wearing clothing made of skins, Tibetans who dressed poorly in skins, canvas, and buckram, and noble ladies of Badakhsham wearing voluminous pleated trousers made from as many as 100 ells of cotton fabric.

Each division of the Mongol imperial guard, *Kashik,* wore uniforms of a distinguishing different hue. The *bahadur,* or life guard, wore black armor and a *kalat* (tunic) faced in red; his horse was black and bore a red harness and saddle, according to Chambers. The mounted archers of the Mongol army wore a uniform, a *kalat* that was either blue faced with red, or brown faced with blue for good weather. It was lined with fur, allocated according to rank, for the winter: officers wore wolf, fox, badger, and monkey fur, in increasing order of status; lower ranks wore dog and goat. Facings on officers' cuffs, collars, and edges of their *kalats* bore gold and silver embroidery. Blue or gray trousers, fur-lined when needed, and heavy-laced, flat-soled leather boots completed the uniform. Each wore a long, loose, raw silk undergarment as protection against lethal arrow wounds since an arrow would push the silk into a wound ahead of it, and the silk would assist in the arrow's removal in a reverse procedure. An illumination in the BN Rashid al-Din manuscript previously mentioned, folios 180v–181ru, shows Mongol archers in battle gear.

In addition to the protective silk undertunics, the Mongols possessed a wide variety of other kinds of armor. Cavalry horses wore head, shoulder, and chest armor, and the khân's elephants had leather armor, according to Marco Polo. The heavy cavalry wore mail coats and oxhide cuirasses or hide-covered scales of iron as well as iron helmets, while the light cavalry fought without armor or wore either a cuirass made of strips of lacquered leather or soft armor consisting only of a quilted tunic; some wore leather helmets. Marco Polo also describes armor made of buffalo skin or other tough boiled leather, including cuirasses and corselets.

The Mongols' standard weapons for light cavalry included a small sword and several javelins, while heavy cavalry equipment consisted of a scimitar, battle-ax or mace, and a twelve-foot lance with a hook below its blade topped by a horsehair pennant; both light and heavy cavalry carried two bows (for short and long range), a minimum of 120 arrows in two quivers, a lasso, and a dagger.

Besides providing warmth in military dress, furs were important in civilian dress. Among those listed by travelers such as Benjamin of Tudela and William of Rubruck are Russian white squirrel, which yields both sable and ermine, and a spotted fur with a high sheen worn by Mangu Khân. Marco Polo mentions ermine, sable, lion fur, and *papiones,* similar to fox, as well as vair and black fox. William of Rubruck recounts the custom of possessing two gowns made from northern furs, one worn fur-side in, and the other with fur turned outward and ordinarily fashioned from wolf, fox, or badger hides.

Hats, also, varied according to status. Portraits of Khubilai Khân and his wife, Chabi, in the National Palace Museum, Taipei, show him wearing a fitted cap with a small turned-back fold around the face edge, while his wife wears a headdress that is a tall edifice elaborately decorated with pearls in a variety of designs, and pearl-decorated bands that go under her chin. Additional pearl clusters and pendulums hang from these bands where earrings would be attached. Women of high status wore the round *botta* head ornament, of light material with a steep pointed tube that towers above it. This construction was covered with silk and decorated with quills, peacock feathers, mallard duck tail feathers, and jewels. William of Rubruck explains that a hat with a hole for this spire held the edifice in place.

**BIBLIOGRAPHY**

Ayer, Jacqueline. *Oriental Costume.* New York: Scribner, 1974.

Baltrušaitis, Jurgis. *Le Moyen Age fantastique: antiquitiés et exotismes dans l'art gothique.* Paris: A. Colin, 1955.

Chambers, James. *The Devil's Horsemen: the Mongol Invasion of Europe.* New York: Atheneum, 1979.

Cuttler, Charles D. "Exotics in 15th-Century Netherlandish Art: Comments on Oriental and Gypsy Costume." In *Liber Amicorum Herman Liebaers.* Ed. Franz Vanwijngaerden, et al. Brussels: Les Amis de la Bibliothèque royale Albert 1er, 1984, 419–434.

Grousset, René. *Chinese Art & Culture.* Trans. Haakon Chevalier. New York: The Orion P, 1959.

Lee, Sherman E. *A History of Eastern Art.* New York: Harry N. Abrams, 1964.

Meiss, Millard. *French Painting in the Time of Jean de Berry: The Boucicaut Master.* New York: Phaidon Publishers Inc., 1968.

Mitter, Partha. *Much Maligned Monsters, History of European Reactions to Indian Art.* Oxford: Clarendon P, 1977.

Rice, David Talbot. *The Illustrations to the World History of Rashīd al-Dīn.* Ed. Basil Gray. Edinburgh: Edinburgh UP, 1976.

[Exhibition catalogue] *Tresors d'Orient: Paris: Paris, 14 juin-fin octobre 1973.* Paris: Bibliothèque Nationale, 1973.

*Laura F. Hodges*

**SEE ALSO**

Benjamin of Tudela; Dyes and Pigments; India; John of Plano Carpini; *Mandeville's Travels;* Marco Polo; Mongol Army; Mongols; Odoric of Pordenone; Textiles, Decorative; Tibet; William of Rubruck

# C

## Cotton World Map (Anglo-Saxon Map)

A map from the tenth or eleventh century that is extremely important because, though drawn in England, it is likely the closest copy known of a Roman world map that is thought to have been a highly influential source for geographical particulars in many other medieval world maps. P.D.A. Harvey suggests that the Cotton "Anglo-Saxon" Map may be "a direct descendant," though "perhaps not a very good copy," of the map that Augustus's son-in-law, Marcus Vipsanius Agrippa, produced in late-first-century Rome, which in turn was possibly based on Julius Caesar's 44 B.C.E. world survey. Consequently, this map does not reproduce the diagrammatic representation of the world—deriving from the tripartite T-O plan (see Maps) or the climate-based zonal map structure—that one sees in a large portion of other *mappaemundi* from the European Middle Ages plan.

East is at the top of the map, with Great Britain clearly positioned in the lower left-hand (northwest) corner. The Italian peninsula is comparatively very large. The map's southern and western edges may be distorted so that it fits the page on which it was drawn: the delta of the Nile, for example, starts in the south, but then the river quickly turns due east; also, the southwestern tip of Britain's exaggerated Cornish peninsula comes very close to northwestern Spain (Harvey claims that this last feature may actually be faithful to the map's Roman original). Mountains are rendered in green, and Middle Eastern and African bodies of water appear in red. Now in the British Library (MS Cotton Tiberius B.V, f.56v), the map derived its name from Sir Robert Cotton (1571–1631), who owned in the seventeenth century the collection of Anglo-Saxon writings of which the map is part.

**BIBLIOGRAPHY**

Harley-Woodward. *The History of Cartography.* Vol. 1. See Gen. Bib.

Harvey, P.D.A. *Medieval Maps.* Toronto: U of Toronto P; London: British Library, 1991.

*Joseph D. Parry*

SEE ALSO

Agrippa's World Map; *Mappamundi;* Maps

## Cresques, Abraham (1325–1387)

Mapmaker of *converso* (Jewish convert) background from Palma de Mallorca. He describes himself as a

Abraham Cresques's Catalan Atlas, oriented to the north. Detail from the extreme north-northeast (upper-right corner) showing the ocean east of Asia and Antichrist, *c.* 1375. Paris, Bibliothèque Nationale. Six double panels 25 inches × 19½ inches (65cm × 50 cm) after facsimile in Georges Grosjean, ed. *Mapamundi: The Catalan Atlas of the Year 1375,* tr. B.M. Charleston, Dietikon-Zurich: Graf, 1977. Reproduced by permission of the Map Division, The New York Public Library (Astor, Lenox and Tilden Foundations).

"master of *mappaemundi* and compasses." Cresques drew portolans and made instruments for Peter IV and John I of Aragon, though the best-known work attributed to him is the magnificently decorated Catalan Atlas of about 1375 presented to Charles V of France or his son; his wife helped him in his mapmaking work and the family tradition was continued by his son, Jafuda (1350–1410).

**BIBLIOGRAPHY**

*Der Katalanische Weltatlas.* Ed. G. Grosjean. Dietikon-Zurich: Graf, 1977.

*Michael Jones*

SEE ALSO

Atlas; Compass, Magnetic; *Mappamundi;* Maps; Portolan Charts

## Crusades, First (1095–1099), Second (1146–1148), and Third (1188–1192)

Papally sanctioned military expeditions, most frequently destined for Palestine. Their leading participants took vows to fulfill specific aims, such as the liberation of Jerusalem, which entitled them to receive a remission of sins in the form of an indulgence. When Pope Urban II preached the First Crusade at Clermont-

Ferrand in November 1095, he unleashed a force that was to change the face of medieval Europe. The concept of religious warfare as a penitential act, coupled with the allure of Jerusalem, the most potent Christian pilgrimage site, proved to be enormously attractive. Urban's appeal prompted a fervid response, and a force, which probably numbered approximately 100,000, set out for the East. When, against all odds, this army actually succeeded in recapturing Jerusalem from the Muslims in 1099, the Latin world saw this as a demonstration that the crusaders really were fighting with God's support. The crusading movement never completely lost the mystique that this initial victory inspired, and it continued to command a unique appeal in the West for a number of centuries.

In the first 100 years, the crusades were mainly preoccupied with defending the Latin settlements in the East that had been established in the wake of the First Crusade. The two largest crusades of the twelfth century, that which occurred in 1147 in response to the loss of Edessa, and that which took place between 1188 and 1192 after the fall of Jerusalem to the Muslim ruler Saladin (1174–1193), have been numbered by modern historians as the Second and Third Crusades. During this period there were, however, a number of smaller crusading expeditions that sought to bring aid to the Catholic peoples settled in the Levant. The popularity of the crusading movement, the size and number of expeditions that it prompted, and the foundation of an isolated Latin foothold in the Holy Land undoubtedly led to changes in the understanding of the Muslim world and prompted growth in Mediterranean travel and trade.

The journeys that the crusader armies had to make to northern Syria and Palestine presented enormous logistical difficulties. The leaders of the First Crusade decided to take the land route to the East, first congregating at Constantinople and then traveling across Asia Minor as a relatively coherent single force. The crusaders must have had some advanced knowledge of the terrain they would encounter since the region lay on the traditional pilgrim route to Jerusalem, and the Byzantine Emperor Alexius I Comnenus (1081–1118) had also provided them with Greek guides. In spite of this, the Latins still suffered serious losses to the depredations of the environment, disease, and, above all, shortages in supplies. One narrative source records that the crusaders suffered so badly from a lack of water during the crossing of the Taurus Mountains in Asia

Minor that "men and women endured wretched tortures, such that the human mind dreads," and on a single day 500 people died. Recent scholarship has demonstrated that, during this journey, the crusaders would have lost almost all of their heavy warhorses, which, it had previously been suggested, would have given them a marked military advantage against the lightly mounted Seljuk Turks. The primary sources reflect the fact that the Latins were obsessed with the shortage of horses, and one eyewitness even wrote that "many of our knights had to go on as foot-soldiers, and for lack of horses we had to use oxen as mounts."

To combat these problems, the crusaders established friendly relations with the indigenous Armenian Christians, who could provide markets for supplies, and during the extended siege of Antioch (October 21, 1097–June 3, 1098), they organized a system of foraging centers to feed the army. In spite of these measures the journey to Jerusalem continued to take its toll, and during the expedition as a whole far more crusaders lost their lives to starvation and disease than in actual battle.

The Second Crusade was an enormous venture, a Catholic offensive on three fronts. Pope Eugenius III (1145–1153) issued crusading indulgences not only for an expedition to the East, but also for an extension of the crusade into Spain and for a German campaign against the Wends. Although the armies traveling to the Holy Land considered sailing to the East from Norman Sicily, they eventually elected to follow the land route. Thus the French contingent under Louis VII and the German force under Conrad III left for Constantinople in June 1147. Although careful preparations for the journey had been made, including the strengthening of roads and bridges along the route, the Latins once again faced the dangers of crossing Asia Minor. On this occasion, however, not only did they experience logistical difficulties, but they also faced a far more concerted Muslim opposition to their advance. Successive waves of first German and then French soldiers were repelled, and in the end only a limited force was able to reach Syria by taking ship from the coast of Asia Minor.

By the time of the Third Crusade, the sea route to the Holy Land had come to be favored. Although the German Emperor Frederick I Barbarossa (1152–1190) led his army across Asia Minor, the contingents from France and England both sailed from western Europe. Moving such large forces by sea presented its own

# C

problems, not the least of which was financial. King Philip II of France (1180–1223) turned to Genoa to provide the necessary ships, forming an agreement that was an important precursor to the fateful treaty made between the city of Venice and the Fourth Crusaders in 1201. Sailing en route to the East with the English fleet, King Richard the Lionheart seized the island of Cyprus from the Greek Isaac II Comnenus in May 1191. This conquest was to prove to be the most enduring legacy of the crusade, since the island, which was to remain in Latin hands for nearly 400 years, lay on a vital trade route between East and West.

Early medieval Europe was not totally ignorant of the geographical and political environment of Syria and Palestine because of the ongoing pilgrim traffic to Jerusalem, but the establishment of a Latin presence in the East, which was to survive for almost 200 years, inevitably led to much greater contact with, and understanding of, the Levantine world. It is clear that the early Latin settlers rapidly realized that they would have to enter into a degree of coexistence with the indigenous peoples of the East. These included Eastern Christians such as Armenians, Nestorians, and Jacobites; Jews; and, of course, Muslims of both the Sunni and Shi'i branches of Islam. The Latins had to develop policies for dealing with both the indigenous communities living under their rule and those inhabiting lands that bordered on their settlements.

In territories under Latin rule, it appears that religious diversity was tolerated to a degree, as the followers of alternative forms of Christianity, as well as of Judaism and Islam, were allowed to practice their faith, albeit with some restrictions. It is important to remember, however, that there was significant regional variation in the distribution of these peoples, so that one must be careful not to make generalizations about their treatment. In the north, the county of Edessa was predominantly populated by Armenian Christians, and the Latins who settled there seem to have entered into a relatively high level of intermarriage with the native population. The Latins of Antioch tolerated the presence of large numbers of Greek Orthodox and Armenian Christians in the northern half of the principality and of Muslims to the south, but this led to a considerable degree of instability within its borders. When the Antiochene army was decimated in the battle of the Field of Blood in 1119, the Latin patriarch of Antioch had to rouse the remaining garrison of the city to prevent the population from rebelling against Frankish rule. The sources demonstrate that in the kingdom of Jerusalem, Muslims and Jews living in cities were forced to pay a poll tax, although native Christians and Jews were permitted to maintain their own civil law courts.

The Latins who settled in the East also entered into a degree of peaceful contact with neighboring Muslim powers. Political and social reality dictated that they could not pursue the cause of holy war interminably, and diplomatic contact with the wider Muslim world meant that mutually beneficial trade links could be developed. Latin rulers might also arrange temporary peace treaties with Muslim powers if it was to their political advantage. When, in 1183, Saladin took Aleppo, Bohemond III of Antioch arranged a three-year truce with the sultan in order to gain time to strengthen his own defenses. On occasion, such contact could even culminate in military cooperation. In 1115 a united Latin army under Baldwin I of Jerusalem and Roger of Antioch joined forces with Muslim troops from Damascus and Aleppo to meet the threat posed by the large army sent by the sultan of Baghdad.

Over time, and through increasing contact, the Latins of the East naturally learned more about Syria and Palestine, and with this knowledge came not only toleration but also a degree of cultural assimilation. Although the evidence is limited, we do know that Frankish settlers adopted some aspects of Eastern lifestyle, including dress, eating habits, and the use of *hamam* (Eastern bathing establishments). One contemporary Latin author, Fulcher of Chartres, noted in the 1120s that "we that were Occidentals have become Orientals." These changes were most noticeable when new Western Europeans arrived in the East either on pilgrimage or crusade. The participants of the Second Crusade were apparently shocked by the Eastern habits of the Franks, while the contemporary Arab writer Usamah ibn-Munqidh (1095–1188) wrote that on one occasion, when he was staying with the Templars in Jerusalem, a Latin who was newly arrived in the Holy Land tried to prevent him from praying in the direction of Mecca. Although there is clear evidence of tolerance and coexistence, however, relations with the Muslim world were still dominated by conflict, and when peace treaties were made, they were generally regarded as temporary expedients rather than as permanent truces.

The course of the early crusades and the establishment of the Latin settlements in the East also affected the pattern of Mediterranean trade. Commercial links between western Europe and the Middle East had certainly existed before the advent of the crusade, but after the First Crusade both the dimension and scope of contacts increased. Although some overland routes did remain open, the most important form of transport was by sea, and because of this, the independent Italian cities of Genoa, Pisa, and Venice came into prominence. The growth of trade benefited both sides. The Latins in the East needed a lifeline to the West, through which they could receive resources, especially manpower, and they also needed to add a naval element to their military capabilities. From an early date the Frankish leaders in the East demonstrated that they were determined to forge close links with the West. Indeed, in 1098, even before the capture of Jerusalem, Bohemond of Taranto granted the Genoese trading rights and a commercial quarter in the city of Antioch. The early Latin settlers also placed considerable importance upon capturing the coastal cities of Syria and Palestine in order to ensure their access to the Mediterranean. The key ports of Latakia, Tripoli, Beirut, and Acre had all been occupied within a decade of the fall of Jerusalem; Tyre was taken in 1124. The potential benefits for the Italian cities were also great. By lending their naval might to the Franks, they gained the opportunity to exploit the extremely profitable trade in Eastern goods, such as glass, sugar, textiles, and, perhaps most important, spices. They were also able to establish an important foothold in the Levant, and the trading concessions and lands they were granted meant that they rapidly developed significant political power in the Latin East.

**BIBLIOGRAPHY**

Cahen, Claude. *La Syrie du Nord à l'époque des Croisades et la principauté franque d'Antioche.* Institut français de Damas. Bibliothèque orientale 1. Paris: Geuthner, 1940.

France, John. *Victory in the East: A Military History of the First Crusade.* Cambridge and New York: Cambridge UP, 1994.

Mayer, Hans Eberhard. *Geschichte der Kreuzzüge.* Stuttgart: Kohlhammer, 1965. Trans. as *The Crusades.* Trans. John Gillingham. London, 1972; Oxford: Oxford UP, 1988.

———. "Select Bibliography of the Crusades." In *A History of the Crusades,* Vol. 6. Ed. H.W. Hazard and N.P. Zacour. Madison: U Wisconsin P, 1989.

Phillips, Jonathan P. *Defenders of the Holy Land: Relations between the Latin East and West, 1119–1187.* Oxford: Clarendon; New York: Oxford UP, 1996.

Riley-Smith, Jonathan S.C. *The Crusades: A Short History.* London: Athlone P; New Haven: Yale UP, 1987.

*Thomas S. Asbridge*

**SEE ALSO**

Acre; Crusade, Fourth; Crusade, Fifth; Eastern Christianity; Edessa; Genoa; *Mandeville's Travels;* Mediterranean Sea; Nestorianism; Pilgrimage, Christian; Pisa; Popes; Saladin; Seljuk Turks; Venice

## Crusade, Fourth (1202–1204)

A crusade that was proclaimed by Pope Innocent III in 1198 and began forming in 1199, when leading barons of northern France took the cross. Because they contracted with the Republic of Venice for three times more ships and food than they ultimately required, the crusaders were forced by circumstance and penury to attack the Christian cities of Zara and Constantinople in 1203. After a series of events culminating in the sack of Constantinople in April 1204, the campaign ended and the Latin Empire was born. Thus, as a result of this crusade, the Byzantine Empire ceased to exist until 1261, when the capital was finally recaptured.

Shortly after his election as pope in 1198, Innocent III proclaimed a new crusade to reclaim Jerusalem. In 1199, at a tournament hosted by Thibaut of Champagne at Ecry, the assembled nobles, which included Thibaut's cousin, Count Louis of Blois, took the cross and made preparations for their departure the following year. Soon other magnates, like Baldwin of Flanders and Hugh of St. Pol, also donned the cross.

The experience of Richard I (the Lionheart) on the Third Crusade (1188–1192) taught the barons that it was much easier to travel to the East by sea rather than risk the dangers of foreign lands with little enthusiasm for itinerant armies of crusaders. Richard had also believed that the key to Jerusalem was Egypt. The barons decided, therefore, to sail directly to Cairo. Since the rank-and-file crusaders would not have favored such a destination, the decision to attack Egypt was kept secret.

Since few of the Frankish nobles had ships, they sent six envoys with sealed blank parchments (the medieval equivalent of blank checks) to contract for vessels at a Mediterranean port. One of these envoys was Geoffroi de Villehardouin (*c.* 1160–*c.* 1213), the marshal of Champagne, who would later write his memoirs—one of the most valuable sources for the crusade. The envoys chose Venice, since they could find more ships there than elsewhere. They arrived in March 1201 and met with Doge Enrico Dandolo (1192–1205). Dandolo, who was in his nineties and blind, helped move

# C

their request through the republic's councils, which finally accepted the proposal. In the end, Venice agreed to provide transport and provisions for 33,500 men and 4,500 horses for one year at a cost of 85,000 silver marks. The vessels were to be ready when the crusaders converged on Venice in June 1202. In addition, Venice agreed to join the enterprise with 100 war galleys, provided that the Venetians received an equal share in the booty. The treaty was signed by both parties and confirmed by the pope.

While the envoys were in Venice, Thibaut of Champagne became ill and died. The leadership of the enterprise was then offered to Marquis Boniface of Montferrat. Powerful in northern Italy, the Montferrat clan also had close ties with the Byzantine Empire and the Latin Kingdom of Jerusalem. Boniface accepted the offer.

The numbers of men who took the cross were large, but not so large as the envoys had projected. That single miscalculation lay behind all of the crusade's later problems. Altogether, the crusaders that arrived at Venice numbered around 10,000: only one-third the number expected. For their part, the Venetians had performed a herculean task with amazing efficiency, enlisting or constructing a huge fleet to carry an army of 33,500. They had also secured vast stores of provisions. But the Franks could not pay for all that they had ordered. Even after turning over all their money, they were still short 34,000 silver marks. Months dragged by as the Venetians and Franks waited for more crusaders to arrive. Few did.

Finally, Doge Dandolo convinced his countrymen to allow the crusaders to leave the lagoon with a promise to pay their remaining debt from captured booty. Yet even this put Venice at considerable risk, given that no one knew when or if sufficient booty would be seized and sent back. In compensation for the loan and the risk, Venice asked the Franks to assist them in a siege of the rebellious city of Zara (Zadar) on the Dalmatian coast. Zara was a Christian city, then under the protection of King Emeric of Hungary (1196–1204), who had himself taken the crusader's vow. If the Franks refused, however, it would mean the dissolution of the enterprise. The crusaders accepted Venice's terms. Shortly afterward, Dandolo himself joined the crusade.

In October, the fleet set sail from Venice and appeared at Zara on November 10. Despite a papal letter threatening excommunication for an attack on the city, the crusaders captured Zara, sacked it, and took up residence there for the winter. The Franks later asked for and received papal absolution for their part in the attack, but the Venetians, who saw no sin in their action, remained excommunicates for the rest of the crusade. Of this they were ignorant, since the pope's formal letter of excommunication was suppressed by the crusade leaders.

During the winter at Zara the crusaders received envoys from the court of Philip of Swabia (rival emperor from 1198 to 1208). Philip's father-in-law was the previous Byzantine Emperor Isaac II Angelus (1185–1195), who had been deposed and blinded by his brother Alexius III (1195–1203). Isaac's son, a young man also named Alexius, escaped from his uncle's guards in 1201 and made his way to the court of his sister, Irene, and brother-in-law, Philip of Swabia. He spent Christmas 1201 there, along with Philip's vassal and the new leader of the crusade, Boniface of Montferrat. Undoubtedly the two talked about events in Constantinople, and probably they discussed the possibility of using the crusade to depose Alexius III and install the young Alexius Angelus. But it was no more than talk. Boniface did not then, nor would he ever, wield more than titular leadership over the crusade.

At Zara, Philip of Swabia's envoys presented to the crusaders the plight of the young Alexius. They begged the knights to come to the aid of this young man bereft of his patrimony by his uncle's tyranny. They implored them to perform an act of Christian charity, not only for the youth, but for the people of Constantinople, who longed to be free from the rule of the usurper. If they would take pity on young Alexius and help him to his throne, he would reward them lavishly. In return for their aid, he promised to pay them 200,000 silver marks, to place the Church of Constantinople under papal jurisdiction, to join the crusade with 10,000 troops, and to maintain a permanent Byzantine garrison in the Holy Land.

For the crusaders, who were cash poor and behind in their schedule, the offer was very attractive. Not only could they pay off their debt to Venice, but they would be financially secure for some time. Constantinople's wealth was legendary in the West: no one doubted an emperor's ability to come up with such a sum. Restoring Christian unity and securing Byzantine assistance in the crusading effort were also powerful inducements. Yet the fact remained that Constantinople was a

Christian city—indeed, the greatest Christian city in the world—and the army had no desire to incur excommunication again. Innocent III, for his part, knew full well that the young pretender hoped to use the crusade to help himself to the throne. The pope had repeatedly forbidden such an action in face-to-face discussions with Boniface, young Alexius, and the leading crusader clergy.

Faced with overwhelming opposition among the crusading host to young Alexius's proposal, the chief barons abandoned debate and signed their names to a treaty committing the crusade to the plan. The rank and file discovered this only gradually, and when they did, many deserted the crusade.

In June 1203, the crusading fleet sailed into view of Constantinople. Now the Frankish crusaders saw the enormous scope of the project they had set out for themselves. Few of them, even those that were well traveled, had believed there was so large a city in the world. Robert of Clari, a poor French knight, exclaimed that the forty largest cities in Western Europe could fit easily within the walls of Constantinople. The population of the city proper was somewhere around 400,000, while the greater metropolitan area was twice that. Inside the vast city, with its hundreds of palaces, churches, monasteries, and rich markets, was a military garrison double or triple the size of the crusade. The walls of the city were enormous—legendary structures that had repelled armies ten times larger than those of the Fourth Crusade.

In July 1203, the crusader army broke the harbor chain and brought its fleet into the Golden Horn. The army then attacked the northwest corner of the city but was successful only in setting a destructive fire within the walls. Fearing a palace coup, Alexius III fled the city. The Byzantine nobility responded by placing Isaac II back on the imperial throne and notifying the crusaders that they had achieved their aims. The Westerners escorted the young Alexius into the city, where Isaac was required to confirm the promises made by his son. The young man was then crowned co-emperor.

Although Alexius IV immediately paid about half of the money he now owed to the crusaders, he was unable to come up with the other half. Finally, he pleaded poverty and asked the crusaders for an extension until March 1204. In the meantime, he would renew the Venetian fleet's contract for an additional year and supply the Westerners with provisions and accommodations outside the city during the winter. Reluctantly, the crusaders agreed. By December 1203, Alexius IV realized that any further attempts to wring money out of the Byzantines to pay the Latins would spell the end of his reign. Therefore, when envoys of the crusade leaders demanded to know whether or not he would keep his covenants, he made it clear that he would not. Having delivered a formal ultimatum to the emperor and then, upon his refusal, having renounced their allegiance to him, the Latins began raiding the area surrounding the city. This situation continued until February 1204, when a high official of the imperial court, the protovestiarios, Alexius Ducas "Mourtzouphlus," led a coup against Alexius IV and imprisoned him. Isaac II had already died, either of fright or old age, and a few days later young Alexius was strangled. Mourtzouphlus was crowned Alexius V in Hagia Sophia.

The crusaders now had little to show for all of their efforts. They could not even afford transportation to Egypt. And so the crusade clergy decreed that since the Byzantines had murdered their lord, and withdrawn themselves from the Catholic Church, the object of the crusade should no longer be Cairo but Constantinople. This decision was in clear violation of earlier papal prohibitions against attacking Constantinople.

On April 9, 1204, the crusaders attacked the harbor walls of the city and were easily repulsed. They tried again on April 12 with more success. A small group of knights, including a fighting cleric named Alleumes of Clari, crawled through a small hole in the city's fortification and put thousands of Greek soldiers to flight. They opened the gates and the rest of the crusaders poured into the city. Although the Latins expected to have to fight for many weeks to subdue the great city, Constantinople surrendered the next morning.

What followed was a three-day sack of unprecedented destruction. Although these Christian soldiers had sworn to leave churches untouched, all of Byzantium's holy places, including Hagia Sophia, were ransacked, defiled, and stripped of everything of value. Although they had promised to respect women, in reality rape was widespread. Even nuns were stripped publicly. When the pope heard of the conduct of his crusaders, he was appalled and enraged. Nicetas Choniates, a Byzantine senator and survivor of the sack, remarked that Constantinople would have fared better had it been conquered by Muslims. With the fall of Constantinople, the Fourth Crusade ended. Most crusaders returned home with their loot. A few remained to support the new Latin Empire.

# C

The Fourth Crusade is one of those historical events that still provoke powerful emotions today. For centuries, scholars have argued the "diversion question." How was it that this enterprise went so seriously off course? There are two schools of thought. "Treason theorists" argue that one or more of the participants plotted to divert the crusade for their own ends. The most oft-cited villains are Boniface of Montferrat and Enrico Dandolo, but there are others. "Accident theorists" contend that the circumstances of the crusade were too complex for anyone to have engineered. Instead, they believe that the crusade was diverted by a difficult series of events and the hard choices made in response to them.

**BIBLIOGRAPHY**

Andrea, Alfred J. "Cistercian Accounts of the Fourth Crusade: Were They Anti-Venetian?" *Analecta Cisterciensa* 41 (1985): 3–41.

Brand, Charles M. "The Fourth Crusade: Some Recent Interpretations." *Medievalia et Humanistica* 2 (1984): 33–45.

Madden, Thomas F. "Outside and Inside the Fourth Crusade: The Treaty of Zara and the Attack on Constantinople in 1204." *The International History Review* 17 (1995): 726–743.

———. "Vows and Contracts in the Fourth Crusade: The Treaty of Zara and the Attack on Constantinople in 1204." *The International History Review* 15 (1993): 441–468.

McNeal, Edgar H., and Robert Lee Wolff. "The Fourth Crusade." In *A History of the Crusades.* Ed. Kenneth M. Setton. Philadelphia: U of Pennsylvania P, 1962; rpt. Madison: U of Wisconsin P, 1969, 2:153–185.

Queller, Donald E. *The Fourth Crusade: The Conquest of Constantinople, 1201–1204.* Rev. edition with Thomas F. Madden. Philadelphia: U of Pennsylvania P, 1997.

———, ed. *The Latin Conquest of Constantinople.* New York: Wiley, 1971.

*Thomas F. Madden*

**SEE ALSO**

Byzantine Empire; Constantinople; Crusades, First, Second, and Third; Egypt; Galley; Holy Land; Jerusalem; Venice

## Crusade, Fifth (1217–1221)

A crusade of strongly multinational character undertaken to recoup the Christian fortunes in the Holy Land. In the late twelfth and early thirteenth century, the crusades had lost ground to a victorious Saladin and suffered embarrassment from the diversion of the Fourth Crusade to capture Constantinople and to lay the foundations of a new Latin Empire in the East. The combination of bitter disappointment, the need to repair severely strained relations between Latins and the Eastern churches, and the continued sorry state of the crusader states influenced Innocent III (1198–1216) to combine plans for a new crusade expedition with his summons of the Fourth Lateran Council in April 1213.

The preparations set in motion in 1213 were the most extensive ever undertaken by a pope. Major administrative efforts went into the selection of crusade preachers and the collection of funds. Efforts were made to bring an end to outstanding conflicts, to prevent the outbreak of new ones, and to enlist all parties in the crusade. At the same time, plans were laid for the Fourth Lateran Council, to be held in November 1215. Innocent III's initial plan for the crusade, contained in his letter "Quia maior," served not merely to inform the faithful but to provide direction for those preaching the crusade. The efforts of these preachers and of papal legates, most notably Cardinal Robert

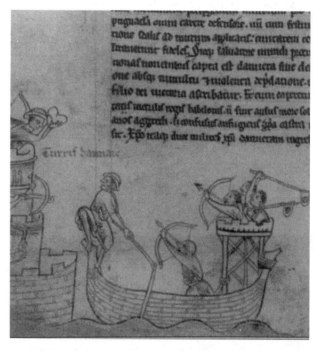

The siege of Damietta. Matthew Paris, *Chronica Majora,* Cambridge, Corpus Christi College MS 16, fol. 59v, *c.* 1250. Permission Master and Fellows, Corpus Christi College, Cambridge.

Courson, soon revealed areas of misunderstanding and conflict in the planning of the crusade. Yet the work of recruitment in this period seems to have been quite successful. The idea of a crusade touched a responsive chord among the lay aristocracy of Latin Europe.

At the Fourth Lateran Council, the crusade was a significant issue in many of the discussions undertaken, including the dispute over the imperial throne, the conflict of King John of England (1199–1216) with his barons, and the status of the Albigensian crusade. The crusade bull "Ad liberandam," appended to the conciliar decrees, shows, however, how effectively the pope worked to win support and even to strengthen his program with a new and more effective tax on behalf of the crusade, now planned to get underway in June 1217. The following months witnessed an intensification of efforts so that, when Innocent III died in July 1216, the newly elected pope, Honorius III (1216–1227), was able to move vigorously to ensure that as little time as possible would be lost.

When June 1217 came, however, recruitment was still going on and only the Rhenish and Frisian crusaders were prepared for departure. They were joined by some English crusaders and sailed to Lisbon, where they supported local efforts against Muslims. Knowing that Frederick II (1212–1250) was not yet prepared to go on crusade, they were in no hurry to arrive in the East. In the meantime, forces led by King András II of Hungary (1205–1255) and Duke Leopold VI of Austria (1195–1230) arrived in Acre in September 1217. They strengthened defenses along the coast and in the interior. Though King András returned home in January 1218, Leopold remained for more than another year. The arrival of the Frisians and Germans in May 1218 was followed by large Italian, French, and English contingents. John of Brienne, king of Jerusalem (1210–1225) by virtue of his daughter Isabella, heiress to the throne, was elected as leader, and the decision to invade Egypt confirmed. The first crusade contingents arrived on the Egyptian coast near Damietta on a narrow island formed by the sea, the Nile, and the al-Azraq Canal.

Cardinal Pelagius of Albano, papal legate to the crusade, was not appointed until June 1218, and arrived in Damietta only in September, with a contingent of Roman crusaders as well as funds from the taxes imposed by the church. Controversy has swirled about this figure, largely as a result of incorrect assumptions regarding his leadership role. The vulnerability of the crusaders resulting from the difficult climatic conditions and disease that carried off, among others, Cardinal Robert Courson, left many deeply discouraged. Yet Pelagius was important in keeping the group together. In late summer 1219, St. Francis of Assisi visited the crusade camp and preached his message of peace and reconciliation to the crusaders. He also visited the Muslim camp. Deeply respected, St. Francis may for a time have raised the spirits of those hoping for some immediate response to their needs. But the siege continued until Damietta fell on November 6, 1219.

The success of the crusaders had led the sultan al-Kamil to offer a compromise settlement on at least two occasions during this period. He would hand over Jerusalem and some other sites in return for the return of Damietta and Christian withdrawal from Egypt. This offer was seriously considered before being rejected on the grounds that it did not provide sufficient security. The critical factor in this stage was the belief that Frederick II, who had already been granted postponements by the pope, would arrive in the East at the head of sufficient reinforcements to make the crusade a success. That this did not happen was due to Frederick's determination to settle his affairs in the West before going on crusade.

Meanwhile, the situation in the East was deteriorating. King John of Jerusalem took a substantial group to Acre early in 1220 because of the growing threat from Syria. Some maligned him, saying that he left for personal reasons, but this is doubtful. Pelagius was awaiting word of the arrival of Frederick and trying to keep the forces together. The critical point was reached when Duke Louis of Bavaria arrived with substantial forces as the representative of Frederick II in May 1221. It was immediately apparent that Frederick would not soon arrive, that the army would, if it did not see combat, disintegrate, and that some decision must be taken immediately. Pelagius wanted action. He sent for King John. Louis of Bavaria favored a limited assault on the sultan's camp. The mass of crusaders, however, wanted to move ahead toward their final objective. It is easy, in hindsight, to spot the weaknesses in each position. But rather than fault the leaders, it is important to point to their limited options. Time and resources were against them. The move southward exposed them to the forces of the sultan, now at al-Mansura, and the flooding of the river, which occurred shortly thereafter. Their effort to overcome both obstacles failed. The army was forced to retreat. The decision

# C

was taken by the imperial representatives, Duke Louis and the bishop of Passau, not by Pelagius. The crusaders were caught and forced to surrender on August 29, 1221. They agreed to return Damietta in exchange for their freedom. What had begun as the most carefully planned crusade, closely identified with the church and the papacy, had failed. At least some laid the blame at the feet of Pelagius; others blamed Frederick. Those who were best informed seem to have been least inclined to levy blame.

## BIBLIOGRAPHY

Donovan, Joseph. *Pelagius and the Fifth Crusade.* Philadelphia: U of Pennsylvania P, 1950.

Powell, James M. *Anatomy of a Crusade, 1213–1221.* Philadelphia: U of Pennsylvania P, 1986.

Riley-Smith, Jonathan. *The Crusades: A Short History.* London: Athlone Press; New Haven: Yale UP, 1987.

Van Cleve, Thomas C. "The Fifth Crusade." In *A History of the Crusades.* Ed. Kenneth Setton. Madison: U of Wisconsin P, 1969–1989, 2:377–428.

*James M. Powell*

## SEE ALSO

Acre; Constantinople; Crusade, Fourth; Egypt; Frederick II; Holy Land; Saladin

## Crusades, Burgundian

A series of Christian campaigns against the Ottoman Turks, organized, financed, and led by the dukes of Burgundy between 1396 and 1464.

The part played by the dukes of Burgundy can probably not be separated from the interest in the crusades that was manifested by the first kings of France from the House of Valois. King Jean II "the Good" (r. 1350–1364) was designated by the pope in 1363 as captain general of the crusade proclaimed that year. But it was not until 1396 that his son, Philip the Bold (named Duke of Burgundy in recognition of his bravery at the Battle of Poitiers in 1356), responded to the call of King Sigismond of Hungary at the same time as other princes. He was the only one of this group to follow through on his promise, consigning to his eldest son, Jean, Count of Nevers (d. 1419), an important contingent of French cavalry that joined with the Hungarian army in descending the valley of the Danube as far as Nicopolis, where the allies put the city under siege. The united forces were surprised by the arrival of Turks, led by Bajazet I (1389–1403). The imprudence

of the cavalry—which insisted on making the first charge—contributed to the destruction of the army, though Jean de Nevers and some of his companions were spared and had to pay a huge ransom.

Philip the Good (1419–1467), son of Jean de Nevers, was no doubt impressed by his father's example; he demonstrated early on his interest in the Orient and the Holy Land, where he sent agents to gather information, as well as in the defense of Europe against the Turks (he sent an ambassador to Hungary in 1436). He armed a flotilla, which left in 1442 to come to the rescue of Rhodes; it was then reinforced by some galleys in an attempt to keep the Turks from passing the straits, though none of this could prevent the disaster of Varna, the Black Sea port at which the Turks, under Murad II, decisively defeated a crusader army and killed Ladislaus II of Poland and Hungary (1444). This flotilla cruised for a certain period in the Black Sea in order to aid the Hungarians.

Some new appeals for a crusade made by Nicolas V and John Hunyadi convinced the duke to announce plans for a crusade in May 1451. But delayed by a war against Ghent, Philip could not take up the cross until 1453 (after the fall of Constantinople), when he solemnly announced his intentions at a banquet and invited his vassals to accompany him. He attempted to involve the king of France, or at least to obtain his support; he went to Germany to enlist the aid of the emperor, but without success. Hunyadi waited in vain for the Burgundian troops at the gates of Belgrade in 1456. He was, however, represented at the meeting called by Pius II in Mantua, after which he sent an army to the pope and armed a new flotilla. Pius's death and the destruction of the flotilla in a storm in 1464 put an end to the enterprise. From then on, the duke limited his activities to sending financial help to Rhodes. His son, Charles the Bold (1467–1477), was moderately interested in the war against the Turks, but he made it only one part of his larger plans. He pursued negotiations with some enemies of the sultan, such as Uzun Hassan, but was unable to show more clearly his interest in the crusades.

It was not without good reason that the popes and other proponents of the crusades had put their hopes in the Burgundian state, as demonstrated by the famous embassy that the Franciscan Lodovico Severi of Boulogne brought to the court of Burgundy in order to solicit support of the duke against the enterprises of Metmed II in 1460 (too late, however, to save most of

C

the territories involved). Philip the Good undertook many diplomatic efforts, furnished naval support, and spent great sums of money with the crusades in mind; he was one of the European princes most aware of the danger of the Ottomans. The other sovereigns, however, did not support his efforts, which were not, perhaps, always completely without self-interest. Philip, in devoting himself publicly to the crusades, reinforced his prestige both in Europe and in Asia.

**BIBLIOGRAPHY**

Müller, Heribert. *Kreuzzugspläne und Kreuzzugspolitik des Herzogs Philipp des Gutes von Burgund.* Göttingen: Schriftereihe des historische Kommission der bayerische Akademie 51, 1993.

Paviot, Jacques. *La politique navale des ducs de Bourgogne. 1384–1482.* Lille: PU, 1995.

Vaughan, Richard. *Philip the Bold.* London: Longmans, 1962.

Walsh, Richard J. "Charles the Bold and the Crusades: Politics and Propaganda." *Journal of Medieval History* 3 (1977): 53–86.

*Jean Richard*

**SEE ALSO**

Constantinople; Ghent; Hungary; Naval Warfare; Ottoman Turks

## Cumans

The designation (Turk. *Quman*) in Greek, Latin, and some Islamic sources (and occasionally in Rus' and Georgian chronicles) of the westernmost grouping of a large and loosely organized Turkic nomadic tribal confederation of Eurasia. In the Islamic world, in neighboring Transcaucasia, and in China, the Cumans were known as the *Qipchaq*s. Indeed, the whole of the territory under their sway, extending from the Danubian borders of Byzantium to the steppes around Khwarazm (present-day western Uzbekistan) and western Siberia was called the "Qipchaq Steppe." The eastern grouping of Qipchaqs was also known by the ethnonym *Qangli*.

A substantial number of the Turkic peoples of present-day Eurasia descend in whole or in part from the tribes of the Qipchaq confederation. The Rus' apparently calqued the Turkic *Quman* ("light, pale") into Slavic as *Polovci* (which was borrowed into western Slavic languages and Hungarian). Similar loan translations of this name can be found in Latin, Germano-Latin, and Armenian sources. The complexity of Cuman nomenclature reflects the disparate origins of the constituent tribal groupings, the majority of which appear to have derived from the Turkic Kimek union of western Siberia. In the early decades of the eleventh century, this union was broken up by a series of migrations of proto-Mongolian peoples resulting from turbulence in and around northern China. By the middle of the eleventh century, they appeared on the borders of Rus', taking over the western Eurasian steppelands from the Pechenegs, who were driven off to the Byzantine Balkan borderlands.

By virtue of their location, the history of the Cumans is intimately intertwined with that of Byzantium, Bulgaria, Rumania, Hungary, Rus', and Transcaucasia; in their diaspora they are also linked to the Islamic world (where they appeared in substantial numbers as *ghulam*s or *Mamluk*s, i.e., slave-soldiers) and Yuan China (functioning here as servitors of the Mongol regime). Once established as masters of the Eurasian steppes, the Cumans were drawn, like other Turkic tribal confederations and states before them, into the diplomatic and military orbit of the sedentary societies to their south. After a period of testing Rus' defenses (ending in the early twelfth century), these nomads came to constitute a constant, if fickle, force in Rus' domestic history, as different Cuman groupings formed alliances (often symbolized by marital ties) with competing factions. They were alternately allies and enemies of the Byzantines, who, however, did not attempt to project their power into the distant and risky steppes where the Cumans resided. The Rus', when united, could make inroads into Cuman territory, and Cuman tribes fleeing Rus' attacks settled for a time in Georgia during the reign of David the Builder (1089–1125), who was married to a Qipchaq princess. Here, they assisted the Georgian monarchy in expelling the Seljuk Turks. Subsequently, other Qipchaq groups took service with the Georgian crown and played a significant role in the affairs of that state until the Mongol conquest (1230s).

The ruling house of Khwarazm also had close dynastic ties with the neighboring Qipchaq chieftains, with occasionally disruptive consequences. The formation of the Second Bulgarian Empire in the late twelfth century was considerably assisted by the involvement of Cuman groupings. Some later Bulgarian dynasties (the Terterids, Shishmanids) were of Cuman origin. Although the Cumans never organized themselves into a state, they managed to integrate themselves into the increasingly

# C

fragmented power system of their neighbors. The absence of a serious external threat prevented the development of a Cuman state and perhaps saved them from the fate of their predecessors in the steppe, all of whom were destroyed by the neighboring sedentary states.

With the Mongol conquest in the 1230s, the Cumans were reorganized and incorporated by the successors of Chinggis Khân into Chinggisid-led military formations that in time became the nuclei of new tribal alignments. In western Eurasia, the Cumans brought about the linguistic Qipchaqization of the Mongol and eastern Turkic elements that formed the ruling strata of the Chinggisid "Ulus of Jochi" (the later Golden Horde). When the Mongol Empire began to divide into rival appanages, the Qipchaq-based Jochids on the Volga soon formed an alliance with the Mamluk state in Egypt-Syria, also based largely on a Qipchaq soldiery. The Uzbek tribal confederation that around 1500 conquered the land that now bears its name and the Kazakh union that broke away from the former in the mid-fifteenth century both derived from the Jochid Qipchaq groupings.

The Cuman-Qipchaqs of the Volga and adjoining steppelands embraced Islam in the course of the thirteenth and fourteenth centuries. Some of their kinsmen in Hungary, Byzantium, Rus', and Georgia were Christianized. The *Codex Cumanicus* (fourteenth century), consisting of several Cuman dictionaries prepared by German and Italian missionaries and merchants, as well as a number of Arabic works stemming from the Mamluk state, provide us with samples of their language.

## BIBLIOGRAPHY

Golden, Peter. B. "Cumanica I: The Qipchaqs in Georgia." *Archivum Eurasiae Medii Aevi* 4 (1984): 45–87.

———. "Cumanica IV: The Tribes of the Cuman-Qipchaqs." *Archivum Eurasiae Medii Aevi* 9 (1995–1997): 99–122.

———. "The Qipchaqs of Medieval Eurasia: An Example of Stateless Adaptation in the Steppes." In *Rulers from the Steppe. State Formation on the Eurasian Periphery.* Ed. Gary Seaman and Daniel Marks. Los Angeles: Ethnographics Press, 1991, pp. 132–157.

Paloczi-Horvath, Andras. *Pechenegs, Cumans, Iasians. Steppe Peoples in Medieval Hungary.* Trans. Timothy Wilkinson. Budapest: Corvina, 1989.

Pritsak, Omeljan. "The Polovcians and Rus'." *Archivum Eurasiae Medii Aevi* 2 (1982): 321–380.

*Peter B. Golden*

## SEE ALSO

Byzantine Empire; Golden Horde; Inner Asian Trade; Inner Asian Travel; Mamluks; Mongols; Nomadism and Pastoralism; Poland; Russia and Rus'; Yuan Dynasty

# D

## Da Gama, Vasco (*c.* 1460–1524)

First European to sail successfully to India. When commissioned by King Manuel I (1495–1521) to lead an expedition using the route around Africa established ten years earlier by Bartolomeu Dias, da Gama was a thirty-seven-year-old Portuguese nobleman, a distinguished soldier, and a trained navigator who had studied astronomy. He was also arrogant, demanding, cruel, intelligent, and compassionate when necessary. Da Gama left Lisbon on July 8, 1497, with four vessels. Two of the ships had been specially built for the voyage, while one was a supply ship to be scuttled after it was no longer needed. The vessels carried approximately 170 seasoned ocean seamen, as well as interpreters who spoke Arabic and some African dialects. He loaded trinkets, beads, and tiny bells to trade with the communities he encountered.

Da Gama's skill as a navigator was demonstrated early in the voyage when he chose to sail far out to sea west and southwest in order to avoid contrary winds and currents near the African coast. He sailed for three months in the mid-Atlantic before turning east. When he sighted Africa, he was only one degree (*c.* 70 miles or 112 kilometers) north of the Cape of Good Hope. On November 18, he rounded the cape and proceeded north, zigzagging up the coast. From Mozambique onward, he encountered Muslim civilization. Since the Muslim ports on the east coast of Africa teemed with oriental goods, including spices, his unsophisticated trade goods and gifts were an insult to the sultans he encountered. Nonetheless, at Malindi, he was furnished an excellent pilot by the sultan to guide him across the Indian Ocean, which he traversed in only twenty-seven days. On May 18, 1497, he made landfall about fifty miles north of Calicut.

Da Gama and his crew spent three months at Calicut, again finding that they had brought worthless goods to trade. In mid-October, they headed for home. The return across the Indian Ocean was difficult (the pilot had mysteriously disappeared), taking three months. Scurvy broke out, killing many of the crew. In March, da Gama rounded the Cape of Good Hope, and he arrived back in Lisbon in early September 1499. He had been gone two years and sailed 27,000 miles. Only fifty-four of his original 170 men survived. Nevertheless, he had opened a sea lane from Portugal to India that others could follow.

Da Gama made two more voyages to India. After the success of his first voyage, da Gama had received titles and a pension. In 1502, he was made an admiral and given a fleet to sail to India to establish Portuguese hegemony in the Indian Ocean. On this voyage, he fought a number of battles with Muslim traders and established a few alliances with Indian rulers. Some of the cruelest acts of his career occurred in these encounters, for he offered no quarter to the Muslims he fought. In 1503, he returned to Portugal partially successful in his mission. On his third voyage in 1524, King João III made him viceroy of India. He died shortly after arriving at Cochin while carrying out his official duties.

**BIBLIOGRAPHY**

Cortesão, Armando. *The Mystery of Vasco da Gama.* Agrupamento de Estudos de Cartografia Antiga 12. Coimbra: Universidade de Coimbra, 1973.

# D

Jayne, Kingsley. *Vasco da Gama and His Successors: 1460–1580*. London: Methuen, 1910; rpt. New York: Barnes & Noble, 1970.

Hart, Henry. *Sea Road to the Indies; An Account of the Voyages and Exploits of the Portuguese Navigators, Together with the Life and Times of Dom Vasco da Gama, Capitao-Mor, Viceroy of India and Count of Vidigueira*. 1950; rpt. New York: Macmillan, 1971.

Ravenstein, Ernest G, ed. and trans. *A Journal of the First Voyage of Vasco da Gama, 1497–1499*. London: Hakluyt Society, 1st series, 99, 1898; rpt. New York: Franklin, 1963.

†*Delno C. West*

**SEE ALSO**

Dias, Bartolomeu; India; Portuguese Expansion; Spice Trade, Indian Ocean

## Damascus

An ancient city that stood at the crossroads of all major trade routes in the preindustrial Middle East; it is reputedly the oldest continuously inhabited city in the world.

Already in existence in the days of Abraham (*c.* 2000 B.C.E.), Damascus was an important Byzantine center in sixth-century Syria, but when the Persians conquered Damascus in 611–613 C.E., the local Nestorian Christians welcomed them. After the Arabs defeated the Persians in 629, Damascus returned briefly to Byzantine control before Arab armies retook the city in September 635. From their capital in Damascus, the Umayyad caliphs sent conquering armies across North Africa into Spain and eastward into India. Tribute flowed into the capital, its irrigation systems were restored, and the city was embellished. The caliph, al-Walīd I (705–715) erected the great Umayyad mosque and received in its courtyard his triumphant armies returning from Spain. Damascus lost political prestige when the 'Abbasids replaced the Umayyads and moved their capital to Baghdad (*c.* 750); however, the city then became an 'Abbasid cultural center, where the caliph al-Ma'mūn (813–833) built an astronomical observatory.

During the ninth century, civil wars engulfed Syria as various factions and ethnicities fought for control. In the tenth century, the Shi'ite Fatimids from Egypt took Syria and garrisoned Damascus with Berber troops. The Seljuk Turks, converted to Sunni Islam, conquered Damascus in 1076 and temporarily restored order.

They allied briefly with the crusaders against Byzantium, but this alliance collapsed when the armies of the Second Crusade unsuccessfully besieged Damascus in 1148. Nū al-Dīn, the Seljuk emir of Syria, made Damascus his capital from 1154 until his death in 1174, when Saladin the Kurd occupied the city. Saladin's rule (1174–1193) began a fruitful coexistence between Egyptian and Syrian cities. His heirs, the Ayyūbids, struggled to control Egypt and Syria, although Saladin's brother temporarily reunited the Ayyūbid state (1200–1218).

Damascus remained a cultural center for Islam under both the Seljuks and the Ayyūbids. Nū al-Dīn, for example, patronized the four schools of law in Damascus, and the Andalusian Arab thinker Ibn al'Arabī (1165–1240) chose to settle in the city, where his tomb later became a pilgrimage site. Under the Mamluk rule that followed (1250–1517), Damascus became the second city of the realm after Cairo. Although the Mongols entered Damascus in 1260, the Mamluks defeated them at Ain Jalut later that year and expelled them temporarily from Syria. When Mamluk forces also conquered crusader Acre in 1291, Damascus celebrated for a month. The Mongols, however, managed to return briefly to devastate Damascus in 1300.

The Mamluk pacification of Syria gave the city more than a century of material prosperity. Its craftsmen produced household goods, luxury textiles, fine leather goods, precision metalwork, glass, and ceramics, while the building trades prospered under the patronage of Mamluk emirs. More than 100 mosques, schools, hospitals, and Sufi convents were built in the city. The 'ulama, scholars and learned men of Islam, cooperated with the emirs and led the city's cultural life. By the fourteenth century, more than 20,000 pilgrims from Anatolia, Iran, Iraq, and Syria gathered annually in Damascus to organize their caravans to Mecca.

Kārimī merchants—a close-knit group of Muslim businessmen—from Damascus and Cairo monopolized the spice trade beginning in the Fatimid era (after *c.* 900). They traveled east to Baghdad, Hormuz, Herat, Samarkand, India, and China; south to Mecca, Yemen, and Ethiopia; and west to Egypt, the Maghrib, and Andalusia. They forged an international network of merchants, created massive fortunes, cooperated with the Mamluks, and contributed to the cultural life of Damascus; but they eventually disappeared in the fifteenth century.

# D

Damascus decayed during the Mamluk civil wars (1388–1412). In 1400, Tamerlane captured the city, where he met the Andalusian traveler and diplomat, Ibn Khaldūn. Tamerlane confiscated much of the city's wealth and deported many of its craftsmen and scholars to Samarkand. Damascus had recovered from earlier devastations between 1312 and 1388, but finally declined due to oppressive taxation, riots, famine, pestilence, and Bedouin depredations in the countryside. The Ottomans took the city in 1517.

**BIBLIOGRAPHY**

Ashtor, Eliyahu. "The Karimi Merchants." *Journal of the Royal Asiatic Society,* series 3, 1956: 45–56.

Fischel, Walter J. *Ibn Khaldūn and Tamerlane, Their Historic Meeting in Damascus, 1401 A.D.* Berkeley and Los Angeles: U of California P, 1952.

Goitein, Samuel D. "From the Mediterranean to India." *Speculum* 29 [2] (1954): 181–197.

Hourani, Albert. *A History of the Arab Peoples.* Cambridge, MA: Harvard and Warner Books, 1991.

Humphreys, R. Stephen. *From Saladin to the Mongols: the Ayyūbids of Damascus, 1193–1260.* Albany: State University of New York P, 1977.

Lapidus, Ira Marvin. *Muslim Cities in the Later Middle Ages.* Harvard Middle Eastern Studies 11. Cambridge, MA: Harvard UP, 1976; rpt. Cambridge, England, and New York: Cambridge UP, 1984.

*Louise Buenger Robbert*

**SEE ALSO**

Ain Jalut; Ayyūbids; Baghdad; Crusades, First, Second, and Third; Mamluks; Muslim Travelers and Trade; Nestorianism; Saladin; Seljuk Turks; Shi'ism; Sunnism; Tamerlane

## Daniel the Abbot (fl. 1106–1118)

The earliest Russian travel writer, known for his journeys to the Levant (*c.* 1106 and 1107), and for his visit to Palestine during the reign of Baldwin I, the Latin king of Jerusalem (1100–1118). The abbot of a Russian monastery, Daniel began the account of his journey at Constantinople. He crossed the Bosporus, sailed through the Dardanelles and into the Mediterranean, and headed to Ephesus, Patmos, and Rhodes. From there he traveled to Jaffa and Jerusalem, entering that city through the western Gate of Benjamin.

His account of the sea journey is an itinerary of the marvelous: the sacred oil that rose from the sea in honor of martyrs near Heraclea, the Tomb of St. John and the Seven Sleepers, the miraculous cross of St. Helena that dangled in space above a Cyrian mountain. But his most vivid pictures are of his time in the Holy Land. He made three excursions while in Palestine: to the Jordan (which he compares to a Russian river, the Snov) and the Dead Sea, to Bethlehem and Hebron, and to Damascus. On this last expedition he accompanied Baldwin, whose armed escort gave him access to places no Christian pilgrim would normally visit. Toward the end of his stay he remained in the Jerusalem House, a Christian hostel, for sixteen months, recording minute observations about Jerusalem from this vantage point near the Tower of David. On his return voyage to Constantinople, his ship was plundered by four pirate galleys; narrowly escaping with his life, he thanked God for his good fortune.

Daniel's depiction of the Holy Land is invaluable as a record of conditions at the beginning of the twelfth century. He writes of the unsettled world of Palestine: Muslim raiders approached the walls of Christian Jerusalem and constantly attacked Christian travelers on the road from Jaffa to Jerusalem; armed escorts were needed for Christians on roads leading out of Jerusalem toward the Sea of Galilee or Nazareth; panthers and wild asses lurked on the west side of the Dead Sea, and lions hunted below the Jordan valley. But he also includes happier details—the date palms by Jericho, the genial relations between the Greek and Latin monasteries—as well as the conventional connections between geography and sacred story—the Sea of Sodom that oozes a vile and stinking breath, the stone column of Lot's wife near Segor. Daniel's is a sharp and observant eye, if at times also credulous and inaccurate. Along with blunders in topography come detailed records of ritual and liturgy; along with errors in distance and confusion of names come accounts of life under the crusader government of Jerusalem.

**BIBLIOGRAPHY**

Beazley, C. Raymond. *The Life and Journey of Daniel, Abbot of the Russian Land.* Trans. John Wilkinson. In *Jerusalem Pilgrimage 1099–1185.* Ed. John Wilkinson. Hakluyt Society, 2nd series, 167. London: Hakluyt Society, 1988, pp. 120–171.

Wright, Thomas, ed. *Early Travels in Palestine.* London, 1848; rpt. New York: AMS, 1969.

*Gary D. Schmidt*

**SEE ALSO**

Constantinople; Dead Sea; Holy Land; Jerusalem; Pilgrimage, Christian; Piracy

# D

## Dante Alighieri (1265–1321)

Native of Florence and author of works with geographical significance, including *The Divine Comedy* (*Divina Commedia*), the *Banquet* (*Convivio*), and possibly *Questions on Water and Earth* (*Quaestio de aqua et terra*).

The notions of geography in Dante's prose writings generally reflect those of his time. They are drawn not from observation but from standard authorities: Orosius, Isidore of Seville, Albertus Magnus, and (more immediately) Brunetto Latini. Dante views the earth as a ball largely covered by ocean, with dry land restricted to the northern, inhabited hemisphere that extends in latitude from Gibraltar (the Pillars of Hercules) in the west to the river Ganges in the east. Although aware of the diversity of opinion on the possibility of life in the antipodes, he affirms that the waters stretching between the hemispheres are impassable, and therefore any conceivable southern region would be devoid of human life. These conventional, even conservative ideas are reflected in his *Convivio,* as well as in the *Quaestio de aqua et terra,* a Latin work (1320) not universally acknowledged to be Dante's own. The *Quaestio* is set in the form of an academic "dispute" that examines whether water, being "nobler" than earth, stands higher than land on the earth's surface. Its author argues, for reasons that are ultimately spiritual rather than physical, that earth rises above water because of stellar (and therefore angelic) influence.

In the poetry of the *Commedia,* however, Dante makes many new "discoveries" that transform the conventional *mappamundi.* Rising out of the supposedly vacant waters of the Southern Hemisphere is a solitary mountain landmass located precisely at the antipodes from Jerusalem. Cut into the rock of its steep slopes are the terraces of Purgatory, while at its summit sits the Garden of Eden. *Purgatorio* emphasizes how the living and the dead share the same globe by frequent references to the twelve-hour time difference between "there" in Purgatory and that Italian "here" where Dante is writing his account: "vespers were there; and where we are, midnight" (15. 6).

Although elements of this geography are found in other sources, the *Commedia*'s combination is strikingly original. Dante resolves the contested location of Eden by putting it in the south, not in the traditional east; he also gives it two rivers instead of the biblical four. Likewise, the poet removes Purgatory from the horrors of the underworld and places it in the bright light of day. No one else had ever joined these two locations so concretely. Nor had anyone else accounted for their double origin in Satan's fall from heaven to the center of the earth (34.112–126).

The *Commedia*'s exploration of the afterlife takes place almost entirely within the physical universe, as Dante visits an underground hell, climbs a purgatorial mountain, and encounters the souls of the blessed on his ascent through the nine spheres of the material heavens. Only his ultimate visit to the City of God in *Paradiso* 30–33 takes him into the Empyrean, and therefore beyond space and time. At several points this imagined journey is related to the common practical experience of medieval pilgrims to Rome or to Jerusalem. Contrasted with religious pilgrimage, however, it is travel inspired not by piety but by *curiositas.* Dante dramatized this impulse in the figure of Ulysses, who (in the striking revision of the hero's traditional route and fate in *Inferno* 26) sails past the Pillars of Hercules, venturing westward across the ocean and coming within sight of the island-mountain in the antipodes, only to be shipwrecked by divine retribution short of a forbidden landfall. The ill-fated 1291 expedition of the Vivaldi brothers may well stand behind this narrative. But the "mad flight" of Ulysses has less to do with actual navigational error than with spiritual transgression, with travel motivated by merely human interests rather than by a desire for the divine.

**BIBLIOGRAPHY**

Alighieri, Dante. *Quaestio de aqua et terra.* In *The Latin Works of Dante.* Trans. Philip Wicksteed. Temple Classics, 1904; rpt. London: J.M. Dent, 1940.

Boyde, Patrick. *Dante Philomythes and Philosopher.* Cambridge: Cambridge UP, 1981.

Hawkins, Peter S. "'Out upon Circumference': Discovery in Dante." In Westrem, *Discovering New Worlds,* pp. 193–220. See Gen. Bib.

Moore, Edward. "The Geography of Dante." In *Studies in Dante.* 3rd series. 1903, rpt. Oxford: Clarendon Press, 1968, pp. 109–143.

Morgan, Alison. *Dante and the Medieval Other World.* Cambridge, England: Cambridge UP, 1990.

*Peter S. Hawkins*

**SEE ALSO**

Albertus Magnus; Antipodes; Brunetto Latini; Four Rivers of Paradise; Ganges; Isidore of Seville; Jerusalem; *Mappamundi;* Orosius; Paradise, Travel to; Pilgrimage, Christian; Purgatory; Rome as a Pilgrimage Site

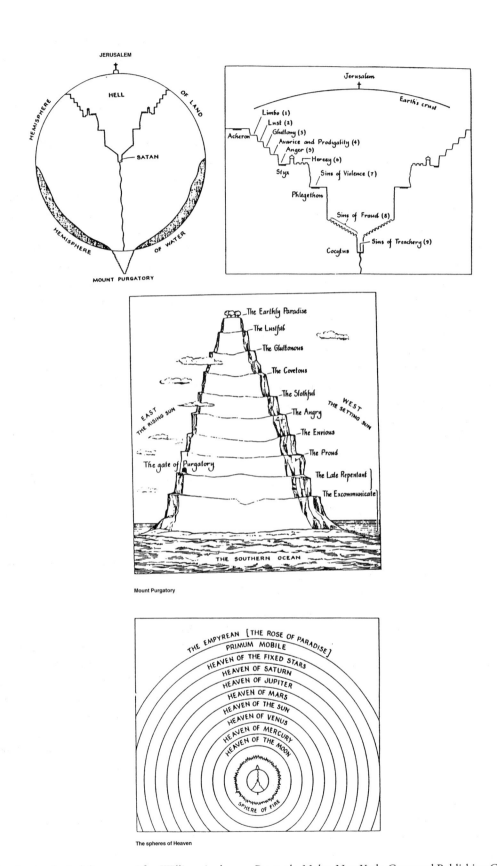

Geographical and cosmological diagrams. After William Andersen, *Dante the Maker*. New York: Crossroad Publishing Co., 1982.

# D

## Daoism

*See* Taoism


## Dead Sea

A saline lake, devoid of animal and vegetable life, in the Judean desert. The Dead Sea (Hebrew *Yam ha-Melach* or "Salt Sea"; Latin *Lacus Asphaltitis* or "Lake of Asphalt"; Arabic *Bahr Lut* or "Sea of Lot") is part of a rift in the Earth's surface extending 4,000 miles (6,500 kilometers) from East Africa to Syria. It lies in the Judean desert between modern Israel and Jordan, with Jericho near its northern end and the obliterated biblical towns of Sodom and Gomorrah to the south. Although the measurements are not constant, the Dead Sea extends about fifty miles (eighty kilometers) on a north-south axis and is about eleven miles (eighteen kilometers) at its widest point. It is larger in wet winters, when runoff from rains through otherwise dry wadis feeds it, smaller in periods of prolonged drought when the few rivers that run year-round do not replace the water lost through evaporation. That evaporation, intensified by the high temperatures in the desert basin, explains why the water of the Dead Sea has the highest salinity and greatest specific gravity of any body of water in the world. The emperor Vespasian (69–79 C.E.) threw manacled slaves into the water to test its buoyancy. At 1,305 feet (398 meters) below sea level, it is the lowest point on earth.

Navigation developed on the Dead Sea in Hellenistic and Roman times. The remnants of the sixth-century mosaic map in the church at Madaba depicts two ships, one sailing northward with a cargo of salt and the other southward with a cargo of wheat. The salt residue of evaporation, found on the shore in fantastic shapes, was collected and sold in Jerusalem. The Nabateans gathered bitumen floating on the sea, which they exported to Egypt where it was used for embalming. The belief that the water possessed curative properties, current since Roman times, persists today. Al-Muqaddasi (fl. 967–985 C.E.), an important Arab traveler and geographer, reports that people assembled on a feast day in August to drink Dead Sea water—which, with five times the salt concentration of sea water, feels smooth and oily and tastes nasty. Navigation increased on the Dead Sea under the crusaders, who levied heavy taxes on transported goods, though the Hospitalers obtained an exemption from them in 1152 and again in 1177.

From Byzantine times Christian pilgrims visited the area, which some called the Devil's Sea. The Arab traveler Yaqut (fl. 1179–1229), responding to the smell of surface sulfur, referred to it as the Stinking Sea. Medieval legends abound. Since no fish can live in the Dead Sea, there are no sea birds—which may account for the legend that no bird could fly over the Dead Sea. The great heat and intense evaporation was thought to produce a noxious miasma. Because of scanty rainfall and the lack of fresh water, there is little vegetation, which may account for the belief that no plants could live in the poisonous air. In fact, the few perennial rivers and warm water springs on both sides of the sea create fertile oases that support semitropical fruits and the production of balsam. The oasis at Zoar, at the southern end of the Dead Sea (probably now submerged), was famous for its palm groves.

### BIBLIOGRAPHY

Karmon, Yehuda. *Israel*. Darmstadt: Wissenschaftliche Buchgesellschaft, 1983.

Orni, Ephraim. *Geography of Israel*. Jerusalem: Israel Universities P, 1971.

Ritter, Karl. *Der Jordan und die Beschiffung des Todten Meeres*. Berlin: Reimer, 1850.

Shkolnik, Ya'acov. *Desert Waterways. Eretz Guide to the Nature Reserves of the Dead Sea Valley*. Givatayim: Eretz Ha'Tzvi, 1991.

Jerome Mandel

### SEE ALSO

Balsam Garden; Madaba Mosaic Map; Military Orders; Muslim Travelers and Trade; Pilgrimage, Christian


## Dias, Bartolomeu (*c.* 1450–1500)

Portuguese sea captain who was the first European to sail around the southern tip of Africa.

The date and place of birth, as well as the early life, of Bartolomeu Dias [Diaz] remain a mystery. He must have been a well-respected sea captain who was trusted at court because in 1487 he was commissioned by King João II (1481–1495) to continue the Portuguese voyages down the West African coast seeking a route around the vast continent.

Dias sailed with a fleet of three vessels, including a supply ship, and fifty to sixty men. He also carried a state-of-the-art map compiled from intelligence reports gathered by the Portuguese spy Pero da Covilhã. The supply ship was left at Angra das Aldeias on the coast of

Angola while the two caravels beat their way south along the African coast. Encountering strong head winds near Cape Province, Dias chose to sail west into the open ocean, where, his experience told him, he should pick up southerly winds. After two weeks following a general course south-southwest, Dias set his course toward the continent again, unaware that he had sailed beyond it. Finding no land after several days, he turned north and, in February 1488, sighted land again. Now the coastline was heading east and north, however, and he knew that he had rounded the tip of the African continent. After several adventures, the ships reached the Keiskama River and turned back due to near mutiny by the sailors. On June 6, 1488, they reached the tip of Africa, which Dias named Cape of Storms. King João later changed the name to Cape of Good Hope.

Dias arrived back in Lisbon in December 1488, having sailed approximately 16,000 miles in fifteen months. He had opened a sea route to the Indian Ocean that would enable Portugal to avoid Venetian and Islamic merchants and gain an advantage in international trade. Dias's trip also disproved Ptolemy's theory that Africa was connected to Asia, and that the Indian Ocean was an inland sea. Dias later joined the expedition of Pedro Álvares Cabral (c. 1467–c. 1520) and was present at the discovery of Brazil, which was claimed for Portugal. He died when his ship sank during a storm near the Cape of Good Hope on May 23, 1500.

**BIBLIOGRAPHY**

Axelson, Eric. *Congo to Cape: Early Portuguese Explorers.* New York: Barnes and Noble, 1973.

Campos, Viriato. *Aclaraco do feito de Bartolomue Dias: Portugues de lei e grande perito na arte de navegar.* Odivelas: Europress, 1987.

*Congreso internacional Bartolomue Dias e a sua epoca: actas.* Porto: Universidade do Porto, 1989.

*Dias and His Successors.* Ed. E. Axelson, C. Boxer, and G. Bell-Cross. Cape Town: Saayman and Weber, 1988.

Fonseca, Luis Adao da. *O essencial sobre Bartolomeu Dias.* Lisboa: Nacional-Casa da Moeda, 1987.

Morison, Samuel Eliot. *Portuguese Voyages to America in the Fifteenth Century.* New York: Harvard UP, 1940.

†Delno C. West

**SEE ALSO**

Da Gama, Vasco; Exploration and Expansion, European; Maps; *Nao*; Navigation; Portuguese Expansion; Ptolemy; Rosselli, Francesco; Spain and Portugal; Venice

## Dicuil (?–c. 825)

An Irish monk and scholar, who taught at the court of Charlemagne around 795–810 and 825. Dicuil is supposed to have been a monk at Hy Abbey, destroyed by the Vikings in 806. He wrote six works of varying importance: *Liber de astronomia* (a computus or guide for fixing the date of Easter); *Epistula censuum* (verses about measures and weights); *De prima syllaba* (a treatise on grammar); *Epistula de questionibus decem artes grammaticae* (lost today); and *Liber de mensura orbis terrae,* a cosmography or description of the world, completed in 825 and his most influential book.

*De mensura* is based primarily on writings of Julius Honorius, Pliny, Solinus, Isidore of Seville, and the mapmakers of Theodosius II. The work, made up of nine chapters, consists of a description of Europe, Asia, and Africa; measurement of the earth; and descriptions of major rivers, islands, seas, and mountains. It includes two reports of special importance: an account of a pilgrimage to the Holy Land, and a narrative of a voyage to islands in the North Atlantic. The first of these describes a monk's journey to Egypt and Palestine as told to Dicuil's abbot Suibneus. He identifies the pyramids of Egypt as Joseph's barns, and recounts a voyage up the Nile to the Red Sea through the ancient canal connecting the Red Sea to the Mediterranean. The second report is based, in part, on Dicuil's own experience; it includes descriptions of the Faeroes or the Orkneys, and observes that clerics had resided for some time on an island called Thule, probably Iceland. Dicuil describes in detail the midnight sun, saying that his sources do not mention the phenomenon. He lists several fabulous animals from classical sources, such as the unicorn and the phoenix, adding an account of the elephant that Harun-al-Raschid presented to Charlemagne.

*De mensura* is the oldest and most detailed geography produced in Carolingian Europe. Dicuil's other works are of lesser quality; they are transmitted only in one manuscript rediscovered in the nineteenth century. The same is true of his computus, which is independent of the one devised by the Venerable Bede and Victorius.

**BIBLIOGRAPHY**

Bergmann, Werner. "Dicuil's 'De Mensura orbis terrae.' " In *Science in Western and Eastern Civilization in Carolingian Times.* Ed. P.L. Butzer and D. Lohrmann. Basel, 1993, pp. 525–537.

# D

Brunhölzl, Franz. *Geschichte der lateinischen Literatur des Mittelalters.* Vol. 1. Munich: Fink, 1975, pp. 306–309, 552.

Dicuil. Liber de astronomia. *An Unpublished Astronomical Treatise by the Irish Monk Dicuil.* Ed. Mario Esposito. *Proceedings of the Royal Irish Academy* 26, Section C, No. 15, Dublin, 1907, pp. 378–447.

———. *Liber de mensura orbis terrae.* Scriptores Latini Hiberniae. 6. Ed. James J. Tierney. Dublin: Dublin Institute for Advanced Studies, 1967.

Vywer, A. van der. "Dicuil et Micon de Saint-Riquier." *Revue Bénédictine* 14 (1935): 24–47.

*Werner Bergmann*

SEE ALSO

Bede; Irish Travel; Isidore of Seville; Pliny the Elder; Red Sea; Solinus, Julius Gaius; Thule

## Diplomacy

The conduct of relations between autonomous political entities (principals), which relies on formal communications or negotiations through accredited envoys. The essential functions of diplomats in medieval times were, as they are now, representing the principal, safeguarding his interests, negotiating on his behalf, and reporting on the negotiations as well as the situation in the host state. A diplomat could either act openly, in good faith, or use illicit and clandestine methods, such as bribery, spreading discord, or playing off factions in the host's court. While unprincipled conduct was frowned on as unworthy of the ambassadorial office, which often carried divine sanction, the result was what truly counted. However, most societies make a clear distinction between diplomacy and spying.

Diplomatic envoys were supposed to enjoy immunity from persecution and attack, ensured by tokens or letters of safe conduct. Envoys carried credentials that identified them and their mission to the host. Their role was limited by the extent of their powers. Envoys could be mere "speaking letters," dispatched to deliver a message from the principal and to bring a response back, but unable to negotiate or reach an agreement. They could, at the other extreme, be plenipotentiaries wielding binding powers to conclude a particular matter. Most commonly, however, envoys had the power only to negotiate, not to conclude. The result of the negotiations had to be ratified by the principal. To make sure that they did not stray from the wishes of the principal, negotiators were issued detailed instructions, which could be updated in the course of each mission. Distance, however, could make updates and reporting very difficult. The negotiations might thus drag on for a considerable period of time and the ratification process stretched them even further. Most diplomatic missions in antiquity and the Middle Ages, however, had little continuity: the mandate of an envoy was terminated once a draft agreement was achieved or the negotiations had broken down.

Diplomats were selected for personal suitability and for the skills or authority they brought to the mission. Noncombatants, in particular women or priests, were often considered particularly suitable for diplomatic missions. Envoys could be either high-ranking members of the dispatching society or persons of relatively low status, such as merchants, foreigners, or members of religious minorities, who possessed special skills, such as language, geographical knowledge, or knowledge of the receiving country, court, or potentate. Often, the staff of diplomatic missions was composed of both types of envoys: the former as prestige and ceremonial figures, the latter as practical and technical support. Some embassies were quite large, counting several hundred people, if the entourage is included. Most, however, were smaller, and those headed by a single negotiator not uncommon, especially where danger and uncertainty were involved.

The envoys usually carried gifts for the host and important members of the host court and were expected to receive gifts in return. The failure to offer adequate gifts could seriously jeopardize a mission. Once the host had acknowledged the arrival of an embassy, he was usually expected to provide for their material needs. This expectation was easily translated into a powerful diplomatic weapon: opulence or miserliness could be used to impress or intimidate envoys.

Ancient and medieval diplomacy had four basic agenda: imperial, political, commercial, and exploratory. The imperial agenda characterized the foreign relations of great territorial empires, such as Rome, Byzantium, and China. Separated from similar political entities by large distances and perceiving themselves as superior centers of power and civilization, they regarded the surrounding states and peoples as inferiors and natural subjects. The main purpose of their diplomatic activity was either to keep their neighbors in a tributary relationship or to prevent them from invading or otherwise endangering the empire. This could be achieved by cultural intimidation, bribery in the guise of benevolent gifts, and playing the neighbors against each other. The Byzantine Empire in particular owed much of its longevity to a judicious use of diplomacy in its foreign affairs.

The political agenda encompassed the mainstream of diplomatic activity. Its purpose was to resolve issues such as peace, frontiers, and alliances. It flourished in areas with large concentrations of political units that were in frequent contact with each other. Medieval Indian states, for example, had a rich tradition of intense diplomatic activity and a highly developed theory of diplomacy and foreign relations. The state, however, was not the sole entity with recourse to diplomacy. In medieval Europe, the right of embassy was exercised by corporations, such as cities or guilds; by various church institutions, such as archbishoprics, bishoprics, abbeys, and universities; and by feudal lords acting independently of their overlords. In the fifteenth century, diplomatic representation increasingly came to be seen as a prerogative of the state. The reason for this development was the dramatic increase in diplomatic activity and the growing acknowledgment that sovereign states, rather than an all-encompassing Christian polity, were the organizing principle of European politics.

Commerce was the most common reason for travel and contact between denizens of different political units and thus it gave rise to the largest number of problems that needed to be settled. The key issues were security of the visiting merchants and their property, justice, scope of commercial activity, and customs or taxes on imports and exports. In Europe, Venetian and Byzantine commercial diplomacy went back to the early Middle Ages. However, it was from the twelfth century onward that commerce became an important or even pivotal topic of negotiations, inextricably intertwined with political negotiations.

The exploratory agenda often involved clandestine or secret diplomacy when the envoys traveled incognito or for a manifestly different purpose. For example, the well-known travels of Leo of Rozmital in 1465–1466, ostensibly an exercise in late medieval tourism, actually constituted an attempt by the Hussite king of Bohemia to forge an anti-Turkish alliance that would bypass the pope. The exploratory agenda also could involve attempts at establishing relations or alliances with distant rulers or even mythical figures. The search for Prester John or the attempts to forge an alliance with the great khân of the Mongols are prime examples.

The most basic functions, institutions, forms, and methods of diplomatic conduct were quite universal and can be traced back to antiquity and beyond. A truly significant innovation, which laid foundation to the present diplomatic practice, occurred only in the second half of the fifteenth century, with the Italian invention of permanent diplomatic representation in the person of a resident ambassador.

**BIBLIOGRAPHY**
Bozeman, Adda B. *Politics and Culture in International Society.* Princeton: Princeton UP, 1960.
Ganshoff, François L. *The Middle Ages. A History of International Relations.* New York: Harper and Row, 1970.
Lloyd, T.H. *England and the German Hanse, 1157–1611. A Study in Their Trade and Commercial Diplomacy.* Cambridge: Cambridge UP, 1991.
Mattingly, Garrett. *Renaissance Diplomacy.* Harmondsworth: Penguin, 1965.
Queller, Donald E. *The Office of Ambassador in the Middle Ages.* Princeton: Princeton UP, 1967.
Roy, Gandhi Jee. *Diplomacy in Ancient India.* Patna: Janaki Prakashan, 1981.
Watson, Adam. *The Evolution of International Society. A Comparative Historical Analysis.* London and New York: Routledge, 1992.

*Ivana Elbl*

**SEE ALSO**
Ambassadors; Byzantine Empire; Guilds; India; La Broquière, Bertrandon de; Mongols; Philippe de Mézières; Prester John; Spies; Venice

## Distances, Measurement of
*See* Measurement of Distances

## Dominican Friars
The Order of Friars Preachers, better known as the Dominicans, after their founder, St. Dominic. Dominican Friars played a major role in dealing intellectually with the non-Christian peoples who lived along the borders of Christian Europe.

The emphasis on intellectual formation was a part of Dominican life from the beginning of the order. St. Dominic, Domingo de Guzman (*c.* 1170–1221), the Spanish priest who founded the order in 1216, did so to counter the Albigenses in southern France. His goal was a well-trained body of friars who lived lives of

# D

evangelical poverty and who could preach the doctrines of the Catholic Church so effectively that the teachers of heresy would be defeated by the power of the priest's words rather than by the might of the crusader's sword. To advance this union of poverty and learning, Dominic established houses of study at the universities of Paris and Bologna, a practice that eventually led to Dominican houses at other medieval universities.

One consequence of the Dominican interest in learned preaching was the establishment of schools to train missionaries in various Asian languages. The first of these schools was established in Spain where the Dominicans had begun to preach among the Jewish and Muslim populations. Another consequence was the publication of materials designed to guide missionaries in debates with Muslims and Jews. Thomas Aquinas's (1225–1274) *Summa contra gentiles* is perhaps the best-known example of this literature.

As missionaries, Dominicans were especially active in the Middle East and Asia. Two Dominicans, Ascelin of Lombardy and Andrew of Longjumeau, participated in the Mongol Mission that Pope Innocent IV (1243–1254) initiated at the First Council of Lyons. Their safe return from the East provided the papacy with additional information about the political and religious situation in Asia. Andrew, who had returned to Europe in 1247, went again to the East in 1248, this time as a member of a Dominican mission sponsored by King Louis IX (1226–1270) of France.

At the beginning of the fourteenth century, the Dominicans established a special organization, the *Societas fratrum peregrinatium propter Christum* (The Society of Pilgrims for Christ) in order to direct missionary activities in the East. Like related developments by the Franciscans, the Dominican *Societas* was an attempt to develop an ecclesiastical institutional structure that would respond to the needs of missionaries in Asia. In 1318, Pope John XXII (1316–1334) divided the administration of the church in Asia between the Franciscans and the Dominicans. The Franciscans retained the archiepiscopal see of Beijing, while the Dominicans were assigned a new archiepiscopal see headquartered at Sultaniyeh in Persia. Working from this center, the Dominicans devoted a good deal of their missionary effort to reconciling the schismatic Christian communities of the East with the Latin Church. They were especially successful in reconciling Armenian Christians.

The Dominicans also played an important role in India. India was of special interest in the Middle Ages because it was known that Christian communities had long existed there. Unlike a small group of Franciscans who had sought to make converts from among the Muslim population of India near modern Bombay, the Dominican Friar Jordan Catalani of Sévérac (d. after 1330) worked among the Christians of St. Thomas, who had existed there since at least the third century. He returned to Europe around 1329, where Pope John XXII appointed him bishop of Quilon in southern India, but it is not known whether he ever arrived there.

By the middle of the fourteenth century, Dominican missionary efforts in the East came to an end. The Black Death reduced the numbers of the friars, and the revival of Islam reduced the possibility of openly preaching the Gospel in many parts of Asia. Few converts were ever made, although there was rather more success in reconciling schismatic communities with the Latin Church. One modern scholar evaluated the late medieval missionary efforts in the East as giving the impression of being "an experiment, of trial and error, of a beginning only in the confrontation of an enormous task" (Baldwin, 516).

**BIBLIOGRAPHY**

Baldwin, Marshall W. "Missions to the East in the Thirteenth and Fourteenth Centuries." In Kenneth M. Setton, *A History of the Crusades.* Vol. 5, *The Impact of the Crusades on the Near East.* Ed. Norman P. Zacour and Harry W. Hazard. Madison: U of Wisconsin P, 1985, pp. 452–518.

Daniel, E. Randolph. *The Franciscan Concept of Mission in the High Middle Ages.* Lexington: UP of Kentucky, 1975.

Moffett, Samuel Hugh. *A History of Christianity in Asia.* Vol. I, *Beginnings to 1500.* New York: HarperCollins, 1992.

Phillips, J.R.S. *The Medieval Expansion of Europe.* Oxford: Oxford UP, 1988.

*James Muldoon*

**SEE ALSO**

Albertus Magnus; Andrew of Longjumeau; Armenia; Black Death; Eastern Christianity; Franciscan Friars; India; Jordan of Sévérac; Louis IX; Lyons, First Council of; Thomas of Cantimpré; Vincent of Beauvais

## Dyes and Pigments

Highly valued substances used in the Middle Ages primarily for imparting color to fabrics, paints, and inks. The trade in dyes and pigments transcended geographical borders perhaps more than any commerce besides silks and spices. Three colors—blue, yellow, and red—dominated the market.

For producing blue, the most important dyes for fabrics came from indigo and woad, the latter of which was grown all over Europe. English records, for example, show woad imports largely from the merchants of Picardy, Lombardy, Languedoc, and Amiens. More expensive than woad, indigo was exported primarily from India via a land route before 1497 and Vasco da Gama's discovery of a route by sea.

The most expensive blues so prized by artists were derived from lapis lazuli, azurite, and turnsole or folium. Persian lapis lazuli produced a blue known as "azure" or "ultramarine azure." In the Middle Ages, the expense of blue from lapis made it as valuable a commodity as gems, so that it was openly displayed and frequently offered as a gift. Less expensive was the blue from the copper ore azurite (a lapis lazuli look-alike mineral) found in European silver mines. Turnsole, a blue-purple pigment derived from a plant, was exported from the town of Grand-Gallargues in southern France, as well as other European and Mediterranean sites.

The most extensively used fast yellow dye was extracted from the weld plant, widely cultivated in England. Additional yellows were obtained from dyer's broom, the sumach plant, Persian berries of the buckthorn (which gives an orange-yellow), and saffron from crocus blossoms obtained from Tortosa in Spain or from Tuscany and brought to the markets in Basel and Nuremberg (the largest saffron market in Europe). Both Basel and the present-day town of Saffron Walden in Essex, England, began home-grown production of saffron.

Other sources of yellow were tumeric, from India and elsewhere in the East, and safflower, which also gives additional dyes of red, orange, and pink, obtained from Asia, the East Indies, and Mediterranean areas.

The most valued red dye was kermes, acquired principally from southern Europe, northern Africa, and eastern lands; it imparted a permanent and lively red color. However, the most commonly used red dyestuff in the Middle Ages was madder, called "Turkey red," which gave a variety of brilliant shades of red. Madder was an Asian and a Baltic export, and a cultivated crop in Holland and France, although a wild madder was native to southwest England.

Other red dyes were cochineal, from Armenia, yielding many reds; lac, from India, Burma, and southern Asia, producing scarlet; and orchil (a lichen) and its variants, originally from the Levant and Far East and introduced to Italy in the early 1300s. England imported a number of these red-dyeing lichens from Norway and the Canary Islands. They were increasingly used to dye silks in Italy after the eleventh century. Another red dye was produced from brazil wood, exported from India, Ceylon, and Sumatra. Marco Polo describes a Chinese variety, called "sappan."

Although all secondary colors could be made by combining primary color dyes, purple and green were sometimes produced by other methods. The costly Tyrian purple from Sidon and Tyre was extracted from Mediterranean whelks or mussels of the genera *purpura* and *murex*. England produced a similar dye from shellfish from the coast of Cornwall and Somerset. Green artists' pigments included terre verte (from crushed celadonite and glauconite), known as "green of Crete"; verdigris (copper acetate) or "green of Greece," from Montpellier; and vegetable greens made from rue, parsley, columbine, black nightshade, the German and Florentine iris, and ripe buckthorn or Rhamnus berries.

Browns and blacks, too, could be made by combining primary colors, or by the use of separate dyestuffs. The three separate dyes for brown were catechu; a dye obtained from betel nut from southeastern Asia and the East Indies; and a dye made from the green shells and roots of walnuts. A black dye, gall black, used specifically for the manufacture of high-grade writing ink, was made from galls or excrescences on oak trees caused by the bite of a fly that laid its eggs in the wood.

Although dyestuffs and pigments came from all over Europe and the East, Constantinople and Venice served as the main entrepôts for the provision of the most exotic of these materials, situated as these cities were to command both Alpine highways and Mediterranean sea-lanes connecting to the caravan routes of the Far East. Indeed, Italy was not only a major center for trade in and processing of the pigments themselves, but became, by the fourteenth and fifteenth centuries, a center for the production of artists' manuals and collections of recipes for paints, dyes, and inks.

**BIBLIOGRAPHY**

Edelstein, Sidney M. "The Thirteen Keys—Hints on Studying the History of Dyeing and Bleaching." *American Dyestuff Reporter* 48.9 (4 May 1959): 35–40.

Friedman, John Block. Appendix A: The Pigment Folium. *Northern English Books, Owners, and Makers in the Late Middle Ages.* Syracuse: Syracuse UP, 1995.

# D

Grissom, Carol A. "Green Earth." *Artists' Pigments: A Handbook of Their History and Characterization.* Ed. Robert L. Feller. Washington, DC: National Gallery of Art, 1986.

Robinson, Stuart. *A History of Dyed Textiles.* Cambridge, MA: Massachusetts Institute of Technology P, 1969.

Rosetti, Gioanventure. *The Plictho: Instructions in the Art of the Dyers which Teaches the Dyeing of Woolen Cloths, Linens, Cottons, and Silk by the Great Art as Well as by the Common.* Trans. of the first edition of 1548 by Sidney M. Edelstein and Hector C. Borghetly. Cambridge, MA: Massachusetts Institute of Technology P, 1969.

Thompson, Daniel V. *The Materials and Techniques of Medieval Painting.* New York: Dover, 1956.

*Laura F. Hodges*

**SEE ALSO**

Canary Islands; Constantinople; Da Gama, Vasco; Gems; India; Saffron; Textiles, Decorative; Venice

# E

## Eastern Christianity

Jesus Christ was born and lived his entire life in Asia. Christianity, as a result, originated in the Middle East and spread out from there. According to the New Testament, the Apostles preached the Gospel in Palestine, Syria, Asia Minor, Greece, Rome, and Egypt.

The first state to adopt Christianity officially was Armenia, in 301, followed in the middle of that century by Ethiopia, which the historiographer Rufinus (410/11), translator and continuator of Eusebius's *Ecclesiastical History,* called "third India." Both countries became Christian states *extra limina Romani imperii* before Roman Emperor Theodosius I accepted Christianity as the official religion of the Roman Empire around 390. For this reason, Asian Christianity has always emphasized its primacy.

Although differences concerning the doctrine of the Holy Trinity in the fourth century might have been resolved, fifth century debates over Christology—or the nature of Jesus Christ—caused irreparable schisms among the Asian and the Eastern Mediterranean Christian communities. Differences in both dogma and mentality resulted in the formation of national churches, a development promoted by the wide variety of vernaculars spoken by early Christians, which impeded mutual communication. After the Council of Ephesus (431), the theological school of Edessa, which believed Christ to consist of two distinct persons, divine and human, while emphasizing his humanity, was rejected as Nestorianism. This decision prompted a countermovement at the theological school of Alexandria, which stressed a single nature to the person of Christ, primarily divine with human attributes. Adher-

ents of this point of view were called Monophysites. At the Council of Chalcedon (451), the view that Christ had two natures inseparably in one person was fixed; Monophysitism was condemned as heresy. Nevertheless, churches that did not accept the Chalcedonian doctrine continued to thrive, as did those of the orthodox ("Chalcedonian") school.

Among the Chalcedonians in the East were several national churches that differed from each other in language, liturgy, and customs, though they were all considered to be orthodox. In addition to the Greek Orthodox Church of the Roman Empire, several other communities, Orthodox as well as Nestorian and Monophysite, deserve mention.

The Melchites (Latin *Suriani*), whose name means "friends of the ruler" (Syriac *malka* "king"), were Hellenized Asians living in the Byzantine Empire, especially in Syria and Egypt, but lacking their own state. Even after the Great Schism of 1054 (when Pope Leo IX's excommunication of Patriarch Michael Cerullarius made the split between the Orthodox and Roman Churches permanent), the Melchites were on good terms with the crusaders and Western Christians of the late Middle Ages.

The Georgians, Christianized in the fourth century, created their own language and alphabet. Although their credal statements linked them, at different times, to the Greeks and the Armenians, they adopted the Chalcedonian orthodoxy in *c.*1000, while continuing to use the Georgian language in their liturgy. These Caucasians, highly regarded as fighters, were thought to be the descendants of St. George, who was venerated by both Greek and Latin Christians.

# E

The Alans, an Iranian nomadic tribe, separated into two groups: one accompanied the Vandals to North Africa during the migration of nations, the other remained north of the Black Sea. Working as mercenaries in the tenth century, they embraced Greek (Byzantine) Christianity. Like the Melchites, they employed Greek in their liturgy; they were also influenced by the Georgians. During the Mongol era (1206–1368), they traveled widely throughout Asia, serving as functionaries and diplomats who specialized in contacts with the West.

The Sogdians (Latin *Soldini* or *Soldani*) were also an Iranian nomadic tribe, living in ancient Sogdiana, between the Oxus (Amu Darya) and Iaxartes (Syr Darya) rivers. Conquered by Alexander the Great, later part of the dominion of the Syrian Diadoches and characterized as Greek-Syrian, they also belonged to the empires of the Parthians and New Persians. They were centered around Maracanda or Afrasiyab (modern Samarkand) in Central Asia. Their Iranian dialect was the *lingua franca* of this part of Asia, and their way of writing, which contained Aramaic (that is, Syrian) elements, was adopted by the Uighurs and later by the Mongols. The Armenian historiographer Hetoum (*c.* 1245–*c.* 1314) records that Sogdians were living in Chorezm and Tarse (Xinjiang), and that they adhered to the Greek creed but used their own language, information also found in reports by many Western travelers to Asia.

The Maronites, whom Western writers sometimes mistook for Chalcedonians, lived harmoniously with the Roman Church after 1180. They accepted Monothelitism, an attempt to reconcile Monophysitism and Orthodoxy that was first proposed in 622, but was curbed by the Arab invasion in Syria and Lebanon.

The Nestorian Church, which took its name from the patriarch Nestorius (*c.* 381–*c.* 451) emerged in the fifth century and had the eastern dialect of Syriac as its official language. From the fifth century on, Nestorian Christians desired to be more than just an appendage of Constantinople. Those who lived outside the Roman Empire, mainly in eastern Syria, were also known as the East Syrian or Assyrian Church (their liturgy is still Syriac). Nestorianism spread from Edessa to eastern Anatolia, Mesopotamia, Iran, the Arabian Peninsula, and India. At the beginning of the seventh century, Nestorians were the most active Christian missionaries in Central Asia, Xinjiang, and China. The famous stone tablet at Xian [or Sian], the ancient Chinese capital Chang'an, with its bilingual inscription, testifies that Christians lived in China as early as 635, and had established an archbishopric there by that time. When Muslim armies conquered Arabia and the Middle East, the Nestorian catholicos remained at his seat at Seleucia-Ktesiphon and became the principal contact for all Christian visitors to the Abbasid caliphate. The Nestorians dominated educated society at Baghdad, imparting Greek culture to the Muslims. A second missionary movement took place at the beginning of the eleventh century, with Nestorians working at Xinjiang and in the Orchon basin, Christianizing the Uighur, Kereyid, Naiman, Merkid, and Önggüd peoples.

The Mongols conquered these nations in the early 1200s, and subsequently they formed a Christian contingent in the Mongol army. Hence, the idea that Mongols supported Western Christians during the later crusades is not mere imagining. To the West, Nestorian Christianity was exotic. Knowledge of their existence along with reports of a Christian emperor called Prester John caused crusaders to believe that a Christian potentate would come from east Asia and help to establish Christian government in the Middle East. The empire of the il-khâns in Persia (1258–1334) briefly seemed to offer a location for their hopes when the Nestorian Mar Jahballaha III, a Mongol by birth, became catholicos in 1280–1281 on a pilgrimage to Jerusalem. But the hope was short-lived. After 1300, Mongol Iran was Islamized; the Mongols governing in China (Yuan Dynasty 1271–1368) never converted to Christianity, despite attempts by Western missionaries to evangelize them.

The Church of St. Thomas of India was known in Europe throughout the Middle Ages. Origen (*c.* 185–*c.* 254) testified that the Apostle Thomas had reached Parthia, which later traditions transformed into India; Cosmas Indikopleustes, in the sixth century agreed. For Rufinus, the Indians are the Ethiopian Aksumites. Some Westerners believed that Indian Christians were Nestorians. Between around 1245 and the 1350s, Westerners such as John of Marignolli visited Christian communities in India, reporting on visits to the church that claimed to have St. Thomas's relics, and some telling of their effort to find Prester John. The Portuguese claimed that the Indian Christians were Nestorians.

Jacobites are members of the Monophysite Church of Syria, deriving their name from the reformer Jakob Bardai (d. 578), bishop of Edessa at a time when Syria was a center of education. Because the Syrian language, an Aramaic dialect (Latin *Chaldaica lingua*), offers a fine vocabulary for abstract ideas, similar to Greek, Syria has long been home to intensive theological discussions. The center of the Jacobites was Antioch. The historian Barhebraeus (d. 1286), living near Mosul, is an excellent witness to the importance of these non-Chalcedonians during the late crusades.

Copts derive their name from the Egyptians. They had their center at Alexandria, where Monophysitism originated. Their language, a descendant of ancient Egyptian with Greek additions (the written form employs the Greek alphabet with additional characters), was used in their liturgy. The Coptic Church found many adherents because numerous Christians living in Egypt did not want to align themselves with Byzantium. After 641, they entered into a covenant of toleration with Umar, caliph of the Moslems. During the Fifth Crusade (1217–1221), they proved to be especially important partners for the crusaders.

The Nubians lived in Upper Egypt and in Sudan, covering the region from Syene (Aswan) to the confluence of the Blue Nile and the White Nile. They were black Christians, often confused with Ethiopians. In Acts of the Apostles 8:27, a "vir Aetiops" is introduced as an official in the court of Kandake (the Candace of the Alexander romances who consorts with the conquerer), which was the title of the Nubian queens. Nubia was Christianized during the sixth century by the Orthodox Byzantine emperor Justinian and his Monophysite wife Theodora: her missionaries worked in the northern kingdom of Nobatia with Bishop Pachoras, while other orthodox missionaries went to the two southern Nubian kingdoms of Makurra and Alwa. Owing to this Byzantine influence, Nubians developed a unique form of Greek, which they used in their liturgy; later they integrated a few characters from the Coptic alphabet. Conquered by the Muslims in the later Middle Ages, some Nubian Christian communities survived as independent kingdoms up to the early sixteenth century. The Nubians are also mentioned in connection with the Fifth Crusade: Oliver of Paderborn prophesied that they would overcome the Muslims.

For classical antiquity, Ethiopia was the southernmost territory known to be inhabited; it lay near the equator. Christianized in the fourth century, the Ethiopians were converted to Monophysitism by nine Syrian missionaries in the sixth century. Around the year 1000, Judaism appears to have been widespread in Ethiopia, but in the twelfth century it was Chris-

tianized again by the Zagwé dynasty. In the late Middle Ages, the country, whose Islamic inhabitants were frequently in conflict with Christians, was governed by powerful Christian rulers. After 1187, the Ethiopians acquired their own church in Jerusalem near the Holy Sepulchre, as a result of which they became better known to Western Christians. The writers of several late medieval works identified the ruler of Ethiopia with Prester John, and after 1400, Western travelers and explorers sought him here rather than in Asia.

Armenians were the most important mediators between Latin Christians and Asia during the time of the crusades. They lived in the Transcaucasian tableland near the lakes of Van, Sevan, and Urmiah. The first nation to declare itself officially Christian, Armenia remained Orthodox until around the year 1000, when it adopted Monophysitism, in response to Byzantium (Greater Armenia). Some Armenians lived in Cilicia (Lesser Armenia) and were closely linked to the crusaders and the Roman Church, especially after 1198 (the beginning of the Fourth Crusade). Some Armenians visited Europe and spoke French; their most prominent voice in the Latin West was the excellent historian Hetoum of Armenia or Gorigos, whose French account of his nation (*c.*1307) was popular; it was widely disseminated in a Latin version as well.

During the first millennium, the West had only vague knowledge of Asian Christianity. Eastern ideology was not always competently or exactly rendered into Latin, and thus Roman-rite Christians frequently considered their Asian counterparts to be be schismatics, or even heretics. During the crusades—especially after the failures of the thirteenth century—interest in them increased. In the later Middle Ages, Western visitors to Asia tried to communicate with Eastern Christians, holding them in high esteem. Written records describe their religious beliefs, warlike bravery, and the exotic products they could supply. The Mongol invasions of the 1230s and 1240s forced Europe to confront Asia and encouraged Latin Christians to look for allies in the battle against non-Christians. Remembering Jesus' command at the end of St. Matthew's gospel, Western Christians also chose to go into all the world to seek other Christians, and this became a motivation for late medieval explorers.

**BIBLIOGRAPHY**
Atiya, Aziz Suryal. *A History of Eastern Christianity.* London: Methuen 1968.

# E

Brincken, Anna-Dorothee von den. *Die "Nationes Christianorum Orientalium" im Verständnis der lateinischen Historiographie von der Mitte des 12. bis in die zweite Hälfte des 14. Jahrhunderts.* Kölner Historische Abhandlungen 22. Cologne and Vienna: Böhlau, 1973.

Frend, W.H.C. *The Rise of the Monophysite Movement: Chapters in the History of the Church in the Fifth and Sixth Centuries.* Cambridge: Cambridge UP, 1972.

Pelikan, Jaroslav. *The Spirit of Eastern Christendom (600–1700).* Vol. 2 of *The Christian Tradition.* Chicago: U of Chicago P, 1975.

Rogers, Francis M. *The Search for Eastern Christians.* Minneapolis: U of Minnesota P, 1962.

Spuler, Bertold. *Die morgenländischen Kirchen.* Leiden and Cologne: Brill, 1964.

——. "Religion. Religionsgeschichte des Orients in der Zeit der Weltreligionen." In *Handbuch der Orientalistik.* I,VII, 2. Leiden: Brill, 1961, pp. 120–324.

*Anna-Dorothee von den Brincken*

**SEE ALSO**

Armenia; Cosmas Indikopleustes; Crusade, Fourth; Crusade, Fifth; Edessa; Egypt; Ethiopians; Hetoum; India; John of Marignolli; Nestorianism; Prester John; Rabban Ata, Simeon

## Ebstorf World Map

The largest *mappamundi* known to have been drawn during the European Middle Ages. Measuring twelve feet in diameter (3.56 x 3.58 meters), the Ebstorf World Map was discovered around 1830, among pre-Reformation liturgical utensils in a lumber room of the (then Protestant) nunnery of Ebstorf 15.5 miles (25 km) south of Lüneburg, Germany, by Charlotte von Lasperg, one of the conventuals. It was brought to Hanover in 1833 or 1834.

The map was painted on thirty goatskins sewn together, but it was disassembled for restoration in Berlin in 1888. During World War II, it was destroyed in the state archives at Hanover during an Allied air raid on the night of October 8–9, 1943. Between 1950 and 1953, four copies were made by the artist Rudolf Wieneke (1890–1955) in original size, form, material, and colors, two of which are publicly displayed in the convent of Ebstorf and the Museum für das Fürstentum in Lüneburg.

The map shows the earth surrounded by the Ocean in circular form. The Mediterranean Sea divides the earth into the three traditional continents of Asia (with the Earthly Paradise at the top), Europe (in the lower left corner), and Africa (to the right).

With its nearly 1,200 map legends, the Ebstorf *mappamundi* is a unique historical and geographical document. It depicts seas, lakes, rivers, mountains, islands, cities, monasteries, and various curiosities. Its sources of information include the Bible (it shows a very detailed Holy Land and the tombs of the Apostles); ancient history (Troy and places associated with Alexander the Great are here); authors like Strabo, Pomponius Mela, Solinus, Orosius, Isidore, Adam of Bremen, and Honorius Augustodunensis; legendary material (for monsters at the edge of the earth); and first-hand experience, especially within Europe. Some rivers (Rhine and Rhône, Danube and Oder, Weser and Main), converge on the map, although in reality they do not flow into each other; rivers may be intended to signify traffic routes.

Differing from most other medieval world maps, Ebstorf shows the earth representing—almost like a huge Eucharistic host—the body of Christ, whose head, hands, and feet mark the four cardinal directions (his head is in the East). In the center of the earth lies Jerusalem, where a depiction of Christ rising from the tomb is located. (Certain parallels can be found in Hildegard von Bingen's second vision in her *Liber divinorum operum,* in the London Psalter Map, and in Piro di Puccio's Genesis in the Camposanto of Pisa.)

The precise date of the Ebstorf World Map is contested; scholars have dated it to various times between 1213 and 1373. Most scholars believe that it was produced between 1230 and 1250; a combination of toponyms connected to Duke Otto I (the Child) of Brunswick-Lüneburg suggest an origin around 1239.

No one has seriously contested the idea that the map was made at or near the Welf [Guelph] court, because it shows eleven relatively unimportant rivers within Welf territory in Lower Saxony, and because of the extraordinary size of the pictures of the Welf residences at Brunswick and Lüneburg, comparable within Europe only to Cologne, Aachen, and Rome. Perhaps the map was painted in the nunnery of Ebstorf and was destined for the ducal residence in Lüneburg (where it never arrived or was lost in the destruction of Lüneburg castle in 1371, leaving only a copy or model at Ebstorf).

The intellectual author (not the painter) of the map was possibly Gervase of Tilbury, whose *Liber de mirabilibus mundi* is the most recently written work the mapmaker used. Gervase, of English origin (Tille-

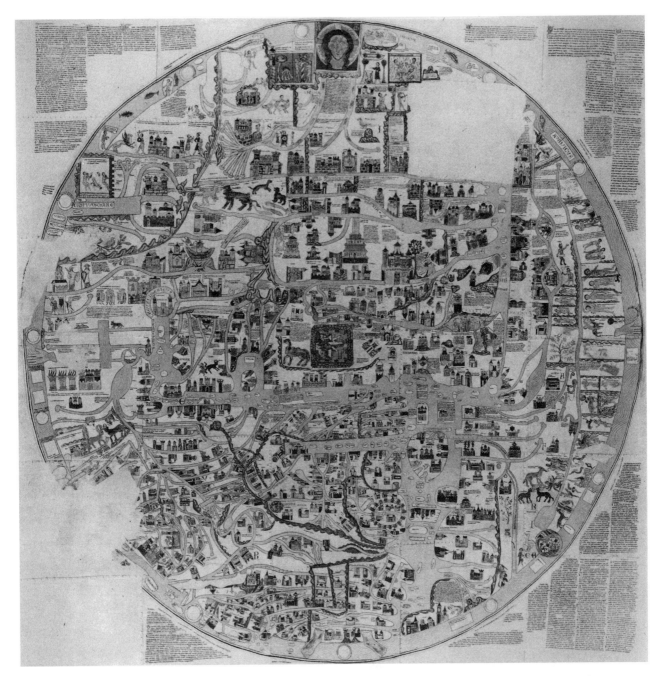

Ebstorf World Map. Lüneburg, *c.* 1240, destroyed 1943. After a facsimile in the Map Division of the New York Public Library. Reproduced by permission of the Map Division, The New York Public Library (Astor, Lenox and Tilden Foundations).

beriensis), was born *c.* 1165 (he referred to himself as *puer* in 1177, and was called *adolescens c.* 1183), earned a master's degree, and taught canon law at the University of Bologna before 1189. He lived at the Sicilian court in 1189, served as judge of the archbishop of Arles in 1201 and of the count of Provence in 1207, and was appointed by Emperor Otto IV of Brunswick

"in regno Arelatis imperialis aule marescalcus" *c.* 1209, which proves his close connection to the Welf court. After the Hohenstaufen and the French defeated the Welfs and the English at the battle of Bouvines in 1214, he lost his office but dedicated his *Liber,* now named *Otia imperialia,* to the defeated emperor to serve as consolation.

# E

Gervase complains about the errors of so-called *mappaemundi* and declares that he added a better one to his work. No surviving manuscript of Gervase's text, however, contains a map, but possibly an offspring of it is preserved in the Ebstorf World Map, which contains several parallels to Gervase's book: the Mediterranean Sea is represented not as a T, but as a Y; Rome is in the form of a lion; episcopal geography is stressed; and the world is in the form of a huge man. Between 1223 and 1234 a "Gervasius" was the provost of the nunnery of Ebstorf. If he is Gervase of Tilbury, as many scholars maintain, this may explain how such an outstanding world map came to be made—or deposited—at Ebstorf.

The Ebstorf World Map must be seen concurrently from various standpoints; from the point of view of geography, it is a map; from that of learning generally, an encyclopedia; as a work of iconography, it is a picture of God's creation; as a work of politics, a sign of lordship; and as a work of piety, it represents a means of meditation.

**BIBLIOGRAPHY**

Kugler, Hartmut, with Eckhard Michael, eds. *Ein Weltbild vor Columbus: Die Ebstorfer Weltkarte. Interdisziplinäres Colloquium 1988.* Weinheim: VCH, Acta humaniora, 1991.

Miller, Konrad. *Mappaemundi, Die Ältesten Weltkarten.* Heft 5: Die Ebstorfkarte. Mit dem Faksimile der Karte in den Farben des Originals. Stuttgart: Roth, 1896.

Rosien, Walter. *Die Ebstorfer Weltkarte.* Hanover: Niedersächsisches Amt für Landesplanung, 1952.

Sommerbrodt, Ernst. *Die Ebstorfer Weltkarte, Hierbei ein Atlas von 25 Tafeln in Lichtdruck.* Hanover: Hahn, 1891.

Wolf, Armin. "News on the Ebstorf World Map: Date, Origin, Authorship." In *Géographie du monde au moyen âge et à la renaissance.* Ed. Monique Pelletier. Paris: C.T.H.S., 1989, pp. 51–68.

———. "Gervasius von Tilbury und die Welfen. Zugleich Bemerkungen zur Ebstorfer Weltkarte." In *Die Welfen und ihr Braunschweiger Hof im hohen Mittelalter.* Ed. Bernd Schneidmüller. Wiesbaden: Harrassowitz, 1995, pp. 407–438.

*Armin Wolf*

**SEE ALSO**
Adam of Bremen; Geography in Medieval Europe; Gervase of Tilbury; Gog and Magog; Honorius Augustodunensis; Isidore of Seville; *Mappamundi;* Mela, Pomponius; Orosius; Psalter Map; Solinus, Julius Gaius

## Economics and Trade

Throughout the European Middle Ages, the volume and patterns of trade depended on a variety of factors, ranging from any one region's natural resources to the intricate play of local and long-distance demand and supply. Trade flows were shaped by economic forces, natural calamities, social relations, politics, and cultural preferences. Market structures, the matrix enabling and constraining commercial interchange, remained profoundly dependent on tradition, established institutions and ties, and set ways of doing business. This does not mean, however, that they were changeless. From 400 C.E. to 1500, Europe experienced the stresses of adapting to profound and often abrupt market structure shifts, both exogenous and inherent to the various European economies, with the inevitable accompaniment of social resistance, foreign and domestic conflict, and increased competition. Changes in population levels, technology, legal practices, property relations, political frameworks, ideologies, and the status of various ethnic and religious groups affected market structures, and thus trade.

In the eastern half of the disintegrating Roman Empire, commerce generally prospered until the later sixth century, and ties were maintained with Central Asia, India, and the Far East. In the West, commercial activity declined as the economy contracted and rural autarchy increased. Western trade in luxuries and special articles, however, remained anchored to the late Roman Mediterranean networks. Seventh-century Marseille continued to import Tunisian oil, Gaza wine, and oriental spices and papyrus. By the early 600s, the Celts, the Anglo-Saxons, and, to some degree, the Franks, were increasingly participating in long-distance commerce as producers, consumers, and middlemen, while Frisian traders linked the Rhineland, Britain, and the Baltic. The Lombard disruption of Italian-Rhenish trade flows had no lasting effect, as routes merely shifted westward to the rivers Rhône and Meuse. Mediterranean pottery found in western Britain documents the persistence of direct but small-scale contacts with Byzantium between 475 and 550.

Despite the turmoil of the Germanic migrations, the decaying infrastructure of Roman roads, bridges, and paved river fords did not seriously hamper overland trade. Although many of the great strategic Roman roadways remained usable until after the fifth century, they made for poor trade routes. Undeviating links between garrison towns and administrative centers, stubbornly braving steep gradients, they were built for soldiers, not merchants. Between smaller settlements, goods had never ceased to travel along pre-Roman tracks, whose use was fostered by the limitations of wheeled transport: until the horseshoe and collar were widely adopted, wagon loads remained light, and trains of pack animals competed easily with wagons. Roman harbors remained mostly in use, and were adapted to changing needs. River navigation continued, above all on the Rhine and the Loire. Some unfortified towns vanished, others were temporarily deserted, and communities surviving within circles of defensive walls shrank in size. But although urban demand contracted, craft production in the key continental towns remained lively, and Syrian, Greek, and Jewish merchants continued to trade there.

A much sharper break in continuity occurred between the 550s and 750, under the impact of plagues that, spreading from Alexandria and Byzantium, ravaged Spain, Italy, and Gaul. Depopulation was compounded by renewed political turmoil, Byzantine attempts to regain the western Mediterranean, and the subsequent Byzantine and Visigothic inability to stem the advance of Islam. Although Muslim conquest ultimately brought large areas into the wide sphere of Islamic commerce, the transition was costly in economic terms. The instability caused by the political, legal, fiscal, and religious changes that accompanied the Muslim advance into northwest Africa (the Maghrib, 647–710) and Spain (711–730) had barely subsided when a massive Berber revolt shook the Maghrib and Spain in 739–741. Sparked by new taxes and by rivalry between the Berber and Middle Eastern troops in Spain, and animated by the austere ideology of Kharijism, a dissident form of Islam, the revolt opened a new period of upheaval. Gradual recovery followed only the founding of such Maghribi Kharijite trading states as the Barghwata principality in Morocco (744), the Midrarid city state of Sijilmassa (757), and the Rustumid imamate of Tahart (761). In Spain, the rise and consolidation in 756–776 of the Umayyad emirate of Córdoba also provided a firmer political framework favoring commerce.

In the meantime, Europe's dynamic center of gravity shifted to the north, where demographic and agrarian growth fostered an economic upswing. Here, trade revived from the late 600s, making the fortunes of new "proto-urban" trading stations and seaports known as *wics*. New regional markets helped open up the hinter-

land, and suburbs settled by merchants developed around walled towns such as Paris, London, and York. New trading outposts along the Elbe and Danube Rivers promoted contact with the Slav populations in the east by the ninth century. Trade also benefited from road maintenance, the adoption of the square sail on northern oared ships, and an increasing use of money, aided by a shift from gold to petty silver coinage. From the late 700s to about 820, the flourishing Carolingian Empire in France and Germany temporarily ensured a more stable and homogeneous environment through political centralization, legal codification, and championing of Christianity.

In southern Europe, corresponding growth began only around 800–850. Although the expansion of Islam did not really close the Mediterranean to Christian trade, direct contacts with the East diminished. The Islamic area, however, exerted a lively demand for raw materials and slaves, and exported Spanish and Oriental luxuries in return. Umayyad Spain and the Aghlabid emirate of Ifriqiya represented powerful economic magnets. Southern Italian towns, in particular Amalfi, poised between the Muslim, Byzantine, and Lombard zones, were asserting themselves as prosperous emporia by 900 C.E. In such northern Mediterranean ports as Marseille, Genoa, and Venice, trade during the ninth and early tenth centuries clearly fell short of the north European ferment. But the gap gradually closed, above all between 850 and 950, even though the economy of southeastern Gaul and parts of southern Italy suffered from Muslim raids mounted during these years from bases in Spain, Sicily (conquered by the Aghlabids between 827 and 902), the Balearics (occupied around 902), Sardinia, and Corsica.

While the foundations of future recovery were slowly being laid in southern Europe, the north experienced a wave of invasions unlike anything seen since late Roman times. Viking raiders turned the northern seas from a source of prosperity into a place of peril. The first great Viking plundering expeditions reached Northumbria in 793, Ireland in 795, the Vendée in 799, and Muslim Spain in the early 800s. In 810, the Danes attacked Frankish trade centers in Frisia, and by 830–840, no continental seaport, from the recently founded Hamburg to the Strait of Gibraltar, through which Viking ships passed into the Mediterranean in 859, was safe. Thrusts directed along the major rivers also took the Scandinavians deep into the heart of

# E

Europe (Cologne, 863; Coblenz, 881; Trier, 882; Paris, 845, 857, 885–886). Under the combined weight of these assaults and of Muslim incursions from the south, the decaying Carolingian Empire lost its cohesion. From 866 onward, the Danes also spearheaded a systematic attempt to conquer England, and in the early 900s, the Norse established a permanent colony in Ireland (Dublin). At the same time, from around 850, nomadic Magyar invaders from the east disrupted the Slav borderlands, and by the early 900s, they reached Burgundy. Between 907 and 955, regular Magyar raids afflicted Germany.

And yet trade in northern Europe rebounded well before the worst was over, despite the complications that resulted from the proliferation of unstable coinages minted by local lords and institutions, the inheritors of weakening Carolingian authority. From 850 to 950, the rise of new periodic markets was favored by a higher mobility of the rural population and by agrarian progress (for example, the spread of water mills, forges, and the horse collar). Disruptive at first, the Scandinavian expansion quickly helped to consolidate a vast maritime network, linked to Byzantium and Asia by way of Russia (a key area of Swedish penetration), and in areas of Viking colonization small urban and artisanal settlements flourished (for example, Norwich or Thetford in England). The Christianization of east and north European elites by German missionaries fostered trade with Germanic lands. Ransoms and booty brought hoarded wealth into circulation, and where capacity constraints did not intervene, the pressure to pay off raiders actually boosted output and transactions. Even defensive infrastructure assisted growth. Local economies were stimulated by the building of redoubts and refuges under Louis the Pious and by Alfred the Great's "burgal hidage" system (a network of some thirty fortified centers, ranging from ancient proto-historic forts like Chisbury, through old Roman towns such as Winchester, to royal manors and monastic centers—Oxford, for instance). Such strongholds became focal points of artisanal production and trade.

In southern Europe, regional development was similarly tied to the founding of strongholds and fortified hilltop villages, a process known as *incastellamento*. By contrast, the maritime activity of ports like Pisa, Genoa, or Venice had at first relatively little impact on the hinterland. This changed once external threats began to subside around 900–930. Urban and rural

growth then interlocked as agricultural surpluses were drawn to urban markets. The decaying unfortified commercial suburbs of such old centers as Narbonne, Carcassonne, or Marseille gradually revived. Lasting from about 930 to 980, this phase prepared the ground for what R.S. Lopez called the "commercial revolution" of the eleventh and twelfth centuries—a sustained expansion of trade accompanied by growing use of coinage and improvements in transport and business techniques.

The "revolution" started in the regions of northern Italy, Languedoc, Catalonia, southern Burgundy, Charente, Poitou, and southern Germany. By the mid-eleventh century it affected other parts of Germany, Navarre, Castile, and Aragon, and finally, late in the eleventh century, Picardy, Berry, Lorraine, and England. Ultimately, two leading foci of growth emerged: north-central Italy (the gateway to Byzantium and the Muslim East) and the Low Countries (a key corridor to the northern maritime space). Both became centers of urbanization and manufacturing. Inside the continental corridor linking the two, there arose by the twelfth century the fairs of Champagne and Brie, which from the 1180s became a meeting ground for Italian middlemen and Franco-Flemish suppliers of light, cheap northern woolen fabrics, such as worsted says and serges, which were in demand in the warmer Mediterranean climate.

The mechanisms underlying the "commercial revolution" were more complex than historians had first thought. Initially, some historical models made the northern itinerant merchant the key agent of change and towns the engine of development (Henri Pirenne), while others stressed the role of Islamic lands, which offered Europe an example of mature commercial techniques and stimulated its underdeveloped economy by purchasing raw materials and supplying luxuries that created consumption habits (Maurice Lombard). But the "revolution's" first phase (from about 980 to the 1070s), which witnessed a widespread revival of European commercial activity, received impetus not only from urban development and long-distance trade, but also from a demographic and agrarian expansion accompanied by changes in settlement and land-holding patterns, as well as in rural power relationships. The process was intertwined with a continuing growth of craft production and regional trade, and with merchants' rising demand for coinage, accommodated by the development of new silver mines in

Germany. Finally, commerce benefited from the Peace of God movement (*c.* 990), which withdrew unarmed clergy and farmers from private feudal warfare, and the Truce of God movement (*c.* 1027–thirteenth century), an attempt by the Church to enforce the cessation of hostilities during holy seasons and days. The Church might condemn the merchant's profit-seeking, but it was willing to protect him as an unarmed traveler who paid lucrative tolls and could be a potential donor.

From the tenth century in the south, and the eleventh century in the north, the clearing of new farmland by peasants chiefly benefited the nobility. Land exploited directly by the lords slowly gave way to dependent small-holdings ringing villages, and seigneurial authority and exactions through bailiffs and stewards expanded. At the same time, the nobility and the Church consolidated large domains better equipped to take advantage of growing urban demand. Both trends increased estate revenue. Sustained by the agrarian upswing and feeding back into it, urban development both contributed to and resulted from commercial and artisanal activity. Moreover, until specialization in production, institutional barriers, and capital requirements concentrated certain activities in towns, rural craft output kept expanding as well. By 1050, this dual ferment had managed to promote steady increases in the supply of raw materials such as wood, iron, copper, lead, flax, wool, skins, and wax. The development was reinforced when, in northern waters, the introduction of the keel in the late 900s enlarged the carrying capacity of ships, promoting traffic in bulky goods such as lumber, grain, wine from southern France, stone from the Baltic, and hides.

The second phase of the "revolution," which witnessed steady expansion of basic trade networks all across Europe and the achievement of Christian naval preponderance in the Mediterranean, began around 1060–1070. It was not, however, a period of uninterrupted growth. In fact, it opened under the shadow of an economic contraction in Germany (a decline that did not affect the rest of Europe until about 1130–1140). New markets nonetheless proliferated, and the Champagne fairs increased in importance once adequate regulatory supports were put in place in 1137–1164. Commerce also benefited from the migration of peasants, artisans, and merchants south toward the Iberian Peninsula and east into the Slavic area. These population movements helped link various regional trade networks. They coincided with the cru-

sades as well as with the Christian advance in the western Mediterranean, which, in reclaiming key regional shipping lanes, arguably surpassed the crusades in commercial significance. The crusades, nonetheless, changed long-distance Levant trade by endowing the upstart western Mediterranean ports of Genoa and Pisa with new privileges in eastern harbors. The newcomers were thus able to challenge such earlier centers of exchanges with the East as Amalfi, Trani, Bari, or Salerno. Venice, with established Eastern interests and a need to placate Byzantium, benefited only belatedly and considerably less.

After a brief pause, the "revolution's" third phase brought renewed economic activity and the spread of new institutions favorable to trade and new business techniques. Commercial growth reached a temporary plateau around 1130–1170, at about the same time as new land development in the West peaked and leveled off (1120–1180). The 1180s, however, ushered in an extensive although geographically uneven period of urban expansion, predicated in the larger towns less on regional agricultural resources and productivity than on political and cultural factors, interregional trade opportunities, and the size of the urban middle class. Increasing division of labor between town and country and a deepening of overland trade networks accompanied the process. The prosperity of the great trade and pilgrimage routes, such as the one linking the four main Champagne fairs at Provins, Troyes, Lagny, and Bar-sur-Aube, stimulated large hinterland areas, fostering a greater commercialization of agriculture. The development of a money-based economy was encouraged by fiscal pressures (church tithes, intensifying royal levies), by cash commutation of peasant services and dues (which progressed everywhere except in the Anglo-Norman area), and by the discovery of new silver lodes in Saxony (1169), Sardinia, Calabria, and Hungary. Reflecting business needs, heavier and larger silver coins, the *grossi,* began to circulate during the late twelfth century.

A variety of institutional refinements promoted predictability and security, lowering transaction costs (a term that covers, for instance, the cost of information-gathering, transportation, weighing and measuring, marketing, and contract enforcement). Commerce benefited from safe-conducts, commercial treaties, the regulation of weights and measures, and the waning of such ancient antimercantile customs as the forfeiture of shipwrecked goods or of the possessions of foreign

# E

merchants who died intestate. Specialized commercial and maritime law increasingly offered quicker justice than the cumbersome civil and ecclesiastical courts, and consuls posted abroad by trading towns began to exercise civil jurisdiction over their compatriots. Associations such as merchant guilds, early craft guilds, and trading town leagues won for themselves the benefits of political influence and better access to capital and information. In northern Europe, the type of merchant league known as *hanse* became prominent. A number of such leagues appeared in the twelfth century, and some of them became lasting institutions. The so-called Hanse of Seventeen Towns, which represented the interests of a group of Flemish and northern French cloth-making centers at the fairs of Champagne, endured from the late twelfth century to the late thirteenth. The understanding that between 1157 and 1161 linked the *hanse* of Germans trading in London, originally headed by the merchants of Cologne, and the recently founded *hanse* of Lübeck, organized for trade with the Baltic island of Gotland, prepared the ground for the creation, in the thirteenth century, of the German Hanse (later the Hanseatic League), which remained a great merchant power throughout the late Middle Ages.

The attitude of the Church toward trade also became more accommodating after 1150, and usury (taking of interest) was increasingly condemned only in word rather than in deed. The legal framework for venture association and investment became more sophisticated as diverse forms of limited and unlimited partnership (known in various places and over time as *rogadia, societas, compagnia, commenda, collegantia*) developed through a mixture of independent invention and Byzantine, Islamic, and Jewish influences. The new accounting approaches of the 1150s led by the late 1200s to experiments with double-entry bookkeeping, which permitted a closer analysis of operations. Currency exchange contracts of the kind notarized by the Genoese in the twelfth century foreshadowed the development of the bill of exchange. Genoese sale contracts offering the option to buy back a cargo at a set price after safe arrival did the same for marine insurance.

Key advances in business technique were limited to major trading centers and remained largely the preserve of the Italians, but the overall effects of favorable institutional trends continued into the thirteenth century. Transfer and deposit banking developed rapidly at the hands of southern money changers and merchant-

bankers. The bill of exchange came to supplement trade credit informally extended by merchants to each other. Improved by Italians frequenting the Champagne fairs and perfected by the late 1200s, the bill combined currency exchange with transfer and credit functions, and avoided risky transport of coin. Meanwhile, silver coins even heavier than the previous *grossi* provided new convenient units for large-scale and long-distance transactions; so did the gold coinages launched by Genoa and Florence (1252) and Venice (1284), which ended the many centuries during which silver had been the dominant coinage. Finally, side by side with the trader traveling independently or involved in partnerships established for a single voyage, there appeared in the south the "sedentary" businessman working from his countinghouse, using common carriers and relying on permanent agents abroad. The insatiable demand of southern towns for foodstuffs and raw materials, and the needs of both the Church and secular rulers for financial services, encouraged the rise of "super-companies," large unlimited partnerships built around a family business core (for example, the Bardi and Peruzzi of Florence), with numerous foreign branches staffed by hired employees known as factors and by junior partners who were often family members.

The thirteenth century also brought further cost and risk reductions in transport. In northern Italy, parts of France, and elsewhere, improvements to roads and navigable waterways speeded up overland trade, while continuing population growth assured an abundance of cheap labor. The "nautical revolution" that began in the thirteenth century shortened the customary winter closure of the seas, reduced risk factors, and yielded economies of scale. The magnetic compass, pilot books (rutters), the first nautical charts (portolans), and the gradual replacement of steering oars by the sternpost rudder made navigation more accurate and, thus, safer. Port facilities improved, and warning beacons and lighthouses multiplied. The Mediterranean lateen-rigged round ships (*naves*) grew ever larger, and so did the northern square-rigged hulks and cogs. Yet for all their increase in size, the latter still remained small compared to the massive southern *naves*, were less complex to build, were more agile, required smaller crews, and were better suited for defense against corsairs. As a result, Mediterranean mariners eagerly adapted cogs to their own needs from 1300 onward.

In terms of trade networks, the 1200s witnessed the development of an ever more intricate and interdependent web of local, interregional, and long-distance markets. The Germanic push eastward integrated into the Western economy large areas of eastern Europe. In the north, the towns of the Low Countries benefited by drawing on the agrarian and natural resources of the Baltic and the British Isles. In the south, the Levant and Black Sea trades supplied not only "spices" (a term that included dyestuffs and medicinal substances, as well as condiments) and luxuries, but also Black Sea grain and vital raw materials (hides, alum, cotton). Trade with North Africa brought to European markets hides, wax, wool, dyestuffs, ostrich feathers, gold, and sharp condiments such as malaguetta from sub-Saharan Africa. The outermost boundary of Europe's commercial contacts, or at least commercial intelligence, now stretched from Iceland in the west to the Sahara in the south and China in the east. Finally, although the peasant remained to some extent a producer resorting to the market only to achieve specific goals, such as getting money to remit feudal agricultural obligations and services, everywhere the market economy made profound inroads into rural life.

Despite this widening and deepening of the commercial sector, signs of progressive saturation appeared in the south before the year 1200, and in the north by 1250–1275. Economic growth continued, but was gradually losing momentum. Between 1260 and 1280, agrarian expansion slowed sharply almost everywhere except in central and eastern Europe, where colonization now had to draw more on local human resources than on immigration. The creation of new, less labor-intensive and more efficient seigneurial domains on marginal lands, the competition for land between grain and livestock producers, the fragmentation of large holdings through inheritance, and the concurrent beginnings of farm enclosure (*apoderamento* in Italy) exacerbated land hunger and rural underemployment. Diminishing returns sapped the countryside's vitality. Grain yields leveled off or declined, landowner and peasant revenues grew more slowly or stagnated, inflation eroded net incomes, and this, together with a rise in status-driven consumption among the land-owning aristocracy, curtailed agricultural investment. By the early 1300s, a colder, more humid, and unstable climate made poor harvests more frequent, finally culminating in the Great Famine of 1315–1322. Population nonetheless continued to expand in many regions, and this further increased impoverishment.

Although many towns reached the peak of prosperity only in the late 1200s and early 1300s, the proliferation of competing urban centers and the slowing expansion of demand began to curtail gains from trade and crafts much earlier. This translated, sometimes as early as the late twelfth century (for example, among the members of the Hanse of Germans trading with London), into a hardening of town policies, an increasingly illiberal attitude by the greater merchant guilds (*gilda mercatoria, universitas mercatorum, hanse*), sharper social tensions between artisans and merchant entrepreneurs, and the proliferation of craft guilds. Both towns and economic interest groups within them reacted vigorously to defend their positions. Generally, they sought to restrict the entry of new economic players, increase their own political power, garner gains from cooperation and control over output, promote exports and limit imports, and put consumers or other guilds at a disadvantage. Their quest for short-term solutions aggravated long-term problems. Wherever new craft guilds had multiplied since the mid-twelfth century, they now tended to clash with the older and more powerful merchant guilds. The latter, to which more prominent businessmen (not necessarily merchants) belonged, either sought to function as urban governing bodies or joined the dominant patrician oligarchies. New money fought old, the guilds of bigger masters fought those of smaller suppliers, and both craft and merchant guilds sought to prevent craftworkers from organizing themselves in any formal way. The strife, along with regulatory ordinances enacted by towns to limit economic benefits to specific groups, had a negative effect on economies in Lombardy and the Rhineland particularly.

Similarly, outside their walls, towns attempted to expand their territorial jurisdiction, divert trade flows to their advantage, and restrain foreign traders. Reactive and often inconsistent, the urban policies seldom involved an outright suppression of rural or small-town economic rivals. But although local urban hegemony did not necessarily hinder regional development, it promoted a segmenting of markets (thus reducing economies of scale and scope and raising transaction costs), blocked competition, and delayed further specialization. Aggressive urban protectionism prevailed wherever central authority was weak or nonexistent, such as in Italy or the Germanic lands. Protectionism was of course a double-edged weapon, preserving some markets while closing others. Realizing this, merchants

# E

sought remedy in bilateral commercial treaties and multilateral leagues, such as the agreement to form a greater German Hanse, reached in 1281 between the leagues of Cologne (the Rhenish League), Hamburg, and Lübeck (the Wendish League). Simmering jealousies, however, made many such alliances inherently unstable.

From 1275–1291 onward, recurrent warfare and political volatility, both in the Mediterranean and north of the Alps, compounded and promoted institutional constraints on trade. After the capture of Acre by the Mamluks in 1291 and the fall of the Latin Kingdom of Jerusalem, the papacy officially condemned all contacts with the Levant. In Europe and throughout the Mediterranean, regional conflicts (for example, the Franco-Flemish wars of 1293–1320; the War of the Sicilian Vespers, 1282–1302; the Ghibelline–Guelf Wars in Italy and their sequels, 1310–1339) required a mobilization of men, transport, and money that diverted resources and hindered traffic. Banditry and plundering, with their accompanying reprisals and lengthy lawsuits, increased transaction costs and risk. So did trade embargoes, war-induced taxation, coinage debasements (reduction of precious metal content per unit of nominal value), restrictions on the export of bullion and coins, and sheer general uncertainty. Danger premiums paid to carriers, the hiring of armed escorts, and the need to use detours or postpone departures because of regional instability all increased the cost of transport. Some sectors benefited from spot demand for war supplies, and speculators thrived on local scarcities. On the whole, however, merchants perceived war more as a threat than a source of profit.

Among the conspicuous casualties of the increasing dislocations were the Champagne fairs. Although the rival Rhine and Rhône-Saône river routes benefited to some extent, overall traffic declined, curtailing the linked demand for manufactures, services, and supplies. This induced a cascading fall in incomes and investment throughout extensive hinterland areas. The rise of permanent branches of Italian companies in the Low Countries and the consolidation of a direct maritime link between Italy and northwestern Europe sealed the fate of the Champagne fairs by the 1320s. The western sea link enriched a number of maritime towns, but this failed to offset the decline in the hinterland, while in the eastbound Levant trade, conditions remained unsettled until the 1340s. Moreover, maritime transport, although relatively faster and cheaper than land carriage during this period, also began to suffer from disruptions. Naval warfare and corsairing raised marine insurance rates, and the pressure to use better armed ships and crews drove up freight rates. Sailing in convoy, adopted above all by the Venetians, improved security at the cost of reduced flexibility, by confining ships to a predetermined course and destination.

During the first half of the fourteenth century, the worsening business climate and massive war loans to governments weakened the largest Italian companies, and low prices during the spell of agricultural recovery that followed the Great Famine of 1315–1322 helped bankrupt big commodity traders. In two great waves, around 1300 and in the 1340s, a string of prominent merchant-banking partnerships of Lucca, Siena, and Florence failed. In a new spirit of caution, many merchants curtailed the scope of their ventures at the cost of missing opportunities, while others diversified into real estate or into interest-yielding state and city loans. Advances in commercial technique focused heavily on marine insurance, double-entry bookkeeping as a tool of closer control over business performance, and other risk-reducing expedients. At the same time, the popular resentment aroused by the proliferation of small banking and money-changing establishments between 1240 and 1300 blended with a new anti-usury campaign by the Church. The diffusion of Italian business and financial methods slowed down, especially in northern Europe, where government and guild legislation eventually limited or temporarily banned the use of bills of exchange, credit transactions, and transfer/deposit banking.

The fourteenth and the first half of the fifteenth century remained under the shadow of warfare, with its attendant economic distortions and blockages. More wars of devastation were fought in Europe from the early 1300s to 1450 than either before this period or from 1450 to 1550. The Anglo-French Hundred Years' War (1337–1453), with its subsidiary confrontations in the Low Countries, Spain, and Brittany, was only one of the numerous external and internal conflicts that disrupted the Mediterranean, the Iberian Peninsula, Germany, the Baltic, and east-central Europe. The Balkans bore the brunt of the Ottoman expansion, and invasions or infighting also afflicted North Africa, the Levant, and the Mongol khânates from the Black Sea to Persia.

The effects of warfare were compounded by a steep demographic plunge that changed the aggregate volume of economic activity, the relative price of labor, the patterns of demand and supply, and the flows of trade. The Black Death plague epidemic of 1348–1351 and later severe outbreaks of the plague (1360–1362, 1374–1375, 1399–1402, 1420, 1437–1438, 1447, 1460–1462) and other diseases (typhoid, dysentery, malaria in the Mediterranean) reduced Europe's population from about 80 million to about 55 million. Densely settled parts of the Near East and North Africa suffered similar losses. This drop was generally accompanied by a less than proportional decline in output and exchanges, and certain sectors, such as the manufacturing and export of English broadcloth or south German fustian (a cotton-linen blend), even experienced long-term growth. Although maritime and long-distance trade tended to decline, regional and local trade increased per capita and in some areas in the aggregate, as regional economies rationalized, integrated, and specialized. The economy fluctuated widely during its period of general downturn, and various regions, branches of trade, and social strata ended up winners or losers during particular cyclic upswings. The period is thus best conceived of not as the "great depression of the late Middle Ages," but as a "secular" (that is, century-long or longer) contraction attended by uneven adjustments in which historical catastrophes often promoted economic improvements.

Economic, demographic, social, and cultural factors favored an increase in demand for luxury items and their middle-range imitations, as well as for higher-quality agro-pastoral commodities such as meat, butter, and cheese. On the one hand, upper- and middle-class ostentatious consumption grew with the inheritance-driven concentration of fortunes. On the other hand, labor shortages put an upward pressure on wages, despite the repressive policies of guilds and governments, allowing some section of the lower classes to emulate the elite in a small way regardless of the wide gap between rich and poor. The productivity of rural labor rose as marginal lands exploited during the demographic peak were abandoned, and as land usage shifted toward cash crops or less labor-intensive pastoralism. With rising productivity and falling aggregate demand, food staples became relatively cheaper, freeing money for discretionary spending. Anxiety about death promoted rapid spending across the social spectrum, causing the upper bourgeoisie and aristocracy in particular to erect ornate tombs, endow chantries, and give large sums to mendicants and other religious groups for perpetual masses.

The growing upscale market and high transaction costs favored the production of luxuries and semi-luxuries (such as better grades of woolen cloth), which bore more easily the cost of trade and created special market niches. Various cheap generic goods formerly traded over long distances were now confined to limited regional outlets. The segmenting of markets, trade flow disruptions, and rising costs also gave an edge to local substitutes for imports. Such imitations often outsold the originals, and even those textile centers that catered to luxury production ultimately lost markets to rivals located closer to the end user. The corresponding efforts by larger entrepreneurs and guilds, especially in old and declining centers, to reorganize production and to control labor and subcontractor costs were socially and politically divisive and painful. To create more predictable microenvironments, business communities increasingly adopted elaborate regulations and continued to enact protectionist laws. Such measures, however, only tended to maintain older production techniques and business methods.

Lively demand for Eastern goods difficult to substitute, such as spices or cotton, perpetuated a negative balance of payments with the East. The eastward drain of coin and bullion was compounded by a declining output of European silver mines, diminishing inflow of gold from sub-Saharan Africa, and the loss of metal through minting, hoarding, and normal wear of coins. Moreover, while bullion flows set off by divergent gold and silver values in different regions exacerbated local shortages of one or the other metal, wartime fiscal measures selectively impeded bullion flows, and periods of recession reduced the velocity of money (the number of times a unit of money turned over to achieve a given volume of transactions). By the 1360s, Europe experienced a relative scarcity of precious metals, which culminated between 1380 and 1410 in a widespread "monetary famine." The pressure was partly eased by the use of trade credit, bills of exchange, bank transfers, and early forms of endorsement. Such expedients, however, were insufficient to create additional money, and weak credit structures hastened cyclic downturns.

Periodic debasements of coinage, practiced by rulers in pursuit of their own fiscal interests, did increase the quantity of money in circulation and temporarily improved the debasing regions' exports. But they also produced inflation (as French and Flemish merchants bitterly complained in the 1430s and 1480s, for instance), and together with occasional strengthenings

# E

(*reinforcement* or reverse of debasement) they undermined confidence in coinage, affected the psychology of consumers and businessmen, and aggravated social discontent. In Flanders, in the 1390s, violent riots followed attempts to force wages down to match the decline in price level provoked by *reinforcements*. Particularly divisive were devaluations of the petty silver currency in which workers were paid. In Florence, in the early 1370s, laborers blamed rising prices on a devaluation of the small silver *quattrino* and on the subsequent rise in the value of the gold florin in terms of silver (which unfortunately depended not only on policy but on the movement of precious metal prices on international markets). Their discontent contributed to the uprising known as the Revolt of the Ciompi (woolworkers) in 1378.

The foundations of renewed long-run commercial growth were, paradoxically, laid in the troubled late fourteenth century. Real incomes of wage earners rose gradually after the initial post-plague inflation of *c.* 1348–1375 (1395 in some areas in northern and east-central Europe), while diversification increased many peasant incomes, despite fiscal and seigneurial pressures, constraining property rights, and inefficient land distribution. The general standard of living improved in the course of the fifteenth century. Seigneurial rents fell in some areas, but the formation of new landed fiefs and new ways of remunerating the nobility's services to monarchs seems to have brought about an extensive growth of seigneurial income. Merchants benefited from regional specialization and integration, which, together with the rise of new manufacturing centers, gradually boosted the fortunes of such less developed areas as southern Germany and the Iberian Peninsula, and allowed others, for instance northern Italy, to catch a second wind.

The south German and northern Italian economic and demographic recovery, which began as early as the 1370s, combined with the commercial expansion of the Holland and Zeeland ports and with growing English cloth exports to promote a revival of north-south overland traffic. By the early 1400s, the Rhine was poised to become the new overland trade artery replacing the Rhône-Saône link (whose decline was marked by the decay of the fairs at Chalon-sur-Saône). Along the Rhine corridor's feeder routes, future international fairs— Antwerp, Bergen-op-Zoom, Geneva, Besançon, and Lyon—were beginning to rise. From the 1460s onward, the Rhineland benefited from a central European copper and silver mining boom, sparked by technological innovation. At the same time, the English debasement of 1464–1465 reduced the exchange rate of the pound sterling, made English cloth more affordable for continental buyers, and thus helped attract German silver to Antwerp. Lively long-distance traffic stimulated further agrarian, manufacturing, and service-sector expansion, and enriched such south German urban centers as Augsburg and Nuremberg. Eastbound overland trade picked up after the Hussite Wars (1419–1436), and the Bohemian-Polish dynastic union under the Jagiello dynasty in 1471 assisted the process by creating a more homogeneous trade zone that also reaped benefits from the relative decline of Austrian trade between the 1450s and the 1480s. Around 1450, the rate of economic growth in Poland and Germany appears to have been higher than in the rest of Europe.

The recovery, like the contraction that preceded it, was uneven. As the Iberian Peninsula was drawn more closely into international trade circuits, signs of dynamic growth were visible throughout Andalusia and in the Douro valley from 1430 onward. Catalonia, nonetheless, plunged into a recession in the 1480s, and Castile suffered from the effects of the civil war of 1464–1474. In southern France, recovery was under way as early as the 1440s, but the economy of the Île-de-France and Normandy remained depressed in the 1450s. In southern Italy, Sicily and parts of the Kingdom of Naples achieved considerable progress in the later 1400s, with the Val Demone, Puglia, Abruzzi, and the Tyrrhenian coast emerging as economically dynamic zones. In Lombardy, political and institutional reforms helped reduce economic fragmentation, and the area further benefited from improvements such as canal-building, which enhanced its role as a crossroads between southern Germany, Genoa, and Venice. By contrast, many regions of central Italy, such as Umbria or Tuscany, continued to lag behind.

The growth of overland and regional trade, whose volume soon surpassed the levels reached around 1300, provided the underpinnings of a new expansion in maritime trade. Despite the Turkish threat to Venetian ties with the Levant from 1463 onward, European exports of textiles to Syria and Egypt increased, and so did the flow of spices and special goods in the opposite direction. Midway between Spain and Flanders, Brittany saw her trade grow thanks to ties with England and to spells of neutrality in the Hundred Years' War. Within some fifteen years of the war's end, a robust revival of commerce was noticeable all along the Atlantic coast of France. In the Baltic, the expansion of the Hollanders' trading rights in 1441 decisively opened up the area to increased competition, while in the North Sea, Holland established supremacy over new herring fisheries. By the century's end, the Portuguese trade with Africa, the Portuguese and Castilian colonization of Atlantic islands, and the opening of maritime routes into the Indian Ocean and to the Americas added a new dimension to this ferment, presaging the expansive growth achieved in the sixteenth century.

## BIBLIOGRAPHY

Dyer, Christopher. *Standards of Living in the Later Middle Ages: Social Change in England, c. 1200–1520.* Cambridge: Cambridge UP, 1989.

Epstein, Steven A. *Wage Labor and Guilds in Medieval Europe.* Chapel Hill and London: U of North Carolina P, 1991.

*Handbook of European History, 1400–1600. Late Middle Ages, Renaissance and Reformation.* Vol. 1. *Structures and Assertions.* Eds. T.A. Brady, H.A. Oberman, and J.D. Tracy. Leiden: E.J. Brill, 1994.

Hodges, Richard A. *Dark Age Economics: The Origins of Towns and Trade, A.D. 600–1000.* New York: St. Martin's Press, 1982.

Lopez, Robert S. *The Commercial Revolution of the Middle Ages, 950–1350.* Cambridge: Cambridge UP, 1976.

Miskimin, Harry A. *The Economy of Early Renaissance Europe, 1300–1460.* Cambridge: Cambridge UP, 1969.

———. *The Economy of Late Renaissance Europe, 1460–1600.* Cambridge: Cambridge UP, 1977.

———. *Cash, Credit, and Crisis in Europe, 1300–1600.* Aldershot: Variorum, 1989.

Munro, John H. *Textiles, Towns, and Trade. Essays in the Economic History of Late-Medieval England and the Low Countries.* Aldershot: Variorum, 1994.

Persson, Karl G. *Pre-Industrial Economic Growth: Social Organization and Technological Progress in Europe.* Oxford: Oxford UP, 1988.

Spufford, Peter. *Money and Its Use in Medieval Europe.* Cambridge: Cambridge UP, 1988.

Verhulst, Adriaan. *Rural and Urban Aspects of Early Medieval Northwest Europe.* Aldershot: Variorum, 1992.

*Martin Malcolm Elbl*

## Edessa

Present-day city of Urfa (Arabic *al-Ruhā'*), located in the plain of Haran, between the Tigris and Euphrates rivers, astride an ancient strategic road from Anatolia to northern Mesopotamia. In the fifth century C.E., Edessa, the leading bishopric in Syria and a center of Syriac Christian culture, became the seedbed of Nestorianism. Occupied several times by the Sasanid Persians, Edessa fell to the Arabs in 638–640, but retained a large local Christian population. Now a frontier town on the approaches to Byzantine territory, it fell into relative decline. In the tenth century, Edessa was dominated by the Bedouin tribe of Banu Numair, and the Cilician Armenian chieftains Philaretus and Thoros asserted control over it by the late eleventh century.

In 1098, during the First Crusade, Edessa was seized by Baldwin of Boulogne (d. 1118), brother of Godfrey of Bouillon. Baldwin, the first count of Edessa, succeeded his brother as king of Jerusalem in 1100, leaving Edessa to his cousin, Baldwin of Le Bourg. The latter fortified the town and strengthened the defenses throughout the surrounding territory. In 1118, Edessa passed to the Courtenays, who persistently fought the Muslim rulers of Aleppo, in particular the *atabeg* of Mosul, 'Imād al-Dīn Zangī. Edessa was finally captured by Zangī in 1144, but although this contributed to sparking off the Second Crusade (1147–1149), the Christian forces made no serious attempt to recapture the town. By 1153, the entire county of Edessa was in the hands of Zangī's son Nūr al-Dīn.

In 1259, Urfa (Edessa) submitted to the Mongol army of Hülegü, marching on Aleppo and Damascus, but its province was nonetheless devastated. During the il-khânid (Mongol) period (1258–1335), Urfa was a center of cotton cloth production. In the fifteenth century, with the revival of trade between Iraq and Syria, and the increase in Indian and Far Eastern traffic through Ormuz (Persian Gulf), Urfa prospered moderately as one of the way stations on the road connecting Tabriz and northern Syria.

# E

**BIBLIOGRAPHY**

Ashtor, Eliyahu. *A Social and Economic History of the Near East in the Middle Ages.* Berkeley: U of California P, 1976.

Runciman, Steven. *A History of the Crusades.* 3 vols. New York: Harper & Row, 1964.

Setton, Kenneth M., ed. *A History of the Crusades.* 6 vols. Madison: U of Wisconsin P, 1969–1990.

*Martin Malcolm Elbl*

**SEE ALSO**

Byzantine Empire; Christianity, Eastern; Crusades, First, Second, and Third; Hülegü; Mongols; Nestorianism

## Edges of the World

English translation of the Latin designation *fines terrae*, which identifies the extreme outlying, yet settled, areas of the world. The concept of "ends" or "edges" of the world by no means contradicts an understanding of the earth as spherical, but rather understands the *oikoumene* (the inhabitable portion of the world) to be a landmass occupying a discrete section of the surface of a globe.

The theory originated with Greek geographers in the sixth century B.C.E., and already during the Hellenistic age it caused maps to acquire framelike edges, representing the extremes of the *oikoumene*, as it was conceived to appear. The colonized world extends to India with its myriad marvels, at the easternmost extreme. Geographers and cartographers debated whether the island of Taprobane is rightly construed to be at the eastern edge of the *oikoumene*, or perhaps adjacent to an antipodal continent. Ethiopia represents the farthest human settlement to the south. The Pillars of Hercules form the *oikoumene*'s boundary to the west, and the north reaches as far as the Orcades Islands (the Orkneys) with ultima Thule (Iceland) at the extreme northwest. Beyond Scythia to the north is the country of the Hyperboreans, who live beyond the cold north winds.

Because the *oikoumene* was first imagined by Western geographers working out of Greece or Rome—that is, comfortably within its boundaries—its edges or ends are regularly characterized as being very distant from the imagined observer or audience. The topography and inhabitants of these regions were also considered to be extremely different from that of the better-known world—if not altogether part of an antipodal, unknown region. Cartographically, the ends of the world are often guarded from the chaos beyond by impressive galleries of monsters that mostly cluster at the southern and western edges of the *mappamundi*.

**BIBLIOGRAPHY**

Brincken, Anna-Dorothee von den. *Fines Terrae. Die Enden der Erde und der vierte Kontinent auf mittelalterlichen Weltkarten.* Schriften Monumenta Germaniae Historica 36. Hanover: Hahn, 1992.

Romm, James S. *The Edges of the Earth in Ancient Thought, Geography, Exploration, and Fiction.* Princeton, NJ: Princeton UP, 1992.

*Anna-Dorothee von den Brincken*

**SEE ALSO**

Antipodes; Ethiopians; India; *Mappamundi;* Monstrosity, Geographical; *Oikoumene;* Scythia; Taprobane; Thule

## Egeria (fl. 384)

One of the earliest recorded pilgrims, after the Anonymous Pilgrim of Bordeaux. Egeria is known to us primarily through her travel journal, *Itinerarium,* in which she relates the pilgrimage of three years' duration that she made to Christian holy places in the Middle East.

The text survives in a sole manuscript from the eleventh century, Codex Arretinus 405 (formerly VI,3), rediscovered and first published by G.F. Gamurrini in 1884. The manuscript is damaged at the beginning and the end. The writer's name is mentioned nowhere in the surviving text; we know who she was, however, thanks to a letter "in praise of the blessed Egeria" written by Valerius Bergidensis, a Galician monk who lived during the seventh century and had access to a more complete text. (A variant reading, Aetheria, which appeared in the first critical edition of Valerius's letter and continues to be used by some scholars, is an erroneous reading, devoid of any paleographical basis).

Egeria was originally from either Galicia (the hypothesis the most often cited) or from southern Gaul, where, in any event, her correspondents seem to have lived. Egeria's status is debated. Some scholars maintain that she belonged to a religious order and was thus a nun who addressed her account to the sisters in her community. Others argue that she was a noblewoman attracted to the ascetic life (as were many aristocrats in her day), and was therefore interested in Eastern monasticism and would have been addressing her account to a specific audience of female friends. The date of her voyage is well established: Paul Devos has provided substantial proof that she arrived in Jerusalem shortly before Easter in 381 and that she left the day after Easter in 384. During these three years she crisscrossed Palestine and Egypt, as far as the Thebaid, visiting and worshiping at many of the biblical and monastic sites.

The surviving text begins in December 383, when she arrived within view of Mount Sinai (today Gebal Mousa), which she climbed; she made her way from Jerusalem to Mount Sinai in twenty-two stages, first following the coastal route (*via maris*) to Peluse, then passing through Clysma (Suez) as she visited the stops supposedly made by the Hebrews during their exodus from Egypt. She then describes her excursion to Mount Nebo in the province of Arabia (now in Jordan), where she saw the tomb of Moses, and a later visit to Carneas, also in Arabia, to worship at the tomb of Job. She also relates her return from Jerusalem to Constantinople, in particular the excursion made from Antioch to Edessa and Harran, followed by a stop at the sanctuary of St. Thecla in Seleucia. She wrote the *Itinerarium* in Constantinople, where she was envisioning still other travels.

It is possible to reconstruct part of her journey within Palestine, Judea, Samaria, and Galilee, thanks to the *Liber de locis sanctis* by Peter the Deacon (twelfth century), who consulted as one of his sources a more complete manuscript of Egeria's book. She traveled by donkey and camel, in the company of clerics and monks who served as guides, occasionally—in unsafe regions of the Sinai peninsula—with a military escort. She was received throughout her journey by bishops and monks, a testimony to her high social rank.

The second part of her account is a long description of the liturgy in use at that time in Jerusalem: daily and dominical rituals, liturgies for Lent and Holy Week, the preparation for baptism, and the Feast of the Dedication. She offers valuable information about shrines in Jerusalem and Bethlehem, and the conduct of a fourth-century pilgrim there.

Egeria's culture is exclusively Christian and largely biblical; her language is a good example of the spoken Latin of her time, simple yet containing certain classical features. Her account, which is spontaneous and unpretentious, reveals her energetic, adventurous, and even daring personality.

**BIBLIOGRAPHY**

*Atti del Convegno Internazionale sulla Peregrinatio Egeriae, Arezzo 23–25 Ottobre 1987.* Arezzo: Accademia Petrarca di Lettere arti e scienze, 1990.

Devos, Paul. "Egeriana." *Analecta Bollandiana* 101 (1983): 43–70; 105 (1987): 159–166, 415–424; 109 (1991): 363–381; 112 (1994): 241–254.

Egeria. *Itinerarium Egeriae.* Eds. E. Franceschini and R. Weber. Corpus Christianorum, Series Latina 175. Turnhout: Brepols, 1975; P. Maraval, Sources Chrétiennes 296. Cerf: Paris, 1982.

*Egeria: Diary of a Pilgrimage.* Trans. George E. Gingras. Ancient Christian Writers 38. New York: Newman P, 1970.

Starowieski, M. "Bibliografia Egeriana." *Augustinianum* 19 (1979): 297–318 (296 titles).

Wilkinson, John, trans. *Egeria's Travels in the Holy Land.* 1971. Rev. edition. Jerusalem: Ariel Publishing House; and Warminster, England: Aris and Phillips, 1981.

*Pierre Maraval*

**SEE ALSO**
Catherine in the Sinai, Monastery of St.; Edessa; Holy Land; Jersualem; Peter the Deacon

# Egypt

Site of an ancient culture and historically one of the world's most important regions, politically and religiously; since the Arab conquest in 641–642, ruled by various Islamic governments. For several centuries following its conquest by the Arabs, Egypt formed a province of larger empires with their centers to the east, but beginning in the mid-tenth century it became the base for a series of independent regimes. Throughout the Middle Ages, Egypt remained an important center of Mediterranean and West Asian commerce.

With the fall of Egypt to the Muslim Arab conqueror 'Amr ibn al-'As in 641–642, Egypt passed permanently from Byzantine control. The Muslim conquest was not entirely unwelcome to Egyptian Copts, whose church had suffered persecution at the hands of the Orthodox establishment during the last centuries of Greek rule; as elsewhere in the Middle East, non-Orthodox Christians and Jews often preferred the more tolerant rule of the early Muslims. The Arab conquerors were comparatively few, and for several centuries Coptic Christians remained a significant majority of the population. While the major urban areas soon became predominantly Muslim (Cairo was a Muslim city from its foundation), it was probably not until later in the Middle Ages that a preponderance of rural inhabitants converted to Islam.

For the first three centuries of the Muslim period, Egypt was ruled by governors representing the ecumenical caliphate: first that of the Prophet Muhammad's companions, based in Medina; then that of the

# E

Woodcut illustration of the pyramids of Egypt, identifying them as the biblical "Granaries of Joseph." Otto von Diemeringen's translation of *The Book of John Mandeville* (Augsburg: Anton Sorg, 1481) fol. 20r. Minneapolis, MN. By permission of the James Ford Bell Library, University of Minnesota.

Umayyads (661–750), who ruled from Damascus; finally that of the 'Abbāsid caliphs (from 749), whose capital was usually Baghdad. Periodically, energetic governors were able to establish *de facto* independence and even (as in the case of Ahmad ibn Tūlūn [r. 868–884]) short-lived dynasties, but their autonomy was never permanent. With the conquest of Egypt by the Fātimid family, representing the Isma'ili branch of Shi'ism, in 969, Egypt became, for the first time since the Ptolemies (330–305 B.C.E.), the base of a large and prosperous empire. Subsequent ruling families and military castes, although of foreign origin, preserved the independence of Egypt until its incorporation into the Ottoman Empire in 1517.

The great port of Alexandria, founded by Alexander the Great in 332 B.C.E., continued to operate as a center of Mediterranean commerce after its conquest by the Arabs. The city's famous lighthouse remained standing and was an object of wonder for many years. The Muslim traveler Ibn Battūta described his visit to the lighthouse in 1326, although when he returned to the city in 1349, he found that "it had fallen into so ruinous a condition that it was impossible to enter it or to climb up to the doorway." Finally, the landmark was leveled by a series of earthquakes in the later Middle Ages.

The city possessed two harbors, separated by the island of Pharos and the causeway connecting the island to the mainland; in the Muslim period, the eastern harbor was reserved for vessels owned by Jews or Christians or coming from Europe or Byzantium, while the western harbor, protected by a great iron chain, was set aside for Muslim shipping. From the tenth century, the number of European merchants in the city increased dramatically; both Ibn Battūta and William of Tyre extolled Alexandria as an emporium in which traders from the East and West came together to exchange their wares. Foreign merchants and their goods were housed in *funduqs* (Italian *fondachi*), and their affairs were monitored by official consuls: Benjamin of Tudela in around 1170 counted twenty-eight European nations or cities with formal representation in the town.

Although the Greek patriarch was forced to leave Alexandria after the Muslim conquest, Alexandria remained an important cultural center for Christians and non-Christians alike. The story that the Muslim caliph 'Umar ibn al-Khattāb (r. 634–644) ordered the destruction of its ancient library, which ironically began circulating among thirteenth-century Arab historians, has now been shown to be false (although it continues to reappear in modern studies); nonetheless, the city's cultural life was inevitably shaped by the Islamic world that now surrounded it. Because of its position on Mediterranean trade routes, Alexandria attracted numerous residents, both Muslim and Jewish, of North African or Spanish origin. Travelers such as Ibn Jubayr (in around 1181) and Ibn Battūta passed through en route to the holy cities of Arabia, and many elected to settle in the town on their return journey. The pressures of the *Reconquista* in Spain and religious and political upheaval in North Africa from the eleventh century drove many refugees eastward; some of them, such as the famous historian Ibn Khaldūn (1332–1406) took up residence in Egypt. The Spanish and North African connection contributed to the presence in Alexandria of a sizeable community of Muslim scholars adhering to the rigorous Mālikī school of law (dominant in North Africa); it was among them that there appeared the first signs in Egypt of the revival of Sunni Islamic culture and identity in the face of the Shi'ite regimes (such as the Fātimids) that had dominated much of the Middle East during the tenth and eleventh centuries. Nonetheless, Alexandria lost its primacy in Egyptian life as a direct result of the Muslim conquest. The original Arab conquerors established their capital in the garrison town of al-Fustāt, just south of the modern city of Cairo. Cairo itself was constructed by the Fātimids as their palace and seat of government, and remained the capital under the Sunni rulers who replaced them.

Egypt, of course, figured prominently in the history of the crusades. Sporadic persecution of Christians under the mentally unstable Fātimid caliph al-Hākim (r. 996–1021), as well as the destruction in 1009 of the Church of the Holy Sepulchre (Jerusalem then being under Fātimid rule), may have contributed to the political atmosphere in Europe that ultimately led Pope Urban II to preach the crusade at Clermont in 1095. Because of the geopolitical importance of Egypt, European expeditions to the Middle East often aimed their blows directly at that country. Their efforts were largely ineffectual, but did at times have important repercussions on internal Egyptian affairs. It was, for example, largely to organize the country's defenses against the crusaders that the last Fātimid caliphs engaged the political and military services of the famous Muslim warrior Saladin (Salāh al-Dīn [r. 1174–1193]), who ultimately overthrew the Fātimids, restored the country to Sunni rule, and made it the base of power for his Ayyūbid dynasty. Louis IX's disastrous crusade of 1249 ended in defeat in the town of al-Mansūra in the Nile delta, but also contributed indirectly to the events that led to the replacement of the Ayyūbid dynasty by the Mamluk (slave-soldier) sultans, who then ruled the country until 1517. The last major crusader attack—that of Peter of Lusignan in 1365—devastated the city of Alexandria, but accomplished little else.

The religious and political tensions associated with the crusades never permanently interrupted commercial and other contacts between Egypt (and other countries of the Muslim Middle East) and Europe. It was in the midst of a crusader campaign near the Egyptian town of Damietta, after all, that St. Francis paid his famous visit to the sultan al-Malik al-Kāmil in 1219. Especially in the later Middle Ages, Egypt became a stopping point for European pilgrims and travelers to the Holy Land. Its major attractions for them included the Monastery of St. Catherine's in Sinai, which contained (and still does) what was thought to be the "burning bush" through which God had spoken to Moses, as well as a variety of sites in the Nile valley associated with the

Holy Family's stay in Egypt, many of which are described in the thirteenth-century treatise on Egyptian churches and monasteries ascribed to Abū Salīh the Armenian. In addition, both Cairo and Alexandria were the homes of thriving Jewish communities throughout the Middle Ages. Jewish merchants, with their personal and cultural contacts with co-religionists on both sides of the Mediterranean, played a critical role in East-West trade, and the records left by one of those communities (preserved in the famous storehouse, known as the Geniza, in a synagogue in al-Fustāt) have proven an important source for reconstructing the history of medieval commerce.

**BIBLIOGRAPHY**

Abū Salih. *The Churches and Monasteries of Egypt and Some Neighbouring Countries.* Trans. B.T.A. Evetts and Alfred J. Butler. Oxford: Oxford UP, 1895; rpt. Oxford UP 1969.

Ashtor, Eliyahu. *Levant Trade in the Later Middle Ages.* Princeton: Princeton UP, 1983.

Butler, Alfred J. *The Arab Conquest of Egypt and the Last Thirty Years of the Roman Dominion.* 1902. 2nd edition. Oxford: Oxford UP, 1978.

Goitein, Samuel D. *A Mediterranean Society: The Jewish Communities of the Arab World as Portrayed in the Documents of the Cairo Geniza.* 6 vols. Berkeley: U of California P, 1967–1994.

Holt, P.M. *The Age of the Crusades: The Near East from the Eleventh Century to 1517.* London: Longman, 1986.

Ibn Battūta. *Travels.* Vol. 1. Trans. H.A.R. Gibb. Hakluyt Society, 2nd series, no. 110. London: Cambridge UP, 1958.

*Jonathan P. Berkey*

**SEE ALSO**

Ayyūbids; Benjamin of Tudela; Catherine in the Sinai, Monastery of St.; Damascus; Eastern Christianity; Fātimids; *Fondaco;* Holy Land; Ibn Battūta, Abu Abdallah; Ibn Jubayr; Louis IX; Mamluks; Merchants, Jewish; Muslim Travelers and Trade; Ottoman Empire; Pilgrimage, Christian; Saladin; Shi'ism; Sunnism

## Elephants

One of the exotic animals brought to medieval Europe from Africa and Asia, typically found in aristocratic menageries that included lions, leopards, cheetahs, camels, buffalo, antelope, monkeys, an occasional giraffe, parrots, and ostriches.

Both African and Asian elephants had been transported to Europe since the classical period. Alexander

# E

the Great's conquest of the East (after 331 B.C.E.) included a clash with King Porus's war elephants at the Battle of Hydaspes (326 B.C.E.); a result of this meeting is that the military "elephant and castle"—the towering howdah of India manned with warriors, borne on an elephant's back—eventually became a familiar iconographic motif in European art. Hannibal crossed the Rhône as well as the Alps with an elephant corps as part of the Carthaginian army on his march against Rome during the Second Punic War (218–202 B.C.E.). The peace treaty that concluded hostilities stipulated that Carthage surrender all its elephants and agree not to train any in the future. The Romans imported wild animals in great numbers from all over the known world for public spectacles; their heavy use of the North African elephant for games in the amphitheatre contributed considerably to its extinction by the fourth century C.E. Several Roman writers note the elephant's

Elephant in Armor. Fresco, Church of St. Nicolas, Clarens (Montreux), Switzerland, *c.* 1450. Photo by John B. Friedman.

Elephant. Cloister Fresco, Nineteenth Arcade, Bressanone, Tirol, *c.* 1450. Photo by Nona C. Flores.

Sea Elephant. Fresco, Church of St. Martin, Zillis (Grisons), Switzerland, 12th century. Photo by John B. Friedman.

talents at circus tricks including tightrope walking; Pliny tells of one animal, often chastised for its slowness in learning, that was found practicing by itself at night (*Natural History,* VIII, 3.6).

Nevertheless, there was little opportunity for a European to view a live elephant during the Middle Ages without traveling abroad: there are fewer than a dozen of the beasts documented as being in Europe between 801 and 1655. Charlemagne received the famous elephant Abul-Abbas from the Baghdad court of Hārūn-al-Rashīd in 801; although the animal's presence is vividly recorded in contemporary chronicles, Carolingian art does not seem to have preserved any records of this royal favorite. By the thirteenth century, Emperor Frederick II's traveling menageries made gifts of exotic animals popular between rulers. Richard of Cornwall's ceremonial entry into the city of Cremona in 1241 was graced by one of Frederick's elephants, which was reported to have been a gift to the monarch from the legendary Eastern ruler Prester John. This elephant is depicted in Matthew Paris's *Historia major* manuscript now in Cambridge (Corpus Christi College, MS 26, fol. 151v) as a piglike creature with a vacuum-hose trunk, flat triangular ears, and saucerlike hooves, bearing a group of musicians in the wooden structure on its back. It is doubtful that Matthew actually saw this elephant; several modern commentators have noted its striking similarity to the elephant in a contemporary English bestiary now in the British Library (Harley MS 3244, fol. 39).

Matthew Paris is also responsible for what may be the most famous medieval elephant illustrations, those of a beast that arrived in England in 1255 as a gift from King Louis IX of France to King Henry III. It was housed with the rest of the royal menagerie in the Tower of London for four years until its death, and its celebrity was recorded by Matthew in the text of the *Chronica majora,* where he reported that "everyone hastened [there] on account of the rareness of the sight," and in two large sketches drawn from life. In one, the elephant is shown with its keeper, and the explanatory caption makes the artist's intent clear: "by the size of the man drawn here, the size of the beast . . . can be estimated" (Cambridge, Corpus Christi College, MS 16, fol. iv). Matthew's other sketch of the Tower elephant, from a manuscript of additions to the *Chronica,* includes a delicately drawn detail of the trunk's segmentations (*Liber Additamenta,* London, British Library MS Cotton Nero D.1, fol. 161v). These draw-

ings represent a considerable advance in the anatomical representation of an elephant, especially when compared to the Cremona elephant illustration—so much so that these drawings are often used by scholars to illustrate the newly awakened artistic "realism" of the thirteenth century.

Matthew's reliance on personal observation of nature is still strongly tempered, however, by his acceptance of medieval authority. On the same page as the scientifically delineated close-up of the trunk that he expressly states is drawn from life, he also includes a statement that the elephant cannot bend its legs because it has no joints, and therefore cannot stand up if it falls. He continues with the story of how hunters partially saw through tree trunks; when an elephant leans against the tree in order to sleep, the tree collapses from its weight and the hunters can kill the helpless animal. This story was widely circulated through the Middle Ages and given credence by its appearance in the *Physiologus,* a second- or third-century text in which the supposed natural characteristics of various animals, birds, and reptiles were described and given religious moral interpretations. This popular text was gradually adapted and expanded into bestiaries. Aristotle had refuted the story of the elephant's lack of knees in his *History of Animals* (II.I), but it reappears in many medieval texts, indeed, so persistently that Sir Thomas Browne was still discussing it in 1645 as the first of the "common and vulgar errors" regarding animals in his *Pseudodoxia epidemica.*

Another popular story circulated via the bestiary was that unicorns often fought with elephants, killing the larger beast by stabbing it in the underbelly with its long horn. Such a battle is depicted in a marginal illustration from the early fourteenth-century English *Queen Mary's Psalter* (British Library, MS Royal 2 B.VII, fol. 100v). The rhinoceros was sometimes identified in the fifteenth and sixteenth centuries as the unicorn of medieval legend. Thus, in 1517, when the king of Portugal received both an elephant and a rhinoceros as gifts from a group of merchants, he put both animals in a specially constructed arena in Lisbon and awaited the outcome of their meeting. The elephant survived, but only by fleeing for its life.

The relative scarcity of elephants in medieval Europe led most artists to guess at the creature's anatomy when depicting it. Though many chose to domesticate the image by adding a trunklike appendage to the muzzle of a familiar animal such as a horse, a dog, a bear, a pig, or

# E

a wolf, others chose instead to emphasize the exotic aspects of the elephant's appearance. They were influenced in this, perhaps, by travelers' descriptions of the elephant and its milieu in foreign lands. In *The Book of John Mandeville* (*c.* 1357), for example, white elephants live on the islands of Prester John in the company of such creatures as colorful serpents six score long walking upright on feet, *orafles* (giraffes), white lions, crocodiles that weep as they eat human flesh, and mice the size of hounds. Marco Polo described the magnificent ceremonial elephants of Khubilai Khân (*c.* 1295), noting the general Eastern practice of using elephants in warfare. He also reports, at second-hand, on the rukh, seen by eyewitnesses in Madagascar, a colossal bird with a wingspan of thirty paces that can pounce on an elephant, carry it to great heights, then drop it so it smashes to a pulp and can be easily eaten.

Most exotic of all were the life-size elephant automatons that became extremely popular with the organizers of ceremonial dinners and public pageants. Such a mechanical elephant appeared in 1454 during an allegorical interlude at a banquet held in honor of Philip of Burgundy at Lille. It bore the master of ceremonies Olivier de la Marche garbed as a nun on its back, and it was led by a giant Saracen; the tableau represented Holy Church under the threat of the Turks. This automaton and its successors were possibly unconscious revivals of a classical prototype: Queen Semiramis, for example, is supposed to have had elephant-dummies made of ox hides that concealed warriors riding on camels.

## BIBLIOGRAPHY

Flores, Nona C. "The Mirror of Nature Distorted: The Medieval Artist's Dilemma in Depicting Animals." In *The Medieval World of Nature*. Ed. Joyce E. Salisbury. New York: Garland, 1993.

Heckscher, William. "Bernini's Elephant and Obelisk." *Art Bulletin* 29 (1947): 155–182.

Lewis, Suzanne. *The Art of Matthew Paris in the Chronica majora*. Berkeley: U of California P, 1987.

*Physiologus.* Trans. Michael Curley. Austin: U of Texas P, 1979.

White, T.H. *The Bestiary, A Book of Beasts*. New York: Capricorn Books, 1960.

*Nona C. Flores*

## SEE ALSO

Animals, Exotic; Bestiaries; Birds, Exotic; Frederick II; Marco Polo; Matthew Paris; Mongol Army; Prester John

## Ethiopians

A nation and ethnic group in southwest Africa; in medieval sources the name often indicates nothing more than a remote and exotic, but otherwise unspecified, group of people.

In some texts, Ethiopians are identified as the people of the ancient Nubian kingdom of Kush, or (after the mid-1300s) as the subjects of the legendary Christian sovereign Prester John; in either case, they were thought to possess magnificent wealth. Classical writers say that the gods greatly loved the Ethiopians and therefore often visited them; later, Christian writers identify Ethiopians as the most pious of people. On the other hand, Ethiopians often came to represent all black Africans and are sometimes described as savage and cruel. The biblical Queen of Sheba (I Kings 10: 1–13) and Candace in the Alexander romance tradition were the best-known Ethiopians in medieval lore.

Beginning with Homer (*c.* 8th century B.C.E.), there is a recurring tradition that says that the name of the region *Ethiopia* is derived from its people's most distinguishing characteristic—namely, that they are black or sunburnt (*Aethiopes*). Later, John of Trevisa (1326–1412) cites Isidore of Seville and provides the same etymology.

Ethiopia. *Secretz de la Nature*, Château d'Aulnoy, Coulommiers (Seine et Marne). Collection Charnacé, unnumbered MS, fol. 26v, *c.*1460. Photo by John B. Friedman.

Augustine (354–430 C.E.), in his commentary on the Psalms (71) where he speaks of the universality of the Christian faith, says that even the Ethiopians, "the most terrible of men," located as they are "at the extreme end of the earth," are capable of receiving God's grace. Here, Augustine echoes Homer, who calls the Ethiopians *eschatoi andron,* the "most remote of men, at earth's two verges, / in sunset lands and lands of the rising sun" (1.25–26). The Ethiopian eunuch in Acts (8:26–40) is the example of the converted Ethiopian par excellence.

More important for early and medieval Christians, the dark skin of the Ethiopian, and ultimately the Ethiopian himself, could also represent the corrupt condition of the human soul. This transformation of the Ethiopian into a metaphor is illustrated by Origen (early third century C.E.), who, in his commentary on the Septuagint version of the Song of Songs (8.5), compares the Ethiopian's natural blackness with the figurative blackness of the unrepentant soul. Origen says that if we remain unrepentant, we are like the Ethiopian— i.e., black and sinful—in our souls.

**BIBLIOGRAPHY**

Kelly, Kathleen. "'Blue' Indians, Ethiopians, and Saracens in Middle English Narrative Texts." *Parergon,* n.s., 11.1 (June 1993): 35–52.

Levine, Donald N. *Greater Ethiopia: The Evolution of a Multiethnic Society.* Chicago and London: U of Chicago P, 1974.

Romm, James S. *The Edges of the Earth in Ancient Thought, Geography, Exploration, and Fiction.* Princeton, NJ: Princeton UP, 1992.

Snowdon, Frank M., Jr. *Blacks in Antiquity.* Cambridge, MA: Harvard UP/Belknap, 1971.

———. *Before Color Prejudice.* Cambridge, MA: Harvard UP, 1983.

Ullendorf, Edward. *The Ethiopians: An Introduction to Country and People.* 2nd edition. London: Oxford UP, 1965; rpt. 1967.

*Kathleen Coyne Kelly*

**SEE ALSO**

Edges of the World; Ham's Curse and Africans; Isidore of Seville; Monstrosity, Geographical; Prester John; Trevisa, John

## Etna, Mount

One of several geographical locations identified in medieval folklore and given learned sanctions as an entrance to the underworld.

In Greek mythology, Zeus imprisoned the giant Enceladus under Mount Etna [Aetna], a volcanic mountain on the island of Sicily. In Roman mythology, Vulcan's forge was located inside Mount Etna. This association of Mount Etna with the infernal was picked up by medieval Christian writers, who located the entrance to hell here.

Various medieval writers identified different Mediterranean volcanic mountains as the gateway to hell. Some apocalypse tales mention Mount Etna or Mount Vesuvius specifically. In the twelfth century, Julien of Vézelay identified Etna as the entrance to hell in a sermon on the difference between hellish and purgatorial fire. In Caesarius of Heisterbach's *Dialogue on Miracles,* written in the early thirteenth century, Mount Etna, along with the nearby Mount Stromboli and Mount Gyber, are identified as the jaws of hell, "because none of the elect but only the wicked are sent into them. . . . Hell is supposed to be in the heart of the earth, so the wicked can not see the light of day."

Book Four of the *Dialogues* of Pope Gregory I (590–604) contains two stories that associate Sicilian volcanoes with hell's entrance. In the first story, a man named Eumorfius sends his slave to his friend Stephen with the mysterious message that "Our ship is ready to take us to Sicily," and he dies upon sending the message. Stephen hears the message and immediately dies as well. Because of the belief that the craters of Sicilian volcanoes led directly to hell, "sailing to Sicily" was a euphemism for dying. Gregory also recounts the legend that the spirits of Pope John and the Roman patrician Symmachus threw the Gothic king Theoderic into the crater of a volcano in the Lipari Islands (a group of small islands due north of Sicily) as punishment for his persecution of Christians.

According to Jacques Le Goff, some medieval Christian writers, such as Peter Damian in his life of Saint Odilo (eleventh century), associated Mount Etna with purgatory. However, the older tradition of a gateway to hell prevailed in the popular imagination and prevented this alternative association from attaining widespread acceptance.

**BIBLIOGRAPHY**

Emmerson, Richard Kenneth, and Ronald Herzman. *The Apocalyptic Imagination in Medieval Literature.* Philadelphia: U of Pennsylvania P, 1992.

Gardiner, Eileen. *Medieval Visions of Heaven and Hell: A Sourcebook.* New York: Garland, 1993.

# E

Le Goff, Jacques. *The Birth of Purgatory.* Trans. Arthur Gold-hammer. Chicago: U of Chicago P, 1984.

*Teresa Leslie*

SEE ALSO
Paradise, Travel to; Purgatory; Purgatory, St. Patrick's

## Etzlaub, Erhard (1460–1552)

Nuremberg mapmaker and navigational instrument maker. Born at Erfurt, Etzlaub became a citizen of Nuremberg, the most flourishing town in Germany at the end of the Middle Ages and a center for chroniclers and cartographers such as Hartmann Schedel (1440–1514), compiler of the *Nuremberg Chronicle* (1484); Hieronymus Münzer (1437–1508); and Martin Behaim (1459–1507), maker of the first globe.

Since the pocket sundials of Etzlaub's workshop were equipped with a compass, he conceived the idea of producing practical roadmaps, a novel conception in Germany. The first of these was a map for young travelers oriented to the south; Nuremberg was placed in the center, and beyond it the surrounding country (on a scale of sixteen German miles with one mile equivalent to 7.5 km) was depicted with the different roads and places noted and a milemeter (or scale) at the map's edge. In the Jubilee Year 1500, he produced a very successful map of the pilgrimage roads leading to Rome, which also was oriented to the south. It was reproduced in woodcut versions and looked like a map of the Roman Empire from Naples to Copenhagen. The instructions for users required a pair of compasses in order to gauge the actual distances to be covered. In 1501, Etzlaub published a map of the roads in the Roman Empire, which from 1512 onward was supplemented with the *Brevis Germaniae Descriptio* of Johannes Cochlaeus; it was the first German geography.

In 1511 and 1513, Etzlaub also made two ivory boxes for sundials, whose covers contain small world maps, oriented to the south and ending at the equator; the notation of the degrees of latitude widen to the lower part, showing that the maker anticipated Mercator projection.

BIBLIOGRAPHY
Harvey, P.D.A. *The History of Topographical Maps. Symbols, Pictures and Surveys.* London: Thames and Hudson, 1980, pp. 85–88, 147–149.

Krüger, Herbert. "Des Nürnberger Meisters Erhard Etzlaub älteste Straßenkarten von Deutschland." *Jahrbuch für fränkische Landesforschung* 118 (1958): 1–286.

Schnelbögl, Fritz. "Life and Work of the Nuremberg Cartographer Erhard Etzlaub (†1532)." *Imago Mundi* 20 (1966): 11–26.

*Anna-Dorothee von den Brincken*

SEE ALSO
Behaim, Martin; Maps; *Nuremberg Chronicle;* Ptolemy; Rome as a Pilgrimage Site

## Europe, Geography in Medieval
*See* Geography in Medieval Europe

## European Exploration and Expansion
*See* Exploration and Expansion, European

## European Geography and Travel, Medieval, Scholarship on
*See* Scholarship on Medieval European Geography and Travel

## European Transportation, Inland
*See* Transportation, Inland (European)

## Exploration and Expansion, European

The European encounter with worlds and peoples outside its own borders has a long history, stretching well back to classical antiquity.

At the height of the Roman Empire (mid-second century C.E.), the Alexandrian geographer Claudius Ptolemy could detail the known world beyond the Roman frontier with some accuracy. Classical writers might have differed in their mathematical calculations regarding the size of the earth, but they generally agreed on its sphericity and on the existence of three continents: Europe, Asia, and Africa. However, the gradual political and military disintegration of the Roman Empire from the third century, its division between Rome and Constantinople, and the loss of old, stable frontiers led not only to Rome's collapse but to a division of Western Europe into a wide spectrum of small polities whose rulers cared little for events in the East. The language of geographical knowledge, Greek, was lost to the West and with it the body of knowledge of Asian and African geography contained in the works of Ptolemy and his Greek contemporaries.

The rise of Christianity after the reign of Constantine I (r. 306–337) led to a gradual disregard for classical geography. Most early Christian theologians rejected pagan antiquity and its learning on doctrinal grounds, creating a need for Christianity to make its own contribution to geographical knowledge. The significance the faith placed on the Holy Land and the practice of pilgrimage served to make Jerusalem a focal point for Christian travelers, from as far afield as Ethiopia and the Caucasus, who had the opportunity to meet and exchange ideas during their devotional journeys. The faith's proselytizing impulse encouraged Christian missionaries and scholars to explore heretofore unknown or rarely visited regions in the name of Christian universalism. From the fourth century, Christendom became increasingly geographically self-aware. A sixth-century Alexandrian merchant, Cosmas Indikopleustes, compiled a *Christian Topography* that presented a world view based not on Ptolemaic observations, but rather on scriptural evidence, describing Christian communities living well beyond the frontiers of the old Roman Empire. In the Eastern Empire, however, classical travel and trading patterns were continued. Links were maintained with India and the Ethiopian kingdom of Axum. Political and economic contacts with China were maintained along the old Silk Road.

The earliest expansion of Europe was into the North Atlantic. While some early texts, such as the *Vita Brendani,* spoke of the sixth-century Irish monk St. Brendan island-hopping across the North Atlantic in a small coracle (a craft made of a wickerwork hull covered by animal hides), it is clear that there was some Irish hermitic settlement in the Faeroe Islands, and possibly Iceland, at least by 800 C.E. By the end of the ninth century, Viking settlement of both regions was in full force. Iceland can be viewed as the first full-fledged European overseas colony, as Norse families established communities and regularly plied the waters between Iceland and the Scandinavian mainland from 900 C.E. Further to the west the inappropriately named Greenland came under Norse settlement under Erik the Red toward the end of the tenth century. Around 987 C.E., Bjárni Herjolfsson was driven off course and sighted new land, which he named Helluland, Markland, and

Vinland, the latter described as particularly bountiful. Leif Erikson won greater credit, according to the *Vinland* sagas, because, in retracing Bjárni's path, he ventured to go ashore and even establish a temporary settlement. His kinsman, Thorfinn Karlsefni, and others from Iceland and Greenland soon followed. The colony, it seems, was abandoned by 1025, though whether due to economic isolation or hostile encounters with the indigenous peoples shall never be known. Norse settlements from the Viking Age have since been discovered at L'anse-aux-Meadows in Newfoundland, though it appears that the site was built only as a short-term trading outpost, rather than a full-fledged colony. At any rate, there seems to be little evidence that the stories of Viking expansion in the North Atlantic had much effect on the transatlantic journeys of the fifteenth and sixteenth centuries. The Vikings also moved south and east, establishing important settlements or colonies in Normandy, Britain, the Mediterranean, and Rus'.

By the mid-eleventh century, a newfound stability in the West laid the foundations for a new stage in European expansion. An increase in population led to a corresponding expansion of towns, trade, and movement of peoples into regions previously uninhabited. Lands held by non-Christians (Lithuanians, Prussians, Sicilian Muslims) were conquered or gradually converted. The expansion of European populations into the Levant was, in essence, an extension of the "internal colonization" that had been taking place in Europe itself. The establishment of Cluniac and Cistercian orders inspired reform of the papacy and motivated its subsequent interest in international affairs and new claims to global authority—in secular as well as religious matters—over Christians and non-Christians alike.

Venice, trading with both Muslim and Greek worlds, soon became the major entrepôt for the importation and distribution of Eastern goods in the West. By the century's end, Genoa and Pisa had also emerged as major players in international trade. Italian city-states thus had substantial trading involvement in the eastern Mediterranean before Pope Urban II preached the First Crusade at Clermont in 1095.

Pilgrims, as well as merchants, had long been a presence in the Levant. Throughout the eleventh century, the volume of pilgrimage from Europe to the holy places increased. Even the Seljuk invasion of Palestine in 1071 did little to stem the tide of travelers, and it was not until the 1090s that the routes were closed,

# E

principally by rulers in the Middle East, a fact that, no doubt, added impetus to Urban's preaching of a crusade.

Quite apart from mercantile and pilgrimage contact, Latin Christians made numerous military incursions into Muslim lands. Most notable of these was the ongoing *Reconquista* in Iberia where, over a period of more than 300 years, Christian armies attempted to push Muslim states off the peninsula. However, the near annihilation of the Byzantine army by the Seljuks at Manzikert in 1071 gave a certain urgency to Urban's call to arms (though it came nearly a generation later).

The crusades saw a confluence of Latin commercial interests, religious reform, and military adventurism. Pleas for assistance from the Byzantine emperor Alexius I Comnenus (1081–1118) were answered by Urban II's call to crusade and his offer of papal indulgences—extended not simply to those willing to fight in the eastern Mediterranean for the liberation of Jerusalem, but also for those fighting Muslim armies in Spain. By the late 1100s, crusading vows were undertaken by those fighting unconverted Lithuanians and Wends in northern Europe as well (and, in the early 1200s, this means of combatting perceived ethnic and religious threats at the margins of, or outside, Europe, was employed at home, when the pope extended crusade indulgences to opponents of heretics in southern France). The victories of the First Crusade and the establishment of Latin polities in the Levant brought news of the East much more clearly into the purview of Western observers. No matter that Latin rule would survive less than 200 years in the Holy Land. At their peak, the crusader states had a population estimated at 250,000, comprising Latin settlers, Eastern Christians of all descriptions, Jews, and Muslims. Few places in the medieval Mediterranean world saw a more eclectic gathering of various religions and ethnic groups than did Acre or Jerusalem. Yet, despite the large numbers of crusaders and pilgrims who made their way eastward from Europe in the eleventh, twelfth, and thirteenth centuries, the vast majority of them returned home again, having fulfilled their vows. Those who did stay did not, for the most part, come to any great understanding of Islam or Eastern Christianity, no matter what "oriental" fashions they might have affected. The crusades were, on one hand, an opportunity lost. They demonstrated the possibilities that existed for Latin expansion—possibilities that were never fully realized. On the other hand, the crusades to the eastern

Mediterranean brought the West into direct and prolonged contact with the heart of the Muslim world and gave it an awareness, no matter how dim, or even warped, of the cultures of western Asia and of those that lay beyond it.

One of the most striking outcomes of contact with the East was the emergence of the legend of Prester John. From the third century, the West had believed that the apostle Thomas had gone to preach the Gospel in India. In 1122/3, the story of Thomas's success was given added credibility when a man, claiming to be a representative of an Indian church, appeared in Rome before Pope Calixtus II (1119–1124). In 1145, the year following the fall of Edessa, Pope Eugenius III (1145–1153) was told of a certain Prester John, a Christian king of the East of great wealth and power, who intended to come to the aid of his coreligionists at Jerusalem. Soon thereafter (*c.* 1165), a letter, addressed to the Byzantine emperor Manuel I Comnenus (1143–1180) and purporting to be from one "presbyter Johannes"—usually called "Prester John" in English—began to circulate in the West. Prester John was, in point of fact, a fictional construct, but one that left a lasting impression on the West. To a Europe mired in crusading failure (Saladin recaptured Jerusalem and other important territory from the Christians in 1187), he would come to represent the potential embodiment of global Christian strength that remained central to European imperial ambition into the sixteenth century.

The greatest sense of expectation of an Eastern ally occurred during the Fifth Crusade at the siege of Damietta, near Cairo (1221), when rumors circulated that a Christian king of the Indies, one King David (alternately identified as Prester John or one of his descendants) had been attacking Muslims in the East, and was en route to help the crusading armies of Latin Christendom. King David did not arrive, but rumors of an advancing army were not without some foundation, being, evidently, based on Nestorian reports of early Mongol incursions into west-central Asia.

The rise of the Mongol polity in Central Asia under Chinggis Khân (1167–1227) had extraordinary consequences for the sedentary peoples of western Asia and Europe. The Mongol conquest of China would eventually provide heretofore unimaginable diplomatic, religious, and mercantile opportunities for the Latin West, perhaps doubly unexpected because of the hostile nature of the earliest European-Mongol encounters. While the initial Mongol presence was barely noted in

Europe, the Hungarian king Béla IV (r. 1235–1270) sent an embassy to Central Asia under a Dominican, Julian, in 1236–1237, who returned with the news that the Mongols intended to attack. The attack, when it did come to Poland and Hungary in 1241, was swift, efficient, and beyond European comprehension. In April, over a period of three days, the flower of eastern European chivalry was decimated at two decisive battles by Mongolian horsemen/archers. The Mongols rode through Hungary and the Balkans with devastating effect. Some horrified Latins thought them the tribes of Gog and Magog, whose release from captivity heralded the end of the world. But the Mongols quickly withdrew—possibly to attend an assembly in Mongolia to elect a new great khân, at which the participation of some leaders in the European invasion was required—and their disappearance was celebrated in the West, albeit with some trepidation, as a miracle. In order to counter the possibility of their return, Pope Innocent IV (1243–1254) dispatched two Franciscan emissaries, John of Plano Carpini and Lawrence of Portugal, to visit the great khân. Leaving Lyons in April 1245, and joined at Wrocław (Breslau) by another Franciscan, Benedict "the Pole," they were allowed to pass unhindered across the steppe to the Mongol camp outside Karakorum, where they witnessed the enthronement of Güyük as great khân on August 24, 1246. In the company were Mongol subjects from across the vast empire: Europeans, Central Asians, and Chinese. Carpini, who would later chronicle his adventures, returned to Lyons in November 1248, bearing a letter from Güyük to the pope expressing amazement that anyone would dare question God's will as expressed through his duly appointed agents, the Mongols. Carpini noted, too, that European internal political dissension would, if left unchecked, be a great temptation for the Mongols.

Carpini was followed, both as traveler and chronicler, by another Franciscan, William of Rubruck, who left from Acre in 1253, to seek out the great khân Möngke at the behest of Louis IX of France (1226–1270). He ventured north to the Volga basin and thence to Möngke's court in the company of a Mongol nobleman; he arrived on December 26, 1253, and remained with the khân's court for seven months, following the *orda* to the capital city, Karakorum, which they reached on Palm Sunday (April 5) 1254. On his return to Palestine in 1255, he chronicled in a letter to King Louis the cultural, religious, and political

goings-on in the Mongol world of the time. His *Itinerarius* can still be viewed as an ethnographic work of considerable sophistication.

The journeys and discoveries of John of Plano Carpini and William of Rubruck opened up a new world for the West. The wealth of China, closed to direct trading since the Roman period, lay open for trade and investigation; the presence of Christians (Nestorians mostly) at Mongol courts, raised the possibility of a great missionizing enterprise; and the potential of channeling Mongol military might against the Muslim world seemed a great boon for the crusader monarchs of the West.

The mission to the Mongols that began in the thirteenth century was part of a much larger evangelizing enterprise to the non-Christian peoples with whom the Latin world had come into contact. When John and William had been sent east, the church had just begun to evangelize among the Lithuanians, Cumans, and others living to the immediate east of Latin Christendom. Asia was, as far as the Latin Church was concerned, a *tabula rasa,* though Nestorian Christianity had succeeded in making some inroads in China and the Mongol lands, and Armenia and Georgia had been Christianized for nearly a millennium. The fact that Mongol khâns had high officials who were Christians (a couple had Christian wives, for that matter) was greeted with great expectation in Latin circles, for while the chances for conversion among the Mongol il-khâns of Iran were assumed to be negligible, the possibility of bringing this powerful people of eastern Asia into the Christian fold played a major part in the Roman Church's evangelical policy through the late thirteenth and early fourteenth centuries.

Throughout the thirteenth century, papal embassies were sent to the il-khânid capital, Tabriz, in the hope of baptizing the ruling il-khân. Dominican and Franciscan houses were established along trade routes across western Asia. Preachers evangelized throughout the western Mongol lands. The Dominican Ricold of Monte Croce, for example, paid careful attention to the local religious customs and practices of Eastern Christians, learned the regional languages, and instructed other potential missionaries to do likewise—a practice that was adopted by some but ignored by others, often at great peril. Execution—which might be interpreted as martyrdom—was a common fate for preachers who violated local strictures governing appropriate behavior. Rumors of the successful

# E

conversion of khâns were a constant source of encouragement and excitement in Latin religious circles, though they rarely had any basis in fact.

Papal interest in China did not take hold until 1291, when Pope Nicholas IV (1286–1292) appointed John of Monte Corvino envoy to China. Traveling via Iran, he arrived in Beijing in late 1293/early 1294. Over the next decade, John's letters to fellow Franciscans detailed his experiences in the Far East. News of his work inspired Pope Clement V to appoint him Beijing's first Catholic archbishop in 1307. Other friars were soon to follow John, and a bishopric was established for the city of Zaiton—a Chinese port with a growing Western population. John himself died between 1328 and 1330, and those who followed him died shortly thereafter. Odoric of Pordenone, another Franciscan, traveled throughout south and southeast Asia before arriving in Beijing in 1325, where he stayed for three years. Odoric, unlike John and his suffragans, was a traveler and not on any official evangelical mission, and his account of his travels reads as such.

India, along with China, was a favored destination of missionaries and, like China, held a semimythological status in the West, due to its years of relative isolation from Latin contact. Notable among the friars who made their way to India was Jordan (Catalani) of Sévérac, traveling in the 1320s, who wrote a short treatise on India and can be credited as the founder of the Latin Church in the subcontinent. Returning to Europe in 1328, Jordan revisited India several years later as the newly appointed Latin bishop of Quilon, with responsibility for evangelizing all India. Before the entry of the Portuguese into the Indian Ocean, one more chronicler left a detailed picture of Asia: the Franciscan John of Marignolli. Sent in 1338 in response to an embassy from China, John traveled a year overland and remained in Beijing as archbishop for approximately seven years, returning to Avignon after a total of fifteen years in the East.

In China, the Latin Church maintained a tenuous existence after the collapse of the Mongol Yuan dynasty in 1368, but few missionaries, merchants, and bishops were available to give the enterprise spiritual and material help. By the time Latin missionaries and Portuguese traders returned to south and east Asia in the sixteenth century, no memory of the medieval missions existed. The hoped-for conversion of Asia did not come to pass, though the West had acquired at least a passing awareness of the political, social, and religious life of the East.

Quite apart from missionaries, Europeans in far greater numbers traveled east in search of wealth and trade in the thirteenth and fourteenth centuries. The European economy had been growing steadily since the tenth century, and Eastern goods were highly valued, though available in very limited supply. Pepper, spices, and silk were imported (usually through Genoese, Florentine, or Venetian entrepreneurs) via Alexandria and other Muslim ports, often in contradiction to papal decree, but land routes to the sources of the goods, through Muslim territories, were closed. Nor did European merchant ships have access to the Indian Ocean until the very end of the fifteenth century. Western merchants had been well established in the Byzantine Empire since the eleventh century, with their own special privileges and communities, but it was the complete redistribution of power in Asia caused by the Mongols between 1220 and 1270 that opened up the Eastern trade to the Latins.

From bases on the Black Sea and at Constantinople, Italian traders developed a large and important trading network throughout the Mongol dominions. Tabriz, the Mongol capital of Iran, became a familiar destination and home to many Western merchants. Often, Italian merchants served the il-khâns as ambassadors and political emissaries to Europe. Some merchants traveled beyond Iran to India, Central Asia, and China. Most notable among these was the Venetian Marco Polo, who allegedly journeyed throughout Asia in 1271 with his father Niccolò and uncle Maffeo, who themselves had been to China during the previous decade. Whether or not Marco's travels, as related in his *Divisament dou monde,* also called *Il Milione,* were in the service of the Great Khân Khubilai, as he claimed, or were independent—or were even undertaken by other merchants altogether—his chronicle affords the reader many unique details of courtly and commercial life in Yuan dynasty China. His attention to the natural resources and principal products of Asia made Western Europeans more keenly aware of the rich commercial potential of the Far East, and his references to thousands of remote islands—including "Cipangu" or (presumably) Japan—entered the European geographical imagination with significant effects in the late 1400s and 1500s. The book attributed to him was widely circulated in the West from the fourteenth century, and was a singularly important influence on future travelers and mariners.

Curiosity about the Mongols and their dominions extended not only to the possible harvest of souls or silk, but also to the role the Mongols might play in European crusading schemes. The potential for alliance was implicit in the full range of Latin-Mongol relations from the mid-1240s onward, and as early as 1248, King Louis IX of France attempted (albeit unsuccessfully) to engage the Mongols in formal diplomacy.

News of the Mongol sack of Baghdad (1258), coupled with stories of the apparent mercy shown to the Christians of the city, was received in Europe as a highly encouraging sign. Shortly thereafter the Mongols were defeated by the Mamluks at the battle of Ain Jalut in 1260. The Mongol il-khâns of Iran began to look to Europeans as potential allies in the wake of their defeat by the Mamluks.

The first positive attempt by the il-khâns to make contact with Europe was made by Hülegü in 1262, who, in a letter to Louis IX, suggested a joint land and naval attack against Egypt by a Mongol-European force. It was not, however, until 1265, with the accession of the il-khân Abagha, that serious consideration was given to cooperation between the West and Iran in a crusading context. The son-in-law of the Byzantine emperor Michael VIII Palaeologus (1253–1282), Abagha spent much of his reign attempting to make such an alliance possible. He sent an embassy to the Council of Lyons in 1274 expressing his desire for alliance. In turn, Pope Gregory X (1271–1276) vowed that any future crusading army would seek the active assistance of the Mongols.

Other embassies followed throughout the 1270s, but with little concrete result. Abagha's son, Argun, also sent a number of embassies to the West, the most notable of which was led by a Chinese Nestorian Christian, Rabban Bar Sauma, who wrote a detailed account of his 1287–1288 voyage to the West.

By the time the crusader outpost at Acre had fallen in 1291, there were three separate embassies en route between Iran and the West, including a Mongol embassy under the leadership of a Genoese, Buscarello de Ghisolfi. Each seems to have been anxious to establish a firm alliance against the Mamluks. Argun's death in 1291 seems to have dimmed Mongol interest for several years until the accession of his son, Ghazan. Ghazan was a Muslim, determined to free Syria from Mamluk control. Informing several Latin leaders of his intentions to invade Syria, he set out in 1299/1300. The story of Ghazan's planned invasion of Syria reached the West in greatly exaggerated form and included stories of his capture and return to the Latins of Jerusalem, even, in some variants, of a conversion of Ghazan to Christianity. The truth of the matter was that no attack on Jerusalem had been executed.

Ghazan's successor, Öljeitü, had been baptized a Christian as a child, though by the time of his accession he was a Muslim. He attempted to maintain the channels of communication that had existed under his father, sending an embassy in 1305 that remained in Europe for three years. The response in Europe was lukewarm, domestic discord holding the attention of the Latin monarchs more than any concrete plans for a crusade of recovery in the Middle East.

The il-khâns eventually converted to Islam, and a treaty of peace was signed with the Mamluks in 1322. While alliance plans continued to be voiced in the West well into the 1340s, there was no longer any response forthcoming from Iran. The dynasty itself collapsed in 1335. Although the possibility that two such different political worlds would ever have been able to coordinate military action over such a great distance was always remote, the mutual advantages that such an alliance afforded continued to remain a mainstay of Western diplomatic overtures to Asia (and indeed to Africa) throughout the fourteenth, fifteenth, and into the sixteenth centuries.

And it was, in fact, to Africa that the Latin world turned to an increasingly greater extent in its attempt to examine the world beyond the Mediterranean, particularly after the fall of the Mongol polity in the 1360s. The Iberian *Reconquista* had brought Christians of the western Mediterranean in conflict with North African Muslims since the eighth century, and by the early thirteenth century, Castilian and Aragonese ships harassed North African ports. Yet, despite rather grand schemes of conquest and annexation devised in Iberian courts, little practical progress was made, despite short-lived crusading operations in Tunisia and Egypt in the mid- to late 1300s.

Latin attentions eventually focused on the West African coast and the horn of northeastern Africa. The trans-Saharan caravan routes that brought gold and salt to the Mediterranean had been known, if not explored, by Latin Christians. Direct access to them had been blocked by Muslim control of the North African coast.

# E

As noted earlier, Ethiopia had been known since antiquity, but it was likewise isolated from the rest of Christendom by the Muslim conquests.

There certainly was active interest in Ethiopia in the West in the latter half of the thirteenth century. Genoese traders apparently operated as far south as Dongola in Nubia. And there was, to be sure, a great deal of secular interest in Ethiopia, expressed in Europe in writings of a variety of observers, including Marco Polo, though there is no proof that any of them actually visited the region. The papacy, too, expressed a great interest in Ethiopia and such papal ambassadors as John of Monte Corvino carried with him letters for the "archbishop" and emperor of Ethiopia, though he clearly never was in a position to deliver them.

In 1310, the veil of mystery was stripped away when an embassy from Ethiopia arrived in Italy—the first of many such embassies to arrive over a period of 250 years. The significance of this particular embassy for Western observers was that its arrival and prolonged stay in Genoa appears to have been the source of Giovanni da Carignano's map, made sometime between 1291 and 1330 (and destroyed in 1943), the first definitive equation of Ethiopia with the land of Prester John—a designation that would remain well into the seventeenth century, and a significant relocation from Asia to Africa of the fictional ruler's territory.

By 1335, as Western interest in the il-khâns had begun to dissipate, interest in Ethiopia remained strong. The conflicts between Muslims and Copts in Egypt in the middle decades of the fourteenth century were reported quite eagerly and copiously in the West. Even after tensions had died down, interest in an alliance in Europe remained strong. In a letter dated 1400, addressed to "the king of Abyssinia, Prester John," Henry IV of England (r. 1399–1413) referred to rumors that the Ethiopians were intent on retaking Jerusalem. Henry's ambassador never went to Ethiopia, but there were Europeans who did, including, from the later years of the fourteenth century, a variety of Italian craftsmen. A Florentine named Antonio Bartoli returned to Europe in 1402 at the head of an Ethiopian embassy. Italians were also present in an embassy in 1408. Little is known of these missions, but it is plausible to assume that Ethiopian kings fancied the notion of pan-Christian unity against the Mamluks and, more important, believed that the importation of Western artisans (sculptors, painters, architects) would enhance their own political power on a broader world stage.

Throughout the course of the fifteenth century, one of the driving forces behind continuing European interest in the Ethiopians as allies was their capacity to inspire utter dread in the Mamluks, who believed that the Ethiopian emperor had the power to stop or divert the flow of the Nile. Fear over the Nile, fear over invasion, and fear regarding internal subversion by native Coptic Christians are repeated themes in Muslim chronicles of the period—themes repeated, with a mixture of awe and glee, by European observers and diplomats who saw this as verification that the Ethiopians were as powerful as the original Prester John had ever been believed to be. Embassies were entertained several times at the courts of Naples and Aragon and at the court of Jean, duc de Berri. And while the intent of these embassies seems to have been to ensure a continuing supply of skilled artisans from France, Italy, and Iberia, the monarchs of the West clearly were looking beyond mere foreign aid and toward the reality of armed alliance in a crusade against Egypt. In 1428, Alfonso V of Aragon even proposed a marital union between Aragon and Ethiopia to secure an alliance. At about the same time, Jean de Lastic, grand master of the Hospitallers, spoke of a pending Ethiopian attack on the Muslim heartland. It was with these expectations that the Portuguese set about searching for "Prester John" in the mid-fifteenth century.

Though it is certain that fishermen from the Iberian Peninsula had been making voyages into the Atlantic from a very early date indeed, the earliest Latin voyage westward of which we have any surviving record is the 1291 sailing of the brothers Ugolino and Guido Vivaldi, who left Genoa in two galleys to search for a route to India "through the ocean." While they disappeared en route, it is almost certain that other voyages and expeditions westward were undertaken in the late-thirteenth and early-fourteenth centuries.

The Genoese explorer Lanzarotto Malocello briefly established a short-lived garrison before 1339 in the Canary Islands. Numerous voyages followed shortly thereafter by travelers from Majorca, Genoa, and elsewhere in the Mediterranean, some seeking fortune and their own kingdoms, like Luis de la Cerda (1344), others seeking souls, such as the Franciscan missionaries who traveled to the Canaries from the 1350s to convert the indigenous "Guanche" population of the islands. It is reasonable to assume from cartographic evidence and the nature of the wind system that Madeira and the Azores had also been encountered by the 1380s. Further exploration in search of gold was undertaken in the first decade of the fifteenth century by the French navigator Gadifer de La Salle (1340–1422), a veteran of crusades both in the Baltic and the Mediterranean, and Jean de Béthencourt (1360–1422), the Norman lord of Grainville, who together established a permanent settlement on Lanzarote in 1402 under Castilian sovereignty. Their settlement was followed by a series of Portuguese voyages through Madeira, the Canaries, and the Azores during the middle third of the fifteenth century, which further increased the detailed knowledge of the Atlantic islands.

The Portuguese also developed the ocean-going caravel, rigged to allow sailing close to the wind and greater maneuverability along the West African coast. The ensuing voyages established the Portuguese as Europe's foremost explorers in the fifteenth century, initially under the patronage of Prince Henry (1398–1460), later termed "the Navigator."

While contemporary scholars continue to debate Henry's motivation—personal political ambition, religious devotion, or genuine scientific curiosity—it is clear that, in Africa and the Canaries, Henry saw the opportunity to tap the lucrative Saharan gold trade. Following the Portuguese capture of the Moroccan port of Ceuta (1415), the Portuguese court professed greater interest in discovering the sources of gold in West Africa, both in order to fuel future crusading ventures against the Muslim world and to enhance the prestige of the Portuguese ruling dynasty on the broader political stage of Latin Christendom.

By the mid-1450s, Henry's interests had shifted from the Canaries to the West African mainland and its bountiful supply of human and mineral wealth. Portuguese voyages came increasingly to be undertaken by professional navigators (often Genoese) rather than members of the court. Through their efforts, the Gambia and Senegal rivers were explored, Cape Bojador was rounded, and contact was made with the great empire of Mali in the continent's interior.

If we are to believe his encomiastic chronicler, Azurara, Henry was motivated to sponsor these voyages in part by a desire to find Christians on the other side of the Muslim world with whom he could ally himself. There can be little doubt that these voyages served permanently to link Iberia with West Africa and the Atlantic islands in a navigational triangle; they also greatly extended European knowledge of the West African coast, thus laying an important foundation for the voyages that would follow.

In 1469, nearly a decade after Henry's death, the Portuguese crown granted Fernão Gomes, a wealthy Lisbon merchant, the right of exploration along the African coast. During the six years that his grant was in effect, Portuguese exploration extended more than 3,000 miles down the west coast of Africa. Small ports and coastal factories were established in order to facilitate an ever-growing and prospering ivory and pepper trade. After Gomes's monopoly was rescinded, the royal house itself, under Henry's grand-nephew, Prince João (later King João II [r. 1481–1495]), undertook the responsibility for launching and patronizing further exploration and exploitation of the resources of Africa. The continuing search for Prester John was a preoccupation of João's imperial policy in Africa. The Treaty of Alcaçovas between Portugal and Castile (1479) had procured Castilian recognition of Portuguese sovereignty in Africa and thus gave the Portuguese primary "responsibility" for maintaining and enhancing diplomatic contact with Ethiopia. Access to Africa was to be restricted to the Portuguese alone. The mark of Portuguese success, as defined by Portugal's entry into the pantheon of Iberian crusaders, would be to find Prester John and to gain his assistance in combating the Islamic menace in the Mediterranean.

Until the latter half of the sixteenth century, Benin was the centerpiece of Portugal's Christianizing policy in West Africa, as well as its efforts to gain access to the gold of the interior. Success was finally achieved after the construction of a fort and trading factory at Elmina, on the Ghana/Benin coast, in the 1480s. The establishment of a major Portuguese trading post in such a strategic location, close to Mali and the trade routes, was very profitable indeed. The volume of the gold that the Portuguese were able to draw away from the trans-Saharan (i.e., Islamic) trade routes seems to have caused significant financial loss to the Islamic merchants of the Levant.

The Portuguese gradually made their way down the African coast, toward the kingdom of Kongo, with which Diogo Cão established contact in 1482. The first Kongo policy, devised by João II and continued by his heir, Manuel I (r. 1495–1521), was to Christianize Central Africa and use Kongo as a base for searching for Prester John. This continuing search for the elusive crusading ally, whose presumed military strength and strategic location was believed to hold the key to a successful crusade, occupied much early Portuguese activity in Mozambique and the East African coast. In early

# E

1488, Bartolomeu Dias (*c.* 1450–1500) made landfall 300 miles past the final cape at the southern tip of the African continent. After mutiny caused the voyage to be abandoned, King João named the cape "Good Hope" because of the promise of India that lay in the distance.

At the same time as Dias's voyage, the Portuguese had also attempted to reach India overland. After a failed journey in 1485/1486, two members of the royal household ventured eastward in 1487 in disguise to the Red Sea. One of them, Pedro de Covilhã, reached India and perhaps East Africa before returning to Cairo in 1490/1491, whence, he claimed, he wrote to the king outlining his trip and the geography of the region in great detail. Afterward, he turned again to the east, only to be taken captive in Ethiopia, where he remained until his death in the 1540s.

Vasco da Gama (*c.* 1469–1525) had not, apparently, heard any of Covilhã's report when he set sail in 1497. João II had died in 1495 and money for further voyages was scarce, but his successor, Manuel I, convinced that the wealth of the Indies and the Christians of the East would allow him to fulfill his own destiny to liberate Jerusalem from Muslim control, was eager to find the sea route eastward around Africa. Da Gama, sailing 6,000 kilometers in the Atlantic, eventually rounded the cape, followed the east coast of Africa, and crossed the Indian Ocean, making landfall at Calicut on the Kerala coast on May 20, 1498.

Once in India, the Portuguese found themselves ill-equipped to enter immediately into the spice trade as they had desired: they lacked suitable goods to trade, behaved inappropriately at religious shrines, and, perhaps most significantly, could provide no suitable reason for local rulers to abandon their long-standing trading ties with Levantine and Gujarati Muslim traders. Da Gama returned to Portugal after two years with only a vestige of his original fleet and crew. Yet, despite their initial failure to establish India as a trading mission, the Portuguese had found themselves in the midst of Asia's most active mercantile network, and subsequent voyages were not as ill-prepared as the first. The Portuguese crown, in time, seized the most important ports of the Indian Ocean basin, establishing a trading empire of great strength and prosperity that brought wealth and prestige to Lisbon and severely damaged the economy of Mamluk Egypt so that, in 1517, it was powerless to stave off an Ottoman conquest.

Mythologies regarding the existence of islands in the western Atlantic and potential crusading allies in Asia, coupled with a belief in the distinctly crusading destiny of Spanish monarchs, all proved to be factors in determining Christopher Columbus's decision to sail westward to find the wealth of the Indies. Familiar with Marco Polo's *Divisament dou monde,* Columbus (1451–1506) looked back on a wide variety of crusading precedents in interpreting his voyages. The conquest of Jerusalem—both spiritual and temporal—was at the heart of Columbus's voyages. Whether it was in the search for allies in the form of the great khân, the search for gold to fill the coffers of his crusading sovereigns, or his eventual desire to create a uniquely Christian paradise, the vision of the Holy Land remained before him. His contact on Cuba with the Carib Indians in Late November 1492, led him to believe that he had encountered the fierce Chinese soldiers of the great khân. During his last voyage, Columbus wrote that he had reached the Chinese province of Mangi, and that the island of Cuba was, indeed, the Chinese mainland. This firm belief that he had reached Asia remained with Columbus until his death in 1506.

Columbus also expressed his desire that none but devout Latin Christians should come to the lands he had reached. This request to keep the New World free from heretics and infidels coincided with another of Columbus's beliefs. The potential wealth to be gained from the lands would, he wrote, give the Spanish crown the ability to reconquer Jerusalem. The desire to possess territory in the Holy Land, Marco Polo's adventures, and the desire to spread the Christian faith to the far reaches of the earth all affected Columbus's definition of his mission in, and after, 1492.

**BIBLIOGRAPHY**

Curtin, Philip D. *Cross-Cultural Trade in World History.* Cambridge: Cambridge UP, 1985.

Fernández-Armesto, Felipe. *Before Columbus: Exploration and Colonization from the Mediterranean to the Atlantic, 1229–1492.* Philadelphia: U of Pennsylvania P, 1987.

Jones, Gwyn. *The Norse Atlantic Saga, Being the Norse Voyages of Discovery and Settlement to Iceland, Greenland, and North America.* 2nd edition. Oxford: Oxford UP, 1986.

Muldoon, James. *Popes, Lawyers, and Infidels: the Church and the Non-Christian World, 1250–1550.* Philadelphia: U of Pennsylvania P, 1979.

Phillips, J.R.S. *The Medieval Expansion of Europe.* Oxford: Oxford UP, 1988.

Riley-Smith, Jonathan. *The Crusades: A Short History.* London: Athlone; New Haven: Yale UP, 1987.

Scammell, G.V. *The World Encompassed: The First European Maritime Empires, c. 800–1650.* Berkeley: U of California P, 1981.

*Adam Knobler*

**SEE ALSO**

## Expulsion, Corporate

The banishment of an entire body of people beyond the physical borders of a state, officially ordered and executed by its legitimate rulers. This type of removal differs from the kindred but distinct phenomena of deportation to another location *within* the same political entity, imposition of exile for political reasons, eviction of a population immediately upon its defeat in an armed conflict, or banishment of individual criminals and deviants.

Corporate expulsion evolved during the Middle Ages and may be considered a characteristic of western European civilization. While deportation occurred mainly within empires, ancient and modern, and the imposition of exile was resorted to by ancient and medieval city-states, corporate expulsion took place within the system of European states that emerged in the central Middle Ages. The relatively small size of the new state, and the advent of ever more efficient state machinery, enabled corporate expulsions from ever larger territories to be carried out as a single act. At the same time, expellees from one place could easily migrate to another, and be easily reintroduced if a ruler decided to do so. Thus, from a systemic standpoint, corporate expulsion could have had beneficial effects, inasmuch as it furthered the diffusion of ideas and techniques, while from the expellees' viewpoint it was a less dire form of persecution than massacre. Because this type of expulsion aimed at the removal of a category of people rather than the physical elimination of all members of a specific group, an individual could often escape expulsion (or return after having been expelled) by publicly pledging a change in behavior.

Typically, a corporate expulsion was set in motion by an edict that spelled out the presumed harmful activities of the category of people earmarked for eviction and specified the period of grace granted before their enforced departure. The earliest extant edict containing these elements is the one by which King Louis IX of France in 1268 drove out of his domain Lombards, Cahorsins, and other foreign usurers, because they had purportedly impoverished the realm by their usury and perpetrated "many bad acts" in their houses; the expulsion was to become effective after three months. Yet, such reasoning appears to have preceded Louis IX's edict by almost a century; for Rigord, one of the main sources on Philip Augustus's expulsion of the Jews from the French royal domain in 1182, introduces his account with a lengthy report on Jewish misdeeds: they Judaized their Christian servants, caused widespread impoverishment by their usury, and desecrated church articles that came into their hands as collateral. Rigord mentions that the span of time between the promulgation of the expulsion order and its implementation was about three months.

Corporate expulsion was aimed most frequently at Jews; but they were not the only target. Christian usurers and Moriscos (Spanish Muslims ostensibly converted to Christianity), Protestants, Jesuits, and Mormons were all expelled at one time or another between the thirteenth and nineteenth centuries.

Religious antagonism was undoubtedly an underlying motive behind most medieval expulsions, but unbelief was not usually presented as its basic reason. The grounds for expulsion given in an edict may, of course, differ from the ones put forward by a contemporary observer. Thus, while the Catholic kings declared in their edict of March 31, 1492, that the Jews were to be expelled from Spain on account of their incessant subversion of Christians (i.e., of the crypto-Jews, or Marranos), the chronicler Andrés Bernaldez maintained that these kings, aware of the grave damage proceeding from the "perpetual blindness" of the Jews, ordered that the Christian doctrine be preached to them, and that

# E

those who subsequently refused to convert should be expelled.

In other civilizations, corporate expulsion appears to have occurred only rarely. Only in Europe was it employed time and again over an extended period, serving as an important and radical tool of governance, with earlier expulsions repeatedly serving as models for later ones. Occurring against a backdrop of sundry biblical, Roman, Germanic, and ecclesiastical precedents of exclusion, corporate expulsion appears to have become institutionalized with the coincidence, from the twelfth century onward, of two major developments. The first of these was the vision of a regenerated, reformed Christian society—a vision that led to more precise delimitation of its spiritual boundaries, coupled with a gripping fear of the evil forces that were perceived as intent on contaminating it. These forces were obsessively demonized: it was in Catholic Europe that the blood libel (the allegation that Jews murder Christian children to obtain blood for ritual use) frequently recurred, from the twelfth century onward; and it was only in Catholic Europe that the Black Death—a hemispheral phenomenon—gave rise to accusations of well-poisoning by the Jews. The other development was the growing tendency of increasingly powerful secular rulers to accentuate their responsibility for the spiritual as well as physical well-being of their realms—a responsibility that they conceived of as a holy obligation and one that required them to deal with threats to that well-being. Thus, the nearly simultaneous emergence of irrational motivation and rational means of execution rendered orderly governmental expulsion a viable mode for coping with perceived internal foes whose physical annihilation was usually precluded by cultural constraints.

## BIBLIOGRAPHY

Kedar, Benjamin Z. "Expulsion as an Issue of World History." *Journal of World History* 7 (1996): 165–180.

Stow, Kenneth R. *Alienated Minority: The Jews of Medieval Latin Europe.* Cambridge, MA, and London: Harvard UP, 1992, pp. 281–308.

*Benjamin Z. Kedar*

## SEE ALSO

Black Death; Canon Law and Subject Peoples; Louis IX; Usury and the Church's View of Business

# F

## Fabri, Felix (1441/2–1502)

The author of a long, detailed, fascinating report of his two pilgrimages to the Holy Land. Felix Fabri was born in Zurich in 1441 or 1442. After the death of his father in 1443, his mother, Clara Issnach, married Ulrich Büller, and moved to Diessenhofen, near Schaffhausen. Fabri may have entered the important Dominican convent at Basle as early as 1452. In 1468, he left Basle to join the Dominican house at Ulm, where he died, probably on March or May 14, 1502. At Ulm he held a position as preacher and probably taught at the convent school. His writings show that important duties within the order were periodically entrusted to him. That he was a man of influence also appears from the fact that he managed to get permission both from the pope and from his order to make two pilgrimages to the Holy Land.

Earlier in his life, in 1467 and 1468, Fabri had made short pilgrimages to see relics at Pforzheim and Aachen. These were followed by his much more ambitious journeys to the Holy Land in 1480 and from 1483 until late January 1484. Fabri recounted his experiences and observations in an expansive work entitled *Evagatorium in Terrae Sanctae, Arabiae et Egypti peregrinationem* (Wanderings in the Journey to the Holy Land, Arabia, and Egypt) (1494), a work written in answer to a request from nuns in Swabia who desired to "become pilgrims in the Holy Land" without leaving their convent. The book runs nearly 1,500 pages (in a modern printed edition), and is written in a lively style, rich with personal remarks. It is in two parts: the first describes Fabri's first pilgrimage from Ulm to Jerusalem and back over the course of 215 days, as well as the initial stages of his second journey from Ulm. The second part details this second pilgrimage, which lasted 289 days, and is of greater interest. The large number of pilgrims who accompanied him and his companions on the ships from Venice or joined them in the Holy Land demonstrates the size of the pilgrimage industry of the time. Fabri and his fellow pilgrims traveled first to Jerusalem, then through Palestine to the Monastery of St. Catherine in the Sinai desert, and across the Red Sea to Cairo. After reaching Alexandria, Fabri and his companions embarked for Venice. The book concludes with the author's homecoming at Ulm.

Fabri interrupts his own account of daily events during the journey with lengthy digressions about the places he visited—or simply heard of—along the way; these digressions, in fact, form the bulk of the book. They derive from a variety of sources, including the Bible, the Alexander romances, Bartholomaeus Anglicus (fl. c. 1250), Thomas of Cantimpré (1201–1270/72), Albertus Magnus (c. 1190–1280), Vincent of Beauvais (c. 1190–1264), and Aeneas Silvius Piccolomini (Pius II [1405–1464]).

Of the many travel books written about pilgrimages to the Holy Land, at least three others date from the period in which Fabri was traveling there. Certainly the most influential because of its early publication and many reprints was the *Peregrinatio in Terram Sanctam* by Bernhard von Breydenbach; far less well known are the *Itinerarium in Terram Sanctam et ad Sanctam Catherinam* by Paul Walther of Guglingen, and *Tvoyage* by Ioos van Ghistele. A thorough scholarly comparison of these reports has never been undertaken.

Fabri was also the author of a guide for a spiritual traveler to the Holy Land (*Sionspilgerin*), a description

# F

of Switzerland (*Descriptio Sueviae* [1487–1488]), and a treatise on the city of Ulm (*Tractatus de civitate Ulmensi, de eius origine, ordine, regimine, de civibus eius et statu* [1488–1489]), which Fabri originally meant to be the conclusion to the *Evagatorium*.

## BIBLIOGRAPHY

Fabri, Felix. *Fratris Felicis Fabri Evagatorium in Terrae Sanctae, Arabiae et Egyptiae peregrinationem*. Ed. Konrad Dietrich Hassler. Bibliothek des Literarischen Vereins Stuttgart, 2–4. Stuttgart: n.p., 1843–1849.

———. *The Book of the Wanderings of Felix Fabri*. Trans. Aubrey Stewart. 4 parts in 2 vols. Library of the Palestine Pilgrims' Text Society 7–10. London: Palestine Pilgrims' Text Society, 1893–1897; rpt. New York: AMS Press, 1971.

———. *Voyage en Egypte*. Trans. Jacques Masson. 3 vols. Collection des voyageurs occidentaux en Égypte, 44. Cairo: Institut français d'archéologie orientale du Caire, 1975.

Feilke, Herbert. *Felix Fabris Evagatorium über seine Reise in das Heilige Land: Eine Untersuchung über die Pilgerliteratur des ausgehenden Mittelalters*. Frankfurt and Bern: Lang, 1976

Scheffer, Lia. "A Pilgrimage to the Holy Land and Mount Sinai in the 15th Century." *Zeitschrift des deutschen Palästinas Vereins* 102 (1986): 144–151.

Weiss, Gerhard. "The Pilgrim as Tourist: Travels to the Holy Land as Reflected in the Published Accounts of German Pilgrims between 1450 and 1550." In *The Medieval Mediterranean: Cross-Cultural Contacts*. Ed. Marilyn J. Chiat and Kathryn L. Reyerson. Medieval Studies at Minnesota 3. St. Cloud, MN: North Star Press, 1988, pp. 119–131.

*Z.R.W.M. von Martels*

## SEE ALSO

Albertus Magnus; Bartholomaeus Anglicus; Breydenbach, Bernhard von; Holy Land; Catherine in the Sinai, Monastery of St.; Pilgrimage, Christian; Pius II; Thomas of Cantimpré; Vincent of Beauvais

## Faeroe Islands

*See* Viking Discoveries and Settlements

## Fairs

Well-organized gatherings of merchants and buyers that not only benefited their time, but had lasting effects on the way the world does business today.

Fairs played many important roles in the Middle Ages by enlarging international trade, distributing goods, developing adjoining agrarian areas, encouraging sophisticated accounting methods, improving travel conditions, disseminating ideas, and providing entertainment. Their success was due to their variety of merchandise and their adaptability to changing demands.

At first located in neutral territory on major trading routes, later held in conjunction with religious festivals, fairs differed from local markets in kinds of goods sold, duration, legal status, and applied mercantile codes. They were important in the economic expansion of the Middle Ages: Flanders cloth bought in France was sold in Italy, and Mediterranean dyestuffs were brought back north for use in future production.

Renowned fairs were held in Germany, Flanders, Italy, France, England, Sweden, and the Middle East. In France, the oldest documented fair is that of St. Denis (710); however, Champagne had the most successful and famous ones during the twelfth and thirteenth centuries.

Blessed by a confluence of rivers that were navigable throughout the year, and traversed by major north-south and east-west trade routes, Champagne was governed by enlightened counts who established set seasons and places for fairs to rotate through their jurisdiction. The earliest was at Châlons-sur-Marne (963); the most famous were at Troyes, Provins, Lagny-sur-Marne, and Bar-sur-Aube. The counts collected reasonable taxes, provided security and courts for disputes, and organized the conduct of the fair, including number of days, sequence of sales, methods of payment, market areas, and temporary storage facilities.

The Champagne fairs began with the Fair of Cloth, where all kinds of fabric were sold. The Fair of Pelts and Furs followed, featuring many items brought from as far as Scandinavia and Russia. Last came the Fair of Weight, at which merchandise was sold by weight (spices or sugar, for example). Concurrent with these fairs were markets for fabricated things such as pots and pans, and for livestock. Neighboring areas took note of what sold and geared production accordingly. The aristocracy also had the opportunity to acquire locally unavailable luxuries known from the crusades, including ivory chess sets, combs, and mirror cases; weapons from Syria and Spain; and the fine silks and ornamented fabrics from Asia Minor of the kind described in medieval romances.

A major function of fairs was the settling of accounts and changing of money, mostly done by Lombards and

Cahorsians. Monies of all denominations and kinds poured into fairs and needed equalization. Letters of credit were issued to obviate carrying large sums home or to the next fair. The need to handle the complex money transactions inspired today's double-entry bookkeeping, separate and alphabetical accounts, a body of codified mercantile law, and the use of Arabic numerals (and thus a decimal system). The instruments of credit and exchange became an important function of fairs, eventually rendering the fair itself superfluous.

Travel to and from fairs led to improved road and bridge construction, as well as the formation of companies of merchants for safety and advantageous negotiation of toll fees or concessions on their journeys. Inns became more numerous and cartage companies were founded. Standardization of weights and measures was another important outcome, including today's Troy weight (taking its name from the fair at Troyes). Finally, fairs provided venues for new ideas and for diversions such as jongleurs, acrobats, animal acts, and tournaments. In England, there were sometimes hangings to titillate the crowd as well.

The Champagne fairs' demise was hastened when the Burgundian duke Philip the Good (1419–1467) began taxing all Flemish goods in order to exert economic and political pressure in his war against Flanders. In addition, expanded maritime transport of goods from the Mediterranean to northern markets that depended on their raw materials allowed merchants to bypass the fairs. Whereas in the early Middle Ages there had been peripatetic commerce, by their end more systematized development had taken place. Banking practices were more refined, and many towns, having grown larger and more prosperous around the fairs, no longer needed their extra trade to be self-sufficient. Champagne remained a banking center, but the fairs themselves were doomed. Finally, with the dawn of the Renaissance and its concomitant undermining of internationalism through a focus on nation-states and boundaries, new complexities arose in travel and trade.

**BIBLIOGRAPHY**
Chatfield, Michael. *A History of Accounting Thought.* Hinsdale, IL: Dryden, 1974.
Lombard-Jourdan, Anne. "Fairs" and "Fairs of Champagne." In *Dictionary of the Middle Ages.* Ed. Joseph R. Strayer. New York: Scribner's, 1984, vol. 4, pp. 582–593.
Moore, Ellen Wedemeyer. *The Fairs of Medieval England: An Introductory Study.* Toronto: Pontifical Institute, 1985.
Pirenne, Henri. *Economic and Social History of Medieval Europe.* Trans. I.E. Clegg. New York: Harcourt, 1963.
Walford, Cornelius. *Fairs, Past and Present: A Chapter in the History of Commerce.* London: Stock, 1883.

*Lois Hawley Wilson*

**SEE ALSO**
Acre; Alfonso X; Bruges; Byzantine Empire; Cockaigne, Land of; Dyes and Pigments; Economics and Trade; Genoa; Inns and Accommodations; Ivory Trade; Law, Commercial; Mecca; Merchants, French; Merchants, Jewish; Pilgrimage Sites, Byzantine; Portuguese Trade; Spain and Portugal; Textiles, Decorative; Transportation, Inland

## Fātimids

A Shi'ite dynasty named after the Prophet Muhammad's daughter Fatima, wife of Ali, whose followers became the Shi'ites as a result of his disputed succession to the caliphate. The Fātimids ruled North Africa (909–1051) and preceded the Sunnite Ayyūbid dynasty in Egypt (969–1171); they also intermittently controlled Syria-Palestine and the Hijaz (northwest coast of Arabia) after 969. Although religio-ethnic-political factionalism and Sunnite opposition to Shi'ism constantly threatened Fātimid hegemony in North Africa, this region was in reality important to the Fātimids mainly as a base for their expansion eastward. A considerable navy (that also acted as a merchant marine in the service of the ruling elite) and control of the northern termini of the trans-Saharan gold trade until around 1051 facilitated the Fātimid conquest of Egypt.

This "conquest" consisted largely of an agreement with the leading tax accountants, land contractors, and merchants whereby the preexisting elite would be left in charge of their respective offices and holdings. As the new administration, the Fātimid dynasty was then in a position to capitalize on the collection of Egyptian agricultural revenues, the basis of Egypt's legendary economic prosperity.

The Fātimid ruling elite channeled Egypt's agrarian wealth into their own commercial endeavors. Caliph al-Mu'izz (953–975), the conqueror of Egypt, and his general, Jawhar, can be described as merchant princes. From their North African base they brought with them to Egypt commercial ties to Amalfi, Pisa, Genoa, Sicily, and Spain. After their installation in Egypt, the Fātimids also came to maintain excellent relations with

# F

the Eastern Roman Empire, despite its repeated attempts to regain northern Syria in the tenth century.

From 1041 to 1070, the Fātimids added the Yemen, and hence Indian Ocean trade coming through the Red Sea, to their sphere of influence. Fātimid propagandists' attempts to reroute Persian Gulf trade away from Mesopotamia and toward the Red Sea and Egypt were aided by the disruption caused by the influx of Turcoman nomads into Mesopotamia at that time.

Trade with the West was also well established during this period, with Italian merchants active in Egypt by the 1060s and Amalfitans there already in 996. Both economic documents and narrative sources indicate the existence of an extensive Egyptian textile industry. Linen exports included honorific robes manufactured in Egypt, as well as humbler fashions. Museum collections today preserve medieval robes of linen with bands of embroidered Arabic inscriptions (tirāz), some robes a mixture of linen and silk, and some embroidered with gold thread. The embroidered inscriptions frequently report the place and date of manufacture. The prevalence of Arabic and pseudo-Arabic embroidered bands along necklines and hems of robes in Renaissance paintings provides graphic evidence of the demand for Egyptian exports.

Fātimid Egypt foundered in the early eleventh century when recurring low water levels on the Nile— beginning in 1024 and recurring from 1045 to 1072—led to civil disturbances and the rise of rival military factions, with Berber, Black, and Turkish groups being the largest and most disruptive. By mid-century the Fātimids had also lost control of North Africa and the trans-Saharan gold trade. During the long reign of al-Mustansir (1036–1074), unpaid and unruly soldiers sacked the palaces and treasury, flooding the international market with imperial gifts from foreign courts. Though the release of these artifacts from the imperial treasury into the marketplace was economically disastrous, it led to a blossoming of new styles in Egyptian craft production, some of which can be seen in the Museo Civico at Pisa.

The train of events following the series of low Nile floods in Egypt—price inflation, famine, plague, decline in trade, civic disturbances, population decline, and nomadic incursions—eventually led also to the loss of territories in Syria-Palestine and the Hijaz. Not only could the military not respond, but it also contributed to disorder, since it did not suffer going unpaid lightly. These developments spread from Egypt to Syria-Palestine and Arabia.

Order was not restored until 1074, when Badr al-Jamālī (1074–1094), governor of Acre, took control of Egypt with his Armenian army and established a military regime. Revenues were used to build walls to defend Cairo from the invading Seljuk Turks. For the next century, until the fall of the Fātimids in 1171, Egypt was administered in accordance with the dictates of military necessity, dominated now by Armenian troops. Given the government's potential for central planning of crops, what little water was available for agriculture should have been allocated to grain cultivation for strategic reasons. And, in fact, al-Afdāl (1094–1121), son and successor of Badr al-Jamālī, reorganized agrarian administration in an attempt to bolster revenue receipts to the government. But sugar cane cultivation also increased during this period.

Al-Afdāl first negotiated with the crusaders and then abandoned remaining Fātimid holdings in Syria-Palestine to them. The Fātimids, like the Byzantines, were threatened not so much by the crusaders as by the continuing influx of Turcomans who had begun arriving in the Holy Land in 1055, and who were the proximate cause of the First Crusade. Throughout the crusades, Fātimid Egypt allied with crusader factions against their coreligionists, the Turks. From 1150 until 1171, the Fātimid ruling class fell into an internecine struggle while the Seljuk Turks in Damascus watched.

The long period of drought and famine in the eleventh century, coupled with the rise of rival military factions, made a decline in the export of Egyptian linen textiles inevitable. Dire economic conditions and instability due to the riots and civil disturbances caused by rival military factions had two deleterious outcomes: first, the decline in flax cultivation, processing, manufacturing, export, and investment (that is, the decline of the entire Egyptian textile industry), and, second, the introduction of imported textiles. By the end of the Fātimid period, Egypt's exports were increasingly reduced to raw materials (processed flax and sugar).

It is important to note that Egypt's commercial focus was historically East and not West: it looked to the Red Sea rather than the Mediterranean. In the early Fātimid period, Egypt's legendary prosperity was due to its integrated agricultural-industrial-commercial production and not to its transit trade. It was only in the late Fātimid and subsequent periods that Egypt began to become an entrepôt for the exchange of non-Egyptian products between East and West.

Tied to Egypt's transformation into an entrepôt was the continual influx of foreign invaders commanding slave, or ethnically different, military elites. These prevented the development of a landed aristocracy and/or commercial class comparable to those that developed during this period in Western Europe.

**BIBLIOGRAPHY**

Bianquis, Thierry. "Une crise frumentaire dans l'Égypte Fatimide." *Journal of the Economic and Social History of the Orient* 23 (1980): 67–101.

Canard, Marius. "Fāṭimids." *Encyclopaedia of Islam,* New Edition, vol. 2. Leiden: Brill, 1983, pp. 850–862.

Frantz-Murphy, Gladys. "A New Interpretation of the Economic History of the Middle East: The Textile Industry." *Journal of the Economic and Social History of the Orient* 24 (1981): 274–297.

Garçin, Jean-Claude. "Ḳūṣ." *Encyclopaedia of Islam,* New Edition, vol. 5. Leiden: Brill, 1983, pp. 514–515.

Goitein, S.D. "La Tunisie du xiᵉ siècle à la lumière des documents de la *geniza* du Caire." *Études d'Orientalism dédiées à la mémoire de Lévi-Provençal* 2. Paris, 1962, pp. 559–579.

———. "Mediterranean Trade in the Eleventh Century: Some Facts and Problems." In *Studies in the Economic History of the Middle East.* Ed. M.A. Cook. London: Oxford, 1970, pp. 51–77.

Grabar, Oleg. "Imperial and Urban Art in Islam: The Subject Matter of Fatimid Art." In *Colloque international sur l'histoire du Caire.* Cairo, 1969, pp. 173–189.

Halm, Heinz. "Miṣr. 3. The Fāṭimid Period 969–1171." *Encyclopaedia of Islam,* New Edition, vol. 2. Leiden: Brill, 1983, pp. 162–164.

*Gladys Frantz-Murphy*

**SEE ALSO**

Amalfi; Ayyūbids; Egypt; Genoa; Gold Trade in Africa; Pisa; Red Sea; Shiʿism; Spain and Portugal; Sunnism; Textiles, Decorative

## Fifth Crusade

*See* Crusade, Fifth

## First Crusade

*See* Crusades, First, Second, and Third

## Fondaco

A hostelry or warehouse in the medieval Mediterranean world in which a traveler or merchant could lodge and store goods while abroad. References to the institution are found in Arabic from the early tenth century and appear in Latin by the eleventh century. The institution of the *fondaco* or *funduq* (plural *fanādiq*) assisted Mediterranean trade and travel, and was similar in purpose to facilities for lodging and storage associated with other trade diasporas, such as the Hanseatic *staelhof* in London. The Latin and Italian word *fondaco* (with variations including *fontico* and *fundaco*) generated many cognates in other Romance languages, having itself been borrowed from the Arabic *funduq*, which in turn came from the Greek *pandocheion.* Each of these terms designated some type of hostelry or commercial facility, although the exact significance of the words varied with time and location.

In general, a *funduq* or *fondaco* was where strangers stayed in a medieval city in the Muslim world and southern Europe. A town might contain many such hostelries, each usually patronized by a different merchant group. In Alexandria, for example, it was normal for Venetian merchants to stay in one hostelry, Tunisian Jewish merchants in another, Muslim merchants importing fruit from Syria in yet another, and so forth. Thus, the institution both preserved boundaries, by segregating non-locals within their own communities, and also promoted contact and commerce. It is unclear whether segregation was due to local law or to the preference of travelers, who may have enjoyed special privileges (as well as the companionship of compatriots) when they stayed in a particular *funduq/fondaco.* For instance, the Christian *fondaci* in Muslim cities often had rights to their own chapel, cemetery, oven, bath, weights, and measures. At night, the doors of *fondaci* were usually locked, and residents were required to remain inside until morning.

There were also less specific uses of the term *fondaco* and its cognates. In Greek, the term *pandocheion* had a more general meaning of "tavern" or "inn," as in the tale of the good Samaritan (Luke 10:34). In the medieval Muslim world, the Arabic word *funduq* could apply to various types of hostelry, not only for commercial purposes but also for the charitable lodging of poor travelers. By the late Middle Ages, the word *funduq* was sometimes used synonymously with *khân* and *caravansarai* in the Near East. In southern Europe, the meaning of the Romance term *fondaco* gradually shifted away from "hostelry" to "warehouse" or "customshouse," although in some places it retained its earlier significance. In Venice, for example, the *Fondaco dei*

# F

*Tedeschi,* established in 1228, preserved the structure and purpose of Muslim prototypes.

The European *fondaci* in Alexandria are well documented in the accounts of European travelers and pilgrims such as Felix Fabri, who stayed in the Catalan *fondaco* in 1483. As described by Brother Felix, the building was "spacious with many rooms . . . [it] had a large courtyard, with numerous chambers all around like a monastery." This fits well with other descriptions of *fanâdiq* and *fondaci* in Muslim and Christian cities, and with architectural data from surviving buildings. Built for both security and storage, they usually had a square central courtyard surrounded by a covered walkway with rooms opening off it. The rooms on the ground floor were used for stabling animals and storing goods, while those on the upper floor (or sometimes floors) were used for lodging travelers. Most Christian *fondaci* in Muslim cities were administered by a consul, who functioned as a host, adviser, judge, advocate, representative of his own government, and liaison between his state and local authorities.

Aside from travelers' accounts, many diplomatic documents provide information on *fondaci.* Commercial treaties drawn up between Muslim rulers and European states such as Venice, Genoa, and the crown of Aragón often contained clauses pertaining to *fondaci.* Muslim legal scholars, chroniclers, and geographers also referred to these hostelries, and it was a commonplace in Arabic geographical writing to describe a flourishing town as having "many baths, markets, and *fanâdiq."* There are also references to *fanâdiq* patronized by Jewish merchants and travelers in the documents preserved in the Cairo Geniza, the hoard of sacred paper stored at the synagogue of Fastat.

## BIBLIOGRAPHY

Bresc, Geneviève and Henri. "'Fondaco' et Taverne de la Sicile médiévale." In *Hommage à Geneviève Chevrier et Alain Geslan: Etudes médiévales.* Ed. Joëlle Burnouf et al. Strasbourg: Centre d'Archéologie Médiévale de Strasbourg, 1975, pp. 95–106.

Gil, Moshe. *Documents of the Jewish Pious Foundations from the Cairo Geniza.* Leiden: Brill, 1976.

Hillenbrand, Robert. "The Caravansarai." In his *Islamic Architecture: Form, Function and Meaning.* New York: Columbia UP, 1994, pp. 331–376.

Jacoby, David. "Les Italiens en Egypte aux XIIe et XIIIe siècles: Du comptoir à la colonie?" In *Coloniser au Moyen Age.* Ed. Michel Balard and Alain Ducellier. Paris: Armand Colin, 1995, pp. 76–89, 102–107.

Mango, Cyril. "A Late Roman Inn in Eastern Turkey." *Oxford Journal of Archeology* 5 (1986): 223–231.

Sharon, M. "A Waqf Inscription from Ramlah." *Arabica* 13 (1966): 77–84.

Simonsfeld, Henry. *Der Fondaco dei Tedeschi in Venedig und die Deutch-Venetianischen Handelsbeziehungen.* 2 vols. 1887; rpt. Stuttgart: Scientia Verlag Aalen, 1968.

Torres Balbás, Leopoldo. "Las alhóndigas hispanomusulmanas y el Corral del Carbón de Granada." *Al-Andalus* 11 (1946): 447–481.

*Olivia Remie Constable*

**SEE ALSO**

Ambassadors; Caravans; Diplomacy; Egypt; Fabri, Felix; Fairs; Hanse, The; Inns and Accommodations; Language Instruction for Western European Travelers; Law, Commercial; Law, Maritime; Mamluks; Merchants, Jewish; Pisa; Spain and Portugal; Transportation, Inland; Venice

## Fornaldarsögur

A group of about forty medieval Icelandic (or Old Norse) sagas that contain stories dealing with the northern world. The *fornaldarsögur* share subject matter with other genres of Icelandic narratives, such as the sagas of Icelanders (or family sagas), the kings' sagas, and the contemporary sagas, but they differ by focusing on a period more remote than the ones treated in these genres, namely the largely mythical age of Scandinavia before the settlement of Iceland in the late ninth century. Sharing supernatural and mythical features with the *riddarasögur,* a genre otherwise characterized by continental European settings, the *fornaldarsögur* are often grouped with these under the common label of "the lying sagas." Manuscripts containing these two genres exist only from the early fourteenth century, but judging from the large number of later manuscripts—they were still being produced in the nineteenth century—they were extremely popular.

During the sixteenth century, all saga genres were forgotten for a while due to a new literary fad, the poetic *rímur.* Rediscovered during the following century, the *fornaldarsögur* at first shared a reputation for historicity with the kings' sagas. As historians realized that the heroes and mythic kings of the former genre were far more ancient than the protagonists of the latter, they were forced to consider how this material survived in the period between the events' occurrence and their recording. As a result, the *fornaldarsögur* came to be considered later and inferior to the kings' sagas, the sagas of Icelanders, and the contemporary sagas.

It has normally been assumed that the *fornaldarsögur* were written during the second half of the thirteenth or the early part of the fourteenth century. By this time, Icelandic authors had finished writing and copying the other genres, thus having covered exhaustively their own contemporary age as well as the immediate past of Norway and Iceland. Free to turn their attention back to ancient times, they now encompassed the Nordic arena in the *fornaldarsögur*, and—in the *riddarasögur*—the larger European and even the global stage. Recently, however, scholars have begun to suggest that at least a subgroup of the *fornaldarsögur*, the so-called heroic sagas—about a dozen narratives within the corpus that share material with ancient vernacular writings from other Germanic peoples verifiable from Latin historiography—may have been established in some form already in the period between 1180 and 1220.

Centered on the Scandinavian world, the *fornaldarsögur* reveal a fairly accurate knowledge of the large geographic features of this area, a specialized legacy of the Viking Age that had entered the general consciousness. That the authors have not learned from personal experience but from reading is suggested by the bookish character of their more detailed information (see, for example, the description of England and Denmark in chapter 37 of *Göngu-Hrolf's Saga*). From this geographic center the authors moved the action westward and eastward. While the heroes' western travels frequently echo the Norse experience of the Greenland and Vinland discoveries, the eastern journeys bring the heroes—most often by ship—from the relatively well-known Baltic region into the lesser known Bjarmaland that merged with the largely mythical Permia in the north and Miklagarðr (the Norse name for Byzantium) in the south. To these countries authors added areas and names known only from mythology, such as Giantland and the Glasir Plains. One text, *Hjálmpérs saga*, invents an unknown land, Mannheimar, or has the hero arrive at several unnamed countries. In these mythical or unknown territories the heroes undergo further tests of their strength and ingenuity. These strategies of geographic invention may have been necessary for isolated Icelandic authors, but it is obvious that the resulting topographical haziness also enhances the narratives' supernatural and unexpected features.

**BIBLIOGRAPHY**

Glauser, Jörg. *Isländische Märchensagas: Studien zur Prosaliteratur im spätmittelalterlichen Island*. Beiträge zur nordischen Philologie, 12. Basel: Helbing/Lichtenhahn, 1983.

Mitchell, Stephen A. *Heroic Sagas and Ballads*. Ithaca, NY: Cornell UP, 1991.

Pálsson, Hermann, and Paul Edwards. *Legendary Fiction in Medieval Iceland*. Studia Islandica 30. Reykjavík: Menningasjóður, 1971.

———, trans. *Gongu-Hrölf's Saga: A Viking Romance*. Edinburgh: Canongate, 1980.

Tulinius, Torfi. *La "Matière du Nord": Sagas légendaires et fiction dans la littérature islandaise en prose du XIIIe siècle*. Paris: Presses de l'Université de Paris-Sorbonne, 1995.

*Jenny Jochens*

**SEE ALSO**

Geography in Medieval Europe; Iceland; Viking Age; Viking Discoveries and Settlements; Vinland Sagas

## Four Rivers of Paradise

Part of the earliest geographical site mentioned in the Holy Bible, the Garden of Eden. In the Middle Ages, sites mentioned in Scripture were believed to exist, but their exact locations were considered lost from human memory. According to Genesis 2:10–14, the four great rivers originated from a fountain at the center of the Garden of Eden or the Terrestrial Paradise to irrigate the earth. The geographic location of Eden and the fount of the rivers was a matter of debate throughout the Middle Ages, but most authorities agreed that Eden was in the East, either on or off the eastern coast of Asia. Others believed it was on an island somewhere in the Ocean Sea. An area designated as the Garden of Eden, and showing the four rivers flowing from it across or sometimes under the earth, was a common feature of medieval *mappaemundi*.

Theological and travel literature often localized the garden, but in geographically inaccessible sites. St. Thomas Aquinas, for example, declared that the site was "shut off from the habitable world by mountains or seas or some torrid region which cannot be crossed." The prophet Ezekiel (28:13–19) had placed it on top of a cosmic mountain, and Dante followed that model in his *Purgatorio*. Johannes Witte de Hese (c. 1395), on the other hand, claims to have been so near the site that he saw the setting sun reflecting on its walls.

In the Middle Ages, the four rivers of paradise had both scientific and religious meaning. To medieval

# F

Four Rivers of Paradise. *Secretz de la Nature.* New York, The Pierpont Morgan Library MS M. 461, fol. 60v, *c.* 1470. Courtesy of The Pierpont Morgan Library. Photo by David A. Loggie.

site has geoeschatological significance in the drama of the history of salvation. Some holy men made spiritual visits to the Garden of Eden and the four rivers of paradise during religious trances, and some, such as St. Brendan, reported having physically gone there. Explorers searched for Eden until the eighteenth century. Columbus thought he was near it when he coasted off the mighty Orinoco River in South America, which, in his Third Letter, he describes as being one of the four rivers of paradise and thus a route to Eden.

## BIBLIOGRAPHY

Lutz, H.F. "Geographical Studies among Babylonians and Egyptians." *American Anthropologist* 26 (1924): 160–174.

Miller, Konrad. *Mappaemundi, die ältesten Weltkarten.* 6 vols. Stuttgart: Roth, 1895–1898.

Niederland, William. "River Symbolism." *Psychoanalytic Quarterly* 25 and 26 (1956–1957): 469–504 and 50–75.

Singleton, Charles. "Stars over Eden." *Annual Report of the Dante Society* 75 (1957): 1–18.

Wright, John Kirtland. *The Geographical Lore of the Time of the Crusades.* See Gen. Bib.

†*Delno C. West*

## SEE ALSO

Beatus Maps; Brendan's Voyage, St.; Cockaigne, Land of; Dante Alighieri; Ganges; Lignum Aloes; *Mappamundi; Mare Oceanum;* Mauro Map, [Fra]; Odoric of Pordenone; Paradise, Travel to; Prester John; Walsperger, Andreas; Witte de Hese, Johannes; Zeitz Map

scientific theorists, the rivers offered a system of hydrology. The rivers sprang from the fountain in Eden, flowed underground, and emerged again as the Tigris, Euphrates, Pison (Ganges), and Gehon (Nile), according to the names assigned to the rivers in the Book of Genesis. These rivers watered the earth, flowed into the "ocean river" where they merged to reenter the earth somewhere, and ultimately were funneled underground through giant caverns back to Eden.

To theologians, the Garden of Eden and its four rivers represented primordial perfection. Abundant and lush in vegetation, with a mild climate, the garden was free from death, sorrow, and troubles, enabling people to live in idyllic harmony with each other and with nature. According to the pseudepigraphal book of Esdras IV, God would cause the location of Eden to be revealed in the "last days" of human history. Thus, the

## Fourth Crusade

*See* Crusade, Fourth

## Franciscan Friars

Members of the Order of Friars Minor, also known as Minorites, founded in 1210 by Francis of Assisi. As missionaries and envoys, they provided European Christians with a great deal of the available information about the peoples of Asia. From the very beginning of the Franciscans, missionary activity among the schismatic Christians of the East, as well as among the Muslim and other non-Christian peoples along the borders of Europe, was an important aspect of their work.

St. Francis (1181/1182–1226) provided his successors with a model of missionary endeavor when he traveled to Egypt in 1219 in an attempt to convert the sultan to Christianity. The image of Francis debating with the Muslim leader provided subsequent generations of friars with one model to emulate. A group of friars who traveled to Morocco at about the same time offered another model when their efforts at converting the Muslims led to their martyrdom.

Underlying medieval Franciscan missionary efforts was the belief that the world was coming to an end and that the friars had an obligation to preach the Gospel of Christ to all mankind before the end. For almost two centuries, the papal bull *Cum hora undecima* ("Now that the eleventh hour of the world has come"), first issued by Pope Gregory IX (1227–1241) in 1239, outlined the Franciscan conception of world mission in apocalyptic terms.

While medieval Franciscans traveled widely to preach the Gospel, their most famous missionary efforts were directed toward converting the peoples of Asia. From the mid-thirteenth century to the early fifteenth century, Franciscans visited Central Asia, China, India, and (possibly) Tibet, in the course of missionary journeys. The number of actual converts appears to have been small, and the Franciscan influence in Central Asia and China waned with the collapse of the Yuan (Mongol) dynasty in China (overthrown by the Ming dynasty in 1368). Nevertheless, this mission had a good deal of long-term significance in the West because several of the missionaries recorded their experiences in letters and histories that circulated widely throughout Europe, at least within ecclesiastical circles.

The earliest Franciscan writings about Asia resulted from Pope Innocent IV's decision at the First Council of Lyons (1245) to send representatives to the Mongol khân in an effort to end Mongol assaults on eastern Europe and to introduce him to Christian teaching. In his *History of the Mongols,* John of Plano Carpini recorded his journey across Central Asia and his meeting with Güyük Khân. Unlike fictional tales of travel to distant lands, Plano Carpini's *History* provided a realistic picture of the Mongol world. The subsequent publication of this book in Vincent of Beauvais's *Speculum Historiale* gave it wide circulation throughout Europe. Other Franciscans who provided Europe with information about Asia include William of Rubruck, who visited the Mongols (1253–1255), and Odoric of Pordenone, who traveled widely in China, India, Sumatra, Java, and Borneo (1318–1330). Odoric's record of his travels is especially important because he describes the existence of several Franciscan communities in China.

Early in the fourteenth century, two letters reached the papal court describing in poignant detail the life of a Franciscan missionary in China. The writer was John of Monte Corvino (1247–c. 1328), a Franciscan who had reached Beijing (Khânbaliq) in 1294. Acting on these letters and responding to Monte Corvino's request for more missionaries to carry on his work, Pope Clement V (1305–1314) named Monte Corvino the archbishop of Tartary and patriarch of the Orient. At the same time, the pope also named several Franciscans as suffragan bishops. They were expected to travel to the East, to consecrate Monte Corvino, and to establish dioceses under his direction. This was the beginning of an Asian ecclesiastical hierarchy that appears to have lasted until the early decades of the fifteenth century.

The end of the mission to Asia in the fifteenth century was a consequence of the Ming dynasty's hostility toward all foreigners, especially those who had entered China along with the Mongols. The Franciscans did not, however, completely forget their houses in China. Minorite sources continued to mention convents in China throughout the fifteenth century.

A second major area where Franciscan missionary activity had long-term consequences was in North Africa and the islands of the Atlantic, especially the Canary Islands. Inspired by the writings and example of Ramon Lull [Llull] (1232–1316), Franciscan missionaries appear to have been associated with the exploration of the Canaries in the mid-fourteenth century shortly after seamen rediscovered these islands. Employing the techniques of peaceful conversion that Lull had taught, the Franciscans eventually found themselves at odds with pirates and slavers. In a manner that foreshadowed the way in which later missionaries were to seek papal protection for the inhabitants of the Americas, the fifteenth-century Franciscans sought such protection for the Canarians, eventually receiving a bull from Pope Eugenius IV (1431–1447) that affirmed the humanity of the Canarians and protected converts from enslavement.

In the final analysis, the religious efforts of the Franciscan missionaries in Asia, North Africa, and the Atlantic islands were not very successful. Few of these peoples accepted Christianity and, by the end of the fifteenth century, there were numerous obstacles to future conversions. In the Atlantic islands, the missionaries who sought peaceful conversion were pushed aside by conquerors and settlers who saw little hope for the Christianizing and Europeanizing of the Canarians.

# F

Yet the Franciscan missionary initiatives had long-term significance in two areas that the friars might not have foreseen. In the first place, Franciscan missionaries provided a great deal of the information about the world beyond Europe that encouraged Columbus and those who followed him to seek a water route to Asia and to find the Christians known to live there. In the second place, the debate about the humanity of the Canarians and the conflict between missionaries and conquerors generated a small literature about the rights of non-Christian, non-European peoples that foreshadowed the much better known sixteenth-century debate about the legitimacy of the conquest of the Americas.

**BIBLIOGRAPHY**

Baldwin, Marshall W. "Missions to the East in the Thirteenth and Fourteenth Centuries." In Setton, *A History of the Crusades.* Vol. 5, *The Impact of the Crusades on the Near East,* pp. 452–518. See Gen. Bib.

Boehrer, George C.A. "The Franciscans and Portuguese Colonization in Africa and the Atlantic Islands, 1415–1499." *The Americas* 11 (1954–1955): 389–403.

Boxer, C.R. *The Church Militant and Iberian Expansion 1440–1770.* Baltimore: Johns Hopkins UP, 1977.

Daniel, E. Randolph. *The Franciscan Concept of Mission in the High Middle Ages.* Lexington: UP of Kentucky, 1975.

Dawson, Christopher, ed. *The Mongol Mission.* See Gen. Bib.

Fernández-Armesto, Felipe. *Before Columbus: Exploration and Colonization from the Mediterranean to the Atlantic, 1229–1492.* Philadelphia: U of Pennsylvania P, 1987.

Moffett, Samuel Hugh. *A History of Christianity in Asia.* Vol. I, *Beginnings to 1500.* New York: HarperCollins, 1992.

Phillips, J.R.S. *The Medieval Expansion of Europe.* Oxford: Oxford UP, 1988.

*James Muldoon*

**SEE ALSO**

Canary Islands; China; John of Plano Carpini; Las Casas, Bartolomé de; Lull, Ramon; Lyons, First Council of; Missionaries to China; Mongols; Odoric of Pordenone; Piracy; Vincent of Beauvais; William of Rubruck; Yuan Dynasty

## Frederick II (1194–1250)

King of Sicily and Holy Roman Emperor.

The son of the German emperor Henry VI and the Sicilian king's daughter Constance, Frederick was born in the east-central Italian town of Jesi and baptized "Frederick Roger" after his famous grandfathers, Frederick Barbarossa and Roger II. Soon orphaned, the red-headed youth became Sicily's king in 1198 under the protection of the papacy. All his life, Frederick led the Ghibelline (Hohenstaufen) political faction in Italy and Germany against the Guelph [Welf] claimants to the imperial throne. Early in his career, he benefited from a series of diplomatic and military successes: winning over to his side the German city of Constance, inventive money-raising in Genoa, an adventurous escape from the Milanese, and the vital assistance of French King Philip II Augustus's defeat of Frederick's rival Otto IV and the English king John at the battle of Bouvines (1214). Frederick became emperor of the *Sacrum Romanum Imperium* at Aachen in 1215; Pope Honorius III presided at his imperial coronation in Rome five years later.

Frederick experienced continuous stormy relations with the popes because they believed the union of the empire with the kingdom of Sicily threatened their land holdings. In particular, Innocent III (1198–1216), Gregory IX (1227–1241), and Innocent IV (1243–1254) wanted to crush him. Frederick was excommunicated several times, though during the 1220s, he attempted to resolve his conflict with the church. After his first wife Constance died in 1222, he married fifteen-year-old Yolande of Brienne (queen of Jerusalem) in 1225, led a crusade, regained control of Jerusalem by a truce with Egyptian sultan al-Malik al-Kāmil in 1229, and took the title of king of Jerusalem.

However, many of Frederick's efforts over the last two decades of his life were spent combating the papacy, the Lombard League of northern Italian cities, and even his own son Henry. Although he won peace with the pope through the Treaty of San Germano in 1230 and a key victory over his foes at Cortenuova (1237), his defeat before Pavia in 1248 continued the long-standing stalemate.

In the 1230s, Frederick opened up the Baltic to German settlement through military and economic expansion. He commissioned his confidante Hermann von Salza, the grand master of the Teutonic Knights, to conquer Prussia as a prince of the empire. German settlers repopulated the area, which became an important source of grain and amber.

Frederick received the sobriquet *stupor mundi,* "wonder of the world," because of his erudition and savoir faire. For example, he had a very large personal library and his itinerant imperial court contained a remarkable collection of exotic animals including elephants, camels, and cheetahs from the Near East and Africa, and birds from as far as Greenland.

In 1224, Frederick founded a university at Naples whose most famous alumnus was Thomas Aquinas. He also established a school in Salerno. His court contained Jewish, Christian, and Muslim poets, translators, and other intellectuals, as well as visitors from Provence, Castile, Tuscany, and Germany. Noteworthy were Jacob Anatoli, Michael Scot, Judah ha-Cohen, Master Theodore, and numerous Sicilian poets. Besides his direct contact with such men, Frederick had a philosophical and scientific correspondence with scholars in Spain, Egypt, Yemen, and Morocco.

Frederick's *Constitutions of Melfi* of 1231 (*Liber Augustalis*) combined Lombard, Byzantine, and Norman legal traditions, church canon law, and Bolognese legal scholarship, bringing a new body of law to Sicily. By means of the laws and the notaries and judges trained at the royal university, Frederick established sound administrative centers at Naples and Messina. His most-recognized architectural creations were the Castello del Maniace at Syracuse, the Castello dell'Imperatore at Prato (near Florence), the hunting lodge at Castel del Monte in Apulia, and the Capua gate and castle. Frederick may only have restored or extended existing sites, but, in so doing, he displayed a practical knowledge of the importance of communication in his architecture, as he did in many other areas. An example is the dominant head of *Justitia* on the Capua gateway. Visitors from the north entering the kingdom of Sicily would clearly know the role of law and justice in the *regno*.

Frederick appears to have had some fluency in nine languages. His consummate intellectual distinction, however, may be the truly innovative and scientific book, *On the Art of Hunting with Birds (De arte venandi cum avibus)*, in which Frederick employed careful observation and empirical study not only to analyze falcons and their prey in a wonderfully illustrated, six-volume work, but also to discuss such little-known subjects as the anatomy and the diseases of birds.

**BIBLIOGRAPHY**

Abulafia, David. *Frederick II, a Medieval Emperor.* Oxford: Oxford UP, 1988.

Kantorowicz, Ernst. *Frederick the Second, 1194–1250.* Trans. E.O. Lorimer. London: Constable, 1931; rpt. New York: Ungar, 1957.

Powell, James M. *The Liber Augustalis or Constitutions of Melfi: Promulgated by the Emperor Frederick II for the Kingdom of Sicily in 1231.* Syracuse: Syracuse UP, 1971.

Van Cleve, Thomas C. *The Emperor Frederick II of Hohenstaufen: Immutator mundi.* Oxford: Clarendon, 1972.

Erhard P. Opsahl

**SEE ALSO**

Animals, Exotic; Birds, Exotic; Camels; Canon Law and Subject Peoples; Crusade, Fifth; Elephants; Gaston Phébus; Innocent IV; Jerusalem; Popes; Teutonic Order

## French Trade

*See* Merchants, French

## Frescobaldi, Lionardo di Niccolò (fl. 1384–1405)

Highly placed Florentine who traveled to Mamluk Egypt and the Holy Land in 1384–1385 under the guise of a pilgrimage but in fact as a military spy. The account of his trip, written in a clear, nonacademic Italian, vividly describes the social and economic life in the Near East.

Frescobaldi was a patrician who renounced his magnate status in 1379 and eventually held several public offices for the Florentine Commune, including that of ambassador to Pope Boniface IX in 1396. He had served in seven military engagements before journeying to the Middle East and later participated at the siege of Pisa (1405).

Considered as a pilgrimage, his journey was unusual in its length (more than eleven months) and route (from Egypt northward to Jerusalem), but it was motivated more by reasons of espionage than religious piety. Frescobaldi was involved in the Florentine-Angevin alliance and knew friends of the recently deceased St. Catherine of Siena. It was no accident that his party chose a fast ship bound for Egypt, the goal of a hoped-for crusade that was frequently discussed, but never mounted, in fourteenth-century Europe. His descriptions of cities include pertinent strategic remarks, such as accounts of their fortifications.

Being socially well-connected, Frescobaldi moved in influential circles and traveled more comfortably—with servants, better lodgings, and better transportation—than did the average pilgrim. His account incorporates standard legendary material with rather

# F

perfunctory descriptions of holy sites, as well as a predominance of accurate observations. He often compares Eastern locales and dimensions to those of Tuscany. He records even the smallest details of life in the Holy Land: places visited, people, customs, fauna, ceremonies, and different Christian denominations, as well as financial instruments, supplies, and provisions used by the travelers. The introspective piety typical of earlier pilgrimage accounts written by clergymen is here replaced by the pragmatism and broader worldview of a politically active citizen.

## BIBLIOGRAPHY

Cardini, Franco. "Three Florentine Travellers to the Holy Land in 1384–1385. . . ." In *Intellectuals and Writers in Fourteenth-Century Europe: The J.A.W. Bennett Memorial Lectures.* Ed. Piero Boitani and Anna Torti. Tübinger Beiträge zur Anglistik 7. Tübingen: Narr, 1986, pp. 191–203.

Delfiol, Renato. "Su alcuni problemi codicologico—testuali concernenti le relazioni di pellegrinaggio fiorentine del 1384." In *Toscana e Terrasanta nel Medioevo.* Ed. Franco Cardini. Florence: Alinea, 1982, pp. 139–176.

———. *Visit to the Holy Places of Egypt, Sinaï, Palestine and Syria in 1384 by Frescobaldi, Gucci and Sigoli.* Trans. Theophilus Bellorini and Eugene Hoade. Intro. by Bellarmino Bagatti. Publications of Studium Biblicum Franciscanum 6. Jerusalem: Franciscan, 1948.

Frescobaldi, Lionardo di Niccolò. *Viaggio in Terrasanta.* Ed. Enrico Emanuelli. Collana di viaggi 1. Novara: Istituto Geografico De Agostini, 1961.

Hyde, J.K. "Italian Pilgrim Literature in the Late Middle Ages." *Bulletin of the John Rylands University Library* 72. 3 (1990): 13–33.

*Gloria Allaire*

SEE ALSO

Eastern Christianity; Egypt; Holy Land; Jerusalem; Mamluks; Pilgrimage, Christian; Pisa; Spies


## Fretellus

The author of a description of the Holy Land who, in the first half of the twelfth century, listed the region's more important localities, stating the distances between them, and briefly mentioning the biblical events believed to have occurred there. Fretellus says very little about the physical traits of the country—a brief passage on alum and bitumen extracted from the Dead Sea constitutes a rare exception—or about contemporaneous events that took place in the Frankish Kingdom of Jerusalem. His treatise takes the form of a guide, rather than an account of a specific pilgrimage.

Fretellus's treatise was extensively used by later writers: John of Würzburg, whose pilgrimage took place in the early 1160s, derived about 45 percent of his main text from Fretellus; Theoderic, who appears to have visited the Holy Land in 1169, did not quote Fretellus verbatim, but about 26 percent of his main text is based on him; the thirteenth-century *Fazienda de Ultra Mar* appears to contain several of his passages.

The author has been identified with Rorgo Fretellus, who was probably a native of the county of Ponthieu (Picardy) and went to the East around 1110. In 1119, he was chancellor to the prince of Galilee and in 1121, chaplain of the Church of Nazareth. Fretellus wrote two versions of his treatise: the first he dedicated in 1137/38 to Henry Zdyck, bishop of Olomouc (Moravia), the second (in which he figures as archdeacon of Antioch) he gave at about the same time (some scholars date it to 1148) to Count Rodrigo Gonzalez of Toledo. Between 1356 and 1362, at Avignon, Cardinal Nicholas Rosselli incorporated the second version in a collection of the Roman Curia.

## BIBLIOGRAPHY

Boeren, P.C., ed. *Rorgo Fretellus de Nazareth et sa description de la Terre Sainte: Histoire et édition du texte.* Koninklijke Nederlandse Akademie van Wetenschappen, Afdeling Letterkunde, Verhandelingen Nieuwe Reeks, Deel 105. Amsterdam-Oxford-New York: North-Holland, 1980.

Hiestand, Rudolf. "Un centre intellectuel en Syrie du Nord? Notes sur la personnalité d'Aimery d'Antioche, Albert de Tarse et Rorgo Fretellus." *Moyen Âge* 100 (1994): 7–36.

Huygens, R.B.C., ed. *Peregrinationes tres. Saewulf—John of Würzburg—Theodericus,* Corpus Christianorum. Continuatio Mediaevalis. Turnhout: Brepols, 1994. Introduction.

Kedar, Benjamin Z. "Sobre la génesis de la *Fazienda de Ultra Mar.*" *Anales de Historia Antigua y Medieval* 28 (1995): 131–136.

*Benjamin Z. Kedar*

SEE ALSO

Dead Sea; Holy Land; John of Würzburg; Pilgrimage, Christian; Theoderic


## Froissart, Jean (1337[?]–1404[?])

Poet, courtier, and chronicler, most famous for his *Chroniques,* a lively and detailed four-volume account in French of the events of the Hundred Years' War from 1326 to 1400. In contrast to earlier writers like Ranulf Higden, who wrote universal chronicles based on traditional materials, Froissart traveled extensively in areas ranging from Scotland to Rome and from the Pyrenees to the Netherlands in order to gather information through personal interviews with those who had participated in, or served as eyewitnesses to, the pivotal events of the century.

Born in the city of Valenciennes in what is today northern France, Froissart early attracted the attention of his compatriot, Philippa de Hainaut, who became Queen Philippa of England and brought him to the English court in 1361 to serve as her secretary. Here he remained for five years, writing poetry and taking advantage of the opportunity to converse with members of one of the most distinguished and varied courts in Europe, which included dozens of high-ranking French hostages and prisoners of war, who were permitted to maintain households and participate in courtly activities. It is during this period that he began gathering material for his *Chroniques,* rewriting and supplementing the material provided by his predecessor, Jean le Bel. When sent on a mission to Scotland (1365), Froissart extended the trip to a three-month stay, which he spent as the guest of King David Bruce, who personally accompanied him on a tour of the kingdom. The section of the book describing this tour offers impressions of the rugged Scottish countryside and describes the cultural differences that distinguish the Scottish military force, ranging from their small horses and high mobility to their poor diet of oatmeal cakes and water.

Other travels under the queen's protection took Froissart to Bordeaux, where he was among the party of Edward the Black Prince at the time of the birth of the future Richard II (1367), and to Milan (where he may have met Petrarch) for the wedding of Prince Lionel (1368). On the latter trip he visited Rome as well,

Jean Froissart offers his book to King Richard II. *Chronicles,* Berlin, Deutsche Staatsbibliothek (Preussischer Kulturbesitz), MS Dep. Breslau 1, Vol. 4, fol. 174r, *c.* 1450. Courtesy Deutsche Staatsbibliothek, Berlin.

# F

before learning of the death of Philippa, an event that ended his connection to England and caused him to return home to Valenciennes.

By 1373, he had completed the first book of the *Chroniques* under the patronage of Philippa's nephew, Robert of Namur, and his fame brought him new patrons, most notably Count Guy of Blois and Duke Wenceslas of Luxembourg and Brabant. For a period of time, Froissart seems to have traveled little, serving as curé of Lestinnes nearby the castles of his two patrons and composing the long verse romance *Meliador*. But on Wenceslas's death in 1383, Froissart was appointed canon of Chimay (where he was not obliged to reside) and personal chaplain to Guy, whom he followed to his castle at Blois. There Froissart wrote the second and third volumes of his *Chroniques* and began the fourth.

In 1388, after having resumed his travels with numerous trips throughout France, Froissart made what was probably his most significant journey, a six-month trip to visit Gaston de Foix [Gaston Phébus] in Orthez. Recognizing that the wars between Spain and Portugal were being reported only from a northern point of view, he wished to get closer to the source. Through a stroke of luck, he met a knight named Sir Espan de Leu [Espan of Lion] on the road from Avignon to Orthez and was able for ten days to hear firsthand accounts of the events associated with each area they passed through, taking notes in the evening and considering questions to ask the next day. The guests in Gaston's court likewise proved to be outstanding sources of information, as did a Portuguese travel companion on the return trip. By this time, everyone from knights to government envoys was eager to talk with the chronicler who would record their deeds for posterity. Froissart mixed freely with participants in the peace negotiations of 1393 at Abbeville and ended his travels with a trip to England in 1395, where he was received warmly and allowed to present a decorated manuscript of his poetry to Richard II.

Although Froissart has been criticized for slanting his accounts to suit his patrons (first pro-English and later pro-French) and for promoting a narrowly pro-aristocratic point of view, his *Chroniques* provide a vivid picture of the way the Hundred Years' War moved throughout Europe and affected the lives of the common people as well as the nobility. Froissart's travel writing includes not only the history itself, but also a whimsical poetic dialog between his horse and greyhound on the trip through Scotland, a *ballade* on the beauties of the southern countryside, and the *Dit du Florin*, a complaint over having been robbed of fifty florins while on the road from Orthez to Avignon. His historical *pastourelles* provide accounts of the major social events he witnessed, ranging from the marriage of the duke de Berry to the state entry of the thirteen-year-old Queen Isabella into Paris. It is perhaps a mark of Froissart's passion for the chivalric life that his *Chroniques* end with the death of Richard in 1400, at which time he seems to have retired from writing and, perhaps, ended his days in Chimay.

**BIBLIOGRAPHY**

Diverres, A.H. "Jean Froissart's Journey to Scotland." *Forum for Modern Language Studies* 1 (1965): 54–63.

Figg, Kristen M. *The Short Lyric Poems of Jean Froissart: Fixed Forms and the Expression of the Courtly Ideal.* Garland Studies in Medieval Literature 10. New York: Garland, 1994.

Froissart, Jean. *Voyage en Béarn.* Ed. A.H. Diverres. Manchester: Manchester UP, 1953.

———. *Chronicles.* Trans. and ed. Geoffrey Brereton. Baltimore: Penguin, 1968.

———. *Dits et debats.* Ed. Anthime Fourrier. Geneve: Librairie Droz, 1979.

*Kristen M. Figg*

**SEE ALSO**

Gaston Phébus; Higden, Ranulf; Horses and Harnesses

# G

## Galley

The principal type of warship in the late medieval Mediterranean; it was used well into the early modern period. Propelled by oars, galleys were long, narrow, of shallow draft, and low in the water.

Rowed vessels using oars arranged on more than one level were typical throughout the ancient period and into the early Middle Ages. The medieval galley was descended from these ancient rowed vessels, but not enough is known to make clear the lines of that descent. It is certain that the medieval galley was a very different vessel from ancient oared vessels: its oars were all disposed in a single plane, it had no waterline ram, and it carried triangular lateen sails rather than the square sails of the ancient vessels. Rowers sat on benches angled from the centerline of the vessel toward the bow. These angled benches allowed several men sitting on one bench to pull their oars in a single plane without interfering with one another. With two men on each bench, each pulling an oar, the galley was referred to as a "bireme"; with three men to a bench, it was a "trireme." Though primarily designed to be rowed, whenever possible galleys proceeded by sail power to spare the rowing crew.

The galley carried a variety of weapons, but in the last analysis it was designed to closely engage other galleys by boarding. A protruding spur, or beak, at the bow was driven over the barricades along the side of an enemy galley and acted as a boarding bridge for marines who engaged the enemy crew in hand-to-hand combat. A galley was most vulnerable when attacked from the side, so fleets normally fought in line so that each protected its neighbor's flank. Because a galley crew could row at top speed for only about twenty minutes before becoming exhausted, timing was crucial in galley battles.

Slender, shallow, and packed from end to end with men sitting shoulder to shoulder, the galley was far from ideal as a cargo vessel. There are only a few references to mercantile use of the bireme galleys of the twelfth and thirteenth centuries. Around 1300, the

View of Venice with galley and cogs. Oxford, Bodleian Library MS Bodley 264, fol. 218, 15th century. Courtesy of the Bodleian Library, Oxford.

# G

addition of a third rower on each bench required a slight increase in the breadth of the hull. This change increased power, but cargo capacity was increased even more. Still, in comparison with pure sailing ships, cargo space remained extremely limited, and efficiency in terms of the number of tons of cargo carried per man was very low. Yet for some cargoes galleys were considered the best transportation available. There was little cargo space, but the large and well-armed crew, sprint speed, and maneuverability that made galleys successful as warships meant that for goods of great value that occupied little space—gold, jewels, silks, valuable spices, and so forth—galleys were the safest form of transportation. The trading cities of Venice and Genoa both required that the most valuable cargoes be shipped on light galleys, the best war ships.

As galleys were used more regularly in commerce, the temptation to increase revenue-producing cargo space, even at the expense of combat performance, was ever present. This led quickly to the development of two types of galleys. To preserve the light, or narrow, galleys (*galee sottile*) that were so important in their navies, both Genoa and Venice, by the 1330s, established regulations that clearly defined maximum dimensions for these vessels and reserved the most lucrative cargoes and routes to them. Great galleys (*galee grosse*) continued to grow in size, but did not add to the number of the crew. As a result, they became more purely sailing ships that combined the defensive advantage of the galley's large crew and some ability to maneuver under oars with a greater capacity to carry goods and passengers.

All galleys were very limited in the provisions they could carry, especially water. Consequently they had to put into port frequently to resupply. Most accounts of galley voyages indicate that they landed every night. For naval fleets made up of light galleys, this meant they operated on a short logistical leash. For merchant galleys these frequent stops could be an advantage. Great galleys became a favorite means of travel for pilgrims and other travelers to whom they offered a chance for fresh food and interesting sights on their frequent stops.

By the middle of the sixteenth century, labor costs had become so great, and sailing ships relatively so much more comfortable and efficient, that merchant galleys were rendered obsolete. War galleys, however, now armed with artillery on their bows, continued to be useful in Mediterranean conditions.

**BIBLIOGRAPHY**

Dotson, John E. "Merchant and naval influences on galley design at Venice and Genoa in the fourteenth century." In *New Aspects of Naval History*. Ed. Craig L. Symonds et al. Annapolis: Naval Institute Press, 1981.

Guilmartin, John F., Jr. *Gunpowder and Galleys: Changing Technology and Warfare at Sea in the Sixteenth Century.* Cambridge: Cambridge UP, 1974.

Lane, Frederic C. *Venetian Ships and Shipbuilders of the Renaissance.* Baltimore: Johns Hopkins UP, 1934. Revised edition, *Navires et Constructeurs à Venise pendant la Renaissance.* Paris: S.E.V.P.E.N., 1965.

———. "From Biremes to Triremes." *The Mariner's Mirror* 49 (1963): 48–50. Rpt. in *Venice and History, the Collected Papers of Frederic C. Lane.* Baltimore: Johns Hopkins UP, 1966.

Morrison, John, ed. *The Age of the Galley: Mediterranean Oared Vessels since Pre-classical Times.* London: Conway Maritime Press, 1995.

Pryor, John H. "The Galleys of Charles I of Anjou, King of Sicily: ca. 1269–84." *Studies in Medieval and Renaissance History,* n.s. (1993): 34–103.

———. *Geography, Technology and War.* Cambridge: Cambridge UP, 1988.

Rodgers, W. L. *Naval Warfare under Oars: A Study of Strategy, Tactics, and Ship Design.* Annapolis: Naval Institute Press, 1940; rpt. 1980.

*John E. Dotson*

**SEE ALSO**

Mediterranean Sea; Naval Warfare; Navigation; Pilgrimage, Christian; Ships and Shipbuilding

## Ganges

River in India with great mythical significance as a boundary marker.

"Asia has at the center of its eastern boundary on the eastern ocean, the mouth of the Ganges River," says the Spanish Christian apologist Orosius in his *Contra paganos*. Like the Indus River, the Ganges is often understood in medieval texts to mark the eastern end of the earth, where the sun rises. It contrasts with "Gades" in the western end of the *oikoumene* where the sun sets. The importance of the Ganges in Hindu religious bathing ritual (whose purpose was often misunderstood by Western observers) made it from early times the home of peculiar "hairy riverine fish-eating peoples" who are often shown in early pictorial accounts of India, like that in the *Secretz de la Nature,* New York, Pierpont Morgan Library MS

M. 471 (and a related manuscript in the Charnacé collection in Paris), swimming and fishing in the river like otters.

Ganges, however, was not just the eastern frontier that Alexander the Great had failed to cross in his march into India; lying at the distant end of the earth, it designated an area rich in natural resources such as gems and ivory, cinnamon and other precious spices, and it was also the land of marvelous animals such as elephants, tigers, and rhinoceri. Though unconquered, wild, even "barbaric," it was also peaceful because, according to tradition, it was subdued by Bacchus.

Isidore of Seville and Vincent of Beauvais, among other medieval writers, held that at the eastern end of the *oikoumene* lay the Earthly Paradise in the area of the Ganges. A contrary view is offered by Dante in the *Inferno* (Canto 26), where Ulysses' "mad flight" led him to violate the western end of the *oikoumene;* he sailed out beyond Gades into the western setting sun, where Dante, breaking with tradition, chose to locate the Earthly Paradise.

**BIBLIOGRAPHY**

Beaugendre, Anne-Caroline, trans. *Les Merveilles du Monde ou Les secrets de l'histoire naturelle.* Paris: Editions Anthèse, 1996.

*Brenda Deen Schildgen*

**SEE ALSO**

Animals, Exotic; Dante Alighieri; Gems; Indus; Isidore of Seville; Ivory Trade; *Oikoumene;* Orosius; Paradise, Travel to; *Secretz de la Nature, Les;* Vincent of Beauvais

## Gaston Phébus (1331–1391)

Third count of Foix, lord of Béarn, and author of a hunting treatise that was based on close observation of animals, both while he was at home in the Pyrenees and during a stay in Scandinavia. Completed in 1389, the *Livre de la chasse* was extremely popular; forty-four manuscripts are known, and the book was adapted into English in the early fifteenth century as the *Master of Game* by Edward, second duke of York. Like the work of his fellow aristocrat Frederick II (1194–1250), whose *On the Art of Hunting with Birds* had brought the experience of wide travels to the study of falcons and their prey, Gaston's book, focusing mainly on the art of hunting with dogs, illustrates how observation of

the world contributed to the aristocratic ideal of erudition in an area of specialized knowledge.

Although the *Livre de la chasse* was based in part on earlier treatises, such as the *De animalibus* of Albertus Magnus, it is remarkable for the fact that Gaston Phébus [Gaston Fébus, Gaston III de Foix] was so reluctant to repeat any information that he himself had not verified. Thus, in discussing diseases and treatments for hunting dogs, he qualifies his description of how to cure rabies by saying that he is reporting claims made by others, not methods to which he can personally attest. This concern for accuracy makes the book useful as a source of information about wildlife in western Europe, since he includes descriptions of the nature and habits of the hart, the fallow deer, two kinds of wild goats (the ibex and Pyrenean chamois), the roe, the rabbit, the bear (still common in the Pyrenees in this period), the wild boar, the wolf, the fox, the badger, the lynx (which he calls "cat-leopard"), and the otter, all of which are carefully illustrated in the magnificent early manuscripts (Paris, BN MS fr. 616; New York, Morgan M 1044; and St. Petersburg, Hermitage). Likewise, his descriptions of cornfields, vineyards, coppices, and woods give a sense of the terrain as seen by one who believes that hunters enjoy their lives more than other people, live longer because of their healthy habits, and, indeed, increase their chances of going to heaven, since they have no time to waste on vices.

Gaston's life provides an excellent example of the role of travel in the careers of medieval aristocrats. On inheriting his domain at the age of twelve, he was directed by his mother to spend an entire year on a ceremonial tour solidifying his position in a troubled realm in much the same way that Louis IX had, a hundred years before, made a series of trips through France to gain support for his crusade. More significantly, in 1357–1358, as he approached the age of thirty, he engaged in a year-long trip to Prussia to join the Teutonic Knights in a military expedition against the non-Christian Slavs of Lithuania. Here he made his reputation by being named to the Table of Honor (*Ehrentisch*), a distinction that identified him as one of the expedition's twelve most courageous knights and bestowed on him a permanent aura of chivalric glory. During the trip home, a voyage achieved entirely on horseback as further proof of physical prowess, he and his party happened to arrive in France just in time to lead an assault on the besieged city of Meaux, where they succeeded in rescuing the wife of the future

# G

Reindeer. Gaston Phébus Hunting Book, New York, The Pierpont Morgan Library MS M.1044, fol. 10v, 1407. Courtesy of The Pierpont Morgan Library.

with up to eighty-point racks, demonstrate clearly enough that the illustrators themselves had never seen such an animal, with BN MS fr. 616 showing a crouching reindeer with a red-deer-like body and antlers so large the animal seems unable to stand, while Morgan 1044 depicts reindeer antlers on the light-colored long-haired bodies of animals resembling mountain sheep.

**BIBLIOGRAPHY**

Gaston Phébus. *The Hunting Book of Gaston Phébus.* Intro. Marcel Thomas and François Avril. Summary and Commentary by Wilhelm Schlag. Graz, 1994; London: Harvey Miller, 1998. [Facsimile in miniature of Paris BN MS fr. 616]

Thomas, Marcel, François Avril, Pierre, duc de Brissac, R. and A. Bossuat. *Gaston Phoebus, Le livre de la chasse.* Graz: 1976. [Complete facsimile ed. of Paris, Bibliothèque Nationale MS fr. 616 with commentary and transcription.]

Tilander, Gustav. *Gaston Phébus, Livre de la Chasse.* Cynegetica 18. Karlshamn, 1971.

Tucoo-Chala, Pierre. *Gaston Fébus, un grand prince d'occident au XIVe siècle.* Pau: Marrimpouey, 1976.

*Kristen M. Figg*

**SEE ALSO**
Albertus Magnus; Frederick II; Froissart, Jean; Teutonic Order

Charles V and a number of other noble ladies from the peasants' revolt known as the Jacquerie, thus assuring Gaston's fame in all the courts of Europe.

As a young man already recognized for his nobility as a hunter, Gaston took the opportunity to enhance his experience in northern Europe by alternating military campaigns with week-long hunting excursions through the Prussian forests. Indeed, even before arriving in Prussia, his party had taken a detour into Scandinavia to hunt reindeer in Norway and Sweden. It was this experience that allowed him, in his *Livre de la chasse,* to include a discussion of the reindeer that later caused the eighteenth-century naturalist Buffon to assume incorrectly that reindeer must have been indigenous to the Pyrenees during this period. The accompanying miniatures, however, which attempt to illustrate Gaston's enthusiastic assertions of animals

## Gems

Important commodities in trade and subjects of literary texts; gems were valued for their rarity and beauty and also prized for their "virtues" in medicinal potions and as charms or talismans. According to medieval lapidaries, certain precious gems had magical powers, such as the ability to confer extraordinary strength or make the bearer invisible.

Gems figured prominently in religious and secular symbol systems. Lists of gems in the Bible most likely influenced the medieval writers who reported the details, real or imagined, about the wealth of oriental monarchs and the opulence of Eastern cities. Descriptions of the palace of the great khân and that of the legendary Christian ruler Prester John, for example, are very clearly influenced by biblical descriptions of Solomon's Temple (I Kings 7:1–31) and the celestial Jerusalem (Revelation 21:10–27).

The gems named most often in lapidaries, encyclopedias, royal inventories, trade documents, imaginative literature, and travel literature are the twelve stones of Revelation (21:19–21), listed here by their Latin names (which do not always correspond to their names in vernacular languages): *iaspis, sapphirus, calcedonius, smaragdus, sardonyx, sardius, chrysolithus, beryllus, topazius, chrysoprasus, hyacinthus,* and *amethystus.* However, medieval authors frequently confused or conflated these gemstones with each other—not surprisingly, given their vague or conflicting color and property descriptions in classical sources and medieval lapidaries.

The true *iaspis* (Mod. E. jasper), a variety of chalcedony, was found in India, Greece, Turkey, and Siberia. The *sapphirus* was found in Thailand, Myanmar (Burma), Kashmir, India, Sri Lanka (Ceylon), and Madagascar. The gemstone known in the Middle Ages as *calcedonius* came from North Africa; it was frequently confused with a variety of other stones. The *smaragdus* (Mod. E. emerald) was found in Egypt, Ethiopia, India, and China. *The Book of John Mandeville* says emeralds are plentiful and cheap in Egypt (the author's source, William of Boldensele, says emeralds are more plentiful in Egypt than anywhere else on earth). The *sardonyx* (ME sardoynes), a kind of agate, was found in India and Arabia. The *sardius* is a variety of carnelian that ranges from pale yellow to reddish orange. The *chrysolithus,* a yellow variety of olivine, was found in Egypt, Ethiopia, India, and China. The *beryllus* was found in the Altai mountains, India, and the Urals. *Topazius* was found in Egypt, the Red Sea Islands, Sri Lanka, India, and Myanmar. The *chrysoprasus,* an apple-green chalcedony, was found in Egypt, Ethiopia, India, and China. The *hyacinthus* (Mod. E. jacinth), a garnet, came from Sri Lanka and Africa. The *amethystus,* a variety of quartz esteemed for its royal purple color, was found in India, Sri Lanka, and Madagascar.

In addition to the twelve stones of Revelation, the following gems are often mentioned in medieval texts. The ruby (related to Latin *rubeus;* OF *rubi, rubis;* ME *ruby*) was commonly believed to come from India, but was actually from Badakhshan, Sri Lanka, Myanmar, or Thailand. Marco Polo claims that the best rubies are found in Ceylon, and repeats the oft-told story that the king of Ceylon owns the largest and most beautiful ruby in the world (which, he says, the great khân covets). Along with the ruby, lapidaries often list a stone *balas,* or use it as an adjective "balas ruby"; sometimes *carbunculus* is a synonym for the ruby. However, carbunculus (ME *charbucle;* OF *charbucle, carbuncle*) was also the name given to a fabulous gem that was believed to shine in the dark or to come from a toad. *Crystallum* (ME *crestal,* OF *cristal*), mentioned frequently in medieval romances as an architectural building material, may have been the rock crystal of the Red Sea area. It was commonly believed that crystal was permanently hardened ice. In the Middle Ages, diamonds (late Lat. *diamas;* OF *diamant;* ME *diamant, diamaunt*) were imported into Europe from India, where they were sometimes found in stream beds. The *Mandeville* author says they are from India, Cyprus, and Arabia, and adds the legend that diamonds can reproduce.

While not gemstones, many polishable vegetable or animal materials were highly prized, and commonly appear alongside gemstones in extended descriptive passages. Amber, the fossilized resin of ancient pine trees and highly valued in the Middle Ages, was washed up on the shores of the Baltic Sea, though in Western Europe, the nature and origin of this substance was a mystery. Coral, prized for its magical properties, was gathered in the western Mediterranean region; Johannes Witte de Hese says that Red Sea coral—which he thinks is an "herba"—cures the sting of local vipers. Thomas of Cantimpré notes that in its natural branched form it has a crucifix-like shape, and thus the polished material was believed to have apotropaic powers for pilgrims like Chaucer's Prioress in the *Canterbury Tales.* Elephant ivory was obtained from East Africa, but medieval Europeans commonly believed that it came from India, after Virgil's account of it in *Georgics;* however, the most common material known as ivory was walrus tusks. The best pearls were generally acknowledged to be those of the Persian Gulf, according to a map legend on the Catalan Atlas and its probable source, Marco Polo, who notes that inferior ones come from the Red Sea. Pearls could also be found off the coasts of Oman and India.

Venetians, Genoans, and Pisans mainly controlled the western segment of the trade in gems, but were dependent on Arab and Byzantine merchants, a factor that made the gems difficult to obtain and extremely expensive. Ironically, some of the gems that were once imported into medieval Europe from the East are now mined commercially in parts of Western Europe.

**BIBLIOGRAPHY**

*English Medieval Lapidaries.* Ed. Joan Evans and Mary S. Serjeantson. E.E.T.S. o.s. 190, 1933; rpt. London: Oxford UP, 1960.

# G

Evans, Joan. *A History of Jewellery: 1100–1870*. 1953. 2nd. edition. Boston: Boston Book and Art, 1970.

Heyd, Wilhelm von. *Histoire du Commerce du Levant au Moyen Age*. 2 vols. Leipzig, 1885–1886; rpt. Amsterdam: Adolf M. Hakkert, 1967.

Hudud al-'Alam. *"The Regions of the World": A Persian Geography 372 A.H./982 A.D.* Trans. V. Minorsky. 2nd ed. London: Luzac, 1970.

*Marco Polo: The Description of the World*. 2 vols. Ed. A.C. Moule and Paul Pelliot. London: G. Routledge, 1938; rpt. New York: AMS Press, 1976.

*Medieval Trade in the Mediterranean World: Illustrative Documents in Translation with Introduction and Notes*. Ed. Robert S. Lopez and Irving W. Raymond. New York and London: Columbia UP, 1955; rpt. New York: Norton, n.d.

*Kathleen Coyne Kelly*

SEE ALSO

Atlas; Chaucer, Geoffrey; Egypt; Genoa; India; Ivory Trade; *Mandeville's Travels;* Marco Polo; Pisa; Prester John; Red Sea; Taprobane; Thomas of Cantimpré; Venice; William of Boldensele; Witte de Hese, Johannes

## Genoa

One of medieval Europe's strongest commercial cities in the twelfth and thirteenth centuries.

Genoa and Pisa had responded to devastating Arab raids in the eleventh century by attacking Muslim seapower in Sardinia and North Africa, thus clearing the way for the development of new markets and exploration. Their merchants, first trading with nearby Corsica and Sardinia, sought in the ports of Tunis and the Maghreb the gold dust brought from central Africa. Genoese were reported after 1300 in Sijilmassa, deep in the Sahara. In 1291, the Vivaldi brothers of Genoa attempted to sail to India through the Straits of Gibraltar and the south Atlantic, but no further record of them is known. In 1312, Lanzarotto Malocello of Genoa discovered the Canary Islands. Manuele Pessagno, serving Diniz (Denis) I, king of Portugal (1279–1325), sailed his Genoese fleet into the Atlantic to claim the Canary Islands, Madeira, and the Azores for Portugal. Genoese merchants also frequented Sicily, having received special commercial privileges from its Norman and Hohenstaufen kings.

Genoa advanced its trade with Iberia by cooperating in the Christian wars against the Moors. Encouraged by the popes, Genoese crusaders assisted the twelfth-century kings of Castile, Aragon, and Navarre in con-quering Almería in Granada and Tortosa on the Ebro River. Ferdinand III of Castile (1217–1252) welcomed foreign merchants in Seville, which he had conquered from the Moors in 1248. Genoa won much wealth from Spanish markets until challenged by Catalonia in the fourteenth century.

The Genoese, while attempting to monopolize the seaborne trade of the cities of Languedoc, also traveled north to the fairs of Champagne. Overland freighting and courier services connected the fairs with Genoa, and their credit instruments presaged the bill of exchange and the check. From 1277, the Genoese began sailing annually through the Straits of Gibraltar, north to Bruges and London. Fourteenth-century Genoese counseled French and English kings.

Traders from Genoa had long visited Alexandria and Damietta in Egypt, despite papal prohibitions against trade with the Muslims. Segurono-Sakran Selvago, a Genoese entrepreneur established in Caffa about 1300, brought shiploads of slaves to the Mamluk sultans of Egypt. By 1370, the volume of trade between Genoa and Alexandria measured two-thirds the total value of all Genoese overseas trade.

Syria attracted Genoese merchant ships as early as 1065. Without their support at the seaports of Palestine, the crusaders could not have preserved the conquests of the First Crusade. Hugh Embriaco of Genoa received Jubail in fief from Raymond of Toulouse after assisting at its capture. Genoese wealth in its Syrian colonies grew with Genoa's maritime importance. Because Genoa had lost privileges in the Holy Land after Saladin's conquests, its ships willingly transported Philip Augustus of France on the Third Crusade in 1190, aided the crusaders at Damietta in 1218–1220, and assisted Louis IX of France on his crusades of 1248 and 1270.

The Ibelin rulers of Cyprus, associated with the Latin Kingdom of Jerusalem, depended on Genoese shipping after 1218. In 1373, the Genoese seized the Cypriot port of Famagusta, holding it until 1407 through a private consortium, the "Maona of Cyprus." They collected customs dues for the Cypriot kings and profited from the Levantine carrying trade. From Cyprus they traded with Lajazzo (Ayas) in Cilician Armenia, gateway to the overland caravan routes into Asia.

The Byzantine emperors first awarded commercial privileges in Constantinople to Genoa in 1155, but encouraged rivalries among the Italian maritime republics. Following the Latin capture of Constantinople in the Fourth Crusade (1204), the Genoese were evicted from the Byzantine markets. In retaliation, Genoese pirates challenged all shipping. Nonetheless, Genoese merchants were uncommon in Greek waters until the Greeks returned to Constantinople in 1261. Manuel Palaeologus, the restored Greek emperor, gave Genoese merchants preponderance in Constantinople and freedom in the Black Sea, after which the Genoese commune in the Constantinopolitan suburb of Pera (Galata) grew to be almost as wealthy as the mother city.

Another Genoese colony at Kaffa in the Crimea exploited the markets of the Golden Horde. Fourteenth-century Genoese traded throughout the Black Sea, entering its great rivers and sailing the Sea of Azov to Tana on the Don, plying the Black Sea's south shore to Trebizond. From Tana, Genoese travelers traveled the Silk Road to China. From Trebizond, Genoese merchants traveled south to Tabriz, capital of Mongol Persia, and further east. They sailed the Caspian Sea for the silk available on its shores. The Mongol il-khân of Persia employed Genoese advisers, one of whom, Buscarello Ghisolfi, the khân sent on embassies to the pope, the kings of France, and the kings of England.

Genoa's Aegean interests centered in the islands guarding the Dardanelles. The Byzantine emperors awarded their Genoese admiral, Benedetto Zaccaria, the fiefdoms of Chios and Phocea. Zaccaria also commanded Genoese ships when Genoa crushed Pisa at Meloria in 1284. He assisted the kings of Castile campaigning against the Muslims of Morocco, Philip the Fair in naval operations against England, and crusading forces in Syria. After his death in 1307, his heirs lost Chios and Phocea, but private citizens of Genoa formed the "Maona of Chios" in 1346, prepared a fleet, and reconquered the islands. When Genoa could not repay them, the "Maona" was given civil, military, and judicial authority over Chios and Phocea. Shareholders took the surname of Giustiniani and held the islands profitably for two centuries. Francesco Gattilusio initiated his family's Aegean fiefdoms in 1355 when he received Lesbos from the Greek emperor. Other Gattilusio holdings included the islands of Lemnos, Thasos, Imbros, and Samothrace, and the Thracian port of Enos.

During these centuries, the Genoese and the Venetians competed for control of Mediterranean commerce. Generally, Genoa controlled the eastern Aegean, while Venice held the western Aegean, but wars and piracy interfered. Between 1256 and 1381, these cities fought four wars.

In addition to losses from war, market fluctuations, and shipwreck, medieval merchants risked confiscation and imprisonment from their foreign hosts, who nevertheless at times also encouraged them with unusual privileges. In each foreign port, the Genoese had their special fortified quarter. Consuls sent from Genoa governed the colonies, while business partnerships controlled their commercial voyages. Profits were as high as 50 percent for merchants who survived the dangers. In the fifteenth century, oversight of Genoa's colonies was increasingly assumed by the Bank of St. George, the creditor of the Genoese state.

Genoese merchants dealt in diverse products in their far-flung commerce. They carried northern European textiles, iron, copper, and lumber to trade abroad. In North Africa they found raw wool, pelts and leather, indigo, and gold. They purchased oriental products—spices, silks, and gemstones—in Egypt, Syria, Constantinople, and, after 1261, in Tana, Trebizond, and Armenia. They also obtained alum and mastic in the Aegean and grain, furs, and wax from the Black Sea. They brought oriental goods to France in exchange for the prized northern woolens.

In response to the medieval expansion of trade, Genoa contributed to its technological development. Twelfth-century Genoese ships, the galley and the round ship, were modified to become the great galleys and the cogs of the fourteenth century. Other inventions—the compass, marine charts, and insurance contracts—were pioneered by Genoese merchants around 1300.

The government of Genoa, led by consuls, podestà, or (after 1339) doges, reflected intense political rivalries within the city. Increasingly after 1350, foreign princes governed Genoa, among whom were King Charles VI of France (1396–1409), Filippo Mario Visconti of Milan (1421–1435), Francesco Sforza of Milan (1464–1478), and King Louis XII of France (1499–1512). These foreign lords alternated with native doges. The city was often disturbed by insurrections led by politicians from the great Genoese families—the Fieschi, Grimaldi, Doria, Spinola versus the Guarco, Montaldo, Adorno, and Fregoso (Campofregoso).

In the later fourteenth century, Genoese voyages became less profitable. Land routes to the Far East became more dangerous as Mongol political unity shattered. Genoese trade also suffered from its wars with Venice and from the general European depression. With commercial decline and civil strife, Genoa lost its independence. Genoa's merchant marine sailed under

# G

foreign flags, and the Genoese invested their wealth in banking rather than in shipping.

**BIBLIOGRAPHY**

Abulafia, David. *The Two Italies, Economic Relations between the Norman Kingdom of Sicily and the Northern Communes.* Cambridge Studies in Medieval Life and Thought, 3.98. Cambridge: Cambridge UP, 1977.

Balard, Michel. *La Romanie génoise: XIIe–début du XVe siècle.* 2 vols. Rome: École française de Rome, 1978; and Atti della Società Ligure di Storia Patria, n.s. 18. 92. Genoa: Società Ligure di Storia Patria, 1980.

Face, R.D. "Techniques of Business in the Trade between the Fairs of Champagne and the South of Europe in the Twelfth and Thirteenth Centuries." *Economic History Review,* 2nd series, X–3 (1958): 427–438.

Heyd, Wilhelm von. *Histoire du Commerce du Levant au Moyen Age.* 2 vols. Leipzig, 1885–1886; rpt. Amsterdam: Adolf M. Hakkert, 1967.

Kedar, Benjamin Z. *Merchants in Crisis: Genoese and Venetian Men of Affairs and the Fourteenth Century Depression.* New Haven: Yale UP, 1976.

———. "Segurano-Sakran Selvaygo: Un mercante Genovese al servizio dei sultani Mamalucchi, *c.* 1303–1322." In *Fatti e Idee di storia economica nei secoli XII-XX: Studi dedicati a Franco Borlandi.* Bologna: Mulino, 1977, pp. 75–91.

Krueger, Hilmar C. "Genoese Merchants, Their Partnerships and Investments, 1155 to 1164." In *Studi in Onore di Armando Sapori.* Milan: Instituto editoriale cisalpino, 1957, pp. 256–272.

———. "Navì e Proprietà Navale a Genova, seconda metà del sec. XII." Atti della Società Ligure di Storia Patria n.s. 25.1; Genoa: Società Ligure de Storia Patria, 1985.

Lopez, Robert S. *Genova marinara nel Duecento: Benedetto Zaccaria, ammiraglio e mercante.* Biblioteca Storica principato, 17. Milan: G. Principato, 1933.

———. *Studi sull'Economia Genovese nel medio evo.* Documenti e studi per la storia del commercio e del diritto commerciale italiano 8. Turin: Lattes, 1936.

*Louise Buenger Robbert*

**SEE ALSO**

Ambassadors; Armenia; Azores; Bruges; Buscarello de' Ghisolfi; Byzantine Empire; Canary Islands; Caravans; Caspian Sea; Cog; Compass, Magnetic; Constantinople; Crusades, First, Second, and Third; Crusade, Fourth; Dyes and Pigments; Egypt; Fairs; Galley; Gems; Gold Trade in Africa; Golden Horde; Holy Land; India; Insurance; Lajazzo; Louis IX; Mediterranean Sea; Merchants, Italian; Piracy; Pisa; Portolan Charts; Saladin; Shipping Contracts, Mediterranean; Sijilmassa; Silk Roads; Spice Trade, Indian Ocean; Textiles, Decorative; Trebizond; Venice

## Geoffrey of Monmouth (*c.* 1100–1154 or 1155)

English author, of Welsh or Breton descent, and a chief source of the Arthurian legend. Geoffrey of Monmouth's *Historia regum Britanniae* (*c.* 1138) was one of the most popular books of the Middle Ages. This often fanciful record of Britain's kings, including Arthur, was "the book which [Geoffrey's] audience . . . had long wished to read" (Roberts 100), filling lacunae in British history and also feeding the twelfth century's taste for encyclopedism and marvels.

Both the prose *Historia* and the later, lesser known, lengthy poem in hexameters, the *Vita Merlini* (*c.*1150), include geographical description, local lore, and eponymous speculation, mixing fantastic and authentic information. The British material is most likely to represent actual experience: the references to some two dozen cities, including Lincoln, London, Winchester, Salisbury, Bath, Exeter, and Caerleon, suggest personal knowledge of them.

The *Historia* opens with a description of Britain. Echoing Bede, Geoffrey says that Britain, "the best of islands," is 800 miles long and 200 miles broad. Its resources include minerals, rich soil, woodlands filled with game, pastureland, and lakes and rivers full of fish. The Thames, the Severn, and the Humber are the "three noble rivers" of the island, carrying "commerce from across the seas from every nation."

Several famous locations are described in the course of the work. Loch Lomond is said to contain sixty islands and to be fed by sixty streams. There are sixty cliffs on the islands, and sixty eagles' nests, and each year these eagles cry out, foretelling the future. The character of this passage, with its repetition of numbers, association with "wise" animals, and prophetic overtones, owes as much to Celtic myth and prophetic tradition as it does to geographical observation.

Stonehenge is introduced when the British king Aurelius (Arthur's uncle) decides to erect a memorial for those killed in the Saxon wars. The prophet Merlin tells the king to bring the "Giant's Ring" from Mount Killaraus in Ireland. He says that the stones were transported to Ireland from Africa by giants. Baths made at the foot of the stones cure the sick, and the water, mixed with herbs, heals wounds. Aurelius sends his brother Utherpendragon, Merlin, and 15,000 men to Ireland, but while the Britons defeat the Irish, they are unable to dismantle the ring until Merlin comes to their aid with his "machinaciones" ("machines"?). Merlin later erects the stones through his "ingenium" ("skill" or "art") near the Monastery of Kaercaradduc, now Salisbury. The Giant's Ring becomes the burial place of Aurelius, Utherpendragon, and Constantine III, and Geoffrey's last reference is to record that the English call it Stanhenge. Despite its fantastic elements, Geoffrey's account appears to accord with the modern archaeological theory that the bluestones were carried by sea and by land from the Prescelly Mountains.

Geoffrey's fondness for eponymous lore is seen in the story of the founding of London. Lud, a pre-Roman king and "a great builder of cities," rebuilds the walls of the town of Trinovantum and orders its citizens to build lavish homes. The town comes to be known as Kaerlud, then Kaerlundein. Lud is buried in the city, near the gateway still called Porthlud or Ludgate.

Much of the geographical material in the *Vita Merlini* is presented by a figure in the poem, the bard-prophet Taliesin, in his lists of islands and bodies of water. These lists are drawn from the *Etymologies* of Isidore of Seville (*c.* 560–636), although the material relating to Britain is sometimes supplemented with other sources or local knowledge. There is also some overlap with the *Historia;* for example, both record the establishment of the hot springs at Bath by Bladud, a pre-Roman British king. The *Vita* adds that the baths are particularly medicinal for gynecological problems.

Strong contemporary interest in miraculous waters may have inspired the list of waters, and the final episode of the *Vita,* in which Merlin is cured of madness by drinking from a new spring in the forest of Caledon, may suggest contemporary interest in Holywell, Denbighshire, center of the cult of St. Winifred (Clarke 149).

Geoffrey may have known Holywell, which was not far from St. Asaph, the Welsh see to which Geoffrey was named (though he never assumed the bishopric) in 1151, but most of the material in the *Vita* is based solely on Isidore rather than on observation or knowledge. The rivers of Campania make barren women fertile and cure madness in men, and in Sicily, one spring induces fertility and the other sterility. The Tiber heals any wound, and Cicero's spring (Puzzoli, near Naples) cures damage to the eye. Two springs in Thessaly are particularly interesting: a sheep drinking from one will

turn white, from the other black; and a sheep drinking from both will have mottled fleece.

There are more exotic locales in the *Vita* as well, including the island of Ceylon, which is said to have two crops a year because it has two springs and two summers. It is notable for its grapes, other fruit, and jewels. The African spring of Zema (in Numidia?) sweetens the voice of whoever drinks from it, while the Ethiopians have a spring whose red waters drive men mad. In the Asphalt Lake of Judea (the Dead Sea), nothing living will sink. Geoffrey's works are not travel literature, as are some of the works of contemporaries such as Gerald of Wales, but they accurately reflect the interests in other places, near and far, characteristic of the period. In addition, his *Historia* exerted a great influence on the later work of Wace, Layamon, Spenser, and Shakespeare.

## BIBLIOGRAPHY

Geoffrey of Monmouth. *Historia Regum Britanniae.* Lewis Thorpe, trans. *The History of the Kings of Britain.* Harmondsworth: Penguin, 1966.

———. *The* Historia regum Britannie *of Geoffrey of Monmouth I: Bern, Burgerbibliothek, MS. 568.* Ed. Neil Wright. Cambridge: Brewer, 1984.

———. *Life of Merlin.* Ed. Basil Clarke. Cardiff: U of Wales P, 1973.

Padel, O.J. "Geoffrey of Monmouth and Cornwall." *Cambridge Medieval Celtic Studies* 8 (1984): 1–28.

Roberts, Brynley F. "Geoffrey of Monmouth, *Historia Regum Britanniae* and *Brut y Brenhinedd.*" In *The Arthur of the Welsh: The Arthurian Legend in Medieval Welsh Literature.* Ed. Rachel Bromwich, A.O.H. Jarman, and Brynley F. Roberts. Cardiff: U of Wales P, 1991, pp. 97–116.

Tatlock, J.S.P. *The Legendary History of Britain: Geoffrey of Monmouth's* Historia regum Britanniae *and Its Early Vernacular Versions.* Berkeley: U of California P, 1950.

*Siân Echard*

## SEE ALSO
Bede; Dead Sea; Gerald of Wales; Irish Travel; Isidore of Seville; Stonehenge and Other Megalithic Marvels

## Geography in Medieval Europe
Derived from the Greek for "writing/depicting the earth," the word *geographia* was rarely employed in medieval Europe—nor did a commonly used synonym circulate in Latin or a major vernacular—but

# G

geographical interests manifest themselves in a wide variety of texts between the early-sixth and the late-fifteenth centuries. These interests include such practical matters as the earth's shape and size, as well as the location and extent of natural features of its surface, including seas, rivers, mountains, and wildernesses; such sociopolitical concerns as tribal or national territories, the position of cities, and the distribution of humans with reputedly extraordinary features; and such theoretical issues as the earth's elemental properties and their effects, its place in the cosmos, the causes of natural phenomena, and a proper aesthetic appreciation of one's surroundings. While component parts of the Greek "geo/graphy" suggest that a description of the world may consist of both verbal and visual elements, medieval European geographical literature before the 1400s infrequently linked the two coherently. To be sure, texts, some of them widely circulating, were occasionally illustrated by maps, but these images were seldom integral to, and their content was not necessarily taken from, the adjacent text. Even brief "readings" (or *legenda*, "legends") about individual places on large-scale world maps (*mappaemundi*) generally served more historical or theological ends.

During the millennium between the dissolution of the western Roman Empire and the transoceanic ventures of Spain and Portugal, European understanding of geography did not markedly develop or supplant ideas that had been advanced by the Greeks, or data that had been accumulated by the Romans. Geography itself was not considered an independent field of study at any time during the Middle Ages; in educational contexts it was a subtopic of geometry or astronomy, and cartography figured largely in historical contexts (geography did not gain recognition as a separate academic discipline until the mid-1800s, about the same time that map departments were established in libraries). In fact, except for a very few usages, the word *geography* entered European discourse only after the appearance in 1475 of a printed version of Ptolemy's great book. Although today this work is conventionally referred to as the *Geographia*, most early publications called it *Cosmographia*, which is how Jacopo d'Angelo styled his Latin translation (*c.* 1407) of what he called Ptolemy's "description of the earth" (*geographiam, hoc est terre descriptionem*); Francesco di Niccolò Berlinghieri's Italian verse description of the world with Ptolemaic maps, published in 1482, was entitled *Geographia*. Indeed, medieval Europe lacked a coherent geographical vocabulary to facilitate discriminations in meaning: *mundus* is as multivalent a word in Latin as is *world* in English (having astronomical, terrestrial, temporal, social, and moral meanings), and it is often difficult to know when a writer is referring to the planet earth, its landmass only, one continent, or some other regional designation. In some contexts, a word or phrase such as *orbis* or *orbis terrae/terrarum* may be impossible to translate. In other respects as well, medieval geography was quite static. While sophisticated, dependable navigational charts were being produced by at least 1200, it is suggestive that the first map of the world ever printed (in Isidore of Seville's *Etymologies* [Augsburg: Zainer, 1472]) was a simple T-O diagram (see Maps), a style then many centuries old and characteristic of the schematic quality of much medieval cartography.

Educational curricula, vocabularies, and maps meet culturally dictated needs. Although generalizations may be profoundly misleading, it can be said with some accuracy that Europeans during the Middle Ages were more bookish than empirical, more skeptical than encouraging of curiosity and exploration, more territorially defensive than expansive. Authoritative sources deemed the earth's equatorial region to be an inaccessible belt of heat, and periodic attacks from unknown invaders approaching from all directions (but collec-

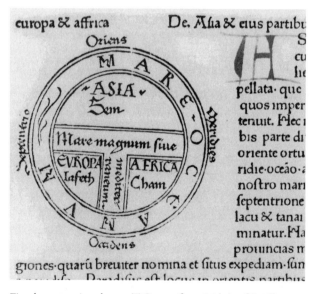

First known printed map. T-O map from Isidore of Seville, *Etymologies* (Augsburg: Günther Zainer, 1472) fol. 177v. Minneapolis, MN. By permission of the James Ford Bell Library, University of Minnesota.

tively referred to as Huns, Saracens, or Turks) reinforced a sense of the wider world's perils. These were among the factors that may have inhibited medieval Europeans (except the Scandinavians) from undertaking journeys of exploration, verifying or understanding the significance of claims of discovery, or greatly challenging the geographical data—or lore—inherited from the classical world.

Yet it would be wrong to characterize medieval Europeans as uninterested in or indifferent to geography. This was an age, after all, when people of consequence often identified themselves by place-names. Artists drew maps and wind roses (circular diagrams of personified winds from various directions) in historical and scientific works, and cosmographical subject matter lent an air of intellectual sophistication to literary texts: this appears to be the purpose of geographical content in Benoît de Sainte-Maure's *Roman de Troie* (c. 1165), Walter of Châtillon's *Alexandreis* (c. 1180), and John Gower's *Confessio Amantis* (1390), in which Book 7 is presented as a summary of a good education, beginning with a survey of the earth's elemental properties and principal divisions. After writing the first sentence of his autobiographical report of a journey to Egypt, Sinai, and the Holy Land in the mid-1330s, William of Boldensele offered a thumbnail sketch of the whole world, placing his Mediterranean voyage in the context of waterways from the Straits of Gibraltar to the Caspian Sea and beyond.

In addition, most encyclopedic compendia written during the Middle Ages include sections specifically dedicated to geographical matter. Among those that circulated widely and had considerable influence are Isidore of Seville's *Etymologies* (uncompleted at his death in 636), Hrabanus Maurus's *De universo* (before 856), Honorius Augustodunensis's *Imago mundi* (c. 1110) and the *Image dou monde* derived from it by Gossouin of Metz (1245/1247), Lambert of St. Omer's *Liber floridus* (1112–1121), Gervase of Tilbury's *Otia imperialia* (1211/1214), Jacques de Vitry's *Historia hierosolymitana* (c. 1221), Thomas of Cantimpré's *Liber de natura rerum* (1228–1244) and Konrad of Megenberg's version of it (*Buch von der Natur* [1349–1350]), Bartholomaeus Anglicus's *De proprietatibus rerum* (1245) and John Trevisa's English translation (*On the Properties of Things* [1398]), Vincent of Beauvais's mammoth *Speculum maius* (c. 1244; final revision c. 1260), Brunetto Latini's *Li livres dou trésor* (c. 1265), Roger Bacon's erudite "preamble" to a *summa* of

knowledge in his *Opus maius* (1266–1267), and Pierre d'Ailly's *Imago mundi* (c. 1410). The subject was important in more focused contexts as well: the first of eight chapters in John of Plano Carpini's *Historia Mongalorum* (History of the Mongols [1247]), based on the author's experience as papal envoy to the great khân in east Asia, treats its subject's "land, . . . its position, physical features, and climate." Clearly, then, at least some geographical knowledge was thought imperative for a well-rounded mind.

At the same time, however, the cursory and non-analytical treatment that a subject may receive in an encyclopedia sometimes led to a spare, derivative, and undeveloped transmission of information. Isidore reviews principal regions (and a few cities) of the world—beginning with Asia, then moving to Europe, "Libya" [Africa], and principal islands—offering brief (not always accurate) explanations of word origins in what at times amounts to little more than a list of toponyms. Nearly 500 years later, Honorius followed Isidore's organization, as well as some of his etymologizing tendencies and many of his details, adding bits of information (or pseudo-information) about some places ("Persida" [Persia] is where the art of magic was first practiced, the city of Rome aptly has the shape of a lion, the Queen of Sheba came from Ethiopia), but his "little book," as he himself describes it, presents a popularized version of geography. Both Isidore and Honorius—as well as many medieval mapmakers—found a place for Troy and Carthage.

The great advances in learning about the earth's surface often associated with the early modern period came about in large part due to developments in technology (including shipbuilding, implements such as the compass, and sea charts) made during the Middle Ages. By and large, however, transmarine travel and trade were risky from the 500s to the 1400s, an obvious obstacle to receiving, transmitting, and developing knowledge about the earth. A more academic impediment was the fact that, as noted above, geography as a discipline had no distinct status in the curriculum. In addition, texts at this time could be disseminated only through scribal copying. Since a handwritten reproduction of even familiar material often was marred by mistakes, geographical toponyms—identifying mountains, seas, rivers, regions, cities, and peoples (sometimes synonymous with regional designations)—were especially vulnerable to corruption. This was particularly true of data that was arguably most important—because unfamiliar—to the reader: details about Asia

# G

or Africa, which had to be rendered from a non-Western language into Latin (or a vernacular) at a time when no system for transliteration existed and linguistic versatility was limited. Thus, the most comprehensive and informative geographical work produced in twelfth-century Europe—al-Idrīsī's *Recreation for Him Who Wishes to Travel* (or *Rogerian Description*), prepared for King Roger II of Sicily around 1154 but composed in Arabic—went essentially unknown. Mathematical details were also subject to copying errors: statistics—the record of distances between cities, across regions, and around the earth—were compromised by the Roman numeral system, which was cumbersome even in small units (88 has eight digits) and lacked a consistent, universally understood method for recording numbers over 5,000. Even after the discovery of the Hindu-Arabic decimal system (and the concept of zero), copyists continued to confuse numerals.

Reliance on etymology, sometimes completely fabricated, to remember facts also intruded on learning and encouraged a moral rather than informational approach to geography. For example, when Mongol armies alarmed Europe by invading Russia and pushing west in the late 1230s, the chronicler Matthew Paris, having learned their tribal designation "Tatar," wrote that they were "rightly called Tartari or Tartarians" because they had "poured forth like devils from Tartarus" (*Chronica majora,* entry for 1240). Others found similarly apt the fact that a Mongol ruler was referred to as *khân,* since this recalled the Latin word *canus,* and the people in general showed an unusual canine rapacity and determination to bite (German texts translate "the great khân" as "der grosse Hund").

The basic theoretical understanding of geography that did circulate during the Middle Ages was largely, though indirectly, based on the accomplishments of ancient Greeks. The noun *geographia,* and the verb from which it is derived, can be traced to Eratosthenes [fl. 250 B.C.E.]. The first identifiable person known to have drawn a map appears to be Anaximander of Miletus (fl. *c.* 570 B.C.E.), and Hecataeus, also from Miletus, produced the earliest surviving methodical description of the earth, based on accumulated data and styled a *periegesis,* or "journey around the world" figured as having two parts, Europe and Asia (the latter including Egypt and Libya). A trading people, the Greeks amassed a remarkable amount of information about places from the Straits of Gibraltar to the northerly regions known as Scythia to the mouth of the Indus, the latter explored by Scylax, *c.* 515 B.C.E.; some two centuries later, Pytheas of Massilia [Marseilles] recorded his explorations in the North Sea beyond the British Isles to the icy waters near "Thule." Equally significant are the intellectual achievements of writers such as Eudoxus of Cnidus (*c.* 408–355 B.C.E.), who developed a sophisticated theory of geographical and astronomical space predicated on a series of concentric spheres surrounding a central earth; and Eratosthenes, who accurately calculated the terrestrial circumference and drew a map employing meridians and parallels (but arranged according to the importance of the area being depicted), an idea that would be "perfected" in the system of latitudinal/longitudinal coordinates Ptolemy of Alexandria developed in the mid-second century C.E. to locate places. The stability and range of the Roman Empire allowed for the gathering of even more facts about the earth's physical makeup; this appealed to governors and citizens more than did conceptual or speculative matter (such as whether an antipodal continent must exist in order to bring harmonious balance to the planet's land areas): geography in the service of the state was decidedly political, an auxiliary science to history and public affairs. It is emblematized in the lower-left corner of the Hereford *mappamundi* (*c.* 1290), which depicts Augustus Caesar, just before the birth of Jesus, commissioning three men to "go into the entire world" and collect data about it, interpreted as the famous "decree" of Luke 2:1.

For Western Europeans after the fifth century, however, Greek was essentially a lost language: thus, the valuable information and stimulating theories produced in the ancient world—except for texts translated into Latin (or into Arabic and thence into Latin), or material excerpted or "borrowed" by later Latin writers—was unknown to medieval scholars and other readers. Nevertheless, several fundamental tenets of classical geography were inherited, and almost without exception recycled, during the Middle Ages. The earth was understood to be an unmoving spherical body at the center (but also the base) of the universe. Its circumference was calculated to be the equivalent of *c.* 25,000 miles (*c.* 40,000 kilometers). (A less accurate estimate—some 33 percent smaller—attributed to Posidonius by Strabo and adopted by Ptolemy, was largely forgotten until the publication of his *Geographia* in the late 1400s, when it was championed by Christopher Columbus.) The inhabited land area on the earth was an extended version of the Greek *oikoumene,* consisting of Asia, Europe, and Africa.

The earth itself had five climate zones (*climata* being the Greek word for these "zones"): the two polar areas were uninhabitable because of extreme cold, the equatorial region was unapproachable because of great heat, and the two intermediate bands were temperate (the northern one was, of course, the location of the *oikoumene,* and some entertained the idea that the southern one might have land as well). For most writers, regions at similar latitudes (in the north) produced similar goods. The four elements—water, earth, air, fire—combined in various ways to produce such natural occurrences as tides, earthquakes, winds, thunder and lightning, and comets.

Such geographical information reached medieval readers via four principal late-classical sources. The eclectic and generally reliable, if rather diffuse, information about the earth's features, as well as its animal and human populations, in Pliny's expansive *Natural History* (before 79 C.E.) was digested by Gaius Julius Solinus (*c.* 230/240), whose *Collectanea rerum memorabilium* (Collection of Memorable Things) preserves the more peculiar details in Pliny by making them the salient features of the earth in a catalogue of wonders that moves west-to-east, from Iberia to India.

Basic data about the earth's size, circumference, climatic zones, and place in the universe were available in Macrobius's lucid *Commentary on the Dream of Scipio* (*c.* 400), approximately half of which treats cosmographical material. The discussion—over sixteen times longer than the visionary passage from a work by Cicero it means to elucidate—is Neoplatonist in character, and even its nongeographical subject matter might influence the way readers conceived the world: Macrobius's idealistic numerology, for example, "explained" how it was in the very nature of things for a body or place to be described in terms of latitude, longitude, and altitude; for matter to consist of a quartet of elements; and for the moon to complete its circuit of the zodiac in twenty-eight days, all because of certain qualities inherent in the numbers three, four, and seven. (His authority could lend an academic sophistication to works of literature, as when Chrétien de Troyes invokes him as the source for a description of a personified Geometry measuring the world, embroidered amid exotica on a robe worn by Erec in *Erec et Enide* [*c.* 1170; ll. 6682ff.].) Medieval manuscript copies of the *Commentary* are frequently accompanied by diagrammatic maps with north at the top.

Between *c.* 410 and 439, Martianus Capella produced a similarly sophisticated epitome of classical learning in *De nuptiis Philologiae et Mercurii* (The Marriage of Philology and Mercury). The work's allegorical setting enabled him to employ a majestic female personification of Geometry to provide details about the earth's sphericity, size, and zones, as well as to guide readers through a long list of place-names as she makes an orderly passage across Europe, northern Africa, and Asia, with a parting glance at territory from Ethiopia to the Canaries and a set of measurements of key distances. It may be noted that within Martianus's fictional construct, Geometry's geographical survey is greeted with scorn by Venus's attendants Pleasure [Voluptas] and Mirth [Iocus], the former of whom questions the purpose of all this "traipsing over so many mountains, rivers, seas, and crossroads" (6.704). She goes unanswered.

A fourth influential late-classical writer employs geography as the foreground for a polemic. Paulus Orosius begins his *Historiarum adversus paganos libri VII* (Seven Books of History against the Pagans), completed in 418, with an overview of the world's regions, moving from Asia (within which he, like many others, includes Egypt), to Europe (as far as the obscure "Thule"), to an Africa that he acknowledges, owing to its small size, might be considered part of Europe; he concludes with a survey of major Mediterranean islands (1.2.1–105, with a possible mention of the Canaries at 1.2.11). Orosius's aim is to enable readers to acquire "knowledge" of the "location" of places that figure prominently in world history, which for him is a succession of "local misfortunes" (1.1.17, 1.2.106). This gloomy, universal judgment is essential to his argument, which is a defense of Christianity against the accusation that Rome's new religion was responsible for the empire's woes, in particular the devastations wrought by Alaric in 410. Encouraged in this project by Augustine of Hippo, Orosius borrowed both from Roman self-aggrandizing historiography and a Judeo-Christian view of human time (based especially on Daniel 2) to shape a narrative explaining that a divinely ordained movement, or "translation," of imperial power and intellectual development—a *translatio imperii* and a *translatio studii*—proceeded from east to west, making the banishment of Adam and Eve from the Earthly Paradise at the earth's oriental extreme the initial moment in an occidental trend that led human civilization "through" Babylon, Persia, and Greece to its ultimate geographical and moral end in a Christianized Rome. The idea proved powerful and

# G

persistent (it has informed the image of America as a "city on a hill" with a "manifest destiny").

Orosian historiography remained a powerful way of reading time in medieval Europe: very popular itself (and adapted in England alone by Gildas [500s], Bede [731], and Geoffrey of Monmouth [c. 1136–1138]), it was updated by Otto of Freising in the 1140s and, with some alteration, given a kind of visual form as the vertical equator on the Hereford *mappamundi,* whose axis links Eden (at the top) with "Babylonia," Jerusalem, Rome (identified in a hexameter appropriate to contemporary poetics), and finally, space beyond the Pillars of Hercules associated in classical thought (and Dante) with the Isles of the Dead; several legends on the map identify places found only in Orosius's geographical chapter. Scribes rarely corrected or improved upon early descriptions of the world. The Iberian Orosius, whose formative years were spent in North Africa, was a Mediterranean man, however, and the Old English translation of his *History* incorporates two accounts of voyages told to King Alfred (871–899), by Ohthere [Ottarr] of Halgoland along the west coast of Norway to the White Sea and by Wulfstan in the Baltic as far as Estonia ["Estland"].

These four writers were certainly sources of raw data throughout the Middle Ages: direct quotations from Solinus and Orosius appear in Honorius Augustodunensis's widely disseminated *Imago mundi* and on various *mappaemundi*. Geographical science is not limited to the contents of a gazetteer, however, and the means by which it is grasped may be as consequential as are facts themselves. For example, by the eighth century, Europeans generally understood the earth's shape to be spherical: it is clearly so described in Bede's *De natura rerum* (before 725), and, a century earlier, Isidore called it round, though whether like a ball or a wheel has been much debated. Yet it is crucial to know on what basis a fact is accepted, since many people hold correct ideas for the wrong reasons. For centuries, an authoritative source about the earth's sphericity was Plato's *Timaeus,* which was circulating in Chalcidius's Latin translation by the fifth century C.E. (key passages resurface in Macrobius's *Commentary*). Borrowing from the Pythagoreans, Plato insisted that the earth was globular because it *had* to be: an ideal universe and its constituent parts would by definition be modeled on the sphere, which is geometry's perfect form. Significantly, Aristotle (or a medieval writer adopting his name) arrived at the same conclusion via a completely different route, stating in *De caelo et mundo* (translated into Latin by Gerard of Cremona before 1187) that the earth's shape may be deduced from the facts that during an eclipse it casts a circular shadow on the moon, and travelers moving from north to south notice new constellations appearing along the horizon. These empirical proofs constitute (in modern terms) scientific rather than philosophical geography.

Not always is it possible to know which approach operates in a particular text. In his *Imago mundi* (c. 1110), Honorius twice likens the earth to a ball (1.1, 1.5), but he offers no evidence for this assertion (perhaps because he is writing a succinct encyclopedia rather than a logical treatise); given the work's date of composition, however, he may have reached the correct conclusion via Plato's speculative route. *The Book of John Mandeville* (c. 1360), on the other hand, bases its description of terrestrial sphericity on (purported) experience (chapter 20). Together, the two texts circulated in hundreds of manuscripts, but in practical terms, since additions to geographical knowledge come from actual investigation rather than armchair travel, the Aristotelian *lesson* of the latter—even if its author did not in fact ever cross the Rhine—was more consequential. The implications of such an epistemology are evident in the richly informative *Itinerarium* of William of Rubruck (1255), in which the writer draws on his own experience as a traveler in Central Asia to question and even to defy the authoritative Isidore of Seville, contradicting his claim—a staple of medieval geographies—that the Caspian Sea has an outlet to a northern ocean, and expressing profound skepticism about his (and Solinus's) report about monstrous races of humans (*de monstruosis hominibus*) inhabiting Asia (chapters 12, 18, 29). William's observations, in turn, made a keen impression on Roger Bacon, whose general knowledge and methodology bear signs of his fellow Franciscan, such as his promotion of the study of geography with the pragmatic aim of furthering evangelism.

As an authoritative book of *scientia* during the Middle Ages, the Bible also contributed several principal ideas to a European understanding of the world. For many writers and cartographers (though not for Augustine of Hippo), the Garden of Eden remained under angelic protection at the eastern extreme of the terrestrial landmass. Here the earth's four major rivers, each with specific properties, had their source (Genesis 2:10–14): these were usually understood to be the

Nile, Tigris, Euphrates, and Ganges (around 1356, the chronicler John of Marignolli, who had been to China, turned the latter into the Hwang-ho). The Nile, identified with "Gihon" in the Genesis passage, was said by some to have gone underground in Asia and resurfaced in Egypt, although both Orosius and Isidore suggested that the river (or a major tributary) ran a subterranean course from *West* Africa.

The classical world's tripartite division of the earth's landmass received Judeo-Christian endorsement in the claim that after the Flood Noah had distributed territory among his sons (Genesis 9:18–19). Firstborn Shem deserved the largest inheritance of Asia, Japhet received Europe, and Africa went to Ham (usually spelled "Cham/Chan," sometimes conflated with his son Canaan, and occasionally identified on maps with a final flourish to the letter that may cause the name mistakenly to be read as "Chaos"). This "biblical geography" was endorsed by widely read theologians such as Peter Comestor (*c.* 1100–1179) in his *Historica scholastica* (*Patrologia Latina* 198: 1087). The assertion that God works salvation "in the midst of the earth" (*in medio terrae*) (Psalm 73 [74]:12 [cf. Ezekiel 5:5]) led writers to imagine Jerusalem as the center of the tricontinental landmass (the city was known *not* to lie on the equator). Makers of *mappaemundi* frequently placed the Holy City at the midpoint of their design; on his enormous cartographical project for the king of Portugal (*c.* 1459), Fra Mauro did not do so, but he included a legend explaining that Jerusalem is central with respect to population density. Finally, a prophecy in the Book of Revelation (20:8) that "Gog and Magog" would join forces with Antichrist at the end of time led some to posit locations for this spectral tribe. An obscure people—they were located vaguely in Ezekiel 38–39, but more specifically in early apocalyptic literature and the Qur'an (18:83–108, 21:97)—their future actions earned them as rightful a place in Honorius's geography as past deeds had for the Trojans (1.10. 1. 20).

References to the earth's "four corners" in Isaiah 11:12 and Revelation 7:7 did not require medieval theologians to envision it as flat and/or square, since the image could be understood in terms of cardinal directions; the depiction of humanity as being *super gyrum terrae* (Isaiah 40:11) was semantically ambiguous. (The period's single articulate flat-earth enthusiast, Cosmas Indikopleustes [*c.* 547], wrote in Greek and was virtually unknown, which is perhaps unfortunate because

some of his ideas, though bizarre, are presented as empirically based.) A rehearsal of the creation story in 2 Esdras, in the Apocrypha, portrays the earth's surface as being six-sevenths land (6:42, 47, 50–52), but classical sources that described much larger oceans were more widely accepted; many accounts avoid assessments of a land-to-sea proportion, although Roger Bacon clearly accepted the Apocryphal text as fact. Other details in geographical treatises came from the canonical Acts of the Apostles—and extra-biblical texts on apostolic travels, such as St. Thomas's mission to "India"—as well as occasional lists of exotic toponyms (such as Isaiah 66:19).

In terms of readership, however, the most important writer about geography for the Middle Ages was the encyclopedist Isidore, bishop of Seville (d. 636), whose *Etymologies* survives today in approximately 1,000 manuscript copies, some containing a map that may be authorial and in any event was a component of the text by the eighth century. This encyclopedia became a standard source of data—not always reliable or clearly presented—about languages, societies, and familial relationships (Book 9); the earth's political and physical geography (Book 14); and cities, the countryside, and measurements of distance (Book 15). Like other medieval compendia noted earlier, Isidore's had the fundamentally catechistic aim of producing informed, astute Christians. His methodology affected such scholars as Remigius of Auxerre (*c.* 841–*c.* 908), whose attempt to elucidate Macrobius's *Commentary* includes his own etymological "explanations" of toponyms.

Other writers reveal a more parochial interest in geography *per se*. The *Cosmographia* of Aethicus Ister, a work that may date from *c.* 700 (it should not be confused with the work of [Julius] Aethicus Cosmographus, who in the 500s produced an excerpted version of Julius Honorius's *Cosmographia,* written during the previous century), is a rarity among medieval texts. Its six books focus almost exclusively on geographical matter, including ethnography, natural history, and physics. The author is a mystery. He purports to be an exile from a culturally moribund Greece who hopes to establish an intellectual community in Istria, but the work is not a translation from the Greek as it claims to be (Latin is the language of its composition), and the writer may have been a native of Dalmatia, or Ireland, or Scythia; he pays particular attention to northern regions. Some have argued that he is identical with the equally obscure Virgil of Salzburg, who was denounced

# G

by Pope Zachary in 748 for believing in antipodal regions (possibly inhabited ones), but whose "heretical" notions did not work to his disgrace, since he became a bishop in 767 and served until his death eighteen years later.

More than just a collection of statistics, Dicuil's *Liber de mensura orbis terrae* (Book on the Measurements of the Whole World), which this Irish scholar completed at the court of Louis the Pious in 825, nevertheless confines itself to world geography, combining details from classical sources with contemporaneous information about Atlantic islands. The author demonstrates a respect for observation and the collection of evidence: he bases his comments about varying periods of darkness and light in northern latitudes on the report of eremitic monks who had visited "Thule" (and during the summer could pick lice out of their clothes at midnight), and he disputes a measurement recorded in Pliny of the sea's greatest depth as being fifteen stades (*c.* 1,200 fathoms) on the grounds that many more soundings would be required for certitude. The eleventh-century figure Guido (scholars once called him Guido of Ravenna and placed him earlier in time) compiled some 3,500 names related to geography, many taken from a seventh-century catalogue of seas, rivers, towns, peninsulas, and islands attributed to the anonymous "Ravenna Geographer."

Perhaps the most intellectually rigorous student of geography during the early Middle Ages was Adam of Bremen (*c.* 1040–*c.*1081), whose *Descriptio insularum aquilorum* (Description of the Islands of the North)—the last of four books in his magisterial *Gesta Hammaburgensis ecclesiae pontificum* (History of the Bishops of the Church of Hamburg)—was written between 1073 and 1076 (revised before 1080), while he was canon at the archiepiscopal cathedral at Bremen, see of the largest diocese in the medieval church, including Scandinavia and Greenland. As critical a geographer as he was a historian, Adam was guided but not intimidated by the usual authorities such as Solinus, Orosius, and Martianus. He questioned their descriptions of monstrous races of humans, relying on information he obtained from travelers to, and natives of, places as remote as the Baltic and Vinland. His report of a voyage undertaken by Frisians beyond Iceland, although it climaxes in their narrow escape from a polar island inhabited by cyclopes, is a rare instance of the use of contemporary expeditions to enrich understanding of the earth's territories. Medieval geography, with its har-

monies and imaginative claims, was often poetical: at times it was, in fact, presented as poetry. An anonymous Frankish metrical cosmography from the 600s presents a succinct Christian view of the world, and the Old High German "Meregarto" (before 1100) dramatically describes its wonders in rhymed couplets.

Geographical writing in the later Middle Ages reflects major changes in the degree and type of contact that the ordinary person might have with the non-European world. Writing shortly after World War I, the astute historian John Kirtland Wright drew a parallel between the enormous increase in North American awareness of the geography of Europe between 1914 and 1918, and the remarkable expansion of European knowledge about Asia and northern Africa during the period of the crusades. Even so, considerable naïveté about lands beyond Europe remains in the encyclopedic works by Honorius and Lambert referred to earlier, and the contemporaneous *Descriptio mappe mundi* (early 1120s) by Hugh of St. Victor. Arguably, however, even this proliferation of geographical material in the generation after the Christian conquest of Jerusalem testifies to growing interest in the outside world. Hugh's book, in fact, devotes itself exclusively to the earth's regions—it covers, in order, Asia, Africa, Europe, and islands—and appears to be assembled as a guide for a mapmaker (unlike Honorius's far more popular *Imago mundi*), and to do so in more pragmatic terms than are found in Hugh's tropological *De archa Noë mystica,* in which the earth is imagined to correspond to the shape of Noah's ark (as reckoned in Genesis 6:15). By the early 1200s, Jacques de Vitry was drawing on his own experience as bishop of Acre for topographical details in his encyclopedic history (noted earlier). The extraordinary wealth of information about the Mediterranean coast—its natural features, cities and villages, and distances between them—found in the *Liber de existencia riveriarum et forma maris nostri Mediterranei,* produced in Pisa, testifies that a sophisticated database was in the hands of portolan chart makers by 1200. After the mid-1100s, more popular, but less trustworthy, works reached many readers, including the *Voyage of St. Brendan,* the *Letter of Prester John,* and stories regarding Alexander the Great and Charlemagne.

Two other kinds of writing mark the twelfth century as a seminal moment in European geographical history. First, translations from Arabic into Latin made available the scientific methodology and learning of Arabs, as well as certain ancient Greek texts. Gerard of Cremona's rendering of Aristotle has been mentioned earlier; his equal in significance is Adelard of Bath (*c.* 1070–*c.* 1142/1146), a widely traveled polymath who in 1126 translated the *Introductorius* of Muhammed ibn Musa al-Khwarizmi, an early-ninth-century text of astronomical tables that introduced unfamiliar, Hindu-Arabic ideas about the world to Europe and helped shape an interest in scientific study in his native England that had a pronounced legacy. Subsequently, William of Conches, a teacher at the cathedral school of Chartres and tutor to the future king Henry II of England, displayed in his *De philosophia mundi* (before 1145) a serious intellectual engagement with the physical phenomena of the universe. William contributes reasoned, often empirically derived explanations of the composition of air, the formation of clouds, the cooler temperatures of the upper atmosphere nearer the sun, and the causes of rainfall, floods, and tides. These interests find their way into the geographical content of later medieval encyclopedias: works by Thomas of Cantimpré, Bartholomaeus Anglicus, Vincent of Beauvais, Brunetto Latini, Roger Bacon, and Pierre d'Ailly (see above). The climate of opinion that welcomed William's "experimentalism" ultimately took the claims of travelers and articulate pseudo-travelers more seriously than those of traditional encyclopedists. Thus, Marco Polo, through Rustichello of Pisa's *Divisament dou monde* (Description of the World [*c.* 1295]), and John Mandeville, through the *Book* attributed to him, gained acceptance as accurate, if garrulous, authorities on Asia and parts of Africa.

A fundamentally new way of imagining and designing space was emerging during this period as well, anticipating the "Ptolemaic revolution" in cartography during the fifteenth century. In his *Descriptio Terre Sancte* (Description of the Holy Land), from 1283, Burchard of Mount Sion proposed to locate significant places in Judeo-Christian history within "quarters" of territory into which he had rather arbitrarily divided Palestine, fanning out from a central point at Acre. While the scheme was not fully realized (and Burchard had to propose a subdivision of the fourth quarter because it included the site-rich area of Jerusalem), it marks a growing interest in systematically, reliably locating topographical features on a sheet of parchment or paper. Soon after, the Venetian Marino Sanudo proposed a sophisticated grid system for the same purpose in his *Liber secretorum fidelium crucis*

(Book of Secrets for True Crusaders), written between 1306 and 1321. Sanudo commissioned the Genoese cartographer Pietro Vesconte to draw a map of the Holy Land, oriented to the east, with an overlay of lines dividing the territory into square "leagues" (seventy-seven running vertically [east to west] and twenty-nine running horizontally [north to south]); this enabled him to write a verbal account of places and fix their locations according to box numbers from the chart. His is the first European book in which a map is essential to the interpretation of a corresponding text. Interestingly, Burchard and Sanudo were devising their spatial formats at about the same time that cartographers produced the much more geographically traditional Ebstorf and Hereford *mappaemundi* (as well as kindred designs that do not survive).

During the early 1400s, what may best be called a school of geography developed around the intellectually vibrant Benedictine foundation at Klosterneuburg, near Vienna. Scholars gathered data about the earth's features, distinguishing among mountains, rivers, and so forth, and assigning coordinates corresponding to imagined lines of latitude and longitude (the accumulated information is known as the Vienna-Klosterneuburg Map Corpus). They presented these data in tabular form, making it possible to produce fairly consistent exempla of a single map image without tracing or copying freehand. Of course, the information was still vulnerable to scribal error and lapse (as may be seen by comparing the data in a manuscript with the legends on one of three surviving derivative maps). The invention and employment of the printing press in the second half of the century eliminated much of this potential corruption and greatly encouraged the proliferation of such knowledge. Thus, as new facts began to flood Europe at the end of the century—before they were even understood to be challenges to fundamental geographical assumptions of the previous millennium—a means for their rapid dissemination was available, which quickly spurred the desire for yet more knowledge, which was also a radical development.

**BIBLIOGRAPHY**

Beazley, C.R. *The Dawn of Modern Geography.* See Gen. Bib.

Bevan, W.L., and H.W. Phillott. "Introduction." In *Mediæval Geography: An Essay in Illustration of the Hereford Mappa Mundi.* London: E. Stanford; Hereford: E.K. Jakeman, 1873; rpt. Amsterdam: Meridian, 1969, pp. xiii–lii.

# G

Brincken, Anna-Dorothee von den. *Fines terrae.* See Gen. Bib.

Crosby, Alfred W. *The Measure of Reality: Quantification and Western Society, 1250–1600.* Cambridge: Cambridge UP, 1997.

Dalché, *Carte Marine et Portulan au XII^e siècle.* See Gen. Bib.

Edson, Evelyn. *Mapping Time and Space: How Medieval Mapmakers Viewed Their World.* London: British Library; Toronto: U of Toronto P, 1997.

Harley-Woodward. *The History of Cartography.* Vol. 1, esp. O.A.W. Dilke, "Itineraries and Geographical Maps in the Early and Late Roman Empires" (pp. 234–257); David Woodward, "Medieval *Mappaemundi*" (pp. 286–370); and P.D.A. Harvey, "Local and Regional Cartography in Medieval Europe" (pp. 464–501). See Gen. Bib.

Lelewel, Joachim. *Géographie du moyen âge.* 5 vols. [Vol. 5 entitled *Épilogue*]. Brussels: Pilliet, 1852–1857; rpt. Amsterdam: Meridian, 1966–1967.

Phillips, J.R.S. *The Medieval Expansion of Europe.* Oxford: Oxford UP, 1988.

Romm, James S. *The Edges of the Earth in Ancient Thought: Geography, Exploration, and Fiction.* Princeton, NJ: Princeton UP, 1992.

Simek, Rudolf. *Altnordische Kosmographie: Studien und Quellen zu Weltbild und Weltbeschreibung in Norwegen und Island vom 12. bis zum 14. Jahrhundert.* Ergänzungsbände zum Reallexikon der Germanischen Altertumskunde 4. Berlin and New York: Walter de Gruyter, 1990.

Wright, J.K. *Geographical Lore of the Time of the Crusades.* See Gen. Bib.

*Scott D. Westrem*

**SEE ALSO**
Adam of Bremen; Aethicus Ister; Ailly, Pierre d'; Albertus Magnus; Antipodes; Atlas; Bartholomaeus Anglicus; Burchard of Mount Sion; Cartography, Arabic; Center of the Earth; Climate; Columbus, Christopher; Compass, Magnetic; Cosmas Indikopleustes; Dicuil; Ebstorf World Map; Exploration and Expansion, European; Four Rivers of Paradise; Gerald of Wales; Geoffrey of Monmouth; Gervase of Tilbury; Gog and Magog; Guido; Ham's Curse and Africans; Hereford Map; Higden, Ranulf; Honorius Augustodunensis; Isidore of Seville; Itineraries and *Periploi;* Jacques de Vitry; John of Marignolli; John of Plano Carpini; *King's Mirror, The;* Klosterneuburg Map Corpus; Lambert of St. Omer; *Mandeville's Travels; Mappamundi;* Maps; Marco Polo; Matthew Paris; Mauro Map, [Fra]; Measurement of Distances; Mela, Pomponius; Navigation; Navigation, Arab; Navigation, Chinese; *Oikoumene;* Orosius; Otto of Freising; Pliny the Elder; Prester John; Ptolemy; Sacrobosco, John of; Sanudo, Marino; Solinus, Julius Gaius; Spain and Portugal; Thule; Travel Writing in Europe and the Mediterranean

Regions; Vesconte, Pietro/Perrino; Vincent of Beauvais; Virgil of Salzburg St.; William of Boldensele

## Geography and Travel, Scholarship on Medieval European
*See* Scholarship on Medieval European Geography and Travel

## Gerald of Wales [Giraldus Cambrensis] (1146–1223)
A proud and colorful clergyman who in three works gives us vivid and invaluable sketches of the land and the people of Ireland and Wales, and who, like such other important twelfth-century figures as William of Malmesbury and John of Salisbury, promotes in his writings the rhetorical superiority of eyewitness narration.

Gerald's *Topographia Hibernica, Itinerarium Kambriae,* and *Descriptio Kambriae* convey in a distinctive, immediate voice both his keen attention to rich natural, topographical, and ethnographical detail, and his abiding curiosity for the miraculous and the marvelous in nature. While Gerald does not necessarily rank among the best scientific minds of the twelfth century, he is one of his age's most engaging "eyewitness" narrators. Aggressively self-promoting, Gerald's sharp focus on the world in which he travels seems frequently guided more by his desire to display his considerable literary and intellectual capacities and by his ambition for the archbishopric of St. David's, than by a loyalty to science *per se.* Nevertheless, his work—which also includes marginal illustrations and a lost map of Wales, as well as lively description and careful sequencing—exhibits impressive precision, which derives, especially in the Welsh works, from firsthand observation, much of it the result of travel.

The *Topographia* (first recension *c.* 1187) derives from a journey Gerald took with Prince John in 1185. The *Itinerarium* (first recension *c.* 1189) is based on a preaching tour he made with Archbishop Baldwin between March 2 and April 24, 1188, to garner support for the Third Crusade (1188–1192). For both of these texts the journey is the explicit organizing principle of the narrative. As he passes by places that attract his attention, Gerald notes the character of the land, certain items of natural history, the habits of birds, fish, and animals he observes, and the manners and customs

222  **Gerald of Wales**

Talking wolf of Ireland. *Topographica Hibernica*. London British Library, MS Royal 13 b. viii, fol. 17v, *c.* 1220. Courtesy of the British Library.

which Gerald re-creates his personal encounters with both the discernible and the ineffable ways of God. In fact, Gerald frequently suggests correlations between the character of the land and the qualities of its human inhabitants. Like many of his contemporaries, Gerald is intent on finding principles of divine order in the visible, particular, and sometimes apparently accidental workings of the phenomenal world. His observations of wildlife, for instance, give him material for moralizing, but they are also occasions for him to meditate on the way one apprehends truth in nature (that is, the relative merits of observation and of *auctoritas*). Gerald claims in his "Second Preface" to the *Descriptio*: "I have pursued my researches into the works of nature farther than most of my contemporaries" (Thorpe 216). He may look at a bird simultaneously to compose a mini-bestiary and to display his learning by textually dueling with a received authority, but he will also re-create the bird's physical features with carefully observed specifics. Even when relating one of his many miraculous stories, Gerald always claims either to have witnessed the event itself or to have encountered in some form a remaining, concrete sign, a tangible connection to the event.

Gerald's care to visualize for his readers the evidence of God's presence in the world suggests his desire to authorize himself as someone who can observe the workings of God in life and the history of creation. His own reading of the sacred models of experience recorded in scripture and other authoritative sources becomes the foundation on which he builds and privileges his own experience and ability to teach others how and what to see in order to find God in every order of creation. One might also see in Gerald's conspicuous presence as narrator, combined with his inclination to set the miraculous in concrete circumstances, his attempt to depict the world as malleable, reflecting his ever-present preoccupation with revising his station upward.

of the land's human inhabitants. Gerald, however, also takes his readers on excursions into marvelous tales in the human and the natural world. The familiar and the strange are both portions of what Gerald considered, according to Robert Bartlett, the "texture" of this world. Some of these "digressions" offer Gerald the chance, for example, to sermonize on doctrine, or to bear witness to the reality of God's interaction with mortals—both his beneficence in the lives of local saints, and his certain, retributive justice for noteworthy sinners. As a rule Gerald is a hostile critic of the Irish, and he is alternately sympathetic and harsh toward the Welsh. Descended from both Norman and Welsh ancestors, Gerald wrote the *Descriptio* (first recension *c.* 1194), as its name suggests, to describe the land and the people of Wales. In a *sic et non* structure (following the "thus and otherwise" form of dialectical disputation), the first book, in addition to discussing the topography, geography, and toponymal etymology of Wales and Cambria, advances a very favorable view of the Welsh themselves; the second book offers pointed criticism of Welsh morals and practices.

One can see especially in the *Topographia* and the *Itinerarium,* but also in the *Descriptio,* that the landscape itself is a kind of timeless, durable frame within

**BIBLIOGRAPHY**

Bartlett, Robert. *Gerald of Wales.* Oxford: Clarendon Press, 1982.

*Giraldi Cambrensis: Opera.* Ed. James F. Dimock. Rolls Series, 21 [5–6]. London: Longman's, 1868.

Gransden, Antonia. "Realistic Observation in Twelfth-Century England." *Speculum* 47.1 (1972): 29–51.

*The Historical Works of Giraldus Cambrensis.* Ed. Thomas Wright. Trans. Thomas Forrester and Richard Hoare. London, 1863; rpt. New York: Bohn Antiquarian, 1968.

*The History and Topography of Ireland.* Trans. John J. O'Meara. New York: Penguin, 1951.

# G

Homes, Urban T. "The *Kambriae Descriptio* of Gerald the Welshman." *Medievalia et Humanistica,* n.s., 1 (1970): 217–232.

*The Journey through Wales/The Description of Wales.* Trans. Lewis Thorpe. New York: Penguin, 1978.

Nichols, Stephen G. "Fission and Fusion: Mediations of Power in Medieval History and Literature." *Yale French Studies* 70 (1986): 21–41.

Roberts, Brynley F. *Gerald of Wales.* Cardiff: U of Wales P, 1982.

*Joseph D. Parry*

**SEE ALSO**

Barnacle Goose; Bestiaries; Crusades, First, Second, and Third; Geoffrey of Monmouth; Irish Travel; Itineraries and *Periploi; Secretz de la Nature, Les;* Stonehenge and Other Megalithic Marvels; Thule; Tides

## Gerbert of Aurillac [Sylvester II] (*c.* 945–May 12, 1003)

Scholar, author of treatises on geometry and astronomy, and later Pope Sylvester II.

Born in the Auvergne, into a family of modest circumstances, Gerbert received his education at St.-Géraud-d'Aurillac Abbey; he taught at the Reims Cathedral school, and in about 983 was appointed abbot of Bobbio Monastery. In 991, he became archbishop of Reims, where he remained until 996, and in 998, he was consecrated archbishop of Ravenna, at the insistence of Emperor Otto III (r. 983–1002), whose tutor and adviser he was. In 999, he was elected pope (the first from France). His tomb and epitaph are in the Church of St. John Lateran, in Rome.

Gerbert's work, both on secular subjects and in the field of church policy, was motivated and fostered by the idea of *renovatio imperii,* Otto III's policy of reviving or reconstructing the ancient Roman Empire within the political and religious context of a Christian theocracy. As a church leader, he greatly strengthened the churches of Poland and Hungary by founding the archdioceses of Gniezno (Poland) and Esztergom (Hungary). He sent a crown from Rome for the coronation of Hungarian King Stephen (István [r. 1000–1038]).

As a scholar, he engaged himself primarily with the quadrivium—the more advanced level of the seven liberal arts—above all with geometry, astronomy, and mathematics. His chief work, *De utilitatibus astrolabii,* comprises, in the first place, a manual on using the astrolabe, an instrument adopted from Arabic science, that can be employed to solve astronomical (and other) problems. Gerbert probably became acquainted with this instrument on an educational trip (about 967) to Catalonia, then controlled by Christians, where he stayed for three years. Gerbert not only used the astrolabe for astronomical purposes, but with it he also determined the time, established geographical latitude, and surveyed land. In his short, final description of the world's important regions and major cities, he classified these according to individual climatic zones as described by geographers and depicted on zonal (Macrobian) maps of the late antique world.

During his lifetime Gerbert was famous for his knowledge of mathematics, and he was suspected of being a wizard. He is said to have introduced Arabic numerals to the West, but this has never been proved.

Gerbert's mathematical treatise, *Regulae de numerorum abaci rationibus,* is unpretentious and gives rules for addition, subtraction, multiplication, and division, calculating with marked stones on the abacus. According to his biographer, Richer of Saint-Rémy, Gerbert built astronomical instruments—among them an armillary sphere—and demonstration models including a celestial globe by means of which he acquainted his pupils with the movements of the stars. Thietmar of Merseburg reports that Gerbert used a horologium (an astronomical clock or perhaps a sundial) to measure the altitude of Polaris.

Gerbert's geometry uses some elements of Euclid's geometry; otherwise it is based on the writings of ancient Roman surveyors. His importance to the progress of occidental astronomy and mathematics may have been overestimated by his contemporaries. Though renowned for his learning, he has not left a large legacy of writings known to have been composed by him.

**BIBLIOGRAPHY**

Bergmann, Werner. "Innovationen im Quadrivium des 10. und 11. Jahrhunderts." *Sudhoffs Archiv Beiheft* 26 (1985): 66–220.

Bubnov, Nikolai. *Arithmetische Selbständigkeit der europäischen Kultur: Ein Beitrag zur Kulturgeschichte.* Berlin: R. Friedländer und Sohn, 1914.

Gerbert of Aurillac. *Gerberti Opera mathematica, 972–1003.* Ed. Nikolai Bubnov. Berlin: R. Friedländer, 1899; rpt. Hildesheim: Ohlms, 1963.

———. *The Letters of Gerbert with His Papal Privileges as Sylvester II.* Trans. and Intro. Harriet Pratt Lattin. New York: Columbia UP, 1961.

Lindgren, Uta. "Gerbert von Aurillac und das Quadrivium: Untersuchungen zur Bildung im Zeitalter der Ottonen." *Sudhoffs Archiv Beiheft* 18 (1977).

Riché, Pierre. *Gerbert d'Aurillac, Le Pape de l'An Mille.* Paris: Fayard, 1987.

*Werner Bergmann*

SEE ALSO

Hungary; Maps; Navigation, Arab; Poland; Ptolemy; Star Maps

## German Literature, Travel in

Travel is one of the most important themes in medieval German fiction. While its direct description is not developed until the later Middle Ages, its outline can already be found by implication as early as the ninth century.

In the *Lay of Hildebrand,* an Old High German poem that dates from the 800s, a Germanic champion, now advanced in years, has traveled widely, although we learn this only through brief, almost casual references to his appearance and through the dialogue he has with the son, who faces him as his opponent. His arm rings are said to have been given him by the lord of the Huns. His son hurls the insult "old Hun" at him partly because he suspects him of craftiness, but also because he sees before him a man wearing the armor, helmet, and other equipment of a Hunnish soldier.

In the first part of their dialogue, the son gives an account of his father's flight eastward, which is later corroborated by the older man's lament that he was forced to roam the world beyond his homeland for thirty years, covering great distances on horseback during a lifetime of wandering. The implied travel history in the *Lay of Hildebrand* represents the earliest example of poetic travel depiction in German.

Longer verse narratives centered on a single hero integrate travel into the story. In the *Song of Alexander* (*c.* 1150; expanded by continuators), Alexander pursues adventures in Europe, Africa, and Asia, conquering a host of real and imaginary countries and places, then explores the ocean (in a diving bell) and the sky (raised toward the kingdom of Heaven on the wings of gryphons). Less international but similarly martial are the travels of Roland in the German *Song of Roland* (*c.* 1170), which takes the hero through most of Europe to the Pyrenees. In these works, travel description is occasionally detailed and follows a generally linear chronology, blending real world locations and legendary places.

Arthurian romances stereotypically show a hero engaged on a quest. In Hartmann von Aue's (*c.*1160–*c.*1205) *Erec,* the hero is accompanied in his travels by the heroine; in *Iwein,* he travels alone. In both romances the travel-histories are to be understood emblematically to stand for a progress through life in which maturity and moral insight are achieved gradually and painfully. The reward for strain and endeavor is mental and emotional equilibrium.

This scheme of travel, imbued with symbolism and signifying specific meaning, was perfected by Wolfram von Eschenbach (*c.*1170 to after 1220) in his *Parzival.* Both the hero and his counterpart, Gawan, move constantly from place to place. Their travel-histories are carefully organized and subtly coordinated; place-names, many of them Wolfram's invention, fix locations so that a second visit, or a subsequent mention, will recall a particular event or suggest a meaning as a geographical pattern develops. Parzival moves from the fictional wilderness in which he was raised to the country of Arthurian fable. He rides to two castles, which represent important stations in his development; at the first he receives the education appropriate for a member of the nobility, and at the second he raises the siege and marries the heiress. His third journey takes him to the Grail Castle. Up to this point, Parzival's travels are skillfully graded: the increasing distance he covers mirrors the growing demand of each encounter. He is guided by supernatural power directly to another preordained goal. At the Grail Castle, however, Parzival loses his way literally and figuratively: after his failure here, God withdraws his hand and Parzival spends years riding at random through unnamed, inhospitable landscapes until Providence relents and calls him back to the Grail.

By contrast, the landscape most tellingly associated with Gawan is idyllic, the *locus amoenus* of classical antiquity. The world through which he rides smiles on him, like his destiny. His travels are blessed by certainty and controlled by God, yet the extent of his journeys is restricted, mirroring the limitations of his mission. Parzival can reach Grail territory, Gawan cannot. Like Parzival's early travels, Gawan's are graded. The increasing architectural wonders of the castles he visits reflect the growing importance of his experiences at each location. Wolfram furnishes references to time, distance, and direction to allow mapping of events.

# G

Two landscape patterns are evident in the course of the narrative, each based on a character's ultimate goal (the Grail Castle for Parzival, the Castle of Marvels for Gawan). These travels in lands of fable are set within a framework of journeys in the real world by Parzival's father, whose fighting career takes him to all three continents, ultimately via North Africa to Toledo, where he rides into the fictional kingdom of the woman who will become the hero's mother. The worlds of reality and fantasy are thus linked and the hero's quest gains worldwide and universal importance.

In Wolfram's later work, *Willehalm,* the real world is dominant. The hero's travels are neither elaborately constructed nor endowed with symbolism, but rather are plausible itineraries. Willehalm has returned to France from the East; here he moves between three major locations (his castle at Orange, the battlefield of Aliscans, and the French court at Munleun [Laon]) in a real world of real place-names (such as Provence, Arles, Orléans, Toulouse, and Paris) whose geography, nevertheless, remains vague. This French real world is then blended with an evocative image of the East, as a Muslim army arrives from Outremer. Wolfram does not describe the Muslim advance as a linear progress from place to place, but he employs a welter of place-names, factual as well as fictitious, to suggest the soldiers' distant origins and wide-ranging journeys. To what degree Wolfram could distinguish fact from fiction in this catalogue remains an open question, nor does it matter aesthetically: the very sound of these exotic place-names conjures up remote and mysterious lands in the imagination of his audiences.

In the anonymous *Nibelungenlied (c.* 1205) too, the real world occupies the narrative foreground. The epic's geography is determined by three major journeys, each of which follows a route between the Burgundian court at Worms and the Hunnish court at "Etzelnburc" (German *Gran*). The first is a diplomatic mission bringing an offer of marriage from the Hunnish court to Worms; the second is the bridal expedition making its way to the Hunnish court; and the third describes the journey of the Burgundians to Gran on the invitation of the queen, their kinswoman. The route these travelers follow is important because it represents in part the connection between Western Europe and Byzantium. The poet presents this reiterated journey with such precision that the "road of the Nibelungs" can still be traced. His place-names are especially dense in territory along the Danube and in Austria, unsurprising in a

poet who was a south German. The first journey is portrayed in general terms: Attila's [Etzel's] envoys leave Hungary, pass through Vienna, Pöchlarn, and Bavaria, arriving twelve days later at the Rhine. The return journey is far more specific: the bride travels to Attila along the Danube via Pförring, Passau, Eferding, Enns, Pöchlarn, Melk, Mautern, and Traismauer (on the river Traisen) to Tulln, where Attila receives his bride. The wedding is celebrated in nearby Vienna, and from here king and queen journey together to Gran via Hainburg. The third journey from Worms to Gran is again sketched only in broad outline: the Burgundians proceed along the river Main, through East Franconia to Grossmehring, Passau, and Pöchlarn. The poet offers little more than a bare itinerary. Such realistic geography does not, however, characterize every journey in the *Nibelungenlied.*

Sigfrid's travels take him to fabulous places: Raised in Xanten, he visits Worms, fights in Saxony, then sails to Isenstein, a mythical place in Iceland. He rules over an imaginary Nibelungland in Norway. Reality and lands of fantasy are merged in the epic; fictional geography is associated with the two figures Sigfrid and Brunhild, who are given an almost superhuman dimension.

The taste among medieval Germans for more literal travel narratives can be measured by the success of the (admittedly fictionalized) *Book of John Mandeville,* translated into German by Michael Velser (from French) around 1393 (printed at Augsburg in 1480), and by Otto von Diemeringen (from Latin) in the mid-1390s (printed at Basel 1481/1482). Both are of high literary quality, and each version survives in approximately thirty-eight manuscripts, making up more than one-quarter of the approximately 275 surviving manuscript copies of the book in any language.

Medieval German authors not only devised travels for their fictional figures; they also traveled themselves, and this is sometimes reflected in their poetry. The most outstanding example of this is Walther von der Vogelweide (*c.*1170–1230), a minstrel who was on the road for most of his life. He claims to have begun his career at the court of the Babenberg dukes but was apparently forced to leave Vienna. Late in life he was given a fief (probably at Würzburg) and thus the opportunity to settle. He spent the intervening years wandering from place to place, earning his livelihood by entertaining. He had access to the greatest courts of his day, imperial, royal, and episcopal. For some time he followed the court of Philip II, crowned in Mainz in 1198, to Magdeburg for Christmas in 1199; two of Walther's songs suggest that he may have been present at both occasions. Walther had other patrons, including Landgrave Hermann of Thuringia (whose castle was the Wartburg) and Margrave Dietrich of Meissen. He may have performed some of his songs at Otto IV's court-day at Frankfurt in 1212. Walther visited the ducal court of Carinthia, the archiepiscopal court at Cologne, the Viennese court, and others. In 1203, he was in the retinue of the bishop of Passau; there is extraliterary evidence of extended journeys in eastern Austria. Walther refers to his many travels in two of his songs, but he was unable to attain his ultimate goals, Rome and the Holy Land.

**BIBLIOGRAPHY**

Brunner, Horst, et al. *Walther von der Vogelweide: Epoche-Werk-Wirkung.* Arbeitsbücher zur Literaturgeschichte. Munich: C.H. Beck, 1996.

Bumke, Joachim. *Wolfram von Eschenbach.* 6th edition. Stuttgart: Sammlung Metzler, 1991.

Cormeau, Christoph, and Wilhelm Störmer. *Hartmann von Aue: Epoche-Werk-Wirkung.* Arbeitsbücher zur Literaturgeschichte. Munich: C.H. Beck, 1985.

Ehrismann, Otfrid. *Nibelungenlied: Epoche-Werk-Wirkung.* Arbeitsbücher zur Literaturgeschichte. Munich: C.H. Beck, 1987.

Hardin, James, and Will Hasty, eds. *German Writers and Works of the High Middle Ages: 1170–1280.* Detroit, Washington, London: Bruccoli Clark, 1994.

Heger, Hedwig. *Das Lebenszeugnis Walthers von der Vogelweide: Die Reiserechnungen des Passauer Bischofs Wolfger von Erla.* Vienna: A. Schendl, 1970.

Jones, George F., *Walther von der Vogelweide.* Twayne's World Authors Series 46. New York: Twayne, 1968.

Wynn, Marianne. *Wolfram's Parzival: On the Genesis of Its Poetry.* Mikrokosmos 9. Frankfurt-am-Main, Berne, New York, Nancy: Peter Lang, 1984.

*Marianne Wynn*

**SEE ALSO**
Attila; *Guerrino il Meschino*; Huns; *Mandeville's Travels*; Travel Writing in Europe and the Mediterranean Regions; Walter of Châtillon

## Gervase of Tilbury (*c.* 1165–*c.* 1234)

Anglo-Norman courtier, geographer, and author of an influential work of historical-geographical content. Born into a noble family at Tilbury (Essex), Gervase probably received his basic education in England. He was a courtier of Henry II (r. 1154–1189), and later of his rebellious son Henry (the Younger), who lived mostly in France (and died in 1183). During 1176–1177, Gervase was a member of Henry II's embassy to the Sicilian court, and on his journey home he may have witnessed the reconciliation between Emperor Frederick I and Pope Alexander III in Venice in the summer of 1177. He studied canon law in Bologna beginning around 1183, and then taught it there himself. In 1189, he was in the service of William II, the last Norman king of Sicily, after whose death (on November 18, 1189), Gervase went to Arles, where he married a relative of the archbishop and joined the court of Emperor Otto IV, who named him (titular) marshal of the Kingdom of Arles. He was also a judge and, perhaps, a chancellor under Otto. In 1209, he attended the imperial coronation at Rome.

After Otto's defeat at Bouvines in 1214, Gervase's fate is unclear. Some sources attest the presence of a "magister Gervasius," a judge (once even a marshal) in Provence. It is likely, however, that Gervase ultimately followed the defeated emperor to northern Germany and received the rather modest office of prior in Ebstorf, near Lüneburg. (Documents attest the presence of a prior "Gervasius," although without the title "magister" during the years from 1223 to 1234). Further evidence that Gervase may have spent the last phase of his life in Ebstorf includes the fact that he sent his great work of history, *Otia imperialia*, to John Marcus (Johannes Gallicus), Otto's secretary and the *praepositus* (prior) at Hildesheim, to be presented to the emperor, and, above all, the connection to the Ebstorf *mappamundi*, which dates from the first half of the thirteenth century and has legends in which traces of Gervase's geographical and cosmological ideas may be found (his *Otia imperialia* is the mapmaker's most contemporaneous source).

Gervase's *Otia imperialia* (also entitled *Liber de mirabilibus mundi* and *Solatium imperatoris*) is a voluminous work dedicated to Otto IV, and probably sent to him in early 1215; an earlier lost version was written for England's Henry the Younger. Gervase's own work may be preserved in at least one (Rome, Biblioteca Apostolica Vaticana MS Vat. lat. 933) of the thirty-odd surviving Latin manuscripts; the text was twice translated into French during the Middle Ages.

*Otia imperialia* is divided into three books (*decisiones*), of which the first, based mostly on Peter

# G

Comestor's *Historia Scholastica*, is, in a sense, a commentary on Genesis (Hexaemeron), with many digressions. Book Two is a history of humankind from the Flood to the author's time, together with a description (chorography) of the inhabited earth (an *imago mundi*). Book Three, perhaps the most interesting, is an unorganized but vivid miscellany of strange and miraculous events and creatures.

From the point of view of the history of central and eastern Europe, and of the Slavs, the second book of Gervase's work contains particularly important information. The description of Europe is based mainly on the *Imago mundi* by Honorius Augustodunensis (c. 1110) and works by Paulus Orosius (his *History*, completed in 418) and Isidore of Seville (c. 560–636). Occasionally, Gervase expands considerably on his sources, perhaps depending on other texts now lost to us, or using oral testimony. Information regarding Poland is "taken from the local inhabitants" ("*ab ipsis indigenis accepi*"). Gervase's description of eastern Europe is the most accurate, credible, and modern one in a period before that of Bartholomaeus Anglicus in *De proprietatibus rerum* (c. 1240).

## BIBLIOGRAPHY

Caldwell, James R. "Manuscripts of Gervase of Tilbury's *Otia Imperialia.*" *Scriptorium* 16 (1962): 28–45.
———. "The Interrelationship of the Manuscripts of Gervase of Tilbury's *Otia Imperialia.*" *Scriptorium* 16 (1962): 246–274.
Duchesne, Annie, trans. Gervais de Tilbury. *Le Livre des merveilles. Divertissement pour un Empereur (Troisième partie)*. Paris: Belles Lettres, 1992.
Leibniz, Gottfried Wilhelm, ed. *Gervasii Tilberiensis Otia Imperialia*. In *Scriptores rerum Brunsvicensium*. Hanover: Sumptibus Nicolai Foersteri, 1707–1710, I: p. 881–1006; II: 751–784. [The only edition of the complete work.]
Richardson, Henry Gerald. "Gervase of Tilbury." *History* 46 (1961): 102–114.
Schnith, Karl. "Otto IV. und Gervasius von Tilbury. Gedanken zu den Otia Imperialia." *Historisches Jahrbuch* 82 (1963): 50–69.
Wolf, Armin. "Ikonologie der Ebstorfer Weltkarte und politische Situation des Jahres 1239. Zum Weltbild des Gervasius von Tilbury am welfischen Hofe." In *Ein Weltbild vor Columbus. Die Ebstorfer Weltkarte. Interdisziplinäres Colloquium 1988*. Ed. Hartmut Kugler and Eckard Michael. Weinheim: VCH Acta humaniora, 1991, pp. 54–116.

*Jerzy Strzelczyk*

SEE ALSO
Bartholomaeus Anglicus; Ebstorf World Map; Honorius Augustodunensis; Isidore of Seville; *Mappamundi;* Orosius

## Ghent [Gand]

A city in present-day Belgium, located at the confluence of the rivers Scheldt and Lys (Flemish *Leie*), the two main arteries connecting Flanders with the wheat-growing plains of northern France. Throughout the Middle Ages Ghent functioned as a major center of industrial production and trade in the Low Countries.

During the era of Roman rule (first century B.C.E.–fourth century C.E.), small groups of craftsmen and farmers settled at *Ganda* (from the Celtic word for river mouth); it can be assumed that they were also involved in regional trade. The whole area was only thinly populated, however, and few settlements survived the withdrawal of Roman troops around 406.

Because of its strategic location, Christian missionaries such as St. Amand (?–c. 676) selected Ganda as their base in the early Middle Ages. Firmly connected to the episcopal centers in northern France by its two important rivers, it served as an ideal gateway to the coastal plains of western and northern Flanders, still largely unexplored by missionaries. St. Amand founded two abbeys at Ganda, dedicated to St. Peter and St. Bavo; they would soon be among the best endowed monasteries in Flanders. In the vicinity of St. Bavo's, a small commercial settlement is attested in the ninth century; half a mile to the north, another small community made up mostly of craftsmen grew around a castle erected in the mid-tenth century by the first count of Flanders. The two communities merged by the year 1000 to form the medieval town of Ghent.

Signs of a vigorous textile industry at Ghent are apparent during this period. For several centuries the two great abbeys held large herds of sheep in the salt marshes of northern Flanders, where they possessed immense lands; yet at the end of the tenth century Ghent imported wool from Tournai, which suggests a demand for still more supplies. One hundred years later Ghent was even importing English wool, the start of a long tradition of intense trade relations fraught with political implications. Although the importance of the cloth industry for Ghent's economic development can hardly be overstated, the city may also owe much of its early growth to the grain trade along the Lys and to its role as a rural market for the region between the two rivers.

Ghent cityscape with rebellion of Philip van Artevelde, 1381, *Chronicles* of Jean Froissart. Berlin, Deutsche Staatsbibliothek (Preussischer Kulturbesitz), MS Dep. Breslau 1, Vol. 2, fol. 287r, *c.* 1450. Courtesy Deutsche Staatsbibliothek, Berlin.

Reliable population figures are available only for the years 1356–1358, when Ghent's economy had clearly passed its peak; however, with approximately 64,000 inhabitants it was then (still) the largest city in Flanders and the second largest city in all Europe north of the Alps (following Paris). For centuries, visitors marveled at its size and sights, while rulers heeded its military and economic power. Ghent acquired—and even cherished—a certain reputation for its frequent revolts against its sovereigns; particularly in the late fourteenth and fifteenth centuries Ghent vehemently opposed the centralizing and fiscal policies of the dukes of Burgundy.

Meanwhile, numerous internal conflicts punctuated the city's history. Until about 1300, these usually resulted from opposition between a small group of landowners monopolizing city government and a coalition of entrepreneurs, craftsmen, and laborers excluded from it. In later centuries, when Ghent's political system theoretically allowed large sections of the population to participate in the decision-making process, social peace might be disturbed by rivalry between weavers and fullers, by conflicting economic interests of various sections in the city community (some depending on cordial relations with France, others on an uninterrupted flow of goods from England), and by the presence of a large, relatively unskilled workforce living on the edge of poverty and vulnerable to both economic crises and demagogic exploitation by more powerful groups.

Ghent survived these tensions thanks to two great assets: its strict regulation of the grain trade over the Lys and Scheldt (which helped to keep food prices within manageable limits at most times) and its control over the so-called *Ghent Quarter*, its hinterland. Much like an Italian city's dominion over its *contado*, Ghent exerted political, judicial, and economic command over a large portion of rural Flanders, which tended to

# G

bear the brunt of any economic adversities the city encountered.

Ghent's medieval history truly came to a close in 1540, when Emperor Charles V (r. 1519–1558) crushed a rebellion by the town in which he had been born and raised, imposing draconian measures to curb its autonomy.

**BIBLIOGRAPHY**

Boone, Marc. *Gent en de Bourgondische hertogen ca. 1384–ca. 1453: Een sociaal-politieke studie van een staatsvormings-proces.* Brussels: Paleis der Academiën, 1990.

Decavele, Johan, ed. *Ghent: In Defense of a Rebellious City: History, Art, Culture.* Antwerp: Mercatorfonds, 1989.

Nicholas, David. *Medieval Flanders.* London and New York: Longman, 1992.

———. *The Metamorphosis of a Medieval City: Ghent in the Age of the Arteveldes, 1302–1390.* Leiden: Brill, 1987.

Verhulst, Adriaan. "The Origins of Towns in the Low Countries and the Pirenne Thesis." *Past and Present* 122 (1989): 3–35.

*Walter Simons*

**SEE ALSO**

Bruges; Crusades, Burgundian; *Fondaco;* Guilds; Inns and Accommodations

## Ghillebert de Lannoy
*See* Lannoy, Ghillebert de

## Giants

Legendary races of human beings or hominids of enormous size, often seen as the objects of wonder in geographical descriptions, and attested to in a variety of texts—scriptural, scientific, and literary—from the ancient world onward. A subject of ancient and medieval anthropology, giants were among numerous "monstrous" or imperfect human races described by authoritative classical sources such as Pliny the Elder (d. 79 C.E.), and by Christian commentators on Scripture. Beliefs that giants were the first race of humans to inhabit the earth are found in Greek, Scandinavian, Native American (Great Plains), and Judeo-Christian traditions.

Genesis 6:4 declares that "giants [*Nephilim*] were upon the earth in those days [before Noah]," and thus belief in their literal existence was widespread and based on biblical witness. Unlike most of the monstrous races described by medieval tradition, giants were usually considered to be extinct. Throughout antiquity and the Middle Ages, discoveries of fossils were described as "giants' bones": St. Augustine (354–430) declared that he had found on the seashore "a man's molar" a hundred times larger than a normal tooth. Stories were also related about giants' tombs. Boccaccio (1313–1375) recounts that at Trapani, in Sicily, peasants discovered a sealed cave containing the seated cadaver of a giant, holding a staff as tall as the mast of a ship.

Most medieval Christian writers agreed with Freculph of Lisieux (d. 852/853) who argued that all or nearly all giants had perished in Noah's Flood. Hugh of Saint-Cher (d. 1263) recorded that the Flood was sent

German giant "Theueto." Thomas of Cantimpré, *De Naturis Rerum.* Valenciennes, Bibliothèque Municipale MS 320, fol. 46v, end of thirteenth or beginning of fourteenth century. Photo by John B. Friedman.

expressly to destroy the giants. Yet the giant-lore in the Old Testament is contradictory, implying that the giants' evildoing had caused the Flood and that only Noah's family survived, yet mentioning postdiluvian giants like Goliath (I Sam. 17:4) and Og, the king of Bashan, the sole survivor "of the race of the giants [*Rephaim*]" according to Deuteronomy 3:11, which reports the preservation of his huge iron bedstead. Some Jewish scholars took this to mean that Og was the only giant to survive the Flood; the influential commentator Nicholas of Lyra (*c.* 1270–1349) derided this interpretation for contradicting Genesis 7:23, which maintains that only Noah, his sons, and their wives survived.

A further problem arose because Genesis 6:4 seems to state that giants were a special race, born from the miscegenation of the "sons of God" and the "daughters of men," an idea developed at length in the influential apocryphal Book of Enoch. While Jewish tradition read the sons of God as fallen angels, Christians generally took them to be the progeny of Adam's good son Seth (the daughters of men being Cain's offspring). After St. Augustine, the sons of Seth theory prevailed in Christian tradition. Dante's giants (*Inferno* 31), and the glosses of his commentators, reflect the orthodox consensus that giants were fully human, not semidemonic, and were extinct. The theory that fallen angels sired the giants was revived after 1400 by Western European theorists who wished to prove that witches could and did have intercourse with demons who had taken on or "assumed" bodies made of condensed air or other elements.

The major exception to this generally pejorative view of giants was St. Christopher; according to Jacobus of Voragine (*c.* 1230–1298), Christopher was a fearsome Canaanite twelve cubits tall. A convert to Christianity, he earned his name (*Christophoros*) by carrying Christ, who appeared to him as a special grace, across a flooded river. In the Eastern church, Christopher was portrayed as a cynocephalus, or dog-head, whose conversion demonstrated the power of the Logos over marginal human beings. His evolution into a giant probably happened through a combination of scribal errors and the widespread custom of making "gigantic" representations of Christopher so that he could be seen from afar and receive the prayers of wayfarers, whose patron he was. Other large-scale medieval effigies, such as those used in British and Flemish civic pageantry, were not always intended as representations of giants, but some followed the same process of gradual redefinition as Christopher.

Giants are common dwellers of remote lands in travel narratives from Homer's *Odyssey,* with its one-eyed giant Polyphemus, through such works as *The Book of John Mandeville,* and in illustrated collections of marvels like the Old English Wonders of the East texts. Certain nations like Germany were also believed to be originally made up of giant citizens, if we can believe Thomas of Cantimpré.

Except for Christopher, good giants are unknown to nonfiction of the Middle Ages; a group of belligerent giants, led by Gogmagog, inhabits Britain and must be destroyed before Brutus and his Trojan followers can settle the island, according to the foundation myth offered by Geoffrey of Monmouth, Wace, and Layomon. In romance, a few giants became good by converting to Christianity. After 1498, good giants became so frequent in patriotic historiography as to threaten the older tradition. With the growth of maritime exploration, rumors of modern giants, such as the inhabitants of Patagonia, evolved. Stories of the Abominable Snowman (*yeti*) in Tibet or "Bigfoot" ("Sasquatch") among Native Americans mark the continued belief in giants inhabiting remote geographical areas in the present day.

**BIBLIOGRAPHY**

Calmet, Augustin. "Sur les géans." In *La Sainte Bible en latin et en françois, avec des notes littérales, critiques, et historiques . . . tirées du commentaire de Dom Augustin Calmet.* 14 vols. Paris: Gabriel Martin et al., 1748–1750. 1.248–1.275.

Céard, Jean. *La nature et les prodiges: L'insolite au XVIe siècle, en France.* Travaux d'Humanisme et Renaissance. Geneva: Droz, 1977.

———. "La Querelle des géants et la jeunesse du monde." *Journal of Medieval and Renaissance Studies* 8 (1978): 37–76.

Cohen, Jeffrey Jerome. *Of Giants: Sex, Monsters, and the Middle Ages.* Minneapolis: U of Minnesota P, 1999.

Friedman, John Block. *The Monstrous Races in Medieval Art and Thought.* Cambridge: Harvard UP, 1981; rpt. Syracuse, NY: Syracuse UP, 2000.

Stephens, Walter. *Giants in Those Days: Folklore, Ancient History, and Nationalism.* Lincoln: U of Nebraska P, 1989.

———. "Witches Who Steal Penises: Impotence and Illusion in *Malleus Maleficarum*." *Journal of Medieval and Early Modern Studies* 28.3 (Fall 1998): 495–529.

*Walter Stephens*

# G

SEE ALSO

Eastern Christianity; Geoffrey of Monmouth; Gog and Magog; *Mandeville's Travels;* Monstrosity, Geographical; Pliny the Elder; *Wonders of the East*

## Godfrey of Viterbo (1125–1192/1200)

Author of *Pantheon* (1187–1191), a world chronicle and "mirror for princes" intended by its author to provide an ancient descent for the Hohenstaufen dynasty and to describe and magnify the great deeds of kings and emperors of the imperial line.

Godfrey was born in Viterbo, an Italian town on the edge of the papal state and empire; he was educated in the famous cathedral school of Bamberg and trained in the papal chancery. In 1152, he entered into the service of Frederick Barbarossa, who was waiting to seize power at King Conrad III's deathbed at Bamberg. Godfrey went on to serve Frederick all his life, partly as chaplain and diplomat, partly as personal secretary and tutor to his children. His *Pantheon,* entitled the *Speculum regum* in its original version, was intended to instruct the young princes. Particularly noteworthy is his attempt to include in his chronicle the characteristics of Christian culture and society as such. For his chronicle structure, Godfrey relies on the *Chronica* of Otto of Freising (c. 1112–1158), and the *Historica Scholastica* of Peter Comestor [c. 1100–1180], which synchronizes pagan and Christian history, leaving out the scholarly disputation and adding numerous tales about kings and emperors.

Godfrey claimed that he wrote his stories on horseback, never knowing the tranquillity of the scholar's cell, but doing his work in the turmoil of battle and the uproar at court. In Frederick's service he traveled widely, once to Spain, often to France, and forty times to Rome. There he met with scholars and ambassadors. He wrote that "Greeks from Constantinople, Saracens from Babylon, Persians and Armenians who came to the imperial or papal court . . . have frequently offered me information and, when occasion arose, delivered their writings into my hands." Even if these words are exaggerated, it is known that diplomats and scholars of the time did collect material and exchange information while en route on their princes' behalf.

The main theme in the work is that, in the course of time, mankind discovered the benefits of civilization: how to cook, build a town, make music, or use medicines to cure the sick. By learning from the skills of others, people built an ordered, civilized society. But they succeeded only because they chose to live under the government of an imperial leader. The first of these was Jupiter, who was civilization personified. His successors include the Trojan and Greek kings and the Roman emperors, whose imperial diadem had been passed down to Frederick Barbarossa in Godfrey's own time. The world traveler Alexander the Great was the first prince on earth who realized the potentialities of world dominion, and thus his life story as told in Godfrey's *Pantheon* emblematizes the history of mankind seeking a civilized society. Sibylline prophecies and the so-called Alexander correspondence are incorporated into the world chronicle to help Godfrey fabricate a life story of Alexander the Great.

According to Godfrey's book, Alexander the Great, on his journey to the Far East, was confronted by the tribes of Gog and Magog, savage peoples who ate wolves, frogs, and even their own parents' bodies. These he decided to wall up behind high mountains, a well-timed intention, since Alexander's action coincided with God's determination to move them. He later encountered the utopian Brahmins, who—for very different reasons—also seemed to be uncivilized to Alexander, since they employed no tools or agriculture. Alexander asked their king, Dindymus, how they organized their government, religion, military activities, trade, and commerce. He himself explained that he ruled over a highly cultured realm, in which he established laws and administered justice. His word was law, and his subjects delighted in architecture, viticulture, music, and delicate cuisine. Moreover, they were acquainted with technical discoveries and military science, though he had nothing to say of trade and commerce. Alexander's fabled encounter with the king of the Brahmins is skillfully molded to portray Alexander as the ideal world emperor, a challenging example for Godfrey's own emperor, Frederick Barbarossa, then planning a crusade to the East, and Frederick's son, Henry VI.

## BIBLIOGRAPHY

Godfrey of Viterbo, *Pantheon.* Ed. J. Pistorius. *Rerum a Germanis Gestarum Historiae,* 2 (Frankfurt, 1613); partial edition in *Monumenta Germaniae Historica. Scriptores,* 22. Ed. G. Waitz. Hanover: Hahnianus, 1872, pp. 107–307.

Hausmann, Friedrich. "Gottfried von Viterbo: Kapellan und Notar, Magister, Geschichtsschreiber und Dichter." In *Friedrich Barbarossa: Handlungsspielräume und Wirkungsweisen des staufischen Kaisers.* Ed. Alfred Haverkamp.

Vorträge und Forschungen 40. Sigmaringen: Thorbecke, 1992, pp. 603–621.

Mulder-Bakker, Anneke B. "A Pantheon Full of Examples: The World Chronicle of Godfrey of Viterbo." In *Exemplum et Similitudo: Alexander the Great and other heroes as points of reference in medieval literature,* ed. Wim J. Aerts et al. Groningen: Forsten, 1988, pp. 85–98.

*Anneke B. Mulder-Bakker*

SEE ALSO

Ambassadors; Diplomacy; Gog and Magog; *Nuremberg Chronicle;* Otto of Freising

## Gog and Magog

An imagined race living in the region of the Caucasus and sometimes identified with the Jews in exegetical and millennialist writing.

This people, while of biblical origin, assumed a life and features of their own in the early Middle Ages. Exegetical, literary, historical, and even cartographic sources demonstrate their impact on Western culture from the seventh to the seventeenth century.

The medieval legend of Gog and Magog was based on the New Testament's distortion of "Gog from the land of Magog" (Ezekiel 38–39) as "Gog and Magog" in Revelation 20:7–8. The peoples thus invented found their way into popular culture, especially the medieval legends of Alexander the Great, who was said to have walled them up behind a great gate of brass. Peter Comestor's identification, in his *Historia Scholastica* (*c.* 1169–*c.* 1173), of Gog and Magog with the Ten Lost Tribes of Israel set the tone for centuries to come: Gog and Magog assumed a central role in a prediction that the Antichrist would be a Jew, born of the tribe of

Gog and Magog. Detail, the extreme north-northeast (left center edge) of the Ebstorf Map showing Gog and Magog. The text reads "Hic inclusit Alexander duas gentes immundas Gog et Magog, quas comites habebit Antichristus. Hii humanis carnibus vescuntur et sanguinem bibunt." (Here Alexander enclosed the two unclean peoples Gog and Magog. Antichrist will control their lords. They devour human flesh and drink blood.) Reproduced from a facsimile in the Map Division of the New York Public Library. Reproduced by permission of the Map Division, The New York Public Library (Astor, Lenox and Tilden Foundations).

# G

Dan (one of the Ten Lost Tribes), who would gather Jews from their dispersion and rebuild the temple at Jerusalem.

The association of Gog and Magog with Jews inverted actual social relations: the unarmed pariahs of Western Europe were reinvented as a dangerous horde of militant orientals. The Mongols and the Turks (to name the most prominent of Christendom's foes) would each be interpreted, in their turn, as Gog and Magog—the former, most famously, by Matthew Paris, and the latter by Martin Luther.

## BIBLIOGRAPHY

Anderson, Andrew Runni. *Alexander's Gate, Gog and Magog, and the Inclosed Nations.* Cambridge, MA: The Mediaeval Academy of America, 1932.

Gow, Andrew. "Gog and Magog on *mappaemundi* and early printed world maps: Orientalizing ethnography in the apocalytic tradition." *Journal of Early Modern History* 2.1 (1998): 61–88.

Manselli, Raoul. "I popoli immaginari: Gog e Magog." In *Popoli e Paesi nella cultura altomedievale: 23–29 aprile, 1981. Settimane di studio del Centro italiano de studi sol'alto Medioevo, 29.* Spoleto: Presso la sede del Centro, 1983, vol. 2, pp. 487–517.

*Andrew C. Gow*

## SEE ALSO

Matthew Paris; Mongols; Ottoman Turks; Red Jews; Seljuk Turks; Ten Lost Tribes, The

## Gold Trade in Africa

A driving force behind the early economic prosperity of the Islamic Mediterranean, and a conduit for European interests in Africa. Gold, as well as other commodities such as slaves, ivory, and hides, was exchanged for salt and copper in central Africa by camel-borne Muslim merchants from North Africa. This gold entered the European economy through Italian merchants, who traded staples and cheap manufactured goods with the cities of the *Maghrib* (northwest Africa), and, later, by the Portuguese, who circumvented the trans-Saharan caravan routes by sail.

Arabo-Islamic expansion in North Africa allowed the gold resources of the *bilād al-Sūdān* ("the land of the Blacks"—stretching across central Africa) to be effectively exploited for the first time. From the eighth century, caravans followed three routes: from Egypt, *Ifrīqiyya* (Tunisia and Algeria), and Morocco, to the African kingdoms of Ghana and Mali, which in succession controlled access to the rich gold fields to the south. In the eleventh century, unrest in *Ifrīqiyya*, and the consolidation of political power in Morocco under the Umayyads of Spain (786–1031), the Almoravids (1054–1147), and the Almohads (1147–1248), led trade routes both to diversify and to gravitate toward the west. Gold continued to reach *Ifrīqiyya*, but the main northern caravan terminus was Sijilmassa, in Morocco. Capital of the often autonomous region of Tafilelt, Sijilmassa was favored by its proximity to the mines of Taghaza, from where salt was carried to Walata on the southern fringe of the Sahara. Sijilmassa was founded in the mid-eighth century and flourished until its sack in 1209. It gradually declined until, after a brief revival under the Marinids (1248–1465), it faded into oblivion.

The wealth of the gold trade is attested to by contemporary travelers who crossed the Sahara: Ibn Hawqal (tenth century), Ibn Battūta (fourteenth century), and Leo Africanus (fifteenth century). Leo reported that the natives of Gao brought so much gold to market that they were unable to trade all of it. These riches attracted the merchants of Genoa and Pisa to *Ifrīqiyya* in the eleventh century and, as the cities of the area became increasingly dependent on Italian trade, the gold effectively bypassed and ceased to benefit their economies. The fourteenth century saw the decline of the Moroccan routes and the revival of the trade via Tunisia and Egypt.

Timbuktu, on the Niger and fifty-one days' trek from Sijilmassa, became the entrepôt of the rich Muslim kingdom of Mali. From its foundation (c. 1100), Timbuktu was a nexus for Saharan nomads and riverine African tribes. Gaining importance under the Mali dynasty (1336–1443), it displaced Walata as the main southern trading center. With the Songhoys (1468–1591), it reached its apogee; famous for its wealth and as a center of Islamic learning and culture. In 1470, Benedetto Dei, a representative of the Portinari bankers of Florence, set up shop in Timbuktu, the first European to do so. Meanwhile, demand for African gold was drawing the attention of the Portuguese. Nuño Tristam rounded the Sahara by ship in 1445, and in the 1480s, São Jorge de Mina was established on Africa's west coast. This fortress outpost offered direct access to the gold-producing Akan forest, and was able to ship 400 kilograms of gold back to Portugal yearly. This opened the resources of central Africa to direct exploitation by Europeans, and the role of Muslim trans-Saharan caravans in this trade declined.

African gold was the engine of Muslim economic prosperity in the Mediterranean, and fueled the political and military successes of Fāṭimid Egypt, Umayyad Spain, and Almoravid and Almohad Morocco. With their salt and copper, Muslim traders brought urbanization and Islam to central Africa and drew its people onto the stages of Islamic and Western history. The wealth of this trade stimulated the interest of Europeans and contributed to a certain economic lethargy in Islamic North Africa; thus, within the fruits of success, it bore the seeds of decline.

## BIBLIOGRAPHY

Abun-Nasr, Jamil M. *A History of the Maghrib in the Islamic Period*. Cambridge: Cambridge UP, 1987.

Brett, Michael. "Ifriqiya as a Market for Saharan Trade from the Tenth to the Twelfth Century A.D." *Journal of African History* 10.3 (1969): 347–364.

Bovill, E.W. *The Golden Trade of the Moors*. London: Oxford UP, 1958.

Levtzion, Nehemia. *Ancient Ghana and Mali*. London: Methuen, 1973.

Niane, Djibril Tamsir. *Le Soudan occidental au temps des grands empires: XIe–XVIe siècle*. Paris: Présence Africaine, 1975.

*Brian Catlos*

## SEE ALSO

African Trade; Caravans; Genoa; Ibn Battūta; Ivory Trade; Muslim Travelers and Trade; Pisa; Portugal and Spain; Sijilmassa

## Golden Horde

The westernmost of the domains established by the descendants of Chinggis Khân's son Jöchi in the early 1200s, also known as the Qipchaq khânate. According to some traditional accounts, the Horde's name, "Zolotaya Orda" in Russian, reflected the impression the glittering Mongol encampment on the Volga River produced on Russian eyewitnesses.

In its heyday, the Golden Horde [Altun-ordu] comprised the Pontic and Caspian steppes, Crimea, the Bulgar country on the Volga and Kama, the northern Caucasus, the Ural basin, and certain territories further east. It also controlled the Russian principalities of Ryazan, Vladimir-Suzdal, Tver, Kiev, and Galicia. Its economy rested on pastoralism and on taxation of caravan trade between Europe, Persia, Central Asia, and China. In the later 1300s, plague weakened the Horde's towns, and in the 1390s, its key administrative and commercial centers were sacked by the Central Asian conqueror Tamerlane [Timur-i-lenk]. In the fifteenth century, the erosion of the Horde's economic base, dynastic rivalries, and clashes between nomads and sedentaries exacerbated separatism. By the mid-fifteenth century, the Horde had fragmented, and its nomadic remnant, the Great Horde, fell in 1502.

The Horde that emerged from the Mongol campaigns of 1237–1241 had a markedly Turkic ethnic character. The armies of its founder, Batu (1227–1255), consisted mostly of Turkic nomads, and the Horde continued to absorb local Turkic speakers. Unlike the Mongols of China or Persia, the Horde never espoused local sedentary culture. The future pattern of the Horde's foreign alliances and rivalries was partly molded by its first serious crisis, under Batu's successor, Berke. Having lost Khwarizm to Alghu, the Chaghatai khân of Turkestan, in 1262–1265, Berke balked at letting Hülegü, the Mongol khân of Persia, control the pastures and caravan routes of Azerbaijan, a region that thereafter was the bane of the Horde's khâns. To outflank Hülegü, Berke sought alliance with Egypt. This helped check the Mongol advance in Syria and promoted Islam within the Horde. In 1262–1266, the conflict with Hülegü disrupted trade with Persia, and the Horde accepted a strategic peace with Byzantium. Berke's successor, Möngke Temür [Mangu Timur] (1266–1280), remained at odds with the Chaghatai, against whom he sided with Qaidu of the house of Ögedëi. He also supported Qaidu's bid for empire against Khubilai Khân, and from this point on the names of the great khâns ceased to figure on the Horde's coins.

Islamization progressed under Tuda Mangu (1280–1287), who was succeeded by Tula-buqa (1287–1290), nephew of Möngke Temür. In Russia, the Horde perfected its system of indirect rule through native princes supervised by resident Mongol representatives (*baskaks*). Real power in the Horde belonged to a Jochid from a junior branch, Berke's old general Nogai, who was finally unseated in 1296–1299 by Toqtai, a son of Möngke Temür. Under Toqtai, relations with Italian merchants worsened, and in 1307–1308, the khân besieged the Genoese colony of Kaffa (Crimea). Tensions persisted until 1312. Toqtai's successor 'Abd

# G

Allah Khân Özbeg (1313–1341), under whom the Horde reached its zenith, formally converted to Islam, strengthening ties with the Mamluks (1323). The conversion did not prevent continued toleration of Christians, however, and good relations with Genoa and Venice were restored by 1316–1332. The Mongol administration of Russia was overhauled, and the *baskaks* were replaced with nonresident envoys (*posoly*). Exploiting Russian internal rivalries, in 1327 the Horde used Muscovite troops to suppress a revolt in Tver (Kalinin Region).

Under Khân Janibeg (1340–1357), the diplomatic influence of Mamluk Egypt intensified, and Islamization accelerated. Relations with the Italians worsened again from 1343 onward, and tensions persisted until 1350. Although Janibeg briefly occupied Azerbaijan in 1355–1358, realizing his predecessors' old dream, the Horde's power was waning, and anarchy prevailed after Berdibeg (1357–1359). The 1370s brought unrest among the Russian princes, a rise in the power of Vladimir-Suzdal as the leading Russian state, and a diminution of tribute payments. Campaigns against the Genoese in Crimea also failed, and the Italians now controlled the area between Sudak and Balaklava.

The Golden Horde was revitalized by Toqtamish (1377–1395), khân of the White Horde (based southeast of the Urals). The Horde's real master at this point was Mamai or Mamaq, a non-Chinggisid khân-maker. Mamai found himself caught between the Russians, who defeated him on Kulikovo Field in 1380, and Toqtamish, who beat him on the river Kalka. Having united the two Hordes, Toqtamish brought the Russian principalities to heel in 1381–1382. Disaster, in the form of an epic confrontation with Tamerlane, was only ten years away, however. Like his predecessors, Toqtamish strove to control Azerbaijan. When Tamerlane seized it, Toqtamish invaded Transoxiana in 1387–1389. Tamerlane counterattacked in 1391, but Toqtamish was able to rebuild his forces and make an alliance with the Mamluk sultan Barquq. In 1395, Tamerlane, therefore, struck again, this time at the urban centers of Hajji-Tarkhan [Astrakhan] and Old and New Sarai, which he destroyed in the winter of 1395–1396, paralyzing the horde's trade. Toqtamish aggravated this paralysis by attacking the Genoese in Crimea in 1396–1397. In 1397–1398, he was ousted in a devastating civil war by the emir Idiqu [Edigei], chief of the Nogai Horde.

Until 1412–1415 real power belonged to Idiqu, and Toqtamish's brother, Shadi-beg (1400–1407) was only a puppet khân. The horde managed to reassert its control over Russia in 1400–1408, only to see the gains eroded during fratricidal struggles between the descendants of Urus, Toqtamish, and other pretenders, even though the khân Ulu Muhammad (1427–1437) still proved able to manipulate Muscovite politics. Expelled from Sarai by Kuchuk Muhammad (1437–1460), Ulu finally seized power in Kazan, where he and his son founded an independent khânate. By then, other splinter khânates were separating from the horde; its western provinces gradually fell to the dukes of Lithuania, and disintegration became irreversible. Outside the horde's diminished core were now arrayed the khânates of Kasimov (dependent on Moscow); Crimea (dependent on Ottoman Turkey from 1477); the "Swift" Horde of Sa'id Amed, between the Don and the Dnieper, scattered in 1455 by the Crimean khân; the Nogai Horde; the khânate of Astrakhan; and the Shaybanid Horde of western Siberia.

The final collapse of the horde's nomadic remnant, now called the Great Horde, occurred under Akhmat Khân (1465–1481), a son of Kuchuk Muhammad. Akhmat found himself pitted in a trial of strength against Ivan III, grand prince of Muscovy. While Akhmat sought the help of the Polish-Lithuanian Commonwealth and the Livonian knights, Ivan III sought that of the Crimean khân Mengli Girei, the Nogai Horde, and the khânate of Kazan. Akhmat waged war unsuccessfully against Moscow in 1471–1472, and sometime thereafter Ivan III ceased paying him tribute. After Ivan's failure to seek reconciliation, Akhmat marched on Moscow in 1480, trusting in the support of Casimir IV of Poland. Pressed by the onset of winter, he finally withdrew from the Ugra River without a decisive battle, and the following year he met his death at the hands of the Shaybanid Horde. His son sought to renew hostilities against Moscow with Lithuanian support, but in 1502, Ivan's ally, the Crimean khân Mengli Girei, attacked Sarai and scattered the last remnants of the Great Horde.

**BIBLIOGRAPHY**

Fedorov-Davydov, German A. *The Culture of the Golden Horde Cities.* Trans. H. Bartlett Wells. Oxford: British Archaeological Reports, 1984.

Grekov, Boris D. *La Horde d'or et la Russie: La domination tatare au XIIIe et au XIVe siècle, de la Mer Jaune à la Mer Noire.* Trans. François Thuret. Paris: Payot, 1961.

Grousset, René. *The Empire of the Steppes.* Trans. Naomi Walford. 1st English edition. New Brunswick, NJ: Rutgers UP, 1970. 1st French edition. Paris: Payot, 1939.

G

Halperin, Charles J. *The Tatar Yoke.* Columbus, OH: Slavica
Publishers, 1985.
———. *Russia and the Golden Horde. The Mongol Impact on
Medieval Russian History.* London: Tauris, 1987.

*Martin Malcolm Elbl*

**SEE ALSO**
Black Death; Chaghatai Khânate; Cumans; Genoa; Hülegü;
Merchants, Italian; Nomadism and Pastoralism; Ottoman
Empire; Russia and Rus'; Tamerlane; Venice

## Gough Map

A unique and important itinerary map of Britain, dating from the mid- to late fourteenth century and measuring 22 by 46.5 inches.

The origin and, for that matter, the specific use of
the map is unknown. Its outline of England's southeast
(top right, since the map is oriented to the east), which
derives apparently from contemporary portolan charts,
is much more precise than the rest of the island's outline. However, the internal relationships between specified locales on the map is, with few exceptions,
impressively correct. Cities and towns are accurately
marked along, or according to, the countryside's highlighted river system. The roads drawn between destinations seem to represent particular itineraries. Distances
of each segment of these itineraries are written in
locally measured miles, which tend to vary somewhat
throughout the country; thus, the map's own differing
numerical quantifiers and also its irregular scale makes
the map as a whole inconsistently balanced. Nevertheless, it presents a much more detailed and, in modern
terms, accurate picture of Britain than does Matthew
Paris's map of the island (*c.* 1250).

As P.D.A. Harvey contends, one must view the
Gough Map as "a collection of itineraries," the accuracy of which "hint[s] at cartographic principles then
unknown outside the Mediterranean" (73). Moreover,
the mystery that surrounds its inception makes its
sophistication all the more intriguing. Even though its
makers and its application remain unknown, this map
powerfully exemplifies the sequential, "narrative" character that inheres in the pictorial, as well as the more
common verbal, maps of the Middle Ages. The map's
first known owner was Thomas Martin, an antiquary
of Suffolk; Richard Gough (1735–1809), author of
several books on British topography, acquired it when
Martin's collection was sold (hence its name). Gough

left his remarkable collection of books and manuscripts
to the Bodleian Library, Oxford, where the map is
today MS Gough Gen. Top. 16.

**BIBLIOGRAPHY**
Alexander, Jonathan J.G. "Mapping the Medieval World."
*Journal of Historical Geography* 16 (1990): 230–233.
Harley-Woodward. Vol. 1 (esp. color plate 40). See Gen. Bib.
Harvey, P.D.A. *Medieval Maps.* Toronto: U of Toronto P;
London: British Library, 1991.
Parsons, E.J.S. *The Map of Great Britain circa A.D. 1360
Known as the Gough Map. An Introduction to the Facsim-
ile.* Oxford: Oxford UP, 1958.

*Joseph D. Parry*

**SEE ALSO**
Itineraries and *Periploi;* Maps; Matthew Paris; Measurement
of Distances; Portolan Charts

## Great Wall

A system of defensive structures, in Chinese called
*chang cheng* ("long walls"), originally constructed
beginning in the fourth century B.C.E. to delineate the
often unstable boundary between the "archers"
(nomads) and the "robed-ones" (Chinese).

For the most part, the wall that can be seen today
dates from the Ming dynastic period (1368–1644) and
was built in the late fifteenth and sixteenth centuries.
The Ming wall has a core of tamped earth faced with
brick and stone. Its average height is eight meters
(approximately twenty-six feet) and its width is
approximately seven meters (twenty-three feet) at the
base and six meters (nineteen and a half feet) at the top.
Fortified watchtowers with embrasures for cannon are
built into the wall at strategic positions. From the Gulf
of Bohai in the Yellow Sea it threads its way westward
for some 4,000 kilometers (2,500 miles) to the Gansu
corridor on the southern edge of Inner Mongolia,
roughly following the northern edge of loess deposits
and the contours of the mountains of northern China.

Earlier dynasties also built walls, but they tended to
be farther north and not as impressive. The Qin ruler
Shihuangdi (r. 246–210 B.C.E.) mobilized huge levies
of forced laborers to construct the first continuous system of defensive walls along the northern frontier. In
doing so, he utilized large sections of already completed defensive structures built during the Warring
States period (406–221 B.C.E.) by states such as Yan

# G

and Zhao. Qin wall-building efforts were directed against the threat posed to China by an increasingly powerful Xiongnu nomadic confederation. When the short-lived Qin collapsed, the Former Han (206 B.C.E.–8 C.E.) and the Later Han (25–220) dynasties continued the Qin practice of building walls to protect China from the danger of Xiongnu attack. Other wall-building dynasties followed, including the Northern Wei (386–557), which was confronted by Rouran power; the Northern Qi (550–577) and Sui (581–618), which were threatened by Turkic nomads; and the Jin (1115–1234) and Ming (1368–1644), which faced a serious challenge from Mongols.

On the other hand, some dynasties, such as the Tang (618–907 C.E.), Song (960–1127), Southern Song (1127–1276), and Qing (1644–1912) did not rely heavily on fortified walls and frontier defenses. They chose instead to utilize institutions of diplomacy, particularly intermarriage, trade, and the exchange of tribute for court bestowals, to promote peace and stability by providing nomads with grain, silk, and other essential goods in exchange for horses, furs, and other products of a pastoral society.

Throughout history, the foreign policy adopted by Chinese courts for dealing with nomadic neighbors fluctuated from peaceful coexistence based on diplomacy and trade, to outright efforts to conquer nomadic rivals, to attempts to seal off frontiers and adopt a policy of isolation. Some dynasties at one time or another explored all three options. As a consequence, depending on foreign policy formulations, the commitment of Chinese courts to maintain the Great Wall and a military presence to fortify it varied dramatically from period to period.

The existence of the Great Wall, or during times of neglect the remnants of earlier parapets, has been for more than 2,000 years a constant reminder of the fundamental incompatibility of the agrarian society of China with the nomadic pastoral society of the steppe. Fearing this incompatibility and also the rowdy nature of frontier society, the Chinese created the Great Wall as a barrier not only to nomadic migration southward, but also to Chinese peasant migration northward. It was utilized to keep disruptive elements in both societies apart.

The Great Wall remains an important historical symbol. For some it provides evidence of China's historical greatness; for others, given the raw power needed to build and maintain the wall, it represents tangible proof of the authoritarian nature of traditional Chinese government; for others it is a key definer of China's northernmost boundary; and for still others, it suggests China's historical preoccupation with its northern frontier and the seemingly constant threat posed to China by nomads. This preoccupation contributed to China's ineffective response to Western encroachment before, during, and after the First Opium War (1840–1842) in China.

**BIBLIOGRAPHY**

Blunden, Caroline, and Mark Elvin. *Cultural Atlas of China.* New York: Facts on File, 1983.

Jagchid, Sechin, and Van Jay Symons. *Peace, War, and Trade along the Great Wall.* Bloomington, IN: Indiana UP, 1989.

Lattimore, Owen. *Inner Asian Frontiers of China.* New York: American Geographical Society, 1940.

Waldron, Arthur. *The Great Wall of China.* Cambridge: Cambridge UP, 1990.

*Van Jay Symons*

**SEE ALSO**
Mongols; Nomadism and Pastoralism; Textiles, Decorative

## Greenland
*See* Viking Discoveries and Settlements

## Gregory of Tours, St.

An influential bishop and historian in sixth-century Gaul important for the propagation of miraculous events at pilgrimage sites in Gaul and for some awareness of early trade with Egypt.

Georgius (later Gregorius) Florentius (538/539–594) was born in Clermont-Ferrand of an aristocratic Gallo-Roman family and became metropolitan bishop of Tours in 573, a position of great responsibility and power. As bishop he had access to many important manuscripts that enabled him to become a well-informed historian. Gaul was ruled by the Merovingian dynasty from around 400 to 751; Gregory's *Historia Francorum* is largely an eyewitness account of four Merovingian kings, Sigibert I (king of Austrasia, 561–575), Chilperic I (king of Neustria, 561–584), Childebert II (king of Austrasia, 575–595), and Guntram (king of Burgundy and Orléans, 561–592).

Gregory's writings fall into two main categories, hagiography and history. The hagiographical writings, including lives of Saints Julian and Martin, focus less on the lives of individual saints than on their shrines and supernatural events reputed to have happened there.

Gregory's historical work consists of the ten books of the *Historia Francorum,* sometimes called the *Historiae,* without which our knowledge of sixth-century Gaul would be greatly impoverished. The work begins with a universal view of the world from the time of the Creation and becomes increasingly centered on France, with only occasional information about neighboring areas. The second half of the *Historiae* covers the years 580–593, ending with the death of Guntram.

Although focused on Gaul, Gregory's *Historiae* occasionally recognizes the wider world. He notes that an ascetic from Nice restricted himself, during Lent, to "Egyptian herbs, which merchants brought home for him," and he pictures ships from the "Indies" anchored in the Gulf of Suez, claiming as well that certain travelers describe many monasteries along the Nile (Thorpe, 92,333, 74–75).

To these books may be added Gregory's *Liber Vitae Patrum,* the incomplete *In Psalterii tractatum commentarius,* and the *De Cursu stellarum ratio,* also known as *De Cursibus ecclesiasticis,* which includes a descriptive list of the wonders of the world and a method for determining the time of singing the night office according to the position of the stars. The *Liber de miraculis beati Andreae Apostoli* and the *Passio sanctorum martyrum septem dormientium apud Ephesum* are also generally held to be by Gregory. His feast day is celebrated on November 17.

**BIBLIOGRAPHY**

Gregory of Tours. *Opera.* Ed. Wilhelm Arndt and Bruno Krusch. MGH Scriptores Rerum Merovingicarum. 1. Hanover: Hahn, 1885.

———. *The History of the Franks.* Ed. and Trans. Lewis Thorpe. Harmondsworth: Penguin, 1974.

James, Edward. *The Franks.* Oxford: Blackwell, 1988.

Wallace-Hadrill, J.M. *The Long-Haired Kings and Other Studies in Frankish History.* London: Methuen; New York: Barnes and Noble, 1962.

*Robert Penkett*

**SEE ALSO**
Egypt; Pilgrimage, Christian

## Guerrino il Meschino

Early-fifteenth-century Tuscan prose narrative by Andrea da Barberino (*c.* 1371–*c.* 1431) fusing the theme of exploration with traditional chivalric material.

The masterwork of the most important Italian chivalric author before Ariosto (1477–1533), *Guerrino* perfectly encapsulates a century and a half of Italian merchant and missionary travel experiences. Medieval in style and content, it is imbued with a proto-Renaissance spirit. Of Andrea's nine prose works, *Guerrino* enjoyed the widest circulation, reaching Padua, Ferrara, Bologna, Venice, Umbria, Naples, and Sicily during the fifteenth century. It was translated into French and Spanish in the early sixteenth century and versified (*c.* 1543) by Tullia d'Aragona. The text survives in fifteen manuscripts and underwent numerous printings from 1473 until 1967, although it lacks a reliable critical edition. According to the manuscripts, its original title was *Il Meschino di Durazzo.*

The author of *Guerrino* was a professional storyteller who recited his texts in the public squares and wrote them down for individual readers. He was well versed in the Italian and French vernacular literatures of his day and produced more skillfully written texts than those of contemporary street singers. Living in Florence, he would have learned much about foreign lands from the city's international bankers, merchants, and pilgrims. Textual evidence in one exemplar of *Guerrino* itself indicates that Andrea had traveled to Rome (Oxford, Bodleian Library MS Canon. Ital. 27, fol. 38v). He may also have visited Paris.

While the framing books of the eight-part *Guerrino* echo the conventions of chivalric literature, the middle portion is an original compendium of late medieval facts and beliefs about Asia, North Africa, and Europe, meticulously giving more than 700 discrete toponyms and identifying rivers, seas, oceans, mountains, cities, regions, and kingdoms. Unlike the fantastic or imprecisely drawn landscapes of many romances, Guerrino's voyage can be charted on a map. His complex itinerary does not follow a single model, but splices together the routes followed by the legendary Alexander the Great with itinerary segments from actual commercial and pilgrimage travels on land and sea. Writing in a quasi-historiographic style, Andrea gives distances or times for travel between points, as well as descriptions of terrain, climate, culture, and local economies. One identifiable cartographic source is Ptolemy's *Geographia,* translated into Latin *c.* 1406 by Jacopo Angelo of Scarperia. For other details, Andrea probably relied on contemporary maps and portolan charts.

The young hero Guerrino—Andrea's own invention—is descended from the royal house of France, and

# G

his adventures occur during the time of the legendary Charlemagne. When Guerrino was still an infant, Turks deposed his father, Milone, from his kingdom at Durazzo and imprisoned him and his wife. Thanks to a nurse the baby escaped, but he was captured by pirates in the Aegean Sea and sold to a Christian merchant from Constantinople. Guerrino became a page at the Byzantine court, befriended the imperial heir, and fell in love with the emperor's daughter. The mockery that he endured as a result of his apparently humble status prompted his arduous journey to discover his lineage. After traveling purposefully throughout the "three parts of the world," Guerrino eventually regains his realm, frees his parents, marries a Persian princess, and sires a new generation of heroes.

Andrea incorporates learned and popular material regarding travel and international commerce seamlessly into a believable fiction. He includes material about the East from classical mythology; the Trees of the Sun and Moon from the Alexander Romance; and Prester John, the Cumaean Sibyl, and St. Patrick's Purgatory from medieval legends. He describes foreign races, notes the pilgrimage sites of different religions, and includes information about matters connected to international trade, such as ports, shipping, the pepper harvest, and exports. Andrea also introduces the "wonders of the East"—exotic beasts (the trained war elephant, rhinoceros, and crocodile) and races (giants, pygmies, cannibals, and wild men)—in a naturalistic tone, but he leaves out highly improbable monsters.

A veritable cultural phenomenon in Italy, *Guerrino's* popularity has endured, although not always for the same reasons that delighted its medieval readership. By the nineteenth century, the story had entered Italian folklore, furnishing material for Neapolitan and Sicilian puppet theaters. It was produced as a play in Argentina (*c.* 1912), and was recently novelized by Gesualdo Bufalino (1993).

## BIBLIOGRAPHY

Allaire, Gloria. "Portrayal of Muslims in Andrea da Barberino's *Guerrino il Meschino*." In *Medieval Christian Perceptions of Islam: A Book of Essays.* Ed. John Victor Tolan. Garland Medieval Casebooks 10. New York: Garland, 1996, pp. 243–269.

———. "The Secular Pilgrimage of an Errant Knight: Andrea da Barberino's *Guerrino il Meschino*." *Romance Languages Annual* 5 (1993): 148–152.

Hawickhorst, Heinrich. "Über die Geographie bei Andrea de' Magnabotti." *Romanische Forschungen* 13 (1902): 689–784.

Osella, Giacomo. "Il Guerrin Meschino." *Pallante* 10, fasc. 9–10 (1932): 11–173.

*Gloria Allaire*

SEE ALSO

Animals, Exotic; Cannibalism; Elephants; Giants; Itineraries and *Periploi;* Merchants, Italian; Ottoman Turks; Pepper; Pilgrimage, Christian; Portolan Charts; Prester John; Ptolemy; Purgatory, St. Patrick's; Rome as a Pilgrimage Site; Wild People, Mythical, and New World Relations

## Guido

Late-eleventh- or early-twelfth-century Italian cosmographer who compiled an encyclopedic work in prose.

The complete *Liber Guidonis* contains a prologue and seven "books" with internal divisions. The book's principal contents are: (1) an early toponymic description of the Italian peninsula, a history and description of ancient Rome, the Antonine itinerary, and a periplus; (2) information about the Roman Empire drawn from Isidore's *Etymologies;* (3) a geographical description of the earth based largely on *Etymologies* 14. 2–5; (4) a history of the world (based on "Hieronymus Presbyter" [Pseudo-Jerome] and Augustine) up to 1108 (the Pisan and Genoese capture of Tunis), and a list of Christian rulers ending with the tenth-century Beneventan prince Pandolfo; (5) the story of Alexander the Great; (6) Pseudo-Dares's *Story of Troy* followed by a version of the *Aeneid;* and (7) the first nine books of Eutropius's *History of Rome* (*Breviarum ab urbe Condita*), in the version by Paul the Deacon (730–799).

The compilation, finished between 1108 and 1119, is in part expository and descriptive, in part simple itinerary, and was illustrated with maps. Only three survive: a map of Italy; a small, modified T-O world map (see Maps); and a map of the ancient world. The second of these is unusual: Africa is compressed due to the amount of space occupied by a large V-shaped Mediterranean separating the continents, and Europe contains nearly as many legends (mostly for regions that are demarcated with lines) as Asia and Africa combined.

In his work, Guido identifies himself by his first name. He was once thought to have been a native of Ravenna, but the textual passages that indicate such an origin have simply been borrowed from an anonymous seventh-century source. He was certainly Italian, either

Pisan or someone associated with the Norman elite in Puglia. Detailed geographical knowledge of Puglia and suppression of information about Bari suggest a person politically sympathetic to Benevento or Trani. Furthermore, codicological evidence indicates that the oldest extant manuscript was copied in southern Italy from a model written in southern minuscule script. He should not, in any case, be confused with Guido da Pisa, the fourteenth-century commentator on Dante's *Divine Comedy*.

**BIBLIOGRAPHY**

De Reiffenberg, F. "Analyses et extraits de manuscrits de la Bibliothèque Royale . . . *Guidonis liber ex variis historiis.*" *Bulletins de l'Académie Royale de Bruxelles* 10.1 (1843): 468–482.

De Smet, Antoine. "Guido de Bruxelles ou Guido de Pise: À propos de l'auteur d'un manuscrit du XII^e siècle." *Cahiers bruxellois* 6 (1961): 159–170.

Miller, Konrad. *Mappaemundi: Die ältesten Weltkarten.* 3: 54–57 and 6: 7–9, 14, 15, 22ff. See Gen. Bib.

Uggeri, Giovanni. "Contributo all'individuazione dell'ambiente del cosmografo Guidone." In *Littérature gréco-romaine et géographie historique: Mélanges offerts à Roger Dion.* Caesarodunum, No. 9 bis. Paris: Picard, 1974, pp. 233–246.

*Gloria Allaire*

**SEE ALSO**

*Antonine Itinerary;* Genoa; Isidore of Seville; Itineraries and *Periploi; Mappamundi;* Pisa

## Guilds

During the Middle Ages, organizations of employers banded together to foster their economic, social, and even spiritual self-interest. Although most urban guild members engaged in artisan craft production, a second type of guild, the merchant guild, also influenced the pace and scope of trade.

In major manufacturing towns like Bruges or Florence, the most important medieval industry, cloth production, was geared for the export market and produced far more cloth than local markets could absorb. The owners of these enterprises, the members of the cloth guilds, had to organize the import of raw materials such as wool, cotton, and silk, sometimes over vast distances. So the famous merino wool from Castile found itself woven on looms in northern Europe and Italy as a result of international trade. The cotton and silk weavers of northern Europe always depended on imported raw materials. In turn, finished cloth had to find a market, and a major one was the Muslim region of the Mediterranean, where there was demand for light woolen cloth and eventually cotton as well. Hence, the urban manufacturing guilds depended on shipping and international trade networks to market their wares. A division of labor within the guild system reflected the nature of this trade, so, for example, in Florence, one guild specialized in importing raw wool from England and Castile, while another guild was in the business of weaving and exporting cloth.

The guild masters were the entrepreneurs engaged in running the shops and small businesses characteristic of the medieval economy, while the apprentices and journeymen and women were regulated by the guild masters but only rarely allowed to be members of the guild. This familiar economic system resulted in the first regular wage labor in Europe for the journeymen and women and lasted well beyond the medieval period. The flexibility of the wage labor system permitted artisans to travel across Europe and take their skills where needed: thus, Flemish weavers brought the best techniques to England, and German miners and metalworkers found employment in Italy. The late medieval business of printing is another example of how migrant employers and workers quickly brought a new trading item to major European cities: by the late 1400s, publishing houses had been established from Portugal to Poland, and from Rome to Copenhagen, with a remarkable traffic in books that passed from one printer to another. Generally recognized standards of training, a feature of the guild system of vocational education, and free movement of labor fostered a rapid diffusion of technological advances across Europe.

The second major way the guild system shaped medieval trade and travel was in the development in some places of specialized merchant guilds, associations of long-distance traders engaged usually in a variety of commodities including grain, cloth, slaves, spices, wines, and many other items. One of the earliest organizations was the merchant's guild in St. Omer. Here the merchants, engaged in the buying and selling of wool and woolens, established their guild as a *de facto* city government. In 1127, the guild received from the count of Flanders freedom from all tolls in the county.

Since traveling merchants faced a series of vexatious tolls as they journeyed across Europe in search of raw

# G

materials and customers, the guild became a privileged circle because it denied any benefits or aid to nonmembers. The fact that members of the clergy, warriors, and foreign merchants were excluded from joining also fostered local class solidarity. The merchants were allowed to bring their own relatives into the guild, which encouraged the passing down of trading skills from one generation to the next. The common economic interests of merchants were enhanced by their collective efforts to secure free passage and other liberties from political authorities. In Venice, where the merchants actually ran city government, no merchant guild was necessary because the city's main business was the fostering of trade by securing favorable treaties and tariffs from its customers abroad. In most medieval trading cities the long-distance traders were the richest and most important people in town; governments, whether the city or some king or lord, usually recognized that it was in their own interests to foster merchants whose capital and taxes were important resources.

Merchant guilds concerned themselves not only with issues such as tolls and customs duties, but also with uniform weights and measures, personal security, and other matters vitally important to traveling merchants. The guilds helped to minimize risk and allowed merchants to make legally enforceable contracts. Merchant guilds also performed the important service of assisting the family of a member who died abroad in recovering his assets. Common mercantile practices became the forerunner of a basic, common business law across Europe. Unlike artisans, merchants did not ordinarily train young men formally in an apprenticeship system but instead hired traveling companions or assistants who learned the business in an informal system of education while on the road or at sea.

In the German cities, merchant guilds, such as the one in Cologne, often dominated town government. The unique feature of these German merchant guilds is the way they banded together across cities and jurisdictions into a common association, the Hanse, to foster overseas trade with Russia, Norway, England, and the Low Countries. Especially after 1250 and the fragmentation of secular power across the German Empire, the Hanse was an effective bargaining agent for the German merchants to get favorable terms of trade from foreign kings, who tried to be effective protectors of their own merchants and consumers. The Hanse established a series of overseas stations where merchants from the German member cities found protection and familiar surroundings.

A merchant guild was only one of several possible ways for traders to foster their self-interest. Taking over a city government or acquiring the patronage of an active monarch or ruler would also work. But when it came to haggling over customs duties or negotiating treaties about privileged trade, the merchants knew best what they needed. Hence, a merchant guild that included all overseas traders, or a specialized powerful guild devoted to one particular item of trade, like the vintners' guild in London or the wool guild in Florence, significantly benefited trade and the medieval economy.

**BIBLIOGRAPHY**

Degrassi, Donata. *L'economia artigiana nell'Italia medievale.* Rome: La Nuova Italia Scientifica, 1996.

Epstein, Steven A. *Wage Labor and Guilds in Medieval Europe.* Chapel Hill: U of North Carolina P, 1991.

Thrupp, Sylvia. "The Guilds." In *Cambridge Economic History of Europe.* Vol. 3. Cambridge: Cambridge UP, 1963, pp. 230–280, 624–635.

*Steven A. Epstein*

**SEE ALSO**

Bruges; *Fondaco;* Ghent; Hanse, The; Silk Roads; Textiles, Decorative; Venice

## Gunpowder

An explosive mixture whose capacity for destruction has made it a valuable item of trade, as well as a device for establishing and maintaining political and economic domination. Gunpowder was invented by Chinese alchemists seeking both the elixir of immortality and the philosopher's stone. Its formula had been determined by the ninth century and perfected for military applications by the eleventh.

The Chinese term for gunpowder is *huoyao,* literally "fire medicine." This is because saltpeter (potassium nitrate) and sulfur, two of the three constituent elements of gunpowder (along with finely powdered charcoal), are important drugs listed in China's first known pharmacopoeia, which dates to Han times (206 B.C.E.—220 C.E.). A Ming dynasty (1368–1644) pharmacopoeia even describes gunpowder as a curative for skin diseases and as an insecticide, desiccant, and disinfectant.

Alchemical experimentation with sulfur during the Eastern Han dynasty (25–220 C.E.) revealed its highly poisonous and volatile nature when heated. In

Destruction of Babylon with a cannon and gunpowder. Werner Rolewinck, *Fasciculus Temporum*. Utrecht: Jan Veldener, 1480. fol. 69r. Courtesy Perkins Library, Duke University. Photo by Laviece Ward.

response, alchemists combined sulfur with other substances (usually potassium nitrate) and burned the mixture until it could produce no more flames, at which point they considered the sulfur "subdued."

During the Tang dynasty (618–907), the Chinese discovered that adding charcoal to an unburned mixture of saltpeter and sulfur produced an instantaneously combustible substance. A Taoist alchemical work dated to about 850 warns against heating a combined mixture of sulfur, saltpeter, and honey (which would have contained carbon). Continuing experimentation showed that increasing the proportion of saltpeter to about 75 percent yielded the greatest explosive force. Around 1040, the Song dynasty scholar-official Zeng Gongliang published the world's first true gunpowder formulae for three types of military weapons.

A popular notion holds that gunpowder, a mere fireworks novelty in China, first saw effective military use in Europe. But the awesome military potentialities of gunpowder were not lost on the Chinese, who between the tenth and fourteenth centuries were using the world's first flamethrowers, bombs, grenades, signal flares, land mines, sea mines, and rockets. The world's first true guns, developed in China between 1250 and 1280, reached Europe by the 1320s.

Many scholars believe that the Franciscan William of Rubruck brought the first gunpowder to Europe in firecrackers in 1256, when he returned from China and Mongolia. The Mongols probably helped to transmit gunpowder technology to Europe during their rampage throughout Eurasia. According to one Chinese source, a Mongol with detailed knowledge of gunpowder weaponry traveled to Europe during the second half of the thirteenth century.

**BIBLIOGRAPHY**

Needham, Joseph. *Military Technology: The Gunpowder Epic*. Vol. 5, Part 7 of *Science and Civilisation in China*. Cambridge: Cambridge UP, 1954–1986.

Zhou, Jiahua. "Gunpowder and Firearms." In *Ancient China's Technology and Science*. Ed. Institute of the History of Natural Sciences, Chinese Academy of Sciences. Beijing: Foreign Languages Press, 1983, pp. 184–191.

*David C. Wright*

**SEE ALSO**

China; Naval Warfare; Taoism; William of Rubruck

# H

## Ham's Curse and Africans

The connection between hereditary servitude and blackness that originated from post-Flood legends of Noah's curse on his son Ham.

Ham was one of the three sons of Noah in the biblical stories of the Flood and its aftermath. In Genesis 9, Noah cursed Ham because he shamelessly mocked his father's drunken nakedness. The curse ensured that Ham's son Canaan and his progeny would henceforth be the servants of the line of Ham's virtuous brothers, Shem and Japheth.

In T-O maps based on Noah's division of the world's three continents among his sons, Ham is usually shown in Africa, suggesting to later thinkers a link between slavery and that continent. The development of an interpretive tradition in which black skin was believed to be a result of Noah's curse provided an enduring biblical justification for the enslavement of Africans. As late as the nineteenth century in the United States it was argued that slavery was a divinely sanctioned punishment meted out to the black descendants of Ham.

When Talmudic and Midrashic scholars in the period between the fifth century B.C.E. and the third century C.E. considered the causes and consequences of Noah's curse, they wondered why Ham's punishment seemed to exceed his offense, and why Canaan and not Ham himself was singled out. They speculated that Ham might have committed some sexual indiscretion on the ark or might have attempted—out of a desire for sexual preeminence in the post-Diluvian world—to castrate Noah; eventually, Ham became a figure of uncontrolled sexuality. A few of these commentators mentioned black skin as among the results of Ham's transgression, but there was as yet no indication that this was hereditary, nor was a connection drawn between servitude and blackness.

The first to make a conceptual connection between Ham, black skin color, and slavery were Muslim writers beginning in the tenth century. Ibn Qutayba and Mas'udi classified black Africans as the cursed descendants of Ham; Tabari explicitly derived slavery as well as blackness, from the curse of Noah. The idea also appeared in the writings of the late-twelfth-century Jewish traveler Benjamin of Tudela, who remarked that the people of Cush are "black slaves, the sons of Ham," and the association remained a commonplace in Islamic thought into modern times.

In Christian Europe, the curse served to explain the origins of several sorts of real and imaginary peoples regarded as strange or threatening, including Africans but also Saracens, Mongols, the exotic semihuman races of the East, and even European peasants. Isidore of Seville categorized Africans, Libyans, Ethiopians, and Egyptians as the main groups descended from Ham, but among the "Ethiopian" peoples he included cannibals, troglodytes, and other fanciful races. Ham also appeared occasionally as the ancestor of Saracens, notably in Pseudo-Aethicus Ister and in some versions of *The Book of John Mandeville*. Invasions by Mongols and Tartars prompted speculation that they were offspring of Ham via the previously enclosed nations of Gog and Magog, now released upon the world in anticipation of the Apocalypse.

In a different but contemporary tradition, speculation based on Genesis 4:15 centered around Cain and his curse as the progenitor of the "monstrous races"

# H

who were thought to inhabit the earth's margins. The two views were often intermingled in the Middle Ages, and the two curses were often used to explain why certain Europeans were slaves or semifree serfs. Thus, the twelfth-century *Vienna Genesis* combined the Cain and Ham traditions to make Cain the ancestor of blacks, while Ham's descendants were the unfree.

The patristic authority of Basil, Ambrose, Chrysostom, and Augustine gave rise to a connection between slavery and human sinfulness: in a world given over to vice, those of weak moral character must be subordinated. Ham was thus not merely a symbol of waywardness and lack of discipline but also a historical, genealogical figure, so that both by character and blood he could be used to justify slavery, a practice otherwise seemingly contrary to divine and natural law, both of which posited an original human equality.

Accordingly, from the Carolingian period until the sixteenth century, Ham was frequently regarded as the ancestor of serfs. For Honorius Augustodunensis (*c.* 1100), serfs were descended from Ham, knights from Japheth, and free men from Shem. In Chaucer's *Canterbury Tales,* the worthy Parson traces servitude ("thralldom") to Canaan (another name for Ham). Ham's sin explained why even Christians could be legally enslaved. Though one finds this argument primarily in literary and didactic works, it also appeared in theological and legal texts, such as the *Summa theologica* of Alexander of Hales (d. 1245), and the *Mirror of Justices,* of about 1289.

All medieval thinkers, of course, did not accept uncritically the connection of Ham and servitude; the idea was questioned as early as the ninth and tenth centuries by Jonas of Orléans and Atto of Vercelli. A particularly vigorous argument against Ham as the ancestor of serfs was offered in the thirteenth century by Eike von Repgow, author of a German legal collection, the *Sachsenspiegel.* Ham could not be the ancestor of European serfs, he argued, as Ham's descendants had settled Africa, apart from the other sons' progeny. One finds a similar argument in Wycliff that since Ham's descendants were Africans, he was the progenitor of free people, even rulers (such as the Pharaohs); therefore Ham has nothing to do with subordination of Europeans.

With the expansion of European commerce and exploration in the fifteenth century, Africa came to be more closely identified with slavery. The curse of Noah served to justify African enslavement rather than European serfdom. What had previously seemed to disprove

Ham's role as the origin of serfs (namely his being the father of Africans) now fit into a justification for the exploitation of Africans. Gomes Eanes de Azurara, a member of the circle of Prince Henry the Navigator, added the curse of Noah to the Isidorian distinction between "white" and "black" Moors (Arabs and black Africans). The punishment of Ham affected the latter, not the former. Away from Africa, however, Ham remained a rather malleable figure: Spanish thinkers of the sixteenth century speculated that the peoples of Cuba or the Orinoco might be Ham's offspring. The first black Protestant minister, Jacobus Capitein, a West African trained by the Dutch as a missionary, wrote in 1742 that slavery was a divinely ordained means for Africans to expiate the sin of Ham.

## BIBLIOGRAPHY

Braude, Benjamin. "The Sons of Noah and the Construction of Ethnic and Geographical Identities in the Medieval and Early Modern Periods." *William and Mary Quarterly* 3rd series 54.1 (January 1997): 103–142.

Evans, William McKee. "From the Land of Canaan to the Land of Guinea: The Strange Odyssey of the 'Sons of Ham.'" *American Historical Review* 85 (1980): 15–43.

Friedman, John Block. *The Monstrous Races in Medieval Art and Thought.* Cambridge: Harvard UP, 1981; rpt. Syracuse, NY: Syracuse UP, 2000.

———. "Nicholas's 'Angelus ad Virginem' and the Mocking of Noah." *Yearbook of English Studies* 22 (1992): 162–180.

Hill, Thomas. "*Rígsíula*: Some Medieval Christian Analogues." *Speculum* 61 (1986): 79–89.

Isaac, Ephraim. "Genesis, Judaism and the 'Sons of Ham.'" *Slavery and Abolition* 1 (1980): 3–17.

Lewis, Bernard. *Race and Slavery in the Middle East: An Historical Inquiry.* Oxford and New York: Oxford UP, 1990.

*Paul H. Freedman*

## SEE ALSO

Aethicus Ister, *Cosmographia;* African Trade; Benjamin of Tudela; Cannibalism; Chaucer, Geoffrey; Ethiopians; Gog and Magog; Henry the Navigator; Honorius Augustodunensis; Isidore of Seville; Las Casas, Bartolomé de; *Mandeville's Travels;* Maps; Mongols; Monstrosity, Geographical; Slave Trade, African

## Hanse, The [Hanseatic League]

From *c.* 1160 to 1660, an association of German merchants, who, by the fourteenth century, had organized into a town-based confederation for mutual commercial advantage and protection. The Hanse remained the single most influential socioeconomic and political phenomenon in medieval northern Europe until its elimination in the seventeenth century. Moreover, its accrued wealth engendered the first bourgeois society in the Western world, establishing the cultural basis for the flowering of the Renaissance in the north. The economic strength of the Hanse was predicated on its ability to conjoin East and West commercially by the exportation of eastern Europe's immense raw material surpluses to the established markets of the West, and, in turn, by the transfer of finished products from the West to the Hanse's eastern clients.

Beginning in the twelfth and thirteenth centuries, the Hanse secured transnational trading concessions from local potentates across the expanse of Europe by producing and distributing products with high demand and superior cost-benefits. To further augment efficiency, the Hansards constructed and colonized new towns devoted to trade throughout northern and central Europe. In this manner, the Hanse, operating from its commercial base at Visby on Gotland, consolidated its position as the cardinal economic producer within the Baltic region. This resulted in the continual penetration of established western European markets by Hanseatic merchants during the course of the later medieval epoch. The commodities of exchange included such products from the greater Baltic region as amber, beer, cereals, furs, livestock, timber, and metals, while northwest Europe provided linens, salt, wines, woolens, and other quality textiles. Hanseatic merchants conveyed their commodities by means of their innovations in ship design, the cog and later the hulk, and by an extensive network of cartways and roads.

The Hanse flourished as a loose political confederation from the thirteenth to sixteenth centuries, expanding in size and scale to include more than 200 towns in locations ranging from the Low Countries and England to Russia and Finland, as well as the lands of the Teutonic Order. Of this number, seventy-two to seventy-seven towns garnered the designation of "active," a title that vouchsafed full legal and voting rights. Hanseatic port towns controlled the economic infrastructure of the confederation while towns in the German and the northern European hinterlands functioned as inland production centers. The preeminent towns of Bremen, Cologne, Hamburg, and Lübeck held sway in the west, while Gdansk (Danzig), Tallinn (Reval), Riga, Rostock, and Stralsund dominated the eastern sphere. Lübeck functioned as the nominal capital.

Counting houses or "factories" on foreign territory reinforced Hanseatic transnational commerce. Principal "factories" included the Steelyard in London, the German Wharf (Quay) at Bergen (Tyskebryggen), St. Peter's Yard in Novgorod, and later the Easterners' House at Bruges; these procured duty-free commercial zones with unrivaled trading privileges. Minor factory sites scattered across Europe, particularly in England and in north-central Europe, bolstered the factory system.

The fluidity of the Hanse discouraged concerted long-term actions in response to infractions of its rules; however, it utilized boycotts and expulsions to maintain its integrity as well as to press its claims. For such actions, Hanseatic Diets issued ordinances that mutually bound its members, although organization was always a problem for the league. On occasion, when negotiations failed, the Hanse fought wars, especially against the Danes and the English.

From the late fourteenth century onward, the Hanse suffered many reversals, but the most damaging was the loss of the Teutonic-controlled lands of eastern Europe to the Poles and Lithuanians. The monopolistic policies of the Hanse aroused ever-sharper opposition in the countries where the Hanse operated, notably in England, Flanders, and Russia, promoting the incursions of hostile, nationalistic merchant interests, which effectively redirected Hanseatic trade in the fifteenth century. Commercial rivalries, once begun between the Hanse towns, only served to erode the Hanse's economic base in the tumult of the late fifteenth and sixteenth centuries in which rapid collapse ensued. The last Diet in 1669 marked the end of the Hanse, but even today a number of the Hanseatic cities of the Middle Ages continue to refer to themselves as "Hansestadt," including not only Bremen, Hamburg, and Lübeck, but also Rostock, whose offical civic designation is Hansestadt Rostock.

**BIBLIOGRAPHY**

D'Haenens, Albert, ed. *Europe of the North Sea and Baltic: The World of the Hanse.* Antwerp: Fonds Mercator, 1984.

Dollinger, Philippe. *The German Hansa.* Trans. D.S. Ault and S.H. Steinberg. Stanford, CA: Stanford UP, 1964.

Fritze, Konrad, Johannes Schildhauer, and Walter Stark. *Die Geschichte der Hanse.* Berlin: VEB Deutscher Verlag der Wissenschaften, 1974. 2nd edition. (West) Berlin: Verlag das Europäische Buch, 1985.

# H

Lloyd, T.H. *England and the German Hanse, 1157–1611*. Cambridge: Cambridge UP, 1991.

Schildhauer, Johannes. *The Hansa: Its History and Culture*. Trans. Katherine Vasrovitch. Leipzig: Druckerei Fortschritt Erfurt, 1985.

Ziegler, Uwe. *Die Hanse*. Bern: Scherz Verlag, 1994.

*Bryan Atherton*

SEE ALSO

Bruges; Cog; *Fondaco;* Gems; Guilds; Hulk; Ships and Shipbuilding; Stones and Timber, Scandinavian Trade in; Teutonic Order; Textiles, Decorative; Transportation, Inland

## Henry of Mainz Map

A *mappamundi* preserved in a twelfth- or thirteenth-century manuscript (Corpus Christi College, Cambridge, MS 66, p. 2). The map, which measures $11\frac{1}{2} \times 8$ inches ($29.5 \times 20.5$ cm), was probably drawn in the later 1100s. In the manuscript codex it precedes historical and geographical treatises (some as excerpts), most notably Honorius Augustodunensis's *Imago mundi* (pp. 2–58), first released around 1110 (a date offered in some sources for the map). The "editor" of "this book" ("qui hunc librum edidit") calls himself Henry, a canon in the Church of St. Mary in Mainz. Unlike most other copies of Honorius's *Imago mundi*, which are addressed to a certain "Christianus," this copy is also dedicated to a "Henricus." This *mappamundi* seems to have been one of the models for the much larger Hereford world map, judging from the clear similarities.

The manuscript is in an English hand; a further English connection can be established via the patron to whom the work is dedicated, Emperor Henry V (r. 1106–1125), husband of Mathilda and son-in-law of the English king Henry I (r. 1100–1135). The manuscript was once in Sawley Abbey.

The outline of Henry's map, including the encircling ocean and coasts, is similar to the Hereford *mappamundi* (*c.* 1290). Various other coincidences occur in geographical features, place-names, formulae of description (for example, "hic habitant Griffe homines nequissimi"; "Gog et Magog, gens immunda"), and objects depicted, such as, in Africa, a basilisk shown as a bird seated between an image of the water deity Triton and the Nile; the pyramids represented as a barnlike structure; a pepper forest located near the Red Sea; and, in Asia, the rampart enclosing a peninsula on which Gog and Magog are confined, consisting of a wall and altars. The conservatism of cartographers is well known, but these similarities and many others suggest that the huge Hereford map was based to a large extent on the mysterious Henry's little *mappamundi*.

Henry's map also has its own historical value. It is one of the first to include Denmark and Russia, and it follows an ancient Greek tradition of placing sacred Delos, rather than Jerusalem, at its center.

BIBLIOGRAPHY

Bevan, W.L., and H.W. Phillot. *Medieval Geography: An Essay in Illustration of the Hereford Mappa Mundi*. London, 1873; rpt. Amsterdam: Meridian, 1969. Introduction, description of map 3 (unpaginated).

Flint, Valerie I.J., ed. "Honorius Augustodunensis. *Imago Mundi.*" *Archives d'Histoire Doctrinale et Littéraire du Moyen Age* 57 (1982): 7–153.

Hahn-Woernle, Brigit, ed. *Die Ebstorfer Weltkarte*. Ebstorf: Kloster Ebstorf, 1987, p. 32.

Harvey, P.D.A. "The Sawley (Henry of Mainz) Map." *Imago Mundi* 49 (1997): 33–42.

Miller, Konrad. *Mappaemundi: Die ältesten Weltkarten*. 3: 21–29. See Gen. Bib.

Santarém, Manuel Francisco de Barros Sousa, Viscount of. *Essai sur l'histoire de la cosmographie et de la cartographie*. Appendix to Vol. 3, 463–498. See Gen. Bib.

*Andrew C. Gow*

SEE ALSO

Egypt; Gog and Magog; Hereford Map; Honorius Augustodunensis; Jerusalem; Maps; Pepper; Red Sea

## Henry the Navigator (1394–1460)

A modern appellation for Infante Dom Henry of Portugal, whom both his contemporaries and many modern historians saw as instrumental in launching the European expansion overseas. Nineteenth-century scholars saluted Henry as a Renaissance hero and one of the founders of modern science. They credited him with major contributions to geography, astronomy, shipbuilding, and scientific education. Many of these claims are unfounded. For example, the "School of Sagres," an academy of astronomy and navigation allegedly founded by Henry to support the explorations, never existed. Later historians, aware of such errors and stressing broader social and economic roots of the Portuguese overseas expansion, tended to downplay Henry's role, sometimes unfairly.

Henry was the third surviving son of Dom João I of Portugal (r. 1385–1433), founder of the Avis dynasty. His father richly endowed him with lands and titles, but Henry's ambitions could not be easily satisfied within the bounds of the small kingdom. His personality and outlook were galvanized by the conquest of the North African city of Ceuta in 1415. For the rest of his life he sought to recapture the emotional climax of that moment and continue the war against the Muslims, building up his personal glory and fortune in the process.

The Portuguese crown was wary, however, of deepening its involvement in Morocco. In 1419, Henry led a relief force to lift the siege of Ceuta, but it was only after the death of João I that he persuaded the new king, his brother, Dom Duarte, to embark on another adventure in Morocco. The expedition against the city of Tangier in 1437 ended in a military and personal disaster for Henry but did not quench his ambitions. He continued fruitlessly to plan new campaigns throughout the 1440s and, following the fall of Constantinople in 1453, he answered enthusiastically the pope's call for a crusade. However, it was only in 1458, two years before his death, that he participated in another successful Moroccan venture: the capture of Qsar al-Saghir, a small city in northern Morocco.

The explorations in the Atlantic, which brought Henry a lasting place in history, occurred in the context of his Moroccan ambitions. He built a land base in the Atlantic by securing Madeira from the crown in 1433, and some of the Azores islands later. He also attempted to gain title to the Canary Islands. Throughout his adult life he organized maritime raids and naval attacks against Muslim shores and shipping, a substitute for land battle in Morocco. The early voyages were principally corsairing expeditions and only secondarily missions of exploration. The majority of Henry's successful explorations took place between 1440 and 1446, when his ships progressed from Cape Blanc to as far as the mouth of the Gambia River. The explorations in and past the Gambia River were continued only ten years later. The final expedition, which reached Sierra Leone, left Portugal in 1460, the year of his death.

It was not until the 1440s that Henry began to view seaborne explorations in Africa as a source of personal glory, under the influence of the praise and admiration his contemporaries began to lavish on him. The humanist Gian Francesco Poggio Bracciolini (1380–1459), for example, compared him to Julius Caesar and Alexander the Great for his exploits in previously unknown lands. However, even then he tried to incorporate these ventures into his dream of conquest, as indicated by the title, tone, and content of their first history, the *Chronicle of the Notable Deeds that Took Place in the Conquest of Guinea at the Order of Infante D. Henrique* by Gomes Eanes de Zurara [Azurara] (*c.* 1410–*c.* 1474).

It would be wrong, however, to replace the image of Henry the Navigator, a Renaissance hero, with that of a fanatical, chivalric crusader. Henry was as realistic, shrewd, and frustrated as many of his peers. Hard pressed by adverse economic and social conditions, he built a base for his ventures with cunning, vision, and perseverance. He amassed not only lands and titles, the most important of which was the governorship of the Order of Christ (1420), but also economic privileges and profitable enterprises. His many clients and retainers held influential posts and were thus able to promote his interests, just as he tirelessly promoted theirs. He wielded tremendous domestic power, especially during the regency of his brother, Dom Pedro (1439–1448). Despite huge debts, Henry's potential bequest to his nephew and adoptive son, Dom Fernando, was so overwhelming that the king imposed himself as the heir instead. However, what brought Henry what he desired most—a lasting place in history—was his belief that fortune lay outside Portugal, in Africa and the Atlantic Ocean.

**BIBLIOGRAPHY**

Diffie, Bailey W., and George D. Winius. *Foundations of the Portuguese Empire.* Minneapolis: U of Minnesota P, 1977.

Elbl, Ivana. "Man of His Time (and Peers): A New Look at Henry the Navigator." *Luso-Brazilian Review* 28 (1991): 73–89.

Russell, P.E. *Prince Henry the Navigator: The Rise and Fall of a Culture Hero.* Taylorian Special Lecture, November 10, 1983. New York: Oxford UP, 1984.

*Ivana Elbl*

**SEE ALSO**
Azores; Canary Islands; Piracy; Portuguese Expansion

## Hereford Map

An elaborately detailed, highly ornamented, and lavishly illustrated map on vellum measuring 65 by 53 inches (1.65 × 1.35 meters), dated *c.* 1290. The Hereford map may have been drawn by, or commissioned

World Map attributed to Richard of Haldingham. Hereford Cathedral *c.* 1280–1300, oriented to the east. The map measures 62½ inches by 52/53 inches (1.58 meters x 1.30 meters). Reproduced by permission of the Dean and Chapter of Hereford Cathedral and the Hereford Mappa Mundi Trust.

that was a curious mixture of authentic reports and literary commonplaces. As such, it can be classified as a "Sallust" map (named for a type of map often attached to Sallust's works)—that is, a more elaborated version of the "T and O" map in which the "T" represents the seas that separated the three continents of Europe, Africa, and Asia, and the "O" contains the world ocean that was believed to surround the continents that comprised the *orbis terrarum habitatio.*

As in many other medieval maps, the world is represented as a flat disk, with the east at the top. Here is painted Christ at the Last Judgment, his angels ranged on either side. His hands are outstretched as if to encompass all of the known world; his feet point north, in the direction of the British Isles (located at the bottom, western portion of the map). Although the painting of Christ lies outside of the "O," Paradise is depicted inside it, directly underneath the figure of Christ; it is surrounded by a stone wall and another wall of fire. Adam and Eve are represented as standing outside the gates of the Garden of Eden. The circular shape of Paradise repeats the O-shape of the world itself. In accordance with tradition, Jerusalem is located

by, one Richard of Haldingham and of Lafford (better known as "Ricardus de Bello"), a prebendary of Hereford, who most likely presented or bequeathed it to Hereford Cathedral.

The first historical record locating the map in the cathedral dates from the early 1600s. Pliny, Solinus, Aethicus Ister, Orosius, Martianus Capella, and Isidore are cited as sources on the map itself, though it is likely that de Bello or his artist/author did not borrow directly from these authorities in all cases, instead acquiring his knowledge second- and third-hand. Many similarities between the Hereford Map and the Henry of Mainz map at Corpus Christi College, Cambridge (MS 66, p. 2), exist, and the ornamentation is similar to that of the London Psalter map. The influence of bestiary and herbal lore, along with accounts of the voyages of Alexander and other real or mythical travelers, can be seen in the hundreds of paintings that decorate the map.

The Hereford map illustrates how medieval maps were often highly schematized, reflecting a written lore

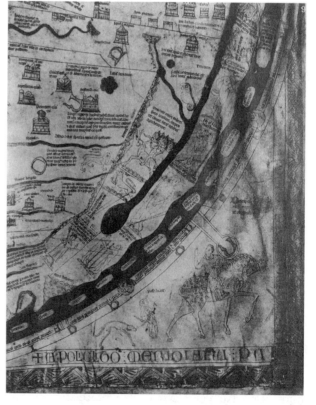

Detail.

in the exact center of the map, and hence the world. It is also depicted as an "O," surrounded by crenellated walls. The Crucifixion is painted just above the city of Jerusalem. Balancing Paradise, located at the eastern limits of the known world, are the Pillars of Hercules, located at the western limits.

The continents of Europe, Africa, and Asia, unrecognizable from their outlines to us today, contain small tableaux drawn from history, legend, and Scripture. Rivers and mountains, along with their names, are indicated; these often have symbolic significance. Metonymic castles and other massive buildings mark the location of cities, such as Babylon, Rome, and London; inscriptions and paintings note the kingdom of Cleopatra, towns founded by Alexander, and an island inhabited by Gog and Magog. Miniatures are numerous, such as the one of a mother tiger foiled by a hunter with a mirror, or another of a griffin fighting with three men over emeralds.

Real and fabulous beasts are depicted, such as the elephant (with a castle on its back), the manticore, the parrot, the camel, the crocodile, the unicorn, and the dragon. Along the extreme edges of the world are ranged the monstrous races, such as the Blemmyae (whose eyes and mouth are located below their shoulders), the Essedones (cannibals), and the Psylli (who test the chastity of their women by exposing their newborn infants to snakes).

While geographical information within the "O" is given in Latin, the language of some of its inscribed frame is Anglo-Norman, the language used to exhort all who view the map (here referred to as *cest estorie* "this story, narrative, history"), to pray for "Richard de Haldingham e de Lafford."

Perhaps designed as an altarpiece (or, at least, used as one at one time), the Hereford map was never intended to be read as a realistic depiction of the known world. Rather, in its representation of the major events of salvation history, the map is a fine example of a Christianized historical geography as reflected in the written encyclopedias of the age.

## BIBLIOGRAPHY

Bevan, W.L., and H.W. Phillott. *An Essay in Illustration of the Hereford Mappa Mundi.* London, 1873; rpt. Amsterdam: Meridian, 1969.

Edson, Evelyn. *Mapping Time and Space: How Medieval Mapmakers Viewed Their World.* London: British Library, 1998.

Harvey, P.D.A. *Medieval Maps.* London: British Library, 1991.

——. *Mappa Mundi: The Hereford World Map.* London: British Library, 1996.

Kline, Naomi Reed. *A Wheel of Memory: The Hereford Mappamundi.* CD-ROM. Ann Arbor: U of Michigan P, 2000.

Miller, Konrad. *Mappaemundi: Die ältesten Welkarten.* Vol 4: *Die Herefordkarte.* See Gen. Bib.

Wogan-Browne, Jocelyn. "Reading the World: The Hereford *Mappa Mundi.*" *Parergon,* n.s., 9.1 (June 1991): 117–135.

*Kathleen Coyne Kelly*

**SEE ALSO**

Aethicus Ister, *Cosmographia*; Birds, Exotic; Camels; Cannibalism; Edges of the World; Elephants; Gog and Magog; Henry of Mainz Map; Isidore of Seville; *Mappamundi*; Maps; Monstrosity, Geographical; Orosius; Paradise, Travel to; Pliny the Elder; Psalter Map, ; Solinus; Julius Gaius; *Wonders of the East*

## Hetoum [Hetum/Hayton] (*c.* 1245–*c.* 1310/1314)

An Armenian monk of a noble family, and author of the important treatise *La flor des estoires de la terre d'Orient* (1307). His name has various spellings, a frequent variant being Hayton, which is often found in copies of his French work. A scion of a collateral line of the Hetoumid dynasty of Cilician (Lesser) Armenia, Hetoum was the son of Oshin, lord of Corycos, whose title he inherited around 1280. He was the nephew of King Hetoum I (r. 1216–1270), in whose court he grew up, and the uncle of King Hetoum II (r. 1266–1307). Hetoum was born sometime before 1245. The date of his death is also uncertain; it probably occurred between 1310 and 1314. He appears to have been a canon regular at the Premonstratensian abbey of Bellapais, Saint Maria de Episcopia on Cyprus, but by this time he had married and had fathered at least six children.

Hetoum's significance lies in his authorship of *La Flor,* conceived as a crusading tract and dictated in 1307 in French to a scribe, Nicolas Falcon, a fellow Premonstratensian, who that same year prepared a Latin translation entitled *Flor historiarum terre orientis.* The work was quite popular, existing in eighteen manuscripts of the French text and twenty-nine of the Latin, as well as in several incunabule editions. At that time Hetoum was in Poitiers, at the papal court of Clement V (1305–1314), whom he tried to convince of the necessity and the feasibility of a joint Armenian-Mongol-French crusade for the reconquest of Jerusalem.

Tartars honor their ruler. *Fleurs des Histoires*, London, British Library MS Add. 17971, fol. 23, *c.* 1440–1450. Courtesy of the British Library.

**BIBLIOGRAPHY**

Dörper, Sven, ed. "Die Geschichte der Mongolen des Hethum von Korykos (1307)." In *Traitiez des estas et des conditions de quatorze royaumes de Aise (1351).* Der Rückübersetzung durch Jean le Long. Kritische Edition. Mit parallelem Abdruck des lateinischen Manuskripts. Wroclaw: Biblioteka Uniwersytecka, R 262; Frankfurt a.M.: Peter Lang, 1998.

Hetoum. *La flor des estoires de la terre d'Orient* and *Flos historiarum terre orientis.* Ed. C. Kohler et al. *Recueil des historiens des croisades.* Documents arméniens 2. Paris: E. Leroux, 1906.

———. *A Lytell Cronycle: Richard Pynson's Translation (c 1520) of La Fleur des histoires de la terre d'Orient (c. 1307).* Ed. Glenn Burger. Toronto, Buffalo, and London: U of Toronto P, 1988.

*Denis Sinor*

**SEE ALSO**

Armenia; China; Mamluks; Mongols

## Higden [Hygden], Ranulf (d. 1364)

A chronicler and Benedictine monk of St. Werburgh's, Chester. Little is known about Higden's life, but he appears to have been a native of Cheshire, and according to a colophon in one copy of his chronicle (Oxford, Bodleian Library MS Laud. Misc. 619), he entered the Benedictine abbey of St. Werburgh's in 1299. There is no evidence that he studied at a university or traveled much outside Chester. The one reliable fact known about the later years of his life is that in 1352, he was summoned by Edward III to appear at court with his chronicles. A note in the Laud manuscript suggests that he died in 1363/1364 after living more than sixty years in religious life.

Higden's major work was his universal chronicle, known as the *Polychronicon* (c. 1342). He also wrote a guide to sermon literature (*Ars Componendi Sermones*), an aid to preaching (*Speculum Curatorum*), and some minor works, including a collection of Latin sermons. His name has been associated with the Chester cycle of Corpus Christi plays, but there is no evidence that he was in any way connected with them. Thus his reputation rests almost entirely upon the *Polychronicon*, which offered to the educated audience of fourteenth-century England a clear and original picture of world history based on medieval tradition, but with a new interest in antiquity and with the early history and topography of Britain related as part of the whole.

*La Flor* is divided into four parts. The first two contain a historical geography of Asia from Syria to India and China (Cathay), with particular emphasis on the lands of Islam. The third, and most valuable, part is devoted to the description of the Mongols. It contains material not found in any other medieval source, including some eyewitness accounts of battles fought between the Mongols and Mamluks. The fourth part is a plea that a new crusade be undertaken. It contains information on the internal conditions of the Mamluk state and precise advice on how the campaign should be launched. Hayton advocated an overland attack on Syria using Cilicia as a base.

In the later Middle Ages, and in the sixteenth and seventeenth centuries, *La Flor* enjoyed great popularity; parts of it were incorporated into collections of Asian travel literature, manuscript as well as printed.

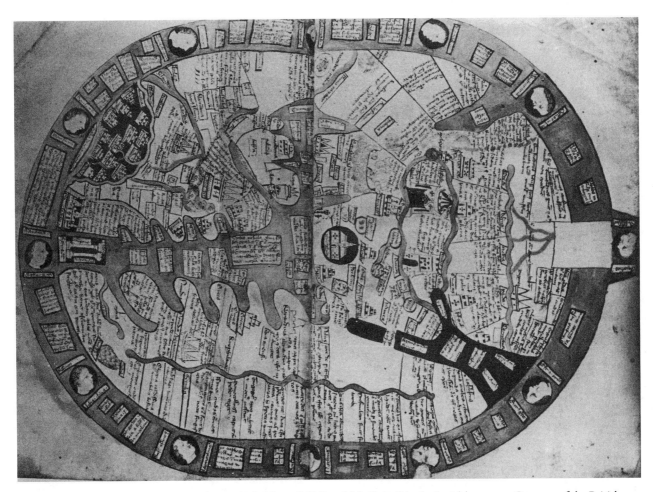

Higden, world map, *Polychronicon*. London, British Library MS Royal 14. C. ix, fols. 1v-2r. 14th century. Courtesy of the British Library.

Higden's historical narrative is particularly notable for its description of the Roman world. An interest in the ancient world had been developing for some time in fourteenth-century England, and Higden claims that at the request of his fellow monks he changed his plan of writing a history of his own country and enlarged the scope of his work. In the *Polychronicon,* he described the development of Rome from it legendary foundation on the banks of the Tiber down to the age of Constantine. His account is most detailed from the time of Caesar, when, in successive chapters, he dealt with the rule of Caesar, the rise to power of Augustus, and the establishment of the empire. In these chapters, Higden commented on the famous figures of the Roman world and noted such events as the birth of Horace, the education of Virgil, and the banishment of Ovid.

A further feature of his account is the description of the world contained in the first book of the *Polychroni-*con. Through the medium of John Trevisa's English translation (1387) and other translations, this section of Higden's work proved to be one of the most popular parts of his chronicle. Higden's description of the world was a traditional one drawn from classical and medieval sources. However, he enlivened his account with such passages as a description of men in India with hollow fingers, crickets in Sicily that sang best when they were dead, and one-eyed perch in Wales. His description of England, of which he had greater knowledge, contained some useful information on the roads, rivers, cities, and dialects of the country. Altogether, this section of Higden's work made compelling reading for its medieval audience.

To illustrate his geographical description, Higden included a world map in the later versions of his chronicle. The most elaborate copy, which may be the closest one to the original, is found in British Library MS Royal 14. C. ix (fols. 1v–2r display an ovular map; a

# H

mandorla-shaped *mappamundi* is on fol. 9v). Higden uses the word *mappamundi* in his text to refer to his verbal geography rather than the cartographical component found in at least twenty-one manuscripts. These are in three different shapes, of which the ovular *mappaemundi* appear to be Higden's own devising, and circular and mandorla-shaped (*vesica piscis* or "fish bladder") examples are later simplifications. The content of the maps is fairly consistent.

The *Polychronicon* went through a number of editions in Higden's lifetime. The Latin text survives in a short, an intermediate, and a long version. Although it was once thought that the intermediate version was the original one, it is clear from Higden's autograph copy in the Huntington Library (in San Marino, California; HM 132) that the short version of the text, written soon after 1327, is the earliest, and that the narrative was then expanded into the later and longer accounts. A medieval text was rarely completed, and Higden was still revising his chronicle at the time of his death.

The Latin text of the *Polychronicon* survives in more than 100 manuscripts; it can thus be said to have had considerable appeal. Many cathedral churches and larger religious houses possessed copies. In the later Middle Ages, copies were also owned by parish churches, Oxford and Cambridge colleges, and individual clerics, as well as by members of the nobility and affluent merchants in London. The influence of the *Polychronicon* is most clearly seen, however, in the continuations that were added to its text during the second half of the fourteenth century, a period that may be termed the age of the *Polychronicon* continuation. The first continuation, covering the period from 1340 to 1377, went through a number of versions and is important because it covers a period that had few competent chroniclers, writers such as Murimuth, Avesbury, and Baker having ended their work in the 1340s and 1350s.

The influence of the *Polychronicon* extended beyond these continuations. The English translations of the Latin text increased knowledge of the book among a lay audience, beginning with the work by John Trevisa. A second translation made in the fifteenth century is found in a single manuscript (British Library Harley MS 2261). Although the influence of the *Polychronicon* was to decline at the close of the Middle Ages, the universal outlook that it reflected lived on among the writers and antiquaries of the Tudor age.

## BIBLIOGRAPHY

Edwards, J.G. "Ranulf, Monk of Chester." *English Historical Review* 47 (1932): 94.

Galbraith, V.H. "An Autograph MS of Ranulph Higden's *Polychronicon*." *Huntington Library Quarterly* 34 (1959–1960): 1–18.

Gransden, Antonia. "Silent Meanings in Ranulf Higden's *Polychronicon* and in Thomas Elmham's *Liber Metricus de Henrico Quinto*." *Medium Aevum* 46 (1978): 231–233, 238–239.

———. *Historical Writing in England: c. 1307 to the Early Sixteenth Century.* London: Routledge and Kegan Paul, 1982, pp. 43–57.

Higden, Ranulf. *Polychronicon Ranulphi Higden, Together with the English Translation of John Trevisa and of an Unknown Writer of the Fifteenth Century.* Eds. Churchill Babington and J.R. Lumby. 9 vols. London: Longman, 1865–1886.

Taylor, John. *The Universal Chronicle of Ranulf Higden.* Oxford: Clarendon P., 1966.

*John Taylor*

## SEE ALSO

Froissart, Jean; India; *Mappamundi;* Maps; Trevisa, John

## Holy Land

In the Middle Ages, the crossroads of east-west and north-south trade routes over the land bridge between Europe, Africa, and Asia from the time of King Solomon; and the object of Jewish pilgrimage since the Babylonian Captivity in the sixth century B.C.E., of Christian pilgrimage since the time of Constantine, and of Muslim pilgrimage since the death of Muhammad. Always referred to as "Eretz Israel" (the land of Israel) by the Jews and renamed "Palestine" by the Romans in an attempt to obliterate the source of rebellion, the Holy Land bore the scars of the great powers that occupied it from 324 to 1516: the Byzantines, the Arabs, the crusaders, and the Mamluks.

When the first Christian emperor of Rome, Constantine (306–337), defeated Licinius at Chalcedon in 324, the small, marginal, and otherwise insignificant Roman province of Palestine became the Holy Land of the burgeoning and ultimately official religion of the Roman Empire. The intense building activity of the emperor, of his mother Helena (who was believed to have found the True Cross), and of many private donors transformed Jewish Jerusalem and the countryside where the events in the life of Jesus occurred or were thought to have occurred.

Earliest known map of Mount Sinai, with shrine of
Saint Catherine. Jacopo of Verona, *Liber Peregrinationis.*
Minneapolis, MN, James Ford Bell Library MS 1424/Co.
vol. 2, fol. 130v. Written at Bonn, August 12, 1424. By
permission of the James Ford Bell Library, University of
Minnesota.

Tens of thousands of Christian pilgrims descended
on the Holy Land together with refugees from the
fifth-century barbarian invasions of Italy, wealthy pious
matrons, and the relatives of those in disgrace at the
imperial court. The pilgrims needed hospices, and the
wealthy built hospitals, homes for the elderly, and
churches as acts of charity. Forts and watchtowers protected the roads where public baths were established for
the convenience of travelers. Anchorites came to dwell
on the fringes of the Judean desert, and monks gathered in colonies.

Among the earliest Christian pilgrim-travelers, who
merely related to scribes their visits to holy places, were
also priests and intellectuals who wrote about their
experiences in Latin *itineraria.* Since almost all were
unfamiliar with the languages and the culture of the
Holy Land, they were dependent upon guides and
translators. The earliest extant itinerary is by the "Bordeaux Pilgrim" (*c.* 330); Egeria wrote another one
about 380; the French bishop Arculf's description of
the holy places, based on his lengthy travels (*c.*
679–682), was both popular and important in that it
was the first to describe the Holy Land under Muslim
rule; the Englishman St. Willibald went to the Holy
Land in 723.

The influx of Christian pilgrims and settlers created
a demand for all kinds of goods. In response to the
strong pressure for more food, agricultural settlements
extended the cultivated areas into the Negev, the desert
region in the south. The Byzantine remains in Negev
towns (which, like the whole country, fell once again
into desuetude after the Byzantine period) attest to the
Nabateans' highly sophisticated methods of collecting
rainwater for irrigation. Remnants of their vineyards
remain. Trade routes crisscrossed the Negev and Sinai,
connecting the Holy Land to Egypt and the Red Sea in
the south and, through Eilat, to Yemen and India in
the east. The Roman roads extended north along the
coast to Sidon and Tyre and northeast to Damascus.
Greek and Jewish merchants kept the sea-lanes open to
the west.

But the fifth-century controversies over church
dogma undermined Christian unity. Justinian's oppressive rule (527–565) led to a revolt by the Samaritans in
the sixth century, the destruction of churches, and the
interruption of trade. The Persians invaded in 614,
occupied Jerusalem, and destroyed all the churches
(including that of the Holy Sepulchre built by Constantine). Although the Persians retreated in 627, no
genuine improvement could be made in the commercial infrastructure of the Holy Land in the short period
before the Muslim incursions from Arabia, which
began in 630. Jerusalem fell in 638, and within two
years the entire region was under the control of the
Arabs. Because all who submitted to Islamic law were
granted their lives, control of their possessions, and
freedom of religious worship (at least during the first
half-century of Arab rule), the devastation that
attended the conquest was quickly set right.

The Holy Land was self-sufficient in cereals; it
imported raw materials, such as timber and metal, and
exported flour, olive oil, wine, dried figs, and raisins,
as well as medicinal products extracted from plants.

# H

Glass vessels and soap made from olive oil were sold in Egypt and Syria. Sugar plantations occupied the Jordan valley and the coastal plain. The Arabs introduced the lemon and the orange to the area. With the consolidation of the Muslim Empire from southern France to India, however, travel became safer, and new, more direct overland trade routes between Europe and the East developed in the ninth and tenth centuries. This subverted the agricultural economy of the Negev. Traffic on the caravan roads through the desert diminished to a trickle, and the desert cities slowly emptied.

Many Byzantine farms were laid waste and the land leased to Jewish tenants, but the Arab rulers imposed heavy taxes on non-Muslim farmers, which ultimately destroyed the agricultural fabric of the country. Moreover, with fewer Christian pilgrims and less capital development, the production of food declined. The local Jewish population settled in the towns, where they took up the trades of dyeing and tanning, which became exclusively Jewish occupations for generations.

Arab pilgrim traffic increased under the Umayyad dynasty, which established its capital at Damascus between 661 and 750. In order to improve their southern possessions and deflect the flow of pilgrims from Mecca, the caliph Abdul-Malik (685–705) built the Dome of the Rock (691) to attract Muslim pilgrims to Jerusalem. Although Arabic literature is rich in many traditions, no separate literary tradition describing visits to the Holy Land (or to Mecca, either) developed that is comparable to that of Christians or Jews. Some mention appears in general Arabic works on geography. Among the most important of these Muslim writers are al-Istakhrī (c. 950), Ibn Hawqal (977), and Muhammad ben Ahmad (985). The most famous itinerary for Muslim pilgrims, "Guide for the Places of Pilgrimage," is an early-thirteenth-century work written by 'Alī al-Harawī, which includes the sites in the Holy Land among those of many other countries.

The Umayyads also built the city of Ramle (712) as the administrative capital of their province, the only city in Palestine founded by the Arabs. Local industries such as pottery and dyeing provided the economic basis for the city's success. By the eleventh century, Ramle figs had become an important export, as had cotton, sugar cane, and (since biblical times) bee-honey and wax, as well as an ersatz honey made from the condensed liquid extract of dates.

In 750, the Abbasids overcame the Umayyad dynasty, moved their capital 500 miles eastward to Baghdad, and geographically marginalized the Holy Land. The Abbasids did, however, build the splendid cistern at Ramle (789) from which twenty-four people could draw water at the same time and which endures to this day. The cistern preserves the earliest example of the systematic use of the pointed arch, which later became a standard feature of medieval European architecture.

As Abbasid power began to wane in the ninth century, the neglected western provinces became semiautonomous principalities under the Tulunids, who ruled in Egypt and Palestine. The Fātimids, who followed the Tulunids, rebuilt the el-Aqsa mosque (1035), and destroyed the Church of the Holy Sepulchre again. Bedouin depredations and earthquakes in 1016 and 1033 contributed to the region's impoverishment. As the Fātimids declined, the increasingly powerful Seljuk Turks systematically robbed and plundered Christian pilgrims to the Holy Land—which led to the European Christian calls for reprisals to free the Holy Sepulchre from the infidel.

Jerusalem fell to French and Norman crusaders in 1099 with great slaughter of the Jewish and Muslim inhabitants. Almost from the beginning the crusaders were on the defensive. The fragmented Muslims gradually united under the Ayyūbids and triumphed under the great Kurdish warrior Saladin, who overwhelmed the crusader armies (1187) and occupied Jerusalem. In 1191, the crusaders recaptured Acre, which became the capital of the second crusader kingdom. But the Mamluks superseded the Ayyūbids and, under Sultan Baybars I and his successors, swept the crusaders from the Holy Land by 1291.

During the two centuries of the crusader period, the Latin Kingdom of Jerusalem was organized on the medieval feudal basis: land, protected by military strongholds, was distributed to vassals who owed fealty in the form of limited military service to the lord. Most crusaders fulfilled their vows and returned to Europe. Those who remained were more concerned with their own survival and security than they were with export. Although colonies of merchants from the Italian seafaring cities occupied the coastal towns and provided the vital commercial sea link to Europe, there is no great evidence of prolonged commercial success in any geographical direction originating from the crusader kingdom. Their pottery—with a greenish yellow glaze and floral or geometric design combined with images of men, beasts, and ships—was the work of local potters;

some handsomely illuminated and illustrated manuscripts were also produced there.

Although debilitated by their limited manpower, the crusaders built almost as many churches as fortresses; to this day, the principal mosques in Gaza, Ramle, Lydda, and other Arab towns are crusader churches reconsecrated to Islam. Castles and churches (the most prominent of which are in Jerusalem) are the primary crusader legacy in the Holy Land. But cultural interpenetration flows both ways. Perhaps the influence of the Holy Land on the crusaders and the future history of Europe was more vital and enduring. The rise in the standard of everyday comfort—at which the East was vastly superior to anything available in Europe—led to increased trade with the East, as well as a demand for new materials and goods like ivory, spices, fine textiles, and the laminated steel and iron weapons called "Damascus."

Conditions in the Holy Land during the crusader period are richly attested by the testimonies of Christian pilgrims and Jewish pilgrims, merchants, and travelers (supported by documents long preserved in the Cairo Geniza and now in Cambridge). Judah Halevi left Spain in 1140 and, although he never arrived in the Holy Land, he records the powerful emotional impetus that underlay pilgrimage to the area. Benjamin of Tudela, Pethahiah of Regensburg, and Jacob ben Nathaniel ha-Cohen toured the area at the end of the twelfth century and provided valuable descriptions of the impoverished Jews before the expulsion of the crusaders in 1291. Judah ben Solomon al-Charizi (c. 1216–1217), Rabbi Jacob of Paris (1238), and Nachmanides (1267) describe the holy places and the condition of the country at the time of the Muslim reconquest.

Of the many Christian travelers to the Holy Land during the crusader period, the report by the ascetic Daniel the Abbot (1106–1108) is among the first written in Russian. Nikulás of Þverá, abbot of a monastery in northern Iceland, visited in 1151–1154, and John of Würzburg in 1165. Other Germans, Willibrand of Oldenburg (1212) and Thietmar (1217), came in the thirteenth century, as did Sabbas, archbishop of Serbia (1225–1227), who wrote in ancient Slavic. The work of Burchard of Mount Sion (c. 1283) is a description rather than an itinerary, written by a longtime resident of the country.

Following his military success in 1291, Baybars I, the Mamluk sultan of Egypt, razed the towns and castles along the coast of Palestine in order to prevent the return of the crusaders and their Christian fleets. Viceroys were established at Gaza and Safed, and Jerusalem was relegated to secondary status, a place of honorable banishment for those disgraced in Cairo. As efficient administrators as they were capable warriors, the Mamluks established a network of caravansaries (inns with large courtyards) to support their system of postal relays between Cairo and Damascus. The connecting roads and bridges were maintained and secure, which contributed to the increasing north-south and east-west trade through the Holy Land well into the Ottoman period when trade in wine, textiles, and dyes improved.

Always too far from the trade routes to succeed at international trade, Jerusalem sustained itself on Jewish, Christian, and Muslim pilgrims, the number and variety of whom increased in the fourteenth and fifteenth centuries, the great period of Christian pilgrimage to the Holy Land. Among those who produced significant writings in their national languages are the Irish monk Simeon Simeonis (1332), the Italian monk Niccolo da Poggibonsi (1345), and the Russian priest Ignatius of Smolensk. In the fifteenth century, the proportion of urban, bourgeois laymen and laywomen and nobles increased. They came from many different countries and left a great number of descriptions and itineraries written in their native languages. From the standpoint of the modern historian, however, Jewish travelers to the Holy Land left more important accounts, because they are often more evaluative and treat matters other than just the holy sites. Among those whose journeys occurred during the time of the Mamluks are Isaac ibn al-Fara, a merchant from Malaga, who visited in 1411, and the Italians Meshullam of Volterra (1481), and Obadiah of Bertinoro in 1488–1490.

**BIBLIOGRAPHY**

Avi-Yonah, Michael. *The Holy Land.* New York: Holt, Rinehart, Winston, 1972.

Benvenisti, Meron. *The Crusaders in the Holy Land.* Jerusalem: Israel UP, 1970.

Dunn, Ross E. *The Adventures of Ibn Battuta, a Muslim Traveler of the Fourteenth Century.* Berkeley: U of California P, 1986.

France, John. *Victory in the East: A Military History of the First Crusade.* Cambridge and New York: Cambridge UP, 1994.

Gil, Moshe. *A History of Palestine 634–1099.* Cambridge: Cambridge UP, 1992.

# H

Goitein, S.D. *Letters of Medieval Jewish Traders.* Princeton: Princeton UP, 1973.

Kafesoglu, Ibrahim. *A History of the Seljuks: Ibrahim Kafesoglu's Interpretation and the Resulting Controversy.* Ed. and trans. Gary Leiser. Carbondale and Edwardsville, IL: Southern Illinois UP, 1988.

Lyons, Malcolm Cameron, and D.E.P. Jackson. *Saladin: The Policies of the Holy War.* Cambridge and New York: Cambridge UP, 1982; rpt. 1997.

Parkes, James W. *A History of Palestine from 135 A.D. to Modern Times.* London: Gollancz, 1949.

Riley-Smith, Jonathan S.C. *The Crusades: A Short History.* London: Athlone; New Haven: Yale UP, 1987.

Wilkinson, John. *Jerusalem Pilgrims before the Crusades.* Jerusalem: Ariel; Warminster: Aris and Phillips, 1977.

*Jerome Mandel*

**SEE ALSO**

Acre; Arculf; Ayūbbids; Baghdad; Baybars I; Benjamin of Tudela; Bordeaux Pilgrim; Burchard of Mount Sion; Byzantine Empire; Caravans; Damascus; Daniel the Abbot; Dyes and Pigments; Egeria; Egypt; Fātimids; Ibn Battūta, Abu Abdallah; Itineraries and *Periploi;* Jerusalem; John of Würzburg; Mamluks; Mecca; Merchants, Jewish; Muslim Travelers and Trade; Nicholas of Poggibonsi; Ottoman Empire; Pilgrimage, Christian; Saladin; Seljuk Turks

## Homo Viator

Literally "man/woman [is] a wayfarer," an image of human beings as travelers in this earthly life. The image is not unique to Christianity—it can be found in many religions—but it has been an important theme in Church theology since the first century.

In one of his psalms, King David implores God to hear his cry: "For I am a stranger with thee, and a sojourner [*peregrinus*], as all my fathers were" (39:12 [Vulgate 38:13]). The trope was first employed in the Bible in a more literal sense by Abraham in Canaan at Genesis 23:4. This sense of alienation from—even contempt for—the world through which one moves, hoping for divine blessing, toward a better place in the next life was quickly carried over into Christian discourse (Hebrews 11:13, written by 95 C.E., and I Peter 2:11).

From the very preface of his *City of God* (413–426), St. Augustine takes the side of those temporarily dwelling (*peregrinans*) in this world, noting later that the true Church is always on a pilgrimage (18.51). But it was Pope Gregory I (the Great), in his *Moralia* (595), a widely read commentary on the Book of Job, who offers a *locus classicus* for the concept, depicting the just person as a wayfarer or pilgrim (*viator ac peregrinus*) in this world and a true citizen of a heavenly homeland. Just as travelers are little conscious of the temporary comfort of an inn where they lodge for a night because they are thinking of their destination, Gregory wrote, so true Christians find only transitory—even dangerous, because it is distracting—happiness on earth.

The image of the faithful believer as a traveler, and not a settled inhabitant, in this world, but at the same time as someone moving toward an immutable order and therefore exhibiting a certain *stabilitas,* was popular among patristic and later writers, especially in the context of Christian asceticism. In the mid-thirteenth century, St. Thomas Aquinas lent it more gravity by including in his incarnational theology the concept of Jesus the man as *viator* (*Summa theologica* I q.113 a.4 ad 1; III q.15 a.10c). Gerhart Ladner has argued that without the "dynamic spell of the *peregrinatio* idea," medieval chivalric ideals—including such manifestations as the Crusades and the literary figure of the knight-errant—"could hardly have developed" (p. 246).

Like many ideas, that of *homo viator* existed in its society among competing experiences and values. Actual travel during the Middle Ages, of course, was dangerous, uncomfortable, and to a degree, suspect. In his *Historia Mongalorum* (c. 1247), John of Plano Carpini recalls that when members of his entourage rode through the German countryside wearing Mongol-style clothes brought back from East Asia, the locals pelted them with rocks. Pilgrims, merchants, and students journeyed in groups, protecting each other in ways that reinforced social bonds and hierarchies. Although Christians were enjoined to be hospitable to strangers and were forbidden to charge foreigners interest, wayfarers were at times branded as vagabonds and socially ostracized: the *Rule of St. Benedict* (c. 540s) identifies four different kinds of monks, the worst of them being *gyrovagi* who "spend their whole lives tramping from province to province . . . always on the move." Such "vagrant" clerics differ completely from the wandering missionary-saints of the next several centuries, particularly those of Ireland, such as Columbanus and Fursa.

Despite the idealization of a wandering life, nomads were generally disliked in medieval culture. Some European pilgrims to the Holy Land, although they may show tolerance for the area's indigenous inhabitants, express suspicion or outright disdain for the itinerant Bedouin. William of Boldensele, writing in 1336, notes their potential strategic importance against the sultan of Egypt, describing them as a people who "neither sow nor reap," but ignoring the implications of this allusion to the Sermon on the Mount (Matthew 6:26). Another apparently unconscious example of the tension in the *homo viator* ethos is found in William of Rubruck's brilliant epistolary travel report to King Louis IX (*c.* 1255), written after his two-year journey from Constantinople to the Mongol capital and back to Tripoli, near Beirut. William did not like many people he encountered, and his first, excoriating observation after stepping into the "other world" of the "Tartars" is that these people "have no abiding city nor do they know of the one that is to come." Since Europe was still reeling from the Mongol attacks of the previous decade, William's tone may not be surprising, but there is a certain irony in his direct citation of a verse attributed to St. Paul (Hebrews 13:14), underscoring the Christian's obligation to be a "stranger and pilgrim" rather than a citizen of this world.

Its rich and complicated texture encouraged diverse readings of *homo viator* during the Middle Ages. It enabled Ulysses to be read as a prototype of the Christian *peregrinus*. It underlies the universality of pilgrimage embedded in the eighteen-line opening sentence of the "General Prologue" to Geoffrey Chaucer's *Canterbury Tales* and explicit in the Parson's determination to show the way, "in this viage," to the celestial Jerusalem. It brings a uniqueness to Dante's literary function as traveler in *The Divine Comedy,* a work that turns Ulysses into a *gyrovagus*. The association of life with wayfaring did not depend on the institution of pilgrimage, as post-Reformation experience proved. The concept of *homo viator* drives the dense allegory of John Bunyan's *Pilgrim's Progress,* and it reinforces the alienation of James Joyce's Stephen Dedalus and Leopold Bloom.

### BIBLIOGRAPHY

Geremek, Bronislaw. "The Marginal Man." In *The Medieval World.* Ed. Jacques Le Goff. Trans. Lydia G. Cochrane. London: Collins and Brown, 1990; rpt. London: Parkgate Books, 1997, pp. 346–373. Originally published as *L'Uomo Medievale.* Rome: Laterza & Figli Spa. 1987.

Ladner, Gerhart B. "Homo Viator: Medieval Ideas on Alienation and Order." *Speculum* 42.2 (1967): 233–259.

Sumption, Jonathan. *Pilgrimage: An Image of Mediaeval Religion.* London: Faber, 1975.

*Scott D. Westrem*

### SEE ALSO

Chaucer, Geoffrey; Constantinople; Dante Alighieri; Egypt; Holy Land; John of Plano Carpini; Louis IX; Ludolf of Suchem; Mongols; Nomadism and Pastoralism; Pilgrimage, Christian; William of Boldensele; William of Rubruck

## Honorius Augustodunensis [sometimes "of Regensburg"] (late 11th–early 12th century)

Author of an influential and widespread "image of the world" (*Imago mundi*), a compendium of geographical, astronomical, calendrical, and historical information.

The identity of "Augustodunum," like that of Honorius himself, remains open to investigation; Autun is now considered erroneous. However, Honorius, who styled himself "Solitarius," has been linked more securely to Canterbury and especially to Regensburg. Honorius released his Latin encyclopedia around 1110 and revised it several times during the following thirty years. The *Imago mundi* became the geographical and historical resource of choice until the appearance of the larger, more comprehensive work of Bartholomaeus Anglicus in the later thirteenth century. During the thirteenth and fourteenth centuries it was adapted, either in whole or in part, into Anglo-Norman French, Old French, Italian, Welsh, and Icelandic. William Caxton's *Mirrour of the World* of 1480/1481 and 1490 translates the French *Image du Monde* of Gossouin (or Gautier) of Metz, which is based solidly on Honorius's work.

Of the extant manuscript copies of the *Imago mundi,* many open with a letter to the author from a certain "Christianus," who has been identified as the abbot of the Irish Benedictine cloister of St. James in Regensburg from 1133 to 1153, and Honorius's response, in which he agrees to "depict the whole world for you" (*"totius orbis tibi depingi"*). Since the *Imago mundi* gives special attention to Bavaria, particularly to Regensburg, Honorius probably completed the book there. However, several twelfth-century manuscripts produced in England that instead have a letter to one "Heinricus" seem to represent earlier versions. Together with a certain interest in England shown in Books 1 and 2, this may mean that Honorius began work on the *Imago mundi* in England, where he apparently lived for a time as a student of Anselm of Canterbury (1033–1109), and completed it when he moved to Germany, changing the dedication in the later versions. The text in Cambridge, Corpus Christi College MS

# H

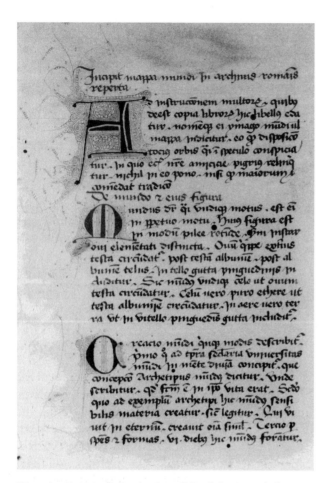

Honorius Augustodunensis, *Imago Mundi* (here entitled *Mappa Mundi*), Minneapolis, MN, James Ford Bell Library MS 1400/Ho, fol. 1, early 15th century. By permission of the James Ford Bell Library, University of Minnesota.

66, originally from Sawley in the diocese of Lincoln, is preceded by a *mappamundi* with similarities to the famous Hereford map.

Honorius was interested more in presenting raw information to be digested than in encouraging inquiry. He says in his prologue that he wrote the *Imago mundi* for "the instruction of the many, who lack copies of books" and he explains that he called his work "image of the world" because "the disposition of the whole world can be contemplated in it as if in a mirror." The title thus looks forward to the "mirrors" of the later Middle Ages, adopting the same specular image and pretense of completeness. By articulating geography and cosmology with chronology and history, the *Imago mundi* attempts to distill and to describe all space and time. It is, accordingly, an

abstract of what Honorius considered most worth knowing about his chosen subjects. In three books, the *Imago mundi* covers (1) the creation and shape of the world, the elements, geography, meteorology, and astronomy; (2) time and its measurement, including discussions of the *computus* and liturgical feasts; and (3) following the six world ages, history down through the Holy Roman Empire. The last section of the text— a chronological list of Roman emperors—has been used to distinguish among Honorius's several putative "editions" of his work. Honorius's prose employs rhyme and meter, and he addresses the reader in a familiar tone, using images of journeying or pilgrimage and avoiding complicated terminology.

Compiling the *Imago mundi* out of the works of late classical and early medieval writers, Honorius adhered for the most part to a traditional, specifically Carolingian, worldview, rather than broach the new learning of the twelfth century. Geographically as well as historically, Honorius's world comprises the Roman and Holy Roman Empires, the biblical Middle East, and a fabulous, often monster-inhabited Asia. The world of the *Imago mundi* is also a world of magic and astrology, in which stones, springs, and animals have special properties that often derive from the influence of the stars and planets. However, Honorius's interest in magic and astrology stays on the side of Christian orthodoxy, which accepted the special properties of things as part of the "scientific" study of nature so long as there was no attempt at divining the future with them. One of Honorius's motives for including a world history in the *Imago mundi* may have been to nullify the implicit fatalism of astrology with an implicitly Christian idea of providence, as was the case with other twelfth-century histories.

Honorius seldom names his sources in the text. Garrigues suggests that an important conceptual source is John Scotus Erigena (*c.* 810–*c.* 877). Honorius's book is, in the manuscript tradition, often attributed to another writer (Orosius, Bede, Henry of Huntington, Anselm of Canterbury) or given an alternative title (*De imagini mundi* or *mappa mundi*). The text also has several *incipits,* complicating attribution further. Factual material in Books 1 and 2 comes chiefly from the works of Pliny, Orosius, Isidore, Bede (probably the vehicle through which Honorius knew Pliny and Isidore), Hrabanus Maurus, and Helpericus; Book 3 draws chiefly from the Bible, Hyginus, Eusebius-Jerome, Orosius, Cassiodorus, Isidore, Bede, the *Histo-*

*ria Miscella,* Frutolf of Michelsberg, and Hermannus Contractus.

**BIBLIOGRAPHY**

Flint, Valerie I.J., ed. "World History in the Early Twelfth Century: The 'Imago Mundi' of Honorius Augustodunensis." In *The Writing of History in the Middle Ages: Essays Presented to Richard William Southern.* Ed. R.H.C. Davis and J.M. Wallace-Hadrill. Oxford: Clarendon Press, 1981, pp. 211–38. Rpt. in Flint, *Ideas in the Medieval West: Texts and Their Contexts.* No. 13. London: Variorum Reprints, 1988.

———. "Honorius Augustodunensis. *Imago Mundi.*" *Archives d'Histoire Doctrinale et Littéraire du Moyen Age* 57 (1982): 7–153.

———. "Honorius Augustodunensis." In *Authors of the Middle Ages: Historical and Religious Writers of the Latin West.* No. 6. Ed. Patrick J. Geary. Aldershot, Hants: Variorum Reprints, 1995, pp. 89–183.

Garrigues, Marie-Odile. "L'œuvre d'Honorius Augustodunensis: Inventaire critique." In *Abhandlungen der Braunschweigischen Wissenschaftlichen Gesellschaft* 38 (1986): 7–136; 39 (1987): 123–228; 40 (1988): 129–190. *Imago Mundi:* 38 (1986): 27–33, 116–118.

Simek, Rudolf. *Altnordische Kosmographie: Studien und Quellen zu Weltbild und Weltbeschreibung in Norwegen und Island vom 12. bis zum 14. Jahrhundert.* Ergänzungsbände zum Reallexikon der Germanischen Altertumskunde 4. Berlin and New York: de Gruyter, 1990, pp. 26–27, 75–83, 396–402.

Twomey, Michael W. "Appendix: Medieval Encylopedias." In *Medieval Christian Literary Imagery: A Guide to Interpretation.* R.E. Kaske, with Arthur Groos and Michael W. Twomey. Toronto Medieval Bibliographies 11. Toronto: U of Toronto P, 1988, pp. 182–215.

*Michael W. Twomey*

**SEE ALSO**

Ailly, Pierre d'; Bartholomaeus Anglicus; Bede; Hereford Map; Isidore of Seville; Orosius

## Horses and Harnesses

During the Middle Ages, the horse had a special role within medieval economy and society because of its versatility. Unlike the contemporary horse, usually referred to by breed name, the medieval horse was named according to specific purpose: *equus, affra, runcinus, palefredus, cursorius, dextrarius,* and *equus magnus.* Thus, information about specific breeds is lacking.

In Latin the terms *equus* (a general word) and *affra* or *avra* denoted work animals. Early in the Middle Ages, the word *runcinus* also applied to a draft horse, but by the fourteenth century, this term was applied to pack animals or inexpensive riding horses. *Palefredi* were relatively costly riding mounts. Though these horses were once thought to have been suitable only for ladies and priests to ride, some historians now believe that they were natural pacers valued for their smooth, even gait. The characteristic motion of the pacer would have rendered long-distance travel on such a horse far more comfortable than on a horse with a standard gait.

Related to the Latin verb "to run" (*cursare*), the term *cursorius* has frequently been misinterpreted in modern times as referring to the warhorse. Although the question has not been thoroughly examined, there seem to be three possible meanings for the word. First, it could have referred to hunting horses. Hunting on horseback was a popular pastime among the medieval nobility, who frequently brought their hawks, dogs, and gamekeepers with them on military campaigns. *Cursorii* might also have referred to swift running horses used by couriers to deliver messages over long distances. Finally, they might have been horses used for cross-country races. Whichever was the case, these were obviously animals selected for speed and not for hauling loads, plowing fields, or bearing warriors into battle.

Warhorses were the most expensive and specialized of all the medieval horse types. Usually referred to as *dextrarii* or *equi magni* (*destrier* in French), they were exclusively stallions and were ridden only in battle, for which their aggressive nature greatly suited them. These horses were extremely unpredictable and probably required considerable training to ensure some measure of control and safety. In general, warhorses belonged only to noblemen. Possession of these animals was linked to the individual's status as a knight and the public display of social position.

The appearance of the term *equus magnus* has led to serious debate over the size of the medieval warhorse; many believe that the expression implies an enormous and heavy animal. As yet, there is no conclusive evidence to indicate that these horses were of any particular size or breed. Pieces of horse armor do not survive from the period before the mid-fifteenth century (though there is a rather full description of some in *Gawain and the Green Knight* from about 1370), and archaeological remains have not produced anything suggesting that horses of remarkable size existed in the Middle Ages.

Over the course of the Middle Ages, horse technology changed in two ways. The most significant

# H

innovation was in carting and hauling, where early harnessing systems were greatly improved by the introduction of the padded horse collar in the tenth century, greatly increasing the horse's efficiency as a draft animal. Before this, the practice had been to attach the horse to the plow or cart by means of a throat latch or leather/canvas strap that encircled the horse's neck. Long leather thongs called traces ran from the latch to the front of the vehicle. Under the strain of hauling, the strap tended to slide up the animal's neck and could cause strangulation. The alternative to this system was the wooden yoke that lay across the backs of the animals' necks or withers. While relatively comfortable and effective for oxen, yokes caused tremendous stress and wear on horses. In addition, yokes required teams of two animals, and because of the rigidity and weight of the device, these two animals had to be of relatively equal height. The horse collar alleviated these problems. Made of padded leather, the collar redistributed the weight of hauling to the horse's powerful front quarters, which maximized the pulling power and prevented the injuries caused by the older systems. Unlike the throat latch or yoke, the horse collar also allowed for the flexibility of hitching teams in tandem or side by side. Teams could range from two animals to as many as six or seven.

Also, by the mid-fourteenth century, changes in military tactics had affected the horse's role. An increased emphasis on militia, archers, and lightly armed horsemen tended to replace the knight mounted on a warhorse as part of a heavy cavalry charge. As the initial charge of heavy cavalry lost acceptance as a military tactic, the role of the knights' horses in battle also decreased. During the Hundred Years' War (1337–1453), the warhorse gradually disappeared from the battlefield. Although costly horses would remain a symbol of social standing, the increasing availability of more ordinary varieties ended the horse's role as an exclusive commodity of the nobility.

## BIBLIOGRAPHY

Barber, Richard. *The Knight and Chivalry.* London: Longman Group, 1970.

Davis, R.H.C. *The Medieval Warhorse.* London: Thames and Hudson, 1989.

Goodall, Daphne, M. *A History of Horse Breeding.* London: Robert Hale Ltd., 1977.

Hyland, Ann. *The Horse in the Middle Ages.* Cambridge: Cambridge UP, 1999.

Langdon, J. *Horses, Oxen and Technological Innovation.* Cambridge: Cambridge UP, 1986.

*Margot Mortensen*

**SEE ALSO**
Economics and Trade; Transportation, Inland

## Hülegü (1217–1265)

Grandson of Chinggis Khân, brother of Möngke Khân, conqueror of Baghdad and Damascus, and founder of the il-khânate of Persia.

In order to complete and consolidate the Mongol conquests, the fourth great khân of the Mongols, Möngke (r. 1251–1259), planned two major military expeditions: the conquest of China and an expedition to the Middle East. The former task was assigned to his brother, Khubilai (the emperor of China 1260–1294, the great khân 1262–1294), the latter to another brother, Hülegü (d. 1265). One of the results of this assignment was that Hülegü set up his own kingdom, the il-khânate of Persia. It is unlikely that Möngke originally intended to grant Hülegü his own domain, but Hülegü's act was approved by the great khân after the fact. Hülegü's achievement as a conqueror and an empire builder is comparable to that of Khubilai, who founded the Yuan dynasty of China. Hülegü established and expanded Mongol rulership over a large part of the Middle East. Under Hülegü, Persia, which had been a mere geographical name for centuries, became a political entity and came into diplomatic contact with the West for the first time since antiquity.

Since Chinggis Khân's invasion of Persia (1219–1222), the Mongols had held suzerainty in its northeast province, but in other provinces the small native lords had maintained their independence. In order to bring the entire region under Mongol control, Hülegü was ordered to suppress the existing politico-spiritual powers in the region, that of the Muslim heretics, the Isma'ilis, and the Abbasid caliphate of Baghdad. By the terror of a small sect known as the Assassins, the Isma'ilis had been exercising control or influence in northern Persia, Iraq, and Syria for more than 150 years. Hülegü confronted them in 1256. The Assassins' grand master soon surrendered, their fortresses were demolished, and most of the Assassins of Persia were wiped out. Hülegü then entered Iraq in 1258 and demanded submission from the caliph. However nominal it may have become, the caliphate had been the central pillar of the Sunnite Muslim community for five centuries. After Caliph al-Musta'sim rejected his demand, Hülegü crushed the caliphate army and besieged Baghdad, forcing the caliph to surrender. Baghdad was looted, and many of the population, including the caliph himself, were killed. Members of the Abbasids escaped to Egypt, where Mamluk sultans thereafter maintained a line of puppet Abbasid caliphs until the Ottoman conquest of Egypt in 1517.

After the destruction of the caliphate, Hülegü proceeded to Azerbaijan, where he established the seat of his dynasty in the northern cities of Tabriz and Maragheh. Hülegü despatched the report of the conquest of Persia and Iraq to the great khân, and also reported his intention to conquer Syria and Egypt. Hülegü invaded Syria and besieged Aleppo, which belonged to the Muslim Ayyūbid dynasty. Hülegü's army was joined by the Christian army led by King Hetoum of Lesser Armenia and his son-in-law, Behemund IV of Antioch. Aleppo fell in January 1260 and was subjected to six days of massacre. Damascus was abandoned by its defenders and surrendered to Hülegü, who was still accompanied by Behemund's army (this association with Hülegü later brought Behemund a sentence of excommunication from the pope). By the early summer of 1260, the il-khân's army had conquered Muslim Syria and penetrated as far as Gaza. At this point, Hülegü received the news of Möngke's death and returned to Persia with the bulk of his army to attend the struggle for succession. The Mamluk ruler of Egypt, who had been offered by Hülegü's envoys the alternative of submission or war, summarily executed the envoys, and marched into Syria to counter the Mongols. The Mamluks, granted by the Franks of Acre a safe passage through the coastal area still held by the crusaders, penetrated into Jordan. The Mamluks defeated the Mongols on September 3, 1260, at Ain Jalut (Goliath's Well) in Palestine, and expelled the Mongols from Syria.

After this, Hülegü's attention was diverted to the northern Caucasian border, where the khân of the Golden Horde Berke (r. 1257–1267) threatened his new kingdom. Berke, the first Mongol khân to convert to Islam, had not only religious but also commercial reasons to ally himself with the Mamluks of Egypt: the Golden Horde was the main supplier of the slaves who constituted the Mamluk army. The inconclusive war between the Golden Horde and il-khânate outlived Hülegü, and lasted until Berke's death in 1267.

Domestically, Hülegü faced rebellions of his vassals, which he suppressed. Hülegü died in 1265 and was followed shortly thereafter by his chief wife, Doquz Khatun, a Kereit princess and Nestorian Christian, through whose influence the court of Hülegü had bestowed favors on the Christians, especially Nestorians. The deaths of Hülegü and Doquz Khatun were sincerely lamented by the Eastern Christians in the Middle East.

**BIBLIOGRAPHY**

Boyle, J.A., ed. *The Seljuq and Mongol Periods.* Vol. 5 of *The Cambridge History of Iran.* Cambridge: Cambridge UP, 1968.

Grousset, René. *The Empire of the Steppes.* New Brunswick, NJ: Rutgers UP, 1970.

Morgan, David. *The Mongols.* The Peoples of Europe Series. Oxford and New York: Blackwell, 1986.

Saunders, J.J. *The History of Mongol Conquests.* London: Routledge, 1971.

Spuler, Bertold. *The Muslim World: A Historical Survey,* Pt. 2, *The Mongol Period.* Leiden: Brill, 1960.

———. *The Mongols in History.* New York, Washington, and London: Praeger, 1971.

*Yoko Miyamoto*

**SEE ALSO**

Acre; Ain Jalut; Armenia; Assassins; Ayyūbids; Baghdad; Damascus; Eastern Christianity; Golden Horde; Mamluks; Mongol Khatuns; Nestorianism; Sunnism; Yuan Dynasty

# Hulk

A tubby, full-ended vessel, either round-bottomed or flat-floored, with characteristic upswept and rounded prow and stern, and one mast carrying a square sail. Like the cog, its more easterly Baltic counterpart, the hulk was one of northern Europe's basic ship types. Primarily a cargo carrier, it also served as a warship. It reached its heyday in the mid-1400s, when it was widely adopted throughout the Baltic and in various parts of Atlantic Europe.

The hulk originated between Calais and the mouth of the Rhine, in the seventh century or earlier. Coins from Dorestad (near Utrecht), struck around 800 C.E., feature hulks, and Frisian mariners used the ships for voyages to England, Norway, and the Baltic. By the thirteenth to fourteenth centuries, however, all the home ports of hulks still lay west of Amsterdam. The cog had meanwhile taken over the Baltic, and by 1300

# H

was spreading throughout Atlantic Europe and into the Mediterranean. Around 1400, hulks in turn began to replace cogs, and by the 1450s they prevailed throughout the Hanseatic area. A hulk was even dispatched by Henry the Navigator from Portugal to West Africa in 1452. In 1482, two hulks carried supplies for the building of the Portuguese fort of São Jorge da Mina, on the Gold Coast (Ghana).

The fifteenth-century hulk was usually too large (up to 500 tons) to be steered effectively by the earlier side rudder, and carried a stern one. Its hull was lapstrake or clinker-built in the northern tradition, with each plank overlapping the top edge of its lower neighbor. The planks ("strakes") typically swept upward in an arc from the hull to support the forecastle and sterncastle. The rounded bottom gave the hulk better structural integrity and improved its seakeeping, its full ends maximized cargo capacity, and its seamwork (plank joining) seems to have been less complicated than that of a cog.

## BIBLIOGRAPHY

Ellmers, Detlev. "The Cog as Cargo Carrier." In *Cogs, Caravels, and Galleons: The Sailing Ship, 1000–1650.* Ed. Robert Gardiner. Conway's History of the Ship. London: Conway Maritime Press, 1994, pp. 29–46.

Fliedner, Siegfried. "*Kogge* und *Hulk*: Ein Beitrag zur Schiffstypengeschichte." In *Die BremerHanse-Kogge: Fund, Kon-*

The seal of New Shoreham, England, second half of the 13th century. After Heino Wiechell. *Das Schiff auf Siegeln des Mittelalters und der beginnenden Neuzeit.* Lübeck: Kultusverwaltung, 1971.

*servierung, Forschung.* Ed. Herbert Abel. Monographien der Wittheit zur Bremen. No. 8. Bremen, 1969, pp. 39–122.

Greenhill, Basil, and Sam Manning. *The Evolution of the Wooden Ship.* London: Batsford, 1980.

Hutchinson, G. *Medieval Ships and Shipping.* London: Leicester UP, 1994.

Wiechell, Heino. *Das Schiff auf Siegeln des Mittelalters und der beginnenden Neuzeit.* Lübeck, Kultusverwaltung, 1971.

*Martin Malcolm Elbl*

SEE ALSO
Cog; Hanse, The; Henry the Navigator; Portuguese Expansion; Ships and Shipbuilding

## Hungary

An area centered in the Danube basin and bounded on the east by the Carpathian Mountains; the region was populated by westward-migrating Magyar tribes in the ninth century.

The Hungarians (Magyars) realized that they would be able to join Latin Europe's social and economic structure only by forming a single political organization and accepting Christianity. Prince Géza (r. 972–997) turned to the German court for missionaries, himself became a Christian, and defeated domestic tribal opposition to the new order; he, his son Stephen (István [r. 997–1038]), and Benedictine monks flocking to his court established the Catholic Church in Hungary. Stephen asked Rome for a crown, which Pope Sylvester II sent for the coronation in 1001. Following West Frankish examples, he organized fort and border districts, centralized the administration, and, by distributing land, created a stratum of landowners, thereby establishing the right to own property privately. He laid the foundation for Hungarian law, on the advice of his council, altering earlier customal laws. Stephen preserved his country's unity against domestic and foreign enemies, and maintained contacts with the papal and Western courts.

A pattern of trade was firmly established in the century that followed him. By the First Crusade the Rhine-Neckar-Danube trade route had developed, and during the Second Crusade, Odo de Deogilo recorded that the river Danube served as an international water route on which merchants shipped wares to and from Esztergom, the capital, seat of the archbishop, and commercial center of the realm. German, Polish, Italian, and Kievan merchants met there to sell their linen, other fabrics, hides, and domestic utensils; in turn, the Hungarians sold them corn, wines, wheat, animals, iron ore, and other metals. The town of Pest, where earlier Bulgarians of the Volga had settled and engaged in commercial activities, also played a role in trade on the Danube. By 1046, it was referred to as *portus,* and later sources refer to Pest as a town with numerous German merchants.

Though the country's economic role in Europe was well established, by the mid-twelfth century, relatively weak Hungarian rulers had to struggle with Byzantine expansionist policy; they eventually appealed to the West as they had before. Géza II (r. 1141–1162) secured some influence over the Balkans, while Béla III (r. 1172–1196) pursued political and cultural diplomacy oriented toward France. Béla married Margaret Capet, the daughter of Louis VII, developed Hungaro-French cultural relations, and invited French Cistercians and Premonstratensian canons to Hungary. He also extended his influence over the Byzantine court, marrying his daughter Margaret to Isaac II Angelos. During his reign Hungarian currency remained strong; he was one of the wealthiest monarchs of his age.

During the reign of Béla IV (1235–1270), the Mongols devastated the land, defeating the king at Muhi (April 11, 1241) and burning Pest, after which the king had to reconstruct the country. He reorganized the administration, founded cities, invited foreign settlers, rebuilt the military defenses, and established marches (*banates*) on the southern border. In his Law of 1267, he updated the constitution. Through his efforts, merchants in Hungary maintained commercial ties with German and Italian cities active in trade and business until the late thirteenth century. Wares from the east and from the southeast arrived in Hungary through Venice and the cities of the Dalmatian seacoast. (It should be noted that Eastern wares and products did not enter Hungary through the Danube; the Lower Danube was wholly impassable for larger galleys, and several reloadings of merchandise would have greatly increased the price of the goods, reducing profit for the merchant.) Merchants from Flanders and the Rhine region traveled through Regensburg, Vienna, and/or Moravia in order to reach Hungary, and Hungarian goods, such as raw gold and raw silver, left Hungary on the same route. By the end of the thirteenth century, however, domestic warfare, thieves, and robbers made travel in the country insecure; in addition, numerous illegally levied tolls collected by regional lords and even more confusing authorized and unauthorized monetary

transactions in the country caused foreign businessmen and domestic merchants to avoid business travel.

In the early fourteenth century, Charles Robert of Anjou, grandson of the daughter of Stephen V (r. 1270–1272), became king (known as Charles I [r. 1308–1342]), and Italian influence gained strength in the country. As Hungarian students frequented the universities of Bologna and Padua, a new social stratum of nobles emerged, together with a system of county-wide royal law courts or legislative sessions.

Charles restored economic connections with the Italians; in 1316, he issued letters of guarantee for merchants visiting from the south. Any merchant who, on entering the country, paid the regulated customs fee and the toll of one-thirtieth of the value of his imported merchandise was free to move about in the country and benefit from the king's legal protection. In his 1318 "Letter of Freedom for the Viennese merchants," the monarch granted similar privileges to them. Reconstruction of the west-German and Flemish trading contacts was more difficult because of the greedy personal politics of the duke of Austria, who insisted that foreign merchants passing through the duchy make a stop in Vienna to display their wares for sale before continuing their journey to the east. For that reason, the Hungarian, Czech, and Polish merchants traveling the Cracow-Brünn-Vienna route had to find an alternative road to travel; beginning in the 1260s, the Hungarians had taken the Buda-Esztergom-Nagyszombat-Holich-Brünn route toward Germany, a route neutralized by deteriorating Hungaro-Czech relations in the 1290s. By the Treaty of Visegrád in 1335, which had an anti-Austrian bias, the kings of Hungary, Bohemia, and Poland effectively regulated merchant traffic on the northern route.

Both Charles I of Hungary and John of Bohemia issued writs of protection to merchants traveling through their territories, regulating the collection and amount of custom dues on the Holich segment of the route; they struck a similar commercial deal with Poland. In Visegrád, Charles also reconciled John of Bohemia with Casimir of Poland. With these arrangements and the establishment of routes from Kassa and Löcse to Cracow and from Kassa through the mining towns in upper Hungary, Zsolna, and Teschen toward Brünn (that is, excluding Vienna), Hungary had, once again, joined the mainstream of international commerce and business trade.

The political scene shifted when Charles's elder son, Lajos (the Great [r. 1342–1382]), led two campaigns

# H

against Naples and occupied it. He aided Poland against the pagan Lithuanians, and prepared for war with the Turks. He combined the administrations of Moldavia and of the Szörény march, and married the daughter of the Head Steward of Bosnia, because he wanted to fight the Serbs, who already occupied the southern portion of Bosnia. When Head Steward Bogdán became prince of Moldavia and formed an alliance with the Serbs and the Bulgarians, Lajos allied himself with the Polish and Bavarian courts, becoming king of Poland in 1370. He defeated Sultan Murad I, humiliated Tsar Simeon of Bulgaria, and confronted the republic of Venice.

During his reign Hungary reached the height of its territorial extension. In addition, the Hungarian currency, the *forint,* based on the gold standard, was stabilized, and a strong Hungaro-Polish-Russian trading network was formed in the northeastern part of the realm, thereby aiding the development of national industry and trade. As for the newly formed Rumanian principalities, Lajos established trading contracts with them through the "Saxon" (German) towns in Transylvania. Lajos made donations to the pilgrimage centers of Mariazell and Aachen, established the University of Pécs in 1367, fought to end domestic violence, and confirmed anew the privileges of the nobility, marking the period as one of great advancement, though the stability of the area was constantly threatened by the advances of the Turks, who destroyed Serbia and occupied Dalmatia in 1389.

After John Hunyadi and the Franciscan John Capistrano halted the Turkish advance into central Europe at Belgrade, the lesser Hungarian nobility elected Hunyadi's son, Matthias I Corvinus, king (1458–1490). Matthias was a Renaissance monarch, surrounded by Hungarian and Italian humanists, such as the historian Antonio Bonfini and the poet Ianus Pannonius. In Buda he established a printing press in 1473; in the royal castle he founded a library of 500 handwritten volumes (*corvinae*) and concluded the construction of the castle in Renaissance style. Under his successors the economic importance of the country declined rapidly, although culture continued to flourish in this, the golden age of Hungarian illuminated manuscripts.

Medieval Hungary was destroyed when the country was defeated by the Turks in 1526 at the battle of Mohács.

## BIBLIOGRAPHY

Bogyay, Thomas. *Stephanus Rex.* Vienna-Munich: Harold, 1975.

Bosl, K., et al., eds. *Eastern and Western Europe in the Middle Ages.* London: Thames & Hudson, 1970.

Fine, John V. A., Jr. *The Early Medieval Balkans: A Critical Survey from the Sixth to the Late Twelfth Century.* Ann Arbor: U of Michigan P, 1983.

———. *The Late Medieval Balkans: A Critical Survey from the Late Twelfth Century to the Ottoman Conquest.* Ann Arbor: U of Michigan P, 1987.

Hóman, Bálint. *Geschichte des ungarischen Mittelalters.* 2 vols. Berlin: de Gruyter, 1940–1943.

Kosztolnyik, Z.J. *From Coloman the Learned to Béla III (1095–1196): Hungarian Domestic Policies and Foreign Affairs.* East European Monographs. New York: Columbia UP, 1987.

———. *Hungary in the Thirteenth Century.* New York: Columbia UP, 1996.

Macartney, C.A. *Hungary.* Chicago: Aldine, 1962.

Marczali, Henrik, ed. *Enchiridion fontium historiae Hungarom.* Budapest: Athenaeum, 1901.

*Z.J. Kosztolnyik*

## SEE ALSO

Byzantine Empire; Crusades, First, Second, and Third; Gerbert of Aurillac; Merchants, Italian; Ottoman Empire; Poland; Russia and Rus'; Venice

## Huns

A nomadic people, presumably of Central Asian origin, who first came to the attention of the Roman West around 376, when their depredations in the northern Balkans forced several Germanic groups to petition for permission to cross the Danube and take refuge in Roman territory.

Nothing remains of the Hunnic language but names preserved in other languages. Since they left few artifacts and no written records of their own, we know them only through the accounts of Greek and Roman historians, all of whom saw them primarily as a dangerous threat to the empire. The only historian who wrote from personal experience was Priscus, whose account of a visit to the headquarters of Attila in 449–450 has come down to us through Cassiodorus and Jordanes. The other accounts are a biased mixture of legend and hearsay. According to the legends, the Huns were the result of carnal intercourse between evil spirits and some witches who had been cast out of Gothic society. They had long dwelt to the east of the Meotic marshes (the modern-day Sivash or Putrid Sea), ignorant of any other peoples until a cow (or a deer in some versions of the story) led them through the marsh and they discovered, and immediately attacked, the people of the Crimea.

The Huns were traditionally herders and warriors. Though they must have traded with both their Roman and their German neighbors, they found it more lucrative to take what they needed by force, threat of force, and deceit. Many Huns also served as mercenaries in Roman armies.

Their mode of fighting was based on their expert horsemanship; they were the first light cavalry. Each warrior kept a string of small, tough horses. In battle, a rider would dash quickly toward the enemy, loose several arrows, and retreat. He would then jump onto a fresh horse and attack again. Since he always had a fresh horse, he could keep on attacking indefinitely. Unable to stand up to them in battle, their neighbors, especially the Eastern Empire, paid them not to attack.

They formed alliances when it suited their purposes, and dissolved those alliances when they were no longer needed. Under Attila's leadership they also often succeeded in playing one neighbor against another, to their own advantage. Acting as allies of Rome, the Huns defeated the Burgundians in a battle on the Rhine in 437, a battle that later provided the historical background for the *Nibelungenlied* and other literary works.

By the time of Attila, the Huns were the predominant power in a very large area stretching from the Balkans to the Baltic, and were ready to move west in search of further wealth and power. Early in 451, a large army of Huns left Pannonia (roughly, present-day Hungary), crossed the Rhine, probably somewhere near Mainz, and attacked Gaul. Trier and Metz fell to their onslaught, and so fierce were the attacks that other cities, such as Strasbourg, which were not even approached, developed in time their own legends about being attacked by the Huns. The Huns besieged Orléans, but a Roman army came to its rescue in time, and the Huns withdrew to the neighborhood of Troyes; after nearly being destroyed, they were finally allowed to retreat. The next year, Italy was the target, but after destroying Aquileia, Pavia, Milan, and other cities, the Huns, faced with famine, abandoned their campaign.

The Huns returned to Pannonia. Attila threatened to attack the Eastern Empire, but he no longer had enough military power to do so, and the empire stopped sending tribute. After Attila died in 453, his heirs were unable to maintain his political control, and despite the absence of either outside attack or internal revolt, the Hunnic nation within a few generations disintegrated and disappeared.

The basis of the Hunnic economy was their animals. They certainly kept horses and sheep, and probably also cattle. There is no evidence of their having practiced agriculture, but there is evidence that they obtained grain by trade or as tribute from subjugated agricultural peoples. Priscus describes in some detail the wooden structures of Attila's headquarters, but such fixed places were probably unusual; most of the Huns lived most of the time in tents. The enormous amounts of gold obtained from Constantinople as tribute or as ransom for captives taken in battle could be used to buy weapons and such luxuries as silk and wine. Captives not ransomed could be sold at slave markets on the Danube frontier. The Huns also traded in horses, and possibly furs, at the Roman frontier markets.

The Huns constituted a serious danger to all their neighbors for about three-quarters of a century, but the stories and legends of later centuries greatly exaggerated their ferocity. Although some writers portrayed the Huns as noble warriors and Attila as a wise, generous, and just ruler, most of the descriptions were the products of historians and theologians who had never seen a Hun, but wrote and preached as though they were still to be feared, in order to make their audiences either more patriotic or more pious. Thus, the Huns became the symbol and exemplar of barbarian cruelty and ruthlessness, and that reputation has persisted in most Western lands until today. The exception is Hungary, where Attila is still a common male name, and where many people regard the Huns as "forefathers" of the Magyars, despite all historical evidence to the contrary.

**BIBLIOGRAPHY**

Bury, John Bagnell. *The Invasion of Europe by the Barbarians.* New York: Russel and Russel, 1963.

Gordon, C.D. *The Age of Attila: Fifth-Century Byzantium and the Barbarians.* Ann Arbor: U of Michigan P, 1972.

Jordanes. *The Gothic History of Jordanes.* Intro. Charles Christopher Mierow. Princeton: Princeton UP, 1915.

Maenchen-Helfen, Otto. *The World of the Huns: Studies in Their History and Culture.* Ed. Max Knight. Berkeley: U of California P, 1973.

Thompson, E.A. *A History of Attila and the Huns.* Oxford: Clarendon Press, 1948.

*James V. McMahon*

**SEE ALSO**

Attila; Cosmas Indikopleustes; Inner Asian Trade; German Literature, Travel in; Nestorianism; Nomadism and Pastoralism

# I

## Ibn Battūta, Abu Abdallah (1304–1368)

Great medieval traveler and author of an extremely detailed Arabic travel account. Ibn Battūta was born in Tangier, Morocco, in 1304. His family included prominent Muslim legal scholars, and he himself undertook the study of Islamic law as taught in the Maliki legal school. In 1325, he left Tangier to make the *hajj,* or pilgrimage to Mecca; he did not return until 1349 after extensive travels throughout the Muslim world, which then extended to the Indian subcontinent and beyond. In addition to the Arabian Peninsula, he traveled through North Africa, Egypt, Palestine, Iraq, and Persia. In 1326, he embarked on a sea voyage to the coast of East Africa, Oman, and the Persian Gulf. In 1330, he departed for India to seek employment as a legal functionary in the sultanate of Delhi. On the way he visited Constantinople and Asia Minor before crossing Transoxiana, Khurasan, Afghanistan, and Sind.

For some years he was appointed a *qādī* (judge) by Sultan Muhammad Tughluq of Delhi. After having suffered shipwreck at the onset of a diplomatic mission on behalf of the sultan to the court of the Mongol emperor of China, Ibn Battūta sailed to Sri Lanka, the Maldive Islands—where he was again employed as a *qādī* for some time—and, finally, China. On his return home to Morocco in 1349, he established himself in Fez, but his urge to travel was not yet satisfied. In 1350, he visited Granada and Andalusia; then, between 1353 and 1355, he undertook a journey across the Sahara to the kingdom of Mali. After Battūta's return to Fez in 1356, the Marinid sultan of Morocco, Abū 'Inān, asked the scribe and writer Abu Juzayy to record Ibn Battūta's

travel account. The traveler was subsequently employed as a *qādī* in a provincial Moroccan town until his death in 1368.

The text compiled by Ibn Juzayy on the basis of Ibn Battūta's notes and oral account, entitled *Tuhfat al-nuzzar fi ghara'ib al-amsar wa-'aja'ib al-asfar* (Precious gift to those interested in the wonders of cities and the marvels of traveling), or, more commonly, *al-Rihla* (The Journey), is not merely a journal or a compilation of notes, but a lively and elaborate report of Ibn Battūta's adventures: it consists of descriptions of countries and cities visited; persons met; historical, anthropological, and economic information obtained; and legends and anecdotes gathered. The account is sufficiently colored by personal experiences to give us a fairly clear sense of Ibn Battūta's personality. Apparently, he was as much driven by religious zeal, and an inclination for asceticism and mysticism, as by personal ambition, authentic wanderlust, and an appreciation for life's pleasures. During his travels he married several times and enjoyed food and luxury, but he also retired more than once in Sufi monasteries to dedicate himself to God. He was probably only a mediocre scholar of Islamic thought, whose ambition forced him to seek employment outside his home country.

Even during his lifetime, the authenticity of Ibn Battūta's travels was contested by some, but the general opinion is that he did, in fact, accomplish the travels that he claims to have made, with the possible exception of his visit to Constantinople and his journey into the interior of China. In addition, the route and time schedule for his travels through Persia and Central Asia include some marked inconsistencies. His descriptions

**I**

of the towns of the Arab Middle East contain some quotations from the famous Andalusian traveler Ibn Jubayr (whose work supplies Ibn Battūta's account with stylistic features that were expected in Arabic travel literature of the time). It is difficult to determine whether these textual problems are authorial or scribal. In any event, the *Rihla* of Ibn Battūta is one of the main sources—and for some areas the only major source—for our knowledge of the Muslim world in the fourteenth century.

**BIBLIOGRAPHY**

Défrémery, C., and B.R. Sanguinetti, trans. and eds. *Voyages d'Ibn Batouta*. 4 vols. Paris, 1853–1858; rpt. 3 vols. Paris: François Maspero, 1982.

Dunn, Ross E. *The Adventures of Ibn Battuta, a Muslim Traveler of the 14th Century*. Berkeley: U of California P, 1986.

Gibb, H.A.R., trans. *The Travels of Ibn Battūta A.D. 1325–1354, Translated with Revisions and Notes from the Arabic Text Edited by C. Défrémery and B.R. Sanguinetti*. 4 vols. Hakluyt Society, o.s., 2nd series, 110, 117, 141, 178. London: Hakluyt Society, 1958, 1961, 1971, 1995.

Hrbek, I. "The Chronology of Ibn Battuta's Travels." *Archiv Orientalni* 30 (1962): 409–486.

*Voyageurs Arabes; Ibn Fadlan, Ibn Jubayr, Ibn Battuta et un auteur anonyme*. Trans. Paule Charles-Dominique. Paris: Gallimard, 1995.

*Richard van Leeuven*

**SEE ALSO**

China; Constantinople; Ibn Jubayr; India; Mecca; Muslim Travelers and Trade

## Ibn Jubayr (1145–1217)

A Muslim pilgrim and traveler. Abu al-Husayn Muhammad Ibn Ahmad Ibn Jubayr, a native of Valencia, Spain, commenced a journey (*rihla*) from Granada on February 13, 1183, that lasted for more than two years, returning on April 25, 1185. He undertook two other journeys, in 1189–1191, and in 1204, which took him to Alexandria, where he died in 1217. As is shown in the almost daily record of his observations, his deeply orthodox piety and undisguised anti-Christian prejudices never interfered with his vivid and objective reporting.

His journey began when he boarded a Genoese ship from Ceuta to Alexandria. After performing the pilgrimage to Mecca, he visited Egypt, Iraq, and Syria, then entered the crusading states in 1184 in the company of Muslim merchants who were still operating freely even during the decisive campaigns of Saladin (1174–1193). Citing the generally tolerant policy of the Latin authorities toward their Muslim subjects and the amity between Christians and their Muslim neighbors, he lamented the fact that the average Muslim under Frankish rule fared much better than his counterpart in the Islamic states. His mistrust of the interaction between cultural groups and the resulting danger to Islamic rigor was to become a recurrent theme of his journals.

On October 18, 1184, Ibn Jubayr sailed from Acre aboard a Genoese ship in the company of more than 2,000 Christian pilgrims from whom he and other Muslims segregated themselves. When the ship was wrecked off the shore of Sicily, it was the intervention of William II that saved the passengers from the consequences of the *jus naufragii,* the so-called law of shipwreck, a custom that allowed the local inhabitants to loot the cargo of a wrecked ship. Continuing his journey, he visited Messina, Palermo, Trapani, and other parts of Sicily, and was astonished at the pervasive influence of Islam and Muslims on the culture of Norman Sicily. Throughout the island, he saw numerous mosques, and met Muslim artisans, merchants, farmers, and landowners. William II's luxurious court looked to him like that of a Muslim monarch. He met state functionaries who confided in him that they were actually secret Muslims—a fact that was well-known to the Christian king.

The benevolence of the Hautevilles toward their Muslim subjects, however, deeply disturbed Ibn Jubayr and the leaders of the Sicilian Muslims. Tolerance, combined with certain privileges reserved for proselytes, tended to seduce many Muslims into conversion to Christianity. In recording complex attitudes of this kind, Ibn Jubayr's observations provide valuable information on the social and economic life of the regions he visited.

**BIBLIOGRAPHY**

Samarrai, Alauddin. "Some Geographical and Political Information on Western Europe in the Medieval Arabic Sources." *Muslim World* 62 (1972): 304–322.

———. "Medieval Commerce and Diplomacy: Islam and Europe, A.D. 850–1300." *Canadian Journal of History* 14 (1980): 1–21.

*The Travels of Ibn Jubayr*. Ed. William Wright. 2nd edition rev. by M.J. de Goeje. Leiden: Brill, 1907; rpt. New York: AMS Press, 1973.

The Travels of Ibn Jubayr. Trans. R.J.C. Broadhurst. London: Jonathan Cape, 1952.

*Alauddin Samarrai*

SEE ALSO

Acre; Crusades, First, Second, and Third; Egypt; Genoa; Muslim Travelers and Trade; Pilgrimage, Christian; Saladin; Spain and Portugal

## Ibrāhīm Ibn Ya'qūb al-Isrā'īli (fl. 960s)

A Hispano-Arab Jewish traveler from the Andalusian city of Tortosa. Very little is known about Ibrāhīm except that he was perhaps a merchant who visited France, Germany, and eastern Europe after the middle of the tenth century. The fact that he met Emperor Otto I in 966 at Magdeburg strongly suggests the possibility that he was also on a diplomatic mission for the Umayyad caliph of Córdoba, al-Hakam II (r. *c.* 961–973). His special interest in medical problems gives the impression that he was a physician. The suggestion that he might have been a slave trader cannot be supported by the evidence.

Ibrāhīm's complete report is not extant, but major portions of it are preserved by Muslim writers, indicating that he wrote his observations in the Arabic script rather than in Hebrew letters. His account contains valuable information about Germany, Bohemia, and eastern Europe. He was the earliest writer to mention Poland ("the Kingdom of Mieszko"), describing the military establishment under Mieszko I (baptized in 966; reigned *c.* 960–992), where the king provided his soldiers and their children with all necessities, including dowries for the daughters. He describes Prague as a commercial center where Rus' and Slavs came from Cracow, and Turkish, Muslim, and Jewish merchants brought their wares, as well as Byzantine gold coins, and carried back slaves, tin, and various kinds of pelts and leatherwork. He observes the use in Bohemia of token money in the form of netlike napkins, undoubtedly for local use only. Ibrāhīm's account includes notices on the social customs and sexual mores of the pagan Slavs: unmarried women were expected to be promiscuous, and a man would dismiss his bride if he found her a virgin; married women, however, would never commit adultery, and widows often killed themselves and were cremated with their husbands.

Ibrāhīm Ibn Ya'qūb also mentions the fauna and flora of the regions he visited, sometimes giving the names of animals and plants in the original Slavonic.

BIBLIOGRAPHY

Ashtor, E. "Ibrāhīm Ibn Ya'qūb." *The World History of the Jewish People.* 2nd series. Vol. 2: *The Dark Ages.* Ed. Cecil Roth. New Brunswick: Rutgers UP, 1966, pp. 305–308.

el-Hajji, Abdurrahman. "Ibrāhīm Ibn Ya'qūb at-Turtūshi and His Diplomatic Activity." *Islamic Quarterly* 14 (1970): 22–40.

Rapoport, Semen. "On the Early Slavs: The Narrative of Ibrahim-Ibn-Yakub." *Slavonic and East European Review* 8 (1929): 331–341.

*Relatio Ibrāhīm ibn Ja'kūb de Itinere Slavico, quae traditur apud al-Bekrī.* Ed. and trans. into Latin and Polish with notes by Tadeusz Kowalski. In *Monumenta Poloniae Historica,* n.s., 1. Cracow: Gebethnera and Wolffa, 1946.

Samarrai, Alauddin. "Medieval Commerce and Diplomacy: Islam and Europe, A.D. 850–1300." *Canadian Journal of History* 14 (1980): 1–21.

*Alauddin Samarrai*

SEE ALSO

Jewish Travelers; Muslim Travelers and Trade; Poland; Russia and Rus'; Spain and Portugal; Thomas of Cantimpré

## Iceland

An island, approximately 39,700 square miles (103,220 square kilometers) in area, located just below the Arctic Circle in extreme northwestern Europe between the Atlantic and Arctic oceans, whose inhabitants contributed significantly to medieval trade, exploration, and culture, especially from the tenth through the mid-thirteenth centuries.

It is impossible to know when Iceland was discovered or when humans first inhabited it. An island called Thule appears in Greek geographical writing around 300 B.C.E., when Pytheas of Massilia [Marseilles] saw it at the edge of a "Frozen Sea." During the next millennium this toponym appears in a variety of texts—from Tacitus's biography of his father-in-law, Agricola, who is said to have glimpsed it in *c.* 80 C.E. while conducting naval maneuvers, to Virgil's *Georgics* (1.30), where "Ultima Thule" symbolizes the seemingly limitless extent of Rome's potential achievements under Augustus Caesar—but the location's characteristic features of "sluggish" seas, constant summer light, and remoteness could equally well apply to any number of places in the far north, from Norway to Greenland. Indeed, Thule

# I

was probably no more geographically fixed in the classical imagination than Timbuktu is in ours.

The earliest reliable usage of "Thule" to identify Iceland is in *De mensura orbis terrae* (*c.* 825), by the Irish Benedictine scholar Dicuil, who described eremitic monks (*papar*) from his native country sailing to the island in the late 700s on journeys of private devotion. Norse settlement of Iceland began around 870 and ended sixty years later when a nationwide assembly, the Alþingi, was established, according to Ari the Learned's *Íslendingabók* (Book of the Icelanders), a work that was written *c.* 1130 and whose distance in time from the events recorded casts some doubt on its chronology (large farms were still being founded in the eleventh century). Most of the early colonists were from western Norway; the Icelandic literary tradition attributes their bold *landnám* (land-taking) in large part to a desire to escape political persecution by the autocratic Haraldr hárfagri (Fine-Hair) Hálfdanarson, who was determined to unify Norway (he succeeded *c.* 890), but important works in this tradition were written during the thirteenth century and may reflect the anxieties of that time, when Norwegian kings were attempting to extend their authority to Iceland (it was, in fact, annexed to Norway and/or Denmark from 1262/1264 to 1944). Such is the case with the famous opening chapters of *Laxdœla saga,* written around 1245, which depict Ketil Flat-Nose, a powerful Norwegian chieftain in the later 800s, refusing to subject himself to Haraldr and deciding to emigrate; his two sons choose to go to Iceland because it has excellent land just waiting to be taken, as well as plenty of stranded whales, salmon, and fishing grounds (Ketil opts to go to Scotland, observing that as an old man he has no desire to see the "land of fish" to which his sons are bound).

Even during the first centuries of Iceland's settlement, when the weather was relatively warm and dry, maritime commerce was essential. Immigrants brought with them, or imported, all domestic animals, as well as cereal grains and luxury goods. In its pristine state the island was evidently covered in brush and small trees, but the sagas make clear that the gathering of driftwood for building materials was from early days an important occupation; ships for offshore fishing and transatlantic trade had to be brought in from abroad. Exports included homespun (cloth woven from high-quality local wool), hides, and furs; after 1300, dried fish from Icelandic waters was an especially popular commodity in European markets.

Trade became a matter of survival after the later twelfth century, when agriculture all but ceased in the northern part of the island as a cooler, wetter climate deleteriously affected it (and much of Europe). Simultaneously, Norwegian merchants came to dominate the market with larger, more efficient ships able to call at only a few ports in Iceland, bringing goods to and from Niþaróss (Trondheim) and then, during the 1200s, Bergen. (In 1152/1153, all Norse settlements in the North Atlantic were incorporated in the new archdiocese of Niþaróss, after which church authorities in Norway involved themselves increasingly in ecclesiastical affairs in Iceland, where Christianity was introduced in 999/1000.) The fact that the Black Death did not reach Iceland even when it was ravaging the other Scandinavian countries during 1349–1350 probably indicates how suddenly and devastatingly the Norwegian shippers were hit by the disease; the calamity ended a period of very active trading. Iceland had its own experience of a "Great Plague" between 1402 and 1404. During the early fifteenth century, English fishermen entered Icelandic waters; by 1440, England was Iceland's principal trading partner, remaining so for at least the next century.

The dominance of other national powers in Icelandic commerce during the later Middle Ages should not obscure the island's earlier status as a leader in maritime achievements, beginning with its very settlement. The discovery and, in some cases, exploration of coastal areas of Greenland (by 930) and North America (after *c.* 986) by Icelanders (or others almost exclusively of Norse background) forms the subject matter of a group

"Irreland" [Iceland] with bears. *Les Secretz de la Nature,* Château d'Aulnoy, Coulommiers (Seine et Marne) Collection Charnacé, unnumbered MS, fol. 45, *c.*1460. Photo by John B.

of texts known collectively as the Vínland sagas (they are based on oral tradition, but the earliest was not written down until around 1200, probably in Iceland). Icelandic annals record the discovery of Spitsbergen (Svalbarþi) in 1194. A monk named Nikulás (identified as Nicholas of Þverá) visited Rome and the Holy Land between 1249 and 1254; his *Leiþarvísir* (Guide) details his route and occasional experiences. Another description of holy sites from Rome to Jerusalem, via Constantinople, versions of which appear in three fourteenth-century manuscripts, may also be Nikulás's work. A brief *Wegur til Róms* (Way to Rome) lists place-names and distances from Lübeck to Rome on a route that crosses the Brenner Pass. Two other travel books are lost: the *Flos peregrinationis* recorded the extensive travels in southern Europe of Gizurr Hallson (d. July 27, 1206), who was Iceland's law-speaker from 1181 to 1200; Björn Einarsson, *Jórsalafari* ("Jerusalem-pilgrim," *c.* 1350–1415), told of his three trips to Rome—the last journey also taking him to Jerusalem, Santiago da Compostella, and Canterbury between 1405 and 1411—in his *Reisubók* (Travel Book), known today only from excerpts in an eighteenth-century manuscript.

Icelanders also demonstrated keen scholarly interest in geography and cosmography, although the scientific literature shows little vestige of a pagan Germanic "worldview." Instead, knowledge was drawn from such encyclopedic works as Pliny's *Historia naturalis* (79 C.E.), Solinus's *Collectanea rerum memorabilium* (*c.* 230/240), Isidore of Seville's *Etymologies* (622–633), Bede's *De natura rerum* (before 725), Hrabanus Maurus's *De universo* (after 840), Honorius Augustodunensis's *Imago mundi* (*c.* 1110), Lambert of Saint Omer's *Liber floridus* (1112–1121), Peter Comestor's *Historia scholastica* (late 1100s), Alexander Neckham's *De naturis rerum* (*c.* 1200), John of Sacrobosco's *Tractatus de sphaera* (1220), and Vincent of Beauvais's *Speculum naturale* and *Speculum historiale* (*c.* 1254). Old Norse texts show no direct awareness of Orosius's history or Beatus of Liébana's cartography. Information from these non-Scandinavian sources was included in Icelandic vernacular texts on geography and ethnography (including catalogues of the "monstrous races" of humans and enumerations of the world's 1,000 peoples and/or seventy-two spoken languages); their dates indicate that twelfth-century (and later) works were already known in Iceland shortly after their composition.

The most important of these texts is the so-called *Stjórn,* a compilation of biblical history commissioned around 1300 by King Hákon Magnússon of Norway, in which a lengthy geographical section is taken largely from Vincent's *Speculum.* A codex known as *Hauksbók* (Haukr's Book), no longer intact and missing approximately seventy of what once were some 210 leaves, was copied out in the early 1300s by (among others) Haukr Erlendsson, an Icelander who was for many years a judge in Norway. The manuscript was originally a kind of florilegium—its content and eclectic form may, in fact, have been inspired by Lambert's *Liber floridus*—containing sagas and Icelandic versions of Latin historical, theological, geographical, and mathematical texts, including a complete translation of Honorius's encyclopedic *Elucidarius* (all or part of his *Imago mundi* was also circulating in Old Norse by *c.* 1300). Another compendium of world geography and history formed the content of a lost thirteenth-century manuscript known as *Gripla.* Of the fourteen known medieval European city maps of Jerusalem, three were drawn in Iceland during the 1300s; one of these is in *Hauksbók.* Three manuscripts preserve five *mappaemundi* made in Iceland during the thirteenth and early fourteenth centuries; three of these depict the earth's climate zones, one combines a simple T-O map with details about elemental properties and the twelve winds, and one is a double-page representation of the inhabited world with some 125 descriptive legends. Four maps of the cosmos, all from the 1300s, are also known. Taken together, the corpus of Icelandic texts shows perhaps the most advanced understanding of the geography of Europe held anywhere during the Middle Ages even if the writers believed that northern Russia and Greenland were connected by land and that "Vinland" and Africa were similarly conjunctive in southern latitudes.

As was the case on the Continent, geographical information was sometimes included in literary works to lend an air of intelligent authority. The remarkable man of letters and political leader Snorri Sturluson (1178/1179–1241) inserts descriptions of the world at or near the beginning of his *Ynglinga saga* (the first section of *Heimskringla* [Circle of the World]) and *Prose Edda* (also known as *Snorra Edda*); in both he offers "Énéa" (derived from Aeneas) as an alternative name for the continent of Europe, and in the latter he quite unusually begins his tour of the *oikoumene* with Africa, before turning to Europe and then Asia, where he locates the center of the world and people who are superior in wisdom, strength, beauty, and ability. Scandinavian geography figures importantly in many sagas,

# I

but awareness of other parts of the world is particularly important in *Nikulás saga,* by the Benedictine Bergr Sokkason (early 1300s); *Orvar-Odds saga* (1275/1300), in which events are set in eastern Europe; the fourteenth-century *Kirialax saga,* which borrows from Nicholas of Þvera's pilgrimage; *Samsons saga fagra* (The Saga of Fair Samson [*c.* 1400]), with ethnographic material like that in Hauksbók; and Dínus saga dramblátá (The Saga of Dínus the Haughty [1300s]), a very popular story of an Egyptian prince (Dínus), who meets his match with an arrogant princess from Bláland ("Blue/black-land," or Ethiopia). In addition, *Konungs skuggsjá* (*c.* 1260), with its cosmographical material, was known in Iceland, and the Augustinian abbot Brandr Jónsson translated Walter of Châtillon's *Alexandreis* into Icelandic, also *c.* 1260.

**BIBLIOGRAPHY**
Byock, Jesse L. *Medieval Iceland: Society, Sagas, and Power.* Berkeley and Los Angeles: U of California P, 1988.
Gelsinger, Bruce E. *Icelandic Enterprise: Commerce and Economy in the Middle Ages.* Columbia: U of South Carolina P, 1981.
Hastrup, Kirsten. *Culture and History in Medieval Iceland: An Anthropological Analysis of Structure and Change.* Oxford: Clarendon Press, 1985.
Maurer, K. "Islands und Norwegens Verkehr mit dem Süden vom IX. bis XIII. Jahrhunderte." *Zeitschrift für Deutsche Philologie* 2 (1870): 440–468.
Simek, Rudolf. *Altnordische Kosmographie: Studien und Quellen zu Weltbild und Weltbeschreibung in Norwegen und Island vom 12. bis zum 14. Jahrhundert.* Ergänzungsbände zum Reallexikon der Germanischen Altertumskunde 4. Berlin and New York: Walter de Gruyter, 1990.

*Scott D. Westrem*

**SEE ALSO**
Beatus Maps; Bede; Dicuil; Geography in Medieval Europe; Honorius Augustodunensis; Isidore of Seville; *King's Mirror, The; Liber Floridus; Mappamundi;* Navigation; Navigation, Viking; Nicholas of Þvera; Pilgrimage, Christian; Pliny the Elder; Sacrobosco, John of; Solinus, Julius Gaius; Thule; Viking Age; Viking Discoveries and Settlements; Vincent of Beauvais; Vinland Map; Vinland Sagas; Walter of Châtillon

## Imago mundi
*See* Honorius Augustodunensis

## Imrama

A medieval Irish narrative genre, an *im(m)ram* (pl. *imrama*) is a tale of a sea voyage that frames the adven-

tures of a hero who, with a few companions, sails from one island to another, encounters many marvels, and eventually returns home. The word *imram* may be translated "rowing about," and the frame tale of this journeying from island to island is central to the genre. This type of tale dates from the seventh or eighth century and is monastic in origin. In the Irish church of the sixth and seventh centuries, monks and clerics embarked on lengthy sea voyages as an act of penitence and devotion, the most famous example being St. Brendan. Tales of these pilgrimages overseas form the basis of the *imram;* the hero undertakes the sea journey either to expiate a sin or to get closer to God by abandoning all land-based ties.

In all, only four Irish tales can be classified as true *imrama: The Voyage of Máel Dúin, The Voyage of Uí Chorra, The Voyage of Snedgus and Mac Riagla,* and the *Navigatio Sancti Brendani Abbatis* (The Voyage of St. Brendan). A fifth tale, *The Voyage of Bran,* is perhaps the earliest of the *imrama,* but is more in the genre of the *echtrae* (pl. *echtrai*), a related tale type that is pre-Christian and Irish in origin. In these tales, the hero undertakes a journey to the Irish Otherworld, either over sea or under land; the pagan otherworldly goal, rather than the "rowing about," informs the structure and theme of the narrative. The *echtrai* very likely influenced the development of the *imrama,* but the *imrama* proper have a distinctly ecclesiastical aspect in their blend of both Christian and native Irish elements.

**BIBLIOGRAPHY**
Dumville, David N. "*Echtrae* and *Immram:* Some Problems of Definition." *Eriu* 27 (1976): 73–94.
Mac Mathúna, Séamus, ed. and trans. *Immram Brain: Bran's Journey to the Land of Women.* Tübingen: Niemayer, 1985.
Oskamp, H.P.A., ed. and trans. *The Voyage of Máel Dúin: A Study in Early Irish Voyage Literature.* Groningen: Wolters-Nordhoff, 1970.
Thrall, William F. "Clerical Sea Pilgrimages and the *Imrama.*" In *The Manly Anniversary Studies in Language and Literature.* Chicago: Chicago UP, 1923, rpt. Books for Libraries Press, 1968, pp. 276–283.

*Dorothy A. Bray*

**SEE ALSO**
Brendan's Voyage, St.; Cockaigne, Land of; Irish Travel

## India

A name used throughout the Middle Ages to signify various territories in the East that were fabulously wealthy and the source of exotic trade goods, including textiles, ivory, pearls, gems, dyestuffs, and such spices as pepper and cinnamon. These goods had been carried to the Mediterranean in antiquity, but trade increased dramatically in the first century C.E., when navigators harnessed monsoon winds to speed ships across the Indian Ocean and back.

Although Roman merchants established colonies in the south of the Indian subcontinent, and Indian rulers sent embassies to Rome, Hellenistic geographers had only vague notions about India's size and location. With Rome's economic decline, trade with India lessened. Islam first reached the subcontinent in the eighth century, and because the Arabs established control over both the Arabian Sea and Iran, Muslim middlemen soon thereafter secured a monopoly on east-west trade. For Europeans, India was a place of fable, a status preserved through wondrous tales and by the legend of St. Thomas, who was reported to have been martyred there in the mid-first century C.E. India's location became more nebulous as well; for medieval and early modern European writers, "India" connoted something like what "Far East" does for English speakers today. Even travelers who visited the subcontinent (modern Pakistan, India, Bangladesh) also spoke of southern Iran, Ceylon, Ethiopia, and East Africa as "India," and its position on *mappaemundi* shifted as geographic lore evolved.

The Indian subcontinent, almost as large as Europe and with a comparable number of peoples and cultures, was never united under one ruler. Despite periodic successes of native dynasties, such as the Guptas in the fourth, fifth, and seventh centuries C.E., India was often politically fragmented and subject to invasions from the north. Expanding Islam conquered Sind (near modern Karachi) in 712, and, beginning with Ghaznavid incursions in the late tenth century, the Indo-Gangetic plain also came under Muslim rule. After 1206, a Turkic sultanate established control over most of northern India while various Indian dynasties competed with each other and against the sultan of Delhi for the rest of the subcontinent.

Because Muslim rulers controlled mountain passes to the north, Indian Ocean islands, and many Indian ports, expanding commerce with the West in the era of the crusades was regulated by Islamic traders and officials. When the Mongols conquered Central Asia and Persia in the mid-thirteenth century, however, a path to India was opened for Western merchants and mission-

India. *Les Secretz de la Nature.* Château d'Aulnoy, Coulommiers (Seine et Marne) Collection Charnacé, unnumbered MS, fol. 36, *c.* 1460. Photo by John B. Friedman.

aries, who traveled through Mongol Persia to the mouth of the Euphrates, thence by sea to India and beyond. Both Marco Polo and the missionary John of Monte Corvino stayed briefly in India in the 1290s. Widely circulated fourteenth-century travel accounts, such as those by Jordan Catalani (or Sévérac) and Odoric of Pordenone, described India at length, mixing fact and legend. Their observations were used to enhance armchair travel narratives, such as the *Book of John Mandeville,* but were also incorporated, along with those of Polo and classical geographers, into fifteenth-century geographic treatises. Although direct access to India was generally denied to European merchants and travelers after the mid-fourteenth century, these earlier travel accounts inspired both Columbus, who sailed across the Atlantic in search of India, and the Portuguese seafarers who succeeded in outflanking Islam by circumnavigating Africa. When direct contact

# I

and trade with India were reestablished, a spate of first-hand reports concerning India and its peoples replaced earlier, fanciful accounts that had fed the imagination of European travelers and merchants since the fall of Rome.

## BIBLIOGRAPHY

Davies, C. Collin. *An Historical Atlas of the Indian Peninsula.* London: Oxford UP, 1946; 2nd edition, 1959.

*India in the Fifteenth Century: Narratives of Voyages to India.* Ed. Richard Henry Major. London: Hakluyt Society, 1852.

Smith, Vincent A. *The Oxford History of India.* Ed. Percival Spear. Oxford: Clarendon, 1919; 4th edition, Delhi and New York: Oxford UP, 1981.

Warmington, E.H. *The Commerce between the Roman Empire and India.* Cambridge: Cambridge UP, 1928; 2nd edition, London: Curzon, 1974.

*James D. Ryan*

## SEE ALSO

Columbus, Christopher; Dyes and Pigments; Ivory Trade; John of Monte Corvino; Jordan of Sévérac; *Mandeville's Travels; Mappamundi;* Marco Polo; Muslim Travelers and Trade; Odoric of Pordenone; Portuguese Expansion; Spice Trade, Indian Ocean; Textiles, Decorative; *Wonders of the East*

## Indians and the Americas

Throughout the Middle Ages, Europeans had little direct information on the native peoples of North America. Those records of actual encounters that did exist—for example, the narratives of expeditions to Vinland in the Icelandic sagas—did not circulate widely; few intellectuals, geographers, or travelers had access to these accounts. This absence of any detailed awareness of North American Indians perforce thwarted the formation of any conceptual category that might define or locate these peoples within (or outside) a European world picture. Yet when the first reports of New World Indians were published in Europe, intellectuals and a broader reading public seemed to recognize and accept the ethnographic descriptions as plausible and accurate. What medieval knowledge or conceptions made Indians intelligible as inhabitants of North America?

The capacity of explorers and writers to grasp and absorb the existence and identities of North American populations reflects the currency and semantic elasticity of the descriptive label "Indians" in late medieval

Columbus, in a small boat, approaches the native peoples of what he called Hispaniola. Christopher Columbus, *Epistola de insulis Nuper Inventis* (Letter to Sanchez) (Basel: Jakob Wolff or Michael Furter for Johann Bergmann, after April 29, 1493) sig. A1v [=fol. 2v]. Reproduced by permission of the Map Division, The New York Public Library (Astor, Lenox and Tilden Foundations).

and early modern Europe. In his *Geography* (early first century C.E.), Strabo claimed that "all who write about India are liars." His remark pinpoints the niche occupied by India in the ancient world and the earlier Middle Ages, as the limit both of the *oikoumene* and of sensible discourse about human civilization. In acknowledging the wild extravagancies that marked others' writings on India, Strabo performs a rhetorical move typical of sober writers who wished to secure readers' confidence in their own accounts. These gestures were reactions against the reports that populated India with monsters, hybrid and humanoid creatures, or radically exotic peoples. Such descriptions of monstrous races in the East persisted throughout the Middle Ages in encyclopedias, wonder books, romances, and travel accounts.

Between the times of Strabo and Columbus, and especially from the twelfth century, medieval scholars, poets, and illustrators attached to "Indians" an array of particular and symptomatic traits. Latin narratives of Alexander the Great's exploits—for example, the *Historia de preliis* (a tenth-century Latin work by Archpresbyter Leo of Naples that survives in more than 120 manuscripts)—borrowed from earlier visual and verbal traditions associated with the marvelous peoples of India, but combined these with newly emerging learned perspectives on natural law, the inherent capacities of the individual, and the unity of the human race. The convergence of these materials, in Alexander stories and elsewhere, produced an encounter of East and West, Europeans and Indians, that conferred a distinctive character on each side as people, race, or nation. The wide dispersion of these texts in vernacular retellings, and in illustrations, ensured that this peculiar character of Indians as strangely familiar was accessible in a variety of cultural registers.

Among the medieval writings that portray Indians in this way are learned texts like Petrarch's *On the Solitary Life* (1346 revised version), political allegories like Philippe de Mézières's *Dream of the Old Pilgrim* (1389), and popular books like *The Book of John Mandeville* (c.1360), which was by far the most widely read travel account of the later Middle Ages and sixteenth century. Johann Hartlieb's *Alexanderbuch* (in manuscript and incunabule copies, 1444–1473) reproduces both the verbal and the visual descriptions of these simple and naked Indians, as do the lavish illustrations produced for the Boucicaut *Mandeville* (Paris, Bibliothèque Nationale MS français 2810; late fourteenth century). By the time of the great voyages, this view of Indians possessed an ethnographic resonance sufficiently broad to sustain its intelligibility when applied to North American peoples. Columbus and his publicists, in effect calling all earlier writers on India liars, transformed existing ethnographic perceptions in producing a "New India." The viability of the term in these circumstances demonstrates that it is no mere misnomer, reflecting the delusions of a fifteenth-century explorer or the gullibility of early modern readers; the potency of "Indians" as an ethnic category has ensured its customary usage for more than 500 years, even to the present entry.

## BIBLIOGRAPHY

Friedman, John Block. *The Monstrous Races in Medieval Art and Thought.* Cambridge, MA: Harvard UP, 1981; rpt. Syracuse, NY: Syracuse UP, 2000.

Hahn, Thomas. "Indians East and West: Primitivism and Savagery in English Discovery Narratives of the Sixteenth Century." *Journal of Medieval and Renaissance Studies* 8 (1978): 77–114.

———. "The Indian Tradition in Western Medieval Intellectual History." *Viator* 9 (1978): 213–234.

Kratz, Dennis M., trans. *The Romances of Alexander.* New York and London: Garland, 1991. [Includes *Historia de preliis* and *Epistola . . . ad Aristotelem.*]

Romm, James S. *The Edges of the Earth in Ancient Thought.* Princeton, NJ: Princeton UP, 1992.

*Thomas G. Hahn*

## SEE ALSO

Columbus, Christopher; India; *Mandeville's Travels;* Monstrosity, Geographical; Philippe de Mézières; Walter of Châtillon; *Wonders of the East*

## Indus

A river in present-day India that, in the Middle Ages, was considered the western border of the known world.

"India is called so after the Indus River, which serves as a border to the occidental regions," wrote Isidore of Seville in *Etymologies* XIV.3, in his discussion of India. For Orosius, one of Isidore's sources, the Indus River was the western border of India, the river Alexander the Great and later Mithridates, the king of the Parthians, had crossed when they conquered northwestern India; it contrasted with the Ganges River, the eastern frontier of India that neither of them had reached. Later encyclopedists, including Vincent of Beauvais and Brunetto Latini, also identify the Indus, itself equated with India, as the western frontier to the eastern end of the *oikoumene* or inhabited world, making it the end of the earth.

When fourteenth-century vernacular writers, like Dante or Chaucer, for example, refer to the Indus, it is a literary *topos* or rhetorical commonplace indicating both India and the reaches beyond *oikoumene,* thus equating it with the eastern periphery of the *orbis terrarum* or orb of the earth. For St. Augustine, it was a place where Indian asceticism and contemplation flourished; this view was later continued by Petrarch in the *Life of Solitude* and by Dante in *Paradiso,* where he speculates about the life of salvation of those just people who have never heard of Christianity (*Par.* XIX). In

# I

contrast to this view of India as a land where contemplatives, identified as Brahmans and gymnosophists, practiced their version of religious life, are the exaggerated descriptions of the Indus as a land of wonders, a tradition dating back to Ctésias, Megasthenes, and Pliny. It is repeated in the medieval encyclopedias, and is further expanded in medieval texts like Pseudo-Callisthenes' *Life of Alexander,* the Alexander romances, and journey literature like Marco Polo's *Divisament dou monde* and *The Book of John Mandeville.*

## BIBLIOGRAPHY

Ctésias. *Histoire de l'Orient.* Trans. Janick Auberger. Paris: Les Belles Lettres, 1991.

Hahn, Thomas. "The Indian Tradition in Western Medieval Intellectual History." *Viator* 9 (1978): 213–234.

LeGoff, Jacques. "L'Occident médiévale et l'Océan Indien: Un horizon onirique." In *Pour un autre Moyen Age: Temps, travail, et culture en Occident.* Paris: Gallimard, 1977, pp. 280–298. Trans. as *Time, Work, and Culture in the Middle Ages,* trans. Arthur Goldhammer. Chicago: U of Chicago P, 1980.

McCrindle, J.W., ed. and trans. *Ancient India as Described in Classical Literature.* Westminster, 1901; rpt. New Delhi: Oriental Books Reprint Corp., 1979.

Schildgen, Brenda Deen. "Dante and the Indus." *Dante Studies* 111 (1993): 177–193.

*Brenda Deen Schildgen*

## SEE ALSO

Brunetto Latini; Chaucer, Geoffrey; Dante Alighieri; Ganges; India; Isidore of Seville; *Mandeville's Travels;* Marco Polo; *Oikoumene;* Orb of Imperial Power; Orosius; Vincent of Beauvais

## Inner Asian Trade

Economic activity in the historic and cultural heartland of the Eurasian continent. Rather than referring to a geographic entity, the term *Inner Asia* is somewhat like the equally vague "Western" or "Eastern Europe" in that it is defined by the particular civilization that developed in the central area of the huge continuous landmass comprising Europe and Asia.

Upon this landmass the great sedentary, city-building civilizations arose on the outer edges and developed into European, Near Eastern, southern (Indian), southeastern, and Eastern (Chinese) cultural spheres. Surrounded by them to the west, south, and east, and bordered in the north by the Arctic Ocean, lies Inner Asia. The toponym "Central Eurasia" would perhaps be a more accurate one, since much of this land lies to the east of the Ural mountains, the traditional eastern boundary of Europe. Inner Asia is, then, that part of the Eurasian continent that has not produced a major sedentary civilization and whose tribes, which during the Middle Ages included Turks and Mongols, were chiefly migratory.

Four Inner Asian natural zones run east-west along latitudinal lines. They are, respectively, from north to south, the tundra, the forest, the steppe, and the desert. The treeless arctic tundra with its frozen marshes is unsuitable for permanent human habitation and hence, for all practical purposes, lies outside the framework of history. The forest zone, called *taiga* from its Russian name, extends over some 6,000 miles, from Scandinavia to the the Sea of Okhotsk, and can support small groups of fishing, hunting, and food-gathering peoples. Because of the climate and lack of resources, no powerful polities have arisen there, nor what we might today call states.

In the premodern age, the Inner Asian steppe zone alone provided suitable conditions for the formation of an effective state. The grassland that covers most of the region—and provided its name—allowed the maintenance of important herds and developed a way of life called pastoral nomadism. Inner Asian nomads traditionally distinguish five categories of domestic animals: horses, camels, cattle, sheep, and goats. Naturally, the horse, because of its military importance, played a dominant role. Only the peoples of the steppe were politically and militarily strong enough to take an important role in Inner Asian history or, indeed, at some periods, in that of the world.

The fourth natural zone of Inner Asia, the desert, cannot support any permanent population; like the tundra then, it has played essentially no role. Accordingly, historians have recovered more "history" from events pertaining only to the forest or the steppe dwellers.

Inner Asian trade, in the proper sense of this word, was not practiced within a single socioeconomic group. All members of a given community had equal access to the commodities provided by the natural resources of the forest or the steppe, and the individual's needs were taken care of by the community through the division of labor; money had no place in these internal economies. Likewise, since external trade relations could exist only between groups producing different goods, there was not much room for exchange of goods between tribes whose natural resources and productive techniques were essentially the same. Thus, in central Eurasia only three major types of trade relations may be distinguished: between the cattle or horse breeder (that is, the pastoral nomads of the steppe) and the sedentary agrarian states on the periphery; between the hunter-gatherers of the forest zone and the sedentary agriculturalists (trade that often passed through the intermediary of pastoral nomads); and transit trade, which, via Inner Asia, served the exchange of goods between sedentary, agrarian populations. Of these trade patterns, the most important was that linking pastoral nomadic economies with the sedentary civilizations of Byzantium, Iran, and China.

In the symbiotic relationship between the Inner Asian pastoral nomads and China, the horse played a key role. Until the use of gunpowder became widespread, large light cavalry forces were virtually irresistible. Because the raising of such an army depended on available adequate pasture, any conflict between pastoral nomadic and sedentary cultures was static. Nomads could conquer territories but were unable to hold them without relinquishing their trump card, the strong cavalry. Thus, their power base was eroded and eventually they were absorbed by and assimilated into—or militarily ejected from—the lands they had conquered. For their part, the sedentary peoples, particularly the Chinese, were unable to maintain a significant and effective force of cavalry on a permanent basis because they depended on pastoral nomads to supply them with horses. In short, the Chinese needed Inner Asian horses to resist Inner Asian nomadic attack, and the nomads needed to choose between selling horses to their potential enemies or making use of them for war.

Because of their undiversified economy, the nomads needed to obtain many goods—especially silk—from China. For many centuries, the nomads seem to have desired silk—though it was of no practical use in their daily lives—for its prestige value. Silk was also the principal trade good with the distant West and was a staple medium of exchange over the vast territories of Inner Asia, though not, as popularly imagined, on "silk roads," which are a modern construct, since there was no single "main thoroughfare" across Central Asia during the Middle Ages. The silk trade was mainly controlled by professional merchants, mostly Sogdians. Tea, another staple Chinese product, became important in trade beyond Inner Asia only in the post-

medieval period. Chinese ceramic wares—which gave rise to the term "china"—were much sought after all throughout Asia and Europe, but were exported chiefly by sea. These luxury goods, however, were really of secondary importance in comparison to grain or rice, linen, and arms in the trade between sedentary and pastoral peoples.

The pastoral nomads' need for grain is often overlooked. Severe weather involving the freezing of pastures—the dreaded *jud* of Mongolia—could ruin empires. Famine, caused by decimation of herds, was a constant threat in nomadic life and accounts for many invasions undertaken by them. Chinese sources are replete with mentions of "barbarian" requests for grain that were sometimes met and at other times not, according to political dictates and the power balance between those who advocated war and those who favored peace. Denial usually resulted in devastating attacks out of desperation by the nomads.

Another major commodity coveted by nomadic eastern Inner Asia was linen, the cheapest and best non-indigenous material for making garments. Surviving documents record complaints that clothing made of hide and fur was simply too warm to be worn in the summer. On the western periphery of the steppe, the Huns appear to have been familiar with the production of linen.

Although engaged in almost continuous warfare—or, perhaps, because they were—the nomad pastoralists were unable to produce arms in the quantity and quality required for their needs. Weapons, then, constituted a much-sought-after merchandise, but one that could be obtained only from the potential enemy. The trade in arms is well documented also on the western periphery of Inner Asia.

In the sixth century, the Byzantine historian Menander noted the Turks' problem in securing adequate supplies of iron, though they themselves were metallurgists. Manufacturers benefit economically from the fact that arms are expendable; swords and spears may break and, even after a victorious battle, the recovery of arrowheads is cumbersome and inefficient. Tombal finds attributed to ninth-century Hungarian nomads indicate that a 20,000-man cavalry force carried about thirty metric tons of metal as arms. At about the same period the Avars made great efforts to purchase Byzantine weapons—principally swords—to be used in their wars against Byzantium.

The emperors of the day—whether Byzantine or Chinese—were understandably reluctant to allow

# I

arms export. In the Han period (206 B.C.E.–220 C.E.), strict regulations had prohibited the exportation to the Hsiung-nu (the dominant power in Mongolia) of strategic goods such as iron and crossbows. There is ample evidence, however, of contraband swords, axes, spades, and knives smuggled out to Inner Asia. Such illicit activity greatly troubled Chinese officials who, nevertheless, were unable to halt it. Of course, political pressure sometimes compelled a sedentary population to provide arms to its enemy. Given reluctantly, such permissions were rescinded as soon as political circumstances permitted.

Most trade between the steppe nomads and sedentary society was more or less efficiently supervised by the latter group. Governments, whether Chinese, Iranian, or Byzantine, made great efforts to limit individual commercial transactions and, as far as possible, to institutionalize trade. This was best achieved by limiting it to well-policed, regular frontier markets that could be opened or closed to regulate the flow of goods toward nomadic neighbors.

Unlike these economic relations between the steppe-nomadic and the sedentary worlds, which played such a dominant role in Inner Asian history and civilization, trade between the forest-dwelling hunters and sedentary societies had no political ramifications. Among the economic activities of the forest zone—fishing, food-gathering, and hunting—fishing played no role in trade. Gathering produced two valuable commodities—wax and honey—which became important export items from Russia in the sixteenth century. The situation was very different with hunting.

Although the primary aim of hunting is to provide food and clothing for the community, its implications for intercultural trade have always been considerable. Within any hunter culture there is a very limited demand for fur, since it is a relatively durable commodity. Moreover, however great the use value of a warm fur coat in the Siberian winter may be, that of a second garment will be much lower, possibly nil, unless there is some external demand for it. By contrast, nomadic horse breeders may be twice as happy with ten horses as they are with five. They will not be afraid of overproduction. Exterior demand may raise or lower the price of the horse, and its exchange value may fluctuate and be superior or inferior to its intrinsic value, but it will always have some use value. The case is quite different with fur. Since the internal market for fur is predeter-

mined by the number of hunters and thus is virtually constant, the incentive for fur harvest results from external demand. Whenever sources speak of forest populations, they always mention fur as their primary, if not only, item of wealth.

Over the centuries, fur constituted the most important staple commodity of Inner Asian export. Indeed, the appreciation of fine pelts is universal and perennial, and there has rarely been a dearth of customers eager to acquire them. As could be expected, most of the fur originated in the forest zone whence it was exported, in small quantities, to the peoples of the steppe and, through their intermediary or by direct trade, and in far greater volume, to the sedentary populations. For example, precious pelts were often included in the tribute-presents offered to China by steppe nomads who had obtained them from the forest hunters. It can even be said that, second only to horses, fur obtained from the hunters constituted the largest single item offered by the nomads for exchange.

Unlike trade in horses, which, because of its political and military importance was usually handled by the states, commerce in furs appears to have been in the hands of entrepreneurs. Evidence to this effect can be found in the mid-thirteenth century *Secret History of the Mongols,* which mentions an encounter between Chinggis Khân and Hassan, a Muslim trader, who was on his way to the river Arghun, driving 1,000 sheep destined to be exchanged for sable and weasel pelts.

As early as the mid-sixth century, the principal income of the Onogurs—a Turkic people possibly connected with the Hungarians and located somewhere in the forest zone west of the Ural Mountains—was derived from fur commerce. This regional trade was mythologized and perhaps from unconscious protectionism made to seem a difficult one. *The Lie of the World,* written probably in 988 by the Arab geographer Ibn Hawqal, notes that the fur sold in Spain originates in the country of the Slavs who, in their turn, get it from the land of Gog and Magog. Thus, the "producers" of fur were located in terms of mythical geography, beyond the pale of civilized humanity, in the land of Gog and Magog, a people so savage they were walled up behind a great gate of brass by Alexander the Great to protect humanity from them. It was in the merchants' interest to exaggerate the difficulties surmounted in obtaining the wares to be sold. They did so quite unashamedly, but there is no reason to doubt that in their trip to the far north they had to overcome very real difficulties.

Marco Polo himself had never visited that northern "Land of Darkness" of which he gives a vivid description based on hearsay in his *Divisament dou monde*. He also describes in vivid detail the grueling journey of thirteen days over marshy land covered with a thin layer of ice. Inaccessible to horses or carts, it may be crossed only by sledges drawn by six dogs who know their way and pull the sledge through ice and mire to the next post where they are replaced by another team. He remarks that merchants undertake such journeys "because there is so great a multitude . . . of precious skins of which very great trade and very great profit are made."

Reaching the vendors is one thing, but to agree with them on a fair price is another. Among the practices of the barter operations, special mention should be made of the so-called dumb-trade, a good description of which is given by the great Muslim traveler Ibn Battūta (1304–1368):

> . . . when the travellers have completed forty stages in this desert, they alight at the Darkness. Each one of them leaves thereabouts the goods that he had brought and they return to their usual camping-ground. Next day they go back to seek their goods, and they find alongside them skins of sable, minever and ermine. If the owner of the goods is satisfied with what he has found alongside his goods, he takes it, but if it does not satisfy him he leaves it, and then they add more skins and sometimes (I mean the people of Darkness) take away their goods and leave those of the merchants. This is their method of selling and buying.

Inner Asian rulers usually welcomed merchants because they provided merchandise that would not have been available otherwise. The Great Khân Ögedei (r. 1229–1241) was particularly fond of them and showed much indulgence toward their foibles. The Persian historian Rashīd al-Dīn (c. 1247?–1318) recorded many such instances. Merchants from all over the world would flock to Ögedei's court because he paid a generous price for their wares without even bothering to look at them. There is reason to believe that most of these merchants were Muslims but we have little information about their identity or the goods they sold.

The key factor in the transit trade—whether Muslim or other—was the mode by which the goods were transported, since much transit profit went to the intermediaries who conveyed the merchandise from its place of origin toward its final destination. Most loads—approximately 400–500 pounds per animal—were carried by Bactrian camels, traveling at a leisurely pace of about two to three miles an hour, covering about twenty-five to thirty miles per day.

Since men and beasts relied on trading posts for rest, the resupply of daily necessities, and, occasionally, the transshipment of goods from one caravan to the other, transit trade passed along well established caravan routes, skirting Inner Asia proper. Because of the very long distances separating one trading post from another, and of the need for local guides familiar with the terrain, few, if any, merchants traveled all along the road from China to the Roman world; rather, goods were passed along in indirect trade. Caravans were in constant danger of being halted by robbers, who generally exacted a heavy ransom before they allowed the merchants to proceed. The effrontery of the bandits is nicely illustrated in a story related by Ibn Fadlān, an envoy of the caliph of Baghdad who, in 921, joined a commercial caravan traveling from Khorezm to the Bulgars of the Volga, important purveyors of fur. Ibn Fadlān describes how his caravan of some 5,000 men was halted by a solitary Turk, "ugly in figure, dirty in appearance, despicable in manner, and base in nature." Having asked for and having been given bread, the Turk declared that he took pity on the caravan and magnanimously allowed it to proceed.

In the thirteenth century, the unification of Inner Asia under Mongol rule brought greater security to the traders and prompted Italian merchants to engage in what was, in effect, transcontinental trade. Italians—some Venetians and Pisans, but mostly Genoese—established trading stations in the Crimea, which became the terminus of their commercial ventures into Inner Asia (and from which the plagues that decimated Europe in the mid-fourteenth century originally came). Thanks to the professionalism of contemporary Italian notaries, there survived a rich documentation on Italian trade, mostly in the Levant, but also further east toward Inner Asia. A fourteenth-century commercial manual written by Francesco Balducci Pegolotti testifies to the careful collection of information used by Italian merchants.

The merchants' choice of trade goods was determined first by their suitability for transport, and second by the price they could command. Bulk merchandise,

# I

such as the grain that was so important in the border trade, was ill-suited to be carried thousands of miles by camel. Thus, they favored commodities of small bulk but high value, such as spices, textiles, porcelain, and gems (or their imitations). Such commodities allowed the merchants to make, as some sources boast, "a hundred-fold profit." It should be noted that, with the exception of fur and narwhal or mammoth ivory, none of the goods traded in this way was of Inner Asian origin.

**BIBLIOGRAPHY**

Boulnois, Luce. *The Silk Road.* New York: Dutton, 1966.

Gibb, H.A.R., ed and trans. *The Travels of Ibn Battūta A.D. 1325–1354.* 3 vols. Hakluyt Society, 2nd series, 110, 117, 141. London: Hakluyt Society, 1958, 1962, 1971; rpt. Millwood, NY: Kraus Reprint, 1986.

Herrmann, Albert. *Die alten Seidenstraßen zwischen China und Syrien.* Berlin: Weidmann, 1910.

Miller, J. Innes. *The Spice Trade of the Roman Empire, 29 B.C.–A.D. 641.* Oxford: Clarendon Press, 1969.

Polo, Marco. *The Travels.* Trans. and Intro. Ronald Latham. London and New York: Penguin, 1958.

Rossabi, Morris. *China and Inner Asia: From 1368 to the Present Day.* New York: Pica Press, 1975.

———. "The 'Decline' of the Central Asian Caravan Trade." In *The Rise of Merchant Empires.* Ed. James D. Tracy. Cambridge: Cambridge UP, 1990, pp. 351–370.

Schafer, Edward H. *The Golden Peaches of Samarkand.* Berkeley and Los Angeles: U of California P, 1963.

Sinor, Denis. "Some Remarks on the Economic Aspects of Hunting in Central Eurasia." In *Die Jagd bei de Altaischen Völkern.* Asiatische Forschungen 26. Wiesbaden: Harrassowitz, 1968; rpt. in Sinor, *Inner Asia and Its Contacts with Medieval Europe.* See Gen. Bib.

———. "Horse and Pasture in Inner Asian History." *Oriens Extremus* 19 (1972): 171–184; rpt. in Sinor, *Inner Asia and Its Contacts with Medieval Europe.* See Gen. Bib.

Vollmer, John E., E.J. Keall, and E. Nagai-Berthrong. *Silk Roads—China Ships.* Toronto: Royal Ontario Museum, 1983.

*Denis Sinor*

**SEE ALSO**

Byzantine Empire; Camels; Caravans; China; Gems; Genoa; Gunpowder; Huns; Ibn Battūta, Abu Abdallah; Inner Asian Travel; Ivory Trade; Karakorum; Marco Polo; Merchant Manuals; Merchants, Italian; Mongol Army; Mongols; Muslim Travelers and Trade; Nomadism and Pastoralism; Pegolotti, Francesco Balducci; Pisa; *Secret History of the Mongols, The;* Silk Roads; Spice Trade, Indian Ocean; Transportation, Inland; Venice; Yuan Dynasty

## Inner Asian Travel

Travel purely for leisure is a relatively modern phenomenon. Medieval travelers setting out on long and often dangerous journeys usually pursued one or several practical aims, such as diplomatic missions (often indistinguishable from spying), religious pilgrimages, or trade. The study of travel in or into Inner Asia suffers from the serious drawback that, for the medieval period, only one indigenous account, in Tibetan, has come down to us. Originally written in the eighth or ninth century in an unidentified Turkic language, it survives in a Tibetan version of the same period. Usually referred to as the *Report on the Kings Residing in the North,* it purports to be the confidential report of five envoys sent by an unknown ruler seeking information on the regions of northern Asia. It contains much valuable, often puzzling information on regions difficult of access.

To travel is one thing, to write about it is another, and not all travelers are inclined to record the details of their journeys. Thus, for example, around 1250, the French knight Baldwin of Hainaut traveled as far as the Mongol capital city Karakorum, but we would have no knowledge of his trip were it not for a remark he made to William of Rubruck concerning the road leading there. By contrast, in 1246 and 1253, respectively, the Franciscans John of Plano Carpini and William of Rubruck reached Karakorum and went on to write invaluable accounts of their journeys, as did Marco Polo, who personally wrote (or at least dictated) a book about his experiences as a merchant.

Greek interest in the northern regions of Inner Asia is documented since the seventh century B.C.E. when Aristeas of Proconnesus wrote his poem *Arimaspea,* of which only a few fragments survive. Herodotus (*c.* 485–425 B.C.E.) had much to say both about Aristeas and the poem purporting to describe his journey, beyond Scythia into the far north where the one-eyed Arimaspians live. What remains of the poem, linked with what the antique sources say about its author, leaves no doubt about the genuineness of some of the information it contains, which must have been provided by a traveler to the region, whether Aristeas or someone else.

A fascinating glimpse into the complex relationship of trade and diplomacy is related by the Byzantine historian Menander. He reports the arrival in Constantinople in 568 of a Turk embassy led by a Sogdian (a member of an Iranian nomadic tribe) eager to establish a direct silk trade between China and the Romans, circumventing the official Iranian intermediaries. (At that time the Turk kaghanate centered on Mongolia ruled over most of Inner Asia.) The following year, a group of Romans joined the returning party and, under the leadership of Zemarkhos, traveled as far as the valley of the Talas where they were warmly received by the Turk kaghan.

Leaving China in 139 B.C.E. on a diplomatic mission, Chang Ch'ien traveled as far as Sogdiana, the area between the Oxus and Iaxartes rivers. He returned to his country in 126 B.C.E. with a vast amount of information on the western regions. His journey greatly enlarged the Chinese horizon and was a major factor in the expansion of trade between China, Iran, and the Roman world.

The spread of Buddhism to China created among the learned monks living there the desire to acquire holy books in India for the purposes of translation and study. Among these travelers should be mentioned Fa-hsien (404–414 C.E.), and Sung Yun (518–521). Informative as their narratives may be, they pale in comparison with the *Record of the Western Regions,* written by the Buddhist pilgrim Hsuan-tsang, who traveled to India between 629 and 645 via Central Asia. On his outward journey through the Tarim basin he took the northern route through Turfan, Kucha, Tokmak, as far as Samarkand, while on his return he traveled on the southern route, via Kashghar, Khotan, and Tun-huang. He describes vividly the flourishing city-states along the caravan routes. He also shows the strength of Buddhism in regions that in later centuries fell under the domination of Islam.

Diplomatic missions to and from China were frequent and were duly recorded in the Chinese annals, though they usually do not give space to the description of the journey itself. A welcome exception are the writings of two envoys of the short-lived Southern Song dynasty to the Mongols, who had not yet emerged as a world power. A *Short Report on the Black Tatars (Hei-Ta shih-lueh),* written in 1237, and a *Detailed Account of the Mongol Tatars (Meng-Ta pei-lu),* written in 1221 and revised in 1227, are based on the notes taken by the ambassadors in the course of their journeys. One of the envoys, Hsu T'ing, is the author of a *Diary of a Journey to the North (Pei-cheng ji-chi)* not yet available in any translation. It should be noted that these texts focus on a description of the Mongols' past and present and, in conformity with Chinese literary conventions, contain virtually no information on the ambassadors' personal experiences.

While still very impersonal, the description of the journey of the Taoist sage Ch'ang-ch'un to the West, as given by his disciple and travel companion Li Chih-chang, belongs to a different category. His *Account of a Journey to the West (Hsi-yu chi)* describes the journey undertaken at Chinggis Khân's behest in 1221–1224 and provides ample information about the itinerary, as well as on the people and the places encountered. Ch'ang-ch'un had been summoned by the great khân, who hoped to obtain from him the secrets of longevity. He traveled with an entourage of several hundred people and, throughout his journey, was received with great honor. On his outward journey, the Taoist sage traveled through Mongolia, Chinese Turkestan, Almaligh, on to Samarkand, and beyond, into northern Afghanistan. Of course, such journeys were also routinely undertaken by merchants, but they left no written records.

The account of the journey of Ch'ang Tê, who set out in 1259 as an envoy from Khubilai to the il-khân Hülegü, Mongol ruler of Persia, was written down in 1263 by Liu Yu. His journey took about a year and its description is a treasure trove of interesting information.

The Latin travel accounts of the Mongol period stand out because of their length and their authors' readiness to report on personal tribulations. Such writers as John of Plano Carpini, William of Rubruck, Andrew of Longjumeau, Simon of Saint Quentin, John of Monte Corvino, and Ricoldo da Monte Croce, all clerics and all active in the second half of the thirteenth or the first half of the fourteenth century, contributed greatly to Western knowledge of Inner Asia. The fame of Marco Polo should not let us forget Maffeo and Niccolò Polo, father and uncle of Marco, who spent eight years (1261–1269) in the Mongol Empire allegedly engaging simultaneously in trade and diplomacy.

Unique in its scope and character is the undertaking of two Nestorian monks, Rabban Sauma and his companion, Markos, who resolved to undertake a pilgrimage to Jerusalem according to an account that has come down to us in Syriac. Rabban Sauma, though probably a native of Beijing, was a Turk Uighur by birth; his companion belonged to the Öngüt, a Turkic-speaking but Nestorian people in what is today northwest China. The two clerics left Beijing probably in 1275 or 1276 and, traveling through Kashgharia, reached Persia, then under the rule of the Mongol il-khân Abagha.

I

They visited Baghdad and many other places in Mesopotamia, though, because of the hostilities between Abagha and the Mamluks, they failed to reach Jerusalem. The two monks then settled in a Nestorian monastery, not expecting the tremendous changes soon to occur in their lives. In 1280, Rabban Sauma was appointed visitor general for China, and in November 1281, under the name of Mar Yaballaha III, Markos was elected head of the Nestorian Church.

The il-khân Arghun (successor of Abagha), anxious to establish friendly relations with the Western powers, entrusted Rabban Sauma with the delicate task of working toward this aim. Early in 1287, Rabban Sauma set out by sea on his great journey and reached Constantinople where he was received by the Emperor Andronicus II (r. 1282–1328). He arrived in Rome on June 23, when the papacy was vacant, so he went first to Paris where he was received by Philip IV the Fair (r. 1285–1314), and then to Bordeaux to meet Edward I of England (r. 1272–1307). Rabban Sauma spent most of the winter of 1287–1288 in Genoa—a city in close commercial contact with the Mongols. At the news of the election of Pope Nicholas IV (1288–1292), Rabban Sauma hastened to Rome where, recognized as an ambassador of the Mongols, he was treated with great respect. He was allowed to celebrate Mass according to Nestorian liturgy and on Palm Sunday received Holy Communion from the hands of the pope himself. Rabban Sauma and his entourage left Rome in April 1288 carrying several letters addressed to the il-khân and to other notables living in his lands.

Surprisingly, Arabs and Persians, who since ancient times played the role of intermediaries between East and West, left few accounts of their exploits in travel by land. Mention has been made of Ibn Fadlan's journey to the Bulgars of the Volga, of which there remains a detailed description. Fragments of travel accounts appear mostly in later geographical treatises. Such is the case of Tamim ibn Bahr, who, in 821, traveled at least as far as the Uighur capital Karabalghasun on the Orkhon River. His observations add much to our knowledge of the history of the region. Ibn Battūta's extensive travels (1325–1353) barely touched Inner Asia.

During the first century of Ming rule over China (beginning in 1368) trade and diplomatic relations between China and the Western countries continued to flourish. The best documented diplomatic missions are those led by Ch'en Ch'eng sent by the Yung-lo emperor to Shah Rukh son of Tamerlane (Tīmūr), and

the counter-embassy dispatched by the latter to China (1419–1422).

Among European travelers of the fourteenth century whose destination was not China, the name of Ruy Gonzales de Clavijo, ambassador of Henry III of Castile to Tamerlane, stands out by reason of the detailed account of his journey (1403–1406), which took him as far as Samarkand. In contrast, little reliable information appears in the recollections of Johann Schiltberger, made a prisoner of the Ottomans at the battle of Nicopolis in 1396. While in Turkish service, at the battle of Ankara (1402) he became Tamerlane's captive, spending nearly thirty-two years in the service of various rulers, wandering from place to place, supposedly even reaching Siberia. Schiltberger's travels were probably prompted by a taste for adventure.

We have information about only a small minority of those who, in search of money or by command, undertook their journeys into or through Inner Asia. For the thousands of merchants moving along its roads, the destination lay beyond its border in Rome, Syria, Persia, India, or China. The crossing itself of this perilous land offered few rewards. To travel for the sake of exploration had no appeal for them.

**BIBLIOGRAPHY**

Bacot, Jacques. "Reconnaissance en Haute Asie Septentrionale par cinq envoyés ouïgours au VIIIe siècle." *Journal Asiatique* (1956): 137–153.

Beal, Samuel. *Si-yu-ki: Buddhist Records of the Western World.* London, 1884.

Dawson, Christopher, ed. *The Mongol Mission.* See Gen. Bib.

Johann Schiltberger. *The Bondage and Travels of Johann Schiltberger, a Native of Bavaria, in Europe, Asia and Africa: 1396–1427.* Trans. B. Telfer and P. Bruun. Hakluyt Society, 59. London: Hakluyt Society, 1859.

*The Mission of Friar William of Rubruck: His Journey to the Court of the Great Khan Möngke 1253–1255.* Trans. Peter Jackson, with notes and introduction by Peter Jackson and David Morgan. Hakluyt Society, 2nd series, 173. London: Hakluyt Society, 1990.

Olbricht, Peter, and Elisabeth Pinks. *Meng-Ta pei lu und Hei-Ta shih-lüeh: Chinesische Gesandtenberichte über die Frühen Mongolen.* Asiatische Forschungen 56. Wiesbaden: Harrassowitz, 1980.

Rabban Sauma. *Voyager from Xanadu: Rabban Sauma's Journey from China to the West.* Tokyo-New York-London: Kodansha International, 1992.

de Rachewiltz, Igor. *Papal Envoys to the Great Khans.* Stanford: Stanford UP, 1971, 89–111.

Riccold de Monte Croce. *Pérégrination en Terre Sainte et en Proche Orient.* Texte latin et traduction . . . par René Kappler. Paris: Honoré Champion, 1997.

*Voyageurs Arabes: Ibn Fadlan, Ibn Jubayr, Ibn Battuta et un auteur anonyme.* Trans. Paule Charles-Dominique. Paris: Gallimard, 1995.

Waley, Arthur. *The Travels of the Taoist Ch'ang-Chun from China to the Hindukush at the Summons of Chingiz Khan.* London: Routledge and Kegan Paul, 1931; rpt. 1963.

*Denis Sinor*

**SEE ALSO**

Abagha; Almaligh; Ambassadors; Andrew of Longjumeau; Buddhism; China; Constantinople; Diplomacy; Eastern Christianity; Hülegü; Ibn Battūta, Abu Abdallah; Karakorum; John of Monte Corvino; John of Plano Carpini; Marco Polo; Mongols; Muslim Travelers and Trade; Nestorianism; Ottoman Empire; Pegolotti, Francesco Balducci; Pisa; Ricold of Monte Croce; Samarkand; Schiltberger, Johann; Scythia; Silk Roads; Simon of Saint-Quentin; Spies; Tamerlane; Taoism; Tibet; Venice; William of Rubruck

## Innocent IV (*c.* 1200–1254; pope 1243–1254)

Born Sinibaldo de' Fieschi (*c.* 1200) at Genoa, the pope who initiated the "Mongol Mission," the first attempt to develop diplomatic relations between Christian Europe and the peoples of Asia in the Middle Ages.

A well-known canon lawyer and papal official before assuming the papal office in 1243, Innocent IV made an important contribution to the theoretical basis for establishing and maintaining relations between Christian and non-Christian societies. In commenting on a letter of Innocent III (1198–1216) that dealt with the vows made by crusaders, instead of discussing the technical issue involved, he raised the fundamental question of the legitimacy of the crusades. By what right could the Christians take the Holy Land from the Muslims who occupied it? Did Christians have the right to seize all the lands that Muslims occupied? Did they have the right to seize any and all lands occupied by non-Christians? Innocent IV concluded that any lands seized from Christians in unjust wars could legitimately be retaken. All other lands that the Muslims or other non-Christians possessed they possessed legitimately, and Christians had no right to deprive them of them. In making this argument, Innocent IV was setting down one of the bases for a general theory of human rights and, at the same time, establishing a legal basis for relations between Christian and non-

Pope Innocent IV at the Council of Lyons. Matthew Paris, *Chronica Majora*, Cambridge, Corpus Christi College MS 16, fol. 187r, *c.* 1250. Permission Master and Fellows, Corpus Christi College, Cambridge.

Christian societies, an early stage of the development of international law.

At the First Council of Lyons (1245), Innocent IV initiated the Mongol Mission when he despatched the Franciscan John of Plano Carpini (*c.* 1180–1252) to the Mongol khân in an attempt to introduce him to the fundamentals of Christianity and to request that he end the Mongol attacks in eastern Europe. John brought with him two bulls from Innocent addressed to the khân (dated March 5 and March 13) urging his conversion to Christianity, to which Güyük responded demanding the pope's submission and threatening reprisals for his failure to do so. In spite of these unsatisfactory results, Innocent IV was thus both a theorist and a practitioner of a Christian theory of international relations. In the sixteenth century, his theories about the rights of infidels provided the basis for the great Spanish debate about the legitimacy of the conquest of the Americas.

**BIBLIOGRAPHY**

Dawson, Christopher, ed. *The Mongol Mission.* See Gen. Bib.

Melloni, Alberto. *Innocenzo IV: La concezione e l'esperienza della cristianità come 'regimen unius per sonae.'* Genoa: Marietti, 1990.

Muldoon, James. *Popes, Lawyers, and Infidels: The Church and the Non-Christian World, 1250–1550.* Philadelphia: U of Pennsylvania P, 1979.

# I

de Rachewiltz, Igor. *Papal Envoys to the Great Khans*. Stanford: Stanford UP, 1971.

*James Muldoon*

**SEE ALSO**

Canon Law and Subject Peoples; Franciscan Friars; Holy Land; John of Plano Carpini; Lyons, First Council of; Missionaries to China; Mongols; Popes; Yuan Dynasty

## Inns and Accommodations

Accommodations for travelers in the Middle Ages covering a wide range of possibilities, of which inns were only one. It was not until the eleventh and twelfth centuries that inns began to regain the importance they had had in the Roman era, but they subsequently spread and flourished.

In the early Middle Ages, religious houses provided the most frequent lodgings for wayfarers and pilgrims. The monastic orders acknowledged their obligation to provide free hospitality to travelers, often with a three-day limit and with certain social distinctions as to where the traveler stayed. Nobles and clerics would be welcomed within a monastery, while poor or unimportant travelers would be lodged in a guesthouse, usually outside the abbey walls. Kings, with their retinues, had the right to require costly hospitality from their lay and their religious vassals. Nobles might find shelter in the castles of friendly members of their class or lodge at religious houses, especially those where previous benefactions ensured a generous welcome. Clerics traveling with their officials could not only claim hospitality from religious houses but even exact a certain quality of food and quarters for their retinue.

From the eleventh century on, European roads were crowded by a growing number of merchants, officials on business, pilgrims, kings, nobility, and clerics. A wider variety of accommodations developed to serve this new traveling public. Hospices, usually built and staffed by members of religious orders, were founded along the most heavily traveled pilgrimage routes, especially in mountainous or isolated areas. Some were very small, but others—such as Mont-joux on the Alpine Great St. Bernard Pass, St. Christine on the Pyreneean Somport Pass, and the oldest and most famous, the Latin hospice in Jerusalem—were large and heavily used. They benefited from gifts by travelers grateful for even the most spartan shelter. Most hospices fell into disuse by the end of the Middle Ages, but the mountain refuges continued to cater to travelers well into the Renaissance.

The growing number of merchants involved in international commerce in the twelfth century, especially from the great Italian trading city-states such as Pisa, Genoa, and Venice, needed not only shops but warehouses for their goods and lodging for themselves and their horses. These separate, all-purpose establishments (*fondaco* in Italian) flourished especially in the Muslim world, but they also existed in Europe. For example in Ghent, merchants engaged in the grain trade from France to Flanders had hostelries with measurers and weighers on the premises, as well as accommodations.

However, from the thirteenth century onward, inns began to overshadow other forms of accommodation and become both more numerous and more prosperous, since, with the increase in a money economy and a more regularized coinage, a greater number of travelers could now afford to pay for lodgings. Italy and southern France boasted the largest network of inns. Northern Europe was less well provided, with inns only in the larger cities, while Spain had few anywhere.

An inn, like an alehouse or tavern, was distinguished by an outside sign proclaiming its function and an identifying name such as The White Horse, or *L'Ecu de Bretagne,* or Chaucer's Tabard. Most were built in cities, where they often clustered near the main gate. They were also found along the main roads and in university towns with their populations of itinerant students and masters.

The term *inn* covered establishments of all sizes, and their prices reflected their size and the amenities they offered. At the bottom of the scale, an inn might be merely two houses knocked together to provide cheap shelter for a few poor travelers, or it could be a large, comfortable, and well-furnished building with a courtyard and adequate stabling for the horses of a merchant's retinue. Such an inn would have a hall, a kitchen, and a varying number of bedrooms, depending on its size. Travelers were normally expected to sleep at least two to a bed, often three or four, or pay a much higher price for single occupancy. Food was usually provided but charged for separately. Many innkeepers did not own the inns they managed, but leased them from wealthy local owners, though some ultimately succeeded in becoming owners. Many were immigrants who catered to compatriots, and husband and wife often worked together. In medieval "estates" literature, innkeepers ("publicans") were of the small artisan or yeoman class.

Literature provides descriptions of inns from the fourteenth century onward, but these were often popular stereotypes. Factual information on the size, cost, and amenities of medieval inns and on their managers can be found in tax registers, contracts, and leases in the archives of cities and towns where they were located, as well as in the records of innkeepers guilds, where these existed. Certainly, by the end of the Middle Ages, inns were the most generally patronized accommodation for all travelers.

**BIBLIOGRAPHY**

Jusserand, J.J. *English Wayfaring Life in the Middle Ages.* Trans. Lucy Toulmin Smith. London: Benn, 1950.

Ohler, Norbert. "Hospitality and Inns." In *The Medieval Traveler.* Trans. Caroline Hillier. Woodbridge, Suffolk: Boydell and Brewer, 1989, pp. 79–96.

Sumption, Jonathan. "Hospitality." In *Pilgrimage: An Image of Medieval Religion.* Totowa, NJ: Rowman and Littlefield, 1976, pp. 198–206.

Wolff, Philippe. "Les Hôtelleries Toulousaines au Moyen Age." In *Regards sur le Midi médiéval.* Toulouse: Privat, 1978, pp. 93–106.

*Margaret Wade Labarge*

**SEE ALSO**

Chaucer, Geoffrey; *Fondaco;* Genoa; Ghent; Jerusalem; Merchants, Italian; Pilgrimage Sites, Spanish; Pisa; Venice

## Insurance

A guarantee or indemnity against personal loss, known in the ancient world and an important factor in medieval commerce.

Although certain kinds of commercial and life insurance can be found in records from Babylonia—and later among the Greeks and Romans—such guards against risk first became widespread and developed sometime during the "commercial revolution" of the Middle Ages, when merchants who no longer saw the need to travel with their merchandise developed a type of contract that came to be known as insurance. The earliest and most important form of insurance for the merchant was marine insurance. Scholars differ over the date of the earliest marine insurance contract (some date it to Genoa in 1347), but most would agree that by the beginning of the fifteenth century, marine insurance had emerged as an established and accepted practice.

Marine insurance most likely developed out of the sea loan (*foenus nauticum*), a common type of contract through which a traveling merchant could minimize his risk in a long sea voyage by contracting a loan with one or more nontraveling merchants. This loan only had to be paid back if the voyage was successful. As the traveling merchant became rare and trade organized around the sedentary merchant much more common, the need for new types of contracts to minimize risk became crucial.

Late in the twelfth century, merchants developed the "insurance loan," which retained some of the characteristics of the sea loan. The insurance loan, like the sea loan, had to be paid back only if the merchandise reached its destination, but the goods had to go unaccompanied. Premium insurance, although influenced by the earlier form just mentioned, was developed by sedentary Italian merchants of the thirteenth century who saw the need for minimizing risk but who did not need to take up debt. Insurance contracts were usually written in the form of a pseudo-sale so that the premium would not be equated with interest. All insurance contracts shared a number of characteristics: several insuring merchants each put up part of a policy; these insurers assumed all risks of the sea, both of God and of man, for the duration of the voyage; and for this insurance the insured paid a fee or premium. The advantage to the merchant was that his investment in merchandise could be protected against a variety of risks without his taking on a large debt.

**BIBLIOGRAPHY**

Maclean, F.J. *The Human Side of Insurance.* London: Sampson Low, Marston & Co., 1931.

Roover, Florence Edler de. "Early Examples of Marine Insurance." *Journal of Economic History* 5 (1945): 172–173.

Westall, Oliver M., ed. *The Historian and the Business of Insurance.* Manchester: Manchester UP, 1984.

*Donald J. Harreld*

**SEE ALSO**

Merchant Manuals; Shipping Contracts, Mediterranean

## Irish Travel

The Irish had acquired a reputation for wanderlust by the early Middle Ages. The Frankish scholar Walahfrid Strabo (*c.* 808–849) spoke of people "from the Irish nation, with whom the habit of traveling to foreign lands (*consuetudo peregrinandi*) has by now become almost second nature."

# I

Like Christians throughout Europe, Irish pilgrims often traveled to Rome and to other holy places both at home and abroad during the entire medieval period. One, a friar named Symon Semeonis [Simeon Simeonis], left a detailed and fascinating description (known from a single manuscript copy) of his travels to the Holy Land in 1323–1324. Within Ireland, "St. Patrick's Purgatory" in Loch Derg, County Donegal, was a popular destination in the later Middle Ages for both Irish and foreign pilgrims. For many Irish ascetics in the early Middle Ages, however, a "pilgrimage" meant not a visit to a shrine followed by a return home, but a permanent condition of voluntary exile. The *Anglo-Saxon Chronicle* records that in the year 891, three Irishmen arrived in Cornwall in a boat without any oars, having left Ireland "because they desired, for the love of God, to be in a state of pilgrimage, they cared not where." Other Irish ascetics traveled to the Orkney and Faeroe Islands and even as far as Iceland, where the first Norse settlers are said to have found books, bells, and croziers left by Irish hermits. Still others followed trails blazed by Columba (Columcille [c. 521–597]), who founded the Monastery of Iona off the coast of Scotland about 563, and by Columbanus (c. 550–615), who founded several monasteries on the Continent, notably Luxeuil (after 593) in Gaul and Bobbio in Italy (in 612).

Subsequent Irish foundations, established under secular and ecclesiastical patrons such as Charlemagne and Charles the Bald, Otto III, and Adalbero II, bishop of Metz, became centers of missionary activity and of Irish cultural influence in early medieval Europe. Among the expatriate Irish scholars who contributed to the revival of learning during the Carolingian period were Dicuil (early ninth century), whose treatise on world geography *Liber de mensura orbis terrae*, completed in 825, included a report of a journey to Egypt by an Irish monk named Fidelis, and Virgil, bishop of Salzburg (?–784), whose speculations regarding the antipodes aroused suspicion of heresy. The reputation of Irish *peregrini* for sanctity at times exceeded reality, and not a few saints of doubtful origin (or even existence) were later presumed to have been Irish, as it were, by popular demand. (Since forced exile was also imposed as a penance for serious crimes, not every wandering Irishman was a scholar, or a saint. At the same time, alleged irregularities in ordination and discipline led to occasional legislation directed against "wandering clerics" of the Irish race.)

Monasteries and hospices continued to be maintained specifically for Irish monks and pilgrims far from their native island down to the end of the Middle Ages—the abbey of St. James at Ratisbon (Regensburg) in Germany was the mother house of an important congregation of Benedictine *Schottenklöster*—but Irish influence had begun to wane by the ninth century, by which time the spiritual prestige of wandering in exile had been diminished by a renewed emphasis on monastic stability.

With scant archaeological remains, literary evidence has to be relied on to construct what is probably a somewhat idealized picture. For travel by water both within and beyond their island nation, the Irish employed a type of vessel called a curragh (Irish *curach*; the word *coracle* properly refers to the similar British craft), made of wickerwork hulls covered with animal hides, and ranging in size from single-hide rowing coracles to substantial sailing vessels fitted with mast, keel, and steering oar (the three Irishmen who landed in Cornwall had traveled in a curragh of two hides and a half). British Celtic hide boats are mentioned by several classical authors, including Caesar (*Civil War* 1.54) and Pliny the Elder (*Natural History* VII.206). In early Irish literature, accounts of marvelous voyages in curraghs constituted a special genre (*imrama*), the most famous example being the Latin "Voyage of Saint Brendan." More conventional planked vessels were also in use, of course (one law tract mentions the *long* and *bárc* in addition to the *curach*), and largely superseded the sailing curragh following the Viking invasions; but small curraghs have remained in use in western Ireland down to the present century (J.M. Synge's vivid description of a harrowing passage in *The Aran Islands* is unmatched).

On land, the elite rode horses and used spoke-wheeled horse- or ox-drawn carts, and there was a system of roads, maintenance of which is provided for in the law tracts. There is no Iron Age archaeological evidence for the war chariots so lavishly described in the epic *Táin Bó Cuailnge* (The Cattle-Raid of Cooley), but a type of "chariot" was certainly known in early Christian Ireland and was probably used for agriculture as well as transport and combat. As a point of penitential discipline, however, the traveling Irish ascetic rarely rode, but walked. Pilgrims set out in groups, sometimes of twelve in imitation of the apostles. Irish monks carried leather book satchels, and several early Irish "pocket" Gospel books have survived.

Maritime trading in the pre- and early Christian periods is evidenced by imported pottery, including a limited distribution of wares from the Mediterranean (both "A ware," now called Red Slip Ware, and "B ware" amphorae) that may have been acquired through secondary exchanges with western Britain, and a more extensive distribution of kitchen or general use "E ware," probably from western France. There is scattered literary evidence for trading contacts with Gaul in the early Middle Ages. According to Jonas of Bobbio, the seventh-century biographer of Columbanus, when Columbanus was compelled to leave Burgundy, he was put aboard a ship "concerned with Irish trade" at the port of Nantes on the Loire. Adamnan's seventh-century *Life of Columba* mentions the arrival of sailors from Gaul in the Gaelic kingdom of Dál Riata in Scotland. The existence of an important wine trade with Poitou by the twelfth century is attested by Gerald of Wales (*Topography of Ireland* 1.5). In the later Middle Ages, wine was imported primarily from La Rochelle, Gascony, and Bordeaux (whence the Irish term *bordgal*, "trading center").

International trading developed in tandem with the gradual urbanization of Ireland following the establishment of trading towns (including Dublin, Limerick, and Waterford) by the Vikings during the ninth and tenth centuries, with Dublin early becoming a center for slave-trading. Following the Anglo-Norman invasion of the twelfth century, Irish overseas trade was controlled by England. Chester and Bristol in England and Rouen in France were among the European ports most involved in Irish trade. Exports included timber, fish (especially herring), cattle hides, marten skins, wool, and cloth (Irish mantles were particularly valued commodities). The Irish imported especially salt, iron, wine, cereals, and honey. In the later Middle Ages, Italian merchant bankers were well established in Ireland.

Less tangible but equally important as the traffic in material goods was cultural traffic in texts and ideas. Irish (Latin) texts and manuscripts were scattered throughout monastic centers in western Europe during the early Middle Ages. A ninth-century booklist from St. Gall, the influential Swiss monastery that was named after a follower of Columbanus, refers to some thirty *libri scottice scripti*: "books in Irish script." Irish scribes and scholars on the Continent played a role in the preservation of classical literature, though it has been exaggerated, and John Scottus Eriugena's knowledge of Greek was the exception rather than the rule.

Cultural influences in the other direction include some tantalizing connections with Near Eastern (Syriac and Coptic) art, apocrypha, and liturgy; Spain has been suggested as an intermediary. Although Ireland had never been a Roman colony, its ecclesiastical culture and literature were heavily influenced by western Britain and Gaul from the time of St. Patrick (?–493). A report in a twelfth-century Leiden manuscript of a fifth-century exodus of Gaulish scholars to Ireland is now generally discounted, but the Christian-Latin literature of late antique and early medieval Gaul did affect the stylistic development of Irish literature, both vernacular and Latin. The impact of classical Latin and medieval continental literature becomes apparent in translations of Virgil, Lucan, and Statius from the twelfth century, and of Franciscan religious texts from the fourteenth. In the wake of the Anglo-Norman invasion, native ecclesiastical reforms, already influenced by Cistercian ideals, were overtaken by English and continental direction, and the Irish church was gradually absorbed—with loss of much of its distinctive character—into the mainstream of European ecclesiastical tradition.

**BIBLIOGRAPHY**

Childs, Wendy, and Timothy O'Neill. "Overseas Trade." In *A New History of Ireland.* Vol. 2: *Medieval Ireland 1169–1534.* Ed. Art Cosgrove. Oxford: Clarendon, 1987, pp. 492–524.

Doherty, Charles. "Exchange and Trade in Early Medieval Ireland." *Journal of the Royal Society of Antiquaries of Ireland* 110 (1980): 67–89.

Gougaud, Louis. *Christianity in Celtic Lands.* Trans. Maud Joynt. London: Sheed and Ward, 1932; rpt. Blackrock: Four Courts, 1990.

Harbison, Peter. *Pilgrimage in Ireland: The Monuments and the People.* London: Barrie and Jenkins, 1991.

Hornell, James. *British Coracles and Irish Curraghs.* London: Bernard Quaritch, 1938.

Hughes, Kathleen. "The Changing Theory and Practice of Irish Pilgrimage." *Journal of Ecclesiastical History* 11 (1960): 143–151.

Ireland, John de Courcy. *Ireland and the Irish in Maritime History.* Dublin: Glendale, 1980.

Kenny, James F. *The Sources for the Early History of Ireland: Ecclesiastical.* New York: Columbia UP, 1929; rpt. with addenda by L. Bieler, New York: Octagon, 1966.

O'Neill, Timothy. *Merchants and Mariners in Medieval Ireland.* Dublin: Irish Academic Press, 1987.

Wooding, Jonathan M. *Communication and Commerce along the Western Sealanes A.D. 400–800.* British Archaeological

Reports, International Series 654. Oxford: Tempus Reparatum, 1996.

*Charles D. Wright*

**SEE ALSO**

Adamnan; Antipodes; Brendan's Voyage, St.; Dicuil; Gerald of Wales; Iceland; *Imrama;* Inns and Accommodations; Navigation; Penance, Travel for; Purgatory, St. Patrick's; Transportation, Inland; Viking Age; Virgil of Salzburg, St.

## Isidore of Seville (*c.* 560–636)

Compiler of a seventh-century encyclopedic work on etymologies that had an enormous influence on medieval culture. He was born into an influential Spanish-Roman family, which was driven off from the province of Cartagena in the mid-sixth century, settling in Seville, where Isidore succeeded his elder brother Leander as bishop. A third brother, Fulgentius, became bishop of Ecija (Astigis).

Isidore was a productive author; seventeen authentic works of his are known. For subjects related to geography the most important work was the *Etymologies* (*Etymologiae sive origines libri XX*), which he began around 620, commissioned by the Visigothic king Sisebut (r. 612–621). This treasure-house of knowledge also contains information he had included earlier in his *Libri differentiarum* and *Libellus de natura rerum*. Although the work remained unfinished at Isidore's death (it was edited and organized into its twenty books by his friend, Braulio of Saragossa), it made him the most famous encyclopedist of the Middle Ages and has caused him to be called the last of the Doctors of the Church in the West. Its title, *Etymologies,* derives from the idea fundamental in his time that the study of word origins helps us to grasp the true nature of things (see *Etymologies* 1.29. 1–2). Books 1–3 are devoted to the seven liberal arts, and the following ones to such subjects as medicine, law, religion, architecture, agriculture, animals, and natural history.

For geography, several sections of Isidore's encyclopedic study are of interest, but particularly Book 9 on languages, races, empires, warfare, citizens, and social relationships; Book 11 on man and monstrous races; Books 13 and 14, dealing with the material universe, including the heavens, atmosphere, water (springs, seas, the great Sea-Ocean, lakes, subterranean channels, and rivers), and the inhabited landmass (or *oikoumene*), islands, promontories, and mountains; and Book 15

World map, Isidore of Seville, *Etymologies*, Madrid, Biblioteca de la Real Academia de la Historia MS 25, fol. 204r, *c.* 946. Courtesy Biblioteca de la Real Academia de la Historia.

on cities and architecture. As Solinus and Orosius had done before, he borrowed from classical authorities and attempted to arrange material rationally and accessibly; he did not base his writing on significant observed experience of his own.

The *Etymologies* were excerpted, often verbatim, from a great many sources, of which a number are now lost. In many cases, Isidore used later compilations of texts rather than their original version. For the geographical information he turned most often to Pliny's *Natural History,* Solinus's *Collection of Memorable Things,* Orosius's *History,* Servius's and Donatus's commentaries on Virgil, Sallust, Justinus, and patristic commentary on the Old Testament. Isidore apparently did not obtain information from maps; however, a T-O map (see Maps) can be found in many manuscript copies of the *Etymologies*. By the later seventh century, many of these maps (which acquire greater sophistication over the centuries) appear at the beginning of Book 14, "On the Earth and Its Parts." As a compilation of older compilations, the *Etymologies* was full of errors. Yet Isidore's enormous authority helped to maintain the belief in all sorts of marvels and fantastic people and monsters to be found in his work. He was consulted not only by scholars, but also by travelers and discoverers. A detailed description of his influence has not yet been made, although Jacques Fontaine's work goes far in this direction.

More than 1,000 manuscripts—some fragmentary—of the *Etymologies* are known today, testifying to the remarkable dissemination of this book. Indeed, during the Carolingian period almost every library owned a copy of the work. But in the later Middle Ages Isidore gradually declined in importance as a source for geographical information; new encyclopedic works began to appear (of which Vincent of Beauvais's *Speculum maius* [*c*.1244/1260] is a major example), and later, new geographical discoveries called into question much of the information found in Isidore and similar sources. William of Rubruck's assertion that "Isidore was wrong" in claiming that the Caspian Sea is a gulf of a northern ocean, in his *Itinerarium* of 1255, is one of the first challenges to the authoritative encyclopedist. Although the *Etymologies* was printed very early in the history of printing (1472 and several subsequent incunabule editions), the editorial efforts of humanists at this same time to return to accurately restored classical sources reduced the importance of later, largely derivative works, even those of so prolific and productive a writer as Isidore.

No translation of the whole work exists, but a new edition of the *Etymologies* (with either English or French translations) is appearing in twenty volumes under the direction of Jacques Fontaine. The series, being published by Budé in Paris (Les Belles Lettres, 1981–), so far consists of Volumes 2, 9, 12, and 17.

### BIBLIOGRAPHY

Fontaine, Jacques. *Isidore de Seville et la culture classique dans l'Espagne Wisigothique.* 3 vols. 2nd rev. edition. Paris: Etudes Augustiniennes, 1983.

———, ed. *De natura rerum* [Traité de la nature]. Bibliothèque de l'Ecole des Hautes Etudes, Etudes Hispaniques 28. Bordeaux: Feret, 1960.

Lindsay, W.M., ed. *Isidori Hispalensis episcopi Etymologiarum sive Originum libri XX.* 2 vols. Oxford: Oxford UP, 1911; rpt. London and New York: Oxford UP, 1985.

Philipp, Hans. *Die historisch-geographischen Quellen in den Etymologiae des Isidorus von Sevilla.* Part 1. Quellenuntersuchung. Part 2. Textausgabe und Quellenausgabe. Quellen und Forschungen zur alten Geschichte und Geographie, 25–26. Berlin: Weidmann, 1912–1913.

Z.R.W.M. von Martels

**SEE ALSO**
Geography in Medieval Europe; Maps; Monstrosity, Geographical; Orosius; Sallust Maps; Solinus, Julius Gaius; Vincent of Beauvais; William of Rubruck

## Isol the Pisan
*See* Bofeti, Pericciolo di Anastasio

## Italian Merchants
*See* Merchants, Italian

## Itineraries and *Periploi*

Genres of medieval travel writing whose purpose is to describe locations and sights along a given route, usually including distances from point to point.

The itinerary and the *periplus* were both developed in classical Europe. The *periplus* (literally "sailing around"), or pilot book, which was known as early as the fourth century B.C.E., helped sailors navigate along established routes by describing coastal landmarks, distances between ports, currents, and wind directions. The *itinerarium,* a road manual that similarly aided "navigation" on land routes, was a development of the Roman Empire, whose complex system of roads created a need for such a guide for long-distance travelers. The *Antonine Itinerary* of 346 lists the names of cities and stations along each of the roads in the empire and the distances between the stations.

In the late antique period, the itinerary became a more descriptive document, as travelers began to produce guidebooks to particular routes. Popular pilgrimage routes, especially to the Holy Land, were the most common subjects. Two fourth-century pilgrims, a nun named Egeria (probably from either Galicia or southern Gaul) and an anonymous traveler known as the Bordeaux Pilgrim, left well-known itineraries describing their journeys to the Holy Land. Like ancient itineraries, their accounts indicate the roads taken and the distances between the places and sights encountered on their travels; unlike earlier itineraries, however, both also include brief descriptions of the landmarks and holy sites visited. Both authors concentrate on describing the significance in Christian history of the places visited in their travels. Later pilgrims' guides became more elaborate and personalized documents and moved away from the strict itinerary format.

Medieval itineraries could describe the travels of kings and aristocrats across their territories, as well as the routes taken by bishops and other religious leaders. The *Itinerary of Richard I of England,* for example, is an important source of information about this twelfth-century king and crusader. Medieval itineraries covered a variety of time spans and distances. Gerald of Wales (1146–1223), a Welsh ecclesiastic known for his historical writings, produced *Itinerarium Kambriae,* a popular account of his five-week progress across Wales in 1188

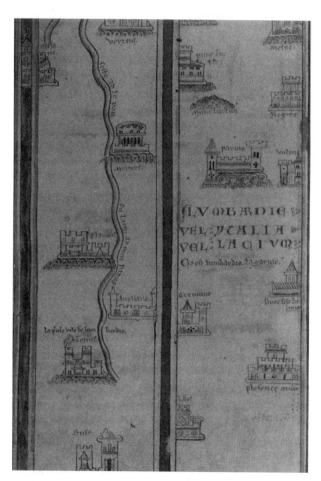

Itinerary from London to Apulia. Matthew Paris, *Chronica Majora,* Cambridge, Corpus Christi College MS 26, fol. ii v, *c.* 250. Permission Master and Fellows, Corpus Christi College, Cambridge.

with Archbishop Baldwin of Canterbury. Benjamin of Tudela, a twelfth-century rabbi, described his thirteen-year journey through Italy, Greece, and the Near East to the western borders of China in an account known as *Massa'ot,* or the *Itinerary of Benjamin of Tudela.*

By the late Middle Ages, itineraries and other travel literature became more personalized and impressionistic. Francesco Petrarch (1304–1374) ostensibly wrote his *Itinerarium syriacum* as a guide to the Holy Land for a friend, but the work is replete with historical and moralistic asides and literary allusions, and thus very different from the sparse lists of distances and locations that made up the earliest itineraries.

**BIBLIOGRAPHY**

Bordeaux Pilgrim. *Itinerary from Bordeaux to Jerusalem.* Trans. Aubrey Stewart. Library of the Palestine Pilgrims' Text Society 1. 1887. Rpt. New York: AMS Press, 1971.

Campbell, Mary B. *The Witness and the Other World: Exotic European Travel Writing, 400–1600.* Ithaca, NY: Cornell UP, 1988.

Gerald of Wales. *The Journey through Wales and the Description of Wales.* Trans. and intro. Lewis Thorpe. New York: Penguin, 1978.

*Teresa Leslie*

**SEE ALSO**

*Antonine Itinerary;* Benjamin of Tudela; Bordeaux Pilgrim; Egeria; Gerald of Wales; Holy Land; *Itinerarium Syriacum;* Peutinger Table; Pilgrimage, Christian

## Itinerarium Syriacum

A pilgrim's guide to the route from Genoa to Jerusalem and Alexandria, based on personal experiences and ancient literary sources, by one of the foremost literary figures of the late Middle Ages, Francesco Petrarch (1304–1374).

In early 1358, while resident in Milan, the humanist and poet Petrarch was asked by Giovanolo da Mandella, nephew of Matteo Visconti (the count of Milan), to accompany his party on a pilgrimage to the Holy Land. Citing the dangers of travel, Petrarch declined, but instead wrote a long letter in which he described what the party would see on the route. He claimed to have composed it in three days, and it covers just over eight pages in the Basel edition of Petrarch's works (1554).

The first half of the *Itinerarium Syriacum* covers the coast and coastal cities from Genoa to Naples. In February 1341, Petrarch had sailed from Marseilles to Naples, and in October 1343, from Nizza to Motrone, then continued overland to Naples; he knew this stretch firsthand. His comments include archaeological observations as well as topographical ones: of the ancient Etruscan city of Tarquinia nothing now remains but "a bare name and ruins"; Anzio had been the ancient capital of the Volscii and Genoa of the Ligurians. He urged Giovanolo while in Naples to visit the royal chapel, recently decorated by Giotto, "my fellow townsman." Beyond Naples, Petrarch depended on his *mappamondo* and classical authors: Pliny the Elder and Virgil for southern Italy, the Aegean, and Asia Minor; the Evangelists for Palestine, Josephus for Jerusalem itself; and Pliny, Cicero, and Suetonius for Egypt. References to classical history and mythology abound, but only once does Petrarch mention a real marvel—an Egyptian spring whose water tastes bitter to Muslims but sweet to Christians.

Presented to Giovanolo on April 4, 1358, the *Itinerarium breve de Ianua usque ad Ierusalem et Terram Sanctam* was probably copied by Boccaccio the following year, and was cited by Benvenuto da Imola in 1375. It survives in at least twenty manuscripts and was first printed in Venice in 1501.

**BIBLIOGRAPHY**

Feo, Michele. "Un Ulisse in Terrasanta." *Rivista di cultura classica e medioevale* 19 (1977): 383–388.

*Francisci Petrarchae Operum, Tomus I.* Ed. Henricus Petri. Basle: H. Peter, 1554. Facsimile edition. Ridgewood, NJ: The Gregg Press Inc., 1965, pp. 618–626.

Koikylides, K.M., and K. Phokylides, eds. *Archaia Latinika, Hellenika, Rossika kai Gallika tina Odoiporika e Proskynetaria tes Hagias Ges.* Jerusalem: Panagiou Taphou: 1912.

Paolella, Alfonso. "Petrarca e la letteratura odeporica del medioevo." *Studi e problemi di critica testuale* 44 (1992): 61–85.

Petrarca, Francesco. *Itinerario in Terra Santa.* Ed. F. Lomonaco. Bergamo: Lubrino, 1990.

Wilkins, Ernest H. *Petrarch's Eight Years in Milan.* Cambridge, MA: Mediaeval Academy of America, 1958.

*Joseph P. Byrne*

**SEE ALSO**

Egypt; Genoa; Holy Land; Itineraries and *Periploi;* Jerusalem; Pilgrimage, Christian; Pliny the Elder

## Ivory Trade

Ivory—the modified dentin found on certain teeth—has been prized worldwide since prehistoric times for its rarity, whiteness, workability, and durability. Elephant incisors are the most common source, although walrus, boar, and narwhal tusks, as well as hippopotamus and sperm whale teeth, also produce ivory.

The world ivory trade has long concentrated on the tusks of the African elephant (*Loxodonta africana*), which have historically been more highly valued than their Indian counterparts (*Elephas maximus*). While only the males of the Indian elephant have visible incisors, both males and females of the African species produce them. African tusks tend to be larger, harder, heavier, and whiter than Asiatic examples, averaging more than six feet and 150 pounds; examples over twelve feet long are known.

Since antiquity elephant tusks have been traded extensively. In the late antique/early medieval period, ivory imports to the Mediterranean area, particularly Constantinople, were considerable. There it was worked into pyxes, relief plaques, and other ecclesiastical objects well into the eleventh century. Antioch and Alexandria also served as major carving centers. The Islamic empires, which extended into Spain, Sicily, and Portugal, made considerable use of ivory for secular objects and inlaid wooden furniture. In the tenth and eleventh centuries, Córdoba was the ivory-carving center of the Islamic world.

Ivory reached the Byzantine and Mediterranean worlds from both India and Africa. Arab traders transported Indian ivory along their Eastern spice routes, and Islamic merchants also controlled East African external commerce through the foundation of residential trading posts from Somalia to Mozambique. Tusks reached them from distant inland areas, passing through many interior trade networks along the way. West African trans-Saharan ivory traffic was also well established in the medieval period. There, too, tusks (and gold) advanced through many mercantile networks before being loaded on caravans eventually to reach Arab hands in North Africa.

This Arab control limited ivory's transport to northern Europe until the eleventh century; walrus ivory served northern carvers instead. It was not until the Romanesque and Gothic periods that a growing supply of elephant tusks spawned industries in Germany, France, Flanders, and England. Artists fashioned luxury goods such as combs, cups, caskets, mirror cases, chess pieces, and weapon handles, as well as book-cover ornaments and small devotional pieces. Siberian supplies of prehistoric mastodon tusks had provided an

Celebration of mass, ivory panel. Frankfurt, Universitäts-bibliothek MS Barth 181, *c.* 875. Courtesy Stadt-und Universitätsbibliothek Frankfurt am Main.

alternative source of ivory for Russian artists. By the tenth century, these teeth, nearly five times as large and much heavier than elephant tusks, supplied raw materials to several Russian carving centers.

In Asia, ivory use was also widespread. Elephants were common in India and Sri Lanka; they also inhabited Myanmar (Burma), Vietnam, Laos, Malaysia, and Sumatra. Local demand on the Indian subcontinent was high; Indians used ivory for jewelry, chess pieces, and as furniture inlay, but also exported tusks to both West and East. By the sixth century, India began importing additional ivory from East Africa, due to the high renewable demand for bridal bangles (burned at funerals). The Chinese sought the commodity from all available sources. Siberian mastodon ivory reached them, and Chinese trade routes brought tusks from as far as Persia and Byzantium. Chinese porcelain found along the East African coast attests to the complex

commercial relationships of the period. China also traded both raw tusks and finished carvings to Japan.

In medieval Africa, elephants were plentiful and enjoyed a wide distribution. Ivory was used locally by many cultures as a prestigious sculptural and ornamental material. In some states, the ruler had special prerogatives concerning its ownership, purchase, or sale. In Nigeria's Benin kingdom, for example, hunters were required to send one tusk of every elephant killed to the monarch, and he had first rights to buy the second.

When the Portuguese first began their sea voyages down the West African coast in the fifteenth century, their interest in ivory, gold, and pepper quickly led to the establishment of trade relationships with coastal peoples. By the 1450s, they had sighted the Cape Verde Islands, and rapidly founded a commercially oriented colony there. The Portuguese contacted Sierra Leone by 1462, Benin by the 1470s, and the Kongo kingdom by 1483. These three areas were major exporters of ivory; their supplies were supplemented by tusks transported from many inland areas. By the close of the fifteenth century, both Sierra Leone and Benin had sent worked objects—as well as raw ivory—to Europe. During the reign of the Portuguese king Dom Afonso (1438–1481), the king held a monopoly on the ivory trade. He in turn maintained a profitable arrangement to resell it all to one merchant. Portugal, which exchanged cloth, metal, and beads for tusks, successfully kept most other Europeans away from its West African commercial partners until the mid-sixteenth century.

The ivory tusks of the walrus (*Odobenus rosmarus* and *O. divergens*), a native of Arctic Circle waters, were widely sought throughout the medieval period. Hunted by Siberians, Inuits, Samme (Lapps), and other northern peoples, it sometimes fetched double the price of elephant ivory. Although certainly rarer, its value seems linked to the belief it would "sweat" in the presence of poisoned food, and could even act as an antidote; the Chinese produced walrus ivory chopsticks for this purpose. Arabs felt it could stanch wounds, and they used it for weapon handles. From northern Russia, Viking traders carried it to Constantinople; from that point, its detective/curative properties assured it a market in China, North Africa, and India. In northern and western Europe, walrus ivory was more widely used than elephant ivory from the ninth to the thirteenth centuries.

The narwhal, too, is a denizen of the Arctic sea. The males of this small whale species (*Monodon monoceros*) produce a single spiraling tusk that can grow to nine feet in length. Since few besides hunters actually saw the animal itself, it was widely believed its tusk belonged to the mythical unicorn and had magical properties. These included the ability to detect and neutralize poison; like walrus ivory, this increased its value and it was traded to many distant parts of the world.

**BIBLIOGRAPHY**

Blake, John W. *West Africa: Quest for God and Gold.* London: Curzon, 1977.

Burack, Benjamin. *Ivory and Its Uses.* Rutland, VT: Tuttle, 1984.

Kunz, George F. *Ivory and the Elephant.* New York: Doubleday, 1916.

Maskell, Alfred. *Ivories.* London: Methuen, 1905.

Ross, Doran H., ed. *Elephant: The Animal and Its Ivory in African Culture.* Los Angeles: UCLA Fowler Museum, 1992.

*Kathy Curnow*

**SEE ALSO**

African Trade; Elephants; Gold Trade in Africa; Muslim Travelers and Trade; Pepper; Russia and Rus'; Spice Trade, Indian Ocean; Whaling

# J

## Jacopo da Verona (fl. 1335)

Augustinian friar and lector, later prior of the Monastery of St. Euphemia at Verona. Author of a detailed account in Latin of his pilgrimage to the Holy Land undertaken in 1335.

Although Jacopo's account, known as the *Liber Peregrinationis* (Book of the Pilgrimage), is not a literary masterpiece, it is an important example of an emerging genre of travel literature in which personal experience is a fitting subject for the writer. In contrast to earlier texts, which were often simple lists of places, mileage, tariffs, and indulgences useful to the pilgrim, the fourteen chapters of this book record details about where the writer preached and celebrated Mass, how he reacted to non–Latin-rite Christians in Palestine and Egypt, and why he has taken the time and trouble to write about his pilgrimage. The original text must have incorporated at least three sketches or maps of different regions: the single extant manuscript, from 1424 (at the University of Minnesota) contains the copy of a map of Mount Sinai, as well as blank spaces for maps—never drawn—of the interior of the Church of the Holy Sepulchre; a triangular area of land bounded by Cairo, Gaza, and Mount Sinai; and, evidently, the Jordan River valley. Jacopo's account gives an idea of the hazards faced by medieval pilgrims: tempests, pirates, robbers, and sometimes hostile Saracens. He was the earliest pilgrim to transcribe the inscriptions on certain crusader kings' tombs.

Jacopo offers credible, eyewitness accounts of most cities and regions, though a few of his descriptions seem drawn from earlier accounts and probably represent places not actually visited. This blending of first-hand information and borrowed material was typical of the medieval composition method.

Jacopo's *Liber* captures the religious fervor of the medieval pilgrim. For example, he avidly describes his own passion for relic hunting: he chipped off many stone fragments from monuments with specially made tools and carried away sacred liquids in small vials. Jacopo treats locations with limited regard for their geographical features, focusing instead on Old and New Testament events that occurred in the vicinity. He records not only what he saw, but also what he heard, touched, smelled, and tasted. For Jacopo, the physical senses clearly heightened the devotional experience, and he attempts to re-create this experience for his reader.

Jacopo records basic observations and beliefs about Muslims, Jews, and the various Eastern Christian sects. He learned some of these facts from inquiries made through his interpreters; other notions are rooted in typical Christian polemical tracts against Islam. Typical of his anti-Muslim stance is his insistence that Arabs are incorrectly called "Saracens" since they have no link to Abraham's wife Sara; as "illegitimate" offspring of the servant Hagar, they are more aptly identified as "Agareni."

In addition to the text's religious content, two chapters might be said to offer "military intelligence": one lists castles and fortifications in the Holy Land, the other describes the sultan's administration and armed forces. The account contains laments for the territory conquered by the Egyptian sultan—especially the city of Acre, taken from the Christians in 1291—and explicit calls for a new crusade.

# J

**BIBLIOGRAPHY**

Braslawski, J. "Jacobus of Verona on the Hebrews in Palestine in the Fourteenth Century." *Bulletin of the Jewish Palestine Exploration Society* 4 (1936–1937): 27–32.

*Liber Peregrinationis di Jacopo da Verona.* Ed. Ugo Monneret de Villard. Istituto Italiano per il Medio ed Estremo Oriente, Il Nuovo Ramusio 1. Rome: Libreria dello Stato. 1950.

"Le Pèlerinage du moine augustin Jacques de Vérone (1335)." Ed. Reinhold Röhricht. *Revue de l'Orient latin* 3 (1895): 155–302.

*Pellegrinaggio ai luoghi santi: Liber Peregrinationis.* Ed. Vittorio Castagna. Verona: Accademia de Agricoltura, Scienze e Lettere de Verona, 1990. [Italian Trans.]

Simeoni, Luigi. "Un frammento del pellegrinaggio de Iacopo da Verona (1335)." *Arte e Storia* (Florence) 3rd series, 25 (1909): 163–165.

*Gloria Allaire*

**SEE ALSO**

Acre; Eastern Christianity; Holy Land; Itineraries and *Periploi;* Pilgrim Souvenirs; Pilgrimage, Christian; Piracy; Spies

## Jacques de Vitry [Jacobus Vitriaco] (*c.* 1165–1240)

Influential cardinal and preacher whose travels through western Europe and the Middle East are recorded in various writings. Little is known about the early life of Jacques de Vitry. It is certain that he studied in Paris and that he was ordained to the priesthood in 1210. His post-Parisian activities took him to Liège (*c.* 1211–1216) where, as an Augustinian canon, he became involved with a lay spiritual movement represented by Marie d'Oignies. In 1213, the papacy commissioned him to preach the Albigensian Crusade. He also preached the Fifth Crusade, which led to his subsequent election as bishop of Acre (1216–1228). As bishop, his duties were varied and tiring, which may have led to his resignation. Between 1225 and 1229, he was auxiliary to the bishop of Liège and carried out various ecclesiastical functions at Cologne, Oignies, and Louvain. In 1229, he was elected cardinal-bishop of Tusculum, near Rome, and it was in this office that he remained until his death on May 1, 1240.

Jacques de Vitry was a prolific writer and his works embrace a range of genres, including hagiography, sermon literature, history, and letters. His *Historia Orien-* *talis* and seven letters, written while serving as bishop of Acre, provide the most information about travel and exploration. The *Historia Orientalis* is an account of earlier crusades, as well as of the people, places, flora, and fauna found in the eastern Mediterranean, Asia Minor, and India. The seven letters provide a diversity of information, such as a description of the early Franciscan movement as well as many details of the Fifth Crusade (1217–1221), such as the siege of Damietta.

The *Historia Orientalis* can be described as a bestiary, travel book, and history rolled into one, in which lions and dragons, Muslims and Amazons all have a place. A good deal of this work is based directly on the *Historia rerum in partibus transmarinis gestarum* of William of Tyre (*c.* 1130–*c.* 1185). Jacques himself lists among his sources Pliny, Solinus, Augustine, Isidore, "histories of the East," and a "mappa mundi." But the work's derivative nature does not detract from its propagandistic function in its scathing portrayal of the life of Muhammad and the origins of Islam. (Jacques could also be highly critical of Christian behavior, as he proved in his *Historia Occidentalis,* in which he inveighs against sin and corruption in Europe.) He is here one of the first Westerners to attempt a balanced, informed description of Eastern Christians. In the *Historia Orientalis,* Jacques presents the Middle East as a biblical travel paradise in which many places of the Hebrew Bible and New Testament come to life. This vivid presentation of the Holy Land arose from Jacques de Vitry's conviction that the crusading movement must continue, and it also cultivated in western Europeans a desire to protect, and even to see, such places as Jerusalem, Nazareth, and Bethlehem. This particular wanderlust is also found in Jacques de Vitry's letters, which at times also borrow from William of Tyre. In a letter to his friends in France, Jacques lamented the fact that, although resident in the Holy Land, he had not yet visited Nazareth "where Jesus Christ lived" and Mount Carmel "where Elias the prophet led the life of a hermit" (*Lettres,* pp. 89–90).

These letters also reveal Jacques de Vitry's trials in his move to the Middle East. The description of his days in Genoa immediately preceding his installation as bishop of Acre demonstrates how a high-ranking cleric would prepare himself for travel. Jacques writes that Genoa was viewed as the ideal place from which to leave for the Holy Land on a crusade since it contained rich and powerful people, had an abundance of ships and galleys, and possessed a multitude of experienced sailors who knew the Muslims well through trade. Moreover, the nature of the journey is described. Jacques and his entourage set sail at the beginning of October for a five-week journey. The Genoese sailors preferred to sail in wintry seas because the food and water would not spoil as it would during the summer months; also, the journey would not be delayed due to lack of wind. Jacques rented five places for himself, his entourage, and his possessions on the ship. In the castle of the ship, he rented one area for eating, studying, and sleeping; in another space he kept his vestments and his provisions for the week ahead; in the third area his servants lived and prepared his food; and in the fourth place he kept his horses. In the belly of the ship he stored enough wine, biscuits, and meats to last nearly three months (*Lettres*, pp. 161–178).

Although the *Historia Orientalis* and portions of the letters offer lyrical and moving descriptions of sacred places in the Middle East, the letters reveal a nostalgia on the part of the author for his native land. His desire to be with his friends and his emphasis on the difficulties of the journey suggest that for Jacques de Vitry, traveling was a lonely business.

**BIBLIOGRAPHY**

Funk, Philipp. *Jakob von Vitry, Leben und Werke.* Leipzig/Berlin: Teubner, 1909; rpt. Hildesheim: Gersternberg, 1973.

*The Historia Occidentalis of Jacques de Vitry: A Critical Edition.* Ed. J.F. Hinnebusch. Fribourg, Switzerland: The University Press, 1972.

*Lettres de Jacques de Vitry (1160/1170–1240) évêque de Saint-Jean-d'Acre. Édition critique.* Ed. R.B.C. Huygens. Leiden: Brill, 1960.

*Libri duo, quorum prior Orientalis sive Hierosolymitanae, alter Occidentalis historiae nomine inscribitur.* Ed. F. Moschus. Douai: B. Bellerus, 1597; rpt. Farnborough, England: Gregg, 1971.

Pryor, John H. "The Voyage of Jacques de Vitry from Genoa to Acre, 1216: Juridical and Economical Problems in Medieval Navigation." In *Derecho de la navegación en Europa.* Ed. Manuel J. Peláez. Estudios interdisciplinares en homenaje a Ferran Valls i Taberner con ocasión del centenario de su nacimiento, 6; Collección de derecho privado especial y ciencias juridicas de la navegación maritima y aeronautica de Promociones Publicaciones Universitarias de Barcelona, 2. Barcelona: Promociones Publicaciones Universitarias, 1987, pp. 1689–1714.

*Carolyn A. Muessig*

**SEE ALSO**

Acre; Amazons; Bestiaries; Crusade, Fifth; Eastern Christianity; Franciscan Friars; Galley; Genoa; Holy Land; Isidore of Seville; Jerusalem; Pliny the Elder; Solinus, Julius Gaius; Thomas of Cantimpré

## Japan, Mongol Invasion of

In order to conquer the Song Chinese efficiently, Khubilai, the founder of the Yuan dynasty of China (1260–1294) and the fifth great khân of the Mongols (1262–1294), found it imperative to subjugate Japan. The Japanese were trading with the Song Chinese and supporting them economically. Khubilai twice sent envoys demanding homage from Japan, but the regent of Japan, Hojo Tokimune (r. 1251–1284), refused both times (1268 and 1271). Khubilai asked his vassal king of Korea to intercede. Knowing that in the event of a Mongol invasion of Japan Khubilai would expect them to supply ships, soldiers, and other military provisions, the Koreans desperately but unsuccessfully tried to persuade the Japanese to cooperate. Thereupon, in 1274, Khubilai sent an army composed of Mongols and subjugated Chinese and Koreans to Japan. The army left from southeast Korea, laid waste to the islands of Tsushima and Iki-shima, and landed in Hakozaki (Hakata) Bay on the most southerly main island of Japan, Kyushu. Japanese lords counterattacked fiercely, and finally a typhoon forced the invaders to leave.

When, in 1276, Khubilai again sent envoys to Japan, the Japanese authorities summarily executed them, thus making a second Mongol invasion inevitable. After the Song resistance was finally suppressed, Khubilai in 1281 sent a large army of Mongols, Chinese, and Koreans to invade Japan. Two fleets embarked from south China and southeast Korea. The invaders landed in Hakozaki Bay, but their advance was checked by a stone wall the Japanese had built along the coast. After almost two months of fighting, a violent typhoon struck, destroying many ships of the invasion fleet, drowning tens of thousands of Khubilai's men, and forcing the surviving ships to depart. Though Khubilai never gave up the idea of conquering Japan, expeditions to Indochina demanded his attention and kept him from mounting another invasion. In Japan, the cost of defense against the Mongols bankrupted the ruling warrior regime, *Kamakura Bakufu*, and contributed to its eventual downfall.

# J

## BIBLIOGRAPHY

Amino, Yoshihiko. *Moko Shurai* [The Mongol Invasions]. Tokyo: Shogaku-kan, 1974.

Hori, Kyotsu. "The Mongol Invasions and the Kamakura Bakufa." Diss., Columbia U, 1967.

Rossabi, Morris. *Khubilai Khan: His Life and Times.* Berkeley: U of California P, 1988.

Susumu Ishii. "The Decline of the Kamakura *Bakufu.*" In *The Cambridge History of Japan,* vol. 3. Ed. Kozo Yamamura. Cambridge: Cambridge UP, 1989.

*Yoko Miyamoto*

## SEE ALSO

Korea, Mongol Invasions of; Mongols; Vietnam and Java, Mongol Invasions of; Yuan Dynasty

## Java, Mongol Invasion of

*See* Vietnam and Java, Mongol Invasions of

## Jerome Map of Asia

A very old regional map depicting mostly Asia but also parts of Europe and the Mediterranean, named for its inclusion in a twelfth-century manuscript of Jerome's *De situ et nominibus locorum hebraicorum* (British Library MS Add. 10049, fol. 64 r.).

The map, which was drawn *c.* 1150, and which measures twenty-three by nine and one-eighth inches (35.6 × 22.9 cm), depicts a geographical area from the Adriatic to the Indian Ocean, and from the Black Sea (Euxinus Pontus) to the Jordan River. East is at the top. The cartographer generally decreases the scale around the margins, enhancing the projection within Asia Minor, so that the map's focal area nearly equals that of the rest of Asia. One well-known characteristic is a patch in the Mediterranean, applied presumably to repair a hole in the vellum, which the cartographer has labeled Crete, in a way that suggests exact representations of space were not a high priority on medieval maps.

Legends name cities, regions, rivers, seas, islands, mountains, and ranges; captions are numerous. Various icons indicate geographical and political features: strings of half-circles mark mountain ranges; semicircular devices show headwaters for most rivers west of the Euphrates; cylindrical shapes (amphitheaters?) and crenellated rectangles locate chief cities. Babylon's marker has a tower; Corinth's has one steeple; Constantinople's has three. Noah's ark rests in the Armenian highlands.

Numerous departures from geographical reality occur throughout: for example, Sardis lies on the Lycus, the Pactolus flows into the Euxine, Patmos also lies in the Euxine near the Tanais (Don) mouth, the Orontes arises in Commagene. The Aegean islands are jumbled. The Indian peninsula's coastline is an undulated arc bending from the Red Sea to the Caspian, a bay on the map's north margin. The Indian Ocean is fed by the Indus, Hipanis (not Hipasis, actually a tributary of the Indus), Ganges, and an unnamed river originating in the Caucasus. On the verso side of the map of Asia is a map of Palestine (here the patch that is Crete becomes the Caucasus Mountains). P.D.A. Harvey has observed erasures and rewriting of place-names. The manuscript and its maps were once in a monastery at Tournai, where they were probably produced.

That Jerome (*c.* 348–420) was familiar with cartography is clear from references he makes to it (*Epist. ad Heliodorum* 60.7 and *Epist. ad Evangelium* 73.5), but whether he personally drew the prototype for the Asia map, whether it stemmed ultimately from Roman regional maps, or whether it was drawn later to illustrate Jerome's works is debated.

## BIBLIOGRAPHY

Destombes, Marcel, ed. *Mappemondes A.D. 1200–1500.* See Gen Bib.

Harley-Woodward. *The History of Cartography.* Vol. 1, pp. 288–292, 322–325. See Gen. Bib.

Harvey, P.D.A. *Medieval Maps.* London: British Library, 1991.

*Roger T. Macfarlane*

## SEE ALSO

Armenia; Caspian Sea; Constantinople; Ganges; Geography in Medieval Europe; Indus; *Mappamundi;* Maps

## Jerusalem

A center of pilgrimage and theological study for Christians, Jews, and Muslims, which underwent four stages of development in the Middle Ages. Although the city was not on main trade routes, its various rulers confirmed their power in expansive building programs.

In the Byzantine period (early fourth century–638 C.E.), Jerusalem was transformed into a Christian city. Since Jews were forbidden to live there, except briefly (614–629 C.E.) following the Persian conquest of Jerusalem, the population of the city was exclusively Christian. From at least the late fourth century, pilgrims were attracted to the city from all over the Christian world. The expansion of ecclesiastical construction, including such edifices as the Church of the Holy Sepulchre, expressed the dominance of Christianity, as did the conscious neglect of Jewish sites, especially the Temple Mount, which was used as a refuse dump.

Caliph 'Umar ibn al-Khattab (Omar [634–644]) had a mosque built on the Temple Mount following his conquest of Jerusalem in the early Muslim period (638–1099), and he permitted seventy Jewish families to live in the city. Though the population remained predominantly Christian throughout this period, under the rule of the Umayyad caliphs, Jerusalem was transformed into a city holy to the Muslims: the Dome of the Rock, constructed by Caliph Abdul-Malik in 692 to supersede the magnificence of Jerusalem's churches, and the al-Aqsā mosque (constructed c. 706–717) were decisive in turning the city into a focal point for Muslim pilgrimage. Christian pilgrims continued to come to Jerusalem as well, mainly from the East, although Gunther, bishop of Bamberg, led 7,000 men to the city from the West in 1065. Jews gathered at the Mount of Olives to commemorate the earlier pilgrimages on Passover, Succoth, and Shavuot mandated in the Torah (Deuteronomy 16:16; cf. Exodus 23:14–17, 34:18–23) and brought support for the heavily taxed Jewish population in Jerusalem and its yeshivah.

When Christian troops under Godfrey of Bouillon took Jerusalem at the start of the crusader period (1099–1291), they slaughtered the Jews and Muslims, who had fought together to repel them, and sold many others into slavery. As capital of the Latin kingdom, the city flourished economically because of the ecclesiastical and governmental administrations there and the new influx of Christian pilgrims. The population grew to more than 20,000. Muslims and Jews were banned from living in Jerusalem, though their pilgrimages continued; Jewish travelers of the late twelfth century found no more than a handful of Jewish dyers living

Bernard von Breydenbach, *Peregrinatio in Terram Sanctam.* (Mainz: Erhard Reuwich, 11 February 1486, n.p. n. sig.) Map of the Holy Land, detail of Jerusalem, with adjacent holy places. Reproduced by permission of the Map Division, The New York Public Library (Astor, Lenox and Tilden Foundations).

near the Tower of David. To confirm Christian rule, many new churches were dedicated and Muslim buildings used for ecclesiastical purposes. Saladin's defeat of the crusaders (1187) allowed Muslims and Jews to move back into the city; a large number of rabbis came from France and England between 1209 and 1211 to settle in Israel. However, the renewed dominance of the crusaders in the city (1229–1244) after the Third Crusade, followed by Muslim and Khwarizmian attacks near the end of the thirteenth century, left the city devastated and depopulated: in 1267, Nachmanides found there only 2,000 Muslims, 300 Christians, and no Jewish community.

Jerusalem was eventually made a province of its own in the Mamluk period (1291–1516), with an administrative head appointed by the sultan. Under the Mamluks, civic construction was carried out on the citadel and water system. The city became a religious center for Islamic studies and was a focal point for Muslim pilgrimages. Sultan Baybars I built a hospice for pilgrims in 1263; numerous Islamic colleges were established between the thirteenth and fifteenth centuries. A heavy tax was imposed on the Jews in 1440 and contention characterized the relations between the Franciscans and the Muslim population, though pilgrimages by both religious communities continued. By the end of the fifteenth century, the population of the city was about 10,000, predominantly Muslim, with roughly 1,000 Christians and 400 Jews.

### BIBLIOGRAPHY

Gil, Moshe. *A History of Palestine, 634–1099.* Cambridge: Cambridge UP, 1992.

Goitein, S.D. *A Mediterranean Society.* 6 vols. Berkeley: U of California P, 1967–1993.

Prawer, Joshua. *Histoire du royaume latin de Jérusalem.* 2 vols. Paris: Éditions du CNRS, 1969–1970.

*Richard G. Newhauser*

### SEE ALSO

Baybars I; Byzantine Empire; Crusades, First, Second, and Third; Franciscan Friars; Holy Land; Jerusalem City Plans; Jewish Travelers; Mamluks; Pilgrimage, Christian; Saladin

## Jerusalem City Plans

Medieval representations of the Holy City, which are among the earliest surviving cartographic images. Ranging from the highly symbolic to the more particu-

larized, their changing forms signal important shifts in both cosmographic outlooks and the interests of mapmakers. P.D.A Harvey observes that "many dozens" of these medieval maps of Jerusalem survive.

The earliest of these images (*c.* 550) appears in a large mosaic map of Palestine and Lower Egypt set into the floor of the Old Church of Madaba, Jordan. Distinct streets and buildings, as well as a notably larger scale, mark off Jerusalem from the surrounding territories and signal its place as a symbolic "center." A map accompanying the pilgrimage account of the Frankish bishop Arculf (his pilgrimage ocurred in 670, but the earliest surviving map dates from the ninth century) presents a diagrammatic view of the Holy City. Characterized by a simple outline of walls and streets and an absence of other pictorial elements, this

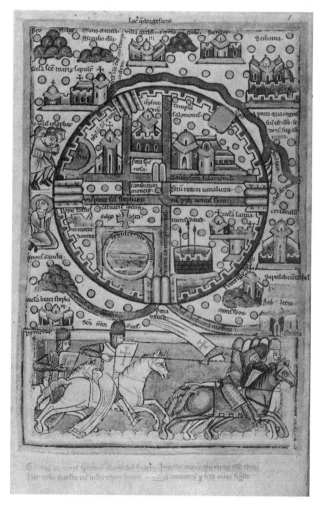

Jerusalem City Plan. The Hague, Koninklijke Bibliotheek MS 76 F 5, fol. 1r, 13th century. Courtesy Koninklijke Bibliotheek.

cartographic type possibly derives from classical survey plans.

Crusader maps from the twelfth century and later retain a diagrammatic form, but their level of precision indicates a more direct knowledge of the city layout. Plans such as that attributed to Pietro Vesconte (*c.* 1320) trace out the principal roads and sanctuaries of Jerusalem. Details of the city's fortifications appear in elevation and suggest the particular concerns of the crusaders. Vesconte's maps are the most topographically accurate representations of the Holy City from the later Middle Ages.

Jerusalem also appears on *mappaemundi* (world maps) of this period, and is often represented by an architectural emblem of the Holy Sepulchre. Generally positioned near the midpoint of these circular maps, the Holy City stands as *umbilicus mundi* (the navel of the world) and, by implication, a microcosm of creation. By the end of the fifteenth century, an interest in precise topographic detail dominated cartographic production, as illustrated by the bird's-eye view of Jerusalem drawn by Erhart Reuwich (of Utrecht) that accompanies Bernard von Breydenbach's pilgrimage account of 1486.

### BIBLIOGRAPHY

Harvey, P.D.A. "Local and Regional Cartography in Medieval Europe." In Harley-Woodward, *The History of Cartography,* 1:464–501. See Gen. Bib.

Kühnel, Bianca. *From the Earthly to the Heavenly Jerusalem: Representations of the Holy City in Christian Art of the First Millennium.* Rome: Herder, 1987.

Röhricht, Reinhold. "Karten und Pläne zur Palästinakunde aus dem 7. bis 16. Jahrhundert, II." *Zeitschrift des Deutschen Palästina-Vereins* 14 (1891): 87–92.

*Elizabeth Rodini*

### SEE ALSO
Arculf; Breydenbach, Bernhard von; Center of the Earth; City Plans; Jerusalem; Madaba Mosaic Map; *Mappamundi;* Maps; Vesconte, Pietro/Perrino

## Jewish Expulsion
*See* Expulsion, Corporate

## Jewish Merchants
*See* Merchants, Jewish

## Jewish Travelers

Letters, itineraries, pilgrimage reports, and comprehensive travelogues record accounts of journeys by Jewish men and women to carry out diplomatic missions for heads of state, engage in commerce or exploration, complete pilgrimages to Jerusalem, visit holy sites in Israel and Jewish communities elsewhere, or flee persecution.

The Torah enjoinder for Jewish men to go to Jerusalem on the festivals of Passover, Succoth, and Shavuot (Deuteronomy 16:16; *cf.* Exodus 23:14–17, 34:18–23) resulted in steady Jewish pilgrimages to the city and other holy sites in Palestine, even after the destruction of the Temple and in spite of the taxation often demanded from Jews by Muslim or Christian rulers. During the period of the Latin Kingdom (1099–1187), Jacob ben Nathaniel ha-Cohen, from Germany, noted that he had to disguise himself as a Christian in order to visit the Cave of Machpelah in Hebron where the patriarchs (Abraham, Isaac, and Jacob, and their wives Sarah, Rebecca, and Leah) are buried.

When Jews were permitted to live in Jerusalem, their well-being was of special interest to other Jews who traveled to the city. Both Elijah of Ferrara, in the early fifteenth century, and Rabbi Obadiah ben Abraham of Bertinoro, at the end of the century, gave full reports of the struggling Jewish community in Jerusalem. Travelers were also drawn to the other holy sites in Israel, in particular to the graves of those mentioned in the Bible and of famous rabbis. Their itineraries are often mere lists of tombs. Samuel ben Samson, who came to Israel from France in 1210, added an account of the ruins of ancient synagogues he had viewed to his itinerary of the graves of the righteous. Estori ha-Parchi, in his *Sefer Kaftor va-Ferach* (composed 1322), likewise describes ancient sites, and gives a depiction of Jerusalem and the state of Jewish culture there.

From the early Middle Ages, Jews traveled to distant parts of the world, bringing back reports of what they had found. In 797, Charlemagne included Isaac the Jew as an interpreter on a mission to the Caliph Hārūn al-Rashīd. In 802, Isaac returned alone to Aachen and brought with him an elephant as a present from the caliph to the emperor. Ibrāhīm ibn Ya'qūb of Tortosa came to the court of Otto I from Spain in 966 and, perhaps on a diplomatic mission for the emperor, traveled to central Europe, returning with the earliest report of the Polish kingdom. Louis de Torres, baptized just before the expedition of 1492, accompanied

# J

Christopher Columbus to the New World and reported the discovery of tobacco.

Jewish travelers were concerned to establish contact between the communities of Jews throughout the world, and they at times expressed, as a messianic theme, the possibilities for Jewish independence. At the end of the ninth century, Eldad ha-Dani appeared in North Africa and Spain claiming descent from one of the Ten Tribes of Israel, who, he said, enjoyed political autonomy. He also claimed to have seen, near Ethiopia, the Sambatyon, a river mentioned in the Talmud that flows with rocks and sand, stopping only on the Sabbath. At the end of the Middle Ages, David Reuveni (d. 1538), likewise claiming descent from one of the lost tribes, attempted to convince European powers to take up arms against the Muslims. The account of his adventurous travels is contained in his "diary," perhaps actually written by others.

The acme of travel literature by Jews came in the twelfth and early thirteenth century. In his *Songs of Zion*, Judah ha-Levi (?–1141) wrote with particular beauty of his travels through Spain and North Africa on his way to Israel. From Spain, Benjamin of Tudela (?–1173) and Judah ben Solomon al-Charizi (?–1235), and from Germany, Pethahiah of Regensburg wrote detailed accounts of their travels as far to the east as Baghdad. Pethahiah traveled overland (1174–1187) through Poland, Russia, Armenia, and Mesopotamia to Israel, describing along the way almost exclusively the Jewish communities and holy sites he visited. Al-Charizi's *Sefer Tachkemoni* also describes the major figures in the Jewish communities its author visited (c. 1216–1217).

Benjamin of Tudela's *Itinerary* (*Sefer ha-Massaot*), which describes his journeys (c. 1166–1173), holds a place of prominence in medieval travel literature because of its factual depiction not only of the Jewish world (including the number of Jews in each city Benjamin visited, their occupations, and the names of the prominent members of the community), but also of attractions of general interest in Rome, Constantinople, Alexandria, Jerusalem, and Baghdad, where Benjamin described the caliph's palace in great detail. Benjamin's work is one of the most important descriptions of the Mediterranean world in the twelfth century.

## BIBLIOGRAPHY

Adler, Elkan Nathan, ed. and trans. *Jewish Travellers*. London: G. Routledge, 1930; 2nd edition, New York: Her-
mon, 1966. Rpt. as *Jewish Travellers in the Middle Ages: 19 Firsthand Accounts*. New York: Dover, 1987.

Benjamin of Tudela. *The Itinerary of Benjamin of Tudela [Sefer Massaot shel Rabbi Binyamin]*. Critical Text, Translation, and Commentary. Ed. and trans. Marcus Nathan Adler. London: Henry Frowde, 1907; rpt. New York: Feldheim, [1965?].

Goitein, S.D. *A Mediterranean Society*. Vol. 1. Berkeley and Los Angeles: U of California P, 1967, esp. pp. 273–352.

Kayserling, Meyer. *Christopher Columbus and the Participation of the Jews in the Spanish and Portuguese Discoveries*. New York: Longmans, Green, 1894; rpt. North Hollywood, CA: Carmi House, 1989.

Prawer, Joshua. *The History of the Jews in the Latin Kingdom of Jerusalem*. Oxford: Clarendon, 1988, esp. pp. 169–250.

Richard G. Newhauser

**SEE ALSO**
Benjamin of Tudela; Columbus, Christopher; Elephants; Holy Land; Ibrāhīm Ibn Yaʿqūb al-Isrāʾīli; Jerusalem; Merchants, Jewish

## Jews, Red
*See* Red Jews

## Johannes Witte
*See* Witte De Hese, Johannes

## John the Fearless, Funeral Cortege of (June 24–July 12, 1420)

A procession, by river and overland, during the summer of 1420, whose careful description offers valuable information about the practical details of travel during the late Middle Ages.

One of the most curious travel documents that has come down to us from the early fifteenth century is an account for services rendered, presented at Lille to the treasury-general of the Burgundian duke Philip the Good (1396–1467; r. c. 1419–1467) by Laurens Pignon, O.P. (c. 1370–1449), his father-confessor. It entails a lengthy description of the disinterment of the body of Philip's father, the second duke of Burgundy John the Fearless (1371–1419; r. 1404–1419), at Montereau-faut-Yonne, and its transportation to and final interment at Dijon.

John the Fearless had been hastily buried at Montereau after his murder on the bridge of Montereau at the hands of the later French king Charles VII and his party. That town fell into royal hands immediately afterward and it was not recaptured by the combined Anglo-

Burgundian army until June 23, 1420. Immediately, Philip the Good sent Pignon and several aides into the town to find John's grave. The place was found in the local Church of Notre Dame and plans were quickly drawn up to identify the body, to preserve it in the best way possible, and to transport it to the Charterhouse of Champmol near Dijon where, Philip remembered, John had wished to be buried near his father, Philip the Bold.

Pignon was mandated to take charge of the entire operation, and his account meticulously describes every detail of those services. On June 24, the late duke's body was suitably salted and spiced and readied for the journey by barge up the Yonne River and by wagon cross-country to Dijon. Early the next day, after a solemn requiem mass, John's mortal remains were accompanied by King Henry V of England (r. 1413–1422), Philip the Good (wearing his trademark black coat), and their retinue on a horse-drawn barge to the village of Cannes. Here the high nobility disembarked in order to continue their military campaign, and things were left to Pignon to complete. The barge continued to ascend the Yonne, putting in at Sens, Joigny, and Auxerre for the nights, reaching Cravant on June 30.

At each town through which the party passed there were religious services, masses, and vigils. From Cravant, the route to Dijon would be by wagon through Avallon, Semur-en-Auxois, and Vitteaux to the final destination at the Charterhouse of Champmol for last rites. At Cravant, the party was held up for eight days to await the necessary supplies that Pignon had earlier required by letter in order to make a funerary procession into Dijon worthy of the deceased duke. On July 12, the entombment was performed, the duchess served a grand dinner, and then, at her request, more masses were said. Pignon notes that from disinterment at Montereau to burial of the corpse at the Charterhouse some 2,000 masses had been said, thirty vigils held, and 200 sets of penitential psalms recited. He carefully specifies that these did not include those paid for by the duchess. His total declared costs came to 4,500 francs.

## BIBLIOGRAPHY

Schnerb, B., "Les funérailles de Jean sans Peur." *Annales de Bourgogne* 54 (1982): 122–136.

Vanderjagt, A.J. *Laurens Pignon, OP. Confessor of Philip the Good*. Venlo: Jean Miélot, 1985.

Vaughan, R. *John the Fearless: The Growth of Burgundian Power*. London: Longman, 1966.

A.J. Vanderjagt

SEE ALSO
Lannoy, Ghillebert de; Transportation, Inland

## John of Marignolli [John of Florence] (*c.* 1290–after 1362)

A Franciscan friar, last of the papally dispatched friars sent to Asia as part of the Mongol Mission that began at the First Council of Lyons (1245).

Born into a noble Florentine family, John of Marignolli entered the Franciscan convent of Santa Croce and appears to have lectured at the University of Bologna. John is particularly important for his mission to Asia (1338–1353), undertaken in response to a delegation representing the Christian Alans in the service of the Mongol khâns who arrived at the court of Pope Benedict XII (1334–1342) at Avignon in 1336. They requested the pope to provide a replacement for John of Monte Corvino (1247–*c.* 1330), a Franciscan who had been appointed archbishop of Khanbaliq (Beijing) in 1307.

Marignolli left Avignon with the Alans in December 1338, not to serve as their bishop but to observe the state of Christianity in Asia. In 1342, he arrived in Khanbaliq, where he spent several years. He departed China in 1347, visited India, and returned to Avignon in 1353. His adventures were evidently quite famous: they appear to have been known to the Holy Roman Emperor Charles IV (r. 1346–1378), who appointed Marignolli his chaplain and historian. In various places throughout the *Chronica Boemorum*, a world history that focused on the Czech homeland of his patron (completed *c.* 1356), Marignolli inserted information and anecdotes based on his Asian travels (these remarks have been gathered together and entitled "Relatio," but Marignolli did not write a travel narrative or report *per se*).

Among other things, Marignolli describes several Franciscan churches, and even the existence of a cathedral (probably built by John of Monte Corvino) in Khanbaliq. In India, he visited a Dominican missionary community operating there, and in Ceylon (Sri Lanka), a local ruler, whom he names "Coya Jaan, a eunuch and an accursed Saracen," robbed him of all the finery he was bringing home from the East.

His experience in Asia may have suggested to him that the future of the Mongol Mission was doubtful. There were already signs that the Mongol Yuan dynasty (1260–1368) was collapsing. It was replaced by the Ming dynasty (1368–1644), which reasserted traditional

# J

Chinese values, including a lack of interest in the world beyond China. The Ming emperors gradually eliminated all elements of the Yuan era, including the Christian missionaries who had entered China under the Mongols.

Marignolli's somewhat scattered remarks about his journey constitute the last description of Asia that the friars of the Mongol Mission produced. Although there were some later attempts to provide friars for the churches that had been established in Asia, they had little success and the mission was gradually forgotten. Marignolli's *Chronicon* survives in one complete and one fragmentary manuscript; it was first published in 1768.

## BIBLIOGRAPHY

Dawson, Christopher, ed. *The Mongol Mission.* See Gen. Bib.

Habig, M.A. "Marignolli and the Decline of Medieval Missions in China." *Franciscan Studies* 26 (1945): 21–36.

John of Marignolli. *Relatio.* In *Sinica Franciscana.* Ed. Anastasius van den Wyngaert. Quarrachi-Firenze: Collegio di S. Bonaventura, 1929, I, 515–560.

Muldoon, James. *Popes, Lawyers, and Infidels: The Church and the Non-Christian World, 1250–1550.* Philadelphia: U of Pennsylvania P, 1979.

Phillips, J.R.S. *The Medieval Expansion of Europe.* Oxford: Oxford UP, 1988.

de Rachewiltz, Igor. *Papal Envoys to the Great Khans.* Stanford: Stanford UP, 1971.

Yule-Cordier. *Cathay and the Way Thither.* See Gen. Bib.

*James Muldoon*

## SEE ALSO

China; Dominican Friars; Eastern Christianity; Franciscan Friars; John of Monte Corvino; Khanbaliq; Lyons, First Council of; Missionaries to China; Mongols; Yuan Dynasty

## John of Monte Corvino (1247–1328)

Archbishop of Khanbaliq, and the first Christian missionary to China.

Born in Monte Corvino (Salerno), Italy, he was a Franciscan missionary to Persia and Armenia. His return to Rome followed the visit there in 1287 of Rabban Sauma, a Nestorian Uighur, sent by Mongol il-khâns in Iran to seek ties. In sending John to China, Pope Nicholas IV (1288–1292) may possibly have been attempting to respond to a putative request by Khubilai Khân that the pope send 100 Christians to evangelize the Mongols, a message supposedly transmitted in 1269 through Niccolò and Maffeo Polo (Marco's father and uncle). According to Marco's account, two Dominicans who had accepted the commission to be missionaries in East Asia turned back at Ayas (Lajazzo) in Armenia. John, who had been active as a missionary in Armenia and Persia between around 1279 and 1283, agreed to attempt to bring Christianity to the Mongols in 1289.

Accompanied by five other Franciscans, John brought papal letters to the patriarch of the Jacobites, King Hetoum II of Armenia, Arghun of the il-khâns, and Mar Yaballaha, patriarch of the Nestorians. In 1291, he left Tabriz for China, with Nicholas of Pistoia, a Dominican, and Peter of Lucalongo, a merchant. He spent thirteen months at Mylapur (Madras) India, baptized about 100 people, and after the death of his companion, Nicholas, saw to his burial at the Church of St. Thomas. He and Peter sailed to Zaiton (present-day Quanzhou) China, and in 1294 reached the Mongol capital Daidu (Beijing), which Turks and Europeans called Khanbaliq; his route may have taken him through the Grand Canal, begun during the Sui dynasty (589–618) and completed by Khubilai. The latter had died, so John presented the pope's letter to the new great khân, Timur Oljeitu (Cheng Zong [1295–1308]).

The khân permitted John to live in the capital and do missionary work, evidently treating him well; but he did not convert, since he "was too far gone in idolatry," by which John means he was a committed Buddhist. John converted "Prince George of Tenduc," an Önggüt Nestorian leader, whom John saw as a descendant of the legendary Prester John; George entered minor orders and assisted John at Mass; after George's death in 1298, John faced a hostile reaction from the Nestorians.

John built three churches. The ruins of one, for the Önggüt at Olon Sume, were found by Japanese archaeologists in the 1930s. The other two (1299 and 1305) were in Beijing, the second "only a stone's throw from the gateway" of the great khân, who, according to John's "Second Letter," delighted in the chants of the daily office sung by forty slave boys whom John bought, baptized, trained, and reared as Franciscan brothers, although at the time of John's writing none of the boys had become a priest.

John claims to have converted and baptized 6,000 people, mostly Alans or Armenians. He translated the New Testament and Psalter into "the Tartar language"—Mongolian or Uighur—but these are lost. His letters of January 8, 1305, and February 13, 1306, sent on to Rome, were, among other things, signs to the church in Europe that he was still alive; they were also pleas for help, especially for psalters with musical notes, other books, and "brethren." Pope Clement V (1305–1314) named him archbishop of Khanbaliq and patriarch of the Orient; his see included the whole Mongol Empire. Seven Franciscans, consecrated suffragan bishops in 1307, were sent to China to invest him. Three survived to do so in 1313. He sent them as bishops to Zaiton. John died in 1328. The death of Andrew of Perugia, third bishop of Zaiton, in 1332, left both sees without a successor.

## BIBLIOGRAPHY

Dawson, Christopher, ed. *The Mongol Mission.* See Gen. Bib.

Habig, M.A. "Marignolli and the Decline of Medieval Missions in China." *Franciscan Studies* 26 (1945): 21–36.

Latourette, K.S. *A History of Christian Missions in China.* New York, 1929.

Muldoon, James. *Popes, Lawyers, and Infidels. The Church and the Non-Christian World, 1250–1550.* Philadelphia: U of Pennsylvania P, 1979.

Phillips, J.R.S. *The Medieval Expansion of Europe.* Oxford: Oxford UP, 1988.

de Rachewiltz, Igor. *Papal Envoys to the Great Khans.* Stanford: Stanford UP, 1971.

Yule-Cordier. *Cathay and the Way Thither.* See Gen. Bib.

*Hugh D. Walker*

## SEE ALSO

Andrew, Son of Guido of Perugia; Armenia; Buddhism; China; Eastern Christianity; Franciscan Friars; Hetoum; India; Khanbaliq; Lajazzo; Marco Polo; Missionaries to China; Nestorianism; Peter of Lucalongo; Prester John; Zaiton

## John of Plano Carpini (*c.* 1180–1252)

Mid-thirteenth-century Franciscan administrator and papal envoy to the Mongols. In addition to being a dedicated and skillful Franciscan administrator, John of Plano Carpini was the first papal envoy commissioned to travel to the seat of the great khâns, actually reaching the khânate capital in Mongolia. On his return to Pope Innocent IV in 1247, he wrote a detailed, somewhat polemical account of the Mongolians—to which he appended a summary of his travel experiences, providing Christian Europe with its earliest account of the Mongols and their extensive military conquests and rapidly expanding empire. John's book, entitled *Historia Mongalorum,* has proven to be one of the best and most widely known sources on the Mongols of the thirteenth century. The text circulated in many manuscripts and was included in the century's most important encyclopedia.

Despite the numerous important offices John held in the church hierarchy—several administrative positions in the newly emerging Franciscan order, papal envoy, papal legate, and archbishop—very little is known of his personal life and activities. The few sources available reveal that John was most likely born in the Tuscan village of Pian di Carpini (*Planus Carpinis* in Latin, now known as Plano della Maggiore) near the city of Perugia. Given the responsibilities he had assumed in the Franciscan order by the early 1200s, he must have been born around 1180. He is known to have died on August 1, 1252, probably in Italy. Nothing is documented about John—his family, youth, or education—until after he entered the Franciscan order.

Since John was born near Assisi, it is not surprising that he soon became a follower and disciple of St. Francis of Assisi, the founder of the mendicant movement and the first head of the Order of Friars Minor until his death in 1226. A first-generation Franciscan, John was early recognized to have leadership talents; he held important administrative offices in the nascent order, being sent to Germany in the early 1220s; he was warden in Saxony in 1222, and became the provincial of all Germany in 1228. Records suggest that he held the office of provincial of Spain for three years, perhaps in the early 1230s. Except for this brief interval, John spent most of his adult life as a Franciscan administrator in Germany, from where he was active in founding new convents and in sending friars into Dacia, Hungary, Bohemia, Poland, Denmark, and Norway. Sources indicate that he carefully watched over his friars and readily defended them before both ecclesiastical and secular princes. He may have been in Germany—perhaps at Cologne—when the Mongols invaded eastern Europe and decisively defeated Polish and German knights at the battle of Legnice on April 9, 1241. However, some scholars suggest that he was an official at the papal curia between 1239 and 1245.

The Mongols never advanced farther west after their incursions in Silesia and Hungary in 1241, but their threat to Europe was still palpable when Pope Innocent IV (1243–1254), a shrewd statesman and the religious

# J

leader of Western Christians, convoked a church council at Lyons in 1245, from which he dispatched the first envoys to the Mongols on April 16, in four separate legations, one of which was entrusted to John. Energetic, intelligent, and knowledgeable about Eastern Europe, he was an ideal selection, although the mission—which involved two-and-one-half years of arduous and dangerous travel—proved to be physically hard on this portly man of around sixty. Carrying two important papal letters—*Dei Patris immensa* and *Cum non solum*—to be delivered to the Mongol court, John left France, following an overland route across northeast Europe. In Wroclaw (Breslau), in Silesia, he was joined by another Franciscan, Benedict the Pole, who served as interpreter and companion on the journey forth and back. (On their return, Benedict wrote his own brief account of their journey.) The friars traveled through Poland and Russia, both of which had been recently devastated by the Mongols; Polish and Russian leaders provided them with advice and gifts, so that they might gain the cooperation of Mongol leaders and pass through Mongol-held territory. John and Benedict left Kiev on February 3, 1246; on April 4, they arrived at Sarai, on the Volga, the capital city of Batu, who had led the Mongol advance westward before 1241 and was the first khân of the western Mongol Empire (or Golden Horde). After having the pope's letters translated into Mongol, Batu ordered the friars to take their embassy to the court of the great khân in Mongolia.

This most formidable part of the journey began on April 8, 1246. John and Benedict accompanied a Mongol caravan north of the Caspian and Aral seas and eastward through the Dzungarian Gap. On July 22, 1246, they reached the imperial camp of Sira Ordu, near Karakorum, the Mongol capital, having traveled about 3,000 miles overland in only 106 days. This astonishing progress speaks well of both the Mongol transportation system and the friars' tenacity. Shortly before their arrival, Güyük had been elected great khân, and along with several thousand other envoys and representatives from throughout the Mongol Empire, John and Benedict witnessed Güyük's formal enthronement on August 12. Since they lacked appropriate gifts, a serious breach of Mongol diplomatic etiquette, they were not granted a private audience with Güyük until November. John made good use of the interval to gather all the information he could about the Mongols and other Asian peoples; he became the first European to report on the Chinese civilization. Güyük was displeased with Innocent's letters, which sharply criticized Mongol behavior in Europe, and he dictated an uncompromising reply, claiming that Mongol world domination was part of a divine plan and insisting on the unconditional surrender of the West. The friars were then dismissed, and they suffered terribly on their winter return trip across Central Asia. They paused several times along the way—in Kiev, Bohemia, and Cologne—returning to the papal court at Lyons in November 1247. According to the Franciscan chronicler Salimbene, John achieved some celebrity as a raconteur, delighting many with the story of his adventures.

In response to requests for information on the situation in Asia, John wrote his ethnographic study, *Historia Mongalorum*: the eight chapters of its first version treat Mongol territories, customs, religion, physiognomy, history, military organization and strategy, and subject peoples, as well as effective martial tactics to use against them. John's focus on military matters reveals a covert aspect of his mission: he had not only had political and evangelical responsibilities, but the pope had also asked him to evaluate the Mongol military machine and determine how best to oppose it. In the second version of his *Historia,* John added a detailed account of his journey, offering valuable geographical and ethnographical data. John was particularly interested in Christians—many of them captives and slaves—whom he encountered among the Mongols and who served as trusted informants. The subject matter and spellings of names in his report indicate that much of John's information came from Russian and Nestorian Christians.

The *Historia Mongalorum* is John's only known literary work and the principal source of his historical reputation. While not a literary masterpiece, the *Historia* is a concise, sober, and detailed report at a crucial historical moment. John's account of Mongol customs and history is one of the better treatments by any Western author. Particularly valuable historically is his record of names: of the Mongol princes and rulers, of peoples conquered by the Mongols, of those still resisting them in the mid-1240s, and of merchants and other Christian witnesses to the truth of his report.

John provided the Christian West with accurate information about Mongol political structures and military organization, although his report is impersonal and repeats geographical misinformation found in authoritative sources at the time, such as the location of several "monstrous races of humans" in Asia. His report is thus inferior to William of Rubruck's *Itinerarium* (written 1255) only in its lack of autobiographical detail and its occasional gullibility, some of it based on oral sources. Like many medieval travelers, he feared that readers would doubt his testimony—thus, he concluded his narrative with a list of witnesses who could verify his claim—but his anxieties proved groundless because readers evidently accepted his book as based on actual experience. Vincent of Beauvais incorporated excerpts from the *Historia*—along with citations from another papal envoy to the khân, Simon of Saint-Quentin, who was unable to reach Mongolia—into his famous *Speculum historiale*. The reports by John and Simon were thus the earliest, most readily available, and most influential eyewitness accounts by Europeans about the Mongols.

Shortly after John's return from the Mongols to Lyons, Innocent IV sent him as a papal legate to King Louis IX, who was about to depart on a crusade to the Holy Land. Later in 1248, the pope appointed John archbishop of Antivavi (now Bari) in Dalmatia. His episcopal tenure was not without problems: John became embroiled in a jurisdictional conflict with the archbishop of Ragusa (now Dubrovnik). The dispute was submitted to the Roman curia for resolution, but John died before the issue was decided.

Although John did not persuade the Mongols to accept Christianity or to abandon their militant behavior, his journey was a remarkable achievement. His *Historia* brought generally factual information about Central and East Asia in the mid-1200s to a European audience that had hitherto relied on legend and speculation. Somewhat ironically, then, his reputation has been overshadowed by that of the more flamboyant Marco Polo.

## BIBLIOGRAPHY

Two versions of John of Plano Carpini's *Historia Mongalorum* exist: ten manuscripts preserve a first recension, which is devoted entirely to a description of the Mongols, and four manuscripts record this same material plus an appended report on the journey. Critical editions of the entire text have been published by d'Avezac (1838); Anastasius van den Wyngaert (1929), and (its most reliable version to date) Enrico Menesto (1989) .

Dawson, Christopher, ed. *The Mongol Mission.* See Gen. Bib.

Guéret-Laferté, Michèle. *Sur les routes de l'Empire mongol: orde et rhetorique des relations de voyage aux XIIIe et XIVe siècles.* Paris: H. Champion, 1994.

Guzman, Gregory G. "The Encyclopedist Vincent of Beauvais and His Mongol Extracts from John of Plano Carpini and Simon of Saint-Quentin." *Speculum* 49 (1974): 287–307.

Menesto, Enrico. *Giovanni di Pian di Carpine: Storia dei Mongoli.* Trans. (into Italian) Maria Christiana Lungarotti. Spoleto: Centro Italiano de studi sull'alto Medioevo, 1989.

Olschki, Leonardo. *Marco Polo's Precursors.* Baltimore: Johns Hopkins UP, 1943, pp. 31–47.

de Rachewiltz, Igor. *Papal Envoys to the Great Khans.* Stanford: Stanford UP, 1971, pp. 89–111.

Saunders, J.J. "John of Plano Carpini: The Papal Envoy to the Mongol Conquerors Who Travelled through Russia to Eastern Asia in 1245–1247." *History Today* 22 (1972): 547–555.

Sinor, Denis. "John of Plano Carpini's Return from the Mongols: New Light from a Luxembourg Manuscript." *Journal of the Royal Asiatic Society* (1957): 193–206.

Skelton, R.A., T.E. Marston, and G.D. Painter. *The Vinland Map and the Tartar Relation.* New Haven; Yale UP, 1965; rev. edition, 1995 (with new introduction), pp. 21–27, 34–51, 104–106, 148–153.

Wyngaert, Anastasius van den, ed. *Sinica Franciscana.* Quarrachi-Firenze: Collegio di S. Bonaventurae: 1929, 1:3–130.

*Gregory G. Guzman*

## SEE ALSO

Benedict the Pole; Bridia, C. de; China; Franciscan Friars; Golden Horde; Hungary; Innocent IV; Karakorum; Lyons, First Council of; Marco Polo; Missionaries to China; Mongols; Monstrosity, Geographical; Nestorianism; Simon of Saint-Quentin; Spies; Vincent of Beauvais; William of Rubruck

## John of Sacrobosco
*See* Sacrobosco, John of

## John of Würzburg (fl. 1160)

A twelfth-century German pilgrim who composed an important description of the Holy Land between the Second and Third Crusades (1146–1148 and 1188–1192).

John of Würzburg tells us the little we know about him in his *Descriptio Terrae Sanctae,* an account of his pilgrimage to the Holy Land in the mid-1100s. Although Titus Tobler dated this journey more precisely to the 1160s, and several scholars have accepted his thesis (or altered it to "*c.* 1170"), the *Descriptio* itself indicates only that the journey occurred after the enlargement of the Church of the Holy Sepulchre in 1149. In contrast, John precisely identifies Würzburg as

# J

his point of origin and dedicates his work to his "dilecto . . . socio et domestico Dietrico." This Dietrich has been identified as Dietrich von Hohenburg, bishop of Würzburg, and, alternatively, with the Theoderic who wrote *De Locis Sanctis* around 1170, but there is no evidence to confirm either identification.

John wrote his *Descriptio* because Bede's account of Jerusalem proved inaccurate following the construction projects of the crusaders. His narrative is thus an important text for the architectural and political history of Jerusalem between the Second and Third Crusades. To be sure, almost half of the *Descriptio* is taken wholesale from the guidebook attributed to Fretellus, but John adds observations about the variety of Christian creeds and practices in the Holy City, and the national rivalries among the crusaders.

The *Descriptio* survives in four known manuscripts from the Middle Ages, the oldest and most complete dating from the late twelfth or early thirteenth century (Munich, Bayerische Staatsbibliothek, Clm. 19418 [from Tegernsee]). The text is structured according to the seven stages of Christ's life: nativity, baptism, passion, descent into hell, resurrection, ascension, and judgment. This structure was completely done away with by Tobler, who put it into what he considered to be a more sensible order, and all editors and translators prior to R.B.C. Huygens have persisted in this alteration.

## BIBLIOGRAPHY

Brincken, Anna-Dorothee von den. *Die "Nationes Christianorum Orientalium" in Verständnis der lateinischen Historiographie von der Mitte des 12. bis in die zweite Hälfte des 14. Jahrhunderts.* Kölner Historische Abhandlungen 22. Cologne and Vienna: Böhlau, 1973.

Grabois, Aryeh. "Le pèlerin occidental en Terre Sainte à l'époque des croisades et ses réalités: La relation de pèlerinage de Jean de Wurtzburg." In *Études de civilisation médiévale, IXe–XIIe siècles: mélanges offerts à Edmond-René Labande à l'occasion de son départ à la retraite et du XXe anniversaire du CESCM par ses amis, ses collègues, ses élèves.* Poitiers: CESCM, 1974.

Huygens, R.B.C., ed. *Peregrationes Tres.* Corpus Christianorum Continuatio Mediaevalis 139. Turnhout: Brepols, 1994.

Tobler, Titus, ed. *Descriptiones Terrae Sanctae ex saeculo VIII, IX, XII, et XV.* Leipzig: J.C. Hinrichs, 1874.

Wendehorst, A. "Johannes von Wurzburg I." In *Die deutsche Literatur des Mittelalters: Verfasserlexikon.* Ed. Wolfgang Stammler-Longosch. Berlin and NY: DeGruyter, 1983, 4:822–824.

*Timothy S. Jones*

SEE ALSO

Bede; Crusades, First, Second, and Third; Fretellus; Holy Land; Jerusalem; Theoderic

## Joinville, Jean de (1224/1225—1317)

Hereditary seneschal of Champagne, friend, confidant, and fellow crusader of King Louis IX of France. The fame of Jean de Joinville rests on his *History of Saint Louis,* an eyewitness account of the Seventh Crusade (1248–1254). His *History* also treats the king's early life and struggles, his last crusade (the Eighth [1270]), and provides information on royal ordinances, the king's advice to his children, and his saintly virtues, behavior, and gifts; but all of these are treated much more cursorily. Written long after the king had died, the narrative inevitably has errors of fact, but these have proved to be quite minor.

Joinville relates at length fascinating and practical details of the crusaders' travels: how preparations were made, the routes that were followed, and the difficulties in hiring ships. The *History* provides an unforgettable picture of the quantities of foodstuffs and wine gathered together at Cyprus, where the army wintered before the invasion of Egypt in 1249. The king's agents "had stacked an enormous number of huge barrels of wine which they had begun to buy two years before the king's arrival, and which they had piled up so high one on top of the other that any one approaching them from the front might have taken them for barns. The wheat and barley had been heaped in great mounds about the fields. The rain had been beating down so long on these heaps that it caused them to sprout, and consequently appear to be covered with grass, so that at a first glance, you might have imagined that they were hillocks" (Joinville and Villehardouin 197).

The dangers and misfortunes that plagued the soldiers—including pathological conditions like fevers, diarrhea, and decaying gums—fascinated Joinville. He also delights in describing the sense of wonder that the crusaders, including himself, felt at new sights, experiences, and customs: watching Norwegians kill lions in the Syrian desert; discovering a fossil; observing three minstrels from Great Armenia, in the entourage of the prince of Antioch, doing elaborate acrobatics while on pilgrimage to Jerusalem. His fascination turns to aversion when he hears about how the pagan Cumans seal their alliances. The blood of the allies is mixed together with water and wine, and the drink is shared. The "blood brothers" now chase a dog between them, brutally slashing it with their swords until it collapses and dies. So will be the fate, the Cumans believe (if we believe Joinville), should either party to the alliance break its faith. The shaming rituals threatened against a knight arrested in a brothel also strike him as worthy of note. The knight was to be led through the streets, nearly naked, tethered by a rope attached to his genitals to the prostitute with whom he has been sleeping. If the humiliation were too much to imagine, the knight might (and in the instance described by Joinville, did) give up his horse and arms—the honorable trappings of chivalry itself—rather than endure the grim parade.

Joinville also relished describing the cluster of problems that affected business, trade, and credit in a world of warriors far from home and their hangers-on. The cavalier attitude toward lesser ranks of men, the hubris indeed toward mere merchants and shopkeepers, for example, of the victorious Christian knights after the taking of Damietta at the mouth of the Nile in 1249 was so great that traders hesitated to do business with the knights, to the considerable injury of the Christian army. The cash-flow problems of crusaders, including Joinville himself, and the cynical exploitation of their dependent position by those with money to lend, constitute another situation that the *History* treats at length.

Business had its more pleasurable side as well. Trade in the markets encountered in the crusader states, where horn, glue, trinkets, camel hair cloth, and a multitude of other products were available for purchase, is a recurring motif in the book. Joinville delights in telling stories about his care in buying pigs, sheep, and wine, the vagaries of winter carriage by sea, and the expense of products sought in the winter season.

One of the most telling stories that Joinville relates, one of many from which evidence of the problems of assimilation across ethnic and confessional lines may be extracted, begins with a tense encounter between Louis IX and a French-speaking convert to Islam who had come to Egypt from Provins in Champagne. Louis could hardly bear to look at him, and despite a kind gesture—a gift of milk and fresh flowers from the Muslim—he dismissed him peremptorily. But Joinville was more curious. The convert, it turned out, had abandoned Christianity for the love of an Egyptian woman and achieved wealth and status in Muslim society—all at the peril, Joinville insisted, of his soul. But the Muslim, depicted by Joinville as insincere and desirous of

returning to the Catholic faith, could not bear the loss of dignity or the embarrassment he would have to endure, if he did return, from Christians who might come to know of his former perfidy. By preserving vignettes like this, Jean de Joinville has left us in the *History of Saint Louis* one of the most memorable records of the age of the crusades.

**BIBLIOGRAPHY**

Delaborde, Henri François. *Jean de Joinville et les seigneurs de Joinville.* Paris: Picard et fils, 1894.

Joinville, Jean de. *Histoire de Saint Louis.* Ed. Natalis de Wailly. Paris: Firmin Didot, 1874.

———. *La vie de Saint Louis.* Trans. Noel Corbett. Sherbrooke, Quebec: Naaman, 1977.

———, and Geoffroi de Villehardouin. *Chronicles of the Crusades.* Trans. Margaret R.B. Shaw. Harmondsworth, England: Penguin, 1963.

*William Chester Jordan*

**SEE ALSO**

Cumans; Louis IX; Marriages between Muslims and Christians, Attitudes toward

## Jordan of Giano (d. after 1241)

A Franciscan friar and chronicler, from Giano, an Umbrian village in the mountains west of Spoleto.

Jordan is best known for his account of the first missions in Germany, which he dictated to Brother Baldwin of Brandenburg in 1262. The chronicle, which begins in 1207, is one of the oldest Franciscan chronicles and is still a principal source for information about the order's early activities, governance, and internal organization.

As a young deacon, Jordan attended the chapter called by St. Francis at the Portiuncule Chapel in 1221. Jordan was recruited against his wishes for a new mission to Germany led by Brother Caesar of Speyer. This group of eleven clerics and thirteen lay brethren included John of Plano Carpini, the famous missionary, and Thomas of Celano, the biographer of St. Francis. Departing Umbria, they traveled by threes or fours to Lombardy, thence to Trent, where some remained. Jordan and the rest continued on foot via Bolzano, Bressanone, Vipiteno, Mittenwald, and Matrei. They established themselves in Augsburg where they were cordially received.

In October 1221, Brother Caesar sent out three missions to various cities including Würzburg, Mainz,

# J

Worms, Speyer, Strasbourg, Cologne, and Regensburg. Jordan and two companions were assigned Salzburg. Thereafter, Franciscans were sent to Franconia, Bavaria, Alsace, and Swabia; a sizeable group went to Saxony. In 1223, Jordan was ordained to help alleviate a shortage of priests. Later that year, missions began in Hildesheim, Brunswick, Goslar, Magdeburg, and Halberstadt. In 1224, Jordan was sent to Thuringia to establish houses for the friars as part of the ongoing expansion.

For many years, Erfurt was his base of operations. In 1225, as *custos* (custodian or guardian) of Thuringia, Jordan sent lay brothers to other cities in that province. In 1230, Jordan bore letters to the minister general in Italy requesting a new minister and a lector for Germany. Jordan was sent to Pope Gregory IX in 1238 to note Saxon grievances against Brother Elias's abusive policies. Two letters written in spring 1241 seem to indicate that Jordan had become vicar of Poland and vice-minister of the provinces of Bohemia and Poland. These letters describe the destruction caused by the "Tartar" invaders, and the inevitable threat to the existence of the Franciscan missions there.

## BIBLIOGRAPHY

Esser, Cajetan, OFM. *Origins of the Franciscan Order.* Trans. Aedan Daly and Irina Lynch. Chicago: Franciscan Herald Press, 1970.

Gurney-Salter, Emma, trans. *The Coming of the Friars Minor to England and Germany: Being the Chronicles of Brother Thomas of Eccleston and Brother Jordan of Giano.* New York: Dutton, 1926.

Jordan of Giano. *Chronica Fratris Iordani a Iano.* In *Analecta Franciscana, sive Chronica aliaque varia documenta ad historiam Fratrum Minorum spectantia. . . .* Vol. 1. Florence: Quaracchi—Collegium S. Bonaventura, 1885, pp. 1–19.

Moorman, John. *A History of the Franciscan Order from Its Origins to the Year 1517.* Oxford: Clarendon, 1968.

*XIIIth Century Chronicles.* Trans. Placid Hermann, OFM. Chicago: Franciscan Herald Press, 1961.

*Gloria Allaire*

## SEE ALSO
Franciscan Friars; John of Plano Carpini; Mongols; Poland

## Jordan of Sévérac [Jordanus Cathala or Jordanus Catalani]

A fourteenth-century Dominican missionary and author of the *Mirabilia descripta* (c. 1330), a work describing the wonders he encountered in his travels throughout the Near East and Indian subcontinent.

Probably coming from Sévérac le Chateau in the Rouergue, Jordan had already been in Persia for some time before he joined a group of Franciscans who, with two Genoese, were about to go on their mission to China (1320). Having sailed from Hormuz, the friars put into port at Thana, near Bombay (at the time a leading port of India), while Jordan went on to visit some Christians at Sofala or Supara, a city near Surat. When he learned of the arrest of the Franciscans, he attempted to come to their aid. He reached Thana too late to assist them (they were martyred April 9–11, 1321), and he had to bury them instead. He remained in this region baptizing numerous catechumens, letting his desire to go to Ethiopia be known to his colleagues in a letter of October 12, 1321. He was, however, still in Thana in 1324, having probably entrusted the remains of the martyrs to Odoric of Pordenone, who bore them to China. He wrote describing the commercial activities between India and Egypt and suggested a naval incursion into the Indian Ocean.

Jordan reappeared in August of 1329 in Avignon, where Pope John XXII named him bishop of Quilon, a see created for him in southern India. About this time he wrote his *Mirabilia descripta,* in which he related the many wonders he had encountered in his voyages from Greece to India, evoking the exoticism of Asia, at least as it was imagined in Western Europe. The content of Jordan's book can perhaps be summarized in his exclamation "Everything is a marvel in this India! Verily it is quite another world!"

Jordan did not leave Avignon before September 1330, carrying letters recommending him to the sovereigns of India and the emperor of Ethiopia, an area included in the diocese entrusted to him. Probably it was for him that the church mentioned by John of Marignolli was built at Quilon, where the Christian princes of the countries underwrote the needs of the missionaries, aided in part by Latin merchants. Nothing is known about the end of Jordan's life; he was later beatified.

Jordan's literary output includes his letters, which served as a draft for the *Passion* of the Franciscans of Thana (recast by Francis of Pisa, a missionary at Sultania), and the *Mirabilia,* which had limited circulation during the Middle Ages.

**BIBLIOGRAPHY**

Jordan of Sévérac. *Mirabilia descripta.* Ed. Coquebert de Montbret. In *Recueil de voyages et mémoires de la Société de Géographie* 4 (1839): 37–64.

Mercati, Angelo. *Monumenta Vaticana veterem diocesim Columbensem respicientia.* Vatican City: Citta del Vaticano, 1923.

Moule, A.C. "Brother Jordan of Sévérac." *Journal of the Royal Asiatic Society* (1928): 349–376.

Loenertz, Raymond-J. *La Société des Frères Pérégrinants. Études sur l'Orient dominicain.* Rome, 1937, pp. 176–182.

Yule, Sir Henry, ed. and trans. *Mirabilia descripta: The Wonders of the East.* Hakluyt Society, 1st series, 31. London, 1863; rpt. New York: Franklin, 1963.

*Jean Richard*

**SEE ALSO**

Dominican Friars; Ethiopians; Franciscan Friars; India; John of Marignolli; Odoric of Pordenone

# K

## Kaifeng

A city in northern Henan Province, China, and a provincial capital until 1954; it is one of China's seven ancient capitals, along with Anyang, Xian, Luoyang, Hangzhou, Nanjing, and Beijing. It has been a political, military, economic, social, and cultural center of China, strategically important because of its topology and climate.

During the fourth century B.C.E., Kaifeng became the capital of the Wei state. At the end of the third century B.C.E., however, it was destroyed by the Qin state (221–206 B.C.E.), which had unified the empire after nearly thirty years of civil war. Located along the southern extent of the Huang He (Yellow River), Kaifeng was linked to four rivers, including the Huai and Yangtze; after the construction of four canal systems it was connected to eight provinces. Frequent flooding of the Huang He resulted in significant deposits of loess on the great plain, which rises only 225 to 255 feet (sixty-nine to seventy-eight meters) above sea level and benefits from moderate rainfall and temperatures averaging 57 degrees F. (14 degrees C.).

From 907 to 959 C.E., regional regimes such as Liang, Jin, later Han, and Zhou (but not the Tang) made Kaifeng their capital. The Northern Song dynasty (960–1127) reunified the empire and reestablished Kaifeng as its capital. The Jin invasion of 1127 forced the Song court to move its capital to Hanzhou in the south. Given various names—Daliang (by the Wei), Junyi (by the Qin), Bianzhou (by the Northern Zhou), Kaifeng (by the Liang), Bianjing and Nanjing (by the Mongols), Dongjing or Dongdu (its official name during the Northern Song dynasty), and Bian-liang or Bianjing (its popular name during this same dynasty)—the city served as capital for more than 450 years under half a dozen dynasties.

Kaifeng was a great commercial center during the Song dynasty, not only for China but for all of Asia. The four major canals drew in vast revenues in grain and commodities. Its population was estimated between 600,000 and 700,000 during the eleventh century. To accommodate so many people, many facilities were built, such as restaurants, wine shops, teahouses, theaters, brothels, as well as temples, mosques, and synagogues. Kaifeng had for centuries the only known Jewish community in China, and a small Jewish population lived here until the early 1900s. An inscription stone still in existence records the fact that Jews lived here from the early centuries C.E. The Mongols took Kaifeng during their conquest of Henan between 1231 and 1234. The city retains archaeological remnants of its political and cultural status under the Song.

### BIBLIOGRAPHY

Boyd, Andrew. *Architecture and Town Planning in China.* New York: St. Martin, 1989.

Gernet, Jacques. *Daily Life in China on the Eve of the Mongol Invasion, 1250–1276.* Trans. H.M. Wright. Palo Alto: Stanford UP, 1962.

Shiba, Yoshinobu. *Commerce and Society in Sung China.* Trans. Mark Elvin. Ann Arbor: U of Michigan P, 1970.

*Key Ray Chong*

### SEE ALSO
China; Mongols

# K

## Karakitai

A Central Asian empire, between 1131 and 1213. Its founder and leaders were ethnic Kitan, a linguistically proto-Mongolic people who had absorbed significant elements of Chinese culture. Their previous empire in Mongolia and northern China, the Liao, endured from 907 until 1125, when it was defeated, replaced, and expanded by the Jurchens and their Jin Empire (1115–1234). At its height, the Karakitai Empire extended from the Altai Mountains in the east to the Aral Sea in the west, and from Lake Balkash in the north to Khotan in the south. As such, the empire included portions of modern Xinjiang (China), Mongolia, Uzbekistan, Tajikistan, Kyrgyzistan, and Kazakhstan.

Karakitai was founded by Yeh-lü Ta-shih, a Kitan general who once served the last Liao emperor against the Jurchen onslaught. In 1124, however, he forsook his emperor and struck out on his own, declaring himself *gur-khân* (universal ruler) and eventually leading a significant remnant of his people westward to Issyk-kul in 1130, where he made his capital at Balasaghun. From there he managed, by 1141, to dominate Samarkand and Bukhara and compel the shah of Khwarazm to acknowledge himself as a tributary.

This hegemony over Muslim Turkic lands by Buddhist polytheists was scandalous to Islamic historians, who treated the history of Karakitai with contemptuous neglect. Chinese historians, however, named Karakitai "Western Liao" and preserved fragmentary records of its history. Thus, the names of the Karakitai leaders are known to us today only in their Chinese transcriptions.

Weakened by internal division during the late twelfth and early thirteenth centuries, Karakitai fell to the Mongols in 1213. But this conquest was difficult even for Chinggis Khân: the *Secret History of the Mongols* celebrates the arduously won victory over the "fine and courageous" warriors of Karakitai.

### BIBLIOGRAPHY

Sinor, Denis. "Western Information on the Kitans and Some Related Questions." *Journal of the American Oriental Society* 115.2 (1995): 262–269.

Wittfogel, Karl, and Feng Chia-sheng. *History of Chinese Society: Liao (907–1125)*. Philadelphia: The American Philosophical Society, 1949, pp. 619–674.

*David C. Wright*

### SEE ALSO

Buddhism; Bukhara; Mongols; Samarkand; *Secret History of the Mongols, The*

## Karakorum [Qaraqorum]

Capital of the Mongol Empire under khâns Ögedei (1229–1241), Güyük (1246–1248), and Möngke (1251–1259). Situated about 200 miles (320 kilometers) west of Ulan Bator, near the Orhon River, Karakorum became important around 1220, when Chinggis Khân (d. 1227) established a military center and arsenal there before his campaign against Khwarazm-shah. Ögedei built his palace there in 1235, raised walls around the town, and made it his center for administration and receipt of tribute. The imperial court occupied Karakorum for only part of the year—during late spring and summer—as part of their seasonal migrations. In 1948–1949, Russian archaeologists found remains of buildings, architectural ornaments, coins, pottery, and metalwork, demonstrating that Karakorum had become a center of trade and industry.

The first European traveler to refer to the place-name was John of Plano Carpini, who stayed near there in 1246, while attending the *quriltai* (princely assembly) at which Güyük was chosen khân. William of Rubruck resided in Karakorum for several months in 1254, finding it "not as large . . . as the village of Saint Denis," whose monastery he estimated to be "worth ten times more" than the khân's palace. Rubruck mentions two quarters (one Muslim, with bazaars where traders gathered, the other Chinese, for craftsmen) within the walls, as well as palaces for court secretaries, twelve "idol temples, two mosques and a Nestorian Christian Church." There he encountered men and women of many nations, including Western craftsmen such as the goldsmith William Buchier ("Master William of Paris"), whom the Mongols had captured and carried east. For the khân's palace Buchier crafted a large silver tree with four silver lions at its base, each of which was fitted with a pipe from which flowed beverages for the court's delectation. After Khubilai (1260–1294) transferred Mongol administration to Khanbaliq (modern Beijing) about 1267, Karakorum became a provincial center. When the Yuan (Mongol) dynasty fell, its last emperor, Toghon Temür, fled to Karakorum in 1368, but after the Mongol Empire collapsed, Karakorum lost importance, its site providing building materials for the construction of a lamasery in the sixteenth century.

### BIBLIOGRAPHY

Dawson, Christopher, ed. *The Mongol Mission*. See Gen. Bib.

*The Mission of Friar William of Rubruck: His Journey to the Court of the Great Khan Möngke 1253–1255.* Trans. Peter Jackson, with notes and introduction by Peter Jackson and David Morgan. Hakluyt Society, 2nd series, 173. London: Hakluyt Society, 1990.

Morgan, David. *The Mongols.* Oxford and New York: Blackwell, 1986.

Phillips, Eustace Dockray. *The Mongols.* New York: Praeger, 1969.

*James D. Ryan*

**SEE ALSO**

John of Plano Carpini; Khanbaliq; Mongols; Nestorianism; William of Rubruck; Yuan Dynasty

## Keel

Ship whose name derived from the single heavy timber, square or nearly square in cross section, which ran in the fore-and-aft plane of the ship from stempost to sternpost and was a common feature of Mediterranean vessels well before the Middle Ages.

All sailing and oared ships in the south had a keel, but in the north, few types had them until Scandinavian shipbuilders added keels to the common rowing barge, creating the typical vessel of the Viking period. The term *keel* came to be used to describe the descendants of those Scandinavian sailing ships that took over many tasks along the west coast of Europe and in the British Isles beginning in the eleventh century and continuing through the end of the Middle Ages. Possibly the absence of a true keel on other contemporary types led to the use of the term to describe the modified Viking ship.

Keels were vessels with a shallow draft carrying a single mast with a single square sail. They were extremely seaworthy and were the best type available for short distance and coastal trading. The vessels could be beached easily, so they could make any stretch of sand into a harbor. With the capacity in many cases to use a few auxiliary oars, they were also highly maneuverable. Their lightness, speed, and modest draft recommended them for naval and especially amphibious operations, as well as piracy. Iberian explorers started their first tentative trips down the African coast in vessels of the same type.

The addition of a keel to the cog in the twelfth century improved its sailing qualities and led to the Viking keels' decline in popularity. The cog proved superior in deep-sea trading within Europe. Because it rode higher in the water and was able to carry many

Keel. A ship of one of the Cinque Ports. Obverse of the seal of Winchelsea, England, 1274. Reproduced by Permission of Winchelsea Corporation.

more men, cogs were also superior in naval battles. Keels did, however, retain many of their earlier functions through the thirteenth and fourteenth centuries, both commercial and naval, while fostering a number of designs of inland and coastal craft that would survive beyond the Middle Ages.

**BIBLIOGRAPHY**

Hutchinson, Gillian. *Medieval Ships and Shipping.* Rutherford, NJ: Fairleigh Dickinson UP, 1994.

Lewis, Archibald R., and Timothy J. Runyan. *European Naval and Maritime History, 300–1500.* Bloomington: Indiana UP, 1985.

Unger, Richard W. *The Ship in the Medieval Economy, 600–1600.* London: Croom-Helm Ltd., 1980.

*Richard W. Unger*

**SEE ALSO**

Cog; Naval Warfare; Piracy; Portuguese Expansion; Ships and Shipbuilding

## Kempe, Margery (*c.* 1373–after 1439)

An English visionary and pilgrim who recounted her journeys in England and abroad in her spiritual autobiography, *The Book of Margery Kempe,* which she

# K

dictated to a priest. In about 1413, after twenty years of marriage and fourteen children, Kempe freed herself from domestic obligation, paying the debts of her husband, John, and thus getting him to join her in a mutual vow of chastity. By 1417, she had accomplished the three great medieval pilgrimages—to the Holy Land, Rome, and Santiago de Compostela. In 1431, after traveling widely in England, she again traveled abroad, to Gdansk (Danzig).

Born in Bishop's Lynn (now King's Lynn), Norfolk, the daughter of one wealthy burgess and the wife of another, Margery Kempe was, as a young married woman, first a brewer and then a miller, but she failed in both endeavors. In 1438, she was named a member of the Guild of the Trinity at Lynn. After the birth of her first child she began to receive visions through which she understood herself to have been chosen by Christ for the benefit of other Christians, to call them into sorrow for sin. To fulfill this ministry she dressed in white (a color of dress not permitted for married, or nonvirginal, women), vowed herself to chastity and prayer, and became a pilgrim.

In obedience to the command of Christ to go to Rome, Jerusalem, and Compostela, and in fulfillment of her own "desyr to se þo placys wher he was born & wher he sufferyd hys Passyon & wher he deyd," in 1413, she traveled to the Holy Land by way of Constance and Venice. In Jerusalem's Church of the Holy Sepulchre, she for the first time experienced the loud "crying" in compassion for Christ's suffering that was to recur for about ten years afterward. While Christians found her behavior unattractive, she reports that "handsome" Muslims were very cordial to her.

Kempe went to Rome in late 1414, spending the winter there. During that time she visited the death chamber of St. Bridget of Sweden, whose *Revelations* had greatly influenced her. Along with her descriptions of mystical experience, she also mentions the linguistic problems she encountered trying to communicate with Italian women. Returning home by way of Assisi, she worshiped in the Church of St. Francis, there viewing the Virgin Mary's veil, and the Portiuncula Chapel, where Francis had worshiped and convoked an important assembly in 1221. In 1417, she sailed from Bristol to make her third great pilgrimage. She took each of these trips in company with other pilgrims, but her volubility, her public insistence on having been chosen by God, and her crying at any reminder of Christ and his Passion caused her companions to treat her scorn-

fully, sometimes robbing her or abandoning her to make her own way home. Her account of her three pilgrimages is typically medieval in that she pays little attention to events that occurred to her in transit. When she does relate travel experiences, it is to serve some purpose (such as to note her rejection by or the isolation she felt from her fellow pilgrims).

Even before taking up her religious vocation and making formal pilgrimages, Margery Kempe had traveled with her husband to shrines in England, sometimes seeking the advice of spiritual authorities such as friars, hermits, and anchorites (including Julian of Norwich), and hearing renowned preachers. After returning from Compostela she continued to travel within England, often again in response to divine direction. She visited, asked counsel of, and sometimes disputed with prelates, friars, and public figures ranging from the mayor of Leicester to the archbishop of Canterbury. Her fits of crying and self-confident responses to criticism led her into frequent conflict, including repeated arrests and examinations for heresy. Nevertheless, often with help from distinguished clerics, she always persuaded her judges of her orthodoxy.

Despite the hardships she suffered on her pilgrimages, Kempe continued to travel until nearly the end of her life. After the death of her eldest son, in 1433 she took advantage of her German daughter-in-law's return to Gdansk to make one last trip. En route, they spent Good Friday through Easter Monday in Norway; on her return, she visited relics displayed at Bad Wilsnack and Aachen. The next year she visited Syon Abbey, the English royal foundation of the Brigittine Order of St. Bridget of Sweden, and obtained the "Pardon of Syon," a papal indulgence given to pilgrims to the abbey during Lammastide.

Following for nearly twenty years a life of spiritual and geographical pilgrimage as a witness to other Christians, Kempe always understood her life as an act of obedience to God. Her account of her journeys provides a useful record of both the range of experiences available to ordinary pilgrims and the kinds of behavior that were and were not expected among religious travelers of her day.

## BIBLIOGRAPHY

Atkinson, Clarissa W. *Mystic and Pilgrim: The* Book *and the World of Margery Kempe.* Ithaca, NY: Cornell UP, 1983.

Goodman, Anthony E. "The Piety of John Brunham's Daughter, of Lynn." In *Medieval Women.* Ed. Derek Baker. Oxford: Blackwell, 1978, pp. 347–358.

Kempe, Margery. *The Book of Margery Kempe.* Ed. Sanford B. Meech and Hope Emily Allen. Early English Text Society, o.s., 212. Oxford: Oxford UP, 1940.

Staley, Lynn. *Margery Kempe's Dissenting Fictions.* University Park: U of Pennsylvania P, 1994.

*Marsha L. Dutton*

**SEE ALSO**

Guilds; Holy Land; Jerusalem; Pilgrimage, Christian; Pilgrimage Sites, English; Pilgrimage Sites, Spanish; Rome as a Pilgrimage Site; Women Travelers, Islamic

## Khanbaliq [Cambalac]

The capital city of the Mongol Empire after 1267. The "city of the khâns" (Turkic) was built, beginning in 1267 C.E., under the express orders of Khubilai Khân, the grandson of Chinggis Khân, in what is present-day Beijing. It was called Dadu, "the great capital," by the Chinese and Daidu by the Mongols. During Khubilai's reign, it became one of the largest and most famous cities in the world.

The decision by Khubilai, the fifth in the line of Mongolian rulers descended from Chinggis Khân, to shift his capital from Karakorum south and east into China signified his commitment to identify his own fortunes with those of his subject Chinese. Khubilai's claim to be the khaghan of all Mongols meant that, in name at least, Khanbaliq became the capital of the entire Mongolian realm stretching westward to the Chaghatai khânate of Central Asia, the il-khânate of Persia, and the Qipchaq khânate in Russia. However, in reality, Khubilai's rule was confined to his own khânate, which included his Yuan dynastic realm in China.

Khanbaliq was built near the earlier sites of the Khitan Liao (ruled in north China from 907 to 1125) capital of Nanjing and the Jurchen Jin (ruled in north China from 1115 to 1234) capital of Zhongdu, and was to some extent modeled after them. Likewise, in 1406, thirty-eight years after the fall of the Mongol Yuan dynasty, the third Ming ruler, Yongle (r. 1402–1424), began construction of what was to become his "northern capital" of Beijing on the Mongol site. Subsequently, Beijing was occupied by Manchu conquerors in 1644 and remained their capital until the Qing dynasty fell in 1912. Beijing has been the recognized capital of China throughout much of the twentieth century. In 1949, Mao Zedong proclaimed it the capital of the People's Republic of China.

Khubilai brought with him no native imperial architectural traditions, and as a result, he borrowed extensively from Chinese traditions to build Khanbaliq. Though his chief architect was the Muslim Yeh-hei-tieh-erh, Khubilai also relied on the counsel of his closest Chinese adviser, Liu Bingzhong, who realized that the use of established imperial forms to build a capital would reassure the conquered Chinese that he did not wish to change or destroy their culture and, at the same time, provide Khubilai with potent symbols of authority. Consequently, the plan for Khanbaliq was based on the classical model for imperial cities found in the very early Chinese text *Zhou Li.*

Khanbaliq was rectangular and enclosed by an immense wall of rammed earth constructed between 1267 and 1268 with a perimeter of 28,600 meters. The wall had eleven impressive gates, two to the north and three in each of the other directions, upon which were built three-story-high towers where defenders watched for impending danger. Emanating from the gates were major north-south and east-west thoroughfares, each approximately twenty-five meters wide. These, in turn, were subdivided by smaller streets to create fifty-four four-sided areas called *fang* (wards or precincts).

Within the outer wall of Khanbaliq, Khubilai created two additional walled enclosures, an imperial city (*huangcheng*), and within the imperial city, also enclosed by walls, a palace city (*gongcheng*). Access to the imperial city was restricted to the royal family or officials working for the court, who entered the city by day to serve the emperor but had to leave by night. The palace city, with a circumference of 3,480 meters, housed buildings for the khân's worship, the holding of imperial audiences, and private affairs.

Striking features of Khubilai's capital were the scenic beauty of the large imperial park in the north-central part, and the sizeable artificial lake running from the west-central part of the outer wall of the city toward its center and then southward into the enclosed imperial city itself.

Khubilai also erected numerous temples in his capital to win the support of Chinese officials. An ancestral temple (*taimiao*) was started in 1263, even before the first of Khanbaliq's walls were erected, where rituals essential to the Confucian veneration of ancestors could be practiced. In 1271, altars of the soil and grain were built where gods could be propitiated to ensure bountiful harvests. A shrine was also built for Confucius as another means to appeal to Chinese scholar-officials.

# K

Unlike earlier Chinese capitals of native Chinese dynasties, which were located along the Yellow River (Hwang Ho) or its tributaries at Xian, Loyang, and Kaifeng, Khanbaliq was built further north where Khubilai could better monitor activities in Mongolia and the larger Mongol realm. Nonetheless, Khubilai's move to north China provides striking evidence of his increasing realization of China's importance to his own political fortunes and his willingness to seek Chinese support for the Yuan dynasty and his emperorship.

The creation of the new Mongol capital in north China also had a dramatic impact on commerce and trade. To feed the growing population of Khanbaliq, grain had to be transported from the lower Yangtze basin to the north China plain. To accomplish this, the Yuan inaugurated a sea transport service and also extended the grand canal system north to Khanbaliq from the Yellow River. This was an immense project that involved hundreds of thousands of workers and was completed in 1289. Eventually, a paved highway was built along the route of the grand canal system from Hangchow to Khanbaliq, a distance of more than 800 miles (1700 kilometers).

The Mongol conquests of Chinggis Khân and his sons made possible for the first time safe travel from Europe and the Mediterranean to China. During this *Pax Mongolica,* European travelers reached China through south Russia and Ili across the steppe, across the Black Sea and through the Inner Asian oases of the silk roads, by sea to Syria, and thence through Baghdad and central Eurasia, or by sea through the Indian Ocean and around southeast Asia to the southeast coast of China. The breakup of the Mongol realm into rival khânates diminished the freedom of merchants to travel. Nonetheless, foreign trade, conducted chiefly by Muslim merchants of central Eurasian origin, enriched Khanbaliq and Yuan China.

**BIBLIOGRAPHY**

Rossabi, Morris. *Khubilai Khan.* Berkeley: U of California P, 1988.
Steinhardt, Nancy Schatzman. "Imperial Architecture under Mongolian Patronage: Khubilai's Imperial City of Daidu." Diss., Harvard U, 1981.

*Van Jay Symons*

**SEE ALSO**

Baghdad; Chaghatai; Chaghatai Khânate; China; Confucianism; Inner Asian Trade; Kaifeng; Karakitai; Karakorum; Mongols; Silk Roads; Yuan Dynasty

## King's Mirror, The

An encyclopedic collection of information about geography, Scandinavian natural science, and etiquette, written in Norway, in Old Norse, between 1249 and 1263.

*The King's Mirror (Konungs Skuggjá)* takes the form of a dialogue, in which a learned father answers a variety of questions from his earnest son. The work's title indicates that it belongs to the tradition of the didactic text—the Latin *speculum regale* being the "handsome" (*fagrt*) alternative title employed for the book in its introduction—whose purpose was to instruct aristocratic young men in the ways of the court. Scholars have theorized that it was written specifically for the sons of King Hákon Hákonarson (1217–1263), but its content suggests that a wider audience was intended, including members of the merchant class, for whom the third part of the book would be particularly relevant. The anonymous author, very probably a cleric, does not ostentatiously present himself as learned, but he must have had a good education and he certainly knew what was expected of royal retainers. It is not known if he studied outside Scandinavia; a considerable amount of his information may have come from oral report. At least sixty-two manuscript copies of the text survive, including one thirteenth-century and one fourteenth-century copy in Iceland, attesting to its popularity.

The book is divided into two sections. The first half deals with secular concerns, presenting informed answers to the son's questions relating to cosmography (why the sea has tides, what climate zones are found on Earth, where the northern lights come from) and natural history (particularly of Ireland, Iceland, and Greenland, each of which is treated in two or more chapters). Knowledge is here essential to personal advancement: the son begins his inquiry by explaining that he would never attempt to gain a place at court without first going abroad to observe foreign customs. The father notes approvingly that people travel for several reasons, among them to obtain wealth or fame and to satisfy "curiosity, for it is also in a man's nature to wish to see and experience the things that he has heard about, and thus to learn whether the facts are as told or not." He specifically urges his son to learn Latin and French, because they are the most widely spoken languages, but not to neglect his own.

The second half of the book addresses the issues of how to behave at court; this section strikes a more pious note by introducing moral exempla drawn from the Old Testament (especially demonstrating good and bad judgments). It also addresses the issue of capital punishment. The author shows some knowledge of Gregory the Great's *Dialogues* (593), Isidore of Seville's *Etymologies* (622–633), and Peter Comestor's *Historia scholastica* (late 1100s).

The secular and homely character of *The King's Mirror* can be gathered from the rather famous anecdote of the candle and the apple (chapter 7), which does not appear in other geographical/cosmographical texts. Attempting to alleviate his son's perplexity about why summer and winter should vary in intensity in different latitudes, the father asks him to imagine a burning candle, set in the middle of a room so that it illuminates the entire space, and then to consider an apple hung so close to the candle that it both heats up and casts a great shadow on the wall. The son is then told to compare this effect to that caused by an apple hung near the wall, which will remain cool and create minimal shadow. The father explains that the earth's spherical shape causes territory to be variously nearer or farther from the sun and its heat; at the same time, given its "path," the sun sheds various amounts of light and may keep one land (Norway) brighter even while other places (Apulia and Jerusalem) experience more darkness while remaining warmer. The analogy is confusing because the apple is not consistently the ball-shaped earth but different parts of the earth, and the shadows representing hours of darkness are, in the analogy, cast by the apple/earth not the sun. Nevertheless, the inquisitive pupil responds enthusiastically that he "sees . . . clearly."

*The King's Mirror* is a charming, if parochial, example of medieval Scandinavian knowledge about the world, society, and natural phenomena.

**BIBLIOGRAPHY**

Bagge, Sverre. *The Political Thought of* The King's Mirror. Mediaeval Scandinavia Supplements 3. Odense, Denmark: Odense UP, 1987.

*The King's Mirror (Speculum Regale—Konungs skuggsjá)*. Trans. Laurence Marcellus Larson. New York: American-Scandinavian Foundation, 1917; New York: Twayne, 1972.

*Konungs skuggsjá*. Ed. Ludvig Holm-Olsen. Kjeldeskrift-fondet. Gammelnorske tekster 1. Oslo: Norsk Historisk Kjeldskrift-Institutt 1945; 2nd rev. edition, 1983.

Shackelford, Jole R. "The Apple/Candle Illustration in *The King's Mirror* and the South English Legendary." *Maal og Minne* (1984): 72–84.

Simek, Rudolf. *Altnordische Kosmographie: Studien und Quellen zu Weltbild und Weltbeschreibung in Norwegen und Island vom 12. bis zum 14. Jahrhundert.* Berlin and New York: Walter de Gruyter, 1990, pp. 131–134, 403–405.

*Scott D. Westrem*

**SEE ALSO**

Climate; Geography in Medieval Europe; Iceland; Isidore of Seville; Language Instruction for Western European Travelers; Tides; Viking Age

## Klosterneuburg [Vienna-Klosterneuburg] Map Corpus

A large body of cartographic material created chiefly during the second quarter of the fifteenth century by a cosmopolitan group of scholars working in a number of centers more or less closely associated with the University of Vienna and the nearby Monastery of Klosterneuburg.

Three intriguing world maps, lost in their "analogue" form but preserved as a series of coordinates in tables, including descriptions and captions, allow us to reconstruct these monastic versions of contemporary cartography. The tables, which were drawn up by a Frater Fredericus in 1449, reproduce the contents of the lost maps according to latitude and longitude. Accompanying German texts supply the traditional contents of *mappaemundi*. The lost common original was produced at Klosterneuburg around 1425, probably with Latin inscriptions and labels.

The derivative maps described in the coordinate tables had been added to by their copyists and enriched with the nomenclature and legends of classical mythology, medieval myth, and astrology that were the stock-in-trade of medieval cartographers. The well-known *mappamundi* of the Zeitz Stiftsbibliothek (MS Hist. fol. 497) derives from the same 1425 original; it is probable that the Benedictine Andreas Walsperger's *mappamundi,* made at Constance in 1448 (Bibliotheca Apostolica Vaticana, Cod. Palat. Lat. 1362b) is closely related to these maps. A large circle of mutual influence and cartographic knowledge over a wide area of southern Germany, centering on monastic houses, can thus be surmised to have existed.

**BIBLIOGRAPHY**

Durand, Dana Bennett. *The Vienna-Klosterneuburg Map Corpus.* Leiden: E.J. Brill, 1952.

*Andrew Gow*

# K

SEE ALSO
*Mappamundi;* Maps; Ptolemy; Walsperger, Andreas;
Zeitz Map

## Knarr

Old Norse name for a type of sailing vessel, generally a merchant ship, although a few poetic sources speak of *knarrs* going into battle. Among the ship types named in the written sources of the twelfth and thirteenth centuries, the *knarr* seems to be a large or medium-sized trading vessel, used for voyages across the North Sea and from Norway to Iceland and Greenland. A special, smaller, type was the "austfareknarr" used for "eastern voyages" in the Baltic.

Two of the wrecks from Skuldelev near Roskilde (Denmark) have been tentatively identified as *knarrs*, Wrecks 1 and 3. Wreck 1 is mainly constructed of pine and was built in western Norway. Wreck 3, made entirely of oak, is Danish. Both date from the early 1000s. They have an open hold amidships for stowing cargo and small decks fore and aft for working the ship. A few oar ports indicate that the ships could be rowed, but the number of oars is too small for regular propulsion, so oars were probably used for maneuvering in and out of harbors and for moving the ship short distances in calm weather. The mast is stepped amidships and carried a square sail spread by a yard along the upper edge.

Written sources clearly indicate that a *knarr* was a more seaworthy vessel than the long, narrow warships. Replicas show that the ships can be sailed with much

Skuldelev 1, Norwegian merchant vessel of pine found near Skuldelev, Denmark. 11th century. Photo by Werner Karrasch. Courtesy of The Viking Ship Museum in Roskilde.

smaller crews than were necessary for a warship with all oars manned. Sailing trials show that the ships sail well, that they can tack against the wind, and that the larger Wreck 1 is a seaworthy vessel. The estimated loading capacity of Wreck 1 is around twenty-four metric tons with a minimum crew of seven or eight men. The smaller Wreck 3 could carry about four and one-half tons of cargo and needed a crew of at least five. During the Viking age, merchants usually paid for cargo space by working as crew members to offset the costs of the voyage, and thus crews might be larger, with many merchants each transporting small amounts of goods.

**BIBLIOGRAPHY**
Falk, Hjalmar. *Altnordisches Seewesen.* Wörter und Sachen 4. Heidelberg: Winter, 1912.
*Maritime Archaeology Newsletter from Roskilde Denmark nr. May 10, 1998.* Roskilde: The Centre for Maritime Archaeology at the National Museum, p. 34.
Olsen, Olaf, and Ole Crumlin-Pedersen. *Five Viking Ships from Roskilde Fjord.* Copenhagen: The National Museum, 1978.
*Arne Emil Christensen*

SEE ALSO
*Langskip;* Navigation; Navigation, Viking; Ships and Shipbuilding

## Korea, Mongol Invasions of

The Mongols first entered Korea in 1218. The kingdom, then known as Koryo (935–1392), accepted for-

Skuldelev 3, a Danish merchant vessel of oak found near Skuldelev, Denmark. 11th century. Photo by Werner Karrasch. Courtesy of The Viking Ship Museum in Roskilde.

mal ties to deter further incursions, but an envoy's death in 1225 led to invasion in 1231. Losing the capital, Songdo (modern Kaesong), the Ch'oe military rulers accepted harsh Mongol demands: the crown prince, 1,000 children from royal and court families, and 2,000 children from provincial families were required as hostages, along with a direct payment of gold, silver, horses, and provisions for one million troops.

The court was moved to Kanghwa Island off the west coast, but this led to further incursions. According to the official history *Koryo-sa,* Koreans lost 200,000 people in the ensuing battles, but the figure seems low. In 1238, King Kojong (r. 1213–1259) was to attend the Mongol court at Karakorum, but he refused, sending Wang Sun as the putative crown prince; Wang Sun subsequently married Möngke Khân's daughter, and became loyal to the Mongols.

In 1259, the real crown prince, Chon, met Khubilai Khân, who sent him back to Korea to succeed Kojong as King Wonjong (r. 1260–1274). The court returned to Songdo, and a century of Mongol rule began (1259–1356), maintained by such factors as intermarriage and blood ties with Koryo's royal and aristocratic families; the taking hostage of the crown prince, and other royal and aristocratic children (which facilitated the continuing policy of intermarriage); and the establishment of strategically located garrisons, led by seventy-two *darugachi* or resident commissioners.

The two Mongol invasions of Japan caused Korea great economic hardship. In 1274, with a population of 300,000, Korea had to build 900 ships and provide 18,000 sailors and 8,000 troops to join 20,000 Mongols; Korean farmers supplied this enormous force. In 1281—out of a total of 140,000 troops and 2,500 ships that sailed in the Mongol fleet—Korea built 900 ships and sent 15,000 sailors and 10,000 troops. Typhoons caused both invasions to fail; only 20 percent of the military got back to the mainland. In 1356, King Kongmin, himself only one-eighth Korean, drove out the Mongols, killing many Koreans with Mongol ties.

Although the Mongol invasions were disruptive, Korean culture flourished in the thirteenth century. Koryo inlaid celadon ceramics were some of the finest ever produced. Koreans developed movable-type printing in 1234 and published a complete set of Buddhist sutras, *Taejanggyong,* with 81,000 woodblocks, each with two pages (1237–1257). Copies are still extant. Korean drum-dance and puppet-drama were both influenced by Mongol storytelling and drama.

BIBLIOGRAPHY
Henthorn, William E. *Korea: The Mongol Invasions.* Leiden: E.J. Brill, 1963.
Kim, Sanggi. *Koryo Sidae-sa* (History of the Koryo Period). Seoul: Tongguk Munhwa-sa, 1961.

*Hugh D. Walker*

SEE ALSO
Japan, Mongol Invasion of; Mongols; Vietnam and Java, Mongol Invasions of; Yuan Dynasty

## Krak des Chevaliers

The strongest and best preserved of the crusader castles in the Levant. Situated on a high plateau in modern-day northwest Syria, the castle of Krak des Chevaliers could command the important roads running from Hama and Homs to the Mediterranean coast. It was first occupied by the crusaders after the conquest of Jerusalem in 1099, but only temporarily. It was captured again in 1110. In 1144, it was given to the Knights Hospitalers of St. John by the count of Tripoli, to serve in defending the eastern border. The Hospitalers built up the fortress into a powerful stronghold over the next century. In 1163, Nur ed-Din attempted to lay siege to the castle but was routed by its defenders. It was the key to the eastern defense of Tripoli from attacks by the Assassins. Like a few other castles maintained by the military orders, Krak des Chevaliers survived the fall of Jerusalem and the victorious campaigns of Saladin after 1187.

The Mamluk sultan Baybars I captured much of Christian-held territory between 1263 and 1268, including Antioch. In response, Louis IX of France again took up the cross, but at the last moment, in June 1270, he decided to detour to Tunis on his way to Egypt. For Krak the decision was fatal. St. Louis died at Tunis in August, and by the time Prince Edward of England arrived the following year Baybars had defeated the Hospitalers and taken the castle. It was later restored and expanded by the Muslims. Fourteenth-century pilgrims, such as William of Boldensele, praise its strength and mourn its passage into Arab hands.

BIBLIOGRAPHY
Deschamps, Paul. *Les châteaux des croisés en Terre Sainte.* Vol. 1, *Le Crac des chevaliers.* Paris: P. Geuthner, 1934.
Kennedy, Hugh. *Crusader Castles.* Cambridge: Cambridge UP, 1994.

# K

Pringle, Denys. *Secular Buildings in the Crusader Kingdom of Jerusalem.* Cambridge: Cambridge UP, 1997.

*Thomas F. Madden*

**SEE ALSO**
Assassins; Baybars I; Louis IX; Mamluks; Military Orders; Saladin; William of Boldensele

## Kumis

The favored drink of the Mongols, as well as of most of the Asiatic nomads (var. kumiz, kimiz, koomis [Russian]; airakh, ayras [Mongolian]), an alcoholic brew of fermented mare's milk. According to the primary sources, medieval Western travelers knew of—but did not care much for—kumis. Sir Henry Yule explained that kumis is made by putting fresh mare's milk into a well-seasoned bottle-necked vessel of horse skin to which sour cow's milk is added. As fermentation occurs over several days, the mix is violently stirred with a staff that remains in the vessel. Everyone in the camp is invited to take a turn at the churn, even foreign guests. This interrupts the process and adds air into the liquid. The product that results in three to four days has a wine-like quality, as well as a peculiar fore- and after-taste.

William of Rubruck, who visited the Mongols between 1253 and 1255, described kumis as having a pungent taste but a pleasant lingering almondlike flavor. He also noted its intoxicating impact, stating that it left his insides warm and could make one's head weak. Obviously, the intoxicating power varies according to the type of brew.

A special kind of kumis, mentioned by William and by Marco Polo, was prepared from the khân's personal herd of 10,000 white horses and mares. Only the khân, and those whom he designated, could drink this kumis. According to Polo, when the khân left his summer palace annually on August 28, the special kumis was spread over the ground so that the earth, the air, and even the false gods would have their share; this ensured that those forces would protect and bless the khân. William reported a different version: the festival was held on May 9, the day of the May moon, during which the herd of mares was consecrated, and the Mongols sprinkled the new kumis on the ground, the first brew of the year. William likened the ceremony to the drinking of new wine or the eating of fresh fruit on various saints' days in the Christian West.

William reported that kumis was so popular that it took the milk of 3,000 mares to satisfy the daily needs of the 300 warriors of the il-khân Batu's camp. Drinking to excess could be a major problem, and several important figures—including Chinggis Khân's warriors—were known to have succumbed to drunkenness. It has been suggested that Marco Polo's failure to discuss tea, the favorite drink of China, in his *Description of the World,* may be due to the prominence of kumis among his Mongol hosts.

**BIBLIOGRAPHY**
Dawson, Christopher, ed. *The Mongol Mission.* See Gen. Bib.
Polo, Marco. *The Book of Ser Marco Polo the Venetian Concerning the Kingdoms and Marvels of the East.* Ed. and trans. Sir Henry Yule. 3rd edition. rev. Henri Cordier. 2 vols. New York: Scribner's, 1921 (first published in 1903).
Ratchnevsky, Paul. *Genghis Khan: His Life and Legacy.* Ed. and trans. Thomas N. Haining. London: Blackwell, 1992.

*Charles W. Connell*

**SEE ALSO**
Marco Polo; Mongol Army; Mongols; Nomadism and Pastoralism; William of Rubruck

# L

## La Broquière, Bertrandon de (*c.* 1400–1459)

A pilgrim to the Holy Land who also traveled in Syria and Turkey during 1432 and 1433.

Fifteenth-century Burgundians were doubly interested in the Near East. In common with many other Christian European leaders, the dukes John the Fearless (r. 1404–1419) and Philip the Good (*c.* 1419–1467) were preoccupied with the crusading ideal of recapturing the Holy Land. Philip was also captivated by "the Orient" because a large part of the political ideology on which he built his political power was indebted to the legend of Jason and the Golden Fleece, a story centered on Turkey and the Black Sea.

With an eye to fitting out a Burgundian crusade, Philip sent his chief carver, Bertrandon de La Broquière [Bertrandon de la Brocquière], on a fact-finding mission to the Holy Land in February 1432. La Broquière and a group of Burgundian companions (including Geoffroy de Thoisy, a Burgundian general, later admiral of the Burgundian fleet that raided the coasts of the Black Sea in 1445) traveled to the Holy Land by the commonly used sea route (Venice, Morea, Crete, Rhodes, Cyprus, and finally Jaffa). As a pilgrim, La Broquière made the usual rounds, meanwhile taking careful observations of the lay of the land and recording them in a little booklet that, after his return to Burgundy in 1433, he turned into a first-person narrative, the *Voyage d'Outremer*.

In the hospital attached to the Franciscan convent of Mount Sion in Jerusalem, he made up his mind to attempt to return to Europe alone overland through Syria and Turkey, a route no one in living memory had survived: "But I thought that anything is possible for a man of average strength and with a rather good resistance to suffering, who has money and health. . . . At this point, I decided to travel the road by land to the kingdom of France or to die trying." The *Voyage* is devoted mainly to the description of this adventure and to the geographic, cultural, and military knowledge that he gleaned from it. La Broquière begins his account with a phrase that shows clearly that this is no mere military espionage report, however: "Wishing to see the world for amusement and distraction . . ."

Remarkable in the *Voyage* are La Broquière's anthropological interests and intellectual curiosity, unusual in a pre-Renaissance traveler. For example, not satisfied by secondhand stories about the Muslims, Islam, and the Prophet Muhammad, he describes with much interest the ceremonies governing the reception in Middle Eastern cities of a Meccan Koran transported on its own camel. La Broquière also seeks a better understanding of religious matters: "Because there had been so much discussion about Muhammad, I went to talk to a priest who had served the Venetian consul in Damascus. I . . . asked him then if he could talk about Muhammad. He said yes, that he knew the Koran well. I begged him humbly to put down on paper what he knew and said that I would take it back to my lord the Duke. He did so willingly and I have brought it." At the very end of his voyage, when La Brocquière reported back to Duke Philip, among his prize possessions were a horse from Damascus, his Saracen clothing, and "the Koran and the Deeds of Muhammed which the chaplain of the Venetian consul in Damascus had given me, written in Latin. This long book my lord gave to Jean Germain, doctor in theology, for inspection." La Broquière

# L

added ironically and wistfully: "I never saw them again."

La Broquière was born in Guyenne around 1400. He entered service to Philip the Good in 1421 and was sent on his first confidential embassy in 1423. Apparently trustworthy, he was appointed "chatellain du Vieil-Chastel" in 1428. After returning from his voyage through Turkey, La Broquière served the duke in many military and consular capacities evidently with continued success, since the duke helped to arrange La Broquière's marriage in 1442 to Catherine, daughter of John, lord of Bernieulles. Philip also appointed him to the military captaincy of the two important garrison towns Rupelmonde and Gouda, and later to those of Neufport and Oostdunes in Flanders.

In the mid-1450s, Philip requested Jean Miélot, his trusted scribe (his ornate calligraphy in a series of *Speculum Humane Salvationis* manuscripts is one of the high points in the art of the handmade book), translator, and illuminator to make a lavish copy of La Broquière's book. Already in the early 1440s there had been some collaboration between Miélot and La Broquière. The former had made a fair copy of the translation into French by the latter of a crusading treatise written by John of Torzelo. In 1457, La Broquière presented the duke with the beautifully written and illuminated *Voyage d'Outremer*. It became part of the collection of works connected to the Voeu du Faisan (Pheasant Banquet) of crusading fame, which was held at Lille in 1454 and was reported to include forty dishes in each course. The works connected to this spectacular banquet were, in turn, closely tied in with books treating the legend of Jason written after the founding of the Order of the Golden Fleece in 1430. The Order and the Voeu were two mainstays of the Burgundian self-image. La Broquière died in 1459 at Lille, where he was interred in the collegiate Church of St. Peter.

## BIBLIOGRAPHY

Izeddin, M. "Deux voyageurs du XVe siècle en Turquie: Bertrandon de la Brocquière et Pero Tafur." *Journal Asiatique* 239 (1951): 159–174.

Paviot, J. "D'un ennemi l'autre: Des Mamelouks aux Ottomans: Voyages de renseignement au Levant XIIIème–XVIIème siècles." In *D'un Orient l'autre: Les métamorphoses successives des perceptions et connaissances.* Ed. J.-C. Vatin. Paris: CNRS, 1991. 2 vols. Vol. 1: 317–328.

Vanderjagt, A.J. "'Qui desirent veoir du monde': Bourgondiërs en de Oriënt." *De Oriënt. Droom of Dreiging:*
*Het Oosten in Westers perspectief.* Ed. H. Bakker, M. Gosman. Kampen: Kok Agora, 1988, pp. 18–37.

*Le Voyage d'Outremer de Bertrandon de la Brocquière.* Ed. C.H. Schefer. Paris: Leroux, 1892.

*The Voyage d'Outremer by Bertrandon de la Brocquière.* Ed. and trans. G.R. Kline. New York: Lang, 1988.

Wilson, Adrian L. *A Medieval Mirror.* Berkeley: U. of California P, 1984.

*A.J. Vanderjagt*

**SEE ALSO**

Costume, Oriental; Crusades, Burgundian; Holy Land; John the Fearless, Funeral Cortege of; Pilgrimage, Christian; Spies; Venice

## Lajazzo [Laias, Layas, Ajas, Ayas]

The principal medieval seaport of Cilician Armenia (Lesser Armenia). Lajazzo [Ayas] lay on the northwestern shore of the Gulf of Alexandretta (Iskenderun Körfezi), near modern-day Yumurtalik. It was a Mediterranean outlet for the products of Persia and Armenia and for westbound trade through the Persian Gulf. In the early fourteenth century, Lajazzo also served as a staging point for officially prohibited trade contacts with Syria and Egypt.

The town became prominent with the consolidation of the Armenian barony of Cilicia in the twelfth century. Under Levon [Leo] II (r. 1187–1219), the first crowned sovereign of Lesser Armenia, Lajazzo became an international port. From it, a key trade route ran through Sivas and Erzincan to Trebizond [Trabzun], and through Erzurum to Tabriz. The alliance between Lesser Armenia and the Mongols forged in 1247 soon exposed Lajazzo to attacks by the Egyptian Mamluks, and in 1266 it was sacked by Sultan Baybars I. Nonetheless, rebuilt under Levon III (r. 1269–1289), Lajazzo was a lively commercial center when Marco Polo passed through in 1271. After the defeat of il-khânid (Mongol) and Armenian forces by Sultan Qalā'ūn in 1281, Lajazzo was torched and remained economically weak during the subsequent Cilician upheavals. It revived again after the Mamluk conquest of the Syrian and Palestinian seaports, which left Lajazzo as the only independent outlet for Asian goods.

In the early 1300s, after the imposition of a stricter papal ban on trade with the Mamluks (1308–1344), Lajazzo became a key Christian entrepôt for merchandise from the Mamluk dominions. Until 1334 it remained the terminus of the Venetian eastbound galleys. In 1322, the Mamluks overran the port, but they gave it up again the following year. The days of Lajazzo's commercial glory were numbered, however. In 1337, it fell permanently to the Mamluks, and it declined rapidly as the weakening of the Persian il-khânid state imperiled overland trade routes. The resumption of direct Italian maritime trade with Egypt and Syria from the 1340s onward ultimately consigned Lajazzo to oblivion as a commercial port.

**BIBLIOGRAPHY**

Boase, T.S.R., ed. *The Cilician Kingdom of Armenia.* Edinburgh: Scottish Academic Press, 1978.

Der Nersessian, Sirarpie. "The Kingdom of Cilician Armenia." In *Byzantine and Armenian Studies.* Vol. 1. Louvain: Imprimerie Orientale, 1973, pp. 329–352.

Edbury, Peter W. *The Kingdom of Cyprus and the Crusades, 1191–1374.* Cambridge: Cambridge UP, 1991.

Mutafian, C. *Le royaume arménien de Cilicie, XIIe–XIVe siècles.* Paris: CNRS, 1993.

*Martin Malcolm Elbl*

**SEE ALSO**

Armenia; Baybars I; Mamluks; Marco Polo; Merchants, Italian; Muslim Travelers and Trade; Trebizond; Venice

## Lamaism

A Western term that refers to the Buddhism of Tibet as well as its offshoots in Central Asia, Mongolia, and China. While not properly reflecting the fundamental character of this tradition, the word *lamaism* does reveal the importance that it has attached to the role of religious adepts, known in Tibet as lamas (*bla-ma*), who act as guides to spiritual liberation.

The development and spread of Lamaism, which was roughly concurrent with the history of medieval Europe, was intimately tied to movements of ideas, peoples, and cultures. Tibet was surrounded by Buddhist neighbors in India, Central Asia, and China, all of whom were to exert influence. Nevertheless, the Buddhism of India ultimately played the decisive role in the formation of Tibetan Buddhism, combining the mature doctrinal and philosophical approach of Mahayana Buddhism with the esoteric ritual tradition known as Tantrism. Buddhism may well have initially filtered into Tibet through informal trade contacts between India and Tibet. The official introduction of the religion, however, took place in two separate stages that involved both Tibetan royal patronage and a considerable traffic in missionaries, students, and pilgrims. Tibetan Buddhism, in turn, was transported beyond Tibet to the peoples of Central and Inner Asia, as well as to China.

Tibet's first official encounter with Buddhism took place during the seventh and eighth centuries when the Yarlung kings were establishing the first Tibetan kingdom in the Yarlung and Tsang river valleys of southern Tibet. Militarily strong and expansionist in outlook, this Tibetan state became a power to be reckoned with by its neighbors who, in making treaties with the Tibetans, often sent their own princesses into the Tibetan court to become royal consorts. The first phase of conversion to Buddhism took place during the reign of Songtsen Gampo [Srong-brtsan-sgam-po (620–649)], when princesses from Nepal and China introduced Buddhism into the court. Consequently, Songtsen Gampo is credited with enlisting the help of Indians to translate Buddhist texts and with the creation of a Tibetan written language adapted from the Indian Gupta script.

A century later, Buddhism became a state religion under the patronage of Trisong Detsen [Khri-srong-lde-brtsan (755–797)], who is perhaps more widely acclaimed for his role in bringing two legendary figures from India. The scholar-monk Śāntaraksita, from the internationally renowned monastic university at Nālānda, and the mystic ritualist Padmasambhava, who was from Kashmir, brought to Tibet their two widely divergent approaches, the combination of which is said to have resulted in the unique nature of Tibetan Buddhism. The presence of Chinese Buddhists in the court at this time reveals not only the extensive official contacts with China, but also the undeniable formative role played by Chinese Buddhism despite its subordinate position when compared to the influence of India.

This same period, from the seventh to ninth centuries, also witnessed Tibetan expansion into Central and Inner Asia. Tibetans gained control of numerous oases along the Silk Road and border cities of China. When they eventually withdrew following the breakup of the Tibetan kingdom after 842, they left behind, in sites such as Dunhuang, an artistic record reflecting their Buddhism. Scattered communities of Tibetans continued to exert influence into the tenth century. Some of these people of Tibetan stock formed the kingdom of Western Xia (Xixia/Hsi Hsia, 982–1224),

# L

which was beholden to the Buddhism of Tibet for its religious tradition.

In the ninth century, the fledgling Buddhism of Tibet suffered persecution under King Lang-darma (Glang-dar-ma). This serious, though temporary, setback was followed by the second phase of conversion to Buddhism that was initiated by the kings of west Tibet in the tenth and eleventh centuries. The accomplishments of this renaissance were closely associated with intensive contacts between Tibet and India. The royal family sent students to study in the great monastery universities of India. Among them was the famous translator Rinchen Zangpo [Rin-chen bzang-po (958–1055)], who upon his return founded numerous monasteries and translated Tantric works. This same royal family also invited the Indian scholar Atīśa (980/90–1055) from the university of Vikramaśīla. He had a decisive influence on the development of doctrine in Tibet. Two Tibetan traveler-scholars of this period, 'Brog-mi (992–1072) and Mar-pa (1012–1096), returned as translators to Tibet after studying in Nepal and India and established their own schools of thought.

In the thirteenth century, Tibet was alone in averting devastating Mongolian invasions by subordinating itself to Chinggis Khân (c. 1167–1227). The close relationship forged between the two peoples eventually resulted in the Mongol conversion to Tibetan Buddhism. Just as had been the case in Tibet, the conversion to Tibetan Buddhism for the Mongols also took place in two phases. The first wave of conversion reached its highpoint during the reign of Khubilai Khân (r. 1260–1294), who founded the Yuan dynasty (1279–1368) in China. Khubilai took the Sakyapa [Saskya] order hierarch Phagspa ['Phags-pa (1235–1280)] as his spiritual preceptor. Besides being credited with the creation of a new Mongolian script, Phagspa was instrumental in introducing Tibetan Buddhist art and architecture to the Mongol court in Dadu (modern Beijing) by enlisting the talents of the eminent Nepalese Anige and a host of other craftsmen. Despite these initial successes, Tibetan Buddhism was confined to royal and aristocratic circles, the majority of the common people remaining faithful to traditional shamanistic practices.

It was during this first phase of conversion that the medieval emissaries and missionary travelers from the West first came in contact with the Mongols. Among these, William of Rubruck, whose journey lasted from 1253 to 1255, debated with Buddhist monks at the court of Möngke Khân (r. 1251–1259). William's description of Buddhism, the first produced by a European, does not provide an entirely clear picture as to the form of Buddhism practiced by these monks, but it suggests that lamas from the Tibetan Buddhist tradition were present at the court.

Following the Mongol expulsion from China after the fall of the Yuan dynasty, the influence of Buddhism waned for two centuries. The second conversion of the Mongols began in the sixteenth century during the rule of Altan Khân (r. 1543–1582), whose incursions into eastern Tibet brought him into contact with lamas. The ensuing relationship had a momentous impact on both cultures. For the Mongols, widespread missionary efforts throughout Mongolia brought the whole Mongol population firmly under the aegis of Tibetan Buddhism and Tibetan culture. For the Tibetans, this contact had significant ramifications for later religious and political life. Mirroring Khubilai's close relationship with Phagspa, Altan Khân in 1578 sought spiritual legitimacy for his leadership over disparate tribes by bestowing the title of Dalai (Great Ocean) on Sonam Gyatso [bSod-nams rGya-mtsho], the third head of the recently founded Gelugpa [dGe-lugs-pa] order. This official recognition aided the eventual ascendance of the Gelugpa over other Tibetan Buddhist orders and in time led to recognition of subsequent incarnations of the Dalai Lama as political rulers of Tibet.

Tibetan Buddhism also continued to have an impact on the court in China. Among the emperors of the Ming dynasty (1368–1644), Yongle [Yung-lo (r. 1403–1424)] was the most notable patron of Tibetan Buddhism. He invited numerous lamas to his court and bestowed on them lavish presents and honorific titles when they came. Since the Mongols remained a real threat, Yongle's motives in enlisting support from these religious leaders were readily apparent. The Manchus, who established the subsequent Qing [Ch'ing] dynasty (1644–1912), had been exposed to Tibetan Buddhism through their extensive relations with the Mongols. As the rulers of China they became benefactors of lamaist monasteries and translation projects while using the religion as a means to further their political objectives in Tibet and Mongolia.

## BIBLIOGRAPHY

Berger, Patricia, and Terese Tse Bartholomew. *Mongolia: The Legacy of Chinggis Khan.* San Francisco: Asian Art Museum of San Francisco, 1995.

*The Mission of Friar William of Rubruk: His Journey to the Court of the Great Khan Möngke 1253–1255.* Trans. Peter Jackson, with notes and introduction by Peter Jackson and David Morgan. Hakluyt Society, 2nd series, 173. London: Hakluyt Society, 1990.

Snellgrove, David, and Hugh Richardson. *A Cultural History of Tibet.* Boston: Shambala, 1968.

Stein, R.A. *Tibetan Civilization.* Stanford: Stanford UP, 1972.

*Daniel Getz*

**SEE ALSO**
Buddhism; India; Mongols; Silk Roads; Tibet; William of Rubruck

## Lambert of St. Omer
*See* Liber Floridus

## Langskip

Old Norse name for a war vessel, literally "long ship." Information about the *langskip* comes largely from written sources, mostly Icelandic, from the twelfth and thirteenth centuries; a few excavated remains of ships interpreted as longships also exist. The written sources indicate that the ships were fast troop transports rather than true warships. Developed naval tactics did not exist in northern Europe during the Middle Ages; sea battles were fought with ships lashed together to make fighting platforms, and the crews fought as they would on land. Warriors doubled as rowers, and the longship had oar ports along most of its length. Like all contemporaneous ships in northern Europe, they had a single mast amidships, rigged with a square sail.

Longships were of different sizes, which the sources indicate by specifying the number of rowing benches (Old Norse *sess*) any one contained. The smallest vessel mentioned that could be called a longship had thirteen seats, while the largest vessel had eighty pairs of oars, according to the sagas. It is unlikely, however, that the flexible clinker-built hulls of the Viking and early medieval periods could have been constructed on such a scale without losing their seaworthiness. For so many oars to be used efficiently, it was necessary to build the longships with a low freeboard, and archaeological finds indicate that the ships had narrow beams, evidently for speed.

Moving armed men swiftly was the primary purpose of longships, and they operated mainly in coastal

Skuldelev 2 and 4, a reconstruction of a vessel for troop transport found near Skuldelev, Denmark. 11th century. Photo by Werner Karrasch. Courtesy of The Viking Ship Museum in Roskilde.

Roskilde 6, a recent find of an exceptionally long—117 feet (36 meters)—troop transport vessel now under reconstruction. Photo by Werner Karrasch. Courtesy of The Viking Ship Museum in Roskilde.

waters. Sagas clearly indicate that these warships were less seaworthy than merchant vessels. Norway, Denmark, and Sweden were divided into levy districts that each built, maintained, and manned a longship for the king's use in war. The system is best known from the Norwegian laws, where the standard size is given as twenty benches. The king and nobility had their own ships, often of greater size.

Two wrecks of such levy ships have been tentatively identified: Skuldelev 5, found in Roskilde Fjord, Denmark, and one of the wrecks found at Fotevik in southern Sweden (Skåne). A very fragmentary vessel found at Hedeby, in northern Germany, and Skuldelev

# L

Wreck 4 are probably examples of large longships that belonged to members of the society's upper class. The Hedeby ship shows an especially high level of quality in materials and workmanship. A recent find in Roskilde, dated to the early eleventh century, is of a ship that was thirty-six meters long.

**BIBLIOGRAPHY**

Crumlin-Pedersen, O. *Pugna Forensis–? Arkeologiska undersökningar kring Foteviken, Skåne 1981–83.* Malmö: Länsstyrelsen, 1984.

Falk, Hjalmar. *Altnordisches Seewesen.* Wörter und Sachen 4. Heidelberg: Winter, 1912.

*Maritime Archaeology Newsletter from Roskilde Denmark nr. 9 December 1997.* Roskilde: The Centre for Maritime Archaeology at the National Museum, pp. 14f.

Olsen, Olaf, and Ole Crumlin-Pedersen. *Five Viking Ships from Roskilde Fjord.* Copenhagen: The National Museum, 1978.

*Arne Emil Christensen*

**SEE ALSO**

*Knarr;* Naval Warfare; Navigation; Navigation, Viking; Ships and Shipbuilding; Viking Age

## Language Instruction for Western European Travelers

Traders and travelers in the Middle Ages could use Latin throughout western Europe, but even as early as the ninth century phrasebooks and dialogue collections appear to help them speak to the classes that might not know the learned international language. The earliest example of such a European vernacular phrasebook is a ninth-century *Altdeutsche Gespräche,* by which western Franks, who spoke a Romance language, could communicate with their Germanic cousins. At the time of the great pilgrimages and of the crusades, short dialogues and word lists were composed to help Western European travelers get by in Greek, Hebrew, Arabic, and Basque.

Beginning in the thirteenth century, the expansion of the phrasebooks in various combinations of vernacular languages points to a change in linguistic practice, in which even educated people used languages other than Latin for business purposes. Henri Pirenne notes a switch from Latin to French among Flemish cloth traders early in the thirteenth century, and others have described the rise of French to the rank of an international language at this time; Marco Polo, Brunetto

Latini, and the author of the *Book of John Mandeville* appear to have chosen it so that their works could reach a wide audience. This move to the vernaculars led to the preparation of a number of vernacular language manuals—including dialogues, guides to orthography, and dictionaries—that are clearly geared toward travelers and traders. Thirteenth- and fourteenth-century examples include French-Flemish and French-English phrasebooks, manuals of orthography and grammar, and classified word lists.

Phrasebooks are represented by such works as the *Livre des Mestiers* and the *Gesprächbüchlein* (French-Flemish), and by a series of "Manières de langage" (French for English-speakers). In the fifteenth century, after German merchants and bankers established the Fondaco dei Tedeschi in Venice, Italian-German collections appear, notably those of Jörg von Nürnberg (1420s) and Adam von Rottwil (1477).

The dialogue format allows the user both to encounter vocabulary in context and to practice interactive skills. For example, the *Livre des Mestiers* presents dialogues that serve as a shell in which the author inserts the classified vocabulary lists presented in earlier *nominalia.* Its vocabulary lessons include names of familial relations, parts of the body, meats, drinks, animals, fish, and birds, before turning to the special needs of merchants: the vocabulary of the cloth trade (types of cloth, measures, and colors), and of other products sold in medieval markets (furs, hides, oil, metals, ores, and grains). The dialogues cover four fundamental interactive contexts: greetings, instructions to a maid, bargaining over the price of cloth, and asking directions.

The French dialogues produced in England in the fourteenth and fifteenth centuries are more dramatic, and less given to extensive lists of vocabulary. They add conversations on finding a room in an inn and asking about the latest news of the Hundred Years' War (1337–1453), as well as instructions on how to care for horses and how to curse highwaymen. They also include more dialogues relating to employer-employee relations, exclusively from the point of view of the employer. The English dialogue collections are found in manuscripts with guides to grammar and orthography, a combination that points to a unified syllabus for classroom use.

The Italian-German collections appear in the first quarter of the fifteenth century. Jörg von Nürnberg's text starts with bilingual lists of vocabulary similar to those found in the Flemish tradition (with the notable addition of religious terms) and continues with grammatical information (lists of verbs and their conjugations, adjectives and their comparative forms). The dialogues that follow are unilingual in German, with occasional brief comments in Italian.

In 1480, William Caxton translated the Flemish section of the *Livre des Mestiers* into English for one of his first publications, ushering in the age of printed collections. This was the beginning of a rapid expansion of language instruction materials. By the end of the fifteenth century, multilingual manuals begin to appear, exemplified by Arnold von Harff's collection of key phrases in nine languages (Croatian, Albanian, Greek, Arabic, Hebrew, Turkish, Hungarian, Basque, and Breton). This expansion formed the basis for the printing of the multilingual phrasebooks attributed to Noel de Berlaimont, which were published in hundreds of editions over the course of the sixteenth century.

**BIBLIOGRAPHY**

Bart Rossebastiano, Alda. "Antichi vocabolari plurilingui d'uso populare." *Gulden Passer* 55 (1977): 67–153.

Bischoff, Bernhard. "The Study of Foreign Languages in the Middle Ages." *Speculum* 36 (1961): 209–224.

Kibbee, Douglas A. *For to Speke Frenche Trewely: The French Language in England, 1000–1600: Its Status, Description, and Instruction.* Amsterdam/Philadelphia: John Benjamins, 1991.

Pirenne, Henri. "L'instruction des marchands au Moyen Age." *Annales d'Histoire Économique et Sociale* 1 (1929): 13–28.

Douglas A. Kibbee

**SEE ALSO**

Brunetto Latini; Caxton, William; *Fondaco;* Lull, Ramon; *Mandeville's Travels;* Marco Polo

## Lannoy, Ghillebert de (1386–1462)

An inveterate traveler connected to the court of the Valois dukes of Burgundy, especially to that of the longest reigning duke, Philip the Good (1396–1467). A soldier and a founding member of the knightly Order of the Golden Fleece in 1430, Ghillebert de Lannoy was also a pilgrim to the Holy Land and at once a spy, an ambassador, a diplomat, a geographer of sorts, and an author of moral-didactic work. His life and accomplishments reveal a sharp practical eye and his master's political shrewdness, as well as religious fervor and wonder at the sights of the world.

Lannoy has left us an autobiographical account of his exploits and adventures entitled *Le voyaiges que fist Messire*

*Ghillebert de Lannoy, en son temps Seigneur de Sanctes, de Willerval, de Tronchiennes et de Wahgnies,* often known as merely *Voyages et ambassades, 1399–1450.* In vivid prose he details his life from his participation in the French assault on the Isle of Wight in 1403 to his journey to Rome in connection with the Jubilee of 1450. As a young man in 1405–1406 he made a first pilgrimage to Jerusalem for obviously religious reasons, terming it "le saint voyaige de Jherusalem." After his return, Lannoy fought the Moors in Spain, took part in the Armagnac struggles in France, and, in 1413, joined the crusade "pour aller en Prusse contre les mescrans." This voyage took him to Prussia and the Baltic states via Friesland, Denmark, Sweden, and Poland. He was knighted at the battle of Massow (near Szczecin [German Stettin]) and returned to France by way of Poland, Bohemia, and Austria.

Duke John the Fearless then made use of Lannoy's skills in various capacities, naming him governor of the

Fortification of Jaffa. Vienna, Österreichische Nationalbibliothek MS 2533, fol. 17r, 14th century. Courtesy Österreichische Nationalbibliothek.

# L

town of Ecluse and ambassador to England on the occasion of the marriage of King Henry V to Catherine of France. Crusading fervor was running high in Burgundy, France, and England, and in 1421, Lannoy was sent to the Near East to study the geographical and political conditions in view of mounting a European crusade to liberate Jerusalem. His route was long and arduous: through northern Germany, Prussia, Poland, Russia, Moldavia, Wallachia, Tataria, and Crimea to Constantinople. From Constantinople he sailed to Rhodes where Lannoy left all his men behind except for three, "pour parfaire plus discrètement mes visitations" in the Holy Land; he then voyaged to Crete, Alexandria, Rosetta, and Cairo.

From his accounts it is clear that this masterful traveler and teller of tales is also a devout, at times gullible, Christian. He adds to his *Voyaiges* a list of all the indulgences he has earned by visiting the various holy places. This list contrasts markedly with his itemizing of the military and geographical conditions of cities he has examined. Departing Cairo, Lannoy visits the desert and proceeds to St. Catherine's monastery in the Sinai, which he had seen previously in 1405–1406. Here again, his perceptions are those of both military engineer and pilgrim: "And there is the church of Saint Catherine built in the way of a strong castle, squarely fortified; and in its three chapels are represented the three laws of Jesus Christ, Moses, and Muhammed. In ours they display the bones of the greater part of Saint Catherine's body." Lannoy then traveled via Damietta to Jerusalem "and to the places pilgrims usually visit." He voyaged home to Burgundy by way of Rhodes, Venice, and Germany where, near the French border, he was arrested by Albert, the Bastard of Lorraine (an illegitimate noble of considerable political power), but freed again by Antoine, the count of Vaudémont.

The crusade never came about, but Philip the Good was able to use the services of this versatile traveler, appointing him to the captaincy of Rotterdam for the organization of the naval defense of Flanders, and sending him with embassies to Scotland, Ireland, and the Council of Basel (1433). Lannoy was part of the famous European Peace Congress of Arras in 1435. In the middle of the 1440s Philip the Good revived the idea of a crusade. To that end Lannoy was sent to King Alfonso V of Naples. Immediately thereafter he made a third journey to Jerusalem, this time following a sea route: Naples, Messina, Stromboli, Morea, Crete, Rhodes, Cyprus, Jaffa, and Jerusalem. At each stop, visits were made to the local authorities to test their willingness to take part in a crusade. Returning through the Aegean Islands up the west coast of Greece, Lannoy visited Naxos and Corfu, and, later, Venice. He then went overland through Austria and Germany until he returned to Philip's court.

After 1450, Lannoy continued in ducal service, but little is known about his final years. Lannoy is the author of the *Instruction d'un jeune prince* (c. 1440), a Burgundian "mirror for princes." He also wrote the *Enseignements paternels,* advice to his son on how to live and behave like a true and gentle knight: "marry well, serve your prince, do your duty in battle." Lannoy's motto was "Vostre plaisir" ("At your service").

**BIBLIOGRAPHY**

*Les Chevaliers de l'Ordre de la Toison d'or au XVe siècle.* Ed. R. de Smedt. Frankfurt-am-Main: Lang, 1994, pp. 42–45.
*Œuvres de Ghillebert de Lannoy, voyageur, diplomate et moraliste.* Ed. Charles Potvin. Louvain: Lefever, 1878.

*A.J. Vanderjagt*

SEE ALSO

Ambassadors; Catherine in the Sinai, Monastery of St.; Crusades, Burgundian; Diplomacy; Egypt; Holy Land; Jerusalem; John the Fearless, Funeral Cortege of; Military Orders; Poland; Rome as a Pilgrimage Site; Spies; Venice

## Las Casas, Bartolomé de (1474–1566)

A Franciscan missionary to the New World and author of ground breaking descriptions and arguments concerning native peoples in the Americas.

In a life spanning ninety-two years and encompassing repeated travel between the Old World and the New, Bartolomé de Las Casas passed through a succession of careers and vocations. Born in Seville (1474) to an adventurer and colonist who accompanied Columbus on his second voyage, nephew to other colonists, Las Casas received a sound education, was ordained a priest, and then sailed to the New World himself at age twenty-seven. There he served as chaplain, *doctrinero* (an aggressive missionary teacher to the peoples of the New World), landowner, farmer, and trader. In 1514, he decided, however, to give up these potentially profitable occupations, and in 1520, he set about organizing a quasi-utopian community of Europeans and Indians in Cumana (off the coast of Venezuela). When a series of massacres doomed this experiment, Las Casas entered the Dominican order; for some four years (1522–1526) he remained a recluse at Santo Domingo, studying canon law and theology, mainly through the writings of the order's great thinker Thomas Aquinas.

After emerging as chaplain and missionary for other settlements on the island, he assumed the role of spokesperson and political activist on behalf of peoples in the New World, intervening with the colonial authorities and writing memoranda and treatises; he became notorious among his opponents for maintaining a large entourage, who carried his theological and archival sources wherever he visited in the New World. Over the course of decades he several times traveled back to the Old World to plead with bishops, ecclesiastical and secular authorities (including the emperor's officials), and the Curia at Rome. In 1544, he became bishop of Chiapas in Mexico, though he later resigned from the see (1547). He returned to Spain to argue and write on the Indians' cause, and to take part in the celebrated dispute with Sepulveda (1550) concerning the rights and status of the peoples of the New World. He died in Madrid (1566), a controversial figure among Europeans but even on his deathbed the champion of native peoples.

In his various activities, and especially in his writings, Las Casas is often represented as a lone voice, eccentric in his thought and without significant precedent in his advocacy of the Indians' stature as human beings with natural rights. The difficulty in defining a historical context for Las Casas's thought arises in large part from the fact that his writings on newly encountered peoples bridge two worlds and two periods of history, the late Middle Ages and the Age of Discovery. The contradictions and the continuities that mark these separate hemispheres, competing worldviews, and successive historical periods insistently mold his writings. For example, Las Casas has often been regarded—by his contemporaries and by modern scholars—on the one hand as a radically innovative thinker who wished to overthrow established powers and colonialist interests, or, on the other hand, as deeply conservative in his support of the Spanish Empire and the exploitation of the New World; likewise, the anomalous features of his thought have sometimes been seen as emanating from the increasing influence of Aristotle in Renaissance thought, and other times as the idealistic fulminations of an academic throwback.

In Las Casas's writings, a welter of concrete detail about indigenous culture and relations between Indians and Europeans is filtered through a clear and distinctive conceptual framework. He seems, almost from his first months in the New World, to have made a written record of what he witnessed, and he drew upon and recycled these vivid experiences in the treatises he produced to the end of his life. Only after his period of study as a new friar, however, did he possess the framework that allowed him to turn these empirical facts into a recognizable anthropology. In his most scholastic work, the *Defense,* Las Casas provides rich details on the social, political, and religious cultures of the Indians; yet, whether he is addressing issues such as conquest and just war, governance and slavery, or land ownership, all of these particulars work in service of constituting an autonomous human stature for the Indians.

Las Casas's unshakable conviction of the Indians' natural human rights—and the injustice of European tyranny—stems directly from arguments and standards associated with medieval intellectual traditions. Las Casas's invocation of a universal natural law that informs all human beings as moral and political creatures, and that makes pagans and Christians equal on earth, reflects the first canon in Gratian's twelfth-century *Decretum,* and the elaborate commentary on it by generations of medieval lawyers. Las Casas's insistence on the full humanity of Indians—based upon their inherent capacity for moral reasoning and language—and their consequent equality with all other humans, including the Spanish, is likewise based upon settled premises of a characteristic medieval anthropology. In his systematic theology, Thomas consolidated the views of earlier thinkers on the ways in which nature ensures the moral sameness of all humankind, and the fourteenth- and fifteenth-century writers whom Las Casas studied confirmed and elaborated these positions.

In deploying a medieval anthropology to make sense of the New World and its peoples, Las Casas was participating in a wider revival of scholastic thought that occurred in Iberia in the fifteenth century (Carro). A glance at the citations in the *Defense* clarifies the profoundly medieval character of Las Casas's ethnographic descriptions: although he repeatedly quotes from Scripture and the Church Fathers, by far his most frequent and trusted authority is Gratian and the accumulated commentaries on the canon law. Moreover, the citations of Thomas far outnumber those of Aristotle, and, where the latter is cited, the location often plainly depends upon its earlier presence in Thomas. Knowledge of these immediate sources demonstrates

# L

that Las Casas's thought was not in itself anomalous, but in fact highly conventional; its potentially radical import stems from his fierce determination that the axioms of medieval moral philosophy and anthropology should apply unswervingly to the newly encountered peoples in the Western Hemisphere. The relatively recent tendency to explain Las Casas in terms of ancient thought or Renaissance revivals of Aristotle (Hanke), or even to dismiss him as bookishly out of touch (Pagden), seriously mistakes the ways in which his writings systematically comprehend the realities of the New World through established frameworks from Europe.

## BIBLIOGRAPHY

Carro, Vanancio D. "The Spanish Theological-Juridical Renaissance and the Ideology of Bartolomé de Las Casas." In Friede and Keen [below], pp. 237–277.

Fernández, Manuel Giménez. "Fray Bartolomé de Las Casas: A Biographical Sketch." In Friede and Keen [below], pp. 67–125.

Friede, Juan, and Benjamin Keen, eds. *Bartolomé de Las Casas in History: Toward an Understanding of the Man and His Work.* DeKalb: Northern Illinois UP, 1971.

Hanke, Lewis. *Aristotle and the American Indians: A Study in Race Prejudice in the Modern World.* Bloomington, IN, and London: Indiana UP, 1959.

———. *All Mankind Is One.* DeKalb: Northern Illinois UP, 1974.

Las Casas, Bartolomé de. *In Defense of the Indians.* Trans. C.M. Stafford Poole. DeKalb: Northern Illinois UP, 1992.

Lottin, Odon. *Le droit naturel chez S. Thomas d'Aquin et ses prédécesseurs.* 2nd edition. Paris: Dillon, 1931.

Pagden, Anthony. *The Fall of Natural Man.* Cambridge: Cambridge UP, 1982.

Rabasa, José. *Inventing America: Spanish Historiography and the Formation of Eurocentrism.* Norman: U of Oklahoma P, 1993.

*Thomas G. Hahn*

## SEE ALSO

Canon Law and Subject Peoples; Columbus, Christopher; Franciscan Friars; Indians and the Americas; New World

## Law, Canon, and Subject Peoples

*See* Canon Law and Subject Peoples

## Law, Commercial [*Lex Mercatoria*]

A customary law quilted from the many legal traditions that affected southern Europe from the Roman period forward. A large part of what we would term commercial law relates to the law of contracts.

After the recovery of Roman law beginning in the eleventh century, first in Italy and then spreading westward in Mediterranean Europe, the use of legal terminology of Roman law origin and the presence and function of legal personnel, including lawyers, scholarly jurists, and notaries, underwent considerable development during the twelfth century. The acts written by notaries were considered legal proof of contractual obligations by the thirteenth century. Notarial acts abounded with formulas inspired by Roman law actions, meant to protect the debtor against overly aggressive action by the creditor. Roman law renunciations, of which Peter Riesenberg and John Pryor both assert the real significance in contract law, included the *exceptio non numeratae pecuniae,* which protected the debtor against a claim by his creditor for restitution in a situation where the debtor had made a recognition of debt prior to receipt of the full funds. Women enjoyed greater ability to engage in business through contracts as a result of the renunciation of the *Senatusconsultum Velleianum,* which had restricted women's ability to assume legal liability for others.

The Middle Ages witnessed the elaboration of sophisticated business techniques in the area of trade and finance. Commercial contracts included partnership techniques, such as the *commenda,* the maritime *societas,* and the *societas terrae;* financial arrangements such as the money exchange contract, the *mutuum* loan, and the sea loan; and, of course, cash and credit sales, stemming from the *emptio venditio* concept of purchase and sale in Roman law.

Commercial law was centered in towns, the essence of which included a market function. The law of markets had its origins again in Roman tradition. Urban tenure by definition was free tenure, variously termed *bourgage* (Normandy), burgage tenure (England), *Weichbild* (northern Germany), and *Burgrecht* (southern Germany). Urban tenure differed from manorial tenure in that it was more easily alienable and carried far lighter obligations. Market law (*Marktrecht*) and the law of strangers (*ius forense*) were urban based. Since matters of concern to merchants were often quite distant from those of feudal, manorial, and royal courts, special courts (the *sceaux rigoreux* in France and piepowder courts in the north) developed to accommodate the faster pace and unique needs of medieval business by dispensing justice rapidly and locally to itinerant merchants and others only temporarily present in a given location. In some municipalities, debtors faced such severe penalties as imprisonment on a diet of bread and water, and seizure and forced sale of their goods at auction.

Special jurisdiction regulated medieval fairs, of which those in Champagne were the most spectacular with their cycle of six fairs spread throughout the year and held in the fair towns of Troyes, Provins, Bar-sur-Aube, and Lagny-sur-Marne. Established under the sponsorship of the counts of Champagne and local religious establishments, their respective courts acted primarily as the venue for disputes between merchants. However, as the fairs expanded in the thirteenth century, the jurisdiction of the wardens became more significant in the enforcement of fair contracts sealed officially with the warden's seal or recorded in the fair registers. Jurisdiction was limited to persons frequenting the fairs. Justice was harsh and rapid; some of the normal protections of the law were eliminated, such as the right to delay a trial or claim that a particular tribunal was incompetent to try the case. The count's court and later the Parlement, when the king of France controlled Champagne after 1285, acted as courts of appeal. Evidence admitted in court included the battle duel, but also witnessed proof, written oaths, the letters of the fairs or those contracts sealed with the fairs' seals, and the fair registers themselves.

In the case of fugitives from fair justice, the warden sent a requisition to the foreign jurisdiction to which the offender was adjudicable, directing the seizure of his goods and their public sale, with the proceeds going to make good on his debts. The fair's jurisdiction was to take precedence over other debts pending, and seisin was guaranteed to the new owners. The foreign jurisdiction was instructed to respond to these requests. If the goods of the fugitive were not of sufficient value, extradition of the guilty party was demanded. Fair sergeants were often sent out to report on the actions of the foreign justice. These procedures invited conflicts between the urban tribunals to which merchants were beholden and the fair warden's justice. Meetings to settle disagreements and, at times, arbitration often decided a case. As a last resort, the fair warden could prohibit attendance at the fairs for the compatriots of the offending party, in the tradition of the law of marque.

More generally, the law of marque functioned in commercial and maritime disputes, in matters of piracy and debt, providing merchants with a means of pressure and reprisal against pirates or defaulting parties. The plaintiffs' home jurisdictions would declare the goods of compatriots of the offenders forfeit to reimburse the wronged plaintiffs. Sovereigns also imposed such sanctions, causing reprisals to evolve, at times, into acts of war, rather than matters of jurisdiction.

Medieval municipal jurisdictions policed commercial transactions and engaged in quality control of local products in the interest of consumer protection and of the good name of a town and its specialties. Enshrined in medieval jurisprudence was the concept of *Fraus omnia corrumpit* (fraud corrupts everything). Commercial fraud was a serious offense. Here, at the heart of the matter, as in the offenses described above, was the issue of loss of trust. Medieval commerce was based on trust and faith in the reliability of business engagements and the honesty of merchants.

## BIBLIOGRAPHY

Bautier, Robert-Henri. "Les foires de Champagne: Recherches sur une évolution historique." *Recueils de la Société Jean Bodin* 5 [*La foire*] (1953): 97–148.

Berman, Harold J. *Law and Revolution: The Formation of the Western Legal Tradition.* Cambridge, MA: Harvard UP, 1983.

Cheyette, Fredric L. "The Sovereign and the Pirates, 1332." *Speculum* 45 (1970): 40–68.

Huvelin, Paul. *Essai historique sur le droit des marchés des foires.* Paris: Rousseau, 1897.

Lopez, Robert S. "Italian Leadership in the Medieval Business World." *Journal of Economic History* 7 (1948): 63–68.

Pryor, John H. *Business Contracts of Medieval Provence. Selected Notulae from the Cartulary of Giraud Amalric of Marseilles: 1248.* Toronto: Pontifical Institute of Medieval Studies, 1981.

Reyerson, Kathryn L. "Commercial Fraud in the Middle Ages: The Case of the Dissembling Pepperer." *Journal of Medieval History* 8 (1982): 63–73.

Riesenberg, Peter. "Roman Law, Renunciations and Business in the Twelfth and Thirteenth Centuries." *Essays in Medieval Life and Thought Presented in Honor of Austin P. Evans.* Ed. John H. Mundy. New York: Columbia UP, 1955, pp. 207–225.

*Kathryn L. Reyerson*

## SEE ALSO

Fairs; Insurance; Law, Maritime; Law of Marque; Notaries; Piracy; Shipping Contracts, Mediterranean

# L

## Law, Maritime

One of the more striking legal innovations during the Middle Ages was the development and refinement of maritime laws. Unlike terrestrial laws, which often had a distinctly regional flavor, maritime laws had a remarkable uniformity throughout the Christian and Muslim worlds. More important, many of the basic concepts that underpin modern maritime laws were developed during the Middle Ages.

The uniformity of medieval maritime law found throughout the Mediterranean was due in large part to the wide dissemination of Rhodian sea law, the *Lex Rhodia,* by the Byzantine Empire. The exact origin of the *Lex Rhodia* has been lost, but it appears to have evolved from Phoenician and Greek maritime customs. An early reference to the code comes from a maritime case argued by Cicero (106–43 B.C.E.) in which he quoted the Rhodian law directly. The earliest written examples are two thirteenth-century copies of a body of Byzantine law called the *Basilica,* which was a reorganization of the codes of Justinian, first promulgated between 529 and 535. Evidence suggests that Rhodian sea law had been absorbed into Byzantine law by the sixth century and was then spread to virtually every seaport on the Mediterranean and Black Sea.

Much of modern sea law devolved directly from the *Lex Rhodia.* For example, its concepts of jettison and contribution have remained virtually unchanged to this day. These concepts, frequently called averaging, stipulate that if cargo or parts of the ship, such as the masts, have to be jettisoned in order to save the vessel, then all persons onboard will "contribute" on a pro rata basis to pay for the losses incurred by the merchants or shipowners who were required to jettison their property. Bottomry, another concept recognized in the *Lex Rhodia,* was in use into the twentieth century until it was made obsolete by modern communications. Bottomry allowed the captain to use the ship as security for obtaining a loan in a foreign port in order to undertake repairs or replace vital equipment. Likewise, the modern rules concerning the valuables of passengers and reimbursement for their loss are identical to those found in the *Lex Rhodia.*

The *Lex Rhodia* also formed the basis for a number of medieval laws. The laws specifying the space to be allotted to various types of passengers, including pilgrims, were copied verbatim by cities, such as Venice, from this law code, as well as the requirement that the *patronus* of a ship consult knowledgeable passengers when considering important decisions concerning the vessel. The Byzantine codes would also be adopted by Muslims as they expanded into the Mediterranean. The Muslims, initially lacking a strong maritime tradition, found in these laws an important underpinning for the explosion of Muslim trade, using them, along with local port laws, with little alteration, except where they conflicted with the *sharī'a* (Islamic sacred law).

While much of the international character of medieval maritime law can be traced to the *Lex Rhodia,* the need for shipowners and merchants to have a consistent body of laws, regardless of which port they put into, was also influential. Since maritime agreements were more often than not between cities rather than states, having a body of laws that was generally consistent, despite the location, was simply good business in that it lessened the likelihood of disputes erupting between the various cities, caused by differing views of correct maritime law. For this reason, cities often copied the laws of others that they deemed appropriate. This habit of adopting other maritime laws, along with the shared Roman and Byzantine heritage, resulted in a distinct commonality among the various corpora of maritime law throughout the Mediterranean.

Regardless of the location, medieval maritime laws shared virtually the same structure and could be generalized into sections including: the rights and responsibilities between the shareholders in a particular vessel and the principal owner, or *patronus,* and their relation to the merchants and passengers; statements concerning the hazards of a maritime venture, the risk that each partner was assuming in such a venture, and the requirement that any binding agreement had to be written and not simply oral; the duties of the *patronus* with regard to the crew and the crew's rights in relation to the owner; responsibilities and obligations concerning shipwreck, piracy, and salvage; penalties for the theft of vital ship equipment, such as anchors or rudders, which might imperil the vessel; the responsibilities of a pilot in guiding a vessel into waters unfamiliar to the master; requirement of an oath by all on board to support one another and the ship until termination of the voyage; the principal of contribution, or the obligation of all on board to participate in the saving of the vessel in a crisis. This last section also covered the reimbursement by all on board of those whose property was lost due to jettison, water damage, or piracy, in an effort to save the ship.

Among the earliest medieval maritime law codes are the laws of Amalfi, often called the *Tabula Amalfitana,* dated 1010. These laws were followed closely by a similar body of law codified by the city of Trani in 1063. Similar codes followed in Pisa, Genoa, Venice, and Marseilles. The medieval maritime laws that developed during this period were important, for they represented a distinct modification of the *Lex Rhodia,* particularly in the area of averaging. Many of the laws that developed in the western Mediterranean during the tenth and eleventh centuries would be introduced to the Levant during the crusades with the establishment of the *fondacos* there by the various city-states. Evidence suggests that these laws influenced the assizes of Jerusalem and, in turn, were brought back to France in the twelfth century to form the basis for the Rolls of Oléron.

Rolls of Oléron developed out of Mediterranean laws and local customs during the twelfth century and were formally codified under Louis IX (r. 1226–1270). The Rolls of Oléron marked an important stage in maritime law, for while they initially evolved to meet the needs of the French wine trade, they came to form the basis for all maritime law in the North Sea and the Atlantic. These laws were rapidly adopted by London and Bristol and were written into the Black Book of the Admiralty by the middle of the fourteenth century. The Rolls of Oléron also spread to Flanders and were later incorporated into the maritime laws of Lübeck, Hamburg, and other North Sea towns. The Hanseatic maritime code would evolve out of a combination of these city codes and the Rolls of Oléron during the fifteenth century.

Another code that contributed to maritime law was that of Wisby [Visby] on the island of Gotland. This town had been an important trading center since the Neolithic period, and its laws, codified in the thirteenth century, are a conglomeration of Norse custom, the Rolls of Oléron, and the sea laws of Lübeck. While the laws of Wisby were not a major departure from previous medieval maritime law, they did introduce a unique concept that is still in use today, that of the load line. Initially, it was simply a single line on the hull marking the maximum point to which the vessel could be allowed to settle as a result of loading cargo. It was quickly adopted as a simple method to deter unscrupulous shipowners from endangering the ship by overburdening it with cargo.

One of the most influential corpora of maritime laws, besides the Rolls of Oléron, to develop was the *Llibre del Consulat del Mar,* commonly referred to as the *Consulat del Mar* or Consulate of the Sea. Major elements of the *Consulat del Mar* can be traced directly to the *Ordenanzas de Ribera* of 1258, promulgated by Jaime I of Aragon (r. 1213–1276). This collection of laws was redacted between 1270 and 1280 in Barcelona to create the *Custums de la Mar,* which would form the basis of the final redaction entitled *Consulat del Mar,* published in 1370. By 1435, it had been included in the Ordinances of the Councilmen of Barcelona and appeared in printed form in 1494. This law code marks a definite expansion of medieval maritime law, particularly in the areas of marine insurance and marine commercial law.

The influence of the *Llibre del Consolat del Mar* on maritime law of the late Middle Ages cannot be overestimated. By the late fifteenth and early sixteenth centuries, this body of law had been translated from Catalan into several languages and adopted throughout Italy. Sections of the code would later be incorporated in the maritime codes drawn up by Louis XIV (r. 1643–1715), and the work was still being translated and used throughout Europe well into the eighteenth century. Not only was it highly influential in the development of maritime law in northern Europe as well as the Mediterranean, but it spread to the New World and Asia with the expansion of the Spanish Empire.

Maritime law represents one of the major contributions of medieval culture to the modern world. The important concepts of bottomry, averaging, and the load line have come down to the present day virtually unchanged since their introduction in the eleventh and twelfth centuries. The basic distinctions between property at sea and on land, and the limitations on the liability of various parties involved in shipping, which underpin modern international maritime law, can be traced directly to developments that took place during the Middle Ages. That so much of medieval sea law has continued in use is a testament not only to the clarity of those laws, but also to the fact that, despite numerous technological advances, the hazards and fundamental requirements of seafaring have changed little, if at all.

**BIBLIOGRAPHY**

Ashburner, Walter. *The Rhodian Sea Law.* Oxford: Clarendon Press, 1909.

De Capmany, Antonio, et al. *Libro del Consulado del Mar.* Barcelona: Cámara Oficial de Comercio y Navegación de Barcelona, 1965.

# L

Jados, Stanley. *Consulate of the Sea and Related Documents.* University [Tuscaloosa]: U of Alabama P, 1975.

McFee, William. *The Law of the Sea.* New York: Lippincott, 1950.

Pardessus, J.-M. *Collection de lois maritimes antérieures au XVIIIe.* Turin: B. d'Erasmo, 1960.

Sanborn, Frederic. *Origins of the Early English Maritime and Commercial Law.* New York: American Historical Association, 1930.

*Lawrence V. Mott*

**SEE ALSO**

Amalfi; Barcelona; *Fondaco;* Genoa; Hanse, The; Insurance; Law, Commercial; Law of Marque; Louis IX; Shipping Contracts, Mediterranean; Venice

## Law of Marque

An international system of dealing with grievances, through which letters of *marque* (*marcharum*) or *reprisal* (*represaliarum*) authorized their possessor(s) to seize property owned by citizens or subjects of a territorial state or civic polity in retaliation for that polity's failure to furnish "justice," in the form of restitution, for a previous injury inflicted by its subjects or citizens (*fatica justiciae*).

From the ninth century until the decline of reprisal during the nineteenth century, Western Europeans active in commerce particularly sought letters of marque to legitimate forays against the compatriots of foreign corsairs or pirates, rendering the license to exercise reprisal legally proximate to the authorization to voyage "for the purpose of corsairing or privateering" (in Latin, *ad cursum*). Reprisal was also invoked as a remedy in cases of foreign robbery, abduction, and commercial disputes over breach of contract and delinquent debt. The range of grievances to which letters of marque could be applied reflected reprisal's mixed origins as a legal institution in the Germanic feud, or *faida,* and the classical practices of *androlephia* (the retaliatory detainment of persons) and *pignoratio* (the Roman practice of seizing property from a delinquent debtor or his guarantors). During their heyday between the twelfth and sixteenth centuries, letters of marque at once afforded Western European polities with a means to contain disputes between allies and to unleash limited war against enemies. By the seventeenth century, the term *letter of Marque* would acquire a new significance, referring to the authorization granted a privateer to attack and seize enemy shipping and contraband cargo. The operation of reprisal was thus closely tied to the evolution of naval warfare in the modern sense, international law, and the sovereign territorial state.

The procedure by which letters of marque were adjudicated and awarded, remarkably uniform throughout Western Europe, may be reconstructed from the evidence of treaties (beginning with the earliest reference to *pignoratio* in an accord between Venice and Lothair I in 840), statutes (beginning with legislation from Novara, dating to 1231), and letters of marque, most dating to the period after 1240, preserved in European archival fonts. The typical request for reprisal was presented before judicial officers within an aggrieved party's native realm or municipality after initial requests for restitution were unsuccessful. In the crown of Catalonia-Aragon, complaints were proffered before the royal curia; in France, before municipal seneschals and the *Parlement* of Paris; in Genoa and Florence, before an office of commerce, or *Officium Mercantie;* in England, before the Court of Admiralty. Petitions generally included a detailed summary of the incident or grievance that had occasioned the plaintiff's demand for restitution, together with an itemized inventory of damages claimed. By the fourteenth century, domestic bureaus began by investigating claims. Approved petitions were then presented before the offender's governing authority by an ambassador of the plaintiff's government. A letter of marque was awarded to the plaintiff by his sovereign or civic ruler if restitution failed to materialize in response to a number of these requests (usually three) within a preappointed time, usually between six and eighteen months. In England, "letters of request" were issued under the royal privy seal, "letters of marque" under the great seal of the English crown.

Although the fifty-second novel of the *Corpus Iuris Civilis,* compiled under the Byzantine emperor Justinian (r. 527–565), had condemned *pignoratio,* medieval jurists such as Joannes Andreas (d. 1348), Bartolus de Saxoferrato (d. 1357), and Giovanni da Legnano (d. 1383) sanctioned reprisal as the legitimate—albeit odious—prerogative of any sovereign authority. The volume of extant juridic and archival evidence for reprisal appears to indicate that medieval sovereigns and civic heads valued letters of marque both as diplomatic weapons and as sources of domestic revenue. Vernacular proscriptive texts such as Honoré Bonet' s *Arbre des batailles* (composed 1387), Philippe de Mézières' *Le songe de vieil pelèrin* (composed 1388–1389), and

Christine de Pisan's *Les faits d'armes* (composed 1408–1409), were nonetheless critical of the way in which reprisal imposed collective penalties and jeopardized commerce.

A dearth of references to the actual operation of reprisal in contemporaneous histories suggests that lay misgivings may have substantively affected the administration of reprisal by the late thirteenth century. Treaties ratified after 1140 typically suspended all current reprisals between ratifying parties. By the mid-thirteenth century, additional restrictions, such as the establishment of mandatory arbitration councils, or the imposition of "grace" periods before new reprisals could go into effect, were also being imposed. Legislation promulgated in Venice and elsewhere exempted foodstuffs from seizure after 1262. By the mid-fourteenth century, letters of marque in Genoa, France, and the kingdom of Catalonia-Aragon were often rendered functionally useless by concurrent awards of safe-conduct to vulnerable foreign merchants and lengthy suspensions of often more than a year. Fifteenth-century Genoese and Venetian legislation, denouncing the injustice of collective judgments, restricted reprisal further, invoking the imperative to protect trade as a rationale. A few merchants appear to have chafed under these restrictions, however. Fourteenth-century Aragonese records, in particular, document the prosecution of individual merchants for the invalid exercise of marque notwithstanding current suspensions.

## BIBLIOGRAPHY

Bartolus de Saxoferrato. "Tractatus Repraesaliarum." In *Consilia quaestiones et tractatus Doctores Bartolicum annotationibus Doctores Bernardi Landriani in quibus nihil praeter jussum quod Thomas Diplovatatius observabit et nunc diligentiori cura quam antea illustravit.* Louvain, 1552, fols. 125r–131r.

Cassandro, Giovanni Italo. *Le rappresaglie e il fallimento a Venezia nei secoli XIII–XVI.* Documenti e studi per la storia del commercio e del diritto commerciale italiano, 14. Turin: Bottega d'Erasmo, 1970.

Giovanni da Legnano. *Tractatus de bello, de repraesaliis et de duello.* Ed. and trans. Thomas Erskine Holland. Oxford: Oxford UP, 1917.

Mas Latrie, M. René de. *Du droit de marque ou droit de represailles au Moyen-Age suivi de pièces justificatives.* Paris: Bau Librairie, 1875.

Timbal, Pierre-Clement. "Les lettres de marque dans le droit de la France médiévale." In *Recueils de la Société Jean Bodin. Tome 10: L'Etranger,* 2: 109–138. Brussels: Editions de la Librairie encyclopédique, 1958.

del Vecchio, A., and E. Casanova. *Le rappresaglie nei comuni medievalie e specialmente in Firenze.* Bologna: Nicòla Zanichelli, 1894.

*Emily Sohmer Tai*

**SEE ALSO**
Genoa; Law, Commercial; Law, Maritime; Naval Warfare; Philippe de Mézières; Piracy; Venice

## Law, Shipping Contracts, Mediterranean
*See* Shipping Contracts, Mediterranean

## Liber Floridus

Elaborately illustrated encyclopedia compiled between 1112 and 1121 by Lambert, canon of the house of St. Omer in northern France (Artois), and containing a number of different maps of the earth and the heavens. The title, which literally means "book of flowers," comes from the medieval idea of the high points in an author's work imagined as "flowers," which a later writer can collect in a *florilegium* or compilation of extracts.

The autograph manuscript of Lambert's *Liber* is conserved today in Ghent (Bibliotheek der Rijksuniversiteit MS 92). Early copies, dating from the twelfth through the fifteenth centuries, are to be found in Wolfenbüttel (Herzog August Bibliothek, MS Codex Guelf, 1 Gud. Lat. [cat 4305]) and eight other locations. The Ghent autograph contains a table of contents with page numbers that does not, however, precisely correspond to the contents of the manuscript as we have it today. Albert Derolez's codicological study has revealed thirteen stages of composition that led to the manuscript's present form (the table of contents reflects Lambert's work up to 1115).

The text of the Ghent manuscript includes such items as biblical and secular chronologies, often organized according to the standard schemata of the Ages of Man; tracts against the Jews by Odo of Cambrai and Gilbert Crispin; word lists in Latin, Greek, and Hebrew; an herbal and a bestiary; and portions of geographical treatises by Macrobius and Isidore of Seville.

Sixty colored miniatures illustrate biblical, scientific, and historical subjects, including Antichrist, Noah's ark, Ecclesia and Synagoga, lunar and solar orbits, palm trees, fig leaves, the lion and the porcupine, Alexander the Great on horseback, the emperor Octavian enthroned, the Monastery of St. Omer with its saintly

**L**

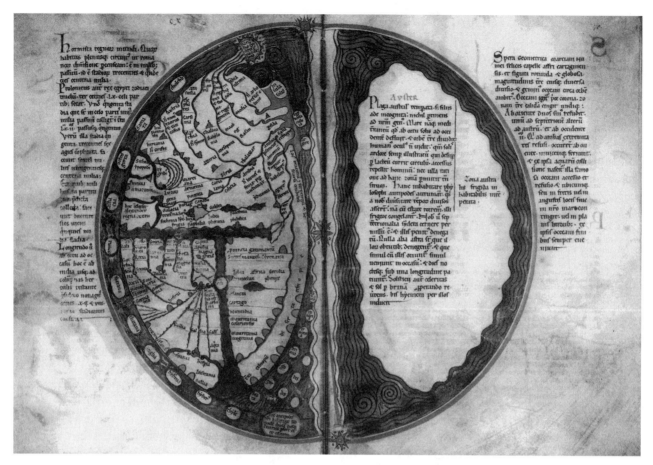

*Liber Floridus.* Hemispherical World Map. Wolfenbüttel, Herzog August Bibliothek MS 1 Gud. lat., fols. 69v–70, 1115/1180. By permission of the Herzog August Bibliothek, Wolfenbüttel.

patron, and Lambert at his writing desk. Among the best-known illustrations is the double-page *mappamundi,* one of at least twenty map images in the Ghent manuscript alone. Although the Wolfenbüttel Macrobian zonal or climate map is the one most often reproduced in modern studies of geography, the Ghent world map most clearly illustrates Lambert's ingenuity in utilizing whatever materials he had at hand. At various times, this meant patching or reusing old folios, interpolating odd pieces of vellum to increase the size of a page, or introducing recent information, such as that on the production of iron, into his encyclopedia during the decade-long course of his project.

Little is known of Lambert, though in addition to the conventional author portrait, the Ghent manuscript also records his personal family tree. Lambert prefaces the work with a dedication to the glory of God, since his compilation is aimed at comprehending the variety and diversity of all creation.

**BIBLIOGRAPHY**

Derolez, Albert. *Liber floridus colloquium.* Ghent: Story-Scientia, 1973.

———. "Lambert van Sint-Omaars als kartograf." In *De Franse Nederlanden, Les Pays-Bas Français.* Rekkem: Belgium: Stichting Ons Erfdeel, 1976, pp. 14–30.

———. *Lambertus qui librum fecit: Ein Codicologische Studie van de Liber Floridus-Autograaf.* Brussels: Palais der Academien, 1978.

*Lamberti S. Audomari Canonici liber floridus codex autographus Bibliothecae Universitatis Gandavensis.* Ed. Albert Derolez. Ghent: Story-Scientia, 1968.

Lecoq, Danielle. "Le mappemonde du *Liber Floridus* ou la vision du monde de Lambert de Saint-Omer." *Imago Mundi* 39 (1987): 9–49.

Mayo, Penelope C. "The Crusaders under the Palm: Allegorical Plants and Cosmic Kingship in the *Liber Floridus.*" *Dumbarton Oaks Papers* 27 (1973): 29–67.

Saxl, Fritz. "Illustrated Medieval Encyclopedias–1. The Classical Heritage"; "Illustrated Medieval Encyclopedias–2. The Christian Transformation." In *Lectures.*

2 vols. London: The Warburg Institute, 1957, 1:228–241; 242–254.

*Sylvia Tomasch*

**SEE ALSO**

Bestiaries; Climate; Honorius Augustodunensis; Isidore of Seville; *Mappamundi;* Maps

## Liber Monstrorum [*Liber monstrorum de diversis generibus*]

A compilation of 117 wonders, portentous monstrosities, and marvels chiefly to be found in India and Africa, probably composed in England between 650 and 750 and disseminated from there to the Continent, at least as early as the ninth century (though the widely held view of the book's Anglo-Latin character has been challenged by Anne Knock). Its Latin style is dense and pyrotechnic with metaphors, with many rare words and constructions, as well as puns and rhetorical figures such as chiasmus.

*Liber Monstrorum* exists in five unillustrated continental manuscripts: Leiden, Bibliothek der Rijks-Universiteit, Voss. lat. MS Oct. 60, ninth–tenth century, probably from Fleury; London, British Library MS Royal 15.B.XIX, tenth century, from Reims; New York, Pierpont Morgan Library MS 906, ninth century, also from Reims; Wolfenbüttel, Herzog-August Bibliothek Gudianus lat. 148, ninth–tenth century, from France; and St. Gall, Stiftsbibliothek 237, probably made at that library in the first quarter of the ninth century. A ninth-century book list from Bobbio mentions other manuscripts, now lost.

The work's three books treat human, animal, and serpent wonders and show a strong preoccupation with travel, nautical metaphors, and exotic locales. Many of these wonders are the sorts of fabulous beings mentioned by Pliny in the geographical sections of the *Historia naturalis,* such as cynocephali and bearded ladies, and in the *Physiologus* and bestiaries. Others, such as Cacus and Geryon, are fabulous, being drawn from Greek and Roman myth by way of Virgil, who is probably the author's most heavily relied-on source and who is himself mentioned as the prince of poets. In addition to these sources, the work incorporates thirteen creatures taken from the late antique Alexander legends of travel to the East, such as the *Epistola Alexandri ad Aristotelem* and the *Letter of Pharasmanes to the Emperor Hadrian.* Patristic sources, including

Isidore of Seville's *Etymologies,* St. Augustine's *City of God* (c.8. book XVI), and the *Historia Adversus Paganos* of Orosius, also contribute to the author's catalogue. The many sources and the way they were used point to a learned compiler employing a well-stocked monastic library, and Michael Lapidge's view is that the *Liber*'s author was a monk at Malmsbury in Wessex.

The *Liber Monstrorum* was associated in the later Middle Ages with Aldhelm of Malmsbury, since a manuscript containing both the *Liber* and Aldhelm's riddles seems to have been known as the work of Aldhelm to the Flemish Dominican encyclopedist Thomas of Cantimpré. The text's most recent student, Andy Orchard, believes that while Aldhelm is not the author, "a colleague, disciple, or imitator working in a 'house style'" probably was.

The author's geographical interest is chiefly in the remote and exotic; indeed, he tells us in his preface he will treat "the secret places of the globe, such as deserts and the islands of Ocean, as well as the lurking spots of distant mountains." Though much of this geography is fabulous, the work does make one of the earliest allusions to the pepper harvest: "between the Red Sea and Arabia pepper grows, which, the land being burned off, men gather blackened and toasted pepper corns." Other actual wonders include knowledge of the crocodile: "on the Nile river are found crocodiles, huge beasts, who stretch themselves out on sunny shores, and will quickly eat people if they waken and notice them nearby."

Like this account, which seems to reflect actual knowledge of the creature in question, the *Liber Monstrorum*'s chapter on the elephant is more realistic than many later treatments: "Elephants, the greatest of all known animals, live among the Bengalese and Indians. Pyrrus brought twenty of them to Rome; through soldiers in howdahs and the weapon of their outstretched trunks they destroy the enemy."

Though most of the peoples mentioned by the author are also fabulous, the Ethiopians are provided with a quasi-scientific explanation for their color based on Macrobian climatic zone theory: "The Ethiopians are all black, scorched by the excessive heat of the equatorial sun, they live in the third zone in the hottest circle of the world, and only survive at all by shadows."

**BIBLIOGRAPHY**

Friedman, John. *The Monstrous Races in Medieval Art and Thought.* Cambridge, MA: Harvard UP, 1981, pp. 149–154 and n. 43, 248–249; rpt. Syracuse UP, 2000.

# L

———. "The Marvels of the East Tradition in Anglo-Saxon Art." In *Sources of Anglo-Saxon Culture*. Ed. Paul Szarmach. Kalamazoo, MI: 1986, pp. 331–332, 336, 338, 340 n. 13.

Knock, Ann. "The *Liber Monstrorum*. An Unpublished Manuscript and Some Reconsiderations." *Scriptorium* 32 (1978): 19–28.

Lapidge, Michael. "Beowulf, Aldhelm, the *Liber Monstrorum* and Wessex." *Studi Medievali* series, 3, 23 (1982): 151–192.

Orchard, Andy. *Pride and Prodigies: Studies in the Monsters of the Beowulf-Manuscript*. Cambridge: D.S. Brewer, 1995, pp. 86–115. [An English translation with en-face Latin edition appears in pp. 254–317.]

Porsia, Franco. "Note per una riedizione ed una lettura del 'Liber Monstrorum.'" *Annali della faculta di lettere e filosophia, Universiti di Bari* 15 (1972): 317–338.

———. "La tradizione manoscritto del 'Liber Monstrorum de diversis generibus': Appunti per l'edizione critica." *Cultura Neolatina* 34 (1974): 337–346.

*John Block Friedman*

**SEE ALSO**

Animals, Exotic; Climate; Elephants; Ethiopians; India; Isidore of Seville; Orosius; Pepper; Pliny the Elder; Red Sea; Thomas of Cantimpré

## Library Collections on Travel

Libraries do not usually treat the literature of travel and discovery as a specialized subdiscipline. Any library that has a strong research collection in medieval history probably has similarly rich holdings of printed books on travel and exploration. Manuscript materials are concentrated in Europe. No American institution can compete with the great national and city libraries of Europe—the British Library (London); the Bibliothèque Nationale (Paris); the Bayerische Staatsbibliothek (Munich); the Österreichische Nationalbibliothek (Vienna); the Laurenziana, Ambrosiana, and Marciana, in Florence, Milan, and Venice, and the Biblioteca Apostolica Vaticana in Rome—for depth and breadth of holdings of medieval manuscripts in any discipline.

There are, however, a number of American libraries with a particular interest in the history of travel. These collections tend to focus on the end of the period covered in this volume, and generally achieve their best coverage for the sixteenth and seventeenth centuries. Such libraries often have their roots in late-nineteenth- and early-twentieth-century collections of Americana—the literature associated with the discovery and early history of the Americas. Since the explorations of the sixteenth century were perceived as being a direct outgrowth of late-medieval travel, collectors often sought such early material as background for their collections of later books. Some of the notable collections of this sort are held by the John Carter Brown Library (Providence, Rhode Island), the Newberry Library (Chicago), the James Ford Bell Library at the University of Minnesota (Minneapolis-St. Paul), the Hispanic Society of America (New York), the William L. Clements Library at the University of Michigan (Ann Arbor), the Henry E. Huntington Library (San Marino, California), and the American Geographical Society collection at the University of Wisconsin, Milwaukee. Among nonspecialized libraries, the rare book collections at Yale University's Beinecke Library, the New York and Boston Public Libraries, the Library of Congress, and Harvard and Princeton Universities have particularly strong holdings of primary materials. Many of these libraries have published catalogs of their rare book collections.

There are fewer such specialized libraries in Europe. Some particularly strong, or well-arranged, collections include the Royal Geographical Society (London), the Herzog-August Bibliothek (Wolfenbüttel, Germany), and the Universiteitsbibliotheek at Leiden (the Netherlands).

*Ben Weiss*

## Lignum Aloes

"Wood of the aloe," also used for "aloe." The Late Latin "aloe" is adopted from the Greek *aloh* and refers: to a plant genus (*Liliaceae*) containing several species, succulent herbs, shrubs, or trees, with erect spikes of flowers and bitter juice; to a drug of nauseous odor, bitter taste, and purgative qualities, made from the juice of these plants; and to the resin or heartwood of the fragrant Agalloch (genera *Aquilaria* and *Aloexylon*). The term *aloe* was used imprecisely in the Septuagint and New Testament to translate the Hebrew *akhalim* and *akhaloth* (the agalloch), probably due to the similarity between the Hebrew and Greek words. Thus, in modern languages *aloe* came to be applied to both the wood and the resin of the agalloch and to the plant genus *Liliaceae*.

Pliny (c. 23–79 C.E.), whose *Natural History* had a profound impact on medieval and early modern travelers and traders, wrote that aloe's chief use was as a purgative for the bowels. When mixed with substances like honey, vinegar, and rose oil, aloe juice acted as a remedy for headache, eye problems, marks and bruises, diseased tonsils and gums, sores in the mouth, bleeding hemorrhoids, hemorrhaging wounds, ulcerated male genitals, condylomata, anal chaps, dysentery, indigestion, and jaundice. It removed hangnails, prevented baldness, and altered the taste and color of wine.

Marco Polo, John Mandeville, John of Marignolli, and Christopher Columbus were all, directly or indirectly, influenced by Pliny, and all wrote of the versatile *lignum aloes.* Geoffrey Chaucer mentions "ligne Aloes" in *Troilus and Criseyde* (5.1317). Polo notes its sacrificial importance to the great khân's Kashmiri and Tibetan enchanters, the Bakhshi; he also states that the khân obtained a 40 percent duty on aloes imports at Zaiton, that the inhabitants of Chamba (Vietnam) paid the khân an annual tribute of elephants and *lignum aloes,* and that Lesser Java abounded in treasures like *lignum aloes* that never reached Europe. William of Boldensele, writing in 1336, states that "lignum aloe," along with the gemstone carnelian, can be found "in and near" the Nile. The passage is somewhat reworked in *The Book of John Mandeville,* where the substance's medicinal value, high cost, and origins in Paradise are also noted; the *Book* later points out that a room on the great khân's chariot is made out of *lignum aloes,* which comes from Paradise via one of the four rivers (Nile, Euphrates, Tigris, Ganges) whose source is there. The same information is to be found in Marignolli (c. 1356), who added that gems came to the inhabited world in the same manner.

On October 21, 1492, Columbus wrote that he would take aboard ten "quintales" of "lignáloe." Although he frequently referred to aloe plants in the journal of his first voyage, he likely confused Pliny's succulent, native to Africa, with the agalloch and the agave (*Agave bahamana Trelease* or *Agave legrelliana*). Indeed, he probably loaded neither the wood of the agalloch nor the succulent, but the agave.

**BIBLIOGRAPHY**

Duke, James A. *Handbook of Biologically Active Phytochemicals and Their Activities.* Boca Raton, FL: CRC Press, 1992.

Pliny. *Natural History.* Ed. and trans. H. Rackham and W.H.S. Jones. Loeb Classical Library. 10 vols. London: Heinemann; Cambridge, MA: Harvard UP, 1948–1984. (Latin and English; see vols. 4, 6, 7.)

*Daniel P. Terkla*

**SEE ALSO**

Columbus, Christopher; Four Rivers of Paradise; Ganges; John of Marignolli; *Mandeville's Travels;* Marco Polo; Pliny the Elder; William of Boldensele; Zaiton

## Liudprand of Cremona (*c.* 920–972)

Bishop, historian, and homilist employed by Emperor Otto I (r. 936–973) on embassies to Rome and Constantinople.

Liudprand belonged to a noble family from Pavia, in Lombardy. The young Liudprand served King Hugh of Italy as page and later became chancellor under Berengar II. In 949, he was sent with his stepfather to Constantinople, ostensibly to learn Greek. Later he quarreled with Berengar and fled to the German court, where he attained high rank. Otto I installed him as bishop of Cremona in 961, and in 968 sent him to the Byzantine court to ask the hand of Theophano, daughter of the Greek emperor Nicephorus II Phocas (r. 963–969), for his son Otto. Liudprand was a suitable representative for this mission, but he was not authorized to negotiate the difficult political questions the Greeks raised. The embassy failed as much due to his own undiplomatic outbursts as to external events beyond his control. He made a third, successful trip to the East late in 971 to reopen marriage negotiations under the new emperor John I Tzimisces (r. 969–976). He died during the return voyage or shortly thereafter.

Besides sermons and the *Historia Ottonis,* Liudprand left two important texts that vividly describe Byzantine court life, ceremonies, intrigues, and cuisine. In *Antapodosis* (*Book of Revenge*), Liudprand vilifies his former lord Berengar, but glorifies the Eastern capital and its marvels, including some that are wonders of machinery, and he praises the wisdom of the emperor. By contrast, his most famous work, the *Relatio de Legatione Constantinopolitana* (968–969), denigrates the Greeks as effeminate, deceitful, and weak. Written at the time when the East and West were becoming more and more divided politically and religiously (the complete break was to come in 1054), Liudprand's *Relatio* is both a Western European self-justification and an anti-Byzantine polemic.

**BIBLIOGRAPHY**

Liudprand of Cremona. *Opera.* Ed. Joseph Becker. Monumenta Germaniae Historica. SS 3. 3rd edition. Hanover: Hahn, 1915.

# L

———. *Relatio de Legatione Constantinopolitana.* Ed. and trans. Brian Scott. Reading Medieval and Renaissance Texts. London: Bristol Classical Press, 1992.

Schummer, Constanze M.F. "Liudprand of Cremona—a diplomat?" In *Byzantine Diplomacy: Papers from the Twenty-fourth Spring Symposium of Byzantine Studies, Cambridge, March 1990.* Ed. Jonathan Shepard and Simon Franklin. Society for the Promotion of Byzantine Studies, Publications 1. Aldershot: Variorum, 1992, pp. 197–201.

Sutherland, Jon N. "The Mission to Constantinople in 968 and Liudprand of Cremona." *Traditio* 31 (1975): 55–81.

*The Works of Liudprand of Cremona.* Trans. Frederic A. Wright. London: Routledge, 1930. Rpt. as *The Embassy to Constantinople and Other Writings.* Everyman's Library. London: J.M. Dent, 1993.

*Gloria Allaire*

**SEE ALSO**
Byzantine Empire; Constantinople; Diplomacy; Eastern Christianity

## Lodestone

A popular name for magnetite ($Fe_3O_4$), a naturally occurring widely distributed iron oxide that has the characteristics of polarity and of attracting iron objects to itself. Important for the development of the magnetic compass, it also appeared as a "marvel" in travel narrative. The magnetic character of the lodestone is probably derived from electric currents near the earth's core. Rocks and minerals brought to the earth's surface through geologic or volcanic action bring the earth's characteristic polarity with them, and once they have cooled, their magnetism is fixed in accordance with the earth's magnetic field.

Knowledge of magnetic rocks existed from very early times. Thales of Miletus mentioned the magnetic properties of certain rocks about 500 B.C.E., and in the first century B.C.E., the Roman poet and writer on natural history Lucretius, in his *De Natura rerum,* noted the attracting and repelling qualities of certain stones. Among early Christian writers, St. Augustine noted the power of the stone to pass its magnetism through one metal ring to another.

The property of the lodestone to attract and repel iron was responsible for a variety of beliefs about its supposedly magical powers in lapidaries or works on stones and in travel writing at almost the same time its magnetism was harnassed in the service of navigation. For example,

even so objective an observer as Albertus Magnus (*c.* 1200–1280) noted (following Thomas of Cantimpré) that the "repelling" character of magnetite was considered useful as a test for a wife's fidelity when placed under her pillow (unfaithful wives at once fell out of the bed) and, when powdered and sprinkled in the four corners of a house, as a means for thieves to scatter the occupants so that they could come in and take what they would. In the *Book of John Mandeville* (*c.* 1360) the land of Prester John is seldom visited by merchants because of great rocks of magnetite "which of its nature draws iron to itself. And because no ships that have iron nails in them can sail that way because of these rocks . . . the ships in that part of the world are all made of wood with no iron."

The most important development regarding the lodestone in the medieval period was the discovery of its ability to impart polarity—direction-finding quality—to metal, leading to the invention of the magnetic compass. This use of the magnetized needle was known to both Chinese and Arab navigators in the twelfth century, but there is no evidence of direct influence from either of these sources on European knowledge of it.

Guyot de Provins in the late twelfth or early thirteenth century wrote of sailors rubbing a needle on a stone called *marinière,* floating the needle in a straw on water, and finding that it would consistently point north. The process was subsequently described by encyclopedists and scientific writers like Alexander Neckham, Vincent of Beauvais, Albertus Magnus, and Roger Bacon, along with more fabulous beliefs. In 1269, Peter Peregrinus de Maricourt wrote instructions for constructing a magnetic compass, and in 1295, Raymond Lully (not related to the Majorcan Raymond Lull) included the magnetized needle among instruments in his *Arte de Navegar.* Clearly, the lodestone and its properties were widely known throughout Europe in the thirteenth century, although the true nature of magnetism would not be understood until much later.

**BIBLIOGRAPHY**

Smith, Julian. "Precursors to Peregrinus: The Early History of Magnetism and the Mariner's Compass in Europe." *Journal of Medieval History* 18 (1992): 21–74.

*John Parker*

**SEE ALSO**
Albertus Magnus; Compass, Magnetic; *Mandeville's Travels;* Navigation; Navigation, Arab; Navigation, Chinese; Prester John; Thomas of Cantimpré; Vincent of Beauvais

## London Psalter Map
*See* Psalter Map

## Lost Tribes
*See* Ten Lost Tribes, The

## Louis IX (1214–1270, r. 1226–1270)

King of France, crusader, and saint. Louis IX went on a number of significant journeys within and outside the kingdom of France in the course of his long rule.

The need to suppress revolts was the most urgent reason for travel in the first half of Louis's reign. From what has been reconstructed of his itinerary, it appears that the king was extremely active in securing his territories during the years 1228, 1230–1231, 1234, and 1242. His most extensive campaign was the invasion of Poitou in the spring of 1242 to put down the rebellion of the count and countess of La Marche, who were supported by King Henry III of England.

Traditional administrative practices provided a second rationale for long trips away from Paris. He did not neglect his capital city, of course, and in fact issued numerous decrees intended to improve conditions there, such as an ordinance in 1256 suppressing royal tolls on fodder. But his concern for provincial life was equally strong. He regularly visited districts in order to scrutinize the work of local authorities and to redress grievances. In the course of such trips, the king stayed at his own provincial residences, was hosted by local officials or by friends, or received hospitality or hospitality payments (Latin, *gista;* French, *gîte*) from nobles, churches, or towns that had an obligation to provide them. Over time, there was a tendency on the king's part to accept smaller amounts of money for this hospitality, whose payment had been a source of constant complaint from his hosts.

The king's most extensive travels took place in conjunction with planning or executing crusades. In 1245, Louis traveled to Lyons to discuss plans for a holy war with Pope Innocent IV, who was temporarily in residence there. A few years later, in 1248, he undertook a series of rapid but extensive ceremonial tours of the royal domain in preparation for his departure on the crusade. Because Louis came to the throne as a minor and in difficult circumstances, he did not make the ceremonial tour many kings undertook at the beginning of their reign; however, he more than

Angels with soul of St. Louis. London, British Library, MS Sloane 2433 C, fol. 7v, 1400. Courtesy of the British Library.

compensated for this deficiency by the pre-Crusade circuit of 1248. The journeys took place from late February through May and covered districts north and south of Paris, to a radius of about 100 miles from the capital.

In June 1248, Louis departed Paris with his entourage, heading southeastward through Champagne, Burgundy, and the Rhône valley to Aigues-Mortes, the royal port that he had fortified and whose economic health he had ensured by a series of charters and agreements requiring merchants on land and sea to trade in its markets. From Aigues-Mortes in August 1248 the king sailed to Cyprus, where he wintered. It was from Cyprus that he launched the invasion of Egypt in May 1249, successfully capturing Damietta at the mouth of the Nile in June. Reinforcements of new crusaders arrived in the months that followed, but the expedition ran into trouble after November 1249 when the army moved south. A full-scale rout by Muslim

# L

forces occurred in April of the next year at the town of Mansura, some forty miles up the Nile from Damietta.

The king's captivity after the disaster at Mansura was brought to an end when he agreed to cede Damietta and pay a huge ransom for the army. On his release in mid-May, Louis traveled by ship to the Holy Land where he spent nearly four years helping to improve the defenses of the crusader states. Although a military failure, the expedition, from start to finish, stimulated a boom in production (of ships, for example) and in trade (of foodstuffs, weapons, and the like) in Italy and in many other Christian territories along the Mediterranean.

It was not until April 1254 that Louis returned to France, landing in Hyères (Provence) in July and making a meandering journey through eastern Languedoc to familiarize himself with the problems and complaints of the region before heading north to Paris. On the northerly route, too, he seized on the opportunity to observe local political conditions.

The Crusade of 1270 (preceded by another ceremonial tour) followed a different route. After leading the army southward for embarkation from Aigues-Mortes, the king departed on July 1 for Sardinia, where there was only a brief layover before the invasion of Tunisia on July 18. During the siege of Tunis, on August 25, 1270, Louis died, but his travels were not quite complete. His heart was reserved as a relic for his brother, Charles of Anjou, who later brought it to Sicily at Monreale. His flesh, after having been boiled off his bones in wine, was interred alongside the bodies of other dead crusaders outside of Tunis. The bones themselves were buried in the royal abbey of Saint-Denis, north of Paris. The cortege followed a route that traversed the Mediterranean to Italy and proceeded (attended by many miracles) up the peninsula, then across to France and at last northward to the king's final resting place and eventual shrine in the royal necropolis. He was canonized in 1297.

## BIBLIOGRAPHY

Jordan, William Chester. *Louis IX and the Challenge of the Crusade: A Study in Rulership.* Princeton, NJ: Princeton UP, 1996.

LeGoff, Jacques. *Saint Louis.* Paris: Gallimard, 1996.

Richard, Jean. *Saint Louis: Crusader King of France.* Ed. Simon Lloyd. Trans. Jean Birrell. Cambridge and New York: Cambridge UP, 1992.

*William Chester Jordan*

SEE ALSO

Egypt; Innocent IV; Lyons, First Council of

## Ludolf [Ludolphus] of Suchem [Suchen or Sudheim] (fl. 1336–1350)

Author of an important travel narrative about the Holy Land written about 1350, and extant in Latin and German manuscripts.

Ludolf is an enigmatic figure: no concrete information about his life is available outside the confines of his book, *De Itinere Terrae Sanctae Liber* (Description of the Holy Land and the Way Thither). In the introduction he identifies himself as "Ludolf, rector of the parish church at Suchem, in the diocese of Paderborn," and he dedicates the book to Balduin [Baldwin] of Steinfurt, bishop of Paderborn. This city is in Westphalia, about fifty miles northwest of Kassel, but the location of Suchem (some versions have it as Sudheim) remains a mystery. Balduin was bishop from 1340 to 1361, but whether he was present in the Holy Land with Ludolf cannot be ascertained. Ludolf states that the journey lasted from 1336 to 1341, but scholars believe he wrote the book in 1350; this is supported by his reference to a recent violent persecution of Jews in Germany, which is known to have occurred in 1348–1349. The oldest surviving manuscript dates to around 1380.

Ludolf specifically mentions having met some Europeans who were companions of "Wilhelmus de Boldensele," although he makes no claim to have met this "knight" (militis). William of Boldensele was a Dominican from Minden who went to the Holy Land perhaps in 1332–1333, on what may have been a diplomatic mission; he wrote an account of his visit in 1336 at the request of an influential cardinal in the papal curia (at Avignon). Ludolf copies many sentences—sometimes whole paragraphs—of William's book, and his meeting with William's companions may be fictional. Ludolf's book is longer and far more interested in wonders and anecdotes than William's. Ludolf provides the first known reference to the "Princes of Vaus," a family with a castle at Acre that John of Hildesheim states received great wealth from the Magi, according to his *History of the Three Kings* (composed 1364–1375). John Mandeville does not borrow from Ludolf in his *Travels,* which was written around 1357.

Ludolf admits that although his account is largely an eyewitness one, he includes oral information given him by others and material from books about places he did

Ludolf of Suchem, *De Terra Sancta et Itinere Iherosolomitano*, first printed edition (Strassburg: Heinrich Eggestein, *c.* 1475), fol. 2r. Minneapolis, MN. By permission of the James Ford Bell Library, University of Minnesota.

not actually see. He opens with a description of the land route to the Holy Land through Constantinople but then concentrates on the sea route that he took. He treats at some length the various perils of sea travel, claiming that he came close to perishing in a storm during the voyage home. Ludolf covers the Mediterranean from Spain to its eastern shore, and he mentions the major islands, Morocco ("Barba"), Italy, Greece, Asia Minor, Cilicia (then called Armenia), Cyprus, the cities of the eastern Mediterranean, and Egypt, although he could not possibly have visited many of these places on a vessel sailing from Italy to a port in the Holy Land (he does not say where he landed). He journeyed in both Egypt and Palestine and wandered extensively through the area, visiting various places mentioned in the Old and New Testaments, many of which were off the beaten track of Holy Land pilgrims. He then went to Damascus and ends his narrative on reaching the coast at Beirut (just as William of Boldensele did).

Ludolf's vivid descriptions of the various monuments and shrines of Christianity and Islam and of life among the people make this a gripping book that even modern readers might enjoy. Ludolf was obviously widely read in his own time, since some fifty Latin manuscripts of his work survive. However, he accepts miracle stories at face value and occasionally he launches into flights of fancy, such as an extended anecdote tracing the movement throughout history of the thirty pieces of silver that Judas received for betraying Jesus. Still, scholars regard this as the most valuable fourteenth-century European account of the Holy Land and an important source for geographical knowledge during the Middle Ages.

**BIBLIOGRAPHY**

Ludolph von Suchen. "De Itinere Terrae Sanctae." Ed. Ferdinand Deycks. *Publicationen des Stuttgarter Literarischen Vereins* 25 (1851). xxiii–xxiii, 1–104.

———. *Ludolph von Suchem's Description of the Holy Land and of the Way Thither.* Trans. Aubrey Stewart. Palestine Pilgrims' Text Society 12. London: Early English Text Society, 1895; rpt. New York: AMS Press, 1971.

———. *Ludolfs von Sudheim Reise ins Heilige Land.* Ed. Ivar von Stapelmohe. Lunder Germanistische Forschungen 6. Lund: Håkan Ohlsson, 1937.

*Richard V. Pierard*

**SEE ALSO**
Acre; Anonymous of the Lower Rhine or of Cologne; Holy Land; *Mandeville's Travels;* Pilgrimage, Christian; William of Boldensele

# Lull, Ramon (*c.* 1232–1316)

A Catalan philosopher, theologian, mystic, poet, and author who traveled widely throughout the Mediterranean world advocating language studies for missionaries and seeking to effect the conversion of Jews and Muslims to Christianity through intellectual persuasion.

Lull [also Llull or Lully] was the only son of French nobles who settled in Palma, Majorca, after Jaime I of Aragon (r. 1213–1276) captured the strategically and commercially important island from the Moors in 1229. He was raised as a courtier and met with some early success writing troubadour poetry. After marrying, starting a family, and rising to the post of administrative head of the royal household, he experienced a religious conversion as a result of a series of visions of Christ on the cross. Determined to reform his life and

# L

dedicate himself to the service of God, Lull began, around 1266, to pursue three goals that would shape the rest of his career: establishing language schools for training missionaries; writing a book against the errors of unbelievers, which by his own admission would be "the best in the world"; and dying for Christ as a missionary. He came under the influence of the Dominican Ramon de Penyafort (1185–1275), who convinced him to spend several years studying a wide variety of disciplines and languages. He was particularly influenced by Augustinian Neoplatonism, Anselm, the Victorines, and the Spiritual Franciscans. The importance of the last is evinced by the widely held assumption that Lull eventually took the habit of the third order of St. Francis. After learning Arabic from his slave, he studied the Qur'an and the writings of the Islamic philosopher and theologian Abu Hamid Muhammed al-Ghazzālī (1058–1111). Lull was proficient enough in Arabic to write the first of his 265 books, the *Book of Contemplation,* in that language.

In 1274, Lull claimed to have experienced an intellectual illumination that enabled him to begin work on his "Art," a universal metaphysical system aimed at establishing intellectual common ground for Christians, Jews, and Muslims. The main purpose of the Art was to prescribe a method for studying the providential governance of creation. After proving its applicability to such fields as logic, jurisprudence, medicine, geometry, astronomy, and politics, Lull tried to demonstrate the inevitable truth of Christian doctrine. He consistently promoted the compatibility of faith and reason, a position requiring him to argue against the rising tide of Averroism at the University of Paris. Until the end of his life, he continued to revise the Art many times in various languages and literary genres for a wide variety of audiences. Notable among his works are two fictional narratives, *Blanquerna* (1283) and *Felix* (c. 1287). On the basis of these Lull is considered one of the creators of literary Catalan.

While writing and teaching his Art, Lull also sought to convince popes and secular rulers to adopt his missionary strategy. In 1276, he persuaded the king of Majorca to open the first school for training missionaries in Oriental languages. Shortly thereafter, Lull himself embarked on a series of unsuccessful missions. As a result of public preaching and debates with Islamic scholars, he was twice expelled from North Africa. He returned to Europe and lectured at universities, including Paris and Naples, while continuing to produce works ranging in scope and style from scientific encyclopedias to catechetical poems. Most important in terms of his approach to missionary work are *Liber de gentili et tribus sapientibus* (*c.*1276), *Libre de passatge* (1291), and *Liber de acquisitione Terrae Sanctae* (*c.*1309). These writings show that Lull gradually, if reluctantly, endorsed the notion of military crusades. After traveling to Cyprus and Armenia in 1301, in response to false rumors of a Mongol invasion of Syria, he began to advocate the unification of all military orders for the sake of the liberation of the Holy Land. At the Council of Vienna in 1311, he successfully advocated this project along with the establishment of language schools. Just before the end of his life, Lull saw chairs in Arabic, Hebrew, and Chaldean instituted at universities in Bologna, Oxford, Paris, and Salamanca.

Lull set out on his final missionary journey to Tunis in 1315. Despite legends of his martyrdom, it seems likely that he died aboard a ship that was returning him to Europe a year later. Buried in Palma, he has been venerated as a saintly figure and his cult received papal approbation in 1847. The history of Lullism is marked by a series of battles between those who question his orthodoxy, associating him with alchemy and cabalism, and others who defend his ascetical, mystical, and encyclopedic methods. His detractors include Rabelais and Swift, while Nicholas of Cusa, Heinrich Alsted, and Leibniz are numbered among his supporters. Recently, scholars have been drawn to his intellectual approach to missiology and his insistence on the relationship between language study and evangelism.

**BIBLIOGRAPHY**

Bonner, Anthony, ed. and trans. *Selected Works of Ramon Llull.* Princeton, NJ: Princeton UP, 1985.

Hillgarth, J.N. *Ramon Lull and Lullism in Fourteenth-Century France.* Oxford: Oxford UP, 1971.

Johnston, Mark D. *The Spiritual Logic of Ramon Llull.* Oxford: Oxford UP, 1987.

Peers, E. Allison. *Ramon Lull, a Biography.* New York: Macmillan, 1929. 2nd edition. New York: Franklin, 1969.

Yates, Frances. "The Art of Ramon Lull: An Approach to It through Lull's Theory of the Elements." *Journal of the Warburg and Courtauld Institutes* 17 (1954): 115–173.

*Scott R. Pilarz, S.J.*

**SEE ALSO**

Dominican Friars; Franciscan Friars; Language Instruction for Western European Travelers; Nicholas of Cusa

## Lyons, First Council of (1245)

An important church council that marked a major step in European understanding of the peoples of Asia. At the council he convoked at Lyons, Pope Innocent IV (1243–1254) dispatched several Franciscan and Dominican friars to the East with the intention of making contact with the rulers of the Mongols, initiating the Mongol Mission.

A major theme of Innocent IV's pontificate was the defense of Europe from the Muslims who were advancing in the eastern Mediterranean and from the Mongols who were attacking eastern Europe. To this end, he sought reunion with the Greek Orthodox Church, preached a crusade against the Muslims, and, at the First Council of Lyons (1245), dispatched two Franciscan friars to find and meet with the Mongol khân.

The most important of these papal representatives was John of Plano Carpini (c. 1180–1252), who carried two letters from the pope that outlined Christian doctrine, suggested a conversion to Christianity, and urged the khân to end his attacks on the peoples of eastern Europe. In response, Plano Carpini brought back with him a letter from the khân ordering the pope and the Christian rulers of Europe to come to Asia, there to submit themselves and their people to Mongol rule. While the friar's journey had little practical consequence for Christian-Mongol relations, his record of the mission, containing careful descriptions of the Mongol way of life, reached a broad audience, particularly because Vincent of Beauvais (c. 1190–c. 1264) included it in his *Speculum Historiale,* a widely circulated encyclopedia.

In the long run, the Mongol mission failed to achieve any lasting relationship between Christians and Mongols for two main reasons. The khân's letter to Innocent IV made it clear that the Mongols expected to dominate European Christians, not deal with them as equals. Furthermore, the subsequent collapse of the Mongol Empire in the fourteenth century meant that travel to and through the East became more difficult, making missionary work almost impossible.

**BIBLIOGRAPHY**

Dawson, Christopher, ed. *The Mongol Mission.* See Gen. Bib.

Muldoon, James. *Popes, Lawyers, and Infidels: The Church and the Non-Christian World, 1250–1550.* Philadelphia: U of Pennsylvania P, 1979.

de Rachewiltz, Igor. *Papal Envoys to the Great Khans.* Stanford: Stanford UP, 1971.

*James Muldoon*

**SEE ALSO**

Dominican Friars; Franciscan Friars; Innocent IV; John of Plano Carpini; Missionaries to China; Mongols; Vincent of Beauvais

# M

## Madaba Mosaic Map

A Byzantine map of biblical lands.

Four maplike documents remain from classical times, three of which are medieval copies. The fourth and only original is a mosaic map of biblical lands in the transept of a sixth-century church in Madaba, now in the Hashemite kingdom of Jordan.

During the Byzantine Empire, Madaba, the biblical Mishor of the Moabites, was a flourishing Christian city with thirteen churches and many houses with mosaic floors, reflecting the pervasiveness of a local industry. The mosaic map in Madaba, dated 560–565 C.E. and depicting biblical lands from southern Syria to central Egypt, was discovered in 1884 and reported to the Greek Orthodox patriarch of Ottoman Jerusalem. New church construction destroyed almost 75 percent of the map, originally about seventy-two feet by twenty-three feet (twenty-two meters by seven meters), before it came to world attention in 1896. The much damaged fragment that remains indicates that the topical features were chosen not only for their intrinsic importance, but also for their significance as sites of events mentioned in the Hebrew Bible, the Gospels, or church history. The Greek text inscribed in the pavement provides biblical and contemporary names, which derive primarily from the *Onomasticon* of Eusebius of Caesarea (*c.* 264–340), sometimes with an added historical note or a verse from the Septuagint. Important places and the areas allotted to the twelve tribes of Israel are lettered in red.

The Madaba map provides the earliest topographical description of Jerusalem. Unlike most later depictions, it is oriented to the east: the map is made to be viewed by a spectator who faces east while examining it. The bird's-eye view shows an oval-shaped walled city in the very center of the map with six gates and twenty-one towers, the colonnaded main thoroughfare (Cardo Maxima, recently excavated and restored by Israel), and thirty-six other identifiable public buildings, churches, and monasteries. Other cities are fragmentary or stylized (a wall with a few towers and rooftops), as are towns, villages, and Negev desert settlements, sixteen of which are not recorded elsewhere. Although the scale is inconsistent, the locations are generally configured on the basis of a Roman road map and enlivened with vignettes of men, ships, beasts, plants, and fish.

**BIBLIOGRAPHY**

Avi-Yonah, Michael. *The Madaba Mosaic Map.* Jerusalem: Israel Exploration Society, 1954.

Donner, Herbert. *The Mosiac Map of Madaba.* Kampen: Kok Pharos, 1992.

Piccirillo, Michele. *Madaba.* Milan: Edizioni Paoline, 1989.

*Jerome Mandel*

**SEE ALSO**
Byzantine Empire; Dead Sea; Jerusalem; Maps; Memory and Maps

## Magnetic Compass

*See* Compass, Magnetic

## Magyar Tribes

A nomadic herding and warring people of Ugric origin who had migrated south from the middle Volga region

# M

between the Iron Age and the sixth century C.E. They lived north of the Black Sea under Khazar rule during the mid-ninth century, benefiting from Khazar trading contracts with the Near East. From their new place of settlement northwest of the Black Sea, where they had developed military and trading relations with Byzantium, they were led across the Carpathian mountains into present-day Hungary in 896 by Arpád, their first elected prince, after the neighboring Pecheneg tribes had totally destroyed their previous settlement. There they were bordered on the west by the Franks, and on the south by Croats. In Byzantine sources they appear as *Turks,* as if to point out their relations in trade and commerce with the Turkish world of Islam during the ninth and tenth centuries.

Before their unification under King Stephen in 1001, the Magyars were divided into a number of distinct clans, of which, according to legend, the Khazars had become preeminent because of their bravery in battle.

## BIBLIOGRAPHY

Bartha, Antal. *Hungarian Society in the Ninth and Tenth Centuries.* Budapest: Akadémia, 1975.

Constantine Porphyrogenitus. *De administrando imperio.* Ed. Gyula Moravcsik. Trans. R.J.H. Jenkins. Budapest, 1949; rev. edition. Washington, DC: Dumbarton Oaks, 1967.

Kosztolnyik, Z.J. *Five Eleventh Century Hungarian Kings: Their Policies and Their Relations with Rome.* New York: Columbia UP, 1981.

Macartney, C.A. *The Magyars in the Ninth Century.* Cambridge, 1930; rpt. Cambridge: Cambridge UP, 1968.

*Z.J. Kosztolnyik*

## SEE ALSO
Byzantine Empire; Hungary

## Majapahit

The east-Java-centered Hindu-Buddhist state that came into existence in the late thirteenth century as the successor to the Singasari and Kadiri *kratons* (courts).

Majapahit entered its "golden age" under the leadership of the chief minister Gaja Mada (r. 1330–1364), who annexed Bali in the early 1340s, and then began a program of military and naval conquest to create an Indonesian archipelago empire (*nusantara*) that Hayam Wuruk (King Rajasanagara [r. 1350–1389]) inherited when he fully assumed the throne in the 1360s.

Majapahit's chronicles, the fourteenth-century *Nagarakertagama* and the fifteenth-century *Pararaton,* claimed that Majapahit ruled over a far-flung realm that included tributary states on the Sumatra, Malay Peninsula, Kalimantan, and eastern Indonesian archipelago coasts. While it is unlikely that Majapahit's kings exercised any degree of centralized control over these regions, it appears that the Majapahit court successfully linked the Indonesian archipelago within its sphere of influence. Majapahit also maintained diplomatic relationships with Vietnam, Cambodia, Thailand, Burma, and China.

Majapahit was both a landed and a trading "empire" that was based in the Brantas (Kediri) and Solo (Bengawan in its lower course) river basin of eastern Java. Majapahit's rulers controlled Java's ample wet rice production, which was exported in bulk by resident merchants and became the medium of exchange for the spices of Indonesia's eastern archipelago "spice islands." These spices in turn made their way through Java's north coast ports into the East-West maritime trade routes. The increased international trade in spices was made possible by Java's internal response to new international opportunities and was witnessed in the development of Javanese market and monetary systems that used Chinese copper coins as the basis of value and exchange. There was parallel evolution of the Javanese state, which was making direct revenue collections, imposing more tolls, raising taxes, and generally increasing its administrative activities. Local inscriptions record a generalized prosperity, with the participation of all levels of society in status-bestowing gifting activities: these include detailed reference to imported cloth, as well as gold and silver transfers. Although not mentioned in the inscriptions, imported Chinese ceramics are found in abundance among the Majapahit archaeological sites.

Majapahit's capital at modern Trawulan was the center of state ritual, which included annual festivals that featured reciprocal gifting between the king and his subjects. New artistic expression in the stone iconography and reliefs of royal and local temples (the largest of which was the Panataran complex near modern Blitar), in Old Javanese *kawi* and *kakawin* literature, and in the performance of Javanese dance, music (*gamelan* gong orchestras), and drama (the Indonesian *wayang kulit* shadow puppet theater was widely popular) demonstrated cultural self-confidence and gave a distinctive Javanese character to Indic-inspired themes.

The memory of Majapahit has lived on in Indonesia, and it is often cited as establishing a precedent for indigenous culture as well as the current political boundaries.

In the fifteenth century Majapahit's influence began to decline; its authority in the Melaka [Malacca] Straits and western archipelago was displaced by the new Malay trading state that was based at Melaka on the Malay Peninsula's western coast. On Java, the Hindu-Buddhist era came to an end around 1527, when new north Java coast port-polities, whose rulers were patrons of Islam, destroyed the court.

**BIBLIOGRAPHY**
Hall, D.G.E. *A History of South-East Asia.* New York: St. Martin's Press, 1981, pp. 90–104.
Hall, Kenneth R. *Maritime Trade and State Development in Early Southeast Asia.* Honolulu: U of Hawaii P, 1985, pp. 232–256.
———. "Ritual Networks and Royal Power in Majapahit Java." *Archipel* 52 (1996): 95–118.
Wicks, Robert S. *Money, Markets, and Trade in Early Southeast Asia.* Ithaca, NY: Cornell UP, 1992, pp. 290–297.
*Kenneth R. Hall*

**SEE ALSO**
Buddhism; China; Malacca Straits; Spice Trade, Indian Ocean; Textiles, Decorative

## Malabar

The southwest coast of India, an important trading and religious center. By Roman times, when knowledge of the Indian Ocean monsoon winds became widespread, sailors and traders who sailed from the Middle East frequented the Malabar Coast (from Arabic Ma'bar, "passage") of southwest India. Malabar's principal appeal was its black pepper, considered to be the best in the world; the area was also the source of cardamom, ginger, cinnamon, and indigo. Malabar Coast enclaves were equally important as vital intermediary ports in the maritime trade between the Middle East and southeast Asia and China.

In the sixth century C.E., the port of Cochin numbered among its residents a well-established Jewish community as well as a Nestorian Christian Church with ties first to Persia and later (after Persia's conversion to Islam) to the Syriac church. By the ninth century, Quilon was the major port of call for seafaring merchants from the West, who reported on its fine bazaars. Its mosque served the Muslim residents (collectively known as Mapillahs) who dominated local commerce and were said to be sufficiently wealthy that any one could buy up an entire ship and its cargo and load it with goods from his own warehouses.

In the first millienium C.E., Malabar became the center of the shipbuilding industry, supplying the Arab *dhows* and Indian *dhangi* that dominated the passage between India and the West. By the sixth century, the coast was subject to a loose confederacy under the Cera kings (hence, today the coast is referred to as Kerala rather than Malabar), members of the dominant Nayyar Hindu caste group, and their Nambudiri Brahmin court advisers. The almost-legendary King Cheraman Perulmal united the region's scattered population clusters in the late eighth century; Cola and other monarchs based on the Coromandel (southeastern) Coast claimed periodic sovereignty over the Cera domain from the eleventh through the thirteenth centuries.

Large Chinese junks began to sail regularly to Malabar ports during the Song dynasty (960–1279), when a community of Chinese merchants established its permanent residences at Quilon, which was in the center of the south coast pepper-producing region. There, Chinese sources report, two trade officials who represented the king negotiated with visiting merchants to guarantee quality and to fix prices on imports, to guarantee that Quilon's pepper growers, as well as foreigners, would receive a fair exchange.

When the Baghdad-centered Abbasid caliphate collapsed in the thirteenth century, the Middle Eastern terminus for East-West maritime trade shifted from the Persian gulf to Aden, with consequence for the Malabar Coast. Mamluk Egyptian merchants (Karimi) based in Aden preferred to trade in Calicut on the northern Malabar Coast, which also became the new center for the resident China traders. Calicut was more strategically situated to act as an intermediary transit and redistribution port of southeast Asian spices and Malabar pepper, Chinese products, as well as Gujarat cotton cloth that was shipped south from a cluster of ports on northern India's Gulf of Cambay. When Ibn Battūta visited in 1342, Calicut was flourishing under a new royal family that was instituted by Samudri Raja ("King of the Seas"—corrupted into "Zamorin"), who extended his authority over surrounding territories with the assistance of the Cairo merchant community. As a result, the Arab merchants became locally dominant at the expense of Chinese merchants. Chinese residential presence on the Malabar

# M

Coast virtually ceased by the early fifteenth century, when, under the revised trade policies of the Ming dynasty (1368–1644), Chinese Indian Ocean traffickers established their new base at Melaka [Malacca] in southeast Asia.

## BIBLIOGRAPHY

Gibb, H.A.R. *Ibn Battūta: Travels in Asia and Africa, 1325–1354.* Hakluyt Society, 2nd series, no. 110. London: Hakluyt Society, 1958.

Mills, John Vivian Gottlieb. *Ying-yai Sheng-lan of Ma Huan (1433).* Hakluyt Society, extra series, 42. Cambridge: Cambridge UP, 1970.

Nilakanta Sastri, K.A. *A History of South India.* Madras: Oxford UP, 1966.

Wolters, O.W. *The Fall of Sribijaya in Malay History.* Ithaca, NY: Cornell UP, 1970.

*Kenneth R. Hall*

## SEE ALSO

China; Dyes and Pigments; Eastern Christianity; Ibn Battūta, Abu Abdallah; Malacca Straits; Mamluks; Nestorianism; Pepper; Spice Trade, Indian Ocean

## Malacca Straits

A narrow passage of water separating the Malay Peninsula (Chersonesus Aurea) on the northeast from the island of Sumatra on the southwest. The strait, about 500 miles (805 km) long, connects the Andaman Sea with the South China Sea. It was, and still is, one of the most important shipping lanes in the world.

Beginning in the seventh century, the Sumatran kingdom of Sri Vijaya controlled the straits. At the height of its power and prestige, Sri Vijayan merchants traded extensively with China and India. Slow decline during the twelfth century led to the subsequent rise of the kingdom of Majapahit, a Javanese maritime empire founded by Vijaya (r. 1293–1309). From 1331 to 1364, chief minister Gaja Mada led the kingdom to a domination of the straits that lasted until the early sixteenth century.

The two largest and most important ports on the strait, Singapore and Malacca (now Melaka), owe their founding to a Sumatran prince married to a Javanese princess. According to the *Malay Annals,* in 1390, Prince Parameswara landed on the island of Temasik, which he renamed Singa Pura, or "Lion City." Archaeological finds on the site of Fort Canning confirm Singapore as a thriving port in the Majapahit Empire. In 1400, however, an invasion drove Parameswara to build a new city named after the Malaka tree. Within fifty years it had become a wealthy and powerful hub of international commerce, with a population of more than 50,000. Cheng Ho [Zheng He], the famous Ming maritime explorer, visited Malacca on his third voyage (1409–1411) and took Parameswara with him to Khangalig (Beijing). In 1414, Parameswara converted to Islam, allying Malacca and the straits with Islamic trading powers. The port was seized in 1511 by the Portuguese, who left the first full descriptions of trade and travel in the area.

## BIBLIOGRAPHY

Hall, D.G.E. *A History of South-East Asia.* London: Macmillan, 1955.

Kennedy, J. *A History of Malaya.* Kuala Lumpur: S. Abdul Majeed, 1962.

Pires, Tome. Trans. A. Cortesão. *Suma Oriental* (1512–1515). 2 vols. London: Hakluyt Society, 1944, Vol. 1.

*Cynthia Ho*

## SEE ALSO

Majapahit; Zheng He, Admiral

## Malaguetta [Grains of Paradise]

A pungent and fruitily aromatic West African spice. Known in the Middle Ages as "grains of paradise" or "xarch nuts," malaguetta was widely used as a condiment and medicinal substance. Now virtually forgotten, it is commonly but erroneously referred to as "malaguetta pepper." General historical literature usually describes it, altogether wrongly, as an inferior substitute for Asian pepper or confuses it with cardamom. Medieval merchants, however, carefully distinguished malaguetta from the above condiments, and unlike their later descendants they valued it more highly than mere pepper.

Grains of paradise are the seeds of several plants of the genus *Aframoma,* family *Zingiberaceae.* The best malaguetta comes from *Aframomum melegueta* (Roscoe), growing in Liberia, on the former Gold Coast, and in the lower Niger River region. The most common source, however, is *Aframomum granum paradisi* (Afzelius), native to the hills of Sierra Leone and other forested parts of West Africa. The spice, which until the opening of the Portuguese trade with Africa in the fifteenth century reached Europe across the Sahara desert, was known to the European consumer either as seeds (grains), or whole seed pods (nuts). Much more expensive than pepper, malaguetta cost as much as fine cinnamon or lesser qualities of ginger. Only saffron, mace, and cloves were more costly.

The first known European reference to malaguetta dates to 1214, and the first documented sale to 1245 (in Lyons). Northwest Europe was the largest consumer, followed by the rest of France, northern Italy, and Catalonia. Either in combination with pepper and cardamom, or as part of ready-made spice mixes, malaguetta was a popular seasoning in soups, sauces, stews, and meat pies. It was also used in mulled wine, or *hypocras,* in honey-based drinks for the sick, and in syrups. As a drug, it was recommended for various fevers and gastrointestinal problems, and many considered it a painkiller.

## BIBLIOGRAPHY

Daniel, William F. "On the Amoma of Western Africa." *Pharmaceutical Journal and Transactions* 14 (1855): 312–318, 356–363; 16 (1857): 465–472, 511–517.

Hieatt, C.B., and S. Butler, eds. *Curye on Inglysch: English Culinary Manuscripts of the Fourteenth Century.* London: Oxford UP, 1985.

Purseglove, J.W., et al. *Spices.* 2 vols. London and New York: Longman, 1981.

Scully, Terence, ed. *The Viandier of Taillevent.* Ottawa: U of Ottawa P, 1988.

Van Harten, A.M. "Melegueta Pepper." *Economic Botany* 24 (1970): 208–216.

*Martin Malcolm Elbl*

## SEE ALSO
Pepper; Portuguese Trade; Spice Trade, Indian Ocean

## Mamluks

A term that as an Arabic word (*mamlūk*) literally means "owned" but is used specifically for the white slaves purchased by Muslim rulers during the Middle Ages who, after a thorough military training, were manumitted in order to become soldiers in their masters' armies. The first to maintain units of Mamluks were the Abassid caliphs of Baghdad, who, in the middle of the ninth century, made them part of their bodyguards in order to protect their rule both from the army, which had strong ties with the local population, and from the provincial governors, who were increasing in strength. From then on, Mamluk units formed an integral part of Muslim armies, and Mamluk involvement

in the affairs of government became an increasingly familiar occurrence in the medieval Middle East. The road to absolute power and uncontested rule lay open before them when the Mamluk establishment gained dominant military and political status during the reign of the Ayyūbid ruler of Egypt, al-Malik al-Sālih Najm al-Dīn Ayyūb (r. 1240–1249). Distrustful of the army he had inherited from his predecessors, al-Sālih Ayyūb built up his own army, rank-and-file soldiers as well as emirs, almost entirely from Turkish Mamluks purchased on the slave markets. These men also came to hold high office in his court.

It was as "Protectors of the Faith" that the Ayyūbids had been accorded legitimacy as Muslim rulers. When at the battle of al-Mansūra, in the spring of 1250, the sultan's Mamluks succeeded in routing the invading crusaders of King Louis IX of France, in spite of the sudden death of their commander al-Sālih Ayyūb, the title went to them. In May of that year, in order to preserve their hold on the senior posts they had attained during their master's life, Mamluk officers from among al-Sālih Ayyūb's elite bodyguard—known as al-Bahriyya—murdered Sultan al-Mu'azzam Tūrānshāh, who had succeeded to the throne, and claimed the rule of Egypt for their own.

With the ascent to power of the Mamluks, the army—which during the Ayyūbid period had been at the beckoning of the ruling stratum—also took over the role of the ruling elite; from its ranks came the sultans who ruled the country for nearly three centuries. They fully subordinated the state's economic resources to their own needs through the *iqtā'* system (the assignment according to rank of revenues from fiefdoms) and because of the dominant cultural and political status they secured for themselves, began eroding the formal, traditional forms of both the civil administration and the religious bureaucracy. The Mamluks established their seat of government at the Cairo Citadel, Qal'at al-Jabal, where they also quartered their troops, thus isolating them from contact with the local population. Furthermore, the Mamluks meticulously held on to their Turkish names, to the Turkish language, to wearing clothes very similar in style to what was worn in their countries of origin, and even to administering their military court in accordance with the *yasa,* the Mongol law code that was not in line with the Muslim law, the *sharī'a.*

When the Ottomans, in 1517, conquered Syria and Egypt, Mamluk autonomous rule ended, though not

# M

the Mamluk institution. Mamluk units were now integrated into the Ottoman garrisons stationed in Egypt, and a process of symbiosis set in that was to last for another 300 years. Only in 1811 were the Mamluks annihilated when Muhammed 'Ali, the Ottoman viceroy of Egypt (r. 1805–1849), massacred them as part of his overall efforts to secure his rule.

Unlike the period before 1250, for which historical information is scant, contemporary sources contain a good deal of detail on the Mamluk system and the way it functioned for the period 1250–1517, when it stood at the center of the political and cultural life of the Mamluk sultanate in Egypt and Syria. Initially, most of the Mamluks purchased as slaves were of Turkish extraction and came from the Qipchaq region, northeast of the Black Sea, which was ruled by the Mongol khâns of the Golden Horde, the Crimea being famous for its slave-trading markets. Thus it was important for the Mamluk sultans to maintain friendly diplomatic relations with both the Byzantine government in Constantinople and the rulers of the Golden Horde. The Byzantines, in 1261, awarded exclusive trade rights for the Black Sea region to Genoese merchants, which facilitated the unhindered passage to Egypt of Mamluk slaves through the Bosporus. With the weakening of the rule over Persia and Iraq of the Mongol il-khâns, sworn enemies of the Mamluk sultans, slave trade resumed along the traditional overland routes through eastern Anatolia, the majority of the Mamluks now being Circassians from the Caucasus region. This difference in ethnic provenance explains the historical division of Mamluk rule into two periods, the *Bahri* period (1250–1382), when Turkish Mamluks were the dominant group in the Mamluk army and provided from their midst those who held the reins of government, and the *Burji* period (1382–1517), when dominance fell to Circassian Mamluks. (A Bahri sultan was restored, but only briefly, in 1389–1390.)

Mamluks were purchased at a young age. On arrival in Cairo, they were quartered in special barracks in the Citadel and divided into peer groups according to age and ethnic origin; smaller groups were then formed for the purpose of instruction, which took place in the military academies also located there. Education consisted of two principal stages: religious studies that continued into adolescence with Muslim sages (*faqīh*, pl. *fuqahā'*) who were enjoined to convert them from pagans into Muslims, followed by a period of rigorous military training that came to an end only when they

had attained the highest level of professional skills in the arts of war. A special ceremony (*'itq*) followed during which the Mamluks were released from servitude and joined the household of the sultan in the Citadel.

At the heart of Mamluk education stood the effort to instill in the young Mamluk a strong sense of solidarity with the other members of his peer group and of loyalty toward his master, called *khushdāshiyya*. It formed a powerful tool enabling the sultan to consolidate his Mamluk faction around him and thus to safeguard the authority and stability of his rule. However, since each new sultan on his ascent to the throne tended to favor his own Mamluk household over the inevitably senior Mamluk faction of his predecessor, this same factional consolidation also spawned the political instability that soon characterized Mamluk rule in general. The result was a situation of chronic tension between senior Mamluk factions who had been ousted from the government offices they held under the previous sultan, and the Mamluk faction of the ruling sultan.

Recurring attempts at overthrowing rulers, often successful, and frequent changes of government led to a state of permanent discontent in the Mamluk army. The rulers' insistence on isolating the army in the Citadel and on maintaining the Mamluks' cultural separation from the local population over which they ruled, as well as the constant influx of new manpower of slave origin, all served to underscore the actual foreignness of the Mamluk elite and to stress that Mamluk rule was largely based on force.

To offset this impression and to improve their standing as Muslims in the eyes of the civilian population, not in the least because they depended on the recognition of their rule as legitimate, the Mamluks went out of their way to show that they acted for the benefit of Islam. Thus, as soldiers in the *jihād*, the Mamluks had succeeded in stemming the advance of the Mongols into the realm of Islam at the battle of Ain Jalut (1260), and later fought zealously to prevent them from crossing the Euphrates. Similarly, they continued the efforts of the Ayyūbids and decimated the crusader presence in Syria and Palestine.

Internally, the Mamluks fostered Islam as a state religion and, in the footsteps of the Seljuks, gave their protection to the Muslim religious institutions and the *'ulamā'* (clerics) who taught there and maintained them. In return for this patronage, the *'ulamā'* (i.e., the intellectual elite), gave the Mamluks the sanction of legitimacy and in their sermons exhorted the population to accept their rule, tyrannical though it was.

The large number of magnificent buildings they erected in Cairo and many other cities, many of monumental proportions and including mosques, *madāris* (colleges where Muslim law was taught), and *khānāqāt* (sufi orders), were to serve all sectors of the population but were, of course, also intended to glorify the contribution Mamluk rulers had made to the welfare of the Muslim community and the propagation of the faith. Though sources indicate that from the middle of the fourteenth century military weakness and misrule characterize the Mamluk system, it is this balance between Mamluk government, the religious establishment, and the populace at large that may in fact explain why and how the Mamluk sultanate could survive into the first decade of the sixteenth century.

**BIBLIOGRAPHY**

Ayalon, D. "The Circassian in the Mamluk Kingdom." *Journal of the American Oriental Society* 69.3 (1949): 135–147.

———. "L'Esclavage du Mamelouk." *Oriental Notes and Studies,* no. 1 (Jerusalem, 1951): 1–66.

———. "Studies on the Structure of the Mamluk Army." *Bulletin of the School of Oriental and African Studies* 15 (1953): 203–228; 16 (1954): 448–476.

Ehrenkreutz, E. "Strategic Implications of the Slave Trade between Genoa and Mamluk Egypt in the Second Half of the Thirteenth Century." In *The Islamic Middle East, 1700–1900: Studies in Economic and Social History.* Ed. A.L. Udovitch. Princeton, NJ: Princeton UP, 1981, pp. 335–345.

Lapidus, I.M. *A History of Islamic Societies.* Cambridge: Cambridge UP, 1994, pp. 353–358.

Levanoni, A. "The Mamluk Conception of the Sultanate." *International Journal of Middle East Studies* 26 (1994): 373–392.

———. *A Turning Point in Mamluk History: The Third Reign of al-Nāsir Muhammad Ibn Qalāwūn (1310–1341).* Leiden: Brill, 1995, pp. 5–27.

*Amalia Levanoni*

**SEE ALSO**
Ain Jalut; Ayyūbids; Golden Horde; Mongols; Yasa

## Mandeville's Travels

The modern editorial title of a remarkable fourteenth-century prose compilation about the East that has survived in some 300 manuscripts (including fragments and excerpts), that circulated in ten languages (Czech, Danish, Dutch, English, French, German, Irish, Italian, Latin, and Spanish), and that, between the late 1470s and 1515, was printed in eight languages (all but Danish and Irish). Scholars now agree that *The Book of John Mandeville,* as it was often called in manuscript, was originally compiled in French sometime around 1360 (the earliest dated manuscript, Paris, Bibliothèque Nationale MS. nouv. acq. fr. 4515, was copied in 1371 for Charles V of France), and that the two principal sources were the German Dominican William of Boldensele's *Liber de quibusdam partibus ultramarinis,* a first-person narrative of a pilgrimage to Egypt and the

Author portrait of John Mandeville from Otto von Diemeringen's translation of *The Book of John Mandeville* (Augsburg: Anton Sorg, 1481), fol. 1v. Minneapolis, MN. By permission of the James Ford Bell Library, University of Minnesota.

# M

Holy Land in the early 1330s, and Friar Odoric of Pordenone's *Relatio,* a first-person account of marvels encountered on a missionary journey to India and China in the 1320s.

There is no consensus on the question of the compilation's authorship, although the matter has been debated since the latter part of the nineteenth century. According to the roughly sixty extant French manuscripts, the author is one John Mandeville, knight, of St. Albans, England, who set out on his travels on Michaelmas (September 29) 1322 and ceased traveling because of "arthritic gout" in 1356 or 1357 (the copies vary on the return date). When it was discovered that the book's claim to be based on the author's own journeys is false, some scholars argued that the name John Mandeville must be a fabrication as well, suggesting that the real author was either Jean de Bourgogne, a physician and the author of a fourteenth-century treatise on the plague, or Jean d'Outremeuse of Liège (1338–1400), the author of a lapidary and two chronicles. In an attempt to refute these claims and restore the book's authorship to an English John Mandeville writing in England, one twentieth-century scholar reconsidered the question in painstaking detail, but in the end could only assert the probability of her case (Bennett 215). More recently, M.C. Seymour, the current authority on the English manuscripts, has advanced "anonymous" as the most likely candidate and claimed that the compilation was originally made on the Continent, possibly in Liège. On the available evidence, the authorship question looks likely to remain unresolved, but it can be said that the textual history of the French manuscripts points more plausibly toward the Continent than England as the place of the book's original writing. The French text unfortunately offers no clues as to where it might have been compiled, asserting only that its ostensible author "came to rest" (*venuz a repos*), but in no particular location, at the end of his travels before putting his account together.

This same textual history has also revealed that the French text exists in three distinct forms—known as the Continental (about thirty-two manuscripts), the Interpolated Continental or Liège (seven manuscripts), and the Insular (about twenty-one manuscripts) versions—each of which gave rise to an independent line of translations. The differences between the Continental and the Insular versions are relatively minor (the most important being found in the account of Sir John's passage through the Perilous Valley), whereas the Interpolated Continental version stands apart from the other two by virtue, above all, of a curious series of interpolations having to do with the Eastern exploits of Ogier the Dane, a figure from the twelfth-century *Chanson de Roland.*

In the Continental and Insular versions, *The Book of John Mandeville* begins with a prologue that defines the text as a guide for real and vicarious pilgrims to Jerusalem accompanied by a description of some of the diverse world to the east of the Holy Land. Both the guide and the description, the English knight says there, are to be based on his recollections of his own travels, and he goes on to add that he should have produced his book in Latin so as to be concise, but that he set it down in French so that everyone might understand it. What follows these enticing opening remarks is a largely third-person depiction of the places and peoples of the world east of Europe beginning at Constantinople and proceeding all the way to the Earthly Paradise, a site that Sir John himself did not reach because he was "not worthy." Roughly the first half of the text is given over to a detailed and sometimes fascinating, sometimes tedious account of the pilgrimage routes and sites between Constantinople and Jerusalem proceeding by way of Egypt. This section of the book uses William of Boldensele's itinerary as a template, but the *Mandeville* author freely rewrites the underlying text, expanding and supplementing it with so much material borrowed from other sources that the resulting pilgrims' guide is at least twice as long as its principal source. The promised guide complete, the text proceeds to the also-promised description of the farther East, especially India and Cathay, as the *Mandeville* author begins using Friar Odoric's "wonder-full" relation as a template, rewriting and supplementing it even more fully than he did William's more sober-minded book.

The most significant change that the *Mandeville* author makes to both his main sources is to depersonalize them: that is, he turns their first-person itineraries into the typical route of any and every traveler ("from Samaria one goes to Galilee"), thereby transforming their individual memoirs into a vicarious textual journey available to all of the book's readers and hearers. Yet even as he depersonalizes the itinerary, the *Mandeville* author has his textual representative, Sir John, appear on the scene at irregular intervals in order to recount highly memorable anecdotes of his "own" unusual experiences. Readers learn, for example, that Sir John served the sultan of Babylon as a soldier in the latter's war against the Bedouins, and that as a reward he was offered a princess in marriage and an accompanying inheritance, so long as he renounced his Christian faith (he would not). The author's English knight also claims to have served the great khân of Cathay in his war against the king of Manzi (southern China)—a war that took place some fifty years before Sir John set out on his textual journey. "Errors" of this sort prove, of course, that the *Mandeville* author could not have done those things that he claims to have done—hence the distinction between the *Mandeville* author (the book's actual compiler) and the English knight Sir John (the book's occasional hero and guiding "I")—but they do not demonstrate that the author never traveled in the East. The most that one can say is that *The Book of John Mandeville* is not based on its author's personal experiences (for example, of a Jerusalem pilgrimage), but is rather an imagined voyage based on others' real travels.

In addition to enhancing both the impersonal and the personal "feel" of his two principal sources, the *Mandeville* author generally makes both of them more compelling reading, augmenting them with factual and legendary information and stories about the places, peoples, flora, and fauna to be found throughout the Eastern world. This supplementary material is drawn from a number of sources, including the Bible, historical writings (Jacques de Vitry's thirteenth-century *Historia Orientalis,* Hetoum's *Fleur des histoires de la terre d'Orient* [1307]), encyclopedias (Vincent of Beauvais's *Speculum historiale* and *Speculum naturale* [c. 1256–1259], Brunetto Latini's *Livres dou tresor* [1260s]), religious writings (Jacobus de Voragine's *Legenda aurea* [before 1267], William of Tripoli's *Tractatus de statu Saracenorum* [1273]), pseudo-historical literature (*Roman d'Alexandre* [mid-twelfth century], *Epistola Presbyteris Johannis* [late twelfth century]), and a scientific treatise (John of Sacrobosco's *De sphaera* [c. 1220]). William of Boldensele's brief reference to the relics of the crucifixion at Constantinople, for example, is greatly expanded with information and legends about the cross borrowed from the *Legenda aurea,* among other sources, while Odoric of Pordenone's perfunctory account of Lamory (Sumatra?), where the friar lost sight of the Pole Star, becomes the occasion for a lengthy proof of the earth's spherical shape and habitability both above and below the equator, the possibility of circumnavigating the earth, and Jerusalem's geographical centrality.

No less striking than these characteristic moments are the *Mandeville* author's reworked accounts of the beliefs and customs of the non-Christian world. Typically undoing the critical commentary of his principal and secondary sources, the author offers his readers portraits of religious "otherness" characterized by a kind of anthropological tolerance, and he often contrasts the piety and devotion of Muslims and pagans with the indifference of his fellow Christians, suggesting several times that if Christians reformed themselves, God would allow them to take the Holy Land back from the "Saracens" (a word restricted in usage to Muslims), who then controlled it. In addition, the *Mandeville* author has Sir John assert that all rational peoples have some knowledge of the one true God, leaving his audience with a vision of a universal proto-Christian religious unity. Almost the sole exception to the book's even-handed depiction of the non-Christian world is its picture of the Jews, who are represented throughout as the past, present, and future enemies of Christians and Christendom.

Given its capacious view of the East—where the Christian pilgrim's horizon has been vastly expanded so as to encompass Marco Polo's marvelous East as well—and given its at once pious and entertaining mix of information, history, anecdote, and legend, it is hardly surprising that medieval and Renaissance audiences found *The Book of John Mandeville* highly appealing. By the early fifteenth century, it had been translated into seven other languages, sometimes more than once, and would make its way into Danish and Irish just before the first printed editions began to appear all over Europe. If the surviving manuscripts are any evidence, there were four important early translations, all of them made probably sometime around 1400 and each of them surviving in nearly forty manuscripts: Michel Velser's German (made from the Continental version); the anonymous "Vulgate" Latin (from the Interpolated Continental version, and so called to distinguish it from the four independent Latin renderings of the Insular version); Otto von Diemeringen's German (from the Interpolated Continental version and possibly the Vulgate Latin); and the anonymous English Defective version (from the Insular version, and so called because of a large gap in the account of Egypt). Velser's German and the English Defective versions render their French sources quite faithfully (although Velser makes several noteworthy interventions to corroborate his text with personal information), while the Vulgate Latin and von Diemeringen's versions freely and frequently diverge from their sources. The Latin

# M

rendering, for example, significantly abridges the entire work, undoes the *Mandeville* author's anthropological tolerance of religious difference, considerably hardening the text's attitudes toward the non-Christian world (yet dispensing with its blatant anti-Semitism at the same time), and has its more pious version of Sir John explicitly argue against Jerusalem's geographical centrality.

From the standpoint of its modern reception, the most important translation of *The Book of John Mandeville* is the English Cotton version (from the Insular version), which may also have been made around 1400 and which survives in a single manuscript only. Initially printed in 1725 in the first scholarly edition of the *Book* in any language, the Cotton version gives the text an impeccable linguistic pedigree by having Sir John claim that he originally composed his book in Latin, then translated it into French, and then translated the French into English—an anonymous translator's authorizing fable in which a few readers apparently still believe. Reprinted many times throughout the nineteenth century, this "authorial" translation fast became *Mandeville* not only to English-speaking readers, but to those on the Continent as well, and it has served as the citation text for virtually every scholarly study of the *Book,* thereby reducing an international work to an English one.

As the foregoing account suggests, *The Book of John Mandeville* is one of the few medieval works to have had an almost continuous readership since it was first composed. Jean, the duke of Berry (1340–1416), Christine de Pisan (1364–1430), and Leonardo da Vinci (1452–1519) are all known to have owned or read the work, as are such Renaissance cosmographers and explorers as Martin Behaim (1459–1507), whose name is associated with the first globe, Abraham Ortelius (1527–1598), Martin Frobisher (1535?–1594), and Richard Hakluyt (1552?–1616). An Italian miller named Menocchio was burned for heresy in 1599 after confessing that the *Book* had influenced his views on the non-Christian world, and in 1755, Samuel Johnson cited the passage on the earth's spherical shape (from the Cotton version) in the introduction to his famous *Dictionary,* while in the same century children across the channel in Holland were using it as a schoolbook. During the nineteenth and twentieth centuries, there have been scholarly editions in all ten of the medieval languages and popular editions in at least five languages. There is every indication that the work will continue to find a varied and international readership.

**BIBLIOGRAPHY**

Bennett, Josephine Waters. *The Rediscovery of Sir John Mandeville.* The Modern Language Association of America Monograph Series 19. New York: Modern Language Association, 1954.

Campbell, Mary B. *The Witness and the Other World: Exotic European Travel Writing, 400–1600.* Ithaca, NY: Cornell UP, 1988, pp. 122–161.

Deluz, Christiane. *Le livre de Jehan de Mandeville: Une "géographie" au XIVe siècle.* Textes, Études, Congrès. Vol. 8. Louvain-la-Neuve: Institut d'Études Médiévales de l'Université Catholique de Louvain, 1988.

Higgins, Iain. *Writing East: The "Travels" of Sir John Mandeville.* Philadelphia: U of Pennsylvania P, 1997.

Howard, Donald R. "The World of Mandeville's Travels." *Yearbook of English Studies* 1 (1971): 1–17.

Lejeune, Rita. "Jean de Mandeville et les Liégeois." In *Mélanges de linguistique romane et de philologie médiévale offerts à Maurice Delbouille.* Vol. 2. Gembloux: J. Duculot, 1964, pp. 409–437.

Letts, Malcolm, ed. and trans. *Mandeville's Travels: Texts and Translations.* Hakluyt Society, 2nd series, 101–102. London: Hakluyt Society, 1953.

Morrall, Eric John, ed. *Sir John Mandevilles Reisebeschreibung in deutscher Übersetzung von Michel Velser.* Berlin, Akademie-Verlag, 1974.

Moseley, C.W.R.D., trans. *The Travels of Sir John Mandeville.* Harmondsworth, England: Penguin, 1983.

Ridder, Klaus. *Jean de Mandevilles "Reisen": Studien zu Überlieferungsgeschichte der deutschen Übersetzung des Otto von diemeringen.* Münchener Texte und Untersuchungen zur deutschen Literatur des Mittelalters 99. Munich: Artemis, 1991.

Seymour, M.C., ed. *Mandeville's Travels.* Oxford: Clarendon P, 1967.

*Iain Higgins*

**SEE ALSO**

Behaim, Martin; Brunetto Latini; Center of the Earth; Climate; Constantinople; Edges of the World; Hetoum; Holy Land; Jacques de Vitry; Jerusalem; Marco Polo; Marriages between Muslims and Christians, Attitudes toward; Odoric of Pordenone; Paradise, Travel to; Pilgrimage, Christian; Prester John; Sacrobosco, John of; Vincent of Beauvais; William of Boldensele; William of Tripoli

## Manichaeism

A universal religion founded by Mani (216–*c.* 277 C.E.) in Mesopotamia during the Persian Sasanian empire (224–651). Merging elements from Zoroastrianism, the

Judeo-Christian tradition, and Mahayana Buddhism, Mani launched an expansive proselytizing faith that reached westward to the Roman Empire and eastward into India, Central Asia, and eventually China. Despite a history of adversity, Manichaeism proved remarkably adaptable and resilient, surviving, in some cases, for centuries in a host of different cultural, linguistic, and religious settings along the East-West trade route.

From its beginning, Manichaeism was a missionary faith intended for a universal audience. Of his teaching, Mani wrote, "My Church, mine shall spread in all cities and my Gospel shall touch every country." Mani himself traveled to India and later spread his message throughout Iran. During his lifetime, missionaries were sent beyond the borders of the Persian Empire to the Roman Empire. An essential factor in facilitating this missionary expansion was Persia's strategic position straddling the commercial routes between East and West. The Silk Road connecting China and Rome was a conduit not only for luxury goods but for religious beliefs as well. In many cases, the Manichaean missionaries who followed the trade routes first into the Roman Empire and later into China were merchants themselves. The Manichaean teaching, which forbad agricultural labor, appeared more favorably disposed to the practice of commerce, the merchant class often serving as its principal audience. This close association, and in some cases identification, between Manichaean missionaries and multilingual merchants ensured the diffusion of the religion over a broad area.

From its inception, however, Manichaean evangelism encountered vehement opposition. Mani was arrested and killed at the instigation of Zoroastrian priests at the Persian court. Similar tribulations awaited the Manichaean Church as it spread westward into the Roman Empire, first at the hands of Roman authorities and later from the Christian Church and the Byzantine Empire. Consequently, by the sixth century, Manichaeism had largely disappeared from the Western world.

The Manichaean experience in the East, although similarly plagued by persecution and suppression, witnessed some notable successes and a longer life. The eastward advance of Manichaeism into Transoxiana coincided with a schism in the sixth century in which the Central Asian adherents known as Denawars no longer recognized the authority of the sect's traditional leadership in Babylonia. East of the Oxus River, the religion acquired a strategically important audience among Sogdians, whose merchants were the principal transporters of goods between East and West. In the sixth century, the Sogdians, who were also conveyers of Buddhism and Zoroastrianism, brought Manichaeism into the Tarim basin, whence it made its way in the following century into Tang China. This process of transmission was intensified in the seventh and eighth centuries as Islam made rapid gains in Persia and Manichaeans fled Iran, seeking haven in the East. During this eastward advance, Manichaeans adapted their religious vocabulary and message to the largely Buddhist milieu in which they found themselves. Manichaean divine powers were identified with various Buddhas and bodhisattvas, and Mani himself eventually was acclaimed as the Buddha of Light.

The Manichaean presence in Central Asia was enhanced in the eighth century when the khaghan of the Uighur Turks, on coming to the aid of the Chinese Tang court during the An Lushan rebellion (755), was converted by Manichaean priests in the Chinese capital of Loyang. Consequently, Manichaeism made significant inroads among the Uighurs, who in turn exploited their position as strategic allies of the Tang to support the religion in China. Through Uighur request, Manichaean temples were permitted by the government in the Yangtze valley. After the demise of the Uighur Empire in 840, Manichaean influence waned, though Manichaeans were present in the Mongol court of Möngke Khân at Karakorum when the Franciscan friar William of Rubruck arrived in 1253.

In Tang (618–907) China, Manichaeism was relegated to the peripheral status of a foreign faith. In 732, it was proscribed by the Tang court for pretending to be a form of Buddhism. Between 842 and 845, as anti-foreign sentiment erupted in the wake of the Uighur decline, Manichaean temples were closed, property was confiscated, books were burned, and priests were defrocked and executed. Buddhism, Zoroastrianism, and Nestorianism suffered a similar fate. Unlike Zoroastrianism and Nestorianism, however, which virtually disappeared after this, Manichaeism survived, transforming itself into a thoroughly indigenous religion as adherents assimilated Taoist characteristics and formed native communites in the thriving coastal commercial centers of Taizhou, Wenzhou, Fuzhou, and Quanzhou (Marco Polo's Zaitun). Notwithstanding persecutions and suppressions of the religion during the Song (960–1279) and Ming (1368–1644) dynasties, Manichaeism endured at least until the beginning

# M

of the seventeenth century, after which it ceased to exist altogether.

**BIBLIOGRAPHY**

Klimkeit, Hans-Joachim. *Gnosis on the Silk Road.* New York: HarperCollins, 1993.

Lieu, Samuel N.C. *Manichaeism in the Later Roman Empire and Medieval China: A Historical Survey.* Manchester, England: Manchester UP, 1985.

*Daniel Getz*

**SEE ALSO**

Buddhism; Byzantine Empire; China; India; Mongols; Nestorianism; Silk Roads; William of Rubruck; Zoroastrianism

## Manzikert

Known in modern Turkish as Malazgirt, a medieval fortified town in eastern Anatolia, on the upper reaches of the eastern branch of the Euphrates, some thirty miles (fifty km) to the northwest of Lake Van. It was near this town that, in August 1071, the Byzantine army suffered a decisive victory at the hand of Turkish Seljuk forces.

During the spring of that year, the Seljuk sultan Alp Arslan (r. 1063–1072) had been campaigning in northern Syria, a prelude to a projected offensive against the Shi'i Fāṭimid state based in Egypt, when he received word that the Byzantine emperor Romanus IV Diogenes (r. 1068–1072) had advanced into eastern Anatolia with a large army. Eastern and, increasingly, central Anatolia had suffered in the previous years from raids carried out by Turkish tribesmen, known as Turcomans, based in the environs of Azerbaijan. On his accession to the Byzantine throne, Romanus had adopted an aggressive policy, which meant carrying the war over the frontier into Muslim territory. In early summer of 1071, he arrived in eastern Anatolia and captured the town of Manzikert, which had recently come under Turkish control. Whether Romanus was taking advantage of Alp Arslan's preoccupations to the south in order to curtail the Turcoman depredations or this was merely a coincidence remains an open question.

Romanus's campaign was seen by Alp Arslan as a breach of a truce between the two rulers, and after vainly entreating the emperor on this point, the sultan had no choice but to abandon his Syrian campaign and turn his attention to this new danger in his exposed rear. It is clear that he was at a numerical disadvantage,

although the numbers given in various sources for the size of the Byzantine army are surely much exaggerated. In spite of its large size, the Byzantine army was a motley collection of troops including many mercenaries: Greeks, Armenians, Slavs, Franks, and even sundry groups of Turkish tribesmen. This army was both unwieldy and racked by demoralization and internal conflicts. Much of this force had been dispatched by the emperor to the south and thus was not with him on the day of the battle. On the other hand, Alp Arslan commanded a small but compact unit of highly trained and loyal Mamluks (slave soldiers), some 4,000, according to one source (Ayalon 44), along with a larger number of irregulars, Kurds, and Turks. The reports of caliphal emissaries exhorting the Muslim troops before the battle need not be rejected out of hand, and would have raised the morale in the Seljuk camp.

The battle seems to have taken place on Friday, August 26, 1071; its actual course is unclear, but initial fighting appears to have been inconclusive. Throughout the combat, the Byzantine emperor was plagued by a trickle of deserters from his army; it is reported that some Turkish troops even went over to the Seljuks. The battle itself was finally decided by a feigned retreat of the Turkish troops that succeeded in drawing the Byzantine forces, already demoralized, into an ambush. Romanus himself was taken prisoner. Alp Arslan treated him well and offered him a relatively mild peace treaty, including the payment of annual tribute and the transfer of several towns in the area, clearly showing that even after his victory, the sultan was not intent on conquering Anatolia, but rather was still focused on his Fāṭimid enemies. In any case, events were soon to render this policy obsolete. Romanus himself was deposed the following year. More important, the Seljuk victory at Manzikert was the major milestone of the Turkish takeover of Anatolia. In its aftermath, the Byzantine frontier in eastern Anatolia, which had more or less maintained itself vis-à-vis the Muslims for more than 400 years, completely collapsed. Turkish tribesmen entered almost all of Anatolia in increasing numbers, leading to the growing Turkification (and Islamization) of the country. In a sense, "Turkey" can be said to have been born at the battle of Manzikert.

**BIBLIOGRAPHY**

Ayalon, David. "From Ayyūbids to Mamlūks." *Revue des études islamiques* 49 (1981): 43–57.

Cahen, Claude. *Pre-Ottoman Turkey.* London: Sidgwick and Jackson, 1968, pp. 26–30.

Friendly, Alfred. *The Dreadful Day: The Battle of Manzikert, 1071.* London: Hutchinson, 1981.

Hillenbrand, Carole. "Malāzgird. 2. The Battle." *Encyclopedia of Islam.* New edition. Leiden: Brill, 1960, 6:243–244.

Vryonis, Spiros. *The Decline of Medieval Hellenism in Asia Minor and the Process of Islamization from the Eleventh through the Fifteenth Century.* Berkeley: U of California P, 1971, pp. 96–104.

*Reuven Amitai-Preiss*

**SEE ALSO**
Byzantine Empire; Fātimids; Mamluks; Seljuk Turks; Shi'ism

## Map, Agrippa's World
*See* Agrippa's World Map

## Map, Anglo-Saxon
*See* Cotton World Map

## Map of Asia, Jerome
*See* Jerome Map of Asia

## Map, Borgia
*See* Borgia Map

## Map, Cotton World
*See* Cotton World Map

## Map, Ebstorf World
*See* Ebstorf World Map

## Map, Gough
*See* Gough Map

## Map, Henry of Mainz
*See* Henry of Mainz Map

## Map, Hereford
*See* Hereford Map

## Map, Madaba Mosaic
*See* Madaba Mosaic Map

## Map, Mauro
*See* Mauro Map, [Fra]

## Map, Psalter
*See* Psalter Map

## Map, Vinland
*See* Vinland Map

## Map, Zeitz
*See* Zeitz Map

## *Mappamundi*

One of the most important forms of medieval cartography, a type of painted map that depicted the surface of the earth by representing both a generalized concept of the universe and particular features such as cities, mountains, and seas.

The term *mappamundi* comes from "mappa" (tablecloth or napkin) and "mundus" (the world). Such maps were noted in catalogues of monastic libraries as early as the ninth century. Their origins are to be sought both in classical antiquity and in the Bible.

Since no painted maps have survived from antiquity, scholars have been able to study only descriptions and later copies, and therefore can merely speculate on the appearance of the originals. Greek philosophers provided the roots of theoretical cartography in their descriptions of nature, while the more practically oriented Romans produced factually specific maps that showed roads and itineraries for military and commercial use. Thus the Greeks created the concept of cosmography, with its components of geography and cartography, while the Romans specialized in studying the inhabited world, known in Greek as the *oikoumene*.

The Hellenistic Greeks also gave the West the idea of a spherical earth, but applications to mapmaking were limited, since a sphere was difficult to represent before the age of perspective. Pythagoras, for example (end of the sixth century B.C.E.) and Parmenides (fifth century B.C.E.) certainly understood the earth as a

# M

sphere, and their opinion was later followed by Plato, Eratosthenes, and Ptolemy. However it was through the works of the Stoic philosopher Krates of Mallos, who wrote commentaries on Homer in the second century B.C.E., that this knowledge was transferred to the West. Krates conceived of the earth as a sphere divided into four insular continents by two zones of ocean intersecting each other, with one going through both poles and the other following the equator. Our north-

ern habitable continent thus corresponds to a southern habitable equivalent, a periecumenical continent at the backside, and an antipodal continent at the southern backside of the sphere, where people are imagined as having feet positioned opposite to those of people in the known world.

Latin sources for the transmission of these ideas to the West were the fifth-century school texts of Martianus Capella (*The Marriage of Mercury and Philology*)

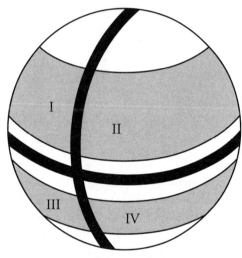

Diagram 1
Sphere according to Krates of Mallos
Habitable Continents I–IV

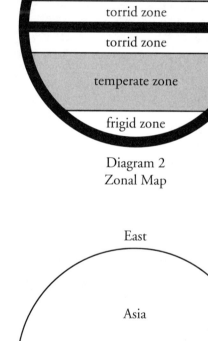

Diagram 2
Zonal Map

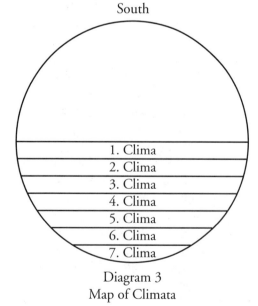

Diagram 3
Map of Climata

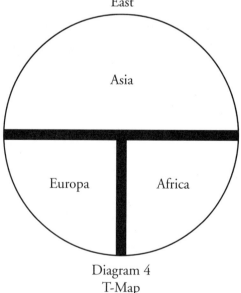

Diagram 4
T-Map

Description of *Mappamundi.* Diagrams 1–4.

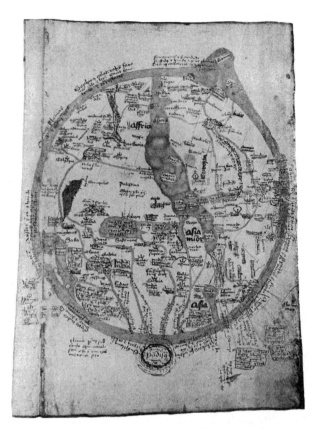

Mappamundi (anonymous) oriented to the west, *c.* 1450. Once Olomouc, Czech Republic Studienbibliothek MS g/9/155; lost after World War II. Reproduced by permission of the Map Division, The New York Public Library (Astor, Lenox and Tilden Foundations) from Anton Mayer, *Mittelalterliche Weltkarten aus Olmütz,* vol. 8 of *Kartographische Denkmäler der Sudetenländer,* Prague: K. André, 1932, plate 1.

and Macrobius (*Commentary on the Dream of Scipio*), both widely consulted throughout the Middle Ages. Macrobius's text is often illustrated in the manuscript tradition by what is usually called a *zone map,* which renders visually the cartographic ideas of Krates. The medieval zone map represents the sphere as divided into five zones, of which the two extreme, at the poles, are not habitable because they are too cold. The two zones next to them are habitable, while the central zone, around the equator, is intensely hot and therefore uninhabitable. Among some Greek cartographic thinkers, the known habitable part of the Northern Hemisphere is further subdivided into seven climates named according to the characteristic places located in each.

Along with the ancient Greek theorists, early biblical commentators contributed to the development of these maps, since Holy Scripture was considered the supreme authority and all scientific statements had to be measured against it. St. Jerome, in translating the Old Testament from Hebrew into Latin, used the word *terra* to name the *oikoumene,* and for the New Testament term *kosmos* he used the word *mundus,* thus distinguishing between the inhabited and uninhabited world. The *oikoumene* is the setting for the fall and salvation of mankind, as well as the life and passion of Christ. Since early world maps were most often incorporated into histories of the world, they tended to represent chiefly the *oikoumene.*

The term *mappamundi,* however, comprises many types of maps, not only world maps. Of the two maps from the twelfth century associated with the name of St. Jerome, one shows the East, the other the Holy Land, and they seem to have been conceived for illustrating the stories of the Old and New Testament. St. Augustine believed Asia to be as big as Europe and Africa together, a concept of proportion that formed the basis for the extremely popular T-O type of world map. T-O maps are oriented with the east at the top instead of north because the east was seen as the direction from which warmth and light came. The term is based on an idea of the world as a disk—the "O"—that was then subdivided into three continents by three major waterways: the river Don (Tanais) between Europe and Asia, the Nile between Asia and Africa, and the Mediterranean Sea between Europe and Africa. It was these waterways that formed the shape of a "T," thus separating Asia at the top from Europe on the lower left and Africa on the lower right. The T-O design became the symbol of the inhabited earth in medieval manuscripts, and, since the Bible did not refer to continents by their geographic names, each landmass in this schema was usually associated with one of the sons of Noah, with Asia as the land of Shem, Africa as the land of Ham, and Europe as the land of Japhet.

Isidore of Seville (d. 636) offers the first synthesis of Christian and classical elements in cartography, and his encyclopedic works contain examples of painted T-O maps. Isidore also originated a variant design for a map in which a circular *oikoumene* was attached like a patch to a spherical earth, which was in turn characterized by arched or curved climatic zones. Isidore's map of this type contained a region marked "Aethiopes" in the south and another designated "Riphei Montes" in the north; other island continents were not marked. A large map now in Rome (Biblioteca Apostolica Vaticana MS Lat. 6018) is oriented from south to east and

# M

presents opposite to the *oikoumene* an island in the southwest called *insula [h]omini incognita* ("island of unknown men"), though this island is not given a great deal of space or detail. The Christian *oikoumene* usually contained a representation of Paradise in the extreme east above India and connected with the rest of the world by the Four Rivers of Paradise.

Another variant *mappamundi* was that found in Beatus of Liébana's commentary on the Book of Revelation. The original manuscript was created between 776 and 786 but is now lost. There are, however, seventeen copies dating from the tenth to thirteenth centuries. The Beatus map was conceived to illustrate the missions of the Twelve Apostles to the ends of the world. A typical map of the Beatus type shows the world as oval and follows the T model, but it shows in the south (the right side of the map) a fourth continent, inaccessible by reason of heat. This fourth continent was placed near the equator or the Sahara desert and was believed to be inhabited by a race of monstrous men who were called *sciopods* because of their custom of using their single giant foot as a sunshade.

One of the most beautifully illustrated twelfth-century encyclopedias was the *Liber Floridus,* composed by the canon Lambert of Saint-Omer between 1112 and 1121. This unique encyclopedia contains numerous map drawings, including, for example, a T-O map held in the left hand of the emperor Augustus, showing him as the ruler of the world; some illustrations depicted the orbits of the planets, and variant forms of the climatic or zone map combined with a T-O map. Lambert seems to have copied an early map that he called the geometrical sphere of Martianus Capella, though this attribution cannot be verified from extant sources. In this map, the planisphere is oriented toward the east, and the *oikoumene* at the left (that is, the Northern Hemisphere) is created by diminishing the uninhabitable zones at the pole and at the equator. It is shaped like a semicircle divided by the T and contains numerous geographical details. The southern hemisphere placed on the right side of the map contains a lengthy text explaining the structure of the map. Paradise is placed in the extreme east outside of the ring of Ocean or O. It is star-shaped and from it emanate the Four Rivers of Paradise. Opposite to it, below in the extreme west, is an island at the western edge of the world, an antipodal zone offering other peoples, times, and seasons.

This period also produced enormous world maps intended for teaching purposes and requiring the skins of many sheep and goats. Among these are the great maps of Ebstorf and Hereford. An example of an extremely miniaturized form of these maps is to be found in a thirteenth-century psalter manuscript now in London (British Library MS Additional 28681, fol. 9). These maps were made for liturgical use. They glorified the Creation and were used for devotional purposes, either in churches, as was the case with the oversized ones, or in private, in individual prayer books.

By the period of the crusades, Jerusalem had typically become the center of the East on Western world maps, which now began to contain pictorial representations of world history projected on the surface of the map in the form of a universal chronicle. For example, they would often show Adam and Eve in Paradise, Noah's ark on Mount Ararat (located in what is now Turkey), Christ in Jerusalem, the tombs of the apostles in various parts of the world (especially India), the location of Troy, and the nations of Gog and Magog, thought to be precursors of the Antichrist, in the Caucasus mountains. In the Jerusalem-centered maps, the world was again represented by the T-O diagram, but instead of the fourth continent, which Isidore and Beatus had placed in the south, there now often appeared a band of monstrous races of men at the extreme edge of Africa. Such *mappaemundi* remained popular throughout the late Middle Ages, but they did not survey the land, and it was not until the discoveries of sea routes to India and America that a real change in universal mapping took place.

## BIBLIOGRAPHY

Brincken, Anna-Dorothee von den. *Fines terrae: Die Enden der Erde.* See Gen Bib.

———. "Mappa mundi und Chronographia: Studien zur imago mundi des abendländischen Mittelalters." In *Deutsches Archiv für Erforschung des Mittelalters* 24 (1968): 118–186.

———. *Kartographische Quellen: Welt-, See- und Regionalkarten.* Typologie des Sources du Moyen-Age Occidental, Fasc. 51. Turnhout: Brepols, 1988.

Brodersen, Kai. *Terra cognita: Studien zur römischen Raumerfassung.* Spudasmata 59. Hildesheim: Olms, 1995.

Campbell, Tony. *Early Maps.* New York: Abbeville Press, 1981.

Crone, Gerald Roe. *Maps and Their Makers: An Introduction to the History of Cartography.* London: Hutchinson, 1966.

Destombes, Marcel, ed. *Mappemondes.* See Gen. Bib.

Edson, Evelyn. *Mapping Time and Space: How Medieval Mapmakers Viewed Their World.* London: British Library, 1998.

Harley-Woodward. *The History of Cartography.* Vol. 1. See
Gen. Bib.

Harvey, P.D.A. *Medieval Maps.* London: The British Library,
1991.

————. *Mappa Mundi: The Hereford World Map.* London:
British Library, 1996.

*The Image of the World: An Interactive Exploration of Ten His-
toric World Maps.* CD-ROM. Produced by Karen Brookfield. London: The British Library, 1995.

Miller, Konrad. *Mappaemundi: Die Ältesten Weltkarten.* Heft
5: Die Ebstorfkarte. Mit dem Facsimile der Karte in den
Farben des Originals. Stuttgart: Roth, 1896.

Whitfield, Peter. *The Image of the World: 20 Centuries of
World Maps.* London: The British Library; San Francisco:
Pomegranate Artbooks, 1994.

*Anna-Dorothee von den Brincken*

**SEE ALSO**
Antipodes; Ararat, Mount; Beatus Maps; Center of the
Earth; Climate; Ebstorf World Map; Four Rivers of
Paradise; Geography in Medieval Europe; Gog and Magog;
Hereford Map; Isidore of Seville; Jerome Map of Asia; *Liber
Floridus;* Mauro Map, [Fra]; *Oikoumene;* Psalter Map;
Ptolemy; Walsperger, Andreas

## Mappamundi, Bell
*See* Bell *Mappamundi*

## Maps

Maps of the world are by far the commonest type of
medieval map known to us, but most are no more than
simple diagrams. Some show the whole sphere of the
earth, seen from the side, divided by horizontal lines
into five or more climatic zones. Three separate traditions of these have been distinguished. One is based on
the fifth-century commentary by Macrobius on
Cicero's *Dream of Scipio,* discussing the nature of the
universe; another is based on the encyclopedic work of
Martianus Capella, also of the fifth century, and often
shows the diagonal ecliptic, with the signs of the
zodiac; and the third, later, group, first appearing in the
eleventh-century work of Petrus Alphonsus, shows
Arab influence in its inclusion of Arin, the mythical
town at the center of the inhabited world. However, in
all three groups there are maps that give more detailed
information: outlines of seas and continents superimposed on the zonal bands, names of towns and regions,
or geographical notes on the surface of the map.

Most medieval world maps are not maps of the whole
earth, like these, but maps exclusively or primarily of the
inhabited world, the landmass of the Northern Hemisphere known to the ancients, forming the three continents of Europe, Asia, and Africa. Often it is shown in
circular form, a kind of projection that may have arisen
from analogy with the zonal maps. Sometimes a fourth
continent, presumed to lie in the Southern Hemisphere,
is shown, separated from the inhabited world by the
impassable ocean around the equator; Africa was thought
to lie wholly in the Northern Hemisphere. All these maps
of the inhabited world that date from before the fifteenth
century derive ultimately from one or more maps made
in the Roman period, of which these distant derivatives
are our only certain evidence, vastly oversimplified, or
travestied by successions of ill-informed copyists, and
often distorted by being forced into circular shape. It has
been suggested that the map that underlies these
medieval maps resulted from a survey of the world
ordered by Julius Caesar in 44 B.C.E. and completed
thirty-two years later; it was from this survey that a map
of the world was then put up by Marcus Vipsanius
Agrippa in a public colonnade at Rome. However, it has
also been argued that the two texts that tell us of this survey are unreliably late and that what Pliny describes as set
up by Agrippa was not a map but a written description.
Whenever the Roman original was produced, enough
tolerably accurate features have survived the process of
transmission on one or another of its medieval derivatives
to show that it must have been a very good map. Besides
coastal outlines, rivers, and mountains, it probably
showed provincial boundaries within the empire, boundaries of regions or nations outside it, and—though this
has been questioned—a significant number of towns.

However, none of the medieval derivatives shows
more than the coastal outlines with a selection of these
features, and many do not even show this. Simplest of
all are the so-called T-O maps, no more than a circle
divided into three parts by waterways that form a T or a
Y to separate the three continents, sometimes slightly
elaborated by such additions as major rivers, the names
of regions, or short geographical notes. T-O maps usually—but not always—are drawn with east at the top.
Certain frequently copied books were regularly illustrated by maps of this kind, among them the
*Jugurthine War* by Sallust (86–34 B.C.E.), the *Etymologies* and *Nature of Things* by Isidore of Seville (*c.* 560–
636), and the *Picture of the World* by Gautier de Metz
(written *c.* 1245).

Some books were illustrated, probably by their
authors, with world maps more elaborate than the T-O

# M

diagrams. Two are especially noteworthy. The so-called Beatus maps illustrate copies of the commentary on the Apocalypse that was written in Spain by Beatus of Liébana in the late eighth century; mostly rectangular in shape, and highly stylized, they show major physical features with some names of regions and towns, with the additions also of the Terrestrial Paradise, showing Adam and Eve, and of notes on the travels of the apostles. The *Liber Floridus,* written by Lambert of Saint-Omer in the early twelfth century, includes a circular world map with details that differ from one copy to another but include some postclassical names such as Norway and Venice. Sometimes a map was attached to a text, normally unillustrated, on the initiative of a copyist, such as the Anglo-Saxon map, which accompanies a copy of Priscian's *Periegesis* (in a Latin translation), and sometimes a map was copied divorced from any text—the eighth-century Albi map, a highly schematic map of the Mediterranean, is an example.

In the course of the twelfth century an important genre of world maps developed, apparently in northern France. Circular in shape, they included not only straightforward geographical details, modern as well as classical, but also what came to be on the larger maps a great mass of general information about distant places, their natural history, and their inhabitants. References were also drawn from Genesis and Exodus, from geographical writers such as Solinus and Isidore, and from literary sources like the Alexander romances. The map became a kind of encyclopedia, arranged geographically, with pictures accompanying the written notes. A short tract—perhaps a lecture—by Hugh of Saint-Victor at Paris described such a map in the early twelfth century; the world map in a French manuscript (now at Munich) of Isidore of Seville's work shows signs of this development, and the largest recorded map of this kind, six meters across, was painted on a wall in the church at Chalivoy-Milon, near Bourges, in the twelfth century (it was destroyed in 1885). However, the genre seems to have been further developed, particularly in England, where the Anglo-Saxon map suggests there may have been unusually good derivatives of the Roman world map. World maps are recorded at Lincoln in the mid-twelfth century and at Durham in 1195, and it was at Durham that the so-called Henry of Mainz world map was drawn in the late twelfth century and attached to a copy of the *Imago mundi* of Honorius Augustodunensis (now in the library at Corpus Christi College, Cambridge). This map contained

little general information, but the thirteenth century produced a succession of maps in this genre either drawn in England or with likely English associations: the Ebstorf map, the London Psalter map, the Hereford map, the Duchy of Cornwall map, which is a fragment of a similar large map, probably of about 1283. The Vercelli map, more sketchily drawn, perhaps about 1218, has been variously ascribed to Italy, southern France, and Spain, but a northern French or English origin is possible. Other maps of the genre that we know only by report include two painted in the 1230s on walls of Westminster Palace and Winchester Castle, both royal residences.

Though some of the maps include a little local information, none contains anything derived from recent distant journeys and, though the Ebstorf map mentions the possibility, none was intended as a guide to travel. The large world maps were meant for display, even ostentation, but they were also meant for edification rather than for simple instruction. They were implicitly representations of God's creation, in all its variety; the Ebstorf, London Psalter, and Hereford maps all include a figure of God, and the Henry of Mainz map has an angel in each corner. The mass of information on the large maps, while interesting and entertaining, was placed in a setting that gave it moral content as well.

An offshoot of the French and English world maps of the twelfth and thirteenth centuries was a group of regional maps developed from the same sources. The Roman map may well have been produced as a series of regional maps, as we find in medieval Islamic atlases, but, if so, no Christian derivative appears to have followed suit. At Madaba, in Jordan, a sixth-century mosaic is a map of the Near East with names in Greek, but from Europe we have no regional maps before the twelfth century. Then, however, there is a map of Europe alone in Lambert of Saint-Omer's autograph manuscript of his *Liber Floridus* and maps of Asia and of the Near East—the so-called Jerome maps—in a manuscript from Tournai of works by St. Jerome. All these are probably simple sections of world maps, and so too—though with added notes—are a map of Europe and the Mediterranean (often called a world map) and a map of Palestine (in three versions) that were drawn by Matthew Paris, chronicler and monk at St. Albans in the mid-thirteenth century. Matthew Paris is one of the few identifiable people in medieval Europe who took an innovative interest in mapmaking.

Of his four maps of Britain, one took its outline from one world map, the others probably from another; but within these outlines he entered towns, rivers, hills, and geographical notes, drawn from other sources that included his own and other people's direct experience. They also included itineraries, notably one of the route from Dover to the north of England. Another of Matthew Paris's productions, again in four versions, was an itinerary in graphic form—effectively a road strip-map—from London to Rome and southern Italy. Another, quite different, map of Palestine by Matthew Paris gives the distances between the coastal towns in terms of days' journeys. Part of the interest of his cartographic work is that it gives us medieval Europe's earliest known association between maps and travel.

A lasting link between maps and travel was first established in the late thirteenth century by the portolan charts. These seem to have developed as aids to navigation, though just how they were used is uncertain and most of those that survive were probably library copies, never taken to sea. Even so, they reflect the way that sea captains, first of Italy and Spain, later of Portugal, extended their knowledge beyond the Mediterranean, along the Atlantic coast to the English Channel then, in the fifteenth century, southward from Morocco to Cape Bojador and beyond. In the general context of medieval maps, the portolan charts are especially important because they introduced to European mapping the concept of scale, a fixed proportion between distances on the map and on the ground—a concept lost since the Roman period. On a map for navigation scale was essential: the sea offered an infinite number of possible routes, and unless a map could show the correct direction and distance between any two points, it would be useless. In travel by land, however, the number of possible routes was restricted to roads and rivers, and a map that showed places in correct sequence along them, with notes of distances, would mostly be as useful as one drawn to scale throughout. In fact it was only in the sixteenth century that maps of areas without coastal outlines came to be commonly drawn to consistent scale.

We see the influence of the portolan charts on the Gough map of Britain, drawn about 1360: the south and southeast coasts, regularly visited by Italian galleys on the so-called Flanders voyages, are of easily recognized shape, whereas the rest of the coastal outline is related to the unimproved world maps of the thirteenth century. Also from mid-fourteenth-century En-

gland is the Aslake map, a large world map of which only a fragment survives; this fragment includes North African place-names and the Canary Islands—discovered in 1336—which must derive from portolan charts. However, most world maps from late-medieval England continued wholly in the tradition deriving from Roman maps; notable among them are the rather crude maps drawn to illustrate the *Polychronicon*, a popular universal history written by Ranulf Higden, a monk at Chester who died about 1364. Many maps of this kind are in the shape of an oval or a mandorla.

With the exception of the Gough map, it is from Italy, not northwest Europe, that we have the most innovative maps of the fourteenth century. Especially important was the work of Pietro Vesconte—the diminutive form "Perrino," which appears on one atlas and one map, may have been used by him or by another member of his family. Although originally from Genoa, he worked principally at Venice, between 1310 and 1330. Besides making portolan charts, he produced in 1321 the earliest known world map to incorporate any part of the outlines borrowed from them; with respect to the Black Sea and the eastern Mediterranean, his world map marks a complete break with tradition. He also produced plans of cities, and a map of Palestine that is of great interest: a grid divides it into squares one league each way and, as a note explains, each town is assigned to a defined square, an extraordinarily early application of scale to a land-based map. The concept is described at some length in the text that accompanies these particular maps, Marino Sanudo's *Secrets for True Crusaders*. A map of Italy drawn at Naples about 1320 may well have been drafted, or at least influenced, by Vesconte; the coastline is taken from portolan charts, but it shows many inland features—mountains, rivers, and towns. The Gough map is the only comparable regional map from the fourteenth century.

The maps of Ptolemy were introduced to Western Europe when his *Geography* was translated into Latin, about 1406. This was the first of several important developments in fifteenth-century mapping. It was not just that Ptolemy offered scale-maps of much more of the world than the portolan charts. Actually, for the areas they both covered, the portolan charts provided a better outline, and in certain areas even some traditional derivatives of Roman maps were more accurate—Ptolemy, for instance, greatly distorted the shape of Scotland. Some world maps drawn in the fifteenth

# M

century largely ignored (or knew nothing of) Ptolemy's maps; one by Andrea Bianco in 1436 is an example and, if genuine, the Vinland map is another. What was especially important about Ptolemy's maps was that they were based on specific geographical coordinates of the places they showed, and extensive lists of toponyms and their precise coordinates—in degrees, minutes, and sometimes seconds—appeared in the long text that accompanied this first atlas in the Western tradition. Whether these coordinates were right or wrong, they provided a secure, permanent framework for the maps, so that the outlines did not lie at the mercy of each successive copyist. Though Vesconte's grid-map of Palestine may be seen as a precursor, the concept was new to medieval cartography.

In the fifteenth century, however, Ptolemy's influence was limited. In the 1420s and 1430s, scholars at Vienna and nearby Klosterneuburg were involved in mathematical and astronomical work that included geographical coordinates, taking as their basis the lists known as the Toledo tables from eleventh-century Arab Spain; a few fragmentary sketches are all that is known of this work, along with diagrams and tables. A copy of Ptolemy's *Geography* made in 1427 included a new map of Scandinavia that was based on an accompanying list of 130 places with their coordinates, and a revised version of the list is known; these were the work of Claudius Clavus, a Dane who was living at Rome, but they are far from accurate. Later manuscripts of the *Geography* include other new maps, similarly based on latitude and longitude, showing the contemporary places of a region to set beside the ancient geography of Ptolemy, and some of these new maps were copied separately, apart from Ptolemy's maps. Most are of Italy, but they include two maps of Germany, one manuscript and one printed, that are attributed to Nicholas of Cusa, cardinal and philosopher; he may have drafted them but they are certainly later, perhaps much later, than his death in 1464.

Effective use of geographical coordinates for constructing maps lay well in the future; only after the mid-1700s did mechanical timepieces make it possible to measure longitude accurately. The portolan charts must have been made by careful measurement of directions and distances, probably steadily corrected over a long period, and the same method was used in the late fifteenth century to construct several notable scale-maps of inland areas that could not use the charts' coastal outline as a framework. Erhard Etzlaub,

instrument maker and surveyor of Nuremberg, published two woodcut versions of a road map of central Europe, from the Baltic to Italy, probably in 1500 and 1501; the coastline came from Ptolemy. A little earlier, Konrad Turst had produced a manuscript map of Switzerland—an impressive achievement, given the difficulties of the terrain—foreshadowing the maps of areas of southwest Germany that were printed in the early sixteenth century.

Meanwhile, however, new discoveries had radically altered both portolan charts and world maps. Some early travels had been slow to appear on maps, and the first surviving map to contain information from Marco Polo's late-thirteenth-century journeys to China was produced by 1375. On the other hand, the Canaries, discovered in 1336, appear on a portolan chart of 1339, and in the fifteenth century the Portuguese discoveries in Africa were quickly recorded on maps—though we have none from Portugal itself—and the successive advances along the coast can be followed step-by-step in surviving charts with, apparently, little time lag. Their progress beyond the equator brought significant change to maps; now, for the first time, lands could be shown in the Southern Hemisphere that were not just imagined or inferred. The Cape of Good Hope, which Bartolomeu Dias reached in 1488, appears on the 1492 globe of Martin Behaim and on the contemporary world maps produced by Henry Martellus at Florence that, though still based on Ptolemy for East Africa and Asia, present an entirely new picture of the shape of the known world. Not all fifteenth-century maps were so up-to-date: the Borgia world map, engraved on a metal plate sixty-five centimeters across, is in the style of the encyclopedic maps of two centuries earlier, and its outline derives from the same Roman sources, barely influenced by portolan charts even in the Black Sea and Mediterranean. At first sight the world map of Fra Mauro, from around 1459, seems the same, though much larger: its surface is covered with a mass of pictures and detailed notes. However, unlike the Borgia map, it incorporates the latest information from the voyages of discovery, and unlike the encyclopedic world maps of northwest Europe, the information conveyed is primarily geographical.

More than a thousand medieval world maps are known (Woodward counts 1,100), and some 180 portolan charts of the fourteenth and fifteenth centuries. Clearly, many more were drawn that are now lost. Even so, we should not suppose that the maps were familiar, frequently encountered objects in medieval Europe. Very few of the world maps were more than simple diagrams, illustrating books known only to a limited, learned readership; of those known that were more than this, most have been specifically mentioned here—their number is very small. The portolan charts were clearly known to others besides professional seamen, but even so, they were primarily tools of navigation, a technique of a particular craft. Where we find a medieval mapmaker moving outside these traditional confines, applying cartography in some new context—such as Matthew Paris's maps of Britain, Pietro Vesconte's grid-map of Palestine—we should see this as an imaginative conceptual leap of great originality. Most people in the Middle Ages were simply not accustomed to using maps, and it was only in the late fifteenth century that we see the first signs of the rapid spread of mapmaking that occurred in the sixteenth. It was only then, too, that the idea of using maps as guides to travel on land began to be accepted; earlier we have only exceptional instances—the Gough map and perhaps one or two others.

All this is fully borne out by the local maps that survive from the Middle Ages—maps of small areas known personally to the mapmaker. Few are known, and that this is because few were made, not just because few have survived, is shown by those in two large monastic archives in England, at Westminster and Durham, where they were clearly the idea of one or two individuals, not a normal part of estate management. In fact, people in the Middle Ages normally seem to have made not even the simplest sketch-map to set out topographical relationships, the positions of features on the ground. Many of the local maps we have belong to strictly limited traditions of maps of particular sorts, and nearly all are oddly concentrated in particular areas. From large parts of Europe we have none at all, and probably none were made. Those we have are, almost without exception, picture-maps: any feature above ground level is shown pictorially, not in outline plan, and there is no attempt at uniform scale. The exceptions are of great interest, though as we know nothing of how or why the maps were made we cannot assess their significance. One is a plan of Venice, of which our three copies date from the fourteenth century, though the original was probably of the twelfth; buildings are shown in elevation but the map's basis seems to be a grand plan drawn to scale. Another, a mid-fifteenth-century copy of a map of about 1422,

shows Vienna, with Bratislava inset; at the foot is a scale-bar, a feature deriving, perhaps directly copied, from portolan charts.

Some medieval local maps have a Roman ancestry, in form or in content. An ideal plan of a monastery, drawn probably at Reichenau in the early ninth century and then sent to St. Gall, where it has remained ever since, is the latest known product of the Roman surveyors' mapmaking tradition: its conventions, perhaps its techniques, are those we find in the few surviving examples of Roman scale-plans. Plans of buildings in the Holy Land, accompanying Arculf's account of his visit in 670, belong to the same tradition, and Roman originals probably lie behind most medieval maps of any part of Palestine. Among these are the maps found in the many manuscripts of Rashi's commentaries on the Hebrew Bible and the Babylonian Talmud: Rashi (Rabbi Shlomo Isaaki) was a French Jewish scholar who died in 1105. Among them, too, are plans of Jerusalem that show the city with circular walls, though others, showing it with straight walls, were more likely based on contemporary information. City plans were, in fact, one genre of local map that developed in medieval Italy, but probably originated from Roman models. The earliest are representations of Verona (tenth century) and Rome (twelfth century), each showing simply the city's principal monuments within its walls; but from the thirteenth century, progressively more detailed picture-maps of cities were drawn, culminating in the fully realistic bird's-eye city views of the late fifteenth. By this time the genre was spreading beyond Italy—it produced plans of Bristol about 1480 and of Rodez in 1495—and the city plans drawn in Italy itself included Cairo, Constantinople, and Jerusalem. It combined with the traditions of the portolan charts to produce the earliest of the *isolarii*, books of islands, which proliferated in the sixteenth and seventeenth centuries: the *Book of the Islands of the Archipelago*, written by Cristoforo Buondelmonti about 1420, contained a descriptive and historical account of the Aegean with a pictorial map of each island and a plan of Constantinople.

It is unsurprising that the city plans, one particular kind of local map, come from one particular part of Europe, but more surprising that local maps in general are confined to limited areas. Thus, some thirty-five are known from medieval England, none from Wales or Scotland; the fifteen from the Netherlands all come from a narrow coastal strip, from Hilversum in the north to

# M

Bruges in the south; from the whole of Europe east of the Rhine and north of the Main we have only two, sketch-maps of lands of the Teutonic Order in Pomerania; from Spain and Portugal there seem to be none at all. Their chronology, however, is more uniform: none are earlier than 1300 except a very few from England and Italy, and most date from the fifteenth century. Within each area there is a great variety of styles, from the detailed picture-map, carefully drawn and colored, to the merest rough sketch; it was the idea of drawing maps that seems to have existed in some regions and not others, not traditions of drawing them in any particular way.

We can only guess why this idea of drawing maps arose in some areas, but there was probably a different reason in each case. Thus, in France, it may have been the use of maps in legal proceedings; in England, architects' growing custom of giving building plans to their clients. But the idea of drawing maps, however introduced, was applied to widely varied purposes: not all the French maps are connected with lawsuits, and only one surviving English one is a building plan. In one group of maps from north Italy, each showing a city with its surrounds, we may see a precocious use of maps for administration by the Venetian government. Very few local maps were drawn as guides to journeys, though one notable example is a plan of the late fourteenth or early fifteenth century showing the roads through Sherwood Forest in England. Few maps, apart from the portolan charts, provide links between cartography and travel in medieval Europe.

## BIBLIOGRAPHY

Beazley, C. Raymond. *The Dawn of Modern Geography.* 3 vols. 1897–1906; rpt. New York: Smith, 1949.

Brincken, Anna-Dorothee von den. *Fines Terrae.* See Gen. Bib.

Delano-Smith, Catherine, and Mayer I. Gruber. "Rashi's Legacy: Maps of the Holy Land." *The Map Collector* (Tring, England) 59 (1992): 30–35.

————, and Roger J.P. Kain. *English Maps: A History.* Toronto and Buffalo: U of Toronto P, 1999, pp. 7–48.

Edson, Evelyn. *Mapping Time and Space: How Medieval Mapmakers Viewed Their World.* London: British Library, 1997.

Harley-Woodward, *The History of Cartography.* Vol. 1. See Gen. Bib.

Harvey, P.D.A. *The History of Topographical Maps: Symbols, Pictures and Surveys.* London: Thames and Hudson, 1980.

————. *Medieval Maps.* London: British Library, 1991.

————. *Mappa Mundi: The Hereford World Map.* London: British Library, 1996.

Pelletier, Monique, ed. *Géographie du monde au moyen age et à la renaissance.* Mémoires de la section de géographie, 15. Paris: Comité des Travaux Historiques et Scientifiques, 1989.

P.D.A. Harvey

SEE ALSO

Agrippa's World Map; Arculf; Beatus Maps; Behaim, Martin; Bojador, Cape; Borgia Map; Bruges; Canary Islands; Cartography, Arabic; Center of the Earth; City Plans; Clavus, Claudius; Climate; Constantinople; Cotton World Map; Dias, Bartolomeu; Ebstorf World Map; Etzlaub, Erhard; Galley; Genoa; Geography in Medieval Europe; Gough Map; Henry of Mainz Map; Hereford Map; Higden, Ranulf; Holy Land; Honorius Augustodunensis; Isidore of Seville; Itineraries and *Periploi;* Jerome Map; Jerusalem; Jerusalem City Plans; Klosterneuberg Map Corpus; Liber Floridus; Madaba Mosaic Map; Marco Polo; Matthew Paris; Mauro Map, [Fra]; Nicholas of Cusa; Paradise, Travel to; Pliny the Elder; Portolan Charts; Portuguese Expansion; Psalter Map; Ptolemy; Rome as a Pilgrimage Site; Sallust Maps; Sanudo, Marino; Scandinavian World Maps; Solinus, Julius Gaius; *Terra Australes;* Teutonic Order; Venice; Vesconte, Pietro/Perrino; Vinland Map

## Maps, Beatus
*See* Beatus Maps

## Maps, Memory and
*See* Memory and Maps

## Maps, Sallust
*See* Sallust Maps

## Maps, Scandinavian World
*See* Scandinavian World Maps

## Marco Polo [Marcus Paulus] (1254–1324)

The son of a Venetian merchant, to whom is ascribed a remarkable account of his travels throughout the medieval Mongol Empire, undertaken during some twenty-four years in the late thirteenth century (1271–1295). The text that records the travels of the Polo family, as well as important information about Asian trade and Mongol history was appropriately entitled *Divisament dou monde* (Description of the World) by the man who actually wrote it, Rustichello of Pisa. While Marco's degree of authorial influence and content is uncertain, he presumably made some notes during his residence in China, and the book that has come, somewhat inaccurately, in modern times to be called his *Travels* is now one of the best known (if not so often read) pieces of travel literature in the history of Western civilization.

Disagreement remains among scholars about what countries Marco actually visited, which routes he followed in his travels to and from the Orient, and how much trust one can place in the accuracy of the descriptions of world marvels. According to the book itself, Niccolò and his brother Maffeo Polo, both Venetian merchants, visited the court of Khubilai Khân in 1267–1268 on a mercantile mission. In 1269, the two brothers returned to Acre with Khubilai's request to the pope that he send a delegation of 100 learned men who could demonstrate the superiority of the Christian religion at the Mongol court. The request—if it can be believed—was ill-timed, for the papacy lay vacant between 1268 and 1271, in which year, according to the book, the Polo brothers returned to the court of Khubilai, taking along with them Niccolò's seventeen-year-old son, Marco. They were accompanied by two Dominicans sent by Gregory X, who had just been elected pope, but they fled before the company had left the Mediterranean region.

In 1292, the Polos left China to travel by the sea route from Cathay to Sumatra, Ceylon, India, and Hormuz, where they took the overland routes through

Marco Polo and companion. Paris, Bibliothèque Nationale, MS fr. 2810, fol. 15v, *c.* 1440. Courtesy Bibliothèque Nationale.

Persia and eventually returned to Venice in 1295. Three years later, Marco became a prisoner of war in Genoa, having been captured in a naval battle while serving as a Venetian commander. It was during his imprisonment, probably until May of 1299, that he met Rustichello of Pisa, a rather successful writer of romances, and their (apparent) collaboration began on the *Divisament dou monde*. Marco evidently lived the remainder of his life obscurely in Venice. His will of 1323–1324 indicated that he acquired a substantial fortune (though not a great one by the standards of his contemporaries), that he left it to his three daughters who survived him, and that he set free a Mongol slave named Peter. Without his chance meeting with Rustichello, whose account of the travels made him famous, Marco's life, as well as his observations of the marvels of the world, would probably have passed unnoticed forever.

Marco Polo left strong impressions of the previously unknown world. His appetite for information was encyclopedic. In his travels he was interested in natural scenery and natural history; exotic plants and wild beasts; ethnic groups, whom he classified according to religion; and cities, which he admired according to their degree of efficiency. Given the book's details of the beauty and height of the Pamir Mountains, the unusual sounds experienced in crossing the Gobi Desert, and the specific—and accurate—splendors of the cities of China (such as the seaport Zaiton), little doubt remains that the *Divisament dou monde* contains accurate, relatively current information. Even for some countries that Marco says he did not visit, such as Japan, the book offers one of the very few pre–sixteenth-century references.

According to the *Divisament*, Marco enjoyed great freedom to travel throughout the Mongol Empire, was treated well, and perhaps served as a trusted administrator for Khubilai Khân in Yangchow in China. However, there are a number of omissions in his account that for centuries have troubled commentators about the book's authenticity. The most famous perhaps are his failure to mention tea, the uniqueness of the Chinese script, or the fact of the Great Wall. These omissions have been explained by assertions that Mongolian was the language of court administration (thus he would not have had time or need to learn Chinese); that kumis was the favorite drink of the Mongols and Marco would not want to insult them by describing the favorite drink of the subject Chinese people; and

# M

that a reference to a walled-in people ("Ung et Mungul"), usually thought to refer to Gog and Magog, actually marks a notice of the Great Wall.

The place of the *Divisament* in medieval travel literature is unique, and that uniqueness grows out of the collaboration between the observer Marco and the storyteller Rustichello. Rustichello organized the book to follow an order and a format fully consonant with the genre of medieval romance. Although there is evidently exaggeration and elaboration, much of the information in the *Divisament* has proven to be accurate and receives its first presentation to the West in the *Divisament*. On the other hand, the Polos were not the first merchants to visit the Mongols; nor were they the last to describe merchant routes to China during Mongol dominance. Christian missionaries, particularly John of Plano Carpini (1245–1247) and William of Rubruck (1253–1255) had described their personal travels in greater detail and had written more accurate descriptions than Marco of the customs of Mongols while they were still nomads living on the Inner Asian steppes rather than living in a conquered civilized center as they did by the time of Khubilai. The Florentine merchant Francesco Balducci de Pegolotti, writing in 1340 or so, described much more concretely how to travel safely on the routes overland from the Black Sea to Khanbaliq (Beijing) during the days of the so-called *Pax Mongolica*. Thus, in preparing the *Divisament*, Rustichello may have consciously tried to set this account apart from its predecessors by focusing on commercial details and offering a generally pro-Mongol point of view (both John and William urged crusades *against* the Mongols).

Most of Marco Polo's readers over the centuries have not cared whether his world was fact or fiction, although his first audience may have been more circumspect: fourteenth-century readers nicknamed him "Il Milione" because he seemed to exaggerate everything—in the thousands—and thus to be less believable. They were fascinated, for example, by the breadth and vision of the *Divisament*'s coverage. From Java and Sumatra to the polar regions of Russia, and from East Africa to China and even Japan, Marco opened the West to a world that was largely unknown. The facts provided by Marco were placed in a context of wonders by Rustichello, who probably envisioned a courtly audience of wealthy aristocrats who would be more interested in tales of amusement than in matters of practical interest to the diplomat, missionary, or merchant. Rustichello chose and cast the details so as

to best titillate and fascinate his medieval readers: he was not interested in presenting a diary, an accurate chronicle of events, or a guidebook. Thus, the organization and order in which the places were described, the common thematic interests that often bound them together, the focus on the wild and the exotic rather than the practical *per se,* all betray Rustichello's intentions to make the facts entertaining as well as interesting. Without this framework, the "world" of Marco, unknown and vast as it was, could have appeared as one more to be feared than to be explored.

The success and influence of the *Divisament* is difficult to assess. It appears to have been less popular among near contemporaries than among readers of later centuries. For example, the number of surviving manuscripts dating from the fourteenth and fifteenth centuries is significant (eighty), but not great. By comparison, sixty-three manuscripts preserve the account of Odoric of Pordenone's travels among the Mongols in the 1330s, and at least 275 record *The Book of John Mandeville* (*c.* 1360). Five hundred manuscripts of Dante's *Divine Comedy* survive from the fourteenth and fifteenth centuries. Though twenty-one Italian and forty-one Latin manuscripts are found among the earliest survivals, the first English translation did not occur apparently until 1579.

Regardless, the stimulation of Marco Polo's vision of the Orient continued to influence important explorers who followed in his wake for centuries. Not only did Abraham Cresques, compiling the Catalan Atlas (*c.* 1375) and the Venetian cartographer Fra Mauro (*c.* 1439) draw information from the *Divisament,* but so did the Portuguese and Genoese explorers Henry the Navigator and Christopher Columbus, who set off to sail westward to India and China in the 1490s.

## BIBLIOGRAPHY

Benedetto, Luigi Foscolo. *La Tradizione Manoscritta del 'Milione' di Marco Polo.* Turin: Bottega d'Erasmo, 1962.

Franke, H. "Sino-Western Contacts under the Mongol Empire." *Journal of the Hong Kong Branch of the Royal Asiatic Society* 6 (1966): 49–72.

Guerra, Giorgio del. *Rustichello da Pisa.* Pisa: Nistri-Lischi, 1955.

Heers, Jacques. *Marco Polo.* Paris: Fayard, 1983.

Olschki, Leonardo. *Marco Polo's Asia: An Introduction to His "Description of the World" Called "Il Milione."* Trans. John A. Scott. Berkeley: U of California P, 1960.

Pelliot, Paul. *Notes on Marco Polo: Ouvrage Posthume.* 3 vols. Paris: Imprimerie Nationale and Adrien-Maisonneuve, 1959–1973.

Phillips, J.R.S. *The Medieval Expansion of Europe.* Oxford: Oxford UP, 1988.

Polo, Marco. *The Book of Ser Marco Polo the Venetian Concerning the Kingdoms and Marvels of the East.* Ed. and Trans. Sir Henry Yule. 3rd edition in two vols. Rev. by Henri Cordier. New York: Scribner's, 1903.

———. *The Travels.* Trans. and Intro. Ronald Latham. London and New York: Penguin, 1958.

*Charles W. Connell*

**SEE ALSO**

China; Columbus, Christopher; Cresques, Abraham; Dante Alighieri; Great Wall; Gog and Magog; Henry the Navigator; Inner Asian Travel; John of Plano Carpini; Khanbaliq; Kumis; *Mandeville's Travels;* Mauro Map, [Fra]; Missionaries to China; Mongols; Odoric of Pordenone; Pegolotti, Francesco Balducci; William of Rubruck; Venice; Zaiton

## Mare Oceanum

According to ancient and medieval geographers, the sea encircling the earth's landmass. This great body of water takes its name from Oceanus, one of the twelve Titans born to Gaea and Uranus, and from very early times was thought to be an impassable river that ran around the earth. Homer called it a "vast and mighty river" and "the father of all things," and he describes it as girdling the rim of Achilles' shield in the famous ekphrasis of *Iliad* 18. It lay beyond the sea, had no source or outlet, and gave birth to all the waters. Strabo (*c.* 64 B.C.E.–23 C.E.) distinguished the Outer Sea from the Ocean that lay further beyond.

The earliest Greek maps—predicated on a spherical earth—show the inhabited world as an island surrounded by water. The typical zonal maps of the world have five zones; the middle, torrid zone is occupied or cut in two by Oceanus flowing between the tropics. In some early spherical representations of the earth, such as the globe of Crates of Mallos (*c.* 150 B.C.E.), the world is divided into four parts by an ocean that extends both from east to west along the equator and from north to south along the meridian. The known seas are but gulfs of the ocean.

These Greek geographical ideas were adopted by some late antique and medieval authors. The Byzantine writer Cosmas Indikopleustes (fl. 540) makes the ocean into a rectangle surrounding a flat earth, but he preserves the four gulfs. Beyond the ocean is another world, where man lived before the Flood. Paradise is distant and unreachable. In the West, Greek ideas were likewise adopted by the Roman Macrobius (fl. 399–422 C.E.) and his contemporaries, the early Christian writers Orosius and Isidore of Seville, whose Asia is bounded in the south by the ocean. Martianus Capella (early fourth century C.E.) asserted that the ocean was navigable, at least around the known world.

Whether the ocean fed the seas or vice versa was a question much debated in the Middle Ages. Peter Abelard (1079–1142) proposed that the earth's sphere floated partially submerged "so that the sea is in contact with one side of it and pours through its veins whence springs and rivers take their rise." The tides were explained by lunar attraction but also by various other causes. Aristotle's explanation that the sea does not overflow due to evaporation was largely accepted, but Alexander Neckam (d. 1217) pointed out that the sea was higher than the beach.

The Ocean River formed the frame of circular representations of the world in antiquity, a tradition continued in the medieval *mappaemundi* of both the T-O and the zonal types (see Maps). The latter have the additional east-west stretch of the Ocean River separating the three continents of Europe, Asia, and Africa from the Antipodes, often much reduced in size by comparison with the antique prototype. The idea of ocean as river lost significance in medieval cartography, and references to the Ocean Sea—*Mare Oceanum* became common; if maps continued to show a ribbon of water at their rim, it was only because their designers saw no need to depict the great portion of the globe that was merely water. Noncircular maps also had a water rim; in later, more elaborate *mappaemundi* it was sometimes dotted with unnamed islands.

As early as the first century C.E., Pomponius Mela and Pliny the Elder claimed that parts of the northern Ocean were navigable, but when Adam of Bremen (*c.* 1040–*c.* 1085) tried to describe the Viking discoveries, he still envisioned the ocean flowing as a river endlessly around the earth, "having Ireland on the left . . . , on the right the cliffs of Norway, and farther off the islands of Iceland and Greenland." As late as 1110, Lambert of St. Omer continued to repeat the Greek idea that no one could cross the equatorial sea.

Although conceived of as the encircling sea, the name "Ocean" usually refers to the western ocean, or the Atlantic. According to the Greeks, the Hesperides guarded the golden apples in the western part of this ocean. Hades was to be reached by crossing the ocean

# M

westward; in the biblical cartography of Hugh of St. Victor (d. 1141), the dead would make their spiritual passage to the Last Judgment across the Atlantic. Contact with the Ocean began just past the Pillars of Hercules (Straits of Gibraltar) where the waters were shallow because of the sinking of Atlantis. Beyond lay various islands, including Britain, Hibernia, and the Tin Islands (Cassiterides); Thule lay to the north, and to the south were the Fortunate Islands, through which some cartographers drew their prime meridian. To the ancient mythical Isles of the Blessed and the Hesperides, several others were added during the Middle Ages: Brasil, Antilia, and others associated with Saints Ursula and Brendan; the westward penetration of the Atlantic, which increased especially in the thirteenth and fourteenth centuries, replaced these with new discoveries, such as the Canaries and Madeira.

Parts of the ocean received regional names; thus some maps referred to the Britannic Ocean (as today we speak of the Irish Sea). The eastern ocean was hardly known, and the part of the map beyond China was often depicted without toponyms. The northern ocean was called vaguely Septentrionalis, Scythian, or Sarmatian ocean, and the southern ocean was called Meridionalis, Ethiopian, or Indian sea. Viking discoveries led to the hypothesis that the Atlantic was a mediterranean sea extending from Vinland to West Africa.

Ptolemy's *Geography* (second century) was unknown to the Latin West during most of the Middle Ages, although it was to have a great impact on European thinking once it was translated into Latin in 1410. Among other innovations, Ptolemy's map showed a landmass in the northeast and made the Indian Ocean into an enclosed sea. Ptolemy had a vague idea, only hinted at in his maps and not articulated well by other European geographers, that the known ocean only enclosed the habitable world and was surrounded in turn by a further landmass.

His views strongly influenced Islamic geography and cartography, and a modified concept of the ocean was universally accepted by Muslim scholars; it was not totally foreign because there was a concept of primary sea in Islamic cosmology as well. The Greek term *Ocean* was translated into Arabic as *al-Bahr al-Muhīt,* "the Encircling Sea," or simply *al-Muhīt.* As in the European tradition, the sea ocean often meant to the Arabs the Atlantic. By the fifteenth century, many of these mythic conceptions of the sea ocean were rendered obsolete by Portuguese exploration and objective cartographic genres such as the portolan charts.

**BIBLIOGRAPHY**

Cassidy, Vincent H. *The Sea around Them: The Atlantic Ocean, A.D. 1250.* Baton Rouge: Louisiana UP, 1968.
Harley-Woodward. *The History of Cartography,* Vol. 1, esp. Chaps. 8–11, 15, and 18. See Gen. Bib.

*Marina A. Tolmacheva*

**SEE ALSO**
Adam of Bremen; Antillia; Antipodes; Brasil; Brendan, Voyage of St.; Canary Islands; Cartography, Arabic; Climate; Cosmas Indikopleustes; Geography of Medieval Europe; Isidore of Seville; *Liber Floridus; Mappamundi;* Maps; Mela, Pomponius; Orosius; Paradise, Travel to; Pliny the Elder; Portolan Charts; Ptolemy; Scythia; Thule; Tides; Viking Discoveries and Settlements; Vinland Map

## Maritime Law
*See* Law, Maritime

## Marriages between Muslims and Christians, Attitudes toward

"Saracen"/Christian marriages, that is, unions between a European Christian and an Asian/Arab Muslim, were events that evoked complex responses in medieval European society. The curiosity they inspired is demonstrated by the way they figure as mainstays to plots in medieval romances written in the three principal literary vernaculars, French, English, and German. The theme shows European fear yet fascination about the East.

Such unions are particularly common in treatments of Charlemagne and his vassals, of Alexander the Great, and of Guillaume of Orange; they also appear in romances about nonhistorical figures, including Parzival and fictitious crusaders. The period of the Crusades (1095 to 1291) saw the creation of many Old French and Middle English poems dealing with the wars in the East, celebrating wars between the Arabs of Spain and the Frankish Christians. Two poems of famous battles are *Les Narbonnais,* inspired by the Frankish capture of Narbonne from the Arabs in 759, and *Le Siège de Barbastre* based on the siege of Barbastro in 1064. Some romances represent a measure of historical reality, since both wars and marriages between Europeans and Muslims did take place. These marriages, however achieved, suggest a rapprochement between the two.

The eroticism of "Saracen" princesses is already hinted at in the Bramimunde episodes of the *Chanson* de Roland. In the fragment *Mainet* (twelfth century), Charlemagne marries Gallienne, daughter of the Muslim king Galafre in Toledo, while in *Anseis de Cartage,* Anseis, Charlemagne's deputy in Cartage (Spain), seduces and marries Gaudisse, daughter of the Muslim king, Marsile. The desire to include foreigners in the European worldview appears also as a topos in some saints' lives. For example, the *South-English Legendary* gives Thomas à Becket a "Saracen" mother, a woman who falls in love with his father, Gilbert, and follows him to England from the Holy Land. Some literary marriages in the poems are problematic, however, because they present heroic figures as lovers from unfavorable perspectives; they also demand that the Saracen woman betray her country and her culture, even mocking her father and civilization before joining the Franks.

The Alexander romance cycles in Anglo-Norman, Old French, Middle English, and Middle High German contain descriptions of Alexander's love affair with Candace, the Ethiopian queen. Her realm is given variously as Ethiopia or Saba, sometimes India, sometimes an imaginary place called Greniz or Gramania. The episode appears in the Anglo-Norman poem *Le Roman de Toute Chevalerie* by Thomas of Kent (1174–1182); in the Old French *Roman d'Alexandre,* written after 1177 by Alexandre de Paris, and *Venjance Alixandre* (before 1181); and the Middle English *King Alisaunder* (before 1330) and *The Wars of Alexander* (fifteenth century). In each narrative, Alexander and Candace have a love affair but do not marry. Ulrich von Eschenbach's *Alexander* (1270–1287) also contains this episode and refers to Belakane's love for Gahmuret from *Parzival.*

So common is the story of the Saracen woman who marries the Christian knight that such a figure has been called "The Enamoured Muslim Princess." Twenty-one of some seventy-four romance-epics deal with marriages of this type. Of twenty-one such women, seventeen are white and marry Frankish knights. Four are black female warriors who do not marry. The same story is told repeatedly. A Saracen princess is the daughter of a rich emir or ruler of a country in Spain (Pamplona, Córdoba, Seville), the East (Babylon, Egypt, or an unknown land, such as "Sobrie" in *Elie de St. Gille,* after 1200), or more familiar territory (Orange in the south of France). Either the Franks attack a city or the Saracens attack the Christian camp, capture Christian knights, and imprison them in the fortress's dungeons. The princess falls in love with a Christian knight, either at first sight or through hearing an account of his chivalrous reputation, and determines to have him. She betrays her father and his kingdom by releasing the Franks from her father's dungeon and showing them how to win the castle.

Through many adventures, the princess sometimes commits murder to achieve her aims. Floripas in *Fierabras* (c. 1170) throws her duenna into the sea and kills her father's chamberlain when they object to her hiding Franks in her room. Rosamonde, in *Elie de St. Gille,* also conceals Franks. In *Aliscans* (late twelfth century) and other poems of the *Guillaume d'Orange* cycle, Orable, who marries Guillaume, is accused of consenting to Guillaume's murder of her children. Josian, in the Anglo-Norman *Boeve de Haumtone* (before 1250) and the Middle English *Beues of Hamtoun* (c. 1300), marries her Saracen fiancé so that she can kill him on the wedding night and thus remove a rival for Bevis. In *Foucon de Candie,* Anfelise, sister of Orable's first husband, and her friend Fausete, both Saracen princesses, betray the Spanish city of Candie to the Christians. In *Guibert d'Andrenas,* Gaiete, daughter of the Saracen king Judas, helps the Franks storm the city because she has fallen in love with Guibert, the hero. A reversal appears in *La Fille du Comte de Pontieu,* where Saracens capture the French countess, and she is married to the sultan of Aumaire. Her son by the sultan engenders the line of the Arab hero Saladin, and thus the French poet attempts to claim French descent for a famous figure.

Later romances also utilize the theme of the enamoured Saracen princess. Huon, in the romance *Huon de Bordeaux* (thirteenth century), enters Babylon on a dare—to knock out four of the emir's teeth, to kiss his daughter, and to pull a hair from his beard—and is promptly thrown in prison. The Emir's daughter, Esclarmonde, promises to release Huon from her father's prison if he kisses her; he refuses, saying that he would never kiss a pagan. Esclarmonde tells the jailor to starve Huon, and after some time she promises to release him if he will marry her. This time he agrees, Esclarmonde frees him, and they escape together. In *Partonopeu de Blois* (both Old French and Middle English from the thirteenth century), Partonopeu marries the Byzantine princess Melior, who is a fairy mistress as well.

Other romances present more congenial relations between young protagonists, often with a conversion theme. In the Old French *Aucassin et Nicolette* (thirteenth century), Aucassin (a Christian) loves Nicolette

# M

(a Saracen slave girl who was baptized as a child). Aucassin's father, objecting to the alliance because Nicolette is a slave, commands her godfather to imprison her, reversing the action of other narratives. This is the first of several separations from Aucassin, but in the end they are united. *Floire et Blanchefleur* (Old French *c.* 1150) and Middle English *Floriz and Blancheflur* (*c.* 1250) also reverse the roles. The two children are born at the same time and given variations of the same name. Floire is a Saracen prince and Blanchefleur is a Christian maid's daughter. The emir sells Blanchefleur, but Floire sets out to find her, succeeds, and the story ends happily.

Some romances are cautionary tales against marriages between Christians and non-Christians, by suggesting that such unions result in monstrous offspring. Wolfram von Eschenbach begins his *Parzifal* (1204) with the romance of Gahmuret the Angevin and Belakane, the black queen of Zazamanc. Their affair produces the Magpie Knight, a strange child with black skin and white spots. In the *King of Tars* (*c.*1280–1340), the Christian princess is married to the sultan of Damascus, himself a strange creature, half-white, half-black. Their child, a formless lump of flesh at birth, becomes a white baby boy when baptized.

The historical record bears witness to several instances of East-West marriages among the Latin kings of Jerusalem. Baldwin I (r. 1100–1118), and Baldwin II (r. 1118–1131) married Armenian women; Baldwin III (r. 1143–1162) married Theodora of Constantinople, and the second wife of Amalric I (r. 1162–1174) was Maria Comnena of Constantinople. Emperor Manuel I (r. 1143–1180) of Constantinople married Mary of Antioch, a cousin of Baldwin III. Sultan Baybars I (r. 1260–1277) had a favorite wife who was a Christian. Alfonso VI, king of Castile and León (r. 1065–1109), who conquered Toledo in 1085, married an Arab woman. The Syrian historian Usamah ibn-Munqidh (1095–1188) tells of marriages between Frankish maids taken captive and Muslim men in his *Memoirs*. Offspring between the Franks and natives in Syria were numerous; they were called Pullani, and the Franks despised them.

Literary treatments of union between the two cultures embody many concerns in the Eurocentric view of the "other" that have persisted to the present day. In almost all cases the "Saracen" converts to Christianity in order to live happily ever after, showing the rightness of Christendom and its presence in the East. The sexual vitality of the Saracen woman or man is irresistible and yet the cautionary note of monstrous offspring is frequently sounded. Thus, though many of these romances treat the idea of union, there is an underlying unease at the idea of its achievement through marriage.

**BIBLIOGRAPHY**

Comfort, W.W. "The Role of the Saracens in Medieval French Epic." *PMLA* 44 (1955): 628–659.

Daniel, Norman. *Heroes and Saracens: An Interpretation of the Chansons de Geste.* Edinburgh: Edinburgh UP, 1984.

de Weever, Jacqueline. "Candace in the Alexander Romances: Variations on the Portrait Theme." *Romance Philology* 43 (1990): 529–546.

———. *Sheba's Daughters: Whitening and Demonizing the Saracen Woman in Medieval French Epic.* New York: Garland, 1998.

Ibn-Munqidh, Usama. *An Arab-Syrian Gentleman and Warrior in the Period of the Crusades: Memoirs of Usamah ibn-Munqidh.* Trans. Philip K. Hitti. New York, 1929; rpt. Princeton, NJ: Princeton UP, 1987.

Lasater, Alice E. *Spain to England: A Comparative Study of Arabic, European, and English Literature of the Middle Ages.* Jackson: UP of Mississippi, 1974.

Menocal, María Rosa. *The Arabic Role in Medieval Literary History.* Philadelphia: U of Pennsylvania P, 1987.

Metlizki, Dorothee. *The Matter of Araby in Medieval England.* New Haven: Yale UP, 1977.

Warren, F.M. "The Enamoured Muslim Princess in Orderic Vital and the French Epic." *PMLA* 29 (1914): 341–358.

*Jacqueline de Weever*

**SEE ALSO**

Armenia; Baybars I; Canon Law and Subject Peoples; Constantinople; Ethiopians; India; *Mandeville's Travels;* Orientalism

## Martin of Troppau, or Martinus Polonus (d. 1278)

Author of a widely read universal chronicle and reference book, *Chronicon pontificum et imperatorum,* which appeared in three editions, in 1268, 1272, and 1277. Born at Opava (German "Troppau") in Moravia, Martin joined the Dominican order at Prague. Documents show him at Rome after 1261 as papal chaplain and *poenitentiarius.* He was elevated to the prestigious position of archbishop of Gniezno (Gnesen) in Poland in 1278 (the city was the site of the coronation of the kings of Poland before 1320), but died on the way there, which may explain why he is often called by the surname *Polonus.*

Besides the chronicle that brought him fame, he is the author of sermons and of a concordance to the *Decretum Gratiani* entitled *Margarita Decreti.* Martin's *Chronicon* follows in form the chronicle style developed by Hugh of St. Victor (*c.* 1096–1141), in which reports of events are presented in two parallel columns, dated twice, both according to the reigns of popes and to the reigns of emperors. Martin paralleled these events on two parallel pages, each page containing fifty years on fifty lines. Thus the deeds of an emperor or emperors were synchronized with those of a pope or popes, producing blocks of text as well as blank space on the parchment. For his last edition of 1277, Martin added material about ancient Rome as well as legends intended to aid preachers in composing their sermons; all this disturbed the visual symmetry of the pages.

Though the events covered in Martin's chronicle concerned only the Latin West and the Mediterranean region, the work was translated into many vernacular languages, including Greek (1299), Persian for readers in the Mongol Empire in Iran (1304–1306), and Armenian (*c.* 1348).

**BIBLIOGRAPHY**
Brincken, Anna-Dorothee von den. "Martin von Troppau." *Deutsches Archiv für Erforschung des Mittelalters* 37 (1981): 694–735; 41 (1985): 460–531; 45 (1989): 555–591; 50 (1994): 613–615.
Martin of Troppau. *Chronicon pontificum et imperatorum.* Ed. Ludwig Weiland. MGH SS 22. Hanover: Hahn, 1868, pp. 377–475.

*Anna-Dorothee von den Brincken*

**SEE ALSO**
Paulinus Minorita of Venice

## Marvels of Rome

Conventional title for *Mirabilia urbis Romae,* a manuscript written about 1143 by a canon (perhaps named Benedict) to guide travelers and pilgrims to the sites of medieval Rome. *Marvels* is a fascinating example of the guidebooks that combine the revival of antique learning with pious Christian concerns. Although it was probably the most influential pilgrim guide to Christian sites throughout Rome, it concerns ruined Roman glories as well as Christian monuments. *Marvels* has several characteristically twelfth-century aims: to act as a guide for the devout pilgrim seeking to retrace the footsteps of Christian martyrs; to praise the monuments of virtuous pagan Roman civic life; and to serve as a learned treatise on the historical traditions signified by the architectural signposts of Roman ruins. At the conclusion of his "tour guide," the author identifies his own purpose: "to bring back to the human memory how great was their beauty in gold, silver, brass, ivory and precious stones."

Ostensibly, the three parts of the text lead the reader on a guided tour of the city of Rome to view spolia and ruins, and to see the imperial context of the Holy City. Benedict's guide purports not only to present the sites, but also to explain them, and in so doing provides modern readers with a unique opportunity to see Rome through medieval eyes.

Divisions of the text of *Marvels* are still critically contested, and inclusions or exclusions of certain incidents illustrate the complex issues in the manuscript history. Part 1 begins with the genealogy of Rome, which introduces both the entire work and this particular section on sites. It goes on to list the pagan ruins of Rome by architectural categories such as walls and gates, linked to very brief notices of important facts in Roman and Christian history.

Part 2 also begins with a prologue in which the pagan emperor Octavian envisions and accepts the revelation of the Blessed Virgin, linking Roman foresight and good sense with Christian truth. It then presents longer narratives about Roman history, each connected to a specific place. The Pantheon, for example, is a site that demonstrates how Rome turned from Cybele, the mother of the gods, to the "Blessed Mary, ever-virgin, who is the mother of all the saints."

The conclusion, Part 3, provides an idiosyncratic perambulation through the city. This section of the text has received more study than the other two because it is more typical of early Christian travel accounts. Because the itinerary is not realistically walkable, it must be considered as an illustration of the author's cultural assumptions and agenda more than anything else. *Marvels* is a helpful text in revealing the large number of classical structures and art works still standing in medieval Rome, disclosing their medieval locations, and providing an insight into medieval attitudes toward antiquity.

**BIBLIOGRAPHY**
Greimas, Algirdas Julien. "English Visitors to Rome in the Middle Ages." *History Today* 28 (1978): 643–649.

# M

Kinney, Dale. "'Mirabilia urbis Romae.'" In *The Classics in the Middle Ages*. Ed. Aldo S. Bernardo and Saul Levin. Binghamton, NY: Medieval and Renaissance Texts and Studies, 1990, pp. 207–222.

Krautheimer, Richard. *Rome: Profile of a City, 312–1308.* Princeton, NJ: Princeton UP, 1980.

*The Marvels of Rome.* Ed. and Trans. Francis Morgan Nichols. 2nd edition. New York: Italica Press, 1986.

*Mirabilia urbis Romae: Codice topografico della città di Roma.* Ed. Roberto Valentini and Giuseppe Zucchetti. Vol. 3. Rome: Tipografia del Senato, 1946.

Wohl, Birgitta. "Mental Images and Late Medieval Maps of Rome." In *Paradigms in Medieval Thought: Applications in Medieval Disciplines: A Symposium.* Ed. Nancy van Deusen and Alvin E. Ford. Lewiston, NY: Edwin Mellen Press, 1990, pp. 173–191.

*Cynthia Ho*

SEE ALSO

Itineraries and *Periploi;* Memory and Maps; Pilgrimage, Christian; Rome as a Pilgrimage Site

## Masons and Architects as Travelers

Architects and masons traveled in the service of aristocratic and ecclesiastical patrons. While mobility characterized the profession during the Middle Ages in both the Byzantine Empire and western Europe, specific projects reveal that travel was contingent on such factors as economics, politics, symbolic expression, and professional status.

Although Byzantine architectural practice is poorly documented, all ranks of builders, from the exalted *mêchanikos* to journeymen masons, traveled extensively to realize imperial projects. Many of Justinian's (r. 527–565) leading architects received their practical experience building fortifications along the eastern frontier with Persia. The *mêchanikos* Isidore of Miletus the Younger collaborated with John of Constantinople in the construction of the outpost of Zenobia on the Euphrates, later returning to the capital to supervise the rebuilding of the dome of Hagia Sophia following its collapse in 558.

Major church construction also led to long-distance travel. To build the Church of the Holy Sepulchre (325), Constantine sent the *presbyter* Eustathios from Constantinople to Jerusalem where he was joined by the Syrian architect, Zenobius. Similarly, Empress Eudoxia furnished plans for the new cathedral at Gaza (402–407), which was erected by Rufinus, an architect from Antioch.

At the lower ranks of the profession, masons, organized into guilds, generally worked within a regional sphere. Yet, when Gregory of Nyssa built his martyrium in around 380, he turned to the bishop of Iconium for masons because of the excessive wages demanded by local workers. And migrant Isaurian masons raised the Monastery of Saint Simeon Stylites the Younger near Antioch (541–565), working voluntarily in the hope of securing the favor of the saint.

In western Europe until the eleventh century, timber dominated construction as stone buildings remained relatively rare. As a result of the shallow pool of skilled masons, monumental projects necessarily drew their workforces from a broad geographical area. Masons journeyed from the Continent to Northumbria, England, in the seventh century to build churches "in the antique manner," and the high demand for

Mason, carving on tomb of St. William of York. York, Yorkshire Museum, *c.* 1400. Formerly in York Minster. Photo by John B. Friedman.

Stylistic architectural borrowing. Bologna, San Stefano, East Facade, 12th century. Photo by Robert Ousterhout.

expert builders brought the famed *magistri comacini* of Lombardy into Germany and France during the tenth and eleventh centuries.

During the Romanesque period, pilgrimage fostered an international exchange of artisans who moved back and forth along the roads connecting shrine churches. Santiago de Compostela and St.-Sernin at Toulouse shared architectural and sculptural workshops, while the domes of St.-Front, Périgueux, which look to prestigious models in Constantinople and Venice, suggest either the presence of Byzantine masons in Aquitaine or French builders' acquisition of new technical expertise through experience abroad. Emulation remained a powerful stimulant behind masons' travels and the transmission of architectural ideas. Numerous "copies" of the Holy Sepulchre at such places as Paderborn (*c.* 1036) and Bologna (after 1141) were based on measurements taken in Jerusalem. In 1224, a lay brother and his son were sent to copy Clairvaux as the blueprint for the construction of the

Cistercian monastery at Aduard (Germany). In 1456, the chapter of Troyes Cathedral dispatched their master mason, Bleuet, to "visit the towers of Reims, Amiens, and Notre-Dame, Paris" in preparation for his new west façade design.

In the Gothic building boom, master masons, summoned by high-ranking patrons, crisscrossed Europe. The Frenchman, William of Sens, went to Canterbury in 1174, Matthew of Arras left Narbonne for Prague in 1344, and the Milan cathedral authorities consulted both French and German masons in the 1390s. The atelier itself was composed of a highly mobile force as shown by Vale Royal Abbey where only 5 to 10 percent of the 131 masons employed between 1278 and 1280 were local men. Occasionally, a master traveled with his workshop, as when the Parisian Etienne de Bonneuil took a team of *"compaignons et bachelers"* to Uppsala, Sweden, in 1287, or Henri de Bruisselles (Brussels) left Troyes Cathedral with *"les ouvriers de la loge."*

# M

From the thirteenth century on, master masons began to assume responsibility for simultaneous projects. Leaving daily construction in the hands of assistants, they shuttled intermittently between building sites. Patrons attempted to control the master's movements by limiting his absences or requiring periods of residence. Thus, when Gautier de Varinfroy was hired as master of Meaux Cathedral in 1253, he was forbidden to spend more than two months at Evreux without the permission of the chapter. In 1312, Jacques de Fauran, master of Narbonne Cathedral, was required by his contract with Gerona Cathedral to return to supervise work every two months.

The variable character of masons' travel can be illustrated by two examples. First, Edward III impressed nearly 1,700 masons into service for the construction of Windsor Castle between 1360 and 1362, some journeying up to 200 miles from the distant counties of Devon and Yorkshire. At the other end of the scale, Martin Chambiges, master of the works at the cathedrals of Beauvais, Sens, and Troyes during his career from 1489 to 1532, apparently exercised a large measure of personal control over his itinerary, for, despite constant entreaties from the Troyes chapter, he visited the city only twice during his thirty-year tenure. Despite such notable exceptions, the medieval mason ordinarily moved at the behest of his patron, his travels directed by the material, technical, and symbolic requirements of the building project.

## BIBLIOGRAPHY

*Les Bâtisseurs des cathédrales gothiques.* Ed. Roland Recht. Strasbourg: Editions les Musées de la Ville de Strasbourg, 1989.

Coldstream, Nicola. *Masons and Sculptors.* Toronto: U of Toronto P, 1991.

Harvey, John. *The Mediaeval Architect.* London: Wayland Publishers, 1972.

Knoop, Douglas, and G.P. Jones. *The Mediaeval Mason.* Manchester, England: Manchester UP, 1933.

Kostof, Spiro. "The Architect in the Middle Ages, East and West." In *The Architect: Chapters in the History of the Profession.* Ed. Spiro Kostof. New York: Oxford UP, 1977, pp. 59–95.

Mango, Cyril. *Byzantine Architecture.* New York: Abrams, 1976.

Mortet, Victor, and Paul Deschamps. *Recueil de textes relatifs à l'histoire de l'architecture et à la condition des architectes en France au moyen âge.* 2 vols. Paris: Picard, 1911–1928.

Murray, Stephen. *Building Troyes Cathedral.* Bloomington: Indiana UP, 1987.

*Michael T. Davis*

**SEE ALSO**
Guilds; Pilgrimage, Christian; Pilgrimage Sites, Spanish; Stones and Timber, Scandinavian Trade in

## Matthew Paris (c. 1200–1259)

Thirteenth-century English monk, historian, hagiographer, and artist best known for his self-illustrated chronicle, the *Chronica Majora.* Matthew became a monk at the Benedictine Monastery of St. Albans in Hertfordshire in 1217 and died there in June 1259.

Considered one of the outstanding medieval chroniclers by both his contemporaries and later scholars, Matthew wrote in a familiar, colorful style and drew detailed illustrations in the margins of the *Chronica Majora.* An innovative cartographer, he included in his illustrations for the *Chronica Majora* and other works four maps of Britain, three maps of Palestine, and a *mappamundi,* as well as four itineraries from London to Apulia, in southern Italy.

Matthew's maps of Britain were innovative in that they are oriented with north at the top, rather than east as was traditional on medieval maps; they also have the four points of the compass marked on the edges. Matthew was one of the first medieval cartographers to display a consciousness of scale and proportion and to produce a map in the modern sense, rather than a rough geographical diagram. Three of his maps of Palestine, drawn to accompany the three volumes of the *Chronica Majora,* do not, however, display the cartographic innovation of his maps of Britain. They are traditionally oriented, with east at the top, and there is no attempt to render scale or proportion. These maps are more interesting for their descriptive legends and drawings of animals and boats than for their geographical content. A fourth Palestine map, bound in a St. Albans Bible, is quite detailed, although rough, and shares with Matthew's maps of Britain both an attention to proportion and scale, and the distinctive top-as-north orientation.

The itineraries are strip-maps, vertical columns of representations of the major stops on the route between England and southern Italy, designed to be read from bottom to top and from left to right. Each

**382  Matthew Paris**

town is represented by a drawing incorporating walls, towers, churches, and, in the case of major cities, other important landmarks.

In addition to the *Chronica Majora,* in which he records the unrest in Western Europe at the threat (and fact) of invasion by the Mongols, Matthew Paris wrote several works of hagiography, including lives of St. Alban, Stephen Langton, Edward the Confessor, and Thomas Becket. Matthew also began a *Deeds of the Abbots of St. Albans,* which was continued by two anonymous successors. His depiction of Mongol cannibalism in one copy of his *Chronica* (Cambridge, Corpus Christi College MS 16, fol. 166) is the first European representation of this Asiatic people.

**BIBLIOGRAPHY**

Lewis, Suzanne. *The Art of Matthew Paris in the 'Chronica Majora.'* Berkeley: U of California P, 1987.

Vaughn, Richard, ed. and trans. *Matthew Paris.* 1958; rev. Cambridge: Cambridge UP, 1979.

———. *Chronicles of Matthew Paris: Monastic Life in the Thirteenth Century.* 1984; rpt. New York: St. Martin's, 1986.

*Teresa Leslie*

**SEE ALSO**

Cannibalism; Elephants; Gough Map; Itineraries and *Periploi; Mappamundi;* Maps; Mongols

## Mauro Map, [Fra]

A *mappamundi* by Fra Mauro, now in the Biblioteca Nazionale Marciana in Venice, representing one of the outstanding achievements of later medieval cartography. Transitional between the Middle Ages and the Renaissance, the map synthesizes European knowledge about the world on the eve of the Age of Discovery. In it are amalgamated different conceptual frameworks and ideas, drawn from a wide variety of sources, including Ptolemy's *Geography,* portolan charts, Arabic documents, and various travel narratives. A penetrating and critical approach blends the strength of religious faith, the tenacity of popular beliefs, and a respect for long-established traditions with the evidence of contemporary geography.

Little is known about the author. Documents dated 1409 and 1433 record that Fra Mauro was a Venetian monk in the Camaldoleusian Monastery of San Michele on the island of Murano. It is known that he made a map of a monastic estate in Istria and that in 1444 he was a member of a commission charged with changing the course of the Brenta River. In 1448, he was apparently at work on world maps, as can be inferred from the monastery's account books, where two collaborators are also mentioned: Francesco da Cherso and Andrea Bianco. He is thought to have died in 1459.

Just when Fra Mauro's cartographic team completed its work is unclear. A date on the reverse of the map (August 26, 1460) follows Mauro's death and probably refers to the map's final framing. It is also assumed that Mauro's map, made in 1459 for the Venetian *Signoria* and finished in the same year, is a copy of a now-lost world map commissioned by Alfonso V, king of Portugal (r. 1438–1481). Alfonso would have supplied the monk with the latest Portuguese sea charts as source material. Indeed, Mauro's map appears to be closely related to a portolan chart now in the Vatican, considered by Roberto Almagià to be a copy of the chart Fra Mauro used. While Almagià dated (on grounds of content) the original *mappamundi* to before 1450, most other scholars disagree, preferring the later date.

The parchment map in the Marciana is colored, but unsigned. It is effectively circular (diameter: west-east six feet [1.96 meters], north-south, five and three-quarter feet [1.93 meters]). The outer frame is approximately six and one-quarter feet square (2.23 meters). Each of the four corner spaces contains geographical and cosmographical scenes, showing (clockwise from top left) the number of heavens; the flood tides and the relationship between ocean and land; the relationship between the elements and the different parts of the globe; and the location of the Earthly Paradise. The map itself is packed with information, both textual and graphic. There are miniature landscapes, towered cities, rivers, trees, and ships. The texts, written in an Italian mixed with Venetian dialect, are of particular interest, for, unlike other medieval cartographical texts, which are usually impersonal, descriptive, and repetitive, Fra Mauro's long explanations (in many cartouches, some written on strips of parchment and glued onto the map) were formulated as personal comments, critical of all doubtful information. In point of fact, Mauro himself—to whom a contemporary coin awarded the accolade *cosmographus incomparabilis*—was no less prone than others to mix classical with up-to-date material derived from the narratives of Marco Polo, John Mandeville,

# M

[Fra] Mauro Map. World Map oriented to the south. Venice, Biblioteca Nazionale Marciana, 1459. 76½ × 75 inches (1.96 meters × 1.93 meters). Courtesy Biblioteca Nazionale Marciana.

and Niccolà dei Conti. At the same time, he also said he made use of firsthand information from Ethiopian churchmen. He must have used Arab portolan charts and sailors' and pilgrims' accounts to describe eastern Africa and northern Europe. With characteristic ease, he solved the problem of Jerusalem's centrality—

becoming increasingly difficult to maintain in the face of European exploration in Asia—by shifting the Holy City westward and justifying this by pointing out that he had considered not just geographical space but population density as well, thus ensuring that Jerusalem remained central to the habitable world.

[Fra] Mauro Map. Detail: Inhabitants of Cathay ("Chataio").

Simultaneously monastic, nautical, and Ptolemaic, Fra Mauro's map presents both a medieval circular framework and early Renaissance characteristics, such as a southern orientation—an Arabic influence—and an accurately defined Mediterranean taken from portolan charts. To get an idea of Fra Mauro's personality it is sufficient to note his attitude toward Ptolemy, the authority most revered by fifteenth-century cartographers. Apologizing for not following the parallels, meridians, and degrees of the *Geography*, Mauro comments that he finds them too constraining to show discoveries unknown to the Alexandrian cosmographer. In case he were to be blamed for not following Ptolemy to the letter, Mauro quotes Ptolemy's own words, where the ancient cosmographer anticipated that his work might be improved with time or as further information became available. With an open mind, Mauro was able to reject the Ptolemaic concept of a landlocked Indian Ocean in the light of what he had heard about Portuguese contacts with Arab traders, and to

embrace the possibility of circumnavigating Africa. Similarly, Mauro's need to make sense of the world around him led him to prefer modern to Ptolemaic toponymy and to abandon the traditional division of the regions of the world. At the same time, Mauro could depict the marvels of Taprobane (Ceylon), Java, and the Fortunate Islands, and the blessed kingdoms of Prester John and the Queen of Sheba, and refer to such mythical beings as cynocephali, cannibals, the phoenix, the Old Man of the Mountain, and St. Patrick's Purgatory. He gets around this paradox by classing these fancies as secrets of nature, in which not everything can be explained or be made known to man, since only the eternal God can measure his own creation. He concedes that the cosmographer's work may never be completely satisfactory: "he who wants to understand has first to believe." Even so, he did doubt the existence of monstrous men in Asia and Africa, and he did not believe that Gog and Magog were an identifiable race, specifically located in a place where they had been

# M

locked up by Alexander the Great while awaiting the Antichrist.

As a measure of his intellectual flexibility, Fra Mauro's solution to the problem of the location and representation of the Earthly Paradise is especially noteworthy. A detailed rubric refers to the authority of Augustine, Bede, and Peter Lombard and offers a summary of the theological and geographical debate on the topic. Mauro explains that the Garden of Eden was a real place somewhere in the East, although "very far from our habitable world and remote from our knowledge." In representing the Earthly Paradise in the map's northeastern corner as a circular garden lying, unexpectedly, outside the *oikoumene,* Mauro also followed tradition in showing that the otherwise inaccessible garden is still part of geographical reality, connected to it by the Four Rivers of Paradise, source of all life, which flow out from the garden to water the whole world. On Mauro's map, the presence of the ocean, surrounding both Paradise and the whole earth, and the Four Rivers—cartographically legitimized—confirms the earthly existence of the Garden of Eden, even though it is not placed within the cartographically represented earth, but rather is found, inaccessible, in a northeastern nowhere.

## BIBLIOGRAPHY

Almagià, Roberto. *Monumenta Cartographica Vaticana.* Vol. 1. Vatican City: Biblioteca Apostolica Vaticana, 1944, pp. 32–40.

Caraci, Giuseppe. "The Italian Cartographers of the Benincasa and Freducci Families and the So-Called Borgiana Map of the Vatican Library." *Imago Mundi* 10 (1953): 23–49.

Destombes, Marcel, ed. *Mappemondes*, pp. 223–226. See Gen. Bib.

Gasparrini Leporace, Tullia. *Il mappamondo di Fra Mauro.* Rome: Istituto Poligrafico dello Stato, 1956 [color facsimile].

Harley-Woodward. *The History of Cartography,* Vol. 1, pp. 286–370. See Gen. Bib.

Iwańczak, Wojciech. "Entre l'espace ptolémaïque et l'empirie: Les cartes de Fra Mauro." *Médiévales* 18 (1990): 53–68.

Zurla, Placido. *Il Mappamondo di Fra Mauro Camaldolese.* Venice: n.p., 1806.

*Alessandro Scafi*

## SEE ALSO

Assassins; Bede; Borgia Map; Cannibalism; Cartography, Arabic; Gog and Magog; *Mandeville's Travels;* Marco Polo; *Oikoumene;* Paradise, Travel to; Portolan Charts; Portuguese Expansion; Prester John; Ptolemy; Purgatory, St. Patrick's; Taprobane; Travel Writing in Europe and the Mediterranean Regions

## Measurement of Distances

Measurement of distances in medieval Europe falls into three metrological categories: land measures, land measures applied to the sea, and sea measures. There were many standards and thousands of local and regional variations. The units presented here are those that became state standards by the later Middle Ages and continued as such until replaced by the metric system during the course of the nineteenth century.

Land measures were by far the greatest in number. In the British Isles the yard (or verge) was three feet (0.914 m), the pace was two steps or five feet (1.52 m), and the perch (or gad, lug, pole, or rod) was sixteen and one-half feet (5.029 m) in England and twenty-one feet (6.401 m) in Ireland. For longer distances the furlong (or stade) and mile were used: the former was 660 feet (0.201 km) in England, forty falls (0.227 km) in Scotland, and 840 feet (0.256 km) in Ireland; the latter was generally 5,000 feet or 1,000 paces (1.52 km) in England until it was finally standardized in the later sixteenth century at 5,280 feet (1.609 km); it was 5,952 feet (1.814 km) in Scotland and 6,720 feet (2.048 km) in Ireland.

In France the *pas* (pace) originally was the distance covered by a soldier in two marching steps, but by the fourteenth century the *pas militaire* was two *pieds* (two feet or 0.650 m), the *pas commun* was two and one-half *pieds* (0.812 m), and the *pas géometrique* (or *brasse*) was five *pieds* (1.624 m). The Parisian *toise* of six *pieds* (1.949 m) was employed extensively throughout France even though there were hundreds of local variations. The *perche* (perch) was fixed under Charlemagne at six *aunes* (ells) or twenty-four Roman *pieds* (7.09 m), and this remained the standard throughout the Middle Ages until replaced by three other standards in the seventeenth century. The French *mille* (mile) originally was 1,000 military paces, but during the Middle Ages the Parisian standard generally was considered equal to 1,000 *pas géometriques* or 5,000 *pieds* (1.624 km).

Italy had no standards used as national models, but five units had extensive road usage in all of the hundreds of communes and republics. The *braccio* (French *brasse*) was originally the length of the two arms extended when measured from the tips of the middle fingers. Standards of five to six *piedi* (feet) were common, but variations from 0.4 m to 0.8 m are found everywhere. Three other shorter measures were the *passo* (pace) varying from 0.670 m to 2.021 m, the *pertica* (perch) from 1.565 m to 6.165 m, and the *trabucco* from 2.611 m to 3.243 m. The Italian *miglio* (mile) was based originally on eight *stadii* (furlongs) of 1,000 paces or 5,000 feet (1.481 km); no national standard existed during the Middle Ages, but standards were found regionally ranging from 1.481 km to 2.519 km.

Some common land distance measures employed in other countries were the *milha* (mile) of Portugal, 1.28 miles (2.06 km); the *perche* and *toise* of Switzerland, 9.84 feet and 11.81 feet respectively (3.00 m and 3.60 m); the *rode* (rod) of Denmark, 10.30 feet (3.14 m), and Norway, 9.74 feet (2.97 m); and the *Ruthe* (rod) of the Holy Roman Empire, varying from 9.38 feet to 15.33 feet (2.86 m to 4.67 m).

The mile was the principal land measure converted for use in medieval sea travel and exploration. In the British Isles the mile when employed on the water was labeled "marine," "geographical," "of the sea," or "nautical," while elsewhere such designations were "de mer," "des cartes marines," and "marine" in France and "della marina," "geografico," and "marittimo" in Italy. In all cases, sea miles were generally from two to five times larger than the corresponding land miles.

The fathom and the league were the dominant linear units used by medieval Europeans for sea travel. In the British Isles the fathom contained six feet (1.829 m), but occasionally seven feet (2.134 m). The league, occasionally used here and in the rest of Europe as a land measure or extended mile, was either 7,500 feet, 7,680 feet, 7,920 feet, 8,910 feet, 9,375 feet, 10,000 feet, or 15,000 feet (2.29 km to 4.57 km), until it was finally standardized in the later sixteenth century at 15,840 feet (4.827 km) or three miles of 5,280 feet each. The familiar knot, a division of the log line by which a ship's rate of speed is measured, and the cable length, a maritime unit based on the length of a ship's cable, had no medieval ancestors and were not even standardized until the nineteenth century.

In medieval France the *lieue* (league) and *demi-lieue* (half-league) dominated. Originating on land as the distance that a man could traverse in one hour of ordinary walking, and used in Gaul before the Roman occupation, the *lieue* was reckoned by the fifth century as 1,500 Roman paces of five feet each (2.216 km). By the end of the eighth century it was increased to three Roman miles (4.411 km). Throughout the rest of the Middle Ages numerous lengths were common, most of them between 2,000 to 3,000 *toises,* with each regional *toise* of varying dimensions. No national standard appeared until the last half of the eighteenth century. The French equivalents in the modern era of the knot and cable length are the *noeud* and *encablure.*

The only standardized leagues found in the medieval Italian states were the Genoese *lega* (league), which consisted of three *miglia* (5.556 km), and the *lega* of Livorno, which had 6,678 11/12 *braccia* (3.898 km). A national standard did not appear until 1803. Several other leagues of medieval prominence, expressed in English miles, were the Portuguese *legoa,* 3.84 miles (6.17 km), and the Spanish *legua,* 3.46 miles and 4.21 miles (5.57 km and 6.78 km).

BIBLIOGRAPHY

Zupko, Ronald Edward. *British Weights and Measures: A History from Antiquity to the Seventeenth Century.* Madison: U of Wisconsin P, 1977.

———. *French Weights and Measures before the Revolution: A Dictionary of Provincial and Local Units.* Bloomington: Indiana UP, 1978.

———. *Italian Weights and Measures: The Later Middle Ages to the Nineteenth Century.* Philadelphia: The American Philosophical Society, 1981.

———. *A Dictionary of Weights and Measures for the British Isles: The Middle Ages to the Twentieth Century.* Philadelphia: The American Philosophical Society, 1985.

———. *Revolution in Measurement: Western European Weights and Measures since the Age of Science.* Philadelphia: The American Philosophical Society, 1990.

*Ronald Edward Zupko*

SEE ALSO

Itineraries and *Periploi;* Navigation

## Mecca

A major trade and pilgrimage city in western Arabia since pre-Islamic times, and birthplace of the prophet Muhammad, as well as of the first caliphs.

Mentioned by Ptolemy in the second century C.E. as Macoraba, Mecca has been controlled since the fifth century by the Quraysh tribe. In the sixth century, Meccans successfully asserted the city's commercial preeminence against Ta'if and defended its religious leadership in Arabia against invading Christian

# M

Ethiopians from Yemen. In 622, Muhammad emigrated from Mecca to Medina, and in 630, he conquered Mecca. The city became the destination of the required Islamic pilgrimage known as the *hajj*, and pilgrim services replaced commerce as the foundation of the local economy.

The chief holy site is the Ka'ba sanctuary toward which Muslims around the world pray. The direction (*qibla*) of the Ka'ba is marked in each individual mosque by the prayer niche (*mihrāb*). In Islamic consciousness Mecca is the center of the world, and this is reflected in Islamic architecture and cartography. The astronomical determination of the *qibla* became a preoccupation of Islamic scientists from the ninth century C.E. / third century A.H. Various schemes were devised to facilitate the practical need of orientation for believers; diagrams were included in medieval Islamic cosmographies. Mecca was also described in travel literature (*rihla*), guides to pilgrimage locations (*ziyārāt*), and praise literature (*fadā'il*).

Before the rise of Islam, Mecca's inhospitable climate and harsh terrain caused its inhabitants to rely on trade as an economic base; routes linking Asia, Africa, Mesopotamia, and the Mediterranean intersected there, and annual fairs held at the end of the date harvest concluded with the common pilgrimage and visitation of the Ka'ba by the members of diverse tribes. The city was constrained by the surrounding hills to a north-south plan; apart from the Zamzam well it had little water but was subject to flash floods. Clans resided in walled and gated blocks of mud-brick houses. Different clans participated in different caravans, which went to Yemen in the winter and to Syria in the summer. The Ka'ba was controlled by the clan of Banu Shaiba, who are still its keepers. After Muhammad's calendar reform, Islamic pilgrimage lost its seasonal character and Mecca became subject to mass visits of pilgrims in the twelfth month of the lunar year. Travelers went to Mecca either on foot or on camels, mules, or donkeys; the use of the horse was reserved for the military. The narrow streets were poorly suited to multitudes of animals brought in for transport and sacrifice at the end of the pilgrimage. As was the case with Medina, entry into the city for non-Muslims was strictly prohibited. Medina and Mecca together constitute the two holiest cities of Islam (*al-Haramān*); on its own, Mecca is titled "the Glorious" (*al-mukarrama*) and "the Ennobled" (*al-musharrafa*).

Mecca and the hajj were powerful means of communication in the Islamic world. The famed caliph of Baghdad, Hārūn al-Rashīd (r. 786–809), performed the pilgrimage there nine times. The tradition of visits by rulers and royal ladies led to expectations of government largesse during the season of pilgrimage. The wealthy endowed buildings and services for visitors and sojourners (*mujāwirūn*). Many noted scholars resided at Mecca, and pilgrims, especially those from afar, liked to stay on for religious studies. The traveler Ibn Jubayr visited there in 1183–1184. Ibn Battūta (1304–1368) started a lifetime of travel by going on hajj, visiting Mecca as a pilgrim and sojourner in 1326, and making four more pilgrimages by 1347. On one occasion he traveled Darb Zubayda, the road between Mecca and Baghdad made famous by the improvements financed by Hārūn al-Rashīd's wife, who herself performed several pilgrimages. The routes from Egypt and Syria converged at 'Aqaba and followed the Red Sea coast. The road from the port of Jidda became the major entry way for pilgrims and goods into the sacred precinct of Mecca (*haram*). Visitors to Mecca often complained of the rapacity of the natives and misrule of the sharifs, but Ibn Battūta found Meccan women "beautiful and chaste." The city and especially the rectangular area around the Ka'ba Haram became a meeting place where marriages were contracted. Mecca also functioned as a slave market and held a fair that peaked immediately on the conclusion of the pilgrimage rites. As a result, the population was highly mixed, with infusions from south and southeast Asia and Africa.

Mecca never served as a political center of Islam. The attempt to secure its political independence from the Umayyads by 'Abd Allāh ibn al-Zubayr failed (680–692). Caliphs appointed governors to both Mecca and Medina, and sometimes Mecca had only a sub-governor. In 930, Mecca was raided by the radical Shi'ite sect of Qarmatians from eastern Arabia, who carried the sacred Black Stone away to Bahrain. After it was returned in 950, the city was governed by 'Alid Hasanid rulers known as *sharīfs*. Until 1186 C.E. (A.H. 582) these were Zaydi Shi'ites; subsequent to interference by Saladin, the Shafi'ite Sunni rite predominated. After the demise of the caliphate in 1258, Mecca and the Hijaz were controlled first by the Mamluks, and from 1517 by the Ottomans.

## BIBLIOGRAPHY

Burton, Richard Francis. *Personal Narrative of a Pilgrimage to El Medinah and Meccah.* 2 vols. 2nd edition. London: Longmans, 1857 (and later editions and reprints).

Crone, Patricia. *Meccan Trade and the Rise of Islam.* Princeton, NJ: Princeton UP, 1987.

Peters, Francis E. *Jerusalem and Mecca: The Typology of the Holy City in the Near East.* New York: New York UP, 1986.

———. *Mecca: A Literary History of the Muslim Holy Land.* Princeton, NJ: Princeton UP, 1994.

Watt, William Montgomery. *Muhammad at Mecca.* Oxford: Clarendon Press, 1953.

Wüstenfeld, Ferdinand. *Die Strasse von Baçra nach Mekka.* Göttingen: Dieterische Buchhandlung, 1871.

*Marina A. Tolmacheva*

**SEE ALSO**

Baghdad; Cartography, Arabic; Ibn Battūta, Abu Abdallah; Ibn Jubayr; Mamluks; Medina; Muslim Travelers and Trade; Ottoman Empire; Pilgrimage, Christian; Ptolemy; Red Sea; Saladin; Shi'ism; Sunnism

## Medieval Europe, Geography of
*See* Geography of Medieval Europe

## Medieval European Geography and Travel, Scholarship on
*See* Scholarship on Medieval European Geography and Travel

## Medina

One of the sacred cities of Islam, located in the Hijaz in western Arabia about 200 miles north of Mecca and 100 miles east of the Red Sea; Muhammad and the first three caliphs of Islam died there.

The name—from the Arabic *al-madīna* "the city"—was given to the old oasis city of Yathrib after the prophet Muhammed and his followers from Mecca settled there in 622. The city is listed by Ptolemy in his *Geography* as Yathrippa. The new name is sometimes explained as an abbreviation of *madīnat al-nabī,* "city of the prophet," but Muhammad apparently called it simply *al-Madīna.* Early sources also give the form *Madīnat al-rasūl,* "city of the messenger." Muhammad's maternal great-grandmother was a native of Medina.

The emigrants (*muhājirūn*) from Mecca and the Arab tribesmen of Medina who had invited Muhammad to the city (called the *ansār,* or supporters), formed the original Muslim community, the *umma;* its early structure is reflected in the document known as "the Constitution of Medina"*(c.* 627). During Mu-

hammad's lifetime there were tensions between these two groups and also among the Arab tribes and clans of Medina. These divisions diminished as the number of Muslims grew and other Meccans and Arabian tribes converted to Islam and joined the *umma.* Among the early settlers of Yathrib were three Jewish tribes; they rejected Muhammad's prophetic mission and were eventually driven out of Medina, killed, or enslaved. As was the case with Mecca, non-Muslims were forbidden to enter the city.

Between 622 and 656, Medina was effectively the capital of the Islamic state, and the conquest of Mecca, Arabia, and much of the Middle East was directed from there, until the caliph 'Ali (r. 656–661) moved to the new city of Kufa in Iraq. The important battle of Uhud (625) took place at the northern edge of the oasis. In 627, the Meccans were repulsed in their attempt to lay siege to Medina (Battle of the Trench). Between 682 and 845, Medina was racked by several uprisings or attacked by the Bedouins, but after that historians rarely speak of it. In 974–975, a wall was built to protect the central part of the city; a second wall of greater extent was added in 1162.

Medieval books praise the city for its fragrant air, the sweet voices of its natives, and its excellent dates, whose export acquired a religious connotation. Medina lay on the trade route from Yemen to Syria and had mercantile connections with Iraq. Its port on the Red Sea was al-Jār (later Yanbu'). After Muhammad's death the city became part of the pilgrimage route; it may be visited either before or after the *hajj* proper. The main sanctuary complex (*al-Haram al-Nabawī*) includes the mosque of the prophet and his tomb within. Under the Umayyads the city became a favored residence for those who retired from politics, and it acquired a reputation for luxury. By the late eighth century, Medina began developing into an intellectual center where scholars, students, and visitors engaged especially in legal and theological studies and Arabic philology. The city and its sites are often described in cosmographies, travel literature, and pilgrimage guides. The famous travelers Ibn Jubayr and Ibn Battūta stayed there and visited the holy sites and important teachers. Many prominent Islamic persons are buried in the cemetery of the Haram, but the graves have been damaged in several disturbances and have undergone restoration. Agriculture remained important until modern times, but pilgrimage and student sojourners became major sources of revenue. Guilds of guide

# M

specialists emerged there, as in Mecca, as well as numerous categories of religious professionals and various attendants. The population is mostly Sunni, predominantly Hanafi. There are Sh'ite minority groups, including an ostracized Twelver Shi'a group called *Nakhāwila* or "palm growers."

**BIBLIOGRAPHY**

Burton, Richard Francis. *Personal Narrative of a Pilgrimage to El Medinah and Meccah.* 2 vols. 2nd edition. London: Longmans, 1857 (and later editions and reprints), Part 2.

Nomachi, Kazuyoshi. *Mecca, the Blessed, Medina, the Radiant: The Holiest Cities of Islam.* New York: Aperture, 1997.

Peters, Francis E. *The Hajj: The Muslim Pilgrimage to Mecca and the Holy Places.* Princeton, NJ: Princeton UP, 1994, pp. 137–143, 257–265.

———. *Mecca: A Literary History of the Muslim Holy Land.* Princeton, NJ: Princeton UP, 1994, pp. 57–105, 285–289, 374–378.

Watt, William Montgomery. *Muhammad at Medina.* Oxford: Clarendon Press, 1956.

Watt, William Montgomery, and R.B. Winder. "al-Madína." *Encyclopaedia of Islam.* 2nd edition. Leiden: Brill, 1960–, vol. 5, pp. 994–1007.

*Marina A. Tolmacheva*

**SEE ALSO**

Ibn Battūta, Abu Abdallah; Ibn Jubayr; Mecca; Muslim Travelers and Trade; Ptolemy; Red Sea; Shi'ism; Sunnism

## Mediterranean Sea

A large body of water bordered by the coastlines of Asia, Africa, and Europe. The Mediterranean Sea's relatively calm and tideless waters, many islands, and hospitable shores had welcomed human habitation and traffic for millennia before Rome declared the Mediterranean (lit. "in the midst of the land") *Mare nostrum,* "Our Sea." It covers some 970,000 square miles (2,512,300 km), stretches 2,500 miles (40,000 km) from east to west, and averages 500 miles (800 km) north to south at its wider points. Its waters actually contain five seas—the Adriatic, Aegean, Ionian, Ligurian, and Tyrrhenian—and seven major islands: Sicily, Crete, Cyprus, Sardinia, Corsica, Rhodes, and Majorca. It is bounded in the west by the Straits of Gibraltar, and in the northeast by the Sea of Marmara, which leads into the Black Sea. The Nile, Rhône, and Po rivers empty into the Mediterranean, creating important deltas. The Italian peninsula and Sicily effectively divide the sea into eastern and western basins, which saw rather different patterns of maritime activity and development during the Middle Ages.

Under Roman rule the Mediterranean had carried nearly unmolested traffic. With the disintegration of the western empire in the fifth century, the Germanic Vandals, operating from Spain and later North Africa, disrupted trade and travel and raided port cities throughout the western sea, using it to advance on Rome, which they sacked in 455. The western Roman fleets had been allowed to decay, but the eastern Roman (Byzantine) fleets remained vigorous and had the advantage of being armed with "Greek Fire." In the 520s and 530s the armies and navy of the emperor Justinian defeated the Vandals and cleared much of the western Mediterranean.

Early Muslim victories in Byzantine Syria and Egypt (630s) provided militant Islam with ports, ships, and trained seamen. Expansion westward meant Islamic control of the western Mediterranean, and the capture of Rhodes and Cyprus relegated the Byzantines to a rather narrow field between the Aegean and Italy. Ninth-century Arab conquests included Crete (823), Sicily (830s), southern Italy (840s), and the Maltese archipelago (870s). These tended to bring revitalizations of agriculture, city life, and trade, and Arabs introduced the Mediterranean world to the magnetic compass, *kamal* (a navigational instrument), lateen sail, and practical higher mathematics. Internal political fractiousness precluded further Arab maritime extension. Scandinavian expansion led to Viking raids of both Moorish and Christian ports in the western Mediterranean, the first northern European incursions into the sea. These were followed in the later eleventh century by the more permanent Norman invasions of southern Italy (beginning 1058) and Sicily (by 1090). Arab power was further eroded by the Turkish conquests in the Levant (a Turkish vassal of Alp Arslan captured Jerusalem in 1071 and Damascus in 1075).

The First Crusade (1095–1099) brought northwestern Europe into the eastern Mediterranean, and effected commercial links between the Levant and the expanding maritime Italian city-states of Genoa, Pisa, and Venice. Western contacts with Constantinople increased, but the city was sacked by errant crusaders and Venetians in 1204, sealing the fate of the eastern empire. From bases in Rhodes (to 1309) and then Malta, the Knights of St. John acted as Christian cor-

# M

sairs harrying Muslim maritime traffic and defending Christian interests until the sixteenth century.

Venice and Genoa extended their trade rivalry by establishing colonies and trade markets in the northeastern Mediterranean. Genoa tended to ship bulky cargoes and dominated the Black Sea trade, while Venetian cargoes were smaller and more precious (cloth, spices) and crossed the southeastern sea. Muslim Turkish aggression, which resulted in the fall of Constantinople (1453), coupled with Christian trade wars, led to Turkish domination of the eastern Mediterranean and a restriction of European trade by the later fifteenth century.

Meanwhile, Catalan Aragon developed its maritime power, competing successfully with Italian and French interests, and came to command the western basin. Iberian discoveries in the Atlantic and a shift of economic power to northern Europe relegated the Mediterranean to a smaller role in world affairs; this serves as one marker of the end of the Middle Ages.

## BIBLIOGRAPHY

Ahrweiler, Hélène, ed. *Géographie historique du monde méditerranéen*. Paris: Publications de la Sorbonne, Université de Paris I, 1988.

Airaldi, Gabriella, et al., eds. *El Mundo mediterráneo de la Edad Media*. Barcelona: Argot, 1987.

Balletto, Laura. "Tra mercanti e mercatura nel Mediterraneo medievale." *Cultura e scuola* 26 (1986): 96–104.

Branford, Ernle. *Mediterranean, Portrait of a Sea*. Toronto: Hodder and Stoughton, 1971.

Braudel, Fernand. *The Mediterranean and the Mediterranean World in the Age of Philip II*. 2 vols. New York: Harper and Row, 1972.

Di Vittorio, Antonio A. "The Seafarers of the Mediterranean." *Journal of Economic History* 10 (1981): 213–221.

Friedland, Klaus, ed. *Maritime Aspects of Migration*. Cologne: Böhlau, 1989.

Galley, Micheline, and Leïla Ladjimi Sebai, eds. *L'Homme méditerranéen et la mer*. Tunis: Salammbô, 1985.

*IX Congreso di storia della Corona d'Aragona: La Corona d'Aragona e il Mediterraneo*. 2 vols. Naples: Società Napoletana di Storia Patria, 1978–1982.

*Joseph P. Byrne*

## SEE ALSO

Compass, Magnetic; Constantinople; Genoa; Merchants, Italian; Navigation; Navigation, Arab; Navigation, Viking; Ottoman Turks; Piracy; Pisa; Shipping Contracts, Mediterranean; Ships and Shipbuilding; Venice

## Mela, Pomponius (fl. 37–42 C.E.)

Roman author unknown except for his composition of a three-book treatise entitled *De chorographia* ("On the Description of Places") or *De situ orbis* ("On the Description of the World"), the earliest (43–44 C.E.; *cf.* 3.44–52) Latin work dedicated solely to geography. Though notable for its prose style, the treatise's derivative and uncritical nature has long vitiated its geographical utility. Mela's attraction to marvelous details outweighed his interest in precise measurements or other numerical data.

Mela did not write from direct observation but gleaned most of his material from authors ranging in date from Herodotus (*c.* 485–425 B.C.E.) to Virgil (70–19 B.C.E.). His worldview (*Chorographia* 1.4) differs little from Eratosthenes', which he probably knew through Virgil (see *Georgics* 1.233ff.) or Varro of Atax. Mela believes the *orbis terrarum* is circled by Ocean and penetrated by four great inlets: Mediterranean Sea, Red Sea, Persian Gulf, and Caspian Sea.

The presentation proceeds counterclockwise from Gibraltar around the Mediterranean basin (Books 1–2), then from Spain's Atlantic coast clockwise around the perimeter of the world (Book 3), mentioning Thule, India, West Africa, and other sites. Mela is the first writer to mention the Baltic Sea, his "Codanus Gulf" (3.31).

The *Chorographia* promotes mythologies that became prominent in medieval geographical lore: griffins (2.1), Amazons and Hyperboreans (1.13), headless Blemyes with their faces on their chests (1.48), and mariners blown past the Caspian Sea to Germany (3.45).

Late classical and medieval scholars held Mela in a higher regard than his work would seem to warrant. Solinus (fl. 230–240) augmented material from Pliny by borrowing from Mela; Macrobius and Martianus Capella also gleaned much from both sources. The number of surviving manuscripts demonstrates that Mela's popularity continued throughout the Middle Ages. Several legends on the Genoese planisphere (1457) assert Mela's authority over Ptolemy. The remarkable Pirrus de Noha map of around 1414 (Rome, Biblioteca Apostolica Vaticana, Archivia di San Pietro H. 31, fol. 8r) accompanies a manuscript of Mela, but much of its content is drawn from elsewhere and its design clearly indicates the influence of Ptolemy, thus presaging the cartographic renaissance of the later fifteenth century and the waning of Mela's authority.

# M

World Map from Mela's *Cosmographia*. Reims, Bibliothèque Municipale MS 1321, fol. 12r. 1417. Document bibliothèque municipale de Reims (France).

**BIBLIOGRAPHY**

Brodersen, Kai, ed. and trans. *Kreuzfahrt durch die alte Welt: Pomponius Mela.* Darmstadt: Wissenschaftliche Buchgesellschaft, 1994.

Parroni, Piergiorgio, ed. *Pomponii Melae* De chorographia *Libri Tres; introduzione, edizione critica e commento.* Storia e Letteratura, 160. Rome: Edizioni di storia e letteratura, 1984.

Ranstrand, Gunnar, ed. *Pomponii Melae* De chorographia *Libri Tres.* Studia Graeca et Latina Gothoburgensia 28. Göteborg: Almqvist and Wiksell, 1971.

*Roger T. Macfarlane*

**SEE ALSO**

Amazons; Caspian Sea; India; Mediterranean Sea; Monstrosity, Geographical; Pliny the Elder; Ptolemy; Red Sea; Solinus, Julius Gaius; Thule

## Memory and Maps

Memory, defined as the vivid and meaningful recollection of sacred history, was a cornerstone of medieval Christianity. From its inception, Christian cartography supported the demands of sacred memory by offering a topographical matrix in which to fix the events of the Bible. As early as the mid-sixth century, the large Byzantine mosaic at Madaba (in present-day Jordan) put mapmaking in the service of sacred lore and instruction. Labels referring to Old and New Testament events present the Holy Land as a site meaningful above all as a frame for the Christian past.

This cartographic image evokes some of the formal devices characteristic of medieval memory training. Deriving originally from classical rhetorical strategies, memory education during this period began with the formulation of an orderly, easily negotiated mnemonic *locus.* This was often diagrammatic in nature, taking the form of a ladder, wheel, architectural space, or cosmological model. The student of memory filled this imaginary frame with significant images intended to stimulate recollection. Controlled navigation of the mnemonic arena allowed for the ordered recovery of an extensive body of learned material and, in a Christian context, served as a foundation for devotional meditation.

As distinctly spatial constructs in a culture of spatially grounded mnemotechniques, medieval maps of the Holy Land bear notable similarities to contemporary systems of memory and recall. Pietro Vesconte's map of the Holy Land (*c.* 1320) is particularly suggestive of such a relationship. Arranged as a grid, its network of lines serves as a guide for locating specific places and the sacred events that occurred there. Vesconte condenses Christian history into a constellation of notable sites and invites viewers to follow an ordered itinerary of the biblical past; the space of the map offers a format for its subsequent recollection.

Traveling among sacred sites was the objective of medieval pilgrims as well, and it is tempting to link pilgrimage maps—notable for their inutility as actual wayfinding tools—with the goal of an imagined or recollected journey through the Holy Land. An important example by the English monk Matthew Paris (mid-thirteenth century) offers a picturesque panorama where geography seems to be at the service of visual diversion and religious education. Diagrammatic cities, fantastic architectural structures, and extensive inscriptions linking particular sites with biblical events fill the

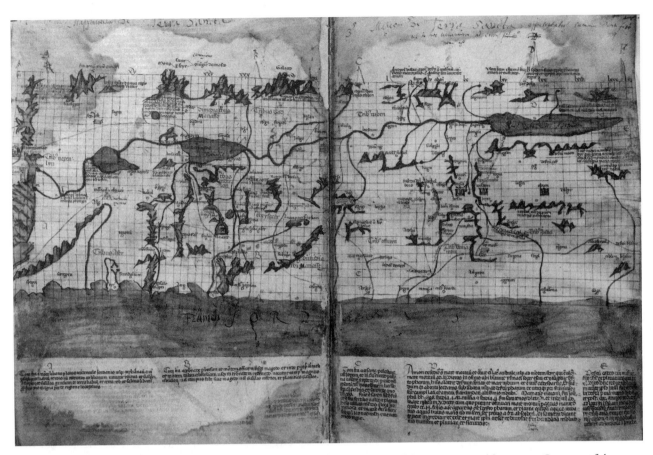

Map of Holy Land by Pietro Vesconte. London, British Library, MS Add. 27376, fols. 188v–189, 14th century. Courtesy of the British Library.

frame of this map. No pilgrim could actually have traveled using such a map as a guide, but it might have been employed to visualize, recall, and meditate upon sacred history via the mnemonic device of an itinerary.

Cartographic images are not alone in linking the geography of Christian history with its recollection. Many medieval pilgrimage texts trace precise paths through the cities and monuments of the Holy Land, using spatial precision to create memorability. Likewise, churches built with formal references to the Holy Sepulchre in Jerusalem allowed for real and imagined itineraries to intersect, and for sacred memory to stimulate devotion. Pilgrims undertaking actual journeys to the lands of the Bible encountered images along the way that helped to situate their own route within a larger Christian cosmography. The tympanum over the central portal at the Church of the Madeleine in Vézelay (*c.* 1120) pictorializes this worldview in a format both diagrammatic and vivid, two of the principal characteristics of medieval mnemonic systems. Such images served to actualize both physical and Christian space, bringing the two together in a memorable format.

Recognizing maps and other maplike structures as memory devices restores an understanding of function to images often misconstrued as "inaccurate" and therefore "untrustworthy." Mnemonic interpretations such as this are rooted in the outlooks of medieval viewers and worshipers, namely: that early maps are above all symbolic rather than representational; that Christian history is inextricably linked with sacred topography; and that spatial formulae provide access to material that demands lucid and inspiring recollection. Religious meditation based on this model emerges as a conceptual journey among various *loci*/biblical events, a spiritual pilgrimage undertaken in order to recall and relive the most significant episodes of the Christian past.

# M

BIBLIOGRAPHY

Carruthers, Mary. *The Book of Memory: A Study of Memory in Medieval Culture.* Cambridge: Cambridge UP, 1990.

———. "The Poet as Master Builder: Composition and Locational Memory in the Middle Ages." *New Literary History* 24 (1993): 881–904.

Connolly, Daniel K. "Imagined Pilgrimage in Gothic Art: Maps, Manuscripts, and Labyrinths." Diss., U of Chicago, 1998.

Halbwachs, Maurice. *On Collective Memory.* Ed. and trans. Lewis A. Cosner. Chicago: U of Chicago P, 1992.

Kupfer, Marcia. "Medieval World Maps: Embedded Images, Interpretive Frames." *Word and Image* 10 (1994): 262–288.

Roy, Bruno, and Paul Zumthor, eds. *Jeux de mémoire: Aspects de la mnémotechnie médiévale.* Montreal: U of Montreal P, 1985.

Yates, Frances. *The Art of Memory.* Chicago and London: U of Chicago P, 1966.

*Elizabeth Rodini*

SEE ALSO

Holy Land; Madaba Mosaic Map; Maps; Matthew Paris; Pilgrimage, Christian; Vesconte, Pietro/Perrino; Vézelay

## Merchant Manuals

Late medieval compendia of mercantile information. Concerned with things a businessman would need to know about international commerce, merchant manuals contain information about conditions throughout the Mediterranean world, and occasionally beyond. Typically, these manuals include material regarding conversion of weights and measures, exchange rates between various currencies, and customs duties and fees. They often advise merchants how to determine quality in certain goods, give information about business conditions in particular markets, and provide other useful guidance. This information is obviously of great interest and utility to modern students of medieval economic history.

The surviving manuals are all either Venetian or Tuscan; one was compiled by a Florentine resident in Genoa. The published Tuscan manuals are attributed to named individuals: Francesco Balducci Pegolotti, Saminiato di Guciozzo de' Ricci, Giovanni di Bernardo da Uzzano, and Giorgio di Lorenzo Chiarini. The Venetian manuals are anonymous. Ugo Tucci has suggested that the manuals had different purposes in the two merchant communities: the Tuscan ones served as reference works in the large firms that dominated the economy of Florence, while the Venetian ones were intended to acculturate youths in the ways of the small to medium-sized companies of that city (Tucci 90). A comparison of the earliest extensive manuals from each city tends to confirm this assessment. The Venetian *Zibaldone da Canal* (Da Canal Notebook) apparently had its origins as a student's arithmetic workbook, perhaps sometime around 1310, and continued to be added to as a kind of commonplace book into the early 1330s. Pegolotti, an important manager in the Florentine Bardi Company (the largest mercantile banking company of its day), worked in various branches of the company in Flanders, Genoa, Cyprus, and elsewhere before he compiled his manual around 1340.

Most of these texts show evidence of common origins, or shared sources. In the introduction to his edition of Pegolotti's manual, Allan Evans investigates these similarities in detail (Evans xxxix–l). The interrelated, but not identical, passages strongly suggest the existence at one time of a larger body of manuscripts. Only Saminiato de' Ricci's manual (1396), written while he represented his family's company in Genoa, seems to bear no relation to any other.

The eclectic nature of the manuals means that they contain material from a wide chronological span. Much of this information was obsolete when the manuals were assembled, as is shown by the section in Pegolotti's work entitled "Acre of Syria for itself when it was in the hands of the Christians," indicating that the manual was compiled after the fall of Acre in 1291, but incorporated earlier data. The inclusion of this material suggests that the manuals were intended to do more than simply serve as reference works. They provided more general information on "merchant culture," acting as a repository of accumulated wisdom.

The oldest surviving fragment of a merchant manual is Pisan in origin and dates from around 1278, while the *Zibaldone da Canal* is the oldest extensive manual; material in it can be dated to the late thirteenth century, about the same time as the Pisan fragment. It seems likely, then, that the genre developed at some time in the thirteenth century and continued into the fifteenth. In the fourteenth century, in addition to Pegolotti's manual and the *Zibaldone da Canal*, another Venetian manual, the *Tarifa zoè noticia dy pexi e mexure di luogi e tere che s'adovra marcadantia per el mondo* ("Tariff, i.e., notice, of weights and measures of places and lands that are used by merchants throughout the world"), originated sometime after 1345. Saminiato de' Ricci's manual is next chronologically, followed by Uzzano's in 1442 (another Pisan work), and the manual attributed to Chiarini from the mid-fifteenth century.

One of the best-known passages from any merchant manual comes near the beginning of Pegolotti's *Pratica della mercatura*: under the heading "Advice on the journey to Cathay [Gittaio] via the road from Tana, going and returning with merchandise," readers are informed that "the road from Tana to Cathay is very safe and that Cathay is a large country with many magnificent merchants" (Evans 21–23.) The wide-ranging nature of the manuals is one of their most valuable aspects. However, they must be used with care. It is difficult to date or determine the provenance of much of the material that the manuals contain with any precision. Furthermore, they often disagree among themselves. Nonetheless, once their limitations are recognized, they can be very useful and informative sources for a wide variety of topics.

**BIBLIOGRAPHY**

Borlandi, Antonia, ed. *Il manuale di mercatura di Saminiato de' Ricci*. Genoa: Di Stefano, 1965.

Borlandi, Franco, ed. *El libro di mercatantie et usanze de' paesi*. Turin: S. Lattes, 1936.

Datini, Francesco di Marco. *La pratica di mercatura datiniana (secolo XIV)*. Ed. Cesare Ciano. Milano: Giuffrè, 1964.

Dotson, John E. *Merchant Culture in Fourteenth Century Venice: The Zibaldone da Canal*. Binghamton, NY: Medieval and Renaissance Texts and Studies, 1994.

Evans, Allan, ed. *Francesco Balducci Pegolotti: La pratica della mercatura*. Cambridge, MA: The Mediaeval Academy of America, 1936; rpt. New York: Kraus, 1970.

Pagnini, Gian-Francesco. *Della decima e di altre varie gravezze imposte dal Comune di Firenze*. Lisbon-Lucca: 1765–1766. Vol. 2, parts 3–4; rpt. Bologna: Forni, 1967.

*John E. Dotson*

**SEE ALSO**
Coinage and Money; Economics and Trade; Merchants, Italian; Pegolotti, Francesco Balducci; Pisa; Venice

## Merchants, French

A class that began to develop in the Merovingian period and became a dominant force in the French economy and culture by the late Middle Ages.

Roman Gaul in later antiquity was a relative commercial backwater when compared with Spain or Italy. Commerce remained localized, and imports were limited. As Roman institutions devolved or crumbled, however, Mediterranean trade—especially with Africa—increased, bringing Greek, Jewish, and "Syrian" merchants into both seaport and inland cities, with Arles the major entrepôt. Sources as widely varying as hagiography, archaeology, and notarial records present what little we know of this early commerce, though there are few surviving references to indigenous merchants, beyond local brokers or shopkeepers, until the seventh century. It is clear, however, that canonical prohibitions against clergy acting as merchants stimulated bishops and monasteries to employ laymen to act in their behalf in both buying and selling necessities of life, and that these were likely to be local Christians.

By the later Merovingian period, long-distance foreign trade was in decline, and the Greek mercantile presence had all but disappeared. In northern France, weights, measures, and coins took on Germanic forms in place of the Roman. Carolingian authorities, like some earlier Merovingians, tried to stimulate trade by establishing and protecting rural and urban marketplaces and providing merchants—both Jewish and Christian—with immunities, exemptions, and protections from both physical and economic molestation. Charlemagne also encouraged merchant associations, which had developed from Roman and Germanic roots, unless these threatened local order. The itinerant imperial court, and later that at Aix, had its own special merchants responsible for victuals and other supplies.

In the years after Charlemagne, much French commerce was controlled by outsiders, including the Viking raider/traders, Mediterranean Muslims, Frisians to the north, and from the eleventh century, Italians. Fairs began to emerge on the model of Dagobert's at St. Denis, and both kings and local lords came to understand the advantage of encouraging merchants and taxing them. Indeed, Philip I was upbraided by Pope Gregory VII in the 1080s for allowing imposts on traveling merchants, and some evidence of urban commercial revival may be seen in Philip's new town charters in the Beauvaisis and around Paris, Laon, and Orléans. In the north, Flemish merchants came to control the lucrative wool and cloth trade with England, and in the south, wine and salt became increasingly important bulk commodities.

Good wines from the classic regions of central France slowly and steadily replaced innately poor local

# M

vintages from marginal soils as they began to be carted north along the still-rudimentary roads or floated south along rivers. The wines of Bordeaux and Auxerre also made their way to England via the Garonne River, reaching an annual peak of nearly 25 million gallons in the early fourteenth century. Most of this was carried by small merchants—both Gascon and English—in small ships. Wholesale buyers of good wines also dealt directly with local brokers in Burgundy.

Merchants of all levels, from international spice traders to artisans with limited stock, increased in number and wealth as the urban revival, which had been fed by the commercial revolution of the twelfth and thirteenth centuries, continued and the population soared. The crusades had reopened trade with the Levant, and agents from Marseilles, Montpellier, Narbonne, and still vital Arles trafficked in spices, dyestuffs, and exotic cloths and edibles such as sugar and rice. Many cities developed special quarters for merchants (as for artisans), and a powerful bourgeoisie played major roles in the French communal movements of the high Middle Ages. From Louis VI on, French kings recognized the importance of this class as allies, counterbalancing the power of the landed nobility, as well as providing needed monetary revenue.

By the later Middle Ages, unprecedented urban fortunes were being made and displayed through sumptuous clothing and housing. In the south, wealthy merchants aped the Italians by purchasing property in the hinterland and marrying into an increasingly impoverished nobility. A more lasting effect, perhaps, was the way that the values of the urban elite came to compete with those of the aristocracy, as displayed in the *Ménagier de Paris* (c. 1392), whose advice to a young wife exemplified the expectations of the serious and frugal urban man of affairs. Though the Hundred Years' War devastated much of the commercial economy, with the aid of the rich merchant of Bourges, Jacques Coeur, Charles VII was able to provide a firm foundation for an economic revival in the later fifteenth century.

## BIBLIOGRAPHY

Boyer, Marjorie N. "A Day's Journey in Medieval France." *Speculum* 26 (1951): 597–608.

Carus-Wilson, Eleanora. *Medieval Merchant Venturers: Collected Studies*. London: Methuen, 1954.

Collas, Alain. "Les gens qui comptent à Bourges au XVe siècle: Portrait de groupe de notables urbains." *Annales de Bretagne et des Pays de l'Ouest* 101.3 (1994): 49–68.

Joris, André. "A propos du commerce mosan aux XIIIe et XIVe siècles." In his *Villes—Affaires—Mentalités*. Brussels: De Boeck, 1993.

Laurent, Henri. "Marchands du palais et marchands d'abbayes." *Revue Historique* 183 (1938): 281–297.

LeGoff, Jacques. *Marchands et banquiers au moyen âge*. Paris: Presses Universitaires de France, 1956.

Marville, Alain. "Les marchands de Marville au XIVe siècle." In *Luxembourg en Lotharingie: Mélanges Paul Margue*. Ed. Paul Dostert et al. Luxembourg: Editions St.-Paul, 1993, pp. 167–175.

Rouche, Michel. "Marchés et marchands en Gaul: Du Ve au Xe siècle." In *Mercati e mercanti nell'alto medioevo*. Spoleto: Presso da sede del Centro, 1993, pp. 395–441.

Wolff, Philippe. *Commerces et marchands de Toulouse (vers 1350–vers 1450)*. Paris: Plon, 1954.

*Joseph P. Byrne*

SEE ALSO

Bruges; Coinage and Money; Economics and Trade; Fairs; *Fondaco*; Ghent; Guilds; Mediterranean Sea; Merchants, Italian; Merchants, Jewish; Spice Trade, Indian Ocean; Transportation, Inland; Viking Age

## Merchants, Italian

A dominant class within Italian society who, guided by their commercial interests, spread to all regions of the world accessible to them, opened new routes, and thus promoted European world exploration and knowledge.

Since the mid-500s, Italy was divided into different zones of influence: while Germanic rulers controlled the interior, in the south and on the coast, Byzantium established permanent rule, thanks to its exceptional navy. Being ruled by a mighty but remote lord, the old harbors of the Italian coast could develop into relatively free towns. From the later seventh century on, the Mediterranean was increasingly dominated by ships from Muslim lands. Maritime cities were urged to defend themselves against the Muslim attacks and built up mighty fleets, serving also as the basis for a growing trade. To improve this trade, the cities gradually turned from self-defense to assaults on Arab power, especially in the western Mediterranean, though not hestitating to make peace and negotiate trade with Muslims if European merchants thought it advantageous.

According to ninth-century sources, Italian merchants from Amalfi, Genoa, Pisa, and Venice had spread all along the Mediterranean coast under Muslim or Byzantine rule: to Spain, Tunis, Tripoli, Alexandria,

Cairo, Cyprus, Antioch, Constantinople, and Trebizond. They founded colonies (*fondachi*), obtained special conditions whenever possible, and sometimes ended up wielding political power. More than 100 Amalfitans were living at Cairo by the tenth century, Venetians held privileges in Byzantium in 992, and an Amalfitan colony under a *consul* at Jerusalem founded a hospital around 1065, some thirty years before the beginning of the First Crusade. After the Norman conquest in the Mediterranean, Amalfi lost independence and sea power, whereas Genoa, Pisa, and Venice continued to gain strength: supporting the crusaders with fleets and local knowledge, they received payment through added privileges. After the twelfth century, Italian merchants clearly dominated the trade of Asian goods between Egypt and Europe. In 1204, Venice convinced the crusaders to conquer Byzantium and thus gained control over the northeastern Mediterranean. The Venetian monopoly was superseded by Genoa in 1261, when the Black Sea became a "Genoese Sea," and the struggle against Byzantium or the Arabs was at times forgotten in internecine struggles among the Italian maritime cities (Pisa was destroyed as a competitor in 1284 when Genoa burned its fleet).

After the Mongols had established their empire between 1220 and 1240, the Italian merchants, already on their way to the East, were well prepared for the new challenge of the large Asian market. In 1245, in the recently conquered city of Kiev, John of Plano Carpini and his fellow papal envoys encountered Genoese, Venetian, and Pisan merchants. The Genoese and Venetian colonies Kaffa and Tana at the northern rim of the Black Sea opened the way to China and India not only for Marco Polo, from 1271 to 1295, but for a large number of merchants. The description of the well-known China route in the handbook (*Pratica della Mercatura c.* 1340) of the Florentine merchant Francesco Balducci Pegolotti shows that this inland city had joined the maritime powers in world trade, founding banks in Tunis in the fourteenth century. The Italian merchants were the most important agents of contacts between Europe and Asia/North Africa during the later Middle Ages, leading to very different consequences: they served as ambassadors for popes, kings, and khâns, and they prepared the way for the missionaries. Asiatic technologies such as silk production were brought to Italy, the large number of imported Asian slaves can be estimated by the half-castes in Italian foundling hospitals, and the outbreak of the bubonic plague in Europe after 1346 can be traced to ships that came from the Genoese colony Kaffa in the Crimea. The needs of Italian maritime merchants promoted new branches of science, including the invention of useful sea charts (*portolani*), the nucleus of modern cartography. Genoese ships had reached the Caspian Sea in the thirteenth century, and before 1317 they sailed down the Euphrates. Noting these achievements, the Dominican William Adam proposed the daring geostrategic idea of starving Egypt by blockading the Indian Sea.

Also in the West, the Italians, especially the Genoese, were participating in voyages of exploration. They reached the Saharan oasis Tuat, and after having wrested control over the western Mediterranean from the Arabs, they sailed into the Atlantic, reaching England and Flanders. They took part in the exploration of the Canaries starting in 1312, and the Vivaldi brothers left Genoa in 1291 in an attempt to circumnavigate Africa.

Each barrier the Italian merchants surmounted revealed others, which in turn required negotiation. Thus, the merchants were always at the forefront of exploring new territory, not neccessarily intending to conquer it but to secure traditing positions there. When Spain, Portugal, and England began to establish colonies in the Atlantic and in the Americas, they employed the knowledge of Italian merchants: the Venetian cartographer for the Portuguese court, Fra Mauro; the Genoese Christopher Columbus; the Florentine Amerigo Vespucci; and the Genoese John and Sebastian Cabot [Cabotto], the early explorers of America in the service of England's King Henry VII.

**BIBLIOGRAPHY**

Ashtor, Eliyahu. *East-West Trade.* Collected Studies series 245. London: Variorum Reprints, 1986.

Basso, Enrico. *Genova: Un impero sul mare.* Cagliari: Istituto sui rapporti Italo-Iberici, 1994.

Citarella, A.O. "The Relations of Amalfi with the Arab World before the Crusades." *Speculum* 42 (1967): 299–312.

Krueger, Hilmar C. "The Italian Cities and the Arabs before 1095." In *A History of the Crusades.* Ed. Kenneth M. Setton. Philadelphia: U of Pennsylvania P, 1958, vol. 1, pp. 40–52.

Schmieder, Felicitas. "Der Umgang der abenländischen Kaufleute mit den Mongolen." In *Europa und die Fremden: Die Mongolen im Urteil des Abenlandes vom 13. bis in das 15. Jahrhundert.* Ed. Felicitas Schmieder. Sigmaringen: Jan Thorbecke, 1994, pp. 152–172.

*Felicitas Schmieder*

# M

## Merchants, Jewish

As a result of their dispersion from Palestine into the various countries of the Diaspora, the Jews were gradually transformed from a predominantly agrarian culture to an urban one in which they practiced commerce and crafts. Accordingly, from very early in the Middle Ages they played an important role as traveling merchants, both in Christian and in Muslim countries. Moreover, due to the uniformity of Talmudic legislation concerning contracts, which facilitated mercantile arrangements between members of Jewish communities geographically distant from one another, Jews enjoyed a particular advantage in international trade, at least until the eleventh century.

In Muslim countries, which had largely urban economies, Jewish merchants were often partners with Arabs and other Muslim associates in larger companies, both in local trade and in long-distance transactions. They were especially active in trading luxury merchandise, such as gems. Some made large fortunes from established hereditary enterprises, as is the case of the Tusturi family during the tenth and eleventh centuries in Egypt. But most Jewish merchants conducted their business while traveling throughout the caliphate, buying and selling products in the various markets and fairs.

The most important company of medieval Jewish merchant-adventurers in the Islamic world was the Rhadanites, named after an Iranian city that was reportedly their place of origin. From the ninth to the eleventh centuries, they conducted business between Central Asia and eastern Europe, especially along the Volga River, and beyond into the Mediterranean region to western Europe, reaching the Rhône River. Their trade included a variety of merchandise, such as fur, timber, spices, gems, arms, and slaves. The Rhadanites were compelled to cease their activities after the triumph of Christianity in newly Kievan Russia (*c.* 1000) where their competitors, the Byzantine merchants, were protected by the government; they were also overwhelmed by the strong competition of the Italian city-states in the Mediterranean Sea.

In the Byzantine Empire, Jewish merchants never played an important role in economic activities, con-

centrating their activities on small local markets, but conditions prevailing in western Europe during the early Middle Ages enabled them to flourish there. The decay of the ancient Roman cities and the rise of feudal society in the newly established "Barbarian" kingdoms left the Jews as the marginalized remnants of an urban culture. Most of these merchants were itinerant mercers, who dealt with local exchange of goods between lords and peasants of the various feudal estates.

Some of them became involved in the import of luxury objects and spices, produced in the East, which they sold to European customers. These merchant-travelers sailed in the Mediterranean, embarking from various ports of Italy and Provence on vessels bound eastward, mainly to Egypt; their local Jewish partners enabled them to contact Middle Eastern dealers and producers located in the Far East, such as China and India. The associates, who were compelled to pay duties and taxes to a variety of governments and feudal lords, created an appropriate system of calculating their expenditures, based on mutual trust and the sharing of the profits of trade.

The activities of Jewish merchants are particularly well documented for historians because when they left Europe to negotiate trade in the Middle East, their communities entrusted them with written queries addressed to the Mesopotamian *Geonim* (the supreme religious authority of Judaism) concerning interpretations of Mosaic law. When they returned, the *Responsa* they brought to their respective communities also contained marginal business notation and memoranda. Thus, because of the habit of writing marginal memoranda and other records on papyri that may also have contained sacred texts (and were thus protected from destruction and merely thrust into rubbish heaps between the walls of buildings such as the Cairo *Geniza*) an enormous amount of information about Jewish mercantile activity and litigation (often adjudicated in community courts, most significantly that of Fustat or Old City of Cairo) is preserved among the documents.

However, the economic status of these Jewish merchants, who can be traced from the eighth to the eleventh centuries, was precarious, due to the competition of their Italian and Catalan counterparts. The rise of the Italian maritime city-states and their virtual monopoly over Mediterranean trade from the eleventh century gradually eliminated Jewish traders from international transactions and compelled them to adopt new professions, such as moneylending, which, during the high and late Middle Ages, became a notorious economic activity of European Jews. Their actual involvement in matters of "credit" qualified as "usury," and this "commerce of money"—the dealing in interest charged on transactions—could nearly equal the amount of profit merchants might enjoy from trade.

The development of towns in western Europe after the eleventh century and the renewal of commerce created new opportunities for Jewish merchants in this area. Their main activities were related to local markets and fairs, including the weekly market day at which the agrarian and urban sectors exchanged their products. In order to allow the participation of Jews, some of these weekly gatherings were not held on Saturdays, especially in those places with important Jewish populations. Their presence was considered indispensable for the development of commercial transactions, including the necessary credit operations. Such regulations demonstrate the important role played by Jewish merchants in particular fields of trade.

The development of regional trade in twelfth- and thirteenth-century Europe, especially in the flourishing fairs, was another opportunity for Jewish merchants, although they played a less important role in this field than in that of local commerce. While their Italian and Hanseatic competitors for all practical purposes held a monopoly over large transactions, including credit operations by the newly created banking systems, Jewish merchants were still crucial to the trade of several regions, especially in the thirteenth-century Christian kingdoms of Spain and in the Rhine Valley. In the latter case, the establishment of the League of the German cities of the Rhineland was followed by the creation of a federation of Jewish communities, named after the initials of its three founding members (as the names might be pronounced or spelled): the *ShUM*—Speyer, Worms, Mainz. This federation included members of Jewish settlements from Basel to Cologne. Its statutes, mainly the regulations of trade, witness to the active role of merchants, both in the interrelationship between local and regional transactions and in the establishment of companies destined to promote larger commercial activities.

In the late Middle Ages, the activities of Jewish merchants declined. The expulsions of the Jews from England (1291) and France (1306) brought about the ruin of once flourishing communities, while the competition of Christian traders in other countries, especially in Germany, relegated Jews to small businesses and compelled many to emigrate. Once resettled in eastern Europe, particularly in Poland, they set up a new commercial class that began to flourish in the fourteenth century. In Western European countries, such as Spain and Italy, they continued to pursue their economic activities, though they were affected by the economic recession of the fourteenth century, which caused them to convert their trade to moneylending operations. This, in turn, stimulated the kind of anti-Semitism that led to the expulsion of Jews from Spain (in 1492), Portugal, and other lands. Similar effects of the crisis were evident in the Muslim world, where Jews were forced to limit their commercial activity to smaller businesses.

## BIBLIOGRAPHY

Ashtor, Eliayhu. *A Social and Economic History of the Near East in the Middle Ages.* Berkeley: U of California P, 1976.

Goitein, Samuel D. *Letters of Medieval Jewish Traders.* Princeton, NJ: Princeton UP, 1973.

Grabois, Aryeh. "Role et fonction de l'usure juive dans le système économique et social du monde médiéval." In Shmuel Trigano, ed., *La société juive à travers l'histoire.* Vol. 3. Paris: Fayard, 1993, pp. 177–205, 501–510.

Poliakov, Leon. *Les <Banchieri> Juifs et le Saint-Siège du XIIIe au XVIIIe siècle.* Paris: S.E.V.P.E.N., 1965

Sombart, Werner. *The Jews and Modern Capitalism.* Trans. M. Epstein. Glencoe, IL: Free Press, 1951.

*Aryeh Grabois*

## SEE ALSO

Byzantine Empire; Expulsion, Corporate; Fairs; Gems; Genoa; Hanse, The; Merchants, Italian; Muslim Travelers and Trade; Pisa; Russia and Rus'; Spice Trade, Indian Ocean; Stone and Timber, Scandinavian Trade in; Usury and the Church's View of Business; Venice

## Military Orders

Religious congregations of knights that arose initially in the twelfth century as a means of maintaining Western control over the crusader states in Syria-Palestine and Anatolia.

The military orders soon became offensive instruments for Catholic Europe's expansion in southwest Asia, North Africa, the Baltic, and Iberia, as well as significant agents of long-distance commerce. The first two and the greatest of them, the Templars (founded *c.* 1119) and the Hospitalers (*c.* 1113), drew members

# M

from all over Europe. Their energies were primarily devoted to the crusader colonies of the Near East, where they occupied strategic strongholds along major routes of travel and trade.

The Poor Fellow-Soldiers of Christ and the Temple of Solomon, more commonly known as the Templars, was the first religious confraternity to assume a military role, having originated as a small band of poor knights sworn to police the pilgrimage routes of the Holy Land. The order, whose rules were written by Bernard of Clairvaux, was officially recognized in 1128. The Knights of the Temple soon became the largest and richest of the military orders, and with their success came deep involvement in trans-Mediterranean banking, as the order passed large sums of money from its European sources of income to its military outposts in the crusader states of the East. The Templars' wealth, power, and reputed arrogance made them a number of enemies, among them King Philip IV of France, and in 1312, Pope Clement V dissolved the order.

In 1136, the Order of the Hospital of St. John of Jerusalem (the Hospitalers) began to assume military functions in addition to its original mission of caring for sick and needy pilgrims in the Holy Land. Managing to survive the collapse of the last crusader state in Syria-Palestine in 1291, the order retreated to Cyprus and then to Rhodes in 1309. From Rhodes it took part in various minor crusades and combated Muslim pirates, while engaging in its own piratical activities and acting as the primary agent organizing pilgrim traffic to the Holy Land. In addition to serving as a forward base for military operations, Hospitaler-controlled Rhodes was an important center for commerce between Europe and the Levant. When Rhodes fell to the Ottoman Turks in 1522, the Hospitalers moved to Malta, where they remained until 1798.

This order escaped the Templars' fate by establishing a sovereign state on Rhodes; Germany's single greatest military order, the German Hospital of St. Mary of Jerusalem (the Teutonic Knights) managed to do likewise in Prussia and Livonia (Latvia). The Teutonic Order began in 1190 as a group of hospital attendants sworn to aid sick and indigent German crusaders in the Holy Land. In 1198, however, they assumed military duties and adopted a rule modeled on that of the Templars. Although their primary responsibilities up to 1291 were in the eastern Mediterranean, as early as 1211 the king of Hungary assigned the Teutonic Knights the defense of a frontier region in Transylvania. When the knights

introduced German colonists and seemed to be on the verge of creating an autonomous state, the king expelled them. In that same year, 1226, Conrad of Mazovia invited the Teutonic Knights to defend his Polish duchy against the pagan Prussians to his east, and Emperor Frederick II (r. 1212–1250) granted the order's grand master the status of imperial prince with the right of governance over all conquered lands.

The conquests began in 1229, with the order using Prussia as a testing ground for knights scheduled to be shipped to the Near East. In 1245, the papacy recognized the Prussian campaign as a perpetual crusade, and by midcentury the Teutonic Knights had carved out an independent state along the eastern littoral of the Baltic Sea, from which they continued to push eastward. To stabilize their recently conquered lands, the knights invited in large numbers of German merchants and farmers, and hundreds of German villages, towns, and cities arose, protected by the order's fortresses.

Following their expulsion from the Holy Land in 1291, the Teutonic Knights moved their headquarters to Venice and from there, in 1309, to Marienburg (Malbork) in Prussia. The knights' involvement in the trading activities of the Hanseatic League, as well as the fertile farms of Prussia, brought great prosperity to the order in the fourteenth century. Between 1309 and 1410 the order waged a century-long "crusade" against pagan Lithuania, Orthodox Russia, and even Catholic Poland. Lithuania's conversion to Roman Catholicism and its union with Poland in 1385–1386 led to the order's crushing defeat at the hands of united Polish, Lithuanian, Russian, and Tatar forces at Tannenberg (Stębark) in 1410. This defeat and the huge indemnity the knights were forced to pay began the order's rapid fall from power. In 1457, Marienburg was abandoned, and the order was secularized in the sixteenth century.

German eastward expansion also produced the Knights of the Sword (c. 1202) and the Knights of Dobrin (1228). Before being absorbed by the Teutonic Knights in the 1230s, these two orders waged crusades against, respectively, the Livonians and the Prussians. The Knights of Dobrin failed miserably, but the Brothers of the Sword conquered Livonia by 1230. Their merger with the Teutonic Knights, therefore, greatly expanded that order's sphere of influence.

The Iberian Reconquest (*Reconquista*) attracted the Templars and Hospitalers, particularly to the kingdom of Aragon, and spawned as well a large number of native military orders, most of which modeled themselves on the rule of the Templars. The three giants of Spain were the orders of Calatrava (*c.* 1158) and Santiago (1170), both of Castilian origin, and the Order of Alcántara founded in León around 1176. The Order of Aviz, originally known as the Order of Evora (*c.* 1146?), was Portugal's sole home-grown military order before the fourteenth century. Like the Templars and Hospitalers, the Iberian military orders commanded frontier fortresses from which they defended potential invasion routes and launched attacks against neighboring Muslim states. They provided the backbone of the army that won the decisive victory of Las Navas de Tolosa (July 16, 1212), which led to the reconquest of all of Iberia by 1248, except for the Muslim kingdom of Granada in the extreme south. Granada's eventual fall in 1492 to the armies of Ferdinand and Isabella was facilitated by the orders of Santiago, Calatrava, and Alcántara, whose border castles combined to overcome the last Moorish outpost in Iberia.

Following the dissolution of the Knights of the Temple, Templar estates and castles in Valencia passed to the new order of the Knights of Montesa (1317); in Portugal they went to the Order of Christ (1319). Beginning in the fifteenth century, the grand mastership of the Order of Christ was reserved for princes of the royal family, the most famous of whom was Henry the Navigator (1394–1460). Prince Henry reformed the order, used its resources to help finance Portuguese oceanic exploration, and secured for it spiritual jurisdiction over the Atlantic and African lands that his sailors explored and colonized. Consequently, his ships bore the order's red and white cross. Henry's contemporary biographer, Gomes Eanes de Azurara, writes that his prince supported exploration largely out of a pious wish to promote a successful crusade against Islam and to convert the heathen—dual objectives of the military orders.

**BIBLIOGRAPHY**

Barber, Malcom. *The Trial of the Templars: Fighting for the Faith and Caring for the Sick.* London: Variorum, 1994.
Burleigh, Michael. *Prussian Society and the German Order: An Aristocratic Corporation in Crisis c. 1410–1466.* Cambridge: Cambridge UP, 1984.
Christiansen, Eric. *The Northern Crusades: The Baltic and the Catholic Frontier, 1100–1525.* Minneapolis: Minnesota UP, 1980.
Forey, A.J. *Military Orders and Crusades.* London: Variorum, 1994.
Luttrell, A.T. *The Hospitallers in Cyprus, Rhodes, Greece, and the West 1291–1440.* London: Variorum, 1982.
———. *Latin Greece, the Hospitallers, and the Crusades, 1291–1400.* London: Variorum, 1982.
O'Callaghan, Joseph F. *The Spanish Military Order of Calatrava and Its Affiliates.* London: Variorum, 1975.
Riley-Smith, Jonathan. *The Knights of St. John in Jerusalem and Cyprus, c. 1050–1310.* London: Macmillan, 1967.
Urban, William. *The Baltic Crusades.* 1975. 2nd edition revised and enlarged. Chicago: Lithuanian Research and Studies Center, 1994.

*Alfred J. Andrea*

**SEE ALSO**

Frederick II; Henry the Navigator; Holy Land; Hungary; Ottoman Turks; Pilgrimage, Christian; Piracy; Poland; Portuguese Expansion; Russia and Rus'; Teutonic Order; Venice

## Minstrels and Other Itinerant Performers as Travelers

Medieval poetry and song show the evidence of extensive cultural interaction on the part of authors and performers. Alternately called *jongleurs,* minstrels, and bards, professional singers not only entertained their audiences, they brought news from distant courts and lands.

Warfare, pilgrimage, and crusade necessitated travel for some medieval writers. Warrior-poets like Count Guilhem IX of Poitiers (1071–1127) and Richard the Lion Heart (1157–1199; r. 1189–1199) composed verse while on crusade in Spain and the Holy Land. Muslim and Arab conquests also led to the opening of new lands for itinerant performers. The *Kitab al-ghani,* or *Book of Songs,* tells of the wandering lifestyles of some Muslim poets and their singing *jariya* (pl. *jariyat*), or slave women. Muslim slave women taken in the siege of Barbastro (Spain) in 1064 were reported by both Muslim and Christian chroniclers to have been exceptional entertainers, and these women were dispersed throughout the courts of Western Europe.

Other performers voyaged by choice, making their living by following the courts of wealthy patrons. The fondness for travel of the troubadour Cercamon, member of the court of Guilhem X of Poitiers, is reflected in his *nom de plume,* which, roughly translated, means "circle the globe." Eleanor of Aquitaine (*c.* 1122–1204) invited her favorite court poets to England where their songs helped shape the English lyrical tradition.

# M

Raymond Bérenger V of Toulouse (r. 1134–1194) took his poets with him when he went to the court of Frederick I Barbarossa (r. 1152–1190) in Turin. Manuscripts tell of *joglars* of the late twelfth century who moved from court to court seeking wealthy and generous lords. Weddings were a magnet for hungry entertainers—laws on record from the south of France to the northern parts of Germany lay out accepted behavior for visiting minstrels seeking short-term work.

The heyday of the traveling entertainer was the twelfth and early thirteenth centuries. The Albigensian Crusade depleted Provence of its poetic talent, and the end of crusades in Spain and the Holy Land left courts without a need to travel. The church also cracked down on the *scurrae vagi,* or wandering *jongleurs,* for singing foolish or flattering songs. Fourteenth- and fifteenth-century persecutions caused Muslims, Christians, and Jews to remain largely in their own communities. The sharing of cultural riches that marked the High Middle Ages was severely dampened.

## BIBLIOGRAPHY

Briffault, Robert S. *Les Troubadours et le sentiment romanesque.* Paris: Les Editions du chêne, 1945; rpt. Geneva: Slatkine Reprints, 1974; trans. Robert S. Briffault, ed. Lawrence F. Koons, *The Troubadours.* Bloomington: Indiana UP, 1965.

Menocal, María Rosa. *The Arabic Role in Medieval Literary History: A Forgotten Heritage.* Philadelphia: U of Pennsylvania P, 1987.

Paterson, Linda M. *The World of the Troubadours: Medieval Occitan Society, c. 1100–c. 1300.* Cambridge: Cambridge UP, 1993.

*Lynn Tarte Ramey*

**SEE ALSO**
Crusades, First, Second, and Third; Crusade, Fourth; Crusade, Fifth; Expulsion, Corporate; Vagrancy

## *Mirabilia urbis Romae*
*See Marvels of Rome*

## Missionaries to China: Suffragan Bishops

Members of the Franciscan order charged with assisting John of Monte Corvino and consecrating him as archbishop, and responsible for the expansion of the Chinese mission in the early fourteenth century. They include Andrew, son of Guido of Perugia (d. *c.* 1332),

third bishop of Zaiton; Andrutius of Assisi (d. *c.* 1307); Gerard Albuini (d. 1318), first bishop of Zaiton; Nicholas of Banzia (d. *c.* 1307); Peregrine of Castello (d. 1322 or 1323), second bishop of Zaiton; Ulrich of Seyfridsdorf (d. *c.* 1307); and William of Villeneuve (d. 1330 or 1331).

These men constituted a group of seven suffragan bishops sent by Pope Clement V (1305–1314) to Khanbaliq (Beijing) in 1307 at the request of John of Monte Corvino, the founder of the Chinese mission; they formed a historical link between William of Rubruck's earlier Mongol mission in 1253–1255 and the later Jesuit missionary activities of the sixteenth and seventeenth centuries.

Andrew, the ranking member of the mission, and his group most likely took the sea route through Ormuz in the Persian Gulf to arrive in India. During a probable sojourn there, three bishops, including Andrutius, died due to the extreme heat, while William apparently returned to Italy. Only Andrew, Gerard, and the aptly named Peregrine reached their assigned goal, arriving at Khanbaliq around 1308, where they fulfilled their mission of ceremoniously investing John as archbishop. Andrew and the others remained at Khanbaliq for almost five years, living by means of an *alafa,* a generous allowance granted by the khân, and forming the core, with Italian merchants and traders, of a Christian settlement there.

During this time, another mission was established at distant Zaiton where a rich Armenian woman endowed it with a great cathedral. Gerard was named the first bishop. During his tenure, the number of Alan Christians in the see swelled to approximately 30,000. On his death in 1318, Andrew was selected to succeed him, but Andrew refused the appointment, which then passed to Peregrine. Andrew's presence at the Zaiton mission during this period is attested by a letter of Peregrine's dated January 1318. Only on the death of Peregrine in 1322 did Andrew finally accept the see.

In January 1326, Andrew wrote from Zaiton to his superiors in the monastery at Perugia. His letter furnishes much of what is known about the medieval Christian Church in China. In his missive, Andrew recalls the sufferings and difficulties faced on the initial voyage eastward and describes the different types of people he encountered there. By 1318, four years before the death of Peregrine, Andrew had decided to transfer to Zaiton, where he was again accorded great honor. The letter concludes with a comment on the coexistence of different religions within the empire. After his death in 1330 or 1332, there appears to have been only one successor to the see, Jacob of Florence, who, together with Friar William of Campania, was martyred in 1362.

Less is known of Nicholas of Banzia than of some of his fellow missionaries. Surviving Latin documents show his city of origin written variously as "Bantia," "Banthra," or "Banthera," the modern Banzia near Genzano, in Apulia. On his trip to the East, he was one of the three bishops who died in India, where he was buried. Nicholas's death is recorded in a letter of 1326 written by Andrew.

Peregrine wrote a letter to his colleagues in the "Vicarate of the East" in Europe dated December 30, 1317. This important document furnishes quite detailed information about the medieval church in China. Somewhat informal and personal in tone, the letter reveals the sense of isolation and "exile" that the three surviving friars suffered and their desire for news from Christendom. Comparing their "flight" abroad to that of the Prodigal Son of Jesus' parable, Peregrine gently reproaches the minister general of his order for neglecting them in their difficult mission. He describes the valuable work John of Monte Corvino had performed before their arrival. Peregrine gives some notion of the cultural and religious diversity in the area: the "schismatic" Nestorians; the Alans, "good Christians," 30,000 of whom were on the khân's payroll; Armenian Christians who were building a church they planned to turn over to John; other Latin Christians, and Muslims. Peregrine makes it clear that the Franciscans were allowed to preach unmolested. His letter names the three Italian friars who assist him in his duties as bishop in Zaiton: they are aged, and do not know the languages well. Peregrine makes an explicit appeal for more brethren to help in the church's work. A final comment hints at the greatness and wealth of the Mongol Empire. The letter also alludes to his old age. Bishop Peregrine died on July 7, 1322 or 1323, as his successor, Andrew of Perugia, noted in a letter dated 1326.

Ulrich is mentioned by name in the original bull of 1307. A letter of 1326, written by Andrew, indicates that it is likely that Ulrich was the third of the suffragan bishops to die en route; no surviving sources document the activities of an "Ulrich" in the Khanbaliq or Zaiton missions.

Although William of Villeneuve received the same bull of election as the others, he apparently did not leave India for China with the other friars in 1307; in letters written the following year, Clement enjoined him to undertake a mission in "Tartary." Ten years later, documents record him—referred to ambiguously as "bishop of Tartary"—at the papal court in Avignon in the company of another Minorite, Jerome, bishop of Kaffa (Feodosiya) in the Crimea. One may surmise that the two bishops serving in the same geographical area had returned to Europe on official business. If William did in fact serve in the East, he did not spend his later career there: in February 1323, William was named bishop of Sagona (Corsica) ; a year later he was in Lombardy with a papal army under the leadership of Cardinal Bertrand Poyet. William moved to Trieste in 1327, where he died and was buried in 1330 or 1331.

**BIBLIOGRAPHY**

Dawson, Christopher, ed. *The Mongol Mission.* See Gen. Bib.

Fedalto, Giorgio. *La Chiesa latina in oriente.* Studi religiosi no. 3. Vol. 1. Verona: Casa Editrice Mazziana, 1973.

Foster, John. "Crosses from the Walls of Zaitun." *Journal of the Royal Asiatic Society* (April 1954): 1–25.

Golubovich, P. Girolamo. *Biblioteca Bio-bibliografica della Terra Santa e dell'Oriente francescano.* Vol. 1. Florence: Quaracchi, 1906.

Moule, A.C. *Christians in China before the Year 1550.* London: Society for Promoting Christian Knowledge, 1930.

Wadding, Luke, ed. *Annales Minorum seu Trium ordinum a S. Francisco Institutorum.* Rev. edition. P. Bonaventure Marrani. Vols. 6 and 7. Florence: Quaracchi, 1931.

Yule-Cordier. *Cathay and the Way Thither.* See Gen. Bib.

*Gloria Allaire*

**SEE ALSO**

Andrew, Son of Guido of Perugia; China; Eastern Christianity; Franciscan Friars; John of Monte Corvino; Khanbaliq; Mongols; Nestorianism; William of Rubruck; Zaiton

## Money

*See* Coinage and Money

## Mongol Army

A multiethnic fighting force, based on nomad cavalry augmented by the manpower, military skills, and techonology of various sedentary societies; the Mongol army overspread much of Asia and parts of Europe beginning in the thirteenth century.

# M

The army of Chinggis Khân (*c.* 1167–1227) at first consisted of Outer Mongolian nomad warriors (similar to those of the rest of Inner Asia). They included all the men in his tribal following, about 70 percent of whom could be mobilized; women and children could operate the pastoral economy. The men were all mounted: pastoralism facilitated horse raising. Warriors, each with a nuclear family, subsisted from their own herds of sheep, goats, various bovids, camels, and horses (horse meat and fermented mares' milk—*kumis*—were favorite foods). A hundred sheep or the equivalent were needed for each warrior and his family; one horse or cow equaled five sheep or goats. The warriors therefore required no pay, although they shared in the spoils of war; taxation primarily redistributed military assets, with surplus horses going to men short of mounts, for instance. Pastoralism simplified logistics: the horses (on the steppe) ate grass and the men ate horses, one a day for 200 men. However, grazing only sustains small horses—ponies—suitable only for light cavalry because of the limited burden (properly 17 percent of body weight: 102 pounds for a 600-pound Mongol pony) and effort they can support; each soldier therefore needed at least five mounts, which he rode in alternation. Moreover, since grazing is slow, the ponies could work only about four hours a day, traveling, for example, some fifteen miles. When accompanied by its families and flocks, the sheep and goats, the army slowed to three or four miles a day.

The Mongol nomads (like the others in Inner Asia) fought primarily with bows and arrows, carrying also a club or ax, but avoiding hand-to-hand combat except against debilitated foes. They could make these weapons themselves, whereas swords and armor, or the metal for them, had to be imported and were available only to the rich. Nor could the nomads' ponies well bear heavily equipped riders. Although they sometimes dismounted to shoot, the Mongols usually fought at the gallop, charging enemies in successive waves and releasing an arrow when close enough (about forty-five yards) for some accuracy and armor-piercing, yet far enough to escape a countercharge; they then turned, circled out of the way and behind the following waves, charged and shot again, repeating this until their half-dozen or so arrows were used up and their ponies tired; then these attackers withdrew to rearm and remount, while others took their place. Hostile nomads, equipped and fighting like the Mongols, might retire to avoid the arrows and to draw the attackers away from their supporting forces, counterattacking when the charge was broken off. The Mongols tried to attack when their enemies lacked space for this maneuvering; on several occasions they drove fleeing enemy cavalry against their supporting forces. The Mongols also pursued an offensive strategy against other nomads, planning to invade before their enemies could ready a defense, and by invading, putting them at a decisive disadvantage. Nomads on their home ground, with their subsistence animals sharing the available grazing with their horses, could not raise as much cavalry from any given district as the Mongols, with their families and flocks left behind and only their horses to graze, could bring against them.

Non-nomad cavalry rarely possessed enough horses to keep up with the Mongols' fast-paced tactics. In sedentary economies, where grasslands were usually converted to cultivation, horses had to be fed from fodder rather than left to graze. This made them expensive and hard for armies to keep in large numbers. Cavalry therefore usually required infantry support, or served as an auxiliary to infantry, losing much of its mobility and tactical flexibility. Transporting fodder and rations also impeded conventional armies. Horses raised on fodder grew larger than the nomads' ponies, of course, and allowed conventional cavalry to try to force hand-to-hand fighting, for which they were usually better armed as well as better mounted than the Mongols. But the Mongols could usually evade shock combat and wear down enemies and their horses. The Mamluks of Egypt and Syria were able, with better equipment, personnel, and training, to outshoot the Mongols, negating their hit-and-run tactics. Against

Mongol mounted warrior. Matthew Paris, *Chronica Majora*, Cambridge, Corpus Christi College MS 16, fol. 145r, *c.* 1250. Permission Master and Fellows, Corpus Christi College, Cambridge.

both nomad and sedentary foes the Mongols also used stratagems of surprise, disinformation, and ambush; pretended retreat or feigned flight was often effective. In all cases, however, the Mongols' chief advantage was derived from superior numbers of men and horses.

This superiority derived from Chinggis Khân's reunification and enlargement of the Mongol tribe, a political association, as usual in Inner Asia, centered on a chief, not a genealogical formation, and not restricted by religion, language, or previous tribal affiliation. Chinggis's leadership qualities attracted a preponderance of the original tribesmen, who overcame the remainder. Subsequently, appealing to the nomads' warriorist ideals of heroism and military accomplishment with a (rhetorically long-familiar) project of world conquest, he won new followers and an enhanced authority, enabling decimal reorganization of the Mongol army and society. Each man, with his family and animals, was assigned to a ten-man unit; ten units of ten made up a unit of a hundred, and so on up to units of 10,000 (the *tümen*). Decimal units facilitated operation, administration, and logistical planning (and inform us of Mongol demographics). They enabled large-unit training, in great battues, encircling and shooting wild animals as practice for how enemies were to be surrounded and killed. Formation of these units also strengthened Chinggis by dividing or amalgamating the odd-sized bands produced by the tribal confusion of the twelfth century, trimming or diluting the power of their erstwhile chiefs. These changes became possible because the chiefs' former tribesmen, attracted by Chinggis and his project, transferred their allegiance to him, becoming his tribesmen, regardless of their previous affiliation. Except at the outset of Chinggis's career, few if any Inner Asian tribes approached the size or unity of his tribe. Most large tribes were only tribal confederations, with a congeries of competitive chiefs more apt to join battle than forces with one another.

By 1206, Chinggis led most of the warriors of Outer Mongolia, about 105,000 men, of whom probably 70,000 could be mobilized, the largest unified cavalry army in Inner Asia. His project later attracted many, perhaps most, of the nomads outside Mongolia (most of them Turks), although many were coerced, as in Mongolia. Chinggis's successors eventually controlled all of Inner Asia's warriors, some 1.5 million men by Mongol census count. By the 1250s, the Mongols could simultaneously field cavalry armies of (nominally) 150,000 men and 750,000 ponies in both the Middle East and China.

Chinggis also recruited non-nomad tribesmen. China, his first objective outside Mongolia, could not be taken by nomads alone. Outer Mongolians numbered about half a million people, while China had a population of about 100 million, many in great walled cities that the Mongols were unable to attack on horseback, and unwilling, given the heavy losses entailed in siege warfare, to assault on foot. Accordingly, Chinggis enlisted Chinese and Manchurian infantry, pregunpowder artillerists, engineers, and (what have been called) "arrow-fodder"—Chinese civilians levied as assault troops for siege operations. Many warriors voluntarily joined Chinggis for a variety of reasons: dissatisfaction with the rulers of China, the transcultural appeal of his project of conquest, or simply the desire to be on the winning side. The civilians were rounded up by Mongol cavalry patrols, against which rural China had no defense after its divided and (mostly) disgruntled nomad subjects in Inner Mongolia were severally subverted or defeated by Chinggis. These Chinese recruits suffered, and inflicted, huge casualties. "Arrow-fodder" were slaughtered wholesale attempting to climb into fortresses. Enemy soldiers and civilians were massacred in their fallen cities to obviate renewed resistance and a second siege risking nomad Mongols, in the absence of enough surviving "arrow-fodder." Famine and disease spread death more widely still.

After the death of Chinggis, the Mongol army in China continued to draw on China's population, still immense despite its enormous losses. For the south China campaign of 1259 against the Song dynasty, 680,000 Chinese, Manchurian, and Korean troops reinforced 150,000 Mongol cavalrymen; subsequently, after its conquest, southern China provided a further 300,000 men for Mongol garrisons. The army that completed China's conquest for Khubilai Khân (r. 1260–1294) was an even more diverse force. Khubilai, like Chinggis (but on a much greater scale), used Chinese infantry supported by Mongol cavalry against the Song foot soldiers (Song had no cavalry). Middle Eastern artificers gave him counterweighted trebuchets superior to the Chinese traction artillery. In addition, Khubilai created a navy, using Chinese and Korean seamen, to overcome Song control of the rivers and ocean. The Mongols fought, and won, the final battle at sea. China was thus taken for the Mongols largely by the Chinese themselves, at a cost estimated at half the population of China.

The Mongol army could not be similarly enlarged on the empire's other fronts. The surviving Chinese

# M

still numbered some 50 million in the late thirteenth century. But Mongol censuses appear to report only 430,000 Russian men, suggesting a population around 2,000,000, from which 40,000 troops might have been raised by ordinary, one-man-in-ten conscription (not the drastic siege levies). The Middle Eastern Mongols counted 220,000 men among perhaps one million settled subjects, who might have provided 20,000 troops. The Mongols had only needed sedentary "arrow-fodder" to conquer these regions because they included, or lay adjacent to, steppes that supported the full weight of the Mongol cavalry. But without large forces of Russian and Middle Eastern infantry, the Mongols could not adapt their army to campaigning beyond the steppe. They could not invade India, nor continue the assault on Europe after their striking successes of 1241–1242.

The Middle Eastern Mongols made changes in their cavalry after defeats by the Mamluks. The Mongols had found that a force large enough to defeat the Mamluks—around 60,000 men—could not be maintained in Syria because the 300,000-odd ponies required by their hit-and-run tactics could not obtain enough water during the arid summers. The Mongols therefore tried to adopt Mamluk methods, procuring more swords and armor, and raising larger horses to carry the increased burden, so as to fight the Mamluks hand-to-hand. They attempted also to copy the archery of the Mamluks, who, from standing mounts, could shoot as many as three arrows in one and a half seconds, whereas a Mongol could shoot only once in the customary galloping attack. With bigger horses and better archers engaging in lower-paced close combat, fewer horses and less water would be needed, and the Mongols might then be able to keep the field in full force and overwhelm the Mamluks. These innovations failed. Bigger horses required fodder besides grazing, creating a different logistical obstacle, and the average Mongol—the ordinary Mongol soldier—could not match the dexterity in archery of the handpicked Mamluk slave-soldiers. In the late fourteenth century, Tamerlane made very effective use of cavalry of this pattern, with fewer horses—three per soldier—and a considerable proportion of armored, if not fast-shooting, riders, but even Tamerlane never reached Egypt.

A number of remarkable but unsuccessful campaigns also took the Mongol army to its limits in East and Southeast Asia. Its victories—even against elephants—in Burma (never before attacked from China), and its five campaigns in Vietnam (involving several Mongol

defeats, one by a surprise attack during the Tet [lunar New Year] celebration), obtained no more than formal "submissions." Indonesians expelled Mongols landed in Java, and the Japanese withstood two invasions. The second attack on Japan, in 1281, perhaps the largest premodern overseas expedition, involved 3,500 ships and 100,000 men from southern China, a Korean contingent of 900 ships, 15,000 sailors, and 10,000 troops, and 30,000 Mongols. The Japanese, behind fortifications at the landing-place, held the Mongols for two months; then the "Kamikaze" typhoon destroyed the fleet and army. By the end of the thirteenth century, the Mongol army had achieved all it could—more than any other has done. It had not conquered the world, but it had won the world's largest empire.

**BIBLIOGRAPHY**

Allsen, Thomas. *Mongol Imperialism.* Berkeley: California UP, 1987.

Hsio Ch'i-Ch'ing. *The Military Establishment of the Yuan Dynasty.* Cambridge, MA: Harvard UP, 1978.

Martin, H. Desmond. *The Rise of Chingis Khan and His Conquest of North China.* 1950; rpt. New York: Octagon, 1971.

Smith, John Masson, Jr. "Mongol Manpower and Persian Population." *Journal of the Economic and Social History of the Orient* 18 (1975): 271–299.

———. "Ayn Jalut: Mamluk Success or Mongol Failure?" *Harvard Journal of Asiatic Studies* 44.2 (December 1984): 307–345.

———. "Mongol Society and Military in the Middle East: Antecedents and Adaptations." In *War and Society in the Eastern Mediterranean, 7th–15th Centuries.* Ed. Yaacov Lev. Leiden: Brill, 1997, chap. 9.

*John Masson Smith, Jr.*

**SEE ALSO**

Japan, Mongol Invasion of; Korea, Mongol Invasions of; Kumis; Mamluks; Mongols; Nomadism and Pastoralism; Tamerlane; Vietnam and Java, Mongol Invasions of

## Mongol Invasion of Japan
*See* Japan, Mongol Invasion of

## Mongol Invasion of Java
*See* Vietnam and Java, Mongol Invasions of

## Mongol Invasions of Korea
*See* Korea, Mongol Invasions of

## Mongol Invasion of Vietnam

*See* Vietnam and Java, Mongol Invasions of

## Mongol Khatuns

Consorts of the khâns, who played major political roles in the Mongol Empire and various khânates that succeeded it. Wives of khâns, particularly the chief wife, enjoyed a special position at court and wielded considerable power.

*The Secret History of the Mongols* and contemporary accounts about the Mongols give extensive information concerning khatuns, each of whom had by right her own household, with numerous retainers and armed men for protection. Prominent at court functions, they struck non-Mongol observers as women of wealth and power. Chief wives usually became regents after their husbands died, administering the empire or khanâte, sometimes for several years, until the new khân's election. The Mongol custom of levirate, whereby a widow became the wife of her dead husband's son (if he was not her own child), also reinforced the position of a widowed khatun in the *ordo* (camp) of her husband, because she became the guardian of future rulers. Under Mongol patrilineal descent, a leader's younger brothers were presumptive heirs, and sons did not usually succeed their fathers immediately. In time, however, widows' sons emerged as candidates for leadership, and khatuns who were adroit politicians maneuvered their children into positions of power in Mongol realms.

Among the most prominent khatuns was Hö'elun, mother of Chinggis Khân. After his father, Yesügei, was murdered by Tatars, the clan rejected her leadership, abandoning her with four children and few resources. Persevering, she maintained her brood, laying the foundation for Chinggis's later rise. The *Secret History,* which paints her as a heroine and model, includes stories emphasizing Chinggis's respect for her advice.

Bortei was Chinggis Khân's chief wife and mother of the four sons (Jochi, Chaghatai, Ögödei, and Tolui) who divided his conquests. She was a princess of the Qonggirat tribe, whose support was vital in Chinggis's rise to power, and from which some of his heirs drew brides. Shortly after their marriage she was abducted by the Merkits, and Chinggis's first real campaign was her rescue. In the *Secret History* she is depicted as a valuable counselor, on several occasions urging Chinggis to eliminate potential enemies. At his death (1227),

Chinggis appointed Bortei regent until the 1229 *quriltai* (princely assembly) to elect his successor convened.

Töregene was chief wife of Ögödei Khân (r. 1229–1241), regent after his death (1241–1246), and mother of Güyük Khân (r. 1246–1248). Ögödei had designated his grandson Shiremün successor, but as regent, Töregene both postponed the *quriltai* to confirm his election and prevented a brother of Chinggis from taking the throne by force. Her maneuvers were instrumental in Güyük's becoming great khân. Persian and Chinese sources call her forceful and dynamic, but they revile her because under her regency Mongol government became more rapacious. Güyük repudiated some of her policies after his election, but until the *quriltai* all state business was in her hands, and no one disputed her authority.

Oghul-Qaimish was Güyük's chief wife, and regent from 1248 to 1251. At his death Güyük was on the verge of war with Batu, khân of the Golden Horde. Even though Batu (Jochi's son) wished Möngke (Tolui's son) to become great khân, in accordance with Mongol law he appointed Oghul-Qaimish regent, and as such she received Andrew of Longjumeau in 1249, taking presents he carried from Louis IX of France as tokens of submission. A plot by princes of the houses of Chaghatai and Ögödei (which she led) was uncovered at the 1251 *quriltai,* and when she refused to pay homage Möngke had her drowned, a sentence carried out in Sorqoqtani-Begi's household.

Sorqoqtani-Begi was the chief wife of Tolui (d. 1231/2), and mother of the great khâns Möngke and Khubilai, and of the first il-khân, Hülegü. She was a Kerait and a Nestorian. After Chinggis suppressed the Keraits (1203), he gave Sorqoqtani-Begi, niece of the dead Wang Khân, to Tolui. Contemporary sources agree that she was brilliant and tolerant of all religions. After Tolui's death (*c.* 1232) she declined to remarry and was given an appanage of 80,000 households to provide for herself and her sons. She was always deferential and adhered to the letter of Mongol law, but when the time was ripe she assisted Batu against Güyük Khân, and with his help her sons supplanted the line of Ögödei. She died in 1252.

Khubilai's chief consort was Chabui, empress of China. She was an ardent Buddhist and champion of Chinese culture at the Yuan court, and mitigated harsh Mongol rule over China's sedentary population. After her death (1281), a kinswoman, Nambui, took her place. When Khubilai became reclusive in his last

# M

years, Nambui became his intermediary, transmitting his decisions and edicts to his ministers.

Doquz Khatun was a granddaughter of the Kerait Wang Khân, and another of Tolui's widows, taken as chief wife by his son Hülegü (d. 1265). A pious Nestorian, she influenced Hülegü to support Christian communities in Persia at the expense of Muslims during the early years of the il-khânate. She died shortly before her son, Abagha (r. 1265–1282) succeeded, but he allowed her niece to continue policies she had established. Under the influence of these women Nestorian and Jacobite churches flourished, and European missionaries had a free hand in Persia.

**BIBLIOGRAPHY**

Boyle, John Andrew. *The Mongol World Empire, 1206–1370.* London: Variorum Reprints, 1977.

*The Mission of Friar William of Rubruck: His Journey to the Court of the Great Khan Möngke 1253–1255.* Trans. Peter Jackson, with notes and introduction by Peter Jackson and David Morgan. Hakluyt Society, 2nd series, 173. London: Hakluyt Society, 1990.

Morgan, David. *The Mongols.* New York and Oxford: Blackwells, 1986.

Rossabi, Morris. "Kubilai Khan and the Women in His Family." In *Sino-Mongolica: Festschrift für Herbert Franke.* Ed. Wolfgang Bauer. Wiesbaden: Harrassowitz, 1979, pp. 153–180.

*Secret History of the Mongols.* Ed and trans. F.W. Cleaves. Vol. 1. Cambridge, MA: Harvard UP, 1982.

Spuler, Bertold. *History of the Mongols, Based on Eastern and Western Accounts of the Thirteenth and Fourteenth Centuries.* Trans. H. and S. Drummond. London: Routledge, 1972.

Vladimirtsov, B. *Le régime social des Mongols—le féodalisme nomade.* Trans. M. Carsow. Paris: Adrien-Maisonneuve, 1948.

*James D. Ryan*

**SEE ALSO**

Abagha; Andrew of Longjumeau; Buddhism; Chaghatai Khânate; Eastern Christianity; Golden Horde; Hülegü; Louis IX; Mongols; Nestorianism; *Secret History of the Mongols, The;* Tolui; Women in Mongol Society

## Mongols (Thirteenth and Fourteenth Centuries)

A tribal, nomadic Inner Asian people who, between 1206 and 1368, conquered and ruled the largest contiguous land empire in recorded history. The five great khâns' goal of world domination affected all the major civilizations of Eurasia militarily, politically, diplomatically, economically, and intellectually throughout most of the thirteenth and fourteenth centuries.

The vast Eurasian landmass has an almost unbroken strip of grassland or steppe stretching approximately 6,000 miles from Manchuria in the east to Hungary in the west. Much of the lush western steppe is at sea level, but the harsh eastern regions are more than a mile above sea level in the area of the Mongolian plateau. While the steppe is interspersed with semideserts and major mountain ranges, there are passable routes, a type of grassy highway, through the desert and mountain barriers. A traveler on horseback can rather easily cover long distances over this grassland. And it was the horse that made life on the steppe politically, economically, and socially viable. Sedentary agriculture was not an option, but the steppe grass did provide excellent pasturage for horses, cattle, sheep, and goats as the people migrated seasonally from pasture to pasture to feed their growing flocks and herds.

Thus pastoral nomadism emerged as the predominant way of life throughout the entire steppeland. The horse, in particular, increased the range, speed, and general mobility of the steppe nomads, whose peaceful movements occasionally encroached on the border lands claimed by sedentary societies and whose cavalry periodically invaded and pillaged those same coastal civilizations to the east, south, and west. The geographic, ethnic, linguistic, and even racial identity of these nomadic invaders is not known in most instances, since the written records of the civilized coastal states frequently labeled them only as Inner Asian barbarians. Most of the larger-scale barbarian invasions occurred when a charismatic and/or ambitious military chieftain unified many different tribes, clans, neighbors, and conquered subjects into a confederation, usually called a horde. Though frequently destabilized by intermittent warfare over pasturage and water rights, the horde could, at least temporarily, be an effective and virtually unstoppable military machine on the battlefield.

The people known to history as the Mongols arose out of this constantly changing intermixture of steppe nomadic groupings. Their exact time and place of origin is not known, but scholars suspect that the Mongols initially migrated southward from the Siberian forest into the Mongolian plateau, which had earlier been the home of other nomadic tribes like the Huns,

Hsiung-nu, Turks, and Kitans. Not originally a steppe people, the Mongols quickly became successful nomadic herdsmen as they adapted to their new surroundings. The early Mongols consisted of a number of different tribes—including Naimans, Merkits, Oirats, and Tatars—who fought each other as readily as all others. Their first experience of political and economic unity occurred around 1000 when the Mongols drove their predecessors, the Turkish Kirgiz, out of Mongolia and defeated the Kitans in northern China—the first Mongol contact with one of the sedentary civilizations. After this early show of strength, the Mongols returned to their traditional way of life on the high Mongolian plateau. Political and military power was in the hands of a type of ruling aristocracy that regularly made and broke alliances as they fought constantly with each other and outsiders.

Whereas the history and activities of most Inner Asian "barbarians" are recorded only in negative terms by the civilizations recently invaded and pillaged by them (illiteracy being an essential part of the definition of barbarism), the Mongols are the only steppe nomads to have produced a written version of their own history. The unique document called *The Secret History of the Mongols* represents the official Mongol tradition of their own rise. In the first few years of the thirteenth century, Chinggis Khân ordered a literate captive to adopt the Uighur script to the Mongol language, making it possible for the Mongol language to be written down for the first time. The *Secret History* is a private record in the sense that it was not intended to be circulated in any form among non-Mongols. It was treated with reverence, bordering on veneration, since it embodied a good deal of early Mongol folklore and contained many of Chinggis's instructions and pronouncements.

The *Secret History* was written in the "year of the rat" some time between the 1220s and 1260s. Since the Mongols used the twelve-animal cycle for chronology, most scholars consider either 1228 or 1240 as the probable date of composition. Chinggis died in 1227, and it would have been logical to commemorate his great deeds as a memorial shortly thereafter. Likewise, it would have been convenient to assemble this venerable work when all of the powerful Mongol princes and military leaders were gathered together to mourn Chinggis's death and to select his successor; never again would so many who knew the details of his entire life and career be assembled and available for questioning.

According to this view, it was years later, possibly in 1240, that a short life of Ögödei, great khân from 1229 to 1241, was tacked onto what was initially a history of the Mongols and a biography of Chinggis. Other scholars opt for 1240 as the date of composition, seeing the section on the reign of Ögödei as part of the original plan.

The *Secret History* is the only reliable source for Chinggis's early life, and even then, its content is probably more correctly characterized as a collection of steppe folktales woven into a type of pseudo-historical document. The interpretation of the *Secret History* presents all kinds of problems since not all obscure passages are clarified nor can all peoples mentioned be identified. It is written in a rhythmic prose suitable for oral recitation. Thus it can be viewed as both a literary epic and a valuable historical source that contains priceless cultural, social, economic, and political information as it depicts the world and life as the Mongols themselves saw it. While the authenticity of many of the details is questionable, there is no real reason to doubt the main lines of this work. Its chief value lies in its description of the early life of Chinggis and the rise of Mongol power, since foreign campaigns receive very little attention.

According to the *Secret History*, the Mongols trace their descent from animals who met and mated at the source of the Onon River by the holy mountain Burkan-Kaldun, the home of the sky god Kökö-Tengri. The first human ancestor, called Dobun the Wise, married a woman from a tribe of forest-dwellers and by her had two sons. But she produced three more sons, allegedly via miraculous impregnation by the sky god Tengri. Mongol folklore stressed this divine parentage because it established an intimate connection with their god—they viewed themselves as a chosen people and thus believed they had a god-given right to conquer and rule the world. As the *Secret History* proceeds from myth and legend to history, it begins to link Mongol affairs with the activities of their neighbors.

Thus the history of the Mongols prior to Chinggis must be reconstructed from this mixed account, as well as from the few periodic references to them in the records of adjacent civilized centers, especially those of China. While dates are vague and nebulous, it was probably in the early twelfth century that some type of unity was established among the various Mongol tribes as military victories led to increased power in the hands of specific leaders, some of whom held exalted titles

# M

like "emperor" or "khân." Memories of the emerging relations between the Mongols and the Chin dynasty of north China, who correctly viewed the Mongols as a threat, are preserved in both the *Secret History* and the Chin *Annals,* although it is difficult at times to establish parallel contemporary leaders and events.

While no well-defined picture of early Mongol tribal organization exists, specific personalities do begin to emerge. One such individual was Yesügei, who died without achieving anything significant except to father a son named Temüjin, known to history as Chinggis Khân. While the exact date of Temüjin's birth is not known, 1167 is the year accepted by most scholars. He was approximately twelve years old when his father Yesügei was killed. The name Temüjin means "smith," a metalworker of some type, so most historical accounts translate his birth name as blacksmith. He was a typical Mongol warrior and warlord, constantly fighting, raiding, and pillaging. At one point Temüjin himself was captured and held prisoner by his enemies. But he was a man of great stamina and resourcefulness. He eventually gained his freedom and set out to eliminate all of his rivals; he was the first leader to unite all of the Mongol tribes. In order to establish the legitimacy of his rule, in 1206 he convened a great national assembly, called a *quriltai,* which declared him the supreme or universal ruler. It gave him the title of Chinggis Khân, the name by which he has been known to history ever since. Because his family was believed to be among the chosen people, his commands were considered as manifestations of the eternal decrees of divine providence—of Tengri, the sky god. This charismatic leader was destined to unite all of the Eurasian steppe into a single vast new empire.

After gathering all the Mongols under his leadership, Chinggis led them in raids that yielded the traditional loot and booty taken from conquered enemies. But under Chinggis's skillful guidance, Mongol aspirations grew larger, with the ultimate objective of ruling over the entire world. With religious, political, and military goals combined, the Mongols dedicated themselves to continuous military campaigns that resulted in rapid and extensive expansion. Once Chinggis convinced the Mongols that he was the instrument of divine purpose and began winning richly rewarding military victories, he experienced no further resistance from his own people. Their total and complete support enabled him to establish the foundation for the largest empire in the world.

Chinggis spent the years after his 1206 enthronement in an ongoing series of military campaigns and conquests. First he attacked the Tibetan Tanguts (also known as the Hsi Hsia), and by 1209 he had reduced them to tributary status. In 1211, he attacked the Chin (Juchen) in northern China, and by 1215 he was in control of their capital, Zhongdu, in the area of modern Beijing. This early victory gave Chinggis the services of Chinese craftsmen who knew how to besiege walled cities and of Chinese bureaucrats who know how to administer civilized agricultural societies. He next conquered his immediate neighbors—the Manchurians, the Koreans, and the Karakitans. Chinggis then moved far from his home base as he next attacked the Khwarizmian shah in the region of north Persia in 1220.

This sudden interest in western Asia was apparently due more to unexpected circumstances than to prior planning. The shah had killed Mongol merchants and/or envoys sent to him by Chinggis; this act violated basic Mongol practice and called for swift and decisive retribution. Chinggis invaded with his full Mongol army and ruthlessly tracked down the Khwarizmian shah and all members of his family. In the course of these conquests, Chinggis and the Mongols totally destroyed the major cities of Bukhara, Samarkand, Merv, and Nishapur, mercilessly massacring the majority of the inhabitants. Only artisans and craftsmen and a few scholars were spared, along with large numbers of women and children who were enslaved. While in the area of the Caspian Sea, Chinggis's eldest son Jochi and the two best generals in the Mongol army crossed the Caucasus Mountains into the southern Russian steppe; the Russians who objected to this Mongol exploratory expedition were quickly defeated in 1223. From this point onward, Jochi claimed the lush southern Russian steppe for himself and his descendants. Chinggis returned to Mongolia where he again led his forces against the Tanguts, who had revolted while he was occupied in western Asia. This was his final military expedition: he died on the campaign in 1227. As he had arranged, his body was returned to Mongolia and buried in a place he had previously selected. The men that escorted and buried his body were then killed to ensure that the exact location of his grave would remain a secret.

Chinggis Khân was much more than just a greedy and successful military chieftain. In addition to uniting his people under his banner and planning and leading the early campaigns, Chinggis also made major and significant contributions to the Mongols' military organization and tactics. As leader of the Mongol army, he instituted a dramatically new structure for his steppe military machine, introducing in particular one simple yet radical change: instead of acknowledging ties of blood and kinship, he organized his followers arbitrarily by numbers based on ten. Ten squads were grouped into a company under an able and experienced battle leader. Larger units of hundreds, thousands, and ten-thousands were structured in the same way. Chinggis thus established the principle that appointment and rank were based on military ability, not on blood and birth. By promoting on ability, he built a virtually unstoppable fighting force that soon overcame all internal Mongol opposition. Each victory meant fresh recruits for his army as he folded the manpower of his defeated enemies into the new military ranking system that he had created, while his constant warfare guaranteed rapid promotion for capable and ambitious men. His armies were able to replenish their numbers and keep on conquering and expanding. Large numbers of Turkish-speaking peoples were soon brought into the army, and they, also, were promoted on the basis of ability. While the Mongols retained most of the top military positions (since they were the most experienced), the number of Turks soon outnumbered Mongols in the ranks.

Chinggis also added to traditional steppe strategy by incorporating new tactics from the civilized societies that he conquered. When his steppe cavalry attacked Chinese walled cities, it faced sophisticated new weapons and tactics, including gunpowder. Chinggis and his Mongols soon learned how to break city walls with siege engines, sappers, catapults, and gunpowder bombs, weapons designed and built by captured Chinese craftsmen whose lives had been spared. Thus Chinggis's well-organized armies were victorious everywhere as he united the fighting manpower of the entire Inner Asian steppe under the experienced command of Mongol generals, while learning to employ the siege strategy and tactics of sedentary civilized societies.

Chinggis improved the system of communications in his empire as well. From the civilized societies that he captured, Chinggis recruited a class of scribes, recordkeepers, and tax collectors who became necessary as the size and scope of the Mongol army and state grew. As the territory he controlled expanded, Chinggis needed to be constantly informed as to what was happening throughout his growing empire; he especially needed to be current on military events and activities. To this end, he introduced a communications system, called the *yam*, that relied on the creation of postal relay stations throughout his vast empire. This mounted courier service included rest stations and fresh horses and riders at regular intervals along the main travel routes so that critical news and information traveled virtually nonstop until it reached the khân. Some scholars maintain that the nineteenth-century American Pony Express was nothing more than a revival of this thirteenth-century Mongol communication system. While it was started by Chinggis, this courier system of relay stations and riders was not fully implemented until during the reign of Ögödei. All ambassadors and envoys to the khân were given safe-conducts and the use of the *yam* relay stations (for food, lodging, and mounts) while traveling to and from the great khâns on official business. The *yam* system not only facilitated the rapid dissemination of news throughout the empire, but also encouraged travel and trade across the vast expanse of land controlled by the Mongols.

Chinggis also made significant contributions in the realm of legal and judicial affairs. He served as a legislator by collecting existing Mongol law and by modifying and supplementing it with his own decrees, thus establishing the legal system or constitution for his empire. His legal code, called the *yasa*, also reflects Chinggis's special relationship with the sky god Tengri. The *yasa* was a comprehensive code that covered virtually all aspects of life—it not only prohibited behavior and decreed punishments (making frequent use of the death penalty) but also defined rules of procedure, jurisdictional delineations, ownership rights, and so on. The *yasa* continued to be the basis of Mongol public order long after Chinggis's death, and sections of it are still observed in some parts of Mongolia.

After Chinggis's death in August of 1227, his third son, Ögödei, was elected by the *quriltai* in 1229 to be the next great khân; he was Chinggis's hand-picked choice to be his successor. While Ögödei thus had precedence over his brothers, each of Chinggis's four sons by his chief wife Bortai inherited specific parts of the empire, as was Mongol custom. The descendants of Jochi, the eldest son, who died six months before Chinggis, received the rich western steppe in Russia; the second son, Chaghatai, got most of Central Asia; and the youngest, Tolui, inherited China. Ögödei and

# M

his family had the area surrounding the capital of Karakorum as well as the title of great khân and its accompanying authority over his three brothers. To keep unity among the four khânates, Chinggis had arranged the transfer of the Mongol officer corps directly to his successor, Ögödei. Thus, all of Ögödei's brothers were dependent on him for the Mongol officers and bodyguards needed to overawe the Turks, Chinese, Tibetans, Slavs, and other subject peoples. In this way Chinggis guaranteed the continued unity of his empire after his death.

Ögödei ruled as great khân from 1229 to 1241. He was not a charismatic leader or military genius like his father. On the contrary, he was a calm and dignified ruler who was shrewd and conscientious in fulfilling his duties. Since he enlarged Karakorum and erected many new buildings, he is usually credited with establishing Karakorum as the permanent Mongol capital city. With larger numbers of people living in Karakorum year-round, he had to organize the importation of food supplies from agricultural China to feed those in his growing capital. He also developed trade and commercial links with China, Tibetan India, and western Asia.

Mongol military victories and expansion continued under Ögödei. In 1234, the last Chin resistance was eliminated, and the Mongols were able to exploit all of northern China. They adopted the administrative style of the Chinese, whose officials had experience dealing with an advanced agricultural society, and continued the Confucian pattern of collecting taxes and running local affairs; Mongol rule was thus not evident in the day-to-day government in China. In 1236, Ögödei directed the Mongol military machine to the west, and by 1241, virtually all Russian princes and cities were conquered. This major military expedition was well-prepared in advance. An army of around 150,000 men was led by Batu, the son of Jochi; in short, the great khân Ögödei let Batu use the main Mongol army to complete the conquest of his patrimony. In 1240, Kiev, the most important city in Russia, was captured, and in 1241, the Mongol army continued into central Europe, where Hungary was its chief objective. In a masterpiece of strategy, the Mongol army split into three parts and attacked Hungary simultaneously from the north, east, and south.

It was clear that no military power in Europe was capable of withstanding the Mongols, who could easily have marched to the Atlantic if they had wanted to do so. Fortunately for Christian Europe and Western civilization, the Mongols voluntarily withdrew in 1242. The death of Ögödei in Karakorum in December of 1241 was part of the reason, as was the fact the there was not enough pasturage in Europe for the large number of Mongol horses accompanying the army. Batu, his cousin and enemy Güyük, and the other Mongol leaders were expected to attend the *quriltai* and participate in the election of the next great khân. Batu never did go to Karakorum, but he did take his military forces to the east in the hope of influencing the decision of the *quriltai*. He established his capital in Sarai on the lush steppe of the lower Volga River, in the vicinity of present-day Volgograd. From there, he and his successors established the khânate of the Golden Horde that ruled over Russia for approximately the next 250 years.

Though Ögödei had died in 1241, his successor Güyük was not enthroned until August of 1246. This five-year interregnum was caused by the serious conflict between Batu and Güyük, the two strongest candidates for the throne. However, in the long run Batu was not able to prevent the election of Güyük as great khân. Güyük's reign was very short, which was fortunate for the Mongols, since Güyük was drunk most of the time during his two-year reign. His death was followed by another three-year interregnum (1248–1250). Thus it was not possible for the Mongols to undertake any major military campaigns for ten years, since the time from 1241 to 1251 was a period of uncertainty—eight years without a great khân and two years of rule by an ineffective alcoholic.

Due to Güyük's poor performance and internal Mongol family politics, the office of great khân was transferred from the line of Ögödei to the family of Tolui. Möngke, the eldest son of Tolui, was elected great khân in 1251. Instead of renewing the attack on Europe, he decided to undertake two major campaigns to complete the conquest of southern China and to defeat the Abbasid caliph of Baghdad in the Middle East. Möngke entrusted these two major and formidable tasks to his two brothers—Khubilai was sent to China and Hülegü ordered to the Middle East. Möngke had a relatively short reign, dying in 1259 before either of the two brothers had completed his assignment.

With his large army, Hülegü marched into the Middle East and ravished Persia, Mesopotamia, and Syria. He captured the Abbasid capital of Baghdad in 1258 and reportedly massacred all of its inhabitants. The hapless caliph was rolled in a carpet and trampled to death by Mongol horses; thus Hülegü avoided shedding royal blood by the sword, an act forbidden by Chinggis's *yasa*. After the capture of the fortified cities of Aleppo and Damascus, it looked as if nothing would stop the Mongols from capturing Egypt and North Africa and thus completing their conquest of the entire Muslim world. But in 1260, the Mongols suffered an unexpected reversal in Palestine as the Egyptian Mamluks defeated a nominal Mongol army at Ain Jalut (also known as Goliath's Spring in the Western sources).

The death of Möngke in 1259, with the ensuing disruption of Mongol unity, was indirectly responsible for this Mamluk victory. Hülegü immediately supported his older brother Khubilai for the office of great khân, but their cousin Berke (a brother of the late Batu), khân of the Golden Horde, opposed them. Berke had converted to Islam and was so outraged by Hülegü's destruction of the caliphate that these two Mongol leaders were drifting toward open hostilities. In anticipation of this impending war with Berke, Hülegü had marched his Mongol forces back into northern Persia, leaving only a weak garrison force of mostly non-Mongol troops in Palestine. The Mamluk victory over this small non-Mongol force in 1260 has been hailed as the critical event that saved Islam from total conquest and marked the beginning of the end of the Mongol Empire, since it represented their first defeat on the battlefield. Religious scholars have seen divine providence in the fact that Islam was unexpectedly saved in 1260 by the death of Möngke just as Christian Europe was saved by the fortuitous death of Ögödei in 1241. But despite this Mamluk victory in 1260, the Mongols still controlled all of the Middle East except Egypt; Hülegü and his successors ruled the Middle East from Persia, where they established the il-khânate or subject khânate. Caught between the hostile Golden Horde to the northeast and the Mamluks to the southwest, the Mongol khâns of Persia, especially Abagha and Arghun, tried to form an alliance with Latin Europe to the northwest, especially with the Christian crusader states in the Levant. Eventually the Mongol khâns in Persia converted to Islam, and they ruled the Middle East until they were overthrown in the mid-fourteenth century.

Meanwhile, Khubilai and the Mongols were bogged down as they faced decades of intermittent but large-scale fighting in south China. By Chinese standards the Song was a weak dynasty, yet these peaceful farmers proved much more difficult to conquer than the traditional warrior Muslims of the Middle East. Khubilai and his generals finally prevailed only by drawing upon their skill in large-scale strategic envelopment movements. First the Mongols went down the Yangtze River to attack the Chinese capital of Hangzhou, and then they outflanked the Song from the west and south, virtually surrounding them. The Mongols captured the great south Chinese seaport of Canton in 1277 and completed the conquest of south China by 1280.

While Khubilai was defeating the Song in China, the Mongol *quriltai* met in 1260 to select the next khân. With the strong support of his younger brother Hülegü, Khubilai was the clear choice for this position. This is not surprising since these two brothers were each in command of large armies in the field. Nevertheless, their younger brother, Arigh Böke, contested Khubilai's election, and it took Khubilai almost five years to end this disturbance. Khubilai was then challenged by his cousin Qaidu, who refused to recognize Khubilai's authority over him in Central Asia.

China was Khubilai's base of power and the only part of the large Mongol Empire where his authority was accepted without question. Throughout his life, Khubilai constantly felt the need to assert the legitimacy of his reign due to his unorthodox accession in a hastily convened *quriltai* at which his brother and chief rival Arigh Böke was not present. Since Khubilai was somewhat insecure about his election, he repeatedly tried to force all other rulers to acknowledge his position of power and superiority as great khân. His ongoing military campaigns show that he kept his basic Mongol warrior identity while, at the same time, he wanted to appear as a traditional Confucian emperor to his Chinese subjects. At first he was fairly successful in balancing his Mongol steppe heritage with his role as a Confucian scholar-ruler: he managed to ingratiate himself with most of the diverse racial, ethnic, religious, and cultural groups within his empire. Khubilai's favorite wife, Chabi, played a significant role throughout his reign, as did his Tibetan, Muslim, and Confucian advisers—Christians, too, if one includes Marco Polo. As he grew older, Khubilai became less personally involved in ruling his empire. Prior to his death in 1294 at the age of eighty, Khubilai's health deteriorated due to excessive amounts of food and drink.

Despite the Mongol military setback in Palestine in 1260 and Khubilai's disputed election in the same year, the Mongol Empire was still an amazing and impressive entity. In addition to the Inner Asian steppe, it included the civilized centers of China, northern India, the Middle East, and Russia. Mongol armies were still

# M

active from the Baltic to southeast Asia, while naval expeditions were attacking Japan and Java. Nevertheless, this gigantic empire was already beginning to crumble, and it became progressively less unified within the next few decades. There are a number of reasons usually given for the disintegration of the Mongol Empire—overextension, assimilation, and internal dynastic rivalries.

In reaching the extremities of Eurasia, the Mongols had overextended themselves. Even with their extraordinary speed, mobility, and communication system, the Mongols could not effectively rule their vast empire, especially since it was more than 6,000 miles east-to-west and more than 1,500 miles north-to-south. The Mongols gained so much so fast that they were soon bogged down in trying to consolidate and rule what they had while continuing their ongoing conquests and expansion. A major problem facing the Mongol khâns was that there were too few Mongols (between one and two million, according to most estimates) to rule their vast empire effectively.

In relation to most of their subject peoples, the Mongols were also too primitive in terms of their development. Thus the barbarian Mongols were vulnerable to assimilation into the more sophisticated and advanced civilizations that they conquered. As soon as they dismounted to enjoy the wealth and benefits of their conquests, they began to adopt the languages, religions, administrative structures, culture, and technology of their more advanced subjects. And once the Mongols were assimilated into the Chinese, Tibetan, Muslim, and Russian civilizations, they lost their sense of themselves as Mongols, identifying with the geographic region of their khânates rather than with their Inner Asian steppe heritage.

Finally, dynastic rivalries between the heirs of Chinggis's four sons added to internal fragmentation at the top. Khubilai, the last of the five great khâns, really had no authority outside of China even though his title was still viewed as giving him priority over all the other Mongol khânates. The fact that Khubilai moved the capital of the great khân from Karakorum to Khanbaliq (modern Beijing) is in itself an indication of the process of the emergence of regional khânates, cultural assimilation, and irreconcilable splits within the royal family itself. While Khubilai was becoming a Chinese emperor, the rulers of the il-khânate in the Middle East accepted Islam; at the same time, the khânates of the Golden Horde in Russia and of the Chaghatai khânate in Central Asia went their own separate ways. Within a short time, the only

remaining pure Mongols were those in Mongolia, and even these came under the outside influence of Buddhism. By the end of the medieval period, they were weak and obscure while the other Mongol khânates had been overthrown in all of the civilized centers.

In spite of their final decline, the Mongols did have a positive impact on the medieval world because of their relative tolerance of intercultural contacts. Mongol control of most of the Eurasian landmass resulted in what is called the Mongol Peace—anyone with a safe-conduct pass could safely travel anywhere in the Mongol Empire. The opening of direct communication between East Asia and Western Europe led to the exchange of goods, peoples, and ideas—the transmission of knowledge in science and medicine, technical innovations like gunpowder, commodities like silk, and even diseases. Both China and Islam rejected most ideas and practices associated with foreign Mongol rule and returned to their traditional cultural worldview and practices as soon as they could, but Westerners proved to be more receptive to borrowing knowledge and technology from the other advanced civilizations. While maintaining a foundation of traditional European ideas and practices, Western civilization integrated foreign knowledge and continued on the path of intellectual growth and technical innovation.

The Mongol Empire, of course, had its most direct and dramatic impact on China and the Middle East, since both of these sedentary centers were ruled by Mongol khâns for about a century. Some scholars maintain that a century of Mongol rule retarded the growth and progress of relatively advanced Chinese and Muslim civilizations; afterward, cultural stagnation continued as the Chinese became xenophobic and the Muslims struggled against external military force. In contrast, because Latin Europe was the farthest from the center of Mongol power in Karakorum, Western civilization experienced less disruption and destruction at the hands of the Mongols, thus allowing Europeans to catch up to and possibly even surpass these other Eurasian societies. Having had the most to gain from the cultural interchanges during the Mongol Peace, Christian Europe prospered and advanced, moving into a position of leadership in the Age of Discovery.

**BIBLIOGRAPHY**

Allsen, Thomas T. *Mongol Imperialism: The Policies of the Grand Qan Möngke in China, Russia, and the Islamic Lands, 1251–1259.* Berkeley: U of California P, 1987.

Grousset, René. *The Empire of the Steppes: A History of Central Asia*. Trans. N. Walford. New Brunswick, NJ: Rutgers UP, 1970.

Halperin, Charles J. *Russia and the Golden Horde: The Mongol Impact on Medieval Russian History*. Bloomington: Indiana UP, 1987.

Jagchid, Sechin, and Van Jay Symons. *Peace, War, and Trade along the Great Wall: Nomadic-Chinese Interaction through Two Millennia*. Bloomington: Indiana UP, 1989.

Juvaini, 'Ala al-Din 'Ata-Malik. *The History of the World Conqueror*. Trans. J.A. Boyle. Manchester, England: Manchester UP, 1958.

Legg, Stuart. *The Heartland*. New York, 1970. Rpt. as *The Barbarians of Asia*. New York: Dorset P, 1990.

Lewis, Archibald R. *Nomads and Crusaders: A.D. 1000–1368*. Bloomington, IN: Indiana UP, 1988.

Morgan, David O. *The Mongols*. Oxford: Blackwell, 1986.

Ratchnevsky, Paul. *Genghis Khan: His Life and Legacy*. Trans. and ed. T.N. Haining. New York and Oxford: Basil Blackwell, 1991.

Rossabi, Morris. *Khubilai Khan: His Life and Times*. Berkeley: U of California P, 1988.

Saunders, J.J. *The History of the Mongol Conquests*. New York: Barnes and Noble, 1971.

*Secret History of the Mongols*. Trans. Igor de Rachewiltz in *Papers in Far Eastern History*. Vols. 4–33 (1971–1986 at irregular intervals). Trans. Francis Cleaves. Cambridge, MA: Harvard UP, 1982. Trans. Paul Kahn. San Francisco: North Point P, 1984.

*Gregory G. Guzman*

**SEE ALSO**

Ain Jalut; Andrew of Longjumeau; Benedict the Pole; Buddhism; Golden Horde; Hülegü; Huns; Inner Asian Trade; Inner Asian Travel; John of Plano Carpini; Karakitai; Karakorum; Marco Polo; Matthew Paris; Mongol Army; Nomadism and Pastoralism; *Secret History of the Mongols, The;* Silk Roads; Simon of Saint-Quentin; Tibet; Vincent of Beauvais; William of Rubruck; Yasa; Yuan Dynasty

## Mongols, The Secret History of the

*See* Secret History of the Mongols, The

## Mongol Society, Women in

*See* Women in Mongol Society

## Monstrosity, Geographical

State of physical or cultural oddity caused by climatic or geographical factors that may be interpreted as the outward sign of moral and cultural deviance.

Beginning with Ktesias (late fifth century B.C.E.) and Megasthenes (fl. 300 B.C.E.) in ancient Greece, travel writers have populated their narratives with monstrous races of men peculiar (from the speaker's point of view) to exotic geographical regions. The Roman author Pliny collected many of these monstrous races in his *Natural History*, from which they passed into the literature and travel lore of the Middle Ages.

According to sources as diverse as Adam of Bremen, Marco Polo, and the author of *The Book of John Mandeville*, monsters dwell at the edges of the world. These are the places where reliable information about geography gives way to incomplete knowledge about various lands, their people, and customs. The farther writers progress from their homelands, the more likely it is that they will populate their narratives with strange phenomena, especially monstrous animals and men. Monstrosity in these travel accounts often results from a writer's attempt to make sense of a new and different environment: in Marco Polo's report of his journey to China, the perfectly ordinary rhinoceros becomes the magical unicorn.

Panotii. Rutland Psalter. London, British Library MS Add. 62925, fol. 57r, *c.* 1260. Courtesy of the British Library.

# M

Blemyae, Rutland Psalter. London, British Library MS Add. 62925, fol. 88v, c. 1260. Courtesy of the British Library.

Monstrosity may also result from the projection of a traveler's fears onto an alien culture or landscape. Dangerous shores are often represented as full of cannibals, who embody the perils that beset travelers and the anxieties they might have about cultures they do not understand; the *Mandeville's Travels* author, for example, describes distant islands full of giants who instantly devour anyone who steps foot on their land. Over time, the fantastic geography where monsters were thought to live was slowly pushed farther away, largely because greater portions of the earth were being charted by Western explorers who failed to find the strange beasts or humanoids described in traditional geographies. From India and Persia, the monsters migrated to Scandinavia, Africa, the far south (the antipodes), and the New World.

Monstrosity often involves some alteration of the "normal" human body. Giantism, very large ears, a single foot, dark skin (in the case of the Ethiopians caused by their imagined proximity to the equator), a head beneath the shoulders, animal limbs, and the mixing of genders are ingredients in the recipe for monstrosity. These physical deformities usually signal that the monster is a breaker of various cultural taboos. When the monster is described as cannibalistic or incestuous, his outside appearance or behavior mirrors his morally transgressive inside. These monstrous distortions reassure writers and their audiences that they themselves possess proper humanity and a superior culture. During the Middle Ages and the Renaissance, Muslims and Native Americans were sometimes represented as monstrous beings. By depicting other cultures as monsters, writers illustrated the threat other ways of life were imagined to pose to the West; this danger in turn was used to justify the taking of lands and lives.

For the most part, monstrosity conditions an aversion: the monster commits the worst possible crimes and thus shows us what not to do. Yet the monster can become an attractive figure, even idealized, as in the case of the Gymnosophisti or cave-dwelling naked wise men encountered by Alexander the Great in India, perhaps because of the monster's nature as something forbidden and outside the circle of the normal. Writers like Jacques de Vitry and the *Mandeville* author fostered a kind of cultural relativism through their often benign depictions of the monstrous races, especially when they used them as a "measure of man" to illustrate contemporary cultural failings.

Geographical monstrosity is ultimately a cultural category that reveals more about the travelers themselves than it does about what they encounter along the road.

## BIBLIOGRAPHY

Campbell, Mary B. *The Witness and the Other World: Exotic European Travel Writing, 400–1600.* Ithaca, NY: Cornell UP, 1988.

Friedman, John Block. *The Monstrous Races in Medieval Art and Thought.* Cambridge, MA: Harvard UP, 1981; rpt. Syracuse, NY: Syracuse UP, 2000.

Wittkower, Rudolf. "Marvels of the East: A Study in the History of Monsters." *The Journal of the Warburg and Courtauld Institutes* 5 (1942): 159–197. Rpt. *Allegory and the Migration of Symbols.* New York: Thames and Hudson, 1977; rpt. 1987, pp. 45–74, 196–205.

*Jeffrey Jerome Cohen*

## SEE ALSO

Adam of Bremen; Animals, Exotic; Antipodes; Cannibalism; Ethiopians; Giants; Jacques de Vitry; *Mandeville's Travels;* Marco Polo; Pliny the Elder

## Moon, Mountains of the
*See* Mountains of the Moon

## Mortuary Roll

A document produced in the scriptorium of a medieval monastic community to commemorate the death of a prominent person associated with the institution. When a monk or nun died, a lay messenger known as a breviator often would be hired to travel to other monastic houses and religious institutions such as cathedral schools to announce the death and ask for prayers for the soul of the deceased. Although he would in most cases carry only a short obituary notice known as a mortuary brief, the death of a prominent person such as an abbot, abbess, or major patron would elicit a more elaborate document known as a mortuary roll. This parchment roll, sometimes called an obituary, precatory, or bede roll, included an elegant obituary of the deceased in an opening section known as an encyclical, which was often beautifully illuminated.

The communities that a breviator with a mortuary roll visited were expected to say prayers for the soul of the dead and to write a memorial of some sort on the roll. Thus the roll grew as the breviator traveled and collected entries, ultimately returning the document to the monastery or nunnery that had issued it. When the initial sheet of parchment was filled, another sheet would be sewn onto the end, extending the roll. A particularly long roll might be made up of a dozen or more such sheets of various lengths. Some surviving mortuary rolls contain entries from hundreds of communities spread over a vast geographical area. The longest roll known to have survived the Middle Ages, circulated to 253 religious institutions throughout northern France and England in the early twelfth century in honor of Abbess Mathilda of Holy Trinity Abbey in Caen, was an impressive seventy-two feet long.

Both the mortuary announcements and the memorial entries from the various communities were written in Latin. Many houses simply added a formulaic "May the soul of this one and the souls of all the faithful dead rest in peace. Amen." Scribes of other communities used the occasion to write beautiful verses or other touching remembrances. At some institutions, especially those with literary reputations, more than one writer would add to the roll. For example, the eleventh-century mortuary roll of Wilfred of Cerdana included fourteen poems from the cathedral chapter at Liège

Ebchester mortuary prayer roll. Durham Dean and Chapter Library MS B. IV. 48, 1464. Courtesy of the Durham Dean and Chapter. Photo by John B. Friedman.

and nine from the Monastery of St. Lawrence in the same city. The entire entry from a single community is referred to as a *titulus,* and the portion of the roll containing these entries is called the *tituli* section.

As early as the eighth century, some monasteries had begun to send letters to other communities announcing the deaths of monks and soliciting prayers for their souls. These were the forerunners of the more formal mortuary briefs and mortuary rolls. The earliest mortuary roll of which some fragments have been preserved comes from Saint-Martial in Limoges and dates from the late tenth century. At first, the circulation of mortuary rolls seems to have centered on France and Catalonia. The idea later spread to Belgium, Germany, Austria, and England.

According to the French scholar Jean Dufour, approximately 160 mortuary rolls are extant, either whole or in part, and the texts of an equal number of rolls no longer extant have also been preserved. Most of

# M

the extant rolls date from the eleventh and twelfth centuries. By the late fourteenth century, the practice of making and circulating mortuary rolls had lost popularity in most regions, perhaps due in part to the disruptions in monastic life at the time of the Black Death, but they were still being produced regularly as late as the fifteenth century in England and Germany. A very late mortuary roll is that of John Islip, abbot of Westminster, who died in 1532; this roll is of particular interest to art historians because it was apparently decorated by Hans Holbein the Younger. The practice of circulating rolls disappeared completely during the Reformation, fading gradually in Europe and ending in England with the dissolution of the monasteries by Henry VIII in 1536.

BIBLIOGRAPHY

Delisle, Léopold, ed. *Rouleaux des morts du IXe au XVe siècle.* Paris: Jules Renouard for La Société de l'Histoire de France, 1866; rpt. New York: Johnson Reprint, 1968.

Dufour, Jean. "Les rouleaux des morts." *Codicologica* 3 (1980): 96–102.

Huyghebaert, N. *Les Documents Nécrologique.* Typologie des Sources du Moyen Age Occidental, fasc. 4. Turnhout: Brepols, 1972.

Leslie, Teresa. *"The Remedy of Holy Prayer": The Mortuary Roll of Abbess Mathilda of Holy Trinity, Caen (d. 1113).* Thesis, West Georgia College, 1993.

*Teresa Leslie*

SEE ALSO
Black Death; Breviator

## Mount Ararat
*See* Ararat, Mount

## Mountains of the Moon

One of the traditional locations of the source of the river Nile, in central Africa. Of the various ancient and medieval stories about the headwaters of the Nile, the account found in Ptolemy's *Geography* (c. 127/151) is closest to being correct. Following the earlier geographer Marinus of Tyre (fl.100 C.E.), Ptolemy placed the source of the river at two large lakes in East Africa that were fed by melting snow from a range of high peaks, the Mountains of the Moon. This account may reflect travelers' reports of the Nile's real headwaters in the area of Lakes Victoria and Albert, near the snow-capped Ruwenzori range.

Ptolemy's was but one of a number of ancient stories about the Nile, and by no means the most influential. Other versions, which had the Nile connected to the major rivers of West Africa, or to the Indian Ocean, were far more widespread during the European Middle Ages. Indeed, the *Geography* had little immediate influence, and was unknown in medieval Europe. The idea of the Mountains of the Moon seems largely to have disappeared until the *Geography* was translated into Arabic around the eighth century. Ptolemy's influence on geographical studies in the Islamic world was extensive but not absolute, and competing traditions existed in Islamic scholarship as well.

The Mountains of the Moon began to appear on European world maps in the mid-fourteenth century. This almost certainly reflects influence from Islamic sources, as the *Geography* itself was not known in Europe until 1397. As knowledge of the *Geography* increased during the fifteenth century—and especially as its atlas maps, which depict the source of the Nile in Africa, were disseminated—the Mountains of the Moon became an almost universal feature on European world maps. Ptolemy's account remained dominant throughout the early modern period, until well into the early nineteenth century.

BIBLIOGRAPHY

Crawford, O.G.S. "Some Medieval Theories about the Nile." *Geographical Journal* 114 (1949): 6–29.

Langlands, R.W. "Concepts of the Nile." *Uganda Journal* 26 (1962): 1–22.

de la Roncière, Charles. *La Découverte de l'Afrique au moyen âge: Cartographes et explorateurs.* Cairo: Société Royale de Géographie d'Egypte, 1924–1927.

*Ben Weiss*

SEE ALSO
Atlas; Ptolemy

## Muslims, Marriages between Christians and, Attitudes toward
*See* Marriages between Muslims and Christians, Attitudes toward

## Muslim Travelers and Trade

Islam encourages certain forms of travel, including the pilgrimage (*hajj*), the pursuit of knowledge (*fi talab al-*

*'ilm*), migration (*hijra*) from lands of infidelity, and visitation of sacred sites (*ziyāra*). Other reasons for travel in the Middle Ages were trade, diplomacy, and espionage. Though many persons traveled within *Dār al-Islām* (the region within which Islam was the principal religion), considerably fewer ventured beyond its frontiers. Indeed, it was mainly trade that opened new regions for Islam and fostered travel to and geographical knowledge about distant countries. *Rihla,* or travel accounts, developed into a literary genre, an art form that encapsulated the believable and the incredible. *Rihla* must therefore be treated with caution as a geographical and historical source.

Muslim travel may profitably be considered first in terms of the chief geographical regions in which it occurred—the Indian Ocean; the Mediterranean; the Sahara and West Africa; and Byzantium and other Christian lands—and then through the accounts of the principal Muslim travelers.

Before the rise of Islam, commerce in the western Indian Ocean had been largely in the hands of Persians. Much of the trade between Arabia and China was carried by Chinese and Persian boats. It was from the Persians that the Arabs learned seafaring in the Indian Ocean, so that they began to frequent Chinese ports in the eighth century.

The peak of early Arab trade with the Far East came in the ninth century. Arab mercantile communities developed along the shores of India and Ceylon, and beyond the Straits of Malacca on the route to China. About 878, the Arab settlement in Khanfu (Canton) was destroyed by Chinese rebels, and direct relations with China were discontinued. After this time, Muslim merchants stopped at Kalah in Malaya, where they met the ships from China, although individual Muslim traders could travel on Chinese ships to Canton.

During the period of the Song dynasty (960–1127), China experienced unprecedented economic growth. As a result, Muslim trade with the Far East grew, with a greater variety of goods shipped to more ports. Muslim mercantile communities developed this time in major Chinese towns along the overland route from Inner Asia and along water routes. Significant numbers of Chinese merchants trading internationally appear to have converted to Islam, in order to be part of the Muslim commercial network.

When the Yuan (or Mongol) dynasty (1124–1368) came into power, their policy of tolerance for other cultures and religions attracted Muslim traders not only to Chinese seaports but to caravan routes across Inner Asia, which led to the establishment of Muslim communities in cities of northern China. The Mongols united so much of Asia that travelers could move securely under a single authority from the Black Sea to the Pacific Ocean. With the fall of the Yuan dynasty and the rise of the Ming dynasty after 1368, native reaction against foreign influences resulted in the withering away of the alien Muslim settlements. Thus, in the middle of the fourteenth century, after the disintegration of the Mongol Empire into a number of quarreling khânates, recurrent anarchy and warfare made the sea route once again preferable. The fifteenth century was the apogee of Arab-Chinese maritime trade.

Trade across the Indian Ocean, which included an important Muslim Indian presence, prospered without a dominant political entity and was free of religious conflicts. At the beginning of the sixteenth century the Portuguese could have joined the Indian Ocean trade peacefully, but they sought a monopoly of trade and built protective garrisons in forts along the Indian Ocean coasts. Only the Red Sea remained in Muslim hands after the Portuguese gained control of most of the Indian Ocean during the early 1500s.

During this later period, Arab *dhows* plying between the Persian Gulf and East Africa carried a wide assortment of goods destined for Muslim coastal towns. Trade with the interior was limited, however, and was carried out by people from the interior. Even the gold trade between Zimbabwe and the port of Sofala, on the coast of Mozambique, was conducted by traders from the interior. There was nothing comparable to West Africa, where Muslim traders penetrated deep into the interior.

While the peak of early Arab trade in the eastern direction had come in the ninth century, it was during the tenth and eleventh centuries, when the Fātimids ruled from Egypt over Syria, the Arabian Peninsula, and the Maghrib, that Egypt became a passageway for international trade and Red Sea trade toward the west developed. Jews and Muslims, part of a single trading community, speaking and writing Arabic, and coming from as far as the Maghrib and Andalusia, were already active in trade with India. Moreover, trade was facilitated by the rise of banking instruments, which were sufficently well developed so that money orders could be transferred easily from one market to another across thousands of miles.

By the twelfth century, the westward expansion of Muslim trade faced certain European challenges.

# M

Merchants from Italy, Catalan, and Provence dominated Mediterranean trade and restricted Muslim shipping to trade along the coasts and the short run between the Levantine coast and Cyprus. Though with the improvement of shipping, pilgrims from Morocco had the choice of traveling by land or by sea on European vessels, they (and all seafarers) had to brave storms, pirates, and hostile navies. Overland pilgrims and other travelers confronted bandits, nomad marauders, and wars between North African states.

Following the crusaders' conquest of Constantinople in 1204, shipping from the individual Italian city-states moved into the Black Sea. The Venetians, and to a lesser extent the Genoese, had mercantile colonies in the Crimea and along the shores of the Sea of Azov, where European traders met the Asians who transported goods around the Caspian Sea and across Inner Asia to link up with the so-called Silk Road.

As with trade to the east and into the Mediterranean, from a fairly early period there was a strong trans-Saharan and West African trade with the Muslim world, especially in gold, described by Muslim travelers. At the end of the ninth century, information about *Bilād al-Sūdān* ("the Land of the Blacks") reached the Muslim world through the Tripoli-to-Chad route. Al-Ya'qūbī, for example, described peoples and kingdoms from east to west. In the middle of the tenth century, with the growth of trade between Morocco and the western Sudan, Ibn Hawqal recorded names of kingdoms from west to east. These were the two most important routes of trans-Saharan trade, growing in size and reaching a peak in the fourteenth century. Berbers were the chief transporters of goods there. From the southern termini of the Sahara to the gold fields, trade was carried on by Mandingo-speaking traders, who set up mercantile colonies at strategic sites and acted as cross-cultural brokers. Europe was then changing from silver to gold as its principal currency, and greater demand stimulated more gold production in the Sudan. West Africa was then producing almost two-thirds of the world's gold supply.

The importance of this growth in African trade led to a corresponding increase in geographical knowledge and cultural contact. In the fourteenth century, Ibn Khaldūn and al-'Umarī were able to record detailed information on Mali without traveling there, gathering reports from Moroccans and Egyptians who lived in Mali and were engaged in commerce or held official religious offices. They also interviewed people from Mali, including royals, who crossed the Sahara on their way to the *hajj*.

By the middle of the fifteenth century, however, the Portuguese had sailed along the Atlantic coast of Africa, and during the next two centuries European factories on the coast contributed to the decline of the overland trans-Saharan trade.

In contrast to the role of trade in encouraging knowledge about Africa, the earliest information Muslims had about Byzantium and other Christian lands was obtained by spies and diplomats. The caliph al-Mansūr (r. 754–775) sent 'Umāra ben Hamza (d. 814) to Constantinople. His account was quoted ninety years later by Ibn al-Faqīh. The caliph al-Wāthiq (r. 842–847) dispatched Muhammad ben Mūsā (d. 873) to Byzantium. This mission was recorded also by Byzantine historians.

The poet Yahyā ben al-Hakam al-Bakrī al-Jayyānī, known as al-Ghazal (770–864), was sent in 845 by the emir of Córdoba, 'Abd al-Rahmān II, to Jutland to negotiate with the Normans, who in 844 had attacked Seville. His account survived in the work of Ibn Dihya, an Andalusian historian of the early thirteenth century. Al-Ghazal had been sent earlier to the Byzantine emperor Theophile, as recorded in the seventeenth century by al-Maqarrī.

In 965, Ibrāhīm ben Ya'qūb al-Isra'ili, a Jewish merchant from Tortosa in Spain, was sent to the court of the German emperor Otto I (the Great). He also visited Britain, and perhaps also Ireland, Iceland, Poland, the Netherlands, and Sicily. Extracts from his accounts, especially on Germany and the Slavs, were preserved in al-Bakrī, al-Qazwīni, Ibn Sa'īd, Abu'l-Fidā', and al-Dimashqī. Abū Muhammad 'Abd Allāh ben Ahmad ben Sulaym al-Uswānī visited the Nubians between 969 and 973 on behalf of the Fātimid chief Jawhar. His account was partially conserved by al-Maqrīzī and Ibn Iyās.

Other Muslims traveled to Christian lands as prisoners of war. After he had been released from the Byzantine prison in mid-ninth century, Muhammad ben Abī Muslim al-Jarmī recorded his experience in captivity. He wrote about the organization and customs of the Byzantines and their neighbors, the Avars, Bulgarians, Slavs, and Khazars. Only fragments of his work survived, in quotations by Ibn Khurdadhbih. Hārūn ben Yahyā was captured by pirates off the coast of Palestine toward the end of the ninth century. During his captivity he visited Constantinople, Thessaloniki, the southern Slav countries, Venice, and Rome, where he collected information concerning France and

England. Parts of his text are quoted by Ibn Rustah and al-Qazwīnī.

Reports by merchants and sailors of travel in the Indian Ocean and to China and India during the ninth century were preserved in *Silsilat al-Tawārīkh,* known also as *Akhbār al-Sīn wa'l-Hind.* It was collected and edited around 916 by Abū Zayd al-Hasan al-Sīrafī. The town of Sirāf was then the most important port on the Persian coast. The first part of this composition is attributed to Suleymān, a merchant who supposedly traveled to China and India. Ibn al-Faqīh quoted Suleymān as his source for the sea route from Sirāf to China. It is more likely that this was not the narrative of one traveler but a collection of accounts by different people. The information about the kings of India was probably based on the report of an envoy sent to India by Yahyā ben Khālid al-Barmakī (d. 805), the vizier of Hārūn al-Rashīd.

The second part of *Akhbār al-Sīn wa'l-Hind* includes descriptions by various travelers to India, China, and southeast China, as well as to the East African coast. There is also information about sea routes, winds, and storms. This part incorporates the story of the merchant Ibn Wahb, from the tribe of Quraysh, who traveled to China in 870 and was granted an audience with the Chinese emperor. The report of Ibn Wahb is of particular importance because it preceded by about eight years the destruction of the Arab settlement in Canton noted above. Abū Zayd al-Sīrafī incorporated in his account impressions of a visit to India by "a trustworthy person" named al-Mas'ūdī, who met al-Sīrafī and mentioned him, in *Murūj al-Dhahab,* as the source for the story of Ibn Wahb.

In the mid-tenth century, Buzurg ibn Shariyār, a captain of the Persian fleet, composed *Kitāb 'ajā'ib al-Hind,* "The Marvels of India," made up of stories collected from sailors about their experience in the Indian Ocean, blending factual accounts and fantastic adventure stories told by armchair travelers. *The Story of Sindbad the Sailor,* also a collection of sailors' accounts, represents another stage in the development of medieval Arab travel literature. Whereas Buzurg's anthology put factual information first and entertainment second, *The Story of Sindbad* reversed these priorities.

About 1009, the navigator Khawashir ben Yūsuf al-Arkī sailed on an Indian boat along the entire coast of east and southeast Africa. The nautical guide he produced was used by writers of the twelfth century, and information about him is preserved by navigators of

the fifteenth century such as Ibn Mājid, who belonged to an illustrious family of Omani navigators. In writing his work of nautical instructions, he added fifty years of personal experience on the Indian Ocean to the legacy of the practical knowledge inherited from his forefathers. A younger contemporary of Ibn Mājid, Suleymān al-Mahrī, wrote another, less original work on navigation in the Indian Ocean.

One of the earliest accounts of travel from the eastern lands of Islam was left by Tamīm ben Bahr al-Muttawwi'ī, who voyaged to the lands of the Turks between 760 and 800. He is quoted by Ibn Khurdādhbih, and through him by Ibn al-Faqīh and Yāqūt. Somewhat later Muhammad ben Mūsā (d. 873), who had already been to Byzantium, was sent on a mission by the caliph al-Wāthiq (r. 842–847) to Tarakhan, the ruler of the Khazars. His contemporary, al-Sallām the Interpreter, an official of the caliph al-Wāthiq, toured central Asia for twenty-eight months on behalf of the caliph. His account survived only in Ibn Khurdādhbih's text.

Al-Ya'qūbī (d. 897 or 905), the earliest traveler whose records were preserved, was born in Baghdad. He visited Palestine, Armenia, and Khurasan, as well as India. He was the first geographer from the East who went west to Egypt and the Maghrib. Likewise, in a slightly later period, the geographical information of al-Istakhrī (second half of the tenth century) is partly based on his own observations during his travels. He visited Syria, Iraq, Persia, Central Asia, and Transoxiana.

A more far-reaching traveler, Al-Mas'ūdī (d. 956), was born in Baghdad and began his travels at an early age. He sailed over all the seas known at the time: the Indian Ocean and the Arabian, Caspian, Black, and Mediterranean seas. He traveled to Persia and to the lands of Central Asia, from Ferghana to the Caspian. He also visited parts of Byzantium. Like al-Ya'qūbī he traveled to the Muslim West, visiting Egypt, North Africa, and Spain. Al-Mas'ūdī claims to have visited China and Java (Zabaj), but most of his materials on southeast Asia can be traced to other sources. He stayed in India for nearly two years, but his account of those lands lacks originality, perhaps because he followed too closely Suleymān's account as presented by Abū Zayd al-Sīrafī. He tested earlier theories and concepts in the light of his own observations and of information he gathered from merchants and sailors.

Early information about inland travel to the north comes in large part from Ibn Fadlān, who participated in an embassy to the Bulgarians of the Volga, sent by

# M

the caliph to "the king of Slavs." The embassy left Baghdad on June 21, 921, and arrived in the land of the Bulgarians on May 12, 922, traveling across the lands of the Khwarizmis, Turks, Petchenegues, Bashkirs, Rus', and Khazars. His account is of great historical, geographical, and ethnographic interest and shows that Ibn Fadlān possessed extraordinary powers of observation and an inquiring mind. He brought back a mass of extremely important information on the Rus' and the Khazars, whom he had been able to see himself or of whom he had heard accounts during his journey. The text we have is an abbreviated version, done by a Samanids vizier in Bukhara. The text in every respect by far surpasses earlier travel accounts that survive in quotations by other geographers. In comparing the text of Ibn Fadlān's *Risāla* with quotations from Ibn Fadlān in Yāqūt, one discovers that a great deal of the documentary and literary value of the original is lost in the quotations.

Interest in travel to the East is most clearly illustrated by Abū Dulaf Mi'sar ben Muhalhil (mid-tenth century), who left accounts of his travels in two epistles (*Risāla*s): one describes a voyage to India, evidently imaginary. The second, relating a journey to Azerbaijan, Armenia, and Iran, was composed shortly after 952–953 and seems to be based on actual experience. In 942, a Chinese embassy reached Bukhara, where Abū Dulaf lived at the court of the Tahirid emirs. He joined the embassy on the way back, and entered China by way of Turkestan (Sinkiang). Then he went over to India and returned via Sijistan to the lands of Islam.

Perhaps the best known early traveler to the African continent was Ibn Hawqal, who was born in Baghdad between 910 and 920. He served the Hamdanids of the Jazira, a Shi'ite dynasty. When in 943 he was forced to leave Baghdad, he chose to travel to the Maghrib, perhaps because of his sympathy to the Fātimids. Though he was pro-Shi'ite, it is difficult to state categorically that he was an Isma'ili missionary (*dā'ī*), as some would claim. He wrote an account in 977, giving information on prices, products, and economic activities, which suggests that he may have been a merchant. From 947 to 953, he traveled in Ifrīqiyya, Andalusia, and down to Sijilmassa, where in 951–952 he collected information about Africa south of the Sahara. Back in the East, Ibn Hawqal visited the court of the Samanids in Bukhara from 965 to 969. In 969, he was in Jurjan, not far from the Caspian Sea, where he gathered information about the population of the Russian

plains. In 970–971, he went to Egypt, which in the meantime had been conquered by the Fātimids. He traveled for the second time to the Maghrib and also visited Sicily.

While the reasons for Ibn Hawqal's travels may have been political or mercantile, other travelers were impelled by religious or purely intellectual motives. For example, Nāsir Khusaru (1003–1088), who was born at Balkh and had served the Seljuks for forty years at Merv, traveled for seven years. He passed the rest of his life as an Isma'ili missionary in the region of Badakhshan. On the other hand, Abū Sa'd 'Abd al-Karīm al-Sam'ānī (1113–1167) traveled in search of knowledge in Bukhara, Nishapur, Isfahan, Baghdad, Aleppo, and Jerusalem; he lived for some time in Hijaz. Significant geographical information on China, the Maghrib, and Central Asia is embedded in his book on genealogies (*Kitāb al-ansāb*). He mentions people who visited China (and therefore have the epithet "al-Sin" attached to their name). His work was an important source for another voyager-intellectual, Yāqūt. Its popularity among scholars is attested by the abridgment of his voluminous work, first by Ibn al-Athīr in the middle of the thirteenth century, and later, in the fifteenth century, by al-Suyūtī, who abridged the abridgement.

Another author interested in religion was 'Alī al-Harawī (d. 1215), who wrote a book on the visitations (*ziyārāt*) of tombs of saints and other holy places. He himself traveled extensively to sacred sites in Aleppo, Damascus, Jerusalem (then ruled by the crusaders), Egypt, Arabia, Iraq, Iran, and India. He also visited Byzantium and saw Mount Etna on Sicily.

Yāqūt (1179–1229), who was Greek by origin (he is known as al-Rūmī), was captured in Byzantine territory and sold to a Syrian merchant, on whose behalf he traded until he was freed in 1199. He then continued to travel widely in the provinces of Iran, Iraq, Syria, and Egypt. In addition to his own experiences and observations, his geographical dictionary preserved accounts of other travelers whose own works had been lost.

Ibn al-Mujāwir (d. 1291) was born in Baghdad. He traveled to India and lived for some time in Multan. He returned by way of Daybul, near Karachi, to Aden. His importance rests mainly on his observations on ethnography and folklore in India. He also had some original information on sea routes from Arabia to India and Java.

A number of accounts of Muslim travel to the Maghrib and Andalusia still survive. In the eleventh century, al-Bakrī was able to produce an excellent description of the land, the peoples, and the kingdoms of the Sudanic belt south of the Sahara, without ever leaving Córdoba. Instead, he relied on accounts of traders and other travelers who crisscrossed the Sahara. In the twelfth century, al-Qazwīnī recorded information about the Sahara and the Sudan from two travelers: 'Alī al-Janahānī al-Maghribī, who described Kakudam, Takrur, and the salt mines, and Abu'l-Rabī' al-Multānī, who detailed the route between Sijilmassa and Ghana. About the same time, Ibn Sa'īd recorded information from Ibn Fātima, who had journeyed in the Sahara, the Sudan, and in East Africa. His information concerned the area near Chad and the Atlantic coast of the Sahara, as well as the caravan routes from Sijilmassa to Ghana.

The work of a pilgrim from Seville, Abu Bakr Muhammad Ibn al-'Arabī (1076–1148), is not extant, but is quoted by Ibn Khaldūn and al-Maqqarī. On his way to and from Mecca in 1096 he studied with 'ulama' and met men of letters in Syria, Baghdad, and Cairo. He returned to Seville after traveling for eight years and became one of the best-known Maliki jurists in Andalusia.

Ibn Jubayr (Abu'l-Husayn Muhammad ben Ahmad, 1140s–1217), the first traveler from the western lands of Islam whose *Rihla* survived, also became a model for the *Rihla* literary genre. Ibn Jubayr's account is precise, vivid, and full of interesting details, written in a style that is descriptive, picturesque, and elegant, yet unadorned. When serving as secretary to the governor of Granada in 1182, Ibn Jubayr was forced to drink seven cups of wine. The governor then rewarded him with seven cups of dinars, which he used to perform the *hajj*. Ibn Jubayr left Granada in February 1183. From Ceuta he embarked on a Genoese ship to Egypt. From Cairo he ascended the Nile by boat, then journeyed by camel to the port of 'Aydhab, where he crossed the Red Sea to the Hijaz. From Mecca he proceeded to Medina, where he joined the caravan of pilgrims to Baghdad. He continued to Aleppo and Damascus in Syria, journeying in the company of Muslim merchants to the crusader kingdom of Acre. He embarked with fifty Muslims on a Genoese ship, which also carried 2,000 Christian pilgrims returning from Jerusalem. The ship was shipwrecked near the shores of Sicily, then under the rule of the Christian Normans. From Sicily he took a ship back to Granada in April 1185, just over two years after his departure. Ibn Jubayr traveled on Christian ships and visited Christian states in crusader Acre and Norman Sicily. But even when he praised the Christian king of Sicily, who had helped to save both Christians and Muslims during the shipwreck, Ibn Jubayr felt it only proper to add: "May God save the Muslims from his misdeeds."

Al-Idrīsī (1100–1166) was nearly equal in fame to Ibn Jubayr as a traveler. He received his early education in Córdoba, and then journeyed in Europe and North Africa. He visited Asia Minor, southern France, and England. He also journeyed through Spain and Morocco. About 1138, he received an invitation from the Norman king Roger II (r. 1097–1154) to come to Palermo in Sicily, where he wrote his *magnum opus*. He presented new, authentic, and detailed information on Europe, the Mediterranean, northern Africa, west Asia and Central Asia, based on information provided by contemporary travelers. He described some regions of northern Europe that had not been mentioned by earlier geographers.

Abū Hāmid al-Gharnātī (1080–1170) was born in Granada and died in Damascus. He first traveled to Egypt in 1114. In 1117 he visited Sardinia, Sicily, Alexandria, and Cairo. He was in Baghdad between 1122 and 1126. In 1130, he was in Iran, and the next year he crossed the Caspian Sea and reached the mouth of the Volga. During this period he performed three journeys to Khwarazm. He was in Hungary in 1150, in Baghdad in 1160, and in Mosul in 1162. He died in Damascus in 1170. In addition to his personal observations he collected information from informants. In Cairo he met a person from the Hijaz who had spent forty years in India and China. A Muslim from Sicily he met in Baghdad provided information about volcanic activity of Mount Etna. His work became very popular because he combined historical facts with wonders. He saw the Pillars of Hercules near Gibraltar shortly before their destruction in 1145 and the obelisk at 'Ayn Shams, near Cairo, before its collapse in 1160.

Ibn Sa'id al-Maghribī (c. 1214–1274) was born near Granada and was educated in Seville. He spent most of his life traveling in search of knowledge. He accompanied his father to the *hajj* in 1240, and visited North Africa and Egypt. On the return journey his father died in Alexandria in 1242. He lived in Cairo until 1250, when he left for Syria and Iraq, staying in Mosul, Baghdad, and Basra. He then went to Aleppo and Damascus and again performed the *hajj*. In 1254 he was at the court of the ruler of Tunis. In 1267, he passed through Alexandria and Aleppo, traveling to Armenia to meet Hülegü Khân

# M

in person. He died in Damascus in 1274, according to one version, or in Tunis in 1286, according to another.

Abū Abdallāh Muhammad al-'Abdarī left his native country of Haha in 1289 and went to Mecca by land across the Maghrib. He described Qayrawan as a center of scholarship, where people from Andalusia and the Maghrib came to seek knowledge and to study crafts. He went back from Mecca through Palestine. Because of his concern with the state of Muslim scholarship, he was extensively quoted by Ibn Battūta, al-Balawī, and biographers, including Ahmad Bābā and Ibn al-Qādī, who found in his notes an important source for the intellectual history of the Maghrib.

Another pilgrim traveler, Al-Tijānī, left Tunis to perform the *hajj* in 1309. His *Rihla* contains additional information about all the regions he visited and about neighboring countries. Ibn Khaldūn considered his *Rihla* very valuable and referred to it frequently for the history of North Africa.

*Rihla* literature developed from the twelfth century as written reports of travelers from the Maghrib and Andalusia. In Spain, Muslims lived close to the Christians; they were forced to seek spiritual refreshment in areas where Islam was the majority culture. Traveling east, mainly to Mecca, was therefore particularly significant for Muslim intellectuals in Spain. As scholars and men of letters, these travelers had a special interest in religious and intellectual life.

The *rihla* literary genre reached its peak with Ibn Battūta. This important author was born in 1304 in Tangiers to a family of legal scholars. He set out for the pilgrimage in 1325, traveling from Tangiers to Alexandria, Cairo, and Syria, where he joined the pilgrims' caravan to Mecca. He made several sorties from Mecca; once to Iraq and Persia, later to Yemen and Aden, then by sea to the coast of East Africa. He returned to Mecca by way of Oman. He then traveled to Asia Minor and crossed the Black Sea to the territories of the Golden Horde in the western plains of Central Asia. From there he made a detour to visit Constantinople. Returning to the Asian steppes, he voyaged eastward through Transoxiana, Khurasan, and Afghanistan, arriving at the banks of the Indus River.

After an eight-year stint in India, most of it as a *qādī* (judge) in Delhi, he was appointed in 1341 by the sultan of Delhi to lead a delegation to the Mongol emperor of China. The expedition ended disastrously in a shipwreck off the southwestern coast of India. For just over two years, he traveled to southern India, Ceylon, and the Maldive Islands, where he served for eight months as a *qādī*. In 1345 he was resolved to go to China on his own. Journeying by sea, he visited Bengal, the coast of Burma, and Sumatra, then continued to Canton. The extent of his visit to China is uncertain, but was probably limited to the southern coastal region. He returned by way of southern India, the Persian Gulf, Baghdad, Syria, and Egypt. From Egypt he made the pilgrimage to Mecca for the last time.

Back in Alexandria, Ibn Battūta sailed to Tunis, where he took a Catalan ship to Sardinia and arrived in Fez via Algiers in 1349, twenty-five years after he had left Morocco. The following year he made a brief trip across the Straits of Gibralter to the Muslim kingdom of Granada. In 1353 he set out on his last journey, to the West African kingdom of Mali. He returned to Fez in 1355. By then he must have been closely associated with the Moroccan court, because before his departure to Mali, Ibn Battūta took leave from the sultan, and he was recalled by the sultan from Takedda.

In 1356, the sultan Abū 'Inān commissioned Ibn Juzayy, a young scholar, to record Ibn Battūta's travels. They worked together for two years. Ibn Battūta retired to a judicial post in a Moroccan provincial town and died in 1368. The younger Ibn Juzayy died before him, in 1356 or 1357, not yet thirty-seven years old.

Ibn Juzayy's task was to edit the traveler's story to conform to the literary standard of a *rihla*. He changed the original form of the eyewitness evidence (*'iyān*) of the traveler to make it part of a literary tradition in which the facts were adjusted to the requirements of scholarly prose and taste. Ibn Juzayy admits that he presented only an abridgment of Ibn Battūta's account. There is no direct evidence that Ibn Battūta ever read the complete manuscript or checked it for errors. Indeed, mistakes in the phonetic spelling of various foreign words suggest that he did not. Moreover, Ibn Juzayy took the liberty to enrich Ibn Battūta's account by drawing on earlier sources without acknowledging them. Sections of Ibn Battūta's *Rihla* on Palestine and Syria, for example, were borrowed from Ibn Jubayr and al-'Abdarī, and sections on Mali from al-'Umarī. Ibn Juzayy skillfully integrated those borrowings into Ibn Battūta's account.

Ibn Battūta seems to have been interested in Sufism, which in the fourteenth century was a central feature of the religious life of Muslims. Scholars like him were attracted to new Muslim communities beyond *Dār al-Islām*. Ibn Battūta could not have secured a prestigious religious post in the central lands of Islam but was appointed *qādī* in the Delhi sultanate.

Ibn Battūta has been hailed as the "Marco Polo of the Muslim world." Like Marco, but traveling some fifty years earlier, Ibn Battūta was able to undertake his extensive journey because the Turco-Mongol states facilitated the movement of merchandise and people. Marco Polo, however, was a stranger in the lands he visited, whereas Ibn Battūta was everywhere at home in the company of Muslims. Marco Polo's work is more accurate and precise in practical information on medieval China and other Asian lands, but Ibn Battūta traveled to more places, and his narrative offers details on almost every conceivable aspect of human life.

## BIBLIOGRAPHY

Chandra, Satish, ed. *The Indian Ocean: Explorations in History, Commerce, and Politics.* Delhi: Sage, 1987.

Constable, Olivia Remie. *Trade and Traders in Muslim Spain.* Cambridge: Cambridge UP, 1996.

Curtin, Philip D. *Cross-Cultural Trade in World History.* Cambridge and New York: Cambridge UP, 1984, pp. 109–135.

Dunn, Ross E. *The Adventures of Ibn Battuta.* Berkeley: U of California P, 1989.

Eickelman, Dale F., and James Piscatori, eds. *Muslim Travellers: Pilgrimage, Migration, and the Religious Imagination.* London: Routledge, and Berkeley: U of California P, 1990.

Ferrand, Gabriel. *Relation de voyages et textes géographiques arabes, persans et turks relatifs à l'Extrème Orient du 7e au 18e siècles.* Paris: Leroux, 1913–1914.

Hourani, George Fadlo. *Arab Seafaring in the Indian Ocean in Ancient and Early Medieval Times.* Princeton, NJ: Princeton UP, 1951.

Kowalska, Maria. "From Facts to Literary Fiction: Medieval Arabic Travel Literature." *Quaderni di Studi Arabi* 5–6 (1987–1988): 397–403.

Kramers, J.H. "Geography and Commerce." In *The Legacy of Islam.* Ed. Thomas Arnold and Alfred Guillaume. Oxford: Oxford UP, 1931, pp. 79–107.

Levtzion, Nehemia, and J.F.P. Hopkins. *Corpus of Early Arabic Sources for West African History.* Cambridge: Cambridge UP, 1981.

Maqbul Ahmad, Sayyid. *A History of Arab-Islamic Geography, 9th–16th Century.* Amman: Al al-Bayt University, 1995.

Miquel, André. *La géographie et géographie humaine dans la littérature arabe des origines à 1050.* Vol. 1 of *La géographie du monde musulman jusqu'au milieu du 11e siècle.* Paris: Mouton, 1967.

Nainar, Muhammad Husayn. *Arab Geographers' Knowledge of Southern India.* Madras, 1942; rpt. Frankfurt: Goethe University, 1993.

Netton, Ian Richard, ed. *Golden Roads: Migration, Pilgrimage and Travel in Mediaeval and Modern Islam.* Richmond, England: Curzon Press, 1993.

Tibbetts, Gerald Randall. *Arab Navigation in the Indian Ocean before the Coming of the Portuguese.* Oriental Translation Fund, n.s., 42. London: Royal Asiatic Society of Great Britain and Ireland, 1971.

———. *A Study of the Arabic Texts Containing Material on South-East Asia.* Leiden: Brill, 1979.

*Nehemia Levtzion*

## SEE ALSO
Acre; African Trade; al-Idrīsī; Baghdad; Bukhara; Byzantine Empire; Caspian Sea; Constantinople; Córdoba; Damascus; Egypt; Etna, Mount; Fātimids; Gold Trade in Africa; Golden Horde; Hülegü; Ibn Battūta, Abu Abdallah; Ibn Jubayr; Ibrahim Ibn Ya'qub al-Isrā'īlī; India; Indus; Marco Polo; Mecca; Medina; Red Sea; Russia and Rus'; Shi'ism; Sijilmassa; Silk Roads; Sindbad the Sailor; Women Travelers, Islamic

# N

## Nao

A generic Castilian term for a ship of medium burden, derived from the Catalan word *nau*. Though *nao* would, over time, gradually be applied to a particular type of vessel, by the end of the sixteenth century it was still a nondescript term for a merchant vessel.

The word first appears in the early thirteenth century and by the second half of the century is in common use. In the law code of Alfonso X (r. 1252–1284), the *Siete Partidas,* the *nao* is listed after the *nave* and the *carraca* in importance with respect to size, even though it is described as having the same number of masts. Even after the naval architecture revolution of the early fourteenth century, in which both the hull design and rigging of ships began to evolve rapidly, the term *nao* continued to be a generic word used simply to designate vessels of modest burden irrespective of the ship's hull design or the rigging type.

By the middle of the fifteenth century, the term *nao* had come to signify a ship of between 100 and 200 tons burden with a high freeboard, forecastle, and sterncastle. Moreover, the definition now included a full-rigged vessel carrying a foremast and main mast with square sails, and a mizzen mast rigged with a lateen sail. Though the high freeboard, broad beam, and deep hold that characterized these ships made them rather slow and gave them poor handling qualities, the large cargo capacity and high sides made *naos* ideal for long voyages in rough seas. After returning from rounding the Cape of Good Hope in 1488, Bartolomeu Dias recognized the inadequacy of his caravels for the long passage to India and helped design two *naos* for the voyage of Vasco da Gama. Probably the most famous *nao* was Columbus's *Santa Maria.* We have little information concerning the vessel other than that Columbus disliked her because, in his estimation, the ship was slow, handled poorly, and drew too much water to be a useful exploration vessel.

By the beginning of the sixteenth century, the *nao* was rapidly increasing in size, and by the end of the century it had a capacity of nearly 1,000 tons. These vessels carried much of the cargo on the *Carrera de Indias*—the large-scale transoceanic trade of Spain and Portugal—and in the course of the century evolved into the large, heavily armed merchant vessel known as the galleon. Yet, despite the increased specialization of ship types, the term *nao* continued to be used loosely to describe merchant vessels and even galleons.

**BIBLIOGRAPHY**

Jal, Auguste. *Glossaire Nautique.* Paris: Chez Fermin Didot Frères, 1848.

Phillips, Carla Rahn. "The Caravel and the Galleon." In *Cogs, Caravels and Galleons.: The Sailing Ship, 1000–1630.* Ed. Richard W. Unger. London: Conway Maritime Press, 1994, pp. 91–114.

Rubio Serrano, José. *Arquitectura de las Naos y Galeones de las Flotas de Indias (1492–1590).* Malaga, Spain: Ediciones Seyer, 1991.

Smith, Roger C. *Vanguard of Empire: Ships of Exploration in the Age of Columbus.* New York: Oxford UP, 1993.

*Lawrence V. Mott*

**SEE ALSO**

Alfonso X; Caravel; Columbus, Christopher; Da Gama, Vasco; Dias, Bartolomeu; Ships and Shipbuilding; Spain and Portugal

# N

## Naval Warfare

From antiquity through the Middle Ages, warfare at sea was conducted chiefly by means of oared vessels known as galleys, propelled by trained oarsmen. Rams were incorporated in the vessel's stem, jutting from the longitudinal structural timbers below the waterline, and made the ship a water-borne projectile. Once the ram had pierced the planking of an enemy vessel, it was designed to fracture so as not to endanger the ramming galley or others in the fleet. (Indeed, the technique was very ancient: a three-pronged bronze ram encompassing some of the ship's prow and dating to the Hellenic age was discovered at Athlit, Israel, in 1980). Once a vessel rammed an enemy ship, marines boarded and fought a hand-to-hand battle, a practice that continued until the fifteenth century, when ships were fitted with cannon.

Due to the inflammable nature of a vessal's sails and wooden structure, fire was an especially effective strategem, which could be unleashed from a distance by the shooting of fire arrows. The Byzantine historian Procopius (c. 499–565) describes the use of fire ships by the Vandals of North Africa against a Roman fleet anchored in a bay in 472. The Byzantine Empire extended the use of fire as an effective weapon at sea with the employment of "Greek fire" by the late seventh century. Its secret formula is thought to have included oil, naphtha or bitumen, quicklime, and saltpeter or potash; the material was discharged from siphons or in clay jars and ignited on contact, even burning on water. Though difficult to control and suitable only for certain environments, it was useful against Muslim raids like that in 655 at the Battle of Masts off the coast of Asia Minor, where Muslim tactics consisted of grappling enemy vessels and cutting their rigging and sails, rendering them helpless. Theophanes' *Chronicle* describes the effectiveness of Greek fire against such tactics in 678 during an Arab attack on Constantinople, and it was especially important in repelling an attack by two Arab fleets in 717–718.

The Roman emperor Justinian (r. 527–565) attempted to recover the western part of the Roman Empire through expeditions against the newly formed Germanic kingdoms. A major success in the ultimately failed effort was the defeat of the Vandal fleets that dominated the western Mediterranean. According to Procopius, the Byzantine fleet of 500 ships included ninety-two fast *dromons*, which he described as "single-banked ships covered by decks, in order that the men

Naval Battle at La Rochelle. Froissart, *Chronicles*, Deutsche Staatsbibliothek (Preussischer Kulturbesitz), MS Dep. Breslau 1, Vol. 2, fol. 48v, *c.* 1450. Courtesy Deutsche Staatsbibliothek, Berlin.

rowing them might if possible not be exposed to the bolts of the enemy."

Viking fleets from the north soon rivaled Byzantine fleets for control of the seas. Viking naval power relied on speed and mobility rather than bulk, even sailing up the rivers of eastern Europe. Viking ships from the ninth century exceeded seventy feet in length, carrying enough men and provisions under a single square sail to range across the Baltic and North seas, over the Atlantic to the Americas, and south into the Mediterranean. Their shallow draft, yet broad beam, and sturdy construction allowed them to navigate the northern seas as well as to strike inland along rivers and streams. Vikings did fight in the open sea, but more commonly they used their vessels to land them near to their targets. Axes, spears, and bows and arrows were used in combat at sea, which usually ended with grappling, boarding, and personal combat.

The Viking's Norman relatives conquered Sicily in the eleventh century. Aggressive and competent seafarers, they challenged all parties at sea. Ships were specially modified for war, particularly for the carriage of horses for chivalric warfare. This was accomplished at the invasion of Anglo-Saxon England by Duke William of Normandy in 1066. The Norman Robert Guiscard (c. 1015–1085) also placed cavalry aboard ships for amphibious assaults in Italy. These tactics were employed by crusaders at several Muslim port cities during the Crusades, notably in the thirteenth century.

Rising naval powers in the Mediterranean beginning in the tenth century included the Italian city-states of Venice and Genoa. Contending for the lucrative trade to the East in silk, spices, and precious metals, they cooperated—and fought—to control this trade. Both states built armed traders and warships. Venetian galleys constructed at the Arsenal, the city's shipbuilding center, plied both the Mediterranean Sea and the Atlantic Ocean. The Venetians and Genoese played major roles in the transport of crusaders to the eastern Mediterranean; they also fought, as well as traded, with Muslims. For the period after 1250, Western Europe possessed superior naval forces due to the construction of new and larger sailing vessels.

Venice and Genoa fought a series of wars after 1253 that featured major fleet engagements in the open sea. Tactics employed by the Genoese included holding a hidden reserve of ships to advance at the opportune moment. Venetian great galleys 120 feet in length and fifteen feet in beam could carry more than 130 tons. The large sailing ships included two-masted lateen-rigged vessels. During the fourteenth century the successful northern European cog influenced the development of a Mediterranean caravel-built vessel with a single square sail like its counterpart. The cocha was a bulk carrier capable of carrying several hundred tons of cargo in its deep, wide hull. The cog employed the sternpost rudder mounted on the stempost and controlled by a tiller in place of a single- or dual-side steering oar. Men positioned in the stem- and sterncastles integrated within the hull lines, or at the topcastle, were well positioned to rain arrows, crossbow bolts, lances, or heavy stones or other objects on their attackers.

By the later Middle Ages, the development of larger sailing ships—often clinker-built (lapstrake planking),

generally of oak—such as hulks, cogs, caravels, and carracks changed the nature of warfare at sea. These larger vessels were not built to be rowed like galleys, but were pure sailing ships. Vessels represented on the seals of port towns throughout northern Europe illustrate these developments. Hulks and cogs were constructed with a main deck and propelled by a square sail supported by a single mast. In the thirteenth century, the line of the deck was modified by the addition of a forecastle (fo'c'sle) and sterncastle. A topcastle was added to the mast. These castles were initially added to merchant vessels to convert them into men-of-war. Bowmen and soldiers (marines) were positioned in the castles—which often had protective crenelations like those in contemporary military architecture—to fight. The height gained from such structures was an advantage in combat at sea, for arrows and other projectiles could be directed at those exposed on enemy decks below. Stones and iron bars were thrown from the topcastle onto the decks of the enemy, usually after the ships had grappled for boarding. Combat at sea was brutal and frequently fatal for the defeated marines and crew, who faced a watery grave. At sea, there was neither concealment nor escape

Larger ships purpose-built for sailing were capable of carrying greater numbers of marines and armaments used in ship-to-ship combat. Arbalests to hurl stones or arrows at the enemy were employed, but they doubtless proved of limited value on a pitching sea. The longbow produced less structural damage but was probably more effective against crews. Crossbows were also effective antipersonnel weapons since their short bowspan and deadly accuracy at short range enabled archers, from the vantage point of the ship's castles, to remain hidden while directing their bolts at officers or key crew members. Armor was worn by medieval knights to fight aboard ship. Numerous illustrations indicate that some of the same armament employed ashore was used at sea. Yet this protection could prove a liability since once over the side, an armor-clad soldier seldom resurfaced.

The Crusades, as well as local wars, prompted large-scale naval operations such as Richard the Lionheart's expedition by sea from the English Channel to the Holy Land, sailing along the Atlantic coast of Europe and into the Mediterranean, where Richard defeated Saladin's fleet near Acre in 1191. Such fleets numbered in the hundreds of vessels on occasion; Edward I raised about 300 ships in 1297 for an expedition to transport 5,800 soldiers to the Continent. The ships used to transport men, supplies, and horses to the Holy Land, especially, required extensive logistical preparation, while amphibious offensive operations, such as the transport and use of war machines to besiege walled fortifications and cities, demanded a specialized naval technology. For example, trumpets were used to signal fleet movements in close ordered formations in addition to the relay of orders by human voice. At night, lanterns served to identify ships and to signal orders.

The Hundred Years' War (1337–1453) required the construction and deployment of large fleets by the French and English as well as their allies. The first naval engagement of the war was the battle of Sluys in 1340. The chronicler Jean Froissart (*c.* 1337–*c.* 1404) states that the French had 260 ships ready at the town of Sluys at the mouth of the river Zwyn. They were prepared to carry an invasion force to England, but Edward III learned of their plans and sailed with a large fleet. The surprised French chained their ships together in the harbor as the English attacked with the wind, tide, and sun at their backs, and the French were caught in the harbor; their inability to maneuver resulted in several groundings and the demise of their invasion plans. The victorious English ships consisted of various types, arranged in three ranks, with troopships supported by vessels carrying archers. Large cogs served as key vessels, including the *Thomas*, the royal flagship. The victorious attackers made the most of their advantage, and French plans for invasion ended in the harbor of Sluys. A decade later at the battle of L'Espagnols-sur-Mer, fought in the English Channel, the English defeated a Castilian fleet.

Technological changes in ship construction in the fifteenth century included the adaptation of vessels to accommodate cannon and other guns. The large caravel-built three-masted carrack carried square sails on the fore and main mast and a lateen sail on the mizzen. Later variants added additional masts and sails. Cargoes of 1,000 tons or greater fit into the multidecked hull. More powerful and maneuverable than ever, these full-rigged ships anticipated the construction of the first true battleships after 1500. The finest existing example of such a ship is Henry VIII's *Mary Rose*, constructed in 1510 with gunports piercing her side planking. The Tudor warship sank with great loss of life while facing a French fleet entering the Solent in 1545;

discovered in the 1970s, she was raised in 1982 for display at the Portsmouth dockyard.

**BIBLIOGRAPHY**

Anderson, R.C. *Oared Fighting Ships: From Classical Times to the Coming of Steam.* Kings Langley: Argus, 1976.

Haywood, John. *Dark Age Naval Power: A Reassessment of Frankish and Anglo-Saxon Seafaring Activity.* London: Conway Maritime Press, 1994.

Hutchinson, Gillian. *Medieval Ships and Shipping.* Rutherford, NJ: Fairleigh Dickinson UP, 1994.

Lewis, Archibald R., and Timothy J. Runyan. *European Naval and Maritime History, 350–1500.* Bloomington: Indiana UP, 1985.

Pryor, John H. *Geography, Technology, and War: Studies in the Maritime History of the Mediterranean, 649–1571.* Cambridge: Cambridge UP, 1988.

Unger, Richard W., ed. *Cogs, Caravels, and Galleons: The Sailing Ship, 1000–1630.* London: Conway Maritime Press, 1994.

*Timothy J. Runyan*

**SEE ALSO**

Acre; Caravel; Cog; Froissart, Jean; Genoa; Gunpowder; Hulk; Navigation; Navigation, Viking; Ships and Shipbuilding; Venice

## Navigation

The study of medieval navigation divides itself naturally into two geographic areas, the Mediterranean Sea and the Atlantic Ocean; and into two periods defined by the available technology, before and after the introduction of the magnetic compass as a marine instrument.

Early medieval navigation in the Mediterranean was heavily influenced by classical technology and tradition. At the height of its power and prosperity, Rome had required a wide variety of goods from the entire Mediterranean area, most of them brought by sea. Roman trade also attracted luxury materials from the Red Sea and Indian Ocean. The former brought into being a maritime competence that served not only Rome but also trade between the provinces. The Red Sea–Indian Ocean commerce brought with it an awareness of a larger world of oceanic trade and the maritime technology associated with it.

Rome's decline reduced the demand for these goods, but the maritime technology was not lost. The routes were known if less traveled, and the large ships used in the Egyptian grain trade—with a length of up to 180 feet, a beam of forty-five feet, and a depth of forty-four feet—were replaced by smaller craft.

The rise of the Byzantine Empire as the hub of the eastern Mediterranean world meant a diminished reliance on maritime trade since Constantinople was served by a vast hinterland to the north with a convenient network of rivers as avenues of supply. Nevertheless, Byzantium did attract maritime trade and was served primarily by ships from Syria and Italian cities including Venice, Naples, Amalfi, and Salerno. Byzantium, of course, had its own fleet of merchant and naval vessels, probably of a light galley type carrying a lateen sail.

The lateen sail, most likely introduced from the Red Sea, was a triangular sheet mounted on either one or two masts. Combined with oars, it powered the galley, which became the dominant ship in the Mediterranean during the medieval period. It was basic to the commerce of the Italian cities and also as a warship against the Muslim fleets, which came to dominate Mediterranean shipping west of the Adriatic from the eighth to the eleventh centuries. The Muslim ships did not vary significantly from their European rivals, all of them adapting to the peculiar needs of the region.

The primary need was for a ship with speed and maneuverability, designed for coastal and inland sailing and adaptable to both commercial and military use. Ships of this type enabled Venice, Genoa, and Pisa, while often contending with each other, to dominate the sea trade from the Bosporus to the Straits of Gibraltar; these cities eventually established colonial outposts in the Black and Caspian seas, where they received Asiatic products and distributed them in Mediterranean trade.

In concurrent use with the galley was a heavier sailing ship that owed much to its Roman predecessors. Powered by square sails mounted on one or two masts, it had little superstructure forward but a high stern. Caravel-planked (that is, with planks laid edge to edge) and steered by a side rudder, this slow but commodious ship was used for transporting horses during the Crusades. Its maneuverability was improved by the addition of a lateen sail, probably the result of Arab influence.

The required knowledge for a Mediterranean pilot in this precompass period was primarily the ability to recognize important landmarks along the route, to estimate distances, and to make soundings to determine depth. Tides were not a significant factor within the Mediterranean. Accumulated knowledge about landmarks and the distances and directions between them was gathered in portolan charts (*portolani*), which were essentially coastal guides, and in *isolarii*, which detailed points of importance among the islands of the Mediterranean. In their earlier forms, these instructions were written texts without a cartographical component.

Voyages out of sight of land required more sophisticated navigational skills. Such voyages would normally be between familiar points, and the navigator would plot his course by wind rose compass. This device was based on the direction of named winds, the circle of the horizon being divided since ancient times into eight or twelve wind directions, and into as many as thirty-two by the thirteenth century. Courses were also plotted by the direction of the sun and the North Star. These techniques were adequate for navigating within the Mediterranean and along the Atlantic seaboard of Europe before the invention of the magnetic compass. In this coastal sailing, the Mediterranean sailors encountered the oceanic navigational skills and maritime techniques developed by the Irish and Scandinavians over a long period.

The earliest medieval European seafarers upon the Atlantic Ocean were Irish monks whose monastic traditions included searching the ocean for places of solitude for individuals and for island sites on which to establish monastic communities. While these voyages are shrouded in legend and sparsely documented, and while the precise extent of their geographic range is unclear, it is certain that Irish monastic voyaging took place between the fifth and ninth centuries.

Drawing on a very ancient technology of leather boats or coracles used by fishermen and transporters of goods in coastal and inland sailing, Irish builders of the long-distance seagoing *curach* brought it to the height of its development in the sixth to eighth centuries. The *curach* was made of ox hides sewn together and stretched over a wooden or wickerwork structure. It had a keel, a steering device, and a mast carrying a sail. It could also be propelled by oars. No exemplar has survived from medieval times, so the dimensions of the ocean-going *curach* are unknown, but one literary source describes a corach carrying seventeen men with provisions for forty days, which suggests a craft of some sixty feet with a beam of twenty feet.

# N

In these boats, and some possibly in vessels built entirely of wood, Irish monks established themselves at Iona (*c.* 563) and other islands off the west coast of Scotland from which they steadily ventured farther abroad. They were in the Orkney Islands by the latter half of the sixth century, and by the end of the seventh were settled in the Faeroe Islands, bringing with them sheep, which became the dominant resource in the islands' economy. By the late eighth century, and possibly earlier, Irish monks had established themselves in Iceland, where they remained for more than a century before being driven out by Norse invasion and settlement.

Beyond these voyages, for which archaeological or literary evidence exists, there were others whose outcome is unknown, but for which literary references suggest a wider knowledge of the Atlantic. The most famous representative of such voyages is St. Brendan (*c.* 484–578), undoubtedly a voyager of considerable reputation in his own time, and one to whom the voyages of many other seekers of remote islands were subsequently attributed. The literary sources for St. Brendan's travels are the *Navigatio Sancti Brendani* and the *Vita Sancti Brendani,* both dating from the tenth century. Some readers of these sources believe they indicate Irish awareness of and visits to Greenland and Jan Mayen Island in the north and the Canary Islands and West Indies to the south.

Another literary source for Irish monastic voyages is Adamnan, abbot of Iona, whose *Vita Sancti Columbae,* surviving in a manuscript written before 713, contains more than a dozen references to islands known to and visited by Irish monks. The *Litany of Oengus* also lists ten sixth-century voyages that recruited from 10 to 150 participants. Another voyage recorded in the Irish *imrama* (accounts of sea travels) is that of Máel Dúin, which was probably first written down in the seventh or eighth century, reporting islands with trees, fruit, and berries. The Irish also used sea voyages as a penance, and banishment to the sea as a form of punishment. For example, in the tenth-century account of their voyage, Snedgus and Mac Riagla report finding men who had been exiled to a remote island for the murder of a king.

The information from these voyages, and undoubtedly from others of which no evidence has survived, was incorporated into *De Mensura orbis terrarum,* written about 825 by Dicuil, an Irish scholar at the court of Charlemagne. This is the nearest thing to a systematic geography to come from this period of Irish history.

Dicuil claimed to have lived on some islands to the north of Ireland and to have read of others. He described the position of the sun at Thule (Iceland) during the summer solstice from the experience of monks there who had reported it to him. Dicuil also alluded to islands to the south of Ireland, but without specific geographical details.

Neither charts for plotting or recording courses nor instruments for determining position at sea have survived from medieval Irish navigation; nor is there any mention of charts or instruments in the literary sources. It is unlikely that either charts or instruments were part of Irish maritime technology. Rather, it is probable that these voyages were guided by experience at sea over time: awareness of the direction of prevailing winds by season, the observed oceanic currents and color of the water in different places, the feeding grounds of whales and shoals of fish, and, most important, the flights of birds in their seasonal migrations and their homing instincts when not migrating. Their direction led navigators to islands and their presence there assured a supply of food on shore for the seagoing monks.

The period of Irish oceanic sailing was brought to a close in the ninth century by the emergence in the North Atlantic of the Vikings, who possessed a superior maritime technology. The "Viking Age," from the late eighth to the late eleventh century, saw Scandinavian seafaring in the North Atlantic surpass anything accomplished by the Irish. While the Scandinavians learned from Irish knowledge of the ocean, their early development of maritime skills was entirely separate from the Irish.

The typical Scandinavian ships of the medieval period evolved from a prehistoric type of craft made of planks fastened to ribs with lashings and caulked with resin. They were propelled by oars. By the fourth century such ships had a length of seventy to eighty feet and sometimes up to one hundred, and a beam of ten and a half feet but without a true keel. They were in coastal service and helped to make the Scandinavians a commercial presence in the Baltic region and along the Frisian, Netherlandish, and Frankish coasts, where they were drawn by the opportunity to trade with the Frankish Empire as well as by the threat of northward expansion of the Franks. Items in trade from the north included furs, walrus tusks, and amber, all luxuries in high demand, originally in Rome and subsequently among the Franks.

This trade also exposed Scandinavian seamen to much more sophisticated vessels, and particularly to the use of the sail; southern merchants brought both goods and maritime technology to the Baltic. The earliest use of sails by Scandinavian ships cannot be established, but they were certainly employed by the eighth century and possibly earlier. The advantage of sails for long-distance navigation is obvious. During the early eighth century Scandinavian long-distance navigation began with Norse voyages to the Shetland and Orkney islands, reaching distances of some 250 to 300 miles (400 to 500 km) from the coast of Norway. They reached the more distant Faeroe Islands later in the eighth century, leading to the colonization of those islands and the departure of the resident Irish monks. Norse colonization of the Shetlands and Orkneys also occurred about 800. Thus began a time of raiding, conquest, and settlement.

The islands to the west of Scotland were raided and settled in the late eighth and early ninth centuries. Ireland was pillaged during the first three decades of the ninth century, and from bases there the Vikings raided the coasts of England, France, Spain, and Portugal, with trade and settlement often following initial contact. They sailed inland as well, up the Seine to Paris in 845, and into the Thames to London in 851.

Knowledge of Iceland undoubtedly came to the Vikings through their contact with the Irish in the Faeroes and the western Scottish islands. They would have needed only to follow the information about distance and direction that was provided to them. The first Scandinavian visitor to Iceland was most likely a Swede named Garðar who circumnavigated the island in about 860–861, spending the winter on its northern coast. Others followed with voyages of exploration and, shortly thereafter, of settlement, so that within sixty years all usable land had been claimed. This settlement came from both the Scottish islands and Ireland, as well as the Norwegian mainland. It involved transporting livestock and supplies as well as immigrants, since production of grazing animals was to become the major industry in Iceland's economy.

The predominant type of ship in the Vikings' commercial, colonial, and piratical enterprise was the *knarr*, which made possible long-distance ocean sailing with the necessary cargoes for trade and settlement. The *knarr* was distinguished from the *langskip*, which was employed more in coastal sailing. Both types were masted and carried a single sail, although they also were fitted with oars. The incorporation of the keel by the early eighth century, together with the mast and sail

about the same time, were primary factors accounting for long-distance sailing on the open sea. The typical *knarr* was about sixty-five feet long with a beam of about twelve feet; it rode deeper in the water than the *langskip,* which had greater length and beam dimensions by ten feet and three feet, respectively. The *knarr* carried a square sail that could be raised and lowered by a halyard and shortened to accommodate strong winds. Originally able to sail before the wind only, the *knarr* subsequently was outfitted with a tacking boom that vastly improved its sailing efficiency. Steering was accomplished by a side rudder attached to the starboard toward the rear of the ship.

By the tenth century, when Iceland was being settled, the *knarr* was a ship of from forty to fifty tons, carrying a crew of perhaps thirty with their gear and cargo for trade, or people and equipment for settlement. It could reach the Shetland Islands from Norway in two or three days. The direct voyage from Norway to Iceland might average two weeks with good sailing, although it could take much longer. The unique quality of this type of ship was its flexibility due to its construction with overlapping planks (clinker-built) lashed to the ribs, which enabled the craft to give with the stress of the sea. Nevertheless, the ocean voyage was fraught with danger, and it must be assumed that many ships were lost. In some instances ships were driven to unintended destinations, and this indeed broadened the areas of ocean known to Scandinavian seamen. Such was the case with the discovery of Greenland.

Sometime between 900 and 930, Gunnbjorn Ulf-Krakason, en route from Norway to Iceland, was storm-driven past his destination and sighted islands off the coast of Greenland at about 65 degrees north latitude. He did not land but returned to Iceland. The existence of those islands remained a part of Icelandic maritime knowledge, and in 982, Eirik [Eiri] the Red made Gunnbjorn's islands his destination. The distance from Iceland was some 450 miles (725 km). Eirik followed the Greenland coast southward and rounded Cape Farewell, settling just to the northwest of it, where he remained for three years. Returning to Iceland, he gathered a group of settlers, some of whom moved farther up the western coast of Greenland to form a new settlement. Thus, by the late 980s, European navigation had extended into the northern part of the Western Hemisphere, bringing settlement, commerce, and religion to that remote region for more than four centuries.

# N

The first half of this period was a time of abnormally warm temperatures, which made navigation in the far north relatively easy. After 1200, the sea ice along Greenland's coast and icebergs farther out to sea became a formidable test for the maritime technology then available, and sailings between Iceland and Greenland became less frequent, leading to the demise of the Greenland colony late in the fifteenth or early in the sixteenth century.

The colony's existence, however, had in the meantime led to further exploration and navigation in the North Atlantic. In 986, just as Greenland was being colonized, a ship captained by Bjárni Herjólfsson intending for Greenland was driven southward by a storm; the men sighted land on the Labrador coast but did not go ashore (for which Bjárni was criticized). Following the coast northward, Bjárni and his crew reached Greenland, inspiring Eirik the Red's son Leif to follow the route in reverse, leading to the discovery of "Vinland," now known to be Newfoundland. An exploring voyage by Leif's brother Thorvald followed, as did a colonizing expedition, but the colony lasted less than two years.

It is unlikely that the Vinland voyages lasted beyond the first decade of the eleventh century, but voyages to "Markland," the forested coast of Labrador, undoubtedly continued in response to the need for wood in Greenland. In any event, the whole episode of trans-Atlantic settlement gave to Scandinavia a knowledge of the North Atlantic, its coasts, and its islands between approximately 50 and 70 degrees north latitude. Navigation within this range was generally from island to island, and not across great distances, but it was supported by a rudimentary art of navigation that was primarily dependent on sea knowledge gained through long experience rather than on instruments.

Some of this sea knowledge is recorded in the *Konungs Skuggsjá* (*King's Mirror*), the earliest known exemplar of which dates from the thirteenth century, but which surely brings together knowledge gathered over the previous five centuries. Among its concerns are the maintenance of ships and equipment as well as the best seasons for sailing in particular seas (readers are encouraged to avoid long voyages between early October and late spring).

The basic skill of Viking sailors was dead reckoning—estimating direction and distance sailed. Yet the ocean they sailed was often beset with fogs and squalls, making this method inexact, and the sagas record many instances of ships being temporarily lost or missing their intended destinations. Though few records survive, undoubtedly many ships were lost at sea.

In order to determine direction so as to set a course, sailors observed the height of the sun and stars—which varied in their locations at particular times and places. Distances were measured in terms of a day's sailing, which could mean twelve or twenty-four hours. Although few written instructions have survived, there must have been well-understood guides for sailing between Norway and Iceland, from Iceland to Greenland, and among the islands of the North Sea. In addition to distance and direction, such instructions would have required an elementary understanding of astronomy: the use of the polestar as an indicator of latitude, in terms not of degrees on a grid (a method of charting unknown to medieval Scandinavians) but of relative position north and south to places known. Similarly, observing either the height of the sun at midday by the length of shadow cast by the mast (or by a "sun board" used for this purpose) or the azimuthal location of the sun on the horizon at sunrise or sunset would have indicated north-south position. These practices would have been learned first, and over a long period of time, on the extensive north-south coastline of Norway. This knowledge was expanded by voyages southward to England, a matter of some ten degrees latitude, the same ten degrees that separated the settlements of southern Greenland from Vinland.

To these elementary navigational techniques the Scandinavians added observation of the natural history of the ocean. This included sightings of birds in migration and the latitudinal range of species not in migration. The color of and currents in the ocean may have been indicators of location learned through long experience. Drift ice would have been a sign of proximity to the Greenland coast. Reflection off the Greenland ice cap, seen above the horizon, would have announced the land to a mariner well out to sea. Fishing shoals, feeding grounds of whales, or prevalence of seaweed may also have been guides to one landfall or another.

At some point the use of the magnetic compass was added to these basic navigational skills. Thormodus Torfaeus, in his *Historia Rerum Norvegicarum* (1711) states that in 1213, Snorri Sturluson was rewarded with a box containing a mariner's compass for a poem he had written on the death of Sweden's Count Byerges. This would have been quite possible, since sailors in southern Europe were using the compass by the 1100s, but it is not evidence that the instrument was widely known in the thirteenth century.

Knowledge of the magnetic properties of the lodestone, a naturally occurring iron oxide or magnetite, goes back to ancient times, but its direction-indicating characteristic was not known in Western culture until the eleventh or twelfth century. Once acquired it was quickly put to maritime use. The compass was also known to the Chinese in the eleventh century, but there is no record of its transfer to Europe.

Guyot de Provins (fl. 1184–1210), noted that a needle rubbed on a lodestone and placed on (or in) a hollow straw that would float it on water would always point north. In the thirteenth century, Jacques de Vitry, Vincent of Beauvais, Albertus Magnus, Roger Bacon, and Dante, among others, noted its use. Petrus Peregrinus de Marincourt in 1269 wrote in detail about the construction of a compass and its use in finding direction. The floating needle (or "wet" compass) was replaced in the thirteenth century by a needle mounted on a pivot. The use of the compass invited greater precision in the design of the wind rose, which in the thirteenth-century Mediterranean navigator's equipment had sixty-four points, with winds named from combinations of half-winds and quarter-winds. Thus at night or on cloudy days direction could be established reliably for the navigator who had no land reference to go by. The magnetic compass led to the refinement of sailing instructions and to portolan and marine charts in which bearings were described or drawn. This information came together in a work titled *Compasso de Navigare* (about 1250), which laid out bearings and distances between ports throughout the Mediterranean, noting also soundings and anchorages, landmarks, and hazards. In 1295, a Majorcan, Raymond Lully (not to be confused with Ramon Lull) wrote an *Arte de Navegar* that mentions needle, astrolabe, and sea charts in use by Majorcan and Barcelonian sailors of his time.

The marine astrolabe came into use at about the same time as the marine compass. This instrument had its origins in the planispheric astrolabe, which was employed by land-based astronomers for measuring the altitude of the sun and stars. It was also used for measuring heights and distances and for telling time. It appears to have come into Europe via the Arabs' invasion of Spain. In adapting it to marine use, Europeans converted it from wood to metal in both the planc and the alidade through which the astral object was sighted. This gave greater stability in taking observations at sea.

The same function of determining elevation could be accomplished with the quadrant or cross-staff, which coexisted with the astrolabe. The quadrant was a quarter-circle made of metal, with small holes bored along the straight edge and a plumb line fastened to the apex. The curved edge was graduated from one to ninety degrees. Sighting the polestar through the holes and noting where the plumb line fell on the graduated scale, the navigator could determine his distance north or south of a particular point, logically the point of departure. The cross-staff was a simple graduated three-foot wooden staff with a movable crosspiece fitted to it. Aligning the eye with the horizon along the staff and the apex of the crosspiece with the polestar gave a reading on the scale indicating relative position north or south of a familiar place.

The alternative to the polestar for determining latitude was the sun's altitude—its angular distance at midday from the celestial equator. Since this varies from day to day through the year, tables charting this mathematical relationship had to be constructed for the navigator's reference. Arab and Jewish mathematicians were instrumental in applying the necessary mathematical techniques to this problem. The *Alfonsine Tables,* named for King Alfonso X of Castile, were an early prototype of this navigational aid and were widely used in the Mediterranean world. The general revival of interest in mathematics during the thirteenth century produced methods that enabled seamen to calculate distance made good along a bearing. Late in the century the Catalan scholar Ramon Lull, in his *Arbor Scientiae,* taught the use of a table to calculate the angle between the true course of a ship and the course actually sailed.

These advances in navigational technique were instrumental in the expansion of commerce that took Mediterranean ships regularly beyond the Straits of Gibraltar, drawn primarily by the trade in wool and woolen cloth that centered on Flanders and Brabant and reached as far north as Novgorod. It was fundamental to the rise in northern Europe of the Hanseatic towns, which were dominant in north European maritime trade from the twelfth to the end of the fifteenth century.

Exposure of Mediterranean shipping to North Atlantic sailing traditions and techniques resulted in a melding of maritime technologies by the fifteenth century. The northern ship, the cog, was usually a single-masted ship, square-rigged, clinker-built in the

Scandinavian tradition, wide-bottomed, and operating with less than half the crew required of a Mediterranean galley of similar tonnage. The cog depended entirely on its sails for power at sea, and it was equipped with defensive towers (castles) fore and aft—positions of height for bowmen. Shallow and clumsy but economically efficient, it appealed to Mediterranean merchants, who brought it into usage there but did not give up the galley, which continued in coastal and inland sailing. The Mediterranean sailors gradually modified the square-rigger from the Atlantic, adding masts and lateen-type sails to permit greater maneuverability. The northern sailors saw these advantages and adopted them also in the fourteenth and early fifteenth centuries. These adaptations progressed through the fifteenth century, many of them resulting from Portuguese exploration of the west coast of Africa under the direction of Prince Henry the Navigator (1394–1460). Following the conquest of Ceuta on the Moroccan coast in 1415, Henry initiated a series of exploratory voyages that continued until his death in 1460. Cape Bojador was rounded in 1435; Rio de Ouro was reached in 1441, and Cape Verde in 1448. The momentum continued after Henry's death: the equator was crossed in 1473, the mouth of the Congo was reached in 1483, and four years later, the Cape of Good Hope was rounded by a storm-driven expedition led by Bartolomeu Dias,who revealed an ocean passage to India.

These were not coasting voyages. Sailing well out to sea, reaching the desired latitude, and then following it to land required new technologies and skills, including the development of ships capable of handling heavy seas and techniques for navigating beyond the equator, out of sight of the familiar polestar.

The common ship for coastal sailing in the early fifteenth century was the caravel, which emerged primarily from Mediterranean and Arab design: it was two-masted, and the foremast carried a lateen sail. As it developed in response to oceanic sailing, it carried three masts and could be lateen or square-rigged. The hull was long, usually seventy feet to eighty feet and possibly up to one hundred feet, with a beam one-fourth to one-third its length. With a low forecastle and low hull the caravel was designed for speed and maneuverability. Its displacement was about 120 tons.

Experience on the high seas demonstrated the caravel's vulnerability in heavy weather, and it was unable to carry large cargoes. For commercial use, the *nao* came into service. This design was not significantly different from that of the contemporary carrack. These ships were three-masted, with the two foremasts rigged square, and the rear (mizzen) mast lateen. They had a length of about one hundred feet and a beam of about thirty-eight feet, with displacement of 400 tons, possibly more. These two types—caravel and *nao* or carrack—dominated the fifteenth-century voyages of the Portuguese and Spanish, and were models for other countries, although western and northern shipmasters devised many adaptations to accommodate particular needs.

Navigating beyond the familiar skies of the Northern Hemisphere required new means for determining latitude. The loss of the polestar as a reference point forced sailors to rely more heavily on the sun to determine latitude. By observing the sun's position at its meridian and the relationship of that position to the celestial equator, and by using mathematical tables of declination, the navigator could determine latitude. The mathematics involved in such calculations was beyond the learning of sailors, so in 1484, King John II of Portugal convened a group of scholars to work out the mathematics in such a way as to provide a guide. They relied principally on the work of Jewish astronomer Abraham Zacuto of Salamanca, who had, in the previous decade, produced a set of tables of declination. The *Regimento do Astrolabio e do Quadrante* resulted from these efforts; though not published until 1509, it was undoubtedly in use in the last two decades of the fifteenth century.

These fifteenth-century improvements in marine technology coincided with studies in geography and cosmography that focused on the size and composition of the earth. The works of Strabo (*c.* 64 B.C.E.–*c.* 23 C.E.) and Ptolemy (fl. 127–145 C.E.), originally written in Greek, were translated into Latin and by 1470 were available in printed form. These, with other classical works, became the basis for a revision of the world geographical view. The thirteenth-century travels of Marco Polo, and the fifteenth-century account of Niccolò dei Conti's voyage to Asia and to the Spice Islands were used in estimating the eastward extension of Asia and its adjacent islands. These studies led to the conclusion by Paolo dal Pozzo Toscanelli (1397–1482), a Florentine scholar, that the coast of China lay some 5,000 miles west of Spain, with Japan 1,500 miles (2,415 km) nearer. Toscanelli was wrong in his estimate of the earth's size and of the eastward extension of Asia, but an

N

oceanic voyage of this distance with the marine technology available by the last decades of the fifteenth century was a credible undertaking. A globe made in 1492 by Martin Behaim (c.1459–1507) showed the Atlantic Ocean to be only slightly wider than Columbus's calculation of it, which was approximately 2,700 miles (4,345 km) between the Canary Islands and Japan, directly west along the twenty-eighth degree of latitude. The convergence of navigational capability and this erroneous concept of the distance between Europe and Asia led to Columbus's first voyage, which began the modern age of maritime trade and exploration.

**BIBLIOGRAPHY**

Ashe, Geoffrey. *Land to the West: St. Brendan's Voyage to America.* New York: Viking, 1962.

Cassidy, Vincent H. *The Sea around Them: The Atlantic Ocean, A.D. 1250.* Baton Rouge: Louisiana State UP, 1968.

Jones, Gwyn. *The Norse Atlantic Saga.* London: Oxford UP, 1964.

Marcus, G.J. "The Navigation of the Norsemen." *Mariner's Mirror* 39 (1953): 112–131.

———. *The Conquest of the North Atlantic.* New York: Oxford UP, 1981.

Parry, John Horace. "The Conditions of Discovery." Part 1 of *The Age of Reconnaissance.* London: Weidenfeld and Nicolson, 1963; rpt. Berkeley: U. of California P, 1981.

Pirenne, Henri. "The Revival of Commerce." In *Economic and Social History of Medieval Europe.* New York: Harcourt Brace, 1963, Chap. 1.

Sawyer, Peter. *The Age of the Vikings.* New York: St. Martin's, 1972.

Taylor, E.G.R. *The Haven-Finding Art: A History of Navigation from Odysseus to Captain Cook.* London: Hollis and Carter, 1956.

*John Parker*

**SEE ALSO**

Adamnan; Albertus Magnus; Alfonso X; Amalfi; Behaim, Martin; Bojador, Cape; Brendan's Voyage, St.; Brittany and Navigational Charts; Byzantine Empire; Canary Islands; Caravel; Carrack; Caspian Sea; Cog; Columbus, Christopher; Compass, Magnetic; Dante Alighieri; Dias, Bartolomeu; Dicuil; Galley; Genoa; Hanse, The; Henry the Navigator; Iceland; *Imrama;* Irish Travel; Jacques de Vitry; *King's Mirror, The; Knarr; Langskip;* Lodestone; Lull, Ramon; Marco Polo; *Nao;* Navigation, Arab; Pisa; Portolan Charts; Ptolemy; Red Sea; Thule; Toscanelli, Paolo dal Pozzo; Venice; Viking Discoveries and Settlements; Vincent of Beauvais; Vinland Sagas

## Navigation, Arab

A tradition known mainly from Arabic sailing instructions for various parts of the Indian Ocean and practiced also in the Red Sea. Extant nautical manuals were composed in the late fifteenth and early sixteenth centuries (by Ahmad ibn Mājid and Sulaymān al-Mahrī), but south Arabians were known to dominate shipping in the western Indian Ocean before the rise of Islam in the seventh century C.E. Sailing routes connecting Arabia with Egypt, East Africa, and India are described in the Greek *Peryplus of the Erithrean Sea* (first century C.E.). In addition to Arabs, subsequent centuries saw Persians, Indians, Malays, and Africans from the Horn and northern Swahili coasts participate in transoceanic shipping as shipowners, captains, merchants, and sailors.

Under the Abbasid caliphate (750–1258 C.E.) oceanic trade revived and expanded to an unprecedented degree, reaching as far as southeast Africa and south China, and promoting conversion to Islam among indigenous coastal populations. From Aden the way to Africa led to Zeila, Mogadisho, Mombasa, Zanzibar, Kilwa, and even the Comoros. Basra, Siraf, and Hormuz were chief ports in the Persian Gulf. Many stories of merchant voyages, some of which gave rise to tales of Sindbad the Sailor and other fables of the *Arabian Nights,* were recorded in the ninth and tenth centuries (*Marvels of India* is the most famous such collection). Some of Marco Polo's return journey from China in the late thirteenth century must have been done on Arab or Muslim vessels. The great Arab traveler Ibn Battūta (1304–1368 C.E.) sailed in Arab ships in the Mediterranean, across the Red Sea, and to East Africa.

The generic Arabic words for "ship" are *markab* and *safīna; dhow* is originally an Indian word [*dau*], used by non-Arabs for lateen-rigged vessels. The common boat on the Red Sea was called *sanbūq.* Smaller boats included *zawraq, qārib,* and *dūnij.* The fast pirate ships of India were known as *bārija.* The basis of ship classification was the form of the hull. The older type is represented by boats now called *būm* and *zārūq:* double-edged, coming to a point at both bow and stern. Such contemporary Arabic names of ships as *baghala, ganja, sanbūq,* and *jihāzi* apply to vessels with square sterns showing European influence. Typical of ships in use in the Indian Ocean was *jalba,* the sewn boat with planks stitched edge-to-edge with ropes of palm fiber. Medieval ships usually had one mast, no deck, two side rudders, and a lateen (triangular) sail, which allowed sailing into the wind. The largest ships

# N

were those destined for China. Sailing speed averaged two to three knots.

Ships were often owned by shareholders. The shipmaster (*nakhoda*) was a merchant. The multiethnic crew included men of various ranks: the boatswain, ship's mate, steersman, lookout, divers (for underwater repairs en route), sailors, and, often, soldiers for protection. The captain (*mu'allim*) was also a pilot (*rubbān*), hired on a per-voyage basis according to his knowledge of the coasts, winds, seasons, and currents, as well as the type of ship he was commanding. He was responsible for navigation and the safety of passengers and goods. He carried his own nautical instructions (most of which he memorized) and instruments: angle measure (*qiyās*), bussole (*huqqa* or *dīra*), lodestone (*hajar*), lot (*buld*), and lantern (*fānūs*). It is not clear whether there were any charts, as such, before the Portuguese era, although navigational books and sailing manuals are mentioned in the early sources. (Extant Arab maps could not have been used for practical navigation.)

The system of orientation used by Arab sailors was based on the rising and setting of certain bright stars and constellations. It may not have been Arab in origin but used Arabic star names. It was representative of the intertropical region and was probably in place by the ninth century C.E. The sidereal rose (*dīra*) has thirty-two rhumbs (*khann*) and is divided into eastern and western halves by Polaris (*Jāh*) and the South Pole (*Qutb*). The remaining fifteen pairs of rhumbs correspond roughly to Ursa Minor, Ursa Major, Cassiopeia, Capella, Vega, Arcturus, Pleiades, Altair, Orion, Sirius, Scorpio, Antares, Centaur, Canopus, and Achernar. By the late Middle Ages the compass was known but rarely used or even carried. Star altitude (*qiyās*) was measured in units called *isba'* (fingers), supposed to correspond to the arc covered by the little finger of an outstretched hand. Its degree value was determined at one-half of the distance from Polaris (at its lowest elevation) to the true pole; it therefore varied with precession. The full circle of 360 degrees corresponded to 210 *isba'* in 1394 but to 224 *isba'* in 1550.

The instrument used for measurements (*kamāl*) was a rectangle of horn or wood with a string through the middle. It was held against the horizon in an outstretched hand, the cord held to the nose or in the teeth by the knot. Knots tied at certain intervals on the cord corresponded to the varying arc, and thus also to the stars or latitudes on a set route. Sometimes a set of boards (*lawh*) represented different arc values on the cord. A later version (*bilistī*) used a rod and slides of different sizes like the Portuguese *balhestilha*.

These measures primarily facilitated a determination of latitude. For longitude a variety of other measurements existed, including something approximating triangulation. For purposes of estimating longitude, one *isba'* equalled eight *zām*, each *zām* (lit. "time unit") corresponding to the distance covered in three hours of average-speed sailing. The bearings (*majrā*) were set by the actual stars visible in the clear skies over the Indian Ocean, not by the mathematically correct rhumbs. Because of the nature of the geography and winds of the Indian Ocean, the pilot's greatest concern was with the latitude of his port. Once this latitude was reached, he could let the wind carry his ship along the parallel to its destination. Another way was to keep a recommended bearing until land was in sight and then make corrections. Prior to sailing, the opening chapter of the Qur'an (*Fatiha*) was recited. At landfall, the crew exclaimed "God is great!" New instruments and methods came into use through European domination of the Indian Ocean, but the expertise of the great fifteenth-century Omani pilot Ahmad ibn Mājid continued to be remembered. Folk Islam treats him as a saint, much as St. Nicholas became a patron saint for Christian sailors, though in this case veneration was based on the real reputation of a not very ancient expert.

Navigation in the Indian Ocean was subject to the monsoon system of seasonal winds. The monsoon regime dominates both the east and the west halves of the Indian Ocean, and controls the sailing calendar. The southwest monsoon (*kaws* or *kusi*) begins in March in East Africa and slowly spreads eastward. It may bring heavy rains and cause heavy ocean swells capable of closing ports. The northeast monsoon (*azyab*) begins from India in early October and reaches Zanzibar in November. Between monsoon periods breezes and other nonmonsoon winds can be used for voyages in other directions. Travel from Arabia to East Africa was best from November to April, and to India in May and also August-September. Typically, the eastbound roundtrip journey from the Persian Gulf to South China Sea took eighteen months.

The Red Sea had been used by the Arabs for early contacts among Arabia, Egypt, and Ethiopia long before Islam. Its role as a conduit between the Mediterranean and the Indian Ocean was already established by the time of Alexander the Great (356–323 B.C.E.). In the early years of Islam, several groups of converts fled persecution in pagan Mecca by traveling to Yemen and then crossing by ship to Ethiopia. In the Muslim era, main traffic consisted of transit trade and pilgrim ships on their annual journey to Mecca. Jedda became the main pilgrim port and the terminus of oceanic routes from the east. Medina was served by al-Jār and Yanbo'. Mocha was the main port in the south. The northeast was served by Aqaba; the west coast had Qulzum and Qusayr in Egypt, and 'Aidhāb, distinguished by a deep harbor. A continuing concern for Muslim governments was provisioning and protection of pilgrims preyed on by pirates based on Dahlak and smaller islands. Muslim shipping on the Red Sea was further disrupted by the crusaders from the north in the twelfth century and by the Portuguese from the south beginning in the early sixteenth century.

Navigation on the Red Sea was aided by the fact that latitudes could be determined by the stars, especially using Polaris, which can be easily seen there. Travel by sailboat, however, was easier from the north than from the south, since the southeasterly winds reach only halfway up the sea and ships carried into the Red Sea from the Indian Ocean must sail against northerly winds. Travel northward past Jedda had to be accomplished in smaller boats. The voyage from the north to the south end, on the other hand, took only thirty days, though the north wind would carry a ship all the way south to the Bab el-Mandeb Strait only from May to September. Sailing was done by coasting and could not be undertaken at night because of the numerous coral reefs and contrary currents.

On the Mediterranean Sea, Arab navigation began in the mid-seventh century C.E. and was from the start supported by the state for military expansion and the protection of trade. Soon after the Muslim conquest of Syria and Egypt, the Arabs attempted to attack the Byzantines by sea. In the early eighth and ninth centuries, Arab navies supported successful invasions against Byzantium, Spain, southern Italy, Sicily, and other islands. The strongest naval bases developed in Egypt (Alexandria, Qusayr) and Tunisia (Tunis). The Levantine coast (Antioch, Tripoli, Tyre, Acre) became heavily involved in naval operations during the Crusades. After the fall of Constantinople to the Turks in 1453 C.E., the Ottomans extended their naval control from the Black Sea to Morocco. The so-called Barbary corsairs, based in North African ports, were privateers licensed by the Ottoman government.

Merchant fleets prospered especially under the Fātimid (909–1171 C.E.) and Mamluk (1250–1517 C.E.) dynasties of Egypt, though during the latter period Arab piracy flourished on Socotra, in the Persian Gulf, and in the Red Sea. Pirate activity increased after the Portuguese, the Dutch, and the English intruded on Middle Eastern shipping and further disrupted trade with Muslim-Christian rivalry and intra-European competition. Piracy was finally suppressed by the power of the British navy in the nineteenth century.

In sum, the basic navigational techniques practiced in Arab Mediterranean countries were learned from the Greeks, Syrians, and Copts. These techniques were refined in the High Middle Ages, when interaction between southern European and Muslim societies led to innovations in shipbuilding and ship armaments, chart and mapmaking, the invention of the compass, and the introduction of the lateen sail from Indian Ocean mariners. After conquering the Arab countries in the early sixteenth century, the Ottomans, who from the fourteenth century onward had assumed many European (Greek and Italian) shipbuilding practices and nautical skills, took over local ports and fleets and extended naval operations into the western Mediterranean as well as the Red Sea, Persian Gulf, and Indian Ocean.

**BIBLIOGRAPHY**

Clark, Alfred. "Medieval Arab Navigation on the Indian Ocean: Latitude Determinations." *Journal of the American Oriental Society* 113 [3] (1993): 360–373.

Fahmy, Aly Mohamed. *Muslim Sea-Power in the Eastern Mediterranean from the Seventh to the Tenth Century A.D.* Cairo: National Publication and Printing House, 1966.

Ferrand, Gabriel. *Instructions nautiques et routiers arabes et portugais.* 3 vols. Paris: P. Guetner, 1921–1928; rpt. 1986.

Hourani, George Fadlo. *Arab Seafaring in the Indian Ocean in Ancient and Early Medieval Times.* 1951; rpt. Princeton, NJ: Princeton UP, 1975.

Soucek, Svat. "Islamic Charting in the Mediterranean." In Harley-Woodward, *The History of Cartography.* Vol. 2, pp. 263–292. See Gen. Bib.

Tibbets, Gerald R. *Arab Navigation in the Indian Ocean before the Coming of the Portuguese.* Oriental Translations Fund, n.s., vol. 42. London: Luzac, 1971; rpt. 1981.

———. "The Role of Charts in Islamic Navigation in the Indian Ocean." In Harley-Woodward, *The History of Cartography.* Vol. 2, pp. 256–262. See Gen. Bib.

Tolmacheva, Marina. "On the Arab System of Nautical Orientation." *Arabica* 27.2 (1980): 180–192.

*Marina A. Tolmacheva*

# N

## Navigation, Chinese

China in the early Middle Ages was chiefly a land power, until the Chinese ventured out into the Nanyang (Southeast Asia) on ships called *junks*. Marco Polo, in the late thirteenth century, mentioned these junks' amazing efficiency, and by the fourteenth century Ming China sent a large number of fleets to promote diplomatic, cultural, and economic relations with countries as far as the Middle East. Their ability to travel to distant lands indicates that the Chinese already had considerable knowledge of, and skill in, shipbuilding and navigation.

Just as the Mongols tried to conquer the whole world with cavalry on the land, so the Ming dynasty (1368–1644), with considerable success, attempted to increase its influence through navigation. From China to Europe, many countries in the path of invading Mongol forces were subjugated. But the Yuan (Mongol) dynasty (1276–1368) had failed to conquer Japan because the Yuan had no advanced knowledge of shipbuilding and navigation, relying heavily on the Koreans to construct the seafaring ships and to sail them.

During the Ming dynasty, however, Chinese shipbuilding and navigational skill improved greatly. War junks of the imperial navy routinely sailed with 400-man crews. Before the Ming, many attempts had been made to further the suzerain-vassal relations between China and neighboring countries for the purpose of diplomacy and trade. Thus, from the sixth to the thirteenth centuries, the Chinese had gained important experience in sailing the high seas.

In the early fifteenth century, Emperor Yongle (r. 1402–1424) commissioned the eunuch-admiral Zheng He to command a large Chinese naval fleet consisting of 300 ships and 27,000 men. Zheng He is believed to have led seven (or eight) naval expeditions that took a total of twenty-eight years, and his fleet went as far as the mouth of the Red Sea beyond the Indian Ocean, almost 100 years before the Portuguese reached India by sailing around the southern tip of Africa. Throughout these voyages Zheng He not only promoted the political and military power of Ming China but also engaged in economic and cultural exchanges among the nations he visited. An extensive seaborne commerce in particular was developed to meet the taste of the Chinese for spices and aromatics and the need for raw materials. Zheng made his first voyage in 1405, visiting Champa (now the central part of Vietnam), Siam, Malacca, Sumatra and Java, Calicut, Cochin, and Taprobane (Ceylon), returning to China in 1407. During this first voyage, Zheng He subjected Calicut, on the west coast of India, and was involved in the war for royal succession in the Majapahit Empire in eastern Java.

In 1409, on his second voyage, Zheng defeated King Alagonakka'ra of Ceylon and took him back to Nanking as a captive. He traveled as far as Calicut and Cochin on this voyage. On his third voyage (1414–1413), Zheng sailed to Hormuz on the Persian Gulf. On the way back, he defeated the royal army in Ceylon. He also liberated Malacca from the control of Siam and Java. On the fourth voyage (1413–1415), Zheng went westward from Calicut to Hormuz; a detachment of the fleet sailed to the east coast of Arabia, visiting Djofar and Aden. A Chinese mission visited Mecca and continued to Egypt. The fleet visited Brava and Malindi, and almost reached the Mozambique Channel. He got involved in a rebellion in the region of Acheh [Atjeh] in Sumatra and quelled it. In 1415, envoys were brought to China from more than thirty countries in south Asia and southeast Asia to pay homage to the Chinese emperor. During the fifth voyage (1417–1419), Zheng's fleet visited the Persian Gulf and the east coast of Africa; on this voyage he ventured farthest from China. The sixth voyage (1421–1422) was launched to take home the foreign envoys from China, visiting southeast Asia, India, Arabia, and Africa. After Emperor Yongle died in 1424, his successor suspended naval expeditions abroad by appointing Zheng He garrison commander in Nanjing. Zheng's last voyage (1431–1433) took him to southeast Asia, India, Arabia, and Africa.

In less than three decades, the Ming Empire mobilized an enormous fleet to pacify some thirty countries in Asia and Africa. Although the Chinese did not establish overseas colonies or trading empires as the Europeans did, they fostered Chinese emigration overseas, particularly to Southeast Asia. This trend persisted well into the nineteenth century.

**BIBLIOGRAPHY**

Clyde, Ahmad. *Cheng Ho's Voyage.* New York: American Trust, 1981.

Duyvendak, J.J.L. "The True Dates of the Chinese Maritime Expeditions in the Early Fifteenth Century." *T'oung Pao* 34 (1938): 341–413.

———. *China's Discovery of Africa.* London: Probstain, 1949.

Levathes, Louise. *When China Ruled the Seas: The Treasure Fleet of the Dragon Throne, 1405–1433.* New York: Simon and Schuster, 1994.

Mote, F.W. "China in the Age of Columbus." In *Circa 1492: Art in the Age of Exploration.* Ed. Jay A. Levenson. New Haven: Yale UP, 1991.

*Key Ray Chong*

**SEE ALSO**

Dias, Bartolomeu; India; Japan, Mongol Invasion of; Majapahit; Malacca Straits; Marco Polo; Portuguese Expansion; Red Sea; Taprobane; Yuan Dynasty; Zheng He, Admiral

## Navigation, Viking

Between 800 and 1050, Viking ships sailed on expeditions of plunder, trade, or colonization across the North and the Baltic seas, followed the coasts of western Europe into the Mediterranean, traveled on Russian rivers as far as the Caspian Sea, crossed the Black Sea for attacks on Constantinople, and carried colonists as far west as the Faeroe islands, Iceland, Greenland, and Newfoundland. The voyages were so far-ranging that scholars have long speculated about how the Vikings navigated their ships; it has been suggested that they had a fairly sophisticated knowledge of astronomical navigation.

The primary sources that contribute to modern understanding of Viking navigational techniques include: (1) a reference in one of the sagas to Norway's King Olaf II Haraldsson (r. 1015–1028) using a "sunstone" to find directions on an overcast day (this sunstone may have been double-refractive feldspar, which polarizes light and shows the direction of the sun after sunset or on lightly overcast days); (2) some sophisticated astronomical writings from twelfth-century Iceland, preserved in manuscripts; (3) a fragment of a small wooden disc with notches around the rim, which some believe to be a bearing dial or possibly a sun compass, found in the ruins of a Norse farm in Greenland.

All of these sources are, however, problematic. No sunstone has ever been identified in archaeological excavation, and thus the saga reference remains ambiguous. The astronomical writings are more recent than the Viking voyages, and in character they are more theoretical—"pure" astronomy—than sailors might use in navigation. The interpretation of the "bearing dial" does not have scholarly consensus. Navigational charts and the compass are later inventions. Sources do not mention the use of a sounding-lead, and none that survive in Scandinavia can be dated to the Viking Age. Thus, it remains a mystery how the Vikings managed their extraordinary navigational feats with such apparent precision.

In coastal waters, landmarks were the prime aid for navigators. The experience gained in the raids of the ninth century enabled Viking pilots to navigate the North Sea and along the coasts of western Europe, sail between ports in the Baltic with confidence, and navigate the rivers of eastern Europe. Natural landmarks would be memorized, and in the late Viking Age the first artificial markers—stone crosses indicating good natural harbors—began to be erected in Norway.

The Vikings divided their world into four cardinal directions whose names in Old Norse suggest that they originated on the west coast of Norway, which runs northeast-southwest. The word for northeast, translated literally, means "landnorth"; northwest is "outnorth," southeast is "landsouth," and southwest is "outsouth."

The only voyages that Vikings undertook on which they lost sight of land for several days were in the North Atlantic, where the longest distances covered were Norway to Iceland, Norway/Iceland to Greenland, and Iceland to Ireland. A detailed knowledge of wind and current systems had probably been built up for the most frequently used sea routes, and the Vikings certainly knew that the polestar indicated true north. Because the sailing season was in the summer, however, it is uncertain how much the Vikings would have been able to depend on stars, at latitudes that would have had almost no darkness from mid-May to late July. The ocean current system, which is generally more stable than wind directions, might have been a more accessible source of information. The description of the route from Norway to Greenland given in one Icelandic source shows that the technique of coastal sailing using landmarks was also employed as a navigational tool in ocean crossings: "From Hernar in Norway sail due west. You should see Shetland on a clear day, and have the Faeroe Islands halfway below the horizon. Sail so far south of Iceland that you do not see the land, but you should encounter seagulls and whales. This takes you to the south tip of Greenland." Sailing across the North Atlantic with the support of three landmarks indicates a great assurance and knowledge of the sea, but it can hardly be called technically sophisticated navigation.

The possibilities for error in such a system were great. When the sun was up, it showed directions according to the time of day, but sailors would also have had to calculate the time of year as well. Because no reliable timepieces existed during the Middle Ages, the time of day had to be estimated and, obviously, longitude was a matter of conjecture. On overcast days, telling directions by the sun was impossible, and after some days of fog and calm, sailors had no means of knowing where they were. The Old Norse expression for the situation is *hafvilla* (lit. "wayward at sea"). Caught in such a predicament, a Viking crew might assemble (as the historical record indicates) and debate what course to set, entrusting the final decision to their most experienced colleague.

**BIBLIOGRAPHY**

Schnall, Uwe. *Navigatin der Wikinger.* Schriften des Deutschen Schiffahrtsmuseums 6. Hamburg: Gerhard Stalling Verlag, 1975

Thirslund, Soren, and C. L. Vebæk. *The Viking Compass Guided Norsemen First to America.* Skjern: Gullanders Bogtrykkeri, 1992.

*Arne Emil Christensen*

**SEE ALSO**
Caspian Sea; Mediterranean Sea; Navigation; Ships and Shipbuilding; Tides; Viking Age; Viking Discoveries and Settlements; Vinland Sagas

## Nestorianism

A sect of Christianity that emerged in the fifth century C.E. This tradition takes its name from Nestorius (*c.* 381–*c.* 451), a patriarch of Constantinople, who embraced a then current theological position holding that two distinct persons, divine and human, existed within Jesus Christ. This position was condemned at the Council of Ephesus (431) and was regarded thereafter as heretical by the church in the West. In contrast, the Church of the East, which was centered within the Sasanian Persian Empire and had the eastern dialect of Syriac as its official language, supported and adopted this position. Consequently, this Church of the East, as

it referred to itself, later became known also as the Nestorian Church.

Having its main theological school located initially at Edessa, and later at Nisibis, and its patriarchal see situated at the Persian capital of Seleucia-Cteshiphon (and subsequently in 762 at Baghdad), the Nestorian Church was strategically situated astride the east-west trade route. This and other commercial arteries of the Persian Empire became conduits for the church's missionary impulse, which was driven by the centrality of the evangelical imperative within the church's theology (based on Matthew 28:19–20). Since the missionary path to the west was barred not only by the anathemas of the Roman and Byzantine churches but also by the bitter and long-standing enmity between Persia and Rome (as well as its successor Byzantium), the Nestorian Church directed its missionary efforts eastward, converting and creating new churches as well as bringing already established Christian communities under the aegis of the Church of the East.

In the sixth century, Nestorian missionaries were sent to the White Huns (Hephthalites) who lived on the eastern fringe of the Persian Empire. Combining evangelization, education, and instruction in agriculture, these early missionaries made considerable inroads among the nomadic Huns. Over the course of subsequent centuries, Nestorian missionaries in Inner Asia established communities of Christians among other nomadic peoples, including Turks, Uighurs, Karaits, and Mongols.

The Church of the East in the sixth century also witnessed increasing ties with the long-established Christian churches of India that claimed a lineage back to the Apostle Thomas. These communities were incorporated into the Persian church's hierarchy and remained Nestorian until Roman Catholic missionary expansion in the sixteenth century.

The alarm with which the Christian West viewed the advent and spread of Islam in the seventh and eighth centuries was not equally shared by the Church of the East. While Persian Christians under Islam found themselves to be a heavily taxed minority, they also initially experienced a degree of freedom and tolerance unknown under Persian Zoroastrianism. Except for a period of persecution under 'Umar II (r. 717–720), the Christian Church through the Umayyad caliphate (661–750) and into the first century of the Abbasid caliphate (750–1258) generally maintained a mutually advantageous relationship with Islamic rulers.

Islamic civilization became the beneficiary of Greek science and learning transmitted through prominent Christians, including Nestorians. Conversely, Christian evangelization benefited from the use of Arab sea routes, particularly that to China. In the eighth century, for example, Nestorian missionaries are recorded to have arrived in China by sea, some of them accompanying Arab envoys on diplomatic missions.

The establishment of a church in China during the Tang dynasty (618–907) represents one of the most notable accomplishments of the Nestorian Church in the first millennium. The early history of this community is documented in the celebrated Nestorian Monument that was erected in 781 at Zhouzhi, located fifty miles southwest of the Tang capital at Chang'an (modern Xian). The monument traces the Chinese church's origins back to the year 635 when Aloben (his Chinese name), the earliest of the Nestorian missionaries mentioned on the monument, arrived in the Tang capital. Earlier Chinese contacts with Christianity might well have taken place, since Nestorian merchants conceivably could have accompanied or followed a Persian embassy that arrived at the Northern Wei dynasty (439–534) capital of Datong in the middle of the fifth century. Nevertheless, solid evidence of significant Christian activity in China is not available until the Tang period. Although Nestorians suffered persecution under the Empress Wu (r. 683–705), Christianity during the Tang period largely enjoyed imperial favor that lasted until the suppression of all foreign religions (Buddhism, Manichaeism, Zoroastrianism, and Christianity) under the emperor Wuzong (r. 840–846). This disastrous episode, along with the chaos that ensued as the Tang dynasty disintegrated, brought to a close the first chapter of Christian activity in China. Christianity could nowhere be found in tenth-century China and was not to reappear there until the Mongol period in the thirteenth century.

For the Nestorian Church, which throughout its history as a minority religion had experienced isolation and persecution, the *Pax Mongolica* (Mongol Peace) established by the far-flung conquests of Chinggis Khân (c. 1167–1227) seemed to offer the bright prospect of large-scale conversion throughout Asia. Although the Nestorian Church never realized even a degree of the universality achieved by Christians in the West during the *Pax Romana* (Roman Peace), significant gains were nevertheless achieved under the umbrella of Mongol tolerance. The papal envoys to the Mongols, John of Plano Carpini and William of Rubruck, repeatedly noted the presence of Nestorians among the Mongols, though they held these Christians in low esteem. (While he reported that the Nestorians baptized more than sixty people at the khân's court on Easter Eve 1254, and admitted to being aided by an Armenian Nestorian named Sergius, William called them usurers, drunkards, and even polygamists.)

These Franciscan envoys also observed the degree to which Nestorians occupied high places in Mongol society. Sorkaktani, the Karait daughter-in-law of Chinggis Khân and a Nestorian Christian, had four sons, three of whom attained significant positions of power in the Mongol order: Möngke as the great khân, Khubilai (r. 1260–1294) as the first Mongol emperor of China, and Hülegü as il-khân of Persia. Not one of these powerful men became a Christian, but all were favorably disposed to Christianity, especially Hülegü, who oversaw a Nestorian revival in Persia, and Khubilai, whose patronage was instrumental in the reestablishment of Nestorian churches in China. The Mongol advance into southeast Asia during this period might also possibly have been accompanied by the establishment of Nestorian communities, but such speculation lacks evidence.

The thirteenth and fourteenth centuries were also a time of renewed contact between the Roman and Nestorian churches. In some cases, the encounter between missionaries sent out by Rome and Nestorian communities was accidental. John of Monte Corvino (1246/1267–c. 1330), appointed the first Roman archbishop of Beijing (Khanbaliq), found a Nestorian church in China that reacted to his presence with hostility and slander. The Dominican missionary Jordanus discovered Nestorians on the Malabar Coast of India and was enjoined by Pope John XXII to bring them back to union with Rome. In other instances, Rome explicitly made overtures for reunion. The Dominican William of Montferrat was sent by Pope Gregory IX in 1235 to the Nestorian Patriarch Sabrisho' V to explore the possibility of reconciliation. While nothing came of this particular mission, there were yet other examples of Nestorian churches that reunited with Rome, the most prominent perhaps being the Church of Cyprus, which was officially accepted into Roman communion in 1445.

The period of promise and renewed expansion of the Nestorian Church that took place under the Mongols ended when their empire declined in the fourteenth century. With the expulsion of the Mongols

# N

from China, the Christian Church there ceased to exist for a second time. The second wave of Mongol/Turkish expansion under the Islamic Timur the Great (Tamerlane; 1336–1405) devastated Nestorian communities across Asia. The fortunes of the church continued to decline through the fifteenth century, and on the eve of European expansion, the only known Nestorian churches were those in Mesopotamia and in India.

Throughout its long history in Asia, the Nestorian Church, much like the medieval church in the West, produced its fair share of explorers, missionaries, and pilgrims who broadened perspectives on the world, spread technologies, and connected widely dispersed peoples. The sixth-century Nestorian merchant-explorer Cosmas Indikopleustes (Cosmas, the Indian Voyager), although in all likelihood not reaching India himself, made the significant claim in his *Christian Topography* that Persian Christians were living in the Indian subcontinent, perhaps even in Sri Lanka. Nestorian missionaries served as agents of civilization through the transmission of technologies and learning. The Byzantine historians Procopius and Theophanes relate a report that Nestorian monks appeared at the court of the emperor Justinian I in 551 with silkworms hidden in a bamboo tube. Sericulture, which had been a closely guarded monopoly of the Chinese, thereafter became a significant industry of Byzantium in the Middle Ages. Out on the steppes, Nestorian missionaries were responsible for creating writing systems for the Huns, Uighurs, and Mongols.

Of all medieval Nestorian travelers, the Uighur monk Rabban Sauma is undoubtedly the best known in the West. Setting out on a pilgrimage to the Holy Land from China in the 1270s, Sauma was accompanied by another Nestorian monk, Mark. After reaching Baghdad, the two men found their path to the Holy Land blocked by warfare. In the course of their stay in Baghdad, Mark was appointed the patriarch of the Church of the East, taking the name Yaballaha III. In 1287, the il-khân Arghun dispatched Sauma as an envoy to the pope and kings of Western Europe to negotiate an alliance to drive the Mamluk Turks out of the Holy Land and the Middle East. Sauma's mission in Europe, which coincided with Marco Polo's visit to Khubilai Khân's China, was in one sense a failure since it did not produce the desired consequences. Yet the highly visible nature of his visit brought him before some of the most powerful people of Europe: an assembly of cardinals in Rome; Philip IV (the Fair) of France

in Paris; Edward I of England in Gascony; and finally the newly elected Pope Nicholas IV on Sauma's return trip through Rome. Not only did he provide prominent Europeans of the late thirteenth century with a firsthand view of the Christianity that existed east of the Euphrates, his journal of his travels, recorded in the Syriac *The History of Yaballaha III*, has presented posterity with a glimpse of medieval Europe as seen from the outside.

## BIBLIOGRAPHY

Budge, E.A. Wallis. *The Monks of Kûblâi Khân, Emperor of China*. London: Religious Tract Society, 1928.

Dawson, Christopher, ed. *The Mongol Mission*. See Gen. Bib.

Manz, Beatrice Forbes. *The Rise and Rule of Tamerlane*. Cambridge Studies in Islamic Civilization. New York: Cambridge UP, 1989.

*The Mission of Friar William of Rubruck: His Journey to the Court of the Great Khan Möngke 1253–1255*. Trans. Peter Jackson, with notes and introduction by Peter Jackson and David Morgan. Hakluyt Society, 2nd series, 173. London: Hakluyt Society, 1990.

Moffett, Samuel Hugh. *A History of Christianity in Asia. Vol. I: Beginnings to 1500*. San Francisco: Harper, 1992.

Montgomery, James A., trans. *The History of Yaballaha III, Nestorian Patriarch, and of his Vicar, Bar Sauma, Mongol Ambassador to the Frankish Courts at the End of the Thirteenth Century*. New York: Octagon, 1966.

Saeki, P.Y. *The Nestorian Documents and Relics in China*. 2nd edition. Tokyo: Toho Bunkwa Gakuin: Academy of Oriental Culture, Tokyo Institute, 1951.

*Daniel Getz*

## SEE ALSO

Armenia; Buddhism; China; Cosmas Indikopleustes; Eastern Christianity; Edessa; Hülegü; Huns; Inner Asian Travel; John of Monte Corvino; John of Plano Carpini; Jordan of Sévérac; Khanbaliq; Malabar; Mamluks; Manichaeism; Mongols; Nomadism and Pastoralism; Silk Roads; Textiles, Decorative; Tamerlane; Zoroastrianism

## New World

Remote or uncharted regions, the understanding of which changed significantly during the course of the Middle Ages.

The ancient and medieval concept of the *orbis terrarum*—the linked landmass of the known or inhabited world, consisting of Asia, Europe, and Africa, and extending to the islands in the Atlantic—in some accounts (such as Plato's *Timaeus*) encompassed a notion of distant or uncharted geographic zones. These territories, linked in Ptolemaic geography with the polar regions at the edge of the *oikoumene,* were referred to as the "Antipodes" or "Antichthones" among Greek and Roman cartographers, philosophers, and satirists. This world-turned-upside-down hardly ever appeared "new" in ancient writings; it functioned simply as an estranging inverse (and thus a reinforcement) of normative Mediterranean identity. Seneca's tragedy *Medea* (lines 364ff.) contains an exceptional formulation that links the otherness of such worlds with novelty: the chorus here observes that recent travel and conquest have discovered new territory ("terra . . . nova") and new worlds ("tellus . . . novos"). This allusion to Roman imperial ambition became a famous commonplace in the fifteenth and sixteenth centuries; next to these lines in his copy of Seneca, Columbus's son Ferdinand wrote, "This prophecy has been fulfilled . . . in 1492." In general, however, ancient writers conceived of the "new" not in terms of spatial discovery but as temporal renovation: Virgil's celebrated Fourth Eclogue epitomizes this in presenting the New Age as the return to a mythic golden age.

Medieval writers nonetheless encountered a variety of "new worlds" as described by the ancients: these might take the form of fantastic or nightmarish "nowheres" (Calypso's Ogygia, or the island of the Cyclopes in the *Odyssey*), of utopian, exotic, or idealized lands (the peoples encountered by Alexander the Great in the East, Latium in the *Aeneid*), or parodic Never Never Lands (Lucian's *True Story*). Medieval texts elaborate the narratives surrounding mythic worlds such as Ultima Thule or the Western Isles, and they portray a spectrum of far-off or fantastical sites, including traditional visions of the Otherworld (*St. Patrick's Purgatory,* the Celtic otherworld of *Sir Orfeo*), or the inverse worlds of *The Land of Cockaigne* and *Aucassin and Nicolette.*

Over and above preternatural journeys or heroic adventure, Christian Scripture provided medieval writers a peculiar idiom for speaking of "a new heaven and a new earth" ("terra nova" in the Vulgate, Revelation 21:1). By the High Middle Ages, writers used this figure with some frequency to visualize the renewal of the individual and of Christian society. In the twelfth century, for example, Isaac of Stella speaks of spiritual life as a "mundus novus" (*Patrologia Latina* 194.1872, 1874); Hildegard of Bingen (1098–1179) declares that

the Lord created a "novus mundus" after the Flood, which Jesus brings to perfection (*Patrologia Latina* 197.235, 241). Peter Lombard (*c.* 1100–1160), Peter Comestor (*c.* 1100–1178), John of Salisbury (*c.* 1115–1180), and Alan of Lille (1120–*c.* 1203) all employ new world imagery ("terra nova"), traceable ultimately to Revelation. Apocalyptic resonances of this sort inflected descriptions of new lands and peoples through Columbus's writings and beyond.

In more literary compositions, writers like Alan and, before him, Bernard Sylvester (d. 1159) had linked the nature of each person, as a "microcosm," to the external world through lengthy catalogues of peoples and places. The potential of the "new man," and his dominion in the physical world, extends in these visions beyond the boundaries of all known geography, so that European identities and aspirations assume a universalizing aspect. Attention to remote and uncharted regions recurs also in chroniclers and historians; Robert Bartlett has pointed out how often their descriptions of "waste" and "empty" locales at the edge of Europe serve as a rationale for expansionism.

Missionaries and other travelers frequently attempted to specify for readers at home—whether pope, emperor, or more ordinary audiences—the novelty and strangeness of non-European settings. In his account of the evangelization of the Mongols, for example, the Franciscan William of Rubruck says, "when I came among [the Tartars in 1253] I really felt as if I were entering some other world" (p. 71). As overseas undertakings of a massive and permanent nature, the crusades set claims for the retaking of an old and familiar world alongside reports of strange new worlds; moreover, they developed practical mechanisms of military expansion and colonial administration that sustained a European presence as strangers in strange lands.

The steady spread of Western interests in the Middle East, Iberia, the Baltic, and eastern Europe, and the development of sea routes to the coasts of Africa and Asia, established a distinctive "frontier mentality" as one of the foundational features of medieval cultural experience. This encompassed not merely the discovery and settlement of new lands, but the grounding ethos that lay behind these patterns of outward movement; Robert I. Burns has made clear how, in history and historiography, medieval preoccupation with more distant worlds has marked every subsequent phase in "the rise of the West," including the settlement of the Americas, North and South.

# N

Medieval curiosity about new worlds was continuous if variable. *The Voyage of St. Brendan* (tenth century or earlier) presents its hero as "consumed with desire" to seek out a new land in the West, rumored to be the land of promise of the saints. In the *Voyage,* the exhilaration of exploring the unknown and exotic itself emerges as a form of religious life, and the survival of this tale in nearly 120 manuscripts makes clear that, however widespread or limited actual expeditions may have been, accounts of the search for strange new worlds enjoyed remarkable popularity. Medieval tales persistently located exotic and unknown lands—for example, the Fortunate Isles—in the "other world" ("alter orbis") off the coast of the European mainland, either among or beyond the British Isles (R.W. Southern). Throughout the Middle Ages, this western fringe of Europe (whether in the North Sea, or the Iberian Peninsula) was associated not merely with new worlds, but with their discovery as well; the myth of the Welsh Prince Madoc's thirteenth-century visit to America illustrates that even through the eighteenth century the Celtic fringe continued to generate such stories.

Beginning just after the year 1000, a number of Icelanders—yet another fringe people—sighted and visited locations in North America, and they eventually established settlements in Newfoundland and perhaps elsewhere. The vernacular accounts of these voyages, in the *Greenland Saga* and *Eirík's Saga,* unequivocally present travel and exploration as a heroic pursuit. Both these narratives, for example, mention the disgrace that befell the merchant Bjárni Herjólfsson who, having discovered new lands by chance, chose not to explore or to bring back detailed descriptions. Unlike the family sagas, which provide vivid histories of local settlement and disorder in Iceland, these voyage narratives celebrate the exploits and stature of their heroes mainly through far-flung travel and discovery.

Although the leading characters in these stories attain preeminence by spearheading interest in new lands, the literary record of such exploration confirms that enthusiasm for new worlds extended far beyond the adventurers themselves. These sagas carry to their farthest point a major theme of medieval Icelandic writings in general, namely interest in frontier societies, and an urge to push the edge of the known world ever westward. It is significant, moreover, that Eirik, the central figure in these discovery narratives, becomes an explorer largely as a consequence of being declared an outlaw; banishment outside the borders of his own

society becomes the incentive to seek new lands. In these sagas, strangeness, knowledge of physical geography, the mystique that comes from reporting unique experiences, and hope for profit and dominion all combine to stir excitement and adventure.

The description of strange and novel locales continued throughout the later Middle Ages in popular narratives that spanned the genres of travel, adventure, and romance such as the *Divisament dou monde* of Marco Polo (*c.* 1295), *The Book of John Mandeville* (*c.* 1360) and the stories of Alexander; in allegories such as Philippe de Mézières's *Dream of the Old Pilgrim* (*c.* 1390), or Christine de Pisan's *City of Ladies* (1405); and in learned encyclopedias such as Pierre d'Ailly's *Imago mundi* (1410) that Columbus extensively annotated. In the aggregate, however, these works present the worlds they encounter as, again, more strange than new, and they take account of recently discovered lands (such as the Canaries and other islands in the Atlantic) only rarely. Medieval cartography paid considerably fuller and more precise attention to peripheries of the *oikoumene.* Versions of Ptolemaic projections labeled areas beyond the known world "terra incognita" (transformed in Waldseemüller's 1507 map to "terra ulterior incognita" or "inventa"). Other traditions of medieval cartography trace the known world through conventional place-names and peoples (including monstrous races), but take little notice of unknown or new lands beyond these established borders.

The much-discussed Vinland map (which a consensus of expert opinion now dates to the middle of the fifteenth century) stands virtually alone among pre-1492 documents in mapping "terra nova," placing it (following the Viking sagas) more or less at the location of Newfoundland. The legends written on the map explicitly repeat this terminology: "a new land is situated in the outermost parts of the world (*noua terra in extremis mundi partibus*), and beyond it no land is found but only the ocean sea" (p. 136); "the companions Bjárni and Leif (Leifr) Eiriksson discovered a new land (*terram nouam*), extremely fertile and even having vines" (p. 140). These descriptions confirm that the concept of new land or new worlds was already in circulation during the later Middle Ages, available for use by cartographers and publicists after 1492, although the phrase appears far from commonplace. Post-1492 maps, early and late, only sporadically use the term *mundus novus* (usually associated with Amerigo Vespucci). The sketch map linked to Bartolommeo Columbus (dated 1503–1520) may be the first to use the phrase *mondo novo*, though it applies the label to the north coast of South America and juxtaposes this to "Asia" (affirming Columbus's own conviction that he had not discovered a new world).

Although these medieval precedents license the use of *new world* as an intellectual and geopolitical category, for the most part Europeans referred to the continents and islands of the Western Hemisphere not by this term, but as a "New India," or, more generally, "the Indies." Such usage is not the outcome of an arbitrary notion of Columbus, or a mark of the relative obscurity of "new world" in both popular and learned lexicons before 1492. Instead, it demonstrates that, by the late Middle Ages in the West, "India" and "Indians" had come to serve as default categories for remote, strange, or singular cultural practices or values. Miranda's naive reaction in *The Tempest*—"O brave new world!"—and Prospero's sophisticated come-back ("'Tis new to thee") make clear how far the very conceptualization of a new world depends upon a continuing dynamic with preexistent categories. In fiction, ethnography, cartography, and other discourses, the delineation and the comprehension of the New World's peculiar features entailed the redeployment of the well-established conventions embedded in European images of Indians.

## BIBLIOGRAPHY

Bartlett, Robert. *The Making of Europe: Conquest, Colonialization, and Cultural Change, 95–1350.* Princeton, NJ: Princeton UP, 1993.

Burns, Robert I. "The Significance of the Frontier in the Middle Ages." In *Medieval Frontier Societies.* Ed. Robert Bartlett and Angus MacKay. Oxford: Clarendon, 1989, pp. 307–30.

Dathorne, O.R. *Imagining the World: Mythical Belief versus Reality in Global Encounters.* Westport, CT, and London: Bergin & Garvey, 1994.

*The Mission of Friar William of Rubruck: His Journey to the Court of the Great Khan Möngke 1253–1255.* Trans. Peter Jackson, with notes and introduction by Peter Jackson and David Morgan. Hakluyt Society, 2nd series, 173. London: Hakluyt Society, 1990.

Skelton, R.A., Thomas E. Marston, and George D. Painter, eds. *The Vinland Map and the Tartar Relation,* 1965; rev. edition, New Haven: Yale UP, 1995.

Southern, R.W. "Europe and the 'Other World.'" In *Medieval Humanism and Other Studies.* New York: Harper & Row, 1970, pp. 133–80.

*The Vinland Sagas: The Norse Discovery of America.* Trans. Magnus Magnusson and Hermann Pálsson. Harmondsworth: Penguin Books, 1965.

Westrem, Scott D., ed. *Discovering New Worlds: Essays on Medieval Exploration and Imagination.* New York and London: Garland, 1991.

Zerubavel, Eviatar. *Terra Cognita: The Mental Discovery of America.* New Brunswick, NJ: Rutgers UP, 1992.

*Thomas G. Hahn*

## SEE ALSO

Brendan's Voyage, St.; Canary Islands; Cockaigne, Land of; Honorius Augustodunensis; Indians and the Americas; *Mandeville's Travels;* Marco Polo; Purgatory, St. Patrick's; Thule; Viking Discoveries and Settlements; Vinland Map; Walter of Châtillon; William of Rubruck

## Nicholas of Cusa (1401–1464)

German theologian, philosopher, canon lawyer, and cardinal who traveled widely and created a prototypical map of central Europe.

Born in Kues on the Moselle, Nicholas (whose surname was Khrypffs) studied with the Brethren of the Common Life at Deventer and at Heidelberg (1416–1418) before traveling to Padua, from whose university he received his doctorate in canon law in 1423. Shortly thereafter he returned to Germany, taking up the study of theology at Cologne, and later becoming the archdeacon of Liège. As a representative from Trier, Nicholas participated in the Roman Church's Council of Basel from 1432 to 1437, at which he gained a powerful reputation and from which he traveled to Constantinople in an attempt to effect a reunion of Orthodoxy with Catholicism.

As a papal envoy Nicholas traveled widely in Germany. He was nominated cardinal in 1448 and officially elevated in 1450. As cardinal and papal legate he traveled throughout Austria and Germany on a mission of church reform, and from 1452, took very seriously the reform and administration of the diocese of Brixen (Bressanone, in Tirol), of which he had been named bishop in 1450. Nicholas subsequently traveled twice to Rome, and died at Todi (Umbria) on the return stage of his second trip.

Nicholas had an interest in European geography that was perhaps fueled by his friendship with Aeneas Sylvius Piccolomini (Pope Pius II). Among other geographic works he owned manuscript copies of Ptolemy's *Geographia* and the Antonine *Itinerary,* as well as several globes. In 1454, he apparently drew up a map of Europe from western Germany to Russia, the Adriatic to the Baltic and North seas; it includes southern Scandinavia

# N

and parts of the Black Sea coast. It is known today only from what is considered a copy made in late-fifteenth-century Florence by the German Henricus Martellus (the Cusanus Martellus map) and from a printed derivative (the Eichstätt map [July 21, 1491]), whose copper plates the humanist and map collector Konrad Peutinger purchased in the 1490s. Cartographic historians consider it a prototype for many central European maps, and it was still being printed a century after its creation.

**BIBLIOGRAPHY**

Bett, Henry. *Nicholas of Cusa.* London: Methuen and Co., 1932.

Campbell, Tony. *The Earliest Printed Maps 1472–1500.* Berkeley: U of California P, 1987, pp. 35–55.

Grass, Nikolaus, ed. *Cusanus-Gedächtnisschrift: Im Auftrag der rechts und staatswissenschaftlichen Fakultät der Universität Innsbruck.* Innsbruck-Munich: Universitätsverlag Innsbruck, 1970.

Nicholas of Cusa. *Opera omnia: Issu et auctoritate Academiae Litterarum Heidelbergensis ad codicem fidem edita.* 11 vols. Hamburg: Meiner, 1959–1983.

*Joseph P. Byrne and Dwight Ferguson*

**SEE ALSO**

*Antonine Itinerary;* Canon Law and Subject Peoples; Eastern Christianity; Maps; Peutinger Table; Pius II; Ptolemy

## Nicholas of Lynn (*c.* 1300–1386)

A noted Carmelite mathematician and astrologer at Oxford born in Lynn (now King's Lynn), Norfolk. Working under the patronage of John of Gaunt (1340–1399), Nicholas produced a *Kalendarium* arranged in four metonic or nineteen-year cycles beginning in 1387 (1387–1462). Nicholas himself indicated that the tables were meant to update and replace those of Walter of Elvedene. The *Kalendarium* is mentioned by Geoffrey Chaucer (*c.* 1343–1400) in his *Treatise on the Astrolabe* ("the [Kalender] of . . . Frere N. Linne"), and he called the Carmelite an expert with that instrument. Fragments of other treatises by Nicholas of Lynn that survive are *De natura zodiaci, De planetarum domibus, De mundi revolutione,* and *De usu astrolabii.*

Scholars have searched the registers of Oxford finding no record of Nicholas of Lynn connected to any of the schools there. Oxford's Merton College had a famous school of astronomy, and Nicholas of Lynn's *Kalendarium* shows use of information provided by scholars there

in the fourteenth century. Beyond this, nothing certain is known about him. Some literary critics have thought that he was the model for Chaucer's "hende" Nicholas in *The Miller's Tale,* but this seems highly speculative since the literary Nicholas was not a friar.

Scholars of late medieval exploration also theorize that he was the author of the now lost *Inventio fortunata,* which tells of a trip to the Arctic region in 1360 by an English Franciscan, expert with the astrolabe, to measure latitudes north of 54 degrees and to study magnetism. The cartographic configuration of the Arctic outlined in *Inventio fortunata* came to dominate early printed maps down to 1700. Information about the contents of *Inventio fortunata* is found primarily in a letter from Gerard Mercator (1512–1594) to the geographer and mathematician John Dee (1527–1608) and in map inscriptions found on world maps drawn by Jacob Ruysch (1507–1508) and Gerard Mercator (1569). Ruysch does not tell his readers exactly where he obtained his information. Mercator used a summary of *Inventio fortunata* from another obscure medieval traveler, Jacob Cnoyen. Cnoyen's travel book has also disappeared. Christopher Columbus and his circle certainly believed that a copy of *Inventio fortunata* was circulating at Bristol at the turn of the sixteenth century when Columbus requested a copy of it.

Undoubtedly someone made a journey to western Greenland in the mid-fourteenth century and wrote a treatise about it that included a lengthy description of the region, though whether or not it was Nicholas of Lynn—or someone he knew—is at present unresolvable. All readers of *Inventio fortunata* state that it was written by a Minorite from England. Nicholas was a Carmelite, not a Franciscan, but the two orders could have been confused by a nonmendicant.

To date, all we know for sure about Nicholas of Lynn is that he lived in the fourteenth century, wrote a *Kalendarium* and other treatises associated with astronomical problems, and belonged to the Carmelite order. All else is speculation.

**BIBLIOGRAPHY**

DeCosta, B.F. *Inventio fortunata: Arctic Exploration.* Bulletin of the American Geographic Society Tract. New York: American Geographic Society, 1881.

Nicholas of Lynn. *The Kalendarium of Nicholas of Lynn.* Ed. Sigmund Eisner. Athens, GA: U of Georgia P, 1980.

Oleson, Tryggvi. "Inventio fortunata." *Annals of the Icelandic National League* 44 (1963): 64–76.

Steinnes, Asgaut. "En Nordpolsdkspedisjon ar 1360." *Syn og Segn* 64 (1958): 410–419.

Taylor, E.G.R. "A Letter Dated 1577 from Mercator to John Dee." *Imago Mundi* 13 (1956): 58–59.

*†Delno C. West*

**SEE ALSO**

Chaucer, Geoffrey; Columbus, Christopher; Navigation; Scandinavian World Maps; Viking Discoveries and Settlements

## Nicholas of Poggibonsi [Niccolo da Poggibonsi] (fl. 1346–1350)

A fourteenth-century Franciscan from a town in the province of Florence, Italy, who wrote a pilgrimage account of the Near East. Little is known of Friar Nicholas's life. He recorded his name in his text, and twice worked it into an acrostic formed by the initials of the first eighty-six chapters. His pilgrimage lasted from early March 1346 to the spring of 1350. Both the outbound and return sea journeys were made via Venice and Cyprus. He traveled with other Minorites, although he barely mentions them: Bonaccorso of Massa, Matthew of Todi, and Jacopo of Gubbio. His stated purpose in making such a lengthy pilgrimage was to see and touch everything, and to record his eye-witness experiences for those constrained to remain home. To ensure accuracy, he "journalistically" jotted notes on small tablets that he carried for this purpose and wrote the account in full on his return.

Nicholas describes various modes of travel employed in addition to walking, including navigation in canal boats and sailing vessels, and overland journeys by camel and other pack animals. Holy shrines, churches, chapels, and monasteries are described in detail, along with comments on which monastic orders supervised them. These sites were associated with the life and passion of Christ as well as with various martyrs. Locations associated with the Virgin Mary show the extent to which popular medieval legends had entered the pious imagination. Old Testament loci are also recounted: Adam's tomb, the places where Noah built the ark, the burning bush where God appeared to Moses, Pharaoh's "granaries" (the pyramids) constructed by Joseph, Samson's palace, David's castle, Absalom's house, and the site of what was Solomon's Temple. Nicholas describes his impressions of different religious ceremonies conducted by non-Roman-rite Christians—Greeks, Nestorians, and Armenians—and by Jews. He is repeatedly awed by dark-skinned Ethiopians and Egyptians. He generally distrusts Muslims and expresses no desire to visit Mecca.

Friar Nicholas's account is not purely meditative. Reflecting his merchant-class milieu, he pragmatically measured places and relics whenever he could *in situ* and includes their dimensions in his relation. He also records the tariffs paid to the "Saracens" in order to acquire access to particular sites, and he notes the specific indulgences granted for visiting them. Despite some similarities with earlier accounts, Nicholas's is in many instances the first to record details such as inscriptions, iconography of mosaics, colors, and architectural features of buildings, many now destroyed.

Friar Nicholas's travelogue survives in twenty manuscripts, mostly from the fifteenth century. It appeared in more than sixty print editions under the erroneous name of "Fra Noè."

**BIBLIOGRAPHY**

Franco, Augusto. "Cenni su Niccola da Poggibonsi." In *Esercitazioni sulla letteratura religiosa in Italia nei secoli XIII e XIV*. Ed. Guido Mazzoni. Florence: Alfani e Venturi, 1905, pp. 298–300.

Golubovich, P. Girolamo. *Biblioteca bio-bibliografica della Terra Santa e dell'Oriente francescano*. 5 vols. Florence: Quaracchi, 1927, vol. 5, pp. 1–24.

Hyde, J.K. "Italian Pilgrim Literature in the Late Middle Ages." *Bulletin of the John Rylands University Library of Manchester* 72.3 (1990): 13–33.

Nicholas of Poggibonsi. *Libro d'Oltramare*. Ed. A. Bacchi della Lega. Bologna: G. Romagnoli, 1881–1882; P.B. Bagatti rev. edition. 1968. Studium Biblicum Franciscanum, Publicazioni 2. Jerusalem: PP. Franciscani, 1945.

———. *A Voyage beyond the Seas (1346–1350)*. Trans. Theophilus Bellorini and Eugene Hoade. Publications of the Studium Biblicum Franciscanum 2. Jerusalem: Franciscan Press, 1945.

*Gloria Allaire*

**SEE ALSO**

Armenia; Eastern Christianity; Ethiopians; Franciscan Friars; Holy Land; Jacopo da Verona; Mecca; Navigation; Nestorianism; Pilgrimage, Christian; Transportation, Inland; Venice

## Nicholas of Thverá [Nikulás of Þverá] (d. 1159/1160)

A monk whose pilgrimage to Rome and the Holy Land in the early 1150s is detailed in medieval Iceland's only

# N

known complete vernacular itinerary, known as *Leiðarvísir* (Guide).

Little is known about the Icelandic pilgrim who is identified in one manuscript *explicit* (written in 1387) as "Abbot Nicholas, who was both wise and famous, blessed with a good memory, learned in many things, sage and truthful." The text attributed to this abbot describes the place of Jesus' crucifixion on Golgotha and the site of his nearby tomb as being within the confines of a single building in Jerusalem; it also refers to Ascalon as a city that is "still heathen." This strongly suggests that its writer visited the Holy Land between the consecration of the crusader-built Church of the Holy Sepulchre on July 15, 1149, and the Christian conquest of Ascalon in August 1153. Based on this chronology, the pilgrim has been identified as Nicholas, abbot (probably the first one) of Þverá, a Benedictine foundation established in 1155 at Munkaþverá on the Eyjafjord in northern Iceland. According to the *Guðmundar sögur biskups* and the *Jóns saga postola IV,* he was a talented man, surnamed Bergþorsson (or Bergsson), who composed a long lay (*drápa*) about St. John the Evangelist. Various annals and one saga record an "abbot Nicholas" dying in 1158, 1159, and 1160; one of the last two dates appears to refer to the pilgrim (the first applies to Nicholas Saemundson, an abbot of Iceland's other Benedictine monastery at Þingeyrar.)

Nicholas's *Leiðarvísir* falls into three sections of roughly equal length. The first begins with a prologue that briefly treats Iceland geography and then recounts the journey from Aalborg in northern Denmark to Cologne, up the Rhine to Basel, over the Alps via the St. Bernard Pass to Aosta, and on through Piacenza and Siena to Rome. He offers an alternative route for travelers from Norway. Nearly one-sixth of the account is devoted to Rome (*Rómaborg*); midway in his description of St. Peter's Church, Nicholas gives the building's measurements in a complete sentence in Latin, suggesting that the work is to some degree a translation. The narrative's second part traces the difficult route across southern Italy (the "kingdom of Sicily") and the voyage from Bari, along the east coast of the Adriatic, past Rhodes and Cyprus, to Acre. The Holy Land, called Judaea (*Jórsalaland*), is the focus of the third section. Nicholas reports on sites in Galilee, but devotes his attention largely to Jerusalem (*Jórsalaborg*), "the most splendid of all the cities of the world . . . [where] wondrous signs of Christ's passion are still seen."

Nicholas's itinerary is practical and succinct: his account of overland journeys consists largely of place-names, distances between them (given variously as miles and days), and an occasional notable feature (Salerno has "the best physicians"; Monte Cassino has a finger of St. Matthew). His treatment of the eastern Mediterranean is also largely a list of toponyms, although he pauses at the site of King Eirík I Ejegod's death (on July 10, 1103) on Cyprus to note appreciatively royal donations that cover the costs for wine drunk by "speakers of Danish" at Lucca and for all food consumed at Piacenza. Nicholas associates almost every site in and around Jerusalem with an event recorded in the Bible, but as a man from a northern latitude he cannot forbear making an observation based on a personal experience near the Jordan river: "if a man lies on his back on level ground and lifts up his knee with his clenched fist on top and raises his thumb from his fist, then the polestar is to be seen above it there, that high but no higher." He also "proves" that "the center of the earth" is in Jerusalem by stating that the sun shines from the meridian on the Feast of St. John the Baptist (June 24). Nicholas's return journey was brisk, a testimony to the relative ease with which travel might be conducted in the mid-1100s. It took him two weeks to sail from Acre to Apulia, another eight weeks to reach the Alps via Rome, and just over four more weeks to return to Aalborg. He is silent about the trip from Denmark to Iceland.

Nicholas's *Leiðarvísir*—a valuable record of 200 place-names, made vivid with anecdotes—is known from two medieval manuscripts (Copenhagen, Arnamagnæanisches Institut, AM 194 8vo [the complete text, written 1387, followed by a separate listing of holy places in Rome and Jerusalem that may also be by Nicholas, and bound with several other works related to geography and ethnography] and AM 736 II 4to [a single leaf, written *c.* 1400, containing the first third of the text]), as well as three eighteenth-century copies.

## BIBLIOGRAPHY

Hill, Joyce. "From Rome to Jerusalem: An Icelandic Itinerary of the Mid-Twelfth Century." *Harvard Theological Review* 76 (1983): 175–203.

Kålund, Kristian, and N. Beckman, eds. *Alfræði Íslenzk: Islandsk Encyklopædisk litteratur.* 3 vols. Samfund til Utgivelse af Gammel Nordisk Litteratur 37, 41, 45. Copenhagen: Møller, 1908–1918, vol. 1, pp. 12–23, 23–32.

Kedar, Benjamin Z., and Christian Westergård-Nielsen. "Icelanders in the Crusader Kingdom of Jerusalem: A Twelfth-Century Account." *Mediaeval Scandinavia* 11 (1978–1979): 193–211.

Simek, Rudolf. *Altnordische Kosmographie: Studien und Quellen zu Weltbild und Weltbeschreibung in Norwegen und Island vom 12. bis zum 14. Jahrhundert.* Berlin and New York: Walter de Gruyter, 1990, pp. 262–280, 478–490.

Wilkinson, John, with Joyce Hill, and W.F. Ryan, eds. *Jerusalem Pilgrimage 1099–1185.* Hakluyt Society, 2nd series, 167. London: Hakluyt Society, 1988, pp. 17–18, 215–219.

Scott D. Westrem

**SEE ALSO**

Acre; Center of the Earth; Holy Land; Iceland; Itineraries and *Periploi;* Jerusalem; Pilgrimage, Christian; Rome as a Pilgrimage Site

## Nomadism and Pastoralism

A way of life characteristic of many parts of Inner Asia and the Middle East during the medieval period, involving people who moved, with their possessions, from place to place to obtain pasture and water for the livestock that provided them with subsistence and protection.

Natural pasturelands covered—and indeed defined—Inner Asia (also known as "Central Eurasia") extending from Hungary to Manchuria, as well as much of the Middle East. Steppe, mountain meadows, and "desert" (technically, land with less than 50 percent vegetation cover) provided grazing, in some places very sparsely, or only seasonally, but abundantly in others: much of Inner Asia yields 600 kg of hay per hectare (approximately 535 pounds per acre). The steppe in Ukraine, northern Caucasia, northern Kazakhstan, and much of Inner Mongolia and Manchuria is, in fact, arable.

Arabian nomads, perpetuating the original Middle Eastern nomadism evidenced from the third millennium B.C.E., moved their animals—sheep where enough water was available, camels otherwise—over wide tracts of nonarable land to obtain sufficient grazing from exiguous vegetation. In the northern parts of the Middle East, and in Turkmenistan, Uzbekistan, Kyrgyzstan, and Chinese Turkestan, an analogous "economadism" obtained, with climate enforcing movement between the winter vegetation of rainy deserts and the summer grasses of mountain meadows. Scant resources compelled a drastic dispersal of the nomad population, and allowed (among the Arabs, Turkmen, and Kyrgyz) only an attenuated society, with communities consisting of camps of a few families. This made for insecurity and a compensating warrior ethos. Genealogically defined clans or "tribes" provided personal identification and grazing and water rights, but they could gather only with difficulty given the centrifugal force of pastoral necessity and the general absence of established leadership. War leaders, chosen ad hoc by consensus, served less as commanders than as facilitators of the further consensus necessary in military undertakings to maintain the voluntary and revokable participation of the nomads in predatory or military undertakings. Arabian nomads, although given great mobility and logistical flexibility by their camels, lacked the horses to field much cavalry (camels make poor combat mounts), and the weaponry, training, and discipline to form effective infantry.

The pastures of Inner Asia, generally much richer than those of Arabia, supplied nomads with a larger variety of animals, a more elaborate society, and far greater military capability. Sheep, goats, and various bovids enabled subsistence, with a nuclear family requiring the equivalent of 100 sheep (at five sheep or goats per bovid); camels served for transportation, not (as in Arabia) subsistence; and horses, available in abundance, provided food (horse meat and *kumis,* fermented mare's milk), transportation, and especially combat mounts. These warhorses—more accurately, war-ponies—shaped Inner Asian nomadism. Much pastureland in Inner Asia can support cultivation or at least sedentary pastoralism: 100 sheep and ten ponies need annual access to only about one-half square mile (1.3 square kilometers) of good steppe pasture. But the small villages of prenomadic Inner Asia could not defend themselves against cavalry, and so, as cavalry proliferated, at about the beginning of the first millennium B.C.E., nomadism in the region developed (more than a millennium after Middle Eastern nomadism). Villages and cultivation were abandoned for mobile herding that enabled both evasion of predators and the formation of large, defensible communities that could be sustained from the more extensive pastures made accessible by nomadic movement. The wholly pastoral economy also gave the new nomads more riders for their horses, since the chores of pastoral subsistence could be managed by women and children, freeing the men for other, especially military, employment. (Arabian camel-nomadism, by contrast, engaged more male

# N

subsistence labor, although still less than needed in cultivation.)

Like their Arabian counterparts, Inner Asian nomads lacked advanced weaponry, except for their bows, but they possessed an advanced weapons system: mounted archery. Pastoralism gave them enough horses to supply every man with mounts and to field all-cavalry armies; it gave them spare mounts enabling fast-paced hit-and-run tactics that exploited their weapons and avoided those of their enemies; and it gave them logistical freedom: the horses supported themselves by grazing, and the soldiers rode some and ate others (one pony could feed about 200 men for a day). Whole nomad peoples could move over the pasturelands like nomad armies, living off of their animals during great emigrations in the same way as on normal migratory rounds.

Richer pastures, greater population densities, and all-cavalry armies produced a more complex nomad society in Inner Asia (excepting the Turkmen and Kyrgyz) than in Arabia. Normal communities were still small, usually encampments of fewer than ten families, but large ones of a few thousand could be maintained by dint of frequent movements. Moreover, armies of tens of thousands of men—and in the case of the Mongols, hundreds of thousands—could be mobilized. These capacities required, and from very early times produced, a system of military command and political leadership centered in autocratic chieftaincy. Like their counterparts in Arabia, the Inner Asian nomads made use of genealogical organizations (clans) for various definitional purposes. But the Inner Asians, unlike the Arabians, also organized themselves for action in political groupings (tribes) centered on chiefs. Such leadership, and the elastic capacity of Inner Asian tribalism to grow by recruitment unlimited by genealogical, linguistic, or religious criteria, could create very large, coherent, and dangerous polities. In Inner Asia, as in Arabia, the nomads embraced a warrior culture, to which the military and political capacity of the Inner Asians gave much greater scope for expression. But nomad power tended to stalemate in endemic intra- and intertribal warfare. Tribesmen sought opportunities to demonstrate their prowess and heroism, usually against their neighbors; would-be chiefs, encouraged by conflicting principles of succession, fought one another; and established chiefs attempted to enlarge their tribes and territories at one another's expense. Weaknesses in settled societies adjacent to the nomads sometimes allowed nomad penetration and domination, as for instance by the Avars and Seljuks. In two cases, Inner Asian nomad power was fully mobilized. The Turks in the sixth century and the Mongols in the thirteenth used the compelling idea of world conquest (already part of Hunnish rhetoric by the fifth century) to unify Inner Asia, and, in the case of the Mongols, to proceed much further toward their ideal goal. Even the Arabian nomads managed to win an empire for Islam when supplied with leadership and inspiration from Medina and Mecca.

The pastures of Inner Asia and the Middle East could support long-distance commerce as well as the migrations and campaigns of nomads. Free grazing eliminated the cost of fodder that limited the range of animal haulage in sedentary societies. Under the Mongols, cargoes could be packed or pulled across the steppe between China and Europe in about five and a half months. But during most of the medieval period this steppe route was closed by nomad interference. Nomads and sedentaries living in proximity to each other tended to develop an economic symbiosis; in Central Asia and the Middle East, for example, nomads traded their animals and animal products, which the intensive cultivators of irrigated land lacked, and sold slaves they took in their internecine and foreign wars, in exchange for the goods of farmers and artisans. In the Far East, however, distance and hostility separated the nomad and Chinese economies. Nomads' animals could not easily be moved off of the steppe to Chinese markets, and China in any case raised its own animals, except for horses. Conversely, Chinese grain could not be supplied to the nomads in significant quantities because of the transportation effort required. Other exchanges were usually stifled by military concerns. China and the nomads vied for control of the arable steppes of Inner Mongolia, and the competition tainted trade relations. China embargoed exports of weapons and strategic metals; the nomads sold China inferior horses at high prices. Both sides made raids on each other in the frontier zone that inflicted commercial as well as strategic damage. These hostilities, active or latent, constricted interregional trade. For reasons of security, the Silk Road had to pass through the wastelands and between the oases of the Tarim basin rather than across the pastures of Mongolia.

## BIBLIOGRAPHY

Barth, Fredrik. *Nomads of South Persia: The Basseri Tribe of the Khamseh Confederacy.* Oslo: Oslo UP; London: Allen and Unwin, 1961; rpt. Prospect Heights, IL: Waveland, 1986.

Cole, Donald P. *Nomads of the Nomads: The Al Murrah Bedouin of the Empty Quarter.* Arlington Heights, IL: Harlan Davidson, 1975.

Dahl, Gudrun, and Anders Hjort. *Having Herds: Pastoral Herd Growth and Household Economy.* Stockholm U Studies in Social Anthropology, 2. Stockholm: U of Stockholm P, 1976.

Khazanov, Anatoli M. *Nomads and the Outside World.* Trans. Julia Crookenden 1983 (Russian). Cambridge Studies in Social Anthropology 44. Cambridge: Cambridge UP, 1984.

Lees, S., and Daniel Bates. "The Origins of Specialized Nomadic Pastoralism." *American Antiquity* 39 (1974): 189–193.

Smith, John Masson, Jr. "Mongol Nomadism and Middle Eastern Geography: Qishlaqs and Tümens." In *The Mongol Empire and Its Legacy.* Ed. Reuven Amitai-Preiss and David O. Morgan. Leiden: Brill, 1999.

*John Masson Smith Jr.*

**SEE ALSO**

Avars; Huns; Inner Asian Trade; Inner Asian Travel; Kumis; Mecca; Medina; Seljuk Turks; Silk Roads; Transportation, Inland

## Notaries

The profession of notary, first termed *tabellio publicus* or *notarius publicus,* had its roots in Roman law traditions. Notaries functioned as recordkeepers for society, preserving public and private law transactions in the form of *instrumenta.* Notaries were paralegal personnel, generally with some university legal training and apprenticeship. In most cities there were also age and residency requirements for entry into the profession.

There were three forms of the notarial act: the brief note, the minute, and the extended form without abbreviations. Minutes with considerable details of specific content, but with many abbreviated legal formulae, make up most of the surviving notarial registers. If requested, the notary would produce an extended version of the transaction or contract, eliminating the abbreviations of the minute.

Italian towns set the pace in legal and institutional developments in Western Europe in the eleventh and twelfth centuries, followed closely by other areas of southern Europe. The revival of Roman law and the emergence of consular governments in the eleventh and twelfth centuries in these areas spawned judicial, governmental, and economic institutions and their documentary records. These records took various forms; by the beginning of the thirteenth century, municipal statutes, chronicles, and charters complemented seigneurial and episcopal cartulary notices, while as early as the mid-twelfth century, Genoa preserved the earliest notarial registers. Registers from the thirteenth and fourteenth centuries remain in the archives of many towns of southern Europe.

Notarial registers contain legally valid instruments written by notaries who had been licensed by public authorities, including kings, bishops, the emperor, and the pope. The notarial instrument might be a will; a cash or credit sale of real property, commodities, or luxury products; an act of litigation; an emancipation; an apprenticeship; an appointment to office; an acquittal; or a statement or letter of one kind or another, solemnly registered by the notary in the presence of witnesses. The notary's register or cartulary served the purpose of a much expanded registry of public deeds, preserving notations of engagements for which written proof, valid in a court of law, might be needed in the future.

**BIBLIOGRAPHY**

Herlihy, David. *Pisa in the Early Renaissance: A Study of Urban Growth.* New Haven: Yale UP, 1958.

Lopez, Robert S. "The Unexplored Wealth of the Notarial Archives in Pisa and Lucca." In *Mélanges d'histoire du Moyen Age dédiés à la mémoire de Louis Halphen.* Paris: Presses Universitaires de France, 1951, pp. 417–432.

Pryor, John H. *Business Contracts of Medieval Provence: Selected Notulae from the Cartulary of Giraud Amalric of Marseilles: 1248.* Toronto: Pontifical Institute of Mediaeval Studies, 1981.

*Kathryn L. Reyerson*

**SEE ALSO**

Genoa; Law, Commercial; Shipping Contracts, Mediterranean

## *Nuremberg Chronicle*

An early printed book officially titled *Liber chronicarum cum figuris et ymaginibus ab inicio mundi (A History of the World from Its Beginning with Pictures and Imaginative Drawings),* compiled from an assortment of texts by the humanist Hartmann Schedel (1440–1514). It was commissioned by Sebald Schreyer and Sebastian Kammermeister and was printed in 1493 by Anton Koberger in Nuremberg, the commercial and intellectual center of late medieval Germany. The *Chronicle* is elaborately illustrated with more than 1,800 woodcuts (in some copies, these are are hand-tinted) by Michael Wohlgemut and Wilhelm Pleydenwurff; Albrecht Dürer probably assisted in the design. Uniting Christian revelation and universal history into a comprehensive, chronological narrative, Schedel's sweeping account was one of the most popular books of the late Middle Ages. More than 3,500 copies in the original Latin and subsequent German translation were printed (1,200 are extant, 800 in Latin and 400 in German), making it a late medieval/ early modern "best-seller."

The *Chronicle* summarizes current knowledge of places and peoples—derived both from humanist sources and from Schedel's own extensive travels—from the seven days of Creation in Genesis through doomsday. Following the scheme of the encyclopedist Isidore of Seville (*c.* 560–636), Schedel divides history into seven ages. For the first six ages, the text freely mixes scriptural narrative, sacred genealogy (from Adam to Christ), mythology, classical literary narrative, early medieval and near-contemporary political and ecclesiastical history, and geography to narrate the history of the world up to the date of publication, 1493. The seventh age predicts and illustrates the future coming of Antichrist and the Last Judgment.

For its depictions of cities and its actual maps, the *Chronicle* was a milestone in the development of cartography. Besides narrative scenes, the book contains panoramic or skyline views of real and mythic cities described by Schedel in the text, including towns in southern Germany and southern Europe, biblical sites, cathedral cities, even "Amazonia." These woodcuts depict realistically rendered landmark buildings visited by the authors as well as projections of pure fantasy.

The same blend of authenticity and fantasy characterizes the maps in the *Nuremberg Chronicle*. At one ex-

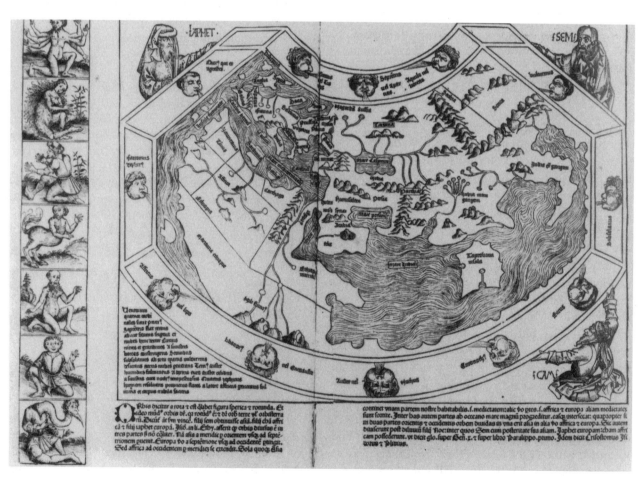

*Mappamundi.* Hartmann Schedel, *Liber Chronicarum.* Nuremberg: Anton Koberger, 1493, fols. 12v–13r.

treme, the *Chronicle*'s description of Germany includes the first printed "modern" map of central Europe, rendered by Hieronymus Münzer after a model by the humanist Cardinal Nicholas of Cusa (the so-called Eichstätt map). At the other extreme, following the biblical narrative of Noah's ark in the second age of history, is a map of the world similar to one in a 1488 Venetian edition of the *Cosmographia* by the Roman geographer Pomponius Mela. Schedel's double-woodcut Ptolemaic *mappamundi* is designed to appear as if held up to view at three of its corners by the sons of Noah, reflecting the biblical theory of world habitation in which the postdiluvian continents of Europe, Asia, and Africa were founded respectively by Japhet, Shem, and Cham (Ham). However, despite the new cartographic knowledge acquired by European navigators in the previous decades, even the contours of Europe are inaccurately rendered on Schedel's 1493 map. Illustrated on fol. 12r and in the left margin of fol. 12v are various antipodean beings, the imagined inhabitants of Ethiopia, Libya, Scythia, and India. Taking their information from Pliny, Solinus, St. Augustine, and Isidore of Seville, the illustrators depict representatives of "monstrous races" such as hermaphrodites, sciapods, wild people, centaurs, crane-men, and six-armed men. Despite Augustine and Isidore's classification of these exotic races as human, Schedel physically places them off, but adjacent to, the map, emphasizing their otherness compared with the normalcy of the humans holding the map's corners.

## BIBLIOGRAPHY

Campbell, Tony. *The Earliest Printed Maps 1472–1500.* Berkeley: U of California P, 1987, pp.152–159 and figs. 33, 34, 45, 46.

Duniway, David Cushing. "A Study of the *Nuremberg Chronicle.*" *Papers of the Bibliographical Society of America* 35 (1941): 17–34.

*Gothic and Renaissance Art in Nuremberg 1300–1550.* New York: The Metropolitan Museum of Art, 1986, pp. 233–234.

Schedel, Hartmann. *Die Schedelsche Weltchronik nach der Ausgabe von 1493.* Epilogue by Rudolf Pörtner. Die bibliophilen Taschenbücher 64. Dortmund: Harenberg, 1978. English version: *The Nuremberg Chronicle: A Facsimile of Hartmann Schedel's Buch der Chroniken, Printed by Anton Koberger in 1493.* New York: Landmark, 1979.

Wilson, Adrian. *The Making of the Nuremberg Chronicle.* Amsterdam: Israel, 1976.

*Lorraine Kochanske Stock*

## SEE ALSO

Amazons; Antipodes; Ethiopians; Ham's Curse and Africans; Higden, Ranulf; India; Isidore of Seville; *Mappamundi*; Mela, Pomponius; Monstrosity, Geographical; Nicholas of Cusa; Pliny the Elder; Ptolemy; Rolevinck, Werner; Scythia; Solinus, Julius Gaius; Wild People, Mythical, and New World Relations

## Odoric of Pordenone

Beatified (July 2, 1755) by Pope Benedict XIV; Blessed Odoric of Pordenone was one of the greatest travelers in the Middle Ages. Born near Friuli, Italy, around 1265, he became a Franciscan friar around 1280 and was ordained a priest around 1290. He did missionary work in southern Russia for more than a decade in the Mongol Qipchak khânate, returned to Italy, then went to Constantinople, Trebizond (Turkey), and Tabriz (Persia) for eight more years of missionary work. In 1322, he left for East Asia, accompanied by Friar James of Ireland and a servant, to join Archbishop John of Monte Corvino in China. Journeying by way of southern Persia, northern Arabia, and present-day Iraq, they arrived at Hormuz, where they set sail for India. At Thana, near Bombay, Odoric gathered relics of Thomas of Tolentino and three other friars who were martyred there in 1320. He visited the Church of St. Thomas at Mylapore (Madras), proceeded east to Sumatra, Java, and Champa (southern Vietnam), and arrived in China at Guangzhou (Canton), around 1323–1324.

Odoric and James went north to Zaiton (Quanzhou, Fujian), visited Bishop Andrew of Perugia, and continued north to Fuzhou, Hangzhou, Nanjing, and Yangzhou, arriving in 1325 at the Mongol capital Daidu (Beijing, Khanbaliq). Odoric assisted Archbishop John of Monte Corvino for three years, then departed before John's death (1328) to return home, seeking more missionaries for China. This journey was overland via Shanxi, Shaanxi, Gansu, Xinjiang or Chinese Turkestan, Central Asia, Persia, Iraq, and Syria, finally arriving at Venice in 1329. En route to Avignon to visit Pope John XXII, he fell ill at Pisa, and returned to Udine. He dictated his travel journal there in May 1330. He died on January 14, 1331.

The narrative of Odoric's journey, called *Relatio* (1330), and translated into French by Jean le Long as *Le chemin de la peregrinacion et du voyage* in 1351, is his great contribution to travel writing, providing a large amount of information on the Mongol court, especially its social and hierarchical relationships, its mix of Christians and Muslims, and even on the khân's daily activities such as hunting and being blessed by the local bishop. The purpose, as the author tells us, was to visit the land of the infidels so as to save souls. The *Relatio*, which is told in the first person, also contains elements of the fabulous travel narrative, such as a report of a journey down one of the Four Rivers of Paradise and the voyage through a perilous valley filled with many kinds of horrors that the narrator survives only by his strong faith. Elements of the *Relatio* were incorporated into and elaborated upon by the author of *The Book of John Mandeville* (*c.* 1360).

### BIBLIOGRAPHY

Jandesek, Reinhold. *Der Bericht des Odoric da Pordenone über seine Reise nach Asien.* Bamberger Schriften Kulturgeschichte 1. Bamberg: self-published, 1987.

de Rachewiltz, Igor. *Papal Envoys to the Great Khan.* Stanford: Stanford UP, 1971.

Strasmann, Gilbert, ed. *Konrad Steckels Deutsche Übertragung der Reise nach China des Odoric de Pordenone.* Texte des Späten Mittelalters und der Frühen Neuzeit 20. Berlin: Schmidt,1968.

De Vignay, Jean. *Les Merveilles de la Terre d'Outremer.* Traduction du XIVe siècle du récit de voyage d'Odoric de Pordenone. Ed. D.A. Trotter. Exeter, England: University of Exeter, 1990.

O

Book of Wonders. Pope John XXII sends Odoric to the Holy Land. Paris, Bibliothèque Nationale MS fr. 2810, fol. 97r, *c.* 1440. Courtesy Bibliothèque Nationale.

Yule-Cordier. *Cathay and the Way Thither.* 2nd series. See Gen. Bib.

*Hugh D. Walker*

**SEE ALSO**

Andrew, Son of Guido of Perugia; Cumans; Four Rivers of Paradise; Franciscan Friars; India; John of Monte Corvino; Khanbaliq; *Mandeville's Travels;* Missionaries to China; Trebizond; Vietnam and Java, Mongol Invasions of; Zaiton

## Oikoumene

The entire inhabited landmass of the earth. Ionian geographers of the sixth century B.C.E. used *oikoumene* as an adjective ("inhabited") modifying the word for earth; eventually it became a noun used to describe a spherical earth, where it meant the section of the globe's surface lit from sunrise to sunset. Usually this area is imagined surrounded by the *fines terrae* or "edges of the world" and framed by the Ocean Sea. The Romans called the *oikoumene* the *orbis terrarum Romanus,* that is, the territory encompassing the Roman sphere of political influence.

Both the Greek and the Roman explanations of the concept were known to the Middle Ages. The Greek theory was transmitted by way of Eratosthenes (third century B.C.E.) and the Stoic Crates of Mallos (second century B.C.E.) to Macrobius (early fifth century C.E.), who made it accessible to the Latin West in his *Commentary on the Dream of Scipio.* According to Macrobius's formulation, the globe is divided in four symmetrical parts by two zones of ocean, crossing each other at right angles; each quarter forms an island continent, not accessible one to another. Only one of them is the *oikoumene,* usually imagined in the Northern Hemisphere, while the *perioikoumenic* continent is opposite, the *anteoikoumenic* is in the south and the *antichthonic* continent is on the back of the Southern Hemisphere. The Greeks imagined these four insular continents as ovals, the Romans as disks.

Christianity soon absorbed these ideas. Medieval conceptions of the earth were homocentric. The writers of the Old Testament imagined the world always as the *oikoumene;* that is why St. Jerome, when he translated the Vulgate, always speaks of *terra,* "earth," while the Greek New Testament *kosmos* is rendered in Latin *mundus.* The Middle Ages were primarily interested in salvation history and therefore used "world" in the sense of *oikoumene; kosmos* was something secondary.

The hemispherical map of Lambert of Saint-Omer's *Liber Floridus* is an example of the *oikoumene* depicted as one insular continent together with the *anteoikoumenic* continent, while Ptolemy presented quite another system, where the ocean is always an inland sea between parts of the *oikoumene.*

### BIBLIOGRAPHY

Lasserre, François. "Oikumene." *Der Kleine Pauly IV, Lexikon der Antike.* Munich: Druckenmüller, 1975; rpt. Deutscher Taschenbuch Verlag, 1979, col. 254–256.

Wright, John Kirtland. *The Geographical Lore of the Time of the Crusades,* pp. 257–261. See Gen. Bib.

*Anna-Dorothee von den Brincken*

**SEE ALSO**

Antipodes; Climate; Edges of the World; Geography in Medieval Europe; Jerome Map of Asia; *Liber Floridus;* Ptolemy; *Terra Incognita*

## Opicinus de Canistris (1296–1355)

A scribe and designer of a set of highly idiosyncratic maps. Opicinus de Canistris spent most of his life in Avignon as a scribe in the papal office of the Apostolic Penitentiary, although earlier he had been a parish priest and had trained as a book illuminator. The author of several religious works, including a famous description of his birthplace of Pavia, he would be little remembered today were it not for the survival of two autograph manuscripts, both referring to a significant and life-threatening illness that, he tells us, struck him on March 31, 1334, and left him partially paralyzed in his right, or writing, hand and unable to continue his official work. Both these documents, now preserved in the Vatican Library, contain diagrammatic drawings that Opicinus made under the influence of this new mystical understanding.

The first of these documents, MS. Pal. lat. 1993, is really a collection of twenty-seven loose parchment sheets, some of them thirty-six inches (ninety-two cm) long, on which Opicinus created a series of large cosmological diagrams. Most of these are geometrically constructed out of circles and suggest a knowledge of contemporary cosmological diagrams and current medical images such as the zodiac man, but also the tradition of diagrammatic exegesis going back to the twelfth century. However, Opicinus creates something entirely new and personal from these sources, combining them into fluid and ever-changing schemata. He utilizes patterns that would have been known to him from his work as an illuminator, such as frontal figures of the Virgin and Child and an elegant, symmetrical image of Christ crucified. Whereas most diagrams produced during the Middle Ages are attempts to fix and clarify, Opicinus uses them to explore and transform. His obsessions are often political, such as the role of the papacy and the church's relationship with the world, but also deeply personal. On one sheet a large circular calendar represents each year in the author's life from his conception. In these designs, too, we see the first of the map constructions in which he superimposes his own anthropomorphic ideas on the outlines of the world as it was then known. These diagrams show a knowledge of portolan charts, accurate nautical maps of the area developed in the late thirteenth century that Opicinus tells us he had seen in Genoa.

The second manuscript, MS. Vat. lat. 6435, was discovered and published only after World War II. This is a small, paper volume and, unlike the large single leaves

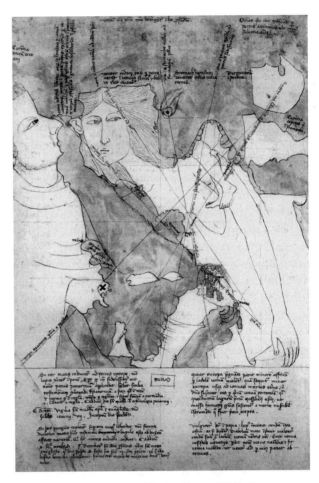

Opicinus de Canistris. World Map. Rome, Bibliotheca Apostolica Vaticana MS Vat. lat. 6435, fol. 53v, c. 1330. Courtesy of the Bibliotheca Apostolica Vaticana.

of MS. Pal. lat. 1993, contains not only schematic drawings but large amounts of text, amounting to a kind of diary of the years following his mystical conversion. Here Opicinus repeats and develops an anthropomorphized map that shows Spain and Italy forming the head and leg of one human figure, with Africa forming the profile head of another. Whereas in the Palatinus manuscript Europe was usually represented as a man and Africa as a woman whispering obscenely into his ear, here the continent of Europe is also represented as female. Certain themes and fantasies recur throughout the maps, such as the Mediterranean styled as the "diabolicum mare" and taking the shape of a devil and what Opicinus refers to as "the Britannic sea between Britain and Spain" looking like a devouring lion.

Geography in Opicinus's schema is not only diabolized but sexualized, with Venice often pictured and

# O

described as a vulva open to a lecherous sea of sperm and Opicinus's birthplace of Pavia always being marked by some portentous image, sometimes a minute replication of the larger copulating continents. Rhumblines do not serve their original navigational purpose but, rather, draw out personal associations between different areas. On the last pages of the Vaticanus manuscript, Opicinus superimposes a grid-map of his own parish in Pavia on that of Europe and North Africa, as usual fascinated by visual correspondences that evoke symbolic meanings.

Scholars who have written about these unique drawings have tended to see in them manifestations of a disordered, even psychotic, personality. However, if one views Opicinus within the mystical tradition of visionary thinkers stretching back to Hildegard of Bingen (1099–1179), there is no need to be so ruthlessly clinical. He then emerges as an individual living in troubled times and struggling to create his own symbolic associations and meanings in an overdetermined universe. In terms of the history of geographical knowledge and exploration, these cartographic fantasies show how geographical exploration of the macrocosm of the world outside expands simultaneously with that of the microcosm of the world within: the map and the self are always combined. Opicinus brings together the most innovative forms of mapmaking, which he sees as directly inspired by God, with an intensely personal cosmology that we are only just beginning to understand.

## BIBLIOGRAPHY

Almagià, Roberto. *Monumenta cartographica Vaticana.* Vol. 1. Rome: Biblioteca Apostolica Vaticana, 1944.

Arentzen, Jörg-Geerd. *Imago Mundi Cartographica: Studien zur Bildlichkeit mittelalterlicher Welt- und Ökumenekarten unter besonderer Berücksichtigung des Zusammenwirkens von Text und Bild.* Münstersche Mittelalter-Schriften 53. Munich: Wilhelm Fink, 1984.

Camille, Michael. "The Image and the Self: Unwriting Late Medieval Bodies." *Framing Medieval Bodies.* Ed. Sara Kay and Miri Rubin. Manchester, England: Manchester UP, 1994.

Kris, Ernst. "A Psychotic Artist of the Middle Ages." In *Psychoanalytic Explorations in Art.* New York: International Universities Press, 1952.

Salomon, Richard Georg. *Opicinus de Canistris: Weltbild und Bekenntnisse eines Avignonesischen Klerikers des 14. Jahrhunderts.* Including studies by Adelheid Heimann and Richard Krautheimer. Studies of the Warburg Institute 1A and 1B. London: The Warburg Institute, 1936; rpt. Nendeln, 1965.

———. "A Newly Discovered Manuscript of Opicinus de Canistris: A Preliminary Report." *Journal of the Warburg and Courtauld Institutes* 16 (1953): 45–57.

Tozzi, Pierluigi. *Opicino e Pavia.* Pavia: Libreria Cardano, 1990.

*Michael Camille*

SEE ALSO
*Mappamundi;* Portolan Charts

## Orb of Imperial Power

A symbol of sovereignty, referring to the classical conception of the universe or world as a globe, which dates at least from the Greek geographers of the fifth century B.C.E. Roman emperors held orbs topped by a winged Victory, wreath in hand, as a badge of office. Christianity replaced this figure with a cross, symbolizing Christ's dominion over the world. Actual orbs, usually made of precious metal and encrusted with jewels, were presented to medieval monarchs at their enthronement. When held by kings, the orb not only represented temporal power, but also alluded to the close and, theoretically at least, reciprocal relationship between church and state. This was particularly true for Holy Roman emperors, who were crowned by the pope and whose consent was required to validate a papal election.

By the fifth and sixth centuries, both Western Roman and Byzantine emperors appear pictorially with orbs. The tradition had reached the Holy Roman Empire by the late tenth century, as seen in numerous illustrations of Otto III (r. 983–1002), including the Aachen Gospels, a famous Carolingian illuminated manuscript. Usually held in the left hand, the orb's counterparts were a scepter or sword gripped in the right; as a state emblem it spread from Germany throughout Europe. The seal of William the Conqueror (r. 1066–1087) shows him with the orb, initiating a long English tradition. Frontal representations of kings holding orbs became medieval conventions for paintings, prints, and coinage in Hungary, Sweden, Poland, Russia, and elsewhere. Occasionally, as in Ambrogio Lorenzetti's fourteenth-century fresco at Siena, *Allegory of Good Government,* Government itself was personified with orb in hand.

Christ with crystal orb. Oxford, Bodleian Library MS Douce 311, fol. 122r, *c.* 1500. Courtesy of the Bodleian Library, Oxford.

Orbs also appear in late medieval and early modern Christian iconography, particularly in northern Europe. Sometimes held by God the Father, angels, or the Virgin Mary, they are more closely identified with Christ. While Jan van Eyck (*c.* 1389–1441) shows the infant Jesus clasping an orb in several works, Christ as *Salvator Mundi* (Savior of the World) most commonly holds the emblem, as paintings from the fifteenth (and early sixteenth) centuries by Rogier van der Weyden, Hans Memling, Hieronymous Bosch, and others demonstrate.

**BIBLIOGRAPHY**
Beckwith, John. *Early Medieval Art.* London: Thames and Hudson, 1969.
Cutler, Charles D. *Northern Painting from Pucelle to Bruegel.* New York: Holt, Rinehart, and Winston, 1968.
Grant, Michael. *The Fall of the Roman Empire: A Reappraisal.* Radnor, PA: Annenberg, 1976.
Gurney, Gene. *Kingdoms of Europe.* New York: Crown, 1982.

*Kathy Curnow*

**SEE ALSO**
Byzantine Empire; Coinage and Money; Hungary; Poland; Popes; Psalter Map

## Orientalism

The process by which Latin Christians of the Middle Ages constructed an image of the Oriental as "other": someone whose way of life could seem either enticing, appalling, or both at the same time but was, in any event, decidedly not European.

Orientalism, as used in nineteenth- and early-twentieth-century English, referred primarily to the study of Arabic and other Near Eastern languages and of Near Eastern history and culture more generally. In eighteenth-century English, however, "orientalisms" were traits of culture believed to be characteristic of "oriental" or Eastern cultures: behind the terminology was the notion that cultures of Asia—from Anatolia to Japan—shared a common outlook that made them different from Western societies.

Such stereotyping existed in antiquity. Egyptians, for example, were distinctly "other" to Herodotus (484–428 B.C.E.) and to Roman travelers of the fourth century C.E. Pliny the Elder's (23–79 C.E.) *Natural History* populated the Far East with fantastic beasts and monstrous races of men. While Pliny coupled this information with reliable scientific and ethnographic information, his book came down to the Middle Ages chiefly in a much abridged digest by Solinus (fl. 230–240), who emphasized the monstrous and the marvelous at the expense of accuracy.

In the tenth and eleventh centuries, as Rome and Constantinople found themselves increasingly at odds theologically and culturally, Byzantium was portrayed as a land of strange and irrational people. Notker of Gall (*c.* 840–912) ascribes to the Greeks, among other bizarre customs, a law that anyone who turns over a fish on his plate while eating it is immediately put to death. The perception of "otherness" was, of course, mutual, as the writings of Anna Comnena (1083–1153) and other Byzantines show. This "otherness" is a product of both doctrinal differences and political and cultural conflict: Notker, after all, was justifying Charlemagne's claim to

# O

the title of emperor, which he considered to have been monopolized by Greeks, whom he portrays as irrational and effeminate. Both Pope Nicholas I (r. 858–867) and Liudprand of Cremona (c. 920–972) bolster their own claims of Roman primacy by portraying the Greeks as dishonest and prone to heresy.

Further east, the world of the "Saracens" is seen as both more dangerous and more intriguing than the Byzantine Empire. For some of the chroniclers of the First Crusade, as for the anonymous author of the *Song of Roland,* Saracens were pagans who worshipped golden idols of Muhammad (one of which, according to several chroniclers, the crusader Tancred found in the temple of Jerusalem in 1099 and destroyed). The pagan warriors in the *Song of Roland* came from strange places where no wheat grew, where men had skin of iron, where demons lived. Yet the Muslim world was also enticing: stories of liaisons between Christian men and Saracen princesses became popular, while Saladin attained to the legendary apex of chivalry.

The world to the east of Islam also had an important place in the Latin imagination. In *mappaemundi,* the edges of the globe—particularly the eastern edges—are the domain of strange and mythical creatures. According to Jean de Joinville (1224/1225–1317), cinnamon, ginger, and other such treasures float down the Nile from Eden, to be fished out by the Egyptians. Stories of voyages to India and China proffer tales of danger and enticement: islands full of pearls, men who share their wives and daughters with guests, men who wash themselves in their own urine, dog-headed people, cyclopes, cannibals. Further east are symbols of Christian hopes and fears: the Christian kingdom of Prester John, Gog and Magog, the Garden of Eden.

What do irrational Byzantines have in common with dog-headed men? Both are part of the stereotype of "Eastern Otherness." This Orient varies in the nature and degree of its strangeness depending on the fears and interests of the individual author, though the tendency (seen most clearly in travel narratives) is for the world to grow gradually stranger the farther east one goes. The East is perceived as different from the West, a distant stage on which to project one's fantasies and fears. This inscrutable East is irrational, frightening, and enticing.

## BIBLIOGRAPHY

Engels, Odilo, and Peter Schreiner, eds. *Die Begegnung des Westens mit dem Osten: Kongreßakten des 4. Symposions des Mediävistenverbandes in Köln 1991 aus Anlaß des 1000 Todesjahres der Kaiserin Theophanu.* Sigmaringen: Thorbecke, 1993.

Friedman, John Block. *The Monstrous Races in Medieval Art and Thought.* Cambridge, MA: Harvard UP, 1981; rpt. Syracuse, NY: Syracuse UP, 1999.

LeGoff, Jacques. "The Medieval West and the Indian Ocean: An Oneiric Horizon." In *Time, Work, and Culture in the Middle Ages.* Trans. Arthur Goldhammer. Chicago: U of Chicago P, 1980, pp. 189–200.

Rodinson, Maxime. *Europe and the Mystique of Islam.* Trans. T. Veinus. Seattle: U of Washington P, 1987.

Said, Edward. *Orientalism.* 1978; rpt. New York: Vintage, 1979.

Tolan, John, ed. *Medieval Christian Perceptions of Islam: A Book of Essays.* New York and London: Garland, 1995.

*John Victor Tolan*

**SEE ALSO**

Byzantine Empire; Cannibalism; China; Constantinople; Costume, Oriental; Eastern Christianity; Edges of the World; Egypt; Gog and Magog; India; Joinville, Jean de; Liudprand of Cremona; *Mappamundi;* Marriages between Muslims and Christians, Attitudes toward; Monstrosity, Geographical; Paradise, Travel to; Prester John; Saladin; Solinus, Julius Gaius; *Wonders of the East*

## Orosius (fl. 420)

A Christian historian and disciple of St. Augustine in the early fifth century. Orosius's fame mainly depends on his epitome of the history of the world, *Historiarum adversum paganos libri VII* (the Seven Books of History against the Pagans), which describes the complete sweep of world history up to the early 400s. It was probably completed about 418.

Orosius was probably born in Brancara (Braga) in Portugal, and died after 418, most likely in Africa. As a young man he had become a Christian cleric (*presbyter*) but had to flee his country because of the incursions of the Vandals. In 414, he reached North Africa, where he discussed his *Commonitorium de errore Pricillianistarum et Origenistarum* with Augustine at Hippo. The following year, encouraged by the eminent theologian, he traveled to Palestine to visit Jerome at Bethlehem. During his stay in Palestine, Orosius became involved in religious controversy, as a result of which he wrote his *Liber apologeticus.* After his return to North Africa he began the work for which he is best remembered.

*The Seven Books of History* were inspired by St. Augustine, who, in his *City of God,* had emphasized the need for a historical work that would prove that wars, plagues, and natural disasters had afflicted mankind more greatly in times *before* the emergence of Christendom, and that accusations by "pagans" that Christianity had unloosed catastrophes on earth were unfounded.

The book divided human history into seven periods from Creation to the fifth century. Short geographical sketches were not uncommon at the beginning of historical works, but Orosius was the first to begin his books on *historia* with a detailed geographical survey of the ancient world (1.2.1–106) so that students would be able to locate specific wars and pestilences (1.1.17). In contrast to the historical sections of Orosius's book, which are written in a sophisticated literary style that aimed at the essence and not the image of things, this geographical "prologue" is dry, though praiseworthy for clarity and intelligence. Orosius first mentions the three continents of the world—Asia, Europe, and Africa—then proceeds to describe each in detail, mostly from east to west, taking into account the unity of the separate parts. His descriptions are, in effect, lists of place names of the principal rivers, gulfs, seas, mountains, peninsulas, cities, and countries in each region. (The large number of toponyms gave rise to considerable textual corruption as manuscripts were copied.) His order is as follows: south Asia, north Asia, north Europe, south Europe, the British Isles, Africa, and finally the islands of the Mediterranean. A subtle distinction between the Roman and the barbarian worlds can also be seen.

The source of Orosius's depiction of the world has not been identified. It is thought that he had an ancient map at his disposal. He was the first to use the term *Asia Minor* in its modern sense, and he offers a few details about world geography that are not known from earlier sources.

Scholars have debated whether Orosius believed the world to be a circle, a sphere, or some other form. He certainly accepted the traditional view that the world's three continents were surrounded by a single "Sea-Ocean," and that a representation of the world would place the east (Babylon) at the top. Jerusalem is not, for Orosius, the center of the earth (as it would become in some later T-O maps [see Maps]); indeed, this heart of Christendom is absent from Orosius's description.

Like Solinus's *Collection of Memorable Things* and Isidore's *Etymologies,* Orosius's *Seven Books of History* exercised a long and profound influence during the Middle Ages. The geographical sections of his work were used *inter alia* by Jordanes, Isidore of Seville, the *Liber glossarum,* the Venerable Bede (in his *Ecclesiastical History*), Dicuil (in *De mensura orbis terrae*), and the author of the anonymous *De situ orbis* (ninth century), and Honorius Augustodunensis (in his *Imago mundi* [*c.* 1110]). The Hereford mappamundi includes a legend that attributes at least some information it contains to Orosius's *De ornesta mundi,* another title the work had in the Middle Ages. From the standpoint of literary history, perhaps the most important translation of Orosius was made into Old English—probably in the late ninth century as part of the educational program commissioned by King Alfred the Great. This rendering is also noteworthy for interpolations to Orosius's text that offer additional information about the geography of Scandinavia and the Baltic attributed to the travelers Ohthere and Wulfstan.

More than 200 Orosius manuscripts are known today, a considerable number. The interest in his geographical description of the world as a source for geographical information declined, however, after the classical geographers were recovered by humanists and new information derived from geographical exploration by merchants and discoverers spread during the late fifteenth century.

**BIBLIOGRAPHY**

Janvier, Yves. *La Géographie d'Orose.* Paris: Société d'édition Les Belles Lettres, 1982.

Orosius, Paulus. *Orosii Historiarum adversum paganos libri VII.* Corpus Scriptorum Ecclesiasticorum Latinorum 5. Vienna: Gerold, 1882; rpt. New York/London: Johnson Reprint, 1966.

———. *The Seven Books of History against the Pagans.* Trans. Roy J. Deferrari. The Fathers of the Church 50. Washington, DC: Catholic U of America P, 1964.

*Z.R.W.M. von Martels*

**SEE ALSO**

Bede; Dicuil; Exploration and Expansion, European; Geography in Medieval Europe; Hereford Map; Honorius Augustodunensis; Isidore of Seville; Maps; Solinus, Julius Gaius; Viking Age

## Otto of Freising (*c.* 1111–1158)

Bishop and historian, the son of Margrave Leopold III of Austria and Agnes, daughter to Emperor Henry IV. Otto studied at the University of Paris where he developed a lifelong interest in Aristotelian philosophy. He

# O

joined the Cistercian order at the Abbey of Morimund in Champagne and briefly served as its abbot. Around 1137, he became bishop of Freising in Bavaria and served there until his death in 1158. As the half-brother of Emperor Conrad III (r. 1138–1152) and uncle of Frederick I Barbarossa (r. 1152–1190), Otto was influential at the German court. He went on the Second Crusade (1147–1149) and made at least two trips to Italy.

His reputation as the leading medieval Christian philosopher of history rests upon his *History of the Two Cities,* a treatment of human events from the Creation to 1146, which contrasted relations between the communities of the faithful ("City of God") and the damned ("City of the Earth"). In relating historical events, Otto emphasizes how God has ordained a gradual *translatio imperii* or movement of centers of power (or empire) from Asia (Babylon and Assyria/Persia) to Europe (Greece and, finally, Rome). He also wrote *The Deeds of Frederick Barbarossa,* a chronicle of Frederick's family that extended to his accession in 1152 and the first four years of his reign. Otto's works were very influential, and passages from his *History,* for example, were combined with Sibylline prophecies by Godfrey of Viterbo in his *Pantheon* to fabricate a life story of Alexander the Great.

Especially important is Bishop Otto's account in Book I of the *Deeds* of his participation in the Second Crusade, which Bernard of Clairvaux (1030–1153) had preached following the Turkish capture of Edessa. He took the cross in February 1147 and traveled in the party of Emperor Conrad and Duke Frederick. Otto provides vivid details of the march down the Danube and the storm that wreaked havoc in their encampment near Constantinople, and he describes vaguely the disastrous final journey to Jerusalem and return to Europe. He acknowledges the "pitiful conclusion" of the Crusade, in that "it was not good for the extension of boundaries or for the advantage of men's bodies," but "it was good for the salvation of many souls." He attributed the failure "to our pride and wantonness."

## BIBLIOGRAPHY

Fellner, Felix, "The 'Two Cities' of Otto of Freising and Its Influence on the Catholic Philosophy of History." *Catholic Historical Review* 20 (1934): 154–172.

Mierow, Charles C. "Otto of Freising: A Medieval Historian at Work." *Philological Quarterly* 14 (1935): 344–362.

Otto of Freising. *The Two Cities: A Chronicle of Universal History to the Year 1146 A.D.* Trans. Charles C. Mierow. 1928; rpt. New York: Octagon Books, 1966.

———. *The Deeds of Frederick Barbarossa.* Trans. Charles C. Mierow. 1953; rpt. New York: Norton, 1966.

*Richard V. Pierard*

**SEE ALSO**
Constantinople; Crusades, First, Second and Third; Edessa; Godfrey of Viterbo; Jerusalem

## Ottoman Empire

A Turkish empire centered at this time in Anatolia and the Balkan Peninsula; its name is derived from that of its founder, Osman (d. 1326). Osman and his descendants began to establish their presence in northwestern Anatolia in the late thirteenth century. By the late fifteenth century, the Ottoman dynasty ruled over the whole of Anatolia, most of the Balkan Peninsula, and several Aegean islands, making it a formidable power in both Europe and Asia. Given its pressure on European borders, the Ottoman state became the target of two Crusades (in 1396 and 1444) and several smaller-scale military operations. At the same time, however, some European powers such as Venice and Genoa recognized the advantages of diplomatic relations and trade agreements with the Ottoman state. Because the Ottoman state was both a geographical meeting place between European and Asian trade routes and a rising political power, it became impossible for any state with commercial or political interests in the East to avoid dealing with the Ottomans on some level.

As the Ottoman state expanded, the focal point of trade in Anatolia shifted westward to the key political centers of Bursa and later Edirne (Adrianople). After 1453, Istanbul (formerly Constantinople) became the commercial and political capital of the Ottoman state. Caravans traveled to Ottoman markets from Iran and eastern Asia bringing such wares as spices, dyestuffs, and textiles; here, these goods, as well as local Turkish products, were purchased by European merchants—particularly Italians. Due to the proximity of the key Genoese ports of Phocea (Foça) and Pera to Ottoman lands, Genoa was the first Italian power to solicit commercial opportunities in these areas, enacting a trade agreement with the Ottomans as early as 1352. Until the mid-fifteenth century, the Genoese enjoyed a monopoly on

Anatolian-produced alum, which was crucial to the dyeing and leather-tanning industries. The Genoese controlled the alum mines of Phocea, and the Ottomans granted them a monopoly over alum produced in Manisa. In addition, Genoese merchants purchased and exported Anatolian cotton and Persian silk to European markets. Slaves were also a major Genoese commodity. Captives from the Black Sea region and Greek areas were shipped to western Europe and Crete, as well as to Egypt for use in the Mamluk sultan's army. In return, Genoa traded such goods as Italian and English cloth, soap, and even wine, since the Islamic prohibition against alcohol was not yet deeply entrenched in Anatolia. To protect its trading privileges with the Ottomans, Genoa often aided them in military operations or observed neutrality.

Venice's relationship with the Ottomans developed later than Genoa's and was marked by greater conflict, culminating in several wars, two of which took place in the late fifteenth century (1463–1479; 1499–1503). In spite of these unsettled conditions, Venetian trade and diplomatic relations with the Ottoman state grew in the late fourteenth and fifteenth centuries. This was a result of the Ottoman annexation of the Turkish emirates Aydin and Menteshe, where Venetians frequented the ports of Theologo (Ephesos) and Palatia (Miletos). Ottoman rulers tended to maintain trade agreements in these areas along the same lines as those established by the emirates. In addition to silk, spices, and alum, Venetian merchants imported large quantities of cereals from Anatolia, the Balkans, and the Black Sea region via Istanbul. Ottoman rulers were thus able to use the grain trade as a bargaining tool in relations with Venice, since these territories were an important source of grain for Venice itself, but especially for its Mediterranean colonies such as Crete, Negroponte in Euboea, and the Peloponnesian towns of Modon and Coron. Venetian exports to the Ottoman state were similar to those exported to Genoa, but the most valuable Venetian commodity was Florentine cloth. Venice dominated this trade with the Ottomans until Florentine traders began replacing them in the mid-fifteenth century.

Florentine traders came to the Ottoman state in increasing numbers during the mid- to late 1460s. At this time, Sultan Mehmed II granted the city substantial trading privileges in order to maintain trade with western Europe during the war with Venice; Genoa's influence in the eastern Mediterranean had greatly diminished by this time. Owing to its recent agreements with the sultan, Florence could now send its valuable cloth directly to Ottoman markets rather than losing much of the profits to Venetian intermediaries. Balkan trade routes to Florence via Ragusa (Dubrovnik) and Ottoman trade with Ragusa itself boosted overland traffic through Bosnia and Herzegovina, which were annexed by the Turks in 1463. The increase in traffic, plus the growth of a local Muslim merchant class, helped to promote urban growth and trade within these regions, allowing towns like Sarajevo to become prominent Ottoman cities by the early sixteenth century.

In addition to merchants, diplomats and other officials often traveled to the Ottoman state during the fourteenth and fifteenth centuries. Because of their commercial interests in Ottoman lands, Venice and Genoa were especially active in this respect. Although most European states were content to send envoys to the Ottoman government on an ad hoc basis before the sixteenth century, Venice had a permanent diplomatic contact residing among the Ottomans as early as 1453, when the Turks conquered Constantinople. This official, or *bailo,* was both the governor of the Venetian colony in Constantinople and an ambassador to the local government. Before 1453, the *bailo* dealt primarily with the Byzantine court, but he also performed diplomatic missions to the Ottomans whenever necessary.

Other Europeans came to Ottoman areas at this time as pilgrims, captives, mercenaries, and renegades. While most pilgrims during this period sailed to Palestine from Venice without taking port in Ottoman territory, a very small number chose to travel overland, passing through Anatolia. Bertrandon de la Broquière made such a journey as a reconnaissance mission for Philip the Good, who had vowed to lead a Crusade. By the end of the fifteenth century, more and more pilgrims elected to stop in Istanbul as a port of call along the sea route. A considerable number of travelers to the Ottoman state were soldiers captured in battle and placed in the Ottoman army or administration. Accounts of their experiences were left behind by Johann Schiltberger, Konstantin Michailowicz, and Giovan-Maria Angiolello. Finally, a number of renegades traveled to Ottoman areas offering their services to the state; this group includes both converts to Islam and those who remained Christian. Renegades are less well documented than other travelers, but there are a few famous examples such as the cannon founder, Urban. Either a Transylvanian or a Hungarian by origin, Urban helped Mehmed II's army develop a powerful cannon that was crucial to the capture of Constantinople.

Despite frequent calls for crusade and concerns about negotiating with the Muslims, many Europeans were indeed traveling to Ottoman lands and interacting with the Turks. Commercial opportunities and the expanding political influence of the Ottoman state drew more and more travelers from the West seeking various fortunes. The mounting influx of European travelers to the Ottoman state was a trend that would burgeon in the sixteenth century with the broadening of international trade and diplomacy, and, of course, the transition of the Ottoman state to a full-fledged empire.

**BIBLIOGRAPHY**

Inalcik, Halil. *An Economic and Social History of the Ottoman Empire.* Vol. 1: *1300–1600.* Cambridge: Cambridge UP, 1997.

Lewis, Bernard. *The Muslim Discovery of Europe.* New York: Norton, 1982.

Schwoebel, Robert. *Shadow of the Crescent.* New York: St. Martin's, 1967.

Yerasimos, Stephane. *Les Voyageurs Dans l'Empire Ottoman.* Ankara: Imprimerie de la Société Turque d'Histoire, 1991.

Zachariadou, Elizabeth. *Trade and Crusade.* Venice: Istituto Ellenico di Studi Bizantini e Postbizantini, 1983.

*Nancy Bisaha*

**SEE ALSO**

Ambassadors; Caravans; Constantinople; Dyes and Pigments; Genoa; Gunpowder; La Broquière, Bertrandon de; Mamluks; Ottoman Turks; Schiltberger, Johann; Spies; Textiles, Decorative; Venice

## Ottoman Turks

Founders of an obscure frontier state that emerged during the 200 years after 1300 as one of the world's great powers, the Ottoman Empire. Because of its geographical position, the Ottoman Empire played a key role in the trade (mainly silk and spices) between Asia, Africa, and Europe.

In the mid-thirteenth century, pushed out of Central Asia by the Mongol expansion, the nomadic Turkish tribe known as Turkmen (Turcomen) moved into Persia, then into Anatolia. The Turkmen adopted the Seljuk Turks' Islamic ways, gathered around *gāzī* (warrior) leaders of different origins, and started raiding Byzantine

territory as a *gazā* (holy war) against infidels who would not accept Islam. Around 1302, one Turkman *bey* (lord), Osman (*c.* 1290–*c.* 1326), defeated a Byzantine army at Baphaeron near Nicomedia. Osman's victory drew other *gāzī*s to his standard, and they became known by their leader's name, as *Osmanlis* (Ottomans). In 1326, Osman's son, Orkhan (*c.* 1324–1362), conquered Bursa, where, by constructing a bazaar, he created a trading center that was to become the most important trading hub of the east-west silk trade.

Under the *Pax Mongolica* (Mongol Peace) of the thirteenth century, the weight of trade between Asia and the Mediterranean shifted from the Red Sea to routes in the Black Sea and Anatolia. The caravans of spices and silk from India, China, and Persia traveled through the Black Sea ports of Tana (Azov), Soldajo, and Kaffa, or via Sultaniya or Tabriz to the Anatolian ports of Trebizond, Samsun, Sayas, Antalya, and Ephesus. Tabriz in Persia was the crossroad of international trade.

Toward the mid-fourteenth century, the fall of the Mongol kingdom of Persia and the rise of anti-Latin feelings thereafter forced European merchants to look for another trading route. Spices, which were important not only for culinary but also for pharmaceutical use, were available through the Red Sea route via Egypt and Syria. But silk traders had established land routes that led from Tabriz to the Anatolian ports of Ephesus, Antalya, and Trebizond. Securing the supply of raw silk was of vital importance to European merchants, because from the thirteenth century luxury silk—along with fine woolen fabrics—became their main source of international trade revenue. With the rise of the Ottomans, and with the Ottoman conquests of principal centers of silk trade in Anatolia, by the end of the fourteenth century the Ottoman capital of Bursa emerged as the most important international trading center for silk. Bursa attracted Genoese, Venetian, and Florentine merchants based in Constantinople and Galata, the two most important cities of trade in the Levant. Though Bursa's prosperity was founded on its silk trade, the city also handled musk, rhubarb, Chinese porcelain, European woolens, and gold and silver coins.

For the Italians, chiefly Venetians and Genoese, the rise of the Ottomans posed a threat to their commercial interests in Levantine and Mediterranean trade. During the thirteenth century, Venetians and Genoese had taken control of former Byzantine trading centers, making Galata, which faced Constantinople across the Bosporus, their trading hub. Venetians dominated the western Aegean and Constantinople, while Genoese took the eastern Aegean and built colonies in the Black Sea. In the face of emerging competition, Venetians took the offensive. They took possession of any coastal region the Ottomans threatened, controlling the most important points in Albania, Morea, and the Ionian Sea; they also occupied the Aegean islands. In response, the Ottoman sultan Orkhan established an alliance with Venice's rival, Genoa, granting Genoese merchants freedom of trade in the empire with capitulations (1352). The alliance was to last, with intermittent anti-Ottoman policies on the Genoese side, until the fall of Galata (1453). Under this alliance, Genoa enjoyed a long-standing monopoly over the main source of alum for the European textile industry and kept colonies in Anatolia, while the Ottomans gained enormous economic profit and naval assistance.

Capitulations were more than trade treaties. In principle, a capitulation was an "amnesty" granted by the head of an Islamic community to non-Muslims who gave the pledge of "friendship and sincere good will." Capitulations guaranteed residency, travel, and trade in Ottoman territory. Non-Muslims who were considered to be hostile to Islam were denied such privileges and could be enslaved by any Muslim in the Ottoman Empire. The Ottomans categorized capitulations as *ahdnames,* a kind of document that is given unilaterally, but that binds the givers before Allah.

Capitulations were granted primarily out of the Ottoman desire to control applicants, gaining allies and neutralizing enemies. Venice obtained its capitulations some time between 1384 and 1387 during Murad I's reign (1362–1389). Despite being at political loggerheads with the Ottomans, Venice badly needed to maintain trade with them because of their economic interdependency. Among other things, Venice and the entire Po Valley were heavily dependent on wheat imported from Anatolia, Macedonia, Thrace, and Thessaly, all under the Ottoman rule. Wheat imports and other commercial privileges often kept Venice from using its powerful navy to help the anti-Ottoman crusades. Venetians and Genoese, in their own rights and also as middlemen for other nationals, virtually monopolized the Ottoman trade with Europe well into the late sixteenth century, when capitulations to other European countries such as France (1569) and England (1580) started to undermine their position.

Though not explicitly stated in the documents, the Ottomans expected their own subjects to receive similar treatment by the holders of capitulations. And in fact, under Ottoman protection, non-Muslim merchants of the empire—Jews, Armenians, Greeks, and Slavs—established thriving merchant colonies in the Italian port cities of Venice and Ancona as early as the fifteenth century.

Though capitulations permitted non-Muslim merchants to travel and trade freely throughout the empire, this freedom was not always practicable. European merchants were forced to reside in special quarters of certain cities. Knowing how Venetians and Genoese had appropriated Byzantine trade centers, the Ottomans did not permit European merchants to establish independent colonies. It was only in the last decades of the sixteenth century that European merchants started to exercise stronger rights in their colonies. Traveling was also difficult. In addition to the hazardous conditions of traveling in general, non-Muslim merchants needed to obtain from the sultan or local governors a special authorization for their safe conduct. While traveling, they were allowed to wear Muslim dress and even carry arms for further protection.

European accounts of travel within the Ottoman Empire are extant but few. The earliest surviving example is by the Aragonese ambassador Ruy Gonzales de Clavijo, who immediately after the battle of Ankara (1402) traveled to the court of Tamerlane (Timur; r. 1369–1405) in Samarkand, passing through Gallipoli, Constantinople, and Anatolia. His contemporary, the Bavarian Johannes Schiltberger, was captured at Nicopolis and subsequently served in the army of Bajazet I until the battle of Ankara. He later composed a memoir (after 1427), which combines his own experience with portions of—or themes from—popular tales about the East.

Capitulations benefited the Ottoman Turks not only politically but also materially. European trade provided the Ottomans with scarce and strategic goods such as tin, lead, steel, gunpowder, chemicals, luxury goods, and, in particular, gold and silver coins. European merchants also paid customs dues (a tax on both imports and exports), which provided a substantial amount of revenue for the imperial treasury. Customs dues varied by the custom zones, the kind of goods, and the legal state of traders. All goods moved over sea were considered to be imports or exports, and thus were subject to customs dues. Goods moved over land were subject to dues only if they were imported by foreign non-Muslims; if imported by Muslim merchants or tribute-paying non-Muslims, they were exempt from dues. Mehmed II (r. 1444–1446 and 1451–1481) changed the rule, imposing customs dues of the same rate on all imports and exports, regardless of transportation route. This unpopular reform was overturned by his successor Bajazet II (r. 1481–1512). Exports to Europe were discouraged, and were subject to the highest customs rate. The export of certain goods—such as wheat, wine, olive oil, iron, arms, and silk—was prohibited for economic and strategic reasons.

Even more important than the trade with Europe was that with the Arab lands. After the collapse of trade through Central Asia in the mid-fourteenth century, Indian and Indonesian trade goods again came mostly through the Red Sea. From Syria and Egypt, the Ottomans imported Indian spices, indigo, Egyptian linen, rice, sugar, and Syrian soap. In exchange they exported timber, iron and iron implements, Bursa silks, cotton textiles, carpets, opium, dried fruits, furs, wax, and pitch. The southern Anatolian ports of Antalya and Alanya were the center for this trade. Antalya was also the center of slave trade, exchanging white slaves from the north for African slaves from the south. The Portuguese began to compete with Muslims in trade with India and Indonesia, penetrating the Red Sea (1503) and defeating a Mamluk fleet in 1509. Sultan al-Ashraf Qānsūh al-Ghūrī appealed to the Ottomans for aid against the Portuguese, resulting in the submission of Egypt and its assimilation into the Ottoman Empire in 1517, after which the Ottoman sultans regarded themselves as protectors of the entire Islamic world. Under Süleyman I (r. 1520–1566), the Ottoman Empire reached a political and cultural peak.

Nonetheless, the decline of the Ottoman Empire started during Süleyman's reign. In addition to various administrative problems, local Arab lords' resistance to Ottoman rule and their collaboration with the Portuguese undermined effective control of trade between Asia and Europe. The rise of other European trading nations—particularly France and England—and the effect of an inundation of cheap silver from the New World shook the Ottoman economy, and the empire after 1600 was a far less influential power on the world scene.

**BIBLIOGRAPHY**

Ashtor, Eliyahu. *Levant Trade in the Later Middle Ages.* Princeton, NJ: Princeton UP, 1983.

Holt, Peter Malcolm, Ann K.S. Lambton, and Bernard Lewis, eds. *The Central Islamic Lands.* Vol. 1 of *The Cambridge History of Islam.* Cambridge: Cambridge UP, 1970.

Imber, Colin. *The Ottoman Empire 1300–1481.* Istanbul: Isis, 1990.

Inalcik, Halil. *The Ottoman Empire: The Classical Age, 1300–1600.* New York and Washington, DC: Praeger, 1973.

———, ed. *An Economic and Social History of the Ottoman Empire, 1300–1914.* Cambridge: Cambridge UP, 1994.

Vaughan, Dorothy Margaret. *Europe and the Turk: A Pattern of Alliances, 1350–1700.* New York: AMS, 1976.

*Yoko Miyamoto*

**SEE ALSO**

Ambassadors; Constantinople; Dyes and Pigments; Egypt; *Fondaco;* Genoa; Gunpowder; India; Mamluks; Merchants, Italian; Nomadism and Pastoralism; Ottoman Empire; Red Sea; Samarkand; Schiltberger, Johannes; Seljuk Turks; Slave Trade, African; Spice Trade, Indian Ocean; Tamerlane; Textiles, Decorative; Trebizond; Venice

# P

## Paradise, Four Rivers of
*See* Four Rivers of Paradise

## Paradise, Travel to

The goal of certain imaginary travel literature, as well as some medieval travelers. Paradise was considered to be an enclosed garden located on a mountain in an idealized geographical region; within its walls normal rules of time and temperature were suspended. Traditionally located in the East, though exactly where varied considerably from source to source during the Middle Ages, Paradise attracted the attentions both of geographers who never left their libraries and of the occasional traveler to Asia.

Brunetto Latini (*c.* 1220–1294) believed the Earthly Paradise—the Garden of Eden of Genesis 2:8–3:24—to be in India, while others placed it in Asia or even Africa. According to Ranulf Higden in his *Polychronicon* (*c.* 1342, translated by John of Trevisa), it is simply "in the uttermost end of the east." Many T-O maps (see Maps) show Paradise as being located in the extreme East. The late-thirteenth-century Hereford map, for example, depicts Paradise as a round island—or at least an isolated space—surrounded by a wall and barred by a fiery gate.

According to the fictitious letter of Prester John to the Byzantine emperor Manuel Comnenus (that began to circulate in Europe around 1160), Paradise was a three-day journey from Prester John's own kingdom—though the letter does not specify just where that kingdom is. A thirteenth-century German itinerary (London, British Library MS Add. 36753) gives the distance between Rome and Paradise: a journey of 1,425 days, via Constantinople, India, and Ethiopia (the circuitous route can be explained by the fact that these last two countries were commonly conflated by medieval Europeans). The fourteenth-century traveler John of Marignolli says that the inhabitants of Ceylon claim that Paradise is "a distance of forty Italian miles" from their island home.

While the entry for *De Paradiso* is tucked neatly between the entries for the real-world destinations of *De Orcada* and *De Parthia* (the Orkneys and Parthia) in Bartholomaeus Anglicus's *De proprietatibus rerum* (*c.* 1245), getting there was apparently not so simple. According to the *Navigatio Sancti Brendani* (composed *c.* 800) when St. Brendan hears of a certain abbot who visited Paradise regularly (returning each time with his clothes imbued with fragrance), he is inspired to search for the promised land of the saints, which, if not Paradise itself, must be very near to it. Although he does reach this blessed island, Brendan is forbidden to cross over into Paradise itself—in spite of his obvious saintliness. In the *Iter ad Paradisum* (*c.* 1150), Alexander the Great goes farther east than any other traveler and reaches the very gates of Paradise; once there, however, he is refused entry because of his great pride and ambition. The author of *The Book of John Mandeville* says that Paradise is too dangerous to travel to, because it is surrounded by violent seas, adding that he himself was not worthy to visit the site. In describing the insurmountable physical obstacles on the way to Paradise, the highest point on the earth, and perhaps alluding to the legend of Alexander, the *Mandeville* author says that "many great lords have many times attempted to

# P

journey via [the four] rivers toward Paradise, but were not able to accomplish the deed." Some died from the exhaustion of rowing against the waves; some went blind and some went deaf from the great noise of the waters; some were drowned and lost in the waves of water; so no mortal can approach except by the special grace of God. In perhaps the most outlandish claim of his imaginative *Itinerarius* (*c.* 1390), Johannes Witte de Hese claims to have sailed past the "root of Paradise," watching the sunset reflect on the island's walls.

The search for the Terrestrial Paradise continued even after the discovery of the New World. Peter Martyr of Angheira reports that, on Columbus's third voyage (1498–1500), the watchman caught a glimpse of it. Columbus himself says that no one can reach Paradise, although he believed he was very near it when he reached the fresh waters of the mouth of the Orinoco. In *The History of the World* (1614), Sir Walter Raleigh summarizes the often conflicting descriptions of the location of Paradise in biblical, patristic, and encyclopedic literature, and argues that it once existed at precisely "35 degrees from the *Aequinoctiall,* and 55 from the North Pole," in Mesopotamia.

## BIBLIOGRAPHY

Delumeau, Jean. *History of Paradise: The Garden of Eden in Myth and Tradition.* 1992. Trans. Matthew O'Connell. New York: Continuum Press, 1995.

*Mandeville's Travels.* Ed. Peter Hamelius. EETS, o.s., 153, 154. 1919, 1923. Rpt. London, 1973, 1961. [Cotton MS]

Oakeshott, Walter. "Some Classical and Medieval Ideas in Renaissance Cosmology." In *Fritz Saxl: A Volume of Memorial Essays from His Friends in England.* Ed. D.J. Gordon. London: Thomas Nelson and Sons, 1957, pp. 245–260.

Patch, Howard Rollin. *The Other World, According to Descriptions in Medieval Literature.* Smith College Studies in Modern Languages, n.s., 1. Cambridge, MA: Harvard UP, 1950; rpt. New York: Octagon, 1970.

Selmer, Carl, ed. *Navigatio Sancti Brendani Abbatis.* University of Notre Dame Publications in Mediaeval Studies 16. Notre Dame, IN: U of Notre Dame P, 1959; rpt. Dublin: Four Courts Press, 1989.

*The Voyage of St. Brendan.* Trans. John J. O'Meara. Dublin: Dolmen Press, 1976; rpt. Atlantic Highlands, NJ: Humanities Press, 1985.

*Kathleen Coyne Kelly*

## SEE ALSO

Bartholomaeus Anglicus; Brendan's Voyage, St.; Brunetto Latini; Columbus, Christopher; Dante Alighieri; Four Rivers of Paradise; Hereford Map; Higden, Ranulf; Itineraries and *Periploi;* John of Marignolli; *Mappamundi;* Measurement of Distances; Prester John; Purgatory; Trevisa, John; Witte de Hese, Johannes

## Pastoralism, Nomadism and

*See* Nomadism and Pastoralism

## Paulinus Minorita of Venice [Fra Paolino Veneto; Paulinus Minorita] (*c.* 1275–1344)

Franciscan diplomat and bishop of Pozzuoli (1324–1344), and author of a universal history in which he displays a far more extensive geographical scope than that of most medieval Europeans.

As an envoy from Venice, his hometown, and a penitentiary at the Papal Curia, Paulinus gained a keen understanding of history and politics that included the Mongolian (Yuan) dynasty in China. In his writing he combined experience from his diplomatic career with his general knowledge and learning of the Western tradition of history writing, or chronography.

Born *c.* 1275, Paulinus was, according to documents, a member of the Franciscan Order at Padua in 1293. By 1301 he was a "lector," in 1304 "custos" at Venice, and between 1305 and 1307 he was inquisitor in the province of Treviso. From 1315 to 1316 and in 1320, Paulinus was the Venetian envoy to the court of King Robert of Naples (r. 1309–1343). After 1321, he was penitentiary and chaplain to Pope John XXII (r. 1316–1324), serving as papal legate to Milan, Venice, Ferrara, and Fano after 1322. Paulinus was named bishop of Pozzuoli in Campania, and after 1326 he was either there or at the court of the king of Naples until his death in 1344.

Paulinus wrote a work in the "mirror for princes" genre at the request of the duke of Crete, Marino Badoer. But certainly his most significant contribution was his universal chronicle, which appeared in three versions, and on which he worked from 1306 until around 1331. The first version, entitled *Nobilium Historiarum Epitoma,* written before 1316, is traditional historiography, following the model of Vincent of Beauvais's *Speculum Historiale;* it treats world events up to the time of Emperor Henry VII (r. 1308–1313) and Pope Clement V (1305–1314). Sometime around 1321–1322, Paulinus became acquainted with the ideas of the crusading propagandist Marino Sanudo (the Elder) whose *Liber Secretorum Fidelium Crucis* the pope had asked him to examine. This led Paulinus to study the world beyond Europe and the Mediterranean Sea, as well as to engage in a prolific and reciprocal interchange with Marino, a fellow Venetian, as Marino testifies in Book 3 of his expansive book, and as Paulinus himself states in his *Satyrica Historia,* compiled after 1321. The *Satyrica Historia* also exists in a shorter version, the *Compendium* or *Chronologia Magna.*

Only small fragments of Paulinus's universal history have been edited, partly because of its complicated manuscript tradition: twenty-two copies are known, and they contain large tables in huge, magnificent codices, such as Paris, Bibliothèque Nationale MS lat. 4939 (*Chronologia Magna*) and Rome, Bibliotheca Apostolica Vaticana, MS Vat. lat. 1960 (*Satyrica Historia*), which are almost three feet high, written in two or more columns of about eighty-two lines, and excellently illustrated. Thus the only truly faithful edition would be a facsimile.

At the courts of Naples and Avignon, and in the great Italian towns, Paulinus encountered worldviews that had been influenced by Mongol invasions, the mendicant missions to Asia, and the dreams (and disappointments) of crusaders, who looked for the support of an Asian Christian power to help them regain territories in the Holy Land. The *Flos Historiarum Terrae Orientis,* written *c.* 1307 by Hetoum of Armenia, offered much information about the geography of eastern Asia. Thus Paulinus added many chapters to his original historical work to produce his *Satyrica Historia,* which he provided with a complicated system of references and special aids for the user, placed at the work's beginning.

In the *Satyrica Historia* as well as in the *Chronologia Magna,* an opening synchronistic table records different events that took place simultaneously. In his chronicle, St. Jerome had employed up to nine parallel columns, but Paulinus far surpassed him by using twenty-six parallel rows on a double opening of a codex. The rows were assigned to individual political entities or groups as follows:

1. Turkestan, or the original country of the Mongols;
2. Cathay (China);
3. Cumania, or Qipchaq;
4. Asia, Persia, or Tabriz (the empire of the Mongolian il-khâns);
5. the Ayyūbids at Damascus;
6. the Ayyūbids and Mamluks in Egypt;
7. Armenia;
8. Antioch;
9. Cyprus;
10. Jerusalem;
11. Venice (almost at the center of historical power);
12. scholars;
13. antipopes;
14. popes;
15. Holy Roman emperors;
16. ecclesiastical councils;
17. Byzantine emperors;
18. kings of France;
19. kings of Sicily;
20. kings of Hungary;
21. kings of Castile;
22. kings of León;
23. kings of Portugal;
24. kings of Aragon;
25. kings of England;
26. kings of Scotland.

The arrangement of the columns follows the model of a cartographic inventory from east to west. In the *Satyrica Historia,* the tables are accompanied by a written "map" (*scriptura*) in which the description of countries also proceeds from east to west. Thus, in his presentation of central Asia, for example, where Paulinus did not dare to deviate from the traditional graphic format, he insists that any reliable map must consist of text as well as of image, so inconsistencies can be discussed in the text and the text can be illustrated by the pictures.

At this place in the text of *Chronologia Magna* there is a magnificent world map, but no explanatory text. In addition, its sections are organized chronologically according to the regnal dates of Roman kings and emperors, with many columns giving information about contemporary events. In the *Satyrica Historia,* however, Paulinus adds a *Provinciale Romanum;* a list of the administrative provinces of the Franciscan order; a treatise on the gods of the pagans and classical poetry that serves as an introduction to the culture of antiquity; an introduction to the game of chess; sixteen different indices, in alphabetical order, on such subjects as scholars, authors, heretics, and place-names; as well as a chronological index to rulers' reigns and a detailed list

# P

of the 238 chapters with their subdivisions, placed before the actual text of the chronography begins.

Paulinus, because of his close ties to King Robert of Naples, was able to ensure that his historiography was embellished with drawings in both ink and pencil, made by some of the finest artists of the time. The manuscripts at the Bibliothèque Nationale and the Vatican (noted earlier) also contain impressive world maps imitating the cartography of the Venetian Pietro Vesconte, which accompanied manuscript copies of Marino Sanudo's book. The maps show a clear influence of portolan charts, but they lack rhumb lines or wind roses.

As there obviously did not exist any preparatory works of such complexity, nor any comparable visual models, Paulinus must have been both an excellent observer and a gifted designer because he had no codices of a similar sophistication to turn to, nor had any other medieval chronicler attempted such a bold, elaborate graphic representation of the world's geographical or historical shape. Paulinus represents a stunning extension of the medieval world's horizons.

## BIBLIOGRAPHY

Brincken, Anna-Dorothee von den. "'. . . Ut describeretur universus orbis.' Zur Universalkartographie des Mittelalters." In *Methoden in Wissenschaft und Kunst des Mittelalters. Miscellanea Mediaevalia* 7 (1970): 249–278.

———. *Die "Nationes Christianorum Orientalium."* Kölner Historische Abhandlungen 22. Cologne and Vienna: Böhlau, 1973, pp. 454–459.

Degenhart, Bernhard, and Annegrit Schmitt. "Marino Sanudo und Paolino Veneto." *Römisches Jahrbuch für Kunstgeschichte* 14 (1973): 1–137.

———. *Vendig: Addenda zu Süd-und und Mittelitalien.* Vol. 2 of *Corpus der italienischen Zeichnungen, 1300–1450.* Berlin: Mann, 1980.

Ghinato, A. *Fra Paolino da Venezia.* Rome: Don Luigi Guanella, 1951.

Holtzmann, Walther, ed. *Bruchstücke aus der Weltchronik des Minoriten Paulinus von Venedig.* Rome: Regensberg, 1927.

Muratori, Ludovico Antonio, ed. *Antiquitates Italicae Medii Aevi.* 6 vols. Milano: Societatis palatinae, 1741. Vol. 4: pp. 951–1034, a fragment, included under the title "Excerpta ex chronico Jordani."

*Anna-Dorothee von den Brincken.*

## SEE ALSO

Diplomacy; Franciscan Friars; Geography in Medieval Europe; Hetoum; Maps; Martin of Troppau; Missionaries to China; Portolan Charts; Sanudo, Marino; Venice; Vesconte, Pietro/Perrino; Yuan Dynasty

## Pegolotti, Francesco Balducci (fl. 1310–1347)

A fourteenth-century Florentine merchant and diplomat, author of a historically invaluable merchant manual, *La pratica della mercatura* (The Practice of Commerce), which provides key insights into the scope and modalities of European long-distance trade on the eve of the Black Death, through the eyes of a ranking employee of the Bardi bank. The Bardi Company provided financial services to the papacy, to the kings of England and France, and to many other European potentates. As a result, it enjoyed a privileged commercial position in many parts of Europe and Asia Minor. It had branches and correspondents in England, the Low Countries, France, Iberia, and the eastern Mediterranean.

Pegolotti, the son of an influential Florentine citizen, was in the service of the Bardi since at least 1310. He was entrusted with many sensitive financial and diplomatic missions, arranging loans, transfers of funds, and large business deals. He traveled extensively and served for prolonged periods of time in Antwerp, London, and Cyprus. In the later stages of his career, in the 1330s and 1340s, he returned to Florence and embarked on an active and successful political career. In 1347, after the Bardi Company had gone bankrupt, he was among the Florentine officials who supervised its liquidation.

Pegolotti's manual is an aggregate of information gathered over some forty years. Its original purpose was to keep track of weights, measures, customs, and exchange rates in the major commercial centers where the Bardi had commercial interests. This included not only Europe but also North Africa and parts of the Near and Middle East. In its own time, such a manual was hardly unique. However, its scope and the fact that it survived, if only as an imperfect fifteenth-century copy of a copy, make it an indispensable tool for historians of late medieval commerce and geography.

## BIBLIOGRAPHY

Pegolotti, Francesco Balducci. *La pratica della mercatura.* Ed. Allan Evans. Cambridge, MA: The Mediaeval Academy of America, 1936, esp. "Introduction," pp. lx–1.

*Ivana Elbl*

## SEE ALSO

Black Death; Diplomacy; Law, Commercial; Merchant Manuals; Merchants, Italian

## Penance, Travel for

Travel as a pilgrimage to a local or distant shrine, often undertaken at the instigation of a confessor, to obtain pardon for sins.

On occasion pilgrimage was undertaken to atone for sins or to request a favor from God by journeying to a specific holy site. The idea of pilgrimage as a means to gain grace from God was widespread in the Middle Ages and could range in character from taking part in a crusade to exploring personal responses in literature, such as the narrative of Margery Kempe. In such texts the journey and the arrival at the destination make up the substance of pilgrimage, which is also a metaphoric or spiritual journey whose destination is the heavenly Jerusalem.

Travel for penance has its roots in the patristic period when many ascetics traveled away from civilization to remote or desert locations in search of a more complete communion with God. For many of these early Christians, there was no specific final destination but rather a life of wandering. But as the act of pilgrimage grew more important during the Middle Ages, certain shrines became foci for penitential travel and among them, some were thought to have a greater value than others. Thus a trip to Canterbury such as that undertaken by Chaucer's pilgrims in the *Canterbury Tales,* being less strenuous and dangerous than a trip to the Holy Land, was counted as less valuable. Popular pilgrimage sites for those enjoined to penance included Canterbury and Walsingham in England, Santiago, Rome, and Jerusalem.

Enjoined pilgrimage could be prescribed by a priest to absolve a person of sin; it could be demanded of the religious as penance for unorthodox religious belief or utterance; and it could be demanded by civil authorities as partial punishment for a criminal transgression by those who were guilty of public rather than private sins. It was felt that public atonement was required for public sins, and such a pilgrimage could be required of even the highest nobility. Pilgrimage for private sins, on the other hand, was more likely to be undertaken as a result of conscience or feelings of guilt.

### BIBLIOGRAPHY

Holloway, Julia Bolton. *The Pilgrim and the Book.* New York: Peter Lang, 1987.
Hopkins, Andrea. *The Sinful Knights.* Oxford: Clarendon Press, 1990.
Howard, Donald R. *Writers and Pilgrims: Medieval Pilgrimage Narratives and Their Posterity.* Berkeley: U of California P, 1980.
Loxton, Howard. *Pilgrimage to Canterbury.* London: David and Charles, 1978.

*Jennifer Lawler*

### SEE ALSO

Holy Land; Irish Travel; Jerusalem; Kempe, Margery; Pilgrimage, Christian; Pilgrimage Sites, English; Pilgrimage Sites, Spanish; Purgatory, St. Patrick's; Rome as a Pilgrimage Site

## Pepper

*Piper nigrum,* the oriental spice par excellence, emblematic of all that was rare, costly, and luxurious about the East. Throughout the Middle Ages it was a gift for a king.

Almost all European travelers to the East comment on the availability and abundance of pepper as a way to emphasize the wonders of the remote lands in which they found themselves. Throughout his travels, Marco Polo often measures the wealth of the inhabitants of a particular region by how much pepper they consume or grow for export. Odoric of Pordenone (1330) maintains that in the realm ("imperio") of Minibar, an area associated with India, pepper grows in a forest that would take eighteen days to traverse, irrigated by rivers full of "cocodrie" or serpents. In typical fashion, the author of *The Book of John Mandeville* (c. 1360) repeats Odoric's information, observing that the serpents protect the pepper forests and distinguishing among "long pepper," "black pepper," and "white pepper."

The botanical information in *Mandeville* is accurate. Black pepper, native to Java and from there introduced into other tropical countries, comes from a perennial climbing shrub whose small fruits, when dried, are the "peppercorns" of commerce. Separated from the dark husks, the kernel of these corns is the milder white pepper. Red bell peppers are an Old World plant (important in the economy of medieval—and modern—Hungary), but the woody-stemmed *Capsicum* peppers are native to the Americas. Allspice, called "pimento," is from the myrtle family and unrelated to—though often confused with—pepper.

### BIBLIOGRAPHY

*Marco Polo: The Description of the World.* 2 vols. Ed. A.C. Moule and Paul Pelliot. London: G. Routledge, 1938; rpt. New York: AMS Press, 1976.

# P

*Medieval Trade in the Mediterranean World: Illustrative Documents.* Ed. and trans. R.S. Lopez and Irving W. Raymond. New York: Columbia UP, 1990.

*Jerome Mandel*

**SEE ALSO**

Exploration and Expansion, European; *Guerrino il Meschino;* Henry of Mainz Map; *Liber Monstrorum;* Malabar; Malaguetta; *Mandeville's Travels;* Marco Polo; Odoric of Pordenone; Portuguese Expansion; Red Sea; Saffron; Spain and Portugal; Spice Trade, Indian Ocean; Zaiton


## Performers, Itinerant
*See* Minstrels and Other Itinerant Performers


## Peter the Deacon [Petrus Diaconus]
Head librarian at the influential Monastery of Monte Cassino in the twelfth century, and the author of a guide to the holy places, *Liber de locis sanctis,* written sometime before 1137.

Peter's *Liber* survives in a single manuscript (Monte Cassino Library, Codex Casinensis 361). Peter himself never visited the East; in the introduction to the book, which he addressed to his abbot, he explains that his information about the holy places was drawn from written sources. Although he does not name these sources, at least three may be singled out: an unidentified twelfth-century work; the Venerable Bede's *De locis sanctis;* and Egeria's *Travels,* written after 384. It seems likely that Peter the Deacon used a manuscript of Egeria's *Travels* that survives today (Codex Aretinus VI,3), which was discovered in Arezzo in 1884 and is known to have come from Monte Cassino. Peter copied entire sections verbatim from the Venerable Bede, following his organization of the text and his choice of explicitly mentioned holy sites. Peter borrows less directly and specifically from Egeria's report, however, summarizing the geographical and historical data in her work but entirely removing her personal touch (he does not employ a first-person narration, as she does). Peter undoubtedly possessed a more complete text of Egeria's book than we have today, and for that reason his *Liber,* minus the sections copied from Bede and those definitely taken from the twelfth-century source, is a helpful aid to reconstructing Egeria's route and drawing a map of the late-fourth-century pilgrimage. In addition, the text is also a witness of geographical and theological ideas of the 1100s.

**BIBLIOGRAPHY**

Weber, R., ed. Extracts in *Corpus Christianorum:* Series Latina 175. Turnhout: Brepols, 1965, pp. 93–98.

Wilkinson, John, trans. *Egeria's Travels in the Holy Land.* Jerusalem: Ariel; and Warminster, England: Aris and Phillips, 1981, pp. 179–210.

*Ora Limor*

**SEE ALSO**

Bede; Center of the Earth; Egeria; Jerusalem; Pilgrimage, Christian


## Peter of Lucalongo
A thirteenth-century Italian merchant who traveled to the Far East.

There has been difficulty in interpreting the designation "Lucalongo," most likely a toponym. It has been suggested that his name may be "Petrus de Luca Longo," which would indicate membership in a Venetian family. After first trading in the Near East, Peter traveled to southern China. His travel companions were the Dominican Nicholas of Pistoia and the Franciscan John of Monte Corvino, noted founder of the Church's missions in China, whose own voyage had originated from Rieti in July 1289. The group probably embarked at Tabriz going by way of the Persian Gulf and the Indian Ocean. They arrived at the Mongol capital Khanbaliq (modern Beijing) in 1291.

Once settled, Peter did business there for several years. He must have prospered, since in about 1305 he bought a tract of land near the khân's palace to provide a building site for John of Monte Corvino's church compound. Apparently, Peter remained a loyal lay supporter of the Franciscan's activities, since John referred to him in a letter of 1306 as "[Dominus] Peter of Lucalongo, a faithful Christian and a great merchant," having donated a house to be used as a church. While little is known about his life, Peter's activities offer an example of the pragmatic support European merchants provided to missionaries in the Far East and demonstrate how the spread of mercantilism and missions went hand in hand.

**BIBLIOGRAPHY**

Dawson, Christopher, ed. *The Mongol Mission.* See Gen. Bib.

Lopez, Robert Sabatino. "European Merchants in the Medieval Indies: The Evidence of Commercial Documents." *Journal of Economic History* 3, Supplement (1943): 164–184; rpt. New York: Kraus, 1959.

Moule, A.C. *Christians in China before the Year 1550.* London: Society for Promoting Christian Knowledge, 1930.

Petech, Luciano. "Les marchands italiens dans l'Empire Mongol." *Journal Asiatique* 250 (1962): 549–574.

Wadding, Luke, ed. *Annales Minorum seu Trium ordinum a S. Francisco Institutorum.* Rev. edition P. Bonaventure Marrani. Vol. 6. Florence: Quaracchi, 1931.

Yule-Cordier, *Cathay and the Way Thither.* See Gen. Bib.

*Gloria Allaire*

SEE ALSO

Dominican Friars; Franciscan Friars; John of Monte Corvino; Khanbaliq; Merchants, Italian

## Peutinger Table [*Tabula Peutingeriana*]

An itinerary map, or *itinerarium pictum,* the only example of its type to survive from the Roman period. Konrad Peutinger (1465–1547), a humanist and antiquarian with interests in classical geographers, acquired the "tabula" that now bears his name in 1508. The Peutinger Table is today Cod. Vindobonensis 324 in the Austrian National Library, Vienna.

Paleography confirms that the polychrome Peutinger Table was created before the mid-thirteenth century, while its contents suggest a fourth-century archetype. Indeed, since the map lists some cities destroyed by the eruption of Vesuvius in 79 C.E., its antecedents may well be as old as the first century. Its measurements, twenty-two feet by thirteen and three-eighths inches (6.75 m × 34 cm), probably permitted it to be used as a scroll, but this format severely diminishes the scale of the north-south axis while elongating the east-west axis.

The Peutinger Table is a road map showing the principal routes of the Roman Empire from southern Britain to the mouth of the Ganges (a cumulative total of some 64,600 miles, or 104,000 km, of roads), along with large rivers and lakes, harbors, mountain ranges, and forests. Locations are marked by miniature icons designating gabled villas, towered walls, baths, granaries, temples, and other landmarks. Distances of stages are given in leagues in Gaul, parasangs in Persian territories, Indian miles in India, but generally in Roman miles. Occasionally, legends, of Christian or pagan import, are written in vacant portions. Three cities are especially distinguished: Antioch, Constan-

tinople, and Rome. This last is marked by a personification of the goddess Roma, seated on a throne, clothed in a red cloak and crown, and bearing in her right hand an orb; twelve roads, each identified by name, surround her like spokes. Constantinople and Antioch are marked by similar personifications, though neither holds an orb.

Dilke asserts that, since the Romans were particularly adept at drawing maps to scale, the Peutinger Table should not be considered typical of ancient Roman maps.

BIBLIOGRAPHY

Dilke, O.A.W. *Greek and Roman Maps.* Ithaca, NY: Cornell UP, 1985, pp 113–120, 193–195; rpt. Baltimore: Johns Hopkins, 1998.

———. "Itineraries and Geographical Maps in the Early and Late Roman Empires." In Harley-Woodward, 1: 234–257. See Gen. Bib.

Levi, Annalina, and Mario Levi. *Itineraria picta: Contributo allo studio della Tabula Peutingeriana.* Rome: Bretschneider, 1967.

Weber, Ekkehard, ed. *Tabula Peutingeriana: Codex Vindobonensis 324. Vollständige Faksimile-Ausgabe im Originalformat.* 2 vols. Graz: Akademische Druck- und Verlagsanstalt, 1976.

*Roger T. Macfarlane*

SEE ALSO

Constantinople; Ganges; Itineraries and *Periploi;* Maps; Matthew Paris; Measurement of Distances; Orb of Imperial Power

## Philippe de Commynes
*See* Commynes, Philippe de

## Philippe de Mézières (*c.* 1327–1405)

Crusade propagandist, tutor, hagiographer, soldier, diplomat, pilgrim, traveler, and author of an important travel narrative, the *Songe du vieil pèlerin,* as well as other works, many of which are still unedited.

Philippe was born in Amiens and spent the first half of his immensely varied career, from around 1345 to 1380, in the service of several important rulers: Lucchino Visconti and Andrew of Naples (1345), Hugh IV of Cyprus (1346), Alfonso XI, king of León and of Castile (*c.* 1350), Peter I of Cyprus (r. 1360–1369), Pope Gregory XI (1372–1373), and

# P

Charles V of France (r. 1373–1380). As a soldier and knight, Philippe served in Italy, in northern France, and perhaps in Spain. He also traveled to the Near East, both as a crusader at the battle of Smyrna in 1346, and as a pilgrim to Jerusalem in 1347, where he was inspired to found a religious order of the Passion. In the service of Peter I, Philippe fought at the sieges of Alexandria in Egypt, Tripoli in Syria, Ayas or Lajazzo in Armenia, and Sataliéh in Turkey during the 1360s. His career in this regard bears a remarkable resemblance to that of Chaucer's Knight in the *Canterbury Tales*.

After his appointment as chancellor of Cyprus in 1361, Philippe often journeyed to Genoa and Venice, whose financial and military support were crucial for the Crusade, as well as to the papal court at Avignon. In the 1360s, Peter I of Cyprus made two grand tours of the kingdoms of Europe in 1362–1365 and 1366–1368 to rally support for the Crusade. During most of the king's first tour, Philippe was at Avignon working for peace between the Visconti rulers of Lombardy and the papacy. His companion there was Peter Thomas, the papal legate to the East and future saint, whose biography Philippe would later write (1366). In 1364, Philippe and Peter Thomas journeyed through northern Italy in support of the peace settlement.

In 1366, Peter I appointed Philippe as his European ambassador for the Crusade. Philippe's writings describe his journey during the 1360s through Swabia, Bavaria, Prussia, Bohemia, Moravia, Austria, and Hungary. His knowledge of the courts, politics, and history of the Germanic cities and states—Westphalia, Brandenburg, Zeeland, Friesland, Frankfurt-am-Main, Königsberg, Nuremberg—and about Scandinavia suggests that he also journeyed widely in northern Europe. During 1368, Philippe accompanied Peter to Naples, Rome, the Tuscan cities, Bologna, Ferrara, Mantua, and Venice.

Philippe was in Venice when Peter I was assassinated in Cyprus early in 1369. He never returned to Cyprus, but after three years of quiet retirement in Venice he was sent to Avignon as Cypriot ambassador to the newly elected Pope Gregory XI (1370–1378). He spent much of 1372 campaigning to gain papal approval for the feast of the Presentation of the Virgin, a project that seems to have served Philippe's crusading interests.

Moving to Paris early in 1373, he entered the service of Charles V, who named him to an eventual regency council in 1374 and made him preceptor of the future Charles VI in 1377. During the 1370s Philippe traveled through France with King Charles. He also performed occasional diplomatic services for Cyprus; he was probably in Milan for the peace negotiations between Cyprus and Lombardy in 1376.

After Charles V died in 1380, Philippe left public service, and, as a layman with the Celestine monks in Paris, he devoted the second half of his life (1380–1405) to writing, in both Latin and French. A tract supported the peace negotiations between Cyprus and Genoa (1381–1383), and his *Épistre au roi Richard* (1395) proposed a military truce between France and England so that both nations could join together in a Crusade. However, Philippe's most interesting literary works during this period are his devotional writings in which he transforms himself into a spiritual traveler and crusader. The *Songe du vieil pèlerin* (1389) is an allegorical fantasy journey through Europe, North Africa, and Asia. At the journey's end, Europe is united, religious schisms are healed, and the kings of Europe lead a fleet to conquer the Holy Land. In his *Oratio tragedica Passionis* (1389–1390), he dedicates his old age to a spiritual instead of a military crusade. His last work, the *Épistre lamentable et consolatoire* (1397), was written after the Christian defeat at Nicopolis (1396). The *Épistre* repeats Philippe's apocalyptic vision of a spiritual conquest of the Holy Land. His proposed religious and military order of the Passion would first accomplish the spiritual renewal that must precede the crusade. The army would consist of three forces gathered from the lands Philippe had visited during his years of propagandizing the crusade.

After a life of travel as crusading knight, diplomat, and spiritual pilgrim, Philippe died in the Celestine monastery in Paris on May 29, 1405.

## BIBLIOGRAPHY

Coleman, William E., ed. *Philippe de Mézières' Campaign for the Feast of Mary's Presentation.* Toronto: Pontifical Institute of Mediaeval Studies, 1981.

Coopland, G.W., ed. *Le Songe du vieil pèlerin.* 2 vols. Cambridge: Cambridge UP, 1969.

Iorga, Nicolas. *Philippe de Mézières (1327–1405) et la croisade au XIVe siècle.* Paris: Bouillon, 1896; rpt. London: Variorum, 1973.

*William E. Coleman*

## SEE ALSO

Ambassadors; Armenia; Chaucer, Geoffrey; Genoa; Holy Land; Jerusalem; Lajazzo; Military Orders; Pilgrimage, Christian; Popes; Rome as a Pilgrimage Site; Venice

## Phocas, John (fl. 1184)

A Greek pilgrim, born in Crete, who visited Palestine around 1178.

The avowed purpose of his unfortunately vague account is to describe the holy places—to "paint a picture, using words on our canvas"—for those who have heard but not seen; Phocas does not wish to imitate "gluttons" who keep the best food for themselves. Such an account, he believes, not only edifies but brings pleasure in that it chronicles that which is a "joy" to see. So Phocas begins in Antioch—a godly city whose wealth surpassed all others in the East—and tells of his journeys to Syria, Phoenicia, and the holy places in and around Jerusalem. While Phocas is chiefly interested in places significant in Christian history, he includes some information of secular importance: a mountain range inland from Tripoli, for example, is home to the "Assassins," who are "Saracens" but neither Christian nor Muslim.

Phocas's account is a mixture of the credulous and the skeptical. He recounts miraculous details from hagiographies, such as extinguished coals lighting in the hand of St. Theodosius and St. Basilius's singing for forty days after the restoration of his tomb. He met the Spanish recluse on the little hill of "Hermoniim" to whom lions brought wood so that he might carve crosses. But Phocas dismisses the claim that a stone monument marks the site of Christ's teaching in Sidon as a report of the vulgar. In Jerusalem, he rejects the belief that a tower on the north side of the city is in fact David's Tower, basing his rejection on the evidence of Josephus.

Phocas's principal interest is in identifying sites associated with scriptural events: the site of the house in Sidon where the widow cared for Elijah, a fountain in Tyre from which Christ and the apostles drank, the ravine in Nazareth where Gabriel appeared to Mary, the house of Joseph, the Mount of Olives, Gethsemane, the desert of Ruba where Christ was tempted, the site on the Jordan river where John the Baptist preached. The accounts are terse affirmations of the existence of the sites, rather than detailed descriptions. The exception to this is Phocas's description of Bethlehem, which verges on the ecstatic. In reflecting on the grotto of Christ's birth, Phocas is deeply moved by the ambiguity of a tiny manger containing one whom all the heavens could not contain. He writes here in the present tense as if he were present at the Nativity and seems to be describing details from paintings, possibly icons.

Phocas's reactions to the churches and clergy of Palestine are mixed, suggesting the tension between the Orthodox and Latin Churches. On the one hand he takes pains to describe the Latin churches he visits, such as that housing the remains of John the Baptist—whose left hand, encased in gold, is kept in a golden vessel—and his parents, Zacharias and Elizabeth. He also describes visits with several Spanish recluses whose marks of sanctity are evident, and he lists the names of several Latin monks who converse directly with God. Yet on the other hand he is not adverse to expressing his personal scorn for the Latin establishments; he writes of the Latin bishop of Lydda as "the intruder," recounting a miracle that took place only "several years ago," in which that bishop tried to open the tomb of St. George of Lydda and was repulsed by fire flashing out from the sepulchre. It is a story in which Phocas seems to delight, for he saves it until the end, and concludes his book with the hope that he will be sweetly refreshed in the imagination by the remembrance of those places about which he has written.

### BIBLIOGRAPHY

Phocas, Joannes. *The Pilgrimage of Joannes Phocas.* Trans. Aubrey Stewart. London: Palestine Pilgrims' Text Society, 1896; rpt. New York: AMS Press, 1971.

———. *A General Description of the Settlements and Places Belonging to Syria and Phoenicia on the Way from Antioch to Jerusalem, and of the Holy Places of Palestine.* Trans. John Wilkinson. In *Jerusalem Pilgrimage, 1099–1185,* ed. John Wilkinson. Hakluyt Society, 2nd series, 167. London: Hakluyt Society, 1988, pp. 315–336.

Runciman, Steven. *A History of the Crusades.* Vol. 2. Cambridge: Cambridge UP, 1952.

Williams, John, with Joyce Hill, and W.F. Ryan, eds. *Jerusalem Pilgrimage 1099–1185.* Hakluyt Society, 2nd series, 167. London: Hakluyt Society, 1988, esp. pp. 22–33.

*Gary D. Schmidt*

**SEE ALSO**

Assassins; Holy Land; Jerusalem; Pilgrimage, Christian

## Pierre d'Ailly

*See* Ailly, Pierre d'

## Pilgrim, The Bordeaux

*See* Bordeaux Pilgrim, The

# P

## Pilgrimage, Christian

The undertaking of a journey as an act of devotion, the performance of which took numerous forms and included a wide variety of sites during the Middle Ages.

The religious practice of pilgrimage, which is, of course, a universal phenomenon, was introduced into Christianity even before the conversion of Constantine, as can be seen from the example of Jerusalem, where the veneration of holy places was already known by 330. From that time on, the Church warned the faithful against attributing too much value to pilgrimage. St. Gregory of Nyssa, who had himself gone to the Holy Sepulchre, advised the faithful that one was no nearer God in the Holy Land than in Cappadocia. This same admonition was given by more than one abbot to his monks. Thus Bernard of Clairvaux retained a pilgrim in his monastery, saying that he was already in the celestial Jerusalem and that he had no need to go seek the terrestrial Jerusalem. This did not, however, prevent Bernard from exalting the spiritual riches of Jerusalem in his work *Praise for a New Chivalry*.

One of the modes of pilgrimage in the early church was abandoned rather early: the visit to ascetic saints, either those in the desert of Nitria or the stylites of Syria. Christians continued to visit members of religious orders in order to ask for prayers or advice; but these visits were not pilgrimages. A true pilgrimage involved travel to the places where saints had lived, or to their tombs or reliquaries.

Pilgrimage has various purposes. One is that the pilgrim can seek out a mystical experience in the process of meditating on the example of a venerated person in the place where he or she lived; pilgrims of this kind sometimes wrote travel narratives in order to help those who meditated without ever leaving home. Few among them, however, shared their own mystical experiences in the way that Margery Kempe and Bridget of Sweden did.

Most often medieval Christians went on pilgrimage to ask for blessings, including cures; springs with curative powers became the destination of pilgrimages after being Christianized. It was common to undergo a pilgrimage in fulfillment of a vow after a prayer had been answered, especially in the case of captives who had been liberated. The fundamental idea was to convince the saints to intercede with God: the pilgrims implored their *suffragia* (intercession).

Early on, pilgrims also began to seek pardon from sins. But the Church was not enthusiastic with regard to this practice, which had been condemned in the Council of 789. The Church required the intervention of a confessor who imposed on the repentant sinner a penance appropriate to the sins committed. The decline of penances paid at a fixed rate was accompanied by the introduction of the custom of commutation of penance, substituting the completion of a pilgrimage for fasting, mortifications, and the like. The Latin Church required that this substitution be authorized by a bishop or even the pope. The papacy favored the introduction in the eleventh century of indulgences, normally comprising a visit to a church where the pilgrim would venerate a certain altar, make an offering to the church, and in turn benefit from the remittance of all or part of the penitence owed in this world or in Purgatory. In the case of the Crusades, an indulgence granted for an undertaking ordered by the pope was identical to a pilgrimage.

A pilgrimage could be a penance in itself, for it imposed a degree of sacrifice and physical effort (*labor itineris*). The penitential manuals of the twelfth century stipulate for certain mortal sins the completion of a pilgrimage to the Holy Sepulchre, and it was widely believed that this was the only pilgrimage that assured pilgrims a plenary indulgence. But St. Peter Damian absolved the Milanese clerics guilty of simony by imposing certain other pilgrimages upon them. And a certain knight from the Midi of France, Bertrand, who had murdered his lord, was given the punishment of living as a pilgrim without ever stopping anywhere, which led him to visit St. Sophia in Constantinople and even to go so far as the shrine of St. Thomas in India.

Pilgrimage can also be a form of asceticism, a means of spiritual perfection achieved by imitating Christ, who had no place to rest his weary head (Matthew 8:20). In this case, pilgrimage is a kind of voluntary exile, one which was especially fashionable among Christians in Ireland, where souls drawn to a life of solitude sought it out in remote islands or among barbarous peoples, to whom they spread the message of the gospel in the manner of St. Brendan and St. Columba.

Among the places where pilgrims went, Jerusalem was without doubt the earliest. Pilgrims went there from the West, as well as from the Greek, Georgian, Armenian, Ethiopian, and Nubian East, facilitating in this way the diffusion of the liturgy of the Holy Land. Places that attracted visitors flourished everywhere, whether they preserved the memory of the life of Christ or the Virgin, of the early history of the Church or biblical episodes. And the Flight into Egypt gave birth to a large number of sites evoking the episode of the Holy Family's sojourn there.

The apostles of Christ attracted no less devotion. In Rome, the apostles Peter and Paul were the object of a longstanding tradition of veneration; but the discovery in the ninth century of the body of St. James in Galicia marked the beginning of a notable pilgrimage as well. Another apostle, Thomas, first venerated at Edessa, was believed to have evangelized India, and even Westerners visited his tomb at Mylapore, where a miracle attributed to him recurred every year (his arm came to life to distribute communion). The tombs of the martyrs, especially those of Rome, were likewise an object of pilgrimages that had as their goals the places where relics were kept. The sites visited by pilgrims were thus innumerable. And the most recent martyrs could also draw crowds. Put to death on December 29, 1170, Thomas Becket was immediately credited with a considerable number of miracles, and by 1179 his tomb was visited by King Louis VII of France, who came to pray for the cure of his son. Saintly monks were also the object of veneration on the part of the faithful, who sometimes came from very far away—and one can imagine that the desire to attract pilgrims was not irrelevant to the efforts undertaken by these communities to make known the saintliness of their founders, or of some great wonder-working abbey. St. Claude was among these, and its reputation was such that the king of France made the trip through the Jura Mountains to visit it.

Marian pilgrimages multiplied from the beginning of the eleventh century (Notre Dame of Le Puy is one of those pilgrimages assigned by Peter Damian to the Milanese). Miraculous images, statues sometimes revealed in a supernatural fashion, or icons like the one that Joinville venerated at Tortosa were often the source of such pilgrimages. At Boulogne-sur-Mer the arrival of pilgrims began immediately after the unveiling of the statue in 1211. Beginning in 1263, the date of the miracle of Bolsena, miraculous occurrences that accompanied the veneration of the Corpus Christi gave birth to new pilgrimages, some of which remained very modest in their geographical range of appeal. Such are those that took place in 1306 and 1331 in the diocese of Autun, at Marigny-sur-Ouche and at Blanot. As soon as the miracle was noted and the inquiry completed, the bishop or the pope accorded an indulgence to those who, on the anniversary of the miracle, came to show their devotion to the holy sacrament by visiting the church. And immediately a pilgrimage was born.

For example the Great Jubilee of Rome in 1300 was born spontaneously from a rumor that a pope had many years earlier bestowed a plenary indulgence upon those who would go to the tomb of the apostles that year. In view of the influx of pilgrims, Boniface VIII confirmed this institution, called everlasting.

It is necessary to consider separately the pilgrimage to Lough Derg where a very ancient tradition affirms that St. Patrick had obtained a special favor for those who went down into its subterranean passage: a revelation of the torments of the afterlife. The reputedly perilous character of this visit made it an exploit reserved for knights, the first who left an account being Oengus O'Brien in 1150.

The nature of pilgrimage sites was thus quite varied and their importance equally so. Some were visited by the faithful from all over the Christian world. Others appear to have been known only in neighboring villages. Nevertheless, the lists drawn up in the courts of justice in the Low Countries at the end of the Middle Ages place the names of the great pilgrimages side by side with those of much more obscure churches and chapels, which causes one to wonder how they came to the attention of the authors of these lists and suggests that we should not underestimate their range of influence.

These lists were prepared for use by judges of the civil tribunals, who sentenced the accused to "forced pilgrimages." These condemnations generally followed a murder, and their goal was to discourage acts of vengeance by removing the murderer from the country for a greater or lesser time, by requiring him to visit sanctuaries where he could pray for the sake of the victim. This practice appears to have begun in the thirteenth century.

Other pilgrims undertook, in exchange for a certain salary, to carry out voyages in place of those who originally had taken vows but found themselves unable to fulfill them. Thus, when King Charles VI of France went mad, other people were sent to visit sanctuaries as representatives of the king and to take offerings there. This, then, was what was called doing a pilgrimage *par vicaire*, "vicariously."

In order to make pilgrim voyages easier, people began early on to make pilgrim guidebooks that were intended to indicate the stops and the modes of travel as well as lists of places to visit. The earliest of these is *The Itinerary from Bordeaux to Jerusalem*. Others took more the form of travel narratives, sometimes with a hagiographic appeal, like the one concerning St. Willibald, but these might also be used by pilgrims to prepare their

**P**

voyages or to enlighten themselves about the places they were going to visit. It was especially around the time of the Crusades that several texts were written that were truly pilgrim guides. They derived in the main from works of St. Jerome on the identification of holy places cited in Scripture. Around 1148 a churchman of the Latin East, Rorgo Fretellus of Nazareth, composed, for the aid of the pilgrims to whom he addressed his book, a *Description of the Holy Land.* It lays out an itinerary across Palestine with distances, and indicates all the spots likely to excite the interest of pious travelers. A little more than a century later, Burchard of Mt. Sion produced another *Description* that for many years was regarded as authoritative. The number of travel narratives increased until one finds what are really only compilations, whose role as guidebooks is more doubtful. Pilgrims used, above all, small pamphlets which they bought in Venice and which gave lists of places to venerate with the indulgences attached to each.

Other texts were composed for visitors to Rome, with an enumeration of the stations of pilgrimage and the *mirabilia* of the city. For Compostela we have the famous *Guidebook for the Pilgrim* which was inserted in the *Book of St. James,* from the twelfth century. But here also these stories of voyages were composed with an eye to use by pilgrims, who are given practical advice—on dress, money, expenses, and precautions to take.

These books may also have served to encourage pilgrims by exalting the merits of the saints that they were going to venerate. Even the *chansons de geste* are thought by some to have served to propagandize shrines.

A pilgrimage required moral and material preparation. Many pilgrims would die along the way and had to put their spiritual lives in order before departure. If certain ones expected to live on charity during the voyage, this was not the case for the authors of extant narratives, who prepared themselves with money and signed a contract with the captain of the ship and with donkey drivers.

The pilgrim distinguished himself by his costume, a waterproof mantle for rain and a broad-brimmed hat bent backward at the front to hold badges that indicated the goal of the voyage or signaled its completion. Upon departure, he accepted from a churchman, as Joinville did from the abbot of St. Urbain, a staff and a shoulder sash. Also he carried a water flask and a scrip, or beggar's bag. Certain pilgrims expected to go barefoot, though this supplementary mortification was discouraged.

Pilgrimage was an act of asceticism; the pilgrim was ordinarily a penitent and he imposed upon himself a discipline very similar to that of penitence, forbidding himself from having luxurious clothing, furs, dogs, and hunting falcons. Nevertheless, some princes and barons did not totally renounce their habits. This was something of a scandal. For pilgrims, even if they were sometimes regarded as slightly disturbing "marginal" figures, could still inspire veneration. Bertrand the Pilgrim was proclaimed a saint, as was Roch, a pilgrim from Montpellier who died of the plague en route to Rome.

Normally the vow of pilgrimage excluded the bearing of arms, and Eudes de Deuil expressed regret that those who accompanied the Second Crusade were not armed. But the three German bishops who were on their way to the Holy Land with a numerous trooop in 1065 were armed and, on the Venetian galleys arranged for their transport, the pilgrims were given weapons when attacked by pirates. Pilgrims were a choice prey for pirates, as the historians of the first years of the Latin kingdom of Jerusalem bear witness.

The pilgrim could travel either alone or in a group. In the second case, walking could be set to the cadence of singing or prayers, but we know very little about this subject. By sea, liturgical life was limited to these practices, for the celebration of mass was prohibited on board, and St. Louis had to obtain a special dispensation in order to keep the Holy Eucharist on his ship. If he died at sea, the pilgrim would be deprived of Christian burial, the sailors not wishing to keep cadavers on board. He would regain the opportunity for normal religious practice once he got to land.

At the site of pilgrimage the rites accomplished were extremely varied. A procession that went around the sanctuary was very common, notably among the Irish Christians. In Jerusalem the procession that guided the pilgrims in retracing the steps of Christ toward the crucifixion and the Holy Sepulchre probably took its definitive form only under the influence of the Franciscans, in the fourteenth or fifteenth century, giving birth to the Stations of the Cross. The custom of nocturnal watches was also peculiar to certain sanctuaries. It required in each case that the pilgrim approach as near as possible to the miraculous image, touch the tomb, kiss the reliquary, or accomplish some other gesture assuring him a corporeal contact with the object of devotion. In order to cure mental illness, the ill person was made to pass underneath a particular sarcophagus.

But an essential element was the participation at offices celebrated by the clergy who served the sanctuary, preferably on certain feast days (thus, at Jerusalem, on Easter). Also, each place of pilgrimage was provided with a religious community that sometimes released its members to accompany the pilgrim toward other sites not permanently staffed. Pilgrim priests celebrated mass in these sanctuaries; but at Compostela the great altar was reserved solely for Canons Cardinal of the Chapter of St. James. Certain sites in the East were not served by clergy of the Latin rite. Still, pilgrims did not visit them any the less, and they encountered there specific ritual practices of other communities, to which they sometimes responded sympathetically.

The act of offering ordinarily accompanied the visit (this was sometimes just a matter of offering a candle.) Those who benefited from blessings—cures, for example—offered an *ex voto*. Thus liberated captives offered their chains to St. Foy de Conques at the moment of accomplishing a pilgrimage made there in fulfillment of a vow. Giving up a precious object to honor a sanctuary was a common act; the Pilgrim of Plaisance who had visited the Holy Sepulchre sometime before the Arab conquest described the accumulation of jewels found there. But other gifts were made that were intended for the maintenance of the sanctuary and the community that served it. Pilgrimages of nobles thus provided an opportunity to increase the capital value of the shrine itself.

When he had finished his pilgrimage the pilgrim retained a feeling of attachment for the site he had visited. He could be intent on leaving the mark of his passage there, in particular by inscribing his name on a wall, as did visitors to the Latin chapel of Sinai where one finds evidence of the visits of pilgrims who told us about their voyage. But it was above all the bond established by confraternities (associations) that permitted pilgrims to prolong their pilgrimage. Thus, when Pope Calixtus II had the idea of transferring to Compostela the archiepiscopal title of a very old archbishopric, he was urged to it by the intervention of the Duke of Burgundy, of the Count of Albon, and of other noble relatives of the pope who were in the Confraternity of St. James by virtue of having completed the pilgrimage. It was the custom for the community serving the sanctuary to offer masses for the benefit of the *confrères*, who could be subject to taxation or be called on to offer their support to the community. This has been thought

to be the origin of the Knights of the Holy Sepulchre, who, since very early times and in any case before 1330, made a practice of conferring knighthood near the tomb of Christ. These confraternities reuniting former pilgrims associated through common devotion multiplied without requiring a direct tie with the sanctuary, but they facilitated visits to it and promoted the cult found there. The confraternities of St. James are the best known.

With pilgrimage is associated the collection of relics that the pilgrims strove to bring back from their voyage. These could be actual fragments of a holy body, but ordinarily pilgrims sought to procure for themselves an object which had merely been in contact with the venerated remains—a piece of the pavement of the Holy Sepulchre, oil from lamps burnt before a tomb and brought back in an ampule, oil flowing from a tomb, as at St. Menas or at Sinai, water from the River Jordan. It was recommended to bring along a jewel or ring with which to touch the venerated tomb; swatches of cloth were put into contact with the shroud to gather its properties.

The mark of having completed a pilgrimage was to carry a characteristic insignia, distinct from that which the pilgrim displayed at the moment of taking his vow (the cross appears to have been adopted by pilgrims leaving for Jerusalem before being used for the Crusades). At Compostela, it was the scallop shell, and a pilgrim could either go find one on the seashore, at Padron, or simply settle for buying one at the market. In Jerusalem, it was the palm, and William of Tyre informs us of the custom which earned for the pilgrim to the Holy Land the name of "palmer." These palms were sold at stores, and they could also no doubt be gathered on the banks of the Jordan. But besides these, there existed other insignia that were ordinarily in the form of badges, worn on the pilgrim's hat. These were representations of the saint or the image of the Virgin venerated in a particular sanctuary; there is evidence of them as early as the twelfth century, when Guernes de Pont-Sainte-Maxence refers to the ampula or the cross that is carried "en signe del viage" ("as a sign of the journey") and "de Rochemadur Marie en plum getée": a medal made of lead representing the Virgin of Rocamadour. Those who went to worship the relics of the Three Kings of Cologne brought back a little metal triptych that represented the Adoration of the Magi. These insignia show great variety and seem to have

# P

been particularly prevalent in Northern France, the Low Countries, and Northern Germany.

The pilgrim could also ask for a certificate confirming the completion of the pilgrimage; this document permitted the bearer to prove that he was not one of the false pilgrims who tried to pass as penitents to escape the police. It was above all necessary for forced pilgrimages, because it proved that the person carrying it had fulfilled the required obligation. But we know that certain disreputable shops, in Venice, fabricated false certificates.

The itineraries usually followed by pilgrims required outfitting. The pilgrimage routes were designated by such names as *iter romanum*, *via Francigena*, or "chemin romeret," for those that led to Rome, and "chemin de sainte Reine" for the one to Alesia. At each stage local residents did their best to provide a resting place for the pilgrims: these were the "maisons-Dieu" where the poor traveler was lodged free of charge and sometimes supplied with alms to pursue his route, while the rich left an offering. Certain points along the route were provided with more important "hospitals"—Roncesvalles in the Pyrenees, St. James of Altopasso in the Appenines, St. Bernard of Montjoux in the Alps—which were often endowed with distant land holdings to assure their financing. Wherever pilgrims were likely to go, inns were provided, such as the houses of Vézelay with their great underground rooms, or the *scholae* in Rome, which in the tenth century, were intended to receive Franks, Frisians, Lombards and Saxons. Monasteries considered it their obligation to welcome pilgrims, and the one at Cap São Vicente, in Portugal, found itself imposed upon to take in Muslim pilgrims from a neighboring sanctuary as if they were Christians. A hospice is thus often found alongside the church of an order or of an abbey. But it was in Jerusalem that the largest of all these, the Hospital of St. John, developed, giving birth to a specific order.

The pilgrim was exposed to many dangers and was defenseless against them; consequently pilgrims became the object of legal protection on the part of the germanic laws—protected by the Peace of God. But in Palestine, due to attacks by Muslim thieves, associations of knights were formed to escort pilgrims, and they created the Order of the Templars.

The pilgrim was also a client for the transportation business from the moment when the sea route began to be used regularly, that is to say from the twelfth century for those whose destination was Jerusalem. The city of Marseilles enacted beginning in the thirteenth century statutes with counterparts in other maritime cities, fixing prices that were calculated according to the accommodations offered and kept relatively low for those less fortunate. In the following century, when pilgrimages recommenced after having been interrupted in 1291 by Muslim interdiction, it was Venice which organized a system of galley transportation for pilgrims, with a whole set of measures to protect them from being cheated. The Dominican Felix Fabri describes in detail the organization of the line of passengers where the different classes, defined by the price each was willing to pay, were provided for. Upon arrival in the East, the Franciscans offered their help to pilgrims to keep them from being the object of unreasonable demands from guides or those who rented beasts of burden. But they were also subjected to the payment of charges levied by Muslim authorities, in particular for entrance to the Holy Sepulchre. Byzantine and even Latin authorities turned the passage of pilgrims to their own advantage, in return, admittedly, for the burden the pilgrims imposed upon them. Elsewhere, the exploitation of pilgrimage for financial gain was less common. In any case, besides its religious function, pilgrimage, if for no other reason than the size of the phenomenon it represented, had a definite role in the medieval economy.

## BIBLIOGRAPHY

Chelini, Jean, and Henry Brauthomme. *Les chemins de Dieu: Histoire des pèlerinages chrétiens des origines à nos jours.* 2nd edition. Paris: Hachette, 1982.

Dansette, Béatrice. "Les pèlerinages occidentaux en Terre Sainte: Une pratique de la Dévotion moderne." *Archivum franciscanum historicum* 72 (1979): 106–133, 331–428.

Favreau-Lilie, Marie-Luise. "Civis peregrinus: Soziale und rechtliche Aspekte der bürgerliche Wallfahrt im späten Mittelalter." *Archiv für Kulturgeschichte* 76 (1994): 321–350.

Ganz-Blätter, Ursula. *Andacht und Abenteuer: Berichte europäischer Jerusalem- und Santiago-Pilger (1320–1530).* Tübingen: G. Narr, 1990.

Oursel, Raymond. *Plerins du Moyen Âge: Les hommes, les chemins, les sanctuaires.* 2nd edition. Paris: Fayard, 1978.

*Pèlerinage et Croisades.* Actes du 118e congrès national des sociétés historiques et scientifiques, Pau, 1994. Paris: C.T.H.S., 1995.

Richard, Jean. "Le transport outre-mer des croisés et des pèlerins." In *Maritime Aspects of Migration.* Ed. Klaus Friedland. Quellen und Darstellungen zur Hansischen Geschichte, n.s., 34. Köln-Wien: Bohlau, 1989, pp. 27–44.

Sigal, Pierre-André. *Les marcheurs de Dieu: Pèlerinages et pèlerins au Moyen Age.* Paris: Colin, 1974.

Sumption, Jonathan. *Pilgrimage, an Image of Medieval Religion.* London: Faber and Faber, 1975.

*Wallfahrt kennt keine Grenzen: Themen zu einer Ausstellung des Bayerischen Nationalmuseums und des Adalbert Stifter Vereins, München.* Ed. Lenz Kriss-Rettenbeck and Gerda Möhler. Munich-Zurich: Schnell und Steiner, 1984.

Jean Richard

**SEE ALSO**

Bordeaux Pilgrim; Edessa; Holy Land; Irish Travel; Itineraries and *Periploi*; Jerusalem; Military Orders; Pilgrim Souvenirs; Pilgrimage Sites, Byzantine; Pilgrimage Sites, English; Pilgrimage Sites, Spanish; Purgatory, St. Patrick's; Rome as a Pilgrimage Site; Taoism; Travel Writing in Europe and the Mediterranean Regions; Vézelay

## Pilgrimage Site, Rome as a

*See* Rome as a Pilgrimage Site

## Pilgrimage Sites, Byzantine

By the end of the fourth century, pilgrimage had become a well-established institution throughout the Christian world, although it never gained official sanction from the Church. In the Byzantine East, pilgrimage was called *proskynesis* (veneration), and the act of worship may have taken precedence over the long and arduous journey. Byzantine pilgrimage did not generate a significant body of literature, and much of what is known about it comes from either saints' *vitae* or the accounts of foreign travelers.

The Byzantine Empire was studded with religious centers of both international and local significance. Pilgrimage was based on the belief that sanctity was transferable through physical contact—that the physical and spiritual worlds come together at certain special places, *loca sancta,* where the powers of heaven could be more easily tapped for earthly benefit or for aid in salvation. From as early as the third century, sites associated with the earthly lives of Christ and the saints were recognized as *martyria,* sanctified by events in their lives or by their tombs. Pilgrimage sites were often given validation by the construction of large architectural complexes, and some included *xenodocheia* or hostels for pilgrims. Visitors could obtain mementos of

their experience, *eulogiai* or "blessings" in the form of relics, earth, stone, oil, water, or a portable work of art associated with the site.

Following in the footsteps of St. Helena, pilgrims of the fourth through seventh centuries, armed with maps and guidebooks, visited numerous sites in the Holy Land associated with events of the Old and New Testament. Most important was the Church of the Holy Sepulchre in Jerusalem, which marked the sites of Christ's Crucifixion, Entombment, and Resurrection. The complex was begun by Constantine in the fourth century and focused on the Anastasis (Resurrection) Rotunda containing the tomb of Christ. Destroyed and reconstructed in the seventh century and again in the eleventh century, the complex remained a center of Byzantine devotion. Pilgrims of the sixth century and later obtained lead ampullae containing oil from the Tomb of Christ that had been touched to the wood of the True Cross. Elsewhere in Jerusalem, pilgrims visited the Pool of Siloam, the Pool of Bethesda (associated with the birth of the Virgin), the church on Sion (with the site of the Last Supper and the relic of the Column of the Flagellation), the site of the Ascension on the Mount of Olives, the Grotto of the Agony in Gethsemane, and the tomb of the Virgin in the Valley of Josephat. The Church of the Nativity in Bethlehem and the site of the Burning Bush on Mount Sinai were also important destinations. At the latter, the Burning Bush was plucked out of existence by pilgrims seeking "blessings." Monasteries of the devout and of the ascetic were also visited by pilgrims as a source of inspiration and "blessings."

Outside of the Holy Land, some important sites grew around venerated local saints. For example, Qal'at Sem'an in northern Syria was made famous by Symeon the Stylite (c. 389–459), whose ascetic extremes attracted a following during his lifetime. After a variety of ascetic feats, Symeon withdrew to the top of a column, from which he continued to preach to pilgrims. After his death, his body was removed to the Cathedral of Antioch, but the column continued to be revered as a relic. A great cruciform church and a monastic complex were constructed around it (late fifth through sixth centuries), with hostels for pilgrims located at the base of the mountain. Already during Symeon's lifetime, pilgrims' tokens made of earth were carried away by the faithful, and these were credited with miraculous cures. Symeon's eccentric asceticism inspired a number of imitators, most notably Symeon the Stylite the Younger (521–592), whose cult, centered at his

# P

church complex near Antioch, followed a similar pattern of development.

Of the tombs of the apostles, that of St. John at Ephesus was the most important. His tomb, located on a hill outside the city, exuded a miraculous healing dust, or *manna*, on his feast days. It was covered by a canopy before *c.* 300, and a great cruciform church was built in the fifth and sixth centuries. A popular trading fair developed around the festival of St. John, at which pilgrims could purchase clay ampullae of *manna*. Ephesus continued to be venerated throughout the Middle Ages by pilgrims who also visited there the tombs of the apostle Timothy, Mary Magdelene, St. Alexander, and 300 holy fathers. The grotto of the Seven Sleepers, near Ephesus, became a popular burial site for pilgrims.

Trading fairs also developed in conjunction with pilgrimage worship at numerous other sites. The Church of St. Michael at Chonae in Asia Minor, which marked the site of a miracle from apostolic times, was a center of pilgrimage and the location of a great trade fair. The Church of St. Theodore at Euchaita in the Pontus was the scene of a crowded fair that coincided with the festival of the saint. Other major commercial centers in Asia Minor possessed important shrines, such as St. Basil at Caesara, the Forty Martyrs at Sebaste, St. Tryphon at Nicaea, and St. Polycarp at Smyrna.

Thessaloniki was famed for the martyr Demetrius, to whom many posthumous miracles were attributed. Although the actual tomb of the saint was elsewhere, Demetrius was believed to reside in Thessaloniki, in a hexagonal ciborium located in the nave of the great basilica (fifth and seventh centuries) that had been constructed on the site of his martyrdom. Cures were often effected through the process of incubation: the invalid would spend the night in the church near the saint's shrine, in hope that the saint would appear and offer a cure. Late in the development of the cult—perhaps as late as the twelfth century—a miraculous aromatic oil became associated with the ciborium. Demetrius is consequently referred to as a *myrobletos*—a myrrh-producing saint, apparently following the example of St. Theodora of Thessaloniki (ninth century). Visitors to Thessaloniki could procure lead ampullae for the myrrh.

Another early figure whose site attracted large numbers of pilgrims was St. Nicholas of Myra (in Lycia on the south coast of Asia Minor), a legendary saint said to have been a contemporary of Constantine the Great, but who achieved prominence only after the ninth century. Veneration centered on his tomb in a church of perhaps the eighth century, which was enlarged in the eleventh and twelfth centuries when the cult was at its height. Nicholas was also a *myrobletos,* and a miraculous myrrh exuded from his tomb and was collected by pilgrims. The patron saint of sailors and travelers, St. Nicholas was believed to be able to calm stormy seas, and his shrine was a popular stop in the eastern Mediterranean for ships en route to the Holy Land. Although Nicholas's body was stolen by sailors from Bari and taken to Italy in 1087, Myra continued to function as a center of pilgrimage.

Saints of the Byzantine Middle Ages also attracted a following, often during their lifetimes, with worship and miracles continuing at their tombs after their deaths. St. Nikon at Sparta (*c.* 930–1000), the Blessed Luke at Stiris (Hosios Loukas, *c.* 900–953), and St. Athanasius of Athos (*c.* 925–1001) had primarily local followings, but the cults drew enough attention to attract imperial patronage. In Asia Minor, new sanctuaries emerged honoring both holy men and the martyrs of the Arab invasions; among these were St. Ioannicius (*c.* 752–846) of Mount Olympus in Bithynia, St. Lazarus (*c.* 972–1053) of Mount Galesius near Ephesus, and the Forty-two Martyrs (d. 838) of Amorium.

The popularity of the Holy Land was diminished after the Arab conquest of the seventh century, compounded by the decline in trade and related economic difficulties. Nevertheless, visitors continued to travel there, such as St. Lazarus in the eleventh century and John Phocas in the twelfth; imperial subsidies continued as well. The diminished significance was offset by the dissemination of relics and the creation of new pilgrimage sites that often had no biblical or apostolic associations.

After the seventh century, Constantinople emerged as the major center of devotion. Already in the fourth century, relics of the apostles had been translated to the Church of the Holy Apostles, which served as the imperial mausoleum throughout the early Byzantine period. Indeed, with the translation of relics, virtually any church could become the object of pilgrimage. Numerous churches in the Byzantine capital obtained relics or miraculous icons associated with the Holy Land. For example, the Blachernae and the Chalkoprateia churches both contained garments of the Virgin; the Hodegon monastery had an icon said to have been painted by St. Luke; the Pantocrator monastery housed the Stone of the Unction, incorporated into the tomb of Manuel I

Comnenus. Other churches housed important relics of Saints Stephen and John the Baptist. At other sites, such as the miraculous spring of the Zoodochos Pege, veneration developed from purely local phenomena. Some shrines specialized in their cures: incubation at the tomb of St. Artemius provided a remedy for diseases of the testicles, whereas the relics of St. Photeine cured maladies of the eyes. Gradually, Constantinople became a "New Jerusalem," filled with relics and holy objects, although many of them were taken to western Europe when the city and its churches were plundered in 1204 by the participants of the Fourth Crusade.

The detailed accounts of Russian pilgrims of the late Middle Ages testify to the continuing spiritual attraction of the Byzantine capital, particularly during the fourteenth and fifteenth centuries. Their itineraries document the wealth of relics still housed in the churches and monasteries of the city. In addition to Constantinople, Russian travelers were also drawn to Jerusalem and the Holy Land, and to the monastic centers on Mount Athos. With the fall of Byzantium in the fifteenth century, Russian shrines and sanctuaries, such as the Monastery of the Caves near Kiev or the remote monasteries of the far north, replaced Byzantine pilgrimage destinations.

**BIBLIOGRAPHY**

*Akten des XII. Internationalen Kongresses für Christliche Archäologie (Bonn 1991) = Jahrbuch für Antike und Christentum, Ergängungsband* 20 (1995). [NB: The conference was devoted to the subject of pilgrimage.]

Majeska, George. *Russian Travelers to Constantinople in the Fourteenth and Fifteenth Centuries.* Washington, DC: Dumbarton Oaks, 1984.

Ousterhout, Robert, ed. *The Blessings of Pilgrimage.* Urbana-Chicago: U of Illinois P, 1990.

Vikan, Gary. *Byzantine Pilgrimage Art.* Washington, DC: Dumbarton Oaks, 1982.

———. "Art, Medicine, and Magic in Early Byzantium." *Dumbarton Oaks Papers* 38 (1984): 65–86.

———. "Pilgrimage." *Oxford Dictionary of Byzantium.* Oxford, 1991, vol. 3, pp. 1676–1677.

Vryonis, Speros, Jr. *The Decline of Medieval Hellenism in Asia Minor and the Process of Islamization from the Eleventh through the Fifteenth Century.* Berkeley-Los Angeles: U of California P, 1971.

Wilkinson, John. *Jerusalem Pilgrims before the Crusades.* Jerusalem: Ariel; and Warminster, England: Aris and Phillips, 1977.

*Robert Ousterhout*

**SEE ALSO**

Byzantine Empire; Constantinople; Crusade, Fourth; Fairs; Holy Land; Inns and Accommodations; Itineraries and *Periploi;* Jerusalem; Phocas, John; Pilgrim Souvenirs; Pilgrimage, Christian; Russia and Rus'

## Pilgrimage Sites, English

Pilgrims were drawn to two principal kinds of sites in England: those devoted to the relics of a local saint, and those devoted to the Virgin Mary. Every cathedral or abbey of course had relics that would draw pilgrims from at least the immediate vicinity. Particularly well-known saints' shrines included those of St. Thomas Becket at Canterbury; St. Cuthbert at Durham; St. Thomas Cantilupe at Hereford; St. Hugh at Lincoln; Edward the Confessor at Westminster Abbey; St. Wulfstan at Worcester; Glastonbury Abbey, associated with Joseph of Arimathea, St. Patrick, St. Dunstan, and King Arthur; the eponymous St. Albans and Bury St. Edmunds; and, more localized, such saints (not always canonized) as Winifred of Holywell, Frideswide of Oxford, Gilbert of Sempringham, Godric of Finchale, and William of Norwich. For the second kind of site, there were important Marian shrines at Walsingham, Caversham, Doncaster, Ipswich, Knaresborough, Penrice, Westminster, Willesden, and Worcester. Other popular pilgrimage sites had relics of Christ, such as the fragment of the Holy Cross at Bromholm Priory in Norfolk, mentioned in Chaucer's *Reeve's Tale* and in Langland, and a vial of the blood of Christ at Hailes Abbey in Gloucestershire, mentioned in the *Pardoner's Tale.*

The two most internationally famous sites were the shrine of St. Thomas Becket in Canterbury Cathedral and that of the Virgin at Walsingham in Norfolk, both visited frequently by foreign visitors and English royals and nobles, as well as more ordinary English men and women. Pilgrims to Canterbury after 1220 had five principal places to visit within the cathedral: the site of St. Thomas's martyrdom in the northwest transept; the high altar, where the saint's body had lain after the murder; the crypt, where he was buried from 1170 until 1220, when the body was translated to its permanent shrine after the rebuilding of the cathedral; the altar of the Crown of St. Thomas (sliced off by one of the murderers' blows) in the easternmost apse called the Corona, built especially for it; and finally the post-1220 shrine itself in Trinity Chapel, east of the high altar. According to D.J. Hall's reconstruction, the shrine had a marble base about six feet high, on which was placed a very large

# P

chest covered with gold plate and jewels, containing the saint's remains; over this was a net of golden wire on which were hung offerings of jewelry. The whole was covered by a huge wooden hood that could be raised and lowered. Erasmus's account of his visit around 1512–1514 includes this impression: "The cheapest part was gold. Everything shone and dazzled with rare and surpassingly large jewels, some bigger than a goose egg" (308). The fifteenth-century *Tale of Beryn,* which purports to show Chaucer's pilgrims at Canterbury, indicates that the cathedral's stained-glass windows were also a focus of attention and that the purchase of pilgrimage tokens or badges was a matter of intense interest.

The pilgrimage site at Walsingham was an Augustinian priory; its principal draw was the famous twelfth-century statue of the Virgin seated with her Child (Dickinson 13), found in "the Holy House," a small wooden building twenty-three feet by twelve feet ten inches, enclosed within an outer building of stone, attached to the north wall of the priory church (Hall 109): this wooden building was itself reputed to be miraculous, built by the hands of angels. Erasmus, who also visited Walsingham between 1512 and 1514, describes his impression: the chapel was dark and fragrant, lit only by scented candles, with the image standing "in the shadows, to the right of the altar" (297); yet "you would say it was the abode of the saints, so dazzling is it with jewels, gold, and silver" (292). Two other points of interest for pilgrims to Walsingham were the high altar in the church, where a vial of the Virgin's milk was to be seen, and the Chapel of St. Laurence, to the east of the church, where there were other relics. There were also two wells within the precincts of the priory, supposedly of miraculous origin, whose water was reputed to have healing power.

Both St. Thomas's shrine and the priory at Walsingham, like many others, were destroyed during the dissolution of the monasteries under Henry VIII (1536–1537), with chests full of gold and silver carried away to the royal treasury. An anonymous sixteenth-century poet lamented of Walsingham:

> Levell levell with the ground the towres doe lye,
> Which with their golden, glitteringe tops pearsed
>     once to the skye. (Dickinson 67)

## BIBLIOGRAPHY

Bowers, John M., ed. *The Canterbury Tales: Fifteenth-Century Continuations and Additions.* TEAMS Middle English Texts. Kalamazoo, MI: Medieval Institute, 1992.

Dickinson, J.C. *The Shrine of Our Lady of Walsingham.* Cambridge: Cambridge UP, 1956.

Erasmus. "A Pilgrimage for Religion's Sake." (*Peregrinatio religionis ergo,* 1526). In *The Colloquies of Erasmus.* Trans. Craig R. Thompson. Chicago: U of Chicago P, 1965, pp. 285–312.

Finucane, Ronald C. *Miracles and Pilgrims: Popular Beliefs in Medieval England.* Totowa, NJ: Rowman and Littlefield, 1977.

Gibson, Gail McMurray. *The Theater of Devotion: East Anglian Drama and Society in the Late Middle Ages.* Chicago: U of Chicago P, 1989, pp. 137–143.

Hall, D.J. *English Mediaeval Pilgrimage.* London: Routledge and Kegan Paul, 1965.

Loxton, Howard. *Pilgrimage to Canterbury.* Totowa, NJ: Rowman and Littlefield, 1978.

*Mary Hamel*

**SEE ALSO**

Chaucer, Geoffrey; Pilgrim Souvenirs; Pilgrimage, Christian; Pilgrimage Sites, Byzantine; Pilgrimage Sites, Spanish

## Pilgrimage Sites, Spanish

Pilgrimage has long been an essential part of Iberian medieval (and modern) Catholicism. In addition to three or four sites of international importance in the Middle Ages, every region had (and still has) a principal shrine, generally dedicated to the Virgin Mary, such as the Virgen del Rocío in Huelva and the Virgen de Guadalupe in Cáceres. On the individual saint's annual feast day, people of the region would undertake the two- to four-day pilgrimage to that shrine to pay respects and pray. In addition, many towns often had a local shrine—situated within a half-day's walk—which served as a focal point of local veneration.

Most famous of all pilgrimage sites in Spain is the town of Santiago de Compostela in Galicia. As the reputed burial place of St. James the Elder, who purportedly worked to Christianize the Iberian Peninsula, Compostela gained the distinction of being one of the top three pilgrimage centers in medieval Christendom (along with Rome and Jerusalem). Dante, in *La vita nuova* (chap. 40), suggests the predominance of Compostela when he writes, "Those who go to the church in Galicia are called 'pilgrims' for James' tomb is farther from his native land than that of any other apostle." "Compostella" and "Templum sancti iacobi" are both noted in legends on the Hereford map (*c.* 1290).

**P**

The legend of St. James has as its nucleus his work on the Iberian Peninsula before his return to the Holy Land where he was martyred. After his death, friends took his body and placed it on an unmanned ship that traveled through the Mediterranean and north along the Atlantic coast until it reached the northwest corner of the peninsula. There, his disciples removed his body and buried it, after a series of miracles that convinced the pagan ruler of James's sanctity. The tomb of the saint lay forgotten until around 881, when it was discovered by shepherds after a series of miraculous events; it was then confirmed by Bishop Theodomir, and relatively soon afterward there are references to the first visitors to the tomb. The first pilgrim of whose name we are certain is Gotescalc, a French bishop who visited Compostela in 950. Hundreds of thousands of pilgrims followed: a trickle in the eleventh century giving way to a flood in the twelfth and thirteenth centuries. Records indicate that pilgrims from all parts of Christendom visited the site: from France, Italy, Ireland, Britain, Germany, Scandinavia, Hungary, and Russia. Diaries, itineraries, and records are extant from the thirteenth century on.

Although it has been common to speak of "The Route to Compostela" (in the singular), in truth there were many ways to reach the pilgrimage site, depending on the starting point, the century in which the pilgrim lived, and the political situation at the time. Since nearly all of Iberia was under Muslim domination during the first years of the pilgrimage, early pilgrims probably traveled along the northern, Cantabrian, coast, which had been reclaimed early on by the Christians. Subsequent military successes managed to push the principal route to the south, until it became codified into The Route as described in Book 5 of the twelfth-century *Liber Sancti Jacobi,* a section of text commonly known as *The Pilgrim's Guide.* The route gathers at four main points in France and funnels into Iberia through two traditional, relatively accessible, passes in the Pyrenees: Somport (Summus Portus) and Ibañeta from St.-Jean-Pied-de-Port to Roncesvalles. From there the two main routes proceeded out of the mountains south and west toward Puente la Reina, where the roads united and became one route west to Compostela. The shrine in the northwest corner of the peninsula lies approximately 625 miles (1,000 kilometers) from Somport, a distance that pilgrims on horseback could traverse in about twelve long days (or in forty to fifty days by foot). Between the Pyrenees and

Compostela rise two substantial mountain ranges, other smaller ones, and the famous plains of Castilla-León, dry and hot during the summer months.

Seven and one-half miles (twelve kilometers) before Compostela, pilgrims paused at the Lavacolla stream to wash themselves, perhaps for the first time since they had begun their trek. Then they continued to the top of the one remaining mountain separating them from the shrine. The first pilgrim from each group to espy the cathedral's towers from the Monte de Gozo was entitled to call himself "king" (or in French "le roy"). Two hours later, having arrived at the cathedral, pilgrims performed a series of ritual acts, including hugging the saint's statue and visiting the crypt. After making confession and attending mass, the pilgrim to St. James received plenary indulgence.

A system of monastery hospices grew up along the route due predominantly to the Cluniac order's efforts. These institutions fulfilled the imperatives of medieval *caritas* (charity): food and lodging for pilgrims, care for sick pilgrims, ransom for pilgrims captured by the infidel, and burial of the dead. In the fifteenth century, the Catholic monarchs King Ferdinand and Queen Isabella funded the construction of a large hospice (now one of the most luxurious five-star hotels in Spain) on the north side of the monumental Plaza de Obradoiro in front of the cathedral. Its four courtyards allowed for the separation of the pilgrims into groups by sex and physical condition (healthy and unhealthy). Pilgrims could receive free lodging and food for three days there, after which they were expected to leave.

Many of Iberia's secondary pilgrimage sites existed on or near The Route and were visited by the pilgrims on their way either to or from Compostela. Each of these sites features some relic or statue of a holy person that is responsible for miracles. In the basilica in Zaragoza [Saragossa], pilgrims could visit the pillar of Jesus' flagellation, which had been miraculously transported there by the Virgin Mary (in her only miracle during her life) in order to encourage James to continue his proselytizing. Other sites required less deviation from the traditional route; they, too, were important for their relics, and tradition made them well known, particularly La Cogolla and Silos, where the relics of two Spanish saints, Millán and Domingo, were located. The works of the twelfth-century poet Gonzalo de Berceo popularized these sites. In Villasirga (along The Route) a statue of the Virgin Mary was

# P

made famous by the *Cantigas* of King Alfonso X ("the Wise" [r. 1252–1284]), in which he narrates miracles that she performed for Compostela-bound pilgrims. In León, the reliquary containing the bones of St. Isidore, brought from Muslim lands in the south in 1056, were placed in a church that also served as a pantheon of the kings of León. Estella, in Navarra, claims an important relic of St. Andrew the apostle, brought there in the late thirteenth century by a bishop of Patras as a pilgrim to Compostela.

Santiago de Compostela and the secondary sites along The Route were by no means the only important destinations in Spain. Oviedo (in Galicia, along the northern, Cantabrian, coast) is of great renown, for it is a very old city, and claims to have the Cruz de Los Angeles relic, drops of liquid from the miracle performed by Jesus at Cana (recorded in John 2:1–11), as well as an ossuary of many New Testament and Spanish saints in the great reliquary chest housed in the Cámara Santa. Although the pilgrimage to Oviedo is at least contemporary with, and possibly older than, the pilgrimage to Compostela, there is little written proof of the great items held in Oviedo. The *Liber Sancti Jacobi* guide completely ignores the town in its description of "musts" to visit. By the thirteenth century, however, Oviedo was second only to Compostela in importance on the peninsula as a pilgrim's destination. Oviedo offered the following saying to remind pilgrims to make the necessary side trip from the main Compostela pilgrimage road: "Who goes to Santiago and not to San Salvador, serves the servant and forgets the Lord."

Montserrat is a famous pilgrimage site located in the Llobregat valley in the Pyrenees Mountains in the province of Barcelona. Legend has it that there was an ancient monastery there by the sixth century where a statue of the Virgin Mary was venerated. When the Moors invaded the peninsula, the statue was hidden, then rediscovered in the ninth century. By the tenth century the cult of this statue was extensive and widespread. The statue now on view is undeniably old but cannot be accurately dated. It is a polychrome wood representation of the Madonna holding an orb, representing the world, in one hand and the infant Jesus in the other. Both Madonna and Son are black, or dark-skinned. Devotion and increased pilgrimages to visit this chapel brought in considerable revenues, and the original chapel was enlarged more than once. The monastery was (re)founded in 1025 by Oliba, abbot of

Ripoll and bishop of Vic. So many pilgrims visited there that by the thirteenth century the Romanesque buildings had to be enlarged. The monastery was reduced to rubble by Napoleon in 1812 but has been rebuilt.

**BIBLIOGRAPHY**

Begg, Ean. *The Cult of the Black Virgin.* London: Arkana-Routledge; Boston: Kegan Paul, 1985.

Davies, Horton, and Marie Hélène Davies. *Holy Days and Holidays: The Medieval Pilgrimage to Compostela.* Lewisburg, PA: Bucknell UP, 1982.

Dunn, Maryjane, and Linda Davidson. *The Pilgrimage to Santiago de Compostela: A Comprehensive, Annotated Bibliography.* New York and London: Garland, 1994.

Jacobs, Michael. *Architectural Guides for Travellers: The Road to Santiago de Compostela.* London: Viking, 1991.

*The Pilgrim's Guide to Santiago de Compostela.* Ed. and Trans. William Melczer. New York: Italica, 1993.

Van Heerwarden, J. "Saint James in Spain up to the 12th Century." In *Wallfahrt kennt keine Grenzen.* Ed. L. Kriss-Rettenbeck and Gerda Möhler. Munich: Schnell & Steiner, 1984, pp. 235–247.

*Maryjane Dunn and Linda Davidson*

**SEE ALSO**

Alfonso X; Barcelona; Dante Alighieri; Inns and Accommodations; Itineraries and *Periploi;* Military Orders; Orb of Imperial Power; Pilgrimage, Christian; Rocamadour; Roncesvalles; Spain and Portugal; Vézeley

## Pilgrim Souvenirs

Mementos, usually of metal, sold to pilgrims at various shrines throughout Europe as evidence that they had completed pilgrimages.

In an attempt to prevent the piecemeal dismantling of shrines by overzealous pilgrims, churches commissioned artisans to produce pilgrim souvenirs in the form of pewter badges and tin ampullae (vials). Pilgrim badges were produced and sold near European pilgrimage shrines from the late eleventh through the sixteenth centuries, becoming visible symbols of the pilgrim and of a completed pilgrimage. Pilgrims pinned or sewed the badges on their broad-brimmed hats or their traveling cloaks. Wearing a badge enabled pilgrims to receive charity and often assured safe passage through enemy territory.

The earliest and most famous pilgrim badge was the scallop shell, from the shrine of St. James at Santiago de Compostela. Strenuous efforts of the Compostela ecclesiastical authorities to monopolize the motif failed, for the scallop shell badge was adopted at various times by other shrines including Mont-Saint-Michel, Rocamadour, Canterbury, and Cologne—thus becoming an emblem of pilgrims and pilgrimage throughout Europe. Other pilgrim badges depicted Christ, the Virgin Mary, and saints identified by their individual symbols. Some, like modern-day souvenirs, had designs that evoked the famous shrines or reliquaries that the pilgrims had visited. These souvenirs imitated the sight of the original, reminding the pilgrims that what they had witnessed and touched was indeed authentic.

Mass-produced in the millions from limestone molds, badges were sold in homes, shops, and churches. They varied in shape from solid geometric plaques to

Pilgrim hat badges from Aachen, Rome, Veronica. Anonymous panel painting of Saints George and Sebaldus. Nuremberg, Germanisches National-museum Inv. Nr. Gm 142, 1487. Courtesy Nuremberg Germanisches National-museum.

Pewter pilgrim badge of the head reliquary of St. Thomas Becket. England, Canterbury Cathedral, 14th century. Collection Brian North Lee. Permission of Brian North Lee.

intricate irregular openwork, and ranged in size from tiny pinheads to several inches square. The same badge was often available in a range of sizes. Badges were also sometimes painted, embellished with elaborate borders, and backed with colored paper or cloth.

Pilgrim souvenirs were inexpensively cast from a pewter or tin mixture that could be melted at a very low temperature, allowing for production without an elaborate foundry. Wealthy pilgrims bought souvenirs made of fine metals embellished with gems, not merely for added distinction, but also because these materials were thought to have intrinsic healing and protective powers. A badge decorated with a sapphire, for example, was thought to protect eyesight and neutralize poison. By the fifteenth century, artisans introduced very thin sheets of brass called "bracteate" to badge making, providing an inexpensive golden sheen. Other

# P

popular media used to create pilgrim souvenirs included papier-mâché, clay, wax, and paper and vellum prints. Pilgrims could also buy horns, bells, whistles, and rattles whose loud noise was believed to ward off evil and lightning.

The market for pilgrim souvenirs and related items was great, and thus this business was highly profitable, with churches and shrines subsidizing building campaigns from the proceeds. Some shrine caretakers controlled the sale of badges by renting out molds and receiving a percentage from every sale, while other shrines operated a completely open market, welcoming any artisan who wished to participate. Some shrines with pilgrim badge monopolies opened their markets to outside artisans during busy periods (such as Holy Week) when their contracted labor could not keep up with the demand of the tens of thousands of pilgrims who crowded into their shrine precinct.

The numbers of pilgrim souvenirs produced, especially during the later Middle Ages, are astonishing. For example, during 1519, the first year of pilgrimage to Regensburg, the shrine was short thousands of badges when 50,000 pilgrims descended on it. Those who received nothing went home bitterly complaining. The following year, the officials were better prepared and sold more than 120,000 badges. These numbers are solid evidence (if late) of the vast scale of medieval pilgrimages, and the finds of varied shrine souvenirs in far-flung spots are indications of the travel patterns of the pilgrims.

Substantial profits led to bitter disputes, sometimes lasting generations, over the privilege of pilgrim badge production. Church officials tried to control the illegal pilgrim souvenir trade by restricting which badges were allowed to touch the shrine or reliquary. Unfortunate pilgrims who purchased the "wrong" kind of badge were turned away and not allowed to touch the shrine with their badge. This diminished the value of the souvenir, for many believed that the power of the saint was transferred to the souvenir when it came into contact with the shrine or reliquary containing the saint's relics.

It was also accepted that power emanated from the association of magical names and holy images used in many pilgrim souvenirs. Names of Christ, the Virgin Mary, the Magi, and other saints enjoyed a reputation of protecting against illness and the threat of sudden death. The images on pilgrim souvenirs could generate the healing power of the saints and their relics.

Popular belief in miracles transformed these humble souvenirs into relics that could cure illness, ensure salvation, and ward off evil. People dipped pilgrim badges into water or wine to be drunk as medicine or daubed on the afflicted body part. Some believed that certain pilgrim badges were effective in reducing the number of years their owners had to spend in Purgatory. Badges (often dozens of them) were cast into bells, chalices, baptismal fonts, and tankards to ward off evil spirits and harsh weather. Pilgrims also used them as amuletic magic charms. Badges have been found buried in the foundations of houses, hung over stall doors, pinned on cattle troughs, and placed in fields to guard against vermin infestations. Ultimately, most pilgrim badges were tossed into rivers, rather like modern-day wishing wells, their owners hoping for even greater rewards.

**BIBLIOGRAPHY**

Bruna, Denis. *Enseignes de Pèlerinage et Enseignes Profanes.* Musée Nationale du Moyen Age: Thermes de Cluny, 1996.

Cohen, Esther. "*In haec signa*: Pilgrim badge trade in southern France." *Journal of Medieval History* 2.3 (1976): 193–214.

Koldeweij, A.M., and H.J.E. Van Beuningen. *Heilig en Profaan: 1000 Laat-Middeleeuwse Insignes uit de Collectie H.J.E. Van Beuningen.* Rotterdam: Rotterdam Papers, 1993.

Köster, Kurt. *Pilgerzeichen und Pilgermuscheln von mittelalterlichen Santiago-Strassen: Saint Léonard- Rocamadour- Saint Giles-Santiago de Compestela.* Schleswiger Funde und Gesamtüberlieferung. Neumünster: Wacholtz, 1983.

Spencer, Brian. "Medieval Pilgrim Badges." In *Rotterdam Papers: A Contribution to Medieval Archaeology.* Ed. J.G.N. Renaud. Rotterdam: Rotterdam Papers, 1968, pp. 137–153.

———. *Salisbury & South Wiltshire Museum Medieval Catalogue II: Pilgrim Souvenirs and Secular Badges.* Salisbury: Salisbury and South Wiltshire Museum, 1990.

*Sarah Blick*

**SEE ALSO**

Anonymous of the Lower Rhine or of Cologne; Gems; Memory and Maps; Pilgrimage, Christian; Pilgrimage Sites, English; Pilgrimage Sites, Spanish; Purgatory; Rocamadour; Vézelay

# Piracy

Robbery at sea that, in the Middle Ages, took two forms: *pirates* attacked merchant shipping indiscriminately, while *corsairs* or *privateers* plundered with the license of territorial states, selectively raiding the shipping and cargo of political and economic rivals. Appointed as *emirs* (the Arabic term) or *admirati* (the term derived from Latin), Muslim and Christian captains utilized piracy as a tactic in naval conflicts throughout the Middle Ages. Pirates and corsairs were seldom easily distinguished, however. Corsairs often abused their authority to plunder allied merchants; pirates enlisted as corsairs in the service of foreign powers.

Mediterranean piracy and trade can be divided into roughly three phases between 800 and 1500. From the ninth to the eleventh centuries, Christian shipping in the Mediterranean was harried by Vikings, by Narentian pirates who sheltered along the Dalmatian coast, and by Muslim corsairs who raided from strongholds in Umayyad Andalusia, Aghlabid and Fātamid North Africa, Fraxinetum (present-day Garde-Frainet, near Nice), Crete (occupied 824–961), and Sicily (occupied 902–1072). While the degree to which Muslim piracy disrupted European trade is disputed, Arab marauding had positive long-term consequences for European overseas trade, spurring the development of sea power in coastal cities such as Pisa, Genoa, and Barcelona.

Between 1100 and 1300, these cities, together with Venice, a former Byzantine colony, rose to prominence as maritime entrepôts in the wake of the Latin crusades. Italians now replaced Arabs as the premier marauders of the Mediterranean, targeting rival Christians as readily as Muslims. The Genoese became particularly notorious, serving as *admirati* for the French, Sicilian, and Portuguese monarchies as well as for the Byzantine Empire and their native Genoa itself. European privateering crippled Muslim shipping and spearheaded Western European economic and territorial expansion into the Byzantine Levant, especially after the Latin conquest of Constantinople in 1204. Catalan, Greek, and Italian corsairs and pirates remained a constant peril along the basin's major shipping lanes, from Monaco to the Aegean archipelago.

Genoese, Greeks, Florentines, and Catalans remained active after 1300, the last raiding in the service of the crown of Catalonia-Aragón, particularly during the reign of Alfonso V ("the Magnanimous," 1417–1455). The fourteenth and fifteenth centuries nevertheless saw a resurgence in Muslim piracy. Launched from Asia Minor, Turkish pirates abounded in the Levant. Barbary pirates, based on the Algerian coast, menaced western Mediterranean shipping after 1400. While

Christian pirates continued to attack one another, the Muslim recrudescence pitted Christian corsairs increasingly against their Muslim counterparts, especially after the Ottoman conquest of Constantinople in 1453.

The sources documenting medieval piracy are rich and diverse, revealing the complexities of piracy's relationship to medieval sea trade. On the one hand, statutes promulgated at Pisa, Genoa, and Venice regulated maritime defense against piracy. The Catalan code of medieval maritime practice, the *Llibre del Consulat del Mar* (c. 1325), addresses piracy's negative impact on commercial practice in several passages. Critical views of piracy may also be gleaned from medieval travelogues, Latin and Byzantine hagiographical works, and merchant correspondence in the Datini archives at Prato. On the other hand, medieval statutes also sanction voyages *ad cursum* or *ad piraticam*—for corsairing or piracy—to undermine commercial rivals.

Archival evidence indicates that corsairs were usually members of the same urban patriciate active in overseas trade. *Admirati* often administered trade alongside naval command. Galleys were interchangeably equipped for commerce or combat. Notarial sources record the sale or delivery of booty captured in privateering raids (varying from slaves to grain and other commodities) to merchants who invested in corsair voyages as open or silent partners. Booty defrayed the costs of armament, contributing to public finance as well as to private coffers. Treaties, the deliberations of governing councils, legal proceedings, and civil law commentaries meanwhile document the practice, from the thirteenth century on, of providing compensation to merchants claiming to have been unjustly attacked *in more piratico,* "in a piratical manner," by corsairs subject to an allied power. The depositions that document these attacks clearly indicate that corsairs and pirates represented equal hazards for peaceful trade. Merchants who failed to receive restitution, however, petitioned for—and occasionally received—*letters of marque,* granting them the right to exercise *reprisal,* or retaliatory seizures, at the expense of their attacker's compatriots.

Latin, Byzantine, and Arabic narrative sources refer plentifully to piracy, but (unsurprisingly) they generally identify only enemy corsairs as "pirates," while lauding their compatriots as naval defenders. The *Cronica* of the Catalan Ramon Muntaner (1265–1328) valuably preserves a corsair's perspective. Literary

# P

works such as Boccaccio's *Decameron* and the Catalan epic *Tirant lo Blanc* vividly document piracy's integration into the medieval Mediterranean economy, depicting Muslim and Christian merchants who combine trade with plunder at sea.

**BIBLIOGRAPHY**

Balletto, Laura. *Genova nel Duecento: Uomini nel porto e uomini sul mare.* Collana storica di fonti e studi 36. Genoa: Università di Genova, Istituto de medievistica, 1983.

Cheyette, Frederic L. "The Sovereign and the Pirates, 1332." *Speculum* 45 (1970): 40–68.

Mollat, Michel, ed. *Course et piraterie: Études presentées à la Commission internationale d'histoire maritime à l'occasion de son colloque international pendant le xiv congrès international des sciences historiques (San Francisco, août 1975).* Paris: Institut de recherche et d'histoire des textes. Centre national de la recherche scientifique, 1975.

Pardessus, Jean Marie, ed. *Collection des lois maritimes antérieurs au XVIIIe siècle.* 6 vols. Paris, 1828–1845; rpt. Turin: Bottega d'Erasmo, 1959.

Predelli, Riccardo, ed. *I Libri Commemoriali della Repubblica di Venezia: Regesti.* 8 vols. Monumenti storici pubblicati dalla reale deputazione veneta di storia patria. Serie prima: Documenti, Vol. 1, 3, 7, 8, 10, 11, 13, 17. Venice: Reale deputazione di storia patria per le Venezie: 1876–1914.

Pryor, John H. *Geography, Technology, and War: Studies in the Maritime History of the Mediterranean, 649–1571.* Cambridge: Cambridge UP, 1988.

Zachariadou, Elisabeth A. *Trade and Crusade: Venetian Crete and the Emirates of Mentesche and Aydin, 1300–1415.* Venice: Istituto ellenico di studi bizantini postbizantini di Venezia per tutti i paesi del mondo, 1983.

*Emily Sohmer Tai*

**SEE ALSO**

Benincasa, Grazioso; Byzantine Empire; Carrack; Daniel the Abbot; Genoa; *Guerrino il Meschino;* Jacopo da Verona; Keel; Law, Commercial; Law, Maritime; Law of Marque; Military Orders; Muslim Travelers and Trade; Navigation, Arab; Pilgrimage, Christian; Pisa; Ships and Shipbuilding; Sindbad the Sailor; Teutonic Order; Venice; Women Travelers, Islamic

## Pisa

Important Italian city-state, mercantile center, and colonial power. The republic of Pisa sent merchants and pirates throughout the Mediterranean and into North Africa, bringing the city great wealth in the twelfth and thirteenth centuries.

After profitable raids on Sardinia, Bône, and Mahdia in the eleventh century, and additional attacks on other Muslim strongholds in Corsica, Sardinia, the Balearics, Sicily, and Tunis in the twelfth century, Pisa established a network of colonies in these ports with particular strength in Tunis. Pisa cooperated with either Muslims or Normans, whoever would grant it the better advantage. Genoa frequently contested these Pisan commercial interests. In 1162, Germany's Frederick Barbarossa promised Pisa extraordinary privileges in Sicilian ports in return for Pisan maritime assistance. Although his promises were not kept, Pisa thereafter steadfastly supported the imperial Ghibelline cause and was thus frequently at war with Florence.

Pisan merchants also frequented eastern Mediterranean ports. The Muslim princes of Egypt granted them a *fondaco* in Alexandria and another in Cairo, the Byzantines awarded them a quarter in Constantinople, and the crusaders gave them privileges in Syrian and Cypriot seaports. The crusading archbishop of Pisa, Daimbert, became the Latin patriarch of Jerusalem in 1099.

In the mid-thirteenth century Pisa began to decline. Lucca and Florence in mainland Tuscany disputed Pisa's control over its surroundings, while the more populous maritime cities of Genoa and Venice successfully challenged Pisa in the Mediterranean. Pisans who survived the naval battle of Meloria (1284) lived out their lives in prisons of the victorious Genoese. Civil strife convulsed Pisa, one of its victims being Ugolino, count of Gherardesca, whose death in the Tower of Famine Dante memorialized in *Inferno* 33. Resurgent malaria and the Black Death weakened the city until Pisa lost its independence to Florence in 1406.

Pisa built its famous Duomo (1068–1118), Baptistry (1153–1278), and Leaning Tower (1174–1350) during its times of great prosperity. Pisans whose influence extended far beyond its borders include the sculptors Nicola Pisano (*c.* 1220–1270/1287) and his son Giovanni (*c.* 1250–*c.* 1314), whose carved pulpits in Pisa, Siena, and Pistoia initiated Gothic sculpture in Italy. Another native of the city, Leonardo Fibonacci (*c.* 1170–*c.* 1240) also known as Leonardo da Pisa, was a mathematician who advocated the adoption of Arabic numerals in Europe in his *Liber abaci* (1202; revised 1228), for hundreds of years a standard European work on algebra and arithmetic. Rusticello da Pisa, a writer of romances, claimed that the extensive information about Asian geography and mercantilism gathered in his book *Divisament dou monde* came from his companion in a Genoese prison in 1298, Marco Polo.

**BIBLIOGRAPHY**

Chistiani, Emilio. *Nobiltà e Popolo nel Comune di Pisa.* Naples: Istituto Italiana per gli Studi Storici, 1962.

Herlihy, David. *Pisa in the Early Renaissance.* New Haven: Yale UP, 1958.

Otten-Froux, Catherine. "Les Pisans en Egypte et à Acre dans la seconde moitié du XIIIe Siècle: Documents nouveaux. *Bollettino Storico Pisano* 52 (1983): 163–190.

———. "Les Pisans en Chypres au Moyen-Age." In *Praktika B'Diethanous Kypriologikou Synedriou.* Tomos B. Leukosia: Mesaionikon Tmama, 1986, pp. 127–143.

———. "Documents inédits sur les Pisans en Romanie aux XIIIe–XIVe siècles." In *Les Italiens à Byzance.* Ed. Michel Balard, Angeliki E. Laiou, and Catherine Otten-Froux. Paris: Sorbonne, 1987, pp. 153–195.

Rossi-Sabatini, Giuseppe. *L'Espansione di Pisa nel Mediterraneo fino alla Meloria.* Florence: Sansoni, 1935.

Schaube, Adolf. *Handelsgeschichte der Romanischen Völker des Mittelmeergebiets bis zum Ende der Kreuzzüge.* Munich and Berlin: Oldenbourg, 1906.

*Louise Buenger Robbert*

**SEE ALSO**

Black Death; Dante Alighieri; *Fondaco;* Genoa; Marco Polo; Piracy; Venice

## Pius II (Enea Silvio [Aeneas Sylvius] Piccolomini) 1405–1464

Pope and humanist who traveled widely, preached one of the last crusades, and wrote the unfinished *Cosmographia,* a geographical compendium covering western Asia and Europe that was heavily influenced by classical authors and by Piccolomini's own journeys.

Born near Siena to an impoverished noble family, Enea was educated in Siena and participated as a secretary in the Council of Basel from 1431 to 1435. He left the council, became Cardinal Albergati's secretary, and traveled to Arras to attend a religious congress. From there he visited the court of James I of Scotland as a diplomat, proceeding part of the way through winter snow on his bare feet in fulfillment of a vow. Enea returned to Basel in 1436, where he supported and became secretary to the antipope Felix V (1439–1449). His classicizing literary efforts brought him to the attention of Emperor Frederick III, whom he served as secretary until 1447.

At this point, Enea left the secular life, being ordained and made bishop of Trieste that same year, and bishop of Siena in 1450. With Nicholas of Cusa he effected a reconciliation between the papacy and the emperor, continuing in papal service as legate to Germany. Spurred by the seige and fall of Constantinople, he fervidly urged a crusade on the Byzantine Empire. His efforts failed, but he was made cardinal and papal counsellor in 1456, and was elected pope in 1458. At Mantua in 1459 he called for a crusade, but met with hostility or indifference from the French and imperial delegates. The following year he wrote a famous letter to Sultan Muhammad II, urging him to convert from Islam to Christianity. Unsuccessful, he returned to his crusade, the preparations for which occupied his last years; indeed, he died in Ancona futilely awaiting the armada's assembly.

Enea's interests in geography and history found their principal expression in two incomplete works known as "Europa" and "Asia," which together are often referred to as the *Cosmographia,* or more properly, *Historia rerum ubique gestarum locorumque descriptio.* Both relate history to geography, though "Europa" is more contemporary and relies heavily on Enea's own experience, while "Asia" is more historical and reliant on classical literary sources. "Europa" was begun before 1458 when Enea, laid up with gout, was asked by a bookseller to revise and finish the *Liber Augustalis,* a history of the empire by Benvenuto da Imola. The result remains fragmentary, sketchy, and uneven: in the 1571 Basel edition of seventy-nine pages, France and "Hispania" each receive only two pages, while Florence and Milan each receive three.

"Asia" originated in a conversation with the duke of Urbino on the road to Tivoli in 1461. In printed editions it precedes "Europa" and opens with speculations about the further reaches of the earth, including the poles and eastern Asia, and the navigability of unknown waters. Cannibals (*anthropophagi*) and Amazons appear, reflecting his use of classical sources. Since his remarks are generally limited to an area bounded by Muscovy and Egypt, the Aegean Sea and Indus River, regions in which he never traveled, he relied very heavily on ancient Greeks and Romans. In discussing

# P

Parthia, for example, he cites Ptolemy, Pliny, Strabo, Pompeius Trogus, and Apollodorus. While the "Europa" was important for later cosmographies by Sebastian Frank and Sebastian Münster, "Asia" influenced cartographers like Johan Ruysch and fed the imaginations of explorers for more than a century (Columbus owned and annotated a copy).

## BIBLIOGRAPHY

Ady, Cecilia M. *Pius II: The Humanist Pope.* London: Methuen, 1913.

Aeneas Sylvius. *Opera.* Basel, 1571; rpt. Frankfurt-am-Main: Minerva, 1967.

Berg, A.W. *Aeneas Sylvius Piccolomini in seiner Bedeutung als Geograph.* Halle, 1901.

Mitchell, R.J. *The Laurels and the Tiara: Pope Pius II, 1458–1464.* Garden City, NJ: Doubleday, 1962.

Pittalunga, Stefano. "Il 'vocabulario' usato da Cristoforo Colombo (Una postilla all'*Historia rerum* di Pio II e la lessicografia medievale." *Columbeis* 1 (1986): 107–115.

*Joseph P. Byrne*

## SEE ALSO

Amazons; Cannibals; Columbus, Christopher; Constantinople; Egypt; Geography in Medieval Europe; Indus; Nicholas of Cusa; Pliny the Elder; Ptolemy

## Plague

*See* Black Death

## Pliny the Elder (23–79 C.E.)

Author of an extremely influential compendium of natural history and geographical information in thirty-seven books, widely excerpted in the Middle Ages, and of other works now lost.

Gaius Plinius Secundus, called Pliny the Elder to distinguish him from a nephew of similar name, was a statesman and military officer in the early Roman Empire. His career allowed him to see firsthand distant parts of the empire; he died observing the erupting Vesuvius, asphyxiated by gases from the volcano. Not all of Pliny's information was firsthand, however, for he was a voluminous researcher into earlier compendia, saying in one of his letters that "no book is so bad that some good cannot be got from it" (3.5). He claims to have extracted 20,000 "facts" from 2,000 works by 100 authors; in fact he cites 473 different authors. He is not very critical of these sources.

The title of Pliny's famous work is often rendered "Natural History" (*Historia Naturalis*) though this title does not fully capture the Greek sense of "historia" as an "inquiry" or "investigation." The *Historia Naturalis* opens with a table of contents and bibliographical excursus and covers cosmology and physical geography, anthropology, zoology, botany, medicine, metallurgy, and mineralogy, with a digression on ancient works of art. The organization of the geographical books is based on the *periplous* or sailing itinerary starting at Gibraltar and moving around the Mediterranean to the Don, across the Riphaean Mountains in Scythia and then back along the northern and western coast to Gibraltar; it then goes in the opposite direction around the Mediterranean to the Don, crosses the mountains again, and returns by the eastern and southern coast of the Encircling Ocean to the starting place.

Pliny's geographical and cosmological information is a mix of the scientific and the fabulous, often yielding strange juxtapositions of incompatible worldviews. Thus he praises the astronomical expertise of Hipparchus, who established a 600-year calendar of eclipses, but can discuss with equal ease celestial portents that were said to be signs of cosmic displeasure at Caesar's assassination. For medieval writers, Pliny's account of exotic tribes and monstrous races—the Hyperboreans of the northern Ocean islands; the Hippopodes, a race of men with the feet of horses; or the Panotii, who clothe themselves only with their enormous ears—exerted great fascination and was repeatedly copied and excerpted to appear on maps and in works of travel.

By the late antique and patristic periods, Pliny was an authoritative source for writers as various as Aulus Gellius, Apuleius, and Tertullian, all of whom flourished in the second century. At least five fragmentary manuscripts from as early as the fifth century survive to attest to the popularity of the *Historia Naturalis;* French and German library catalogues through the twelfth century listed several copies of the work. Probably the most important descendant of Pliny's sprawling work is Solinus's *Collectanea rerum memorabilium* (*c.* 230/240), more than three-quarters of which is entirely Pliny's material; it has survived in more than 150 manuscripts. The early-fifth-century writers Macrobius, Martianus Capella, and St. Augustine, as well as Isidore of Seville in the seventh century, all knew both Pliny's encyclopedia and Solinus's version of it.

Bede cites Pliny several times and his original argument against a flat earth in *De natura rerum* (46) clearly depends on Pliny's; his account of the Northern Hemisphere's ten zones is also taken directly from Pliny. Dicuil (?–c. 825) used him, as did Thomas of Cantimpré (1201–1270/1272) and Vincent of Beauvais (c. 1190–1264). Robert of Cricklade's *Defloratio Historia Naturalis Plinii Secundi* shows that Pliny was read in the classrooms of Oxford in the late twelfth century; Pierre d'Ailly (1350–1420) cites him on occasion, though he explicitly declines to perpetuate the fantasies the work conjures up. A fourteenth-century manuscript of Pliny's work was lavishly illustrated by Pietro of Pavia.

While Pliny's popularity was no doubt increased by his reports of strange humanoids and fantastic animals, the Middle Ages did not read the work only for its monsters. Pliny endorses the concept of a spherical earth largely covered with water upon which the dish-like *orbis terrarum* is fixed. His earth may be circumnavigated. As water drops form spheres, so too the earth is drawn into a globe, though irregular in shape, like a pine cone. The Antipodeans, like the inhabitants of the known world, are drawn to the center, and are thus kept from falling off. Pliny respectfully affirms Eratosthenes's measurement of the earth's circumference, though he does not fully understand it. Though Pliny's passion for encyclopedic abundance often perpetuated rumors and myths, his Latin text offered a wealth of ancient geographical knowledge to a Western readership that would not have access to his Greek sources for centuries.

## BIBLIOGRAPHY

Chibnall, Marjorie. "Pliny's Natural History in the Middle Ages." In *Empire and Aftermath: Silver Latin II*. Ed. T.A. Dorey. London and Boston: Routledge and Kegan Paul, 1975, pp. 57–78.

Dihle, A. "Plinius und die geographische Wissenschaft in der römischen Kaiserzeit." In *Tecnologia, economica, e società nel mondo romano*. Atti del Convegno di Como (27–29 Sett. 1979). Como: Banca Popolare Commercio e Industria, 1980, pp. 101–137.

Hünemörder, Christian. "Das Lehrgedicht: 'De Monstris Indie' (12. Jh.). Ein Beitrag zur Wirkungsgeschichte des Solinus und Honorius Augustodunensis." *Rheinisches Museum für klassische Philologie* 119 (1976): 267–284.

*Pliny, Natural History, with an English Translation*. Ed. and trans. Horace Rackham et al. 10 vols. Cambridge, MA: Harvard UP, 1938–1963.

Sallmann, K. "Plinius der Ältere 1938–1970." *Lustrum* 18 (1971): 5–299; 345–352.

Serbat, Guy. "Pline l'Ancien: Etat présent des études sur sa vie, son oeuvre et son influence." *Aufstieg und Niedergang der römischen Welt* 32.4 (1986): 2069–2200.

Thomson, J. Oliver. *History of Ancient Geography*. Cambridge: Cambridge UP, 1948.

Winkler, Gerhard, and Roderich König, eds. and trans. *C. Plinius der Ältere, Naturkunde*. Munich: Heimeran and Artemis, 1973–1993.

*Roger T. Macfarlane*

**SEE ALSO**

Ailly, Pierre d'; Antipodes; Bede; Climate; Dicuil; Geography in Medieval Europe; Isidore of Seville; Itineraries and *Periploi;* Mediterranean Sea; Monstrosity, Geographical; Scythia; Solinus, Julius Gaius; Thomas of Cantimpré; Vincent of Beauvais; *Wonders of the East*

## Poland

Region north of the Carpathian mountain range and south of the Baltic Sea. Like other Slavic peoples living on the eastern border of the Frankish Empire—the Czechs, the Moravians, the Slovenes of the Nyitra region and of Pannonia, the Croats, and even some Serb clans—the Poles had submitted to Charlemagne and attempted to secede from the empire after his death. While the Czechs met with limited success in forming their own state because of being under the jurisdiction of the archbishop of Mainz, the Moravians and Croats were more successful. The Poles, in their separation from the empire, experienced periods of both political weakness and economic success.

Proselytized by German clerics, the peoples of this region accepted Christianity during the mid-tenth century. The Piasts, a people of Viking origin and the rulers of the Polish tribes, had as feudal vassals submitted to German rule. However, Boleslav the Brave (992–1025) freed the Polish Church from dependence on the German ecclesiastical hierarchy and obtained political independence as well, having himself crowned king of Poland in the year 1000. Soon, the Poles had established close working relations with the Hungarian court: Boleslav the Brave married one of the sisters of Stephen I of Hungary, and further dynastic relations were established between the Piast and Arpád families.

Medieval trade and commerce followed, in part, a north to south and, in part, a west to east trade pattern, the latter route going through east-central Europe—Bohemia, Hungary, Silesia, southern Poland, and southern Russia, in that geographical and chronological

# P

order—providing the conditions for a booming economic activity. Among the Czechs and the Moravians, the German merchants, who were encouraged and protected by nearby German rulers, played a key role in interregional commercial business development, in activities that included mining silver and gold in Silesia and conducting high level trade in what came to be regarded as the Carpathian mountain belt. In this process they aided the development of cities like Prague and Brno.

Piast rule became increasingly burdensome to the Poles. Following Viking and Slavic customs, Piast monarchs continually divided the country among their sons, and because of earlier German political and ecclesiastical dominance, many German settlers had entered the country and even Germanized certain regions of it. The Poles further suffered from Mongol invasions in the thirteenth century, especially at the battle of Legnice [Liegnitz] on April 9, 1241, following the burning of Cracow; their country was thoroughly devastated, as were the lands of the Kievan-Rus' and of the Hungarian kings.

Nonetheless, Silesia began its commercial rise in the fourteenth century both because of its mines and because it served as a road junction in northern-southern and western-eastern interregional trade, especially toward northeastern Poland and the western Russian lands. Hungary's law codes inform us that the country's interregional trade and commercial interest were mainly agricultural: it exported grain, cattle, and horses, both as meat animals and as specially bred horses for the military, as well as silver and copper from mines in Transylvania.

In Poland, Cracow had become the most important urban center of trade, commerce, industry, and banking by the early tenth century. German businessmen and Armenian, Jewish, and Greek merchants arrived in Cracow to import and export goods, carry out fiscal transactions, earn a profit, and settle, though later Cracow had to share some of those activities with the town of Lvov in trading with Moldavia and southern Russia. Indeed, southern Poland became the main international trade route toward the Russian south through the estuary of the Danube, the Polish route penetrating inner Russian lands through the Black Sea maritime connection by way of the rivers Dnieper and Don. Polish historical sources—chronicles and official documents written mostly in Latin—refer to important and steady economic business relations between Kiev and Cracow. Polish participation in Russian economic life

became even stronger when Casimir III the Great (r. 1333–1370) occupied Russian lands in 1347, creating an economic reality that changed little even during the Mongolian occupation of southern Russia between the mid-thirteenth and the late fourteenth centuries.

During the fourteenth and fifteenth centuries, Poland entered an era of progress; it flourished with the aid of Hungarian kings Charles Robert (r. 1308–1342) and Louis of Anjou [Lajos I] (r. 1342–1382). Casimir the Great was able to add the region of Halich to Polish territory, but he was the last member of the Piast dynasty, and the Poles elevated Louis of Hungary to the Polish throne. Thus, Poland and Hungary entered into a union with each other, and Poland joined Louis's east-central European kingdom. After Louis's death the union came to an end, but his daughter Jadwig [Hedwig], the inheritor of the Polish crown, married Prince Vladislas Jagiello of Lithuania, who converted to Christianity and united Poland and Lithuania into a huge empire; the Jagiellos ruled Poland for more than a century. In the 1400s, they broke the strength of the Teutonic Knights, who had occupied Prussian territories, taking from them the western Prussian region, thereby opening a corridor through Gdansk (Danzig) to the Baltic Sea. The east Prussian region, however, remained under Prussian control. It was the knights who had Germanized the Prussians of Baltic-Slavic origin and converted them to Christianity.

The Jagiello dynasty gave several rulers to Hungary and Bohemia; among them, Vladislav I of Hungary (r. 1440–1444) reestablished union between Poland and Hungary and actively tried to eject the Turks from southeastern Europe; in this he received almost no help from other European powers and he was killed in battle against elite Turkish forces at Varna, on the Black Sea.

**BIBLIOGRAPHY**

Bosl, K., et al., eds. *Eastern and Western Europe in the Middle Ages*. London: Thames and Hudson, 1970.

Gieysztor, Alexsander, ed. *A History of Poland*. 2nd edition. Warsaw: Panstwowe Wydawnictwo Naukowe, 1979.

Manteuffel, Tadeusz. *The Formation of the Polish State*. Trans. Andrew Gorski. Detroit: Wayne State UP, 1982.

*Z.J. Kostolnyik*

**SEE ALSO**

Hungary; Military Orders; Mongols; Ottoman Turks; Russia and Rus'; Teutonic Order

## Polonus, Martinus
*See* Martin of Troppau

## Popes

Ecclesiastical leaders holding the title bishop of Rome and head of the Western Christian church. Curiously, although medieval popes saw themselves at the head of a church with a mission to all mankind, and at the head of a society, Christendom, under constant threat from the Muslims, they only rarely played a direct role in dealings with the peoples outside Europe.

While the popes encouraged both crusading and missionary efforts, they rarely negotiated with Muslim or other non-Christian rulers, and they almost never sponsored and directed missionary work. Instead, papal efforts in these areas were often restricted to issuing statements that encouraged others to act.

The most famous example of the papal role in the Crusades was Urban II's call for a crusade at the Council of Clermont (1095). His passionate appeal to recover the Holy Land led to the First Crusade, which climaxed with the capture of Jerusalem in 1100. Subsequent popes also called for crusades along all of Christendom's frontier and authorized indulgences for those who went. As late as the fifteenth century, Pius II (1458–1464) was still seeking crusaders. This theme even influenced Christopher Columbus, who dreamed of employing the wealth of the New World to support one last great (and successful) crusade to regain the Holy Land.

Innocent IV (1243–1254), the initiator of the Mongol Mission at the First Council of Lyons (1245), sent representatives (most prominently John of Plano Carpini) to meet with non-Christian rulers of Asia, but these contacts had little practical effect.

Even with regard to peaceful missionary efforts, the papacy largely played a secondary role, licensing missionaries, especially Franciscan and Dominican friars, granting them letters authorizing their efforts, outlining the terms on which schismatic Christians could be reconciled to the Latin Church, and settling disputes that arose, for example, from the marriage practices of newly Christianized societies. The role of the papacy in expansion is perhaps best exemplified in the story of Marco Polo's father and uncle who presented Pope Gregory X (1271–1276) with Khubilai Khân's request for 100 learned men to accompany them on their return journey to his court. The pope could find only two friars willing to go, and they gave up before they got any farther than Asia Minor.

In 1307, the papacy did play a direct role in missionary work in Asia, when Pope Clement V (1305–1314) created an institutional structure that would provide a basis for organizing Christianity there. At the request of John of Monte Corvino (1247–c. 1328), a Franciscan who had traveled to Beijing (Khanbaliq), Clement V named Monte Corvino the archbishop of Tartary and patriarch of the Orient. At the same time, the pope also named several Franciscans as suffragan bishops. They were expected to travel to the East, to consecrate John of Monte Corvino, and to establish dioceses under his direction. Although several of those appointed died en route or never left Europe, three of them reached their destination, thus establishing an ecclesiastical hierarchy in Asia that survived until the early decades of the fifteenth century. Subsequently, this archbishopric was divided into two jurisdictions, a Franciscan one at Peking and a Dominican one at Sultaniyeh in Persia.

The role of the papacy in late medieval missionary activity and the problems that it faced foreshadowed the situation in the sixteenth century when Columbus's voyages revealed to Europe the existence of the Americas. Above all, the problems of financing missionary efforts, of organizing ecclesiastical administrative structures, and of translating Christian theology into other languages and cultural traditions—issues faced by medieval church leaders—reappeared on a vastly larger scale in the Americas and then in Asia at the beginning of the modern era.

**BIBLIOGRAPHY**

Baldwin, Marshall W. "Missions to the East in the Thirteenth and Fourteenth Centuries." In *The Impact of the Crusades on the Near East.* Ed. Norman P. Zacour and Harry W. Hazard. Vol. 5 of *A History of the Crusades,* pp. 452–518. Gen. ed. Kenneth M. Setton. See Gen. Bib.

Brundage, James A. *Medieval Canon Law and the Crusades.* Madison: U of Wisconsin P, 1969.

Muldoon, James. *Popes, Lawyers, and Infidels: The Church and the Non-Christian World, 1250–1550.* Philadelphia: U of Pennsylvania P, 1979.

de Rachewiltz, Igor. *Papal Envoys to the Great Khans.* Stanford: Stanford UP, 1971.

Ryan, James Daniel. "Nicholas IV and the Evolution of the Eastern Missionary Effort." *Archivum Historiae Pontificiae* 19 (1981): 79–95.

*James Muldoon*

# P

## Portolan Charts

Navigational or sailing directions in a portable, book-like format. Such works have come to be known as *portolani* (or portolans in English), probably because they were used in conjunction with written sailing directions in book format that were also known as portolans. Most extant manuscript books containing written directions come from the late fifteenth century; very few surviving portolans date from before 1450 (although some of these exist in several copies). The same holds true for early sailing charts: of the approxi-

mately 180 medieval charts and bound atlases that have survived, only a few dozen were compiled before 1400. Undoubtedly hundreds more portolans—in both written and cartographic form—existed, but were destroyed through exposure to the elements in their actual use at sea or were replaced when new navigational knowledge rendered older, inaccurate sailing instructions obsolete and dangerous to retain.

While we know that the ancient Greeks used written sailing directions, the origins of portolan charts remain obscure. Although we have no charts from classical times, navigators surely must have consulted some sort of master chart when venturing out along the Mediterranean coastline. These charts, however, probably did not have the lines radiating out from central wind roses we have come to expect on portolan charts. It is more likely that ancient charts included prominent features such as coastal mountain peaks and towers, which guided navigation, as well as hazards such as sandbars and rocky promontories.

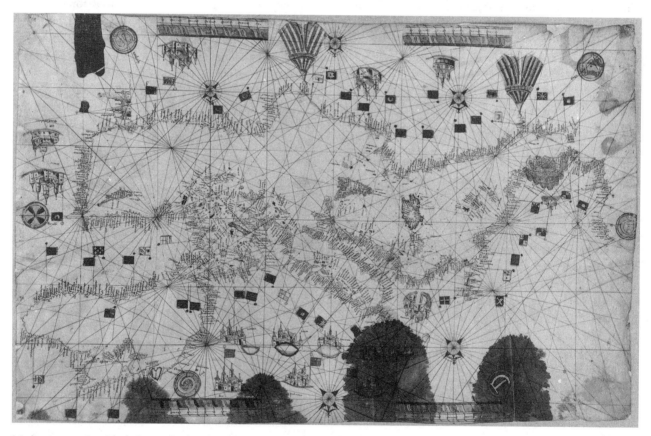

Mediterranean Sea, Black Sea, and Adriatic Sea, anonymous atlas from Catalonia. Hispanic Society of America, K 28, *c.* 1500. Reproduced by permission of the Hispanic Society of America.

Zuane Pizzigano, *Pizzigano Nautical Chart,* Venetian (57×90 cm). Minneapolis, MN, James Ford Bell Library MS 1424/mPi, 1424. By permission of the James Ford Bell Library, University of Minnesota.

Almost all portolan charts were drawn on vellum (calfskin) or parchment (sheepskin), which are quite durable, receive ink and paint fairly easily, and are flexible enough to be rolled for transport and storage. Navigational charts of the western Mediterranean were sketched for navigators as early as the twelfth century in Italy. The earliest surviving portolan chart is the "Carte pisane" (Paris, Bibliothèque Nationale Rés. Ge. B 1118) drawn between 1275 and 1291—a simple, functional navigational tool; this model was followed by other cartographers for most of the early charts now extant.

Portolan charts, based on practical knowledge rather than theoretical applications, corrected a traditional error in the east-to-west measurement of the Mediterranean by reducing its extent by almost one-third.

Although navigators must have known from experience that the classical sources were incorrect, portolan charts graphically documented this fact and perhaps encouraged some sea captains to veer out of the familiar maritime routes into more adventurous territory.

By the end of the thirteenth century, ships from the Mediterranean countries regularly traveled north around the Iberian Peninsula to reach Flemish markets. These commercial voyages brought Italian and Catalan navigators into close contact with the Portuguese when their vessels dropped anchor in Lisbon's commodious harbor. Catalan cartographers benefited from an expanded market for portolan charts during the fourteenth century. Captains were required by royal mandate to have such charts aboard; for example, King Pedro IV of Aragón (r. 1336–1387) commanded that every ship be provided with a minimum of two portolan charts. Such an order must have stimulated mapmaking within his own realm since Aragón at that time included the port cities of Catalonia, the territory of Valencia, the Balearic Islands, Sicily, and the kingdom of Naples. From this fourteenth-century impetus in production some thirty-three Catalan and Italian charts have survived.

Advances in medieval science encouraged the far-ranging voyages that eventually led to circumnavigation of the earth and an expanded view of the world, neither of which could have been accomplished without the portolan charts developed much earlier. King Alfonso X (r. 1252–1284) of Castile fostered an important circle of scholars during the thirteenth century, and the king himself formulated the *Alphonsine Tables.* Two significant astronomical questions discussed in this text were the angle between the plane of the equator and the earth's solar orbit (the ecliptic), and the precise length of time required for the sun to complete a revolution around the earth (medieval cosmology positing a geocentric universe). Both of these measurements were crucial to determining a ship's coordinates on the open sea by solar observation.

The solution to such problems relating to practical navigation led to a much better understanding of coastal areas in the Atlantic and other large bodies of water in which sailors lost sight of landmarks for increasingly longer periods of time. This knowledge was rapidly transmitted to the flat surface of the portolan charts. It is important to remember, however, that portolans were drawn without a cartographic projection that sought to compensate for curvature of the

# P

earth's surface. Since they were therefore accurate only in small-scale versions, a large sea or ocean coastline was often drawn in several small charts bound together in an atlas.

While scientific progress, including inventions such as the mariner's compass and the lateen (triangular) sail, contributed to the proliferation of portolan charts, some charts were apparently created purely for visual grandeur. Elaborately decorated with costumed monarchs, indigenous flora and fauna, and highlights in gold paint, these were usually created as presentation pieces for royal collections. Probably the most famous of these is the Catalan Atlas, which was in the library of King Charles V of France by 1375, and which also happens to have the first known example of an ornamental compass rose on a portolan chart. (This atlas is actually a hybrid, uniting features of both portolans and *mappaemundi*.)

Other iconographic aspects of portolan charts connect them with the great medieval *mappaemundi*. These include religious imagery such as the Crucifixion, the Virgin, Golgotha, and various saints and holy shrines, along with captions describing holy events. On portolans, however, this imagery is not very common and frequently has the character of a decoration—albeit a very pious one—at the edges of the chart (often where it is tapered, at the "neck" end of the animal skin on which it is drawn). More scientific imagery with medieval cartographic roots appears in topographic features and depictions of the winds. If *mappaemundi* focused inward on a structured, closed society, portolan charts, whose boundaries could be adapted to reports of new lands and new possibilities, eventually expanded Western Europe into a new world.

## BIBLIOGRAPHY

Bagrow, Leo, and R.A. Skelton. *History of Cartography.* Trans. D.L. Paisey. 2nd edition. Chicago: Precedent, 1985.

Campbell, Tony. "Census of Pre-Sixteenth-Century Portolan Charts." *Imago Mundi* 38 (1986): 67–94.

———. "Portolan Charts from the Late Thirteenth Century to 1500." In Harley-Woodward, Vol. 1, pp. 371–463. See Gen. Bib.

Cortesão, Armando. *History of Portuguese Cartography.* Vol. 2. Lisbon: Junta de Investigações do Ultramar-Lisboa, 1971.

Mollat du Jourdin, Michel, and Monique de La Roncière. *Sea Charts of the Early Explorers.* Trans. L. le R. Dethan. New York: Thames and Hudson, 1984.

Nordenskiöld, A.E. *Periplus, an Essay on the Early History of Charts and Sailing-Directions.* Trans. Francis A. Bather. Stockholm: P.A. Norstedt & Sons, 1897.

Sider, Sandra, with Mitchell Codding and Anita Andreasian. *Maps, Charts, Globes.* New York: The Hispanic Society of America, 1992. Esp. "A Brief History of Portolan Charts," pp. xii–xv.

*Sandra Sider*

**SEE ALSO**

Alfonso X; Benincasa, Grazioso; Brittany and Navigational Charts; Bruges; Compass, Magnetic; Cresques, Abraham; Ghent; *Mappamundi;* Maps; Mauro Map, [Fra]; Navigation; Portuguese Expansion; Roselli, Petrus; Vesconte, Pietro/Perrino

## Portugal

*See* Spain and Portugal

## Portuguese Expansion

A term referring to the overseas explorations, commercial activities, and warfare that Portugal embarked on in the fifteenth and sixteenth centuries and that resulted in the establishment of Portuguese control over many vital sea-lanes in the Atlantic, Indian, and Pacific oceans. Despite many challenges, the Portuguese hegemony endured until the first half of the seventeenth century, when it was shattered by the Dutch, English, and French.

The beginnings of the Portuguese overseas expansion are rooted in the Iberian tradition of reconquest and in the serious economic and social pressures that resulted from severe monetary problems and the plague-induced demographic decline. The nobility was particularly affected, as its revenues shrank and its opportunities became severely curtailed.

The most cherished objective of the Portuguese expansion was the conquest of Morocco. The capture of the city of Ceuta in 1415 marked the first major Portuguese success outside Europe. Despite a temporary setback at Tangier in 1437, the Portuguese managed to gain a firm foothold in Morocco in the second half of the fifteenth century, and at the beginning of the sixteenth century, they came close to controlling much of the Moroccan coast. However, in the 1530s and 1540s, most of these gains were lost, and in 1578, Morocco was the scene of a military disaster that led to the loss of Portugal's independence to Spain between 1580 and 1640.

The Atlantic explorations were long secondary to the war in Morocco. While some progress was achieved in the 1420s and 1430s, with the settling of the Madeira archipelago, the discovery of the Azores, and the circumnavigation of Cape Bojador (1434), it was only in the 1440s and 1450s that significant headway was made along the African coast. By 1446, the Portuguese reached Gambia, and by 1461, Sierra Leone. At that point, however, the pace of exploration had slowed down, only to pick up again in the 1470s when commercial forces, foreign interloping, and a personal interest of the crown prince Dom João combined to inspire new ventures. In 1471, the Gold Coast was reached, and between 1472 and 1474, the Gulf of Guinea was explored, and the islands of São Tomé, Príncipe, and Fernando Pó discovered. In 1474–1475, Lopo Gonçalves and Rui Sequeira crossed the equator and pushed as far as Cape Santa Catarina at 2 degrees south latitude. At the same time, the Portuguese were venturing into the North Atlantic and reached either Greenland or Newfoundland.

The overseas expansion intensified when Dom João ascended to the Portuguese throne in 1481. For the first time, there was a Portuguese monarch with deep personal interest in overseas matters other than Morocco. Dom João II possessed a clear and grandiose vision that involved not only Africa but also Asia. He moved quickly to reorganize the crown overseas enterprise and to secure key areas, especially the Gold Coast, against foreign intervention; he promoted settlements on the Atlantic Islands and embarked on a systematic series of explorations. In 1483, Diogo Cão reached Congo and continued as far as 15 degrees south latitude, in modern-day Angola. On his second voyage, 1485–1486, Cão advanced as far as Walvis Bay, 22 degrees 10 minutes south latitude. In 1487/1488, Bartolomeu Dias successfully rounded the southernmost tip of Africa, proving the existence of a sea passage to the Indian Ocean.

At that point, however, the explorations temporarily ceased. The renewed war in Morocco, the death of the crown prince (1491), and the king's illness may all have been contributing factors. It is also possible, however, that the intelligence on the Arabian Sea basin and the Malabar coast, gathered by the overland expedition of Pero de Covilhã and Afonso de Paiva between 1487 and 1489, might have persuaded Dom João that the sea route to India, while possible, was not practical. In any case, his willingness to go to war with Castile over

the results of Columbus's 1492–1493 voyage proves that he did not abandon interest in either the overseas expansion or establishing links to India. The 1494 Treaty of Tordesillas between Portugal and Castile eventually resolved the conflict, guaranteeing the Portuguese Africa, Asia, and, as it turned out, part of South America as their exclusive area of operation.

It was, however, left to Dom João's successor, Dom Manuel I (r. 1495–1521) to preside over the most successful period of the Portuguese expansion, 1497–1513. While it took the Portuguese some eighty years to circumnavigate Africa, they needed less than a decade to explore the Indian Ocean and to reach their ultimate destinations: the Spice Islands and China. The momentous voyage of Vasco da Gama (1497–1499) opened to the Portuguese most of the East African coast and brought them to the Malabar Coast of India, which not only produced much pepper but also served as an entrepôt area for goods from east and southeast Asia. In 1500, the Portuguese first landed in Brazil. In 1503, they had explored much of the Arabian coast; in 1505 they arrived in Sri Lanka and began to explore the Bay of Bengal; in 1509 they first landed in the Malay Peninsula and Sumatra; in 1511 they reached the Moluccas (the famed Spice Islands, the sole source of cloves); and in 1513, China. Although many exploratory voyages, both by sea and by land were subsequently undertaken, and Japan (Marco Polo's "Cipangu") was first visited only in the early 1540s, the first two decades of the sixteenth century determined the geographical scope of the Portuguese expansion.

The Portuguese, unlike the Spanish, did not establish a territorial empire, except in Brazil. They concentrated on controlling access to trade routes and trading areas through a judicious combination of naval presence, a network of fortifications, and a system of trading outposts (*feitorias*). This strategy was very effective in preventing other European powers from gaining access to Portuguese-controlled waters and, for a few decades, in significantly altering the commerce in the Indian Ocean. Already in the 1520s, however, cracks were beginning to show, and after 1550, the Portuguese grip weakened considerably.

Overseas expansion had a dramatic impact on Portugal. The crown was greatly enriched. It came to rely on overseas territories for much of its revenue, as much as 80 percent at the peak of its spice trade. It no longer needed to cooperate with its nonnoble subjects to obtain revenues, and it lost much of its previous interest

# P

in supporting the domestic economy. Thus the overseas ventures provided opportunities for fame and wealth for both the warrior nobility and social climbers while, in many ways, the expansion pushed back the clock of social evolution in Portugal. However, contemporaries viewed sixteenth-century Portugal with awe and envy. Its international standing skyrocketed with the news of military victories, geographical discoveries, and the influx of valuable commodities, which included gold, spices, slaves, valuable textiles, and various exotic goods. Overseas ventures came to be seen as a ticket to prosperity and a requirement for any aspiring European power.

**BIBLIOGRAPHY**

Diffie, Bailey W., and George D. Winius. *Foundations of the Portuguese Empire, 1415–1580.* Minneapolis: U of Minnesota P, 1977.

Godinho, Vitorino Magalhães. *Os descobrimentos e a economia mundial.* 4 vols. Lisbon: Presença, 1984–1987.

———. *Mito e mercadoria, utopia e prática de navegar, séculos XIII–XVIII.* Lisbon: Difel, 1990.

Subrahmanyam, Sanjay. *The Portuguese Empire in Asia, 1500–1700: A Political and Economic History.* London and New York: Longman, 1993.

Thomaz, Luis F. "Expansão portuguesa e expansão europeia—reflexões em tormo da génese dos descobrimentos." *Studia* 47 (1989): 371–415.

———. "Le Portugal et l'Afrique au XVe siècle." *Arquivos do Centro Cultural Português* 26 (1989): 151–256.

———. "Factions, Interests, and Messianism: The Politics of Portuguese Expansion in the East, 1500–1521." *Indian Economic and Social History Review* 28 (1991): 97–109.

*Ivana Elbl*

**SEE ALSO**

Azores; Bojador, Cape; Columbus, Christopher; Da Gama, Vasco; Dias, Bartolomeu; Gold Trade in Africa; India; Malabar; Pepper; Portuguese Trade; Slave Trade, African; Spain and Portugal; Spice Trade, Indian Ocean; Textiles, Decorative

## Portuguese Trade

The establishment of trade as an important feature of Portuguese economy proceeded simultaneously with the emergence of Portugal as an independent state in the twelfth century, especially where foreign trade was concerned. The internal commercial framework emerged gradually in the thirteenth and fourteenth centuries, as a money economy slowly penetrated the formerly autarkic estates of northern Portugal and as

the *Reconquista* added important urban centers, such as Evora, in the south. Most regional fairs and local markets received their charters in the late thirteenth and early fourteenth century. In the second half of the fourteenth century, domestic trade was further encouraged by rapid population growth in the cities.

Foreign trade was largely maritime and oriented toward northwestern Europe, although trade links with North Africa and the Mediterranean were also well established, and numerous overland routes linked Portugal to Castile. Foreign trade intensified greatly in the late fourteenth and especially fifteenth centuries when Portugal, as a result of depopulation of the rural areas and of declining revenues of the nobility, turned to cash crop production.

The main Portuguese exports fell into two basic groups: consumables and raw or semifinished materials. In the category of consumables, Portugal exported fruit, both fresh and preserved; wine; honey; olives; olive oil; fish; some brown sugar and molasses; and quality salt in large quantities. The raw materials included cork; wax; hides and leather; tallow and grease; peltry; and high-quality kermes dye. These goods found ready markets in the major trading cities of the Atlantic seaboard of France, in England, and in Flanders. Portuguese salt found its way to the Baltic Sea.

In return, Portugal looked to foreign markets for cloth, the most important of its imports; precious and base metals; arms and armaments; luxury and fancy goods; and increasingly from the middle of the fourteenth century, for grain. Cloth could be had from Flanders, England, and northern France, although Castile also supplied substantial quantities by overland routes. Metals arrived from England, Galicia, Morocco, and—via Flanders—from Germany. Arms were brought from Flanders and from Italy, in particular Milan. Imported grain, on which Portugal became dependent from the later fourteenth century onward, came from the Mediterranean, Andalusia, Brittany, Normandy, and the Baltic, again often via Flanders.

Foreign trade to northwestern Europe was largely in Portuguese hands. Portuguese merchants, supported by a flourishing shipping industry, operated in Flanders, England, and France since the late twelfth century and were well established in many port cities in the thirteenth and fourteenth centuries. In the late fourteenth and fifteenth centuries, the Portuguese merchant communities secured long-term safe conducts and letters of privilege improving their security in the host countries and codifying their trading advantages. The Grand Charters of Privileges granted to the Portuguese merchants and shippers by the duke of Burgundy in 1411 and 1434 were the most important of these because they secured their legal standing in the area pivotal to Portuguese commerce: Flanders.

Visiting or resident foreigners also played an important role. Foreign traders are documented in Portugal from the end of the twelfth century. Among them were the Italians, Castilians, Basques, French, and English. Italian merchants controlled the bulk of Portuguese imports from the Mediterranean. The Genoese were traditionally the most important and best established in Portugal, followed by the Venetians in the second half of the fourteenth century and, increasingly, the Florentines in the fifteenth. The English were regular visitors since the fourteenth century at the latest. The Flemish were a relatively late arrival: after some early contacts in the twelfth century, Flemings began visiting Portugal with some frequency again only in the second half of the fourteenth.

Starting with Dom Fernando I in the 1370s, the Portuguese kings made an effort to attract and protect foreign merchants in Portugal, even though they tried to keep them from entering the retail trade. The generous privileges were at first aimed mostly at the various powerful Italian nations. The Flemings, for example, had to wait until 1457 for a formal charter of privileges. Individual foreign merchants or merchant families were often granted large exclusive contracts: the Lomellini, a Genoese family with branches in many European countries, controlled the exports of cork from Portugal for most of the second half of the fifteenth century.

The steady support of the Portuguese crown was an important factor in the growth and flourishing of Portuguese foreign trade. From as early as the thirteenth century, there is evidence that the crown sought to protect the interests of Portuguese traders abroad, by both diplomatic and military means, and to encourage Portuguese foreign trade through policy. In 1293, for example, King Dom Dinis [Denis] (r. 1279–1325) sought to establish a *bolsa* (association) of all Portuguese traders abroad, which would provide them with a social base, commercial intelligence, and emergency assistance in the various locations where they traded. While the broader project seems to have failed, in Flanders the *bolsa* played an important role until the end of the fifteenth century. In 1377, a similar project, this time focusing on Portuguese shipping, was attempted by Dom Fernando.

The importance of foreign trade to the crown and to Portuguese nobility was greatly accentuated by the crisis of revenues brought about by depopulation of the countryside following successive waves of plague and by the severe devaluation of currency in the second half of the fourteenth and first half of the fifteenth century. Both the crown and the nobles became important exporters during this period, trading in their own name and represented abroad by ship patrons or factors in their service. In the 1440s and 1450s, for example, the king, the queen, Dom Fernando (the king's brother), the duchess of Burgundy (the king's aunt), the duke of Bragança and his sons, and the counts of Ourem and count of Arraiolos all traded actively between Portugal and Flanders, often with several ships.

One of the byproducts of the search for additional revenue was the overseas expansion, which in the second half of the fifteenth century significantly altered the character of the Portuguese foreign trade. Sugar from the Atlantic islands; gold, slaves, spices and aromatic substances, ivory, exotic animals, and pelts from Africa; and, at the beginning of the sixteenth century, spices and textiles from Asia transfixed the attention of the crown and shifted its interests and those of the powerful foreigners away from the traditional Portuguese commodities. This shift in interest seems to have negatively influenced the mainstream of Portuguese foreign trade and weakened the position of the Portuguese merchants, in favor of foreign interests, in the early modern period.

## BIBLIOGRAPHY

Elbl, Ivana. "Nation, Bolsa, and Factory: Three Institutions of Late Medieval Portuguese Trade with Flanders." *International History Review* 14 (1992): 1–22.

Fereira, Anna Maria Pereira. *A Importação e Comércio Têxtil em Portugal no século XV (1385–1481).* Lisbon: Imprensa Nacional—Casa da Moeda, 1983.

Heers, Jacques. "L'expansion maritime portugaise à la fin du Moyen-Age: La Méditerranée." *Revista de Faculdade de Letras de Lisboa* 22, 2nd series, 2 (1956): 5–33.

Marques, A.H. de Oliveira. *Hansa e Portugal na Idade Media.* Lisbon: Tip. A. Tomas dos Anjos, 1959.

———. "A circulação e a distribuição dos produtos." In *Portugal na Crise dos Séculos XIV e XV.* Lisbon: Presença, 1987, pp. 123–180.

Ribeira, Vítor. *Privilégios de Estrangeiros em Portugal (Ingleses, Franceses, Alemães, Flamengos e Italianos).* Coimbra: Academia das Ciências de Lisboa, 1917.

Trindade, María José Lagos. "Marchands Etrangers de la Méditerranée au Portugal pendant le Moyen Age." In

# P

*Estudos de história medieval e outros.* Lisbon: FLUL, 1981, pp. 209–230.
———. "O comércio externo portugues antes da Expansão." In *Estudos de história medieval e outros.* Lisbon: FLUL, 1981, pp. 165–176.
Verlinden, Charles. "Le problème de l'expansion commerciale du Portugal au Moyen-Age." *Biblos* 23 (1948): 453–467.

*Ivana Elbl*

**SEE ALSO**
Animals, Exotic; Bruges; Diplomacy; Dyes and Pigments; Fairs; Genoa; Ghent; Gold Trade in Africa; Ivory Trade; Mediterranean Sea; Merchants, Italian; Pisa; Slave Trade, African; Spice Trade, Indian Ocean; Textiles, Decorative; Venice

## Prester John

A legendary Christian priest-king who was believed to rule over vast dominions in the lands beyond Muslim-held territory. For more than 400 years, Prester John and his Eastern kingdom of wealth and power fueled the medieval European imagination, at some times satisfying political and religious needs and at others a taste for exotica. From the mid-twelfth to the late sixteenth century, the prospect of finding Prester John's marvelous kingdom in India, the Far East, or, later, Ethiopia, was a measure of the strength of popular fantasies positing the existence somewhere of such a blessed realm.

Otto of Freising records in his *Historia de duabus civitatibus* (History of the Two Cities) that in 1145 he witnessed a meeting between Bishop Hugh of Jabala (Lebanon) and the newly elected Pope Eugenius III (1145–1153) at which the bishop described Prester John's desire to liberate the Holy Land from Muslim control. According to Hugh, Prester John was a descendent of the Magi, a Nestorian king of great wealth, and the leader of an army held in check by the Tigris River. Hugh, pleading on behalf of the besieged Eastern church, mentioned Prester John only in order to dispel reports of the priest-king's great power, and thereby to compel the pope to launch a crusade independent of the aid of an Asian ally. Shortly after the meeting, Eugenius III issued a bull urging a new crusade.

The details of Hugh's account had no influence on the famous *Letter of Prester John,* which began to circulate throughout Europe around 1160. Both documents, nevertheless, were condensations of a rich oral and literary tradition concerning the East composed chiefly of stories associated with Alexander the Great, St. Thomas of India, Moses and the Ten Lost Tribes of the Jews, and the vast literature on the marvels of the East. The fabulous *Letter,* as Albéric of Trois Fontaines notes in his chronicle for the year 1165, was addressed to Byzantine emperor Manuel I Comnenos (r. 1143–1180), German emperor Frederick I Barbarossa (r. 1152–1190), and other European kings. In the *Letter,* Prester John ("Presbyter Johannes") is depicted as a magnanimous and devout Christian who rules over seventy-two provinces, including the Amazons, the Bragmani (a race of Indian sages), and the Hebrew tribes. His empire, extending from "Lower India" through "Middle India" to "Upper India" is rich with marvels: gemstones carried to his kingdom by one of the Four Rivers of Paradise; a fountain of youth; magical rings and herbs; a thirteen-story tower with a magical mirror atop it; palaces of ebony, gold, and precious stones; and natural wonders, such as a vast pepper forest, an uncrossable sea of sand, a river of stones, salamanders that produce silk, fish that exude purple dye, and representatives of the many monstrous races. Prester John's wonders are so many and his dominion so vast that the *Letter* concludes with the challenge: "If you can count the stars in heaven and the sand of the sea, then you can calculate the extent of our kingdom and our power."

In the medieval imagination, India was not only a place of marvels but a place of morals. Prester John's kingdom is characterized by absolute social solidarity, moral excellence, and unified commitment to defeating the enemies of Christendom. In his letter he vows to bring aid to the failing crusaders from behind the Muslim front, and offers himself as an example of the harmony of Christian and secular leadership at a time when, in Europe, the discord of church and empire was pronounced. As late as the Fifth Crusade (1221), a papal letter identifies Prester John with King David of India, said to be underway to Egypt with an immense army. King David turned out to be no Christian savior, but the Mongol enemy, Chinggis Khân. But belief in Prester John's power of deliverance continued. In the thirteenth-century *Jüngerey Titurel* of Albrecht von Scharfenburg, the Grail is moved from the immoral West to Prester John's realm for safekeeping.

The immensely popular *Letter of Prester John* survives in more than 250 Latin and vernacular manuscripts, including twenty-five Old French, fifteen Italian, five Middle High German, four Hebrew, three Welsh, two Irish, one Scottish, and forty-six Slavonic copies. With translation came accretion: the *Letter* received the last of five major interpolations at the end of the thirteenth century, and by the time the *Letter* became one of the first books to be printed, Prester John and his kingdom had become little more than elements in a grab bag of Eastern exotica. The appeal of Prester John throughout the Middle Ages seems to have been closely tied to his double role as fantasy figure: marvelous object and Christian ideal. The author of the *Letter,* a Latin churchman who lived in or had intimate knowledge of the East, counted on the document's appeal to his readers' desire for both entertainment and instruction.

Despite Prester John's status as a fictional figure, medieval travelers and modern historians searched far and wide for the elusive priest-king. Medieval and early modern travelers such as John of Plano Carpini (1246), William of Rubruck (1253), Marco Polo (*c.* 1299), John of Monte Corvino (1305–1306), Odoric of Pordenone (1330), "Sir John Mandeville" (*c.* 1360), Johannes Witte de Hese (1389), Dom Pedro of Portugal (1425), Niccolò dei Conti (1435–1439), Pero de Covilhñā (1487), and Edward Webbe (1590) intended to find Prester John, and several claimed to have encountered him.

In medieval cartography, Prester John appears first in Asia on a map of Paulinus of Venice (Paris, Bibliothèque Nationale MS lat. 4939, fol. 9; *c.* 1320), then, increasingly in the fifteenth century, in Africa. The first writer to place the priest-king's kingdom in "Ethiopia" is Jordanus Catalani or Sévérac (*c.* 1321). The mobility of Prester John's kingdom is due in large part to increased knowledge of India and to confusion over the location of the three Indias, one of which was associated with Ethiopia, itself not a definitively located place in the medieval imagination. Similar confusions, this time semantic and philological, account for competing views in modern historiography of Prester John's origin and function. Those supporting the "Asiatic thesis" find a historical prototype in the Karakitan ruler Yeh-lü Ta-shih, and in the name "Johannes" they find Gurkhan, the ruler's title. Though the "African thesis" was discredited as early as 1839, another group of historians derives "John" from the Ethiopian royal title *zan*. Others have tried to find a historical antecedent in figures like the Dalai Lama, John the Evangelist, and the Georgian general John Orbelian.

Yet the legacy Prester John and his kingdom left is above all fictional. He makes appearances or is alluded to in works by Dante, Boccaccio, Chaucer, Philippe de Mézières, Ariosto, Rabelais, Shakespeare, Cervantes, Montaigne, Voltaire, Nerval, Lamb, Wilde, Buchan, T. S. Eliot, and Charles Williams.

**BIBLIOGRAPHY**

Gosman, Martin, ed. *La lettre du Prêtre Jean: Les versions en ancien français et en ancien occitan: Textes et commentaires.* Groningen: Bouma, 1982.

Knefelkamp, Ulrich. *Die Suche nach dem Reich des Priesterkönigs Johannes.* Gelsenkirchen: Müller, 1986.

Slessarev, Vsevolod. *Prester John: The Letter and the Legend.* Minneapolis: U of Minnesota P, 1959.

Ullendorff, Edward, and C.F. Beckingham. *The Hebrew Letters of Prester John.* Oxford: Oxford UP, 1982.

Zaganelli, Gioia. *La Lettera del Prete Gianni.* Parma: Pratiche, 1990.

Zarncke, Friedrich, ed. "Über eine neue, bisher nicht bekannt gewesene lateinische Redaction des Briefes des Priester Johannes." *Berichte über die Verhandlungen der königlich sächsischen Gesellschaft der Wissenschaften zu Leipzig. Philologische-historische Classe* 29 (1877), pp. 111–156.

———. "Der Priester Johannes." *Abhandlungen der philologisch-historischen Classe der königlich sächsischen Gesellschaft der Wissenschaften* 7 (1879), pp. 831–1028; and 8 (1883), pp. 1–184.

*Michael D. Uebel*

**SEE ALSO**

Amazons; Byzantine Empire; Chaucer; Crusade, Fifth; Dante Alighieri; Dyes and Pigments; Eastern Christianity; Ethiopians; Four Rivers of Paradise; India; John of Monte Corvino; John of Plano Carpini; Jordan of Sévérac; Karakitai; *Mandeville's Travels;* Marco Polo; Mongols; Monstrosity, Geographical; Nestorianism; Odoric of Pordenone; Otto of Freising; Paulinus Minorita of Venice; Pepper; Philippe de Mézières; Ten Lost Tribes, The; William of Rubruck; Witte de Hese, Johannes

## Psalter Map [London Psalter Map]

An anonymously created Christian world map (*mappamundi*) bound into and illustrating a psalter, or book of the Psalms, designed and painted in England *c.* 1250; it measures five and five-eighths inches (14.3 cm) by three and three-quarters inches (9.5 cm), and forms part of British Library MS Additional 28681, fol. 9r.

The Psalter map is one of a group of twelfth- to fourteenth-century world maps that are similar in design. These include maps by Henry of Mainz, Pietro Vesconte, Ranulf Higden, and the Ebstorf, Hereford, and Aslake *mappaemundi.* All but Vesconte's have

# P

English associations. Like the Ebstorf and Hereford maps, the Psalter map is of the T-O type (see Maps), which owes its origins to ancient Greek cartography. Its picture of the inhabited section of the globe (*oikoumene*) is set within a circular frame, the "O." Inscribed within this frame is a "T," composed of the Mediterranean (the vertical bar), which is topped and crossed by the rivers Don and Nile (the horizontal bar). This dominant hydrographical feature separates the three known continents from one another: Asia fills the upper semicircle, Europe the lower left quadrant, and Africa the lower right quadrant. Like many medieval T-O maps, the Psalter map is oriented to the east. The great Ocean River marks the map's circumference; and, following a cartographic tradition dating back to the first century B.C.E., the monstrous races are shown, in demarcated territories, at the south and southwest (right) edge of the map. Twelve heads representing the winds face the circumference near the circumambient Ocean. At the bottom of the earth (beneath an image

of the Pillars of Hercules and the head of the west wind) lie two dragons who either support—or are weighed down by—the earth.

Even if it were not bound into a collection of the Psalms, the overtly didactic Christian program of the Psalter map would be clear. Christ overarches its world and holds in his left hand an orb inscribed with a golden "T," literalizing and visualizing the connection between his creation of the world and that of the artist/cartographer. Censed by a pair of angels, he holds his right hand in the classic posture of benediction and gazes straight at the viewer. Like other medieval world maps, the Psalter is centered on Jerusalem, City of God on earth (Ezekiel 5:5). Directly east of the Holy City and touching the farthest reaches of the world is the Earthly Paradise. Its circular walls enclose portraits of Adam and Eve, and from its base issue five major rivers (rather than the conventional four of Genesis 2:10–14): the Ganges, the Euphrates, the Tigris, the Gihon, and the Phison. In the northeast is a semicircular ring, probably representing the wall Alexander the Great built to encircle the tribes of Gog and Magog, although no legend or depiction makes this identification explicit. Below this sits Noah's ark, perched atop Mount Ararat. The brightly colored Red Sea is easily identifiable. A second T-O map, consisting only of place-names, is found on fol. 9v.

**BIBLIOGRAPHY**

Campbell, Tony. *Early Maps.* New York: Abbeville Press, 1981.

Crone, Gerald Roe. *Maps and Their Makers: An Introduction to the History of Cartography.* London: Hutchinson, 1966.

Harley-Woodward. *A History of Cartography.* Vol. 1. See Gen. Bib.

Harvey, P.D.A. *Medieval Maps.* London: The British Library, 1991.

*The Image of the World: An Interactive Exploration of Ten Historic World Maps.* CD-ROM. Produced by Karen Brookfield. London: The British Library, 1995.

Stefoff, Rebecca. *The British Library Companion to Maps and Mapmaking.* London: The British Library, 1995.

Whitfield, Peter. *The Image of the World: 20 Centuries of World Maps.* London: The British Library; San Francisco: Pomegranate Artbooks, 1994.

*Daniel P. Terkla*

World map from a Psalter. London, British Library MS 28681, fol. 9, 13th century. Courtesy of the British Library.

**SEE ALSO**

Ailly, Pierre d'; Ararat, Mount; Ebstorf World Map; Four Rivers of Paradise; Ganges; Gog and Magog; Henry of Mainz Map; Hereford Map; Higden, Ranulf; Isidore of

## Ptolemy

An astronomer, astrologer, and geographer in Alexandria (*c.* 100–180 C.E.), and author of an astronomical text of major influence during the Middle Ages and a "geography" that revolutionized medieval cartography in the 1400s.

During the Middle Ages, the knowledge accumulated by the Greeks over eight centuries of research and work was not entirely forgotten. Many Greek scientific texts were preserved, most of them in Constantinople; from Greek they had been translated into Syrian, Arabic, or Hebrew, then converted into Latin from Arabic or Hebrew. Ptolemy remained famous for the entire Middle Ages throughout the Mediterranean basin, although his work was not completely known in medieval Europe until the fifteenth century.

Active during the reign of the Roman emperor Antoninus, Ptolemy composed comprehensive treatises that organized and clarified the work of Greek scientists from the time of Thales of Miletus (*c.* 624–547 B.C.E.).

Ptolemy's first work, entitled *Mathematica Syntaxis* (more commonly called *Almagest,* a title derived from an Arab word meaning "the greatest"), and consisting of thirteen books, treated the cosmos—earth and sky, fixed stars, and planets—according to the geocentric hypothesis. The treatise's method of explaining *phainomena* (or "what appears to us"), often referred to as "Ptolemy's system," had in fact been used by most Greek scientists attempting to attain practical results, notably in geography. According to the geocentric hypothesis, the earth is a motionless globe, located in the center of the celestial sphere that rotates around its axis: it is a mere point compared to the enormous size of the sky. The extremities of the axis of rotation are the celestial poles on the celestial sphere, the terrestrial poles on the earth; beneath each of the main celestial circles—equator, tropics, polar circles—falls the corresponding terrestrial circle that bears the same name. The horizon and the meridian are the only great celestial circles that stay motionless, related as they are to the observer's place on the earth. From the inclination of the axis on the horizon of a place, it was easy to deduce the height of the pole, the sections of the

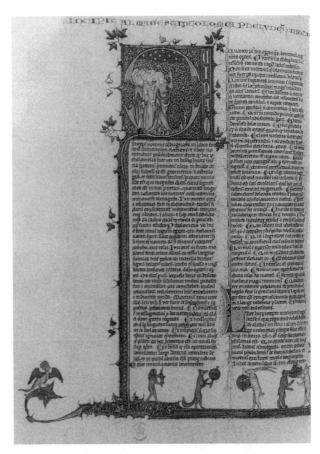

Astronomers, *Almagest.* London, British Library MS Burney 275, fol. 390v, *c.* 1300. Courtesy of the British Library.

tropic by the horizon (hence the length of the longest day), and the ratio of the gnomon to its shadow for this place. In his *Mathematica Syntaxis,* Ptolemy shows how to calculate the main features of each latitude; he does not rely greatly on observation. Ptolemy grants, as his predecessors had done, that the earth's habitable landmass—the *oikoumene*—lies entirely north of the equator.

Ptolemy later wrote another *Syntaxis,* divided into four books (thus commonly called *Tetrabiblos*), dealing with the influences on the earth and on human beings of celestial bodies, including stars, the zodiac, and planets. He classified the nature and power of each celestial body according to its position in the sky, and drew an astrological map of the known world, which he, like his predecessors, believed to occupy less than one-half of the Northern Hemisphere.

One of Ptolemy's last books was the *Geographical Survey,* which he wrote specifically to provide mapmakers

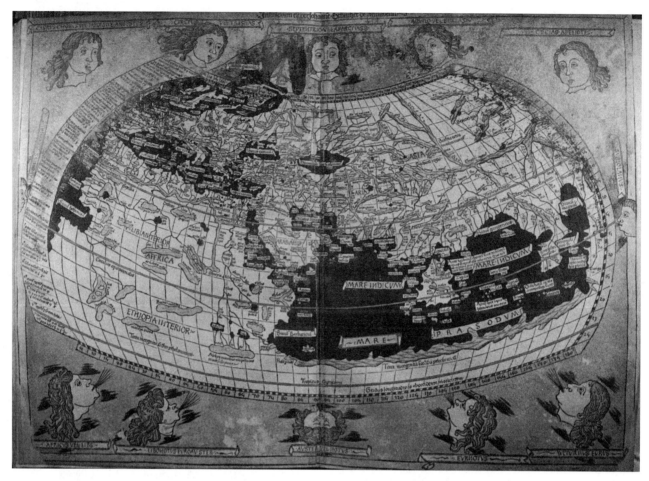

Woodcut world map showing Ptolemaic projection, oriented to the north, with twelve winds. *Cosmographia.* (Ulm: Lienhart Holle, 16 July 1482) np. n. sig. Reproduced by permission of the Map Division, The New York Public Library (Astor, Lenox and Tilden Foundations).

with data and instructions to use in their craft. Borrowing from (and criticizing) the research of his near contemporary, Marinus of Tyre (fl. C.E. 120), he extended the earth's landmass south of the equator to 16 degrees 25 feet south latitude and calculated its extent in longitude at 180 degrees, from the Canary Islands in the west to the "silk-land" in the east, although in the east, land continues beyond 180 degrees "longitude." Unfortunately, Ptolemy rejected the accurate measurement of the earth's circumference derived by Eratosthenes (c. 275–194 B.C.E.), accepting instead the erroneous—if convenient—figure advanced by Posidonios (c. 135–50/51 B.C.E.), who fixed the earth's circumference at 180,000 stadia, making the value of each degree of meridian equal to 500 stadia. (Eratosthenes had calculated the earth's circumference at 259,000 stadia; Hipparchus, using this value, divided the meridian in 360 degrees of 700 stadia each.)

On an earth with a circumference and eastward extent of landmass such as that advanced by Ptolemy, it would seem possible to sail west from Cádiz to reach the east coast of Asia within a few weeks—the amount of time a vessel's stored provisions could sustain its crew. Ptolemy's conclusions were accepted by Christopher Columbus, and prompted his transatlantic voyage in search of Cathay.

Ptolemy's work, especially the *Almagest,* was influential in varying degrees in various places during the Middle Ages, but it must be remembered that in the West, the *Almagest* was inaccessible to readers who knew no Greek between the second and the twelfth centuries, and the *Geography* was unavailable between the second and the fifteenth centuries. In Alexandria, it was abundantly commented on by the mathematicians Pappus (fl. 300) and Theon of Alexandria (fl. 360). In

Constantinople, capital of the Roman Empire after 324 and an important intellectual center beginning in the time of Constantius II (r. 337–361), Greek texts were collected for the imperial library. In Edessa (Syria), a school was founded in 323; one century later the Nestorians, expelled from the Byzantine Empire, gathered there, bringing with them many Greek manuscripts. The scientific and technical treatises, in particular, were soon translated into Syriac, and, as a result, the original Greek copies disappeared. After the Arabs conquered Syria (635), their considerable interest in Greek science caused them to translate these scientific texts from Syriac into Arabic.

Baghdad, founded in 762 during the caliphate of al-Mansūr (754–775), was provided by Caliph al-Ma'mūn (r. 813–833) with a "House of Wisdom" (832) that enabled learned scientists to work together. This house possessed a translation office, a rich library, and an observatory. Al-Ma'mūn acquired as many Greek scientific texts as he could from Byzantine Emperor Michael II (r. 820–829) and had them translated into Arabic: a copy of the Arabic translation of the *Almagest* made in 827 is today in the Bibliotheek der Rijksuniversiteit, Leiden. In order to simplify the study of the *Almagest,* al-Farghānī (fl. 833–861), in Baghdad, wrote a summary of it, the *Rudimenta Astronomiae.* Another translation was completed by Abu Yusuf Ya'qūb ibn Ishāq al-Kindī (fl. *c.* 850) and revised by Thābit ibn Qurra (836–901); it is preserved in at least five manuscripts (in Tunis, Paris, and the Escorial); the oldest copy, at Tunis, is dated October 1085.

Al-Ma'mūn's caliphate coincided with what is often called the first Byzantine renaissance, a period when Greek texts, which had hitherto been written in uncial (block capital) letters, began to be copied using a small-letter or minuscule alphabet. Humanist scholars sponsored the copying of many scientific treatises: they included Leon the Philosopher (also called Leon the Astronomer), bishop of Thessaloniki (840–843) and head of the university there; Photius, patriarch of Constantinople (858–886); and Arethas of Patras (born *c.* 850), archbishop of Cesarea. Ptolemy's *Syntaxis Mathematica* survives in two ninth-century manuscripts (Paris, Bibliothèque Nationale MS gr. 2389 and Rome, Biblioteca Apostolica Vaticanus MS Gr. 1594), one of which, the Vatican copy, belonged to Leon the Philosopher. MS gr. 313 at the Biblioteca Nazionale Marciana (Venice), probably copied in the tenth century, was sent by the Byzantine emperor Manuel I Comnenus (r. 1143–1180) to King William I of Naples and Sicily (r. 1154–1166), who had it translated into Latin around 1160, in Palermo.

Arabs who settled in Spain brought with them many scientific books, especially translations of Greek texts into Arabic, disseminating their taste for astronomy and mathematics. In Seville, the astrologer Geber ben Afflali (probably Johannes Gebir Hispalensis) wrote a *Commentary on the Almagest.* The *Toledo Tables,* a list of geographical coordinates based on the prime meridian in the Canaries, was composed *c.* 1080, principally by al-Zarkali (*c.* 1029–*c.* 1087) some five years before the Christians recovered the town and acquired the Arabs' scientific treasures. In order to make this important information accessible to the West, a translation office was created in Toledo, with the aim of producing Latin versions of Arabic texts previously translated from Greek. Thus the Italian Gerard of Cremona (1114–1187) came to Toledo, learned Arabic, and completed a Latin translation of the *Almagest* in 1175 (it was printed in Venice in 1515). Gerard's work, together with many other Latin translations of Greek works known in Arabic copies, greatly contributed to the diffusion of Greek science in the Western world.

European scholars built on this knowledge to produce scientific works of their own: the Englishman John of Holywood, also known as Sacrobosco (*c.* 1200–1254), professor of mathematics at the University of Paris, wrote *De sphaera* (The Sphere), a very popular handbook inspired by Greek elementary astronomy and geography. This handbook was often copied during the Middle Ages and spread throughout Europe; it was printed many times. The *Almagest* was also translated into Latin directly from Greek in 1451, at the request of Pope Nicholas V (1447–1455), by his secretary George of Trebizond (1396–1484), but this translation was judged a poor one by contemporaries.

Ptolemy's *Geography,* a more technical book consisting of specific instructions for the drawing of maps and thousands of coordinates for place-names, was not so well known as the *Almagest* during the Middle Ages. It was translated into Arabic, probably three times in the ninth century C.E. (these versions are all lost), and the historian and geographical writer al-Mas'ūdī (d. 956 C.E.), in his *Meadows of Gold* (1.8), describes the brilliantly colored maps illustrating the text. Arabic geographers used Ptolemy's data but corrected information when they thought it necessary; they developed their own ideas and drew maps of their own. In Europe, the

# P

scholar Maximus Planudes (*c.* 1260–1310), actively collected manuscripts of scientific texts for his library at the monastery at Chora in Constantinople and was eager to get a copy of Ptolemy's *Geography;* the one he found consisted of text only, but Planudes had a set of maps drawn according to Ptolemy's instructions. Emperor Andronicos II Palaeologus (r. 1282–1328) admired the text and its accompanying maps so much that he had a copy made for himself by Athanasius, the former patriarch of Alexandria (in Constantinople from 1293–1308). From then on, many copies were done, mostly in the East.

In the early 1400s, when the Turks were threatening Constantinople, Byzantine Greeks and Italians from Venice, Florence, and Rome united to prevent the destruction of Greek texts. Many manuscripts were brought from Constantinople to Italy, either by Greeks who chose to live in the West or by Italians interested in reviving Greek learning, which had been more or less lost to medieval Europe. Manuel Chrysoloras, a Greek scholar and ambassador sent in 1397 by the Byzantine emperor to request the assistance of the Venetian republic against the Turks, chose to settle in Italy; he was the first to teach Greek at the University of Florence. In the early years of the fourteenth century, he began a Latin translation of a Greek text of the *Geography* that he had brought with him. He soon began to rely on one of his best pupils, the Florentine Jacopo Angelo [Jacobus Angelus], to complete the task, and Angelo's translation, entitled *Cosmographia,* was finished in 1406; maps with Latin legends were drawn by 1415. Throughout the fifteenth century, scribes and cartographers working mostly in Florence competed with each other to produce beautiful copies of the *Geography,* with exquisitely drawn and colored maps, which served as noble gifts for kings and wealthy Europeans.

The text first appeared in printed form (without maps) at Vincenza by Hermannus Liechtenstein on September 13, 1475. On June 23, 1477, the first edition with maps (twenty-six copper plates) was published in Bologna by Dominicus de Lapis (it is erroneously dated 1462 in the colophon), followed on October 10, 1478, by Arnold Buckinck's version in Rome (a copy of which Christopher Columbus used when he planned his voyage west). A Florentine Platonist, Francesco Berlinghieri, composed a free translation of the *Geography* in *terza rima;* entitled *Le Sette Giornate,* it was printed at Florence by Nicolaus Laurentii before September 1482. This printing is particu-

larly significant in being the first to include additional maps ("tabulae modernae") using newly acquired geographical knowledge. This 1482 edition included "new" maps of Spain, France, Italy, and the Holy Land (the latter oriented to the East).

Subsequent printings increased the number of these modern maps. In 1482, for example, Lienhart Holle of Ulm included a map of Scandinavia (missing from Ptolemy's world) in an edition accompanied for the first time by woodcut maps (including the first printed map to be signed by "Johannes Schnitzer de Armssheim"). Johann Reger's edition, also published at Ulm, appeared on July 21, 1486, and made use of the woodcut maps Holle had printed; he included an alphabetical register of place-names at the end of the volume and added a treatise entitled "De locis de mirabilibus mundi." Petrus de Turre's printing at Rome on November 4, 1490 (with twenty-seven copperplate maps reused from the 1478 edition), is the last of the fifteenth century.

As the number and variety of these manuscripts and editions would indicate, the works of Ptolemy profoundly influenced the development of geographical and cosmological knowledge—practical and theoretical—throughout the entire Middle Ages. Through his *Almagest,* which covered the entire cosmos, and his *Geography,* which treated the earth and its landmass, Ptolemy contributed to the dissemination of the geocentric hypothesis, the assumption of a spherical earth, and a method of investigation that had allowed the Greeks to attain a theoretical knowledge of the whole earth, although they had experienced only a small part of it.

**BIBLIOGRAPHY**

Aujac, Germaine. *Claude Ptolémée, astronome, astrologue, géographe: Connaissance et représentation du monde habité.* Paris: C.T.H.S., 1993.

Harley-Woodward. *A History of Cartography.* Vol. 1, pp. 177–199. See Gen. Bib.

O'Leary, De Lacy. *How Greek Science Passed to the Arabs.* 1949. Rpt. London: Routledge and Kegan Paul, 1980.

Pedersen, O. *A Survey of the Almagest.* Odense, Denmark: Odense UP, 1974.

Ptolomaeus, Claudius. *Geographia.* Ed. K. Müller. 2 vols. Paris: A. Firmin-Didot, 1883–1901.

———. *Geography.* Trans. E.L. Stevenson. New York: The New York Public Library, 1932.

———. *Almagest.* Trans. G.J. Toomer. London: Duckworth, 1984.

*Syntaxis Mathematica.* Ed. J.L. Heiberg. 2 vols. Leipzig: Teubner, 1898–1903.

*Tetrabiblos.* Ed. and trans. F.E. Robbins. Cambridge, MA: Harvard UP, 1940; rpt. 1980.

*Germaine Aujac*

SEE ALSO

Baghdad; Canary Islands; Cartography, Arabic; Columbus, Christopher; Edessa; *Mappamundi;* Maps; Measurement of Distances; Nestorianism; Sacrobosco, John of

## Purgatory

An intermediate place or condition between Heaven and Hell where souls are purified of their venial (i.e., pardonable) sins, or remain to complete the temporal punishment for their mortal sins, after departing from their present earthly life before Judgment Day. It was used as the locus for action in a variety of travel narratives of a literary kind.

In the Middle Ages, three biblical texts were regarded as proof of the existence of Purgatory: 2 Maccabees 12:41–46 was cited for the belief in the forgiveness of sins after death and the efficacy of prayers for the faithful departed; Matthew 12:31–32 was thought to assume the remission of sins in the Otherworld; and 1 Corinthians 3:11–15 (the most frequently quoted text) provided the image of "a refining fire."

The concept of purgation these texts presented was developed by the Church Fathers. In the medieval West, Caesarius of Arles (*c.* 470–542) built on Augustine's certainty of purifying pains in his *De Civitate Dei* 21.13 and 24. The least of these pains were considered to be more terrible than anything experienced in this life. Caesarius distinguished between minor sins, which might be expurgated by good works on earth or purged by fire in the Otherworld, and capital sins, for which souls would suffer eternally in the fires of Hell.

Gregory the Great (590–604) contributed much to the cathartic imagery of Purgatory, including a narrow bridge and a black river from which arise smoke and an intolerable stench, and that is inhabited by terrible creatures. Other topographical features include ladders and mountains on which souls, as they try to ascend, are assailed by demons, and extremes of cold and heat.

The distinction between Hell and Purgatory was not always clear. Bede (*c.* 673–735) was among the first writers to record visions of the Otherworld in which a special place was set aside for souls undergoing purgation. Other accounts of visions, however, often confused the two places. It was not until the twelfth century that Purgatory began to appear on maps of the Otherworld and the Latin phrase *purgatorium* replaced *purgatorius ignis.* Even then, scholastics remained uncertain as to its location. LeGoff traces the history of the concept of Purgatory and draws attention to the understanding of it as a distinct and separate place in the Otherworld in the late twelfth century. The twelfth-century Cistercian Henry of Sawtry's treatise, *De Purgatorio Sancti Patricii,* refers to Purgatory as a separate place in the Otherworld with an entrance in this world.

During the thirteenth and fourteenth centuries, descriptions of Purgatory were generally allegorical, of which Dante's *Purgatorio* is the greatest and best-known example. Pictorial representations of Purgatory developed in the fourteenth century, preserving features that had been associated with it since the early Middle Ages.

BIBLIOGRAPHY

LeGoff, Jacques. *La Naissance du Purgatoire.* Paris: Gallimard, 1981. *The Birth of Purgatory.* Trans. A. Goldhammer. Aldershot, England: Scolar, 1984.

Morgan, Alison. *Dante and the Medieval Other World.* Cambridge: Cambridge UP, 1990.

*Robert Penkett*

SEE ALSO

Bede; Dante Alighieri; Etna, Mount; Paradise, Travel to; Purgatory, St. Patrick's

## Purgatory, St. Patrick's

The name given to a cavern and important pilgrimage site on Station Island in Lough Derg, County Donegal, Ireland. According to legend, Christ appeared in a vision to St. Patrick (385–461) in the first half of the fifth century and showed him a deep pit, which was believed to be an entrance to the Otherworld. The faithful who spent a day and a night alone in penitence in the pit were promised complete remission of all their sins and exemption from the torments of Hell after death, passing through Purgatory to experience the joys of Paradise.

By the twelfth century, St. Patrick's Purgatory was well known on the Continent. In 1120 it was described by David, the Irish rector of Würzburg. In the middle of the century an Irish knight, Owein, was condemned to do penance on the island. The knight later accompanied the Cistercian Gilbert of Luda (Louth Park), on a

Hibernia with bishop regarding Patrick's Cave. *Les Secretz de la Nature.* Château d'Aulnoy, Coulommiers (Seine et Marne) Collection Charnacé, unnumbered MS, fol. 36, *c.* 1460. Photo by John B. Friedman.

visit to Ireland, acting as interpreter and bodyguard. He told the monk of his journey to the Otherworld through the pit. Owein visited four fields of punishment that were all at the same altitude, fell into the mouth of Hell, crossed a river of fire and sulfur by a high, narrow, slippery bridge, entered the Terrestrial Paradise, climbed a mountain, and was shown the gate of the Heavenly Paradise.

Gilbert related this story to the Anglo-Norman Cistercian Henry of Sawtry, who recorded the account in his treatise *De Purgatorio Sancti Patricii,* written late in the twelfth or early in the thirteenth century. This text was frequently copied and translated.

Shortly after the dissemination of this text, English, French, Hungarian, and Portuguese Christians made pilgrimages to St. Patrick's Purgatory; they stayed first on nearby Saints' Island for nine days before rowing to Station Island, where they remained for the requisite

length of time, then returned to Saints' Island, where they did penance for a further nine days.

The island's fame was further increased by Jocelin of Furness's *Vita Sancti Patricii,* written between 1180 and 1183, in which the cavern is fancifully situated on Mount Cruachin Aigle, Connaught, Ireland; a thirteenth-century manuscript of Giraldus Cambrensis's *Topographia Hibernica* similarly alters the cavern's location.

Many influential historians and hagiographers, such as Roger of Wendover, Matthew Paris, Caesarius of Heisterbach, and Jacob of Voragine, made insular and continental readers aware of the cavern and its legends, and it is also mentioned in Vincent of Beauvais's great encyclopedia, *Speculum Maius.*

In 1470, Thomas, abbot of Armagh, received the priory of Station Island, where a community of Augustinian canons had lived since 1130. By 1479 the community had almost died out. The cavern was closed by edict of Pope Alexander VI on St. Patrick's Day, 1497. The site, however, has continued to attract thousands of pilgrims and tourists each year up to the present day.

**BIBLIOGRAPHY**

Marie de France. *L'Espurgatoire Seint Patriz.* Ed. Yolande de Pontfarcy. Louvain: Peeters, 1995.

*St. Patrick's Purgatory.* Ed. Robert Easting. Oxford: Oxford UP, 1991.

*Robert Penkett*

**SEE ALSO**

Etna, Mount; Gerald of Wales; Irish Travel; Matthew Paris; Paradise, Travel to; Pilgrimage, Christian; Purgatory; *Secretz de la Nature, Les;* Vincent of Beauvais

**Qaraqorum**
*See* Karakorum

**Qipchaqs**
*See* Cumans

# R

## Rabban Ata, Simeon (fl. 1230s–1240s)

A thirteenth-century Nestorian prelate known by his honorific title "Rabban Ata," "rabban" being the Chaldean word for "monk." Rabban Ata lived for many years at Tabriz in Syria. His expertise as a physician gained him great influence at Ögödei Khân's court (1229–1241), and he remained in the good favor of the khâns throughout his entire life. Thanks to Mongol religious tolerance, Nestorians (and other Christians) were allowed to exist unmolested alongside persons of other faiths. Rabban Ata was granted the right to supervise the application of their prescriptions of tolerance, and did much to help other Christians of the region. He played an important role in the diplomatic negotiations that led to a period of increased cooperation between occidental and oriental Christians.

Between 1235 and 1240, Rabban Ata used his influence to benefit Christians living under Mongol rule in Cilician Armenia as well as in the rest of the Middle East. The Armenian *catholicos* (patriarch) Nerses III allowed him to make an inspection visit in his diocese. Later, Rabban Ata was visited by the Dominican papal envoy Ascelin as this group (which included among its members Simon of Saint-Quentin, who wrote an account of this embassy) passed through Tabriz on its way back to Pope Innocent IV in 1247.

At the time of the Council of Lyons (1245), Pope Innocent IV sent the letter *Cum simus super* to church dignitaries in all countries affirming the primacy of the Roman Church. The papal envoy to Syria, Andrew of Longjumeau, conferred for twenty days with Rabban Ata, whom the document calls "vicar of the Orient." Rabban Ata sent a response to the pope, asking him to protect Nestorians living in the Latin Orient from the discriminatory policies of the Roman Church. He also urged Innocent to put an end to the conflict with Emperor Frederick II (1212–1250), a disruption that threatened the unity of Christendom even as another Mongol advance into Europe seemed imminent.

As Rabban Ata grew old, the khân of Persia, who ruled most of the traditional Middle East, assigned a convent to him as a gift, but exactly when the prelate died is unknown.

### BIBLIOGRAPHY

Grousset, René. *The Empire of the Steppes: A History of Central Asia.* Trans. Naomi Walford. New Brunswick, NJ: Rutgers UP, 1970.

Pelliot, Paul. "Les Mongols et la Papauté." *Revue de l'Orient chrétien* 23 (1922–1923): 3–30; 24 (1924): 225–335; 28 (1931–1932): 3–84.

Sinor, Denis. "The Mongols and Western Europe." In *Inner Asia and Its Contacts with Medieval Europe.* Ed. K.M. Setton. London: Variorum Reprints, 1977, pp. 513–544.

*Gloria Allaire*

### SEE ALSO

Andrew of Longjumeau; Armenia; Diplomacy; Frederick II; Hülegü; Innocent IV; Lyons, First Council of; Mongols; Nestorianism; Simon of Saint-Quentin

## Rabban Sauma

*See* Inner Asian Travel; Nestorianism

# R

## Red Jews

An imaginary people called "red" as a sign of their falsity and deceit. In the German-speaking world, from the late thirteenth to the sixteenth century, they embodied and articulated the popular medieval association between Jews and the savage apocalyptic destroyer tribe of Gog and Magog. The Red Jews played a central role in exegetical and prophetic literature concerning the Last Things. A xenophobic projection of German Christians preoccupied by the imminent end of the world, the Red Jews appear only in vernacular texts. Their very name, a term of opprobrium, reflects an "orientalizing" process; it is an early and powerful example of racist and anti-Semitic ethnography in medieval Europe.

Extracted from the Hebrew and Christian Bibles, reworked in exegetical and popular literature since late antiquity, the Gog and Magog legend and the story of the Ten Lost Tribes of Israel were eventually confused with each other, probably for the first time by Peter Comestor (*c.* 1110–1179) in his popular and long-lived *Historia scholastica* (*c.* 1165). This identification of legendary Jews with legendary destroyers was consonant with the steadily deteriorating state of Christian-Jewish relations at this time. There is an interesting correspondence (and a possible source) in popular Jewish belief, according to which the Ten Tribes would, at the end of time, free the remnant of Israel from bondage in the Diaspora; furthermore, Christians identified the Messiah awaited by the Jews as Antichrist from a very early date. This view of the Ten Tribes from differing perspectives helped solidify the popular Christian association all over Europe between Jews and future apocalyptic destroyers. Not surprisingly, such "apocalyptic" disasters as the Mongol invasions in the thirteenth century and the Black Death in the fourteenth century were frequently associated with Jewish connivance or agency.

From the late thirteenth to the early seventeenth century, the Red Jews represented both Gog and Magog and the Ten Tribes. Once the associates of the coming Antichrist—people whom more cautious theologians such as St. Jerome refused to identify with any particular nation—had been labeled as Jews, Christian authors proceeded to fabricate an apocalyptic itinerary for them and to invest them with concrete, personal characteristics. The term *rôt* (red), which in Middle High German meant not only the color but also "false, wicked, deceitful" (cf. *rotwelsch*—thieves' cant—a mid-

thirteenth-century coinage contemporary with that of the *rote Juden*), was applied for the first time to Jews in the rather rough and ready continuation (*c.* 1270) of the courtly poem *The Younger Titurel*. The Jews thus denoted were clearly wicked. In other Middle High German texts, they were not only menacing but also physically repulsive, endowed with oriental features and impervious hides. They were identified as the peoples Alexander had enclosed behind walls formed by the Caucasus Mountains to keep them from destroying the rest of the world.

From the thirteenth century on, the Red Jews appeared as apocalyptic destroyers in German-language works of all sorts, from courtly and late-courtly epics to popular exegetical works, German translations of travelogues such as Michael Velser's version of *The Book of John Mandeville*, chronicles, and Reformation-era pamphlets. In 1531, Luther referred to them in his sermon on 38–39 Ezekiel, but like Johannes Agricola, in his *Proverbs* of a few years earlier, he dismissed the Red Jews as a fable—even while tracing the ancestry of the Turks through the "Tatars" to the Red Jews. The rise of critical biblical scholarship and the expulsion of most Jews from the German-speaking lands by the time of the Reformation combined to undermine this tale and relegate it to the realm of fable and myth.

In the second half of the sixteenth century and the first decades of the seventeenth century, the Red Jews crop up again in broadside ballads and in satirical contexts that mock the credulity of common folk. After this time, the term is limited to Jewish usage, into which it passed as part of the medieval Jewish inheritance of Yiddish. Thus, until the twentieth century, Eastern European Jews often referred to the legendary Ten Tribes (understood as the military arm of the coming Messiah who would free dispersed Jewry from bondage among the Gentiles) as the Red Jews, though clearly this use of the term was devoid of the negative connotations that it originally possessed.

**BIBLIOGRAPHY**

Gow, Andrew Colin. *The Red Jews: Antisemitism in an Apocalyptic Age, 1200–1600.* Leiden and New York: Brill, 1995.

Mellinkoff, Ruth. *Outcasts: Signs of Otherness in Northern European Art of the Late Middle Ages.* 2 vols. Berkeley, Los Angeles, Oxford: U of California P, 1993, vol. 1, pp. 150–157.

*Andrew C. Gow*

R

SEE ALSO

Black Death; Expulsion, Corporate; Gog and Magog; *Mandeville's Travels;* Mongols; Orientalism; Ten Lost Tribes, The; *Wonders of the East*

## Red Sea

From biblical times to the sixteenth century, the Red Sea (Latin *Sinus Arabicus* or *Mare Rubrum;* Greek *Erythraean Sea;* Arabic *al-Bahr* or *al-Ahmer*) provided the main sea route for European traders between the Mediterranean and the east coast of Africa (modern Egypt, Sudan, Ethiopia, and Somalia), the southwest corner of Arabia (Yemen), and the west coast of India. Until modern times the Red Sea was erroneously identified with the Reed Sea (Hebrew *Yam Suf*) the Israelites crossed on the Exodus from Egypt (Exodus 14:1, 9, 21–22).

At its northwest extreme, the Indian Ocean opens through the Bab el-Mandeb Strait on the Red Sea, the warmest and most saline of all open seas. About 1,450 miles (2,330 kilometers) long, generally between 125 and 155 miles (200–250 kilometers) wide, and covering a total area of some 178,000 square miles (461,000 square kilometers), the Red Sea is divided at its northern extreme into two gulfs, which are separated by the uninhabitable wilderness of Sinai. The Gulf of Suez on the western side provides the shortest route to the Mediterranean, connected via the Bitter Lakes to the Nile by an ancient canal repaired at various times by Darius I (r. 542–486 B.C.E.), the Ptolemies (r. 323–246 B.C.E.), and the Romans. In disrepair during the Middle Ages, the canal was abandoned; cargo was unloaded at Suez and carried by camel caravan to Cairo and Alexandria. On the eastern side, the Gulf of Aqaba (or Eilat) provided an important navigation route for the kings of Israel and Judah, their Phoenician allies, and the Nabateans, also supporting trade with the Dravidic tribes on the west coast of India during the Hellenistic and Roman periods. Cargo unloaded at Elath (Ailath, Aila, Ezion-geber) could be transported westward to the Mediterranean ports or northward to Be'ersheva, Hebron, Jerusalem, and Damascus.

Constantinople became an international and cosmopolitan capital in the fourth and fifth centuries C.E. As a revolution in bulk containers occurred (from pottery amphorae to wooden casks) and as improvements in ship construction took place, Byzantium played a major role in the commerce of the Indian Ocean. The growth of Syrian and Egyptian commerce in the sixth and seventh centuries, however, cut into Byzantine prosperity. And as Arab commerce expanded along with Islam, Muslim merchants operated freely throughout the Mediterranean Sea and Indian Ocean. The Persian Gulf, rather than the Red Sea, offered the most convenient access to the East for all but the Egyptians, who also controlled the north-south commerce with the east coast of Africa through the Red Sea. Under the caliphate of Baghdad (750–1258 C.E.), long-distance commerce—dominated by Syrians, Greeks, and Jews—fabulously enriched Baghdad. No doubt the Muslim historian exaggerated when he said that in the ninth century "not a Christian plank floated" in the Mediterranean. In any event, from the tenth century on, the Italian seafaring city-states increased their control over the Mediterranean.

In the eleventh century, the military exploits of the crusaders disrupted east-west trade. Since Muslim sultans refused to allow foreign merchants to cross their lands and protected the Egyptian monopoly on Red Sea commerce, crusaders entered into partnership with Muslims, receiving their transported goods at coastal ports. The twelfth century was the great century of Venetian commercial power. Their most important cargo was "spices" (*species* or *spezerie*), a generic term that included all kinds of exotic commodities, from the small, black peppercorns of India and Indonesia to incense, musk, medicines, drugs, dyes, and sugar.

After the Mamluks triumphed in the thirteenth century, their tolerance for foreign traders on the east-west land routes diminished the risky oceanic traffic through the Red Sea. Such traffic again became desirable, however, when the political decay of the Mamluk Empire in the fifteenth century permitted Arab marauders to tax and destroy the caravans on the land link between Suez and Alexandria. Portuguese attempts to block Red Sea traffic in support of their route circumnavigating Africa (following Vasco da Gama's voyage in 1498) were futile but hastened the collapse of Mamluk Egypt. The Ottomans who replaced them in 1517 revived the route by allowing the Venetians to enjoy a near monopoly on Red Sea trade toward the end of the Middle Ages. By the late sixteenth century, the trade in sugars, spices, and dyes from the East through the Red Sea was again disrupted by cheaper products brought from the Atlantic islands, Brazil, and Mexico.

The route from Cairo to the Monastery of St. Catherine in the Sinai—and to Mecca in Arabia—caused

# R

thousands of Christian, Jewish, and Muslim pilgrims to see (and in some cases to sail across) the Red Sea on their route to holy sites. Some Christian pilgrims pause in their accounts to explain that the water of the Red Sea is not red, but rather that its rocky bottom was. Its corals were also admired: Johannes Witte de Hese (c. 1390) claimed they were an antidote to poisonous serpents. European cartographers often used scarlet or vermillion ink to color the Red Sea, a convention that continued into the early modern period.

## BIBLIOGRAPHY

Goitein, Samuel D. *A Mediterranean Society: The Jewish Communities of the Arab World as Portrayed in the Documents of the Cairo Geniza.* Berkeley: U of California P, 1967.

Hourani, G.F. *Arab Seafaring in the Indian Ocean in Ancient and Early Medieval Times.* Princeton, NJ: Princeton UP, 1951.

Lewis, Archibald. *The Sea and Medieval Civilizations.* London: Variorum Reprints, 1971.

Richards, D.S. *Islam and the Trade of Asia.* London: B. Cassirer, 1970.

Scammel, G.V. *The World Encompassed: The First European Maritime Empires c. 800–1650.* Berkeley: U of California P, 1981.

Thompson, James Westfall. *Economic and Social History of the Middle Ages (300–1300).* New York: Ungar, 1928; rpt. 1959.

*Jerome Mandel*

## SEE ALSO

Baghdad; Byzantine Empire; Catherine in the Sinai, Monastery of St.; Constantinople; Da Gama, Vasco; Damascus; Dyes and Pigments; Egypt; Jerusalem; Mamluk; Mecca; Mediterranean Sea; Muslim Travelers and Trade; Ottoman Empire; Spice Trade, Indian Ocean; Venice

## Ricold of Monte Croce (d. 1320)

Italian Dominican and missionary to the Middle East, many of whose ethnographic and religious observations were new and unique, and whose treatise on Islam became widely diffused and remained extremely influential for centuries.

Originally from the Monte di Croce area of Florence, Ricold was well educated when he entered the Dominican order in 1267 and became a lecturer in Italian convents. Late in 1288, he embarked on a pilgrimage to the Holy Land whose sacred places he later described with accuracy and great devotion. In 1289, he traveled through Turkey to Persia and Baghdad, where he stayed for several years, studying the Qur'an and discussing theology with Muslims. After the fall of Acre in 1291, Ricold remained behind in Baghdad as the sole Dominican; in his work he lamented the slave market being filled with Christian captives. He was called back to Italy before 1301 to "clarify some dubious points" in his writings. Although he had intended to return to the East, he never succeeded in doing so, becoming prior of the intellectually rich Convent of Santa Maria Novella in Florence.

Ricold's *Itinerarius* (sometimes styled *Liber peregrinacionis*) contains his personal impressions of the peoples he encountered. He engaged in discussions with many "Eastern Christians," including Nestorians, Jacobites, and Maronites; he accurately and fairly recorded their principal beliefs concerning the nature of Christ and their rituals for baptism and the preparation of the eucharistic Host. Ricold was also interested in their customs such as female circumcision, although he "could not well understand what they circumcised." In his *Ad naciones orientales* (c. 1300), the chapters on the Eastern Christians are detailed and logically presented expositions and refutations of their theology, which has led modern scholars to champion Ricold as an expert in these matters. But much of his text is actually a verbatim rendering of a work by Thomas Aquinas. When it came to theological details, Ricold apparently preferred to rely on authority rather than on his own experience.

Ricold's descriptions of Turks ("living in subterranean caves like moles") and Kurds are short and harsh: they are barbarous and wild people. His significantly longer chapters on the Mongols, however, provide much original information that was previously unknown to the Latin West. They contain Middle Eastern stories and legends about Mongol history from the rise of Chinggis Khân (c. 1200) to the conquest of Baghdad in 1258 and to the western Mongols' conversion to Islam in the early 1290s. The Mongols are depicted as broad-faced with eyes like fissures, giving them the appearance of apes, especially their old men and women. They honored excessive drinking, rape, and theft, but they detested lying; they showed total obedience to their superior even to the point of death. Ricold was the first westerner to describe horse impalement and other Mongol burial rites. Mongols differed from all other nations in that they had no sacred book but lived according to natural instincts, and Ricold expressed the (vain) hope that they would therefore be easily converted to Christianity. He was fascinated to observe that Mongol women enjoyed equality with Mongol men, and he described their dress, their equestrian expertise, and their active role in armies, while among other ethnic groups he hardly mentions women at all. In Persia he met the Mongols' Buddhist priests ("baxites"). They believed in "365 tümän gods" (in Turkish, tümän means "10,000"), but they were sincere and able to perform miracles, although one reputedly able to fly actually only levitated.

Outside Baghdad, Ricold spent some time in a community of Sabeans (or Mandeans), a closed Jewish-Christian sect influenced by Persian religious elements; they revered John the Baptist but denied the divinity of Jesus. Ricold wrote the first known description of their beliefs and their rituals, which were dependent on access to running water. He was allowed to inspect their holy scriptures that, so far as we know, were read by no other outsider to the community before the early twentieth century.

Ricold's long work on Jewish theology shows no influence of any personal encounter with Jews. It is well organized and pedagogically suited for future missionaries, but it adds nothing new to the traditional *adversus iudaeos* genre known since St. Augustine (*c.* 400), whom Ricold quoted at length together with the twelfth-century convert Peter Alfonsus and Ricold's fellow Dominican Raymundus Martin.

Ricold's greatest achievement was his theological treatise on Islam, the *Contra legem sarracenorum*. He began work on it in Baghdad, where he learned Arabic, but completed it in Italy. According to Ricold, Islam was a heresy within Christianity; its adherents displayed a deliberate aversion to truth. He attempted to prove that the Qur'an was confusing, filled with contradictions and apparent falsities, apt to cause its believers to commit violence, and opposed to biblical revelation. Ricold concluded that Islam is a demonic invention meant to destroy Christianity. In contrast to Christ, Muhammad never performed any true miracles but only convinced simpleminded Arabs by means of fantastic tales—or by the sword—of his nightly journey to heaven. Ricold's treatment of this story is thought to be one of the sources for Dante's description of Muhammad in the *Inferno*.

Ricold's work on the Qur'an is based on Christian sources but also on an intense personal study of the Arabic text and the work of Muslim theologians. His entirely negative evaluation of Islam is not surprising when one considers his firm belief in the truth of Christianity, but it contrasts markedly to his far more tolerant—even enthusiastic—attitudes toward individual Muslims. In his *Itinerarius,* he also denied that the Qur'an had any validity but only after having described Muslims as sincere and friendly, always interested in discussing religious matters and consistently showing great reverence for God and Jesus. One gets the impression that Ricold actually found the company of Muslims pleasant and enjoyed the free exchange of religious ideas even if he could not personally—or publically—accept their faith.

Ricold's *Contra legem sarracenorum* was widely copied during the Middle Ages; it was a prime source for Nicholas of Cusa in the 1450s, and it was printed in 1543 on the initiative of Martin Luther together with an openly anti-Islamic translation of the Qur'an that was the only translation available to Europeans until 1698. The negative view became known, while Ricoldo's *Itinerarius,* with its much more balanced attitude, circulated in only a few manuscripts and was not printed until 1873. Two medieval vernacular translations of Ricold's *Itinerarius* are known, however: one in Italian and another, by Jean le Long of Ypres, in French; this latter translation, completed in 1351, is part of an anthology of translated works—the others being the travel/geographical books by Hetoum, William of Boldensele, and Odoric of Pordenone—and survives in six manuscripts.

**BIBLIOGRAPHY**

Panella, Emilio. "Ricerche su Riccoldo da Monte di Croce." *Archivum Fratrum Praedicatorum* 58 (1988): 5–85.

Ricold of Monte Croce. *Itinerarius.* In *Peregrinatores Medii Aevi Quatuor.* Ed. J.C.M. Laurent. Leipzig: Hinrichs, 1873, pp. 105–141.

———. *Ad nationes orientales.* Ed. A. Dondaine. "Ricoldiana: Notes sur les oeuvres de Ricoldo da Montecroce." *Archivum Fratrum Praedicatorum* 37 (1967): 119–179.

———. *Contra legem sarracenorum.* Ed. Jean Marie Mérigoux, "L'ouvrage d'un frère Prêcheur florentin en Orient à la fin du XIIIe siècle: Le 'Contra legem Sarracenorum' de Riccoldo da Montecroce." *Memorie Domenicane,* n.s., 17 (1986): 1–144.

———. *Pérégrination en Terre Sainte et en Proche Orient.* Texte latin et traduction . . . par René Kappler. Paris: Honoré Champion, 1997.

*Kurt Villads Jensen*

**SEE ALSO**

Acre; Baghdad; Dante Alighieri; Dominican Friars; Eastern Christianity; Hetoum; Holy Land; Mongols; Nestorianism; Nicholas of Cusa; Odoric of Pordenone; William of Boldensele

# R

## Rivers of Paradise

*See* Four Rivers of Paradise

## Rocamadour

A small town in southern France, a few miles north of the Via Podiense, one of the four main pilgrimage routes to Santiago de Compostela in Galicia (Spain). Both the town and its church are dedicated to the Virgin Mary, and its primary significance is as a pilgrimage center.

While the town's early history is sketchy, during the Middle Ages it was referred to as the fourth great pilgrimage site in Christendom: pilgrims traveled there to worship at the shrine containing the relics of a local hermit, St. Amadour, whose uncorrupted remains were discovered in 1166. Some medieval sources claimed that the remains were actually those of Zacchaeus, the chief tax collector who looked down at Jesus from a sycamore tree (Luke 19:1–10) and, according to legend, married St. Veronica. Rocamadour was not entirely dependent on Compostela pilgrims making a separate side trip to visit the shrine, since it was also located on a heavily traveled north-south road running from Paris to Toulouse. Judging by the number of miracles recorded as occurring to merchants, they must have made up a substantial percentage of the visitors.

Among the famous visitors to the shrine were St. Bernard of Clairvaux (1090–1153), St. Dominic (*c.* 1170–1221), Louis IX of France (r. 1226–1271), and King Henry II of England (r. 1154–1189), who in 1159 was supposedly cured of an illness after praying to the image of the Dark Virgin housed in the church, which is dedicated to the Virgin Mary. Rocamadour was also the destination of many lesser-known pilgrims who were required (or who chose) to make a penitential pilgrimage. Rocamadour has a detailed history of regulations pertaining to the making of pilgrim badges, trading in which became so restricted in Rocamadour that it was a virtual monopoly of a few families.

### BIBLIOGRAPHY

Cohen, Esther. "*In haec signa:* Pilgrim badge trade in southern France." *Journal of Medieval History* 2.3 (1976): 193–214.

Delaruelle, Etienne. "La spiritualité du pèlerinage de Rocamadour au moyen âge." *Bulletin de la Société des études littéraires, scientifiques et artistiques du Lot* 87 (1966): 69–85.

Rocacher, Jean. *Rocamadour et son pèlerinage.* 2 vols. Toulouse: [privately published], 1979.

*Maryjane Dunn and Linda Davidson*

### SEE ALSO

Louis IX; Penance, Travel for; Pilgrim Souvenirs; Pilgrimage, Christian; Pilgrimage Sites, Spanish

## Rolevinck, Werner (1425–1502)

Carthusian monk and author of many books, including, most significantly, *Fasciculus Temporum,* whose dissemination in the late 1400s marks the spread of printing and its technical developments throughout Europe. Born in Laer in Westphalia, Rolevinck entered the Carthusian order at St. Barbara's in Cologne at the age of twenty-two, in 1447. By 1460, he had written books and sermons that were circulated and admired in monastic circles. The Benedictine abbot of St. Martin's Monastery at Sponheim, Johannes Trithemius, visited Rolevinck in 1495 and described him as an "extraordinarily diligent and prolific author of thirty or more books." Rolevinck died of plague in 1502.

Rolevinck wrote for an audience of clerics and monks, and he was aware from the earliest days of printing how this new process of disseminating information could revolutionize society and the Church, as he notes in the second published version of his *Sermo de presentacione beate virginis Marie* (Cologne: Arnold Ther Hoernen, 1470). In the preface to a later edition of the *Sermo,* he observes that the printing press will facilitate the work of God "because in no other way is it possible to communicate more easily and quickly with more people." Although Rolevinck clearly understood the impact of printing on the circulation of his sermon, he would have been amazed at the commercial success of the book for which he is chiefly known today: a world history entitled *Fasciculus Temporum,* one of the first best sellers of early printing.

The *Fasciculus Temporum,* literally "the little bundle of the things of time," was first printed in 1474 in Cologne, when the art of printing was barely thirty years old and was practiced in only a few places in Europe. Nevertheless, even in its first edition the book was produced with such complex printing techniques as woodcuts, highly schematic page layouts, and two-color printing. The text itself is a history of the world, starting with Creation (the "first age") and continuing into the mid- to late 1400s. The graphic layout, using circles and horizontal lines to trace the passage of time and the genealogy of biblical and royal families, is, as the author promises in the preface, "in a form like a painting in just a few pages." This concise, schematic,

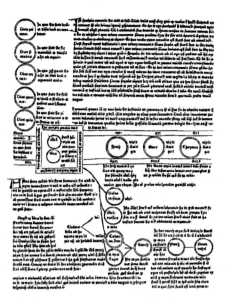

Timeline, *Fasciculus Temporum*. Cologne: A. Ther Hoernen, 1474, fol. 37v. Courtesy New York Public Library.

Monster from a foreign land. *Fasciculus Temporum*. Rougemont [Switzerland]: Henricus Wirtzburge de Vach, 1481, n.f. Photo by Laviece Ward.

illustrated format with its central, horizontal time line helped to make the book a commercial success in the world of late-fifteenth-century printing by offering a history of the world that was accessible to a wide variety of readers.

Early printers recognized the *Fasciculus* as a good speculative venture. From 1474 to 1500, it was issued in twenty-five editions in Latin and seven editions in translation—the first into Dutch, followed by two into German and four into French. After 1500, the *Fasciculus* was reprinted three times in French and five times in Latin. Between 1472 and 1726 it was issued a total of thirty-nine times.

The spread of printing throughout Europe can be traced by mapping the towns in which the *Fasciculus Temporum* was printed during the 1400s. German printers who left Cologne in the 1470s and 1480s settled in Holland, Switzerland, Italy, Spain, and France; one of the first books to issue from their presses was the *Fasciculus*. Often it was the first history, and also the first illustrated book, printed in any given town (for example, Louvain, Basel, Seville, Lyons, or Venice). Each printer in turn attempted to sell his edition by appealing to the local audience, either by translating the work into the vernacular or by setting it with appealing illustrations. Printers of the *Fasciculus* developed a strategy of providing an illustration of the town in which the work was printed, and thus the book is important in disseminating the images of foreign cities throughout Europe. The first edition (1474) included a woodcut representing the city of Cologne (with its cathedral unfinished); it was the first such image to appear in a printed book. Copies printed at Venice depicted the doge's palace and the Great Canal; those produced in Louvain, Utrecht, and Lyons depicted local market squares and churches. Woodcut views of scores of other cities were included in these printings, but with less emphasis on topographical accuracy: the same woodcut could be used to portray several different cities. In the edition printed by Erhard Ratdolt at Venice (1485), for example, the same woodblock is used to designate Cologne, Jerusalem, Vicenza, and the Roman Adriatic harbor of Sipontus.

Printers also provided woodcuts that depicted current technology, such as gunpowder, large cannons, and machines used in the construction of buildings and walls for towns and castles. Other illustrations appealed to interest in exploration, science, and marvels by depicting lunar eclipses, comets, and monstrosities such as dog-headed or fish-tailed humans who inhabited distant lands. Both the text (in Latin and translations) and the images of the *Fasciculus* document the creative efforts of early printers to sell a book to an audience far larger than any ever envisioned by its scholarly, cloistered author.

**BIBLIOGRAPHY**

Baer, Leo. *Die Illustrierten Historienbücher des 15. Jahrhunderts: Ein Beitrag zur Geschichte des Formschnittes.* Strassburg: Heitz and Mündel, 1903.

Murray, Alexander G.W. "The Edition of the *Fasciculus Temporum* Printed by Arnold Ther Hoernen in 1474." *Library,* 3rd series, 4 (1913): 57–71.

# R

Rolevinck, Werner. *Fasciculus Temporum.* Cologne: Arnold
Ther Hoernen, 1474.

Ward, Laviece. "Early Italian Printing and the Carthusian
History, *Fasciculus Temporum.*" In *San Bruno e la Certosa
di Calabria: Atti del convegno internazionale di studi per il
IX centenario.* Ed. Pietro De Leo. Soveria Mannelli, Italy:
Rubbettino, 1995, pp. 104–121.

———. "The *Fasciculus Temporum* and Early Printing in
Spain." In *Congrés Internacional, Scala Dei, Primera Car-
toixa de la Península Ibérica* I. Barcelona: L'Onde Car-
toixà, 1996, pp. 1–16.

*Laviece Ward*

SEE ALSO

City Plans; Gunpowder; Monstrosity, Geographical; Venice

## Rome, Marvels of
See Marvels of Rome

## Rome as a Pilgrimage Site

By the seventh century C.E., an established destination
for travelers from continental Europe and England. As
the capital of the great, if moribund, Roman Empire,
home to a worldwide religious bureaucracy, and an
active cult center, Rome was assured its place as the
center of pilgrim and tourist activity in the Western
world. Two sometimes compatible, sometimes conflicting, sets of sights lured visitors on pilgrimage: the
ruined glories of the pagan Roman past and the sacred
relics of Christianity.

After the public practice of pagan cults was banned
in 346, some temple buildings were put to a new use:
the Pantheon, for example, was Christianized in 609.
In other cases, pagan sites were dismantled or
despoiled, their stone used in new building projects,
usually churches. Thus pagan and Christian destinations were often combined in one site. Christian pilgrims visited the main churches and spaces connected
with early Christianity but often seemed more interested in monuments of the pagan past. This led Gregory the Great (590–604) to urge the destruction of all
antiquities since they distracted the pious from their
pilgrimages. (Gregory also did much to liberate Rome
from political authority at Ravenna, and thus helped
reestablish the city's power). A late-eighth-century
guide, the *Codex Einsidelensis,* which was created for
the Christian visitor with strong antiquarian interests,
records pagan and Christian inscriptions and randomly
lists ancient and Christian monuments from an imagined itinerary.

Two later tour guides detail the sights enjoyed by
well-educated travelers interested in the glories of
ancient Rome that had acquired Christian significance.
Benedict's late-twelfth-century *Marvels of Rome* describes
both secular wonders and Christian places, with greater
emphasis on the former. A slightly later English visitor
to Rome, Magister Gregory, illustrates in his *Marvels
of Rome* the revival of scholarly interest in, and nostalgic
yearning for, the ancient world, which was then prevalent in Western European scholarly circles. In contrast,
many strictly pious pilgrims used the *Indulgentiae eccle-
siarum urbis Romae* as guides. These texts provided pilgrims with information on churches, relics, and
indulgences in Rome and ignored the antique remains.

Antique monuments constituted the most important
characteristic of Rome, appearing on all medieval maps
and in almost all tour guides. Two such buildings
anchored medieval Rome: the Mausoleum of Hadrian,
Christianized as Castel Sant' Angelo, and the Theater of
Marcellus. Other famous places included the Pantheon,
the Colosseum, the triumphal arches of Constantine and
Septimus Severus, the Columns of Marcus Aurelius and
Trajan, several ancient Roman aqueducts (many of which
were still in use during the Middle Ages), the Baths of
Caracalla and Trajan, and the Theater of Pompey.

Whereas pagan Rome faced east, overlooking the
Forum, the town of medieval Rome looked west, an
approach that was not developed until Michelangelo's
monumental plan. The medieval city's lack of natural
center was exacerbated by the sprawl of the major Christian sites, many outside the city of Rome. Important
Christian pilgrim goals were the early basilicas of St.
Peter's, St. Paul Outside the Walls, St. Mary Major
(Maria Maggiore), and St. John Lateran. In addition, the
papal construction program beginning in the late eighth
century, financed by the great influx of pilgrims, built
churches and restored Christian antiquities. The Catalogue of Turin lists 414 churches in medieval Rome.

Although Rome was always a center of pilgrim activity, the flood of travelers into the city rose greatly during
the thirteenth century. The permanent population of
Rome was relatively small, around 35,000, and it was the
transient population that provided income to the
Church and local merchants. Problems arising from
housing, feeding, and defending the pilgrims are
reflected in Angelo Malabranca's 1235 senatorial edict in
protection of pilgrims. In 1240, when Gregory IX

announced indulgences for anyone who visited St. Peter's and St. Paul's, he escalated an already burgeoning fervor for penitential pilgrimage to Rome. Other important sites were the churches making up the Forty Stations. Toward the end of the thirteenth century, pilgrims received one year and one quarantine (a Lenten season of forty days) of indulgences for attending any one of these stations, and many pilgrims would stay in Rome for the whole of Lent, attending all forty. Travelers not only attended to church business and toured the city, but they also shopped for objects new and old. Pilgrims could buy tin badges, with the images of Saints Peter and Paul, from the canons of St. Peter's, who had a papal monopoly. John of Salisbury (c. 1115–1189) tells the tale of Henry of Blois, bishop of Winchester, who collected classical statuary in Rome in 1150 to ship home to England.

Perhaps as many as 2,000,000 pilgrims visited Rome in February of 1300 for the first Jubilee. Numerous chronicles record the crush of travelers, the shortages of basic amenities, and the profits made by the city. Jubilees were intended to increase tourist traffic, which they did, and consequently, other countries tried to stem the flow of money. Although many English traveled to Rome, and an English hospice was even founded there in 1362, Edward III (r. 1327–1377) denied many pilgrims' departures to keep English money at home. Because of the first Jubilee's success, subsequent popes declared them at shorter intervals and offered greater penitential rewards, even though the papacy resided at Avignon for most of the fourteenth century, leaving Rome in economic and political turmoil. A revival of the institutions of ancient Rome was attempted, unsuccessfully, by Cola di Rienzi (1313–1354). Still, because of its offering to diverse audiences, travel to Rome remained relatively unabated into the Renaissance.

## BIBLIOGRAPHY

Brentano, Robert. *Rome before Avignon: A Social History of Thirteenth-Century Rome.* New York: Basic Books, 1974.

Gregorius, Magister. *Marvels of Rome:* Trans. John Osborne. Toronto: Pontifical Institute of Medieval Studies, 1987.

Hetherington, Paul. *Medieval Rome: A Portrait of the City and Its Life.* New York: St. Martin's Press, 1994.

Hulbert, J.R. "Some Medieval Advertisements of Rome." *Modern Philology* 20 (1922–1923): 403–424.

Krautheimer, Richard. *Rome: Profile of a City, 312–1308.* Princeton, NJ: Princeton UP, 1980.

*The Marvels of Rome.* Ed. and trans. Francis Morgan Nichols. New York, Italica Press: 1986.

*Cynthia Ho*

## SEE ALSO

Inns and Accommodations; Itineraries and *Periploi; Marvels of Rome;* Pilgrim Souvenirs; Pilgrimage, Christian; Pilgrimage Sites, Byzantine; Pilgrimage Sites, English; Pilgrimage Sites, Spanish

## Roncesvalles

An ancient village in Navarra (Spain) located at the foot of the Ibañeta Pass (Puerto Ibañeta, elevation 1,483 feet [452 meters]), some five miles (eight kilometers) from the French border. Roncesvalles is famous as the site of Roland's famous battle and death (778), described in the *Chanson de Roland* and the *Cantar de Roncesvalles.*

The area has been occupied since prehistoric times, as witnessed by the many dolmens found there. The Romans laid a road connecting Burdeos (France) with Astorga (Spain) that passes through Roncesvalles. This road proved extremely popular with the advent of pilgrimage to Santiago de Compostela; the three northernmost routes from France joined together in Ostabat and then crossed the Pyrenees going up from Saint-Jean-Pied-de-Port, crossing the Ibañeta Pass (where since the late eleventh century there had been a large hostel for pilgrims, the Hospital of San Salvador).

Roncesvalles grew in importance with the establishment of its own Augustinian foundation and Hospital of Santa María in the second half of the eleventh century, during the reigns of Alfonso VI of León and Castilla (1065[1072]–1109) and Sancho Ramírez of Aragón (1063–1094), with the support of the diocese of Pamplona. The oldest extant building dates from the twelfth century and is the Capilla del Espíritu Santo (also known as the Silo de Carlomagno). It is constructed over a cave and served as the burial area for pilgrims who died at the hospital. Other sites dating from the medieval period are the Colegiata de Nuestra Señora de Roncesvalles (founded between 1194 and 1215), and the Iglesia de Santiago (thirteenth century), a small, well-preserved church typical of those found along the pilgrimage route.

## BIBLIOGRAPHY

García, Fermín Miranda. *Roncesvalles: Trayectoria patrimonial (siglos XII-XIX).* Pamplona: Gobierno de Navarra, 1993.

*Maryjane Dunn*

# R

**SEE ALSO**
Inns and Accommodations; Military Orders; Pilgrimage, Christian; Pilgrimage Sites, Spanish

## Roselli, Petrus (fl. 1447–1468)

A maker of nautical charts on Majorca. Nothing certain is known about Petrus Roselli's life. Claims have been made for his nationality as either Italian or Spanish. He may have been an Italian, like his predecessor Angelino de Dalorto (fl. 1325–1330) or Salvat de Pilestrina, who studied on Majorca, an important cartographic production center. He may have belonged to a group of *conversi* or Jews who emigrated from Italy in the twelfth century.

Extant charts signed by Roselli are dated 1447, 1456, 1462, 1464, 1465, 1466, 1468. Another is unsigned and undated, but displays a distinctive ornamental frame that is his trademark. In a legend for the chart of 1447, Roselli states that it was produced at Majorca "de arte baptista Becarij"—an apparent tribute to the Genoese cartographer Battista Beccario (fl. 1426–1435). This unusual statement has been interpreted as evidence of a Genoese school of cartography. Similarly, Roselli is acknowledged by a possible pupil, the Catalan Arnaldo Domenech, who calls himself Roselli's "disciple" on a chart made in the 1480s. Rather than indicating an actual apprenticeship to a master mapmaker, however, these statements of homage may be simple acknowledgments of a particular model or style a cartographer followed.

Although Roselli's origins and training are still under debate, he is credited with various stylistic innovations. He doubled the number of rhumb lines that extend from the center of a wind rose (the unembellished point at which rhumb lines come together) from sixteen to thirty-two. This feature appears in charts he produced between 1456 and 1468, and is useful in dating his earlier sea charts. His 1462 portolan introduced an improved outline of the northern European coastline from Flanders to Jutland, showing Ireland more true to scale and accurately articulating Scotland's coast. His 1464 chart extends farther northeast in the Baltic Sea than any previous portolan did, and it shows more of Africa than did his models. It is also the earliest known example of a chart's "neck" decorated with a Madonna and Child. His portolan of 1465 shows still more African cities and also is decorated with the Madonna. Like his Catalan models, this portolan

included inland features; inland cities appear as two-dimensional drawings labeled with their names in the Italian manner. Flags bearing various devices or emblems indicate major political powers.

**BIBLIOGRAPHY**

Campbell, Tony. "Portolan Charts from the Late Thirteenth Century to 1500." In Harley-Woodward, vol. 1, pp. 371–463. See Gen. Bib.

Errera, Carlo. "Un particolare notevole in una carta nautica del secolo XV." *Rivista Geografica Italiana* 9 (1902): 643–644.

Harvey, P.D.A. *Medieval Maps.* London: British Library, 1991.

Mesenburg, Peter. *Kartographie im Mittelalter: Eine analytische Betrachtung zum Informationsgehalt der Portulankarte des Petrus Roselli aus dem Jahre 1449.* Karlsruhe: Fachhochschule Karlsruhe, Fachbereich Vermessungswesen und Kartographie, 1989.

Winter, Heinrich. "Petrus Roselli." *Imago Mundi* 9 (1952): 1–11.

*Gloria Allaire*

**SEE ALSO**
Atlas; Maps; Portolan Charts; Ptolemy

## Rosselli, Francesco (*c.* 1447—after 1507 and before 1527)

A late-fifteenth-century Florentine cosmographer, miniaturist, and map engraver, who produced the earliest known printed world map that includes New World discoveries. Born into one of Florence's leading families, Francesco was the younger brother of the well-known painter Cosimo Rosselli. In 1470–1471, Francesco worked for the Cathedral of Siena as an illuminator. Between around 1480 and 1484, he worked at the court of the learned King Matthias I Corvinus of Hungary (r. 1458–1490), where he produced a map of Hungary (now lost). By the early 1490s, he had returned to Florence where he opened a printing shop. He utilized the new copperplate technology to execute precise multiple copies of drawings by master mapmakers. By 1508, Rosselli was in Venice, where he apparently remained for a few years. He died in Florence—although scholars differ considerably about the date—and his business passed to his son, Alessandro.

Rosselli was not a cartographer in the modern sense of the word, but he is the first specialized map engraver and dealer known to us by name. He collaborated with famous cartographers such as Henricus Martellus and

Giovanni Matteo Contarini. Only two extant maps bear Rosselli's name; although several attributions to him have been made, not all are securely datable. His world maps belonged to a phase of mapmaking that incorporated recent world discoveries into the Ptolemaic standard. Certain details in Rosselli's outlines suggest that he depended on actual travelers' reports, possibly going back to Marco Polo (c. 1298). An early world map (c. 1492) illustrates the voyage of Bartolomeu Dias and is the only surviving printed map to reproduce geographical concepts held by Columbus before his famous voyage. In 1506, Rosselli engraved an important world map on a fan-shaped projection, drawn by Contarini (hence known as the Contarini world map). Despite its inaccuracies, this is the earliest known printed map that shows any territory in the Americas. He is generally credited with having developed the ingenious method of oval projection, seen in his world map of around 1508.

Rosselli also produced panoramic representations of localities with their architectural features seen in elevation. Such maps were intended for permanent display. These bird's-eye-view maps were first produced in Italy and became widely popular throughout Europe. An important, detailed view of Florence (c. 1482) survives; similar engravings of Constantinople and of Pisa are recorded but been lost. A view of Rome drawn shortly before 1490 is also lost, but probably resembled a large panorama at the ducal palace in Mantua.

**BIBLIOGRAPHY**

Almagià, Roberto. "On the Cartographic Work of Francesco Rosselli." *Imago Mundi* 8 (1951): 27–34.

Campbell, Tony. *The Earliest Printed Maps 1472–1500.* Berkeley: U of California P, 1987.

Ettlinger, L.D. "A Fifteenth-Century View of Florence." *Burlington Magazine* 94 (1952): 160–167.

Heawood, Edward. "A Hitherto Unknown World Map of A.D. 1506." *Geographical Journal* 62 (1923): 279–293.

Hind, Arthur M. *Early Italian Engraving: A Critical Catalogue with Complete Reproduction of All the Prints Described.* Part I. *Florentine Engravings and Anonymous Prints of Other Schools.* 4 vols. New York: Knoedler, 1938; rpt. Nendeln (Liechtenstein): Kraus, 1970, vol. 1, pp. 304–309.

*Gloria Allaire*

**SEE ALSO**

City Plans; Columbus, Christopher; Constantinople; Dias, Bartolomeu; Hungary; Maps; Marco Polo; Pisa; Ptolemy; Rome as a Pilgrimage Site

## Russia and Rus'

A political entity that arose in the ninth and tenth centuries when Scandinavian Vikings called Varangians established trading stations in the forest-steppe region to the east and south of modern Kiev and merged with the Slavic inhabitants of the eastern European plain. Their focus on the Dnieper River as a major trade route eventually resulted in the establishment of Kievan Rus'.

The origin of Rus' ranks among the most controversial subjects in medieval Russian history. Scholars expressing a pro-Scandinavian or "Normanist" (referring to "Northmen") point of view, have contended with pro-Russian Antinormanists over the identity, the date, and the origins of the Rus'. The Normanist view that the Rus' represented a group of Scandinavian Vikings who eventually established Kiev and made it the capital of a political entity of that name has gained greater acceptance than the Antinormanist contention (based more on Marxist ideas of historical development than on historical evidence) that they were Slavs who had always lived south of Kiev. The *Russian Primary Chronicle* (854/862) describes Varangian incursions at the invitation of the Slavs, and coin-hoard finds show that in the early ninth century, Viking groups from northern Russia apparently went inland in search of Arabic silver *dirhems,* which they reexported to Scandinavia.

Further support for a Normanist origin of Rus' comes from both eastern and western sources. Ibn Fadlan, an ambassador from the caliph of Baghdad to the Volga-Bulgars (921–922), maintains that the "tall, ruddy, and fairhaired" Rus' traded slaves and furs for Arabic money, used Frankish swords, and practiced ship burial, characteristics suggestive of Viking identification. Rus' emissaries in the treaty of the Kievan prince Igor with Byzantium in 944 had Scandinavian names, and Liudprand of Cremona identifies the Rus' with the Normanni, a contemporary Western term used to denote Vikings.

Commerce seems to have played a large part in the history of Rus'. Recent research suggests that Varangian trading centers, which arose in the forest-steppe zone beginning in the mid-eighth century, brought the local forest resources into the long-distance trade system in the early tenth century and developed into political and ecclesiastical centers by the eleventh and twelfth centuries. The capital of the Rus', Kiev, was strategically located for maritime trade in the Baltic and the Black Sea, as well as for east-west land trade. Byzantine

# R

coin hoards document the completion of a trade route "from the Varangians to the Greeks" in the late tenth century. This is corroborated by the *Russian Primary Chronicle*'s reference to the integration of the Russian north into the Kievan realm by Prince Vladimir in the 970s and 980s. In 988, Vladimir converted to Greek Orthodox Christianity and married a woman from the Byzantine imperial house commonly identified with Emperor Basil II's sister. As a result of his conversion, the Orthodox faith and Byzantine art and architecture were disseminated in Kievan Rus'.

Under Yaroslav the Wise (d. 1054) and his successors, the Kievan state enjoyed its greatest commercial prosperity and military success. Laws were codified and churches were built. Rus' developed a lucrative trade in sable and fox furs. As the buying power of Byzantium decreased, Kiev became a transit point in Russia's fur trade with both Europe and the Turks.

The decline of Kievan Rus' starting in the middle of the twelfth century resulted from demographic, economic, and political changes in the region. Constant dissension among the rulers and increasing attacks on its territory in the south by neighboring nomadic tribes, such as the Cumans, resulted in a population exodus to the northeast. Kiev's economic potential was weakened because Venetian and Genoese mercantile expansion had eroded the trade route from the "Varangians to the Greeks." The dire results of the Fourth Crusade (1202–1204), in which Westerners took over Constantinople, further undermined the political and economic relations between Byzantium and Rus'. During this period, as well, the Russian fur trade shifted from a north-south to a west-east axis. The relatively unified Kievan state began to fragment into many smaller spheres of influence with Novgorod becoming independent in 1136, profiting from trade relations with Lübeck, a member of the Hanse. In the south, Vladmir became the capital of a principality after the Kievan grand prince Andrey Bogolyubsky had abandoned the capital, Kiev, and razed much of it in 1169.

Russia fell victim to the Mongol invasion in the 1240s, though it is difficult to assess the exact long-term impact of the Mongols. Some have held the Mongols responsible for the destruction of Kievan Rus' and particularly of the capital in 1240 and the rise of the autocracy in Muscovite Russia; others more recently have emphasized that the Golden Horde primarily affected only the economic, political, and institutional spheres of Russian society between the 1240s and 1480 since the religious barrier between the two societies curtailed overwhelming Mongol cultural influence on Russia. While the Russian princes had to travel to the Horde to receive the khân's permission to rule, after the initial conquest, Russian-Mongol relations were relatively peaceful. The Mongols carefully nourished commerce in the region, provided tax exemptions for the Church, and used Russian princes as tax collectors. The emerging princes of Moscow borrowed Mongol institutions—including the taxation systems, army organization, and diplomatic protocol—to create the foundation of the Muscovite autocracy.

The complex reasons for the rise of Moscow are partly economic, partly geopolitical. Ivan I of Moscow (r. 1331–1340), called "Moneybag," was able to exploit his city's favorable trade location in the midst of arable lands and near major river transportion for trade with Constantinople and Crimean ports. By shrewd manipulation of his distant Mongol overlords and their taxation system, and friendly relations with the Church, he came to dominate the Moscow region. The consolidation of the Russian realm continued when Dmitry Donskoy defeated the Mongols at Kulikovo in 1380.

By 1480 the Moscovites had effectively repulsed Mongol raids. After Ivan III (r. 1462–1505) conquered the huge trading empire of Novgorod in 1477–1478, Muscovite Russia became an important power among the European states, completing a major political and economic shift from Kiev in the north.

## BIBLIOGRAPHY

Halperin, Charles. *Russia and the Golden Horde.* Bloomington: Indiana UP, 1987.

Martin, Janet. *Treasure of the Land of Darkness.* Cambridge and New York: Cambridge UP, 1986.

Mühle, Edward. *Die städtischen Handelszentren der nordwestlichen Rus': Anfänge und frühe Entwicklung altrussischer Städte (bis gegen Ende des 12. Jahrhunderts).* Quellen und Studien zur Geschichte des östlichen Europa 32. Stuttgart: Steiner, 1991.

Noonan, Thomas. "Why the Vikings First Came to Russia." *Jahrbücher für Geschichte Osteuropas* 34 (1986): 321–348.

Ostrowski, Donald. *Muscovy and the Mongols: Cross-Cultural Influences on the Steppe Frontier 1304–1589.* Cambridge: Cambridge UP, 1998.

Pritsak, Omeljan. "The Origin of Rus'." *Russian Review* 36.3 (1977): 249–273.

Riasanovsky, Nicholas. "The Norman Theory of the Origin of the Russian State." *Russian Review* 7.1 (1947): 96–110.

*The Russian Primary Chronicle.* Eds. and trans. Samuel Hazzard Cross and Olgerd P. Sherbowitz-Wetzor. Cambridge, MA: Medieval Academy of America, 1953.

Vernadsky, George. *Kievan Russia.* Vol. 2 of *A History of Russia.* New Haven: Yale UP, 1976.

*Isolde Thyrêt*

**SEE ALSO**

Byzantine Empire; Coinage and Money; Constantinople; Crusade, Fourth; Cumans; Golden Horde; Hanse, The; Liudprand of Cremona; Mongols; Teutonic Order; Viking Age

# S

## Sacrobosco, John of (*c.* 1190–1258)

Author of books on the algorithm, computus, and astrolabe, and, most importantly, *De sphaera,* a short textbook on elementary astronomy and geography, completed around 1220.

John of Holywood or of Sacrobosco, the Italian form of his name, may have been born in Yorkshire, England, but spent most of his life in Paris, where he was first a student of the arts, and afterward a doctor of philosophy and professor. At his death he had a sphere carved on his tomb in the cloister of the convent of St. Mathurin in Paris. His *Tractatus de sphaera* (or *Opusculum sphaericum*) was widely copied and commented on and remained popular well into the seventeenth century because of its clarity, simplicity, and utility.

*De sphaera* is divided into four chapters. The first one offers two definitions of the sphere, borrowed from Euclid (fl. 300 B.C.E.) and Theodosius of Bithynia (*c.* 170–150 B.C.E.). It describes the main features of the cosmos according to a geocentric hypothesis: the sphere of the heavens rotates regularly around the axis of the poles; the spherical earth stays motionless in the center of the celestial sphere, geometrically reduced to a point. The second chapter describes the main celestial circles that constitute the structure of the "material sphere," imitating the structure of the cosmos: the equator, the zodiac, the colures, the meridian, and the horizon are great circles; the tropics and the polar circles, smaller in size when projected on the earth, limit the five terrestrial zones. The third chapter deals with the rising and setting of the constellations, with the length of the solstitial days according to latitude,

and with the division of the inhabited world into *climata* defined by the length of the longest day. In the very short final chapter, Sacrobosco alludes to certain hypotheses such as eccentric circles and epicycles propounded by Greek astronomers to justify the apparently irregular motion of the planets; he then draws figures showing how solar and lunar eclipses take place.

Though not an innovative work, *De sphaera* is a highly influential compilation of the basic teachings of the Greek astronomical and geographical science becoming available to the Latin West in the second half of the twelfth century through the Latin translations from Arabic made by Gerard of Cremona and Plato of Tivoli. These Italian scholars, who settled in Spain at a time when Arabic science and civilization were in full bloom, were anxious to turn into Latin the Arabic translations of the Greek scientists, not only Euclid and Ptolemy, but also less famous geometers such as Autolycos of Pitane and Theodosius of Bithynia, whose teachings offered a simplified approach to the great Ptolemy.

Sacrobosco's *De sphaera* included, besides the elements of astronomy and mathematical geography, a great many references to Greek and Arabic scientists—such as Aristotle, Euclid, Eratosthenes, Ptolemy, and Alfraganus [al-Farghani]—and to Latin poets such as Ovid, Virgil, and Lucan. Alfraganus, the chief astrologer at the court of al-Ma'mūn (813–833) in Baghdad, had written a work called in Latin *Elementa,* an abstract in thirty chapters of Ptolemy's *Almagest,* translated into Latin in the twelfth century by John of Seville and Gerard of Cremona; this summary was very popular but was replaced by the more convenient work of Sacrobosco.

# S

From 1366 on, Sacrobosco's *De Sphaera* was a compulsory textbook in many European universities, remaining in use until as late as 1700. It was one of the first printed books on astronomy and mathematical geometry, and was reprinted many times after the first edition of Venice, which had appeared by 1472; more than sixty-five editions appeared before 1550 and a total of 180 between 1472 and 1639. Important commentaries on the *De Sphaera* were those by Pierre d'Ailly (1350–1420) and Robertus Anglicus. The Florentine Gregorio (Goro) Dati (1362/3–1435/6) translated Sacrobosco's textbook into Italian *octava rima* as *La Sfera;* printed as early as 1475 in Venice (only three years after the appearance of the Latin text), it also had a great success.

**BIBLIOGRAPHY**

d'Alverny, Marie-Thérèse. "Translations and Translators." In *Renaissance and Renewal in the Twelfth Century.* Ed. Robert L. Benson and Giles Constable. Cambridge, MA: Harvard UP, 1982, pp. 421–452.

Campbell, Tony. *The Earliest Printed Maps 1472–1500.* Berkeley: U of California P, 1987.

Duhem, Pierre. *Le Système du monde: Histoire des doctrines cosmologiques de Platon à Copernic.* Vol. 3. Paris: Hermann, 1958.

O'Leary, De Lacy. *How Greek Science Passed to the Arabs.* 1949; rpt. London: Routledge and Kegan Paul, 1980.

Pederson, O. "In Quest of Sacrobosco." *Journal of the History of Astronomy* 16 (1985): 175–221.

Thorndike, Lynn. *The Sphere of Sacrobosco and Its Commentators.* Chicago: U of Chicago P, 1949. [This work contains an edition and translation of the work.]

*Germaine Aujac*

**SEE ALSO**

Ailly, Pierre, d'; Baghdad; Climate; Ptolemy

## Sæwulf (fl. 1103)

Author of a pilgrimage account, entitled *Peregrinatio Sigewulfi,* which offers the earliest description of the Holy Land after the First Crusade and a detailed itinerary of the sea journey from Italy to Joppa [Jaffa].

Nothing is known of Sæwulf apart from his short and fragmentary account of a journey to the Holy Land. The name itself is Anglo-Saxon, but it may be descriptive rather than proper. William of Malmesbury records (4.146) that a merchant of the same period retired to Malmesbury Abbey in his old age, but there is no conclusive evidence that the two are identical. Internal evidence indicates that Sæwulf made his journey from July 1102 to May 17, 1103. The account survives in a single late-twelfth-century manuscript (Cambridge, Corpus Christi College, MS 111).

The chief interest of Sæwulf's travel narrative is its description of the voyages to and from the Holy Land. Sæwulf made his outward journey on a trading vessel sailing from Monopoli, near Bari, along the coasts of Greece and Asia Minor and the islands of the Aegean and eastern Mediterranean on a voyage that was apparently quite tempestuous. The voyage concluded in the harbor at Joppa, where Sæwulf vividly describes a storm that destroyed twenty-three ships and took more than 1,000 lives on the morning after he had gone ashore. The return journey took a direct route from Joppa to Constantinople, but the text breaks off before Sæwulf reaches the city.

Sæwulf's account of the Holy Land itself is largely stock description, concentrating on Jerusalem and its immediate vicinity, but it includes such interesting observations as the danger of being attacked by "Sarracen" robbers on the road from Joppa to Jerusalem. As the narrative moves farther from Jerusalem, however, it becomes even less idiosyncratic or personal, suggesting only a secondhand knowledge of these regions. Indeed, in addition to rather frequent citations of Bible verses, Sæwulf's account includes striking echoes of the Venerable Bede's *On the Holy Places* (702–703), and a work known as the Ottobian Guide (1101–1103 [Rome, Biblioteca Apostolica Vaticana, Cod. Ottobianus latinus 169]). The narrative ends rather peremptorily at Raclea, near Constantinople, where, Sæwulf notes, Paris abducted Helen.

**BIBLIOGRAPHY**

Pryor, John, ed. "The Voyage of Sæwulf." In *Peregrinationes Tres.* Ed. R.B.C. Huygens. Corpus Christianorum: Continuatio Medievalis 139. Turnholt: Brepols, 1994.

William of Malmesbury. *De Gestis Pontificum Anglorum: Libri quinque.* Ed. N.E.S.A. Hamilton. Rerum Britannicarum Medii Aevi Scriptores 52. London: Longman, 1870.

*Timothy S. Jones*

**SEE ALSO**

Bede; Constantinople; Crusades, First, Second, and Third; Holy Land; Jerusalem

## Saffron

An expensive spice that has been an important item in East-West trade for centuries. Saffron has long been coveted (1) as a food flavorer, particularly in Mediterranean foods such as bouillabaisse, paella, breads, and other rice and fish dishes; (2) as a dyestuff, ranging in color from yellow to bright orange; and (3) as a medicine, with saffron tea being used as a tonic. Saffron consists of the dried stigmas, either whole or powdered, of the flower of the plant *Crocus sativus,* which blooms for a single two-week period each year, generally in late autumn. It takes approximately 70,000 flowers to yield one pound of saffron since only three orange-red stigmas are harvested from each blossom.

The word "saffron" is derived from an Arabic word *za'faran,* which means "yellow." It is believed to have been indigenous to Greece, Asia Minor, and Persia, spreading both eastward to the Kashmir region of India around 500 B.C.E. and westward along the Mediterranean during the ninth and tenth centuries. Muslims introduced the cultivation of saffron into Spain by the early tenth century. Saffron was brought to Italy, France, and Germany by returning crusaders during the thirteenth century, and to England during the fourteenth century.

The medieval saffron trade was global: saffron from Valencia and Catalonia dominated markets in Europe, while saffron from Tuscany sold in Byzantine and Levantine markets. For example, merchants from San Gimignano dominated the distribution of saffron in the Kingdom of Jerusalem during the thirteenth century. Southern French towns, particularly Montpellier, played major roles in the redistribution of saffron to northern French markets in the fourteenth century. During the fourteenth and fifteenth centuries, Cracow merchants imported saffron from Spain into Poland and Bohemia and then reexported it to Flanders. Saffron was such an important and lucrative commodity that many medieval communities, including Montpellier, Barcelona, and Nuremberg, imposed regulations and controls on the inspection and sale of saffron to guard against its adulteration.

**BIBLIOGRAPHY**

Abulafia, David. "Crocuses and Crusaders: San Gimignano, Pisa and the Kingdom of Jerusalem." In *Outremer: Studies in the History of the Crusading Kingdom of Jerusalem Presented to Joshua Prawer.* Ed. B.Z. Kedar, H.E. Mayer, and R.C. Smail. Jerusalem: Yad Izhak Ben-Zvi Institute, 1982, pp. 227–243.

Parry, John W. *Spices.* New York: Chemical Publishing Co., 1969.

Rosengarten, Frederick, Jr. *The Book of Spices.* Philadelphia: Livingston, 1969.

*Debra A. Salata*

**SEE ALSO**
Barcelona; Dyes and Pigments; Pepper; Spice Trade, Indian Ocean

## Saint Brendan's Voyage
*See* Brendan's Voyage, St.

## Saint Catherine in the Sinai, Monastery of
*See* Catherine in the Sinai, Monastery of St.

## Saint Gregory of Tours
*See* Gregory of Tours, St.

## Saladin [Salāh al-Dīn Yūsuf b. Ayyūb] (A.H. 564–589 / 1138–1193 C.E.)

Sultan of Egypt and Syria, who led military ventures that won back for Islam much of the territory in the Holy Land occupied by Western crusaders. Saladin was born at Tekrit into a Kurdish family in service to 'Imād-al-Dīn Zangī of Mosul; Saladin served 'Imād-al-Dīn's son, Nūr al-Dīn Emir of Syria. At this time, political and moral authority was divided between the Fātimid caliphate of Cairo and the Abbasid caliphate of Baghdad; regions and cities were held by independent warlords, and wide divisions separated the general population from the military men who wielded power. The crusader states, with their small populations, represented an additional irritating complication, a potential if not an actual threat.

After serving for ten years in Nūr al-Dīn's court at Damascus, Saladin accompanied his uncle Shīrkūh to Egypt on an expedition, during which Shīrkūh seized effective power in Cairo in 1169; Shīrkūh died almost immediately, and Saladin succeeded him in command. He played a dual role as Fātimid vizier and as Nūr al-Dīn's subordinate until the caliph's death in 1171 and Nūr al-Dīn's in 1174. Saladin proclaimed himself sultan of Egypt, with authority over Mesopotamia, and initiated the Ayyūbid dynasty. Part of the rest of his career was spent in a power struggle with the Zangids, in the course of which he successfully established his

# S

power in Syria, where he took Damascus and later Aleppo with the aid of his brother Tūrānshāh. He failed, however, to subdue the city of Mosul completely, or to win unqualified approval from the Abbasid caliphs.

Saladin represented himself as the champion of Islam against the crusaders, a role whose potentialities had been developed by Nūr al-Dīn, and his intermittent campaigns against the crusader states culminated in the battle of Hattin (near Tiberias) in 1187, in which he destroyed the field army of the Latin Kingdom of Jerusalem; he went on to capture Jerusalem and take most of the crusader strongholds. Tyre, however, provided the crusaders with a base, and Saladin's victories prompted the calling of the Third Crusade in 1189, during which the western armies were able only to capture Acre. Although the engagements between Christian and Muslim forces were to a degree politically indecisive, they greatly influenced cultural life in the West owing to the famous encounter between England's King Richard the Lionheart (r. 1189–1199) and Saladin. The sultan's ensuing reputation for generosity and chivalry earned him a place of honor in medieval romance, and even Dante located his soul in Limbo. The crusaders were not strong enough to recapture Jerusalem but neither could Saladin clear them from the coast. This stalemate led to a truce in 1192, the Peace of Ramleh [Ramla], shortly after which Saladin died.

During the late 1100s, trade was an important source of revenue, which Saladin needed for his military campaigns. The armament industry and the slave trade flourished, and anecdotal evidence indicates that trade routes remained open even while wars were being fought nearby, and that huge profits could be made from military supplies (although risks of loss were also high). During the Third Crusade (1189–1192) there was considerable interference with Mediterranean shipping, but Saladin enjoyed the benefits of an open trade route between Egypt and India (via the Red Sea, thanks to the extension of his control over Yemen).

Saladin unquestionably changed the pattern of Middle Eastern history, not so much because he established his own dynasty (the Ayyūbids were short-lived) but, immediately, because he gave the coup-de-grâce to the ailing Fātimid dynasty. He also made Europe aware that retaining crusader states would involve enormous effort and expense. As a corollary to this, he demonstrated the increasing importance of an efficient, if expensive, professional army, which later contributed

to the refinement of the Mamluk system; this, arguably, led to a profound change in the economic and social resources of Egypt and Syria.

## BIBLIOGRAPHY

Ehrenkreutz, Andrew S. *Saladin.* Albany: State U of New York P, 1972.

Gibb, H.A.R. *The Life of Saladin: From the Works of Imad ad-Din and Baha ad-Din.* Oxford: Clarendon, 1973.

Lyons, Malcolm Cameron, and D.E.P. Jackson. *Saladin: The Politics of the Holy War.* Cambridge and New York: Cambridge UP, 1997.

*Malcolm C. Lyons*

## SEE ALSO

Acre; Ayyūbids; Baghdad; Crusades, First, Second, and Third; Damascus; Dante Alighieri; Egypt; Fātimids; Jerusalem; Mamluks; Red Sea

## Sallust Maps

A subcategory of the T-O type of *mappamundi* (see Maps), found in some sixty surviving medieval manuscripts of *De bello Jugurthino* by Gaius Sallustius Crispus (86–c. 34 B.C.E.). Sallust's book is the chief source for information about Rome's war against Jugurtha, king of Numidia (r. 111–105 B.C.E.); it includes an ethnogeographical excursus on northern Africa (chapters 17–19), a passage that is typically accompanied in the manuscript tradition by a map that illustrates, in a schematic way, the location of many place-names in the text.

Sallust maps tend to be somewhat more detailed than the T-O maps found in many manuscript copies of Isidore's *Etymologies* (at the beginning of Book 14). Marcel Destombes (1964) distinguishes between Sallust maps that contain some twenty names and those with fifty or more; in either case, Sallust maps are remarkable among medieval *mappaemundi* for their range of coverage of Africa. The locations of chief cities, such as Rome, Carthage, Troy, and Jerusalem, are indicated by either legends or sketches of turreted fortifications and steepled churches. The Nile and Egypt are often shown in Asia—a geographical concept common in medieval sources—beyond "*Catabathmos*," the sloping plain east of Cyrene that Sallust regards as Africa's boundary (17.4).

Sallust maps are usually oriented to the east, although some examplars are oriented to the south (Paris, Bibliothèque Nationale MS Lat. 6088, fol. 33v) or the west (Paris, Bibliothèque Nationale, MS Lat.

6253, fol. 52v). Though Asia generally occupies half of the circle that depicts the earth's total landmass, some Sallust maps make Africa the largest continent (Paris, Bibliothèque Nationale MS Lat. 5751, fol. 18r).

Codices with Sallust maps—they are found in around one-third of the 200 extant manuscript copies of *De bello Jugurthino*—range in date from the ninth to the fourteenth centuries. Jerusalem's absence on one of the oldest exemplars (Leipzig, Universitätsbibliothek, Cod. 1607, fol. 1) led Konrad Miller to conclude that the Sallust map archetype had a classical, not Christian, origin.

BIBLIOGRAPHY
Destombes, Marcel, ed. *Mappemondes,* pp. 37–38, 65–73. See Gen. Bib.
Miller, Konrad. *Mappaemundi: Die ältesten Weltkarten.* 6 vols. Stuttgart: Roth, 1895–1898, vol. 3, pp.110–115.
Woodward, David. In Harley-Woodward, vol. 1, pp. 286–370, esp. 301, 334, 343–344, 346, 355, 357. See Gen. Bib.

*Roger T. Macfarlane*

SEE ALSO
Egypt; Isidore of Seville; Jerusalem; *Mappamundi;* Maps

# Samarkand

A city on the Silk Road in the valley of the Zeravshan.

Samarkand was known to the ancient Greek and Roman authors as Maracanda, the capital of Sogdiana, which had been conquered and destroyed by Alexander the Great in 329/328 B.C.E. By the early Middle Ages, the city had regained its prominence, as is testified by Chinese sources (in particular the account of the seventh-century traveler Hsuan-tsang). Conquered by the Arabs in 712, Samarkand was a major center of the world of Islam by the ninth century. At the same time, it served as the seat of a Christian Nestorian bishop (until at least the mid-eleventh century) and was the site of other religious communities, the most important of which was Jewish (according to Benjamin of Tudela, who visited Samarkand *c.* 1170, this community included many "wise and learned men"). Islamic geographical literature of the tenth century, when the city was ruled by the Iranian Samanid dynasty, includes detailed descriptions of its architecture, treasures, and population.

During the eleventh and twelfth centuries, Samarkand was ruled by members of the Turkic Muslim dynasty of Karakhanids; after 1089, the khâns of

Samarkand were nominated by the Seljuks. The Seljuk dominance ended with the appearance of a new power in the area, the partially sinicized nomadic horde of the Karakitai. In 1141, the Karakitai gurkhan Yeh-lu Ta-shih defeated Seljukid Sultan Sanjar and his Karakhanid vassal Mahmud Khân near Samarkand. Yeh-lu ta-shih later became one of the prototypes of the legendary Prester John (in whose *Letter* the name Samarkand appears). The Karakhanids continued to rule under Karakitai overlordship until 1212, when the city passed to Muhammad Khwarazmshah. His rule ended in 1220 with the destruction of the city by Chinggis Khân. Marco Polo's *Divisament dou monde* (*c.* 1298) includes a description of Samarkand under Mongol rule. The travel account by the Castilian envoy Ruy Gonzales de Clavijo (1403–1406) testifies to the new grandeur of Samarkand, which the city acquired after Tamerlane in 1369 had made Samarkand his capital and extended his empire from this point for nearly forty years.

BIBLIOGRAPHY
Barthold, W. *Turkestan Down to the Mongol Invasion.* London: Luzac, 1928. 4th edition. London: E.J.W. Gibb Memorial Trust, 1977.
Chekin, L.S. "Samarcha, City of Khazaria." *Central Asiatic Journal* 33 (1989): 8–35.
Knobloch, Edgar. *Beyond the Oxus.* London: Benn, 1972.
Muminov, I.M., ed. *Istoriia Samarkanda.* Vol. 1: *S drevneishikh vremen do Velikoi Oktiabr'skoi sotsialisticheskoi revoliutsii.* Tashkent: Fan, 1969.

*Leonid S. Chekin*

SEE ALSO
Benjamin of Tudela; Karakitai; Marco Polo; Mongol Army; Mongols; Nestorianism; Prester John; Seljuk Turks; Silk Roads; Tamerlane

# Sanudo, Marino [the Elder, also called Marino Sanudo Torsello] (*c.* 1270–*c.* 1343)

Propagandist, chronicler, cartographer.

Belonging to the San Severo branch of the illustrious Sanudo family, Venetians distinguished for their military, commercial, literary, and scientific achievements, Sanudo as a young man traveled as his father's business agent to Negroponte, Naxos, and other eastern ports. Later he frequented the courts at Palermo, where he became the protégé of Cardinal Richard Patroni of Siena, and at Rome. In 1304, back in Venice, he served

# S

in the war against neighboring Padua. The experience of residing in Acre (1285–1286) just before its fall had an important formative influence on him, and the desire for a new crusade, prevalent among his contemporaries, motivated the intense propagandist activities that occupied him for the rest of his life.

Sanudo wrote with the authority of personal experience: his descriptions of the Holy Land show a pragmatism and insight that reflect their author's extensive commercial and political dealings with various regions throughout the Mediterranean and even to the seas north of Europe. His monumental *Liber secretorum fidelium crucis* apparently underwent two earlier "drafts" before reaching its known form. Its first redaction, known as *Conditiones Terrae sanctae,* was begun in 1306 and presented to Pope Clement V in 1309. This unedited treatise proposed a blockade of land and sea routes as a means of cutting the economic power of the Egyptian sultan: goods from India could be shipped by other routes, products then being purchased in Egypt could be cultivated in Europe, and a Christian armada could guard Mediterranean ports.

Sanudo began expanding his *Conditiones* into a three-part work in 1312. After years occupied with continued commercial voyages that probably often included an unofficial diplomatic component, he presented the enlarged, second redaction to the Avignon pope John XXII in 1321 under the title *Opus Terra sanctae.* The new second "book" proposed the creation of a professional army to be paid for by the Church and supported by the Venetian navy. This plan proposed first to conquer Egypt—the real power preventing access to the Holy Land—in a land invasion with the help of Abyssinian Christians and Persian Mongols. The book is noteworthy for its detailed campaign plan (how to construct warships and war machines, what type of *condottiere* to employ, recruitment of sailors, numbers of troops, rations, payment, and the like). Sanudo also displays an extensive knowledge of waterways and topography. The third section of the *Opus* was a sweeping history of the Holy Land, based on Jacques de Vitry's *Historia Hierosolymitana,* but with many original comments.

The final version of the *Liber secretorum* was written in Avignon between 1321 and 1323. This is the best known of his works, perhaps because already in his day several manuscript versions were produced and disseminated to European heads of state. For instance, Brussels, Bibliothèque Royale MSS 9347–8 and 9404–5

were dedicated to Philip VI of France in 1332, and Oxford, Bodleian MS Tanner 190 was addressed to Robert of Boulogne, count of Auvergne. This book included illustrations of warfare and important maps of the world, the Near East, and Jerusalem probably drawn by Pietro Vesconte. The map of the Holy Land contains a grid with each square representing two leagues, an important aid for the military tactician.

Nearly forty of Sanudo's letters and memoranda survive and most have been published. He wrote to popes, cardinals, prelates, Italian rulers, the French king, and the Byzantine emperor encouraging the project of a new crusade. Like his contemporary, Dante Alighieri, he lamented the political division of the Italian peninsula and criticized the popes for fomenting discord within Christendom. He encouraged a holy war not only to free the Holy Land, but as an expedient to establishing peaceful relations among Christian princes.

From 1328 to 1333, Sanudo wrote a chronicle of Morea, a valuable source for understanding the Aegean lordships in the later thirteenth century. It survives today only in an Italian translation, *Istoria del regno di Romania.* In 1331 or 1332, he participated in treaty talks with Robert of Naples, and he was at Constantinople in 1334 continuing to encourage preparations for a crusade. He died in 1343 or shortly after.

## BIBLIOGRAPHY

Cerlini, Aldo. "Nuove lettere di Marino Sanudo il Vecchio." *La Bibliofilìa* 42 (1940): 321–359.

Dilke, Oswald and Margaret. "Mapping a Crusade." *History Today* 39.8 (1989): 31–35.

Laiou, A. "Marino Sanudo Torsello, Byzantium and the Turks: The Background to the Anti-Turkish League of 1332–1334." *Speculum* 45 (1970): 374–392.

Sanudo, Marino. *Liber secretorum fidelium crucis super Terrae Sanctae recuperatione et conservatione.* Hanover: Typis Wechelianis, 1611. Facsimile printed by Jerusalem: Massada, 1972.

———. *"Istoria del regno di Romania sive regno di Morea."* In Carl Hopf, ed., *Chroniques greco-romanes inedites ou peu connues.* Berlin: Weidmann, 1873; rpt. 1966, pp. 99–170.

*Gloria Allaire*

## SEE ALSO

Acre; Constantinople; Dante Alighieri ; Diplomacy; Egypt; Holy Land; India; Jacques de Vitry; Jerusalem; Measurement of Distances; Mediterranean Sea; Mongols; Rome as a Pilgrimage Site; Venice; Vesconte, Pietro/Perrino

## Scandinavian Trade
*See* Stones and Timber, Scandinavian Trade in

## Scandinavian World Maps
Among the approximately 8,000 medieval Icelandic manuscripts that have been preserved, maps play only a minor role: three manuscripts contain between them a total of five *mappaemundi* (plus four postmedieval copies). In addition to these western Scandinavian maps, a twelfth-century map, probably originating at Lund (Sweden) is known. This scarcity of maps does not, however, signify a lack of interest in geographical knowledge among medieval Scandinavians. Prose texts testify rather to the opposite: in Icelandic manuscripts alone, there are four different redactions of more or less complete cosmographies, which survive in twenty-five manuscript copies. In addition, there are even more texts of a less detailed geographical nature, as well as itineraries from Iceland, Norway, Sweden, and Denmark. The relative paucity of maps must therefore be attributed to other factors, the most important of which may be the limited function of *mappaemundi*, which served primarily to give either a rough view of the round earth's landmass and its division into three continents, or a schematic view of the world's climatic zones.

Three of the five medieval Icelandic *mappaemundi* (plus three of the later copies) are zone—or climate—maps, showing the division of the earth into two uninhabitable frigid polar zones, an uninhabitable hot equatorial zone, and two habitable temperate zones in between, the southernmost of which is labeled "southern inhabitable zone." Three of the maps, namely the closely related copies in the manuscripts Copenhagen Arnamagnaean Collection AM 736 I, 4to, 1v (early fourteenth century, copy in Copenhagen Kongelige Bibliotek Ny Kongelige Samling NkS 359, 4to, p. 15, eighteenth century) and AM 732b, 4to, 3r (early fourteenth century), divide the earth's northern habitable region into three continents (Asia, Europe, and Africa), while a small map in Copenhagen Kongelige Bibliotek, Gamle Kongelige Samling MS GkS 1812, 4to, 11v (thirteenth century; copy in AM 252, fol. 59v, *c.* 1700), shows no such division of the Northern Hemisphere. This latter map is a copy of similar maps in William of Conches's cosmographical treatise, *De philosophia mundi* (written *c.* 1130), from which the text is adapted (the text is incorrectly attributed to Bede in the manuscripts).

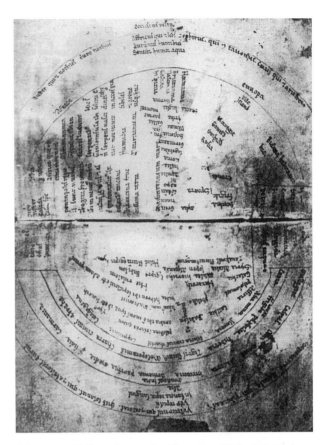

*Mappamundi.* Copenhagen, Det Kongelige Bibliothek Gml. Kgl. Sml. 1812, fols. 5v-6r., 1250. Courtesy Det Kongelige Bibliothek.

One of the three maps to be found in a medieval Icelandic computistic-cosmographic miscellany, GkS 1812, 4to, is a very simple T-O map (see Maps) (6v; copy in AM 252, fol. 58r), which gives only the names of three continents; this *mappamundi* is actually only the very center of a cosmological diagram that also shows cardinal directions, winds, seasons, the ages of man, and the months of the year with accompanying zodiacal signs.

Far more interesting is another T-O map in the same manuscript, covering a double page (5v–6r; copy in AM 252, fol, 62r) and containing well over 100 names, about seventy of which are names of countries, almost all in Latin. This tendency toward chorography (lists of countries) shows some similarity with the Old Norse prose cosmographies mentioned earlier, although there is no clear link between this map and any prose redaction. Compared with continental *mappaemundi*, the map contains an unusually detailed chorography of the Scandinavian countries: "Tile" (for Thule), "Island," "Norvegie," "Gautland," "Sviþiod," "Biarmar habitavit

# S

hic," even "Rusia" and "Kio" (Kiev), and it also specifically identifies monstrous races that are found on much larger *mappaemundi*: "Monstras india" are located at the map's eastern extreme, while the legend "Getulia where children play with serpents in Africa" is a garbled version of the legend of the Getuli (who expose the newborn to snakes to test their legitimacy). Unlike continental *mappaemundi* of similar detail, there are no images on this map, nor are the continents even demarcated, making this a rather prosaic exemplar.

The map from Lund, now Berlin Ms. Theol. lat.149, fol. 27r, is the oldest surviving Scandinavian world map. It is a T-O map in the Sallust map tradition. Together with rota-style representations of the seven planets, it fills one page (with no text) in a copy of the Latin *Annales Colbacenses* (now Berlin, Staatsbibliothek Preusischer Kulturbesitz). The author, who writes in a German hand, includes in Europe placenames only for Rome, Bari, Achaia, Constantinopole, Greece, Cologne, England, "Dacia," and "Suithia," which points to his classical learning on the one hand, and to the close connections among Lund, Cologne, and England on the other hand. This map also lacks any iconography beyond the basic T-O scheme.

The so-called Vinland map continues to arouse controversy. The map's layout and contents contradict all other medieval *mappaemundi,* especially in showing Greenland as an island: Scandinavian maps up to the seventeenth century and all medieval prose texts testify to the belief that Greenland was linked both to Siberia in the east and Vinland in the west. Quite apart from the depiction of Greenland as an island—a startlingly modern idea—the map's northern orientation, the lack of a T-O scheme, and the resulting positioning of continents all make it extremely unlikely that the Vinland map is an example of medieval Scandinavian cartography.

## BIBLIOGRAPHY

Mel'nikova, Elena A. *Drevneskandinavskie geograficeskie socinenija: Teksty, perevod, commentariij.* Moscow: Nauka, 1986.

Simek, Rudolf. *Altnordische Kosmographie: Weltbild und Weltbeschreibung in Norwegen und Island vom 12. zum 14. Jahrhundert.* Berlin and New York: DeGruyter, 1990.

———. "Skandinavische Mappae Mundi in der europäischen Tradition." In *Ein Weltbild vor Columbus: Die Ebstorfer Weltkarte: Interdisziplinäres Kolloquium 1988.* Ed. Hartmut Kugler with Eckhard Michael. Weinheim: VCH, Acta humaniora, 1991, pp. 167–184.

*Rudolf Simek*

SEE ALSO

Antipodes; Bede; Climate; Edges of the World; Iceland; *Mappamundi;* Maps; *Oikumene;* Sallust Maps; *Terra Incognita;* Viking Discoveries and Settlements; Vinland Map

## Schiltberger, Johann (*c.* 1381–1430)

Bavarian soldier captured at the battle of Nicopolis (1396), who spent more than thirty years as a slave of Eastern potentates; after his escape and return to Europe, he wrote an account of his experiences that excited attention a century after his death.

As a fifteen-year-old squire from Freising, Schiltberger accompanied his lord, Leinhart Reichhartinger, on a crusade against the Turks. Wounded and captured when forces led by the sultan Bajazet I (r. 1389–1403) surprised—and decimated—the crusading army as it attempted to cross the Danube at Nicopolis (September 26, 1396), he was spared from the massacre of some 3,000 prisoners ordered by Bajazet. Led to Bursa (Brusa), he was put into the service of the sultan as a foot courier and took part in the campaign at Karaman. After Schiltberger failed in an attempt to escape, Bajazet sent him to Egypt in an entourage that he put at the disposition of Sultan an-Nasir-ud-Dīn Faraj (r. 1399–1405). When Bajazet was himself conquered by Tamerlane (1402), Schiltberger became Tamerlane's slave and followed him to Samarkand. Over the next twenty-five years, Schiltberger served a series of local rulers who were kin to, or vassals of, Tamerlane or succeeding khâns: he passed into the control of Tamerlane's son Shāhrukh, then his brother Miranshāh (who perhaps took the young squire to Baghdad), Miranshāh's son Abū Bakr, and Tzeggra (a Mongol prince disputing his inheritance in the Golden Horde). Tzeggra took him as far as Siberia (1415–1416); after Tzeggra's death, a final master led him to Kaffa (Feodosiya) in the Crimea and to Georgia.

Discovering how near he was to the Black Sea, Schiltberger fled with five of his companions. They identified themselves as Christians to the captain of a ship, and they were delivered finally to Constantinople. Schiltberger was received by the emperor and the patriarch; he returned to Freising, by way of Poland, in 1428. He seems to have ended his life in the service of the duke of Austria, whose guard he commanded.

Schiltberger's experience is thus that of a soldier-slave who served Eastern potentates. Although there would certainly have been personal advantages had he renounced his faith, he never appears to have done so, and he carefully noted his contacts with all the Christians he encountered. No one knows exactly the conditions under which he composed the account of his adventures, which are written in a Bavarian dialect; perhaps he dictated them. His narrative style and structure are simple, but he displays considerable knowledge of social and political conditions in the East that were unfamiliar to his contemporaries. He followed his account with a brief description of the countries he had seen, though sometimes only superficially; he regretted this, for example, in the case of Jerusalem. In addition to these geographical descriptions, he also offered a tableau of the morals and beliefs of Greeks, Muslims, and Armenians; occasionally, he used other written sources, as, for example, in his account of the Monastery of St. Catherine in the Sinai, which is heavily dependent on *The Book of John Mandeville,* probably in a German translation. His narrative thus takes its place among the "descriptions of the world" so appreciated in the Middle Ages, but it is his personal experience that renders it so valuable. Schiltberger's book survives in four fifteenth-century manuscripts and was frequently printed during the sixteenth and seventeenth centuries.

**BIBLIOGRAPHY**
Halm, Christian, ed. *Deutsche Reiseberichte.* Vol. 1 of *Europäische Reiseberichte des späten Mittelalters: Eine analystiche Bibliographie.* Gen. ed. W. Paravicini. Frankfurt am Main: Lang, 1994, pp. 56–62.
Langmantel, Valentin, ed. *Hans Schiltbergers Reisebuch.* Bibliothek des Literarischen Vereins in Stuttgart 172. Tübingen, 1885.
Telfer, J. Buchan, trans. *The Bondage and Travels of Johann Schiltberger, a Native of Bavaria, in Europe, Asia and Africa 1396–1427.* Hakluyt Society, 1st series, 59 (o.s.). London: Hakluyt Society, 1879.

*Jean Richard*

**SEE ALSO**
Armenia; Baghdad; Catherine in the Sinai, Monastery of St.; Constantinople; Egypt; Golden Horde; *Mandeville's Travels;* Mongols; Ottoman Turks; Poland; Samarkand; Tamerlane

## Scholarship on Medieval European Geography and Travel

By the late 1400s, scholarly attention was already being devoted to geographical treatises and travel books written during the previous several centuries. The printing press not only revolutionized cartographic science by enabling Ptolemy's *Geography* to circulate widely—editions were printed in 1475 (without maps), 1477, 1478, 1482 (twice, each one with updated "modern maps" [*modernae tabulae*]), 1486, and 1490—but before 1500 it also brought to a larger audience more traditional geographical ideas in works such as Isidore of Seville's *Etymologies* (the edition of 1472 contains the first map printed in Europe, a simple T-O design [see Maps]), John of Sacrobosco's *Tractatus de sphaera,* Vincent of Beauvais's *Speculum historiale,* Pierre d'Ailly's *Imago mundi,* and travel-related books by (or attributed to) Burchard of Mount Sion, Ludolph of Suchem, John Mandeville, Marco Polo, and Johannes Witte de Hese.

Humanists of the day turned their attention to such works, applying methodologies aimed at recovering more "original" texts and assembling thematically linked material in collections (for example, the *Hodoeporica* [1502] of Conrad Celtes [1459–1508], himself subject to wanderlust). During the 1550s, the Venetian diplomat Giambattista Ramusio (1485–1557) released his monumental anthology, *Delle navigationi et viaggi,* three volumes of accounts of journeys of discovery that were organized geographically: the first and third (1550, 1556) focus on recent Portuguese and Spanish exploration in Africa/Southeast Asia and the "West Indies," respectively; the second (misdated 1559) turns to older books on northeast Asia, including those by Marco Polo and Hetoum, from around 1300. Although Polo's *Divisament dou monde* had been printed several times before 1500, Ramusio's Italian version includes passages not found in any known manuscript—he claimed to have had access to a Latin one "of marvelous antiquity"—but they are now among the more famous elements of the Polo story, and thus this edition may be said to have established the book within the canon of Western travel literature.

Richard Hakluyt (1552?–1616) published his *Principall Navigations, Voiages, and Discoveries of the English Nation* in 1589 to promote geographical knowledge as well as to garner support for English commercial and colonial interests. Many English travelers—beginning with Helena, mother of Constantine (c. 255–c. 330)—receive the equivalent of encyclopedia entries here, but one "primary source" included in its entirety is *The Book of John Mandeville* (entitled *Liber Johannis Mandevil*). This is the single text Hakluyt printed in Latin,

# S

which may reflect an abandoned plan to produce a more scholarly work, rather than a deliberate attempt to keep sailors from getting wrongheaded ideas from it, as has been argued. When Hakluyt issued a second, three-volume edition (1598–1600)—with the telling insertion of *Traffiques* as the third element in the title's series of nouns—he omitted Mandeville's *Liber,* but it returned in abbreviated form in *Hakluytus Posthumus, or Purchas His Pilgrimes* (1625), by Hakluyt's anointed successor, Samuel Purchas (1577?–1626), who was somewhat more interested in theology than commerce, and whose title page depicts Mandeville with King Solomon and Columbus as avatars of men eager to acquire knowledge about the world.

Quite different concerns motivated other scholars. Heinrich Canisius, a professor at the University of Ingolstadt, printed for the first time the pilgrimage narrative of William of Boldensele (1336), along with an account of Frederick I Barbarossa's exploits on the Third Crusade (1189–1190), in his five-volume *Antiqvae Lectionis* (1601–1604), a collection of texts assembled specifically to counter the "discord" created by Protestant "imposters and deceivers." Prompted more by meticulousness than polemics, the seventeenth-century Franciscan Francesco Quaresmius searched archives in Jerusalem for old manuscripts recording pilgrimage indulgences in his attempt to determine the precise spiritual value of visits to Holy Land shrines.

The treatment of maps as artifacts can be traced to the edition of Ptolemy's *Geography* printed at Strasbourg in 1513; in the atlas section *tabulae antiquae,* drawn according to the coordinates given in the second-century text, were grouped separately from *tabulae modernae,* which displayed more current geographical knowledge. In 1598, Markus Welser produced an engraving of a twelfth- or early-thirteenth-century road map—evidently a copy of a fourth-century original—that had belonged to Konrad Peutinger (now called the Peutinger Table); Welser's work is the first known facsimile of an ancient map made in Europe. And yet the extraordinary amount of new geographical knowledge and the revolution in cartographical style in late-fifteenth-century Europe constituted so profound a shift in perspective that medieval treatises and maps were not even regarded as "precursors"; although some were collected, protected, and even catalogued, they were seldom studied for their own merits. In 1713, Johann Gottfried Gregorii observed in his *Curieuse Gedancken von den vornehmsten und accuratesten alt-*

*und neuen Land-Charten* that old maps were becoming as rare as antique coins in Germany, but as his title suggests, they were valued as curiosities rather than as sources of information. The earliest known reference to the Hereford map is a telling single phrase in Thomas Dingley's description of Hereford Cathedral in his *History from Marble* (c. 1682): "a map of ye world drawn on vellum by a monk."

Travel reports fared similarly. In his *Traicté de la Navigation* (1629), Pierre Bergeron produced one of the first serious attempts to analyze European journey narratives written between around 1100 and his own day, but he could not resist being dismissive of such fourteenth-century figures as Odoric of Pordenone, John Mandeville, and Johannes Witte de Hese for their failure to distinguish between what they heard and what they personally observed, as a result filling their books with the stuff of fable, "which is a general problem with everyone from that period." More dispassionate and codicologically aware—and less condescending—readings of medieval travel books make up the insightful two-volume *Litteratur der älteren Reisebeschreibungen* (1807–1810), by Johann Beckmann, a professor of economics at the University of Göttingen.

The nineteenth century witnessed the inauguration of geography as a discrete subject for serious study. National geographic societies were established in France (1821 [*Société de géographie de Paris,* the world's oldest such organization in continuous existence]), Germany (1828), Great Britain (1830), Russia (1845), the United States (1851), Austria-Hungary (1856), Italy (1867), the Netherlands (1873), Portugal (1875), Romania (1875), Belgium (1876), Denmark (1876), Spain (1876), Sweden (1877), Finland (1888), and Norway (1889). Formal instruction in the subject began around the same time with the establishment of university chairs (or the equivalent) in geography in the United States (1854, at the College of New Jersey [Princeton]), Italy (1859), Norway (1871), the Netherlands (1874), Denmark (1883), and Sweden (1895). The British Museum's map collections became a separate administrative unit of the institution in 1844. (Outside Europe, a leader in the acquisition and dissemination of such knowledge was Egypt, which had a national geographical society and a college curriculum in geography by 1875.)

Unsurprisingly, geography's new status altered the way scholars evaluated earlier work on it and related disciplines. In a letter written in 1839, the Portuguese scholar Manuel Francisco de Barros e Sousa, second viscount of Santarém (1791–1856), coined the word "cartography" to identify the study of *early* maps, reflecting a need for language with which to develop a new science. Two years later he published the first edition of his *Atlas,* which, while not the earliest collection of medieval maps in facsimile, remains a milestone because of the methodology Santarém employed in arriving at a chronological arrangement of his subject. His contemporaries also made significant contributions to the field, especially Edme-François Jomard (1777–1862), who headed the map department created in the Bibliothèque Impériale in 1828, and who published a medieval atlas of his own in serial form between 1842 and 1862; and Joachim Lelewel (1786–1861), the author of the first modern history of medieval geography (1852–1857), a work that gave considerable attention to Arab-Islamic contributions. Santarém was superseded by Konrad Miller (1866–1944), whose six-volume *Mappaemundi* (1895–1898) included transcriptions of map legends and benefited from improvements in printing methods.

Not all scholars were so enthusiastic about medieval cartography as a science. Oxford's University Lecturer in the History of Geography and in Historical Geography, Charles Raymond Beazley (1858–1951), in his magisterial, three-volume, 1,827-page, *Dawn of Modern Geography* (1897–1906), wrote that "a bare allusion to the monstrosities of *Hereford* and *Ebstorf* should suffice," and then he dispatched two of the more detailed cartographic achievements of the Middle Ages with a single sentence. Michael Corbet Andrews, in 1926, agreed: "[M]edieval *mappaemundi* have no place in the development of the modern map, upon which they exercised no influence; they seldom represent the best contemporary geographical knowledge; the original material is not easily accessible, nor is there a sufficient number of accurate reproductions." Nevertheless, Andrews contributed greatly to the establishment of a taxonomy for categorizing *mappaemundi* (he knew of 600), drawing on the classification system of Théophile Simar (1912) and influencing that of Marcel Destombes in his *Mappemondes A.D. 1200–1500* (1964), a catalogue that enumerated some 1,100 surviving world maps in manuscripts (it was part of a proposal, announced in 1949, to account for *all* medieval maps, but volumes covering nautical charts and local maps never appeared). Simar's taxonomy was also adopted by

John Kirtland Wright, librarian of the American Geographical Society, in his *Geographical Lore of the Time of the Crusades* (1925), a sweeping study of medieval Arabic and European political and physical geography that, as a digest of the subject, is as unsurpassed as is Pierre Duhem's ten-volume *Le système du monde* (1913–1959) on the development and dissemination of cosmological ideas.

Andrews's system has been revised but not fundamentally challenged in important late-twentieth-century contributions to the study of medieval cartography, in particular those of Jörg-Geerd Arentzen (1984), who focused on the relationship between a map's text and image; and David Woodward (1987), whose "Medieval *Mappaemundi*" is a succinct but probing analysis of the cultural milieu, intellectual character, and technical achievements of world maps before 1500, part of an ambitious multivolume *History of Cartography* project announced in 1983 by Woodward and J. Brian Harley (1932–1991). Between 1970 and 1990, the field was further expanded by such scholars as Anna-Dorothee von den Brincken (on cartographical ideologies and correspondences), Tony Campbell (on portolan charts and early printed maps), Patrick Gautier-Dalché (meticulous editions of geographical works, with exceptional commentary), P.D.A. Harvey (on local and world maps), and Rudolf Simek (on medieval, especially Scandinavian, cosmology).

Nineteenth- and twentieth-century scholarship on pilgrimage accounts and other travel narratives followed a rather similar route, producing editions, formulating taxonomies, and gradually bringing such texts increased attention and an enhanced reputation. In 1890, Reinhold Röhricht published an invaluable and still reliable census of manuscripts and early printed editions of Jerusalem pilgrimage accounts. Nevertheless, some of these works have never been edited, while a good many others are available only in editions from the nineteenth century that were based on whatever manuscript(s) might have been available. Surprisingly few texts have been produced in critical editions that account for all identified exemplars. (An exception is the collection of thirteenth- and fourteenth-century reports by Franciscans about East Asia produced by Anastasius van den Wyngaert[1929]). Most editors have resisted intrusive interpretation, an exception being the Belgian scholar Paul Hamelius's presentation of the Middle English Cotton Version of what he called *Mandeville's Travels* (1919–1923), with notes portraying the author as a

# S

clumsy plagiarist and antipapal conspirator; it was published by the Early English Text Society, which has lent the quirky edition an august authority for decades.

The nineteenth-century traveler and polymath Sir Henry Yule had a quite different effect on the objects of his attention: dedicated to the essential veracity of works by, or attributed to, Marco Polo (*c.* 1298), Odoric of Pordenone, Jordan of Sévérac (both *c.* 1330), and others, Yule brought to them unusual archaeological, geographical, historical, and linguistic expertise, and hence scholarly weight. (Polo's book received more academic attention following Luigi Foscolo Benedetto's elaborate critical edition of the French original [1928], a two-volume study of alternative readings from many early versions of the work by A.C. Moule and Paul Pelliot [1938], and background studies by Leonardo Olschki [1943, 1960].) English translations commissioned during the late 1800s by the Palestine Pilgrims' Text Society, although seldom based on critical editions and now quite dated, introduced a wider audience to medieval pilgrimage narratives; indeed, a few fascinating, observant, literate works not included in any of the society's volumes—such as those by Jacopo of Verona (*c.* 1335) and William of Boldensele (1336)—are sometimes overlooked in the scholarly literature.

By the late twentieth century, some scholars had turned their attention to determining if medieval travel literature might be said to constitute a literary genre, and if so what features characterize it. Taxonomies—or at least some attempt to categorize existing texts and themes—were advanced by Gerd Tellenbach (1977), Jean Richard (1981), Mary B. Campbell (1988), and Michèle Guéret-Laferté (1994), among others. Campbell and Guéret-Laferté identified rhetorical tropes and strategies in discrete groups of travel books; Christiane Deluz (1988) adopted a similar approach to a single text (and its sources): *The Book of John Mandeville.* In the learned study *Writing East* (1997), Iain Macleod Higgins analyzed the *Book* as an example of sophisticated "medieval multitextuality" by tracing how its author transformed the words and ideologies of many sources and how its translators and scribes continually reformed it.

In fields related to medieval geography and travel, the work of Felipe Fernández-Armesto (1987) and J.R.S. Phillips (1988) on European expansion, as well as Rudolf Wittkower (1942) and John Block Friedman (1981, 2000) on the visual and textual representation of non-Europeans (particularly of the "monstrous races") deserves particular mention.

Despite major contributions to medieval geography/cartography and travel during the later 1900s, many texts—descriptions of the world, maps, accounts of pilgrimages and other journeys—remain unedited, incompletely edited, ignored, or even unknown. There is ample reason to expect scholars to make discoveries and to challenge assumptions in all these areas for many years to come.

## BIBLIOGRAPHY

Andrews, Michael Corbet. "The Study and Classification of Medieval Mappae Mundi." *Archaeologica* 75 (1925–1926): 61–76.

Beckmann, Johann. *Litteratur der älteren Reisebeschreibungen.* 4 vols. in 2. Göttingen: Röwer, 1807–1810.

Bergeron, Pierre de. *Traicté de la Navigation et des voyages des descovverte & conqueste modernes.* Paris: I. de Heuqueville et M. Soly, 1629.

Campbell, Tony. *Early Maps.* New York: Abbeville Press, 1981.

Dingley, Thomas. *History from Marble Compiled in the Reign of Charles II by Thomas Dingley, gent.* Intro. John Gough Nichols. Camden Society, 94, 97. Westminster: Camden Society, 1867–1868; rpt. New York: Johnson, 1968, 1:clx, 78.

Dunbar, Gary, ed. *Modern Geography: An Encyclopedic Survey.* Garland Reference Library of Humanities 1197. New York and London: Garland, 1991.

Gregorii, Johann Gottfried. *Curieuse Gedancken von den vornehmsten und accuratesten alt- und neuen Land-Charten.* Frankfurt and Leipzig: Ritscheln, 1713.

Harley-Woodward, *The History of Cartography.* Vol. 1, especially Harley, "The Map and the Development of the History of Cartography" (pp. 1–42); Woodward, "Medieval *Mappaemundi*" (pp. 286–370). See Gen. Bib.

Harvey, P.D.A. "Local and Regional Cartography in Medieval Europe." In Harley-Woodward, pp. 464–501. See Gen. Bib.

Milanesi, Marica. "Giovanni Battista Ramusios Sammlung von Reiseberichten des Entdeckungszeitalters 'Delle Navigationi e Viaggi' (1550–1559) neu betrachtet." In *Reiseberichte als Quellen europäischer Kulturgeschichte.* Ed. Antoni Maczak and Hans Jürgen Teuteberg. Wolfenbütteler Forschungen 21. Wolfenbüttel: Herzog August Bibliothek, 1982, pp. 33–44.

*Scott D. Westrem*

Ludolf of Suchem; *Mandeville's Travels; Mappamundi;* Maps; Marco Polo; Monstrosity, Geographical; Odoric of Pordenone; Peutinger Table; Pilgrimage, Christian; Ptolemy; Sacrobosco, John of; Witte de Hese, Johannes; Spain and Portugal; Travel Writing in Europe and the Mediterranean Regions; Vincent of Beauvais

## Scythia

In medieval geography, a region in the northeast extreme of the known world; in modern terms it would correspond to the steppe of Eurasia (mainly Inner Asia and the areas north of the Black Sea).

The Scythians, a nomadic people who spoke an Iranian language, were known to Mediterranean societies from the seventh century B.C.E., when their expansion reached as far as Palestine. Their domination of the Eurasian steppe led to the designation of this entire region as "Scythia" in ancient Greek sources. Scythian decline in the third century B.C.E. was hastened by the rise of the Sarmatians, another group of Iranian nomads. The last Scythian stronghold, in the Crimea, survived until the second half of the third century C.E., when it was destroyed by the Goths, but the traditional nomenclature persisted. In the literature of the Middle Ages, the name "Scythians" was widely applied to ethnically and temporally unrelated nomadic groups, including Hungarians and Mongols. The ethnographic descriptions of these later peoples were often modeled on ancient representations of the Scythians, who had been alternatively stereotyped as "fierce barbarians" and "noble savages."

Aside from their alleged barbarism, the Scythians were also known to the medieval West for being an exceedingly ancient people ("more ancient than the Egyptians"); as a result, some Europeans regarded the Scythians as a "prestigious" people, and tried to establish genealogical links with them. Thus, the *Declaration of Arbroath,* the letter sent by the barons of Scotland to Pope John XXII on April 6, 1320, claims that the Scots came "de Maiori Schithia"—from Greater Scythia. This declaration followed the tradition of the ninth-century *Historia Brittonum,* which claimed Scythian origins for the Irish.

The various ways in which "Scythia" and "Scythians" were perceived in ancient sources played an important role in their treatment by geographers and cartographers in the Christian and Muslim world. Arab geographers described "Inner Scythia" (the land of the Turkic peoples) using Ptolemy's *Geographia.* For the Byzantines, the name *Scythians* was a generic term that they applied to any barbarous peoples north of the empire, including Turkic nomads and the Rus'. The East Slavic *Primary Chronicle* understood the term *Velikaia Skif* (Great Scythia) as the Greek generic name for eastern European tribes united by Rus', and also identified the Scythians with the Khazars. Scandinavian geographers translated Latin *Scythia* as "Great Sweden," and understood it to be the mythical homeland of the Scandinavians.

More generally in the medieval West, Scythia was broadly understood to be coterminous both with "Germania" in the west and with "India" (also broadly conceived) in the southeast. In the east and north it is washed by the great Sea-Ocean. In the theoretical geography of antiquity and the Middle Ages, it was a commonplace to compare the Scythians to Egyptians or Ethiopians, as inhabitants of respectively northern and southern latitudes. To subdivide the vast territories generally considered to be Scythian, geographers in the medieval West singled out Lower Scythia ("Scythia inferior"), the easternmost province of Europe, which stretched between the Tanais (Don) and the Danube rivers (the Don formed the border between Europe and Asia in medieval geography). In addition, the Roman Empire, in the early fourth century, included "Scythia minor" as one of its provinces, located south of the Danube estuary. Perhaps by analogy with this "minor Scythia," some early medieval authors (including Jordanes in the mid-sixth century) defined the expanse of "great" Scythia as "Scythia magna" or "Scythia maior."

**BIBLIOGRAPHY**

Aalto, Pentti, and Tuomo Pekkanen. *Latin Sources on North-Eastern Eurasia.* 2 vols. Wiesbaden: Harrassowitz, 1975–1980.

Carile, Antonio. "Byzantine Political Ideology and the Rus' in the Tenth–Twelfth Centuries." *Harvard Ukrainian Studies* 12/13 (1988–1989): 400–413.

Chekin, L.S. "Lower Scythia in Western European Geographical Tradition at the Time of the Crusades." *Harvard Ukrainian Studies* 15 (1991): 289–339.

*Leonid S. Chekin*

**SEE ALSO**

Cartography, Arabic; Ethiopians; Hungary; India; Inner Asian Trade; Inner Asian Travel; *Mare Oceanum;* Mongols; Nomadism and Pastoralism; Ptolemy; Russia and Rus'

## Second Crusade

*See* Crusades, First, Second, and Third

# S

## Secret History of the Mongols, The

A complicated thirteenth-century literary text, entitled *Yuan Chao Bi Shi* in Chinese and *Monggol-un niuca tobca'an* in Mongol, that is an important primary source about the Mongols, relating their history and traditions from their legendary beginnings to the reign of Ögödei. Its title, *Secret History*, reflects the fact that it was written by Mongols, for Mongols, and not intended for circulation in the outside world. It is the only text in which members of a steppe nomad culture describe their own activities and culture.

The *Secret History* is the main source for the early life of Temujin, known more commonly by his title, Chinggis Khân. Without it, little would be known about him or the struggles among the Mongolic tribes during the last half of the twelfth century. Continuous tribal warfare led to Chinggis's emergence as the most powerful leader in the eastern steppes. At the great *quriltai*, or grand assembly, of 1206, the Mongolic people became a tribal nation, the Mongols, and Temujin was given the title Chinggis Khân, "Universal Emperor."

The earliest copy of the *Secret History* that survives is a fourteenth-century Chinese transliteration of the original: Chinese characters are used to express the sounds of Mongol words rather than to translate their meaning into another language. It is accompanied by an abridged Chinese translation. The text is, thus, very awkward and difficult, requiring knowledge of both languages. Many words have obscure meanings or origins, reflecting the fact that the Mongol written language was in its infancy when this work was written.

Scholars disagree on whether the language of the original was Chinese or Mongolian or Uighur, since Mongols used Uighur scribes during this era. It was written in the "year of the rat," which fell most likely between Chinggis's death in 1227 and 1264, when Khubilai became the great khân. The history of how the text was transmitted through the centuries is extremely complicated.

The first five chapters of the *Secret History*, dealing with Temujin's early life, are written in epic form. The remainder of the work is a narrative history of the struggles among the Mongolic tribes and Temujin's emergence as their primary leader, up to the time of his successor, Ögödei. The epic qualities of his early life, such as his presumed supernatural ancestors—the Blue Wolf, Fallow Doe, and "Duwa Soqor," described as a cyclops with great vision and foresight—enhance the colorful aspects of Temujin's life but make it difficult to distinguish factual history and imaginative literature.

For instance, Temujin's birth holding a blood clot in his hand as a portent of greatness fits the genre of epic. References to his having "a fire in his eyes and a light in his face" cast the text in a similar vein. However, his difficulties with his father's *anda* ("sworn brother"), To'oril, and his own *anda*, Jamuqa, are harder to assess, since their description partakes of both epic and historic qualities; they are also common to tribal conflicts of that era.

The *Secret History* probably originated as an oral account of how Temujin conquered the other tribes, forged them into a nation, and, as Chinggis Khân, embarked on a religious quest to bring universal peace through world conquest. Since it was Chinggis who ordered the creation of a written Mongol language, the oral tradition was probably written down fairly early in Ögödei's reign.

Of equal significance, from a historical standpoint, are details of clan and tribal structures, and social and other Mongol customs depicted in the *Secret History*. Without it, little would be known about the customs of the Mongolic peoples during the late twelfth century. Because of its textual difficulties, translations of the *Secret History* are few and have involved laborious effort. For many years, the only complete Western translation was in German (Haenisch), with partial translations in French (Pelliot) and Russian (Kozin). Waley and Sun's English translation renders only the Chinese text. A full English translation by Cleaves provides more complete insight into this work and understanding of its importance.

*Hugh D. Walker*

**BIBLIOGRAPHY**

Cleaves, Francis Woodman. *The Secret History of the Mongols.* Cambridge, MA, and London: Harvard UP, 1982.

Haenisch, Erich. *Die Geheime Geschichte der Mongolen.* Leipzig: Harrassowitz, 1941.

Hung, William. "The Transmission of the Book Known as 'The Secret History of the Mongols.'" *Harvard Journal of Asian Studies.* 14. 3,4 (1951): 433–492.

Pao, Kuo-yi. *Studies on the Secret History of the Mongols.* Bloomington: Indiana UP, 1965.

**SEE ALSO**

Mongols; Yuan Dynasty

### Secretz de la Nature [Merveilles du Monde], Les

A geographical work treating fifty-six real and imagined countries, islands, or vague regions, including discussion of actual and mythical peoples of the world, arranged alphabetically and existing in four illustrated manuscripts and several printed editions. The text is a *compilatio* of antique material from Pliny and Solinus as well as of lore from later writers such as Gervase of Tilbury and Odoric of Pordenone. Jean du Vignay and Harent of Antioch were once mentioned as possible authors, but in fact the work is a translation into French of Pierre Bersuire's (d. 1363) *Reductorium Morale*, Book XIV. Unlike *The Book of John Mandeville* with its Eastern emphasis, the *Secretz* concentrates as much on Europe as on Asia and rather more on peoples like the Frisians than on mythical groups like Gog and Magog.

Accurate and detailed accounts of material culture such as churches and cathedrals, agricultural practices, and the origins of writing are combined with legends of cannibals, Amazons, and sciopods, silk-bearing trees, strange stones, and odd spices. Christian miracles exist alongside pagan idols and religious practices.

The earliest manuscript of *Les Secretz* includes an additional seventeen chapters treating human wonders, prodigies, and monstrosities, and wonders relating to human ingenuity. The text is accompanied by a series of "menu pictures" illustrating each entry, where every wonder or feature of interest mentioned in that region appears within the picture space to guide the reader in conceptualizing the place. Though the texts are the same in each of the earlier manuscripts, the illustrations are simplified in the last surviving codex. Such menus then serve as mnemonic "maps" of the culture and nation in a series of quickly graspable stereotypes, as well as providing the armchair pilgrim traveler with information on names of churches especially hospitable or worth visiting.

The manuscripts of *Les Secretz* appear to derive from an archetype composed in France about the end of the fourteenth century. The first of these manuscripts in order of probable production is Paris, Bibliothèque Nationale MS fr. 1377–1379, a codex whose colophon notes that it was written for a Master Renaud, a merchant of Bourges, in March of 1427. Its miniatures have been attributed to the Master of Marguerite d'Orléans.

Next in age to the Renaud volume is a codex now owned by the Charnacé family of Paris. The book is illustrated by the Master of the Geneva Boccaccio, active in 1460. Charles Sterling has associated this master with the painter Colin d'Amiens, connected with the Loire region and perhaps more specifically with Angers. Closely related in style and age to the Charnacé volume is New York, Pierpont Morgan Library MS M. 461, which differs from the other manuscripts in including an author's preface, and a rather sumptuous but generic author portrait of a cleric on folio 3. It is also illustrated by Colin D'Amiens. The last known manuscript is Paris, Bibliothèque Nationale MS fr. 22971, dating from about 1480. Recently, this manuscript has been identified as the production of Robinet Testard, who worked for Charles d'Angoulême and his wife, Louise de Savoie.

Twelve editions of the work, titled *Secrets de l'histoire naturelle,* appeared between 1504 and 1534 from the shops of Paris and Lyons printers, attesting to its continuing popularity in the Renaissance.

Writers or works mentioned include Albert the Great, Augustine, Cicero, the *Gesta Romanorum,* Gerald of Wales, Herodotus, Isidore, Josephus, Pseudo-Methodius, Odoric of Pordenone, Orosius, Ovid, "Postumanus," Pliny, Seneca, Solinus, Titus-Livy, and Virgil. Many exempla are drawn from Scripture. Gervase of Tilbury's *Otia Imperialia* provided material on contemporary political divisions and regions of France such as Poitou and Provence.

The translator justifies what may seem an irreligious fascination with secular marvels by claiming Christian and educational purposes for his book in the Preface to MS Morgan M. 461:

> In order that the names of places and of countries be not too long, and because through time and mutations of realms, religions, and languages they are changed and forgotten such that the marvels cannot now be understood, I have classified them under the rubrics of regions. And I undertook this heavy charge when I considered the good outcome it could have, which moved my spirit to translate this little book from Latin into French, that those reading it could have knowledge of the marvels and diversities of the world, and by this knowledge to know the creator in the created and to love Him.

The artists illustrating *Les Secretz* show a distinct aristocratic and contemporizing bias, emphasizing the

# S

social and human at the expense of the geographical. For example, Robinet Testard in Paris, Bibliothèque Nationale fr. 22971 shows Europe as an emblem of Burgundian luxury and civility, though the text for his picture consists of a direct quote from Ptolemy contrasting the effects of European and African climates on the inhabitants of those regions.

The text for "Irrlande," by which the author intended Iceland, shows the work's character:

> A very cold country, full of frozen rivers and covered with ice until the end of time. This region is inhabited by horrible animals called bears which break the ice with their teeth and claws and spying fish in the water beneath seize them with a swipe of the paw and eat them. And they would willingly do this to the people there except that they stay well away from the bears.

Colin D'Amiens places the bears in the foreground on a frozen river with the Icelanders a group of watchful armed men well in the background. In the illustration for the actual text of an entry on Ireland, this artist also provides an important visual witness for how St. Patrick's Purgatory was conceived.

**BIBLIOGRAPHY**

Beaugendre, Anne-Caroline. *Les Merveilles du Monde ou Les Secrets de l'histoire naturelle*. Paris: Bibliothèque Nationale and Anthèse, 1996.

Friedman, John Block. *The Monstrous Races in Medieval Art and Thought*. Cambridge, MA: Harvard UP, 1981; rpt. Syracuse, NY: Syracuse UP, 2000.

Reed, Richard B. "A Bibliography of Discovery." In Theodore Bowie et al., eds., *East-West in Art: Patterns of Cultural and Aesthetic Relationships*. Bloomington and London: Indiana UP, 1966, pp. 136–153.

Sterling, Charles. *La Peinture médiévale à Paris 1300–1500*. Paris: Bibliothèque des arts, 1987–1990.

*John Block Friedman*

**SEE ALSO**

Albertus Magnus; Amazons; Bartholomaeus Anglicus; Cannibalism; Climate; Gerald of Wales; Gervase of Tilbury; Gog and Magog; Iceland; Isidore of Seville; *Mandeville's Travels;* Mela, Pomponius; Monstrosity, Geographical; Odoric of Pordenone; Purgatory, St. Patrick's; Pliny the Elder; Ptolemy; Solinus, Julius Gaius; *Wonders of the East*

## Seljuk Turks

Nomadic horsemen whose leaders founded both a great empire in the eleventh century, extending from the Bosporus to the Chinese border, and, after its collapse, successor states from Iran to Anatolia.

The Seljuks took their name from an Oghuz Turk commander, Seljuk, whose lineage ruled in those regions for more than three centuries. The majority of the Turkic herdsmen (called Turkmen or Turkomans) who formed the power base for Seljuk and his descendants were of the Oghuz tribe, but the Seljuk [Saljuq] Turks also included other peoples who moved from the northern steppes into Transoxiana seeking pasturage. They spread south, east, and west, using their military prowess to create a Sunni dictatorship that was established in the name of the caliph and accepted by the Muslim population at large.

Around the year 960, Seljuk led a large band of Turkmen south to the bank of the Iaxartes (Syr Darya), on the border of Muslim Transoxiana, where he and they converted to Islam. Becoming a *ghazi* (a warrior for the faith), Seljuk renounced allegiance to the *yabghu* (the Oghuz paramount chief). About 986, Turkmen commanded by Arslan, one of Seljuk's sons, were invited by the Samanids to settle in Transoxiana as defense against recently arrived Karakhanids. By the death of Seljuk in around 1009, numerous bands of Turkmen, with their flocks and families, had settled in Transoxiana under the leadership of his sons and grandsons, the most important of whom were Arslan, his brother Musa, and their nephews Chaghri and Toghril. They were hard pressed for adequate grazing lands, however, because three forces, the Samanids, Karakhanids, and Ghaznavids, contested dominion over Transoxiana. As fresh recruits from the steppe swelled their numbers, the Turkmen entered Ghaznavid-controlled Khurasan (northeast Iran) in 1035. They successfully defended themselves against Ghaznavid armies sent to drive them out (1035–1040), and, using Khurasanians, set up a Persian bureaucracy to administer their new state, with Toghril (Toghril Bey r. 1040–1063) as nominal overlord. Under Toghril, the Seljuks systematically conquered additional lands, further disrupting trade long hampered by *Ghazi* raiding. Their incursions into Armenia and Anatolia induced the Byzantine Empire, by a truce in 1051, to abandon eastern Armenia and upper Mesopotamia to Toghril, and all travel in the Levant, even pilgrimage, became extremely hazardous.

The Seljuks could assume a leading role in the Muslim world at this time because they were orthodox Sunni. The Ghaznavids, the Buyids (or Buwayhids, a Persian dynasty who dominated Iraq and Mesopotamia), and the Fātimids (who controlled Egypt, Palestine and Syria) were Shi'ite. As soon as the Seljuks were firmly established, the caliph appealed to them for liberation from heretical overlords. Toghril entered Baghdad in 1055, ended Buyid control, and was proclaimed sultan by a grateful caliph. As sultan he exercised political authority over non-Turkish peoples, but he was merely clan head for Turkmen, who gave primary loyalty to warrior chieftains of their individual bands. Accordingly, Seljuk history was punctuated by intermittent civil war, as sons, grandsons, and great-grandsons of Seljuk, each commanding Turkmen companies across the growing empire, sought to establish independence or, perchance, to win recognition of overlordship and the sultanate. In 1063, for example, when Toghril died childless, Alp-Arslan (r. 1064–1072), a son of Chaghri, had to defeat two of his brothers and an uncle before becoming sultan and resuming Seljuk conquests. His defeat of a Byzantine army at Manzikert in 1071 opened Anatolia to Turkish domination. It was this, and subsequent Turkmen interference with pilgrim access to Jerusalem, which set the stage for the preaching of the First Crusade in 1095.

Under Alp-Arslan's son Malik-Shāh (r. 1072–1092), the Seljuk Empire reached its fullest extent. Great-grandsons of Seljuk had seized most of Byzantine Anatolia, and by 1087, Anatolia, Armenia, and all areas south of the Caucasus were under their control. Seljuk Turks were unable to dislodge the Fātimids from Egypt, but Malik-Shāh's brother Tutush administered Syria and Palestine from Damascus. By 1090, the Seljuk Empire stretched to the Great Wall of China. Meanwhile, in 1088, forces launched south brought the Hijaz (western Arabia), Yemen, and Aden under Turkish rule. Thereafter, only the Assassin sect resisted Turkish dominion within the Malik-Shāh's vast realm.

The creation of this empire brought some stability, which allowed trade and commerce to revive in Central Asia, but Seljuk rule changed the face of Islam there. Under the influence of Iranians, who organized and administered the Seljuk empire, Persian supplanted Arabic in all usages save prayer. Two able viziers, 'Amid-al-Mulk al-Kunduri (r. 1055–1064), who served Toghril, and Nīzam-al-Mulk (r. 1064–1092), who served both Alp-Arslan and Malik-Shāh, were the chief architects of Seljuk administration. The latter, author of a *Treatise on Government*, engineered the triumph of Malik-Shāh (a child when Alp-Arslan died) over other Seljuk princes, and became ruler, in fact, of the Seljuk Empire. Resurgent Islamic orthodoxy was strengthened under Seljuk rule. Schools for study of Islamic law (the *madrasa*) became common throughout their domain, and many richly endowed mosques and hospitals were established with Seljuk patronage.

Trade was again adversely affected when the larger Seljuk Empire broke up in 1092, after Vizier Nīzam-al-Mulk and Sultan Malik-Shāh were assassinated. Malik-Shāh's successors ruled in Iraq and Khurasan until 1194, but disorder, contests for the sultanate, and internal weakness limited their authority to those territories. Seljuk successor states were established in three regions: in Anatolia until 1308, in Syria until 1117, and in Kirman until 1187. The rest of the empire broke away completely in disorder and fragmentation, conditions that inhibited peaceful trade but benefited European crusaders, who arrived in the Middle East only five years after Malik-Shāh's demise.

**BIBLIOGRAPHY**

Barthol'd, Vasili V. *Turkestan Down to the Mongol Invasion.* Tr. H.A.R. Gibb. London: Gibb Memorial Series, n.s., 5, 1928. 4th edition. Philadelphia: Porcupine, 1977.

Cahen, Claude. "The Turkish Invasions: The Selchükids." *A History of the Crusades.* Vol. 1. *The First Hundred Years.* Ed. K.M. Setton and M.W. Baldwin. Philadelphia: U of Pennsylvania, 1958, pp. 135–176.

———. "The Turks in Iran and Anatolia before the Mongol Invasions." *A History of the Crusades.* Vol. 1. *The Later Crusades,* 1189–1311. Ed. K.M. Setton et al., pp. 660–692. See Gen. Bib.

Kafesoglu, Ibrahim. *A History of the Seljuks: Ibrahim Kafesoglu's Interpretation and the Resulting Controversy.* Ed. and trans. Gary Leiser. Carbondale and Edwardsville: Southern Illinois UP, 1988.

Klausner, Carla L. *The Seljuk Vezirate: A Study of Civil Administration, 1055–1194.* Cambridge, MA: Harvard UP, 1973.

Saunders, J.J. "The Seljuk Turks and Their Place in History." *History Today* 12 (1962): 336–345.

*James D. Ryan*

**SEE ALSO**

Armenia; Assassins; Baghdad; Byzantine Empire; Fātimids; Great Wall of China; Manzikert; Nomadism and Pastoralism; Shi'ism; Sunnism

# S

## Sempad the Constable (c. 1208–1276)

Son of Constantine of Lampron, brother and adviser to King Hetoum I (r. 1216–1270), constable of Armenia, ambassador, and chronicler.

Sempad [Smbat] was sent on an embassy to the Mongol khân in 1247 or 1248 by Hetoum I, one of the first rulers to acknowledge the Mongol threat. His mission was ostensibly to congratulate Güyük on his accession, but he was also sent to demonstrate allegiance against Muslims at the khân's court. Sempad was received cordially and he returned in 1251 with a guarantee of protection for Cilician Armenia. This alliance held until 1260, when the Mongols retreated into Persia before the Mamluks.

Although Sempad did not apparently gain as much knowledge of the Mongol Empire as did his contemporaries John of Plano Carpini or William of Rubruck, he traveled at least as far as Samarkand. From this city, he wrote a letter to his brothers-in-law, Henry I, king of Cyprus, and John of Ibelin, count of Jaffa, describing his journey. While not as detailed or historically accurate regarding the Mongols as other accounts were, Sempad's letter was important for the influence it had on European-Mongol relations. Its contents concerning the destruction and massacres carried out by vast armies of "Tartars" corroborated news received from other European emissaries. Its claim that the Mongols were descended from the three Magi of Matthew 2:1–12 and its references to a Christian population flourishing under Mongol protection and to a Christian king in "India" (probably an echo of the Prester John legend) encouraged European optimism about a possible East-West alliance against the Muslims.

Sempad's *Chronicle* is the most important historical account of Cilician Armenia. He also revised the law code of Mkhit'ar Gosh. The *Assizes of Antioch* is preserved only in his Armenian translation.

Sempad fathered a son, Vasil, nicknamed "the Tatar," during a marital union with a Mongol princess descended from Chinggis Khân. In 1266, during the Egyptian invasion of Cilicia, Sempad led the defending army. He died later, at Sis, from a foot wound received while pursuing the Mamluks near Marash.

### BIBLIOGRAPHY

Bournoutian, George A. *A History of the Armenian People.* Vol. 1. Costa Mesa, CA: Mazda, 1993.
Der Nersessian, Sirarpie. "The Armenian Chronicle of the Constable Sempad or of the 'Royal Historian.'" *Dumbarton Oaks Papers* 13 (1959): [141]–168.
———. "The Kingdom of Cilician Armenia." In *A History of the Crusades.* 2 vols. Ed. K.M. Setton. Madison: U of Wisconsin P, 1969, 2:630–659.
*Diary of General Sempad.* Ed. Khoren Lazarian. San Lazzaro, Venice: Armenian General Benevolent Union, 1956.
Richard, Jean. "La lettre du Connétable Smbat et les rapports entre Chrétiens et Mongols au milieu du XIIIème siècle." In *Armenian Studies—Études Arméniennes: In memoriam Haïg Berbérian.* Ed. Dickran Kouymjian. Lisbon: Calouste Gulbenkian Foundation, 1986, pp. 683–696.
Yule-Cordier, *Cathay and the Way Thither.* See Gen. Bib.

Gloria Allaire

**SEE ALSO**

Ambassadors; Armenia; Diplomacy; Hetoum; India; John of Plano Carpini; Mamluks; Mongols; Prester John; Samarkand; William of Rubruck

## Seville

A key inland port of Iberia, on the Andalusian river Guadalquivir. In the eleventh century, Seville became the leading center of Muslim southern Spain, and from 1091 it served as a bridgehead for North African armies fighting in the Iberian Peninsula. Conquered by Christians in 1248, it remained a major commercial node and naval arsenal, and became the favorite residence of several Castilian kings. In the later 1400s, Seville rose to fame as a base for the Spanish expansion across the Atlantic.

Already important in Phoenician times, in the fourth century C.E., Roman Hispalis (Seville) replaced Corduba (Córdoba) as the metropolis of Roman Baetica. In 425, Seville fell to the Asding Vandals and Alans, in 441 to the Suevi, and in 567 to the Visigoths. Conquered by the Muslims in 712–713, it served as the capital of Muslim Spain (al-Andalūs) until 717. The early history of Muslim Seville was marked by attempts to gain independence from Córdoba, and by strife between the Yemenite (south Arabian) and Kalbite (Syro-Arab) Muslim settlers. The Yemenite clan of Banū Hajjāj made Seville virtually autonomous from 895/913, and the decline of the Umayyad caliphate a century later propelled to power another Yemenite family, the 'Abbādids. The 'Abbādids reached their peak under al-Mu'tadid (r. 1042–1069), who annexed Córdoba in 1069, and al-Mu'tamid (r. 1069–1090), who controlled all of southern Spain except Granada by 1085. Seville nonetheless became tributary to Castile in the 1060s, and was saved for Islam only by the North African Almoravids (al-Murābitūn) between 1086 and 1091. Their rule brought renewed prosperity, but also relative cultural stagnation. As Almoravid power crumbled, Seville fell to the Almohads (al-Muwahhidūn) in 1146. The Almohad regime eventually brought new riches, demographic growth, and a great building boom. Just prior to the Christian reconquest, Seville had some 65,000–80,000 inhabitants.

Seville threw off the weakening Almohad rule in 1229, and sought other Muslim overlords. Their support failed the city, however, and it capitulated to Ferdinand III of Castile in 1248. Repeopling by Christians proceeded slowly, and by 1275–1280, Seville had only some 14,000 inhabitants. The military intervention of the new Marīnid rulers of Morocco in Spain and in the Straits of Gibraltar, as well as conflicts between the burghers and the urban military aristocracy (*caballeros*), hampered recovery until about 1325. The subsequent easing of Muslim pressure, the Christian victory in the struggle for the straits, and greater political stability under Alfonso XI (r. 1312–1350) favored economic revival. Thriving on transit trade between the Mediterranean and the Atlantic, Seville also served as a gateway for the traditional products of Andalusia. Prosperity was followed, in 1355–1369, by a depression aggravated by plague and warfare. A key naval base, the city was heavily involved in the late-fourteenth-century Castilian conflicts with Aragón and Portugal. The crisis sealed the burghers' loss of power to the *caballeros,* allied from 1369 with Andalusia's high nobility (*hidalgos*).

The demographic and economic recovery of Atlantic Andalusia in the fifteenth century was marred by partisan unrest in support of the sons of Ferdinand of Antequera, the Infantes de Aragón (r. 1416–1420, 1436–1441). The high nobility tightened its control over Seville, with the families of Guzmán and Ponce de León dominating the city from 1445 onward. Seville's cathedral was built between 1402 and 1511. A pivot of renewed warfare against Granada since 1406, Seville was at the forefront of the campaigns between 1455 and 1464, which resulted in the conquest of Gibraltar. These were followed by a severe economic contraction in 1462–1469, which coincided with the destabilizing attempts by Henry IV to build up a local power base for his favorite, Juan Pacheco. The tight control exercised by the Guzmán and Ponce de León families

spared Seville much unrest, but between 1471 and 1474, the lineages began to support rival pretenders to the crown, plunging the city into turmoil.

The accession of the Catholic monarchs Ferdinand and Isabella ushered in policies designed to curtail the high nobility's role in city politics. Commerce with North Africa came to supplement Seville's economic activities by the mid-1400s, and the Canary Islands, as well as interloping in Portuguese West Africa (until 1480), began to offer fresh avenues. Until 1492, the struggle for Granada continued to strain Seville's resources, but the city nonetheless managed to prosper. The local university was founded in 1502. Finally, the Spanish conquests in the Americas and the establishment of the Seville House of Trade (*Casa de Contratación*) in 1503 transformed Seville into Spain's gateway to the Americas.

## BIBLIOGRAPHY

Ballesteros Beretta, A. *Sevilla en el siglo XIII.* Madrid: J. Pérez Torres, 1913.

Bosch Vilá, Jacinto. *La Sevilla Islámica, 712–1248.* Seville: Universidad de Sevilla, 1984.

Collantes de Terán Sánchez. *Sevilla en la Baja Edad Media: La ciudad y sus hombres.* 2nd edition. Seville: Servicio de Publicaciones del Excmo. Ayuntamiento, 1984.

González Jiménez, M., M. Borrero Fernández, and I. Montes Romero-Camacho. *Sevilla en tiempos de Alfonso X.* Seville: Ayuntamiento de Sevilla, 1987.

Ladero Quesada, Miguel A. *La ciudad medieval (1248–1492).* 3rd edition. Vol. 2 of *Historia de Sevilla.* Seville: Universidad de Sevilla, 1989.

Lévi-Provençal, E., and Emilio García Gómez. *Sevilla a comienzos del siglo XII: El tratado de Ibn 'Abdūn.* Madrid: Moneda y Crédito, 1948.

*Martin Malcolm Elbl*

SEE ALSO

Black Death; Canary Islands; Córdoba; Mediterranean Sea; Spain and Portugal

## Shi'ism [Shī'ism]

The more esoteric and smaller of the two major Muslim sects. Shi'ism (which takes its name from Arabic *Shiat 'Alī,* "the party of Ali"), exerted less influence on medieval travel and trade than did its counterpart, Sunnism.

Sunni and Shi'ite Muslims split into two factions at the death of Muhammad (632 C.E.), when the latter

# S

group supported Muhammad's son-in-law 'Alī to succeed the Prophet as the political and religious leader of Islam. A central tenet of Shi'ite theology to this day is belief in the *imamate*, a chain of religious leaders descended from Muhammad, his daughter Fātima, and his son-in-law 'Alī.

Because Shi'ites were fewer in number and lacked an established political structure for much of the medieval period (their clergy still does not have a formal hierarchy), records about them—especially their role in trade, travel, and the development of geographical knowledge—are scarce; accounts of Muslim travel come largely from Sunnis. There are no outstanding figures like Ibn Battūta in their ranks who composed major accounts of their journeys as traders or pilgrims. Nor can they be assigned to a specific geographical area during this time; rather, they established small "centers of resistance" within predominantly Sunni areas. Shi'ism itself was divided into several different subgroups, which did not always interact peacefully. Shi'ites did travel, of course, but they did so on a much smaller scale, chiefly in the course of mounting political movements and maintaining contact with coreligionists in other regions.

Pilgrimage was always difficult for Shi'ites. Not only did they have to endure the harsh traveling conditions that other pilgrims bore, but the Sunni rulers of the various cities and villages on the pilgrimage route harassed them, levying higher taxes for their merchants and making it difficult for them to conduct business or find lodging, and Sunni pilgrims ridiculed their customs. This ill treatment reached its height after the medieval period, but its origins can be seen from the earliest days of Shi'ite pilgrimage. Pilgrimage to Mecca—the *hajj*—was evidently safer under the rule of the Fātimids, the Ismā'īlī Shi'ite dynasty based in Egypt (909–1171 C.E.), but the Fātimids may, ironically, have made pilgrimage more difficult for later Shi'ites, because their high taxation of pilgrims fostered Sunni resentment.

Shi'ites were safer while conducting their less important pilgrimages to the various shrines throughout what is now Iraq and Iran. Shi'ites consider the graves of Muhammad's descendants to be sacred and visit these shrines often. If one could not travel all the way to Mecca, Islam's holiest site, and Medina, the location of Muhammad's grave, another destination might be chosen, such as An-Najaf, where 'Alī was buried, or Karbala (both sites are in present-day Iraq), the site of the martyrdom of 'Alī's son (and Muhammad's grandson) Husayn.

Shi'ites also made pilgrimages to Meshed (Mashhad, in Iran), an important trading center and the burial site of the imam al-Rida (as well as the Sunni caliph Hārūn al-Rashīd). It was already a sanctuary in the tenth century, when the traveler Ibn Hawqal (whose account is pre-Shi'ite) described its walls (977 C.E.). Tensions between Sunnis and Shi'ites can be measured by reports of medieval Shi'ite pilgrims who bowed before the grave of al-Rida and kicked the tomb of Hārūn al-Rashīd.

Sunni Muslims also visited sites sacred to Shi'ites, as Ibn Hawqal reports and as is even more evident in the lengthy travel account by Ibn Battūta (c. 1357). Ibn Battūta, while accompanying the caravan returning from Mecca to Baghdad, joined a group of pilgrims traveling to An-Najaf, where he apparently stayed for a few days. During thirty years of travel, however, he generally avoided Shi'ites whenever possible, considering their beliefs fanatical and ill-conceived; thus, like other Sunni writers, he cannot be trusted to give a reliable account of Shi'ites, although his description of the mosque at An-Najaf is thorough and apparently accurate.

Muhammad, in order to gain control of Mecca, left it for nearly a decade (622–630 C.E.); his departure, the Hejira (Arabic *hijra*), marks the beginning of the Muslim calendar), establishing a *dar al-hijra*, or place of emigration, in Medina. The radical Ismā'īlīs Shi'ites adopted Muhammad's practice of "emigration" over a relatively short distance, forming bases of operation from which to attack Sunni-dominated villages. Thus there were *dar al-hijras* established throughout the Muslim world as the Ismā'īlīs tried to gain control. The "emigration" that constitutes the birth of Islam became a model for political conquest after the Prophet's death.

Another, more subtle means of employing short journeys for political ends was used by the *manaqibi*, or itinerant singer, who wandered from city to city, singing the praises of 'Alī in an effort to convert the Sunni majority to Shi'ism. Although most of the poems have been lost, reports of this practice appear in the histories.

Shi'ite travel generally took place on a small scale. While merchants, scholars, and pilgrims certainly made journeys, Shi'ites often experienced hardships because of their faith. Some attempted to disguise their identity while traveling, although this practice was generally discouraged. Others used travel to further political and religious ends. Shi'ite travel during the Middle Ages was thus deeply affected—and sometimes motivated—by Shi'ism's place as a minority sect with a long history of effective political activism within Islam.

**BIBLIOGRAPHY**

Barthold, W. *An Historical Geography of Iran.* Trans. Svat Soucek. Ed. C.E. Bosworth. Princeton, NJ: Princeton UP, 1984.

Boyle, J.A., ed. *The Saljuq and Mongol Periods.* Vol. 5 of *The Cambridge History of Iran.* Cambridge: Cambridge UP, 1968.

Le Strange, Guy. *The Lands of the Eastern Caliphate: Mesopotamia, Persia, and Central Asia from the Moslem Conquest to the Time of Timur.* Cambridge: Cambridge UP, 1905; rpt. Lahore: al-Biruni, 1977.

Momen, Moojan. *An Introduction to Shii Islam: The History and Doctrines of Twelver Shi'ism.* New Haven: Yale, 1985.

Peters, F.E. *The Hajj: The Muslim Pilgrimage to Mecca and the Holy Places.* Princeton, NJ: Princeton UP, 1994.

*Bonnie D. Irwin*

**SEE ALSO**

Baghdad; Fātimids; Ibn Battūta, Abu Abdallah; Mecca; Medina; Minstrels and Other Itinerant Performers; Muslim Travelers and Trade; Sunnism

## Shipping Contracts, Mediterranean

Legal documents that developed during the Middle Ages to record agreements regarding capital investment and labor for voyages, shipbuilding and chartering, and purchase of cargo and passenger space.

On the one hand, few medieval contracts confined themselves exclusively to maritime traffic or naval warfare. On the other hand, many contracts dealt with shipping, as well as overland commerce and other forms of economic activity. Some had been Roman law contracts. Many others had parallels in Roman, Byzantine, Arabic, and Jewish commerce and law. It is rarely possible to demonstrate that any one ethnic or political group with its own legal system directly adopted or adapted another community's legal contracts, but in many cases striking similarities suggest either mutual influence or a common response to problems.

The contract form known as *columna* appears to have been a type of collective maritime commerce practiced in south Italy at least as early as the eleventh century. In this type of contract, seamen, shipowners, and merchants formed a partnership and all contributions of capital, equipment, and labor were listed in a column of a register. Profits and losses were shared pro rata according to the value of each partner's contribution. As maritime traffic became more sophisticated from the eleventh century, such collective operations became obsolete. As a result, no actual document recording a *columna* survives. It is known only from the law codes.

From the eleventh to thirteenth centuries, the contract most fequently used for maritime traffic in general, and shipping in particular, was the *commenda,* or *collegantia* (Venice), or *societas* or *accomendatio* (Genoa). It had points of similarity to the Jewish '*isqa,* Roman *societas,* Muslim *qirad,* and Byzantine χρεοκοινωνια contracts, but was itself an eclectic creation of the medieval Latin West. Unlike Roman *societates,* it was a real contract, concluded by the delivery of capital to the traveling partner. Essentially, it was a sleeping partnership in which one partner provided capital but stayed at home while the other did the labor (including travel). This kind of contract had a unilateral form in which the traveling partner provided no capital, usually bore no liability for loss of capital, and received one-quarter of any profit; it also had a bilateral form in which the traveling partner also provided some capital, normally one-third, and usually bore liability for one-third of any capital loss, receiving, in turn, one-half of the profit. Large numbers of *commendae* were contracted with capital in ships, fractions of ships (quarters, halves, and so on), or *loca* in ships (from around the turn of the twelfth century, it became common to divide the value of ships into shares, *loca,* of equal value). These could be bought and sold on the market, issued as the capital of *commendae,* or leased out.

The earliest surviving contracts for building ships are for the crusades of King Louis IX of France (r. 1226–1270). They take the form of promises and agreements (*promissiones et conventiones*) by the contractors to Louis's agents. Under Roman law, a *promissio* was a formless agreement creating an obligation that could be used when a specific, nominate contract did not exist for a particular type of undertaking. *Conventio* was the general term for the agreement between the parties found in any type of contract. Medieval contracts for building ships were therefore couched in terms of *promissiones et conventiones* because Roman law had no specific contract for them.

# S

Ships, fractions of ships, or *loca* in ships could be bought and sold like any other commodity. In Roman law the contract of purchase and sale had been one contract: *emptio venditio*. However, in the medieval West purchase and sale tended to be distinguished. If the buyer promised to pay for commodities delivered, the contract was a purchase, *emptio*. If the vendor acknowledged receipt of the price and promised to make delivery, the contract was a sale, *venditio*. No matter what the case, the contracts were consensual, concluded by agreement on the price.

Ships could also be chartered. *Loquerium, locarium,* or *locatio* were words for leases in general but *naulum/nolum* (from Greek ναυλοσ "passage money," and ναυλοω "to lease a ship out") became a synonym for *loquerium* in the case of ship charters. Notaries used the verbs *naulare/nolare/nolizare* to describe the chartering of ships. As with shipbuilding contracts, the charter contract was consensual, concluded by agreement on payment of the charter money and the terms of the voyage. Charters might include dispositions for cargoes, but merchants could also make freight contracts without actually chartering a ship, either making the voyages with their goods or simply consigning them for delivery at a specified place. These were usually framed either as a *promissio* by the ship's master to carry the freight or as a *confessio,* an acknowledgment creating a liability by the ship's master, of receipt of the freight and specification of the terms of delivery. In the fourteenth century such contracts developed into bills of lading.

People traveling as passengers—and not as merchants with cargo—leased space by contracts of charter (*naulum*) analogous to the charter of ships. They might lease anything from several *loca,* to whole cabins, a portion of the deck, or one place, *platea,* the smallest unit of space allocated to steerage passengers on the 'tween decks in the hold.

Early medieval law codes suggest that contracts between shipowners and sailors were partnerships and that sailors were remunerated by shares of profit. But by the thirteenth century such arrangements were obsolete, except in coastal navigation (cabotage) and privateering. In maritime commerce shipmasters now engaged sailors for wages. Contracts took the form of *promissiones* or *conventiones* by sailors to serve for, or by the masters to engage sailors for, specified voyages for specified wages. It is peculiar that such informal Roman law forms of contract should have been used for this purpose rather than the nominate contract, *locatio conductio operarum,* which was used during the Middle Ages for other forms of hire of labor.

Two commercial contracts were linked inextricably to shipping: the sea loan and the sea exchange. The Roman sea loan, *fenus nauticum,* in which the loan had to be repaid only if the ship arrived safely with its cargo, survived into the Middle Ages. It was common in the eleventh and twelfth centuries, the usury or interest on the loan being accepted because the lender assumed the risk of the voyage. But this was ended by Pope Gregory IX's decretal *Naviganti* of 1227–1234, which condemned sea loans as usurious because the lender assumed the risk only for the voyage and not for the business. Sea loans disappeared thereafter but continued in a different guise. Contracts now stipulated currency exchanges—repayment was made in a currency different from that in which the loan had been made—making no reference to usury or interest, and by this means the profit-taking could be concealed. Even though the Church remained deeply suspicious of exchange contracts in general, it could not legally sustain the charge of usury against them. Sea exchange contracts continued to be drawn up throughout the Middle Ages.

Maritime insurance contracts developed very slowly; their early history is unclear, leading to scholarly debate about when true insurance can be identified. Since the concept of maritime insurance was in fact a medieval invention, its earliest forms appear in legal documents as loans, sales, exchanges, and other contracts. It was not until the mid-fourteenth century that a mature form of a contract appeared in which risk was assumed by underwriters in return for a prepaid premium.

## BIBLIOGRAPHY

Boiteux, L.A. *La fortune de mer: Le besoin de sécurité et les débuts de l'assurance maritime.* Paris: SEVPEN, 1968.

Dotson, John E. "Freight Rates and Shipping Practices in the Medieval Mediterranean." Diss., Johns Hopkins University, 1969.

Jackson, R.P. "From Profit-Sailing to Wage-Sailing: Mediterranean Owner-Captains and Their Crews during the Medieval Commercial Revolution." *Journal of European Economic History* 18 (1989): 605–628.

Lattes, A. *Il diritto marittimo privato nelle carte liguri dei secoli XII e XIII.* Vatican City: Typographia Polyglotta, 1939.

Lopez, Robert S., and Irving W. Raymond. *Medieval Trade in the Mediterranean World: Illustrative Documents Trans-*

*lated with Introductions and Notes.* New York: Columbia UP, 1961; rpt. 1990.

Pryor, John H. *Business Contracts of Medieval Provence: Selected Notulae from the Cartulary of Giraud Amalric of Marseilles, 1248.* Toronto: Pontifical Institute of Mediaeval Studies, 1981.

Scialoja, Antonio. *Saggi di storia del diritto marittimo.* Rome: Foro Italiano, 1946.

Zeno, Riniero. *Documenti per la storia del diritto marittimo nei secoli XIII e XIV.* Turin: Lattes, 1936.

*John H. Pryor*

**SEE ALSO**

Insurance; Law, Commercial; Law of Marque; Louis IX; Mediterranean Sea; Ships and Shipbuilding; Usury and the Church's View of Business

## Ships and Shipbuilding

The vessels Europeans used during the Middle Ages came from two divergent traditions, one southern and the other northern. Despite the existence of these established regional traditions, there was always a wide variety of ships and boats suited to specific conditions or functions, offering shippers a broad range of choices in how they carried out their tasks. The physical problems of travel dictated that many trips and the transportation of most cargo over any distance would be on board ship rather than overland. Mistakes in ship design and construction were obviously costly—in human and commercial terms—and so shipbuilders relied on a body of traditions inherited in the early Middle Ages.

In southern Europe the tradition, inherited from the Romans, was mortise-and-tenon construction. Planks abutted one another and were held in place by tenons, shouldered wooden stubs, which were fitted into mortises, rectangular recesses that shipwrights chiseled into the sides of the planks. The tenons were secured by nails or dowels forced through the sides of the planks and the wooden tenons sitting in the mortises. All parts of the ship were built in the same way. The result was an extremely strong but stiff hull and a vessel of up to 1,400 tons.

The Roman method of shipbuilding continued but gradually deteriorated during the early Middle Ages. The number of tenons—which were very tedious to cut—decreased until finally, by the late tenth century, there were none left. Hull planks were simply tacked onto internal frames. The hull relied on the internal skeleton rather than the skin for strength. Less stiff, but

Full-rigged ship, a three-masted carrack. Engraving by the Flemish master "W. A.," *c.* 1450. After Robert Gardiner ed. *Cogs, Caravels and Galleons: The Sailing Ship 1000–1650.* London: Conway Maritime Press, 1994, p. 77.

lighter and easier to build, these vessels had a construction style that opened new possibilities for design, although the method of building the skeleton first increased the risk of leaks and damage. Sailors understandably worried about whether their ships would last and were reluctant to compromise safety. They also wanted to be certain that any given vessel was suitable for the task at hand. Ships had to earn a profit for their owner, however unpredictable and unstable the trading and travel environment might be. Shipbuilders had to balance efficiency with durability.

Roman ships fell into two large categories: galleys (or, more generally, oared vessels with sails) and sailing ships. Both types continued to be used well into the Middle Ages. Galleys served as fighting ships and transported valuable commodities. They carried a single square sail on a single mast located amidships. Roman galleys also had a small square sail slung under the bow to help in controlling the ship. As with all Mediterranean vessels,

# S

one or two side rudders at the stern were used to steer. The Byzantine Empire maintained war galleys, and their size grew significantly in the tenth and eleventh centuries, largely because of naval competition in the eastern Mediterranean with the Islamic states to the south and east. The *dromons* or runners of the Byzantine navy acquired a second, upper bank of oars and thus they were bigger than Roman war galleys. The increased size meant little improvement in carrying capacity or range since crews expanded with the larger number of oars.

Sailing ships, on the other hand, became much smaller during the early Middle Ages. The giant cargo vessels of the first and second centuries disappeared. In fact, ships only one-tenth their size were probably rare. The smaller vessels lost the typical square sail that all but the smallest craft had in the Roman Empire. Lateen or triangular sails became the source of propulsion for all vessels, including those with oars. Though more difficult to handle, lateen sails made it possible to sail closer to the direction of the wind and so increased maneuverability. After this initial decline, sailing ships, beginning in the tenth century, grew in size and carrying capacity. The lateen-rigged sailing ship, with a ratio of length to breadth of around three to one, proved to be the workhorse of the Mediterranean commercial revival.

In northern Europe ships radically differed in construction from the Roman type. In Scandinavia and along the southern shores of the Baltic and North seas, shipwrights built their ships with overlapping planking, called clinker or lapstrake construction, which produced a strong hull that was nevertheless flexible in small craft. Each plank was fitted to the one below. The builder added internal ribs, if there were any, after he finished the hull. A Celtic variant or perhaps forerunner of the complete clinker-built boat was one with some planks, those on the bottom abutting one another, but with overlapping strakes on the sides.

There were, broadly speaking, four different categories of these clinker-built vessels. The cog was a Celtic type in use probably even before the Romans invaded northern Gaul. In the first century B.C.E. it was a coastal vessel for the southern shores of the North Sea and also the Baltic. The cog's flat bottom, made of abutting planks, enabled it to operate in shallows and over sandbars. The clinker-built sides offered strength. With sharply angled posts at bow and stern, the small cog also had relatively good carrying capacity.

The hulk was Celtic in origin too, built of heavy planks that curved (it was shaped like half of a banana), giving it real advantages on rivers and in estuaries. The hulk was by no means exclusively a river boat, though, and made voyages across the North Sea in the eleventh century and probably earlier.

The punt, another Celtic river craft, had a flat or nearly flat bottom and straight sides to accommodate barrels and other bulky goods transported by river in the north, where (unlike southern Europe) many streams were navigable for considerable distances and served as avenues for existing commerce. Punts were often maneuvered by poles, but, like the hulk, could be equipped with sails. Rafts with logs lashed together—either to ship the logs themselves or to carry cargo—were also used on rivers. Such simple river craft never disappeared and continued to be important for the transport of people and goods throughout the Middle Ages.

A fourth type of vessel, the Scandinavian rowing barge, was transformed, perhaps during the seventh or eighth century, into the Viking ship by the addition of a true keel and a single square sail. Vessels of this type were essentially constructed in the same manner, whatever their function, although shipbuilders were specializing somewhat by the ninth century, producing cargo ships with a stiffer hull than raiding or fighting ships had. The latter were also known as longships because their ratio of length-to-breadth was greater. The cargo type proved highly seaworthy, crossing the open ocean, which its predecessors and other types could not manage. The largest, called a *knarr,* was three times longer than wide, had bluff bows, and was capable of sailing to the islands of the North Atlantic and to Greenland and the lands south of it. Cargo ships reached carrying capacities of fifty tons and perhaps as much as eighty-two feet (twenty-five meters) in length. Smaller versions traveled the coasts of western Europe. Lighter versions with higher length-to-beam ratios carried goods and men up and down Russian rivers to the Caspian Sea and Constantinople.

As different types of vessels sailed more frequently to more distant places, improvements in their designs resulted from contacts among mariners, so that by 1300 a new range of improved ships emerged. The cog added a rudder on the sternpost, replacing the side rudder typical of all European vessels in both the north and the south. In about the twelfth century, the cog got a keel like that of Scandinavian longships. Equipped with a single square sail, the improved cog proved to be a reliable deep-sea sailing vessel, capable of carrying larger cargoes more safely than any competing type.

The boxlike hull of the cog made longer voyages economically feasible, though problems of maneuvering such ships of 200 tons and more made it advisable to choose courses away from the coast.

Cogs were the principal cargo carriers for the Hanse cities, trafficking regularly from the eastern Baltic to Britain and northern France. They rose to ninety-nine feet (thirty meters) in length, but breadth was limited to a maximum of thirty-one feet (9.5 meters). Thus cogs were always tubby. To improve the cog's sailing qualities, thirteenth-century shipbuilders adopted several features of the hulk, creating a composite type. The new vessel, which was called a hulk in one place and a cog in another, still had a sternpost rudder, a single square sail, and posts sharply angled to the keel, but its more rounded hull was better equipped to deal with tides. The beginning of the trade in grain, which was exported from southern Baltic ports to the Low Countries, depended on this more reliable and relatively economical carrier. The cog-hulk combination was also used in the export of furs and wax from the East and served as well for moving bulkier goods like fish and salt within and beyond the North Sea. Like earlier cogs, however, these ships could be loaded and unloaded only from a quay, which restricted their ability to make landfall.

Coasting or river traffic in the north was conducted by the descendants of Scandinavian cargo ships, loosely called keels. Their typically shallow draft and ability to be beached made them ideal for smaller ports and for use close to shore. They served as dispatch vessels, ferries, fishing boats, and cargo ships. They were not practical for every purpose—cogs were preferred by wine traders, for example—but they remained vital to North Atlantic shipping. Keels also functioned as fishing boats. When used inland, they were often rowed and had a shallow draft. On the high seas they carried sails and had much greater capacity. The latter kind of keel increased in number as the northern European fishing industry moved out to deeper waters. Expansion of fishing and long distance overseas transportation led to more innovation in ships used in these industries than in boats, like the punt, employed in river traffic. These innovations, in turn, influenced trade. As traffic in Baltic grain, for example, became more profitable, farmers in the Oder and Vistula river valleys joined a trading network that extended to the Low Countries and Britain.

By 1300, improvements in ship design had also taken place in southern Europe. To increase a vessel's size, shipwrights could add a second lateen sail. Capacity increased to 600 tons and length to 115 feet (35 meters) and more by the thirteenth century, expanding trade in bulk goods. Coming about with lateen sails required a 180-degree rotation of the yard, pivoting it on the point where it was attached to the mast, so the distance from the end of the yard to its middle could never exceed the distance from the top of the mast to the deck. This limited the size of the sail and, thus, the size of the ship.

There were smaller variants on the lateen-rigged round ship of the Mediterranean. Such ships, often with just one mast and sail, proved effective for fishing, coastal traffic, and even long voyages since they had maneuverability equal to or greater than bigger boats. The round ships proved capable through the twelfth and thirteenth centuries of maintaining contact with ports in Italy, southern France, and the Holy Land, and they were vital to the Crusades. Even after the collapse of the crusader states, these ships sailed between the western and eastern Mediterranean as well as the Black Sea, carrying everything from luxury goods to bulky grain.

While round ships in general tended to grow in size, Mediterranean galleys got smaller and faster as shipwrights made them lower and lighter, and, in the thirteenth century, replaced the two banks of oars with one. They angled the twenty-five to thirty benches so that three rowers, each with his own oar, could sit next to each other. This increased power while lowering the profile. Lengths reached 130 feet (40 meters) but beam was typically under 16 feet (5 meters). Galleys gained speed but lost the ability to carry anything but expensive, lightweight goods, transforming them into "specialist" ships. During the thirteenth century, galleys used as warships were built in government-owned yards (arsenals) in Mediterranean ports. They had almost no cargo-carrying capacity and could not be used commercially; hence only governments would build them.

In contrast, the great galley, first built at the Arsenal at Venice around 1300, was a compromise between the low-oared vessel and the slower, ponderous round ship. Designed originally as a warship, it evolved during the fourteenth century into a lateen-rigged cargo ship with a higher length-to-beam ratio than other cargo ships. It was also equipped with a bank of oars, which meant that it could enter or leave a port under almost any circumstance. The size of such ships was limited, reaching 150 tons but rarely more. Crews were large and, thus, galleys were more expensive to operate than sailing ships.

# S

Commercial shipbuilding yards were typically temporary, a section of beach set aside for the duration of a single enterprise. Arsenals, on the other hand, were the largest industrial establishments of the later Middle Ages, with permanent buildings, regular salaried employees, and stores of spare parts. While arsenals built some commercial vessels, their principal function was to turn out, repair, and maintain warships. The new low, swift galleys had no commercial function, so governments had to establish their own yards to build them. Those yards produced both warships and cargo ships. Only in the later Middle Ages did commercial shipbuilding sites gain greater permanence, and then chiefly in the north. For example, the principal ports of the Hanseatic League set aside a small district of their towns for shipbuilding and associated trades, but such arrangements were exceptional. Even at the end of the Middle Ages, the construction of commercial ships was still an occasional activity undertaken by a few men in diverse places.

In the Mediterranean the great galley continued throughout the Middle Ages to carry valuable cargoes and to transport pilgrims between Venice and the Holy Land. Large oared ships had cabins to house female passengers, while male passengers and crew found accommodations between the decks. Voyages were not rapid—galleys made frequent stops—but they were reliable, predictable, and relatively comfortable and safe. The great galley was employed regularly for voyages to northern Europe, proving capable of surviving the Atlantic during summer months, its oars keeping it out of coastal danger. The cost of a galley voyage was high, so only luxury goods (such as alum, spices, and citrus fruits) were carried north, in trade for high-quality cloth and wool from England and Flanders, which in turn benefited the newly established Italian textile industry.

The introduction of guns on board ships in the late Middle Ages changed all types of galleys, just as, over time, the presence of cannon on vessels would alter the design of ships dramatically and lead to specialized differentiation between warships and cargo ships. Small galleys became even more exclusively fighting ships during the fourteenth and fifteenth centuries. As armaments increased, more space was required for the guns, gunpowder, and artillerymen. For sailing ships the change began only in the closing years of the fifteenth century when large guns became reliable enough to threaten other ships. Not until the sixteenth century,

however, could guns alone determine the outcome of sea battles.

In spite of advances in shipbuilding, Mediterranean vessels did not fare well in the open Atlantic, at least before about 1300, nor could they compete with local ships in the Indian Ocean. Traders who trafficked outside of Europe had to use other types of craft, most commonly products of Arab maritime technology. Traveling merchants from Italian ports (like the Polos), would have carried their goods across the Arabian Sea in some variant of the *dhow*, with one or two lateen sails and a hull construction that differed from that of European vessels. (Hulls were often sewn together and in no case would they have been of frame-first construction). Although it is certain that European traders were familiar with the sailing vessels from East Asia—such as those employed in present-day Indonesia—they seem to have brought home little if any of that technical knowledge.

On the other hand, northern European technology transformed Mediterranean ships during the fourteenth century. The crusaders brought northern ships, such as the Scandinavian longship and the cog, into the Mediterranean. Although the cog was well known in the Mediterranean by 1200, its use was apparently limited to transporting crusaders from England and the Low Countries to the Holy Land. The rig and form of the hull caused difficulties for cogs trying to return to the Atlantic and made them poor candidates for maneuvering among the many islands of the Mediterranean. It was thus only through a cross-fertilization of techniques and knowledge, as well as demands for a new range of vessels with greater capabilities than any before, that rapid advances occurred in the design and construction of all European ships, yielding superior new types in the fourteenth century.

Sometimes clumsy, the cog still had a large capacity for its length. Mediterranean builders changed the hull construction, employing the skeleton-building typical of the region. External planks now abutted one another, making the ship relatively lighter and more flexible. They also changed the rigging, adding a lateen sail toward the stern, on its own second mast. The result was the carrack. This tubby sailing ship was ideal for carrying bulk cargoes economically. It was more maneuverable than earlier cogs, with two sails (one of them a lateen). It had more carrying capacity for each unit of length than earlier Mediterranean round ships, yet it rode higher in the water than other contemporary vessels, thus intimidating potential pirates. Towering over existing keels, they were also effective fighting ships in northern waters. What is more, the carrack was able to travel with little difficulty from south to north, transporting such goods as sweet Cretan wines directly to the British Isles.

In the late fourteenth century the carrack evolved into the full-rigged ship, generating a much more versatile type by altering hull construction and, even more important, rigging. Hull-first building was replaced by strong internal frames and ribs. The square mainsail and the lateen mizzen at the stern were joined by a small square sail at the bow, effecting a logical balance that gave captains much greater control over their vessels. With three sails they could hold a course better and also maneuver more easily in and out of port. Sailors could deal with each sail in turn. With extra canvas at the bow and stern, the mainsail could be reduced in size with no loss in motive power. This in turn meant that the crew could be smaller. Combined with the greater hull space of the carrack design, this gave full-rigged ships a bigger payload than any predecessor for each unit of length.

Until the modified and improved design of the full-rigged ship came into widespread use, lengthy voyages of exploration were logistically impossible. In planning such voyages, captains had to calculate the amount of food and water and other supplies needed to sustain each crew member, that is, how much of a ship's overall tonnage was required to "serve" each man aboard. Reducing sailors' needs was difficult, and thus the number of tons served per crew member—two or three tons on medieval intra-European voyages—had to rise before distant voyages could become practical, much less profitable. Full-rigged ships were more economical to operate and more reliable than their predecessors. European shipbuilders originally made changes to improve safety and earnings. In the process they opened up new possibilities. A greater payload made it possible for ships to carry more and bigger guns, and although it was costly to do so, cargo ships could carry some armaments and the increasingly specialized warships could be even more heavily armed.

The full-rigged ship enabled Europeans to venture farther afield. Voyages of exploration predated the new designs but were not very successful. In the fourteenth century the Portuguese crown embarked on a deliberate program, at times suspended or interrupted, to explore the west coast of Africa. At first explorers used a vessel called a *barca,* which was probably a keel, based on earlier Scandinavian types. The *barca's* tonnage ranged from approximately twenty-five to fifty, with a length of between sixty-nine and eighty-nine feet (twenty-one and twenty-seven meters). It had partial decks and a single mast with a square sail. Some may have had a second, small mast at the stern, which also carried a square sail. It was a common type, not particularly different in any way from fishing boats that worked along the coast of Morocco or made voyages to the Canary Islands.

As distances increased and vessels had to stand out from the shore, explorers started to use a variant of a Mediterranean fishing boat, the caravel, which is first mentioned as part of a voyage of 1440 and later came to dominate the fleets sent out from Portugal to Africa. The caravel carried two or three lateen sails, each on its own mast. The hull was long, narrow, and light, with little freeboard and little draft—and thus it resembled the whaling, fishing, and river boats of the coast of the Bay of Biscay. Smaller caravels had only a half deck or were completely open. There was no forecastle, which gave it a rakish look, while the lack of upperworks also decreased resistance in a crosswind. Caravels used for voyages of exploration were relatively small, at most sixty tons to seventy tons and about 66 feet to 115 feet (twenty to thirty-five meters long). Lateen sails combined with the hull form made it highly maneuverable, especially along coasts with changeable winds and unknown hazards.

In the fifteenth century, the caravel grew in size and acquired more decking. It proved especially good for voyages to the Atlantic islands, but on longer runs it was inferior to the full-rigged ship. On his first voyage, Columbus stopped in the Canary Islands to rerig one of his caravels, replacing all but one lateen sail with square ones, thus making it a full-rigged ship. Vasco da Gama did something similar on a voyage to the Indian Ocean in 1502. By the end of the fifteenth century vessels used for exploration were almost all full-rigged ships, although some traders used caravels to go to the New World. For trips around the Cape of Good Hope to India, the Portuguese used carracks. Three-masted, and later four-masted, ships became massive, reaching as much as 2,000 tons by the late sixteenth century.

The two-masted carrack plied northern European waters by the first years of the fifteenth century, and a three-masted version followed soon after. These carracks probably came originally from the west coast of

# S

Europe and were quickly known in the Bay of Biscay and the North Sea. At the time, the cog-hulk combination dominated long-distance trade and was only slowly supplanted by the new design, in part because northern shipwrights did not know how to build skeleton-first hulls. The change and development already under way in the north, indicated by the adaptation of the cog, may also have slowed acceptance of the full-rigged ship. However, in the course of the late fifteenth and the sixteenth centuries the new type took over the bulk and long-distance trades, first in the Low Countries and Britain and later in the Baltic. Other vessels remained in use. Cogs returned to their earlier functions along the coasts. They became smaller but retained their basic hull design and rig. Keels continued to be used along the coasts, in rivers, or through marshlands.

Changes in smaller vessels also occurred in the north. Shipwrights in the Low Countries modified existing designs to create the *buss* for the herring fishery and the *hoeker* for the cod fishery. In around 1400, inland vessels began to carry the simple *una* rig, which had two sails on a single mast. One sail, to the stern, was held up by a yard or sprit at a 45-degree angle to the mast. The second hung down from the forestay, the rope forward of the mast that held it in place. The two sails then were in the same plane as the keel of the ship and could be adjusted easily or shifted from side to side to take maximum advantage of wind from any direction. The sails could be handled independently by a small crew; indeed, one man could handle a small boat with such a rig. This new design effected more efficient river and lake transportation, laying the groundwork for later improvements in the rig of large cargo ships, river and coastal vessels, and, ultimately pleasure craft.

By the end of the Middle Ages, European ships paradoxically enjoyed both a greater variety and more common features than ever before. Many different forms of vessels were still being used. Some were specific regional or local types, known to only a few builders and users, specifically made for unique tasks and/or waters, while others were variants on the main types adapted to local needs. Shipwrights used existing technology to respond to local conditions. Still, by 1500, European ships and shipbuilding had acquired a kind of uniformity, a common tradition. The full-rigged ship and its variants made voyages of exploration possible while remaining the principal vessel for intra-European trade and travel.

## BIBLIOGRAPHY

Bass, George, ed. *A History of Seafaring Based on Underwater Archaeology.* London: Thames and Hudson, 1972.

Friel, Ian. *The Good Ship: Ships, Shipbuilding and Technology in England, 1200–1520.* Baltimore: Johns Hopkins UP, 1995.

Gardiner, Robert, ed. *Cogs, Caravels, and Galleons: The Sailing Ship, 1000–1650.* Vol. 3 of *History of the Ship.* London: Conway Maritime Press, 1994.

Hattendorf, John B., ed. *Maritime History in the Age of Discovery: An Introduction.* Malabar, FL: Krieger, 1995.

Hutchinson, Gillian. *Medieval Ships and Shipping.* Rutherford, NJ: Fairleigh Dickinson UP, 1994.

Lane, Frederic C. *Navires et Constructeurs à Venise pendant la Renaissance.* Paris: SEVPEN, 1965.

Lewis, Archibald R., and Timothy J. Runyan. *European Naval and Maritime History, 300–1500.* Bloomington: Indiana UP, 1985.

Pryor, John H. *Geography, Technology, and War: Studies in the Maritime History of the Mediterranean, 649–1571.* Cambridge: Cambridge UP, 1988.

Scammell, G.V. *The World Encompassed: The First European Maritime Empires, c. 800–1650.* Berkeley: U of California Press, 1981.

Unger, Richard W. *The Ship in the Medieval Economy, 600–1600.* London: Croom-Helm Ltd., 1980.

*Richard W. Unger*

**SEE ALSO**

*Barca;* Canary Islands; Caravel; Carrack; Cog; Da Gama, Vasco; Galley; Gunpowder; Hanse, The; Hulk; Keel; *Knarr; Langskip;* Mediterranean Sea; Naval Warfare; Navigation; Navigation, Arab; Navigation, Viking; Venice

## Sijilmassa

The medieval capital of Tafilalt, Morocco's largest Saharan oasis, in the southeastern province of Ksar es-Souk. Its extensive ruins lie on the outskirts of modern-day Rissani, by the Wādī Zīz. Throughout the Middle Ages, Sijilmassa served as one of the key gateways for caravans headed across the Sahara to the western Sudan, and as an important marshaling point for Moroccan pilgrims to Mecca.

Sijilmassa developed as a settlement of Miknāsa Berbers, between 722 and 758 C.E. In 976–977, the ruling Miknāsa dynasty was replaced by a Zanāta Berber lineage, the Banū Khazrūn, who at first held Sijilmassa for the Umayyads of Córdoba, and later ruled in their own right. By 1020, the emirate of Sijilmassa reached its peak. It prospered thanks to its command over caravan trails linking the western Sudan, the

Maghrib, and Egypt. In 1055–1056, Sijilmassa fell to the Almoravids (al-Murābitūn), but it soon regained virtual independence under their Saharan branch. In 1146–1148, the city reluctantly submitted to the Almohads (al-Muwahhidūn). From 1255 onward, the ʿAbd al-Wādids of Tlemcen strove for control of Sijilmassa against the Marīnids of Fez, whose troops finally conquered and sacked the city in 1274. Sijilmassa quickly recovered, however, and prospered again.

From 1315–1316 until 1332–1333 and a prolonged siege by the Marīnid sultan Abū ʾl-Hasan, Sijilmassa was the seat of a junior branch of the Marīnid dynasty. The descendants of this branch attempted to reclaim the city throughout the fourteenth century, mostly with ʿAbd al-Wādid support. In 1351–1352, the traveler Ibn Battūta found Sijilmassa still thriving. But the commercial contraction of the later fourteenth century, political changes in the western Sudan, shifts of desert trails, and possibly drought undermined the city's economic base. Sijilmassa finally succumbed to the social and political turmoil that followed the death, in 1393, of the Marīnid sultan Abū ʾl-ʿAbbās, and its inhabitants scattered among individual fortified settlements in the oasis.

**BIBLIOGRAPHY**
Colin, G.S. "Sidjilmāsa." In *Encyclopedia of Islam.* Leiden and London, 1913–1938, vol. 4, pp. 432–434.
Devisse, J. "Sijilmāsa: Les sources écrites, l'archéologie, le contrôle des espaces." In *L'histoire du Sahara et des relations transsahariennes entre le Maghreb et l'Ouest africain du moyen âge à la fin de l'époque coloniale, Actes du 4ème Colloque Euro-Africain, Erfoud (Maroc), 20–25 Octobre 1985.* Bergamo: Walk-Over, 1986, pp. 18–25.
Jacques-Meunié, D. *Le Maroc Saharien des origines à 1634.* Paris: Librairie Klincksieck, 1983.
Lessard, J.-M. "Sijilmassa: La ville et ses relations commerciales au XIe siècle, d'après El Bekri." *Hespéris-Tamuda* 10 (1969): 5–36.

*Martin Malcolm Elbl*

**SEE ALSO**
Caravans; Córdoba; Egypt; Genoa; Gold Trade in Africa; Ibn Battūta, Abu Abdallah; Mecca; Muslim Travelers and Trade

## Silk Roads

Interconnected caravan routes through Central Asia, from China to the Mediterranean, in use as a continuous trade route well before the beginning of the Christian era. Open in whole or part throughout the Middle Ages, the silk roads fed urban and commercial life in Central Asia and beyond.

Although the Chinese sought jade and other precious commodities from Central Asia, long-distance trade developed only after silk was introduced to the West. Scraps of silk in Egyptian grave wrappings date its arrival in the Mediterranean to the dawn of the first millennium B.C.E., but the exotic fabric, whose luxurious texture gave it such value, remained rare in the West until the late second century B.C.E. Only after armies of the Han dynasty (202–220 C.E.) pushed through the Hexi [Hohsi] Corridor, into Xinjiang [Sinkiang], was the way for trade open. The Han enclosed the Hexi's habitable strip behind the Great Wall, establishing cities on the fringes of Xinjiang's Takla Makan desert. These included Yumen Kuan (the "jade gate"), Tunhuang (where the Caves of the Thousand Buddhas still attract tourists today), and Lou Lan (now a ruin, the "City of the Dead"), on the shores of the salt Lop Nor. Beyond the Hexi Corridor lay the world's highest peaks and bleakest deserts, where oasis and mountain settlements, connected by trade routes, were already established. Such links in an expanding commercial highway let China become a magnet for traders seeking silk. At first China enjoyed a monopoly, for silk's source was a closely guarded secret. Even after techniques of sericulture were smuggled west in the sixth century C.E., China still manufactured the best silk, and continued to draw trade.

From East to West, the principal caravan routes ran north and south of the Takla Makan, rejoined at Kashgar (modern K'ashih), the eastern gate to the Pamirs, and there split north and south over that high plateau and its peaks. The southern route led to Balkh (Bactra in ancient times, today Vazirabad, Afghanistan), near the headwaters of the Amu Darya (Oxus), and there branched in three directions: south, over the Hindu Kush to the Indo-Gangetic plain; north, through the "Iron Gate" into Transoxiana (Sogdiana); or directly west into Persia. The northerly route from Kashgar across the Pamirs led to Fergana, Kokand, Tashkent, Samarkand, and Bukhara, the fabled bazaar cities of Transoxiana. Transoxiana could also be reached from China by striking north from Yumen Kuan to Hami, then west past the Turfan Depression, north of the Tien Shan, through Almaligh (south of Lake Balkash), to Tashkent. This shorter "summer route" was used when weather and political conditions permitted, but

# S

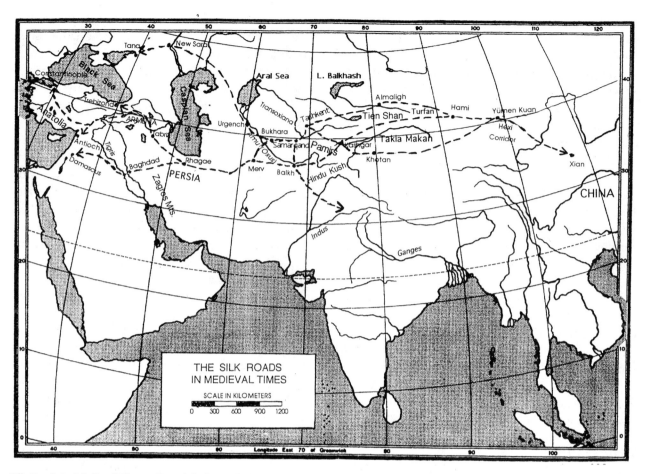

Silk Roads in Medieval Times. Copyright James D. Ryan.

it was often made impassable by war between nomadic tribes.

From Transoxiana the silk roads passed west to Merv (modern Mary, in Turkmenistan), then south of the Elburz Mountains to Rhagae (Rai, near modern Tehran). There the route divided again, leading either north, through Tabriz and Erzerum (in Armenia), into Anatolia; or west, through Ecbatana (modern Hamadan) and across the Zagros Mountains to Baghdad (near the site of ancient Seleucia and Ctesiphone). From Baghdad, traders could set out across the desert, through Palmyra (Tadmor) to Damascus, Tyre, or Sidon; or they could travel north along the Tigris into eastern Anatolia. Several roads ran through Anatolia, leading to ports like Trebizond on the Black Sea, to Tarsus and Antioch on the Mediterranean, or due west toward Constantinople. Lastly, during the Mongol era (1206–1368) an alternate path was opened, north from Bukhara, through Urgench, then around the Caspian Sea to New Sarai, then across the steppes to Tana or the Crimea.

The silk roads played a significant role in cross-cultural exchange. Traders seeking profits also brought ideas and technology both east and west. Europe received oranges, peaches, roses, and azaleas, repaying China with grapes, figs, cucumbers, alfalfa, and sesame. The silk roads were also highways for missionaries who spread Manichaeism, Christianity, Islam, and Buddhism. Travel along the silk roads probably reached its peak during the *Pax Mongolica,* following conquests made by Chinggis Khân (r. 1206–1227). After the accession of Khubilai Khân (r. 1260–1294), who completed Mongol domination of China, East Asia was open to Western merchants and missionaries. The Polos were among the earliest Europeans to visit China (Niccolò and Maffeo from 1260 to 1269, joined by Marco on a second trading mission from 1271 to 1295), but by the time Marco dictated his *Divisament dou monde* (c. 1298), many merchants were already in the East, and missionaries like John of Monte Corvino (1247–1328), first Latin archbishop of Khanbaliq

**560    Silk Roads**

(Beijing), had followed in their wake. Eastern travel became so common that Francesco Balducci Pegolotti could compile a detailed and accurate merchant guide to the silk roads, *The Practice of Commerce* (*c.* 1340), based on reports from returning travelers. Not all traffic was beneficial, however; the Black Death also moved along these routes from Asia to Europe.

Europe's golden age of commerce on the silk roads came to an end in the fourteenth century because of devastation caused by the plague, the conversion of most Mongols to Islam, and the overthrow of the Yuan dynasty in 1368 by the more xenophobic Ming dynasty. For centuries thereafter, trade with the East was in the hands of Muslim middlemen as Europe searched for alternate routes to Asia. Once the Portuguese opened ocean links between eastern Asia and Europe in the sixteenth century, the silk route, and the oasis cities nourished by its trade, withered and decayed. Many were ruins when rediscovered by nineteenth-century explorers like Baron Ferdinand von Richthofen (1833–1905), who traversed the Central Asian route in mid-century and dubbed it "die Seidenstrasse." Other adventurers, historians, and archaeologists uncovered forgotten cities that had lined the silk roads, some buried under desert sands, and indicated this highway's important role in trade and cross-cultural exchange. Among these were Sven Hedin (1865–1952), whose excavations of terra-cotta artifacts at Khotan (1896) touched off a race for antiquities, and Sir Aurel Stein (1863–1943), whose four decades of excavations helped bring the civilizations that flourished along the silk roads to the attention of the twentieth century.

**BIBLIOGRAPHY**

Boulnois, Luce. *La route de la Soie.* 1963; 3rd edition, revised. Geneva: Olizane, 1992. *The Silk Road.* Trans. Dennis Chamberlain. New York: E.P. Dutton, 1966.

Frank, Irene M., and David M. Brownstone. *The Silk Road: A History.* New York and Oxford: Facts on File Publications, 1986.

Hopkirk, Peter. *Foreign Devils on the Silk Road: The Search for the Lost Cities and Treasures of Central Asia.* Amherst: U of Massachusetts P, 1984.

Stein, Aurel. *On Ancient Central-Asian Tracks: Brief Narrative of Three Expeditions in Innermost Asia and Northwestern China.* Ed. Jeannette Mirsky. New York: Pantheon Books, 1964.

Yule-Cordier. *Cathay and the Way Thither.* See Gen. Bib.

*James D. Ryan*

**SEE ALSO**

Almaligh; Armenia; Baghdad; Black Death; Buddhism; Bukhara; Caravans; Caspian Sea; China; Damascus; India; Inner Asian Trade; John of Monte Corvino; Khanbaliq; Manichaeism; Marco Polo; Mongols; Pegolotti, Francesco Balducci; Portuguese Expansion; Samarkand; Textiles, Decorative; Trebizond; Yuan Dynasty

## Simon of Saint-Quentin (fl. 1240s)

Dominican papal envoy to the Mongols in the Middle East who wrote an account (known today only in excerpts) about his encounter with Mongols in 1248.

Simon of Saint-Quentin was a member of one of the four official embassies that Pope Innocent IV sent to establish diplomatic contact with the Mongols in 1245, in the wake of their destructive incursion in Russia and eastern Europe during the previous decade. Hoping to acquire a sense of Mongol military strength—both to ensure Europe's defense and to assess the possibilities of a joint European/Mongol crusade against the Muslims in the Holy Land—the pope selected Friar Ascelin to lead a Dominican mission to any Mongol army that it could find in the Middle East. One of Ascelin's companions, Simon, wrote a brief account of this embassy; his narrative, the *Historia Tartarorum,* is the only record of the expedition. The text of Simon's *Historia* has been lost except for those parts incorporated by Vincent of Beauvais into the last three books of his *Speculum historiale.*

Historians know almost nothing about Simon; his book reveals surprisingly little personal information. Scholars continue to hope to find a copy of his complete account, but few have studied him seriously. A Dominican friar, evidently a missionary in the Middle East, Simon was presumably selected to accompany Ascelin because of his knowledge of Middle Eastern languages: he probably knew Arabic and Persian, possibly Turkish, but not Mongol.

Simon had a flair for writing engaging history. His text combines a colorful travelogue with a report of Ascelin's papal embassy. Perhaps because he was not reporting directly to the pope in answer to an official commission, Simon felt no need to structure his account as rigidly as those of other envoys; it is anecdotal, focusing on dramatic events and exotic people, as it collects interesting experiences and episodes from a variety of sources, principally Georgians, Armenians,

# S

and Latin mercenaries serving the Turkish sultan of Iconium.

Simon's account reflects certain biases of his age. He was intransigent in matters of Christian dogma and practice, rejecting all deviations from Latin rites and theology that had been adopted by Eastern Christians. He also had a rather low opinion of the Mongols, stressing their worst practices while overlooking any good qualities. Simon's dislike for the Mongols, which he shared with many contemporaries, probably stemmed from his own personal experience. The Dominican embassy of which he was a member spent more than a year under Mongol jurisdiction, including nine weeks in the army camp of the Mongol general Baiju, during which time the friars suffered both humiliation and deprivation; treated as prisoners rather than envoys, they were sentenced to death no less than three times.

The *Historia Tartarorum* provides valuable information on Mongol culture as well as a general outline of their conquest of the Middle East up to 1247. Simon describes their military practices and invasion tactics, stressing their deceitfulness and cruelty, and he becomes more specific as the Mongol armies moved westward against Khorezmians, Persians, Georgians, and Armenians. The Turkish sultanate of Iconium receives the most attention—its conquest is covered in twice as many chapters as any other. Simon furnished the Latin West with its first reliable description of the Seljuk Turks, especially the revolts and conflicts that characterized their political history in the mid-1200s. Some of his observations are found nowhere else. Simon describes in detail, for example, the decisive Mongol victory over the sultanate in 1242, offering reasons for the Turkish defeat and recording the tribute the Seljuks agreed to pay the Mongols in their 1245 peace treaty. Simon's *Historia* is thus significant in the history of European exploration literature because it was the earliest and most complete Western account of Mongol conquests in the Middle East before the invasion of Hülegü. That the Turkish material was new to Western Christians is clear from the fact that Vincent incorporated so much of it into his *Speculum historiale,* placing it in a context that both gave the information authority and brought it to a learned audience.

Simon was an excellent Latinist who employed complicated syntax, frequently translating what he heard from his sources in the form of direct quotations in order to preserve their discourse. His scholarly abilities may explain why it was he who wrote an account of this embassy rather than the pope's appointed leader, Ascelin, whose arrogance, tactlessness, and lack of diplomacy repeatedly angered the Mongols.

The Dominicans succeeded neither in establishing political relations with the Mongols nor in converting them. Because it produced Simon's informative and accurate *Historia,* however, the embassy was not a total loss.

## BIBLIOGRAPHY

Guzman, Gregory G. "Simon of Saint-Quentin and the Dominican Mission to the Mongol Baiju: A Reappraisal." *Speculum* 46 (1971): 232–249.

———. "Simon of Saint-Quentin as Historian of the Mongols and Seljuk Turks." *Medievalia et Humanistica,* n.s., 3 (1972): 155–178.

———. "The Encyclopedist Vincent of Beauvais and His Mongol Extracts from John of Plano Carpini and Simon of Saint-Quentin." *Speculum* 49 (1974): 287–307.

Kaeppeli, Thomas. *Scriptores Ordinis Praedicatorum Medii Aevi.* Rome: S. Sabina, 1980, vol. 3, p. 348.

Simon of Saint-Quentin. *Historia Tartarorum.* Ed. Jean Richard as *Simon de Saint-Quentin: Histoire des Tartares.* Paris: Paul Geuthner, 1965.

*Gregory G. Guzman*

SEE ALSO

Armenia; Dominican Friars; Eastern Christianity; Holy Land; Hülegü; Innocent IV; Mongols; Seljuk Turks; Vincent of Beauvais; William of Rubruck

## Sinai
*See* Catherine in the Sinai, Monastery of St.

## Sindbad the Sailor

Legendary Arab merchant and seafarer, the hero of seven fabulous voyages as recounted in the *Arabian Nights* (also called *Tales from the Thousand and One Nights*).

The tales told about Sindbad apparently represent a fusion of many sources: mythic narratives from Persian, Indian, and Mediterranean traditions are mingled with incidents based on medieval travelers' tales of wonder and factual information derived from geographical and navigational treatises. These sources were all widely available in Arabic verse texts during the caliphate of Harun al-Rashid (786–809 C.E.), the putative period of Sindbad's exploits.

The fictional personality of Sindbad reflects the ideal qualities of merchant-adventurers during the height of Muslim commercial expansion throughout the Indian Ocean basin. Just a simple trader in his early voyages, Sindbad capitalizes on his resourcefulness and hard-won experience to gain the skills typical of a *mu'allim,* or navigator of the highest reputation, one able to pilot a ship over open ocean using celestial navigation. Allowing for both the storyteller's interpolation of fanciful detail and the deliberate exaggeration typical of merchants who wish to dramatize the hardships they have undergone while trading in exotic luxury goods, many of the locales Sindbad visits can be recognized as actual ports of call on the trade routes from the Persian Gulf port of Basra eastward toward the western coast of India, the island of Ceylon (Sri Lanka), the Malay Peninsula, and the archipelago that is present-day Indonesia. The tales contain descriptions of actual topographical features and landfalls (such as "Adam's Peak" on the island of Serendeeb, or Sri Lanka, during the sixth voyage).

Beneath the surface of mythic exploit and fantastic invention that characterizes the Sindbad narratives is a solid array of factual information that attests to the courage and resourcefulness of medieval Arab seafarers. While the modern reader will dismiss as archetypal folktales Sindbad's encounters with monsters such as the gigantic Roc, a carnivorous bird that preys on elephants, or the whale mistaken by sailors for an island, the real physical dangers that the adventurer endures— he survives typhoons, shipwrecks, starvation, and tropical illness, and is the victim of theft, piracy, and enslavement—underscore the risks taken by merchants to bring to Baghdad and other cities of the Abbasid realm such commodities as gemstones, ivory, perfumes, camphor, and sandalwood, which the tales include among the luxury goods in Sindbad's inventories. Sindbad's despair at being cast away on hostile foreign shores during his early journeys doubtless reflects the sense of isolation felt by the novice traveler in unfamiliar and sometimes xenophobic environments. On the other hand, as the survivor of misfortune, he is treated with compassion and generosity by his fellow merchants, an openhandedness he reciprocates with lavish gifts to the poor of Baghdad on the successful conclusion of each voyage.

Because of their knowledge of foreign languages and customs, as well as their cultivation of personal friendships with men of power and wealth in distant cities—a basis of trust vital for commercial undertakings—Arab merchants were frequently asked by rulers to serve as messengers or diplomatic agents, in exchange for a partial subsidy of the expenses of their voyage. They doubtless engaged in intelligence activities as well: Sindbad concludes each of his latter voyages with a report to the caliph of his travels and encounters, and he is closely questioned concerning the political and military strength of the cities he has visited. Such information could provide the basis for state decisions: on his final voyage, Sindbad is ordered to transport diplomatic gifts to the king of Serendeeb, with whom he is given authority to negotiate a treaty of reciprocal trade and friendship.

**BIBLIOGRAPHY**
Hourani, George Fadlo. *Arab Seafaring in the Indian Ocean in Ancient and Early Medieval Times.* 1951. Rev. and expanded edition, Princeton, NJ: Princeton UP, 1995.
Severin, Tim. *The Sindbad Voyage.* New York: Putnam, 1982.
*Tales from the Thousand and One Nights.* Trans. N.J. Dawood. Harmondsworth, England: Penguin, 1973.

*Allan T. Kohl*

**SEE ALSO**
Baghdad; Diplomacy; Gems; Ivory Trade; Muslim Travelers and Trade; Navigation, Arab; Spice Trade, Indian Ocean; Spies

## Slave Trade, African

The demand for servile labor is an ancient institution, and African participation in this institution as both laborers and providers of labor dates from classical antiquity. People of African descent became the primary slave population of the slave-using world only after the sixteenth century, when the transatlantic slave trade developed along with the population and exploitation of the Americas by Europeans. A significant trade in Africans, however, existed throughout the Middle Ages, both within the African continent and as exports to northern Mediterranean societies, western Asia, and the Indian Ocean basin.

Historical sources for the medieval African slave trade are predominantly external to the continent and vague with regard to the slaves' ethnic and geographic origins. The existence of the Asian trade can be inferred from Asian travelers' accounts as well as from the human evidence of people of African descent living in various communities in western Asia and the Indian

# S

subcontinent. However, statistical data for the entire period are not abundant, making it difficult to seize on the trade's scale, chronological fluctuations, and longevity. Prices for African labor varied greatly according to time period, place of origin, distance from point of origin (since a greater distance decreased the likelihood of escape), and the slaves' skill level, physical appearance, and health.

The majority of Africans in the Middle Ages lived in locally organized or stateless societies in which slavery was rare or nonexistent, and most slaves were obtained by purchase far from the Africans' original homes by those who would use their labor. The vast majority of African slaves were obtained at the start of their odyssey through war, raiding, or kidnapping—a traumatic act of violence.

Within sub-Saharan Africa, slaves were vital as porters for trading goods and became commodities themselves, as slaves, when they reached a final sales destination. They also served as domestics, craftsmen, farm laborers, and miners, and, in the Persian Gulf, as pearl divers. And, like the Mamluks in Egypt and elsewhere, soldier-slaves were also used within Africa both for defense of states and to capture other potential slaves. Since medieval Africa had a very low population base, another important use for slaves was to supplement the population of slave-holding societies and to serve as concubines, producing more new citizens for the state. In African social systems an advantage in the purchase of a concubine over that of a free wife was that the master would then have complete control of the resulting offspring with no interference or competing claims from in-laws.

Evidence of a trade in African slaves across the Sahara exists from classical antiquity. Throughout the Middle Ages major routes developed, rose, and declined in usage following political developments to the north and south of the desert as well as changing demands in the Mediterranean and western Asian world for African labor. African slaves were used in the active cross-desert trade, as well as in the Saharan salt and copper mines and for date and vegetable production in the Saharan oases.

Slavery was an accepted institution throughout the medieval world, and Islamic societies were no exception in the practice of trading in and using slaves. Most of the central Islamic world, in the Arabian Peninsula and Fertile Crescent area, had slaves of African (and non-African) descent before the prophecy of Muhammad.

Thus, the existence of the slaves as an institution in the Islamic world and the trade in them was not a function of Islam's development as a religion. However, Islam did accept slavery and develop an extensive religious jurisprudence regarding the enslavement of people, their treatment while in bondage, and the encouragement and procedures of manumission. A number of Arabic manuals recount these precepts and indicate the presumed skills of various ethnic groups (African and non-African) that were frequently used as slaves. Islamic cities and states in the Middle Ages documented large slave populations, many of African ancestry. The famed Zanj revolt in southern Iraq in the eighth century is only the most well-known example of large concentrations of African laborers in medieval Asia.

Besides the military, domestic, and artisanal occupations mentioned above, African slaves were used in the Islamic world in diplomacy, for slaves were sent as gifts establishing friendship between individuals as well as between rulers and as payment of tribute. The early Islamic conquest of North Africa included raiding for Berber and black African slaves south into the Sahara, and demands for slave tribute to supply the eastern Muslim world. There is no doubt that the trans-Saharan trade in slaves grew enormously after the establishment of Islam in North Africa, though the slave trade throughout the Mediterranean—in both the Christian and Islamic worlds—was brisk in the medieval period.

Islamic Egypt was a heavy user of sub-Saharan African slaves as domestic labor, as soldiers in various all-African regiments, and as labor for mines in the Egyptian/Sudanese desert. Scholars have long recognized the *baqt*, an institution that has been described variously as a trade treaty regulating exchange of Nubian slaves for provisions or a treaty requiring a yearly tribute payment in slaves between the Nubians of the Sudan and the Arabs based in Fustat, Egypt. More recent research would seem to indicate that the *baqt* was not imposed on the Nubians nor does it represent a regular event from which numbers of Nubians filing north can be calculated, as has been suggested by some scholars attempting to arrive at totals for the slave trade.

Arab merchants from Egypt were also frequent travelers to the south, in the area of modern-day Sudan, from which large numbers of sub-Saharan Africans, frequently called *an-Nuba,* were exported to fill a huge demand for African slaves throughout the Islamic world. It has been suggested that the trade in slaves out of medieval Nubia may have caused a heavy population drain on the area. Extant correspondence also exists between the sub-Saharan Islamic state of Bornu in the fourteenth century and the Mamluk sultan in Cairo regarding complaints against Arab slave traders in Bornu who were capturing free Muslim subjects of the Bornu ruler for sale in Egypt and points east.

The trade in Africans as military slaves was established in the Islamic world from a very early period. The ninth-century Aghlabid dynasty in Ifrīqiyya and the contemporary Tulunids of Egypt relied heavily on these foreign military slaves, whose loyalty to their military commanders was presumed due to their cultural isolation from the civilian population. The trade in non-African military slaves into Africa from the Black Sea region led to the establishment of the Mamluk "slave dynasty" that controlled Egypt between 1250 and 1517. Specifically, African slave troops played their most powerful role in the eleventh century during the Fātimid rule of Egypt, becoming the primary infantry force for the Fātimid caliphate until their destruction by Saladin [Salāh al-Dīn] in 1169. In addition, African military slaves were used on the Indian subcontinent in Gujerat, Bengal, and the Deccan, and by the Rasulid dynasty of Yemen (1229–1454).

The most expensive slaves in slave-holding societies were eunuchs. African boys were castrated outside the Islamic world, most frequently in southern Ethiopia. Once healed, the new eunuchs would then be traded north through Egypt or east to the Red Sea coast and beyond for use in domestic households and as trusted government servants in various states. As northern and western Africa became Islamicized, an internal eunuch trade developed with supply sources from the areas of modern-day southern Chad and the Central African Republic.

There is evidence of Africans traded as slaves as far north as Ireland in the Middle Ages. Provence also received African labor between the thirteenth and fifteenth centuries, but the most well-documented European use of African slave labor was in the southern Italian city-states as domestics and particularly for plantation labor on various Mediterranean islands and on the Iberian Peninsula. At the end of the Middle Ages, owing to Islamic military power, the Black Sea slave markets became difficult of access for Christian traders, producing an expansion in the trade in African slaves north to the Mediterranean markets.

From the early fourteenth century, the Portuguese crown was interested in obtaining African slaves and issued licenses to privateers to operate in Morocco for that purpose. In this early trade, slaves were obtained from the Canary Islands as well as from Morocco. As the Portuguese began their maritime expansion down the Moroccan coast and further into the sub-Saharan coastal region in the fifteenth century, they continued to purchase and raid for slaves, gradually establishing, by the mid-1550s, a regular trading system with African suppliers that, as time went on, increased in scale the further south they went. Portuguese maritime traders were able to tap into, and draw from, a long-established trans-Saharan trading system, providing the opportunity for African traders to deal with a separate and competing trade network.

The Portuguese obtained a papal monopoly on the Atlantic coast slave trade in Africa during the last decades of the fifteenth century, with the majority obtained from Senegambia. At the end of the century, the Portuguese also had a significant trade with the Kingdom of Benin, with the slaves passing through the trading fort at São Jorge da Mina, built in 1482 on the Gold Coast. A few years later, a royal office was created in Lisbon for overseeing the royal trade in slaves, including a licensed reexport slave trade, mostly into Spain where a large and organized black slave community developed. Most slaves in Italy were acquired from the trans-Saharan routes. By and large, slaves in Europe were owned by the aristocracy, church leaders and institutions, and some government officials.

Though not negligible, the Indian Ocean trade in Africans did not involve the numbers attained by the other trade routes for the delivery of Africans during the Middle Ages. Independent traders from throughout the western Indian Ocean region operated in small *dhows* bringing African slaves as far as China and all points between, but they were more a luxury and curiosity than a crucial labor source for the Asian societies that purchased them.

**BIBLIOGRAPHY**

Ayalon, David. "On the Eunuchs in Islam." *Jerusalem Studies in Arabic and Islam* 1 (1979): 67–124.

Fisher, Allan G.B., and Humphrey J. Fisher. *Slavery and Muslim Society in Africa.* Garden City, NJ: Doubleday, 1971.

Hunwick, J.O. "Black Slaves in the Mediterranean World: Introduction to a Neglected Aspect of the African Diaspora." *Slavery and Abolition* 13.1 (April 1992): 5–38.

Mark, Peter. *Africans in European Eyes: The Portrayal of Black Africans in Fourteenth and Fifteenth Century Europe.* Syracuse, NY: Syracuse UP, 1974.

# S

Phillips, William D., Jr. *Slavery from Roman Times to the Early Transatlantic Trade.* Minneapolis: U of Minnesota P, 1985.

Popovic, Alexandre. *La Révolte des esclaves en Iraq au IIIe/IXe siècle.* Paris: Paul Geuthner, 1976.

Renault, François. *La Traite des noirs au proche-orient médiéval.* Paris: Paul Geuthner, 1989.

Saunders, A.C. de C.M. *A Social History of Black Slaves and Freedmen in Portugal: 1441–1555.* Cambridge: Cambridge UP, 1982.

Spaulding, Jay. "Medieval Christian Nubia and the Islamic World: A Reconsideration of the *Baqt* Treaty." *International Journal of African Historical Studies* 28.3 (1995): 577–594.

*Kathryn L. Green*

**SEE ALSO**
African Trade; Canary Islands; Caravans; Egypt; Fāṭimids; Gold Trade in Africa; Mamluks; Muslim Travelers and Trade; Portuguese Expansion; Portuguese Trade; Saladin; Spain and Portugal

## Smbat the Constable
*See* Sempad the Constable

## Solinus, Julius Gaius (fl. *c.* 230/240 C.E.)

Author of an influential geographical compilation, *Collectanea rerum memorabilium* (Collection of Memorable Things), a digest of Pliny's *Natural History.*

Though marred at times by an inelegant and willfully obscure style and manner of presentation, the *Collectanea* was an exceedingly rich compendium of marvels and fables, especially for geography, eventually replacing in popularity the sources on which the author had drawn. It is a lengthy work, running to fifty-six sections and 216 pages in its modern edition and containing the names of about 1,900 places and persons, both historical and mythological.

Solinus's exact date and place of birth are unknown. On the basis of internal evidence he is thought to have been Italian (perhaps from Rome) and to have lived between the later second century and the fourth century (though most probably during the mid-third century). Nor is there agreement about his full name. A group of tenth-century manuscripts call him Gaius Julius Solinus; earlier manuscripts and sources refer to him as Julius Solinus, or merely Solinus.

The single work for which he is remembered today, his *Collectanea rerum memorabilium,* also appears under the titles *De mirabilibus mundi* and *Polyhistor* (this name, meaning roughly "Many Stories," also became a nickname for the author himself). Recent scholarship prefers the last title, since *De mirabilibus mundi* was used by the author only in the first edition of the text (perhaps dedicated to Constantius II); when the author wanted to replace this edition with a better one, he changed the original title to *Polyhistor* (as is explained in the second dedicatory letter to Aventus, wrongly interpreted by Mommsen as a later interpolation). The title *De mirabilibus mundi* apparently arose from confusion between the two different states of the text.

The work provides a description of miraculous and extraordinary phenomena of the known world. Its lengthy first book treats the foundation of Rome and its further history (chiefly mythical) until the reign of Augustus. It includes extensive information about the Roman calendar—taken largely from the now lost *De anno Romanorum* of Suetonius—and a short discourse on the human race. Then Solinus gives accounts of the various parts of the world, beginning with Italy (which he treats at considerable length), Greece and adjacent parts, Germany (broadly conceived), Gaul, Britain, Spain, and Africa, then moving on to Arabia, Syria, Asia Minor, and Assyria, followed by "India" (for the "Far East") and Parthia (inhabited by monstrous races of humans, and many kinds of animals, real and imaginary). He concludes with the islands Gorgades and Hesperides, both situated in the Atlantic and home to "monstra." This loose geographical framework was convenient for the author's main purpose: relating all the world's wonders.

Solinus does not indicate his sources but it is now clear that about three-quarters of his work (chiefly the lore of plants, animals, gems and natural wonders) derives from Pliny's *Natural History.* For human manners and customs and local peculiarities of regions, he relied on Pomponius Mela, though some of his facts, particularly those pertaining to the British Isles, are apparently unique to Solinus.

The *Collectanea,* though a compilation, was enormously important as a source for other geographical and historical compilers to use in late antiquity and the Middle Ages. Solinus was drawn on by Ammianus Marcellinus (*c.* 390); the *Liber genealogus* (*c.* 455); St. Augustine in his *City of God;* Martianus Capella's *Marriage of Mercury and Philology* (*c.* 500); Priscian; the authors of Virgil and Lucan *scolia;* Isidore of Seville's *Etymologies;* Aldhelm; Bede; Dicuil's *De mensura orbis terrae* (*c.* 820); the anonymous *De situ orbis* (*c.* 850); the Hereford *Mappamundi* (he is directly cited in twelve different map legends and the clear source of more than twenty others); Lupus of Ferrières; Walafrid Strabo; Heric of Auxerre; and many other medieval writers on travel, geography, history, and ethnography. Above all, he had a significant influence on Isidore of Seville, whose *Etymologies* incorporated a large portion of Solinus and passed his information on to crusaders, discoverers, and others interested in distant countries, monsters, and all kinds of wonderful things in the East (and elsewhere). *Collectanea* is preserved today in at least 350 known manuscripts, of which at least twenty-five are epitomes and excerpts in prose and poetry.

New discoveries of far and unknown countries that began in the later Middle Ages gave rise to a different understanding of geography and how to encompass written descriptions of the world. More and more critics accused Solinus of inaccuracy—both in his content and in his employment (or distortion) of information from earlier classical sources. One indication that the classical authors had regained respectability by the late 1400s is that Solinus was often printed with—but following—Pomponius Mela's *De chorographia* (see the translation into English in 1587 by Arthur Golding in the bibliography below). Yet this decline of Solinus's influence was a gradual process; approximately eighty-five printed editions were published after 1473, of which at least fifty appeared during the sixteenth century alone. Moreover, many well-known scholars studied Solinus's book, including such humanist leaders as Joannes Camers [Giovanni Ricuzzi Vellini] (1448–1546) and Filippo Beroaldo (1453–1505).

**BIBLIOGRAPHY**

Büren, Veronika von. "Une édition critique de Solin au IXe siècle." *Scriptorium* 50 (1996): 22–87.

Golding, Arthur, trans. *The Excellent and Pleasant Worke of Caius Iulius Solinus.* A facsimile edition [of the edition of 1587] with intro. by George Kish. Gainesville, FL: Scholars' Facsimiles and Reprints, 1955.

Milham, Mary Ella. "C. Julius Solinus." In Paul Oskar Kristeller, *Catalogus translationum et commentariorum.* Washington, DC: Catholic U of America P, 1986, vol. 6, pp. 73–85.

Mommsen, Theodor, ed. *C. Ivlii Solini, Collectanea rervm memorabilivm.* Berlin: Weidmann, 1958.

Schmidt, Peter Lebrechts. "Solins Polyhistor in Wissenschaftsgeschichte und Geschichte." *Philologus* 139 (1995): 23–35.

Walter, Hermann. *Die 'Collectanea Rerum Memorabilium' des C. Iulius Solinus: Ihre Entstehung und die Echtheit ihrer Zweitfassung.* Wiesbaden: Steiner, 1969.

Z.R.W.M. von Martels

**SEE ALSO**

Animals, Exotic; Bede; Dicuil; Ebstorf World Map; Gems; Geography in Medieval Europe; Hereford Map; Isidore of Seville; Mela, Pomponius; Monstrosity, Geographical; Pliny the Elder; *Wonders of the East*

## Solomon and Saturn

Two Old English poems written in the second half of the tenth century about debates between the biblical King Solomon and Saturn, here uniquely represented in Old English poetry as a Chaldean prince (*Caldea eorl*). Poem I's 165 lines (Menner's edition) contain Solomon's dramatic, if didactic, personification of the Pater Noster's power to dispel demons. Poem II, approximately twice the length of Poem I, comprises a more dialogic contest of wit and wisdom between the two men. Often couched in riddling language and ranging widely between the bizarre and the proverbial, Poem II touches on Germanic concerns about fate, old age, and exile; Christian themes of the fall of Lucifer, the afterlife, a heavenly Jerusalem, and guardian angels; Hebraic lore about differences between fate and foreknowledge; and esoterica concerning the nature of fire and the *uasa mortis* (II, 246–272), a four-headed, whale-bodied, vulture-feathered, griffin-footed bird that lives in "the middle region of the Philistines."

Of particular interest from the standpoint of the geographical lore of Anglo-Saxon England is the list of places Saturn visited to garner his vast knowledge: he ranged widely throughout Asia from the Indian Ocean (*Ind[ea] mer[e]*) to the lands of Syria and "Palestinion" and into Asia Minor's "Cappadocia," "Piþinia," and "Pamphilia." He traversed Marculf's native land, Saul's kingdom, Porus's borders; plumbed Lybia's learning; and observed the Greeks' skills (*creca cræftas*) and the race of Arabians (*cynn Arabia*). Faring into "Persea," "Macedonia," and "Mesopotamie," he visited the treasure halls of Medes (*Meda maþumselas*), the dwellings of the Philistines (*Filistina flet*), the stronghold of Crete (*fæsten creca*), the forest of Egypt (*wudu Egipta*), the waters of Midian (*wæter Mæthea[n]*), and the cliffs of Horeb (*cludas coreffes*). He knows "Niniuen" (Nineveh) and

# S

the cities where Christ walked, including "Hieryhco," "Galilea," and "Hierusa[lem]."

This impressive list of toponyms is probably meant to demonstrate Saturn's worthiness as Solomon's opponent since it does not present a schematic geography. Place-names are not organized by their geographical affinity, but by their poetic appropriateness to the alliterative style; hence, *Persea rice* (Kingdom [of] Persia) is linked to *Palestinion; pamphilia* to *Pores gemœre* (Porus's borders); and *Macedonia* to *Mesopotamie*. Because the poet organizes the catalogue according to metrical and alliterative requirements rather than copying it directly from a single text, the list's order presents an opportunity to speculate about—but, given the linguistic differences, probably not to identify specifically—the compiler's source materials, such as Aethicus Ister's *Cosmographia* and the *Nomina locorum ex beati Hieronimi presbiteri et Flaui Iosephi collecta opusculis* often attributed to Bede (see O'Keeffe). The poems survive in two incomplete manuscripts at Corpus Christi College, Cambridge. MS 41, a fragment, contains ll. 1–93 of Poem I; and MS 422 contains a portion of Poem I and Poem II.

## BIBLIOGRAPHY

Kemble, John, ed. and trans. *The Dialogue of Solomon and Saturnus, with an Historical Introduction.* 1848; rpt. New York: AMS Press, 1974.

Menner, Robert J., ed. *The Poetical Dialogues of Solomon and Saturn.* MLA Monograph Series 13. 1941; rpt. New York: Kraus, 1973.

O'Keeffe, Katherine O'Brien. "The Geographic List of Solomon and Saturn II." *Anglo-Saxon England* 20 (1991): 123–141.

Shippey, T.A., trans. "The Second Dialogue of Solomon and Saturn." In *Poems of Wisdom and Learning in Old English.* Cambridge, England: Brewer, 1976, pp. 86–103.

*Robert K. Upchurch*

**SEE ALSO**

Aethicus Ister, *Cosmographia;* Bede

## Spain and Portugal: Trade and Commerce

During the sixth and seventh centuries, the Iberian Peninsula was a backwater in international commerce. After the Islamic conquest in the eighth century, however, the area gradually became an important economic transit zone between the Muslim world and western Europe, continuing as such for the next four centuries.

From about the twelfth century, the expanding Christian kingdoms in the north of the Iberian Peninsula developed trading links with northwest Europe, and this area became a part of the European Atlantic trade network. The Christian "reconquest" of most of Iberia during the thirteenth century coincided with increased activity by Christian merchants in Iberia and a corresponding decline in the number of Muslim merchants, although some Jewish traders remained active in the area up to the end of the Middle Ages. By that time, Christians, now in control of the entire peninsula, were geographically and politically well placed to become a link between the Atlantic and the Mediterranean worlds.

Within Iberia, trade developed slowly. During the twelfth century, periodic markets were supplemented by permanent commercial centers and "great fairs." While there was some continuity in the products traded, new commercial organizations began to evolve by the twelfth century and new commodities, such as merino wool, became important by the late Middle Ages. By the fourteenth century, Iberian ships began voyages of trade and exploration along the West African coast and into the Atlantic, leading ultimately to the discovery of a sea route to India and the Americas.

During Visigothic dominance over the Iberian Peninsula during the sixth and seventh centuries, trade had been minimal. Cities declined and manufactures were limited largely to armaments and essential farming and household implements, although Byzantine rule over southern Iberia during the sixth century stimulated some limited trade across the Mediterranean. There are references to Greek merchants landing on the peninsula in the seventh century and to trade between Visigothic Iberia and Marseilles. The Visigothic ruler, Leovigild (568–586) issued gold coins. Legal texts of the period refer to money changers and moneylenders. Some Visigothic rulers sought to limit the role of Jewish merchants in their domains. Egica (r. 687–702) imposed particularly heavy sanctions on Jewish merchants. However, evidence on trade is scarce before the Muslim invasions of the early eighth century.

The period from the early eighth to the end of the eleventh century was a new phase in the development of Iberian commerce. During this period, much of the Iberian peninsula was under the rule of the Muslims, who called the region *al-Andalūs.* Al-Andalus was far more economically developed than the small Christian states in the north of the peninsula, and, as a rule, changes in political fortunes within al-Andalus had minimal impact on the growth of trade. For example, in the eighth and early ninth centuries, al-Andalus was part of the Umayyad caliphate based in Damascus, and trade developed with the North African coast, Palestine, and Syria. Cities flourished. The population of Córdoba, for instance, rose from about 25,000 in the early eighth century to 75,000 in the ninth century. The fall of the Umayyad caliphate (750 C.E.) and the simultaneous rise of the Abbasid caliphate centered on Baghdad had limited impact on this commerce since al-Andalus remained an autonomous region governed by a member of the Umayyad family. While trade with African and Near Eastern ports continued, new commercial linkages formed with Byzantium and the Frankish Empire remained weak, and trade connections between al-Andalus and the Christian kingdoms in northern Iberia strengthened only gradually. Commercial growth was somewhat slow during the ninth century due to the sluggish development in Mediterranean trade as a whole, not the change in political structures.

On the other hand, the establishment of an independent Umayyad caliphate based in Córdoba in 929 stimulated Iberian trade. Within a few years, Umayyad forces gained control of several ports on the North African coast, giving the caliphate access to the supply routes of gold from West Africa. Trade with the Christian kingdoms grew. In the ninth century, the belief that the body of St. James had been found at Santiago de Compostela led to the development of a pilgrim center there; during subsequent centuries, the growth of pilgrim traffic was accompanied by increased trade. The collapse of the Umayyad caliphate in 1031 enabled the Christian kingdoms of the north to expand southward, although by 1086, the Almoravid revival incorporated much of old al-Andalus into an empire that also included a large part of northwest Africa. Thus, despite political changes throughout the period from the eighth to the eleventh century, Iberian international trade was largely oriented toward the eastern Mediterranean and Africa. However, Viking incursions on Atlantic coastal areas in the ninth and tenth centuries led to some contacts with northern Europe, and by the eleventh century, connections with Flanders and England supplemented the long-standing trade links between Spanish and French ports in the Bay of Biscay.

During the Middle Ages, although the areas under Islamic rule were more urbanized than was the Christian north, most people still lived in small villages. Rural markets provided places where local agricultural and craft products were exchanged. These markets were cyclical; markets, for example, were held on Wednesdays in some places and on Tuesdays in others. They were also relatively unregulated. Products of the urban and rural economies were usually exchanged in the somewhat larger periodic markets located just outside the city gates, and some towns also developed public markets in the main square. Many goods were transported by pack animals, but in some regions, where the old Roman network of roads existed, horse-drawn wagons were used. In most areas, rivers were of limited use for transport because the water levels fell sharply during the summer. Tolls were charged at frontier towns and customs duties at ports. A Muslim law of the eighth century specified customs duty as 2.5 percent for Muslims, 5 percent for local non-Muslims, and 10 percent for foreigners, but these rates were subject to negotiation. In al-Andalus, merchants cleared their cargo through the *dīwān* (customs bureau) and lodged at the *funduq* (hostelry and warehouse).

Seaborne trade was conducted in small ships that hugged the coast; there was great reluctance to conduct travel and trade during the winter. The early ships were mostly round vessels (*nefs*) that used square sails and had two steering oars in the rear. Later, lateen sails also began to be used. According to eleventh-century texts, these ships could carry up to 400 passengers. Valuable cargo was carried in galleys propelled by oars and a supplementary sail. Galleys were more limited than sailing vessels in their storage capacity, but they were favored for trade in areas where pirates operated because they were not dependent on winds for locomotion. The northern cog was not common in Iberian trade though it was seen in the northern Spanish ports.

By the end of the eleventh century there was a shift from periodic to permanent markets, although permanent stalls often coexisted with more transient weekly markets. Stalls specializing in goods of one type came to be located in a single street or cluster of shops. Weights and measures were regulated by a market inspector, or *muhtasib*, who also inspected buildings and sanitation. *Muhtasibs* in seaports also monitored foreign trade. Wool, linen, and silk textiles (silk worms were imported to al-Andalus in the eighth century) were produced both for export and domestic consumption in the south; Granada, Valencia, and Almería were known for their cloth. Cattle raising took place in the north, but high-quality leather production centered on Córdoba, and the area's fine, supple cordovan leather

# S

was in demand throughout Western Europe. Toledo was well known for its cutlery and weaponry (especially swords). The best paper was produced at Játiva, though Almería and Denia also exported it. Al-Andalus was also famous for its gold and silver crafts. Gold, silver, copper, iron, and lead were all mined in Granada. Mercury was mined at Almadén, north of Córdoba, copper and silver in Alentejo, iron west of Córdoba and near Seville, and tin in the Algarve. In Valencia, oranges were the chief crop. Other exports included olive oil (chiefly from Seville), dried figs (from Málaga and Seville), and slaves. In the tenth century, Pechina (near Almería) was the chief port in the southeast. Wheat, rye, and barley were produced in the Meseta area chiefly for subsistence and local trade, but the vineyards at La Rioja, Porto, and La Mancha became famous throughout Western Europe.

Imports to the peninsula included spices from the East such as pepper, cinnamon, cloves, and saffron; aromatic substances like camphor, musk, aloes, and ambergris; dyes such as indigo, lac, and a variety of other products including brazilwood, wool, flax, slaves, and gold. Persia continued to supply a small quantity of high-quality silks. Some of these products were reexported to northwest Europe. Iberia's Mediterranean neighbor, Morocco, supplied wood, alum, and antimony in exchange for copper and cloth, with trade centered mainly in Seville. Tunisian towns were entrepôts for traders from al-Andalus and the eastern Mediterranean until the Hilali invasion of the mid-eleventh century. After that, trade between Iberia and the eastern Mediterranean became more direct.

Urban centers continued to grow. Córdoba's population exceeded 100,000 by the tenth century. Seville, whose population grew to 82,000 in the eleventh century, became the major commercial center in the south. Toledo grew to 37,000 by the eleventh century, but the largest city in the west, al-Ushbana (Lisbon) had just over 5,000 inhabitants. Town life in the Christian north emerged out of military and administrative centers, but adjacent market centers began to grow in the tenth and eleventh centuries. In twelfth-century cities like León, Zamora, and Salamanca, the new commercial areas became fused with the old administrative centers.

The coinage in early medieval Iberia was silver, but the inflow of Sudanese gold in the tenth century enabled the Umayyad caliph, Abd al-Rahmān III (r. 912–961), to mint gold dinars. Ramon Berenguer I (r. 1018–1035), count of Barcelona, was the first

Christian ruler to coin money; his coins were imitations of the Muslim dinars. The right of coinage was generally reserved for kings, although Alfonso VI of Castille-León (r. 1065–1109 [king of Castille from 1072]) authorized the bishop of Compostela to issue coins. Leónese bullion *deniers,* Muslim gold *dinars* and silver *dirhams,* and even Byzantine gold *nomismata* freely circulated in Christian Iberia. In 1172, Alfonso VIII of Castile (r. 1158–1214) issued *morabitinos* or *maravedis* (copied from the *al-Murābitūn,* the Almoravid coin). Afonso Henriques, who founded Portugal in the mid-twelfth century and ruled as king from 1139 to 1185, also coined *morabitinos,* which soon became the basic coinage in Christian Spain. His simultaneous coining of *deniers* (*dinheiros*) and half-*deniers* (*mealhas*) reflects the continuing mediating role of the Iberian Christian kingdoms in trade between the Muslim world and Western Europe.

Christians and Jewish merchants conducted much of the trade between the Muslim south and the Christian north. Muslim merchants did not travel frequently to Christian areas, although the 1166 revenue register of Evora refers to Moorish merchants. On the other hand, Jewish merchants traded between the Iberian Peninsula and the eastern Mediterranean as early as the ninth century. Islamic rule brought better conditions for Jewish merchants, though their position in al-Andalus was never entirely secure as evidenced by the violent anti-Jewish riots in Granada in 1066. The arrival of the Almoravids reduced their opportunities further. Another bloody anti-Jewish riot occurred in Granada in 1090, and Jewish traders suffered sporadic discrimination from the Almohads in the twelfth century. The Jewish quarter in Córdoba was sacked in 1135. By the twelfth century, some Jewish merchants moved from Islamic into Christian areas, where they played a key role in the growth of trade in the later Middle Ages. Hispanic Christian merchants were also becoming more active by the end of the eleventh century. One should not exaggerate these religious divisions, however. Merchants of different faiths worked together and often traveled aboard the same ships, although it was rare to see them pool their resources for common ventures.

New trends in Iberian commerce in the twelfth and thirteenth centuries reflected developments in international trade. During this period, Italian city-states gained a dominant role in trade in the northern Mediterranean. By the twelfth century, products from the Islamic world were flowing to Western Europe through the Italian cities of Pisa, Genoa, and Venice. Iberian ports in the north thus had to rely more on exporting products from the peninsula itself. On the Biscay coast, San Vicente de la Barquera, Santander, Laredo, and Castro-Urdiales developed trade in iron, timber, and fish with Bayonne and Bordeaux. Trading links with England and Flanders were strengthened. In 1226, Henry III of England (r. 1216–1272) gave more than 100 safe conducts to Portuguese traders in his territories. In 1283 and 1288, the Corporation of London appointed special brokers to handle incoming merchandise from Portugal. In 1280, special privileges were given to "Spaniards" in Bruges, but Castilian involvement in the Anglo-French wars of the thirteenth century harmed Castile's trade with England. Cloth (ranging from costly scarlets to cheap Cornish cloth) was the major import from northwest Europe, but other manufactured goods—including basins and mugs of tin and pewter, belts, caps, mirrors, knives, cushions, and candles—came into Iberian ports. The goods exported to northwest Europe in exchange included iron from the Basque regions, wine from Bordeaux, and some wool. Small quantities of merchandise including cotton, sugar, silk, dyes, and spices were transshipped through the Iberian peninsula, but their significance was minimal.

The Mediterranean trade links with the Iberian ports were still the most important external trading linkage. By the thirteenth century, the increasingly accepted practice of lending money for interest and the development of bills of exchange further stimulated international trade in the region. However, Italian traders began to play an important role in this area as well. By the second half of the twelfth century, Genoa and Pisa signed agreements that guaranteed safe conduct for their ships and lower customs dues in Almohad ports. After Ferdinand III of Castile-León (r. 1217–1252 [king of León from 1230]) captured Seville in 1248, the Genoese obtained similar privileges from him. By the end of the thirteenth century, the Venetian Flanders fleet had begun to call at Lisbon and Seville. By the next century, the Genoese had colonies in Seville, Cádiz, Jerez, Murcia, Cartagena, and Lisbon; the gold *florin* of Florence was widely used as currency. Barcelona became an important center of trade. Other ports that prospered included Valencia, Alicante, Cartagena, and Murcia, but Almería declined after its conquest by Christians in the twelfth century. Bilbao, founded around 1300, swiftly became a bustling trading center known particularly for its wool exports. By the thirteenth century, fishing and the coastal trade had stimulated the development of marine fleets that began to compete with foreign ships for the carrying trade. Shipyards in Barcelona had the capacity to construct or repair up to thirty ships at a time. Alfonso X of Castile (r. 1252–1284) ordered the construction of shipyards at Seville, while Dinis (r. 1279–1325) encouraged shipbuilding in Lisbon.

Trade expanded within the Iberian Peninsula as well. The pilgrim traffic to Compostela increased steadily, and by the mid-twelfth century, the markets of Burgos, León, and Huerca were well known. Products from al-Andalus were traded there. Cattle rearing developed further in Andalusia, Algarve, and Alemtejo. From the thirteenth century, the great fairs of Castile began to develop. Alfonso X established two fairs in Seville, one extending for thirty days around Pentecost (a movable feast) and another for thirty days at Michaelmas (September 29). Fairs established by royal charter were limited in number but saw extensive wholesale trading. In time, other regional fairs grew in Valladolid, San Zoil de Carrion, Brihuega, and Alcalá de Henares. In Portugal, fairs developed mostly in the thirteenth century, though the Ponte de Lima fair was in existence by 1125. Rulers interested in their revenue possibilities provided security and regulated prices, credit, and sanitation at these fairs. In Catalonia, public buildings were constructed to facilitate the development of markets and fairs.

The twelfth and thirteenth centuries also saw the development of new commercial arrangements in Iberia. By the thirteenth century, Catalan traders used the *commenda*. Essentially, it was a sleeping partnership in which one partner provided capital but did not travel while the other provided labor and did the traveling. In the unilateral form, the traveling partner provided no capital, usually bore no liability for loss of capital, and received a quarter of any profit. In the bilateral form, the traveling partner also provided some capital, normally a third, and usually bore liability for a third of any capital loss, and received a half of the profit.

In the fourteenth century, there developed the *societas maris*, by which two or more merchants would get together for a single venture: one would travel with the goods and all would share profits at agreed proportions at the end of the voyage. Trading companies for a fixed term, usually five years, came into being in Iberia in the fifteenth century.

# S

New commercial organizations grew as well. In 1296, Santander, Laredo, Castro Urdiales, and San Vicente de la Barquera joined with San Sebastián, Fuenterrabia, Bermeo, and Guetaria to form the *Hermandad de las villas de marina de Castilla con Vitoria*. The objectives of the *Hermandad* included freeing the towns from paying tolls to the bishop of Burgos, monopolizing the export of iron, and escaping the jurisdiction of the *almirante de Castilla* in Burgos. This indicated the growing importance of the merchants in the northern ports. The *Hermandad*, however, did not systematically exclude alien traders, who faced fewer restrictions in Iberia than in the Hanseatic League. In Portugal, the first *bolsa de commercio* was set up in Lisbon with royal approval in 1295. The *bolsa* was an agreement among Portuguese merchants trading with Flanders, England, and France that provided for an insurance system for all vessels loading in Portugal or chartered by Portuguese companies to go abroad. Part of the sum collected was sent to Flanders to defray legal costs and other expenses, but most of it remained in Portugal.

Artisan confraternities and guilds developed. Confraternities were primarily religious and social in nature; they mobilized members for support in times of need and defended the economic interests of the members. Guilds tried to monopolize crafts. Except in Catalonia, rulers generally viewed the guilds with suspicion and tried to prevent their development. In 1257, Jaime I of Aragón (r. 1213–1276) allowed merchants to draw up ordinances regulating maritime customs. In 1283, Pedro III of Aragón (r. 1276–1285) granted a charter establishing the Consulate of the Sea. This charter provided for the annual election of two consuls who would preside over the guild and settle disputes. Pedro IV (r. 1336–1387) also chartered such groups in Majorca (1343) and Barcelona (1347). The consulates served as maritime courts as well.

The thirteenth century also saw changes as a result of the Christian reconquest. During the thirteenth century many Muslim merchants and artisans left areas conquered by the Christians for North Africa, and Iberian trade became a predominantly Christian concern. However, Jewish converts to Christianity (known as *conversos*) played an important role in commerce within Iberia, although in some areas they were occasionally exposed to violence as in the anti-*converso* riots in Toledo in 1449.

Catalan trade developed swiftly in the thirteenth century. The seizure of Majorca (1229–1235) and

Valencia (1238) by Aragón strengthened the kingdom's dominance over trade on the eastern coast of Iberia. In 1227, Jaime I decreed that goods from Barcelona must be exported in Catalan ships if they were available. Catalan traders lived in Alexandria as early as 1219. Links forged with Tunis, Sicily, Sardinia, and ports in the eastern Mediterranean gave Catalans access to spices, gold, silk, and slaves, which were exchanged for woolen cloth, olive oil, rice, and fruits. Catalans traded extensively with the Muslims despite papal prohibitions and, by the mid-fourteenth century, dominated Alexandria's trade with the Iberian Peninsula. However, their participation in the Atlantic trade was slight.

By the late fourteenth century Catalan trade was in a serious decline. Trade in Barcelona decreased fivefold between the mid-fourteenth and the mid-fifteenth centuries. This decline is variously attributed to the collapse of private banks (1381–1383) and an increasing aversion to risk-taking by the Catalan merchant community. The rise of the Turks, Genoese competition, and the Black Death were contributing factors. Catalonia's total population fell by more than 20 percent between 1378 and 1497. In the fifteenth century, Catalan woolen cloth faced competition from better quality English cloth. Continued prosperity in neighboring Valencia, where the Genoese obtained supplies, might indicate that Catalonia's decline was also due to its inability to gain a share in the new trade flowing through the Straits of Gibraltar into the Atlantic.

By the end of the fourteenth century, the Iberian Peninsula had become the southern frontier of the Christian European trading system, and harbor cities such as Seville and Málaga became important ports of call between the Atlantic and the Mediterranean. Trade with northwest Europe continued to develop through the ports in northern Spain as well. In 1351, Edward III of England (r. 1327–1377) concluded an agreement with the *Hermandad* promising protection to Castilian merchants visiting his ports. In 1353, he made a similar agreement with the merchants of Lisbon and Porto. Increasing numbers of Castilian and Portuguese merchants were at Bruges. When Rouen, Bordeaux, and Bayonne came under his control in 1363, Charles V of France (r. 1364–1380) promised protection to Castilians in these ports.

However, royal policy was not always favorable to merchants. The rulers of Castile and Portugal, for instance, often imposed restrictions on the export of gold, silver, cereals, horses, cattle, goats, sheep, pigs, and other products. King Fernando of Portugal (r. 1367–1383) claimed priority in loading for his own merchant ships. In 1373, the *Cortes* complained that Fernando requisitioned wheat at five *soldos* and sold it at a 1,000-percent profit. Fernando also tried to discourage farmers from abandoning their fields to engage in trade by threatening to seize untilled land. On the other hand, his decree of 1377 provided that residents of Lisbon building a ship of at least 100 tons could cut timber from the king's forest; were exempt from the tithe on sailcloth, iron, or wood; and were free of all taxes on the first cargo. In 1380, these privileges were extended to those who built ships of more than fifty tons; in 1381, the policy was extended to residents of Porto. By the fifteenth century there were Castilian, Catalan, Basque, and Portuguese factors at Bruges dealing with increasing commerce between Iberia and Flanders.

There was both continuity and change in the products traded. With the Christian reconquest, the flow of gold from Africa slowed to a trickle and the export of silk declined. However, trade in other products such as dried fruit and cordovan leather continued. Olive oil was in great demand overseas. Spain also became one of Europe's main producers of mercury. The production of iron expanded: by 1500, Spain produced almost one-third of Europe's iron.

A major change in the late Middle Ages was the expansion in sheep rearing in the Spanish *meseta*. By the early fourteenth century, Castilian wool was a major export. The migration of sheep (*trashumancia*) led to the establishment of the *Mesta* to regulate and control sheepwalks. Cattle ranching developed in the reconquered lands as well. Woolen cloth was exported to Italy, northern Europe, and North Africa. Depopulation due to the Black Death, which led to a shortage of labor and the growing demand for wool in Europe, were the major forces that propelled further change. The number of sheep doubled to some 2.7 million in 1467. Major sheep owners, who were the grandees of Spanish society, owned up to 40,000 sheep. In the late fourteenth century, a powerful guild of wool exporters at Burgos recruited members from other cities such as Toledo and Segovia to promote exports. The Castilian rulers, on the other hand, were more interested in fostering a domestic cloth industry. For example, in 1462, Enrique IV (r. 1454–1474) allowed only one-third of the raw wool produced in his kingdom to be exported.

Regional fairs continued to prosper. *Feiras francas*, at which merchants paid no taxes or duties, were rare in the fourteenth century but became common in the fifteenth; from the mid-fifteenth century, the fairs of Medina del Campo became famous throughout Western Europe. The fair was the center for the wholesale trade in wool, and after 1450, Medina del Campo was also the financial capital of Castile.

The late fifteenth century also saw a temporary but significant halt in the rise in the price of bullion that had been taking place for some 200 years. New techniques of extracting silver and the availability of African gold via the Atlantic sea route contributed to this development. The currency stabilized in the mid-fourteenth century, with the Spanish *real* and the Portuguese gold *cruzado* having a ready market. Significant efforts were made to standardize weights and measures. King Manuel I of Portugal (r. 1495–1521) decreed in 1499 that all measures and weights should conform to the copper patterns made and kept in the city hall in Lisbon.

Meanwhile, Iberian exploration of the Atlantic islands and the African coast proceeded, although the history of that exploration, often provided in unreliable primary sources, is complicated and, at times, shrouded in mystery. The Canary Islands were rediscovered around 1341, apparently by a Genoese, Lanzarotto Malocello, who may have been operating for the Portuguese; the Canaries were given to Castile (by papal bull) in 1344, but ownership continued to be contested at least until 1479. By the 1400s the Canaries were exporting sugar to Castile. The Madeira Islands were occupied by the Portuguese in the 1420s. In 1439, a royal charter exempted all merchandise from Madeira from customs dues, and from 1450 to 1470, the island of Madeira exported more than 1,500 tons of grain annually to Portugal, although by the 1470s sugar had become the dominant crop. By the early 1490s, Madeira exported more than three million pounds (1,350,000 kilograms) of sugar annually. Settlement of the Azores, "discovered" by the Portuguese in 1427, began in the 1440s. The Azores produced dyestuffs, wheat, and cattle in the 1470s, but efforts to produce sugar there failed. The Cape Verde Islands, discovered and settled in part by Italians sponsored by Portugal, suffered from attacks by Castilians, who sacked Santiago Island in 1476; little trade developed there, but they were important in Portugal's voyages of discovery along the West African coast.

Exploration of the mainland African coast was pioneered by the Genoese and the Catalans, but the

# S

Portuguese soon took the lead. In 1434, Gil Eanes sailed beyond Cape Bojador. Soon after, he and Goncalves Baldaia reached Río de Oro, where they traded for gold. In the 1440s, Nuno Tristão explored the mouths of the Senegal, Gambia, and Salum rivers. The voyages continued after the 1440s partly because they proved to be profitable. The Portuguese found it easier to obtain slaves from the West African coast than from the Canaries or Morocco. The first black slaves were brought from north Mauritania in 1441. Between 1441 and 1448, a total of at least 1,000 were brought in, and in the 1450s the rate escalated to 700 to 800 slaves a year. Most slaves were sold within Europe for domestic and artisan labor, although some were put to work on sugar plantations in the Atlantic islands.

Until the mid-fifteenth century, any person was legally permitted to equip a vessel and sail to Africa, but one-fifth of all spoils were owed to the Portuguese crown. In 1443, however, Prince Henry (1394–1460), also called the Navigator, was granted both a monopoly on exploration and the right to a share in the spoils. He granted permits to other entrepreneurs. If Henry made no investment at all, he got one-fourth of all profits, but if he equipped the ship, he received one-half. Profits were high, generally above 100 percent—sometimes as high as 700 percent—of investments. By the 1440s, the first permanent station was set up on the island of Arguin (off the coast of Mauritania). In the 1450s, a second was established some miles to the south. Meanwhile, the Portuguese crown set up the Casa de Ceuta to supervise trade with Africa, and by 1445, another office at Lagos (Portugal; later moved to Lisbon) to supervise trade with Arguin. Portugal reached Guinea and Sierra Leone during the 1450s. When Henry died in 1460, his trading privileges reverted to the crown. Recent historical writing, while assigning Prince Henry considerable credit for encouraging exploration, makes clear that only one-third of all Portuguese voyages undertaken between 1415 and 1460 were taken on his initiative.

In 1468, the Portuguese crown granted a monopoly of trade with the African coast to Fernão Gomes, a Lisbon merchant, for five years, provided that he explore at least 100 leagues (320 miles or 550 kilometers) of coastline a year. In 1473, this contract was extended for another year. João de Santarem and Pero Escolar reached the Gold Coast in 1471, and Fernando Po sailed into the Bight of Biafra in 1472. Lopo Goncalves and Rui de Sequeira reached Gabon in 1474–1475. In 1474, Prince João (later King João II, 1481–1495) laid out a comprehensive plan of discovery leading to a search for a new route to the East. The Portuguese war with Castile (1475–1479) led to intrusions by Castilian ships on the Guinea coast, but the Treaty of Alcacovas (1479) gave the Portuguese a monopoly of all lands south of the Canaries in exchange for a renunciation of all claims to the Canaries themselves. Diogo Cão's first expedition (underwritten by João II) reached 15 degrees south latitude in Angola; on his second voyage (1485–1486), Cão sailed to 22 degrees south latitude. The mouths of all the large rivers of West Africa were explored before the end of the century. In 1488, Bartolomeu Dias rounded the Cape of Good Hope and reached Natal. Meanwhile, Pero de Covilhão and Afonso de Paiva were sent overland to Asia in 1487. Covilhão reached India and returned to Cairo, where he sent a report to the king, and then proceeded to Ethiopia, where he lived until his death in 1526.

The Portuguese conducted some westward exploration into the Atlantic, but it is uncertain how far they traveled. By 1474, João Vaz Corte Real and Alvaro Martins Homem seem to have reached Greenland or Newfoundland (which they called "Terra dos Bacalhaus" [Codfishland]), but evidence for their voyage is inconclusive.

Exploration of the Atlantic islands and the West African coast opened up a new trading area and made the Iberian Peninsula a major transshipment point of African goods to Europe. From Guinea came gold, gum arabic, civet, red pepper, cotton, ivory, and parrots. In exchange, cloth, red coral beads, silver, and blankets were exported to Africa. Iberia had reestablished itself as an economic transit zone. The voyages of exploration enabled Iberian seamen to accumulate extensive knowledge of the winds and currents of the Atlantic, information that was of great use in the succeeding period of voyages of discovery to the New World.

**BIBLIOGRAPHY**

Childs, Wendy R. *Anglo Castillian Trade in the Later Middle Ages.* Manchester, England: Manchester UP, 1978.

Constable, Olivia Remie. *Trade and Traders in Muslim Spain: The Commercial Realignment of the Iberian Peninsula, 900–1500.* Cambridge: Cambridge UP, 1994.

De Oliveira Marques, A.H. *Ensaios de Historia Medieval Portuguesa.* Lisbon: Portugalia, 1965.

Dufourcq, Charles Emmanuel, and J. Gautier-Dalché. *Histoire Economique et Sociale de l'Espagne Chrétienne au Moyen Age.* Paris: Colin, 1976.

Glick, Thomas F. *Islamic and Christian Spain in the Early Middle Ages.* Princeton, NJ: Princeton UP, 1979.

Magalhães Godinho, Vitorino. *A Economia dos Descobrimentos Henriquinos.* Lisbon: Sa da Costa, 1962.

Roth, Norman. *Jews, Visigoths, and Muslims in Medieval Spain: Cooperation and Conflict.* Leiden: Brill, 1994.

Ruiz, Theofilo F. *Crisis and Continuity: Land and Town in Late Medieval Castile.* Philadelphia: U of Pennsylvania P, 1994.

*Chandra Richard de Silva*

**SEE ALSO**

Alfonso X; Azores; Baghdad; Barcelona; Black Death; Bojador; Bruges; Canary Islands; Coinage and Money; Córdoba; Dias, Bartolomeu; Dyes and Pigments; Fairs; *Fondaco;* Galley; Genoa; Gold Trade in Africa; Guilds; Hanse, The; Henry the Navigator; Insurance; Ivory Trade; Lignum Aloes; Measurement of Distances; Merchants, Jewish; Pepper; Pilgrimage Sites, Spanish; Piracy; Pisa; Portuguese Expansion; Portuguese Trade; Saffron; Seville; Shipping Contracts, Mediterranean; Ships and Shipbuilding; Slave Trade, African; Spice Trade, Indian Ocean; Textiles, Decorative; Transportation, Inland; Venice; Viking Age

## Spice Trade, Indian Ocean

The Indian Ocean was the principal arena of Old World trade in spices, although China, Europe, and Africa also played an important role, as producers and especially as consumers. The Indian Ocean linked together the main spice-producing areas—Southeast Asia, India, and the Middle East—and provided viable distribution routes to a commerce that had to bridge distances that appear daunting even to modern eyes. Indonesian spices, for example, would travel some 7,500 miles (more than 12,000 kilometers) before reaching Suez, and cinnamon from China had to travel 10,000 miles (16,000 kilometers) to the same destination. Trading across such distances was made feasible by the natural advantages of sea travel in the Indian Ocean, in particular the monsoon winds, and by well-established networks of entrepôts and regional exchange.

Spice trade in the Indian Ocean dates from very early times. Cloves from the Molucca Islands, for example, were found at archaeological sites in northwestern India dating to the third millennium B.C.E. Cinnamon and cassia, originating from China, are referred to in the Old Testament. Asian literature of the first and second millennium B.C.E. refers to widespread use of the condiments, medicines, and incenses associated with the Old World spice trade. The writings of ancient Greeks and Romans show familiarity with most spices from the Indian Ocean basin. The spice trade of the medieval period thus reflected a long-established tradition in both supply and demand.

The ancient and medieval idea of "spices" was much more encompassing than the modern Western notion of spices as those food condiments that do not come from common garden herbs. In the premodern period, any rare article with culinary, aromatic, and medicinal application might be classified as a "spice." In the past, the aromatic and medicinal function of spices overshadowed their role as seasoning, unless, of course, the surviving sources neglected to dwell on an activity as base as cooking. Often, however, a single spice could perform all three functions, or at least two of them: culinary and medicinal. This applies to most of the spices commonly used in the West today: pepper, ginger, cinnamon, turmeric, cardamom, cloves, nutmeg, and mace. Spices with a predominantly aromatic function—aloewood, benzoin, camphor, frankincense, myrrh, sandalwood—are less well known today, but their past importance should not be underestimated.

Southeast Asia was undoubtedly the richest source of spices. The presence of cloves, nutmeg, and mace, which grew exclusively on a few small Indonesian islands, accounts for much of this exalted position. The clove, considered by medieval Europe the "queen" of spice, is a dried, unopened flower bud of an evergreen tree, *Eugenia caryophyllata,* which used to grow only on five small islands in the Moluccan archipelago. Nutmeg and mace are parts of the fruit of another rare evergreen tree, *Myristica fragrans,* native to the Banda archipelago.

The area was also home to more widely occurring spices, in particular ginger, cinnamon, cassia, amomum, pepper, galingale, and turmeric. Ginger, the rhizome of *Zingiber officinale,* may have been native to eastern Java, but its cultivation had spread to other parts of Southeast Asia, China, and India at a very early date. Cambodian ginger was considered the best. South Asian cinnamon, the "Malayan bark," was the fine bark of young branches and tips of the tree *Cinnamomum macrophyllu* and related species, which grew in Cambodia and the Malay Peninsula, on Borneo, Java, Sumatra, the Moluccas, and in the Philippines. Cassia, *Cinnamomum cassia* and related species, is native to Southeast Asia and widely grown there. Amomum, the seeds and rhizome

# S

of *Amomum kepulaga* and a number of related species of the *Zingiberaceae* family, was widely cultivated throughout the area. Pepper, *Piper nigrum,* was imported to Southeast Asia from southern India, and was widely cultivated on Sumatra, in the Malay Peninsula, and in Thailand. Galingale (galanga), a dried rhizome of *Alpinia galanga,* was found on Sumatra and in the Malay Peninsula. Turmeric, the tuber of *Curcuma domestica* and related species of the *Zingiberacae* family, grew widely in Southeast Asia, although Malayan turmeric was the one most commonly exported.

Southeast Asia also produced rare aromatic woods. Aloewood (*Aquilaria malacensis* and related species) grew widely in Cambodia, the Malay Peninsula, Borneo, the Philippines, and the Moluccas. Cambodian and Malayan aloewood enjoyed a particularly high reputation. Benzoin, the resin of *Styrax benzoin* and related species, was widespread throughout the area, particularly in Cambodia, Sumatra, and Java. Camphor, a crystalline substance derived from the dead wood and leaves of the tree *Dryobalanops aromatica,* was available in Borneo, Sumatra, and the Malay Peninsula. Lakawood, derived from the climber *Dalbergia parviflora,* was native to the Malay Peninsula, Sumatra, Java, and Borneo. Sandalwood (*Santalum album*), one of the most important sources of incense, occurs in eastern Indonesia, from east Java to Timor, and is easily cultivated.

Some of the more common spices of Southeast Asia also grew in southern China. The most important of these were cassia and cinnamon (*Cinnamomum cassia*), the "Chinese wood," very likely the most common cinnamon of antiquity. China also grew and exported an abundance of ginger (*Zingiber officinale*), amomum (*Amomum kepulaga* and others), and galingale (*Alpinia officinarum*). Aloewood and camphor were also available in China, but not in sufficient quantity to satisfy demand.

India offered varieties of many Southeast Asian spices and aromatic woods. Indian aloewood (*Aquilaria agalocha* and related species) grew in northeastern India, southern India, and Sri Lanka. Sandalwood (*Santalum album*) is indigenous to dry parts of southern India and is cultivated in northern parts of the subcontinent. Amomum (*Amomum subulatum*) grew in northern India, Nepal, and Bengal. Turmeric (*Curcuma domestica*) was at a very early day transplanted to India from its home in Southeast Asia. Its cultivation became so widespread that it came to be seen as an indigenous Indian spice. India also produced several varieties of cinnamon. On the southern slopes of the Himalayas grew *Cinnamomum tamala* and several related species; in southern India, particularly on the Malabar Coast, *Cinnamomum iners* and other species; in Sri Lanka, *Cinnamomum zeylanicum* or *Cinnamomum verum,* which, as the latter name implies, has been in modern times considered the "true" cinnamon. However, in comparison with the Chinese and Southeast Asian varieties, the Indian cinnamons seem to have played a relatively minor role in ancient and early medieval trade. There are no indications of cinnamon exports from Sri Lanka before the third century C.E., and the island seemingly did not become a key producer until the fifteenth century.

The most important spice native to India was pepper. In northern India and in the mountainous parts of southern India there grew long pepper (*Piper longum*), called so because the seeds were contained in a spike-like pod. Black pepper (*Piper nigrum*), the most common pepper variety, grew both wild and cultivated in southern India, particularly in Malabar. Black pepper is the dried, unripe seed of the climber pepper plant. White pepper is derived from the ripe seed, stripped of its outer layer.

India also produced many other spices and aromatic products. One of the best known—and exclusive to India—was cardamom, the dark, pungent, and very aromatic seeds of *Elletaria cardamomum,* native to the Malabar coast. Sesame (*Sesamum indicum*), was grown in northern India for its seeds and the oil pressed from them. The other Indian spices are less familiar today and were appreciated mainly for their aromatic and medicinal qualities. Bdelium was the aromatic resin of the thorny shrub *Commiphora mukul,* which grew in dry parts of western India. Cyperus was the aromatic root of *Cyperus rotundus.* Putchuk, or costum, was the aromatic root of *Saussurea loppa,* a perennial herb native to Kashmir. Spikenard was the fragrant spike and rhizome of *Nardostachys jatamansi,* a valerian-type herb indigenous to the central Himalayas. Calamus or "sweet flag" was the root of a perennial herb *Acorus calamus,* which grows in many mountainous parts of central and southern India. The aromatic "sweet rush" or ginger grass referred to the root of *Cymbopogon schoenanthus* and similar species, which grow in many parts of northern and southern India and in Sri Lanka. Zedoary (*Curcuma zedoaria*) was widely exported in the later Middle Ages; it was, in a sense, the consummate "spice," being used as a condiment, a perfume, and a medicinal stimulant.

The western shores of the Indian Ocean offered highly prized aromatic substances. The most valuable were balsam, frankincense, and myrrh. All three were available both from the Arabian Peninsula and from East Africa. Balsam is the gum of the desert shrubs *Commiphora kataf* and *Commiphora opobalsamum*. Myrrh is the gum of another member of the *Commiphora, C. Myrrha.* Myrrh is native to both Arabia and East Africa, although the latter was the predominant source. The myrrh from the Horn of Africa was valued the most. Frankincense, by contrast, is associated mostly with the Arabian Peninsula, although it is also found in East Africa and Socotra. It is the resin of the shrubs of the *Boswellia* family, of which *Boswellia carterii* was thought to be the best source. Persia also offered some aromatic gums, namely all-heal (*Ferula galbaniflua*), asafoetida (*Ferula assa-foetida*), sacopenium (*Ferula persica*), and sarcocolla (*Astralagus fasciculifolius*), but these were not as highly regarded as frankincense, balsam, and myrrh. The Arabian Peninsula and East Africa also became early producers of ginger, transplanted there from Southeast Asia.

Spices were distributed from their areas of provenance along trade routes determined by a combination of geographical factors and areas of demand. The basic links were Southeast Asia–China; China–India; Southeast Asia–India; Southeast Asia–East Africa; India–Middle and Near East–North Africa–Europe; Middle East–Southeast Asia–China. The routes involving Indonesia necessarily had to rely on maritime traffic. Spice trade from mainland Southeast Asia, India, East Africa, and China usually used a combination of sea and land routes.

Spatial logistics of the trade in the Indian Ocean defined the actual routes. In Southeast Asia, there were two defining points: the Straits of Malacca (between the Malay Peninsula and Sumatra) and the Sunda [Soenda] Straits (between Sumatra and Java); these waterways controlled access to the Indonesian archipelago as well as the regional trade with the Spice Islands (Moluccas and Bandas). As a result, the political situation in Sumatra, Java, and the Malay Peninsula always influenced but did not dominate the flow of the Southeast Asia spice trade. The oscillating attitude of the Chinese to foreign trade also played a role.

From Southeast Asia, the maritime traffic not destined for China could be directed either to the Bay of Bengal, Sri Lanka, the Malabar Coast, or East Africa. The Sri Lanka and East Africa routes appear to have been of great importance in antiquity and in the early centuries of the first millennium C.E. The importance of East Africa, however, appears to have waned later in the millennium. The Malabar Coast, a pivotal exporter of its own spices, was the dominant entrepôt for westbound Southeast Asian spices in the medieval period. From the Malabar Coast, spices were taken by ship either in the direction of the Red Sea, by way of Aden, or the Persian Gulf, where there existed many ports, among which Ormuz [Hormuz] eventually emerged as the dominant one. From Arabia and the head of the Persian Gulf, spices traveled overland to Alexandria, Damascus, Beirut, and other cities in the Near East, from where a portion went to North African and European markets.

Spice trade in the Indian Ocean was wide open. While some groups might have been more strongly represented than others, access to the trade was not barred to anyone with means to carry it on. Malay sailors and traders predominated on the ancient route between Southeast Asia and east Africa. The Arabs controlled much of the traffic in the Arabian Sea, until complemented by the Romans in the first century C.E. In the third century C.E., the Persians supplanted the Romans, gradually venturing as far as Southeast Asia and China. Late in the Gupta period (*c.* 320–*c.* 550), Indian ships increasingly followed the existing cultural links to Southeast Asia. The rise of Islam brought the western Indian Ocean traffic into Muslim hands, but not exclusively. During the Tang (619–907) and especially the Song (960–1279) dynasties, the Chinese came to play an important role in the trade of the eastern part of the Indian Ocean, a role that decreased under the Ming (1368–1644).

In the late Middle Ages, under the pressure of political changes, the spice trade became concentrated heavily in a few crucial entrepôt areas: Malacca, Malabar, Ormuz, and Aden. This fact proved pivotal when the Portuguese arrived in the Indian Ocean at the beginning of the sixteenth century and made their bid for the control of its sea-lanes and thus its trade. An attempt to control the sea-lanes was a novelty in a region where most powerful states were land-based and land-oriented. Portuguese geopolitical strategy, naval power, and artillery made it possible, temporarily, to seize the spice trade by controlling or blockading the four pivotal points: Malacca, Malabar, and the

# S

entrances to the Red Sea and Persian Gulf. The Portuguese hegemony was short-lived: their grip began to weaken in the 1520s, and by 1550, had largely faded away.

**BIBLIOGRAPHY**
Chaudhuri, K.N. *Trade and Civilization in the Indian Ocean.* Cambridge: Cambridge UP, 1985.
Godinho, Vitorino Magalhães. *Os descobrimentos e a economia mundial.* Vol. 2. 2nd edition. Lisbon: Presença, 1985.
Hall, Kenneth R. "Economic History of Early Southeast Asia." In *The Cambridge History of South-East Asia.* Vol. 1. *From Early Times to c. 1800.* Ed. N. Tarling. Cambridge: Cambridge UP, 1992, pp. 173–275.
Mahindru, S.N. *Spices in Indian Life (6500 B.C.–1950 A.D.).* New Delhi: Sultan Chand & Sons, 1982.
Miller Innes, J. *The Spice Trade of the Roman Empire, 29 B.C. to A.D. 641.* Oxford: Clarendon P, 1969.
Pearson, M.N., ed. *Spices in the Indian Ocean World.* Aldershot, Hampshire, England: Ashgate Publishing, 1996.
Purseglove, J.W., et al. *Spices.* London and New York: Longman, 1981.
Sarkar, H.B. *Trade and Commercial Activities of Southern India in the Malayo-Indonesian World (up to A.D. 1511).* Calcutta: KLM, 1986.

*Ivana Elbl*

**SEE ALSO**
Balsam Garden; China; Damascus; India; Lignum Aloes; Majapahit; Malabar; Malacca Straits; Pepper; Portuguese Trade; Red Sea

## Spies

Espionage was a vital form of information-gathering in the Middle Ages, often performed by those who traveled in another capacity. As in antiquity, medieval spies were recruited with three main objectives: naval and land-based military reconnaissance; domestic surveillance of suspect compatriots; and the gathering of information concerning the political and commercial affairs of rival and allied polities. Internal surveillance remained an important aim of espionage in the Byzantine Empire, the territories of the Umayyad, Abbasid, and Fātimid caliphates, and the Mongol khânates of China and Russia, all of which maintained networks of intelligence officers operated in conjunction with state-maintained postal services. Political fragmentation and the evolution of the territorial state over the period between 1000 and 1500, by contrast, engendered a growing emphasis on the arena of "foreign" intelligence

in the West. Merchants, physicians, and, above all, diplomatic envoys attained particular importance in the collection and transmission of intelligence under these changing conditions.

The impact of espionage on the course of medieval history appears to have been considerable. Procopius attributes the undoing of several key figures at the court of the Byzantine emperor Justinian (r. 527–565) to the machinations of spies in the service of the Empress Theodora. Similar cloak-and-dagger activities, described by the Byzantine chroniclers Georgios Monachos (fl. mid-ninth century), Symeon the Logothete (Symeon Magister, *c.* 912–987), and the authors of the "Continuation of Theophanes" (*Theophanes Continuatus,* spanning the period from 813 to 916), are said to have scuttled a massive conspiracy against the emperor Leo VI (r. 886–912). The thirteenth-century *quassad* or "secret service" of the Mamluk sultan Baybars I is said to have uncovered the activities of enemy Mongol and Frankish spies and foiled an attack planned by King Heytoun of Lesser Armenia. In 1349, merchant informers helped to thwart the rebellion of King James III of Majorca against King Peter IV the Ceremonious of Catalonia-Aragón (r. 1336–1387). Resort to counterintelligence strategies was therefore common. The seventh-century Code of the Lombard King Rothair (643) decreed capital penalties for any subject who hid a spy. Emissaries of the Abbasid caliphates abroad were forbidden to consort with local women for fear of resulting breaches in security. Fourteenth- and fifteenth-century English and Venetian legislation went further, restricting written and oral communication with foreigners.

Modes of relaying acquired intelligence were also developed. The ninth-century Byzantine scholar Leo, surnamed "the Mathematician" (*c.* 790–869), devised a telegraphic message system, whereby information could be relayed to Constantinople from borders adjacent to Arab territories by means of synchronized beacons; spies in the service of the Seljuk, Mamluk, and Ottoman Turks would later employ carrier pigeons. Code, or cipher, was employed in Arab, Italian, and Burgundian diplomatic correspondence by 1400. Improving communications and the establishment of resident ambassadors throughout Europe nevertheless entrenched a ubiquitous resort to espionage after 1450.

Narrative, archival, and even pictorial sources attest to the real and perceived importance of such espionage in the conduct of medieval warfare. Theoretical works, such as *Siyāsat-Nāme* (Book of Government) of the Persian Nīzam al-Mulk (1018–1092), grand vizier to the Seljuk sultans Alp Arslan (r. 1063–1072) and Malik-shāh (r. 1072–1092), as well as *Le songe de vieil pelèrin* of Philippe de Mézières (1327–1405) and *Les faits d'armes* of Christine de Pisan (1364–1431), reiterate classical recommendations concerning the engagement of spies in wartime—indeed, *Le Jouvencel* of Jean de Bueil (1406–1477) advises rulers to spend one-third of their income on spies. The Bayeux Tapestry (executed in 1078) depicts the operation of Anglo-Saxon scouts during the Norman conquest of England (1066). The *History* of Gregory of Tours (538–594); the *Royal Frankish Annals* (compiled 787–831); the *Itinerarum regis Ricardi* (detailing the third Latin crusade); the *Annales genuenses* of Caffarus and his continuators; and the romance of the Scottish poet John Barbour (1316–1395) all refer plentifully to the use of spies in conflicts. Genoese and Venetian archival records preserve instructions furnished to captains and admirals appointed by these maritime communes to obtain intelligence concerning the strength of enemy fleets during the War of the Straits (1350–1354). Froissart's indications that spying played a crucial role in military preparations on both sides during the Hundred Years' War (1337–1453) are corroborated by evidence preserved in the British Public Record Office of disbursements by the English crown to French and Flemish squires specifically designated as *exploratores*—a classical Latin term for *spy*.

Burgeoning ties of commerce and diplomacy accorded the merchant and the envoy roles of equal or greater importance than the military scout in medieval intelligence-gathering. In *De administrando imperio,* the Byzantine emperor Constantine VII Porphyrogenitus (r. 913–959) describes the operation of bureaus that monitored foreign powers with the particular assistance of diplomatic representatives and subject and immigrant merchants. Building on the legacy of their mentors, the Byzantines, the Venetians by the fourteenth century required all emissaries dispatched on the diplomatic and commercial affairs of the republic to furnish written and oral *relazioni* of their findings to the Venetian senate on their return. The ideal situation of the medieval ambassador as observer and potential informer, so readily exploited by dispatching governments, understandably excited fear and anxiety in those who received them. Liudprand of Cremona's colorful account of his near imprisonment at the court of the Byzantine emperor Nicephorus II Phocas in 969; John of Plano Carpini's dismay at the prospect that Mongol emissaries might accompany him home from his mission to the great khân (1245–1247); and the trenchant *Mémoires* of Philippe de Commynes (1447–1511) all attest to a contemporary perception that ambassadors and spies were often one and the same.

To supplement their discoveries, envoys and their masters often turned to court physicians, servants, and especially to merchants, praised by Philippe de Mézières as the best sources for intelligence in the medieval world. During the War of Chioggia, or Tenedos, between the maritime republics of Venice and Genoa (1378–1381), merchants sympathetic to the Venetian cause communicated details of Genoese naval preparations to Pietro Cornaro, the Venetian ambassador in Milan, who relayed them back to Venice. At least one of Cornaro's informants was a bona fide spy, who worried that his insufficient involvement in commerce might arouse suspicion. The Tuscan merchant Luchino Scarampi, by contrast, combined the functions of finance, diplomacy, and espionage, loaning money to King John I of Catalonia and Aragón (r. 1387–1396) while representing—and spying for—the Genoese at his court.

**BIBLIOGRAPHY**

Alban, J.R., and C.T. Allmand. "Spies and Spying in the Fourteenth Century." In *War, Literature, and Politics in the Late Middle Ages.* Ed. C.T. Allmand. New York: Harper and Row, 1976, pp. 73–101.

Amitai-Preiss, Reuven. "Mamluk Espionage among Mongols and Franks." *Asian and African Studies* 22 (1988): 173–181.

Arthurson, Ian. "Espionage and Intelligence from the War of the Roses to the Reformation." *Nottingham Medieval Studies* 35 (1991): 134–154.

*Carte reali diplomatiche di Giovanni I il Cacciatore, re d'Aragona riguardanti l'Italia.* Ed. Francesco C. Casula. Pubblicazioni dell'Istituto di storia medievale e moderna dell'Università degli studi di Cagliari in collaborazione con l'Archivio della Corona d'Aragona. Colección de documentos inéditos, vol. 48. Padua: CEDAM, 1977.

Constantine VII Porphyogenitus. *De administrando imperio.* Ed. and trans. Gyola Moravcsik and R.J.H. Jenkins. Washington DC: Dumbarton Oaks, 1967.

Cornaro, Pietro. *Dispacci di Pietro Cornaro: Ambasciatore a Milano durante la guerra di Chioggia.* Ed. Vittorio Lazzarini. Monumenti storici pubblicati dalla reale deputazione veneta di storia patria. 1st series: Documenti 20. Venice: Deputazione di storia patria per le Venezie, 1939.

# S

Dvornik, Francis. *Origins of Intelligence Services: The Ancient Near East, Persia, Greece, Rome, Byzantium, the Arab Muslim Empires, the Mongol Empires, China, Muscovy.* New Brunswick, NJ: Rutgers UP, 1974.

Queller, Donald E. "Newly Discovered Early Venetian Legislation on Ambassadors." In Donald E. Queller and Francis R. Swietek, *Two Studies on Venetian Government.* Geneva: Droz, 1977, pp. 7–98.

*Emily Sohmer Tai*

**SEE ALSO**

Ambassadors; Baybars I; Byzantine Empire; Commynes, Philippe de; Diplomacy; Fātimids; Froissart, Jean; Genoa; Hetoum; John of Plano Carpini; Liudprand of Cremona; Mamluks; Mongols; Ottoman Empire; Philippe de Mézières; Seljuk Turks; Venice

Constellation Cetus, Aratus, *Phaenomena.* London, British Library MS Harley 2506, fol. 42v, 10th century. Courtesy of the British Library.

## Star Maps

Diagrams illustrating treatises on cosmography and pictures of constellations usually illustrating astronomical texts. Star charts were practically nonexistent in the Middle Ages. In general, medieval astronomers were concerned either with large theoretical questions about the structure of the universe, or with the specific task of predicting the location of heavenly bodies, a task necessary for the computation of calendars, which was itself a matter vital to the dating of movable Christian feasts, such as Easter. During the early Middle Ages, Europeans drew most of their astronomical knowledge from such nontechnical Roman literature as the *Natural History* of Pliny the Elder (23–79 C.E.), and did not have the necessary skills to observe and calculate the positions of the stars with great precision. Even those few who did were not generally concerned to do so, preferring to rely on existing texts and tables. The technical sophistication of European astronomers expanded enormously beginning in the tenth and eleventh centuries, when contact with Muslim Spain allowed them to acquire measuring instruments such as the astrolabe, and highly technical ancient astronomical texts, most notably Ptolemy's *Almagest* (second quarter of the second century C.E.) and recent commentaries on that text by Muslim scholars.

Those pictures of the heavens that survive from the Middle Ages fall generally into two categories: cosmographical diagrams and pictures of constellations. The former are schematic drawings of an earth-centered universe that accompany cosmographical treatises such as John of Sacrobosco's *De Sphaera* (c. 1220/1230).

Drawings of constellations are sometimes found in astrological texts such as the *Aratea* of Germanicus Caesar (15 B.C.E.–19 C.E.), a Latin translation of the *Phainomena* of the Greek poet Aratos (315–245 B.C.E.), magnificently illustrated in the Carolingian period in such manuscripts as London, British Library MS Harley 647 and Leiden, Bibliotheek der Rijksuniversiteit, Voss. lat. Q 79. Such drawings may or may not contain accurate depictions of the stars that make up the constellation. Accurate or not, they almost always serve as illustrations to the text rather than as practical guides to the stars.

Maps of all sorts have very low survival rates from the Middle Ages. It is very possible that some star charts were made, particularly in the fifteenth century, when there was growing interest and expertise in both mathematical astronomy and celestial navigation. To date, none has surfaced.

**BIBLIOGRAPHY**

Kren, Claudia. "Astronomy." In *The Seven Liberal Arts in the Middle Ages.* Ed. David L. Wagner. Bloomington: Indiana UP, 1983, pp. 218–247.

Mütherich, Florentine, and Joachim E. Gaehde. *Carolingian Painting.* New York, George Braziller, 1976.

Saxl, Fritz, Hans Meier, and Patrick McGurk. *Catalogue of Astrological and Mythological Illuminated Manuscripts of the Latin Middle Ages.* London: The Warburg Institute, 1953, 1966, vols. 3 [1, 2] and 4.

Snyder, George Sergeant. *Maps of the Heavens.* New York: Abbeville Press, 1984.

*Ben Weiss*

SEE ALSO
Pliny the Elder; Ptolemy; Sacrobosco, John of

## Stonehenge and Other Megalithic Marvels

Prehistoric stone monuments in western Britain and western France that helped to shape the attitudes of actual and armchair travelers to these regions. These areas were thus, like India, Africa, and the Holy Land, widely recognized as locations for marvels. For example, Ralph Niger, discussing in his *Chronicum* (1199) the four "wonders" of Britain, observed that "second among them is Stonehenge where stones of a miraculous size and length are erected in the fashion of doorways, nor can anyone imagine by what art so many stones are raised to such heights."

In the Bodleian Library, Oxford, MS Bodley 614, a collection of monster and wonder *mirabilia* of *c.* 1000, is a marvel accompanied by an illustration. It shows a group of distraught-looking women and a ring of stones. The Latin text explains that "there are also to be seen in the extremest part of France [Brittany] seven women leading a dance . . . in the form of a circle." The Latin text continues, "now these were sisters who with their mother led a dance on a feast day. The priest Urri was about to celebrate mass and . . . he cursed them that they would have to dance forever, and so they have done. One empty place is seen in the ring, where the mother tore herself free at the moment of the curse and now the adjacent sisters have their arms stretched out but not touching." This marvel, however, is not confined only to Brittany. It is duplicated, the text notes, in Britain, "where a similar dance of young women is to be found." Brittany was associated with giants, sorcery, and other forms of the specifically anti-Christian supernatural, as were Cornwall, Wales, Yorkshire, Northumberland, and Scotland.

The dancing women referred to in the manuscript text are megalithic stone circles. The "marvel" specifically located in Britain is probably to be identified with the "Merry Maidens," a ring of nineteen stones in Cornwall believed to be young women petrified for

Menhirs and Dolmens. Kermario, Carnac, Brittany. Photo by John B. Friedman.

# S

dancing on Sunday. The gap in the circle left by the mother presumably refers to a stone already fallen or removed from the ring.

These visible remains of the megalithic past, today a great tourist attraction, were for medieval readers and travelers sources of fear as well as navigational utility. One of the most important medieval texts claiming pagan and evil origins for a megalith is Geoffrey of Monmouth's extremely popular *History of the Kings of Britain* (c. 1138), whose account also appears in Wace's *Roman de Brut* (1155) and Layamon's *Brut* (c. 1199/ 1229), among other places. Geoffrey tells how King Aurelius plans to build an eternal monument on the plains of Salisbury. His masons confess themselves inadequate and only Merlin has both the skill to construct the monument and the vision of the future necessary to foretell its permanence.

Merlin counsels the king to send for the *Chorea Gigantum,* the Giants' Dance (or ring), a great stone structure in Ireland on Mount Killaraus (Kildare): "in that place there is a stone construction which no man of this period could ever erect, unless he combined great skill and artistry. The stones are enormous and there is no one alive strong enough to move them. If they are placed in position round this site, in the way in which they are erected over there, they will stand for ever." Merlin further observes that the stones "are connected with certain secret religious rites and they have various properties which are medicinally important. Many years ago the Giants transported them from the remotest confines of Africa and set them up in Ireland at a time when they inhabited that country."

The stones were shipped to England, and Aurelius summoned clergy to bless, Christianize, and rededicate them on Pentecost. Merlin thus erected Stonehenge on the Salisbury plain (exactly as it had been set up in Ireland) near the Monastery of Kaercaradduc. The Giant's Ring becomes the burial place of Aurelius, Uther Pendragon, and Constantine III. Geoffrey's last reference is to record that the English call it Stanhenge (VIII.10–13). Archaeologists currently believe that the blue stones used in the building of Stonehenge were carried by ship and stone sledges 170 miles from the Prescelly Mountains in Pembrokeshire; this idea seems in keeping with Geoffrey's sense that the stones were transported from some distance away to the Salisbury plain.

In its reference to a ring of stones as a dance, this oldest and most elaborate story of Stonehenge's origins belongs with the account of the marvel in Bodley 614.

The source of Geoffrey's legend of the Giants' Ring is unknown. Henry of Huntingdon (1084–1185) alludes to its size and awe-inspiring quality in his *Historia Anglorum* (1154), but says nothing of its origins. Geoffrey thus either apparently invented the story or found it in a source no longer extant.

Aside from Stonehenge, a group of stones in Oxfordshire—one of the *mirabilia* in the *Abbreviationes Chronicorum* associated with the name of Pseudo-Ralph of Diceto (c. 1148)—was similarly supposed the work of giants: "great stones were arranged together in some pattern by the hand of man—but in what time or by what people or for what purpose or reason that was done this is unknown."

Gerald of Wales (1146–1223), in his *History and Topography of Ireland,* also mentions Stonehenge as a topographic wonder in discussing the Irish place of origin for the stones used to build it. As a travel writer, he is especially interested in the giant builders' superhuman skill; however, he also shows an actual acquaintance with and appreciation of Stonehenge. "Employing truly remarkable skill and ability," Gerald notes of the builders, "it is amazing how so many great stones were ever brought together or erected in one place, and with what skill upon such great and high stones others no less great were placed. These latter seemed to be hanging, as it were, and suspended in space, so as to rest rather on the skill of the craftsman than on the base of stones beneath."

In Brittany, large numbers of prehistoric stone monuments called *menhirs,* an Old Breton word meaning "long tall stones," and stone burial chambers—two slabs with a capstone laid horizontally—called *dolmens,* in appearance somewhat like Stonehenge but built on a smaller scale, dotted the landscape, most frequently along the southwest coast in the *départements* of Finestère and Morbihan.

A menhir typically was a large rectangular block of stone, quarried by the action of water-swollen wooden wedges or sometimes by the heat of large fires, suddenly doused with water, producing splits in the mass of rock. The blocks were tooled, sometimes by the pounding action of rock mauls, into fairly smooth shapes and sunk vertically in the ground, often to a considerable depth. Their function seems primarily to have been to mark graves, though it is thought that they also had astronomical purposes when they were originally constructed (5000–2000 B.C.E.).

Such stones often were carried long distances and erected, by means still unclear, in long fairly parallel rows often stretching one-third mile (one-half kilometer), called *alignements*. There are seventeen of these in Finestère and twelve in Carnac in the Gulf of Morbihan. The fields of stones near the town of Carnac occupy about three-quarters of a mile (one kilometer) in extent and contain 2,934 menhirs ranging from 1.5 feet to 12 feet (.5 meter to 4 meters) in height. Such enormous stones may originally have covered as much as a mile and one-quarter (about two kilometers), but were often pillaged for building materials.

These monuments must have played an important role in travelers' perceptions, though little textual evidence remains. In Old Breton, the suffix "peulven" in place-names like Kerampeulven or Rupeulven means *menhir*. Such stone monuments were early associated with idolatry, paganism, the activities of giants, sorcerers, and the like, but they were also (as these names indicate) assimilated to the community as boundary markers, as is evident in monastic cartularies like that from the Abbey of Redon made in 848, itemizing land that extends "from one part down the slope of Mount Clergeruc to the great stones." The phrase "great stone" or stones and a name attached to a stone indicated menhir.

Mariners rounding the rocky and dangerous coast of Brittany used megalithic monuments as navigational landmarks from very early times. The *Periegesis* (literally a *periplum* or "sailing around") associated with the name of the Greek geographer Scymnus of Chios (100 B.C.E.) seems to have referred specifically to the great menhir at Locmariaquer in Carnac, now broken in four pieces. Called the Fairy Stone, this hexagonally shaped granite pillar originally measured about sixty-two feet (18.9 meters) in height and the ensemble is missing a piece that would have brought the total height to a bit more than seventy feet (21.34 meters), making it the tallest known menhir in Brittany.

The writer of the *Periegesis* says "at the extremity of the country of the Celts, that is France, is found the column of the north, which faces an ocean of resounding waves. The westmost Celts and the Vannais live near this column." This menhir and others near it apparently served sailors entering the Gulf of Morbihan as landmarks, though it was already broken in 1483. The sea chart or "rutter" made by Pierre Garcie *dit* Ferrande (1483) notes the great tumuli or burial barrows of Mané Lud and Mané Er-Hroek just adjacent to the Fairy Stone.

A map of southwestern Brittany made around 1550, but clearly influenced by earlier maps, and now in London (British Library MS Sloane 557, fol. 26r), shows as landmarks the churches and cathedrals of the various dioceses, but at the eastern edge of the Gulf of Morbihan what may have been a Christianized menhir is labelled "La Croisse."

One monument that must certainly have been legendary to medieval mariners is the islet of Er-Lannic in the commune of Arzon, which lies in the principal channel of the gulf of Morbihan. It contains two circles of menhirs, about six to sixteen feet (two to five meters) high; the northern circle is uncovered and covered by the tide—which can be as high as thirteen feet (four meters)—and the southern one is completely submerged. It is possible that this small island was the prehistoric site of what the Greeks would have interpreted as a temple. Diodorus of Sicily (fl. 60–30 B.C.E.) cites Hecataeus of Miletus and other geographers, who say that "opposite the country of the Celts, is an island as great as Sicily inhabited by the Hyperboreans. The inhabitants honor Apollo more than the other gods. A magnificent circular temple is dedicated to him on the island." Allowing for exaggeration of size and location, this "temple" could have been the circles of Er-Lannic, which would have been completely visible on a hillside slope in the Roman period, as is evident from the hydrographic history of the region, as well as the changes wrought by wind and erosion. Ancient dikes now submerged indicate that the present tidal level for the area is some thirty to thirty-six feet (nine to eleven meters) higher than it was in antiquity. The difference between high and low tide is about twenty-four feet (7.4 meters), so that the look of the coast at very low tides today reflects in its outlines the medieval coast at high tide.

As both objects of wonder and landmarks by which to navigate, prehistoric stone structures strongly affected the lives of medieval people traveling in these areas by sea and by land.

**BIBLIOGRAPHY**

Burl, Aubrey. *Rings of Stone: The Prehistoric Circles of Britain and Ireland.* New Haven, CT, and New York: Tickner and Fields, 1980.

Ferguson, Arthur B. *Utter Antiquity, Perceptions of Prehistory in Renaissance England.* Durham, NC, and London: Duke UP, 1993.

Giot, Pierre-Roland, et al. *Préhistoire de la Bretagne.* Rennes: Ouest France, 1979.

Gransden, Antonia. *Legends, Traditions, and History in Medieval England.* London and Rio Grande, OH: Hambledon Press, 1992.

# S

Grinsell, Leslie V. *The Legendary History and Folklore of Stonehenge.* West Country Folklore 9. St. Peter Port, Guernsey, C.I.: Toucan Press, 1975.

Jondorf, Gillian, and David Dumville, eds. *France and the British Isles in the Middle Ages and the Renaissance.* Woodbridge, Suffolk: Boydell and Brewer, 1991.

Joussaume, Roger. *Dolmens for the Dead: Megalith Building throughout the World.* Ithaca, NY: Cornell UP, 1988.

Mitchell, John. *Megalithomania: Artists, Antiquarians, and Archaeologists at the Old Stone Monuments.* Ithaca, NY: Cornell UP, 1982.

Taylor, Eva G.R. *The Haven-Finding Art;* rpt. New York: American Elsevier Publishing Co., 1971.

Thom, A., and A.S. Thom. *Megalithic Remains in Britain and Brittany.* Oxford: Oxford UP, 1978.

John Block Friedman

**SEE ALSO**
Brittany and Navigational Charts; Geoffrey of Monmouth; Geography in Medieval Europe; Gerald of Wales; Itineraries and *Periploi*

## Stones and Timber, Scandinavian Trade in

A key element of commerce mainly in the northern Baltic regions but also throughout Europe. In northern Europe, the increasing demand of the growing urban centers for food and building material gave rise to regular trade in heavy goods in the second half of the twelfth century. During the following centuries trade in stones and timber developed into a large-scale industry. Yet, in spite of its volume, the technical difficulties involved, and its undoubtedly great economical significance, this trade is little known today. The scanty documentary evidence that does exist largely relates to timber; as for stone, we have to rely almost exclusively on the evidence of the stones themselves.

Geological analyses have identified a number of sites and limited areas where different kinds of stone were quarried for export purposes: for example, soapstone in southeast Norway, and sandstone and limestone on the Baltic islands of Gotland and Öland. By far the most important center was Gotland, which probably more than equaled the contemporary central- and west-European industries of Baumberg, Caen, Namur, and Purbeck both in terms of the volume and the diffusion of its output.

Gotland's rich supply of silurian sandstone and limestone, suitable for a wide variety of purposes, together with its location at a commercial crossroads, made the island an easily accessible and comparatively cheap source of good stone for all the countries along the Baltic coast. The majority of exports were either fully or partially finished goods: baptismal fonts, altar slabs, gravestones, and architectural elements such as plinths, quoins, mullions, columns, capitals, and floor tiles.

Among the first products of Gotlandic stonework to be shipped overseas in the twelfth century was a famous series of Romanesque baptismal fonts, sculpted in sandstone. The beginning of the following century witnessed an almost complete abandonment of soft sandstone in favor of harder limestone (more suitable for exterior architectural uses), and the introduction of serial production of the items mentioned above. For nearly 200 years, or at least up to the end of the fourteenth century, Gotland dominated this sector of the stone market in the whole Baltic area; thereafter the production dwindled and became less diversified.

The main part of the output went to developing regions that lacked a local supply of good architectural stone, namely to various parts of Sweden, Denmark, and the southern shores of the Baltic, from Schleswig-Holstein to Prussia. Certain products, especially baptismal fonts and grave slabs, penetrated the coastal zones and often found their way deep into the European and Scandinavian mainlands, or left the Baltic by way of the Danish straits and were shipped as far as Bergen in Norway and Bruges in Flanders. It is not yet possible to calculate the total volume of the export, but a general idea of its diffusion can be conveyed by a map showing the distribution of some 750 medieval baptismal fonts of Gotlandic limestone.

The long-range trade in timber from Norway and Sweden—mainly in the form of boards, planks, and beams—focused on the thriving merchant cities on both sides of the English Channel. The earliest documentary evidence is found in England, where a number of Norse vessels landed their cargo of boards in Grimsby in 1230; in 1253, Henry III purchased 3,000 boards from Norway for paneling at Windsor Castle. During the following century, timber from Norway and Sweden appears fairly regularly in the customs accounts of a number of ports on the east coast of England and Scotland. Some of the Swedish timber, bought by merchants in Visby (on Gotland), Wismar (in Mecklenburg), and other Hanseatic ports, may also have been intended for customers on both sides of the channel. The same is true for the vast quantities of Pomeranian timber, mainly oak, which at least from

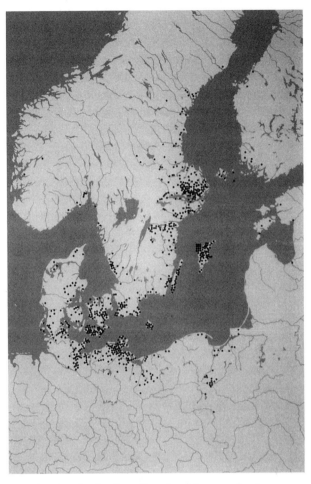

Gotlandic limestone baptismal font. Rimbo Church, Uppland, Sweden *c.* 1250.

Map showing distribution of baptismal fonts made of Gotlandic limestone.

the beginning of the fourteenth century was imported to Denmark and Sweden.

That the growth of trade in stone and timber was facilitated by the formation and expansion of the Hanseatic League seems clear, but to what extent it was also controlled by that organization is an open question. From the fact that timber is very rarely mentioned in the toll-rolls of Lübeck (concerned only with Hanseatic ships), it has been argued that at least short- and middle-range trade within the Baltic was handled largely by local peasant-merchants or other free agents. The almost total absence of documentary evidence for the import and export of stones may be interpreted as pointing in the same direction, but it is also possible that stone escaped customs duties for other reasons, for instance, by being classified as ballast.

**BIBLIOGRAPHY**

Berggren, Lars. "The Export of Limestone and Limestone Fonts from Gotland during the Thirteenth and Fourteenth Centuries." In the proceedings of the conference *New Markets for New Goods. The Emergence of Large-scale Trade in Northern Europe 1150–1400.* Fridhemsborg, Malmö/ Sweden, 19–21 February 1997. Ed. Lars Berggren, Nils Hybel, and Annette Landen. Toronto: The Pontifical Institute of Medieval Studies, 2000.

Bugge, Alexander. *Den norske trælasthandels historie.* Vol. 1. *Fra de ældste tider indtil freden i Speier 1544.* Skien: Fremskridts boktrykkeri, 1925.

Kjærheim, Steinar, et al. "Trelasthandel." *Kulturhistoriskt Lexikon för Nordisk Medeltid* 18. 2nd edition. Copenhagen: Rosenkilde and Bagger, 1982, pp. 587–599.

Landen, Annette. "Dopfuntar så in i Norden." *Kulturmiljövård* 5 (1993): 40–45.

# S

———. "Gotländsk stenexport." In *Medeltid.* Ed. Erik Osvalds. Lund: Historiska Media, 1997, pp. 81–93; 2nd ed., 1999, pp. 67–78.

———. "Die Mittelalterliche Taufe der Dorfkirche in Neuberg bei Wismar." *Mecklenburgische Jahrbücher* 114 (1999): 5–15.

Møller, Elna, et al. "Sten." *Kulturhistoriskt Lexikon för Nordisk Medeltid* 17. 2nd edition. Copenhagen: Rosenkilde and Bagger, 1982, pp. 144–151.

*Lars Berggren and Annette Landen*

SEE ALSO
Bruges; Hanse, The

## Sunnism

The largest branch of Islam, whose name derives from an Arabic word meaning "tradition," linked originally with a conviction of the legitimacy of the succession of the first four caliphs as Muslim leaders following Muhammad. In the medieval Muslim world, travel and trade were tied closely to religion, and the Sunnis, being the dominant and most populous sect, were the more prominent geographers and travelers.

Muhammad left Mecca for Medina in 622. This Hejira (Arabic *hijra*), or emigration, caused travel to be united with faith from the very beginning of Islam. Muhammad's triumphant return on what is known as the Farewell Pilgrimage in 632 C.E (the first year of the Muslim calendar) established the traditions of the *hajj* (pilgrimage), further emphasizing travel as an activity of a pious Muslim. In a matter of decades Islam spread more widely, in terms of geography, than Christianity did over several centuries. During the medieval period the Dār el-Islām (the "House of Islam," those lands inhabited with Muslim populations) was not a single political unit, or a linguistic one, but its inhabitants shared a common faith. The Middle East had long been a center of travel, due to its location at the intersection of three continents; Islam strengthened this tradition by encouraging those in more remote areas to visit the sacred and commercial places at the known world's "center." Sunni Muslims thus journeyed to and from Asia, Africa, and, to a lesser extent, Europe, primarily for three reasons: conducting political business, negotiating commerce, and making a pilgrimage.

Along with conversion and conquest came the need for, and acquisition of, various ancient Greek and Persian geographical treatises, which helped to guide Muslims in both travel and prayer. Geographies were sometimes altered as they were translated into Arabic so that they coincided with Islamic ideas. The most significant of these revisions were carried out by the Balkhi school, which sought verification in the Qur'an for all intellectual theories and subsequently "corrected" the Persians' center of the world by moving it to Mecca, an adjustment that was neccessitated by the *qibla* (the ordained direction of prayer toward the Holy City). Sunni geographers also sought out Greek and Persian astronomical texts to determine the *qibla* more precisely from any point in the expanding Muslim world.

Many roads already led to the Middle East at the time of Islam's foundation in the seventh century C.E., and they facilitated the development and maintenance of political ties. As the Muslim Empire grew, the roads were mapped and postal stations were established. These improvements aided communication and thus helped to maintain unity throughout the geographical expanse. Indeed, one of the earliest Sunni contributions to geographical knowledge of the time came from one of the officers of the postal service. The *Book of Routes and Provinces,* written around A.H. 231/846 C.E. by Ibn Khurdādhbih (*c.* A.H. 240–*c.* 300; *c.* 820–*c.* 911 C.E.) provided detailed descriptions of the various stations and of the routes between them. His interest, however, was limited to the boundaries of Islam, and in this he resembled his fellow Muslims, who rarely ventured beyond the borders of their faith.

Islam had no bias against the legal and upright acquisition of material wealth (Muhammad had, after all, been a merchant), and Sunni Muslims carried out trade by sea and land. Until the arrival of Portuguese explorers in Indian waters in the early 1500s, no one knew the seas from Africa to the subcontinent better than Muslim sailors. On the other hand, Muslims avoided the Atlantic, which they considered such a danger that Qur'anic scholars recommended suspending the civil rights of anyone foolhardy enough to travel there.

The pilgrimage caravan was a great unifying force among the Sunnis: merchants, scholars, political leaders, and common laborers traveled in groups, joining caravans from other regions as they journeyed to sites they all believed to be holy. Pilgrims from distant lands would set out long before the assigned time of the *hajj* in the last month of the year so that they could make many stops along the way, trading goods and information. In fact, many merchants paid the entire cost of their pilgrimage through trading.

During the Abbasid dynasty (750–1258 C.E.), the political and commercial center of the Sunnis was located in Baghdad. Because Islam's holiest place was Mecca, the road between these two cities was especially well traveled and maintained. Moreover, since Abbasid caliphs, like all pious Muslims, made the pilgrimage, the route was marked by inns and other accommodations of a quality befitting distinguished travelers. Caliph Hārūn al-Rashīd (r. 786–809) and his wife, Zubayda, are particularly known for improving the pilgrimage road, building caravansaries, cisterns, and reservoirs between Kufa in Iraq and Mecca. Zubayda herself was responsible for so many of these improvements that this section of the route became known as "Zubayda's Way."

The three most famous travelers among medieval Sunni Muslims all began their journeys as pilgrims and, not surprisingly, they richly documented their experiences on the *hajj*. The Persian Nāsir Khusaru from Balkh (1003–1068 C.E.) made his pilgrimage in 1050, Ibn Jubayr from Córdoba (1140s–1217 C.E.) in 1184, and Ibn Battūta, a native of Tangiers (1304–1368 C.E.), in 1326. Each traveled a different route in a different century, providing us with a panoramic sense of the medieval *hajj*. Ibn Battūta so enjoyed the experience of travel on his pilgrimage that he spent the next thirty years on journeys over land and sea that took him an estimated 73,000 miles (some 118,000 kilometers).

Sunnis also traveled to obtain knowledge, itself a spiritual enterprise. Both the Qur'an and the sayings of Muhammad encourage learning, and some Muslims interpret this to be a mandate to journey wherever knowledge is available. Muhammad is reported to have said, "Seek knowledge, even in China." While not all Sunni Muslims took this recommendation as seriously as Ibn Battūta did, many did travel to Baghdad, Cairo, Damascus, and Mecca to study with recognized religious authorities. Because knowledge and faith are so intertwined for Muslims, there was no need to venture outside the Dār el-Islām. Most Sunnis were thus assured not only of increasing their knowledge of Islam and the world, but also of finding comfort in familiar customs and a common faith, even in unfamiliar lands.

**BIBLIOGRAPHY**
Bovill, E.W. *Caravans of the Old Sahara.* London: Oxford UP, 1958. 2nd edition. *The Golden Trade of the Moors.* London: Oxford UP, 1968.
Dunn, Ross E. *The Adventures of Ibn Battuta, a Muslim Traveler of the Fourteenth Century.* Berkeley: U of California P, 1986.
Gellens, Sam I. "The Search for Knowledge in Medieval Muslim Societies: A Comparative Approach." In *Muslim Travellers: Pilgrimage, Migration, and the Religious Imagination.* Ed. Dale F. Eickelman and James Piscatori. Berkeley: U of California P, 1990, pp. 50–68.
Kramers, J.H. "Geography and Commerce." In *The Legacy of Islam.* Ed. Thomas Arnold and Alfred Guillaume. Oxford: Clarendon Press, 1931, pp. 79–106.
Peters, F.E. *The Hajj: The Muslim Pilgrimage to Mecca and the Holy Places.* Princeton, NJ: Princeton UP, 1994.
*Bonnie Irwin*

**SEE ALSO**
Baghdad; Caravan; Cartography, Arabic; Damascus; Egypt; Ibn Battūta, Abu Abdallah; Ibn Jubayr; Inns and Accommodations; Mecca; Medina; Muslim Travelers and Trade; Navigation, Arab; Shi'ism; Women Travelers, Islamic

# Sylvester II
*See* Gerbert of Aurillac

# T

## Table, Peutinger
*See* Peutinger Table

## Tamerlane (1336–1405)

Central Asian ruler. A Barlas Turk, born near Kash near Samarkand in Transoxiana, he claimed descent from the Chinggisid line of Mongols.

Tamerlane [or Tamburlaine; Arab./Pers.: Tīmūr: Turkic: Temür] was apparently granted the epithet "Lang" ("lame") as the result of a deformity in his legs. Having served the ruler of Khazghan with some distinction in his youth, he was rewarded with the governorship of Kash in 1361. By 1380, through a careful manipulation of regional disputes, he successfully mounted a conquest of Balkh (1370), and Jata and Khwarazm (1369–1380). He began to undertake the conquest of Persia in 1380–1381 with an invasion of Khorasan. In rapid succession he then defeated and effected the submission of the Iranian highlands, the rulers of Mazandaran on the Caspian coast, the Muzaffarids in Shiraz and the western Iranian provinces, and the Jalayarids in Mesopotamia by 1387.

Tamerlane's conquests, which were in truth a series of massive plundering expeditions, continued unabated in the next decade, with victories in the Caspian region, and in Mesopotamia and Edessa. In 1395, he definitively broke with his former ally Toqtamish, ruler of the White Horde, who had invaded Tamerlane's territory. In response, Tamerlane launched a full-scale invasion of the Qipchaq lands of the Golden Horde, deposed Toqtamish, occupying Moscow, defeated the Qipchaq Turks, and occupied Georgia. In 1398, he commenced a successful invasion of northern India, sacking the city of Delhi in December of that year; he thus brought into subjection the entire territory from the Indus to the lower Ganges.

In the West, Tamerlane became most renowned for his operations in Anatolia and Syria, culminating in 1402 with his defeat and capture of the Ottoman sultan Bajazet I at the battle of Ankara. Throughout 1402–1403, Tamerlane conducted successful longrange diplomacy with a variety of Western princes, many of whom came to look on him as an ally in their desultory holy wars against the Ottomans, in spite of his sack of Smyrna in 1403.

By 1404, Tamerlane had returned to his court at Samarkand, in order to plan a campaign in China. It was at this point that his court was visited by Ruy Gonzalez de Clavijo, whose *Embajada al Tamerlan* remains to this day one of the most detailed accounts of the mores and affairs of Tamerlane and his court. The ruler died in January 1405 shortly after crossing the Oxus. His body was returned to Samarkand, where he was buried with great ceremony.

Many Western and Eastern chroniclers characterized Tamerlane's reign as marked by ferocity and brutality, though his portrayal in early modern European literature and drama came increasingly to mark him as a noble, proud, and good ruler and warrior. Muslim chroniclers, including many who had previously served rulers subjugated by Tamerlane, wrote in increasingly lurid detail of the crueler aspects of his conquests: the massacre of captives in India, the collection of 70,000 enemy heads in Isfahan, and the construction of towers made from skulls on numerous

# T

occasions. This being said, Tamerlane proved a great patron of the arts and architecture, and his city of Samarkand flourished with many endowments and monumental buildings.

Tamerlane was not a gifted statesman, nor did his grand empire endure long past his death, but he was a clever and accomplished ruler of a diverse group of fractious tribes. He came to represent for the West during the early modern period the very model of justice, as his multiple representations in European literature have shown. Increasingly, since the late eighteenth century, his cruelty has been highlighted as emblematic of "barbarous hordes" as historians of nineteenth-century Britain and Russia desired to contrast the actions of past Central Asian rulers with their own "enlightened" imperial rule. He thus became the model for the West's construction of the "Oriental despot." Yet recent scholarship has attempted to restore some semblance of humanity to the history of a man who became known in popular literature for his cruelty. Following the establishment of independent states in Central Asia in 1991, Tamerlane was revived as a national hero and as the progenitor of Uzbek national sovereignty.

## BIBLIOGRAPHY

González de Clavijo, Ruy. *Embassy to Tamerlane, 1403–1406*. Trans. Guy Le Strange. New York: Harper & Brothers, 1928; rpt. Frankfurt am Main: Johann Wolfgang Goethe University, 1994.

Hookham, Hilda. *Tamburlaine the Conqueror*. London: Hodder and Staughton, 1962.

Ibn Arabshah. *Tamerlane, or, Timur the Great Amir, from the Arabic Life of Ahmed ibn Arabshah*. Trans. J.J. Saunders, 1936; rpt. Lahore: Progressive Books, 1976.

Ibn Khaldūn. *Ibn Khaldun and Tamerlane*. Ed. and trans. Walter Fischel. Berkeley: U of California P, 1952.

Knobler, Adam. "The Rise of Tīmūr and Western Diplomatic Response, 1390–1405." *Journal of the Royal Asiatic Society*, 3rd series, 5.3 (1995), pp. 341–349.

Lentz, Thomas W., and Glenn D. Lowry. *Timur and the Princely Vision: Persian Art and Culture in the Fifteenth Century*. Washington, DC: Smithsonian Institution for Arthur M. Sackler Gallery, 1989.

Manz, Beatrice Forbes. *The Rise and Rule of Tamerlane*. Cambridge: Cambridge UP, 1989.

Roemer, Hans R. "Timur in Iran." In *The Cambridge History of Iran*. Ed. Peter Jackson and Laurence Lockhart. Cambridge: Cambridge UP, 1986, vol. 6, pp. 42–97.

Woods, John E. "The Rise of Timurid Historiography." *Journal of Near Eastern Studies* 46.12 (1987): 81–108.

———. "Timur's Genealogy." In *Intellectual Studies on Islam: Essays Written in Honor of Martin B. Dickson*. Ed. Michael M. Mazzaoui and Vera B. Moreen. Salt Lake City: U of Utah P, 1990, pp. 85–125.

*Adam Knobler*

**SEE ALSO**
Caspian Sea; Edessa; Ganges; Golden Horde; India; Indus; Mongols; Ottoman Empire; Ottoman Turks; Russia and Rus'; Samarkand; Inner Asian Trade; Inner Asian Travel; Yuan Dynasty

## Taoism [Daoism]

A Chinese religio-philosophical system that served as the major indigenous alternative and challenge to the mainline tradition of Confucianism.

Taoist philosophical ideas originated in Zhou [Chou] dynasty (1030–221 B.C.E.) texts like the *Daode jing* [*Tao-te ching*], traditionally attributed to the shadowy sage Laozi [Lao Tzu] and the *Zhuangzi* [*Chuang Tzu*] by the author of the same name. In contrast to the Confucian tradition that was concerned with the fulfillment of societal obligations, the observance of decorum, and individual moral cultivation through learning, Taoism rejected social conventions and emphasized a return to a life of spontaneity, naturalness, and simplicity patterned after the cosmic Way (Tao), the fundamental metaphysical principle that undergirds reality and gives rise to all things. While Confucianism commonly appealed to the bureaucratic scholarly elite, philosophical Taoism was often embraced by scholar hermits who shunned public life and sought a solitary existence in remote places, often mountains. In the Later Han dynasty (25–220 C.E.), a full-fledged Taoist institutional religion emerged that was characterized by a pantheon in which Laozi was apotheosized, a scriptural canon, a complex liturgical system, and a clergy. This religious tradition, while deriving some basic ideas from the early texts, at the same time adopted a considerably different approach to reality that reflected popular religious aspirations, including the attainment of immortality, the curing of illness, and the securing of mundane benefits.

In the promotion of trade, travel, and exploration, Taoism had a mixed record. On the one hand, Taoism, like Confucianism, lacked a missionary vision and therefore was largely confined to the Chinese cultural sphere of East Asia—this, despite the impression given by the third-century Taoist religious text, *Scripture of the Conversion of the Barbarians (Huahu jing)*, which claimed Laozi had departed into the western region where he preached to and converted the Buddha. This text, however, was not so much an expression of Taoist evangelical zeal as a reflection of the defensive stance taken by Taoists against Buddhism as it was making substantial inroads in China. Despite the absence of a missionary impulse, Taoism in both its philosophical and its religious expressions nevertheless exerted an influence, indirect as well as direct, on trade, travel, and exploration in East and Southeast Asia.

One of the momentous events in the encounter of major civilizations in world history was the introduction and adoption of Indic Buddhism in China. Taoism, mainly in its philosophical form, played a pivotal role in this process, ultimately serving as a bridge for the entry and assimilation of Buddhism into Chinese civilization. In the third and fourth centuries of the Common Era, as Buddhist Scriptures were first being translated into Chinese, Taoist concepts were employed to translate many abstruse Buddhist ideas. The Chinese gentry of this period, who were engaged in exploring Taoist ideas through the "Mysterious Learning" (*Xuanxue*) movement, embraced Buddhism when they discovered a striking correspondence between the main concepts of their philosophy and the central ideas found in the newly translated Mahayana *Perfection of Wisdom Scriptures* (*Prajñā-pāramitā*). This process in turn encouraged Chinese scholars to seek further for additional scriptures and greater clarification from the western regions.

In a more direct way, Taoism contributed to travel and commerce by promoting pilgrimage and by fostering a greater knowledge of China and its environs through the production of geographical literature and maps. Just as pilgrimage in medieval Europe had a mutually beneficial relationship with commerce and travel, so too, in China, especially from the Song period on, increased pilgrimage to comparatively remote sacred sites both benefited from expanded commercial and travel routes and acted as a stimulus for further commerce and the improvement of travel. In helping to create a sacred geography of China that was centered around numinous peaks in which the immortals were thought to reside, Taoism fired the popular imagination that inspired countless pilgrims to frequent these holy places.

Pilgrims who visited these sites and Taoist figures who sought out other out-of-the-way places produced travel diaries and geographical descriptions of these localities. Taoist adepts also contributed to China's knowledge of the outside world. Most prominent in this regard was Qiu Changchun (fl. 1221), famed alchemist and second patriarch of the Way of the Realization of Truth Movement (*Quanzhen dao*) who, in 1219, traveled to the court of Chinggis Khân, located at that time in Afghanistan. Many geographical details of Qiu's arduous journey were recorded by his secretary, Li Zhichang, in the *Changchun zhenren xiyou ji* (Western Journey of the Taoist Changchun). Cartography also benefited from Taoist advances in astronomical knowledge. Taoists of the Tang period (618–906) appear to have produced maps that linked celestial coordinates to earthly ones.

Together with Confucianism and Buddhism, Taoism played an important part in creating a universal East Asian cultural milieu. The cultures of Korea and Japan assimilated Taoist philosophical ideas as well as Taoist religious beliefs and practices. In Korea, religious Taoism was accorded an honored position by the state in the Koryŏ (918–1392) and early Chosŏn (1392–1910) periods. In Japan during the Nara (710–784) and Heian (794–1185) periods, Taoist texts, philosophical concepts, and religious beliefs were introduced by emissaries, students, and Buddhist monks returning from China. Taoist ideas and customs, which initially enjoyed popularity in the aristocratic class, were, in time, also assimilated by other sectors of the population.

Taoism was as much a beneficiary of commerce and travel as it was a contributor. As traveling merchants and officials posted to other places in China brought their gods with them, local devotions were gradually transformed into national cults. Taoist beliefs and practices were transported beyond China's borders to East and Southeast Asia by Chinese seafarers and colonists. Most notable in this regard was the cult of the goddess Mazu [Ma-tzu], which from the Song period (960–1279) on was disseminated throughout the coastal areas of China and beyond.

**BIBLIOGRAPHY**

Bentley, Jerry H. *Old World Encounters: Cross-Cultural Contacts and Exchanges in Pre-modern Times*. New York: Oxford UP, 1993.

# T

Gernet, Jacques. *A History of Chinese Civilization.* 2nd edition. Cambridge: Cambridge UP, 1996.

Graham, A.C. *Disputers of the Tao: Philosophical Argument in Ancient China.* La Salle, IL: Open Court, 1989.

Naquin, Susan, and Chün-fang Yü, eds. *Pilgrims and Sacred Sites in China.* Berkeley: U of California P, 1992.

Needham, Joseph. *Science and Civilisation in China.* Vols. 2, 3. 1953; rpt. Cambridge, England: Cambridge UP, 1962.

Waley, Arthur. *The Travels of an Alchemist.* London: Routledge, 1931.

*Daniel Getz*

**SEE ALSO**

Buddhism; China; Confucianism; India; Pilgrimage, Christian

## Taprobane

The Greek name for an island south of India (commonly identified as Ceylon, present-day Sri Lanka), known because of Alexander's martial exploits in the East (330 B.C.E.), but rarely visited.

On a map (long since lost) drawn by Eratosthenes (*c.* 275–194 B.C.E.), Taprobane, as much a legend as a geographical certainty, was situated at the southern limit of the earth's landmass, the northern extent of which was defined by Thule, another island shrouded in legend, known through Pytheas of Massilia (Marseilles), a contemporary of Alexander the Great who traveled north of Britain around 325 B.C.E. Eratosthenes, who accurately calculated the circumference of the earth, believed that the inhabited world extended as far south as Taprobane and the Somali coast, which he located at approximately 12 degrees north latitude, although Sri Lanka (Ceylon) lies, in fact, much farther south, between 6 degrees and 10 degrees north latitude. What was said about Taprobane lacked precision: it was supposed to be a large island, as large as Britain, seven sailing days from India. Onesicritus, one of Alexander's chief military officers, whom Strabo called "the admiral of wonders," claimed it was twenty days away, and his was one of several sources that inhabited the island with elephants and maneaters. We know from Pliny (23–79 C.E.) that some early writers mistook Taprobane for the northern edge of a fourth "antipodal" continent.

Ptolemy (*c.* 100–180 C.E.) believed the earth's landmass extended to 16 degrees 30 feet south latitude, and he situated Taprobane on both sides of the equator. In his atlas (a collection of reconstructions based on Ptolemy's geographical data), the last of the "regional" maps represents Taprobane alone, depicting it as an extensive island with two mountains and five rivers, lying between 13 degrees north latitude and 4 degrees south latitude, surrounded by numerous small islands. On the Ptolemaic world map, Taprobane lay south of India, whose coastline he drew nearly flat, on an east-west axis. For these reasons, Taprobane, as described in classical texts such as Solinus's *Collectanea* [53.1, 54.1; *c.* 230/240] is usually understood to refer to today's Sri Lanka, although its size and reported marvels suggest some confusion with other islands of East Asia.

Marco Polo (*c.* 1298) and other travelers made places in the East somewhat better known to the medieval West. Polo refers to a large island with a circumference of some 2,400 miles (3,860 kilometers) east of the coast of India. He calls this island "Seilan," but the focus of his description—a huge ruby owned by the local king, as well as the exotic local products—suggests that it is the same place others named Taprobane (a toponym that is not found in his account). Traveling from China to Avignon between 1347 and 1353, John of Marignolli made port in "Seyllan," where a local tyrant robbed him of all his precious possessions; John maintained that the earthly paradise was very near the "Illa Taprobana" (associated with great riches and wonders and site of a majestic seated king and an elephant) depicted on the Catalan Atlas (*c.* 1375), but that it was situated in the eastern-most part of Asia, whereas Ceylon (? Illa Jana) was located near India; the same is true of the Fra Mauro *mappamundi* (1459) and the Martin Behaim globe (1492). A similar doubling can be found in *The Book of John Mandeville,* whose Silha is a huge island ("800 miles" in circumference) replete with dragons and crocodiles, the site where Adam and Eve wept for their expulsion from Paradise; Taprobane, meanwhile, was farther east, beyond the land of Prester John, to whom the people are subject.

In medieval geographical treatises, Taprobane is in essence a classical legacy, passed on by Isidore of Seville (*c.* 560–636) in *Etymologies* 14.6.12. Honorius Augustodunensis (*c.* 1110) places the island in the Indian Ocean, states that it has ten cities, and observes that its climate (two summers and winters per year) makes it a verdant place. Similar information is found in Hugh of St. Victor's *Descriptio mappaemundi* (1128/1129). From Isidore, too, Taprobane made its way onto the Hereford map ("Taphana insula"; *c.* 1280), as well as the Henry of Mainz map (late 1100s), where it is called "Tabana," and the Ebstorf map (c. 1240).

Thus Taprobane had more or less the same fate as Thule, its sister-island at earth's northern margin. Both became famous as indicators of the limits of human life. Few people, if any, visited them, so legends freely developed and their "actual" locations shifted. Thule, which may originally have been Iceland, was also associated with Norway and the Shetland islands; Taprobane entered Western geography almost certainly as Sri Lanka, but in the late Middle Ages the word identified Sumatra (or Java or Borneo).

**BIBLIOGRAPHY**

Aujac, Germaine. *Claude Ptolémée, astronome, astrologue, géographe; connaissance et représentation du monde habité.* Paris: Ed. du C.T.H.S., 1993.

Gambin, M.T. "L'Ile Taprobane: Problèmes de cartographie dans l'Océan Indien." In *Géographie du Monde au Moyen Age et à la Renaissance.* Ed. Monique Pelletier. Paris: Ed. du C.T.H.S. 1989, pp. 191–200.

*The Geography of Strabo.* Trans. Horace Leonard Jones. London: Heinemann; Cambridge, MA: Harvard UP, 1917–1932, vols. 1 and 7.

Harley-Woodward. Vol. 1, pp. 182, 198, 270, and plates 9, 18, 19, 20. See Gen. Bib.

Kish, G. *La carte: Image des civilisations.* Paris: Seuil, 1980.

*Ptolemy's Geography.* Trans. F.L. Stevenson. New York: New York Public Library, 1932.

*Germaine Aujac*

**SEE ALSO**

Antipodes; Behaim, Martin; Ebstorf World Map; Henry of Mainz Map; Hereford Map; Honorius Augustodunensis; Isidore of Seville; John of Marignolli; *Mandeville's Travels*; Marco Polo; Mauro Map, [Fra]; Prester John; Ptolemy; Solinus, Julius Gaius; Thule

## Ten Lost Tribes, The

Members of the ten northern tribes of ancient Israel who were taken into captivity in the eighth century B.C.E. and never returned to Palestine.

The biblical kingdom of Israel, composed of twelve tribes that possessed land, split into two states after the accession of Rehoboam I (c. 930 B.C.E.); the "northern" kingdom (also known as Samaria), consisting of ten tribes, was the first to be conquered by foreign enemies and dispersed. From the time of their forced emigration to Assyria in the eighth century B.C.E., the Ten Lost Tribes of Israel have occupied the imagination of Jews eager for the return of the Messiah, sustaining an ideal of freedom and independence and supporting a belief in the return to Zion; they have also entered into Christian theology, and, occasionally, anti-Semitism.

King Tiglathpileser III of Assyria (r. 744–727), mentioned in 2 Kings 15:29 (and named "Pul" in 2 Kings 15:19), regularly deported population groups from conquered nations in order to inhibit rebellions and break the bond uniting deities, people, and land. This practice continued under succeeding kings of Assyria and Babylon. When Sargon II (r. 722–705) destroyed Samaria in 721, he scattered the leaders of resident tribes widely throughout the vast Assyrian Empire. The "southern" kingdom, Judea, was conquered by Sargon II, and its people were also deported to Babylon (Jeremiah 52:28–30 cites three separate deportations in 597, 586, and 561). The Persian king Cyrus allowed the Jews in Babylon to return to their native land in 537 B.C.E. By this time, however, the ten tribes of the north were lost; during the succeeding centuries they acquired a kind of mythic status as an image of Jewish redemption and the triumphant return of a nation of Israel.

Isaiah (11:11), Jeremiah (31:7–8), and Ezekiel (37:19–22) preserved the idea of separate Jewish identity for the ten tribes in exile and affirmed the belief that they would return to Palestine. Although the belief was reiterated in the Talmud, rabbis Eliezer ben Jose (fl. second century C.E.) and Akiba ben Joseph (c. 50–c. 135) expressed strong doubts. Nonetheless, their survival in exotic and distant lands was a subject of folktale and legend. Josephus (c. 37–? C.E.) located them beyond the river Sambatyon ("the Sabbath river"), for which later commentators claimed mysterious powers. They described it as a raging river that hurls stones on six days of the week but honors the Sabbath by resting on the seventh day—precisely the day the exiled Jews could not travel to cross it. Thus, as long as they remained pious, it was impossible for them to return.

Medieval travelers and explorers, both Jewish and non-Jewish, attempted to locate the Ten Lost Tribes. In the ninth century, Eldad ha-Dani, a traveler from Babylonia to North Africa and Spain, claimed that his native land was home to four of the lost tribes and that they maintained an independent kingdom in Havilah, "the land of gold," near Ethiopia. His colorful account contradicted the view of some Christians that Jewish political independence ceased with the destruction of

# T

the second Temple in 70 C.E. and encouraged idealistic belief in a free Jewish community existing somewhere in the world. The twelfth-century traveler, Benjamin of Tudela, a more respected authority than Eldad ha-Dani, contributed to the myth when he reported the belief of Persian Jews that four of the tribes lived in Nishapur (in the northeast of present-day Iran).

Christian writers also speculated about the survival of the lost tribes. Peter Comestor (*c.* 1100–1178) linked the biblical story to the Alexander legend, identifying a people the Macedonian hero found imprisoned near the Caspian as the "offspring of the captive tribes." His idea made its way into Vincent of Beauvais's *Speculum historiale* in the 1250s. Ricold of Monte Croce suggested that the Mongols might be descended from the lost tribes, and he advanced a linguistic argument to support it (*c.* 1291). The association between Gog and Magog and the ten tribes—in German vernacular text, sometimes "Red Jews"—is found in texts from the thirteenth through the fifteenth centuries. None is more pernicious, perhaps, than *The Book of John Mandeville,* which portrays Gog and Magog, confined in the Caucasus region, as heirs to the lost tribes, who will break forth at the end of time and link up with fellow speakers of Hebrew throughout the world to massacre Christians.

During the fifteenth century, letters, tales, and emissaries from Jerusalem to the far-flung Jewish communities circulated reports about the existence of the ten tribes that inflamed Messianic expectations and generated the desire to return to Palestine. The Messiah, it was said, commanded huge armies of the ten tribes that would return in triumph to the Holy Land, conquer Mecca, and serve in the apocalyptic wars at the end of time. In 1488–1489, Obadiah of Bertinoro confirmed that the ten tribes warred against Prester John in Ethiopia. In 1528, the Jerusalem kabbalist Abraham ben Eleazar ha-Levi associated the ten tribes with the wars of the Falashas in Ethiopia, and shortly thereafter, the false Messiah David Reuveni claimed kinship with the king of three of the lost tribes that had settled in Arabia. Rumors and reports of the Ten Lost Tribes have continued to circulate in the modern period, sometimes identifying them with inhabitants of unexpected places, including South America, the United States, and Great Britain.

## BIBLIOGRAPHY

Anderson, Andrew Runni. *Alexander's Gate, Gog and Magog, and the Inclosed Nations.* Monographs of the Mediaeval Academy of America 5. Cambridge, MA: The Mediaeval Academy of America, 1932.

Eldad HaDani. *Relation d'Eldad HaDanite, voyageur du IXe siècle.* Paris: Dondey-Dupré, 1838.

Godbey, A.H. *The Lost Tribes, a Myth.* Durham, NC: Duke UP, 1930.

Gow, Andrew Colin. *The Red Jews: Antisemitism in an Apocalyptic Age, 1200–1600.* Studies in Medieval and Reformation Thought 55. Leiden: Brill, 1995.

Law, David A. *From Samaria to Samarkand.* Lanham, MD: UP of America, 1992.

*Jerome Mandel*

**SEE ALSO**
Benjamin of Tudela; Ethiopians; Gog and Magog; *Mandeville's Travels;* Prester John; Red Jews; Ricold of Monte Croce; Vincent of Beauvais

## Terra Australes

A theoretical landmass in the Southern Hemisphere.

The origin of the idea of a large continent in the Southern Hemisphere lies in classical antiquity's concern for symmetry and balance, producing a geographical concept of an equal amount of land in the Northern and Southern Hemispheres of a spherical earth. Aristotle suggested it, Crates and Virgil helped to popularize it. Ptolemy (100–180 C.E.), in his *Geographia,* supported the idea, but with a land connection between southern Africa and eastern Asia. The earliest clear articulation of a separate landmass was the "anticthones" of the Roman geographer Pomponius Mela (first century C.E.) who placed it to the south of Africa. Solinus in his *Collectanea* (230/240 C.E.) referred to the land of the Antipodes, noting that some had erroneously identified it with Taprobane (Ceylon). Early Christian writers such as Lactantius (*c.* 300) and Cosmas Indikopleustes (sixth century) rejected the idea of the Antipodes as not conforming to a scriptural interpretation of the Creation.

The major transmitter of the concept of the southern continent into Western Christian geographic thought was Macrobius, a widely read fifth-century school author whose "Commentary" on the Dream of Scipio Africanus allowed for the existence of such a landmass in the Southern Hemisphere and considered the possibility that it was populated. Isidore of Seville (seventh century) in his *Etymologies* acknowledged the idea of "fabled Antipodes" but, like St. Augustine, clearly considered the notion a fable. The Church held that if there were inhabitants of *terra australes* they could not have been formed at the Creation, but could only be monsters of a nonhuman kind.

In cartography, the southern continent appeared prominently in the world map of the Spanish priest Beatus of Liébana (eighth century), which continued to be reproduced into the thirteenth century. He bounded Africa on the south with an ocean that was north of the equator, and to the south he placed the antipodean continent, but without indicating any inhabitants. Later painters of the map, however, often placed there sciapodes—men who each had a single umbrella-like foot. Similarly, the canon Lambert of St. Omer, in his map accompanying his *Liber Floridus* (c. 1119), gives some prominence to *terra australes,* which he noted had "nothing to do with our race."

Many maps of the fifteenth century did not include it, and it did not attract the attention of late fifteenth- and early sixteenth-century explorers, but it reappeared on maps in the later sixteenth and sevententh centuries as Terra Australes Incognita. It was not eliminated as a geographical concept until the second circumnavigation of Captain James Cook (1772–1775), which traversed the area in which the continent presumably existed.

**BIBLIOGRAPHY**

Spate, O.H.K. *The Spanish Lake.* Vol. 1. Minneapolis: U of Minnesota P, 1979.

*John Parker*

**SEE ALSO**

Antipodes; Beatus Maps; Cosmas Indikopleustes; *Liber Floridus;* Mela, Pomponius; Ptolemy; Solinus, Julius Gaius; Taprobane; *Terra Incognita*

## Terra Incognita

Land existing outside the *oikoumene,* unknown to but habitable by man. Since the word *terra* in the Bible always refers to the *oikoumene* or inhabited earth, *terra incognita* is land that is not yet investigated or known by experience because it is a zone separated from the *oikoumene.*

Pomponius Mela (fl. 37–42 C.E.), in his *Chorographia* (1,4), refers to territory located beyond a torrid (equatorial) region and therefore "incognitus." Mela's world, divided from north to south in five zones, makes of *terra incognita* an unknown landmass separated from Asia/Africa/Europe by a belt of great heat at

the equator that cannot be traversed. This view was made popular on maps in manuscripts of Macrobius's fifth-century *Commentary on the Dream of Scipio,* which embodied the doctrine of Crates of Mallos (fl. 150 B.C.E.), who believed in a spherical earth, divided into five girdles, or zones. The two zones at both poles were thought to be cold and uninhabitable, while the part in the middle at the equator was said to be extremely hot and likewise inhospitable to human life; only the two zones in between, one in the Northern, the other in the Southern Hemisphere, were habitable, but, because they were separated by the equatorial belt, people living in the northern habitable part would not be able to reach the southern part. Nevertheless, medieval geographers and cartographers visualized the southern continent and called it *terra temperata nobis incognita* ("temperate land unknown to us").

The seventh-century encyclopedist Isidore of Seville, in his *Etymologies* (14.5.17), characterizes this space as a fourth continent after Asia, Europa, and Africa—*solis ardore incognita,* "not yet explored because of [the zone of] great heat." A map in the Isidorean tradition (dated *c.* 775) in a manuscript now in Rome (Biblioteca Apostolica Vaticana MS Vat. Lat. 6018 fols. 64v–65) depicts an *insola incognita* as the fourth continent. All the maps accompanying copies of Beatus of Liébana's *Commentary on the Apocalypse of St. John* (written 776–786) also show this *deserta terra incognita,* this one inhabited by sciapodes, a monstrous race of humans who use a single huge foot as a sunshade. Lambert of Saint-Omer (fl. 1112–1121) depicted in some of the many maps inserted in his autograph copy of the *Liber Floridus* the antipodal continent called *terra incognita.* An early fifteenth-century map contained in the initial "O" of Pomponius Mela's *orbis situm* in a manuscript at Reims (Bibliothèque Municipale MS 1321, fol. 13) even presents three *terrae incognitae,* one at the edge of the *oikoumenical* earth in northern Europe, another in northern Asia, and the third in southern Africa, as Cardinal Fillastre, the manuscript's commissioner, knew from Ptolemy how to define the boundaries. All such maps assume the location of the *terra incognita* at the poles or the equator; apparently no one expected to find it west or east of the *oikoumene.*

**BIBLIOGRAPHY**

Brincken, Anna-Dorothee von den. "*Terrae Incognitae.* Raum und Raumvorstellungen im Mittelalter." *Miscellanea Mediaevalia* 25 (1998): 557–572.

# T

Dalché, Patrick Gautier. "L'Oeuvre géographique du cardinal Fillastre († 1428)." *Archives d'histoire doctrinale et littéraire du Moyen-Age* 67 (1992): 319–383.

*Anna-Dorothee von den Brincken*

**SEE ALSO**

Antipodes; Beatus Maps; Climate; Edges of the World; *Liber Floridus;* Isidore of Seville; Mela, Pomponius; Monstrosity, Geographical; *Oikoumene*

## Teutonic Order

A military religious order founded in 1190 as the German Hospital of St. Mary of Jerusalem for the care of German crusaders. In 1198, responding to the pressing need for warriors to defend Christian strongholds in Palestine, the order modified its duties to include military service, a change that Pope Innocent III swiftly approved. This "German Order" (a more accurate translation of *der Deutsche Orden*) grew quickly to take its place alongside the Templars and Hospitallers.

When it became apparent that the Holy Land lacked space to deploy the growing number of knights, men-at-arms, priests, and hospital personnel being attracted to the order, Grandmaster Hermann von Salza sought out new fields of activity on the borderlands of east-central Europe. First in Transylvania (1211–1224), then in Prussia (1230), and finally in Livonia (1237), the Teutonic Order went beyond its primary role of defending Christendom to create states independent of all outside authority except the papacy and, to a considerable extent, the Holy Roman Emperor.

Modern research demonstrates that the Teutonic knights do not fit the negative stereotypes promulgated during the past two centuries. The knights and priests were deeply religious, represented many nationalities (though for the sake of practicality, every member was expected to speak some version of the German language), and possessed estates, convents, and hospitals from Sweden to Italy. The simple knights, priests, and serving brothers were largely of nonnoble origin, though they usually chose nobles as officers; they were forerunners of neither the Second Empire nor the Third Reich. They were active in trade and exceptionally pragmatic in war and diplomacy, attracting the company of the leading nobles of western and central Europe for incursions into pagan Lithuania. They fought much less often against Roman Catholic Poland and Orthodox Russian states.

With exceptions only in Riga and occasionally Danzig (Gdansk), the Teutonic Order enjoyed an excellent relationship with the merchants who lived in their lands or traded there; cooperation with the Hanseatic League was especially close. The grandmasters were careful to guarantee the safety of roads across Poland for crusaders assembling at Marienburg and for merchants; they negotiated treaties assuring German merchants' rights to cross Masovia to Brest and thence down to the Black Sea; they made agreements even with the pagan rulers of Lithuania for the mutual protection of traders; they were staunch supporters of the Hanseatic cities in exercising their treaty rights to trade in Novgorod, Pskov, and Polozk; and they helped suppress piracy on the Baltic Sea. In addition to filling the order's coffers with taxes and buying their grain, wood, honey, and amber, their merchant allies provided them with first-class intelligence about trade routes through neighboring countries, the customs of the peoples, and the personalities of the rulers. Unfortunately, little of this information was written down for posterity.

The chroniclers of the order did, however, write descriptions of the native peoples and the countryside; among them was Aeneas Silvius (later Pope Pius II, 1458–1464), who became interested in the practices of the formerly pagan peoples of the area while serving as papal legate there. In the late fourteenth century, the commander of Königsberg (Kaliningrad) collected from scouts a description of the various routes into Lithuania. This *littauische Wegeberichte* was supplemented by the reports of subsequent visitors, such as Ghillebert de Lannoy (1414), so that together they provide the best information we have on the region prior to the Reformation.

One interesting medieval explorer, Gerhard of Cleves, came through the territories of the Teutonic Order in 1438, stopping periodically to lend his prestige and talent to the resolution of local disputes. The count's intent was to travel to Jerusalem via Novgorod and Byzantium, thus opening up a new pilgrimage route that bypassed the Turks. However, he was robbed by Karelian natives shortly after crossing into Russia and spent several months vainly trying to organize the military forces necessary to take revenge and recover his goods.

The financial disasters in the years after the Treaty of Thorn (1422) completed the political decline that began at the battle of Tannenberg (Grunwald) in 1410. The order's sorry state in these decades made it impossible to counter its enemies' propaganda as effectively as had been the case when the grandmasters ruled over a vibrant economy and commanded the most powerful military machine in the region. The Reformation, though ending the order's long connection to Prussia, began a new military and chivalric relationship with the house of Habsburg that lasted until the twentieth century. The order continues to exist, with its headquarters in Vienna.

**BIBLIOGRAPHY**

Arnold, Udo, ed. *Zur Wirtschaftsentwicklung des Deutschen Ordens im Mittelalter.* Quellen und Studien zur Geschichte des Deutschen Ordens 39. Marburg: Elwert, 1989.

Boockmann, Hartmut. *Der Deutsche Orden: Zwölf Kapitel aus seiner Geschichte.* Munich: Beck, 1981.

Christiansen, Eric. *The Northern Crusades: The Baltic and the Catholic Frontier, 1100–1525.* Minneapolis: U of Minnesota P, 1980.

*Gli Inizi del cristianesimo in Livonia-Lettonia* and *La cristianizzazione della Lituania: atti del colloquio internazionale di storia ecclesiastica . . .* Ed. Michele Maccarrone. Vatican: Libreria editrice Vaticana, 1989.

Sarnowsky, Jürgen. *Die Wirtschaftsführung des Deutschen Ordens in Preussen (1382–1454).* Köln: Böhlau, 1993.

Urban, William. *The Samogitian Crusade.* Chicago: Lithuanian Research and Studies Center, 1989.

———. *The Baltic Crusade.* 1975; 2nd edition, revised and enlarged. Chicago: Lithuanian Research and Studies Center, 1994.

*William Urban*

**SEE ALSO**

Gaston Phébus; Hanse, The; Lannoy, Ghillebert de; Military Orders; Pius II; Pilgrimage, Christian; Piracy; Poland; Russia and Rus'

## Textiles, Decorative

Important trade items in the Middle Ages, most notable of which were patterned silk fabrics and knotted pile carpets made from wool.

East Asian silk was the most desirable textile import to Europe from the period of the Roman Empire (30 B.C.E.–395 C.E.) onward through the Middle Ages, either as woven fabric or as raw material in cocoon form. In the late medieval period, densely knotted and colorful woolen carpets from Asia Minor also became coveted and prestigious trade goods; they appear in Flemish manuscript miniatures and panel painting as signs of fashion and affluence.

During most of the Middle Ages, before drawlooms and skilled weavers were brought to Italy, the Latin West depended heavily on imported silks for ritual use in vestments, furnishings, the cult of relics, and burials. By the fourteenth century, the fledgling silk industry in Tuscany began to compete with Chinese and Central Asian *panni tartarici,* lively figured silks arriving by the reopened eastern trade routes during Mongol rule (*c.* 1206–1368). The silk and gilt-silver velvets of fifteenth-century Florence and Venice, with motifs derived from Middle Eastern prototypes, appealed to the sophisticated tastes of neighboring Ottoman, Spanish, and northern European elites.

Lightweight and resistant to the hazards of travel, silk was an ideal long-distance trade commodity. On pilgrimages to the Holy Land in the fourth and fifth centuries, wealthy Christians could purchase Syrian or Egyptian figured silks to hold sacred relics. The Silk Road ports were then controlled by the Sasanids (224–651), and although Byzantium was able to acquire superior Chinese silk via the northern trade routes, Justinian I (r. 527–565) was eager to replace this costly import with domestic sericulture. At the time of the seventh-century Islamic conquests, silk production was well established both in the Middle East and in Spain under the Umayyads (756–1031).

Since silks were produced on looms around the Mediterranean and across Asia for more than half a millennium, patterned examples are often difficult to assign to either Byzantine or Islamic origins, and many are frankly imitative. Some textiles display specific Christian content, but most feature vegetal, animal, and figural imagery with origins in ancient mythology. Secure dating is also problematic due to such conservative traditions, and because these textiles frequently had existed for generations before they were deposited in reliquaries or tombs. Thus, the "Elephant silk" from the tomb of Charlemagne in the cathedral at Aachen has been attributed to late eleventh-century Constantinople, but could well have been added by Frederick II as late as 1215.

It is known that many of the extant medieval silks in European treasuries were diplomatic gifts, woven on Constantinopolitan imperial workshop looms that were capable of producing extraordinary silks up to nine feet (three meters) in width. The frequently quoted displeasure of Bishop Liudprand of Cremona (d. 972), unable to pass through Byzantine customs with his acquired purple silks, is an indication that the precious and supposedly restricted dye made from the murex, a kind of shellfish, and known as imperial purple, may also have been commercially available. In a

# T

similar, apparent paradox, the silks with Kufic inscriptions woven on the looms of Almería in Islamic Spain under the Berber dynasties (1088–1232) featured prominently as shrouds and burial textiles for Christian Spanish royalty, and as fabrics for the vestments of Spanish clergy, whose joint mission it was to reclaim the Iberian Peninsula from the Muslims.

Technological advances in medieval silkweaving took place outside Europe; the new compound weave structure, lampas, allowed a broader textural range than the previous compound twill, samite. Lampas appeared fully developed in early twelfth-century silks in the region of Baghdad, possibly parallel with developments in al-Andalūs. It was also at this time, during the crusades, that Frankish nobles in the Latin kingdoms acquired tastes for silks and other luxuries on an unprecedented scale. The sack of Constantinople in 1204 had further consequences for Europe's textile manufacture, because it brought dispossessed weavers to Lucca, establishing the first Italian silk industry there. Other city-states followed in keen competition, first Florence, then Venice and Genoa.

Lush pile fabrics in wool were produced in Egypt in the early centuries C.E., and recent archaeological finds have shown that knotted pile carpets were already fully developed around 500 B.C.E. Experts have disagreed on where in western or Central Asia such knotted carpets originated—perhaps, like compound weave structures, they represent shared and parallel practices. The Armenians of Asia Minor had a long tradition, reaching back to the legendary Phrygian caps, of producing and trading dyestuffs, especially the cochineal reds of insects, kermes, and plant roots (particularly madder). Indigo for blue was grown in Egypt and Syria, although India exported a superior quality. In comparison with silk, the relatively heavy carpets were less well suited to true long-distance trade. The pragmatic Venetian, Pisan, and Genoese merchants took on the richly colored rugs in the nearby Anatolian ports since this was easier commerce than going farther east where similar carpets were probably also produced.

Early Anatolian rug fragments survive in three distinct styles: animal carpets; dragon and phoenix carpets; and so-called small-patterned Holbein carpets. It does not seem possible to prove that these carpets were made by a particular demographic group. To establish a precise chronology is an equally thorny issue; only a few Anatolian early carpet examples have been radiocarbon dated; the earliest among them has been assigned to the seventh-to-tenth century. If Marco Polo's thirteenth-century travel account can be taken at face value, we may believe that the best carpets were produced by Anatolian weavers—Armenians, Turks, and Greeks working together in harmony. The supposed influence of the Seljuks in Anatolia (1071–1194) on the decorative arts and architecture has been revised recently; this dynasty, once thought to have brought about considerable artistic change, was already in sharp decline from the twelfth century.

Interestingly, there is evidence that newly arrived patterns also crossed textile disciplines, since the asymmetrical cloud motif of an early fourteenth-century Chinese silk appears to be the model for a fifteenth-century Mudejar carpet. This practice can also be observed elsewhere in medieval art, particularly manuscript painting, embroidery, and tapestry design.

## BIBLIOGRAPHY

Becker, John. *Pattern and Loom: A Practical Study of the Development of Weaving Techniques in China, Western Asia and Europe.* Copenhagen: Rhodos, 1987.

Franses, Michael. "The 'Historical' Carpets from Anatolia." In *Orient Stars: A Carpet Collection.* Ed. E. Heinrich Kirchheim. London: Hali, 1993, pp. 262–273.

Geijer, Agnes. *A History of Textile Art: A Selective Account.* London: Pasold Research Fund, 1979.

Lombard, Maurice. *Études d'économie médiévale III: Les textiles dans le Monde Musulman du VIIe au XIIe siècle.* Paris and the Hague: Mouton, 1978.

Muthesius, Anna. *Byzantine Silk Weaving A.D. 400 to A.D. 1200.* Vienna: Fassbaender, 1997.

Schorta, Regula. "Zur Entwicklung der Lampastechnik." In *Riggisberger Berichte 5, Islamische Textilkunst des Mittelalters: Aktuelle Probleme.* Riggisberg, Switzerland: Abegg-stiftung, 1997, pp. 173–180.

*Désirée Koslin*

## SEE ALSO

Armenia; Baghdad; Byzantine Empire; Caravans; China; Constantinople; Dyes and Pigments; Egypt; Genoa; Holy Land; Inner Asian Trade; Luidprand of Cremona; Marco Polo; Ottoman Empire; Pilgrimage, Christian; Pisa; Seljuk Turks; Silk Roads; Venice

## Theoderic (fl. 1170)

A German pilgrim of the late twelfth century, Theoderic composed a valuable description of Palestine in the last years of the crusader kingdom.

Theoderic's pilgrimage to the Holy Land occurred around 1172. His account, *De Locis Sanctis,* provides a valuable description of the crusader kingdom some fifteen years before Saladin's conquest of Jerusalem. Except for what little personal information we can glean from the text, we know nothing of Theoderic. He may have been from Würzburg or Hirsau; the text refers to a companion named Adolf from Cologne (who was buried in Jerusalem on Palm Sunday). The evidence neither proves nor disproves that he was the "socio et domestico Dietrico" to whom John of Würzburg dedicated his *Descriptio Terrae Sanctae.*

Introducing himself as the "dung of all monks, a Christian," Theoderic states that he has written an account, based entirely on personal experience or "the true account of others," to satisfy those unable to make the journey. According to Theoderic, these readers can bring Christ to mind by reading a description of holy places; by doing so they will love him, pity him, and long for him, leading them to absolution, grace, and the kingdom of heaven. Thus his book has a spiritual as much as a geographical purpose.

Theoderic reveals a detailed knowledge of construction and building materials, as well as a fascination with the architecture of the Holy Land; he compares the roof of the Church of the Holy Sepulchre to the cathedral at Aachen. Thus, *De Locis Sanctis* is a major source for the medieval topography of Jerusalem, and descriptions of art, architecture, and agriculture. The account suggests little interest in marvels or miraculous events, although Theoderic reports witnessing the coming of the "Holy Fire," lighting a liturgical lamp in a church in Jerusalem (not always the Church of the Holy Sepulchre) on Holy Saturday.

*De Locis Sanctis* survives in two manuscripts of the fifteenth century, each of which includes several texts related to the Holy Land. Scholars became aware of the second of these only in 1985; R.B.C. Huygens's edition is the first to make use of both manuscripts.

**BIBLIOGRAPHY**

Dolbeau, François. "Théodericus, De locis sanctis: Un second manuscrit, provenant de Saint-Barbe de Cologne." *Analecta Bollandiana* 103 (1985): 113–114.

Hazard, Harry W., ed. *The Art and Architecture of the Crusader States.* Vol. 4 in *A History of the Crusades.* Ed. Kenneth M. Setton. See Gen. Bib.

Huygens, R.B.C., ed. *Tres Peregrinationes.* Corpus Christianorum: Continuatio Mediaevalis 139. Turnholt: Brepols, 1994.

Stewart, Aubrey, trans. *Guide to the Holy Land.* Palestine Pilgrims' Text Society. London: 1891; rpt. New York: AMS Press, 1971.

*Timothy S. Jones*

**SEE ALSO**

Crusades, First, Second, and Third; Holy Land; Jerusalem; John of Würzburg; Pilgrimage, Christian; Saladin

## Third Crusade
*See* Crusades, First, Second, and Third

## Thomas of Cantimpré (1201–1270/1272)
Compiler of a popular Latin encyclopedia of natural history in twenty books, called *De naturis rerum* or *On the Natures of Things.*

Thomas of Cantimpré was born in 1201 at Lewes, near Brussels, of a noble family, his father having fought under Richard the Lionheart in Palestine. As a schoolboy in Liège from 1206 to 1216, Thomas heard Jacques de Vitry—who had written a popular work on the Holy Land and its flora and fauna—preach and was apparently captivated by the exotic natural history mentioned in Jacques's sermons. At sixteen, Thomas entered the Augustinian abbey at Cantimpré, then in 1232, presumably because he felt his vocation was more to be scholar than priest, he joined the Dominicans at Louvain, and to further his education, went to Cologne, where he studied with Albert the Great. From 1237, he was in Paris at the Convent of St. James and probably studied at the University of Paris until 1240. He knew both German and French, and also some English. At the age of forty-five he returned to the convent at Louvain as subprior and reader, eventually attaining the rank of preacher-general in a monastic province composed of Germany, Belgium, and France. He probably died on May 15, 1270 or 1272.

While at Paris (between 1237 and 1240), Thomas completed his encyclopedia, which quickly became very popular, surviving in 144 manuscripts (not all of these complete), as well as a large number of excerpts and adaptations of individual books and sections, particularly those on stones and monstrous races of men. Some of the manuscripts, for example Valenciennes,

Bibliothèque Municipale MS 320, as well as the adaptations, were illustrated with depictions of the subjects of individual entries rather in the style of a modern encyclopedia.

Though similar in its scientific outlook to its near contemporary competitors, the *De proprietatibus rerum* of Bartholomaeus Anglicus (*c.* 1200–1272) and the *Speculum naturale* of Thomas's fellow Dominican, Vincent of Beauvais, Thomas's work differed in one important respect, in that he wrote his text, at least in part, for preachers, to whom he offered not just accessible scientific information but also improving moralizations deriving from it. The *De naturis rerum* was translated into Middle Dutch by Jacob van Maerlant in the second half of the thirteenth century and into Middle High German by Konrad von Megenberg in the second half of the fourteenth. There is no English translation.

In his material on natural—and unnatural—history (Books 3, 4–9, and 13), Thomas treats foreign and local wonders, and even maritime activities such as whaling (considered in a somewhat marvelous way). In his third book, on monstrous races of men, he catalogues both exotic and home-grown wonders: "men are to be found in the East of middle stature and their eyes gleam like fires" and "in France are to be seen hermaphroditic men who are both male and female."

Besides these monstrous races of men, Thomas also speaks of several individual beings of a marvelous sort in Italy and Germany. For example, a certain colossus was so huge that when he was killed, the river Tiber could not contain his body, and the sea for a great distance into the estuary was stained red by his blood. A temple and statue were erected in his honor in Rome and named Colossus after him. A similar marvel is that of a German giant, Theuto. (Thomas claims that there there are many such giants in Germany). His tomb was near the Danube river in a town called St. Stephen about two miles from Vienna. The tomb was ninety-five cubits long and the bones therein exceeded human imagination. The skull, for instance, was so great that someone holding two swords pommel to pommel could sweep them around inside the skull without the sword tips anywhere touching the inner walls. And his teeth were wider than a man's palm.

Thomas's comments on the whaling industry may well describe a form of this activity practiced in Ireland; it is one of the very few Western accounts of the craft. Fishermen, noting a place where a whale is to be found, gather there in many boats; they make a concert of pipes and flutes to attract it, since the whale delights in music. And when the fishermen see it swimming near the ships they stupify it with the modulations of their music. Stealthily they approach, and with an instrument like an iron harpoon with barbs or pointed teeth, they stab it in the back and then flee in all directions. After a time, the whale feels the wound and makes for the sea floor, where, rubbing its back on the bottom, it forces the iron deeper into the wound and salt water enters, killing the beast. It floats to the surface and the whalers with ropes and lines draw it to shore with much dancing in order to celebrate such a copious bounty.

This account of whaling bears some relation to descriptions of Irish whaling by the tenth-century Jewish traveler Ibrāhīm Ibn Yaʿqūb and the eleventh-century Moorish geographer Udhri, where the fishermen clap their hands and even sing to attract and frenzy the whales or dolphins; then they leap on their backs to drive in the hook or harpoon.

Based mainly on received authorities like Pliny's *Natural History,* Thomas's work was an important source for geography and Eastern travel to his contemporaries, for it presents monstrous races of men, mythical stones, springs, and rivers in foreign lands (such as the magical Fontaine de Baranton in the Forest of Brocéliande, in Brittany, well known from Arthurian legend), and a variety of exotic animals, birds, fish, and sea mammals often with associated legends. His audience probably consisted of lawyers, court officials, doctors, merchants, and poets, as well as fellow clerics.

## BIBLIOGRAPHY

Abeele, Baudouin van den. "Bestiaires encyclopédiques moralisés: Quelques succédanés de Thomas de Cantimpré et de Bartholemy l'Anglais." *Reinardus* 7 (1994): 209–228.

Boese, Helmut, ed. *Thomas Cantimpratensis Liber de natura rerum.* Berlin/New York: De Gruyter, 1973.

Debroux, Anne. *Thomas de Cantimpré (vers 1200–1270): L'homme et son oeuvre écrite: Essai de bibliographie.* Louvain: Aneth, 1979.

Friedman, John Block. "Albert the Great's Topoi of Direct Observation and His Debt to Thomas of Cantimpré." In *Pre-Modern Encyclopaedic Texts: Proceedings of the Second COMERS Congress, Groningen, 1–4 July, 1996.* Ed. Peter Binkley. Leiden: Brill, 1997, pp. 379–392.

Hünemörder, Christian. "Antike und mittelalterliche Enzyklopädien und die Popularisierung naturkundlichen Wissens." *Sudhoffs Archiv* 65 (1981): 339–367.

Walstra, G.J.J. "Thomas de Cantimpré, *De naturis rerum*—État de la Question." *Vivarium* 5 (1967): 146–171; 6 (1968): 46–61.

*John Block Friedman*

**SEE ALSO**

Albertus Magnus; Bartholomaeus Anglicus; Dominican Friars; Giants; Ibrāhīm Ibn Ya'qūb al-Isrā'īli; Jacques de Vitry; Monstrosity, Geographical; Pliny the Elder; Vincent of Beauvais; Whaling

## Thomas of Tolentino (c. 1260–1321)

Important early Franciscan reformer and missionary from a small town near Spoleto, Italy.

Thomas was a leader of the Spirituals, a group of zealous Franciscans in the Marches of Ancona who protested an edict by Gregory X (1271–1276) permitting Franciscans to hold property. For his opposition, he was twice imprisoned by the church authorities as a heretic and schismatic. Later exonerated, he was sent by the new minister general of the order with other Spirituals to Armenia in 1290 at the request of King Hetoum (Hayton) II. This group of friars included Angelo da Gingoli (Angelo Clareno), Angelo da Tolentino, Mark of Montelupone, Peter of Macerata, Liberato of Macerata, and another Peter of unknown origin. In 1291, Thomas and Mark of Montelupone returned as envoys of Hetoum to Pope Nicholas IV (1288–1292). Letters dated January 1292 show that Nicholas sent them on to Philip IV of France (r. 1285–1314) and Edward I of England (r. 1272–1307). An account by Clareno describes the persecutions these friars suffered at the hands of Syrians in Armenia (1290–1293), and in Greece (1295–1305).

In 1302, Thomas returned to Italy to request a new mission. At this time, or possibly during his years in Armenia, he met Giacomo da Monte Rubbiano (the name is uncertain), an elderly missionary well acquainted with the East. Thomas is documented as being in the company of twelve friars during a six-month sojourn in Greece in early 1303. He probably also preached in Persia for a time; his presence in Tabriz in 1306 is recorded. He returned to Europe in summer 1307 bearing a letter from John of Monte Corvino, Franciscan missionary in Khanbaliq (Beijing), to Pope Clement V (1305–1314), then in Gascony. Thomas probably did not personally journey to China, but was merely the last in a series of letter carriers. His comments to the pope on the importance of John of Monte Corvino's work in Asia may have helped in the creation of the metropolitan see of Khanbaliq with John consecrated its first archbishop (1313).

His activities during the next decade are unknown, but in 1320, he and three other Franciscans—James of Padua, Peter of Siena, and the lay brother Demetrius of Tiflis—accompanied the Dominican Jordan of Sévérac (Jordanus Catalani) on his trip toward China. They embarked from Ormuz [Hormuz] in the Persian Gulf, and not finding a ship sailing for Quilon, their desired destination, they traveled via Thana, on the island of Salsette, near Bombay (the same route John of Monte Corvino had taken when he preached in India in 1291). While Jordan, who spoke Persian, went on to Supera (Sofala) to preach, Thomas and his colleagues remained behind in Thana where they were sheltered by a tiny Nestorian community. As a result of a domestic dispute in their host's house, the local authorities became aware of the Franciscans' presence. They were ordered to participate in a theological debate, which they willingly did; the ensuing polemics precipitated their executions.

The four missionaries were arrested and put to death on April 9 and 11, 1321. When Jordan returned to Thana, he had their bodies removed for burial in the Church of Saint Thomas at Supera. A few years later, their relics were exhumed by Odoric of Pordenone and taken to the Franciscan convent at Zaiton. Jordan and several close contemporaries described their martyrdom in letters and chronicles that cast their story in a hagiographic light. As Odoric relates events, Thomas called Muhammad "the son of perdition, placed in hell with the devil, his father—and not he alone but all who keep to [the Muslim] faith, for it is pestiferous and false." The crowd echoes the people calling on Pilate to crucify Jesus in crying out: "Let them die! Let them die!" The account does not completely accord with historical records, but it was the version of the martyrdom that circulated widely in medieval Europe.

**BIBLIOGRAPHY**

Golubovich, P. Girolamo. *Biblioteca bio-bibliografica della Terra Santa e dell'Oriente Francescano.* Vols. 1 and 3. Florence: Quaracchi, 1906, 1927.

Moorman, John. *A History of the Franciscan Order from its Origins to the Year 1517.* Oxford: Clarendon, 1968.

Richard, Jean. "Les missionnaires latins dans l'Inde au XIVe siècle." *Studi veneziani* 12 (1970): 231–242; rpt. in *Orient et Occident au Moyen Âge: Contacts et rela-*

# T

*tions (XIIe–XVe s.)* London: Variorum Reprints, 1976, section 25.

Wadding, Luke, ed. *Annales Minorum seu Trium ordinum a S. Francisco Institutorum.* Rev. ed. P. Bonaventure Marrani. Vols. 4, 5, 6, and 9. Florence: Quaracchi, 1931.

Yule-Cordier. *Cathay and the Way Thither.* See Gen. Bib.

*Gloria Allaire*

**SEE ALSO**
Hetoum; John of Monte Corvino; Jordan of Sévérac; Khanbaliq; Nestorianism; Odoric of Pordenone; Zaiton

## Thule

An island some distance from Britain, marking the world's farthest extreme, to the north and west, for the ancient Greeks. Isidore of Seville (*c.* 560–636) calls Thule "the farthest island in the Ocean in the northern and western waters, beyond Britain. It takes its name 'from the sun' [*sole*], because here the sun makes its summer solstice [i.e., seems to be standing still in summer]" (*Etymologies* 14.6.4).

Thule was visited by Pytheas of Massilia (Marseilles), a Greek mariner who voyaged north of Britain around 330/325 B.C.E. Since Pytheas was otherwise noted for astronomical discoveries, some believe his journey was one of scientific exploration; others maintain he sought a trade route for British tin and Baltic amber. His voyage greatly expanded Hellenistic knowledge of the remote north. Virgil coined the term "Ultima Thule" in a passage that defines the breadth of Rome's burgeoning empire (*Georgics* 1.30). For later authors, Thule was "no less fabulous than famous" (Gerald of Wales, *Topographica Hibernia* 2.17, first recension, *c.* 1117) and marked the end of the known world. The term has since become a synonym for limitation—either a territory practically beyond human ken or a goal almost beyond reach.

Pytheas's record survived only in fragments, known from citations in Strabo and Pliny (see his *Natural History,* 2.77 and 4.16). Medieval geographers regarded Thule as an island six days north of Britain (Dicuil, *De mensura orbis terrarum* 7.2.3, *c.* 825); beyond it, the sea was ever-frozen (Martianus Capella 6.666, Isidore *Etymologies* 14.6.4, Bede *De natura rerum* 9). The phenomenon of the midnight sun, which Pytheas observed, is reported by later sources (Solinus, *Collectanea,* p. 65 [*c.* 230–240]; Dicuil, *De mensura* 7.2.3; and Honorius Augustodunensis in *Imago mundi* 1.31

[*c.* 1110]). According to a legend, invalids had themselves carried to Thule, where they could die in peace (Gossuin de Metz, *Image du Monde* 1.6, translated by Caxton as *Myrrour of the Worlde,* fol. 52).

In 83 C.E., Agricola thought he saw Thule from the Orkneys (according to Tacitus in his biography [10]), although he almost certainly saw the Shetlands. Silius Italicus (d. 101 C.E.) confused Thule with Britain itself, and Procopius (fifth century) associated it with Scandinavia (*De bello Gothico* 2.14; see also Bede, *In Regum librum xxx questiones* 25.19). Dicuil tells of Irish priests who had explored Thule in the late 700s (7.2.6). The modern identity of ancient Thule is much disputed, with scholars variously promoting the Orkneys, Shetlands, Faeroes, Norway, Iceland, and Greenland. Since ancient and medieval writers were themselves uncertain about where or what "Thule" was, any of these identifications might be correct.

**BIBLIOGRAPHY**
Aujac, Germaine. "L'île de Thule, mythe ou réalité: Étude de géographie grecque." *Athenaeum,* n.s., 76 (1988): 329–343.

Hawkes, Charles Francis Christopher. *Pytheas: Europe and the Greek Explorers.* J.L. Myres Memorial Lecture 8. Oxford: Blackwell, 1977.

Mund-Dopchie, Monique. "La survie littéraire de la Thulé de Pythéas: Un example de la permanence de schémas antiques dans la culture européenne." *L'Antiquité Classique* 59 (1990): 79–97.

Whitaker, Ian. "The Problem of Pytheas' Thule." *Classical Journal* 77 (1981–1982): 148–164.

*Roger T. Macfarlane*

**SEE ALSO**
Bede; Caxton, William; Dicuil; Edges of the World; Geography in Medieval Europe; Gerald of Wales; Iceland; Isidore of Seville; *Mare Oceanum;* Mela, Pomponius; New World; Scandinavian World Map; Solinus, Julius Gaius; Taprobane

## Tibet

A country situated in Inner Asia on the elevated heights of the Tibetan plateau. Medieval Tibet covered a vast expanse of approximately 900,000 square miles between India and China at altitudes averaging some 16,000 feet (4,880 meters). Vague knowledge of the Tibetan plateau circulated in the West during classical antiquity, while a few border peoples on the plateau had some contact with China and India even earlier. However, firm relations between Tibet and the non-Tibetan world date only from the early seventh century.

The earliest documented contact between Tibet and the world beyond the plateau came during China's Sui dynasty (581–618), when a few Tibetan and Chinese missions were exchanged. Major relations with China date from the Tang dynasty (618–907), which was nearly contemporaneous with the Tibetan imperial period. During this time, Tibetan exports to China included animals and animal products (such as horses and musk), as well as salt, precious stones, and various objects crafted from gold. The main import from China was silk. During its imperial era, Tibet gained periodic control over crucial parts of the Silk Roads, including the important oasis cities in present-day Xinjiang, and was able at times to dominate the trade passing between China and the West. Tibet is known to have imported iron and steel products from Central Asia, while exporting musk widely throughout Eurasia. During this period too, precise, firsthand geographical information about the Tibetan plateau was first recorded by Chinese writers.

After the collapse of the Tibetan Empire (following the assassination of the Tibetan emperor in 842), the loss of Tibetan power led to a decline in international intercourse with central Tibet, although small Tibetan states on the northeastern part of the plateau continued to play an active intermediary role in trade between East and West in the tenth and eleventh centuries. In addition, the decline of Buddhism in India and its intensified development in Tibet precipitated increased interaction with Tibet on the part of neighboring Buddhist rulers and peoples. The later rulers of the Tangut state (also known as China's Xixia dynasty [1038–1227]) developed contacts with Tibet, and their successors, the Mongols (Yuan dynasty [1227–1360]) followed suit. This naturally resulted in greater knowledge about the plateau and a renewal of international trade with Tibet. During the reign of Khubilai Khân (1260–1294), Tibet and (Mongol) China were linked by official post routes, while paper money printed by the Mongols reached Tibet, indicative of the two countries' commercial ties. In 1281, an expedition was sent from China to locate the source of the Yellow River (Hwanghe), thus adding to Chinese geographical knowledge about the Tibetan plateau.

During the period of the Mongol Empire, Europeans also acquired new information about Tibet. Although none of the Europeans who traveled to the Mongol court seems actually to have visited Tibet, many of them encountered Tibetans elsewhere within Mongol territory. The records of voyagers such as William of Rubruck (1253–1255), Marco Polo (c. 1298), and others contain accounts relating to Tibetan customs and religion. William of Rubruck, for example, notes the natural wealth of the territory: people who need gold dig in the ground until they have found what they need; they do not hoard it. Though often inaccurate, such reports did provide the impetus for European interest in and exploration of Tibet in later centuries. Interestingly, William's report of a religious debate—with Christians, Muslims, and Buddhists—before Möngke Khân (1251–1259) are paralleled by an extant Tibetan account produced by a prominent Tibetan monk at the same emperor's court, describing his own triumph over Christian debaters.

In China, the overthrow of Mongol power and its replacement by the xenophobic Ming dynasty (1368–1644) did not mark an end to Chinese interest in Tibet. The first Ming emperor sent several Chinese monks to Tibet, at least one of whom was specifically ordered to make maps of the country. Commercial relations with Tibet likewise continued. With lessened interaction between Tibet and its southern and western neighbors (due to the degeneration of Buddhism in India), by the beginning of the fifteenth century Tibet's major international commercial ties were with Ming China, which traded silks, silver, and especially tea for horses, wool, precious stones, and other items from Tibet. Trade was carried on under the guise of "tribute," as well as through the border trade markets set up by the Ming for the exchange of two of the major items in this commerce: Chinese tea for horses supplied from Tibet. Both the "tribute" arrangements and the border trade markets were intended to allow the Ming to control the trade, but China's need for horses and the prospect of great profits in the Tibetan trade produced a large amount of illicit private commerce along the Sino-Tibetan frontier into and after the fifteenth century.

**BIBLIOGRAPHY**

Beckwith, Christopher I. "Tibet and the Early Medieval *Florissance* in Eurasia: A Preliminary Note on the Economic History of the Tibetan Empire." *Central Asiatic Journal* 21 (1977): 89–104.

# T

Franke, Herbert. "The Exploration of the Yellow River Sources under Emperor Qubilai in 1281." In *Orientalia Iosephi Tucci Memoriae Dicata*. Ed. G. Gnoli and L. Lanciotti. Rome: Istituto Italiano per il Medio ed Estremo Oriente, 1985, pp. 401–416.

Satō Hisashi. "The Route from Kokonor to Lhasa during the T'ang Period." *Acta Asiatica* 24 (1975): 1–19.

*Elliot Sperling*

**SEE ALSO**

Buddhism; China; Khubilai Khân; Marco Polo; Mongols; Silk Roads; William of Rubruck; Yuan Dynasty

## Tides

Medieval understanding of the tides was based primarily on the *Introductorium in astronomiam* of Albumasar, a ninth-century Arabic text translated into Latin in the twelfth century. Albumasar supplied the medieval student with the theory that the moon caused ebb and flood tides; he discussed the tidal effects of the moon's phases and its relation to the sun; and he commented on the effects of wind and topographical features on tides. Other theories, such as Al-Bitruji's notion that the tides were caused by the general circulation of the heavens, also came to the Middle Ages through Latin translations of Muslim writers. When Chaucer says that his Shipman could "rekene wel his tydes," however, we should not imagine a mariner calculating the ebb and flow of the tides from a shipboard copy of a theoretical treatise in Latin. Rather, the Shipman would have used a simple booklet, written in English and known as a "rutter."

Sailing during the Middle Ages was not undertaken for pleasure but for business. The captain of a seagoing vessel, carrying cargo and perhaps passengers for some considerable distance, needed a rutter that would supply him with information not only about tides but also harbors, hazards, landmarks, and coastal streams. The English word *rutter* comes directly from the French *routier*, or "route" book, which emphasizes the general purpose of such volumes—tidal knowledge being a means to an end and not an end in itself. Equivalent names in Portuguese (*roteiro*) and Spanish (*derrota*) reinforce this concept, while the Italian *portolano* or "port book," the Dutch *leeskaart* or "reading chart," and the German *Seebuch* or "sea book" also show these booklets circulated in a variety of forms and several vernaculars, meant to provide all the information needed to leave one port in England or Europe and arrive in another.

Few rutters survive from the Middle Ages, and, given the conditions under which they were used, this is scarcely surprising. The genre is best known from printed versions, the first of which appeared in 1490, and even printed versions are rare because of the hard use to which they were subjected. The information about tides in such volumes is meager. Some printed rutters recount a simple rule of thumb by which one could find the day of the new moon in any month, and, if the time of high tide for the port on that day was known, calculate the time of high tide for a specific day following the new moon by adding forty-eight minutes for each twenty-four hours that had passed. Such rough-and ready methods were no doubt widely used in commerce. While detailed and accurate information about high and low tides at different places had been compiled in the Middle Ages, for example, by Gerald of Wales in his thirteenth-century *Topographia Hiberniae*, such learned Latin treatises would not have been found on shipboard. Gerald knew that when the tide was ebbing in Dublin it was beginning to rise in Bristol, but the seafaring man needed only to know when the tide was sufficient where he planned to land or to set sail. The earliest known tidal table also dates from the thirteenth century, and was compiled for London Bridge. Regrettably, it is a table based on a single observation and then built up theoretically from the rule of thumb already noted. It is therefore not very accurate and would not have been particularly helpful to a navigator.

As well as knowing when high tide would occur, the medieval shipman had to know the flow of the tidal stream or current within a large harbor. Since such streams sometimes flow as fast as a ship can sail, the direction of their flow within the harbor was especially important. Thus, in the anonymous rutter published by Lester as "The Earliest English Sailing Directions," the sailor is cautioned that for one English harbor the tidal stream runs south-by-southwest on the north side of the harbor, but southwest-by-south on the southern side.

In the Middle Ages, clocks were uncommon and time was reckoned without a keen sense of accuracy. Thus, although some knowledge about high tides and tidal streams was important for sailors to possess, even with such knowledge sailing was not a precise science. The first English rutter cited earlier advises sailors to go south "a glass or two," meaning one or two emptyings of an hour glass, in order to avoid certain rocks; it also advises taking soundings along a certain coastal area at night, but then cautions that "the most wisdom is to abide till it be day." Many tidal "problems" were no doubt "solved" simply by waiting for the tide to change, and by acting on direct observation both of the flood tide and its direction. Neither the captain nor his crew was paid by the hour, but rather for bringing a boat safely to harbor.

The finest scholarly treatment of medieval tidal theories is in Pierre Duhem's *Le Système du monde*.

**BIBLIOGRAPHY**
Burwash, Dorothy. *English Merchant Shipping: 1460–1540.* Toronto: Toronto UP, 1947.
Duhem, Pierre. *Le Système du monde.* 10 vols. Paris: Hermann, 1913–1959.
Lester, Geoffrey A. "The Earliest English Sailing Directions." In *Popular and Practical Science of Medieval England.* Ed. Lister M. Matheson. East Lansing, MI: Colleagues Press, 1994, pp. 331–367.
Taylor, Eva G.R. *The Haven-Finding Art: A History of Navigation from Odysseus to Captain Cook.* London, Sydney, and Toronto: Hollis and Carter, 1956; new edition Cambridge: Cambridge UP, 1971.
Waters, D.W. *The Rutters of the Sea.* New Haven and London: Yale UP, 1967.
Wright, J.K. *Geographical Lore of the Time of the Crusades.* See Gen. Bib.

*Chauncey Wood*

**SEE ALSO**
Chaucer, Geoffrey; Gerald of Wales; Navigation; Navigation, Arab; Portolan Charts

## Tīmūr
*See* Tamerlane

## Tolui (*c.* 1193–1232/3)

Fourth son of Chinggis Khân by his chief wife, Bortei, and father of the Toluid line of Mongol khâns. Although not chosen to succeed Chinggis, Tolui surpassed his brothers in military prowess, and possibly generalship. Chinggis kept Tolui at his side in early campaigns against northern China and the Khwarazm-shah; nevertheless, he distinguished himself by capturing several fortified towns. Tolui assumed a larger role, beginning about 1220, during campaigns in Khwarazm (present-day western Uzbekistan) to stamp out resistance to Mongol rule. Forces led by Tolui devastated such important cities as Merv, Nishapur, and Herat, visiting slaughter and appalling destruction on Transoxiana and Khurasan

(eastern Persia). As Chinggis's chief assistant in military affairs, Tolui was hailed as "great *noyon*" (khân's companion). According to Rashid al-Din, "no prince conquered as many countries as he." Chroniclers characterized him as a fearless, brilliant general, but also as a hot-headed alcoholic.

When Chinggis endowed each son with an *ulus* (patrimony), Tolui, as youngest, in accordance with Mongol custom, was promised his father's original *ordu* (grazing lands and people dwelling thereon—the "hearth"), where the bulk of Mongol forces were still quartered. After his father's death (1227) Tolui was virtual regent for two years before summoning the *quriltai* (princely assembly) that implemented Chinggis's will by electing Tolui's elder brother Ögödei, as great khân. In the subsequent final campaign against northern China, Tolui led the Mongol host until his death in 1232–1233 (at about the age of 40). He left his chief wife, Sorqoqtani Begi (Seracian or Sorocan), with four young sons and an uncertain political future. Nevertheless, his reputation as warrior and hero, coupled with her remarkable political acumen, allowed two of Tolui's children later to assume the office of great khân (Möngke [1251–1259] and Khubilai [1260–1294]), and another to found the ilkhânate in Persia (Hülegü [1258–1265]).

**BIBLIOGRAPHY**
Barthol'd, Vasili V. *Turkestan Down to the Mongol Invasion.* Trans. H.A.R. Gibb. London: Gibb Memorial Series, n.s. 5, 1928. 4th edition. Philadelphia: Porcupine, 1977.
Jackson, Peter. "The Dissolution of the Mongol Empire." *Central Asiatic Journal* 22 (1978): 186–243.
Morgan, David. *The Mongols.* Oxford: Blackwell, 1986.
Rashid al-Din. *The Successors of Genghis Khan.* Trans. J.A. Boyle. New York: Columbia UP, 1971.

*James D. Ryan*

**SEE ALSO**
Hülegü; Mongol Army; Mongol Khatuns; Mongols

## Torsello, Marino Sanudo
*See* Sanudo, Marino

## Toscanelli, Paolo dal Pozzo

Noted Florentine physician, mathematician, astronomer, and leading cosmographer of his day (1397–May 1482).

# T

Born into a family of rich Florentine merchants and bankers, Toscanelli studied medicine (he is sometimes referred to as Paul the Physician) at the University of Padua, the principal seat of scientific learning in Italy. Here he acquired a sound theoretical education, which he combined with a Florentine appreciation of pragmatism and practical experience. He was a scientist with a businessman's eye for calculations. Toscanelli numbered among his close friends and acquaintances important humanists like Nicholas of Cusa, Filippo Brunelleschi, Angelo Poliziano, Cristoforo Landino, and Leon Battista Alberti; he also knew Marsilio Ficino and Giovanni Pico, although he disagreed with them on the subject of astrology.

If little has survived of Toscanelli's own writings, we know from the tributes of his contemporaries that he was held in great regard. Toscanelli was interested in a wide variety of subjects, including optics and agriculture. One surviving manuscript shows that his observations on comets were remarkably accurate for his day. Highly empirical, he founded his geographical theories more on contemporary travel accounts and his own research than on classical sources such as Ptolemy. He is reported to have interviewed travelers and visitors recently returned from Asia and Africa: he knew Marco Polo's *Divisament du monde* (*c.* 1298) and Niccolò dei Conti's account of Asia based on his travels (1435–1439), written by his contemporary, Poggio Bracciolini.

Early biographers of Toscanelli credit him with having theorized about the possibility of reaching the Indies via the Atlantic, and of making his idea known to King Alfonso V of Portugal (r. 1438–1481) and Christopher Columbus (1451–1506). In 1474, Toscanelli is said to have written a letter defending the notion that one could sail west from Europe and reach the spice regions of "Cathay" to Portuguese canon Fernão Martins de Reriz, a familiar at court and later cardinal. The information was meant for the king. Toscanelli and Martins had been friends of Nicholas of Cusa for many years; both had been present at his death in 1464. A world map supposed to have accompanied the letter and now also lost, greatly underestimated the true expanse of the Atlantic, showing "Cipangu" (Japan) lying 3,000 nautical miles (some 3,450 miles or 5,555 kilometers) west of the Canaries and at about the same latitude. Having learned of this letter and map, Columbus wrote to Toscanelli from Lisbon some years later (*c.* 1480) requesting a copy of the map. A transcription of Toscanelli's response survives in a book (*Historia Rerum Ubique Gestarum* by Aeneas Silvius [Pope Pius II]) that Columbus once owned. The veracity of this correspondence has been disputed, and even if authentic, Toscanelli's miscalculation of the earth's circumference probably only confirmed Columbus's own ideas rather than implanted them as has been claimed.

The text of the letter encourages Columbus to undertake such a westward voyage for several reasons: commercial (the East was rich in precious commodities); practical (a voyage across the Atlantic, as Toscanelli misconstrued it, would be quicker than the route around Africa); and pious (Christian Europe would be able to resurrect its mission to Asia, which had been abandoned in the fourteenth century, and mount a crusade to reconquer the Holy Land).

Years after his death, Toscanelli's fame as a scientist had not waned; in 1493, Ercole d'Este, duke of Ferrara, sent to Toscanelli's heir in Florence seeking to obtain his manuscripts and maps.

## BIBLIOGRAPHY

*La Carta perduta: Paolo dal P.T. e la cartografia delle grandi scoperte.* Florence: Alinari, 1992.

Flint, Valerie I.J. *The Imaginative Landscape of Christopher Columbus.* Princeton, NJ: Princeton UP, 1992.

Garin, Eugenio. "Ritratto di Paolo dal Pozzo Toscanelli." *Belfagor* 3 [anno 12] (1957): 241–257; rpt. in *Ritratti di umanisti.* Florence, 1967, pp. 41–66.

Morison, Samuel Eliot. *Journals and Other Documents on the Life and Voyages of Christopher Columbus.* New York: Columbia UP, 1963.

Phillips, J.R.S. *The Medieval Expansion of Europe.* Oxford and New York: Oxford UP, 1988.

Revelli, Paolo. *Cristoforo Colombo e la scuola cartografica genovese.* Genoa: Consiglio Nazionale delle Ricerche, 1937.

*Gloria Allaire*

## SEE ALSO

Columbus, Christopher; Geography in Medieval Europe; Marco Polo; Missionaries to China; Nicholas of Cusa; Pius II

## Trade

*See* Economics and Trade

## Trade, African

*See* African Trade

## Trade, Inner Asian
*See* Inner Asian Trade


## Trade, Ivory
*See* Ivory Trade


## Trade, Muslim Travelers and
*See* Muslim Travelers and Trade


## Trade, Portuguese
*See* Portuguese Trade


## Trade, Scandinavian, in Stones and Timber
*See* Stones and Timber, Scandinavian Trade in


## Trade, Slave
*See* Slave Trade, African


## Trade, Spice, Indian Ocean
*See* Spice Trade, Indian Ocean


## Transportation, Inland (European)

Travel and transportation were central features of life in Europe throughout the Middle Ages, and the modern perception that medieval people seldom ventured very far from home is uninformed. Although the speed and extent of movement were certainly less than they are today, the motives for travel and transport were no more limited then than now, whether it was for trade, employment, war, family matters, politics, communications, or curiosity. Indeed, medieval Christianity's emphasis on pilgrimage as a valid—even necessary—religious practice, added a dimension to travel largely missing today.

As medieval people were drawn into an increasingly vigorous market economy, especially from the so-called commercial revolution that began in the thirteenth century, travel to and from neighboring towns—and even places further afield—became common. As trade grew more energetic in most European regions, where clusters of towns often set up circuits of markets held on different days of the week, people were able to

widen their geographical horizons routinely. Thus, ample evidence shows that far from being constricted by a narrowly parochial worldview, medieval people frequently wandered far from home.

Much of this travel and transport went by necessity over inland routes. Although sea travel was certainly cost effective for moving bulk goods—and an absolute necessity for trade with Europe's various islands—it was an option of rather limited applicability for most of the people of Europe, either because they lacked access to the sea, or because shipping was inappropriate to their needs and inclinations. People tended to prefer inland transport in part because of the delays, dangers, and fears connected with sea travel, but also because shipping at the time was heavily oriented toward merchants, which made it inimical to small-scale carrying. Moreover, it reflects a growing confidence in an inland transportation system that was gradually expanding

Barge, crane, and canal transshipment of wine. Kraneplatz, Bruges, Hours by Simon Bening. Munich, Bayerische Staatsbibliothek Clm. 23638, fol. 1-1v, 1530.

T

Carter, from Eike von Repgow's legal collection *Sachsenspiegel*, Heidelberg, Universitätsbibliothek, MS Cod. Pal. Germ. 164, fol. 20r, 1375. Courtesy Heidelberg, Universitätsbibliothek.

over the medieval period, particularly as the various European states improved the security of land travel. Thus, as one example, although sea or coastal travel was a natural solution for transportation needs along the southern Italian peninsula in the Middle Ages, it was supplemented by a well-used road along the coast from Rome to Naples.

Inland transport was of two types: (1) overland transport (usually but not necessarily via roads) and (2) travel along waterways, both natural (rivers) and artificial (canals). To a large extent the relationship between the two modes of travel was geographically determined. Road travel was obviously difficult in wet and low-lying land (marshes), in heavily forested land, or in areas with large lakes or estuaries. River travel was hampered where

rainfall was minimal or land sloped so quickly as to create natural barriers such as rapids or waterfalls. Social and economic concerns could also determine the predominant mode of travel. The needs of long-distance trade could conflict with a local economy. In the later Middle Ages, for example, this was clearly expressed in quarrels that frequently erupted between boat owners wishing to use waterways and mill- and fishing-weir owners who wanted to control water flow for their own purposes. Sometimes, of course, the aims of the two groups were complementary: it has been suggested that fishing and mill weirs made navigation along the upper Thames during the Middle Ages possible by regulating water levels (acting in a sense as locks). Generally, though, weirs and water transport were incompatible. As a result, over time, some river routes were kept open for water transport, while others were given over totally to mills and fishing weirs.

Which option was chosen depended in part on the character of the regional economies. Thus, the inhabitants of an area such as eastern England, where the economy was stimulated by the larger cities (London, for example) and by proximity to the Continent, were concerned to keep a large number of river routes open to ports. Where economic networks were weaker—in western England, for instance—river systems could be rendered unnavigable by mills and weirs. Similarly, the maintenance of viable waterways could be reinforced by the establishment of important international routes, where river systems flowing to different seas were connected by portages, such as the Dnieper-Western Dvina (linking the Black and Baltic seas) or the Rhône-Saône-Meuse (linking the Mediterranean and North seas). The building of canals (or, later in the Middle Ages, locks) could also extend and supplement river systems, but by and large, canals were of minor importance and figured substantially only in a few areas, such as the Low Countries, the Lagoon of Venice, and the fen district of England.

Despite the maintenance of many important inland waterway systems, land transport became increasingly popular during the Middle Ages. One reason was the technical improvement in horse harness, in particular the development of a padded horse collar that revolutionized vehicle hauling over most of Europe. Scholarly research has considerably qualified the magnitude of this so-called revolution by pointing to signs of efficient horse-hauled transport during the late Roman period, especially in Gaul, but nonetheless, road transport at the end of the Middle Ages looked very different than it had a thousand years earlier. The practice of using oxen for farm or road vehicle hauling, which had been preeminent in most of Europe in the early Middle Ages, was found at the end of the period almost exclusively in difficult terrain; elsewhere it was replaced by hauling by horses (or, in drier climates like Spain, mules). Many historians have noted that this shift coincided with the so-called commercial revolution of the twelfth and thirteenth centuries. Horse-hauling suited vibrant, commercially oriented economies, like that in Flanders, by providing a faster and more flexible method of transport to suit the quickening commercial pace. Indeed, in these areas, sizable amounts of land began to be set aside for the cultivation of oats and other horse "fuels," a change from the previous, more ox-oriented era, where pasture had played a stronger role in providing fodder for transport animals.

The advances in vehicle hauling by no means excluded other modes of transport. Packhorses provided a significant supplement to vehicle transport, as indeed, they had during the days of ox-hauling, particularly for perishables such as fish, or for valuable commodities such as cloth. Pack-animal trains—such as those recorded crossing the Alps from Genoa to Champagne in the thirteenth century or those entering Southampton in the fifteenth century with cloth from Yorkshire and Lancashire—were a common sight in many parts of Europe, particularly in hilly terrain. Often the pack loads for the horses (or, in some places like Spain, donkeys and mules) were simply tied onto the animal's back, although gradually more sophisticated crooks and panniers for positioning and securing the loads began to appear. Porterage—the carriage of goods by humans—should not be underestimated as a mode of transport either. Large numbers of porters were routinely hired for loading and unloading ships and boats; in rural areas, poorer peasants, as part of their services for lords, sometimes had to carry fragile items like eggs on foot.

The increase in vehicle hauling was accompanied, unsurprisingly, by developments in the construction of vehicles. Relatively light but durable carts, with spoked wheels and extendable sides to accommodate bigger loads, became more and more common from the late Roman period. Made of ash or other woods of high tensile strength, they were capable of carrying relatively light loads efficiently, a principal requirement for horse-powered hauling. Ox-hauled, two-wheeled vehicles (English "wains") tended to be heavier and were often made of oak. Four-wheeled vehicles were slower to develop, primarily because it was difficult to design a moveable forecarriage that would give wagons a reasonable turning radius. This problem was not effectively solved until the postmedieval period, with the development of dished or outward-splayed wheels or small front wheels that could turn under the bodies of the vehicles. As a result, wagons played a limited role in goods haulage and were mostly used as gaudy coaches for the aristocracy; they were, in effect, the limousines of the Middle Ages.

Vehicles were obviously only as effective as the traveling surface allowed them to be. Roman roads were justly famous for providing good travel surfaces, and the fact that many of them continued to form parts of the medieval road network testifies to their durability and continuing popularity. But as time passed, this old network fell into disrepair; moreover, the routes taken by Roman roads, many established for military purposes, often did not suit newer patterns of trade and settlement. Medieval roads were less well maintained; most were little more than dirt tracks. Contemporary records attest to much worse conditions in winter, when wet weather could turn the roads into mud. The remains of medieval roads today, in the form of "hollow-ways" (that is, depressions in the landscape caused by the centuries-long passage of carts and other traffic) graphically demonstrate the rudimentary nature of the road surface. The spectacular cases of road mishaps—for example, drownings in potholes created by people digging up the road illegally for materials like marl or fullers' earth—also hampered transportation.

It would be naive, however, to think that medieval people were oblivious to the need for an efficient road system. What they lacked was supervision of the road system as a whole, such as that provided by the Roman Empire. In medieval Europe, road upkeep was generally the responsibility of communities or individual landholders, and the degree of their vigilance varied. Yet some did try to improve, or at least to maintain, road conditions. Roadside ditches were cleared to allow proper runoff and prevent the washing out of roads. Causeways were built or sections of roadway were lined with logs, permitting routes to cross wetland areas. Some road surfaces were paved with stones, especially at the approaches to towns.

The most striking improvement in the medieval inland transport system, however, was in bridge construction. The importance of these structures was never

# T

forgotten in medieval Europe; they were key to the strategic movement of troops and the efficient transport of goods. In the military restructuring that took place in England during the reigns of the Anglo-Saxon kings (beginning with Alfred the Great [871–899]), bridge maintenance became one of "the three obligations" (*trinoda necessitas*) required of free landholders, along with participation in the militia (or *fyrd*) and contribution to borough fortification. Economic expansion or restructuring also encouraged bridge making. In building their water mills, many owners appear simultaneously to have constructed bridges over the adjacent stream or river; they did so not only out of self-interest, providing access to customers, but also out of community need, even legal obligation. Construction of mill weirs often flooded river fords and other traditional crossing points; some court cases imply that community pressure was brought to bear on mill owners to erect bridges to replace these lost crossing points. Thus, in western Europe in particular, bridge construction increased in frequency; in many countries (such as England), there were as many bridges in the mid-1300s as there would be in the 1700s. The quality of these bridges varied considerably, ranging from impressive stone structures that are still standing to simple, narrow wooden bridges of a few feet wide. As in the Roman period, fords and ferries often supplemented bridges in providing crossing points. Fords were more common in eastern Europe, where forests and bogs dominated the landscape.

Thus, a road network—however rudimentary in places and lacking overarching supervision—was established. In getting from place to place by land, it is clear that people had a range of options. The itineraries of medieval kings—some of them clearly detailed in surviving records—show the road network's intricacy. No community on the mainland was unreachable by road, though many roads were in poor condition. Certain routes had priority status, such as the "king's road" (*via regis*) in England and the "public road" (*strata publica*) in France or Italy, which took precedence as major thoroughfares. Routes were classified, in various sources, as cartways, packhorse trails, or foot paths (the last term also applied to most bridges). Droving roads for animals also existed; they were fairly wide and offered access to grazing land along the way. Rates of travel along these routes could be impressive: horse-hauled vehicles might travel some thirty miles a day, and packhorses were even quicker. Driving animals (to

slaughterhouses, for example) was a slower business; herds generally covered around ten miles a day.

For all its inferiority to modern road networks, the medieval system of transport routes was sufficient to serve the needs of the time. Although sources routinely record complaints about the roads, conditions were not so poor that governments were inclined—or spurred—to undertake substantial reforms. Monitoring of the road system thus occurred only to a limited and inconsistent degree. Community pressure could be effective in maintaining roads, however. Besides reporting and prosecuting cases of outright vandalism (such as the illegal digging up of roads), communities provided the upkeep of bridges and roads. This was sometimes supplemented by government inquiry (the English crown, for example, investigated the bridges across the river Lea, north of London, in 1278–1279).

Inland water routes, where they were not hindered by mills and other obstructions, also flourished. English agricultural records from around 1300 demonstrate how farm production could be mobilized by access to cheaper inland water transport, which made rural regions part of lucrative metropolitan or international markets. Goods that entered these markets not only brought producers increased profits, but this profitability was reflected in the higher value of lands in these areas. Boats of many types serviced these inland waterways, ranging from simple log rafts to more sophisticated clinker-built vessels, with sails and (sometimes) oars. Most tended to be flat-bottomed keelboats, which could navigate in shallow rivers and might haul some ten tons of goods, making them more efficient than road transport, which in terms of ton-per-mile cost was generally between two and five times more expensive.

Maintaining the larger inland waterways was not generally a problem. Many river systems (including the Volga, Dnieper, Danube, Elbe, Oder, Rhine, Rhône, Seine, and Thames rivers) were powerful enough to require little upkeep. The banks of smaller rivers and streams needed attention to prevent flooding in the surrounding countryside. Although mills and fishing weirs caused some problems for river flow (and, obviously, navigation), a balance was usually struck between the needs of the larger trading community and those of a local economy. Some towns, specifically established as heads of navigations or important inland ports (Henley-upon-Thames, Rouen, Avignon, Cologne), defined the inland water transport system for many countries; they also marked the boundary between areas concerned with local economic matters and places more involved with the wider economy. Investment in harbors, quays, cranes, and so forth, could be considerable at these inland water entrepôts and at seaports that were the intersections of inland and international routes. Timber or stone waterfronts characterized these towns, replacing the previously existing beaches.

Routes—by land or water—once established, required an infrastructure that would enable them to function effectively. Among other things, travelers and traders needed information, security, accommodation, and storage. The importance of information cannot be underestimated. Medieval people were far more dependent on local populations in conducting their journeys than are modern travelers: asking for directions would have been much more common and a sense of the spatial relationship of places was probably not well developed. At the same time, local maps of roads and river systems existed during the Middle Ages—a good example is the Gough map of England, dating from around 1360 (Oxford, Bodleian Library, MS Gough Gen. Top. 16); but they were not common. Although medieval documents generally give accurate measurements of distances between places, particularly local ones, whatever sense medieval people had of space and local geography was based far more on experience or report than on formal education. Thus, traveling into unknown regions posed obvious problems. Guideposts or milestones were infrequently set up and would have been of little use in largely illiterate societies. The sociability that we associate with medieval travel (whether from works of fiction such as *The Canterbury Tales* or historical records like *The Book of Margery Kempe*) no doubt resulted from the need for both road directions and personal security.

Travel—whether overland or by water—was hazardous. Highway robbery was all too common throughout Europe, varying obviously according to geography and prevailing sociopolitical conditions. Mounted soldiers and archers accompanied shipments of money or valuables, at times resembling small armies; in England in 1319, for example, it took eight mounted soldiers, twelve archers, and 180 footmen to conduct a large sum of money from Stamford to Boston, through an area notorious for its robbers. Even when law and order prevailed, travel had its dangers. English coroners' rolls during the late thirteenth and early fourteenth centuries record substantial numbers of "traffic accidents," involving carts overturning, crushing their occupants, flinging them into nearby ditches or rivers where they drowned, or crashing, in one case killing a man whose stallion was galloping after a mare in heat. River traffic was also dangerous; in 1343, forty passengers drowned when an overloaded boat capsized on the Yare in England. On longer trade routes, merchants succumbed to disease, attack, foul weather, and accidents; merchant burial grounds—for example, along the Volga and Dnieper—were common, and many pilgrims to the Holy Land mention the Field of Blood (Akeldama) near Jerusalem, a cemetery for the faithful who died abroad.

Of course, not all travel was unpleasant. Historical records indicate that great sociability could be found along inland transportation routes. Inns and taverns obviously brought together travelers, often from many different places. Accommodations were available in private houses and commercial hostelries, the latter (called *hospitii* or *fondaci*) springing up particularly along well-traveled routes or in principal trading towns, often sponsored by religious institutions or political entities (such as the city-states of Venice or Genoa). The need for social control—keeping an eye on strangers—no doubt encouraged the establishment of such foundations, but more practical issues came into play as well: travelers could exchange useful information about routes, road conditions, the current political climate, and worthwhile scenic attractions. Rowdiness and drunkenness might bring roadside inns into disrepute, but such inns were critical to the maintenance of long-distance trade.

Just as important as inns to house travelers were facilities to store goods, which were needed all along a route but especially at a seaport terminus of an inland transportation route, where goods might be stockpiled for some time until favorable winds or sea conditions prevailed. Vaulted stone cellars built during the Middle Ages are mentioned in historical records, particularly with reference to the logistics of military campaigns; they were important for storing provisions, especially perishables. Most storage facilities were relatively small-scale, however, serving domestic rather than commercial needs. Except in the commercially developed north of Italy, goods distribution by means of a postal or parcel system was largely unknown: medieval entrepreneurs relied on personal connections to transport facilities, arranging contracts with individual transporters by sea or land.

This decentralized state of affairs was reflected in the personnel required for the transportation system, which was comprised of a mixture of professional and part-time workers. Professional carters were employed on the large farms of lords (especially in England where direct demesne farming was common until the late fourteenth century) and among the professional companies that routinely carried goods across the Alps from Italy to Germany. In large cities, "brokers" found carting services for customers. The degree to which professional carting dominated the vehicle trade is uncertain, however, and it appears that part-time trade in carting flourished, run by farmers who offered their services during slack times in the farming year and who might also be commandeered by the state for such purposes as supplying armies. Manorial and other records indicate that peasants owned most existing vehicles, so it is likely that part-time transportation was a sizable and fairly profitable sideline industry. Packhorse travel was probably organized on more professional lines, especially for long-distance hauling of fairly expensive goods, such as cloth, transported from Genoa to Champagne in the thirteenth century or from Westmorland to Southampton in the fifteenth. Part-time peasant carriers also played a role here, as indicated by the customary packhorse services that peasants owed English lords. (Packhorse carrying probably declined as vehicle hauling expanded: the latter became the more common service requirement during the twelfth and thirteenth centuries). Finally, porters were a common sight, either carrying goods on their back or using wheelbarrows, as depicted in medieval manuscript illustrations done by Simon Bening and his workshop, where gardeners are shown transporting pots of carnations grown indoors in winter and moved outside in the spring. It was hard work and poorly paid, but clearly employed large numbers of people.

On the water, carriage was likely to be more professional still. Boat owners were regularly hired by the English crown to carry goods along the Thames or across narrow bodies of water such as the Solent. The amount of capital invested in a boat, usually several times an average person's annual income, would have encouraged (or forced) its owner to use it full-time. On inland waterways, transportation was a physically demanding enterprise: rowing and hauling, particularly for upstream travel, made the job labor intensive. Large numbers of loaders and porters would have been needed, and so it is likely that many medieval people made their living from transport.

Inland transport was thus well developed throughout medieval Europe; historians agree that it formed a "mature network," that is, one that had generally reached a consistent level of performance. Even if investment in the transportation network appears to have been rather small—though some canals, causeways, and mountain roads received significant state and community investment—the medieval transportation system was sufficient to meet the time's economic and social needs. While medieval society was often slow to react to problems (the shift from ox- to horse-hauling took well over a century, for example, and problems in the inland water transport system lingered longer still), people recognized the importance of an efficient transport system at least enough to make frequent complaints about the deficiencies of the roads and waterways as they existed.

Developments in transport were connected with general economic trends. Thus, it is no accident that the great "commercial revolution" of the thirteenth century coincided with the changeover to horse-hauling. It is impossible to state which change began first, but the economic growth of the period does demonstrate that transport adjusted well to new circumstances. Governments also found that the existing transportation network was adequate to military and other needs: the Hundred Years' War, for example, does not appear to have been significantly impeded by problems in transporting men and supplies over large distances. Whether the transportation system was eventually stretched beyond its limits is uncertain; the economic downturn that began in the early 1300s does not seem to have resulted from transportation problems, but rather from money supply shortages, failures in crop production, and perhaps a faltering in investment.

The greatest problem of inland transport in medieval Europe may not have been its scale but its structure or quality. Of course, the relative lack of professional carriers and the low level of capital investment in transportation systems were bound to have implications. Canals, paved roads, and causeways were not built at a rate or on a scale that characterized Europe's attention to its infrastructure during the seventeenth century and later, or Rome's in the days of the empire. Nonetheless, the construction and protection of bridges, in particular, is evidence of considerable attention to local development. Transportation was a critical element in the medieval economy. It employed large numbers of people and was a vital component in societal change and development.

**BIBLIOGRAPHY**

Edwards, J.F., and B.P. Hindle. "The Transportation System of Medieval England and Wales." *Journal of Historical Geography* 17 (1991): 123–134.

Harrison, D.F. "Bridges and Economic Development, 1300–1800." *Economic History Review,* 2nd series, 45 (1992): 240–261.

Hindle, B.P. "The Road Network of Medieval England and Wales." *Journal of Historical Geography* 3 (1976): 207–221.

———. "Seasonal Variations in Travel in Medieval England." *Journal of Transport History,* n.s., 4 (1977–1978): 170–178.

Langdon, John. "Horse Hauling: A Revolution in Vehicle Transport in Twelfth- and Thirteenth-Century England?" *Past and Present* 103 (1984): 37–66.

———. *Horses, Oxen, and Technological Innovation.* Cambridge: Cambridge UP, 1986.

———. "Inland Water Transport in Medieval England." *Journal of Historical Geography* 19 (1993): 1–11.

———. "Modes of Transportation in Preindustrial Societies." *Proceedings of the 18th International Congress of Historical Sciences.* Montréal: Comité International des Sciences Historiques, 1995, pp. 397–409.

Lefebvre des Noettes, R. *L'Attelage et le cheval de selle à travers les âges.* Paris: A. and J. Picard, 1931.

Leighton, Albert C. *Transport and Communication in Early Medieval Europe: A.D. 500–1100.* Newton Abbot, England: David and Charles, 1972.

Lopez, Robert S. "The Evolution of Land Transport in the Middle Ages." *Past and Present* 9 (1956): 17–29.

Masschaele, James. "Transport Costs in Medieval England." *Economic History Review,* 2nd series, 46 (1993): 266–279.

McGrail, Sean. *Ancient Boats in N.W. Europe: The Archaeology of Water Transport to A.D. 1500.* London: Longman, 1987.

Postan, Michael. "Transport." In Vol. 2 of *Trade and Industry in the Middle Ages: The Cambridge Economic History of Europe.* Cambridge: Cambridge UP, 1952.

*John L. Langdon*

**SEE ALSO**

Chaucer, Geoffrey; Economics and Trade; Fairs; *Fondaco;* Genoa; Gough Map; Holy Land; Horses and Harnesses; Inns and Accommodations; John the Fearless, Funeral Cortege of; Kempe, Margery; Pilgrimage, Christian; Ships and Shipbuilding; Venice

## Travel, Astrological Influence on

*See* Astrological Influence on Travel

## Travel in German Literature

*See* German Literature, Travel in

## Travel, Inner Asian

*See* Inner Asian Travel

## Travel, Irish

*See* Irish Travel

## Travel, Library Collections on

*See* Library Collections on Travel

## Travel to Paradise

*See* Paradise, Travel to

## Travel for Penance

*See* Penance, Travel for

## Travel Scholarship, History of

*See* Scholarship on Medieval European Geography and Travel

## Travelers, Islamic Women

*See* Women Travelers, Islamic

## Travelers, Masons and Architects as

*See* Masons and Architects as Travelers

## Travelers, Muslim, and Trade

*See* Muslim Travelers and Trade

## Travel Writing in Europe and the Mediterranean Regions

Between the late fourth and the early fifteenth centuries, a surprisingly large number of people traveling long distances for a wide variety of reasons saw fit to record their journeys, or at least to leave written traces of them. Travel writing as we would recognize it in the modern era did not, however, exist in the West, since

**T** the idea of traveling for sheer pleasure or curiosity was alien to medieval experience: medieval travel writing in Europe could be said to have reached its close when Petrarch made his famously pointless ascent of Mount Ventoux, a gesture of pure sensibility. What did exist were several genres and miscellaneous texts that together give historians and literary scholars a chance to extrapolate answers to some of the questions modern travel writing answers more directly. These texts include pilgrimage accounts (Christian, Muslim, and Jewish), guide books (religious and commercial), chronicles (particularly of the Crusades), business and diplomatic letters, occasional book-length accounts of merchant and of missionary travel, passages in personal letters, "wonder books," and, late in the period, anomalously adventurous "récits" (as they would be more clearly identified in France) such as the *Rihla* of the Berber traveler Ibn Battūta (1304–1364) or the *Boke* of the imaginary English knight Sir John Mandeville (*c.* 1360).

Since the personal and business letters often examined by historians for information on lands in which the writers were traveling (and on the writers' attitudes toward them) are only inadvertently "travel writing," there is no reason to treat them at length; the same is true of crusade chronicles, whose chief purpose seems to have been to celebrate the acts of certain political or dynastic figures important to the writer or his community. Some eyewitness crusade chroniclers were inspired to represent their own experience as travelers within works otherwise more historical than geographical (or autobiographical) in aim: Fulcher of Chartres's chronicle (1101–1128) of the First Crusade is at the same time the chronicle of Fulcher's own adventure in expatriation, and Joinville's account of the Fourth Crusade (his *Vie de Saint Louis* [1309]) is also personal and experiential in nature. Both crusade narratives include material on the human and animal wonders traditionally located east and south of Europe. The Cilician Armenian Hetoum's *La Flor des Estoires de la tere d'Orient* (1307), detailing the rise of the Mongol Empire and its relations with Armenia, the crusader states of "Outremer," and the Latin West in the later thirteenth century, is also written by a traveler with much firsthand experience of the scene of action. As for letter writers directly focused on their own commercial or diplomatic business (or their domestic needs as in the case of the Pastons), their documents can be found in many archives and collections printed from such archives: especially interesting are the letters of Jewish traders stored in the Cairo Geniza and published (in English translation) in a number of works by S.D. Goitein.

The major and characteristic contribution of the Middle Ages to the history of travel writing was, of course, the eyewitness account of pilgrimage, written throughout the period and often at some length. Jewish and Muslim pilgrimages gave rise to written records, but the most plentiful and the most fundamentally dependent on the author's function as witness are the accounts of Christian pilgrimage. These begin in the fourth century, with letters written home to friends by Christians visiting the sites of biblical narrative in the Holy Land, and, indeed, they are still being written. The early letters are sometimes exhortations to absent friends to come closer to the places so often visited in pious imagination; these letters also serve as intermediaries between the biblical text, with its divinely authored narrative of long-dead, legendary persons, and the living present tense that grounds the reality of spiritual history for a religion whose central myth is the Incarnation. The fourth-century pilgrim Paula (a wealthy Roman matron who had left her wealth and position behind to join St. Jerome's community of the faithful in Palestine) stands on certain spots already inscribed in the Bible and "remembers" the biblical stories rather than describing the physical facts of the scene before her eyes: "Behold, in this little nook of the earth the Founder of the heavens was born; here he was wrapped in swaddling clothes, beheld by the shepherds, shown by the star, adored by the wise men" (LPPTS vol. 1). The words of the living witness are mnemonic devices, even as is her actual experience of travel. What is to be remembered is definitively located in the sacred past.

Descriptions of the visitors' immediate responses to holy places became increasingly important as the numbers of Holy Land pilgrimages and pilgrimage accounts increased. The seventh-century Merovingian bishop Arculf is recorded by Adamnan (author of the important work *De locis sanctis*) as having seen Christ's actual footprints in the church on Mount Olivet, where "crowds of the faithful daily plunder the earth trodden by the Lord, [and] still the spot suffers no perceptible damage." In the eighth century, Jacinthus provides startlingly precise detail about the layout of the holy places in what was by then a rather crowded theater of piety: "As we went down from the choir, on the left of the stairs by which we went down is one wall of a well (and the other is joined to the choir-screen): over this well the star stood which led the Magi from the east. From the well to the place where our Lord was born is one-and-a-half paces. . . ." (Wilkinson 123). One of the most famous and balanced of all the early accounts is the late-fourth-century *Peregrinatio* of the Gallician pilgrim Egeria (known also as Aetheria and St. Sylvia): it combines the mnemonic qualities of Paula's letter with scrupulous attention to architectural and ritual detail in the description of Jerusalem.

Masterpieces in this genre from the later Middle Ages include the peregrinations of Benjamin of Tudela (a Jew who in the late twelfth century journeyed beyond the Holy Land to India and China), Burchard of Mount Sion (fl. 1280–1285), William of Boldensele (1336), and Ludolph of Suchem (1350), and, in the fifteenth-century, Piero Tafur (an Andalusian) and the voluble Felix Fabri (1480 and 1483). The memoirs of the English mystic Margery Kempe (1373–1489) include a considerable narrative of her Holy Land pilgrimages, focused much more on interior experience than are the accounts of the male pilgrims.

Guidebooks to major pilgrimage sites in Jerusalem, Rome, and Santiago de Compostela, as well as Mecca and Medina, abound. They do not usually include an individualized narrator or reference to personal experience. (The late-twelfth-century *Narracio de mirabilibus* of Gregorius is a nice exception, but it concentrates on Rome's classical heritage and could be said to belong more to the "wonderbook" tradition than to the genre of guidebooks). Both Christian and Muslim guidebooks to the holy sites prescribe ritual behavior as well as offer descriptions of place: "Thence you come to the doors, and in the midst of the choir is a place called the Center of the World, where our Lord Jesus Christ laid his finger, saying, "This is the center of the world." And there is an indulgence for seven years and seven Lenten seasons" (*Guidebook to Palestine*, LPPTS vol. 6). "Then one should go to the Rocks which are to the rear of the mosque, adjacent to the Gate of the Tribes, and pray in the place which is called the Throne of Solomon" (*The Book of Arousing Souls to Visit Jerusalem's Holy Walls*). Travel as understood by the guidebooks is an experience infinitely repeatable and identical for all travelers, and its chief purpose is pious ritual.

Missionary accounts of travel abroad belong mostly to the period of Christian contact with the Mongol Empire and include several first-person narratives of an apparently modern kind: as the writer is traveling in regions that have no prescribed significance and require no ritual observances, he (these accounts are all by men) is forced to examine his experience in secular and even personal terms. The most sensitive and ethnographically detailed of these accounts is the *Itinerarium* of the Franciscan William of Rubruck (1255), written shortly after the Seventh Crusade (1248–1254) in the form of a long letter or report on the author's mission to the king of France, Louis IX (r. 1226–1270), in whose service his quasi-diplomatic journey to the court of Möngke Khân at Karakorum had been undertaken. Other important missionary reports about Asian territories, mostly Franciscan, include those of John of Plano Carpini (the first) and his traveling companion Benedict the Pole (both 1247), John of Monte Corvino (two letters from China, dated 1305–1306), Odoric of Pordenone ([1330] from whom the Mandeville-author borrowed much of his material on the farther East) and John of Marignolli (who related some personal experiences between 1339 and 1352 in a chronicle written *c.* 1355). We have what Christopher Dawson calls "a Mongol counterpart" to William's narrative in the Syriac *History of the Life and Travels of Rabban Sawma, Envoy of the Mongol Khans to the Kings of Europe,* which details the journey of a Nestorian monk, Rabban Sauma (a Mongolian Turk from Khanbaliq), who was sent to Rome by Argun Khân in 1286.

Merchants were perhaps the busiest and most numerous travelers of the later Middle Ages, although their records are rarely close to the narrative or representational kind we could loosely call travel writing. Some long-distance mercantile travel did result in important representational works, chief among them, of course, the *Divisament dou monde* of the Venetian Marco Polo (dictated to a writer of French romances during his three-year imprisonment in Genoa, after his capture in the city's naval battle with Venice in 1298). Polo's travels across the eastern lands of the Mongol Empire have rarely been equaled in extensiveness, though he was very much the merchant in his perceptions. The Florentine merchant Francesco Balducci Pegolotti's *Practica della mercatura* (*c.* 1340) was, as its title suggests, more a commercial guidebook than the account of a journey; it records the routes, currencies, exchange rates, duties, principal imports and exports, and business customs useful for trade with such distant parts as Khanbaliq, Tabriz, and Dunfermline. The journey to Central Asia, India, and Africa of Niccolò dei Conti, as preserved in Book 4 of the humanist Poggio Bracciolini's *Vicissitudes*

# T

of Fortune (later printed separately as *India Recognita*), was concluded in 1441; the account pays as much attention to fauna, flora, and human customs as to mercantile opportunities.

One last major medieval genre that overlaps with the somewhat anachronistic category of "travel writing" is the wonder book, which is perhaps more a mode than a genre: wonder books may take as their subject all kinds of places conventionally handled by other and separate genres. Friar Jordan of Sévérac's *Liber mirabilis* (1330) recounts his experience of missionary work in fourteenth-century India in the form of a list of wonders; Gregorius's *Narracio de mirabilibus* (mentioned earlier) does the same for his pilgrimage to Rome. It is within this context, no doubt, that such works of *curiositas* as *Mandeville's Travels*, the *Itinerarius* of Johannes Witte de Hese (c. 1390), or the great Ibn Battūta's *Rihla* were first read. Its origins are very ancient, going back at least to the *Indika* of Ctésias (fourth century B.C.E.) and continuing with the paradoxographies of late antiquity and the many branches of the Alexander romance, especially that concerned with Alexander's fictional "Letter to Aristotle." Its most consequential instance may be the twelfth-century "Letter of Prester John," which established the (imaginary) existence of a distant and wealthy empire of eastern Christians. As late as 1436, Niccolò dei Conti was claiming, according to Piero Tafur, who met him in the Sinai Peninsula, to have been married by Prester John to one of his subjects. Books of travel to distant places, whatever their genre or purpose, have always come under a certain amount of readerly suspicion, and writers have always found the theater of the distant culture a good place within which to set up the therapeutic mirror of satire: it is significant that the most frequently copied, longest-lived, and best-loved work of medieval travel writing, popularly known as *Mandeville's Travels,* is in many ways a fiction, and a fiction suffused with social commentary on the territories of home.

## BIBLIOGRAPHY

Adler, Elkan Nathan, ed. *Jewish Travellers in the Middle Ages: Nineteen Firsthand Accounts.* London: Routlege, 1930; rpt., New York: Dover, 1987.

Campbell, Mary B. *The Witness and the Other World: Exotic European Travel Writing, 400–1600.* Ithaca, NY, and London: Cornell UP, 1988.

Dawson, Christopher, ed. *The Mongol Mission.* See Gen. Bib.

Hennig, Richard, ed. *Terrae Incognitae: Eine Zusammenstellung und kritische Bewertung der wichtigsten Vorcolumbischen Entdeckungsreisen.* 4 vols. 2nd edition. Leiden: Brill, 1944–1956.

Howard, Donald. *Writers and Pilgrims: Medieval Pilgrimage Narratives and Their Posterity.* Berkeley: U of California P, 1980.

*Itineraria et alia geographica.* 2 vols. Corpus Christianorum: Series Latina, 175–176. Turnhout: Brepols, 1965.

Palestine Pilgrims' Text Society. *Library of the Palestine Pilgrims' Text Society* [LPPTS]. 12 vols. London, 1884–1897; rpt., New York: AMS Press, 1971.

Parks, George B. *The Middle Ages (to 1525).* Vol. 1 of *The English Traveler to Italy.* Stanford: Stanford UP, 1954.

Richard, Jean. *Les Récits de voyages et de pèlerinages.* Typologie des sources du moyen âge occidental 38. Turnhout: Brepols, 1981.

Wilkinson, John, ed. and trans. *Jerusalem Pilgrims before the Crusades.* Jerusalem: Ariel, and Warminster: Aris and Phillips, 1977.

*Mary B. Campbell*

## SEE ALSO

Adamnan; Arculf; Armenia; Benedict the Pole; Benjamin of Tudela; Burchard of Mount Sion; Crusades, First, Second, and Third; Crusade, Fourth; Egeria; Fabri, Felix; Hetoum; Holy Land; Ibn Battūta, Abu Abdallah; Itineraries and *Periploi*; John of Marignolli; John of Monte Corvino; John of Plano Carpini; Joinville, Jean de; Jordan of Sévérac; Karakorum; Kempe, Margery; Louis IX; Ludolf of Suchem; *Mandeville's Travels;* Marco Polo; *Marvels of Rome;* Mecca; Medina; Merchant Manuals; Merchants, Jewish; Odoric of Pordenone; Pegolotti, Francesco; Pilgrimage, Christian; Pilgrimage Sites, Spanish; Prester John; Rome; William of Boldensele; William of Rubruck

## Trebizond

Black Sea entrepôt (modern Trabzon) and medieval empire (1204–1461). Trebizond was founded around 756 B.C.E. and flourished as a trading center in Roman times. Blessed by a fertile hinterland, it was rich in minerals and well positioned to capitalize on East-West trade. In addition to exporting local products (silver, iron, alum, timber, wine, cloth, and hazelnuts), Trebizond became an important market for trade in silks and spices, a lucrative industry developed by Italians in the fourteenth century.

Effectively independent of Constantinople by 1073, Trebizond was known to Muslim writers as a source of cloth and as a place from which Muslim traders carried goods to Iconium, Mesopotamia, Persia, and Transoxiana. The city was isolated by the successes of the

Seljuks in Asia Minor, but revived as the capital of Alexius I (r. 1204–1222), member of the imperial family (Comnenus) of Byzantium who fled when Constantinople fell to the West in the Fourth Crusade (1204). Under Alexius's successors, trade expanded and, although it gradually passed out of local hands and into the control of Italians, the city profited from the heavy tariffs that it levied. Manuel I (r. 1238–1263) introduced a reliable silver coin, the asper, and saved the empire of Trebizond by submitting to the Mongols as a vassal. After Hülegü's destruction of Baghdad (1258), transit trade from central Asia increased.

The Genoese established a quarter by 1250, and gained a virtual monopoly by 1261. When the Byzantine Empire was restored, Trebizond maintained its independence but at times had to pay tribute money. Galfried de Langele, an envoy of Edward I of England (r. 1272–1307), stayed with the Genoese during his visit (1291–1293) at the time of Trebizond's greatest prosperity. The fourteenth century was marked by recurrent battles between Trebizond and the Genoese over tariff levels. In 1319, Venice secured trading rights. By the 1340s, the city was in decline: there was civil strife and, as Mongol hegemony waned, trade routes became increasingly insecure. In 1461, nine years after the conquest of Constantinople, the Ottoman sultan Mehmed II (r. 1451–1481) captured Trebizond. He killed the last Comnenus emperor and all other males in the family (sparing one); most of the population was deported and the city sank into decline.

## BIBLIOGRAPHY

Janssens, Emile. *Trébizonde: en Colchide.* Brussels: Presses Universitaires, 1969.

Miller, William. *Trebizond: The Last Greek Empire.* New York: Macmillan, 1926.

Vasiliev, A.A. "The Empire of Trebizond in History and Literature." *Byzantion* 15 (1940–1941): 316–377.

*Brian Catlos*

## SEE ALSO

Baghdad; Byzantine Empire; Genoa; Hülegü; Merchants, Italian; Mongols; Ottoman Empire; Seljuk Turks; Silk Roads; Textiles, Decorative; Venice

## Trevisa, John (c. 1342–1402)

Fourteenth-century translator of important encyclopedic and historical works; his translations made geographical information available to readers of Middle English.

The historical record is silent on Trevisa's early years, but he was probably born around 1342 in Cornwall on land belonging to the Berkeley family of Gloucestershire. Thomas III, Lord Berkeley, may have taken an interest in the young man and financed his education. It is certain that Trevisa began a long relationship with Oxford University in 1362 when he entered Exeter College, remaining to become a fellow at Queen's College in 1369. Though expelled around 1378 amid internal political squabbles, he maintained a connection and rented rooms off and on as late as 1396. Thomas IV appointed him vicar of Berkeley (c. 1374), and a record of his replacement indicates that he died before May 21, 1402.

Trevisa is best known for his translations of the encyclopedia *De proprietatibus rerum* by Bartholomaeus Anglicus (fl. 1250), the apocryphal *Gospel of Nicodemus,* a *Dialogus inter Militem et Clericum* on spiritual and temporal power sometimes ascribed to William Ockham, Richard FitzRalph's scathing sermon against the friars *Defensio curatorum* (preached to Pope Innocent VI in 1357), Aegidius Romanus's advice on governance *De regimine principum,* and Ranulf Higden's *Polychronicon,* a great history of the world completed around 1342.

In addition to being a translator, Trevisa was himself something of a traveler. In his translation of the *Polychronicon,* he makes occasional mention of his travels undertaken before April 18, 1387, when the book was completed. He mentions, for example, that he had seen the hot baths at Aachen and used those at Aix-les-Bains, that he changed money at Breisach on the Rhine, and that Higden is wrong about there being only one kind of French, for there are as many dialects of French in France as there are of English in England. Clearly, he must have crossed the Channel and passed through the Low Countries to Aachen and Cologne, where he traveled up the Rhine, stopping at Breisach (just west of Freiburg). From here his itinerary is uncertain; he may have gone directly to Aix-les-Bains or stopped there on his return.

Trevisa shows no personal knowledge of Tours when he mentions their coinage, and when he describes the Coliseum as the place of the images of provinces and lands, he simply repeats without correction what Higden had written much earlier in the *Polychronicon.* Finally, his comment that the Alps are high hills in

# T

Lombardy does not suggest personal experience at the time he was translating Higden's work, though there is evidence that Trevisa traveled abroad again in 1388 and 1390.

**BIBLIOGRAPHY**

Edwards, A.S.G. "John Trevisa." *Middle English Prose: A Critical Guide to Major Authors and Genres.* New Brunswick, NJ: Rutgers UP, 1984, pp. 133–146.

Fowler, David C. *John Trevisa.* Authors of the Middle Ages 2: English Writers of the Late Middle Ages. Aldershot: Variorum, 1993.

Hanna, Ralph, III. "Sir Thomas Berkeley and His Patronage." *Speculum* 64 (1989): 878–916.

Lawler, Traugott. "On the Properties of John Trevisa's Major Translations." *Viator* 14 (1983): 267–288.

Lidaka, Juris G. "John Trevisa and the English and Continental Traditions of Bartholomaeus Anglicus' *De proprietatibus rerum.*" *Essays in Medieval Studies* 5 (1988): 71–92.

Trevisa, John, trans. *Polychronicon Ranulphi Higden monachi Cestrensis: Together with the English Translations of John Trevisa and of an Unknown Writer of the Fifteenth Century.* Ed. Churchill Babington and Joseph Rawson Lumby. *Rerum britannicarum medii aevi scriptores* [Rolls Series] 41. 9 vols. London, 1865–1885; rpt. Nendeln, Liechtenstein: Kraus, 1964.

*Juris G. Lidaka*

**SEE ALSO**

Bartholomaeus Anglicus; Coinage and Money; Higden, Ranulf; Rome as a Pilgrimage Site

## Turks, Ottoman
*See* Ottoman Turks

## Turks, Seljuk
*See* Seljuk Turks

# U

*Ultima Thule*
*See* Thule

## Usury and the Church's View of Business

The Roman Church, whether through popes who issued binding laws or theologians whose teachings varied in logic and authority, took a spiritual and institutional interest in fostering justice and fighting sin. No pope or scholastic in the Middle Ages was in any meaningful sense an economic thinker or even especially knowledgeable about business. General and specific teachings about sin and justice sometimes impinged on the world of buying and selling, lending and borrowing, employing and working. Nowhere was Christian teaching more involved in the business of laypeople than in the knotty problem of usury.

Of all business practices, borrowing money was particularly problematic from the Church's perspective because it raised moral questions. Was any charge for a loan proper and moral under any circumstance? Ancient traditions provided some answers. Hebrew Scriptures prohibited taking any usury—anything exceeding the principal—from a "brother" (coreligionist), but permitted it from a stranger or "foreigner" (Leviticus 25:36–37; Deuteronomy 23:19–20). In the Beatitudes, Jesus stated that his followers should "lend, expecting nothing in return" (Luke 6:35), apparently a direct prohibition of making any profit on lending money. Even hoping for a gain was wrong: the intention of the lender must be charitable; taking advantage of the distress of one's brother or sister was a sin against justice.

Aristotle, in his *Politics,* held that money was sterile, that it was only a means of exchange and hence its increase through usurious practices was unnatural. Roman law used the word "usury" to describe the act of demanding anything more than the principal of a loan, and used the word "interest" to describe payments made for damages and exceptional circumstances that might arise in a loan. It is necessary to distinguish carefully between these words and their uses. For Christian theologians usury was a sin of avarice and always wrong, although in very unusual circumstances some payment beyond the principal was licit. Medieval canon law eventually incorporated all these traditions and taught that a usurer, by demanding more than he loaned, sins against God, the teachings of the Church, and even nature by selling time, which belonged to everyone (or at least to God). Hence the early medieval theological speculations about whether or not a merchant could be saved rested on real moral doubts about using money through loans to make more money.

By the thirteenth century authoritative voices strengthened and extended the teaching on usury. Popes and church councils condemned usury and considered its ill-gotten gains to be theft: such gains must be restored. A decretal letter of Pope Gregory IX (1227–1241) struck at the sea loan and seemed to remove risk as one of the conditions allowing for interest. St. Thomas Aquinas (*c.* 1225–1274) defended partnerships in which both parties risked capital in a joint venture, but he offered what became the most respected theoretical assault on usury. Thomas did not believe a market for money was possible because it did not change in value and could not be sold. He considered

# U

Banking and usury, "Treatise on the Vices." London, British Library MS Add. 27695, fol. 8r, late 14th century. Courtesy of the British Library.

charge and the interest was considered a gift. But usury, the loaning of money with the hope of profit, was a sin according to both canon law and the civil laws of medieval European cities and states.

These rules, along with less noticed guidelines on just prices, fair wages, the spiritual perils of foreign travel, and the legitimacy of guilds, affected commerce in ways difficult to measure. Despite the rules on usury, abundant business contracts from across Europe testify to numerous ways in which merchants advanced credit and loaned money for interest, sometimes concealing the real purposes in the written documents, other times not. Dante placed the usurers deep in his Hell (*Inferno* XVII), punished by flames and burning sands for their sins against nature. Some merchants, fearing such a judgment, drew up wills in which they tried to restore any ill-gotten gains by giving money to the Church, although many others failed to mention any usury. One effect of the Church's teaching was that the Jews, excluded from so many trades and professions, increasingly found themselves in the unpopular business of loaning money at interest. On the one hand, moneylending by Jews, the only people in Christendom who were, in theory, allowed to intend to take usury, undoubtedly served pragmatic needs of society (including the financing of many a military campaign). On the other hand, the Jewish "practice" of usury reinforced anti-Semitic prejudice. The realities of commercial life were such that while usury became a dirty word, an economy that required credit could not survive without it and businesses found ways to circumvent (if not to ignore) the prohibition.

The legacies of Church teaching on usury were that Christian society disapproved of people who made their living by extending credit, believed that at a certain point interest rates were outrageous and unjust, and favored economic enterprises based on shared investment rather than debt. A few theologians, most notably the spiritual Franciscan Peter John Olivi (c. 1248–1298) questioned the prevailing synthesis by proposing new ideas on utility, capital as not merely money, and interest as present "in potential" in all productive uses of capital. Some of these ideas found a qualified acceptance in Bernardino of Siena (1380–1444) and Antoninus of Florence (1389–1459), but the Thomistic ideas continued to prevail to the end of the Middle Ages. The prohibition on interest charges was first removed (in Europe) in 1545.

money to be a "consumptible or fungible," that is, it was consumed or extinguished in its use. Hence the value of using money could not be separated from the value of owning it. Thus a lender should not charge for the use of his money, because the inseparable ownership and use now belonged to the borrower. This reasoning, resting on canon law and Aristotelian thought, remained the dominant teaching on usury for the next two centuries. Another thirteenth-century canonist, Henry of Segusia (Hostiensis), believed that *lucrum cessans,* the loss of profit (what today would be called the "opportunity cost" to the lender), in some cases justified interest, but this remained a minority view for a long time. The Church did allow "partnerships," that could yield profit to one party, as, for example, the exchange of money from one currency to another for a fee, or even interest on loans where the loan was made free of

**BIBLIOGRAPHY**

Mueller, Reinhold C. *The Venetian Money Market: Banks, Panics, and the Public Debt 1200–1500.* Baltimore: Johns Hopkins UP, 1997.

Noonan, John T., Jr. *The Scholastic Analysis of Usury.* Cambridge, MA: Harvard UP, 1957.

de Roover, Raymond. *Money, Banking, and Credit in Mediaeval Bruges.* Cambridge, MA: Mediaeval Academy of America, 1948.

———. *The Rise and Decline of the Medici Bank, 1397–1494.* New York: Norton, 1966.

Shatzmiller, Joseph. *Shylock Reconsidered: Jews, Moneylending, and Medieval Society.* Berkeley: U of California P, 1990.

Spicciani, Amleto, Paolo Vian, and Giancarlo Andenna. *Pietro di Giovanni Olivi: Usure, compere e vendite: La scienza economica del XIII secolo.* Milan: Europìa, 1990.

*Steven A. Epstein*

**SEE ALSO**

Economics and Trade; Expulsion, Corporate; Merchants, Jewish; Shipping Contracts, Mediterranean

# V

## Vagrancy

Geographical mobility, coupled with social and economic dislocation. Vagrancy is an aimless wandering from one place to another without any predetermined destination. The vagrant is a person who does not regularly use social institutions; has neither residence, profession, nor master; and therefore poses a threat to the established order. The pilgrim, the traveling merchant, even the soldier, are not considered vagrants nor stigmatized as such.

Throughout the Middle Ages (and afterward), vagrancy was condemned in a variety of contexts. In fact, most of what we know about medieval vagrancy stems from censorious texts. The earliest condemnation, referring to wandering monks, is enunciated in the monastic Rules of the Master and of Saint Benedict (late fifth–early sixth centuries). The Rules of the Master describes what are termed *gyrovagi* (men who wander around) in great detail as gluttons, parasites, men of no faith or discipline, who make their way from one monastic cell to another, eating and drinking each one dry in turn. Benedict, the first authority specifically to insist on monastic stability, was more succinct: *gyrovagi* were the worst kind of monks, of whom the less said, the better. This attitude stood in contrast to a venerable monastic tradition, typical especially of early Eastern and later Irish monasticism, which encouraged monks to go on "perpetual pilgrimage," thus remaining detached from any specific "worldly" location.

When the Benedictine Rule became the required model and code for all monasteries in the Carolingian Empire in the early ninth century, the principle of stability triumphed over the ideal of pilgrimage. But Car-olingian rulers were not concerned only with the uncontrolled mobility of monks and nuns; both capitularies and conciliar legislation repeatedly condemned secular as well as ecclesiastical vagrancy. The *vagantes* were identified with crooks and swindlers, who practice their arts on the innocent; with false beggars, who pretend to be on a penitential journey; with "naked men in irons" (people who had been thus punished by the authorities); and with monks and priests who had committed a crime and embraced a life of vagabondage instead of accepting their punishment. The slur of vagrancy was also cast on those monks who attempted to renounce their vows and leave their monastery.

First appearing in fairly large numbers in the eleventh century, the *vagantes* were, 100 years later, more clearly classed with actors, jugglers, and dancers, who were thought to be morally pernicious—or at least suspect—people. They were usually clerics in minor orders, who eventually became identified with the growth of scholarly institutions throughout Europe. While most of the university student population was sedentary, some—especially the poorer among them—wandered from place to place. The drinking songs and literary parodies produced by those wandering scholars (such as the *Carmina Burana*) reflect a world of Latin learning combined with a deliberate inversion of conventional morals. These writings—often referred to as Goliardic songs (perhaps from "Bishop Golias" [Goliath], a legendary master of an "order" of vagrants)—praise drinking, dicing, and whoring, while presenting these activities in pseudo-pious forms. Most are anonymous, although "Primus" (Hugh d'Orléans [fl. early twelfth century]) and the

# V

"Archpoet" (fl. 1160–1165) are credited with having composed some particularly fine verses.

Wandering scholars of dubious reputation probably remained a constant reality in late medieval Europe, as the shady figure of François Villon (1431–?) indicates, but their presence was swallowed in the growing numbers of lower-class, illiterate, lay vagrants who became a common feature of the fourteenth and fifteenth centuries. Two factors caused an upsurge in vagrancy. First, problems in societal structure, such as the growing rigidity of professional guilds, forced many journeymen and unemployed people to go on the road. In England, landownership styles dispossessed peasants, forcing them off their land. Second, the catastrophes of the fourteenth century—wars, famines, the Black Death, economic depression—caused the dislocation of large populations. In the fifteenth century, a Parisian chronicler estimated that there were 80,000 vagrants in the city. Even if the figure is inflated, it is evidence of a considerable problem.

Throughout Europe, urban authorities viewed vagrants with suspicion. Any suspect of a crime who could not prove a fixed residence was adjudged to be infamous (that is, notoriously criminal, whose guilt needed no further proof), and hence liable to torture for the purpose of extracting a full confession. Given the scarcity of labor in the wake of the Black Death, vagrancy was also identified with idleness and voluntary unemployment. Legislation forcing all able-bodied men and women to accept work at preplague wages or to suffer a variety of penalties was promulgated in England (Statute of Labourers [1349]), in France (Ordinance of John the Good [1351]), and in Castile (Ordinance of Pedro I [1351]). The original penalty for idleness was expulsion in France, but by the 1360s and 1370s, vagrants were threatened also with prison and corporal punishment. These measures, which became increasingly stringent over time, were accompanied by a deliberate reduction of charitable activities directed at the migrant poor. By 1496, vagrants in France were automatically sent to the galleys. At the same time, English vagrants were punished with three days of bread and water, whipping, and forced return to their place of origin. In Germany and Switzerland, urban statutes repeatedly forbade the giving of charity to the foreign poor, who were to be expelled from the city unless they had found employment.

By the end of the fifteenth century, vagrancy was firmly associated with criminality, mendicancy, and idleness. The appearance, in 1500, of the earliest *Liber Vagatorum* in Strasbourg, heralded a new type of literature: that which classified the various types of "false beggars," all of them criminals and vagrants, characterizing them all as cheats hoping to gull innocent people into giving them charity. Many of them, like the earlier wandering scholars, were (or claimed to be) religious in various orders.

The social profile of late medieval Europe's vagrant population, as seen in court records, vagrancy literature, and city ordinances, seems to have been changing toward the end of the fifteenth century. While the earlier vagrant population was predominantly male, single, and young, by the end of the Middle Ages the proportion of women, children, and elderly among the vagrants increased, a clear sign of the growth and institutionalization of the phenomenon. By the early modern era the vagrant population of Europe consisted of a fully grown subculture with its own jargon, social structures, and cultural norms.

## BIBLIOGRAPHY

*Concilia Aevi Karolini.* Ed. Albert Werminghoff. Hanover: Monumenta Germaniae Historica, 1906–1908.

Geremek, Bronislaw. *Truands et misérables dans l'Europe moderne (1350–1600).* Paris: Gallimard, 1980.

———. "Le refus du travail dans la société urbaine du bas moyen âge." In *Le Travail au Moyen Age: Une approche interdisciplinaire.* Ed. Jacqueline Hamesse and Colette Muraille-Samaran. Louvain: Institut d'études médiévales de l'Université Catholique de Louvain, 1990, pp. 379–394.

Schnapper, Bernard. "La répression du vagabondage et sa signification historique du XIVe au XVIIIe siècle." *Revue historique de droit français et étranger* 63 (1985): 143–157.

Waddell, Helen. *The Wandering Scholars.* London, 1927; rpt. London: Constable, 1990.

*Esther Cohen*

SEE ALSO

Black Death; Galley; Minstrels and Other Itinerant Performers

## Vasco da Gama

*See* Da Gama, Vasco

## Venerable Bede

*See* Bede

## Venice

A city built on 118 small islands in a lagoon of the Gulf of Venice at the northwest extreme of the Adriatic Sea; its remarkable success in navigation and commerce made it one of the most influential political and trading powers of medieval Europe.

Venetians have always been seafarers. From their first settlements on islands in the shallow upper Adriatic in the late sixth century, they traveled to Constantinople and to Egypt, where they feuded with the Prasini family in the seventh century. In 828, according to legend, two Venetian merchants in Alexandria stole the body of St. Mark the Evangelist, concealing it from Muslim authorities in a barrel of pork. They brought their precious relic to Venice, where it was triumphantly placed in a new private chapel near the ducal residence. Later doges rebuilt the chapel as the Basilica of San Marco (1063–1071).

The Byzantines considered Venice to be a part of their empire. Magistrates and directives came into Venice by sea from Constantinople. Early doges received Greek brides and Byzantine titles. Venetians assisted Greek squadrons against hostile Saracen incursions in the Adriatic in 827, 829, 840, and 846. Tenth-century Byzantine emperors cautioned Venice not to trade in slaves nor sell to Muslims.

Eleventh-century Byzantines depended on Venetian naval strength in waters of the western Mediterranean. In 1081, Venetian ships opposed the Norman adventurer Robert Guiscard (1015–1085) as he besieged the Byzantine town of Durazzo (Durrës). A grateful Emperor Alexis I Comnenus (r. 1081–1118) rewarded Venice with trading privileges and exemption from tolls. Thereafter, documents reveal Venetians bringing slaves, lumber, and iron to markets in the East in exchange for silks, spices, and precious stones.

During the First Crusade (1095–1099), Genoese and Pisan ships ferried crusaders to Palestine, and after they captured Jerusalem, a Venetian fleet led by the doge (Vitale Michiel I) sailed to the Holy Land. Venetian expeditions in 1110 and 1122–1125 also assisted the crusaders, who granted them commercial privileges. In foreign seaports, Venetian merchants established colonial outposts, known as *fondaci;* the largest colony was in Constantinople, where some 10,000 Venetians lived in 1171.

In the twelfth century, Venice began to act independently from Byzantium. Venetian commerce grew as the city's vessels carried goods in the eastern Mediter-

Venice from Werner Rolewinck, *Fasciculus Temporum,* Venice: G. Walch. 1479, fol. 38v. Courtesy Annmary Brown Library, Brown University. Photo by Laviece Ward.

ranean, as well as crusaders and pilgrims to the Holy Land. In 1201–1202, responding to a request from French crusaders for transport to the Holy Land on the Fourth Crusade, Venice constructed a fleet of approximately 500 ships, equipped, provisioned, and manned for a large crusading host. When fewer crusaders than promised arrived in the city with insufficient funds in 1202, the soldiers paid their way by recapturing Zara (Zadar) for Venice, although for sacking the city the crusaders were excommunicated by Pope Innocent III. Shortly thereafter, the crusaders and Venetians accepted the invitation of a deposed Byzantine prince to help him and his deposed father regain the throne, for which he would guarantee money, supply Greek soldiers to fight on the crusade, and place the Greek church in obedience to Rome. When the Greeks did not accept the agreement and turmoil threatened Constantinople, the crusaders, led by doge Enrico Dandolo (r. 1192–1205), captured and sacked Constantinople in April 1204.

Venetian and French crusaders divided the spoils and their presumed authority over the former Byzantine Empire. They installed a Latin emperor in Constantinople; Venice dominated the sea-lanes and began to sail the Black Sea. Official Venetian expeditions took possession of Dalmatian and Ionian ports. Marco Sanudo conquered the Cyclades and established a dynasty on Naxos while the Ghisi family ruled the Sporades. After purchasing Crete from Boniface of Montferrat, Venice gradually conquered that island from its Greek inhabitants and Genoese pirates. Negroponte, on the island of Euboea, became a Venetian base. Thus was founded the Venetian commercial empire.

But the Greeks under Michael Palaeologus, with Genoese aid, recaptured Constantinople in 1261, and

# V

the Mamluks conquered Acre, the last stronghold of the Latin Kingdom of Jerusalem, in 1291. This resulted in a momentous change: new trading procedures and terms, as well as technological innovations in navigation and shipbuilding brought about a commercial revolution; Mediterranean merchants traveled to even more remote ports. Venetians sailed to Constantinople, then into the Black Sea, stopping at Kaffa (Feodosiya) or Soldaia in the Crimea, and then east to Tana on the Sea of Azov. Travel farther east was by land caravan. The Polos took this route in 1271. Another land route ran south of the Black Sea port of Trebizond to Tabriz and Ormuz [Hormuz], then across the Arabian Sea to India. A third avoided the Black Sea altogether, taking Venetians across the Mediterranean to Cyprus and Ayas (Lajazzo) in Cilician Armenia. From there, travelers could go overland to Tabriz, south to Ormuz, and by sea to India. Marco Polo returned to the Mediterranean by this route in 1235. Venetian merchants continued to frequent Egypt. Oriental goods were brought to Egypt from India, across the Arabian and the Red seas, to Egyptian ports. Whenever warfare interrupted their voyages to the Black Sea or Egypt, merchants sailed from Venice to the seaports of Syria and sometimes traveled overland to Damascus. Goods came to Damascus on caravans from Mecca, sometimes from its port of Jidda, after the voyage from India.

Venetian colonies could be found not only in Mediterranean seaports, but also inland at Kiev, Damascus, Tabriz, Trebizond, Tana, and even in Cathay in the late thirteenth and fourteenth centuries. Individual Venetians traveled far for business opportunities. Niccolò Guistinian headed a Venetian trading embassy to the Tartars in 1333 and established the Venetian colony at Tana. Giovanni Loredan and four other Venetian nobles traveled to Delhi in 1338. Alvise da Mosto sailed down the west African coast for Prince Henry the Navigator in 1455, trading horses for black slaves, and discovering the Cape Verde Islands when he was blown off course. Giacomo Garzoni and Paolo Trevison traveled to Ethiopia in 1482.

Venetians also traveled west. Tunis, whose commerce had been dominated by Pisa, became a center for the Venetian purchase of grain and gold in the late thirteenth century. After Genoese ships sailed through the Straits of Gibraltar north to the Low Countries in 1270, the Venetians followed. Early in the fourteenth century, Venetian great galleys sailed to Bruges and Antwerp, carrying Levantine spices and silks from the Mediterranean to exchange for Flemish textiles and English wool. These convoys, known as *muda*, were composed of state-owned merchant galleys auctioned off annually to the highest Venetian bidder, who then captained the ships and sailed as profitably as possible to and from the stated destination. Credit instruments in Venice were dated and made payable upon the safe return of the *muda*. Galley lines were also established for voyages to Constantinople and the Black Sea, to Beirut, to Alexandria, and to Barbary. In the fifteenth century, these fleets provided dependable transportation throughout the Mediterranean and into the Atlantic, as far as the Straits of Dover. During the fifteenth century, the ships carrying pilgrims from Europe to the Holy Land were overwhelmingly Venetian.

Genoa challenged Venice for control of the Mediterranean sea-lanes in four wars—in 1257–1270 (over Acre), in 1294–1299, and in 1359–1365 (to control Tenedos). The last of the four wars, the War of Chioggia (1378–1381), ended when the Genoese, besieging Venice from the neighboring village of Chioggia, were in turn blockaded by Venice from the Adriatic and the lagoons. After the starving Genoese sued for peace, both parties were exhausted; Venice recovered and even extended its control over the Aegean, but Genoa did not.

A limited patriciate of Venetian merchant oligarchs controlled the commerce as well as the government of their republic in the fourteenth and fifteenth centuries. With exclusive elective powers, they chose the magistrates and colonial governors, the routes and schedules of the merchant galleys, and the business policies of Venice. Their Council of Ten judged the performance of the city's civil servants. An elected doge presided in ceremonial splendor over this wealthy commercial empire, which continued to exist for 300 years after Columbus's voyages to America.

By the end of the fifteenth century, Venetian shipping was retreating before the formidable opposition of the Ottoman Turks. Constantinople fell to Sultan Mehmed the Conqueror in 1453. Venice lost its second war with the Turks (1463–1479) because the Turks could marshal greater forces than could Venice. The republic paid a huge indemnity and renounced Scutari, Negroponte, and several Aegean islands. Consequently, by 1500, the Ottomans replaced the Venetians as the strongest maritime power in the Mediterranean.

**BIBLIOGRAPHY**

Kretschmayr, Heinrich. *Geschichte von Venedig,* 3 vols. Gotha, 1905; rpt. Stuttgart: Aalen, 1964.

Lane, Frederic C. *Venice, a Maritime Republic.* Baltimore, MD: Johns Hopkins UP, 1974.

Luzzato, Gino. *Storia Economica di Venezia dall'XI al XVI Secolo.* Venice: Centro Internazionale delle Arti e del Costume, 1961.

Queller, Donald E., and Thomas F. Madden. *The Fourth Crusade.* 2nd edition. Philadelphia: U of Pennsylvania P, 1996.

Robbert, Louise Buenger. "Venice and the Crusades" In *The Impact of the Crusades on the Near East.* Ed. Norman P. Zacour and Harry W. Hazard. Vol. 5 of *A History of the Crusades,* pp. 379–451. Ed. Kenneth M. Setton. See Gen. Bib.

Thiriet, Freddy. *La Romanie vénitienne au moyen âge: Le Dévelopment et l'exploitation du domaine colonial vénitien (XIIe–XVe siècles).* Paris: Boccard, 1959.

*Louise Buenger Robbert*

**SEE ALSO**

Byzantine Empire; Crusades, First, Second, and Third; Crusade, Fourth; Crusade, Fifth; *Fondaco;* Lajazzo; Marco Polo; Mediterranean Sea; Merchants, Italian; Muslim Trade and Travel; Naval Warfare; Ottoman Empire; Pilgrimage, Christian; Trebizond

## Vesconte, Pietro/Perrino (fl. 1311–1330)

One of the first professional cartographers. It is not known if Pietro ("Petrus") is identical with a certain "Perrinus Vesconte," who produced maps dated 1321 and 1327. Perrino may be simply the diminutive form of his name, or it may designate a son or nephew. A native of Genoa, Vesconte lived in Venice by 1318 and produced some of his works there. Vesconte's art would have benefited from the extensive seafaring experiences of the Genoese and Venetians, whose coastal cities contributed much to the science of mapmaking in the thirteenth and fourteenth centuries. The last documented mention of Pietro shows him in Genoa in 1347.

Unlike most early maps, several works by Pietro/Perrino are identifiable by their signatures and dates. One sea chart and seven atlases have been attributed to Pietro; one chart and an atlas to Perrino. Of these surviving works, scattered among various European collections, eight are signed.

Pietro Vesconte was a cartographer of great skill and imagination who employed earlier techniques and introduced many innovations as well. Recognizable features of his maps have led some scholars to hypothesize a Genoese school of map production. Vesconte was the first to show precise outlines of the Mediterranean and Black seas: the former was drawn with an accuracy that was not exceeded until the eighteenth century. He achieved this with the aid of a compass and by relying on earlier portolan (sea) charts, but he did not devise a system of projection. Some Vesconte maps are covered with rhumb lines, a technique borrowed from portolans. Important Vescontian advances include many new features: an improved north-south alignment for the British Isles; the overall addition of 119 toponyms to the mapmakers' repertoire; and the use of stippling to indicate shoals. Some of his surviving exemplars were mounted on wooden boards, probably to protect them and facilitate their use.

Pietro's earliest work, also the earliest extant dated map, is a portolan chart from 1311. It depicts the eastern and central parts of the Mediterranean. Other works by Vesconte include an atlas composed of six maps, dated 1313, which shows the entire Mediterranean and the western coasts of Europe as far as the British Isles and Holland, and atlases that were assembled in Venice between 1313 and *c.* 1325. A small atlas from 1321 is signed by Perrino. At this period in cartographic history, individual maps in atlases were drawn to different scales, a practice that Vesconte followed.

Pietro's maps were appended to Marino Sanudo's *Liber secretorum fidelium Crucis* (*c.* 1307–1321), a sprawling work that argued (among other things) for another crusade to capture the Holy Land. One can only speculate about whether Pietro collaborated directly with Sanudo. The *Liber* survives in seven manuscript copies and was also printed. It includes a world map (*c.* 1320); maps of the Black Sea, the Mediterranean, the west coast of Europe, and Palestine; and city plans of Jerusalem, Acre, and Antioch, all by Vesconte. His world map maintains the old circular format with the east to the top, but he has eliminated fantastic elements that appear on some *mappaemundi* and has included Scandinavia. Vesconte's map of Jerusalem is more accurate in shape, although not in scale, than the other circular medieval plans of that city. Like other Italian maps of Pietro's day, these city maps feature two-dimensional drawings of landmarks rather than simple street grids. His map of Palestine, however, uses a grid to show distances between cities, a great

# V

conceptual advance. Sheets in the 1482 Berlinghieri and Ptolemy atlases derive from this map. An early seventeenth-century edition of the *Liber secretorum* featured engravings of Vesconte's maps. The latest known Vesconte work is a map of western Europe (*c.* 1330).

## BIBLIOGRAPHY

Campbell, Tony. "Portolan Charts from the Late Thirteenth Century to 1500." In Harley-Woodward. *The History of Cartography.* Vol. 1, pp. 371–463. See Gen. Bib.

Harvey, P.D.A. *Medieval Maps.* London: British Library, 1991.

Revelli, Paolo. *L'Italia nella Divina Commedia: Con la riproduzione diplomatica del planisfero vaticano—palatino di Pietro Vesconte . . . .* Milano: Treves, 1922.

———. *Cristoforo Colombo e la scuola cartografica genovese.* Genoa: Consiglio Nazionale delle Ricerche, 1937.

Sanudo, Marino. *Liber secretorum fidelium crvcis.* Vol. 2 of *Gesta Dei per Francos.* Ed. Jacques Bongars. Hanover: Typis Wechelianis, apud heredes Ioannis Aubrii, 1611.

Vesconte, Pietro. *Carte nautiche.* Intro. by Lelio Pagani. Bergamo: Grafica Gutenberg, 1977.

*Gloria Allaire*

## SEE ALSO

Acre; Atlas; City Plans; Genoa; Jerusalem; *Mappamundi;* Maps; Portolan Charts; Ptolemy; Sanudo, Marino; Venice

## Vézelay

An ancient city in the central (Burgundian) region of France. Benedictine monastic activity began in Vézelay [Vézeley] at least as early as the ninth century; the community later came under Cluny's rule. Its importance as a pilgrimage site was based on the cult of St. Mary Magdalene that evolved during the eleventh and early twelfth centuries, largely due to the personal devotion of Abbot Geoffroy (1037–1052), who convinced Pope Leo IX (1048–1054) to name her as one of the patrons of Vézelay. Later eleventh- and twelfth-century manuscripts invent a complex history of how the remains of Mary Magdalene were translated there in the eighth century, after having earlier been carried from the Holy Land to Aix-en-Provence by the monk Badilio. The convoluted history of her remains is described in Geary (74–78).

The *Liber Sancti Jacobi Pilgrim's Guide* lists Vézelay as the starting point of the "Via Lemovicense" (the Burgundian route), which brought pilgrims from Belgium, Champagne, and Lorraine to Compostela, Spain. Others

Mission of the Apostles with marvels. France, Vézelay Church Tympanum, 1122. Photo by John B. Friedman.

made a local pilgrimage to pray at the shrine, without following the entire route through Spain. In 1044 Bernard of Clairvaux preached the Second Crusade from the church at Vézelay. Richard the Lionheart (r. 1189–1199) and King Philip Augustus (r. 1180–1223) were other famous pilgrims, stopping at the church in 1190 as they were bound for Jerusalem during the Third Crusade. A sense of the Church's role on the pilgrimage routes can be gained from the tympanum above an inner entrance to the nave, on which are sculpted representations of various "monstrous races" in a context that clearly presents them as humans capable of (indeed, needing) salvation; they show the pilgrims that the power of the Word extends to even the most distant places.

## BIBLIOGRAPHY

Cohen, Esther. "Roads and Pilgrimage: A Study in Economic Interaction." *Studi Medievali.* 3rd series, 21.1 (1980): 321–341.

Friedman, John Block. *The Monstrous Races in Medieval Art and Thought.* Cambridge, MA: Harvard UP, 1981; rpt. Syracuse, NY: Syracuse UP, 2000.

Geary, Patrick. *Furta Sacra.* 1978. Rev. edition Princeton, NJ: Princeton UP, 1990.

Hall, Melvin. "Vézeley, Hill of Pilgrimages." *National Geographic* 103.2 (February 1953): 229–247.

*Maryjane Dunn and Linda Kay Davidson*

## SEE ALSO

Crusades, First, Second, and Third; Monstrosity, Geographical; Pilgrimage, Christian; Pilgrimage Sites, Spanish

## Vietnam and Java, Mongol Invasions of

In order to conquer south China, Mongols took the city of Yünnan and sought transit via Dai Viet (modern North Vietnam), in 1257, to enter Guangxi and trap the southern Song in a pincer movement. Tran Thai-Tong (r. 1225–1258) refused, so the Mongols invaded and burned the capital, Thang-long (Ha-noi). Lack of supplies, tropical climate, and a counterattack by Tran Hu'ng Dao drove them back to Yünnan. Further war was delayed by Khubilai Khân's succession and the invasion of Korea in 1259 and Japan in 1274 and 1281. Tran Thanh-Tong (r. 1258–1278) and Nhan-Tong (r. 1279–1293) refused demands to come to the Yuan court, or to send sons and brothers as hostages and men as troops.

In 1281, Nhan-Tong reconsidered and sent a royal family member, Tran Di Ai, to the Yuan court, where he was named king and sent home with 1,000 troops. After he was killed, Mongols invaded Champa (present-day South Vietnam) in 1281 and 1283; long an enemy of Dai Viet, Champa forced the Mongol troops northward. Then, the Mongol leader Toghan and 500,000 troops invaded Dai Viet from China in 1284, sacking Thang-long and killing many people. Dai Viet's military leader, Tran Hu'ng Dao, retaliated with a force of 200,000 troops, as King Nhan-Tong and the court fled to Thanh-hoa. While Toghan took the rich Hong delta, other Mongols advanced north. However, Tran Hu'ng Dao defeated the Mongol forces with 50,000 troops, made his way to the capital, and, by July, 1285, took more than 50,000 prisoners. Tradition says Toghan escaped by hiding in a bronze drum.

Khubilai was forced to abandon a planned third invasion of Japan in order to seek revenge against Dai Viet. In 1287, Toghan and 300,000 troops burned Thang-long, but fled when their supply ships were sunk. When a Mongol fleet of 500 ships entered the Bach Dang River, Tran Hu'ng Dao used a traditional strategy. Sharp poles put in the river bed at low tide sank 100 ships, and 400 others were captured when the tide ebbed again. Tran Hu'ng Dao put his troops' backs to the river, and forced them to swear to defeat the Mongols or die in the effort. Toghan withdrew in 1288, and plans for a further invasion died when Khubilai died in 1294. Vietnam was the only place where the Mongols were defeated militarily.

During the same period, Mongols were also making incursions in other areas of Southeast Asia. Troops from Yünnan took the Kingdom of Pagan in Burma in 1287. Mistreatment of Mongol envoys to Java in 1289 by King Kertanagara led to invasion in 1293. The king died before the invasion took place, and Crown Prince Vijaya joined with the Mongols to overthrow a usurper. However, Vijaya later betrayed his Mongol allies, and thus their invasion of Java ultimately failed.

**BIBLIOGRAPHY**

Kim, Tran-trong. *Viet-Nam Su-Luoc.* Saigon: Tan-Viet, 1964.

Le, Thanh Khoi. *Histoire du Vietnam: Des origines à 1858.* Paris: Sudestasie, 1981.

Masson, André. *Histoire du Vietnam.* Paris: Presses Universitaires de France, 1967.

*Hugh D. Walker*

**SEE ALSO**
Ambassadors; Diplomacy; Japan, Mongol Invasion of; Korea, Mongol Invasions of; Mongols; Yuan Dynasty

## Viking Age

The name identifying the epoch in northern Europe from the end of the eighth century to the middle of the eleventh century. During this period advances in shipbuilding among Scandinavian peoples were largely responsible for a remarkable increase in trade, travel, and exploration.

Before the eighth century the small communities of Scandinavia were self-sufficient and without a social class that required luxury goods obtainable only from abroad. Nonetheless, relying on their physical strength in rowing, Nordic men had long explored local shorelines. From the seventh century, sails woven from wool—an important female contribution to the Viking achievements—and the simultaneous development of the keel made possible the harnessing of wind power, thus enabling Viking men to travel to more distant places. In the process they familiarized themselves with European geography, to which they added the northern coast of Russia, the eastern Baltic, and Iceland, Greenland, and North America. Annual forages for booty followed by permanent settlement in newly discovered (or conquered) areas resulted in regular travel, as the immigrants and their descendants maintained ongoing connections with their mother countries. Exposing voyagers to new cultures and tastes, exploration and travel, in turn, engendered diverse trade. During the Viking Age, therefore, the north

# V

established regular trading routes with both Western and Eastern Europe. When the Vikings ended their expeditions, they also abandoned exploration and travel as objectives, but trade survived and became an integral part of northern medieval life.

Ship burials in Norway and Denmark and illustrations on Swedish runic stones make it possible to follow the development and varieties of the northern ship. Although sails were known to the Romans, northern Europeans relied on rowing until the seventh century. The Sutton Hoo ship burial suggests that the Anglo-Saxons rowed—rather than sailed—to Britain. The sail was introduced when a rowing ship reached a length of around 100 feet (30 meters); its chief assets, lightness and flexibility, made the Viking ship not only the greatest invention of the period but also a cultural emblem of outstanding grace and beauty. Propelled by wind and stabilized by its keel, the Viking ship enabled men to sail into the open waters of seas and oceans. Light enough to be pulled up on land, it could be transported to inland waterways that allowed access to new oceanic travel. The most outstanding specimens are found in two Norwegian burial sites, the ninth-century Oseberg ship and the tenth-century Gokstad ship, discovered in 1880 and 1904, respectively. Used mainly as warships, this type of craft was still being built in the eleventh century, as demonstrated by the Bayeux tapestry depicting the fleet that brought the Normans to England and by two of the Skuldelev ships purposely placed to block the harbor of Roskilde in Denmark. This group, discovered in 1962, also included two merchant ships of a different design, broader, heavier, and capable of carrying considerable cargo. Around 1200, the cog appeared, which combined traits from previous vessels used on the Rhine and along the Frisian coast with the features of the Viking ship. The cog was not as capacious as the largest Nordic ships, but in the hands of the Hanseatic merchants of the later Middle Ages, it became the premier vessel on the North and Baltic seas.

The Vikings employed these various kinds of boats for their increasingly longer travels. An important impetus for the Norwegians was a shortage of arable land at home. When these new boats became available, Shetland and Orkney—a mere day-and-a-half's journey from Bergen or Stavanger—became manageable destinations. Archaeology of burial sites suggests that Norwegian immigration had already occurred there in the seventh century. From the end of the following century, Vikings explored, attacked, and in some cases colonized much of northern Europe. The Norwegians went to Ireland, the Danes to England and France. Heading east, the Swedes settled and traded in Russia and were enlisted as elite soldiers of the Byzantine emperor (the Varangian Guard). Vikings also discovered and colonized new territories: Iceland, settled mainly by Norwegians in the late-ninth century, entered the European community; Greenland, in turn discovered by the Icelanders, harbored Norse settlements for about five centuries; the Greenlanders established a colony in the New World in the early eleventh century, but it lasted for only a few generations.

Mixing adventure, conquest, and war, the Viking expeditions also enabled men to amass great loot, with which they sustained traditional gift-giving and honed newer trading skills. Substantiated from archaeology, this kind of travel and trading is also illustrated in later literary accounts, such as *Egils saga*. Of particular interest is the voice from the late ninth century belonging to Óttarr [or Othere], himself active in these endeavors. In the service of Alfred the Great, king of Wessex in the 890s, Óttarr offered valuable information about his home in northern Norway, his extensive travels east into the White Sea to northern Russia, south along the Norwegian coast and to Skíringssalr in Vestfold, west to Jutland and south to Hedeby, and east and north to Birka in Sweden. The king had the report of this "Ohthere" inserted into the Anglo-Saxon translation of Orosius's *History*.

The main trading route of the period went west to east, beginning in the Rhine area; it stretched like a bow toward the north, reaching Hedeby, Birka, and Lake Ladoga in Russia before turning southward toward Byzantium by way of the Black Sea and further east toward the Arabic world along the Caspian Sea. Óttarr's account indicates that the trade route also incorporated territory as remote as northern Norway and Russia. An important connection between Europe and the Arabic world was secured in this period by the Vikings, as attested by numerous hoards of Arabic coins on Scandinavian soil. In Sweden, no fewer than 80,000 specimens have been unearthed, 70 percent on the island of Gotland. The north and east offered fur, hides, lumber, falcons, slaves, vessels made of soapstone, walrus ivory, and homespun; the west and south exchanged woolen and silk cloth, swords, pottery, glass, jewels, wine, and silver.

When the Viking Age came to an end around 1000, a commercial revolution was already underway in

Western Europe, although this important transformation did not make its impact in the north until the twelfth century. As the demand for diverse foodstuffs expanded in the growing towns of Western Europe, it was largely met by men from the north. As a result, goods mass-produced by northerners entered long-distance trade in earnest. Dried fish, herring, butter, meat, grain, and metal from the north were traded for salt, cloth, wine, beer, flour, and malt from the south. This trade was largely in the hands of the Hanseatic League (active *c.* 1160–1660), with whose appearance a new chapter in the history of northern trade begins.

**BIBLIOGRAPHY**

*Egils saga.* Trans. Hermann Pálsson and Paul Edwards. Harmondsworth, England: Penguin, 1976.

*Medieval Scandinavia: An Encyclopedia.* Ed. Phillip Pulsiano. New York and London: Garland, 1993; especially Mikael Andersen, "Transport," Alan Binns, "Ships and Shipbuilding," and Arnved Nedkvitne, "Trade."

Orosius, Paulus. *The Seven Books of History against the Pagans.* Trans. Roy J. Deferrari. The Fathers of the Church: A New Translation. Vol. 50. Washington, DC: Catholic U of America P, 1964.

Roesdahl, Else, and David M. Wilson, eds. *The Vikings.* Trans. Susan M. Margeson and Kirsten Williams. London: Penguin, 1991, pp. 78–128, 187–197.

———. *From Viking to Crusader: Scandinavia and Europe 800–1200.* The 22nd Council of Europe Exhibition. Copenhagen: Nordisk Ministerräd, 1992–1993.

Sawyer, Peter, ed. *The Oxford Illustrated History of the Vikings.* Oxford and New York: Oxford UP, 1997.

*Jenny Jochens*

**SEE ALSO**
Byzantine Empire; Caspian Sea; Cog; Hanse, The; Iceland; Keel; Navigation; Navigation, Viking; Orosius; Russia and Rus'; Scandinavian World Maps; Ships and Shipbuilding; Stones and Timber, Scandinavian Trade in

## Viking Discoveries and Settlements: The Faeroe Islands, Iceland, Greenland, and Vinland

A significant result of the Viking expeditions was the incorporation—permanent or temporary—of hitherto unknown (or little-known) territories into the Western cultural community. The process of Viking discoveries and settlements can be traced from archaeology and from Old Norse texts, among which the most impor-tant are the Icelandic *Landnámabók* (Book of Settlements), a catalogue of the original Viking settlers on Iceland and their descendants, and *Eiríks saga rauða* (The Saga of Eirik the Red) and *Grœnlendinga saga* (The Saga of Greenlanders), narratives that describe the Norse discovery of Greenland and the New World. Made possible by the Viking ship, colonization efforts were most successful in Iceland. Here the initial settlement is normally associated with the Norwegian king, Haraldr I Halfdanarson [Haraldr hárfagri] (Harold Fair/Finehair; r. *c.* 870–*c.* 940], whose long harsh reign—according to other Icelandic sagas—induced many people to leave Norway during the last decades of the ninth century. Norwegians had settled on the nearby Orkney and Shetland Islands since the seventh century, however, and a pattern of emigration and settlement (in northern European territory) had long been established.

Little is known about the Viking settlement in the Faeroes, which occurred early in the 800s. The first Norse settler is supposed to have been Grímr kamban, whose name suggests mixed Norse and Celtic origin. His descendants were among the first visitors to, and original colonists of, Iceland. Grímr's presence in the Faeroes would thus fit the report of Dicuil (Dicuilus), the learned Irish scholar at the court of Charlemagne, in his *De mensura orbis terrae* (825) that Irish monks left the Faeroes early in the ninth century because of Norse invasions. In the second half of the ninth century, a Norwegian Viking by the name of Naddoddr is known to have settled on one of these islands.

The Faeroes provided the last of the stepping stones that allowed relatively short journeys into the North Atlantic on a maritime route that had been explored systematically by Norwegians since the eighth century. By contrast, the Vikings reached the more distant landmasses of Iceland, Greenland, and Vinland accidentally, as they were blown off course on their voyages to or from well-known places. Exploration and settlement of these new areas followed immediately or gradually. Naddoddr, "a great viking," was, for example, on his way to the Faeroes when winds drove him instead to the east coast of Iceland. Finding no sign of human habitation, he was disinclined to stay there; experiencing a great blizzard as he was leaving, he named the island Snowland. The next Viking to set foot on Iceland may have been Garðar Svávarson, a Swede who landed on the southeast coast as he was returning from the Shetlands; during the next year he circumnavigated

# V

the island and named it Garðarshólmr (Garðar's Isle). The Norwegian Flóki Vilgerðarson also spent a year here in the mid-ninth century; among his companions was Þórólfr smjǫr (Butter), the grandson of Grímr kamban; his own grandson (Þorsteinn Sǫlmundarson) was later named among the original settlers. Impressed by the amount of ice in a northern fjord, Flóki gave the country the name by which it has been known ever since (Old Norse *Ísland*). True colonization started with the two foster brothers, Ingólfr Arnarson and Hjǫrleifr Hróþmarsson; Ingólfr is considered the founding father of Iceland. After an initial visit to the country, they returned home and spent a year preparing for their permanent settlement. If Irish monks had established themselves in Iceland (the question is currently under debate), the arrival of the first Norwegian settlers caused them to abandon it about 870.

Among the settlers who arrived in Iceland during the first third of the tenth century was a certain Gunnbjǫrn, who "drifted in a westerly direction from Iceland" and discovered small islands off the east coast of Greenland that became known as Gunnbjarnarsker (Gunnbjǫrn's Skerries). Snæbjǫrn, a great-grandson of an original settler, attempted to find these islands with the purpose of colonization, but his expedition was a failure. Only late in the tenth century, when Iceland had been fully settled and famine was threatening, did Greenland look more promising. The two most important names in the Norse explorations are Eiríkr Þorvaldsson (popularly known as Erik the Red) and his son Leifr, who are associated with the discovery of Greenland and Vinland, respectively. Eiríkr was probably born in Norway but had been established in Iceland so long that one text identifies him as Eiríkr from Breiðafjorðr (a fjord in western Iceland). Outlawed for murder, he decided to spend the three years of his exile (possibly 982–985; probably a decade later) looking for the land sighted by Gunnbjǫrn. He discovered Greenland and was impressed by the potential for settlement on its west coast. Encountering new problems as soon as he returned to Iceland, he decided to colonize the new land. He named it Greenland, astutely acknowledging that "people would be much more tempted to go there if it had an attractive name." The scheme worked. The following summer, twenty-five ships left Iceland, carrying entire families with livestock and all the necessities to start life in a new country. Only fourteen of these vessels ever reached their destination.

For half a millennium, the Norse community in Greenland maintained a thriving culture. For a brief period in the early eleventh century they also established an outpost on the North American continent. According to a few lines in *Eiríks Saga*, Leifr, Eirikr's son, was the accidental discoverer of "lands which he did not even know existed." Far more developed—and favorable to Leifr—is the story as told in the *Saga of Greenlanders*. Here, only a fall from his horse prevented Eiríkr from participating in his son Leifr's expedition to find new land, and Leifr thus became the first European recorded to have set foot in or set sail to the Americas. The saga reports that Leifr was following a route taken shortly before by Bjarni Herjólfsson, who had sighted land. Bjarni, a merchant who was attempting to follow his father from Iceland to Greenland, experienced bad weather and sailed off course. When he and his crew were again able to navigate, they saw land three separate times and were able to sail close enough to the coast to determine that it was not Greenland. Despite entreaties, however, Bjarni refused to land; later, safely in his father's new home, he related what he had seen, providing sufficient detail to enable modern scholars to identify tentatively his sightings in sequence as Newfoundland, the Labrador coast, and Baffin Island. His stories stirred excitement as well as outrage that he failed to explore the new land. Acquiring Bjarni's ship and hiring a crew of thirty-five men, Leifr Eiríksson followed a similar route, reaching the three places Bjarni had spotted and going ashore. He and his men built shelters, spent the winter, and returned to Greenland the next summer, bringing with them grapes, which prompted him to call the country Vinland. Subsequent expeditions maintained the colony for a few decades, but in the end, internal division among the colonists and problems with the natives caused the settlement to be abandoned. In the 1960s, archaeological discoveries at L'Anse-aux-Meadows in Newfoundland confirmed the literary accounts of Viking colonization. More a gateway for trade than a settlement, the site may not have been the place settled by Leifr. Nonetheless, evidence for the presence of Vikings in North America in the eleventh century was sufficiently strong for President Lyndon Baines Johnson to proclaim a "Leif Erikson Day" in 1965.

Most of the early explorers were undoubtedly men, but it deserves notice that a few women were among the early adventurers and settlers. Among Garðar Svávarson's crew, for example, were his companion Náttfari and a slave couple. The four got separated and

Garðar returned home, but the three others stayed, and the unnamed slave woman thus became the first housewife in Iceland. Flóki was accompanied by his two daughters, of whom one died in the Shetlands and the other was married in the Faeroes. Eiríkr's illegitimate daughter Freydís, who may have been born in Greenland, made an independent expedition to Vinland. Immigrating to Greenland, Þorbjǫrn Vífilsson was joined by his daughter Guðríðr and her foster mother, Halldís. Halldís died on the way, but Guðríðr married twice in Greenland. She traveled with her first husband from the settlement in the east to his home on the west coast; later she accompanied her second husband to Vinland where she gave birth to a son. When the colonization experiment ended, the family returned, first to Greenland and eventually to Iceland. After her husband's death Guðríðr made a pilgrimage to Rome, returning to Iceland, where she became a nun. While she was not an original explorer, she must have been one of the most well-traveled people of the early eleventh century.

**BIBLIOGRAPHY**

*The Book of Settlements.* [*Landnámabók.*] Trans. Hermann Pálsson and Paul Edwards. Winnipeg: U of Manitoba P, 1972.

Clausen, Birthe L., ed. *Viking Voyages to North America.* Roskilde: The Viking Ship Museum, 1993.

Ingstad, Helge. *Westward to Vinland: The Discovery of Pre-Columbian Norse House-sites in North America.* Trans. Erik J. Friis. New York: Harper & Row, 1969; rpt. 1972.

Jochens, Jenny. "Vikings Westward to Vinland: The Problem of Women." In *Cold Counsel: The Women of Old Norse Literature and Myth.* Ed. Sarah M. Anderson and Karen Swenson. New York: Garland, 2000.

Jones, Gwyn. *A History of the Vikings.* New York: Oxford UP, 1968, pp. 145–311.

Seaver, Kristen A. *The Frozen Echo: Greenland and the Exploration of North America ca. AD. 1000–1500.* Palo Alto, CA: Stanford UP, 1996.

*The Vinland Sagas: The Norse Discovery of America.* Trans. Magnus Magnusson and Hermann Pálsson. London: Penguin, 1965.

*Jenny Jochens*

**SEE ALSO**
Exploration and Expansion, European; Iceland; Navigation, Viking; Viking Age; Vinland Sagas

## Viking Navigation
*See* Navigation, Viking

# Vincent of Beauvais (*c.* 1190–1264)

Dominican compiler and encyclopedist. In the mid-1240s to 1250s, Vincent of Beauvais, an erudite Dominican, produced a huge compendium, offering an overview of classical and ecclesiastical knowledge available at that time. It thus acts as a "great mirror" of medieval thought. Vincent divided his *Speculum maius* into separate units (discussed below), of which his *Speculum historiale* has particular importance to students of medieval European knowledge of the world, since it includes substantial excerpts from works by mendicant friars who traveled in the 1240s as papal envoys to the Mongols, who had just conducted a devastating invasion of eastern Europe.

Vincent left behind a large body of works on theology, pedagogy, and science (broadly understood), but very little is recorded about his personal life. He apparently was born and died in his native Beauvais. He joined the Dominican order around 1220 and studied at the University of Paris. Vincent may have been transferred to the new priory established in his hometown of Beauvais some ten years later. Vincent developed very close connections to the nearby Cistercian Abbey of Royaumont and to King Louis IX of France, who had founded Royaumont in 1228 and whose favorite residence was in the vicinity. This friendship brought Vincent royal favor and financial assistance.

Vincent had developed a scheme to organize all existing sacred and profane literature into a systematic collection that would make the wisdom of earlier authors more easily accessible to his fellow Dominicans. On hearing of Vincent's growing compilation of quotations and excerpts, Louis IX wanted a copy for himself and offered the financial assistance needed to complete the undertaking. Originally, the *Speculum maius* contained only two parts, the *Naturale* (treating aspects of the physical world) and *Historiale* (offering a universal history from Creation to 1254). Vincent later reorganized and added material, producing a third part, the *Doctrinale* (covering theoretical and practical arts and sciences). Sometime between 1310 and 1325, a fourth part, the *Morale,* drawn chiefly from the *Summa theologiae* of Thomas Aquinas, was anonymously added. All printed editions contain these four sections, although Vincent is responsible only for the first three.

The *Speculum maius* was both popular and influential, as is evident from the numerous extant manuscripts, excerpts, and summaries, as well as from medieval

# V

translations of all or part of it into French, Catalan, Spanish, Dutch, and German. It was printed four times in the fifteenth century, once in the sixteenth, and once in the seventeenth. The 1624 Douai edition, reprinted in facsimile in 1964–1965, is the most readily available and most frequently cited version. The lack of a modern critical edition, however, makes it difficult to analyze confidently the organization, sources, and contents of Vincent's great encyclopedia.

The date of composition for the *Speculum* is a complicated issue because Vincent reorganized and modified his material several times. The first draft is usually dated 1244 and the last about 1260. The *Historiale* in particular underwent significant change. Scholars have identified five different versions: the Dijon, Klosterneuburg, Vienna, St. Jacques, and Douai texts. The universal chronicle in this part of the encyclopedia covers human history from the creation of Adam and Eve to 1254. While much of the Old and New Testament material is borrowed from earlier accounts, Vincent becomes a very valuable original source for information about matters with which he was personally familiar: the conflict between the papacy and the empire, diplomatic responses to the Mongol threat, and the court of his patron, Louis IX.

Scholars of medieval European expansion and discovery are especially grateful to Vincent for incorporating into the last three books of his *Historiale* excerpts from works written by two papal envoys to the Mongols: the Dominican Simon of Saint-Quentin and the Franciscan John of Plano Carpini. Vincent gave these two books a wider audience. Indeed, Simon's *Historia Tartarorum* is known today only from the excerpts included in the *Historiale*. Simon's account of the Seljuk Turks and the first Mongol embassy to Europeans—proposing a Mongol-Christian alliance against the Muslims to King Louis on the island of Cyprus in 1248—are unique among the period's sources.

John's text brought to Vincent's encyclopedia valuable information about the geography and peoples of Central Asia and especially about Mongol history and society. Vincent also faithfully retained fabulous reports of monstrous peoples that Simon and John perpetuated in their histories.

While Vincent's careful orchestration of divergent sources displays a logical and rational mind, the content of the *Historiale* also reveals a somewhat credulous compiler who intermingles superstition, fable, myth, and miracles with verifiable factual data and scientific knowledge as he cites from more than 400 sources with amazing regularity and accuracy.

## BIBLIOGRAPHY

Aerts, W.J., E.R. Smits, and J.B. Voorbij. *Vincent of Beauvais and Alexander the Great: Studies in the* Speculum Maius *and Its Translation into Medieval Vernaculars.* Groningen: Forsten, 1986.

Duchenne, Marie-Christine, Gregory G. Guzman, and J.B. Voorbij. "Une liste des manuscrits de *Speculum historiale.*" *Scriptorium* 41 (1987): 286–294.

Guzman, Gregory G. "The Encyclopedist Vincent of Beauvais and His Mongol Extracts from John of Plano Carpini and Simon of Saint-Quentin." *Speculum* 49 (1974): 287–307.

Kaeppeli, Thomas. *Scriptores Ordinis Praedicatorum Medii Aevi.* Rome: Istituto Storico Domenicano, 1993, vol. 4, pp. 435–458.

Lusignan, Serge. *Préface au* Speculum maius *de Vincent de Beauvais.* Montreal: Bellarmin, 1979.

Paulmier-Foucart, Monique, and Serge Lusignan. "Vincent de Beauvais et l'histoire de *Speculum maius.*" *Journal des Savants* (1990): 97–124.

Paulmier-Foucart, Monique, Serge Lusignan, and Alain Nadeau, eds. *Vincent de Beauvais: Intentions et réceptions d'une oeuvre encyclopédique au Moyen Age.* Montreal: Bellarmin, 1990.

Vincent of Beauvais. *Speculum quadruplex: Naturale, doctrinale, morale, historiale.* 4 vols. Douai, 1624; rpt. Graz: Akademische Druck u. Verlagsanstalt, 1964–1965.

Voorbij, Johannes Benedictus. *Het "Speculum Historiale" van Vincent van Beauvais: Een studie van zijn ontstaansgeschiedenis.* Groningen: Universiteitsdrukkerij, 1991. [For an English summary of this seminal Dutch study, see the *Vincent of Beauvais Newsletter* 16 (1991): 3–8.]

*Gregory G. Guzman*

**SEE ALSO**
Dominican Friars; John of Plano Carpini; Louis IX; Mongols; Simon of Saint-Quentin

# Vinland
**See** Viking Discoveries and Settlements

# Vinland Map

Although its authenticity is much debated, the Vinland map may be the earliest map to show part of North

America, and the only such map to predate Christopher Columbus's first voyage of 1492. The map's origins, however, are unknown, as are its history and provenance until a very brief time before its acquisition by Yale University in 1959. Cartographic and linguistic inconsistencies, the map's mysterious history, conflicting scientific analyses of its ink, and the map's very uniqueness have fed thirty years of debate, which remains unresolved, about whether it is a genuine fifteenth-century document or a recent forgery.

Drawn in faded brown ink, the map covers two facing pages of parchment. In a limited sense, it resembles a conventional medieval world map in that it depicts the earth's landmass as consisting of Europe, Africa, and Asia, with decreasing accuracy as the map moves away from the Mediterranean Sea. Unlike most *mappaemundi*, however, the Vinland map is oriented to the north. Its general outline is related to that of a 1436 world map drawn by Andrea Bianco in Venice. The eastern outlines of Asia may derive in part from the text bound into the manuscript with the map, an otherwise unknown travel account called the *Tartar Relation* written by C. de Bridia, who attributes his information to the envoys from Pope Innocent IV who journeyed to the Mongol khân between 1245 and 1247.

At the extreme northwest of the map are Iceland and Greenland; farthest west—and outside the implied oval that contains the rest of the map—is a large island labeled Vinland. Vinland was the name given to mainland North America by the Vikings during their exploration and brief colonization of northern Newfoundland (and perhaps regions further south) around 1000 C.E. In addition to place-names, the map bears a number of short paragraphs, including one (the longest) describing the discovery and settlement of Vinland and a visit there by a bishop around 1117. Greenland and Iceland remained well-known throughout the Middle Ages, but the colony on Vinland was short-lived, and the Old Norse texts that describe it had a very limited circulation (and a date of composition that is uncertain). If the map is genuine, it provides the only evidence that knowledge of Vinland was both discussed and disseminated as late as the fifteenth century.

The map was originally bound together with an unquestionably genuine mid-fifteenth-century manuscript of the *Speculum historiale* (Mirror of History) by Vincent of Beauvais, and the *Tartar Relation,* an account of John of Plano Carpini's fourteenth-century journey to Central Asia. At some time (probably around the turn of this century), the texts were separated and rebound. The sheet that contains the Vinland map was originally at the front of the *Speculum historiale,* but was separated from that text and bound with the *Tartar Relation.* There is, however, no firm record of either the manuscripts or the map until 1957, when Laurence Witten, a rare book dealer in New Haven, Connecticut, bought the volume containing the Vinland map and the *Tartar Relation* from an itinerant book dealer based in Spain named Enzo Ferrajoli. Ferrajoli refused to name his source for the book. By chance, the manuscript of the *Speculum historiale* also found its way to New Haven as part of the private collection of Thomas Marston, Yale's curator of manuscripts. The two manuscripts were reunited and purchased for Yale's Beinecke Library with funds provided by Paul Mellon.

The library kept its acquisition secret for several years while a team of scholars prepared a lavish study. The authors of *The Vinland Map and the Tartar Relation,* published in 1965, generally agreed that the map is genuine and was drawn around 1440, probably in or near Basel. The physical evidence of the manuscript's handwriting and paper support that date and location. Several of the authors also tried to tie the creation of the map to intellectual exchange at the general council of the Catholic Church held at Basel between 1431 and 1439.

The publication of the map was greeted with great excitement and enthusiasm, but the very importance of such a discovery may have fostered the skepticism with which it was almost immediately received. Early criticism focused on the map's uniqueness; its curiously accurate depiction of the unnavigable northern coastline of Greenland; the fact that both Greenland and Vinland lie outside the oval that seems to define the border of the rest of the map; and seeming inconsistencies between all other accounts of the discovery of Vinland and the version found on the map. Defenders of the map's authenticity claim that it is being held to standards of consistency few medieval documents of any sort could meet.

Further complicating the issue are the conflicting results from two tests of the map's ink. Hoping to break the scholarly stalemate, Yale allowed chemical tests of small samples of ink in 1972. The tests suggested that the ink contains a high proportion of Anatase, a titanium precipitate not available until the 1920s. Yale immediately accepted the evidence and

# V

declared the map a fake. The map's defenders remained unconvinced, and the map was subjected to more tests in 1985. By using a nondamaging proton beam, the new tests did not require ink to be removed from the manuscript, and were, consequently, more extensive than the first set. The new results found virtually no titanium in the ink at all. The body of opinion seems to lie with the newer results, but, as the team that conducted the tests has been careful to point out, the new results merely contradict the 1972 test, providing no evidence about the date of the map itself.

The debate continues. Heartened by the new scientific tests, Yale has reissued its 1965 edition and study of the map (and the *Tartar Relation* by C. de Bridia). Meanwhile, Kirsten Seaver has for the first time identified a plausible forger in Josef Fischer, an early-twentieth-century historian of cartography. In the end, the debate about the map has absorbed more attention than has the map. As a number of reviewers pointed out shortly after the map's initial publication, authentic or not, the map is merely a confirmation of what was already known. For nearly a century, there has been almost universal acceptance that Norse explorers reached North America around 1000 C.E. There has also been agreement that, however fascinating the episode, it had no long-term effects, although most scholars also believe that by the later Middle Ages, European fishermen and other navigators knew that a large land area existed to the west of Greenland. Like the Norse sailors, the Vinland map—if real—left no legacy until our own time.

## BIBLIOGRAPHY

Monmonier, Mark. "The Vinland Map, Columbus, and Italian-American Pride." In *Drawing the Line: Tales of Maps and Cartocontroversy.* New York: Henry Holt, 1995.

*Proceedings of the Vinland Map Conference.* Ed. Wilcomb E. Washburn. Chicago: U Chicago P, 1971.

Seaver, Kirsten. "The Vinland Map: Who Made It and Why? New Light on an Old Controversy." *The Map Collector* 70 (Spring 1995): 32–40.

Skelton, R.A., et al. *The Vinland Map and the Tartar Relation.* New Haven, CT: Yale UP, 1965; 2nd revised edition New Haven: Yale UP, 1995.

*Ben Weiss*

## SEE ALSO

Bridia, C. de; John of Plano Carpini; *Mappamundi;* Maps; Viking Discoveries and Settlements; Vincent of Beauvais; Vinland Sagas

## Vinland Sagas: *Grœnlendinga Saga* and *Eiríks Saga Rauða*

Belonging to the genre of the "sagas of Icelanders "(or "family sagas"), the *Groenlendinga* saga and *Eiríks saga rauða* describe the Norse discoveries of Greenland and, in particular, of Vinland, an area believed by modern scholars to have been located somewhere on the east coast of North America. *Grœnlendinga saga* (GS) does not exist as an independent text but is extant only as two interpolations in a work known as the *Longest Saga of Óláfr Tryggvason* (chapters 342 and 427–433), found in the large manuscript known as *Flateyjarbók,* copied in the late fourteenth century. Modern editors of *GS* normally preface these fragments with a chapter that sketches Eiríkr's discovery of Greenland taken from *Longest Saga* (chap. 220), in the version found in *Flateyjarbók* (where it is chap. 340). *Eiríks saga* (ES) is preserved in two different manuscripts dated *c.* 1300 and *c.* 1400. Scholars have determined that they derive from a common source, probably written early in the thirteenth century.

Because the two narratives have striking differences, their relative chronology is important. The dating of *GS* is particularly difficult because most of the text exists in only one version; since the mid-1900s, scholars have generally accepted that *GS* was written in the late twelfth century. The author of *ES* may have known this older text, but it is also clear that the two narratives tapped different oral traditions characteristic of northern and western Iceland, respectively.

The two sagas concur that Eiríkr rauði (Erik the Red) discovered Greenland and started a Norse colony there in the late 900s. Their differences primarily concern the discovery of Vinland. According to *GS*, an Icelandic merchant by the name of Bjarni Herjólfsson was the first to sight three landmasses that modern scholars have identified as Newfoundland, the coast of Labrador, and Baffin Island. Relying on Bjarni's information and using his boat, Erik's son, Leif, started an expedition from Greenland. In reverse order he found the lands Bjarni had spotted, landing briefly in the first two places and settling for the winter in the last, which he called Vinland. Four more expeditions were made from Greenland by Leif's relatives. The second did not reach the New World, but the others arrived with remarkable accuracy at Leif's houses in Vinland.

In *ES*, Bjarni is not mentioned, and Leif was the accidental discoverer of the New World, a story told in a few lines. Reporting only two additional expeditions, this text is illustrative of the vagaries of sailing in northern climes. Wishing to visit King Óláfr Tryggvason of Norway, Leif was thrown off course from Greenland and landed on the Hebrides. Staying for most of the summer, he succeeded in reaching Norway in the fall. Having spent the winter with the king, he wished to return to Greenland the following summer but was again thrown off course and landed in the New World before finally managing to return to Greenland. The second expedition, led by Leif's brother Þorsteinn, made a great circle in the direction opposite the one intended, getting close to Iceland and Ireland before returning to Greenland. The third expedition, led by Þorfinnr karlsefni, was the most successful. Exploring the northeastern coast of the New World, the group named close to a dozen places and in the end located what they thought was Leif's Vinland.

Erik and Þorfinnr karlsefni are the two most important men in *ES,* but the most significant person is Þorfinnr's wife, Guðríðr Þorbjarnardóttir. She was known not only for her own qualities but particularly because she became the ancestress of several Icelandic bishops. Whereas *GS* provided an historical account of the discovery of Vinland, the additional purpose of *ES* may have been an attempt to secure a saint for the bishopric in Hólar in the person of Bishop Bjǫrn Gilsson, one of Guðríðr's descendants, who occupied the see from 1147 to 1162.

### BIBLIOGRAPHY

Halldórsson, Ólafur. "The Conversion of Greenland in Written Sources." *Proceedings of the Eighth Viking Congress.* Ed. Hans Bekker-Nielsen et al. Odense: Odense UP, 1981, pp. 203–216.

———. "Lost Tales of Guðríðr Þorbjarnardóttir." *Sagnaskemmtun: Studies in Honour of Herman Pálsson.* Ed. Rudolf Simek et al. Vienna: Böhlau, 1986, pp. 239–246.

Jóhannesson, Jón. "The Date of the Composition of the Saga of the Greenlanders." *Saga-Book of the Viking Society* 16 (1962): 54–66.

*The Vinland Sagas: The Norse Discovery of America: Grænlendinga saga and Eirik's saga.* Trans. Magnus Magnusson and Hermann Pálsson. Harmondsworth, England: Penguin, 1965.

Wahlgren, Erik. "Fact and Fancy in the Vinland Sagas." *Old Norse Literature and Mythology: A Symposium.* Ed. Edgar C. Polomé. Austin: U of Texas P, 1969, pp. 19–80.

*Jenny Jochens*

**SEE ALSO**

Fornaldarsögur; Iceland; Navigation, Viking; Viking Discoveries and Settlements

## Virgil of Salzburg, St. (d. November 27, 784)

Learned Irish churchman who came to the Continent in 743–744; Virgil was responsible for churches in the Salzburg area as abbot of the Monastery of St. Peter by 747, consecrated bishop of Salzburg on June 15, 749, and canonized in 1233.

From 745, Virgil was a missionary in Bavaria, an area that lay under the overall ecclesiastical authority of Archbishop Boniface (*c.* 675–754), the Anglo-Saxon "Apostle to the Germans." Indefatigable in his efforts to convert the Bavarians (and later the Carinthian Slavs), Virgil was a source of irritation to Boniface because of some of his apparently heretical ideas. Pope Zachary's response in 748 to one of Boniface's complaints about Virgil was later understood to demonstrate the progressive views of the Irishman in matters of cosmology. The letter states that Virgil should be condemned if it could clearly be shown that "he believes that below the earth there is another world, with other men—complete with sun and moon" ("*alius mundus et alii homines sub terra sint seu sol et luna*").

At the beginning of the seventeenth century, Johannes Kepler assumed from this text that Virgil believed in the existence of populated areas below the equator, and thus presented him as an early Copernicus persecuted by church authorities for his enlightened views (Flint). A more recent development in this line of reasoning argued that Virgil had written the work known as the *Cosmography of Aethicus Ister* as a parody of his accusers' views (Löwe).

It is likely that Virgil of Salzburg believed there were people living "below the earth," though not necessarily in a way that would have sounded familiar to Pliny, Macrobius, or Martianus Capella (that is, in a southern hemisphere). Seventh-century texts written in Ireland indicate that in early Christian Ireland the native belief in another world "below"—the dwelling place of the immortals, from which they could enter into our world at any time—was thought to be confirmed by several New Testament allusions to peoples "below the earth." Early medieval Irish scholars followed the patristic pattern of remaining uncommitted as to the shape of the

# V

earth, and were probably inclined to continue in the natural belief that the earth is flat, but by the 700s, there was greater awareness of the Latin secular tradition, so that belief in a spherical earth became more widespread.

Starting in the tenth century, Irish texts clearly show that the idea of a subterranean world had become conflated with the secular notion of antipodean people living on a wonderful island in the Southern Hemisphere. But the assimilation of secular ideas from the Continent must have begun sooner, influenced at least in part by a passage in Servius's commentary on the *Aeneid,* which identifies the underworld with the dwelling place of the antipodeans (Carey). Because the Bible itself uses the phrase "below the earth," Irish scholars could overcome the objections to the very possibility of the existence of antipodeans, namely that the complete inaccessibility of those regions beyond the ocean or on the other side of the torrid—and thus impassible—equatorial zone made it impossible for descendants of Adam ever to reach there. It could reasonably be argued that if Scripture referred to peoples below the earth, then they must exist, and therefore, secular claims for the existence of antipodeans were legitimate. It is possible that Virgil of Salzburg brought such ideas from Ireland, and in this he would have been at variance with the normal Christian scholarly views of his day, which claimed that even if there was land in the Southern Hemisphere, it could not be inhabited. On the other hand, the *Cosmography of Aethicus Ister,* written probably in the Salzburg area in the late 700s, does not even assume a spherical earth (Smyth), and it could well be that Virgil was simply referring to the older Irish idea of another world "below" the surface of the presumably flat earth, which he believed to have been given scriptural support.

## BIBLIOGRAPHY

Carey, John. "Ireland and the Antipodes: The Heterodoxy of Virgil of Salzburg." *Speculum* 64 (1989): 1–10.

———. "The Irish 'Otherworld': Hiberno-Latin Perspectives." *Éigse: A Journal of Irish Studies* 25 (1991): 154–159.

Flint, Valerie I.J. "Monsters and the Antipodes in the Early Middle Ages and Enlightenment." *Viator* 15 (1984): 65–80.

Löwe, Heinz. "Ein literarischer Widersacher des Bonifatius: Virgil von Salzburg und die Kosmographie des Aethicus Ister." *Abhandlungen der Akademie der Wissenschaften und der Literatur in Mainz. Geistes- und Sozialwissenschaftlichen Klasse* 11 (1951): 899–988.

Smyth, Marina. "Das Universum in der Kosmographie des Aethicus Ister." In *Virgil von Salzburg: Missionär und Gelehrter.* Ed. Heinz Dopsch and Roswitha Juffinger. Beiträge des Internationalen Symposiums vom 21–24. September 1984 in der Salzburger Residenz. Salzburg: Salzburger Landesregierung, 1985, pp. 170–182.

*Marina Smyth*

**SEE ALSO**

Aethicus Ister; Antipodes; Beatus Maps; Climate; *Oikoumene;* Purgatory, St. Patrick's

## Walsperger, Andreas (fl. *c.* 1448)

A Benedictine monk about whom nothing more is known than that he drew an interesting *mappamundi* at Constance in 1448. This colored depiction of the world, which has a diameter of 16½ inches (42.5 cm), or 22⅜ inches (57.5 cm) including the border (cosmological) rings, is preserved at Rome (Biblioteca Apostolica Vaticana, Pal. Lat. 1362b).

The Walsperger map is of particular interest because it represents an early attempt to reconcile the classical and medieval cartographic and cosmological traditions. On the map, but below the depiction of the world itself, Walsperger writes: "In this figure is contained a *mappa mundi,* or geometrical description of the world, made according to the *Cosmographia* of Ptolemy proportionately to the latitudes, longitudes, and divisions by climates, and a true and complete chart for the navigation of the seas."

The result is an eclectic mix of Ptolemaic and medieval cartography that has a number of remarkable features. Red dots represent Christian cities, and black dots indicate the sites of "infidel" settlements. The Terrestrial Paradise is represented in the east by a medieval castle, out of which the Four Rivers of Genesis 2:10–14 flow. But recent—even revolutionary—geographical knowledge has also seeped in: the Indian Ocean is no longer closed, as it is on most older maps and in the Ptolemaic tradition, but is connected to the surrounding Sea-Ocean by a channel. More a political than a topographic map, the names of towns and countries predominate over those of mountains and rivers. A scale with instructions for its use (to determine "by how many miles a region or a city is separated from other ones") and the map's inscription within a compass (*circulus*) betray a practical, worldly approach to cartography quite different from the medieval norm (for *mappaemundi,* at least). The map's orientation to the south suggests an Arabic influence, but this format

World Map by Andreas Walsperger, Rome, Biblioteca Apostolica Vaticana MS Pal. lat. 1362B, unfoliated, 1448. Courtesy Biblioteca Apostolica Vaticana.

is not unusual for some rather sophisticated world maps produced in fifteenth-century Europe. Dana Bennett Durand argued compellingly that the Walsperger map is one of a group of maps that belong to an independent tradition of medieval cartography called the "Vienna-Klosterneuburg School," circular world maps for which coordinate tables survive in one fifteenth-century manuscript.

While the Walsperger map has some features of a modern map, characteristics of a medieval *mappamundi* can also be seen: fabulous creatures and monsters of classical and medieval origin are described in legends, including a story of Alexander according to which the Macedonian enclosed not just "unclean peoples," but the Ten Lost Tribes of Israel behind a great wall, here identified with the biblical destroyers Gog and Magog. (The association can be traced as far back as Christian of Stablo [c. 865] and became better known through Peter Comestor in his *Historia scholastica* [c. 1165].) The legend "Gog and Magog. Land of the Red Jews, imprisoned within Caspian Mountains" appears below the figure of a cannibal depicting "Andropofagi [who] eat human flesh." Prester John, the great khân, and other figures from medieval legend and science also appear.

The main difference between the Walsperger map and earlier *mappaemundi* is that Christian ideological content is much less evident. The overall effect is of transition from one worldview to another; the empirical approach of the Renaissance "age of exploration" jostles hard against inherited verities, but has not yet banished them. In this regard, Walsperger's map is quite similar to the larger and much better known 1459 *mappamundi* of Fra Mauro.

**BIBLIOGRAPHY**

Destombes, Marcel, ed. *Mappemondes.* See Gen. Bib.

Durand, Dana Bennett. *The Vienna-Klosterneuburg Map Corpus of the Fifteenth Century.* Leiden: Brill, 1952, vol. 1, pp. 209–213.

Gallez, Paul. "Walsperger and the Discovery of Patagonian Giants." *Imago Mundi* 33 (1981): 91–95.

Gow, Andrew Colin. *The Red Jews: Antisemitism in an Apocalyptic Age, 1200–1600.* Leiden: Brill, 1995.

Harley-Woodward. *The History of Cartography,* vol. 1, pl. 21 and note. See Gen. Bib.

Westrem, Scott. "Against Gog and Magog." In *Text and Territory: Geographical Imagination in the European Middle Ages.* Ed. Sylvia Tomasch and Sealy Gilles. Philadelphia: U of Pennsylvania P, 1998.

*Andrew C. Gow*

**SEE ALSO**

Cartography, Arabic; Four Rivers of Paradise; Geography in Medieval Europe; Gog and Magog; Klosterneuburg Map Corpus; *Mappamundi;* Mauro Map, [Fra]; Prester John; Ptolemy; Red Jews; Ten Lost Tribes, The

## Walter of Châtillon (fl. 1160–1190)

One of most celebrated poets of the twelfth century, whose *Alexandreis* reveals the author's interest in the East and in world geography.

Despite Walter of Châtillon's reputation as an extraordinary poet in Latin, we know little about his life. He was born near Lille, then in the county of Flanders. After studying at schools in France (probably at Paris, possibly at Reims or Orléans), he taught at a number of schools in northern France, including one at Châtillon. After studying at Bologna, he joined the court of William, archbishop of Reims, who eventually made Walter a canon, probably of Amiens. In addition to numerous lyrics in Latin on a wide variety of subjects (religious, erotic, and satirical) and a treatise against the Jews, Walter wrote his best-known work, the *Alexandreis* (between 1171 and 1181), which he dedicated to Archbishop William. *The Alexandreis,* a ten-book epic in dactylic hexameters, takes its form, diction, and style from the classical epic tradition. Its primary model is Lucan's *Bellum civile,* its primary historical source, Quintus Curtius Rufus's *Historia Alexandri Magni.*

Although the *Alexandreis,* which covers the life of Alexander the Great, is more restrained than some versions of the story in the Alexander romance tradition, it nevertheless reveals Walter's considerable interest in the East. By contrast to the Alexander romance, the *Alexandreis* follows Curtius's more "realistic" depiction of the East. Alexander does not confront any of the monstrous races or exotic peoples described in the romance. For example, rather than encountering the Brahmans, the legendary inhabitants of India famed for their ascetic life and philosophy, Walter's Alexander meets the Scythians. His Scythians, however, presented as idealized primitives living in accordance with Nature's dictates, have much in common with the Brahmans of the romance.

Walter's Alexander seems to be a paradigm for crusaders—in particular for crusading kings such as Philip Augustus (r. 1180–1223). Critics have argued that he serves, on the one hand, as a positive model of prowess to be imitated and as a negative warning against pursu-

Alexander ascends to the heavens drawn by griffins. Parish Church, Remagen, Germany, 13th century. Photo by John B. Friedman.

*Alexandreis* was widely known during the Middle Ages—it survives in some 200 manuscripts and was familiar to such prominent vernacular poets as Dante and Chaucer (whose Wife of Bath alludes casually to Darius's tomb in her "Prologue" [ll. 497–499])—the poem has been largely (and undeservedly) forgotten.

**BIBLIOGRAPHY**

Kratz, Dennis. *Mocking Epic: Waltharius, Alexandreis, and the Problem of Christian Heroism.* Madrid: José Porrúa Turanzas, 1980.

Lafferty, Maura K. "Mapping Human Limitations: The Tomb Ecphrases in Walter of Châtillon's *Alexandreis.*" *Journal of Medieval Latin* 4 (1994): 64–81.

Ratkowitsch, Christine. *Descriptio Picturae: Die literarische Funktion der Beschreibung von Kunstwerken in der lateinischen Grossdichtung des 12. Jahrhunderts.* Vienna: Verlag der Österreichischen Akademie der Wissenschaften, 1991.

Walter of Châtillon. *Alexandreis.* Ed. Marvin L. Colker. Padova, Italy: Antenore, 1978.

———. *Alexandreis.* Trans. R. Telfryn Pritchard. Toronto: Pontifical Institute of Medieval Studies, 1986.

———. *Alexandreis.* Trans. David Townsend. Philadelphia: U of Pennsylvania P, 1997.

*Maura K. Lafferty*

**SEE ALSO**
German Literature, Travel in; Godfrey of Viterbo; Hereford Map; *Mappamundi;* Marriages between Muslims and Christians, Attitudes toward; *Wonders of the East*

ing the wrong things in the Holy Land: wealth and fame rather than the salvation of his soul.

A catalogue of the lands of Asia in Book 1 and a description of a map carved on the inside of the dome of the tomb of the Persian emperor Darius in Book 7 define the natural limitations of the world. This map is a typical medieval *mappamundi* of the tripartite type: the *orbis terrarum* has a circular form and is oriented to the East, with Asia filling the top half of the circle, Europe and Africa the two quarters on the bottom. The world is ringed by a surrounding Ocean. Like contemporary *mappaemundi,* Walter's includes places and peoples of significance from all periods in biblical, ancient, and medieval history. Walter presents as unnatural Alexander's ambition to cross the Ocean, to see the regions of the extreme East, and to conquer the peoples of the Antipodes. When Alexander begins to fulfill this ambition by invading the Ocean, the goddess Nature intervenes and arranges his death. Although Walter's

## Warfare, Naval
*See* Naval Warfare

## Wey, William (1406–1476)
English pilgrim and author of an itinerary of travel to the Holy Land. Born in Devonshire and educated at Oxford, by 1430 he was a fellow at Exeter, and after 1442 he became one of the original fellows of Eton. Early in 1456, he undertook the first of three pilgrimages, a visit to the shrine of St. James at Compostela, a relatively short journey to the Continent and back. In May of 1457, he took a leave of absence from Eton and began a longer, thirty-nine-week pilgrimage to the Holy Land, reaching Jerusalem in June and remaining there through July. In February 1462, Wey left for his final trip to the Holy Land, traveling extensively through Europe on his return.

After his final pilgrimage, Wey resigned his fellowship and took monastic vows with the Augustinian canons at Edington, Wiltshire. He remained there the rest of his life, leaving at his death some relics and wooden miniatures of the holy places he had visited on his journeys. He left behind also a pilgrimage narrative of what came to be called *The Itineraries of William Wey*. First edited in 1857, this English-Latin account of Wey's three pilgrimages was particularly descriptive of the Holy Circulus, the journey of the Stations of the Cross that the Franciscans had instituted in Jerusalem, in which pilgrims stopped at historical and supposed sites of Jesus' journey to Calvary. The account also contained a detailed and rather large bannerlike map seven feet long by sixteen and one-half inches wide (2.3 meters by .3 meter) that might have been composed by Wey himself.

The *Itineraries*, like other pilgrimage narratives of its kind, was intended both to describe Wey's own journey and to explain to other potential pilgrims how they too might journey to the Holy Land. It began, typically, with introductory suggestions for travelers on what they might expect both en route to and within Palestine. In fact, the opening four sections are written in English and advise on such matters as currency exchanges, necessary equipment, lodging, travel arrangements and shipping, bedding, medicine, and food and drink. Some of Wey's material is in verse, such as his descriptions of the Stations of the Cross, probably derived from another anonymous verse pilgrimage account.

Wey's itinerary suggests that he was both exact and observant as a pilgrim. In Venice he counted eighty-four ships in the harbor and notes that thirty-two are English. In writing about his first pilgrimage to Compostela, he adds incisive material about religious life in Spain. Nothing escapes his eye—not even the dangers of riding one's mule too close to the mule in front or too close to the mule in back. Though not as well known as some of the lengthier pilgrimage narratives, such as that of Felix Fabri, Wey's itinerary provides an important record of a late medieval pilgrimage to the Holy Land in a period of somewhat more settled social and political conditions.

BIBLIOGRAPHY

Howard, Donald R. *Writers and Pilgrims: Medieval Pilgrimage Narratives and Their Posterity.* Berkeley: U of California P, 1980.

Williams, G. *The Itineraries of William Wey, Fellow of Eton College, to Jerusalem,* A.D. *1458 and* A.D. *1462; and to Saint James of Compostella,* A.D. *1456.* Roxburgh Club 76; 88. London: Roxburgh Club, 1857, 1867.

*Gary D. Schmidt*

SEE ALSO

Fabri, Felix; Franciscan Friars; Holy Land; Itineraries and *Periploi;* Jerusalem; *Mappamundi;* Maps; Pilgrimage, Christian; Pilgrimage Sites, Spanish; Travel Writing in Europe and the Mediterranean Regions; Venice

## Whaling

Whales were frequently hunted and scavenged along the coastlines of prehistoric and medieval Europe, as archaeological remains and the historical record indicate. Whales provided a variety of raw materials and resources, which contributed to prehistoric and early medieval coastal economies and, later, market economies throughout western and northern Europe. Whale meat, blubber, hide, teeth, and baleen were used for food, fuel, ropes, shelter, clothing, ivory, tools, and accessories. Ambergris was an immensely popular whale product valued for medicinal use, often acquired as driftage and imported from the coast to inland markets. Whale bone was perhaps the most versatile cetacean resource, used in a vast array of tools and crafts, from weaving tools, clubs, and chopping blocks to gaming pieces, small caskets, and grave goods. One eleventh-century Arab traveler reported that the inhabitants of the smaller islands of Britain used whale bones and vertebrae instead of wood in building. Whale bone objects survive in countless prehistoric and medieval archaeological sites around Europe, particularly in early medieval Scandinavia and Scotland.

Cetacean products were important commodities in medieval European trade and commerce. Whale meat, bone, and baleen were sold in markets, such as the eleventh-century market of the Abbey of St. Vaast-d'Arras in France, and whale bone also served as an item of royal and papal tribute, particularly in northern Europe. Certain regions of medieval Europe were notable for their whale use. Norse and early Scandinavian peoples took whales from the waters of the North Atlantic and from the North, White, and Baltic seas as early as the Bronze Age. Whales were so important to medieval Norse society that the thirteenth-century Icelandic work the *Konungs Skuggsjá* described twenty-one different folk categories of whales known by the Norse in the North Atlantic. The Norman and Basque regions of France and Spain also had active whaling communities, and harpoon-based whaling industries began in these regions as early as the eleventh century.

References to whale hunting are found in travel narratives with increasing frequency from the ninth century. The Norwegian traveler Ohthere graced the court of King Alfred of Wessex (r. 871–899) with stories of whale hunting Ohthere observed in his native Norway, and during his travels in the North Atlantic and the White Sea. Ohthere paid particular attention to the contribution of marine mammals to northern economies, reporting that northern Scandinavian peoples paid tribute in whale hides, whale bone, and fine walrus tusks. Other medieval authors reported on the pursuit of whales in the waters around Britain and Ireland. The Arabic author al-Qazwīnī, citing the eleventh-century account of the early Spanish geographer al-'Udhrī, described offshore whaling along the coast of Ireland. Al-Qazwīnī detailed the whaling methods and the hunting tools of the Irish, and their use of the slaughtered animals. Marco Polo's thirteenth-century account of the whaling cultures of the Arabian Sea described the dangers of offshore whaling, as well as the contribution of cetacean products to the island economies. Polo noted that the Arabian Sea was teeming with whales, and that the inhabitants of numerous islands hunted large whales in the open sea. These accounts of medieval whaling provide information not only on hunting strategies, whale behavior, and the economic contribution of cetacean products, but they also tell us about the nature of whaling societies.

The technology of whale hunting was rudimentary during the Middle Ages. It has been argued that active whaling did not commence in Europe until the Basque industries of the later Middle Ages, and that until then only stranded whales were utilized. Archaeological and historical evidence, coupled with ethnographic analogies from nonindustrialized whaling cultures, indicates that coastal whaling was practiced in many regions of Europe since prehistory. Injured or dying whales could easily be rounded up and beached when they were a short distance from the coast. Small cetaceans, such as pilot whales, were encircled with nets and boats and driven ashore to be harpooned. Dozens to hundreds of whales could be slaughtered in such a drive. Marco Polo and al-Qazwīnī both described open sea whaling strategies, which were much more advanced than typical coastal hunting methods, but these accounts are somewhat fanciful, and should be examined with a skeptical eye. Whale hunting and butchering tools in

the early Middle Ages were multifunctional implements, such as harpoons, lances, and knives, that could be used in a variety of other hunting activities. More specialized whaling implements may have been developed in the later Middle Ages with the full-fledged whaling industry of the Basques.

**BIBLIOGRAPHY**

Clark, Grahame. "Whales as an Economic Factor in Prehistoric Europe." *Antiquity* 21 (1947): 84–104.

Ellis, Richard. *Men and Whales.* New York: Knopf, 1991.

Lund, Niels, ed. *Two Voyagers at the Court of King Alfred.* York, England: William Sessions, 1984.

*Vicki Ellen Szabo*

**SEE ALSO**

Iceland; Ivory Trade; *King's Mirror, The;* Marco Polo; Navigation; Ships and Shipbuilding; Thomas of Cantimpré; Viking Age

# Wild People, Mythical, and New World Relations

Late medieval Europe's concept of mythical "Wild People" shaped preconceptions about the ethnography of the races that early modern explorers expected to encounter at their intended destination, Asia, and influenced early written accounts and visual depictions of the indigenous inhabitants of the New World.

The Wild People were an imagined ethnographic group constructed by medieval Europe. The mythical Wild People had affinities with or prototypes in figures of "wildness" derived from many sources in ancient literary texts and mythologies. The generic "Wild Man" was known by a variety of names throughout Europe: *agrios, homo sylvestris, hombre salvagio, uomo selvaggio, l'homme sauvage,* the wodewose, and the *wilde mann.* Models or analogues for the Wild Man and his female cohort, the Wild Woman, included Enkidu from the *Epic of Gilgamesh;* Cain, Ishmael, Esau, Nebuchadnezzar, Lilith, and the Lamia from the Old Testament or Apocryphal tradition; John the Baptist and Mary Magdalen from the New Testament; satyrs, sileni, centaurs, Amazons, and maenads from Greek myth; Silvanus and Maia from Roman myth; Orken, Wildmännl, and the Waldfäken from Nordic-Germanic folklore; Cernunnos, Dagda, and Suibne from Celtic and Irish myth; and John Chrysostom and Mary of Egypt from early Christian eremitic traditions.

Spanish Wild Man sculpture. West Façade, La Casa Grande, Hearst Castle, 15th century. Photo by Lorraine Stock. Reproduced by permission of Hearst San Simeon State Historical Monument, Department of Parks and Recreation, San Simeon, CA.

By the end of the Middle Ages, characteristics from this array of sources had crystallized into a fairly consistent profile of imagined appearance, behavior, temperament, and iconography that Europeans projected on the Wild People. Classified among the usually oriental "monstrous races," the Wild People lived an outdoor existence, dwelling in crevices, caves, or trees in the most remote parts of the forest beyond the margins of established, civilized society. They were reputedly skilled hunters, and their legendary strength and dominance over the flora and fauna of the natural world were represented in images of the Wild People wielding natural weaponry, such as a huge club or an uprooted tree, riding stags rather than the horse of a medieval knight, or holding fabulous beasts such as griffins and unicorns in a posture of submission. The physical

characteristic that most differentiated this race from their "normal" human counterparts was their extreme hirsutism. Long, unkempt hair and a shaggy beard crowned their rough coat of brown or green fur. Sometimes this was accompanied by a girdle of leaves and moss circling the Wild Man's torso, while knees, elbows, and feet were bare. His female companion was covered with sparser fur, her bared breasts often exposed erotically.

Constructed as the cultural antithesis of "civilization," the Wild People were attributed with inordinate, uncontrolled aggression (flouting the structured rules of chivalric combat) and aphasia, a limited or complete incapacity to speak, which projected on them a socially unacceptable, subhuman irrationality. This "madness" extended to their reputation for an unrestrained libido and insatiable, freely indulged sexuality, a reversal of Christian/chivalric morals, mores, and attitudes toward eroticism. As late-medieval visual images attest, to satisfy his legendary insatiable sexual appetite, the Wild Man abducted and raped human women, while the Wild Woman shape-shifted and seduced human men. Exploiting the Wild People's association with both insanity and hypersexuality, medieval authors appropriated their extreme behavior and projected it on literary characters who were either gifted with prophetic power (Merlin in Geoffrey of Monmouth's *Vita Merlini* and Heldris of Cornwall's *Roman de Silence*), or afflicted with the torments of thwarted passion (Chrétien de Troyes's *Yvain*, Gottfried von Strassburg's *Tristan*, and Thomas Malory's *Lancelot*). These characters abandon the artifices of the civilized state and adopt various aspects of the Wild Man's "natural" lifestyle— seeking seclusion in the deep forests, stalking animals and eating raw (rather than cooked) meat, berries, and woodland plants, and trading their courtly clothing for nakedness.

That medieval Europe both was repelled by and on some level identified with the Wild People reflects the complex provenance of these mythic figures. Represented as both menacing symbols of "non-civilization" and idealized "Noble Savages," they evoked terror, admiration, even imitation. In the late Middle Ages, the now-legitimized Wild People, as both bearers and subjects of heraldic and family crests, even became popular icons of fertility and dynastic promise.

Because Wild People were purportedly of oriental origin and because late medieval visual/literary depictions of them proliferated, it is unsurprising that European explorers, searching for new routes to Asia, expected to encounter such monstrous races as the Wild People and the Amazons in the New World. Early written reports and visual depictions of the inhabitants of the Americas drew heavily on the familiar medieval image of the Wild People. European preconceptions were, to a degree, confirmed by some of the actual customs of Native Americans, as reported by Columbus and his successors. Mirroring the more negative and "savage" construction of the Wild People, the New World inhabitants (whose tribes were rarely differentiated from each other) thus carried clubs, inhabited caves, hunted for their food, wore virtually no clothing except for the leafy girdles and head garlands depicted in some popular images of the European Wild People, and used no iron weapons. Moreover, they seemed sexually promiscuous (to European eyes) and were reputed to practice such "savage" customs as cannibalism. Other reports, emphasizing the gentleness, innocence, and generosity of these indigenous "Americans," reflected the tendency of Renaissance humanism to view the Wild People, through the idealizing lens of primitivism, as exemplars of the now lost, classical Golden Age or, in Christian terms, the state of innocence before the Fall in Eden. Late medieval images of the family life of the now-domesticated Wild People (themselves modeled on depictions of Adam and Eve in Paradise and the domestic life of the Holy Family) influenced early sixteenth-century engravings of New World native family groups. The complex blend of fear and wonder implicit in Europe's cultural conflation of the medieval Wild People with the indigenous New World inhabitants culminated in Montaigne's early seventeenth-century essay *On Cannibals,* which influenced Shakespeare's characterization of "wild" Caliban in *The Tempest.*

## BIBLIOGRAPHY

Bartra, Roger. *Wild Men in the Looking Glass: The Mythic Origins of European Otherness.* Trans. Carl T. Berrisford. Ann Arbor: U of Michigan P, 1994.

Bernheimer, Richard. *Wild Men in the Middle Ages: A Study in Art, Sentiment, and Demonology.* Cambridge, MA: Harvard UP, 1952; rpt. New York: Octagon, 1970.

Chiappelli, Fredi, et al., eds. *First Images of America: The Impact of the New World on the Old.* 2 vols. Berkeley: U of California P, 1976.

Doggett, Rachel, ed. *New World of Wonders: European Images of the Americas, 1492–1700.* Washington, DC: The Folger Shakespeare Library, 1992.

Dudley, Edward, and Maximillian E. Novak, eds. *The Wild Man Within: An Image in Western Thought from the Renaissance to Romanticism.* Pittsburgh, PA: U of Pittsburgh P, 1972.

Husband, Timothy, ed. *The Wild Man: Medieval Myth and Symbolism.* New York: The Metropolitan Museum of Art, 1980.

Sprunger, David A. "Wild Folk and Lunatics in Medieval Romance." In *The Medieval World of Nature: A Book of Essays.* Ed. Joyce E. Salisbury. New York: Garland, 1993, pp. 145–163.

*Lorraine Kochanske Stock*

**SEE ALSO**

Amazons; Columbus, Christopher; Indians and the Americas; Monstrosity, Geographical; New World

## William of Boldensele (fl. 1330–1336)

Dominican author of an influential *Liber de quibusdam ultramarinis partibus* ("Book of Certain Overseas Regions"), completed in 1336. His readable Latin account of a pilgrimage to Egypt and the Holy Land was freely taken over in two later and livelier books: Ludolph von Suchem's *Itinerary* (1340s), and the probably pseudonymous *Mandeville's Travels* (c. 1360).

William of Boldensele was the pen name of Otto von Nyenhusen or Neuhaus, who is known to have entered the Dominican cloister of St. Paul at Minden, to have left without permission in 1330, and to have made his journey not long afterward—one of the first such pilgrimages since the fall of Acre, the last Christian stronghold in Palestine, in 1291. Little else is known about the author beyond what can be learned from his book and its two separate introductory letters.

One of the letters is addressed to Cardinal Hélias Talleyrand de Périgord, cardinal in the papal curia at Avignon and a supporter of a crusade planned by the kings of France and Aragón. The other letter, dated September 29, 1337 and accompanying a requested copy of the manuscript to a Cistercian abbot in Bohemia, calls the work a "little book on the state of the Holy Land."

That is certainly part of what the work is, but its concerns are by no means limited to the Holy Land alone, and the text is actually organized around William's itinerary and experiences, taking the form of a pious, and somewhat chatty, first-person narrative of a grand holy tour. The itinerary begins near Genoa and proceeds by sea through the eastern Mediterranean—with calls only at Genoese possessions en route, the

Venetian territories being avoided—first to Constantinople and then to Egypt; from there it continues overland past Mount Sinai through the Holy Land to Jerusalem and places farther north, ending in Beirut. In following the author's footsteps (and one equestrian journey across the Sinai desert), the reader not only receives a concise digest of historical and legendary information about important sites—the information typically being presented with a certain critical intelligence—but is also witness to a parade of such curiosities as plantains, a giraffe, and three "living" elephants. Counterbalancing both the data and the novelties are several notable devotional reflections on significant elements of the author's faith, including the work's closing metaphorical fusion of the pilgrim-author's desire to return home to a Christian port with every Christian's obligation to aspire to the spiritual harbor of Christ. In addition, William is not shy about being the star of his own narrative; he makes sure his readers know about his substantial retinue and his special favors from the sultan of Egypt. Likewise, he takes care to present himself as an exemplary Christian pilgrim, lamenting a ruined church, for example, or drawing attention to his diligence, or quoting his Muslim interpreter's rebuke when he wants to visit the Dead Sea into which Sodom and Gomorrah had sunk: "You have come as a pilgrim in order to visit places blessed by God; you ought not to approach those that have deserved the curse of the Most High."

The appeal of such a book to more literary-minded writers like Ludolph and the *Mandeville*-author is obvious, and the number of surviving copies and versions—twenty-three Latin manuscripts, all of which derive from the version of the *Liber* sent to Bohemia; six manuscripts of a slightly modified French translation (1351) by Jean le Long of Ypres; and one Middle High German fragment (*c.* 1350–1375) of chapters 2 and 3—suggests that the *Liber* enjoyed a small but respectable favor.

## BIBLIOGRAPHY

Beckers, Hartmut. "Der Orientreisebericht Wilhelms von Boldensele in einer ripuarischen Überlieferung des 14. Jahrhunderts." *Rheinische Vierteljahrblätter* 44 (1980): 148–166.

Deluz, Christiane. "La 'géographie' dans le Liber de Guillaume de Boldensele, pèlerin de Terre Sainte 1336." In *Voyage, quête, et pèlerinage dans la littérature et la civilisation médiévales.* Aix-en-Province: le C.U.E.R.M.A., 1976, pp. 25–38.

Schnath, Georg. "Drei niedersächsische Sinaipilger um 1330: Herzog Heinrich von Braunschweig-Grubenhagen, Wilhelm von Boldensele, Ludolf von Sudheim." In *Festschrift Percy Ernst Schramm zu seinem siebzigsten Geburtstag. . . .* 2 vols. Eds. Peter Classen and Peter Scheibert. Wiesbaden: Franz Steiner, 1964, vol. 1, pp. 461–478.

William of Boldensele. "Des Edelherrn Wilhelm von Boldensele Reise nach dem gelobten Lande." Ed. C.L. Grotefend. *Zeitschrift des historischen Vereins für Niedersachsen.* 1852. Hanover, 1855, pp. 209–286. (Text 236–286).

———. *Liber de quibusdam ultramarinis partibus et praecipue de terra sancta de Guillaume de Boldensele, 1336, suivi de la traduction de Frère Jean le Long, 1351.* Ed. C. Deluz. Thèse de doctorat de troisième cycle. Sorbonne [Paris, 1972], pp. 292–355.

*Iain M. Higgins*

SEE ALSO

Acre; Animals, Exotic; Constantinople; Dominican Friars; Egypt; Elephants; Genoa; Holy Land; Itineraries and *Periploi;* Jerusalem; Ludolf of Suchem; *Mandeville's Travels;* Pilgrimage, Christian; Venice

## William of Rubruck (*c.* 1215?–*c.* 1270?)

Franciscan missionary who traveled to the court of the Mongol Khân Möngke at Karakorum in 1254 and left an important record of his journey.

Little is known about Rubruck. He was most likely born between 1210 and 1230 in Rubruck, near Cassel in French Flanders, not in Ruysbroeck in Brabant, as earlier thought. Although Flemish may have been his native language, he spent much of his life in France, was as fluent in French as in Latin, and was apparently familiar with the geography of central France, which he often used to compare distances while recording his journey to Asia. Nothing is known of his education. His Latin style was not elegant, nor did he demonstrate much familiarity with literature beyond the Vulgate, quoting just once from Virgil's *Aeneid* in his account of his journey. But he was a keen observer, with a strong sense for detail, and many of his observations were the first to be recorded by a Westerner.

Some scholars believe Rubruck accompanied King Louis IX on his crusade that embarked from southern France in 1248, but it is more likely that the Franciscans had dispatched him prior to that date and that he connected with the king's party after it arrived on Cyprus. Rubruck says nothing of why or how he came to know Louis IX or why he was selected for the journey.

Louis IX had heard that Sartaq, son of Batu Khân, the overlord of the western Mongol kingdom, was a Christian convert, and the king wished to develop a Christian base among the Mongols. Thus, Rubruck's mission was not so much diplomatic as evangelical. Bearing letters of introduction from the king and some gifts, he left Acre in April and traveled to Constantinople to gather additional supplies and information before departing for the Crimea, the destination nearest to the known camp of Sartaq. He was accompanied by Bartholomew of Cremona, another friar companion whom he had met in Constantinople, as well as an interpreter, who proved to be of little value.

Rubruck's journey took him along the traditional eastward trade route from Constantinople to the Crimea, from there to his first encounter with the Mongols just east of Soldaia, then on to the Volga camp of Batu Khân, and then over the steppe to the Mongol capital at Karakorum. He spent the first half of 1254 in Möngke's court before beginning his return along the same route back to Batu's court at Sarai near the north end of the Caspian Sea. Next, he traveled a new route southward to Tabriz, then through Armenia across the Euphrates river, and eventually westward into southern Turkey, where he was able to find sea transport to Cyprus to rejoin King Louis IX. By August of 1255, he completed the circle in Tripoli, having traveled more than 8,000 miles in the Mongol world.

Rubruck himself considered the mission a failure because he converted few Mongols and could not persuade Möngke to acknowledge the pope or Christianity. He expressed his frustration in remarking that "I had neither the opportunity nor the time to put the Catholic Faith before him, for a man may not say more in his presence than he [the khân] desires, unless he be an envoy."

However, Rubruck's account was quite different from that of his well-known predecessor, John of Plano Carpini. Although the routes of the two friars were very similar, and both experienced personal hardships in travel and arrogant rejection by the khâns, their reports focused on different aspects of Mongol life and customs. Because the Mongol Empire had curtailed its westward expansion and was rumored to be converting to Christianity, Rubruck did not have to provide the same kind of military reconnaissance of the enemy as had been necessary eight years before; thus he could pay attention to details of geography and culture that his predecessor had not.

The more than thirty-eight chapters of Rubruck's extraordinary account of his journey are filled with personal memories of the dangers encountered and his repulsion at Mongol personal habits. Despite this, he admired their powers of endurance and military expertise, as well as the geographic extent of their empire, on which he commented in a most original way. He was the first to disprove Isidore of Seville's claim that the Caspian was a gulf of the ocean; to correctly identify the sources and directions of the Don and the Volga rivers; and to mention Korea to the West. He was equally keen in observing the cultures, being the first to identify the Seres with the people of Cathay, the first to make objective remarks on Chinese medicine, and the only Western writer to recognize the ideographic nature of Chinese writing. In addition, he correctly noted the parentage of the Slavic language, and is still a major Western source for understanding the Cumans, who inhabited the Crimea at the time of his journey. Finally, the medieval West owed much of its knowledge about the oriental religions to Rubruck's observations. His is the earliest account of Buddhism, and he provided valuable material about the shamans, as well as the first notice of the role of incarnation among the Lamas.

The influence of William of Rubruck's *Journey* is disputed. On his return in 1255, Louis IX was no longer in the Near East, and it was not until about 1257 that he returned to France. Roger Bacon was fascinated by Rubruck's experience and used his narrative as a main source for his writings on comparative religion. Some would also argue that Rubruck's work stimulated missionary efforts to the East. However, few manuscripts of his work survive and they are all of English provenance. Thus, the extent of his influence on continental Europeans is less clear. There were many other travelers to China after Rubruck's return, especially Franciscan missionaries, and an archbishopric was even established in Khanbaliq (the site of modern Beijing); but we have no direct evidence that these missionaries read his account. Other new knowledge began to filter into the West, which, like Rubruck's own account, should have done much to dispel the myths and fables that had long shaped the Western understanding of the mysterious East. However, the travel literature of thirteenth- and fourteenth-century Franciscan missionaries and merchants, including John of Plano Carpini, William of Rubruck, and Marco Polo, did not bring about a major transformation of the Western understanding of the Mongol and Chinese worlds they encountered, only serving to underline the irony of Rubruck's accomplishment.

**BIBLIOGRAPHY**

Boyle, J.A. "The Il-khans of Persia and the Princes of Europe." *Central Asiatic Journal* 20 (1976): 25–40.

Dawson, Christopher, ed. *The Mongol Mission.* See Gen. Bib.

Kappler, Claude and René, eds. and trans. *Guillaume de Rubrouck Envoyé de Saint Louis Voyage dans L'Empire Mongol 1253–1255.* Paris: Payot, 1985.

*The Mission of Friar William of Rubruck: His Journey to the Court of the Great Khan Möngke 1253–1255.* Trans. Peter Jackson, with notes and introduction by Peter Jackson and David Morgan. Hakluyt Society, 2nd series, 173. London: Hakluyt Society, 1990.

*Charles W. Connell*

**SEE ALSO**

Acre; Bartholomew of Cremona; Buddhism; Caspian Sea; China; Cumans; Franciscan Friars; Isidore of Scville; John of Plano Carpini; Khanbaliq; Lamaism; Louis IX; Marco Polo; Missionaries to China; Mongols; Travel Writing in Europe and the Mediterranean Regions; Yuan Dynasty

## William of Tripoli (fl. late 1200s)

A Dominican friar in Acre in the Holy Land, who wrote about Islam and who might have accompanied Marco Polo at the beginning of his journey to the East.

Modern scholars have described William as a successful missionary to Muslims in the Middle East who allegedly recommended the peaceful conversion of Muslims through dialogue as an alternative to crusading. This evaluation stems from the conclusion of what ranked as William's best-known work, *De statu Sarracenorum*, thought to have been written in 1273: ". . . and so, by the simple preaching of God and without philosophical arguments or military arms, [Muslims] will, like simple sheep, seek the baptism of Christ and enter the flock of God. This said and wrote he, who by the instigation of God has already baptized more than a thousand." This remarkable statement has no parallel in any other record describing medieval Latin Christians in the Middle East.

The image of William as a congenial—and extremely successful—missionary was undermined by Peter Engels in his critical edition of *De statu Sarracenorum* in 1992. Engels proved that the text traditionally attributed to William was an elaboration, probably written after 1273 in western Europe, which differs considerably from the original and which is not a manual for missionaries but an attempt to inform Europeans about fundamental Muslim beliefs. The famous conclusion was added to give the text greater authority, but it is an unfounded, improbable invention of the compiler. *De statu* was widely read in later medieval Europe; portions of it were incorporated in the extremely popular *The Book of John Mandeville* (c. 1360) and have been cited as evidence for the "tolerance" of that work.

William's original text, entitled *Notitia de machometo*—and unknown to modern readers before Engels's edition—was written in 1271 at the request of Tebaldo Visconti, an Italian archdeacon of Liège who was then in the Holy Land, and who wanted written information about Islam. Visconti was elected Pope Gregory X later that year (1231–1276). The work is divided into three parts, treating the life of Muhammad and the early history of the Muslim conquest; the Qur'an; and a defense of the Christian faith based on arguments and citations from the Qur'an. To this is added a few chapters on Muslim society and rituals, one describing a mosque. The work is serious and very well informed, although it is uncertain whether William knew Arabic. He was especially interested in Quranic verses that praise Jesus and Mary, contrasting these to the near-absence of Muhammad in the holy book. The work was not much distributed in Europe, but it was used by Nicholas of Cusa in the 1450s.

Though less harsh than that of many of his contemporaries, William's attitude toward Islam was still far from being an irenic criticism of crusading. *Notitia* ends with the phrase: "Everybody preach, prophecize, and expect the Saracens to be divided into three parts, of which the first will fly to the Christians, the second will perish under the sword, and the third will perish in the desert. Amen."

Twentieth-century biographical accounts of William have been elaborate and detailed but are mostly unfounded. It is certain that he was in Europe during 1264, seeking help for the Latins in the Holy Land. According to the "Prologue" of Marco Polo's *Divisament dou monde*, the three Polos had an audience with Pope Gregory X in Acre, immediately after his election to the papacy, at which he blessed their journey to the East and chose two Dominicans, "the wisest in all that province," to accompany them. They were given authority to ordain priests and bishops as well as to grant absolution to the degree that the pope himself could. One of these friars was named "William of

Tripoli." The papal commission was almost certainly exaggerated, if it occurred at all, and if the friar is identical with the author of the *Noticia,* it is no great honor to him: according to the *Divisament,* the two friars got as far as Ayas (in Asia Minor) before they became afraid for their lives and abandoned the Polos, in the company of the grand master of the Templars.

**BIBLIOGRAPHY**

Wilhelm von Tripolis. *Notitia de machometo: De statu Sarracenorum.* Ed. Peter Engels. Corpus Islamo-Christianum, Series Latina 4. Altenburg: Oros, 1992.

*Kurt Villads Jensen*

**SEE ALSO**

Acre; Dominican Friars; Lajazzo; *Mandeville's Travels;* Marco Polo; Nicholas of Cusa

## Witte de Hese, Johannes [Jan Voet] (fl. 1389–1392?)

A cleric whose late-fourteenth-century pilgrimage took him to eastern Asia, where he had unlikely adventures, according to a travel narrative, attributed to him, that enjoyed moderate popularity in the fifteenth and sixteenth centuries.

Several fifteenth-century manuscripts preserve a Latin text, which lacks any introductory rubric or title, beginning "In the year of our Lord 1389, I, Johannes Witte de Hese, a priest in the diocese of Utrecht, was in Jerusalem, in May, visiting the holy sites there." The ensuing narrative of some 4,400 words purports to record the adventures of this Dutch cleric-pilgrim—the diocese of Utrecht in the late 1300s was roughly coterminous with modern Holland—on overland and sea journeys throughout Asia during some two-and-one-half years, returning him to Jerusalem at the end of the narrative. The work was printed ten times between *c.* 1490 and *c.* 1507, each edition styling it *Itinerarius* (hence its modern title). It was translated into Middle Dutch around 1450.

According to the text, Johannes Witte de Hese "continued [his] pilgrimage" from Jerusalem evidently (and impossibly) by following the Jordan River to the Red Sea, where he sampled grotesque flying fish while en route to Egypt to visit sites associated with the infancy of Jesus. He crossed the Sinai desert to the Monastery of St. Catherine, where he observed several wonders, and at nearby Marach [Marah] he watched a unicorn purify

water poisoned nightly by serpents. Returning to the Nile via "the land of Ur of the Chaldeans, where the Red Jews live," Witte boarded a ship at Damiad [Damietta], then sailed along the coast of Ethiopia, "called Lower India," near territory where pygmies fight storks (though the tradition more usually referred to cranes). He managed to survive the voyage past one sea of sand (*Mare Arenosum*) and another with an iron-attracting lodestone bottom (*Mare Iecoreum*), as well as short, stocky "Monoculi," who stride into the water and devour unlucky sailors. At Andranopolis, in "Middle India," he encountered many Christians and admired the urban architecture; nearby, he and companions who enter the story unannounced were taken captive by brigands of the great khân (*Grandicanis*), who ultimately liberated them, "because [they] were pilgrims of St. Thomas," at the frontier of "Upper India."

After more marine obstacles, Witte arrived at Edessa, where he saw the spectacular palace of Prester John. It stands atop some 900 columns, which must be sturdy because the square building measures two German miles on each side and rises seven stories, each level exhibiting various marvels and dedicated to a specific Christian entity (in order: prophets, patriarchs, virgins, martyrs and confessors, apostles, the Virgin Mary and angels, and the Trinity). Among the palace's wonders are a bell, fashioned by St. Thomas himself, that exorcises demons, and a looking-glass that reveals everything going on in the world. In Edessa, Witte also found the Four Rivers of Paradise and an all-male population visited three times a year by women from "Terra Feminarum," a nearby island. Four days away by foot lies Hulna, the island city that houses the shrine of St. Thomas; the sea parts for pilgrims as they go to celebrate the saint's feast day. Witte recalls the liturgy, in which the patriarch holds the saint's arm, which distributes the eucharistic Host only to worthy communicants; he states emphatically that he witnessed the hand withdraw the sacrament from three sinners when he was there "in 1391." Stones set in the church's tower shine so brightly that they direct mariners who are fourteen days out to sea (for slow vessels, roughly the distance from New York harbor to Savannah, Georgia).

After departing from Prester John, Witte sailed "in the remotest parts of the sea" for nearly a one-and-one-half years, roaming the verdant "Root of Paradise," watching the sun set splendidly against the walls of the Terrestrial Paradise, pausing at Purgatory to win the release of three souls, narrowly escaping death when an island he is cooking on turns out to be a whale that submerges, hearing Sirens, and approaching Gog and Magog, before returning to Jerusalem, which he refuses to describe because it is well-known territory. Although the text is spare in giving compass directions, Witte appears consistently to tend eastward—he makes only one reference to winds carrying him to the north—and thus the account evidently describes the circumnavigation of a globe with three continents.

The *Itinerarius* has characteristics that link it to other medieval travel accounts, both real and imaginary: an asseverating narrator, distances given in days' journeys (generally in threes, fours, and multiples of six), interest in public architecture, and fascination for natural and mechanical marvels. Like the putative narrator of *The Book of John Mandeville,* Johannes Witte de Hese has a name that is similar to, but not definitively identifiable with, people in the historical record (including students at the University of Cologne, as well as aldermen and a cathedral canon in the city of Utrecht around 1400). Information in the text appears to come from the *Letter of Prester John, Herzog Ernst,* and the *Legend of St. Brendan,* but borrowings are not literal enough to establish actual quotation.

The *Itinerarius* survives in five manuscripts (the earliest is reliably dated 1424), seven incunables (*c.* 1490–1499), and four early printed editions (1504, 1505, *c.* 1507, 1565); three additional manuscript copies were made from an incunable. The first edition (at Cologne) directly or indirectly underlies versions produced by six other printers at Antwerp, Deventer, and Paris. During its first century-and-one-half of circulation, the Latin text underwent three extensive revisions, so that the earliest manuscript and the last printing seem to present wholly different narratives. The changes are largely stylistic rather than substantive, however, turning the original into something more literary rather than less fantastical (one early manuscript *adds* first-person claims of authenticity; two early manuscripts and the [related] first incunable edition cast part of the narrative in the third person). The context of the *Itinerarius* in manuscript codices and citations from it by humanists suggest that it initially enjoyed a respectful reception. Criticized during the seventeenth and eighteenth centuries for its "medieval gullibility," the work has since the later 1800s been seen in the context of early Dutch literary culture and the development of travel literature as a genre. The mid-fifteenth-

century Middle Dutch translation, which renders the earliest state of the Latin text, is known from three manuscripts that identify the traveler as Jan/Johan Voet. They offer valuable information about early Dutch dialects.

Reference works catalog the putative traveler-author of the *Itinerarius* under many different names: Jean/Joannes/Johannes [de] Hees/Helt/Hese/Hesse ("Witte," a surname found only in three early manuscripts, is generally not known). Scholars who give 1489 as the date of the journey follow an error found in one of three later printed editions; the association of Johannes Witte de Hese with Maastricht is specious. The work's ultimate significance rests less on its accuracy or literary quality than on its record of how a northern European with moderate education might have imagined Asia during the later Middle Ages, as well as on the light it sheds on the early history of printing.

**BIBLIOGRAPHY**

Beckmann, Johann. *Litteratur der älteren Reisebeschreibungen.* 4 vols. in 2. Göttingen: Röwer, 1807–1810.

Friedman, John Block. *The Monstrous Races in Medieval Art and Thought.* Cambridge, MA: Harvard UP, 1981; rpt. Syracuse, NY: Syracuse UP, 2000.

Gregor, Helmut. *Das Indienbild des Abendlandes (bis zum Ende des 13. Jahrhunderts).* Wiener Dissertationen aus dem Gebiete der Geschichte 4. Vienna: Geyer, 1964.

Rogers, Francis M. *The Quest for Eastern Christians: Travels and Rumor in the Age of Discovery.* Minneapolis: U of Minnesota P, 1962.

Vries, Mathias de, ed. "Fragment eener Nederlandsche Vertaling van het Reisverhaal van Joannes de Hese." *Verslagen en Berigten uitgegeven door de Vereeniging ter Bevordering der Oude Nederlandsche Letterkunde* 2 (1845): 5–32.

Wasser, Ben A.J. *Nederlandse pelgrims naar het heilige land.* Zutphen: Terra, 1983.

———. "Die Peregrinatie van Iherusalem: Pilgrimsverslagen van Nederlandse Jerusalemgangers in de 15e, 16e, en 17e Eeuw: Ontstaan en Ontwikkeling." *De Gulden Passer: Bulletin van de Vereeniging der Antwerpsche Bibliophielen* 69 (1991): 5–72.

Westrem, Scott D. "A Medieval Travel Book's Editors and Translators: Managing Style and Accommodating Dialect in Johannes Witte de Hese's *Itinerarius.*" In *The Medieval Translator* 4. Ed. Roger Ellis and Ruth Evans. Exeter, England: U of Exeter P, 1994, pp. 153–180.

———. *Broader Horizons: Johannes Witte de Hese's* Itinerarius *and Medieval Travel Narratives.* Cambridge, MA: The Medieval Academy of America, 2000.

Zarncke, Friedrich. "Der Priester Johannes." *Abhandlungen der Philologisch-Historischen Classe der Königlich Sächsischen Gesellschaft der Wissenschaften* 7–8 (1879, 1883), vol. 7, pp. 827–1028; vol. 8, pp. 1–186.

Scott D. Westrem

**SEE ALSO**

Brendan's Voyage, St.; Catherine in the Sinai, Monastery of St.; Edessa; Ethiopians; Four Rivers of Paradise; Gog and Magog; India; Jerusalem; Lodestone; *Mandeville's Travels;* Mongols; Paradise, Travel to; Pilgrimage, Christian; Prester John; Purgatory; Red Jews; Scholarship on Medieval European Geography and Travel; Travel Writing in Europe and the Mediterranean Regions

## Women in Mongol Society

Women in Mongol society enjoyed a greater recognition of their economic value, and consequently held a higher social position, than did their contemporaries in China, the Arab world, or Europe. In the mid-thirteenth century, John of Plano Carpini and William of Rubruck both noted women's special position in Mongol society, sentiments echoed a century later by Ibn Battūta. Although surviving records tell more about noble women in Mongol society than about other steppe dwellers or members of lower classes, considerable information on women's place in nomadic societies has been preserved.

Mongol women were partners with their men in the tasks demanded by nomadic herding on the Eurasian steppe. Their labor was crucial to the economic well-being of the families and clans that constituted the tribe, the basic social unit. Women's responsibilities included the household, where they cooked, sewed, processed felt, churned butter, and made cheese. They also moved the camp from one seasonal grazing area to another, loading the *gers* (or *yurts,* felt tents) and household possessions on wagons, driving these with the herds, and making camp again. Duties such as herding and milking cattle, sheep, and goats were shared with men. Although there was a recognized division of labor (for example, men butchered livestock while women cut and tanned the hides), Chinggis's *yasa* (the Mongol law code, which probably recapitulated established steppe custom) prescribed that women carry out all the duties of men during their frequent absences for war or the hunt. Because women were not insulated from warfare on the open steppe and might be called on to defend the camp and herds, they too were trained in riding and archery. A few Mongol women even hunted or rode to war with the men, but their ability to assume complete responsibility for the camp, which allowed the total mobilization of the tribe's men, was actually more important to Mongol martial success.

Steppe tribes were exogamous, and although wives might be stolen, families generally contracted marriages over several generations from a particular tribe, cementing long-term alliances. Mongol women, unlike their counterparts elsewhere in East Asia, had legal and customary privileges. John of Plano Carpini reported that Mongols put to death both men and women caught committing adultery, adding that "if a virgin commit fornication they kill both the man and the woman." Although Mongol men were allowed to have more than one wife (khâns had up to four wives, each with her own household, in addition to concubines), prospective grooms had to make a generous bride-payment and maintain each wife in a separate household within the camp; thus, the average Mongol probably could not afford to live a polygamous life. Even in the case of plural marriage or concubinage, however, no offspring were illegitimate and all had inheritance rights. In addition, on the death of a khân, his widowed chief wife was generally made regent until a new leader could be chosen; some khatuns (or consorts) reigned over the Mongol Empire or within a khânate for several years.

Women did not enjoy completely equal status with men, however. While women could own property, men generally inherited wealth through the complex patrilineal system that characterized Mongol society. Levirate, the remarriage of a widow with a dead husband's son or brother, was the rule. Widows were not permitted to remarry outside the family because, in Mongol belief, widows would be claimed by their former husbands in the next life. To preserve the family and to provide for widows, the youngest son married his father's widow(s) (except for his own mother), or a younger brother wed an elder brother's widow(s). On a practical level, this custom persisted because it was very difficult for a woman alone to manage a household and raise children.

Privileges accorded to Mongol women should not blind one to their fundamentally unequal status. Mongol men, no less than their contemporaries in other societies with more complicated social systems, saw women more as objects than as equals. The *Secret History of the Mongols* abounds with references to women as booty to be won in war; hence Chinggis Khân's definition of the greatest joys a man can know: "To conquer his enemies and drive them before him. To ride their horses and take away their possessions. To see the faces of those who were dear to them bedewed with tears, and to clasp their wives and daughters in his arms." For the khân and his steppe followers, women, like possessions, were prizes to be won or lost in the contests waged by men.

**BIBLIOGRAPHY**
Dawson, Christopher, ed. *The Mongol Mission.* See Gen. Bib.
*The Mission of Friar William of Rubruck: His Journey to the Court of the Great Khan Möngke 1253–1255.* Trans. Peter Jackson, with notes and introduction by Peter Jackson and David Morgan. Hakluyt Society, 2nd series, 173. London: Hakluyt Society, 1990.
Morgan, David. *The Mongols.* Oxford: Blackwell, 1986.
Rossabi, Morris. "Kubilai Khan and the Women in His Family." In *Sino-Mongolica: Festschrift für Herbert Franke.* Ed. W. Bauer. Wiesbaden: Harrassowitz, 1979, pp. 153–180.
Ryan, James D. "Christian Wives of Mongol Khans: Tartar Queens and Missionary Expectations in Asia." *Journal of the Royal Asiatic Society* 8.3 (1998): 1–11.
*Secret History of the Mongols.* F.W. Cleaves, trans. and ed. Vol. 1. Cambridge, MA: Harvard UP, 1982.
Spuler, Bertold. *History of the Mongols, Based on Eastern and Western Accounts of the Thirteenth and Fourteenth Centuries.* Trans. H. and S. Drummond. London: Routledge, 1972.
Vladimirtsov, B. *Le régime social des Mongols—le féodalisme nomade.* Trans. M. Carsow. Paris: Adrien-Maisonneuve, 1948.

*James D. Ryan*

**SEE ALSO**
Ibn Battūta, Abu Abdallah; John of Plano Carpini; Mongol Khatuns; Mongols; Nomadism and Pastoralism; William of Rubruck; Women Travelers, Islamic; Yasa

## Women Travelers, Islamic

Medieval Muslim women of various social classes traveled relatively infrequently, but sometimes they did journey great distances. They left no descriptions of their journeys, and we learn of them from books composed by male authors. Among the best sources are the *Marvels (Wonders) of India* by Buzurg ibn Shahriyar (953 C.E.), the *Rihla* (Journey) of Ibn Jubayr (d. 1217), and the *Travels* of Ibn Battūta (d. 1368).

Islam arose in Arabic society where nomadic migration, travel for commerce, and pilgrimage were common. Women participated in these activities alongside men, but the hazards and discomfort of travel made it undesirable. Concerns for safety, privacy, and prestige led women to avoid travel. Islam spread among many non-Arab nomadic societies where women's spatial mobility was less restricted. Despite the rise of veiling and seclusion, which especially affected free urban Muslim women, travel away from home remained accessible to them and was socially acceptable, though certain laws and rules of propriety had to be observed. In general, Muslim women were not to travel beyond the realm of Islam and had to have a male escort subject to legal specifications. Free women had the right to refuse to accompany their husbands on their journeys. Slave women were normally not given the choice, but in principle, servants could not be compelled to travel with their master against their will.

Most women traveled for social or religious reasons. Brides traveled to join prospective husbands; wives accompanied husbands and journeyed to visit their natal families while married or to return home if widowed or divorced. Ibn Battūta's first marriage was negotiated with her father in the woman's absence while passing through Tunis in a caravan; the bride then was sent to Tripoli where the caravan had moved in the meantime. This match was quickly abandoned, and Ibn Battūta found another candidate in the daughter of a fellow-traveler from Fez; she too had to be sent for.

Travel was fraught with danger. Disease, lack of water, and nomad depredations threatened at all times. Pilgrims joined caravans because it was both customary and also more secure. In caravans destined for Mecca the number of women was greater than usual; for protection they usually stayed in the middle of the caravan. In case of attack, women, even those of high rank, could be robbed, raped, enslaved, or held for ransom. Piracy was rampant, and shipwrecked passengers were at the mercy of their rescuers. Only the largest ships had cabins that could be used as accommodations for ladies or families of paying passengers. On land, curtained litters carried by camels, horses, or two to four donkeys were available for women's comfort and privacy. Queens and princesses traveled well protected and supplied, and were able to extend protection to male travelers like Ibn Battūta.

Perceived need was sufficient cause for women to travel without men or under unusual circumstances. The pre-Islamic custom of women accompanying men to the battlefield continued for a while under Islam, and the first Muslim sailors were encouraged to bring their wives on board. There were other secular occasions for travel, including affairs of state for highborn ladies. Princesses often married abroad. Ibn Battūta traveled to Constantinople in the train of a Byzantine princess who was married to a Muslim Mongol ruler and was returning home to give birth. In the thirteenth and fourteenth centuries, Mongol princes and their wives, including those who accepted Islam, were expected to travel long distances to the annual meeting in Central Asia. On occasion, royal women served as unofficial diplomats whose proclaimed mission was pilgrimage. Sometimes, travel was forced by danger. After a short reign over Egypt (1250), Queen Shajarat al-Durr attempted to find security in Jerusalem. Princess Radiya of Delhi (r. 1236–1240) was deposed, raised a rebellion, and was killed in flight.

Reasons for women's travel included a range of religious purposes, such as emigration (*hijra*), pilgrimage to Mecca (*hajj*), visits to holy places (*ziyāra*), and search for education. These high goals made it possible for single ladies, married women without their husbands, and groups of women to travel without opprobrium. The first emigration of Muslim converts from Mecca to Ethiopia included several women, among them Muhammad's daughter Ruqaiya and her husband, the future Caliph 'Uthman. Among the emigrants from Mecca to Medina there were some wives who had converted and left their pagan husbands behind. After Islam's success was ensured, a number of Meccan women traveled the distance of 200 miles to Muhammad at Medina to bring him the "women's oath."

Islam legitimized travel for all Muslims on the occasion of pilgrimage to Mecca (*hajj*). Required once in a lifetime, this journey gave women considerable freedom. The wife did not need her husband's consent for it (although if she went against his wish, she was not entitled to support for her travel), and during *hajj* ceremonies she was not subject to his authority, nor did she need to veil (in fact, was prohibited to cover) her face. Pilgrimage could occupy from several months to several years of a person's life. Among scholars who pursued religious education by extending their stay in Mecca or Medina were a few women. One of them was Shaykha Zaynab (1248–1339), nicknamed "the goal of the world's travel," a reference to the many people who journeyed great distances to study with her. Another was Sitt Zahida (d. 1326), famous for her piety and served by a group of male mystic devotees.

Some famous queens and princesses performed the pilgrimage, marking their devotion with charitable works and pious endowments along the way. The consort of the Abbasid caliph al-Mahdi Khayzuran made her first pilgrimage of 787 as a slave concubine; in 788, she came to Mecca from Baghdad as queen-mother (of the caliph Hārūn al-Rashīd, [r. 786–809]). To celebrate her triumph, she purchased Muhammad's former house in Mecca and converted it into the sacred Mosque of the Nativity. Hārūn al-Rashīd's wife Zubayda, a four-time pilgrim, had caravansaries and watering stations built along the road between Mecca and al-Kufa in Iraq, which was named in her honor *Darb Zubayda*. Shaghab, mother of the caliph al-Muqtadir (r. 908–932), donated one million dinars each year from her estates in support of pilgrimage and created many endowments in Mecca and Medina. Ibn Jubayr reported the lavish pilgrimage of Malika Khatun, the wife of the ruler of Aleppo, Nūr al-Dīn (r. 1174–1181). Sitt Hadaq, a high-placed woman at the court of a Mamluk sultan of Egypt and pilgrim to Mecca in 1328, commemorated her return from pilgrimage by erecting a mosque in Cairo. The mother of the Egyptian Mamluk sultan al-Ashraf Sha'ban II, Baraka Khatun, was honored by a magnificent pilgrimage procession in 1368, called the "Year of the Sultan's Mother."

**BIBLIOGRAPHY**

Eickelman, Dale F., and James Piscatori, eds. *Muslim Travellers: Pilgrimage, Migrations, and the Religious Imagination.* Berkeley and Los Angeles: U of California P, 1990.

Faroqhi, Suraiya. *Pilgrims and Sultans: The Hajj under the Ottomans, 1517–1683.* London, New York: Tauris, 1994.

Morinis, Alan. *Sacred Journeys: The Anthropology of Pilgrimage.* Westport, CT, and London: Greenwood, 1992.

Netton, Ian Richard, ed. *Golden Roads: Migration, Pilgrimage and Travel in Mediaeval and Modern Islam.* Richmond, Surrey: Curzon, 1993.

Peters, F.E. *The Hajj: The Muslim Pilgrimage to Mecca and the Holy Places.* Princeton, NJ: Princeton UP, 1994.

Roded, Ruth. *Women in Islamic Biographical Collections: From Ibn Sa'd to Who's Who.* Boulder, CO: Lynne Rienner, 1994.

Tolmacheva, Marina A. "Ibn Battuta on Women's Travel in the Dar al-Islam." In *Women and the Journey: The Female Travel Experience.* Ed. Bonnie Frederick and Susan H. McLeod. Pullman, WA: Washington State UP, 1993, pp. 119–140.

———. "Female Piety and Patronage in the Medieval Hajj." In *Women in the Medieval Islamic World.* Ed. Gavin R.G. Hambly. New York: St. Martin's Press, 1998, pp. 161–179.

*Marina A. Tolmacheva*

**SEE ALSO**
Baghdad; Caravans; Ibn Battūta, Abu Abdallah; Ibn Jubayr; Mamluks; Mecca; Medina; Muslim Travelers and Trade; Pilgrimage, Christian; Piracy; Sunnism; Shi'ism

### Wonders of the East

Common name for an Old English prose translation of a Latin description of marvelous animals and monstrous races derived from other Latin texts, such as the *Letter of Pharasmanes* (Fermes) to Hadrian on the wonders of the East. Though both surviving Old English versions retain Latin spellings—MS Tiberius B.V. records the Old English version and a recension of the Latin source in alternating paragraphs (see below)—most toponyms (such as Antimolima, Lentibelsinea, Locotheo, and Gorgoneus) remain unidentifiable. All the marvels mentioned, however, are localized between Babylonia and the Red Sea.

The text refers to many kingdoms or islands, only one-third of which are specifically named; all are identified by proximity to Babylon or Babylonian lands, the Nile and the "Bryxonte," the Red Sea, or simply "where the sun rises." The movement, for example, from Liconia-in-Gallia to a place "beyond the Bryxonte, east of the river" to an area "on the Bryxonte" to "another island south of the Bryxonte," to "another kingdom on the south side of the ocean" to "another place" to a "certain island in the Red Sea" suggests the author follows no particular geographical scheme, as Honorius Augustodunensis does in his *Imago mundi* (c. 1110), although it implies a familiarity with a type of map similar to the Ebstorf or Hereford *mappaemundi*.

Of the seventeen monstrous races included, six have names: the dog-headed "Conopoenas" (Old English *healfhundingas*); the "Homodubii" (used twice: for long-haired men who live on raw fish and for gentle-voiced creatures, part human and part ass); the cannibalistic black giants called the "Hostes"; the half-human/half-soothsayer, cannibalistic "Donestre"; and the Ethiopians (Old English *silhearwan* [T]/*sigelwara* [V]). In addition to other races of tricolored men, men with eyes and mouths in their chests, and an exceedingly swift race of men with enormous ears, two unnamed races of monstrous women are included: one race of huntresses and one of boar-tusked, ox-tailed giants whom Alexander annihilates (because, as the Old English text reads, they were "offensive in body and ignoble").

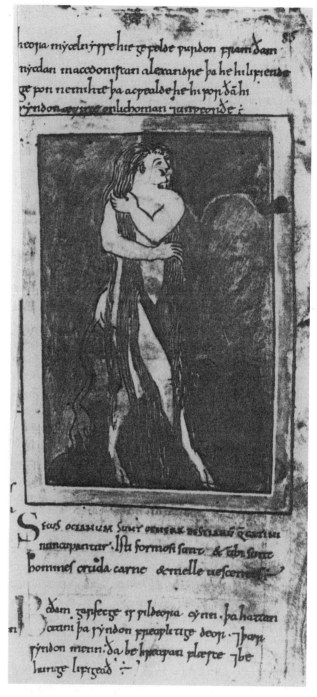

Women with tusks, long hair and horse feet. London, British Library MS Cotton Tiberius B.V, fol. 85r, *c.* 11th century. Courtesy of the British Library.

The collection of animals ranges from marvelous gold-digging ants, ram-horned serpents, dragons, griffins, and the phoenix—all staples of classical and patristic lore—to real, but no less fascinating, elephants, to the strange ass-eared, bird-footed, wooly Lertices. Sites of interest include "the works of Alexander," the Lakes of the Sun and Moon, a temple built in the days of Bel and Jove, jewel-bearing trees, and "the biggest mountain between the Median mountain and Armenia."

One of the two surviving manuscripts (London, British Library MS Cotton Tiberius B.V.; fols. 78ᵛ–87ʳ), part of an early eleventh-century miscellany that also includes the Cotton "Anglo-Saxon" map (fol. 56ᵛ), is a dual-language version beautifully illustrated with thirty-seven colored miniatures. The second manuscript (MS Cotton Vitellius A. xv.; fols. 98ᵛ–106ᵛ) is accompanied by no Latin text, slightly abbreviated, and less finely illustrated, with twenty-nine uncolored drawings; it is written in the first hand of the *Beowulf* manuscript and bound in a codex with *Beowulf* and *Judith* between a fragment of the *Life of St. Christopher* and the *Letter of Alexander the Great to Aristotle* (in the same tenth- or eleventh-century hand).

**BIBLIOGRAPHY**

Campbell, Mary B. *The Witness and the Other World: Exotic European Travel Writing, 400–1600.* Ithaca, NY: Cornell UP, 1988.

Knappe, Fritz A., ed. *Das angelsächsische Prosastück Die Wunder des Ostens.* Berlin: Bernstein, 1906.

McGurk, Patrick, et al., eds. *An Eleventh-Century Anglo-Saxon Illustrated Miscellany: British Library Cotton Tiberius B.V, part 1.* Early English Manuscripts in Facsimile 21. Copenhagen: Rosenkilde and Bagger, 1993.

Malone, Kemp, ed. *The Nowell Codex: British Museum Cotton Vitellius A. XV, Second MS.* Early English Manuscripts in Facsimile 12. Copenhagen: Rosenkilde and Bagger, 1963.

Orchard, Andy. *Pride and Prodigies: Studies in the Monsters of the Beowulf Manuscript.* Cambridge, England: Brewer, 1995.

Rypins, Stanley, ed. *Three Old English Prose Texts in MS Cotton Vitellius A.XV.* EETS, o.s., 161. London: Oxford UP, 1924 [for 1921].

Scheil, Andrew P. "Bodies and Boundaries: Studies in the Construction of Social Identity in Select Late Anglo-Saxon Prose Texts." Diss., U of Toronto, 1996.

Swanton, Michael, ed. and trans. "Wonders of the East." In *Anglo-Saxon Prose,* 2nd edition. London: Dent, 1993, pp. 227–233.

*Robert K. Upchurch*

**SEE ALSO**

Cotton World Map; Ebstorf World Map; Ethiopians; Hereford Map; Honorius Augustodunensis; *Mappamundi;* Monstrosity, Geographical; Pliny the Elder; Red Sea; Stonehenge and Other Megalithic Marvels

# Y

## Yasa

The body of Mongol law, whose promulgation was attributed to Chinggis Khân (d. 1227), the founder of the Mongol Empire. The word itself is a Turkish derivative (rendered *yāsā* or *yāsa* in Arabic and Persian) from the Mongolian *jasagh,* and refers to both a single statute and the entire legal corpus. The term will be used here in the latter sense unless otherwise indicated.

The origins and nature of the *yasa* have been a subject of some debate in recent decades. Earlier scholars believed that it was a unified and systematic code of law enacted in 1206, at the time of the great *quriltai* (assembly) during which Chinggis Khân was officially proclaimed the supreme ruler of all the Mongols. These scholars attempted to reconstruct a detailed version of the code by piecing together the individual statutes found in a variety of sources, particularly *The History of the World Conqueror* by Juwaynī (d. 1283). In a series of articles that appeared in the early 1970s, David Ayalon questioned the credibility of Juwaynī's evidence, at least as far as it presented a comprehensive or even representative list of the *yasa*'s contents, and conclusively showed that the versions presented by other Muslim writers (including the hitherto much-vaunted Maqrāzī [d. 1442] and the apparently independent report by the Syriac writer Bar Hebraeus [d. 1286]) were in large measure ultimately derived from Juwaynī's work. Later, David Morgan suggested that given the lack of explicit contemporary evidence, it might be questioned whether Chinggis Khân himself issued this code or whether this was only a post facto attribution to him by his descendants, searching to legitimize their own laws and actions, especially their struggles with rival kinsmen.

Most of this research was based on Persian, Arabic, and Latin sources, but in 1993, Igor de Rachewiltz, drawing on studies by Russian and Chinese scholars and working mainly with sources in Chinese and Mongolian (particularly *The Secret History of the Mongols* [1228?]), demonstrated that the *yasa,* consisting "of a number of binding injunctions and normative rules concerning matters of governance, military administration, the administration of justice, the division of spoils, etc.," was indeed formulated by Chinggis Khân, albeit over time and not in a systematic way. The *yasa* was meant to be a body of fundamental laws, and thus can be distinguished from *jarligh*s, or ad hoc orders on specific issues. While there is no direct indication that the *yasa* was put in writing at this early date, there is circumstantial evidence indicating that this was the case. It was left to Chinggis's son and successor Ögödei (r. 1229–1241) to systematize the various laws, statutes, and orders into a unified code. Ögödei initiated the custom of proclaiming anew the *yasa,* which henceforth was known as the "Great *Yasa,*" at the enthronement of each great khân. The Great *Yasa* was not immutable, and as early as Ögödei's reign some changes were made, although they did not affect its tenor. The enforcement of the *yasa* was the responsibility of the ruler as well as specially appointed officials known as *jarghuchi*s, investigating magistrates who enjoyed the right to conduct courts-martial and order executions.

The full text of the Great *Yasa* is not extant, but since its provisions were promulgated among conquered

# Y

populations, notices regarding its contents have come down to us in a number of sources in different languages. Not surprisingly, the statutes contained in *The Secret History of the Mongols* deal mainly with military matters, as do many of those found in later sources. Two laws are recorded by John of Plano Carpini, papal envoy to the great khân's court in 1246: one mandates capital punishment for anyone who declares himself khân and the other dictates that the Mongols "are to bring the whole world into subjection to them, nor are they to make peace with any nation unless they first submit to them . . ." John, however, does not use the word *yasa*, but refers to "laws and statutes" ("*leges et statuta*"), so it is not certain that he is referring to the Great *Yasa*. In any event, this is an an attempt to institutionalize an important aspect of the Mongol imperial ideology by giving it the status of law.

One statute regarding trade is found in a later Mamluk source, Ibn Fadlallâh al-'Umarî (d. 1349): "One who is entrusted three times with merchandise and loses (or squanders) it [each time] is to be executed." This echoes the well-known interest of the Mongol elite in promoting international commerce, in which they often participated as investors in trading partnerships (*ortaq*s). The available material, however, offers no evidence of a developed body of Mongol law regulating trade, such as can be found in Islamic jurisprudence. A statute of the *yasa* defines the basic characteristics of the *Jam*—the postal system based on horse relays that was of prime importance for communications within the far-flung Mongol Empire as well as for travel and trade. It must be noted, however, that these statutes, recorded by later sources, were not necessarily part of the original *yasa* of Chinggis Khân, but may have been added by his successors.

The dissolution of the united Mongol Empire (c. 1260), did not lead to the disappearance of the *yasa*. Rather, the rulers of the various Mongol successor states often referred to the *yasa* of Chinggis Khân, not the least in their struggles with each other. For example, Berke—the ruler of the Golden Horde in what is now southern Russia—wrote to the Mamluk sultan Baybars in 1263 and complained that his cousin Hülegü, ruler of the il-khânid state in Persia, had contravened the *yasa*. Here, as is often the case, it is not clear whether the reference is to the entire corpus of law or to only one particular statute or even to an order of Chinggis Khân. In fact, in the Islamic world at least, the term *yasa* came

increasingly to be used to mean a "command" or "order" of an individual Chinggisid ruler.

Although the Mongols in Persia eventually converted to Islam in the late thirteenth century, there is evidence that they remained loyal to the *yasa* of Chinggis Khân, at least as they understood it. Ghazan Khân (r. 1295–1304), who became a Muslim with much pageantry on his accession to the il-khânid throne, saw no contradiction between his newfound religion and his adherence to the *yasa*. This was one reason why he and the Persian Mongols in general were labeled heretics by the Syrian religious scholar Ibn Taymiyya (d. 1328), who, in a famous judicial decision, called on the Mamluks and Muslims in general to continue fighting them. It appears that within a generation or so interest in the *yasa* waned in the il-khânid state, but it continued to be have some force in the various Mongol or quasi-Mongol successor states in Central Asia. It remains an open question how much these later notices to the *yasa* actually refer to the Great *Yasa* of Chinggis Khân, or to a hodgepodge of Mongol traditions and laws (some perhaps going back to the great conqueror) with more recent innovations.

**BIBLIOGRAPHY**

Amitai-Preiss, Reuven. "Ghazan, Islam and Mongol Tradition: A View from the Mamluk Sultanate." *Bulletin of the School of Oriental and African Studies* 59 (1996): 1–10.

Ayalon, David. "The Great Yasa of Chingiz Khân: A Re-examination." *Studia Islamica* 33 (1971): 97–140; 34 (1971): 151–180; C1 (36): 113–158; C2 (1973): 107–156; reprint in D. Ayalon, *Outsiders in the Land of Islam.* London: Variorum, 1988.

Haider, M. "The Mongol Traditions and Their Survival in Central Asia (XIV–XV Centuries)." *Central Asiatic Journal* 28 (1984): 57–79.

Morgan, David O., "The Great *Yāsā* of Chingiz Khān and Mongol Law in the Ĭlkhānate." *Bulletin of the School of Oriental and African Studies* 49 (1986): 163–176.

de Rachewiltz, Igor. "Some Reflections on Činggis Qan's Jasaγ." *East Asian History* 6 (1993): 91–104.

Vernadsky, George. "The Scope and Contents of Chingis Khân's *Yasa*." *Harvard Journal of Asiatic Studies* 3 (1938): 337–360.

*Reuven Amitai-Preiss*

**SEE ALSO**

Baybars I; Hülegü; Inner Asian Trade; Inner Asian Travel; John of Plano Carpini; Mamluks; Mongols; *Secret History of the Mongols, The*

## Yuan Dynasty

First proclaimed by Khubilai (r. 1215–1294), grandson of Chinggis Khân, in 1271, the Yuan dynasty became the first alien dynasty to rule all of China. Mongol rule of China continued until 1368. Although his authority was challenged by other Mongol princes, Khubilai was also nominal ruler of the entire Mongol Empire.

The conquest of China by the Mongol great khân began in 1234 with the fall of the Jurchen Jin state in north China. In 1271, after a prolonged struggle with his cousin Kaidu and Kaidu's allies in Central Asia, Khubilai announced the founding of his dynasty, named *Yuan,* a term meaning "origin" that within the context of the classic Chinese text, the *I Ching* or *Book of Changes,* signified "the primal force" or the "origins of the universe." He then marched south and in 1279 defeated the Southern Song dynasty to become the first emperor of a conquest dynasty to rule the whole of China as well as the Inner Asian steppes.

Until his death in 1294, Khubilai established a pattern for ruling China that was little altered by his descendants. He clearly understood China and brilliantly devised accommodations that might meet both Mongolian imperial needs and Chinese expectations. Khubilai realized that he ruled China solely because he had conquered the Chinese. Dramatically outnumbered by his sometimes hostile Chinese subjects, he faced the problem of recruiting an efficient governmental bureaucracy, yet the nomadic background of Mongol herdsmen ill prepared them for administrative responsibilities in a vast, mostly sedentary state. Moreover, Khubilai did not want to dilute the martial spirit and organization of the Mongols on which he depended, as would likely occur if they were to depart from the tribal and nomadic nature of Mongol life.

Because Khubilai was highly suspicious of the loyalty of his Chinese subjects, he divided the people of China into four ethnic classes which, in order of descending privilege, were the Mongols themselves; the *semu jen* ("various kinds of people") or western and central Asians; the *Han jen,* which included the northern Chinese, Jurchen, Khitan, and other peoples living in the territory previously controlled by the Jin state; and the *nan jen,* or southern Chinese who inhabited areas previously ruled by the Southern Song. Khubilai then abolished the traditional Chinese civil service examinations so that powers of appointment rested solely with him, and he turned primarily to *semu jen* (Persians, Uighurs, Qipchaqs, and others) to help him govern China. (Later emperors reverted to this time-honored appointment system because of discontent among the Chinese.)

At the national level, Khubilai utilized the traditional tripartite Chinese division of authority among civil, military, and censorial offices to administer China. A central secretariat (*Zhong-shu sheng*) managed civil affairs. Its head consulted with Khubilai on major decisions, which were implemented by six ministries (personnel, revenue, rites, war, punishment, and public works) supervised by a prime minister of the right (*you cheng-xiang*) and a prime minister of the left (*zuo cheng-xiang*). A separately functioning privy council (*Shu-mi yuan*) was responsible for military affairs, and the censorate (*Yu-shi tai*) monitored the activities of officials throughout the realm to ascertain their continued loyalty, honesty, and incorruptibility. Both Chinese and Mongolian were official languages of government, requiring the employment of many interpreters and translators.

At the local level, Khubilai diverged from traditional Chinese practices. China was divided into provinces, each administered by a prime minister (*cheng-xiang*) assisted by officers drawn from branch offices (*xing-sheng*) of the secretariat, and further divided into 180 circuits. Special representatives (*darughachi*), usually non-Chinese officials, were sent to monitor the activities of local officials and to assure continued Mongol dominance. Taxation followed Chinese precedents: people paid taxes in kind and in money; the corvée supplied a labor force for large public works projects. Mongols and *semu jen* were exempt from all taxes, as were clerics from all religions.

Khubilai governed China from two capitals. The principal capital was Khanbaliq, "the city of the khâns" (Turkic), which was called Dadu, "the great capital," by the Chinese and was built beginning in 1267 on the site of present-day Beijing. The summer capital was Shangdu, "the upper capital" (Coleridge's Xanadu), some 200 miles (320 kilometers) north in the steppes of Inner Mongolia, present-day Dolon Nor [Tolunnoerh]. Generally, the Yuan court resided in Khanbaliq from late autumn to early spring and then retreated to Shangdu to spend late spring, summer, and early fall. Yuan rulers annually withdrew from China to reaffirm to their non-Chinese subjects the universality of their

# Y

rule and to participate in the horseback riding and hunting activities so essential to their military prowess.

In addition to institutional measures based on bald political and military power, Khubilai also employed more subtle means to win the support of the local populace. He was generally tolerant toward Chinese religions and was a patron of Chinese art, literature, and theater. Khubilai and his successors were also proponents of improving China's infrastructure, particularly its roads and canals, and showed a keen interest in fostering native agriculture. Consequently, there were important cultural and technological advances in China under Yuan rule.

Though Khubilai discriminated against the Confucian scholar-official elite of China by denying them the opportunity to take civil service examinations, he nonetheless initiated a number of projects to garner their support. These included the building of an imperial ancestral temple (*Tai-miao*) and preparing ancestral tablets for the practice of dynastic ancestor worship, as well as recruiting scholar-officials to translate Confucian classics into Mongolian and to write the dynastic histories of the Liao and Jin dynasties.

Khubilai actively recruited Muslims in China to staff his government, so it is not surprising that he showed great tolerance toward them. Khubilai allowed Muslim minorities in China to form virtually self-governing communities where they could speak their own languages and follow the dictates of Islam.

Khubilai was also sympathetic to his Buddhist subjects, and was especially supportive of the Tibetan monk, the 'Phags-pa lama. He helped the 'Phags-pa lama gain a dominant position in Tibet, and, in return, this Tibetan cleric provided Khubilai with the religious sanction he coveted by identifying Khubilai with the Boddhisattva of Wisdom, Manjusri, and also by portraying him as Cakravartin, the universal emperor. Court rituals associated with Buddhism were initiated, and Buddhist clergy participated in ceremonies to protect the state. Khubilai granted Buddhist monks tax-exempt status for much of his reign and supplied funds for the construction of new Buddhist temples and monasteries. The Buddhist canon in Chinese was printed with woodcut illustrations.

In 1258, Khubilai favored the Buddhists in an ongoing dispute with Taoists. Though he sided with the Buddhists, he did not proscribe Taoism and showed moderation in dealing with its adherents. He provided Taoists with monies to build temples and accorded Taoist priests the same tax exemptions offered to Buddhist monks. Taoism, however, was partly outlawed in 1281.

Cultural and technological advances that occurred during the Yuan were fostered by the court through its commitment to encouraging trade and continuing discourse with other countries, as well as by its active recruitment and support of artisans and craftsmen. Late-thirteenth-century travelers such as Marco Polo (*c.* 1298) were amazed at the cosmopolitan nature of Khubilai's China. Scholars have noted that the diversity of peoples, range of costumes and manners, variety of arts and crafts, and breadth of philosophies and doctrines in Yuan China equaled those found anywhere else in the world at that time and those found in the great capital of the Tang dynasty, Changan, throughout the seventh and eighth centuries.

During the Yuan period, artisans and craftsmen were accorded high status and given freedom to innovate and experiment. Many were provided with government salaries, rations of food and clothing, and exemptions from corvée labor in return for their service. The Mongols encouraged the creation of a hereditary artisan class; by the late thirteenth century, about 300,000 families were classified as artisan households. The dynasty promoted ceramic production to secure fine porcelains for the court, for tribute exchange, and for trade with other countries. Yuan potters, less constrained by Song canons of taste, created new blue-and-white porcelains as well as white porcelains and some celadons of exceptional quality.

There is still debate regarding the Yuan impact on Chinese painting. The most renowned of Khubilai's supporters among the painters was Zhao Mengfu, who argued that under the Mongols he found greater freedom of expression and less interference than had been offered by the Song Imperial Academy. Amateur painters, often disenchanted scholars, emerged during the Yuan period and sometimes in discreet ways expressed their hostility to the Mongols through their painting. Significant new forms of calligraphy and of brush-and-ink landscape painting emerged.

Although a long and popular dramatic tradition existed in China from the eleventh century, during the period of Mongol rule, scripts and productions were produced in greater number and with greater sophistication than ever before. At least 160 plays from this period survive, and more than 500 more were written and performed, although they are no longer extant; the most famous collection of Yuan theatrical literature is the Yuanquawan. Plays were written by professional playwrights and unemployed Chinese scholars. Dynastic leaders encouraged theater by serving as patrons for playwrights and by staging a number of performances at court. Yuan espousal of the use of colloquial Chinese also facilitated the writing of plays because writers could better replicate the speech patterns of ordinary persons and present a broader range of characters. There was also little censorship, and other forms of government interference were uncommon. Audiences found Yuan dramas appealing because they mixed short sketches with songs, dances, and acrobatics. This period also saw the development of the novel, written in the vernacular rather than in the Chinese literary language.

Notable technological achievements that occurred during the Yuan dynasty include the reopening and expansion of the Grand Canal to provision the new capital in Dadu. The Yuan also built roads and expanded and improved the postal relay system. Designed to transmit official mail, relay stations were available to traveling officials, military men, and foreign emissaries as well as for the transport of foreign and domestic tribute. Though not originally intended, relay stations were ultimately utilized as hostels by merchants and therefore became increasingly important to commerce. Significant progress was also made in shipbuilding during the Yuan, setting the stage for seven impressive naval expeditions sponsored in the early fifteenth century by the Ming emperor Yongle (r. 1403–1424) to south Asia and even to the coast of Africa.

Khubilai showed great interest in further developing agriculture. He established the Office for the Stimulation of Agriculture (*Chuan-nong si*) to monitor and report on developments in farming, sericulture (silk), and water control, and from this office dispatched officers to help peasants better cultivate their land. Granaries were built to store grain for emergency use. Cotton production increased, and sorghum was introduced to north China.

Khubilai also created the Institute of Muslim Astronomy (*Hui-hui si tian jian*) with an observatory at Daduin (1279) and the Imperial Academy of Medicine (*Tai-yuan*); medical treatises were translated into Persian in 1313. He showed a great interest in cartography and encouraged the mapping of China's frontier regions; an atlas of China was produced between 1311

and 1320. Another achievement of the Yuan court was the establishment of a paper currency (backed by a silver reserve) that was utilized on a wider scale than ever before. This system functioned well when the economy was productive, though as uprisings weakened the Yuan authority over time, paper money became less acceptable. The Yuan also conducted international relations with success, establishing diplomatic contact with Asia and Africa; they waged unsuccessful campaigns to conquer Japan (1274, 1281) and Java (1281,1292).

A number of factors contributed to the ultimate demise of the Yuan. First, Khubilai and subsequent Yuan rulers failed to establish a stable mechanism for imperial succession. Khubilai was succeeded by his grandson Temür (Ch'eng Tsung), who ruled for thirteen years (1294–1307), but during the following twenty-six years, eight emperors ascended the Yuan throne. The final Yuan ruler, Toghon Temür (Shun Ti) reigned for thirty-five years until he was driven out of China in 1368 (he died two years later). Second, weak central leadership enabled factional struggle in the bureaucracy to increase and corruption to grow unchecked. Powerful bureaucratic factions emerged, which often pitted imperial clansmen against court bureaucrats, or officials based in China with strong bureaucratic support against officials with firm connections to the steppe and military power. Factional struggles often centered around ideological issues related to governmental centralization and growing Mongol Sinicization that posed a threat to Mongolian and central Eurasian elites. Third, an unprecedented string of natural disasters, ranging from unusually severe winters to major floods and droughts, uprooted and impoverished people, making them inclined to rebel. Finally, the growth of Confucian-minded activists—such as Liu Ji, who joined with the future Ming founder, Zhu Yuanzhang—mobilized the populace with promises of tax equalization and moral regeneration once the Mongols were overthrown.

The Yuan period is a significant one in Chinese history, an interval of alien rule between the Chinese Song and Ming dynasties. Ray Huang suggests that the mood of growth and expansion found during the Tang and Song periods and initially embraced by the Mongols was abandoned by late Yuan rulers. The Mongols also instituted more authoritarian methods of government and became increasingly reliant on China's agrarian base. It is clear that the tone and nature of

# Y

government under the Ming (1368–1644) contrasted sharply with that of the Song, and one can ascribe this in no small part to the cumulative effects of Mongolian rule. Interestingly, scholars who have studied the Mongol impact on the evolving Russian state also note the dramatic differences between Kievan Rus' in the pre-Mongol period and the more authoritarian, structured, and agrarian-oriented Muscovite state that followed.

## BIBLIOGRAPHY

Allsen, Thomas T. *Mongol Imperialism: The Policies of the Grand Qan Möngke in China, Russia, and the Islamic Lands, 1251–1259.* Berkeley: U of California P, 1987.

Cahill, James. *Hills beyond a River: Chinese Painting of the Yuan Dynasty.* New York: Weatherhill, 1976.

Chan, Hok-lam, and William Theodore de Bary, eds. *Yüan Thought: Chinese Thought and Religion under the Mongols.* New York: Columbia UP, 1982.

Crump, James I. *Chinese Theater in the Days of Kublai Khan.* Ann Arbor: U of Michigan P, 1990.

Dardess, John W. *Conquerors and Confucians: Aspects of Political Change in Late Yuan China.* New York: Columbia UP, 1973.

De Hartog, Leo. *Genghis Khan, Conqueror of the World.* New York: St. Martin, 1989.

Endicott-West, Elizabeth. *Mongolian Rule in China: Local Administration in the Yuan Dynasty.* Cambridge, MA: Harvard UP, 1989.

Franke, Herbert, and Denis Twitchett, eds. *The Cambridge History of China.* Vol. 6. Cambridge, England: Cambridge UP, 1994.

Hsiao, Ch'i-ch'ing. *The Military Establishment of the Yuan Dynasty.* Cambridge, MA: Harvard UP, 1978.

Huang, Ray. *China: A Macrohistory.* Armonk, NY: Eastgate, 1988.

Lee, S.E., and W.-K. Ho, *Chinese Art under Mongol Rule.* Cleveland, OH: Cleveland State UP, 1968.

Rossabi, Morris. *Khubilai Khan.* Berkeley: U of California P, 1988.

*Van Jay Symons*

## SEE ALSO

Buddhism; China; Confucianism; Japan, Mongol Invasion of; Khanbaliq; Marco Polo; Mongol Army; Mongols; Nomadism and Pastoralism; Russia and Rus'; Taoism; Vietnam and Java, Mongol Invasions of; Yasa; Zheng He, Admiral

# Z

## Zaiton

The Persian name for present-day Quanzhou [Ch'üan-chou], in the southern Chinese province of Fukien, one of the greatest ports in the medieval world; important for its commerce with the Near East and Europe.

In 1087, under the Song dynasty, Zaiton was the seat of a maritime trade bureau. By 1283, its population numbered about 455,000. The voluminous cargo that passed through this port included pepper, gemstones, pearls, and ceramics. Zaiton provided access to inland cities via roads and waterways and was a strategic port from which the Mongols launched unsuccessful invasions of Japan (1281) and Java (1292).

In the late thirteenth and much of the fourteenth centuries, merchants from many nations traded at Zaiton, with Muslims predominating. The presence—even welcome—of foreigners and the safe traveling conditions were due to the tolerance of the khâns. Marco Polo, Andrew of Perugia, Peregrino of Castello, Odoric of Pordenone, John of Marignolli, and Ibn Battūta all described the port in their writings between c. 1298 and c. 1356.

In part with the financial assistance of European merchants, Franciscans under John of Monte Corvino built a cathedral at Zaiton. The mission included living quarters for the use of Christian merchants. Odoric transferred the remains of the four Franciscans martyred in India (at Thana) in 1321 to the Franciscan mission here.

Architectural finds prove the existence of foreign inhabitants at Zaiton: tombstone inscriptions are written in Syrian, Chinese, Arabic, and Latin. The expulsion of the Mongols in 1368 and the xenophobic policies of the ensuing Ming dynasty (1368–1644) marked the end of Chinese relations with the medieval West.

### BIBLIOGRAPHY

*The Cambridge History of China.* Ed. Herbert Franke and Denis Twitchett. Vol. 6. Cambridge, England: Cambridge UP, 1994 (see "Ch'üan-chou").

Goodrich, L. Carrington. "Recent Discoveries at Zayton." *Journal of the American Oriental Society* 77 (1957): 161–165.

———. "Westerners and Central Asians in Yuan China." *Oriente Poliano: Studi e conferenze tenute all'Is. M.E.O. in occasione del VII centenario della nascità de Marco Polo, 1254–1954.* Rome: Istituto italiano per il Medio e Estremo Oriente, 1957, pp. 1–22.

Hambis, Louis. "Les Cimetières de la région de Zaiton." *Académie des Inscriptions et Belle-lettres (France). Comptes rendus des séances.* Paris: Klincksieck, 1960, pp. 213–221.

Long, So Kee. "Financial Crisis and Local Economy: Ch'üan-chou in the thirteenth century." *T'oung Pao* 77 (1991): 119–137.

Yule-Cordier. *Cathay and the Way Thither.* See Gen. Bib.

*Gloria Allaire*

### SEE ALSO

Andrew of Perugia; Franciscan Friars; Ibn Battūta, Abu Abdallah; Japan, Mongol Invasion of; John of Marignolli; John of Monte Corvino; Marco Polo; Missionaries to China; Mongols; Odoric of Pordenone; Pepper; Thomas of Tolentino; Vietnam and Java, Mongol Invasions of

# Z

## Zeitz Map

One of a small number of surviving fifteenth-century maps that combine features of most European *mappaemundi* with elements of Arabic cartography and geographical data compiled at the Monastery of Klosterneuburg, near Vienna.

Oriented to the south and having a vertical diameter of eight and seven-eighths inches (22.5 cm), the Zeitz map was traced from an apparently lost original by a German scribe in 1470, and included in his copy of Nicholas Germanus's version of Ptolemy's *Cosmographia*. In addition to the standard grid-based maps that are usually joined to Ptolemy's text, it incorporates three *tabulae modernae* (of Spain, Italy, and northern Europe), which were drawn on the basis of the contemporary geographical information in the codex (Zeitz, Stiftsbibliothek, MS Lat. Hist. fol. 497, fol. 48r; Zeitz lies some thirty miles [fifty kilometers] south of Leipzig). The Zeitz map has been trimmed on its left and right edges, with loss of text and design at both sides; this includes the extreme eastern territory in which a large representation of the Earthly Paradise, and its Four Rivers, appears on the Walsperger map, as well as far western regions in the Atlantic, where parts of two islands, but no explanatory legend, are visible (one of these is probably "Canaria," a single location standing for the Canaries).

The Zeitz map belongs to the same cartographical tradition as the Bell and Walsperger maps: all three attempt to place towns precisely by means of an ink dot, show a Mediterranean coastline that is influenced by the portolan charts used by navigators, and extend the east coast of Africa as do Arabic maps (the west coast has a similar extension). Unlike them, the Zeitz map has no exterior frame of concentric circles or non-geographical designs of any kind, neither architectural designs indicating major cities nor drawings of population groups. It lacks the distance and degree scales, as well as the "Antarctic Pole," of the Walsperger map. Throughout its southern half, legends are more detailed, even discursive, than those of the Bell or Walsperger maps, in some cases helping to explain the latter, whose information is more terse (about a race of west African people whose single foot shields them from heavy rains, for example, or their goat-headed neighbors). Except for notices in Scandinavia and off the northern coast of Scotland, traditional Europe contains only place-names, most of them in Italy, France, Iberia, and Britain; trading cities on rivers (Belgrade, Budapest, Kraków); or ports in the Hanseatic League (Riga, Gdansk, Trondheim).

Underlying the Zeitz map is an attempt to locate places based on a set of coordinates compiled by geographers operating at or near Vienna in the early 1400s; it thus represents an early attempt, before the publication of Ptolemy, to produce a world map on which space is apportioned mathematically rather than hierarchically (or simply conveniently). Its unique inclusion of "Warna castrum" south of the Danube river delta (marking Varna, the site of an Ottoman victory in 1444) and its placement of "Ethiopia, in which Prester John reigns" *west* of the Red Sea demonstrate the mapmaker's desire to make current concerns a matter of cartographical record; conversely, its inclusion of the monopedes in South Africa, the "especially evil Scythians" east of the river Don, and even "Gog and Magog—Red Jews" (with its anti-Semitic implications in fifteenth-century Europe) is characteristic of maps constructed to perpetuate more traditional classical and theological assumptions.

### BIBLIOGRAPHY

Destombes, Marcel, ed. *Mappemondes*, pp. 212–217, 247 [54.17]. See Gen. Bib.
Durand, Dana Bennett. *The Vienna-Klosterneuburg Map Corpus of the Fifteenth Century: A Study in the Transition from Medieval to Modern Science*. Leiden: Brill, 1952, esp. pp. 213–217; plate XVI.

*Scott D. Westrem*

### SEE ALSO

Bell *Mappamundi;* Borgia Map; Canary Islands; Cartography, Arabic; Four Rivers of Paradise; Geography in Medieval Europe; Gog and Magog; Hanse, The; Klosterneuburg Map Corpus; *Mappamundi;* Maps; Monstrosity, Geographical; Portolan Charts; Prester John; Ptolemy; Red Jews; Red Sea; Walsperger, Andreas

## Zheng He, Admiral (c. 1371–1433)

Diplomat, military commander, and leader during the early Ming dynasty of seven major maritime expeditions, which extended Chinese political, cultural, and commercial influence throughout southeast Asia and beyond into the Indian Ocean basin. The descendant of a prominent Muslim family of Mongol origin in Yunnan, Zheng He [Cheng Ho, or Ma San-pao, or Ma Ho] was captured as a youth and castrated for eunuch service in the court of Prince Zhu Di, son of the founding ruler of the Ming dynasty. Of imposing appearance, and repeatedly demonstrating his loyalty as both shrewd negotiator and skilled military leader, Zheng He rose rapidly in the favor of Zhu Di, who usurped the throne in 1402 and reigned thereafter as Emperor Yongle (1402–1424).

Determined to establish himself after his precarious rise to power, Yongle entrusted Zheng He with the construction and command of a great fleet, the original purpose of which was to consolidate Yongle's international prestige through a demonstration of overwhelming power in neighboring states. For his first voyage, Zheng He assembled a vast armada of 317 ships, including "horse ships," supply ships, and troop transports, along with several great nine-masted "treasure ships." The fleet's complement of 27,870 men included not only soldiers and sailors, but also scholars, scientists, and artisans. Sailing fron Nanjing and Liujia in 1405, the first expedition visited Champa (Vietnam) and various ports in the Indonesian archipelago before passing through the Straits of Malacca en route to Sri Lanka and Calicut, in southern India. Resolving local political disputes through a combination of military power and diplomacy, Zheng He enhanced China's prestige as a force for regional stability. At the same time, he promoted the economic advantages of trade, offering Chinese silks, porcelain, and horses in exchange for rare woods, incense, and ivory.

After Zheng He's successful return in 1407, bringing diplomatic gifts, political hostages, and tribute from foreign rulers to the imperial court, he was commissioned to undertake six subsequent expeditions into the "Western Seas." During his fourth voyage (1413–1415), he sailed beyond India, reaching Hormuz on the Persian Gulf. The fifth (1417–1419) and sixth (1421–1422) voyages continued even farther, touching at Aden and several East African ports, including perhaps Malindi and Mogadishu. Gifts to the emperor brought by the returning fleet included exotic animals, such as a pair of giraffes that were put in the newly constructed Forbidden City at Beijing. Yet the expeditions, despite their spectacular results, proved an enormous drain on China's resources. On the accession of Emperor Xuande in 1425, conservatives in the imperial court increasingly pushed for an end to foreign ventures. Zheng He's death at sea in 1433, followed by the death of Xuande two years later, brought the great era of Chinese maritime expansion to an abrupt end.

BIBLIOGRAPHY

Levathes, Louise. *When China Ruled the Seas: The Treasure Fleet of the Dragon Throne, 1405–1433.* New York: Simon & Schuster, 1994.

Mote, F.W. "China in the Age of Columbus." In *Circa 1492: Art in the Age of Exploration.* Ed. Jay A. Levenson. New Haven, CT: Yale UP, 1991, pp. 337–350.

Needham, Joseph. "Nautics." In *Science and Civilization in China.* Cambridge: Cambridge UP, 1971, vol. 4, p. 3, section 29.

*Allan T. Kohl*

SEE ALSO

Animals, Exotic; China; Ivory Trade; Malacca Straits; Navigation, Chinese

## Zolus the Pisan

*See* Bofeti, Pericciolo di Anastasio

## Zoroastrianism

An Iranian religion founded by Zoroaster [Zarathustra], who is now thought to have lived in the latter half of the second millennium B.C.E. Initially established to reform the Indo-Iranian religion brought to the region by Aryan invaders, Zoroastrianism gradually accommodated itself to the beliefs and rituals of that older religion, and in the process, became the national religion of Persia. While the early spread of Zoroastrianism throughout Iran was made possible through missionary efforts, once the religion acquired a national identity, it failed to develop the same universal evangelistic orientation found in Christianity, Buddhism, and Manichaeism, religions with which Zoroastrianism shared the trade routes of the Middle East and Central Asia. Thus, despite its appearance in other parts of Asia during the medieval period, Zoroastrianism, with few exceptions, remained an ethnically bound religion that did not significantly depart from the confines of Persian merchant and refugee communities.

The limited impact made by Zoroastrianism in missionary proselytization was far outweighed by its pivotal role in the commerce of religious ideas. Judaism, Christianity, Islam, Manichaeism, Mahayana Buddhism, and the belief systems of some Inner Asian peoples are all thought to have been beneficiaries of teachings and practices derived from Zoroastrianism. Zoroaster's unique religious vision replaced polytheism

# Z

with the worship of one creator god, Ahura Mazda, and posited a dualistic struggle between forces of good and evil that was reflected both in a cosmic drama and in the ethical life of human individuals. Zoroastrian beliefs assimilated by other traditions included the notion of an immortal soul judged according to its deeds, the idea of heaven and hell as places of reward and punishment, the belief in angelic beings as well as the personification of the forces of evil, the concept of stages in cosmic history, anticipation of a world savior to be born of a virgin, and an apocalyptic ordeal culminating in a final judgment and bodily resurrection. Zoroastrian religious practice is largely preoccupied with rites of purification, most prominent of which is the tending of a sacred fire kept in temples.

Centuries after the beginnings of Zoroastrianism in eastern Iran, missionaries were successful in converting western Iranian peoples, the Medes and the Persians, who established the first Persian Empire under the Achaemenid dynasty (550–331 B.C.E.). During this period, Zoroastrianism as an imperial religion exerted its influence well beyond the borders of Iran, affecting most notably postexilic Judaism and coming to the attention of the Greeks. The conquest of Alexander the Great ushered in a period of Hellenization in which Zoroastrianism, although still present, was largely overshadowed. This continued through the Seleucid (312–171 B.C.E.) and Arsacid (171 B.C.E.–224 C.E.) periods. The reestablishment of a Persian Empire under the Sasanids witnessed the growth of a strong national consciousness, which at times verged on xenophobia. Zoroastrianism was embraced as an official national religion and other foreign religious traditions were sporadically persecuted.

Although Zoroastrianism of the Sasanid period (224–651 C.E.) is known for its transformation into a national religion, it nevertheless continued to exert an influence beyond the Persian Empire. The western Tujue, a nomadic Turkic people located on the Persian Empire's northeast borders who maintained relations with the Byzantine Empire on Persia's western side, were noted by the Byzantine scholar Theophylus Simocattes for their veneration of fire and their worship of Ahura Mazda. This same period also witnessed Persian merchant caravans transporting the Zoroastrian faith across the oases of the Central Asian Silk Roads into China. This movement was aided by the Sogdians, a people living on the northeast borders of Persia who were also instrumental in conveying Manicheaism and Buddhism along the same route.

The Arab conquests of the seventh century marked the beginning of the eclipse of Zoroastrianism by Islam. In the wake of the Islamic takeover of Persia, many Zoroastrians fled either east or south. Those departing eastward followed the merchant routes across Central Asia into Tang (617–906) China where they established émigré communities. The prominent position of these refugee and merchant communities in the Tang capital of Chang'an is reflected in the establishment of Zoroastrian temples by the Chinese court. This efflorescence ended in the 840s with a suppression of all foreign religions by Emperor Wuzong (r. 840–846), which left Zoroastrianism and Nestorianism largely defunct. Nevertheless, historical sources all the way into the Southern Song period (1127–1279) record the existence of Zoroastrian temples.

The southerly exodus of Zoroastrians from Iran brought many to the western coast of India where they set up communities in Gujarat and became known as Parsis [Parsees]. Although they lost contact with fellow-believers in Iran and did not reestablish significant communication until the fifteenth century, the Parsis remained true to the tradition. The Dominican friar Jordanus, who visited this community in 1350, made note of their dualism, their worship of fire, and the Zoroastrian custom of exposing their dead on top of (or within) open air towers.

## BIBLIOGRAPHY

Boyce, Mary. *Zoroastrians: Their Religious Belief and Practices.* London: Routledge and Kegan Paul, 1979.

Duchesne-Guillemin, J. "Zoroastrian Religion." In *The Cambridge History of Iran.* Vol. 3.2. Cambridge, England: Cambridge UP, 1983.

Grousset, René. *The Empire of the Steppes.* New Brunswick, NJ: Rutgers UP, 1970.

*Daniel Getz*

## SEE ALSO

Buddhism; Byzantine Empire; Caravans; Manichaeism; Muslim Travelers and Trade; Nestorianism; Silk Roads

# General Bibliography

Alington, Gabriel, and Dominic Harbour. *The Hereford Mappamundi: A Medieval View of the World.* Leominster: Fowler Wright Books, 1996.

Arentzen, Jörg-Geerd. *Imago Mundi Cartographica: Studien zur Bildlichkeit mittelalterlicher Welt- und Ökumenekarten unter besonderer Berücksichtigung des Zusammenwirkens von Text und Bild.* Münstersche Mittelalter-Schriften 53. Munich: Fink, 1984.

Ashtor, Eliyahu. *A Social and Economic History of the Near East in the Middle Ages.* Berkeley: U of California P, 1976.

Bagrow, Leo. *History of Cartography.* Revised and enlarged by R.A. Skelton. Trans. D.L. Paisey. Cambridge, MA: Harvard UP, 1964; 2nd edition. Chicago: Precedent, 1985.

Barber, Peter. "Visual Encyclopedias: The Hereford Map and Other Mappae Mundi." *The Map Collector* 48 (1989): 2–8.

———. "Old Encounters New: The Aslake World Map." In *Géographie du monde au moyen âge et à la renaissance.* Ed. Monique Pelletier. Paris: Editions du C.T.H.S., 1989, pp. 69–88.

———. "The Evesham World Map: A Late Medieval English View of God and the World." *Imago Mundi* 47(1995): 13–33.

Barber, Peter, and Michelle Brown. "The Aslake World Map." *Imago Mundi* 44 (1992): 24–44.

Beazley, Charles Raymond. *The Dawn of Modern Geography: A History of Exploration and Geographical Science.* 3 vols. Vols. 1 and 2: London: Murray, 1897, 1901; vol. 3: Oxford: Clarendon Press, 1906; rpt. New York: Peter Smith, 1949.

Beckingham, Charles F., and Bernard Hamilton, eds. *Prester John, the Mongols, and the Ten Lost Tribes.* Aldershot: Variorum, 1996. Selective bibliography on pp. 291–304.

Benedetto, Luigi Foscolo, ed. *Marco Polo: Il Milione.* Florence: Olschki, 1928.

Benjamin, Sandra, ed. and tr. *The World of Benjamin of Tudela: A Medieval Mediterranean Travelogue.* London; Cranbury, NJ: Fairleigh Dickinson UP, 1995.

Birch, Debra J. *Pilgrimage to Rome in the Middle Ages.* Suffolk and Rochester, NY: Boydell, 1998.

Brincken, Anna-Dorothee von den. "Mappa mundi und Chronographia: Studien zur imago mundi des abendländischen Mittelalters." *Deutsches Archiv für Erforschung des Mittelalters* 24 (1968): 118–186.

———. *Fines terrae: Die Enden der Erde und der vierte Kontinent auf mittelalterlichen Weltkarten.* Monumenta Germaniae Historica, Schriften 36. Hanover: Hahn, 1992.

Buridant, Claude, ed. *Libri duo, quorum prior orientalis, siue Hierosolymitanae: alter, occidentalis historiae nomine inscribitur. La traduction de l'Historia orientalis / Jacques de Vitry.* Paris: Klincksieck, 1986.

Campbell, Mary B. *The Witness and the Other World: Exotic European Travel Writing, 400–1600.* Ithaca: Cornell UP, 1988.

Campbell, Tony. *The Earliest Printed Maps 1472–1500.* Berkeley and Los Angeles: U of California P, 1987.

———. "Portolan Charts from the Late Thirteenth Century to 1500." In Harley-Woodward, pp. 361–463.

Castañeda, Paulino, gen. ed. *Obras completas / Bartolomé de las Casas.* Madrid: Alianza, 1988–1998.

*The Christopher Columbus Encyclopedia.* Ed. Silvio Bedini. 2 vols. New York: Simon & Schuster, 1992.

Dalché, Patrick Gautier, ed. *La "Descriptio Mappe mundi" de Hugues de Saint-Victor.* Paris: Études Augustiniennes, 1988.

———. *Carte Marine et Portulan au XIIe siècle: Le Liber de Existencia Riveriarum et Forma Maris Nostri Mediterranei (Pise, circa 1200).* Collection de l'École Français de Rome 203. Rome: École Français de Rome, 1995.

Davidson, Linda K., and Maryjane Dunn-Wood, eds. *Pilgrimage in the Middle Ages: A Research Guide.* New York: Garland, 1993.

Dawson, Christopher, ed. *The Mongol Mission: Narratives and Letters of the Franciscan Missionaries in Mongolia and China in the Thirteenth and Fourteenth Centuries: The Makers of Christendom.* New York: Sheed and Ward, 1955; rpt. *Mission to Asia.* Medieval Academy Reprints for Teaching 8. Toronto: U of Toronto P, 1992.

Deluz, Christiane. *Le Livre de Jehan de Mandeville: Une "géographie au XIVe siècle.* Université Catholique de Louvain Publications de l'Institut d'Études Médiévales 8. Louvain-la-Neuve: Institut d'Études Médiévales de l'Université Catholique de Louvain, 1988.

Destombes, Marcel, ed. *Mappemondes A.D. 1200–1500; Catalogue préparé par la Commission des Cartes Anciennes de l'Union Géographique Internationale.* Vol. 1. of *Monumenta Cartographica Vetustioris Aevi A.D. 1200–1500.* Ed. Roberto Almagià and Marcel Destombes. *Imago Mundi,* suppl 4. Amsterdam: N. Israel, 1964.

Dilke, O.A.W. *Greek and Roman Maps.* Ithaca: Cornell UP, 1985.

Duhem, Pierre. *Le système du Monde aux XIIIe et XIVe siècles.* Nouvelle Bibliothèque du Moyen Âge 28. Paris: Champion, 1994.

*The Encyclopedia of Islam.* New edition. Vols. 1–2. Leiden: Brill, 1983–1986.

Flint, Valerie I.J. "Monsters and the Antipodes in the Early Middle Ages and the Enlightenment." *Viator* 13 (1984): 65–80.

———. *The Imaginative Landscape of Christopher Columbus.* Princeton: Princeton UP, 1992.

———. "The Hereford Map, Its Authors, Two Scenes, and a Border." *Transactions of the Royal Historical Society,* 6th ser. 8 (1998): 19–44.

Friedman, John Block. *The Monstrous Races in Medieval Art and Thought.* Cambridge: Harvard UP, 1981; rpt. Syracuse, NY: Syracuse UP, 2000.

Gardiner, R., ed. *Cogs, Caravels, and Galleons: The Sailing Ship, 1000–1650.* Conway's History of the Ship. London: Conway Maritime Press, 1994.

Le Goff, Jacques. *The Birth of Purgatory.* Trans. Arthur Goldhammer. Chicago: U of Chicago P, 1984.

Goitein, S.D. *A Mediterranean Society: The Jewish Communities of the Arab World as Portrayed in the Documents of the Cairo Geniza.* 6 vols. Berkeley: U of California P, 1967–1994.

Gosman, Martin. "Otton de Freising et le Prêtre Jean." *Revue belge de philologie et d'histoire* 61 (1983): 270–285.

Greenblatt, Stephen. *Marvelous Possessions: The Wonder of the New World.* Chicago: U of Chicago P, 1991.

Greenhill, Basil, and Sam Manning. *The Evolution of the Wooden Ship.* London: Batsford, 1980.

Hakluyt, Richard, ed. *The Principall Navigations Voiages and Discoveries of the English Nation . . . Imprinted at London [:Bishop and Newberie], 1589: A Photo-Lithographic Facsimile.* Intro. David Beers Quinn and R.A. Skelton. Hakluyt Society, e.s., 39. 2 vols. Cambridge, England: Cambridge UP, 1965.

Hamelius, Paul, ed. *Mandeville's Travels, Translated from the French of Jean d'Outremeuse.* 2 vols. Early English Text Society, o.s. 153–154. London: Oxford UP, 1919–1923, rpt. 1960–1961.

[Harley-Woodward] Harley, J.B., and David Woodward, eds. *The History of Cartography.* Vol. 1: *Cartography in Prehistoric, Ancient, and Medieval Europe and the Mediterranean.* Vol. 2: *Cartography in the Traditional Islamic and South Asian Societies.* Chicago and London: U of Chicago P, 1987.

Harvey, P.D.A. *Medieval Maps.* London: The British Library, 1991.

Haslam, Graham. "The Duchy of Cornwall Map Fragment." In *Géographie du monde au moyen âge et à la renaissance.* Ed. Monique Pelletier. Paris: Editions du C.T.H.S., 1989, pp. 33–44.

Heyd, Wilhelm von. *Histoire du Commerce du Levant au Moyen Âge.* 2 vols. Leipzig, 1885–1886; rpt. Amsterdam, 1967.

Higgins, Iain Macleod. *Writing East: The "Travels" of John Mandeville.* Philadelphia: U of Pennsylvania P, 1997.

Hildinger, Erik, tr. *The Story of the Mongols Whom We Call the Tartars—Historia Mongalorum quos nos Tartaros appellamus: Friar Giovanni di Plano Carpini's Account of His Embassy to the Court of the Mongol Khan.* Boston: Branden, 1996.

Hutchinson, G. *Medieval Ships and Shipping.* London: Leicester UP, 1994.

Jomard, Edme-François. *Les monuments de la géographie; ou, Recueil d'anciennes cartes européennes et orientales publiées en fac-simile de la grandeur des originaux.* Paris: Duprat, 1842–1862.

Kamal, Youssouf. *Monumenta cartographica Africae et Aegypti.* Rev. ed. Fuat Sezgin. Frankfurt am Main: Institute für Geschichte der Arabisch-Islamischen Wissenschaften an der Johann Wolfgang Goethe-Universität, 1987.

Kappler, René, ed. and tr. *Ricold de Monte Croce, Pérégrination en Terre Sainte et au Proche Orient; lettres sur la chute de Saint-Jean d'Acre.* Textes et Traductions des Classiques Français du Moyen Âge 4. Paris: Honoré Champion, 1997.

Kedar, Benjamin Z. *Crusade and Mission: European Approaches toward the Muslims.* Princeton: Princeton UP, 1984.

Kliege, Herma. *Weltbild und Darstellungspraxis hochmittelalterlicher Weltkarten.* Münster: Nodus, 1991.

Kugler, Hartmut, with Eckhard Michael, ed. *Ein Weltbild vor Columbus: Die Ebstorfer Weltkarte. Interdisziplinäres Colloquium 1988.* Weinheim: CH, Acta Humaniora, 1991.

Larner, John. *Marco Polo and the Discovery of the World.* New Haven: Yale UP, 1999.

Lewel, Joachim. *Géographie du moyen âge.* 5 vols. Vol. 5: *Épilogue.* Brussels: Pilliet, 1852–1857; rpt. Amsterdam: Meridian, 1966–1967.

Lewis, Bernard. *Race and Slavery in the Middle East: An Historical Inquiry.* Oxford and New York: Oxford UP, 1990.

Lopez, Robert S. *The Commercial Revolution of the Middle Ages, 950–1350.* Cambridge: Cambridge UP, 1976.

*Marco Polo: The Description of the World.* 2 vols. Ed. A.C. Moule and Paul Pelliot. London: G. Routledge, 1938; rpt. New York: AMS Press, 1976.

Martels, Z. *Travel Fact and Travel Fiction: Studies on Fiction, Literary Tradition, Scholarly Discovery and Observation in Travel Writing.* Leiden: Brill, 1994.

Meyvaert, Paul. "An Unknown Letter of Hulugu, Il-Khan of Persia, to King Louis IX of France." *Viator* 11 (1980): 245–259.

Miller, Konrad, *Mappaemundi: Die ältesten Weltkarten.* 6 vols. Stuttgart: Roth, 1895–1898.

Moffett, Samuel Hugh. *A History of Christianity in Asia.* Vol. 1: *Beginnings to 1500.* New York: Harper Collins, 1992.

Mollat [Du Jourdain], Michel. *Études d'histoire maritime (1938–1975).* Torino: Bottega d'Erasmo, 1977.

Moretti, Gabriella. *Gli antipodi: Avventure letterarie di un mito scientifico.* Parma: Pratiche editrice, 1994.

Morgan, David. *The Mongols.* Oxford and NY: Blackwell, 1986.

Morison, Samuel. *Admiral of the Ocean Sea: A Life of Christopher Columbus.* 2 vols. Boston: Little, Brown, 1963.

Muldoon, James. *Popes, Lawyers, and Infidels: The Church and the Non-Christian World, 1250–1550.* Philadelphia: U of Pennsylvania P, 1979.

Mütherich, Florentine. "Geographische und ethnographische Darstellungen in der Buchmalerei des Frühen Mittelalters." In *Popoli e Paesi nella cultura altomedievale: 23–29 aprile 1981.* Spoleto: Presso la Sede del Centro, 1983. Vol. 2, pp. 709–745.

Olschki, Leonardo. *Marco Polo's Precursors.* Baltimore: Johns Hopkins UP, 1943.

———. *Marco Polo's Asia: An Introduction to His "Description of the World" called "Il Milione."* Trans. John A. Scott. Rev. Leonardo Olschki. Berkeley: U of California P, 1960.

Pagden, Anthony. *European Encounters with the New World.* New Haven: Yale UP, 1993.

Palestine Pilgrims' Text Society. *The Library of the Palestine Pilgrims' Text Society.* 13 vols. London: Committee of the Palestine Exploration Fund, 1885–1897; rpt. New York: AMS Press, 1971.

*Pauly-Wissowa Realencyclopädie der classischen Altertumswissenschaft.* Herausgegeben von Konrat Ziegler. Register der Nachträge und Supplemente von Hans Gärtner und Albert Wünsch. Munich: A. Druckenmüller, 1980.

Pelliot, Paul. *Recherches sur les Chrétiens d'Asie Centrale et d'Extrême-Orient.* Paris: Imprimerie Nationale, 1973.

Peters, F.E. *Jerusalem: The Holy City in the Eyes of Chroniclers, Visitors, Pilgrims, and Prophets from the Days of Abraham to the Beginnings of Modern Times,* Princeton: Princeton UP, 1985.

Phillips, J.R.S. *The Medieval Expansion of Europe.* Oxford and New York: Oxford UP, 1988.

Pirenne, Henri. *Economic and Social History of Medieval Europe.* New York: Harcourt Brace, 1956.

Purchas, Samuel. [*Hakluytus Posthumus*] or *Purchas His Pilgrims.* London: Fetherstone, 1625; rpt. in 20 vols. Glasgow: MacLehose and Sons, 1905–1907.

de Rachewiltz, Igor. *Papal Envoys to the Great Khans.* Stanford: Stanford UP, 1971.

Richard, Jean. "Isol le Pisan: Un Aventurier Franc Gouverneur d'une Province Mongole." Rpt. in *Orient et Occident au moyen âge: Contacts et relations (XIIe–XVe s.).* London: Variorum, 1976, pp. 186–194.

Richard, Jean. *Les récits de voyages et de pèlerinages.* Typologie des sources du moyen âge occidental 38. Turnhout: Brepols, 1981.

Riley-Smith, Jonathan. *The Crusades: A Short History.* London: Athlone; New Haven: Yale UP, 1987.

Rogers, Francis M. *The Search for Eastern Christians.* Minneapolis: U of Minnesota P, 1962.

Röhricht, Reinhold. *Bibliotheca Geographica Palaestinae: Chronologisches Verzeichniss der auf die Geographie des Heiligen Landes bezüglichen Literatur von 333 bis 1878.* Berlin: Reuther, 1890; rpt. [expanded by David H.K. Amiran] Jerusalem: Universitas Booksellers, 1963.

Rossabi, Morris. *Kubilai Khan: His Life and Times.* Berkeley: U of California P, 1988.

Roux, Jean-Paul. *La Religion des Turcs et des Mongols.* Paris: Payot, 1984.

Ruberg, Uwe. "Mappae mundi des Mittelalters im Zusammenwirken von Text und Bild." In *Text und Bild: Aspekte des Zusammenwirkens zweier Künste in Mittelalter und früher Neuzeit.* Ed. Christel Meier and Uwe Ruberg. Wiesbaden: L. Reichert Verlag, 1980, pp. 550–592.

Runciman, Steven, ed. *A History of the Crusades.* 3 Vols. Cambridge, Cambridge UP, 1954; rpt. Cambridge, 1998.

Santarém, Manuel Francisco de Barros e Sousa, Viscount of. *Atlas composé de cartes des XIVe, XVe, XVIe, et XVIIe siècles.* Paris, 1841. 2nd edition. *Atlas composé de mappemondes, de portulans et de cartes hydrographiques et historiques depuis le VIe jusqu'au XVIIe siècle.* Paris: Thunot, 1849; facsimile rpt. with additions by Helen Wallis and A.H. Sijmons, Amsterdam: Muller, 1985.

Saunders, J.J. *The History of Mongol Conquests.* London: Routledge, 1971.

Scammell, G.V. *The World Encompassed: The First European Maritime Empires, c. 800–1650.* Berkeley: U of California P, 1981.

Schur, Nathan. *Jerusalem in Pilgrims' and Travellers' Accounts: A Thematic Bibliography 1300–1917.* Jerusalem: Ariel, 1980.

Setton, Kenneth M., gen. ed. *A History of the Crusades.* Madison: U of Wisconsin P, 1969–1990.

Simar, Théophile. *La géographie de l'Afrique centrale dans l'antiquité et au Moyen Âge.* Brussels: Vromant, 1912. Also published in *Revue Congolaise* 3 (1912–1913): 1–23, 81–102, 145–169, 225–252, 289–310, 440–441.

Simek, Rudolf. *Heaven and Earth in the Middle Age: The Physical World before Columbus.* Trans. Angela Hall. Suffolk and Rochester, NY: Boydell, 1996.

Sinor, Denis. *Inner Asia and Its Contacts with Medieval Europe.* London: Variorum Reprints, 1977.

Smith, Catherine Delano-, and Roger J.P. Kain. *English Maps: A History.* Toronto and Buffalo, NY: U of Toronto P, 1999, pp. 1–40.

Spufford, Peter. *Money and Its Use in Medieval Europe.* Cambridge: Cambridge UP, 1988.

Spuler, Bertold. *History of the Mongols, Based on Eastern and Western Accounts of the Thirteenth and Fourteenth Centuries.* Trans. H. and S. Drummond. London: Routledge, 1972.

Strayer, Joseph R., gen. ed. *Dictionary of the Middle Ages.* New York: Scribner's, 1984.

Tattersall, Jill. "Sphere or Disc? Allusions to the Shape of the Earth in Some 12th-Century and 13th-Century Vernacular French Works." *Modern Language Review* 76 (1981): 31–46.

Taviani, Huguette, et al. *Voyage, quête, pèlerinage dans la littérature et la civilisation médiévales. Actes du colloque organisé par le C.U.E.R.M.A. les 5, 6, 7 mars 1976.* Senefiance 2. Aix-en-Provence: Edition CUERMA; Paris: H. Champion, 1976.

Tellenbach, Gerd. "Zur Frühgeschichte abendländischer Reisebeschreibungen." In *Historia Integra: Festschrift für Erich Hassinger zum 70. Geburtstag.* Ed. Hans Fenske, Wolfgang Reinhard, and Ernst Schulin. Berlin: Duncker and Humbolt, 1977, pp. 51–80.

Tilmann, Sister Jean Paul, tr. *An Appraisal of the Geographical Works of Albertus Magnus.* Ann Arbor: U of Michigan P, 1971.

Tomasch, Sylvia, and Sealy Gilles, eds. *Text and Territory: Geographical Imagination in the European Middle Ages.* The Middle Ages Series. Philadelphia: U of Pennsylvania P, 1998.

Westrem, Scott D. ed. *Discovering New Worlds: Essays on Medieval Exploration and Imagination.* New York and London: Garland, 1991.

White, T.H. *The Bestiary: A Book of Beasts, Being a Translation from a Latin Bestiary of the Twelfth Century.* New York: Putnam, 1960.

Wilkinson, John. *Jerusalem Pilgrims: Before the Crusades.* Jerusalem: Ariel; and Warminster: Aris and Phillips, 1977.

Wittkower, Rudolf. "Marvels of the East: A Study in the History of Monsters" and "Marco Polo and the Pictorial Tradition of the Marvels of the East." In *Allegory and the Migration of Symbols.* London: Thames and Hudson, 1977, 1987, pp. 45–74 (and 196–205), 75–92 (and 205–206). (Originally published in 1942 and 1957.)

Woodward, David, and Herbert M. Howe. "Roger Bacon on Geography and Cartography." In *Roger Bacon and the Sciences.* Ed. Jeremiah Hackett. Leiden, NY, and Cologne: Brill, 1997, pp. 198–222.

Wright, John Kirtland. *The Geographical Lore of the Time of the Crusades: A Study in the History of Medieval Science and Tradition in Western Europe.* American Geographical Society Research Series 15. New York: American Geographical Society, 1925; rpt. [new intro. Clarence J. Glacken] New York: Dover, 1965.

Wright, Thomas, ed. *Early Travels in Palestine.* London, 1848; rpt. New York: AMS, 1969.

Wyngaert, Anastasius van den, ed. *Itinera et Relationes Fratrum Minorum Saeculi XIII et XIV.* Vol. 1 of *Sinica Franciscana.* Quaracchi-Florence: Collegium S. Bonaventure, 1929.

[Yule-Cordier] Yule, Henry, ed. and trans. *Cathay and the Way Thither: Being a Collection of Medieval Notices of China.* Rev. edition Henri Cordier. Hakluyt Society, 2nd series, 37; Nendeln, Lichtenstein: Kraus, 1967.

———, ed. and trans. *The Book of Ser Marco Polo, the Venetian, Concerning the Kingdoms and Marvels of the East.* 2 vols. London: Murray, 1871. 3rd rev. edition. Henri Cordier. London: Murray, 1903, 1921, 1929. New York: Scribner's, 1921, rpt. 1929; NY: Airmont 1968.

# Index

Page numbers set in **bold** indicate the page where the main entry for the topic appears, and an *i* following a page number indicates that an illustration can be found on that page.

Angelus, Jacobus, 10. *See also* d'Angelo, Jacopo.
Angiolello, Giovan-Maria, 465
angle measure, 438
*Anglo-Saxon Chronicle,* 288
Anglo-Saxon map. *See* Cotton world map
Anglure, Ogier d', 44
Ani, 32
Ani, Cathedral of, 33
Saint Anianus, 38
Anige, 328
*Anima Mia,* 50
animals
  bestiaries, 61–62
  birds, exotic, 63–64
  camel, 89–90, 94–95
  exotic, **23–25**
  of Frederick II, 23, 24, 63, 90, 177, 201
  horses and harnesses, 261–262
  mythical. *See* monstrosity, geographical; mythical creatures
  and nomadism, 451
  *See also* individual type of animals
Ankara, battle of, 284, 467
*Annales Colbacenses,* 538
*Annales Marbacenses,* 26
*Annals,* 410
Anne de Beaujeu, 24
Anonymous Russian, 127
Anonymous of Lower Rhine or Cologne, **25–26**
Anonymous of Piacenza, 29
Anselm of Canterbury, 259, 260
*Antapodosis (Book of Revenge)* (Liudprand of Cremona), 343
Antarctic Circle, 9, 56
anteclimates, 10
antelope, 62
anteoikumene, 27
anthrax, 65
Antichrist, 219, 233
antichthone, meaning of, 27, 130, 458
Antillia, **26–27**
antimony, 570
Antioch
  fall of, 51, 135
  Jacobites, 159
antipodes, **27–28,** 27*i*
  Albertus Magnus on, 12
  ancient Greeks on, 27
  Beatus of Liébana on, 28
  *Book of John Mandeville* on, 28
  Cosmas Indikopleustes on, 594
  on Ebstorf world map, 28, 62
  Gervase of Tilbury on, 28
  Isidore of Seville on, 28, 594
  Lambert of Saint-Omer on, 27, 28

on London Psalter map, 28
and *oikoumene,* 27, 130
on Hereford map, 28, 62
and *terra Australes,* 594–595
*Antiqua Lectionis* (Canisius), 540
Antivavi, 309
*Antonine Itinerary (Itinerarium provinciarum Antonini Augusti),* **29,** 291
*Antonini Placentini Itinerarium (Antoninus Travel),* **29–30**
Antoninus of Florence, 620
Antoninus Pius, 29
Antonius Martyr, 29
Antwerp, 77
  fair of, 170
Anyang, 315
Anzio, 293
apes, 23–24
*apocrisiarii,* 19
Apocrypha, 219
*apoderamento,* 167
Apostles
  on Beatus maps, 52–53, 366, 368
  Holy Land sites, 484
  locations for Gospels, 157
Apple Orchard (Almaligh), 15
apprenticeship system, 242
Apuleius, 494
Apulia, 17
Aqaba, 439
Aqsā, -el, mosque, 256, 301
Aquileia, 267
*Arabian Nights,* Sindbad the Sailor, 562–563
'Arabī, Ibn al-, 146
Arabs
  and Albertus Magnus, 12
  and astrolabe, 224
  on astrology and travel, 35
  and Black Death, 66
  in Egypt, 173–175
  and exotic animals, 25
  Mediterranean area conquests, 390
  naval warfare, 439
  navigation of, 437–440
  nomadism of, 415–452
  as pirates, 491
  on tides, 604
  trade with Africa, 5, 7
  trade with Ottoman Empire, 468
  *See also* cartography, Arabic; Islam; Muslim travelers and trade
'Arabshah, Ibn, 44
Aragon, 92, 164
d'Aragona, Tullia, 239
Aral Sea, 101
*Aran Islands* (Synge), 288

Ararat, Mount, **30–31**
*Aratea of Germanicus Caesar,* 580
Aratos, 580
Araxes, 30
arbalests, 429
*Arbor Scientiae* (Lull), 435
*Arbre des batailles* (Bonet), 338
*Arca Noe* (Kircher), 30
architecture
  Armenian, 33
  cistern at Ramle, 256
  and city plans, 110–111
  and Frederick II, 201
  Holy Land cathedrals, 4, 31, 54–55
  masons/architects as travelers, 380–382
  Monastery of St. Catherine, 102
  Persian, 43
Archpoet, 624
Arctic Circle
  Adam of Breman on, 3
  of al-Idrīsī, 15
  on *mappamundi,* 9
  walrus hunt, 294
Arculf, **31**
  Adamnan's travel narrative of, 3–4, 31, 54, 255, 614
Arentzen, Jörg-Geerd, 541
Arethas of Patras, 509
Arghun, envoys to, 67, 83–84, 185, 284, 306
Arghuri, 30
Arhat, 80
Ari the Learned, 272
Arigh Böke, 413
*Arimaspea* (Aristeas of Proconnesus), 282
*Arin,* center of the earth, **103–104**
Ariosto, 239
Aristeas of Proconnesus, 282
Aristotle
  and Albertus Magnus, 11, 12
  on animals, 23, 24, 177
  on earth's shape, 218
  on oceans, 375
  on usury, 619
Arles, 227
Armenia, **31–33**
  Armenian Church, 32
  carpets of, 32, 598
  exports of, 32
  and Hetoum, 251–252
  missionaries in, 306
Armenian Christians, 135, 136, 154, 159
Armorica, 75
Arnarson, Ingólfr, 632
Arpád, 352
*Ars Componendi Sermones* (Higden), 252
Arsacid dynasty, 32
Arsenal, 429

St. Foy de Conques, 481
France
    Black Death, 65
    Brittany, map of, 75–76
    and Canary Islands, 90–91
    fairs of, 192–193
    map development in, 368
    measurement of distances in, 386,
        387
    merchants of, 395–396
    Rocamadour, 522
    trade, development of, 164
    Vézelay, 628
    and Vikings, 630
Francesco da Cherso, 383
Francis of Assisi
    and Crusades, 141, 175
    founding of Franciscans, 198–199
Francis of Pisa, 312
Franciscan friars, **198–200**
    barefoot travel of, 50
    contributions of, 200
    envoy to Mongols, 49–50, 57–58,
        183
    missionaries to China, 22–23, 184,
        199, 305–306
    missionaries to Germany, 311–312
    missionaries to Mongols, 21, 49–50,
        57–58, 74, 108, 183, 199, 285, 305,
        307–309, 402–403
    missionaries to New World, 332–334
    missionary activity of, 199–200
Franco-Flemish wars, 168
Frank, Sebastian, 494
frankincense, 575, 577
Franks
    and Avars, 39
    in Jerusalem, 202
    and Muslims, 270
Frater Fredericus, 321
*fraus omnia corrumpit,* 335
Freculph of Lisieux, 230
Fredegarius, 90
Frederick I Barbarossa, Holy Roman
        Emperor, 135, 200, 227, 232, 504
Frederick II, Holy Roman Emperor,
        **200–201**
    and coinage, 119
    and Crusades, 141
    and exotic animals, 23, 24, 63, 90,
        177, 201
Fregoso family, 211
Frescobaldi, Lionardo di Niccolò,
        **201–202**
Fretellus, Rorgo, **202,** 480
Frideswide of Oxford, 485
Friedman, John Block, 542
Frisia, 163

Frobisher, Martin, 360
Froissart, Jean, **202–204**
*Fuero real,* 13
Fuerteventura, 91, 92
Fulcher of Chartres, 136, 614
Fulgentius, 290
*funduqs,* 174
furlong, 386, 387
furs, 211, 247, 267, 272
    clothing of, 133, 280
Fustāt, al-, 175, 398
fustian, 132, 169
Fuzhou, 361
Fyn, 111

gad, 386
Gades, 89, 106
Gadifer de La Salle, 90–91
Gaikhatu, 84
Gaius Sallustius Crispus, Sallust maps,
        534–535
Gaja Mada, 352, 354
Galata, 211, 467
Galbert of Bruges, 76
Galfried de Langele, 617
Galicia, 235
galingale, 576
St. Gall, 289
gall black, 155
galley, **205–206,** 205*i,* 211, 431,
        553–554
    great galley, 555–556
Gallia Senonensis, 48
*Gallic Wars* (Caesar), 93
Gallicus, Johannes, 227
Galway, 71
Gambia River, 7, 187, 249
Gamurini, G.F., 172
Ganda, 228
Ganges, 198, **206–207,** 219
*ganja,* 437
Gao, 5, 7, 234
Garcie, Pierre, 76
Garðar, 433
Garðarshólmr, 632
Garden of Eden
    of Beatus maps, 53
    in Dante's writing, 148, 277
    Four Rivers of Paradise, 197–198,
        198*i,* 218–219
    of Hereford map, 250
    location of, 30
garnet, 209
Garzoni, Giacomo, 626
Gaston de Foix, 204, **207–208**
Gate of Benjamin, 147
Gate of the Gates, 101
Gattilusio, Francesco, 211

Gaul
    and Attila, 37, 38
    history of, 238–239
    and Huns, 267
    and Ireland, 289
    and trade, 395
Gautama (Buddha), 79–80
Gautier de Varinfroy, 382
Gautier-Dalché, Patrick, 541
*Gawain and the Green Knight,* 261
Gawan, 225–226
Gaza, 257
*gazā,* 466
Gdansk, 247
Gebal Mousa, 173
Gehon River, 198
gems, **208–209,** 275, 282
    on Asian clothing, 132, 133
Genesis
    flood. *See* Noah's flood
    Four Rivers of Paradise, 197–198,
        218–219
    Garden of Eden, 30, 53, 218
    on giants, 230, 231
Geneva fair, 170
Geniza, 175, 257
Genoa, **210–211**
    galley, use of, 206
    and gold trade, 211, 234
    and Golden Horde, 235–236
    and international trade, 163, 165, 166,
        181, 209–211, 391, 397, 571
    navigational inventions, 211
    and navigation, 187
    pirates from, 491
    trade with Ottoman Empire, 464–465,
        466–467
    and Trebizond, 617
*genovino,* 119
geocentric hypothesis, 507
Geoffrey of Langley, 83
Geoffrey of Monmouth, **212–213**
    descriptions of Britain, 212–213, 582
    on giants, 231
    on Wild People, 644
Geoffroi de Villehardouin, 137
Geoffroy de Thoisy, 325
*geographia,* 216
*Geographia* (Berlinghieri), 214
*Geographical Lore of the Time of the
        Crusades* (Wright), 541
*Geographus Nubiensis* (Nubian
        geographer), 14
geography in medieval Europe, **213–221**
    and Adam of Bremen, 2–3, 220
    and Aethicus Ister, 4–5, 219–220
    and al-Idrīsī, 14–15, 216
    and Albertus Magnus, 11–12

hats, of Mongols, 133
Hattin, battle of, 534
*Hauksbók (Haukr's Book)* (Erlendsson), 273
Hautevilles, 270
Havilah, 593
Hawqal, Ibn, 99, 234, 256, 280, 422
    on African gold trade, 234
Hayam Wuruk, 352
hazelnuts, 616
Hebraeus, Bar, 657
Hebrides, 72
Hebron, 55, 303
Hecataeus, 216, 583
Hedin, Sven, 561
Hegesippus, 55
Heian, 591
*Hejira,* 419, 550, 586
    *See also* pilgrimage, Muslim
Helche, 37
Heldris of Cornwall, 644
St. Helena, 86, 483
    and True Cross, 147, 254
hell
    Dante's view, 132, 148, 207, 259
    and Mount Etna, 179
Helluland, 112, 181
Helpericus, 260
Henan, 315
*hennin,* 132
Henri de Bruisselles, 381
Henriques, Afonso, 570
Henry I, king of England, 23, 248
Henry II, king of Cyprus, 67
Henry II, king of England, 227
Henry III, king of Castile, 284
Henry III, king of England, 23, 90, 177, 571
Henry IV, king of Castile, 128
Henry IV, king of England, 186
Henry V, Holy Roman Emperor, 248
Henry VI, Holy Roman Emperor, 200
Henry VII, king of England, 430
Henry of Blois, 525
Henry E. Huntington Library, 342
Henry of Huntingdon, 260, 582
Henry of Mainz map, 17, **248,** 368
Henry the Navigator, **248–249**
    Azores, discovery of, 40–41
    and Cape Bojador, 68
    and future navigation, 436
    and Order of Christ, 401
    and Portuguese expansion, 187, 248–249
    profits from trade, 574
Henry of Sawtry, 511, 512
Henry of Segusia, on usury, 620

Henry the Younger, of England, 227
Heraclea, 147
Heraclius, Byzantine emperor, 39
Herat, 605
Hereford, 485
Hereford Cathedral, 250
Hereford map, **249–251,** 250*i,* 366
    Amazons of, 17
    antipodes of, 28, 62
    on geographical information, 216
    and Orosian historiography, 218
    sources for, 8, 29, 248
Herjolfsson, Bjárni, 181, 434, 446, 632, 636
*Hermandad de las villas de marina de Castilla con Vitoria,* 572
Hermann von Salza, 596
Herod the Great, 44
Herodotus, 93, 282
Herzog-August Bibliothek, 342
Hesperides, 375–376
Hetoum, **251–252**
    on Eastern Christianity, 158, 159
    travel writing of, 251–252
Hetoum I, king of Armenia, 251, 263, 548
Hetoum II, king of Armenia, 251, 306
Hexi Corridor, 559
Hibernia, 376
hide boats, Celtic, 288, 431–432
Hierro, 91
Higden, Ranulf, **252–254**
    geographical work of, 253–254, 369
    on Paradise, 469
    translator of, 617
Higgins, Iain Macleod, 542
Hijaz, 388, 547
    Fātimids in, 193, 194
*Hildebrandslied (Song of Hildebrand),* 38
Hildegard von Bingen, 160, 445
Himyarit, 130
Hinayana Buddhism, 80
Hinduism, and Ganges, 206
Hipanis, 300
Hipparchus, 113, 494
Hippopodes, 494
hippopotamus, 24
Hispalis, 127, 548
Hispanic Society of America, 342
Hispaniola, 121
*Historia adversus paganos libri VII* (Orosius), 8, 17, 217, 462–463
*Historia Anglorum* (Henry of Huntingdon), 582
*Historia animalium* (Aristotle), 23, 177
*Historia de preliis* (Leo of Naples), 277
*Historia ecclesiastica* (Bede), 4

*Historia Francorum* (Fredegarius), 90
*Historia Francorum* (Gregory of Tours), 238–239
*Historia hierosolymitana* (de Vitry), 215
*Historia major* (Paris), 177
*Historia Mongalorum* (John of Plano Carpini), 20, 199, 215, 258, 307–309
*Historia naturalis* (Pliny), 23
*Historia Orientalis seu Hierosolymitana* (de Vitry), 18, 123, 298–299
*Historia Ottonis* (Liudprand of Cremona), 343
*Historia regum Britanniae* (Geoffrey of Monmouth), 212–213, 582
*Historia rerum Norvegicarum* (Torfaeus), 434
*Historia rerum in partibus transmarinis gestarum* (William of Tyre), 298
*Historia rerum ubique gestarum* (Piccolomini), 120
*Historia scholastica* (Comestor), 219, 228, 232, 233, 518
*Historia Tartarorum* (Simon of Saint-Quentin), 561–562, 634
*Historia tartarum (Tartar Relation)* (de Bridia), 58, 74–75
    and Vinland map, 635
*Historiae Philippicae* (Pompeius), 17
*Historiarum adversus paganos* (Orosius), 8
*History of Saint Louis* (Joinville), 310–311
*History of Cartography,* 541
*History* (Herodotus), 93
*History of the Life and Travels of Rabban Sawma* (Sauma), 615
*History from Marble* (Dingley), 540
*History of Rome (Brevarum ab urbe Condita)* (Eutropius), 240
*History of Three Kings* (John of Hildesheim), 346
*History of the Two Cities* (Otto of Freising), 464
*History of the World* (al-Din), 131
*History of the World Conqueror, The* (Juwaynī), 657
*History of the World, The* (Raleigh), 470
*Hjálmpérs saga,* 197
*Hodoeporica* (Celtes), 539
hoeker, 558
Hö'elun, 407
Holland, trade, development of, 170, 171
Holle, Lienhart, 112
hollow-ways, 609
Holy Fire, 60
Holy House, 486

on *terra incognita,* 595
on Thule, 602
Islam
    Assassins, 33–34
    and canon law, 94
    center of world in (Arym), 9
    and Chaghatai, 105, 106
    in China, 660
    Christian converts to, 128
    Egypt, 173–174
    Fātimids, 193–195
    first community, 389
    on Ham's curse, 245
    and Holy Land, 135, 255–256,
        301–302
    and India, 275
    law, 51
    and Mamluks, 355–357
    Mecca in, 387–388
    Medina in, 389–390
    missionaries, 33–34
    and Mongols, 185, 235, 236, 263, 413,
        658
    Muslim Spain, 46, 54, 128
    Muslim/Christian intermarriage, 94,
        **376–378**
    Muslim/Christian relations and
        Crusades, 136
    and Ottoman Empire, 466
    Ricold of Monte Croce on, 521
    Shi'ism, 33–34
    and slavery, 564
    Sunnism, 82
    Turkic tribes, 106, 466
    *See also* Muslim travelers and trade
Island of Seven Cities, and Antillia,
    26–27
Island of Sheep, 72
Island of Smiths, 72
Isle of the Blest, 57, 376
Isle of Wight, 331
*Islendingabók (Book of the Icelanders)*
    (Ari the Learned), 272
Isles of the Dead, 218
Islip, John, 418
Isma'ili Shi'ism, 34, 262
Isol the Pisan, 67
*Isolario,* 36, 431
    of Bartolomeo da li Sonetti, 50–51
    of Buondelmonti, 50, 371
Issnach, Clara, 191
Istakhrī, al-, 99, 256, 421
Istanbul, 464
Istria, 4
Italy
    Amalfi, 16–17, 163
    Attila, conquests of, 37

Black Death, 65, 66
    and Byzantine Empire, 85
    coinage, 119
    embassies of, 20
    and Ethiopia, 186
    *fondaco,* 195–196, 286
    and Huns, 267
    map development of, 369–371
    measurement of distances in, 386–387
    and Mediterranean Sea, 390
    merchant manuals, 394–395
    merchants of, 296–397
    naval warfare, 429
    pirates of, 491
    shipping contracts, 551
    and Tabriz, 1
    trade, development of, 163, 164, 165,
        170, 396–397
    trade with Asia, 281–282, 397
    trade with Spain/Portugal, 571
    *See also* specific city-states
*Itinerarium burdigalense* (Bordeaux
    Pilgrim), 68–69
itineraries and *periploi,* **291–292**
    *Antonine Itinerary,* 29, 291
    "Antoninus Travel," 29–30
    of Benjamin of Tudela, 59–60, 126,
        292
    of Bordeaux Pilgrim, 68–69, 172, 291
    of Egeria, 172–173, 291
    of Gerald of Wales, 222–223, 292
    Gough Map, 237
    *Marvels of Rome,* 379
    of Petrarch, 292–293
    Peutinger Table, 475
    of Ricold of Monte Croce, 520–521
    *See also* Holy Land descriptions; travel
        writing
*Itineraries of William Wey* (Wey), 642
*Itinerarium* (Egeria), 172–173
*Itinerarium Kambriae* (Gerald of Wales),
    222–223, 292
*Itinerarium syriacum* (Petrarch), **292–293**
*Itinerarium in Terram Sanctam et ad
    Sanctam Catherinam* (Walther), 191
*Itinerarius* (Ricold of Monte Croce), 520,
    521
*Itinerarius* (William of Rubruck), 183,
    218, 291, 615, 647–648
*Itinerarius* (Witte de Hese), 18, 470,
    649–650
*Itinerary* (Benjamin of Tudela), 59–60,
    126, 304
*Itinerary of Richard I of England,* 292
*ius forense,* 334
Ivan I, czar of Russia, 528
Ivan III, czar of Russia, 528

Ivan III, prince of Muscovy, 236
Ivan IV, 101
ivory trade, **293–295**
    and Africa, 7, 209, 293, 294
    and India, 275, 293, 294
*Iwein* (von Aue), 225
Iyās, Ibn, 420

Jabob's staff, 55
Jacob of Florence, 23, 403
Jacob of Paris, 257
Jacob van Maerlant, 600
Jacobite Christians, 20, 136, 158–159
Jacobus of Voragine, 231, 359
Jacopo da Verona, **297–298**
    travel writing of, 297
Jacopo of Gubbio, 449
Jacquerie, 208
Jacques de Fauran, 382
Jacques de Vitry, **298–299**
    travel writing of, 18, 123, 215, 220, 298
Jaén, 128
Jaffa, 51
Jagiello dynasty, 170
Jagiello, Vladislas, 496
Jaime I of Aragón, 572
Jalāl al-Din, 104
Jalāyirids, 44
*jalba,* 437
*jam,* 658
Jamālī, Badr al-, 194
St. James, 479
St. James the Elder, 486–487
St. James of Compostela, 318, 381
    insignia of site, 481, 488–489
    legend of St. James, 487
    pilgrimage site, 13, 480, 481, 486–488
    route to site, 487, 522
St. James at Ratisbon, abbey of, 288
James of Florence, 16
James Ford Bell Library, 342
James of Padua, 601
Jamuqa, 544
Jan Mayen Island, 432
Janibeg, Khân, 236
Japan
    Buddhism in, 80, 81–82
    Mongol invasion of, **299,** 406
Japhet, 219, 245, 246
Jār, al-, 389
*jarghuchis,* 657
*jariya,* 401
*jarlighs,* 657
Jarmi, Muhammad ben Abī Muslim al-,
    420
Jasconius, 71
Játiva, 570

Jaume I, king of Aragon, 337
Java, 576
    Majapahit, 352–353
    Mongol invasion of, 406, **629**
javelins, 133
Jawhar, 193, 420
Jean, duc de Berri, 186, 360
Jean, count of Nevers, 142
Jean de Bourgogne, 358
Jean de Lastic, 186
Jean d'Outremeuse, 358
Jean II, king of Burgundy, 142
Jean IV de Béthencourt, 90–91, 92, 187
Jedda, 439
Jerome
    on cannibals, 93
    center of earth of, 103–104
    map of Asia, **300**, 365, 368
    on *oikoumene,* 365
Jerusalem, **300–302**, 301*i*
    and Alexander the Great, 2
    as center of earth, 103–104, 219, 303,
      366
    as Christian city, 300–302
    city plan, 111, **302–303,** 302*i*
    and Crusades, 135–136, 137, 301
    Jews in, 301–302, 303
    Madaba mosaic map of, 351
    Mamluks in, 302
    on *mappaemundi,* 303
    Muslims in, 135, 255, 301–302
    Persian conquest, 255, 300–301
    *See also* Holy Land
Jerusalem House, 147
Jesus Christ
    and Balsam Garden, 44
    Eastern Christian view of, 157
    and Ebstorf world map, 160
    and Hereford map, 250–251
    Holy Land sites related to, 55, 483
jettison, 336
Jewish travelers, **303–304**
    Benjamin of Tudela, 59–60, 304
    Ibrāhīm ibn Ya'qūb, 271
    pilgrimage to Holy Land, 301, 303
    travel writings of, 304
Jews
    in Baghdad, 43
    blood libel allegation, 190
    and canon law, 94
    in China, 315
    in Constantinople, 126
    corporate expulsion of, 66, 189–190
    in Egypt, 175
    federation of communities (ShUM),
      399
    and Gog and Magog, 233–234, 518
    in Jerusalem, 301–302

    in Malabar, 353
    merchants, 398–399, 570, 572
    occupations of, 59, 256
    persecution and Black Death, 66, 190
    Red Jews, 518
    in Spain, 46, 189, 568, 570
    Ten Lost Tribes, 593–594
    and usury, 399, 620
Jia Dan, 126
Jidda, 388
*jihād,* 356
*jihāzi,* 437
Jin dynasty, 124, 238, 316
Joan II, King of Barcelona, 46
João I, king of Portugal, 249
João II, king of Portugal, 68, 145, 150,
    151, 187–188, 574
João de Santarem, 574
Job, tomb of, 173
Jocelin of Furness, 512
Jochi, 407, 410
Jochids, 144, 235
*joglars,* 402
John, king of England, 141
John, king of Jerusalem, 141
John, king of Portugal, 55
St. John, tomb of, 484
John I of Aragon, 134
John I Tzimisces, emperor of Greece, 343
John III Vatatzes, Byzantine emperor, 49
John V, Byzantine emperor, 86
John VIII, Byzantine emperor, 86
John XXII, Pope, 154, 312
John of Bohemia, 265
John of Brienne, 141
John Carter Brown Library, 342
John of Constantinople, 380
John the Fearless, 90, 331
    funeral cortege of, **304–305**
John of Hildesheim, 26, 346
    on Balsam Garden, 44
John of Marignolli, **305–306**
    in Almaligh, 16
    on aloe, 343
    on banana, 45
    mission to Mongols, 184, 305–306
    on Paradise, 469
    on Taprobane, 592
John of Monte Corvino, **306–307**
    archbishop of Khanbaliq, 306, 307
    bishop of Beijing, 109
    in India, 275
    mission to China, 184, 199, 306–307
    mission to Ethiopia, 186
    mission to Persia, 67
John of Norwich, 24
John of Plano Carpini, **307–309**
    and Benedict the Pole, 57–58, 74

    de Bridia on, 74
    history of Mongols, 20, 199, 215, 258,
      307–309
    mission to Mongols, 57–58, 74, 108,
      183, 199, 285, 349
    on *yasa,* 658
John of Sacrobosco, 112, 273, 359
John of Salisbury, 222, 445
John of Spain, 35
John of Torzelo, 326
John of Trevisa, 24, 90, 178
John of Wallingford, 104
John of Würzburg, **309–310**
    sources for work, 202
    travel writing of, 309–310
Johnson, Samuel, 360
Joinville, Jean de, **310–311,** 462, 614
Jojin, 82
Jolof, 7
Jomard, Edme-François, 541
Jonas of Bobbio, 289
*jongleurs,* 401, 402
Jónsson, Brandr, 274
Jordan, 263
    Madaba mosaic map, 351
Jordan of Giano, **311–312**
Jordan of Sévérac, **312**
    mission to India, 154, 184, 601
    travel writing of, 275, 616
Jordanes, 37, 266, 666
Jörg von Nürnberg, 330
*Jórsalafari (Jerusalem-pilgrim)* (Einarsson),
    273
Josephus, 593
Jubail, 210
Jubayr, Ibn, 423, 587
Jubilee of 1300, Rome, 479, 525
*jud,* 279
Judah ha-Levi, 304
Judea, 60
*Jugurthine War* (Sallust), 367, 534
Saint Julian, 238
Julian of Norwich, 318
Julien of Vézelay, 179
Julius Caesar, 8, 93
Julius Honorius, 4, 12, 219
*Jüngerey Titurel* (Albrecht von
    Scharfenburg), 504
junks, 440
*Junta dos mathematicos,* 55
Junyi, 315
Jurchen Jin, 319
Jurchens, 316
Jurgurtha, 534
*jus naufragii,* 270
Justin II, 39
Justinian, 84, 102, 159, 255
    and Byzantine law, 336

*mare oceanum,* 375–376
medieval, development of, **367–372**
and memory, **392–393**
New World, first map, 526–527
of Opicinus de Canistris, 459–460
portolan charts, 369, 370–371,
  498–500
of Ptolemy, 36, 216, 369–370
of Sanudo, 221
scholarship on, 540
strip maps, 382–383
of Vesconte, 36, 221, 369, 627–628
voyage and discovery, impact of, 370
Maqarrī, al-, 420, 423
Mar Yaballaha III, 84, 158, 284, 306
Mar-pa, 328
Maracanda, 535
Maragheh, 263
Marand, 30
Marche, Oliver de la, 178
Marches of Ancona, 601
Marciana, 342
Marco Polo, **372–374**
  on aloe, 343
  on Asian clothing/fabrics, 132, 133
  authorship of book, 373, 374
  on Caspian Sea, 101
  in China, 108, 184
  on exotic animals, 24, 25, 178
  on exotic birds, 63
  on fur trade, 281
  on gems, 209
  in India, 275
  and Khubilai Khân, 108, 178, 184,
    373–374
  and kumis, 324, 373
  omissions in work of, 373–374
  on Taprobane, 592
  travel writing of, 108, 184, 188, 221,
    281, 373–374, 615
  on whale hunting, 643
Marcus, John, 227
*Mare Caspium,* 101
*Mare Hyrcanium,* 101
*Mare nostrum,* 390
*mare oceanum,* 375–376
*Margarita Decreti* (Martin of Troppau),
  379
Margrave Dietrich of Meissen, 227
Margrave Leopold III, 463
Margus, 37
*marhala* (caravan stages), 15
Maria Comnena of Constantinople, 378
Saint Maria de Episcopia, 251
Mariazell, 266
Marie d'Oignies, 298
Marienburg, 400
Marigny-sur-Ouche, 479

Marinids, 234, 559
*marinière,* 344
Marinus of Tyre, 418, 508
maritime law. *See* law, maritime
St. Mark the Evangelist, 625
Mark of Montelupone, 601
*markab,* 437
market law, 334
Markland, 112, 181, 434
Markos, 283, 284
*Marktrecht,* 334
marmoset, 24
Maronites, 158
Marpa, 81
Marranos, 189
marriage, between Muslims and
  Christians, **376–378**
*Marriage of Mercury and Philology*
  (Capella), 114, 364–365
Marseilles, 163, 164, 396
Martellus, Henricus, 526
Martianus Capella, 28, 78, 114, 217,
  364
  on oceans, 375
  sources for work, 391
*Martin Behaim's Erdapfel,* 56
Saint Martin, 238
Martin, Thomas, 237
Martin of Spain, 36
Martin of Troppau, **378–379**
Marvazi, 127
*Marvels of India* (Shahriyar), 652
*Marvels of Rome,* **379,** 524
St. Mary Magdalene, 628
Mary, mother of Jesus, pilgrimage sites,
  44, 483, 484, 485, 487–488
*Mary Rose,* 430
Mary of Antioch, 378
Saint Mashtots', 33
masons and architects, as travelers,
  **380–382**
Massagetae, 93
*Master of Game* (Edward, duke of York),
  207
mastic, 211
Masts, Battle of, 428
Mas'udi, al-, 245, 421
Materea, 44
mathematics
  and Gerbert of Aurillac, 224
  and Nicholas of Lynn, 448
  and Ptolemy, 508–509
St. Mathieu, 75
Mathilda, Abbess of Holy Trinity Abbey,
  73, 417
Matthew of Arras, 381
Matthew Paris, **382–383**
  Brittany on map of, 75, 382

on cannibalism, 383
on exotic animals, 177
on Gog and Magog, 234
map innovations of, 368–369,
  382–383, 392–393
on Mongols, 216
work of, 21, 177, 382–383
Matthew of Todi, 449
Matthias I Corvinus, king of Hungary,
  266
Mauro, Fra, 75, 219
Mauro map, 76, **383–386,** 384*i,* 385*i*
Maurus, Hrabanus, 215, 273
Mausoleum of Hadrian, 524
Maximilian, emperor of Germany, 77
Mazu, 591
measurement of distances, **386–387**
  and Arab cartography, 15, 100
  and Gough map, 237
  land measures, 386–387
  and map development, 369, 370
  miles, 15
  and portolan charts, 369
  Roman, 29, 386, 387
  sea measures, 387
Meaux, 207
Meaux Cathedral, 382
Mecca, **387–388**
  and Arabic cartography, 99
  and Muhammad, 387, 388, 550
  pilgrimage to, 146, 256, 550
*mêchanikos,* 380
*Medea* (Seneca), 445
Medici Atlas, 112
Medici, Lorenzo di, 24
*Medieval Mappaemundi* (Woodward),
  541
Medina, 173, 388, **389–390**
  and Muhammad, 389, 586
  pilgrimage site, 389–390, 550
Medina del Campo, 573
Mediterranean Sea, **390–391**
Megasthenes, 278, 415
Mehmed I, Ottoman ruler, 20
Mehmed II, Ottoman ruler, 142, 465
Mehmed the Conqueror, 626
Mela, Pomponius, **391–392**
  geographical work of, 391
  map of, 391, 391*i*
  sources for work, 391
  on *terra Australes,* 594
  on *terra incognita,* 595
Melaka, 353, 354
Melchites, 157
*Meliador* (Froissart), 204
Meloria, 211
Meloria, battle of, 492
Memling, Hans, 77, 461

Procopius, on naval warfare, 428
procurators, role of, 19
Promised Land, and Brendan's voyage, 71–72
*promissio,* 551, 552
*proskynesis,* 483
Provins fair, 165, 192
Provins, Guyot de, 123
Pryor, John, 334
Psalter map, **505–506**
Pseudo-Callisthenes, 278
Pseudo–Ralph of Diceto, 582
*Pseudodoxia epidemica* (Browne), 177
psittacines, 63
Psylli, 251
Ptolemais, 2
Ptolemy, **507–510**
   *Almagest,* 113, 507, 508, 509
   and Arab cartography, 99, 509
   on astrology and travel, 35
   cosmology of, 507
   *Geography* of, 10, 15, 75, 101, 112, 214, 369–370, 507–510
   latitude/longitude coordinates, 36, 99, 113, 216
   on Nile, 418
   on ocean, 376
   on spherical earth, 364
   on Taprobane, 592
   on *terra Australes,* 594
   translations of work, 509–510
Ptolemy Euergetes, 130
Ptolemy II Philadelphus, 2
public road, 610
publicans, 287
Puccio, Piro di, 160
Puglia, 170
Pullani, 378
Punic War, Second, 176
punt, 554
Purchas, Samuel, 540
Purgatory, **511**
   St. Patrick's, **511–513**
   in Dante's writings, 148, 197
   meaning of, 511
purple, dyes for, 155
putchuk, 576
Putrid Sea, 266
Puzzoli River, 213
Pythagoras, 27, 363
Pythagorean Wheel, 35–36
Pytheas of Massilia, 216, 271, 592
   on Thule, 602

*qāḍī,* 269
Qaidu, 105, 235, 413
Qal'at al-Jabal, 355
Qal'at Sem'an, 483

*Qangli,* 143
Qarakhanids, 82
Qaraqorum, Karakorum, **316**
*qārib,* 96, 437
Qarmatians, 388
Qazwīnī, al-, 421, 423
   on whale hunting, 643
*qibla,* 98, 100, 388
Qin, 238
Qing dynasty, 238
Qipchaq khanate, Golden Horde, 235–236
Qipchaq Steppe, 143
*Qipchaqs,* 143
Qiu Changchun, 591
*qiyās,* 438
Qonggirat, 407
Qsar al-Saghir, 249
Qu dynasty, 238
quadrivium, and Gerbert of Aurillac, 224
Quanzhou, 175, 361, 663
quarantine, Black Death, 66
Quaresmius, Francesco, 540
quattrino, 170
Quay, 247
*Queen Mary's Psalter,* 177
*questionary,* 35
*Questions on Water and Earth (Quaestio de aqua et terra)* (Dante), 148
Quilon, 184, 312, 353
Qulzum, 439
Qung dynasty, 328
Quraysh, 387
*quriltai,* 316, 410
Qusayr, 439
Qutayba, Ibn, 245

Rabban Ata, Simeon, **517**
*Rabenschlacht (The Battle of Ravenna),* 38
La Rabída, 120
Radiya, princess of Delhi, 653
Ragusa, 66, 465
Rahmān III, 'Abd al-, 128, 420, 570
raisins, 255
Raleigh, Sir Walter, 470
Ramle, 256, 257
Ramon de Penyafort, 348
rams, 428
Ramusio, Giambattista, 539
Rashi (Shlomo Isaaki), 371
Rashid al-Din, 67, 131, 281
Rashīd, Hārūn al-, 43, 151, 177, 303, 388, 550, 563, 587
rats, and Black Death, 64, 66
Ravenna, 224
Ravenna, Guido of, 240–241
Ravenstein, E.G., 56
Raymond Bérenger V of Toulouse, 402

Raymond II, count of Tripoli, 34
Raymond of Toulouse, 210
Real, João Vaz Corte, 574
*Recognoverunt proceres* of 1284, 46
*Reconquista,* 174, 182, 185
   and military orders, 400–401
   trade effects, 568, 572–573
*Record of the Western Region* (Hsuan-tsang), 283
*Records of the Western Region (Da Tang Xiyü)* (Xüanzang), 81
red, dyes for, 155
Red Jews, **518**, 594
Red Sea, 438, **519–520**
   and Ayyūbids, 40
   and trade, 519–520
Red Slip Ware, 289
*Reductorium Morale* (Bersuire), 545
Regensburg, 259
Reger, Johann, 112, 510
*Regimento do Astrolabio e do Quadrante* (Abraham Zacuto of Salamanca), 436
*Regulae de numerotum abaci rationibus* (Gerbert of Aurillac), 224
Rehoboam I, 593
Reichhartinger, Leinhart, 538
Reie River, 76
Reims, 224
*Reisubók (Travel Book)* (Einarsson), 273
*Relatio* (Benedict the Pole), 58
*Relatio de legatione Constantinopolitana* (Liudprand of Cremona), 20, 343
*Relatio* (Odoric of Pordenone), 358, 457
relics. *See* pilgrim souveniers
religion
   Buddhism, 78–82
   Christian. *See* Christianity; Roman Catholic Church
   Confucianism, 124–126
   and corporate expulsion, 189–190
   Eastern Christianity, 157–159
   Lamaism, 327–328
   Manichaeism, 360–362
   Taoism, 590–591
   Zoroastrianism, 665–666
*renovatio imperii,* 224
*Report on the Kings Residing in the North,* 282
reprisal, law of marque, 338–339
*Responsa,* 398
Resurrection, Holy Land site, 55, 483
Reuveni, David, 304, 594
Reuwich, Erhard, 74, 303
Reval, 247
Revelation, twelve stones of, 209
Revolt of the Ciompi, 170
Rhadanites, 398

Mongols in, 410, 412, 528
Moscow, rise of, 528
origin of, 527
and Scythia, 543
trade and commerce, 527–528
and Vikings, 527, 630
*Russian Primary Chronicle,* 527, 528
Russian travelers
and Caspian Sea, 101
Daniel the Abbot, 147
travel to Byzantium, 87, 127
Rustah, Ibn, 421
Rusticello da Pisa, 493
and Marco Polos' travel record, 221,
373, 374
*ruthe,* 387
rutters (route books), 166, 604
Ruy Gonzáles de Clavijo, 25, 127, 284,
467, 535, 589
Ruysch, Jacob, 448, 494
Ryazan, 235

Sabbah, Hasan ibn, 33–34
Sabbas, 257
*Sachsenpiegel,* 246
sacopenium, 577
Sacrobosco, John of, 9, 509, **531–532**
geographical work of, 359, 531–532
sources for work, 531
Saemundson, Nicholas, 450
Sæwulf, **532**
Safed, 257
safflower, 155
saffron, 155, 355, **532–533,** 570
*safina,* 437
Sa'īd, Ibn, 100
saints. *See* individual saints by name
Sakyapa, 328
Saladin, **533–534**
and Ayyūbids, 39–40, 256
and Crusades, 39–40, 136, 140, 182,
302
in Damascus, 146, 534
in Egypt, 175
Salamanca, 570
Salamanca Commission, 120–121
Salerno, 16, 165
Salīh, Abū, 175
Salimbene, 308
Salisbury, 213
Sallām the Interpreter, 421
Sallust maps, **534–535**
nature of, 250, 367
salt, 234, 235, 247, 289
Salvat de Pilestrina, 526
*Salvator Mundi,* 461
Salza, Hermann von, 200
Sam'ānī, Abū Sa'd 'Abd al-Karīm al-, 422

Samanids, coins of, 82
Samaria, 593
Samaritans, 2, 59, 255
Samarkand, 1–6, 15, 82, 105, 283, **535**
and Tamerlane, 589–590
Samarra, 43
Sambatyon River, 304
Saminiato di Guciozzo de' Ricci, 394, 395
Samme, 294
Samo, 39
Samothrace, 211
*Samsons saga fagra (The Saga of Fair
Samson),* 274
Samsun, 83
Samudri Raja, 353
Samuel ben Samson, 303
San Germano, Treaty of, 200
San Miguel, 41
San Vincent de la Barquera, 571
San Zoil de Carrion, 571
*sanbūq,* 437
Sancho IV, 128
Sancho Ramírez, king of Aragón, 525
sandalwood, 575
Sangha, 79
*Santa Maria,* 427
Santa Maria Islands, 41
Santander, 571
Sāntaraksita, 327
Santiago of Compostela. *See* St. James of
Compostela
Santiago Island, 573
Sanudo, Marco, 625
Sanudo, Marino, **535–536**
on Balsam Garden, 44
on crusades, 36, 221
travel writing of, 221, 369, 536, 627
São Jorge de Mina, 234, 264, 565
sappan, 155
*sapphirus,* 209
Saracens, 12, 178, 245, 297
and orientalism, 461
Saracen/Christian marriage, 376–378
Sarai, 236, 412
sarcocolla, 577
Sardinia, 163, 165, 210
Sardis, 300
*sardius,* 209
*sardonyx,* 209
Sargon I, king of Akkad, 43
Sargon II, 593
Sarmatians, 543
Sarmatrian ocean, 376
Sasquatch, 231
Sassou, 130
Satanazes, 27
*Satyrica Historia* (Paulinus Minorita of
Venice), 471

Sauma, Rabban Bar, 185, 283–284, 306,
444, 615
Sauwer, 93
Sawley Abbey, 104, 248
Saya, 27
scale, in map development, 369, 370, 382
Scandinavia
Atilla, stories of, 38
Black Death, 66, 272
*fornaldarsögur* sagas, 196–197
geographer of, 3, 18, 220
and Iceland, 272
*King's Mirror,* 320–321
measurement of distances in, 387
ships of, 554
stones/timber trade, 584–585
world maps of, **537–538**
*See also* Viking age; Viking
discoveries/settlements
Scarampi, Luchino, 579
*sceaux rigoreux,* 334
Schedel, Hartmann, 180, 453
Scheldt River, 228, 229
Schiltberger, Johann, 127, 284, 465, 467,
**538–539**
Schmeidler, Bernhard, 3
scholarship on medieval European
geography and travel, **539–542**
collections of original texts, 539
geography as subject of study, 540–541
on *mappaemundi,* 541
maps as artifacts, 540
of pilgrimage accounts, 541–542
with religious focus, 540
taxonomies, 542
travel writing analyses, 540
on voyages of discovery, 539
*See also* surviving manuscripts
School of Sagres, 248
Schreyer, Sebald, 453
sciapod, 53–54, 366, 595
scimitar, 133
Scot, Michael, 35, 201
Scotland, measurement of distances in,
386
Scourge of the Crusaders, Saladin as,
39–40
scriptoria, functions of, 33
*Scripture of the Conversion of the
Barbarians* (Huahu jing), 591
*scurrae vagi,* 402
Scylax, 216
Scythia, 172, 216, **543**
Scythian ocean, 376
Scythians, 17, 93
Sea of Azov, 211
sea exchange, 552
Sea of the Khazar, 101

Turkestan, 235
Turkmen, 466, 546
Turks
    Cumans, 143–144
    and Golden Horde, 235
    in Hungary, 266
    Mamluks as, 51, 355–356
    and Mongols, 105, 106, 409, 411
    Muslim, 106
    as nomads, 466
    oldest world map of, 104
    Onogurs, 280
    origins of Ottoman Empire, 466
    as pirates, 491
    *See also* Seljuk Turks
turnsole, 155
Turst, Konrad, 370
Tusculum, 298
Tutush, 547
Tver, 235, 236
*Tvoyage* (van Ghistele), 191
Twelver Shi'a, 390
typhoid, 169
typhus, 65
Tyre, 2, 137, 255
Tyskebryggen, 247
Tzeggra, 538
Tzinista, 130

*uasa mortis,* 567
Ugolino of Gherardesca, 492
Ugra River, 236
Uhud, battle of, 389
Uighurs, 95, 104, 105, 158, 306, 361,
    544
Ujjain, 104
'ulamā, 356
Ulf-Krakason, Gunnbjǫrn, 433
Ulm, 191, 192
Ulrich of Seydrisdorf, 22, 402
Ulrich von Eschenbach, 377
Ulu Muhammad, 236
*ulus,* 104, 605
Ulus of Jochi, 144
Ulysses, in Dante's writings, 148, 207,
    259
Umar, 159
'Umari, Ibn Fadlallāh al-, 100, 658
Umayyads
    in Damascus, 146, 174, 256
    in Holy Land, 256, 301
    in Mecca, 388
    in Medina, 389
    in Morocco, 234
    in Spain, 569
*umbilicus mundi,* 303
*umma,* 389

unicorn, 151, 177, 251
    similarity to exotic animals, 24
uniforms, of Mongol army, 132–133
*Universal History* (al-Din), 67
Universiteitsbibliotheek, 342
Uppsala, 3
Urban II, Pope, 134, 175, 181, 497
urban tenure, 334
Urfa, 171
Urus, 236
Ushant, 75
Ushbana, al-, 570
usury, 166, **619–620**
    and corporate explusion, 189
    and Jews, 399, 620
    and sea loans, 552
Uther Pendragon, 213, 582
Uturgurs, 38
Uzbekistan, 82, 105, 143

vagrancy, **623–624**
    itinerant performers, 401–402, 623
Val Demone, 170
Vale Royal Abbey, 381
Valencia, 569, 570
Valerius Bergidensis, 172
Valladolid, 571
Valley of Josephat, 483
Vandals, 85, 390, 428, 548
Varangians, 527
Varna, 142
Varro of Atax, 391
Vasil the Tatar, 548
Vaspurakan, 32
vehicles, for inland transportation, 609
Velser, Michel, 226, 359, 518
Vendée, 163
Venice, **625–626**
    and Byzantine Empire, 625–626
    city plan, 111
    coinage of, 119
    and Crusades, 137–138, 625
    galley, use of, 206
    and international trade, 163, 165, 181,
        209, 391, 397, 626
    merchant guilds of, 242
    trade with Ottoman Empire, 465,
        466–467
*Venjance Alixandre,* 377
Vercelli map, 368
verdigris, 155
Verdun, Treaty of, 39
verge (yard), 386
St. Veronica, 522
Vesconte, Pietro/Perrino, **627–628**
    city plans, 303
    maps of, 36, 221, 369, 392, 393*i,* 627

Vespasian, 150
Vespucci, Amerigo, 397, 446
Vézelay, **628**
*Vicissitudes of Fortune* (Bracciolini),
    615–616
Victoria, Lake, 5
*Vie de Saint Louis* (Fulcher of Chartres),
    614
*Vienna Genesis,* 246
Vienna-Klosterneuburg Map Corpus,
    221, **321,** 640
Vietnam
    Buddhism in, 80
    Mongol invasion of, 406, **629**
Vífilsson, Þorbjǫrn, 633
Vijaya, 354
Viking age, **629–631**
    *fornaldarsögur* sagas, 196–197, 446,
        630, 631, 632
    naval warfare, 428–429
    and New World concept, 446
    ship burials from, 329, 630
    ships and navigation, 322, 329–330,
        432–434, **441–442,** 629–630
    time period of, 629
    trading route, 630
    Viking plunder, 163–164
Viking discoveries/settlements, 181,
    **631–633**
    Faeroe Islands, 631
    Greenland, 433–434, 630, 632–
        633
    Iceland, 433, 630, 631–632
    in Russia, 527, 630
    Scottish islands, 433
    Vinland, 632–633
Vilgerðarson, Flóki, 632
Villani, Giovanni, 117
Villasirga, 487–488
Villon, François, 624
Vincent of Beauvais, **633–634**
    on Amazons, 17
    on barnacle goose, 47
    on exotic animals, 24, 25
    on Ganges River, 207
    on magnetic compass, 123
    sources for work, 309, 349
    on Ten Lost Tribes, 594
    works of, 25, 74, 108, 199, 215,
        633–634
Vinci, Leonardo da, 111
*Vinland,* 181
Vinland, 3, 112
    sagas of, 273, **636–637**
    Viking settlement, 181, 434,
        632–633
    on Vinland map, 635